Seventh Edition

Psychological Testing

ANNE ANASTASI
Department of Psychology, Fordham University

SUSANA URBINA
Department of Psychology, University of North Florida

Pearson

Authorized adaptation from the United States edition, entitled *Psychological Testing, 7th Edition,* ISBN 9780023030857, by Anastasi, Anne; Urbina, Susana published by Pearson Education, Inc, Copyright © 1997.

Indian Subcontinent Adaptation

ISBN 978-93-325-7558-5

First Impression, 2017
Thirteenth Impression, 2025
Fourteenth Impression, 2026

Published by Pearson India Education Services Pvt. Ltd, CIN: U72200TN2005PTC057128.

Head Office: 1st Floor, Berger Tower, Plot No. C-001A/2, Sector 16B, Noida - 201 301, Uttar Pradesh, India.

Registered Office: 6th Floor, Tower A, Unit A and B, International Tech Park, CapitaLand Chennai, 200 Feet Radial Road,Zamin Pallavaram, Old Pallavaram Chennai – 600117, Tamil Nadu, India

Website: in.pearson.com; Email: companysecretary.india@pearson.com

Digitally printed in India by Trinity Academy for Corporate Training Ltd, New Delhi in the year of 2026

This book is dedicated to the memory of
John Porter Foley, Jr., who made significant
contributions to each successive edition.

A.A

S.U

Contents

Preface

The 1990s have witnessed a continuation and expansion of the upsurge of interest in psychological testing that was evident in the 1980s. This growth is indicated by the development of new tests—some representing novel approaches—as well as by the revisions of earlier tests and continued research on existing tests. In selecting instruments for mention or discussion, a primary goal was to expose readers to the rich variety of measurement tools available in the field today, as well as to some historically significant tests and techniques; any attempt to cover the field—or even a significant segment of it—in a comprehensive fashion would have been clearly beyond the scope of this book.

Increasing attention is being given to the individual who is tested. The test user is encouraged to search for the causes of the individual's performance in that person's experiential history and reactional biography: What about the individual's background may help to understand that person's test responses and enhance the value of scores in predicting subsequent behavior—in school, at work, and in other contexts of everyday-life activities? It follows that the *test user* has increased responsibility in selecting appropriate tests and methods of presenting testing to the individual; in interpreting scores; and in communicating and using test results. Because of such considerations, this textbook is designed especially with the goal of providing a foundation for proper test use.

Effective test use requires some basic familiarity with test construction. Such information is needed in order to evaluate different tests, choose tests appropriate for particular purposes and individual examinees, and to interpret scores properly. Although this book is not addressed specifically to the test constructor, it nevertheless includes enough information about how tests are developed to meet the needs of the test user.

This edition also provides simple explanations of some widely used and rapidly developing concepts and procedures, which are likely to affect psychometric practices in the 21st century. Examples include computerized adaptive testing, meta- analysis, structural equation modeling, the use of confidence intervals in place of the traditional statistical significance, cross-cultural testing, and the increasing use of factor analysis in the development of ability and personality tests. A practical application of the factor-analytic approach has been to provide norms that permit interpretation of scores at different levels of specificity or generality, so that a test user can apply the level that is most suitable for the particular person or situation.

Two significant long-term trends are abundantly evident in testing today; instead of devoting separate chapters to these, we chose to discuss them wherever they were pertinent, throughout the entire book. The first trend is the constantly increasing influence of computerization in test development, test construction, and test administration, in addition to the well-established uses of computers in test scoring and score processing. The velocity of technological advances is so startling that it seems to outpace progress in substantive areas of psychology. Technology, however, also contributes mightily to progress in both the research and theoretical fronts. For instance, a great deal of integration and cross-fertilization of areas within the psychological literature is rapidly taking place, fostered by the ease with which information can be accessed, processed, and communicated among investigators around the world. The recasting of cognitive and personality traits as interacting and inseparable aspects of the individual—who is, in turn, inextricably tied to her or his physical self, life events, and environment—is one of the most salient, and promising, instances of this tendency toward integration.

A second trend that affects psychological testing in very significant ways is the growing encroachment of political and legalistic concerns in the area. While this is a divisive and potentially pernicious influence on the field, it may also have some positive ramifications in terms of fostering creativity and increased vigilance with respect to the intended and unintended consequences of the use of tests. Citations of a number of public laws (P.L.) that have had an impact on testing practices are given throughout the text—along with their titles and the years they were enacted; their content can be found in the United States *Congressional Record* as well as other periodical publications available in the reference departments of most libraries.

Although the first six editions of this text had a single author, this edition is a true co-authorship. The two authors jointly planned the reorganization of chapters and the major topics to be covered. The specific revision and re-writing of chapters was allocated as follows: Anastasi was responsible for chapters 1–7 and 10–12; Urbina for chapters 8, 9, and 13–18; Urbina also undertook major administrative and correspondence functions. Nevertheless, each author read a draft of the other's chapters and suggested improvements, which were usually implemented. It also should be noted that the goal of balancing the order of precedence for the feminine and the masculine genders—in pronouns and other words—was achieved by using the alphabet as a guide. Thus, "her" precedes "his," "he" precedes "she," "female" precedes "male," "man" precedes "woman," and so on.

Obviously this book could not have been written without access to the research and publications of many psychologists, both present and past, from different parts of the United States and other countries. Their names appear throughout the text: in the citations of their publications, in the acknowledgements of the sources of figures and tables, and in the composite list of references at the end of the book. Within this impressive group, a few individuals nevertheless stand out because of their ever-ready cooperation and the extent of their contributions. Conspicuous among them are Dianne Brown from the Science Directorate of the American Psychological Association, Aurelio Prifitera and Joanne Lenke of the Psychological Corporation, Lorin Letendre of Consulting Psychologists Press, Carol Watson of National Computer Systems, Douglas Jackson of Sigma Assessment Systems, Elizabeth McGrath and John Oswald of the Riverside Publishing Company, and Wayne Camara of the College Board. In addition, the assistance of staff members of the Fordham University and University of North Florida libraries, in meeting the varied challenges involved in the preparation of this book, is gratefully acknowledged.

Anne Anastasi
Susana Urbina

ABOUT THE INDIAN EDITION

Psychometric testing in India has seen a multifarious growth in recent times. Earlier, these tests were widely used as diagnostic tools in clinical, therapeutic, and social context. However, psychometric tests are now being used by all types of organization, from educational to professional, for the purpose of selection of candidates or employees and to provide them with development opportunities by understanding their requirement for training and testing the knowledge acquired thereafter.

The books available in the market on the subject provide well written and simple explanations of some of the widely used and rapidly developing psychological assessments which are likely to affect psychometric practices in the 21st century. However, most of these books neither have up-to-date information on the recently revised versions of important assessment test nor the local Indian contexts and conditions. The information on tests used in Indian organizations has rarely been quoted. Keeping these reasons in mind, *Psychological Testing, 7e*, has been adapted in order to make it contemporary and relevant in the Indian context, without disturbing the original structure and content. Information on the latest revisions and editions of some of the important tests like Wechsler Scales, Ravens' Progressive Matrices, Bayley Scales of Infant Development, Strong Interest Inventory have been provided. In this edition, readers will get an insight about the relevance of these widely-used, internationally-developed tools in the Indian market and how these can be further applied. Certain complex concepts have been explained with the help of Indian examples. Special attention has been paid to showcase certain important psychological assessments that are widely used in the country.

An interesting addition to the text are the intriguing insights about generational changes in performance on intelligence tests. After going through these students may learn to appreciate the different perspectives around intelligence testing. Moreover, discussion on the influence of cultural diversity on intelligence has also been included.

Furthermore, this revised version provides information about the ethical and social considerations of using psychological assessments in the Indian context which serves as an added advantage as these aspects are rarely mentioned in the other books. Moreover, the information on the Indian psychological agencies and best practices in the domain of psychometrics are also included.

To conclude, this Indian adaptation provides a good blend of global and indigenous examples to explain the technical concepts of psychological testing. This edition hopes to increase recognition and acceptance of psychological testing, equip the readers with right tools and technologies, and encourage further growth in psychometric testing in the immediate future.

Tanvi Chaturvedi

PART 1

Functions and Origins of Psychological Testing

Chapter One

Nature and Use of Psychological Tests

Psychological tests are tools. To reap the benefits that tests can provide, one must keep this essential fact in mind. Any tool can be an instrument of good or harm, depending on how it is used. Testing has been growing at an increasing pace, and it is contributing effectively in more and more areas of daily life.[1] But this growth has been accompanied by some unrealistic expectations and misuses. Test users need to know how to evaluate tests. How good is this test for the particular purpose for which it is being used? What kind of information can it provide about the person who takes it? How can its results be integrated into the network of data leading to action decisions? It is primarily with such questions in view that this book has been prepared. The book is not designed for the test specialist but rather for the general student of psychology. Today, some basic knowledge about tests is needed—not only by those who construct or give tests but also by anyone who uses test results as one source of data in reaching decisions about oneself or others.

USES AND VARIETIES OF PSYCHOLOGICAL TESTS

Traditionally, the function of psychological tests has been to measure differences between individuals or between the reactions of the same individual under different circumstances. One of the earliest problems that stimulated the development of psychological tests was the identification of mentally retarded persons. To this day, the detection of intellectual

[1] For lucid illustrations of the potential contributions of psychological tests, with real-life examples, see Dahlstrom (1993b).

deficiencies remains an important application of certain types of psychological tests. Related clinical uses of tests include the examination of persons with severe emotional disorders and other types of behavioral problems. A strong impetus to the early development of tests was likewise provided by assessment needs arising in education. This was the case in the famous Binet tests that ushered in intelligence testing. At present, schools are among the largest test users. The classification of children with reference to their ability to profit from different types of school instruction, the identification of outstandingly slow or fast learners, the educational and occupational counseling of high school and college students, and the selection of applicants for professional schools are among the many educational uses of tests.

The selection and classification of industrial personnel represent another major application of psychological testing. From the assembly-line operator or filing clerk to top management, there is scarcely a type of job for which some kind of psychological test has not proved helpful in such matters as hiring, job assignment, transfer, promotion, or termination. To be sure, the effective employment of tests in many of these situations, especially in connection with high-level jobs, usually requires that the tests be used as an adjunct to skillful interviewing, so that test scores may be properly interpreted in the light of other background information about the individual. Nevertheless, testing constitutes an important part of the total personnel program. A closely related application of psychological testing is to be found in the selection and classification of military personnel. From simple beginnings in World War I, the scope and variety of psychological tests employed in military situations underwent a phenomenal increase during World War II. Subsequently, research on test development has been continuing on a large scale in all branches of the armed services.

The use of tests in individual counseling has gradually broadened from a narrowly defined guidance regarding educational and vocational plans to an involvement with all aspects of the person's life. Emotional well-being and effective interpersonal relations have become increasingly prominent objectives of counseling. There is growing emphasis, too, on the use of tests to enhance self understanding and personal development. Within this framework, test scores are part of the information given to the individual as aids to her or his own decision-making processes.

It is clearly evident that psychological tests are currently being employed in the solution of a wide range of practical problems. One should not, however, lose sight of the fact that such tests are also serving important functions in basic research. Nearly all problems in differential psychology, for example, require testing procedures as a means of gathering data. As illustrations, reference may be made to studies on the nature and extent of individual differences, the organization of psychological traits, the measurement of group differences, and the identification of biological and cultural factors associated with behavioral differences. For all such areas of research—and for many others—the precise measurement of individual differences made possible by well-constructed tests is an essential prerequisite.

Similarly, psychological tests provide standardized tools for investigating such varied problems as life-span developmental changes within the individual, the relative effectiveness of different educational procedures, the outcomes of psychotherapy, the impact of community programs, and the influence of environmental variables on human performance.

The many kinds of tests designed for these diverse purposes differ also in other major characteristics. They vary in the way they are administered, as in the individual testing of each person by a trained examiner, the simultaneous testing of large groups, or the administration of tests by computers. Tests also differ in the aspects of behavior that they cover. Some concentrate on the assessment of cognitive traits, or abilities. These may range from broad aptitudes—such as readiness to profit from college work—to highly specific sensorimotor skills required to perform a simple manual operation. Other tests provide measures of affective variables, or personality, such as emotional or motivational traits, interpersonal behavior, interests, attitudes, and values.

In the face of such diversity in nature and purpose, what are the common differentiating characteristics of psychological tests? How do psychological tests differ from other methods of gathering information about individuals? The answer is to be found in certain fundamental features of both the construction and the use of tests.

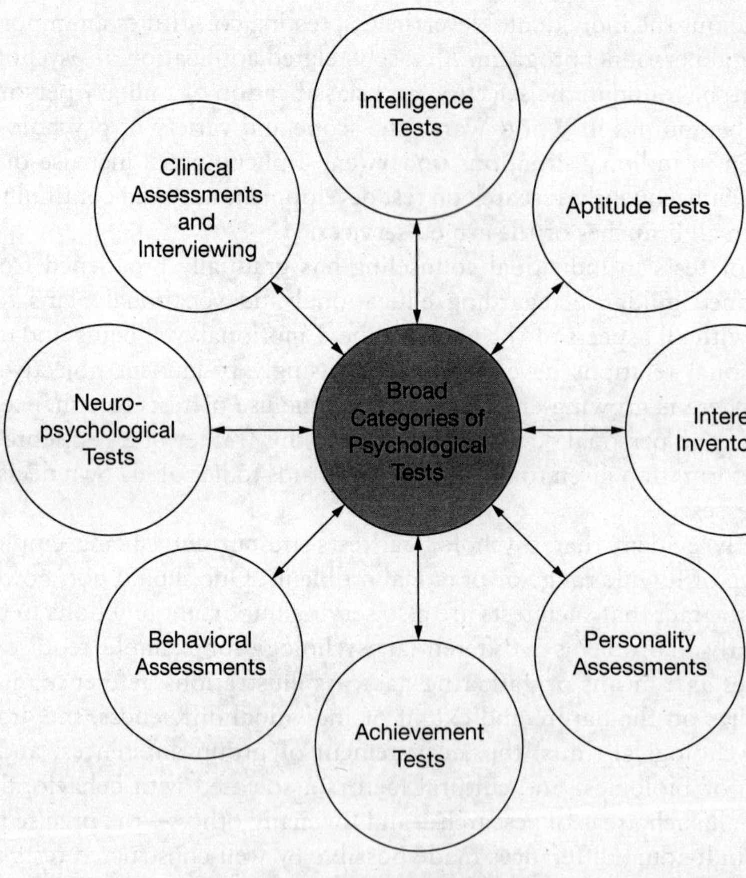

Figure 1-1. Broad Categories of Psychological Tests

Intelligence Tests	Measure an individual's potential for scholastic or other occupations. Typically assess the ability in areas, such as verbal comprehension, perceptual organization, reasoning, arithmetic, and information. For example, Stanford-Binet IQ test, Wechsler Intelligence Scale for Children (WISC), Wechsler Adult Intelligence Scale (WAIS), Raven's Progressive Matrices (RPM)
Aptitude Tests	Measure an individual's capability for a relatively specific task or type of skill such as mechanical abilities, manual dexterity, reading comprehension, spelling and language usage, and abstract reasoning. For example, Differential Aptitude Tests (DAT), Scholastic Assessment Test (SAT)
Interest Inventories	Measure an individual's preference for certain activities and topics, and thereby help to determine the occupational or career choices. Most of the interest inventories are based on Holland's occupational themes – Realistic, Investigative, Artistic, Social, Enterprising and Conventional (RIASEC) and measure interests in a broad range of occupations, work activities, leisure activities and academic subjects. For example, Strong Interest Inventory, Career Decision Making (CDM) System
Personality Assessments	Measure the traits or attributes that are intrinsic to a person's individuality and helps in predicting the future behavior. Such tests come in several formats including checklists, inventories and projective techniques. For example, Sixteen Personality Factor Questionnaire or 16PF Questionnaire (16PF), Myers Briggs Type Indicator (MBTI), DISC assessment and Revised NEO-Personality Inventory (NEO-PI)
Achievement Tests	Measure an individual's degree of learning, success or accomplishment in a subject matter. Such tests determine the degree to which an individual has absorbed, applied, and mastered a certain subject. Such tests commonly have several sub-tests, such as reading, mathematics, language, science, and social studies
Behavioral Assessments	Identify the antecedents and consequences of the behavior. These objectively describe and calculate the frequency of behavior. Such assessments are widely used in identifying the emotional and behavioral difficulties in children. For example, Beck Depression Inventory (BDI) and Beck Youth Inventories (BYI). The principles of behavioral assessments are also widely used in an occupational setting and its outcomes are usually interwoven with various selection and development interventions
Neurop-sychological Tests	Measure an individual's cognitive, sensory, perceptual, and motor performance to determine the extent, locus and behavioral consequences of brain damage. For example, Cambridge Neuropsychological Test Automated Battery (CANTAB), Dean-Woodcock Neuropsychology Assessment System (DWNAS) and Luria-Nebraska neuropsychological battery
Clinical Assessments and Interviewing	Screen and diagnose the psychological problems in children and adults and help to identify the cognitive, emotional, adaptive, social, and personality-related issues that obstruct individuals to lead a better quality of life. These tests are used by mental-health professionals such as psychologists and allied professionals to learn about an individual's psychological disorders, learning potential, specific learning disabilities, attention problems, as well as social, emotional and behavioral issues and their severity to develop effective intervention plans. For example, Bayley Scales of Infant and Toddler Development, Beck Anxiety Inventory (BAI), Millon Clinical Multiaxial Inventory (MCMI) and Minnesota Multiphasic Personality Inventory (MMPI)

WHAT IS A PSYCHOLOGICAL TEST?

Behavior Sample. A psychological test is essentially an objective and standardized measure of a sample of behavior. Psychological tests are like the tests in any other science, insofar as observations are made on a small but carefully chosen *sample* of an individual's behavior. In this respect, the psychologist proceeds in much the same way as the biochemist who tests a patient's blood or a community's water supply by analyzing one or more samples of it. If the psychologist wishes to test the extent of a child's vocabulary, a clerk's ability to perform arithmetic computations, or a pilot's eye–hand coordination, he or she examines their performance with a representative set of words, arithmetic problems, or motor tests. Whether or not the test adequately covers the behavior under consideration obviously depends on the number and the nature of items in the sample. For example, an arithmetic test consisting of only five problems, or one including only multiplication items, would be a poor measure of the individual's computational skill. A vocabulary test composed entirely of baseball terms would hardly provide a dependable estimate of a child's total range of vocabulary.

The *diagnostic* or *predictive value* of a psychological test depends on the degree to which it serves as an indicator of a relatively broad and significant area of behavior. Measurement of the behavior sample directly covered by the test is rarely, if ever, the goal of psychological testing. The child's knowledge of a particular list of 50 words is not, in itself, of great interest. Nor is the job applicant's performance on a specific set of 20 arithmetic problems of much importance. If, however, it can be demonstrated that there is a close correspondence between the child's knowledge of the word list and his total mastery of vocabulary, or between the applicant's score on the arithmetic problems and her computational performance on the job, then the tests are serving their purpose.

It should be noted in this connection that the test items need not resemble closely the behavior the test is to predict. It is necessary only that an empirical correspondence be demonstrated between the two. The degree of similarity between the test sample and the predicted behavior may vary widely. At one extreme, the test may coincide completely with a part of the behavior to be predicted. An example might be a foreign-vocabulary test in which the students are examined on 20 of the 50 new words they have studied; another example is provided by the road test taken prior to one's obtaining a driver's license. A lesser degree of similarity is illustrated by many vocational aptitude tests administered prior to job training, in which there is only a moderate resemblance between the tasks performed on the job and those incorporated in the test. At the other extreme one finds projective personality tests such as the Rorschach inkblot test, in which an attempt is made to predict from the respondent's associations to inkblots how he or she will react to other people, to emotionally toned stimuli, and to other complex, everyday-life situations. Despite their superficial differences, all these tests consist of samples of the individual's behavior. And each must prove its worth by an empirically demonstrated correspondence between the examinee's performance on the test and in other situations.

Whether the term "diagnosis" or the term "prediction" is employed in this connection also represents a minor distinction. Prediction commonly connotes a temporal estimate—for example, individuals' future performance on a job being forecast from their present test performance. In a broader sense, however, even the diagnosis of present condition, such as mental retardation or emotional disorder, implies a prediction of what the individual will do in situations other than the present test. It is logically simpler to regard all tests as behavior samples from which predictions regarding other behavior can be made. Different types of tests can then be characterized as variants of this basic pattern.

Another point that should be considered at the outset pertains to the concept of *capacity.* It is entirely possible, for example to devise a test for predicting how well an individual can learn French before he or she has even begun the study of French. Such a test would involve a sample of the types of behavior required to learn the new language, but would in itself presuppose no knowledge of French. It could then be said that this test measures the individual's "capacity" or "potentiality" for learning French. Such terms should, however, be used with caution in reference to psychological tests. Only in the sense that a present behavior sample can be used as an indicator of other, future behavior can we speak of a test measuring "capacity." No psychological test can do more than measure behavior. Whether such behavior can serve as an effective index of other behavior can be established only by empirical tryout.

Standardization. It will be recalled that in the initial definition a psychological test was described as a standardized measure. Standardization implies *uniformity of procedure* in administering and scoring the test. If the scores obtained by different persons are to be comparable, testing conditions must obviously be the same for all. Such a requirement is only a special application of the need for controlled conditions in all scientific observations. In a test situation, the single independent variable is often the individual being tested.

In order to secure uniformity of testing conditions, the test constructor provides detailed directions for administering each newly developed test. The formulation of directions is a major part of the standardization of a new test. Such standardization extends to the exact materials employed, time limits, oral instructions, preliminary demonstrations, ways of handling queries from test takers, and every other detail of the testing situation. Many other, more subtle factors may influence performance on certain tests. Thus, in giving instructions or presenting problems orally, consideration must be given to the rate of speaking, tone of voice, inflection, pauses, and facial expression. In a test involving the detection of absurdities, for example, the correct answer may be given away by smiling or pausing when the crucial word is read. Standardized testing procedure, from the examiner's point of view, will be discussed further in a later section of this chapter dealing with problems of test administration.

Another important step in the standardization of a test is the establishment of *norms.* Psychological tests have no predetermined standards of passing or failing; performance on each test is evaluated on the basis of empirical data. For most purposes, an individual's test score is interpreted by comparing it with the scores obtained by others on the same test. As its name implies, a norm is the normal or average performance. Thus, if normal 8-year-old children complete 12 out of 50 problems correctly on a particular arithmetic reasoning test, then the 8-year-old norm on this test corresponds to a score of 12. The latter is known as the raw score on the test. It may be expressed as number of correct items, time required to complete a task, number of errors, or some other objective measure appropriate to the content of the test. Such a raw score is meaningless until evaluated in terms of suitable interpretive data.

In the process of standardizing a test, it is administered to a large, representative sample of the type of persons for whom it is designed. This group, known as the standardization sample, serves to establish the norms. Such norms indicate not only the average performance but also the relative frequency of varying degrees of deviation above and below the average. It is thus possible to evaluate different degrees of superiority and inferiority. The specific ways in which such norms may be expressed will be considered in chapter 3. All permit the designation of the individual's position with reference to the normative or standardization sample.

It might also be noted that norms are established for personality tests in essentially the same way as for aptitude tests. The norm on a personality test is not necessarily the most desirable or "ideal" performance, any more than a perfect or errorless score is the norm on an aptitude test. On both types of tests, the norm corresponds to the performance of typical or average persons. On dominance–submission tests, for example, the norm falls at an intermediate point representing the degree of dominance or submission manifested by the average person. Similarly, in an emotional adjustment inventory, the norm does not ordinarily correspond to a complete absence of unfavorable or maladaptive responses. A few such responses occur in the majority of "normal" individuals in the standardization sample, and this number of maladaptive responses would thus represent the norm.

Objective Measurement of Difficulty. Reference to the definition of a psychological test with which this discussion opened will show that such a test was characterized as an objective as well as a standardized measure. In what specific ways are such tests objective? Some aspects of the objectivity of psychological tests have already been touched on in the discussion of standardization. Thus, the administration, scoring, and interpretation of scores are objective insofar as they are independent of the subjective judgment of the particular examiner. Any one test taker should theoretically obtain the identical score on a test regardless of who happens to be the examiner. This is not entirely so, of course, because perfect standardization and objectivity have not been attained in practice. But at least such objectivity is the goal of test construction and has been achieved to a reasonably high degree in most tests.

There are other major ways in which psychological tests can be properly described as objective. The determination of the difficulty level of an item or of a whole test is based on objective, empirical procedures. When Binet and Simon prepared their original, 1905 scale for the measurement of intelligence, they arranged the 30 items of the scale in order of increasing difficulty. Such difficulty was determined by trying out the items on 50 normal and a few mentally retarded children. The items correctly solved by the largest number of children were, *ipso facto*, taken to be the easiest; those passed by relatively few children were regarded as more difficult items. By this procedure, an empirical order of difficulty was established. This early example typifies the objective measurement of difficulty level, which is now common practice in psychological test construction.

Not only the arrangement but also the selection of items for inclusion in a test can be guided by the proportion of persons in the trial samples who pass each item. Thus, if there is a bunching of items at the easy or difficult end of the scale, some items will be discarded. Similarly, if items are sparse in certain portions of the difficulty range, new items can be added to fill the gaps. More technical aspects of item analysis are considered in chapter 7.

Reliability. Reliability refers to the degree to which a test is consistent and stable. In other words, reliability is the extent to which a test is effectively measuring what it is intended to measure. A test is said to be reliable if it is consistent within itself and across time.

As used in psychometrics, the term "reliability" basically means consistency. Test reliability is the consistency of scores obtained by the same persons when retested with the identical test or with an equivalent form of the test. If a child receives an IQ of 110 on Monday and an IQ of 80 when retested on Friday, it is obvious that little or no confidence can be put in either score. Similarly, if in one set of 50 words an examinee identifies 40 correctly, whereas in another, supposedly equivalent set she gets a score of only 20 right, then neither score can be taken as a dependable index of her verbal comprehension. To be sure, in both illustrations it is possible that only one of the two scores is in error, but this could be demonstrated only by further retests. From the given data, we can conclude only that both scores cannot be right. Whether one or neither is an adequate estimate of the individual's ability in vocabulary cannot be established without additional information.

Before a psychological test is released for general use, a thorough, objective check of its reliability should be carried out. The different types of test reliability, as well as methods of measuring each, will be considered in chapter 4. Reliability may be checked by comparing the scores obtained by the same test takers at different times, with different sets of items, with different examiners or scorers, or under any other relevant testing condition. It is essential to specify the type of reliability and the method employed to determine it, because the same test may vary in these different aspects. The number and nature of persons on whom reliability was checked should likewise be reported. With such information, test users can predict whether the test will be about equally reliable for the group with which they expect to use it, or whether it is likely to be more reliable or less reliable.

Validity. Undoubtedly the most important question to be asked about any psychological test concerns its validity—that is, the degree to which the test actually measures what it purports to measure. Validity provides a direct check on how well the test fulfills its function. The determination of validity usually requires independent, external *criteria* of whatever the test is designed to measure. For example, if a medical aptitude test is to be used in selecting promising applicants for medical school, ultimate success in medical school would be a criterion. In the process of validating such a test, it would be administered to a large group of students at the time of their admission to medical school. Some measure of performance in medical school would eventually be obtained for each student on the basis of grades, ratings by instructors, success or failure in completing training, and the like. Such a composite measure constitutes the criterion with which each student's initial test score is to be correlated. A high correlation, or *validity coefficient,* would signify that those individuals who scored high on the test had been relatively successful in medical school, whereas those scoring low on the test had done poorly in medical school. A low correlation would indicate little correspondence between test score and criterion measure and hence poor validity for the test. The validity coefficient enables us to determine how closely the criterion performance could have been predicted from the test scores.

In a similar manner, tests designed for other purposes can be validated against appropriate criteria. For instance, in an organizational context, one of the primary reasons why tests are used is to predict an employee's potential for future success. In such scenarios, a test is said to be valid when a high correlation exists between scores on the test and more criteria, or between scores on the tests and measures of job performance such as performance appraisal ratings and 360 degree feedback. By collecting test scores and criterion scores, the confidence on test scores to predict job success can be determined.

The reader may have noticed an apparent paradox in the concept of test validity. If it is necessary to follow up the test takers or in other ways to obtain independent measures of what the test is trying to predict, why not dispense with the test? The answer to this riddle is to be found in the distinction between the validation group on the one hand and the groups on which the test will eventually be employed for operational purposes on the other. Before the test is ready for use, its validity must be established on a representative sample of persons. The scores of these persons are not themselves employed for operational purposes but serve only in the process of testing the test. If the test proves valid by this method, it can then be used on other samples in the absence of criterion measures.

It might still be argued that we would need only to wait for the criterion measure to mature, to become available, on *any* group in order to obtain the information that the test is trying to predict. But such a procedure would be so wasteful of time and energy as to be prohibitive in most instances. Thus, we could determine which applicants will succeed on a job or which students will satisfactorily complete college by admitting all who apply (or a random sample of them) and waiting for subsequent developments! It is the very wastefulness of this procedure—and its deleterious emotional impact on individuals—that tests are designed to minimize. By means of tests, the person's present level of prerequisite skills, knowledge, and other relevant characteristics can be assessed with a determinable margin of error. The more valid and reliable the test, the smaller will be this margin of error.

The special problems encountered in determining the validity of different types of tests, as well as the specific criteria and statistical procedures employed, are discussed in chapters 5 and 6. One further point, however, should be considered at this time. Validity tells us more than the degree to which the test is fulfilling its function. It actually tells us *what* the test is measuring. By studying the validation data, we can objectively determine what the test is measuring. It would thus be more accurate to define validity as the extent to which we know what the test measures. The interpretation of test scores would undoubtedly be clearer and less ambiguous if tests were regularly named in terms of the empirically established relationships through which they had been validated. A tendency in this direction can be recognized in such test labels as "scholastic assessment test" and "personnel classification test" in place of the vague title "intelligence test."

WHY CONTROL THE USE OF PSYCHOLOGICAL TESTS?

"I wish to purchase Raven's Progressive Matrices. My daughter has to take it next week for admission to Grade XI and I would like to give her some practice so that she can pass."

"To assess our employees on the job competencies, we need a culture-free IQ test that measures each employee's innate potential and learning agility".

"Last night, I answered the questions of an intelligence test published in a magazine and I got an IQ of 80! - I think such psychological tests are silly."

"My roommate is doing her graduation in psychology. She gave me a personality test and I came out as a neurotic. I have been too upset to go to class ever since."

"You gave a personality test to our employees for understanding their behaviors and motivations. We would like to have the scores for each of the questions and their correct answers for our records."

These remarks are not imaginary. Each remark is based on a real incident, and the list could easily be extended by any psychologist. Such remarks illustrate the potential misuses or misinterpretations of psychological tests in such ways as to render the test worthless or to hurt the individual. Like any scientific instrument or precision tool, psychological tests must be properly used to be effective. In the hands of either the unscrupulous or the well-meaning but uninformed user, such tests can cause serious repercussions. There are primarily two reasons for controlling the use of psychological tests:

(a) To ensure that the test is used and administered by a qualified practitioner or a competent authority and that the scores are properly used.
(b) To prevent a general familiarity with the test content that would invalidate the test.

The need for a qualified practitioner is imperative when it comes to using psychological tests. There are three major aspects of a testing situation: a) selection of the test, b) administration and scoring, and c) interpretation of scores. For all these aspects, a qualified practitioner is required.

For instance, if you are considering hiring a consultant or a practitioner for an organization or business, it is important to evaluate his or her qualifications and experience beforehand. Professionals working in this field should, generally, have a research degree (an M.Phil. or a Ph.D.) in industrial or organizational psychology, or a related field along with several years of hands-on experience in the related areas. These consultants or practitioners may be found in psychology or business departments at universities and colleges. Others serve as full-time consultants, either working independently or as members of consulting organizations.

Typically, professional consultants in this domain will hold memberships in the American Psychological Association (APA), the British Psychological Society (BPS), the National Academy of Psychology (NAOP), or some other professional organizations. Most of these practitioners will either hold Certificates of Competence in the use of ability tests (formerly Level A) and personality tests (formerly Level B) given by deemed professional organizations such as the BPS and the European Federation of Psychological Association (EFPA), the NAOP, or the Certificates of Competence in the use of a specific test that are provided by the relevant test publishing and consulting organizations. For example, in India, Anahat is the official Indian representative and provides certifications for CPP's range of psychometric instruments like the Myers Briggs Type Indicator® (MBTI®), the FIRO-B®, and the CPI260™. Similarly, Pearson TalentLens develops and publishes tests, and provides certifications for their own range of psychometric instruments like the Watson-Glaser Critical Thinking Appraisal (W-GCTA), SOSIE personality assessment, and Golden Personality Type Profiler (GPTP).

The need for a qualified practitioner or consultant is vital because tests cannot be chosen like lawn mowers from a mail-order catalog. They cannot be evaluated by name, author, or other easy marks of identification. It requires no psychological training to consider factors such as cost, bulkiness, availability of supporting test materials, ease of transporting test materials, testing time required, and ease and rapidity of scoring. Information on these practical points can usually be obtained from a test catalog or from the company websites of the test publishers and should be taken into account in planning a testing-based intervention. For the test to serve its function, an evaluation of its technical merits in terms of characteristics, such as validity, reliability, difficulty level and norms, is essential. For example, is the test valid for the test user's intended purpose? Is it reliable and fair? Is it cost effective? Is the instrument likely to be viewed as fair and valid by the test takers? Such information is presented in the Technical Manual and the User's Guide of each test. With this information, a qualified practitioner or consultant can help the test users determine the appropriateness of tests for their particular purpose and its suitability for the type of persons on whom they plan to use them.

Furthermore, a qualified practitioner or a consultant is required to ensure that the test is properly administered, scored and interpreted as per the stated guidelines in the Technical Manual and the User's Guide of the test. Either the test users employ a consultant or they get themselves trained from these qualified practitioners and consultants to ensure that the test is deployed correctly. The qualifications and training required for a test user will depend on the nature and complexity of the test. The greater the complexity of the test, the more training a user will require. However, even simple-to-understand tests need trained staff to ensure valid results. Test users should be given ample time to learn their responsibilities before they administer and use a test.

Good test users use only those instruments that have proven efficacy for the task and follow the ethical guidelines for their use. They are able to identify the types of tests and questionnaires that provide the information they are looking for and are able to evaluate the quality and the research evidence supporting different measures, out of which they choose the most effective one. The users should consider how the scores will be interpreted and in what ways will they be used. For example, some background data regarding the individual being tested are essential in interpreting any test score. The same score may be obtained by different persons for different reasons. The conclusions drawn from such scores would therefore be quite dissimilar. Test users also need to provide appropriate information to the test takers, so that they can take an informed decision. For example, a test taker needs to know in general terms what the test will show about them and how the information will be used. The test user needs to make every effort to ensure that the test is taken under appropriate conditions and that the test taker receives feedback on the results if he or she wants.

Qualified Examiner. The need for a qualified examiner is evident in each of the three major aspects of the testing situation: selection of the test, administration and scoring, and interpretation of scores. Tests cannot be chosen like lawn mowers, from a mail-order catalog. They cannot be evaluated by name, author, or other easy marks of identification. To be sure, it requires no psychological training to consider such factors as cost, bulkiness and ease of transporting test materials, testing time required, and ease and rapidity of scoring. Information on these practical points can usually be obtained from a test catalog and should be taken into account in planning a testing program. For the test to serve its function, however, an evaluation of its technical merits in terms of such characteristics as validity, reliability, difficulty level, and norms is essential. Only in such a way can test users determine the appropriateness of any test for their particular purpose and its suitability for the type of persons with whom they plan to use it.

The introductory discussion of test standardization earlier in this chapter has already suggested the importance of a trained examiner. An adequate realization of the need to follow instructions precisely, as well as a thorough familiarity with the standard instructions, is required if the test scores obtained by different examiners are to be comparable or if any one individual's score is to be evaluated in terms of the published norms. Careful control of testing conditions is also essential. Similarly, incorrect or inaccurate scoring may render the test score worthless. In the absence of proper checking procedures, scoring errors are far more likely to occur than is generally realized.

The proper interpretation of test scores requires a thorough understanding of the test, the test taker, and the testing conditions. What is being measured can be objectively determined only by reference to the specific procedures through which the particular test was validated. Other information—pertaining to reliability, nature of the group on which norms were established, and the like—is likewise relevant. Some background data regarding the individual being tested are essential in interpreting any test score. The same score may be obtained by different persons for very different reasons. The conclusions to be drawn from such scores would therefore be quite dissimilar. Finally, some consideration must also be given to special factors that may have influenced a particular score, such as unusual testing conditions, the temporary emotional or physical state of the test taker, and the extent of the test taker's previous experience with tests.

Role of the Test User. A significant development in psychological testing in the 1980s and 1990s was the increasing recognition of the key role of the test user (Anastasi, 1990b). In this context, the test user is anyone who uses test scores as one source of information in reaching practical decisions. The test user may or may not be the examiner who administers and scores the test. Examples of test users are teachers, counselors, administrators in school systems, and personnel workers in industry or government. Most criticisms of tests are directed, not to intrinsic features of the tests, but to misuses of test results by inadequately qualified users. Some misuses stem from a desire for shortcuts, quick answers, and simple routine solutions for real-life problems. Time pressure from work overload may encourage reliance on such expedients. Probably the most frequent cause of test misuse, however, is insufficient or faulty knowledge about testing (Eyde, Moreland, Robertson, Primoff, & Most, 1988; Moreland, Eyde, Robertson, Primoff, & Most, 1995; Tyler & Miller, 1986).

Special committees of national professional organizations, working jointly with test publishers, have been giving increasing attention to the prevention of test misuse. A notable example is the project conducted by the Test User Qualifications Working Group, familiarly known by the delightful acronym TUQWoG (Eyde et al., 1988). The chief goal of TUQWoG was to develop an empirical, data-based set of essential qualifications for users of different types of tests that test publishers could incorporate into their test purchaser qualification forms. Through five years of intensive, nationwide research, the TUQWoG project developed an impressive database. Some publishers have already begun to use the results in their purchaser qualification forms. A second working group was subsequently formed whose purpose was to use the available TUQWoG database to develop guidelines and training materials for test users. Known by the modified acronym of TUTWoG (With a T for training), it had as its first product a casebook of common test misuses to guard against (Eyde et al., 1993). The cases are based on specific instances of misuses actually observed in a variety of settings that were submitted in the project's wide-ranging survey. A later summary is given by Moreland et al. (1995).

Security of Test Content and Communication of Test Information. For the test results to be fair and valid, no test taker should have an opportunity to view a test beforehand. In case of paper-pencil test, ensuring security of test content is not restricted to test developers or test publishers. It is applicable for the users of the test as well. Ideally, all material related to the test must be stored in locked rooms or cabinets when not in use, and accounting must be done for all materials that are used during the testing session. Test takers should not take any item from the testing room, including rough papers used by them during the test. In an organizational or business set-up, most of the tests are computerized. The test users create a unique login identification key along with a unique password for each of the test taker to ensure security of the test content. In such cases, all databases should be secure and password protected, whether on a computer or an internet server. When computerized tests are used over a long period of time, it becomes increasingly likely that some test questions will leak out. To maintain security, test developers must periodically introduce new alternate forms of test questions.

It must be ensured that the security of specific test content should not interfere with the effective communication of testing information to test takers, concerned professionals, and the general public. Such communication serves several purposes:

1. It tends to dispel any mystery that may be associated with testing, thereby helping to correct the prevalent misconceptions about what tests are designed to do and what their scores mean. Several publications of the major test publishers are designed for this purpose.

2. It provides technical procedures on how tests are to be constructed and evaluated, and presents the relevant data about reliability, validity, and other psychometric properties of the test. This type of information is typically included in the Technical Manual and the User's Guide prepared for each test and is available to anyone interested.
3. It familiarizes the test takers with the testing procedures, dispels anxiety, and ensures that each test taker will perform to the best of his or her ability. Several explanatory booklets have been prepared for this purpose, some being general in nature while some meant for specific tests. These materials will be discussed later in this chapter.
4. It provides feedback to the test takers regarding their own performance on any test they have taken. Psychologists have given considerable attention to the most useful and meaningful ways of conveying such information in different contexts. Appropriate procedures are examined in chapters 17 and 18.

TEST ADMINISTRATION

The basic rationale of testing involves generalization from the behavior sample observed in the testing situation to behavior manifested in other, nontest situations. A test score should help us to predict how the client will feel and act outside the clinic, how the student will achieve in college courses, and how the applicant will perform on the job. Any influences that are specific to the test situation constitute error variance and reduce test validity. It is therefore important to identify any test-related influences that may limit or impair the generalizability of test results.

A whole volume could easily be devoted to a discussion of desirable procedures of test administration. But such a survey falls outside the scope of this book. Moreover, it is more practicable to acquire such techniques within specific settings, because no one person would normally be concerned with all forms of testing, from the examination of infants to the clinical testing of psychotic patients or the administration of a mass testing program for military personnel. The present discussion will therefore deal principally with the common rationale of test administration rather than with specific questions of implementation. An excellent example of implementation can be found in the comprehensive discussion of the individual assessment of children given by Sattler (1988, chap. 5).

Advance Preparation of Examiners. The most important single requirement for good testing procedure is advance preparation. In testing there can be no emergencies. Special efforts must therefore be made to foresee and forestall emergencies. Only in this way can uniformity of procedure be assured.

Advance preparation for the testing session takes many forms. Memorizing the exact verbal instructions is essential in most individual testing. Even in a group test in which the instructions are read to the test takers, some previous familiarity with the statements to be read prevents misreading and hesitation and permits a more natural, informal manner during test administration. The preparation of test materials is another important preliminary step. In individual testing and especially in the administration of performance tests, such preparation involves the actual layout of the necessary materials to facilitate subsequent use with a minimum of search or fumbling. Materials should generally be placed on a table near the testing table so that they are within easy reach of the examiner but do not distract the test taker. When complex apparatus is employed, frequent periodic checking and calibration may be necessary. In group testing, all test blanks, answer sheets, special pencils, or other materials needed should be carefully counted, checked, and arranged in advance of the testing day.

Thorough familiarity with the specific testing procedure is another important prerequisite in both individual and group testing. For individual testing, supervised training in the administration of the particular test is usually essential. Depending upon the nature of the test and the type of persons to be examined, such training may require from a few demonstration and practice sessions to more than a year of instruction. For group testing, and especially in large-scale projects, the preparation may include advance briefing of examiners and proctors, so that each is fully informed about the functions he or she is to perform. In general, the examiner reads the instructions, takes care of timing, and is in charge of the group in any one testing room. The proctors hand out and collect test materials, make certain that instructions are followed, answer the individual questions of test takers within the limitations specified in the manual, and prevent cheating.

Testing Conditions. Standardized procedure applies not only to verbal instructions, timing, materials, and other aspects of the tests themselves but also to the testing environment. Some attention should be given to the selection of a suitable testing room. This room should be free from undue noise and distraction and should provide adequate lighting, ventilation, seating facilities, and working space for test takers. Special steps should also be taken to prevent interruptions during the test. Posting a sign on the door to indicate that testing is in progress is effective, provided all personnel have learned that such a sign means no admittance under any circumstances. In the testing of large groups, locking the doors or posting an assistant outside each door may be necessary to prevent the entrance of latecomers.

It is important to realize the extent to which testing conditions may influence scores. Even apparently minor aspects of the testing situation may appreciably alter performance. Such a condition as the use of desks or of chairs with desk arms, for example, proved to be significant in a group testing project with high school students, the groups using desks tending to obtain higher scores (T. L. Kelley, 1943; Traxler & Hilkert, 1942). There is also evidence to show that the type of answer sheet employed may affect test scores (F. O. Bell, Hoff, & Hoyt, 1964). Because of the establishment of independent test-scoring and data-processing agencies that provide their own machine-scorable answer sheets, examiners sometimes administer group tests with answer sheets other than those used in the standardization sample. In the absence of empirical verification, the equivalence of these answer sheets cannot be assumed. In testing children below the fifth grade, the use of *any* separate answer sheet may significantly lower test scores (Cashen & Ramseyer, 1969; Ramseyer & Cashen, 1971). At these grade levels, having the child mark the answers in the test booklet itself is generally preferable.

Even more significant at any age level are the possible differences between paper-and-pencil and computer administration of the same tests. Considerable attention has been devoted to the effect of such a difference in test administration on norms, reliability, and validity, in relation to the nature of the test and the population of test takers. Special professional guidelines have been formulated to aid test users in assessing the comparability of test scores obtained under the two types of administration (Butcher, 1987; Hofer & Green, 1985).

Many other, more subtle testing conditions have been shown to affect performance on ability as well as on personality tests. Whether the examiner is a stranger or someone familiar to the test takers may make a significant difference in test scores (Sacks, 1952; Tsudzuki, Hata, & Kuze, 1957). In another study, the general manner and behavior of the examiner, as illustrated by smiling, nodding, and making such comments as "good," or "fine," were shown to have a decided effect on test results (Wickes, 1956). In a projective test requiring the respondent to write stories to fit given pictures, the presence of the examiner in the room tended to inhibit the inclusion of strongly emotional content in the stories (Bernstein, 1956). In the administration of a typing test, job applicants typed at a significantly faster rate when tested alone than when tested in groups of two or more (Kirchner, 1966).

Examples could readily be multiplied. The implications are threefold. First, follow standardized procedures to the most minute detail. It is the responsibility of the test author and publisher to describe such procedures fully and clearly in the test manual. Second, record any unusual testing conditions, however minor. Third, take testing conditions into account when interpreting test results. In the extensive assessment of a person through individual testing, an experienced examiner may occasionally depart from the standardized test procedure in order to elicit additional information for special reasons. In such a case, the test results can no longer be interpreted in terms of the test norms. Under these circumstances, the test stimuli are used only for qualitative exploration; and the responses should be treated in the same way as any other informal behavioral observations or interview data.

Introducing the Test: Rapport and Test-Taker Orientation. In test administration, "rapport" refers to the examiner's efforts to arouse the test takers' interest in the test, elicit their cooperation, and encourage them to respond in a manner appropriate to the objectives of the test. In ability tests, the objective calls for careful concentration on the given tasks and for putting forth one's best efforts to perform well. In self-report personality inventories, the objective calls for frank and honest responses to questions about one's usual behavior; in certain projective tests, it calls for full reporting of associations evoked by the stimuli, without any censoring or editing of content. Still other kinds of tests may require other approaches. But in all instances, the examiner endeavors to motivate the respondents to follow the instructions as fully and conscientiously as they can.

The training of examiners covers techniques for the establishment of rapport as well as those more directly related to test administration. In establishing rapport, as in other testing procedures, uniformity of conditions is essential for comparability of results. If a child is given a coveted prize whenever she solves a test problem correctly, her performance cannot be directly compared with the norms or with that of other children who are motivated only with the standard verbal encouragement or praise. Any deviation from standard motivating conditions for a particular test should be noted and taken into account in interpreting performance.

Although rapport can be more fully established in individual testing, steps can also be taken in group testing to motivate test takers and relieve their anxiety. Specific techniques for establishing rapport vary with the nature of the test and with the age and other characteristics of the persons tested. In testing preschool children, special factors to be considered include shyness with strangers, dis tractibility, and negativism. A friendly, cheerful, and relaxed manner on the part of the examiner helps to reassure the child. The shy, timid child needs more preliminary time to become familiar with the surroundings. For this reason, it is better for the examiner not to be too demonstrative at the outset, but rather to wait until the child is ready to make the first contact. Test periods should be brief, and the tasks should be varied and intrinsically interesting to the child. The testing should be presented to the child as a game and his curiosity aroused before each new task is introduced. A certain flexibility of procedure is necessary at this age level because of possible refusals, loss of interest, and other manifestations of negativism.

Children in the first two or three grades of elementary school present many of the same testing problems as the preschool child. The game approach is still the most effective way of arousing interest in the test. The older schoolchild can usually be motivated through an appeal to the competitive spirit and the desire to do well on tests. When testing children from educationally disadvantaged backgrounds or from different cultures, however, the examiner cannot assume that they will be motivated to excel on academic tasks to the same extent as children in the standardization sample. This problem and others pertaining to the testing of persons with dissimilar experiential backgrounds are considered further in chapters 9, 12, and 18.

Special motivational problems may be encountered in testing emotionally disturbed persons, prisoners, or juvenile delinquents. Especially when examined in an institutional setting, such persons are likely to manifest a number of unfavorable attitudes, such as suspicion, insecurity, fear, or cynical indifference. Special conditions in their past experiences are also likely to influence their test performance adversely. As a result of early failures and frustrations in school, for example, they may have developed feelings of hostility and inferiority toward academic tasks, which the tests resemble. The experienced examiner makes special efforts to establish rapport under these conditions. In any event, he or she must be sensitive to these special difficulties and take them into account in interpreting and explaining test performance.

In testing any school-age child or adult, one should bear in mind that every test presents an implied threat to the individual's prestige. Some reassurance should therefore be given at the outset. It is helpful to explain, for example, that no one is expected to finish or to get all the items correct. The test taker might otherwise experience a mounting sense of failure as he or she advances to the more difficult items or is unable to finish any subtest within the time allowed.

It is also desirable to eliminate the element of surprise from the test situation as far as possible, because the unexpected and unknown are likely to produce anxiety. Many group tests include a preliminary explanatory statement that is read to the group by the examiner. An even better procedure is to provide each test taker in advance with materials that explain the purpose and nature of the tests, offer general suggestions on how to take tests, and contain a few sample items. Such explanatory booklets are regularly available to participants in many large-scale testing programs, such as those conducted by the College Board.

Adult testing presents some additional problems. Unlike the schoolchild, the adult is not so likely to work hard at a task merely because it is assigned. It therefore becomes more important to "sell" the purpose of the tests to the adult, although high school and college students also respond to such an appeal. Cooperation of test takers can usually be secured by convincing them that it is in their own interests to obtain a valid score—that is, a score correctly indicating what they can do rather than overestimating or underestimating their abilities. Most persons will understand that an incorrect decision, which might result from invalid test scores, would mean subsequent failure, loss of time, and frustration for them. This approach can serve not only to motivate test takers to try their best on ability tests but also to reduce faking and encourage frank reporting on personality inventories, because respondents realize that they themselves would otherwise be the losers. It is certainly not in the best interests of individuals to be admitted to a course of study for which they lack the prerequisite skills and knowledge or assigned to a job they cannot perform or would find uncongenial.

Common Instructions for Most of the Personality Assessment – Sample. Here are some questions to see how you feel about certain situations. There are no "right" or "wrong" answers because you have a right to your own views. To get the appropriate advice, you should answer these questions accurately and honestly:

- Answer every question without hesitation and as honestly as possible. Do not mark what seems "the right thing to say" to impress others.
- Give the first natural answer that comes to your mind, and do not spend too much time on any one question.
- Do not skip any question. Answer every question, although some questions may not apply to you very well or may not interest you, yet give your best guess.
- Remember that answers given here are kept confidential. Answers to each question are not inspected. So, give answers which are true for you. It is best to mark what you really think.

SITUATIONAL FACTORS THAT AFFECT TEST PERFORMANCE

Psychological testing is a dynamic process influenced by many factors. Although qualified practitioners and consultants strive to ensure that test results accurately reflect the attributes being assessed by following administration guidelines. Nevertheless, at times, the characteristics and the motivation of the test taker may affect the test performance. For instance, a bright student may perform poorly on a speeded ability test because of test anxiety; an intelligent candidate may perform poorly on an IQ test because of his discomfort with abstract reasoning questions; a sane murderer might seek to appear mentally ill on a personality inventory to avoid prosecution; a student of average caliber might undergo coaching to perform better on an aptitude test; an applicant may attempt to give socially desirable responses on a selection test to get a job. Some people are not motivated and are indifferent towards their performance on psychological tests. In all of these instances, the test results may be inaccurate because of the distorting and filtering of the test taker's characteristics such as text anxiety, malingering and coaching.

Test Anxiety. The test anxiety construct is considered as a situation-specific trait accounting for individual differences in the extent to which people find the test-taking environment as threatening (Spielberger & Vagg, 1995). One of the most common reasons for test anxiety is that one's performance is judged by others, leading to a fear of failure among the test takers. Spielberger's (1966) notion of 'ego threat' includes threats to self-esteem and the consequences of performance success or failure, in addition to potential derogatory judgment by others. Furthermore, Zeidner (1998) outlines three components of test anxiety that explains this concept:

- Cognitive: The negative thoughts and depreciating self-statements that occur during assessments (e.g. 'If I fail this exam, my whole life is a failure') and the performance-inhibiting difficulties that may arise from anxiety (e.g. recalling facts and difficulty in reading and understanding questions)
- Affective: The person's appraisal of their physiological state (such as tension, tight muscles, and trembling)
- Behavioral: Poor study skills, avoidance and procrastination of work

Test anxiety is a serious problem for many students. In India, the main documented cause of anxiety among school children and adolescents is the parents' high expectations for academic achievement (Deb, 2001). Furthermore, in India, this is amplified as scores on various tests are the main determining criteria for securing admission to best senior secondary schools, a preferred academic stream, and an occupation of choice. Moreover, competition among students for quality education and high profile jobs is high as the demand surpasses supply. Therefore, there is a constant pressure on them to perform well in all spheres of life.

An extensive body of research has indicated that test anxiety is negatively correlated with school achievement, aptitude test scores, and measures of intelligence. Test anxiety among students has been negatively associated with test performance, achievement of degrees, and the selection of occupations (Topp, 1989). Students at all levels who suffer from test anxiety choose and pursue careers which involve infrequent evaluations, and which, consequently, may not fully challenge their cognitive abilities (Krohne and Laux, 1982). However, the interpretation of these correlational findings is not straightforward. There may be a possibility that students develop test anxiety because of a history of performing poorly in tests. That is, the decrements in performance may precede and lead to cause the text anxiety. In support of this interpretation, Paulman and Kennelly (1984) found that independent of their anxiety, many test anxious students display ineffective test taking in academic settings. Such students would perform poorly in tests irrespective of their anxiety. In some situations, it may be fair to say that test anxious students have poor study habits that predispose them to poor test performance. The test anxiety of such test takers could be partly due to their lifelong frustration over mediocre test results.

Several investigators have compared test performance under conditions designed to evoke "anxious" and "relaxed" states. Mandler and Sarason (1952), for example, found that ego-involving instructions, such as telling test takers that everyone is expected to finish in the time allotted, had a beneficial effect on the performance of low-anxious persons, but a deleterious effect on high-anxious persons. Other studies have likewise found a relation between testing conditions and such individual characteristics such as anxiety level and achievement motivation (Lawrence, 1962; Paul & Eriksen, 1964). It appears that the relation between anxiety and test performance is non-linear—a slight amount of anxiety being beneficial while a large amount is detrimental. Individuals who are customarily low on anxiety benefit from test conditions that arouse some anxiety, while those who are customarily high on anxiety perform better under more relaxed conditions.

Research on the nature, measurement, and treatment of test anxiety has been continuing at an ever-increasing pace. With regard to the nature of test anxiety, two important components have been identified namely emotionality and worry. The emotionality component comprises feelings and physiological reactions such as tension and increasing heartbeat. The worry or cognitive component includes negative self-oriented thoughts, such as expectation of doing poorly and concern about the consequences of failure. These thoughts draw attention away from the task-oriented behavior required by the test and thereby disrupt performance. Both these components are measured by one of the key test anxiety inventories called the Test Anxiety Inventory developed by C. D. Spielberger and his co-workers in 1980. In India, several inventories based on the same principles have been developed. Some of these inventories are State Trait Anxiety Test by Sanjay Vohra, Anxiety Scale (English and Hindi) by D. N. Srivastava and G. Tiwari, and Sinha's Comprehensive Anxiety Test.

Treatment of test anxiety has been one of the important concerns in test anxiety research. Just as there have been different ways of conceptualizing the problem of test anxiety, there have also been different ways of approaching its treatment. With the early understanding of test anxiety in terms of a physiological or emotional phenomenon, treatment efforts were directed towards reducing the physiological arousal through behavioral methods. Later, treatments moved more in the direction of cognitive and combined approaches. There is a serious lack of research on test anxiety reduction programs for primary, secondary, and high school students, and this concept is quite new in India. However, a meta-analysis study (Ergene, 2003) indicated that on measures of anxiety reduction, the average individual completing treatment was found to be better than 74 percent of those individuals who did not receive treatment. The treatment of test anxiety has been quite successful in reducing the test anxiety level of clients. The most effective treatments appear to be those that combine skill-focused approaches with behavior or cognitive approaches. Furthermore, individually conducted programs along with programs that combined individual and group counseling produced the greatest changes.

Test anxiety is a complex phenomenon with multiple causes and the relative contribution of different causes varies with individuals. To be effective, treatment programs should be adapted to individual needs. Further, test anxiety is only one manifestation of a more general set of conditions that reduce the individual's effectiveness as a learner.

Malingering. Sometimes, the test takers try to perform in an inadequate or unrepresentative manner to give responses that puts them in a favorable light. For instance, in case of a job selection test, a candidate may respond according to how they think a successful candidate would respond; an individual who is seeking benefits from rehabilitation from social agencies will consciously fake and perform poorly in personality and ability tests. Most of the well-developed assessments have questions that have a built-in lie detector or has questions for which the preferred responses are not obvious. Furthermore, it is advisable to gather evidence outside the testing situation such as corroboration of others, situational assessments, or task-performance methods to validate the results of the tests. It is best to inform the test takers that an assessment is able to detect lying and an attempt to sabotage the results will not prove beneficial. There are various other sources of malingering and it will be discussed in the later chapters.

Coaching. Coaching refers to either undertaking training to improve the scores on a test or take practice tests that consist of the questions in a format that are similar to the main test. Coaching and its effect on the test scores are more relevant in the domain of aptitude tests or qualifying examinations. Prospective applicants to graduate colleges and professional schools are, understandably, interested in improving their scores on qualifying examinations. For example, a consequence of the increasing importance of large-scale nationwide testing for management courses, such as Graduate Management Admission Test (GMAT), Common Admission Test (CAT) and Management Aptitude Test (MAT), has been the publication of test coaching booklets and establishment of training centers that purport to increase a person's score on these tests. Whether coaching has a significant effect on scores of these and other qualifying examinations has been a topic of debate for many years. It is an important issue, if it can be proved that coaching can improve test results, for aspiring candidates who do not have the means to afford coaching will be deprived of the opportunity seized by their more affluent peers. Furthermore, it will put an additional pressure on the middle income group parents to provide training to their children in these coaching institutions, leading to many other psychological and societal problems.

In case of SAT, literature review of studies conducted during the past two decades has shown that intensive drills on questions, similar to those on the SAT, may yield gains of 25 to 32 points on both the verbal and the mathematical sections. However, students who retook the SAT have shown gains that are nearly as high (Donlon, 1984). It may be fair to assume that the 25–32 point gain may arise due to correctly answering two to four questions in the mathematical section and one to two questions in the verbal section.

If these findings are applied in the Indian context, it will be observed that most of the applicants experience anxiety over mathematical or numerical subjects than other subjects; and hence, brushing up on specific areas such as geometry and algebra, and speeded calculation techniques just before taking a qualifying exam may be the reason for enhanced scores. Furthermore, the test taking procedure can also be a likely cause for increase in performance scores. Skipping difficult questions and coming back to them after completing the rest of the questions in that section, looking for reasonable answers by reading comprehension passages, making informed guesses, etc. may not work wonders in the long run but are likely to improve the scores. In any case, the test developing agencies are aware of the impacts of coaching and they usually upgrade the existing questions or develop new type of questions that are not susceptible to coaching and short-term drills or instructions (Powers, 1993).

The decision to seek coaching for any qualifying or entrance examination is still the one that students and their parents must make individually, but this deliberation ought to be based on the best evidence available.

EFFECTS OF TRAINING ON TEST PERFORMANCE

In evaluating the effects of training or practice on test scores, a fundamental question is whether the improvement is limited to the specific items included in the test or whether it extends to the broader behavior domain that the test is designed to assess (Anastasi, 1981a, 1981b). The answer to this question represents the difference between coaching and education. Obviously, any educational experience the individual undergoes, either formal or informal, in or out of school, should be reflected in her or his performance on tests that sample the relevant aspects of behavior. Such broad influences will in no way invalidate the test, insofar as the test score presents an accurate picture of the individual's standing in the abilities under consideration. The difference is, of course, one of degree. Influences cannot be classified as either narrow or broad but obviously vary widely in scope, from those affecting only a single administration of a single test, through those affecting performance on all items of a certain type, to those influencing the individual's performance in the large majority of activities. From the standpoint of effective testing, however, a workable distinction can be made. Thus, it can be stated that a test score is invalidated only when a particular experience raises the score without appreciably affecting the behavior domain that the test is designed to measure.

Coaching. The effects of coaching on test scores have been widely investigated. Several early studies were conducted by British psychologists, with special reference to the effects of practice and coaching on the tests formerly used in assigning 11-year-old children to different types of secondary schools (Yates et al., 1953–1954). As might be expected, the extent of improvement depends on the ability and earlier educational experiences of the test takers, the nature of the tests, and the amount and type of coaching provided. Individuals with deficient educational backgrounds are more likely to benefit from special coaching than are those who have had superior educational opportunities and are already prepared to do well on the tests. It is obvious, too, that the closer the resemblance between test content and coaching material, the greater will be the improvement in test scores. On the other hand, the more closely instruction is restricted to specific test content, the less likely is improvement to extend to criterion performance. Many coaching studies, moreover, yield ambiguous and uninterpretable results because of serious methodological shortcomings (Anastasi, 1981a; Bond, 1989; Messick, 1980a). Chief among these shortcomings is the failure to employ a non-coached control group that is truly comparable to the coached group. Students who enroll in commercial coaching programs, for example, are self-selected and tend to differ from those in the control group in initial ability, motivation, and other personal characteristics that affect test performance. In experimental designs that employ pretests and posttests, furthermore, it is difficult to ensure that test takers are equally motivated to do well on both tests; this is especially true if one test is given in a regular administration, the other in a special administration for practice or for research purposes only.

The College Entrance Examination Board has been concerned about the spread of ill-advised commercial coaching courses for college applicants. To clarify the issue, the College Board has conducted several well-controlled experiments to determine the effect of such coaching on the Scholastic Aptitude Test (SAT) and has surveyed the results of similar studies by other, independent investigators (Donlon, 1984; Messick, 1980a, 1981; Messick & Jungeblut, 1981). These studies covered a variety of coaching methods and included students in both public and private high schools. Samples of minority students from both urban and rural areas were also investigated. The conclusion from all these studies is that intensive drill on items similar to those on the SAT is unlikely to produce appreciably greater gains than occur when students are retested with the SAT after a year of regular high school instruction.

It should also be noted that in their test construction procedures, such organizations as the College Board and the Graduate Record Examination Board investigate the susceptibility of new item types to coaching (Evans & Pike, 1973; Powers, 1983; Powers & Swinton, 1984; Swinton & Powers, 1985). Item types on which performance can be appreciably raised by short-term drill or instruction of a narrowly limited nature are not retained in the operational forms of the test. An obvious example would be the type of problem that requires a simple, insightful solution, that, once attained, can be applied directly to solving all similar problems. When encountered in the future, such problems would thus test recall rather than problem solving skills. Another example is provided by complex item types using novel or unfamiliar material and requiring lengthy and involved instructions (Powers, 1986).

Coaching, in the narrow, traditional sense, is designed to develop highly restricted skills that may be of little use in life activities. Similarly, the practice of "teaching to the test" tends to concentrate on the particular sample of skills and knowledge covered by the test, rather than on the broader knowledge domain that the test tries to assess. The so called "truth in testing," or disclosure, laws that require the general release of test forms after a single administration also encourage a focus on test-specific skills of limited applicability. Finally, insofar as coaching may be available to some test takers and not to others, it tends to introduce individual differences in narrowly defined test-taking skills, thereby reducing the diagnostic value of the test.

Test Sophistication. The effects of test sophistication, or sheer test-taking practice, are also relevant in this connection. In studies with alternate forms of the same test, there is a tendency for the second score to be higher. Significant mean gains have been reported when alternate forms were administered in immediate succession or after intervals ranging from one day to three years (Donlon, 1984; Droege, 1966; Peel, 1951, 1952). Similar results have been obtained with normal and intellectually gifted schoolchildren, high school and college students, and employee samples. Data on the distribution of gains to be expected on a retest with a parallel form should be provided in test manuals, and allowance for such gains should be made when interpreting test scores.

Nor are score gains limited to alternate forms. The individual who has had extensive prior experience in taking standardized tests enjoys a certain advantage in test performance over one who is taking her or his first test (Millman, Bishop, & Ebel, 1965; Rodger, 1936). Part of this advantage stems from having overcome an initial feeling of strangeness, as well as from having developed more self confidence and better test-taking attitudes. Part is the result of a certain amount of overlap in the type of content and functions covered by many tests. Specific familiarity with common item types and practice in the use of objective answer sheets may also improve performance slightly. It is particularly important to take test sophistication into account when comparing the scores obtained by persons whose test-taking experience may have varied widely. For computer-administered testing, attention should be given to the test taker's familiarity with this form of test administration (Hofer & Green, 1985).

Short orientation and practice sessions can be quite effective in equalizing test sophistication (Anastasi, 1981a; Wahlstrom & Boersman, 1968). Such familiarization training reduces the effects of prior differences in test-taking experience as such. Since these individual differences are specific to the test situation, their diminution should permit a more valid assessment of the broad behavior domain the test is designed to measure. This approach is illustrated by the College Board publication entitled *Taking the SAT I: Reasoning Test,* a booklet distributed to all college applicants who register for this test. The booklet offers suggestions for effective test-taking behavior, illustrates and explains the different types of items included in the test, and reproduces a complete form of the test, which students are advised to take under standard timing conditions and to score with the given key. A similar booklet, *Taking the SAT II: Subject Tests,* illustrates and explains items from different subject-matter tests.

The Graduate Record Examinations (GRE) also provide test familiarization materials. The *Information Bulletin* distributed to all applicants includes an explanation of sample items from the General Test, as well as a complete previously administered test with its scoring key. Additional test forms are published regularly for this test in book form *(Practicing to Take the GRE General Test).* Similar practice booklets are available that provide individual GRE tests in several subject-matter areas.

The upsurge of test familiarization materials appearing in the 1980s and 1990s is not limited to the printed medium but includes transparencies, slides, films, videocassettes, and computer software. Many of these materials have been developed and are distributed by Educational Testing Service. A few are designed for use with specific tests, as illustrated by a slide show to accompany *Taking the SAT* and others on the interpretation of scores on the SAT and on the College Board achievement tests. A computer program to aid in understanding SAT scores is also available. A relatively elaborate test-preparation software package has been developed for students planning to take the GRE General Test. By means of an interactive computer program, this package provides sample items; a simulated, timed testing situation; explanations for incorrectly answered items; and an analysis of the test taker's strengths and weaknesses.

Other materials (print, films, multimedia packages, computer software) are designed for more general test-taking orientation, spanning a range from primary school children to adults. An example is *On Your Own: Preparing for a Standardized Test* (1987), a video disk for use by high school students individually or in groups. A simple, comprehensive guide in book form is *How to Take a Test: Doing Your Best* (Dobbin, 1984). Test orientation aids have also been prepared by a few major commercial test publishers and by government agencies. The latter is illustrated by the set of materials for use with the General Aptitude Test Battery (GATB) of the U.S. Employment Service.

Instruction in Broad Cognitive Skills. Some researchers have been exploring the opposite approach to the improvement of test performance. Their goal is the development of widely applicable intellectual skills, work habits, and problem-solving strategies. The effects of such interventions should be manifested in *both* test scores and criterion performance, such as college courses. In accordance with the distinction introduced at the opening of this section, this type of program is designed to provide education rather than coaching. Some of these investigators have been working with educable mentally retarded children and adolescents (Babad & Budoff, 1974; Belmont & Butterfield, 1977; A. L. Brown, 1974; Budoff & Corman, 1974; Campione & Brown, 1979, 1987; Feuerstein, 1979, 1980; Feuerstein, Rand, Jensen, Kaniel, & Tzuriel, 1987). Others have concentrated on college and professional school students from educationally disadvantaged backgrounds (Linden & Whimbey, 1990; Whimbey, 1975, 1977, 1980).

Many of the training procedures employed in these programs are designed to develop effective problem-solving behavior, such as careful analysis of problems or questions; consideration of all alternatives, relevant details, and implications in arriving at a solution; deliberate rather than impulsive formulation or choice of a solution; and the application of high standards in evaluating one's own performance. These are obviously strategies that should improve one's intellectual functioning not only on tests but also in academic work and in many other everyday-life activities that depend on school learning. A crucial question, however, pertains to the degree of transfer and generalizability of effects beyond the types of contents and settings employed in the training. Results thus far reported are promising. But the programs are still in an exploratory stage, and more research is needed to establish the breadth and durability of the improvement attained.

Overview. We have considered three types of pretest training that are quite dissimilar in their objectives. How do these types of training affect the validity of a test and its practical usefulness as an assessment instrument? The first was coaching, in the sense of intensive, massed drill on items similar to those on the test. It was noted that well-constructed tests choose item types so as to minimize their susceptibility to such drill; and they also protect the security of specific test items. Insofar as such coaching might improve test performance, it would do so without a corresponding improvement in criterion behavior. Hence, it would thereby reduce test validity. The test would become a less effective measure of the broad abilities it was designed to assess and a less accurate means of ascertaining whether the individual has developed the skills and knowledge prerequisite for success in the criterion situation.

Test orientation procedures, on the other hand, are designed to rule out or equalize differences in prior test-taking experience. Like the effects of coaching, these differences represent conditions that affect test scores as such, without necessarily being reflected in the broader behavior domain to be assessed. Hence, the test orientation procedures should make the test a more valid instrument by reducing the influence of test-specific factors.

Finally, training in broadly applicable cognitive skills, if effective, should improve the trainee's ability to cope with subsequent intellectual tasks. This improvement will and should be reflected in test performance. Insofar as both test scores and criterion performance are improved, such training leaves test validity unchanged; but it enhances the individual's chances of attaining desired goals.

SOURCES OF INFORMATION ABOUT TESTS

Psychological testing is in a state of rapid change. There are shifting orientations, a constant stream of new tests, revised forms of old tests, and additional data that may refine or alter the interpretation of scores on existing tests. The accelerating rate of change, together with the vast number of available tests, makes it impracticable to survey specific tests in any single text. More intensive coverage of testing instruments and problems in special areas can be found in books dealing with the use of tests in such fields as counseling, clinical practice, personnel selection, and education. References to such publications are given in the appropriate chapters of this book. In order to keep abreast of current developments, however, anyone working with tests needs to be familiar with more direct sources of information about tests.

One of the most important sources is the *Mental Measurements Yearbook* (MMY) established by Oscar K. Buros and edited by him through 1978. Since 1985, the MMY has been published by the Buros Institute of Mental Measurements at the University of Nebraska. This series of yearbooks covers nearly all commercially available psychological, educational, and vocational tests published in English. The coverage is especially complete for paper-and-pencil tests. Each yearbook includes tests published during a specified period, thus supplementing rather than supplanting the earlier yearbooks. The earliest publications in this series were merely bibliographies of tests. Beginning in 1938, the yearbook assumed its current form, which includes critical reviews of the tests by one or more test experts, as well as a complete list of published references pertaining to each test. Routine information regarding publisher, price, forms, and age of persons for whom the test is suitable is also regularly given. The current plan is to publish a new MMY every two or three years, with a supplement published between year books.

The test entries of the MMY, together with the critical reviews, are now available electronically through SilverPlatter (see Appendix B). The database begins with the entries in the ninth MMY and is updated every six months. Another publication of the Buros Institute is *Tests in Print,* now in its fourth volume (TIP-IV, 1994), edited by L. L. Murphy, Conoley, and Impara. This publication provides cumulative coverage of all known commercially published tests in English, together with factual information and reference lists. Each successive edition of *Tests in Print* can also be used as an index to all the MMYs that preceded it.

Another major source of information about published tests is the *Test Collection Bibliographies* prepared by Educational Testing Service (ETS). Annotated test bibliographies are available in specific content areas. Coverage is comprehensive, including all types of tests, as well as tests designed for particular uses and for special populations, such as physically disabled persons. Each test entry provides factual information, including author, publication date, publisher, target population, purpose of the test, and any sub-scores or variables measured. Test bibliographies for particular areas can be purchased for a nominal fee from Test Collection, ETS (address in Appendix B). This is one of several ETS publications providing current information on tests and testing.

Besides published tests, there is a vast store of unpublished tests that are described or reproduced in books, journals, or unpublished reports. Of interest chiefly to research workers, such tests have been surveyed in various compendiums (e.g., Goldman & Mitchell, 1995). Current information about unpublished tests is available through *Tests in Microfiche,* distributed by Test Collections, ETS. A new set of these tests is added each year, and an index of each set can be obtained. Individual tests or sets may be purchased by qualified users. A clear and concise guide for finding information on both published and unpublished tests is available from the Science Directorate of the American Psychological Association *(Finding Information,* 1995). This source is regularly updated; anyone requesting a copy will automatically receive the latest version.

For the test user, the most direct source of information about particular current tests is provided by the catalogs of test publishers and by the manual that accompanies each test. A comprehensive list of test publishers, with addresses, can be found in the latest *Mental Measurements Yearbook*. For ready reference, the names and addresses of publishers whose tests are cited in this book are given in Appendix B. Catalogs of current tests can be obtained from the major publishers on request. Manuals and specimen sets of tests can be purchased by qualified users.

The test manual should provide the essential information required for administering, scoring, and evaluating a particular test. In it should be found full and detailed instructions, scoring key, norms, and data on reliability and validity.

Moreover, the manual should report the number and nature of persons on whom norms, reliability, and validity were established and the methods employed in computing indices of reliability and validity. In the event that the necessary information is too lengthy to fit conveniently into the manual, references to a technical manual or other printed sources in which such information can be readily located should be given. The manual should, in other words, enable test users to evaluate the test before choosing it for their specific purposes. It should be added that some test manuals still fall short of this goal. But the larger and more professionally oriented test publishers are giving increasing attention to the preparation of manuals that meet adequate scientific standards. An enlightened public of test users provide the firmest assurance that such standards will be maintained and improved in the future.

A succinct but comprehensive guide for the evaluation of psychological tests is to be found in the *Standards for Educational and Psychological Testing,* prepared by the American Psychological Association (APA), in collaboration with two other associations concerned with testing, the American Educational Research Association (AERA) and the National Council on Measurement in Education (NCME). First published in 1954, the *Standards* were revised in 1966, 1974, and 1985. A further, extensive revision is in progress by the three participating associations.

In India, a catalog on various indigenous tests, foreign tests, and unpublished tests is available. This catalog serves as a reference guide to the two thousand tests in education, psychology, and allied areas. It is available in the National Library of Educational and Psychological Tests (NLEPT), located in the Department of Educational Psychology and Foundations of Education, NCERT, New Delhi. Most of these tests can be purchased from the Prasad Psycho Corporation, New Delhi. Also, the well-established foreign tests, which are widely used and adapted in India, are also readily available online on their respective test publishers' and test distributors' websites.

The need to establish *Testing Standards*[2] that concern not only the technical quality of the tests but also the effect of testing on the welfare of the individual began to surface in the 1980s (see Fig. 1–2, p. 30). That this concern represents a continuing trend is indicated by the nature of the most recent revision of the *Testing Standards*. Figure 1–3 on p. 31 contains a proposed list of *Standards* prepared by a committee from the three associations in 1996. Clearly, concern with adapting the selection of tests—as well as concern with the interpretation and use of their scores—to available knowledge about the test-taker's experiential history shows a continuing rise. It is noteworthy that a whole section (Part II) of Figure 1–3 is entitled "Fairness in Testing." Test users are becoming increasingly aware that the improper application of tests can harm the individual and decrease the effectiveness of her or his contribution to society. Popular criticisms of the misuse of tests may well have contributed to this growing awareness by testers, which should decrease such misuses. This in turn should increase public recognition of the potential benefits of test use.

---

[2] For brevity, we shall henceforth follow the common practice of identifying them as "*Testing Standards*" throughout this book.

STANDARDS FOR EDUCATIONAL AND PSYCHOLOGICAL TESTING

Part I. Technical Standards for Test Construction and Evaluation

1. Validity
2. Reliability and errors of measurement
3. Test development and revision
4. Scaling, norming, score comparability, and equating
5. Test publication: technical manuals and users' guides

Part II. Professional Standards for Test Use

6. General principles of test use
7. Clinical testing
8. Educational testing and psychological testing in the schools
9. Test use in counseling
10. Employment testing
11. Professional and occupational licensure and certification
12. Program evaluation

Part III. Standards for Particular Applications

13. Testing linguistic minorities
14. Testing people who have handicapping conditions

Part IV. Standards for Administrative Procedures

15. Test administration, scoring, and reporting
16. Protecting the rights of test takers

Figure 1-2. Topics covered by the *Standards for Educational and Psychological Testing* (AERA, APA, NCME, 1985).

PROPOSED LIST OF STANDARDS FOR EDUCATIONAL AND PSYCHOLOGICAL TESTING

Part I. Test Construction, Evaluation, and Documentation

1. Validity
2. Reliability, errors of measurement, and test score information function
3. Test development and revision
4. Scaling, norming, standards, and score comparability
5. Test administration, scoring and reporting
6. Test documents

Part II. Fairness in Testing

7. Fairness and bias
8. Protecting the rights of test takers
9. Testing people whose first language is not English
10. Testing individuals with disabilities

Part III. Testing Applications

11. General Principles of test use
12. Psychological testing and assessment
13. Educational testing and assessment
14. Employment testing, licensure and certification
15. Testing in program evaluation and public policy

Figure 1-3. Topics chosen for revised edition of *Standards for Educational and Psychological Testing* (AERA, APA, NCME, 1996). Manuscript in preparation.
(Reproduced by permission of the Joint Committee on the Standards for Educational and Psychological Testing [Dianne Brown, Project Director].)

Chapter Two

Historical Antecedents of Modern Testing

A brief overview of the historical antecedents and origins of psychological testing will provide perspective and should aid in the understanding of present-day tests.[1] The direction in which contemporary psychological testing has been progressing can be clarified when considered in the light of the precursors of such tests. The special limitations as well as the advantages that characterize current tests likewise become more intelligible when viewed against the background in which they originated. This chapter is concerned only with the antecedents and the early development of the testing movement as a whole. More recent developments are discussed in later chapters, in connection with particular types of tests, such as ability tests (chaps. 8–12) or interest tests (chap. 14), as well as areas of test use, such as educational, industrial, clinical, and counseling (chap. 17).

The roots of testing are lost in antiquity. There have been repeated accounts of the system of civil service examinations prevailing in the Chinese empire for some 2,000 years (Bowman, 1989). Among the ancient Greeks, testing was an established adjunct to the educational process. Tests were used to assess the mastery of physical as well as intellectual skills (Doyle, 1974). From their beginnings in the Middle Ages, European universities relied on formal examinations in awarding degrees and honors.

[1] A more detailed account of the early origins of psychological tests can be found in F. L. Goodenough (1949) and J. Peterson (1926). See also Boring (1950) and G. Murphy, and Kovach (1972) for more general background, DuBois (1970) and McReynolds (1975, 1986) for more recent accounts of the history of psychological testing, and Anastasi (1965) for historical antecedents of the study of individual differences. An overview of ongoing trends in psychological testing can be found in Anastasi (1993).

To identify the major developments that shaped contemporary testing, however, we need go no farther than the nineteenth century. It is to these developments that we now turn.

EARLY INTEREST IN CLASSIFICATION AND TRAINING OF MENTALLY RETARDED PERSONS

The nineteenth century witnessed a strong awakening of interest in the humane treatment of mentally retarded and insane persons. Prior to that time, neglect, ridicule, and even torture had been the common lot of these individuals. With the growing concern for the proper care of people with mental problems came a realization that some uniform criteria for identifying and classifying these cases were required. The establishment of many social institutions for the care of mentally retarded persons in both Europe and the United States made the need for setting up admission standards and an objective system of classification especially urgent. First it was necessary to differentiate between insane and mentally retarded individuals. The former manifested emotional disorders that might or might not be accompanied by intellectual deterioration from an initially normal level; the latter were characterized essentially by intellectual defect that had been present from birth or early infancy. What is probably the first explicit statement of this distinction is to be found in a two-volume work published in 1838 by the French physician Esquirol (1838), in which more than 100 pages are devoted to what is now termed "mental retardation." Esquirol also pointed out that there are many degrees of mental retardation, varying along a continuum from normality to "low-grade idiocy." In the effort to develop some system for classifying the different degrees and varieties of retardation, Esquirol tried several procedures but concluded that the individual's use of language provides the most dependable criterion of her or his intellectual level. It is noteworthy that current criteria of mental retardation are also largely linguistic and that present-day intelligence tests are heavily loaded with verbal content. The important part verbal ability plays in our concept of intelligence will be repeatedly demonstrated in subsequent chapters.

Of special significance are the contributions of another French physician, Seguin, who pioneered in the training of mentally retarded persons. Having rejected the prevalent notion of the incurability of mental retardation, Seguin (1866/1907) experimented for many years with what he termed the physiological method of training; and in 1837 he established the first school devoted to the education of mentally retarded children. In 1848 he emigrated to America, where his ideas gained wide recognition. Many of the sense-training and muscle-training techniques subsequently employed in institutions for mentally retarded individuals were originated by Seguin. By these methods, severely retarded children are given intensive exercise in sensory discrimination and in the development of motor control. Some of the procedures developed by Seguin for this purpose were eventually incorporated into performance or nonverbal tests of intelligence. An example is the Seguin Form Board, in which the individual is required to insert variously shaped blocks into the corresponding recesses as quickly as possible.

More than half a century after the work of Esquirol and Seguin, the French psychologist Alfred Binet urged that children who failed to respond to normal schooling be examined before dismissal and, if considered educable, be assigned to special classes (T. H. Wolf, 1973). With his fellow members of the Society for the Psychological Study of the Child, Binet encouraged the Ministry of Public Instruction to take steps to improve the condition of retarded children. A specific outcome was the establishment of a ministerial commission for the study of retarded children, to which Binet was appointed. This appointment was a momentous event in the history of psychological testing, of which more will be said later.

THE FIRST EXPERIMENTAL PSYCHOLOGISTS

The early experimental psychologists of the nineteenth century were not, in general, concerned with the measurement of individual differences. The principal aim of psychologists of that period was the formulation of generalized descriptions of human behavior. It was the uniformities rather than the differences in behavior that were the focus of attention. Individual differences were either ignored or accepted as a necessary evil that limited the applicability of the generalizations. Thus, the fact that one individual reacted differently from another when observed under identical conditions was regarded as a form of error. The presence of such error, or individual variability, rendered the generalizations approximate rather than exact. This was the attitude toward individual differences that prevailed in such laboratories as that founded by Wundt at Leipzig in 1879, where many of the early experimental psychologists received their training.

In their choice of topics, as in many other phases of their work, the founders of experimental psychology reflected the influence of their backgrounds in physiology and physics. The problems studied in their laboratories were concerned largely with sensitivity to visual, auditory, and other sensory stimuli and with simple reaction time. This emphasis on sensory phenomena was in turn reflected in the nature of the first psychological tests, as will be apparent in subsequent sections.

Still another way in which nineteenth-century experimental psychology influenced the course of the testing movement may be noted. The early psychological experiments brought out the need for rigorous control of the conditions under which observations were made. For example, the wording of directions given to the participant in a reaction-time experiment might appreciably increase or decrease the speed of the person's response. Or again, the brightness or color of the surrounding field could markedly alter the appearance of a visual stimulus. The importance of making observations on all experimental participants under standardized conditions was thus vividly demonstrated. Such standardization of procedure eventually became one of the special earmarks of psychological tests.

CONTRIBUTIONS OF FRANCIS GALTON

It was the English biologist Francis Galton who was primarily responsible for launching the testing movement. A unifying factor in Galton's numerous and varied research activities was his interest in human heredity. In the course of his investigations on heredity, Galton realized the need for measuring the characteristics of related and unrelated persons. Only in this way could he discover, for example, the exact degree of resemblance between parents and offspring, brothers and sisters, cousins, or twins. With this end in view, Galton was instrumental in inducing a number of educational institutions to keep systematic anthropometric records on their students. He also set up an anthropometric laboratory at the International Exposition of 1884 where, by paying threepence, visitors could be measured in certain physical traits and could take tests of keenness of vision and hearing, muscular strength, reaction time, and other simple sensorimotor functions. When the exposition closed, the laboratory was transferred to South Kensington Museum, London, where it operated for six years. By such methods, the first large, systematic body of data on individual differences in simple psychological processes was gradually accumulated.

Galton himself devised most of the simple tests administered at his anthropometric laboratory, many of which are still familiar either in their original or in modified forms. Examples include the Galton bar for visual discrimination of length, the Galton whistle for determining the highest audible pitch, and graduated series of weights for measuring kinesthetic discrimination. It was Galton's belief that tests of sensory discrimination could serve as a means of gauging a person's intellect. In this respect, he was partly influenced by the theories of Locke. Thus, Galton wrote: "The only information that reaches us concerning outward events appears to pass through the avenue of our senses; and the more perceptive the senses are of difference, the larger is the field upon which our judgment and intelligence can act" (Galton, 1883, p. 27). Galton had also noted that persons with extreme mental retardation tend to be defective in the ability to discriminate among heat, cold, and pain—an observation that further strengthened his conviction that sensory discriminative capacity "would on the whole be highest among the intellectually ablest" (Galton, 1883, p. 29).

Galton also pioneered in the application of rating-scale and questionnaire methods, as well as in the use of the free association technique subsequently employed for a wide variety of purposes. A further contribution of Galton is to be found in his development of statistical methods for the analysis of data on individual differences. Galton selected and adapted a number of techniques previously derived by mathematicians. These techniques he put in such form as to permit their use by the mathematically untrained investigator who might wish to treat test results quantitatively. He thereby extended enormously the application of statistical procedures to the analysis of test data. This phase of Galton's work has been carried forward by many of his students, the most eminent of whom was Karl Pearson.[2]

CATTELL AND THE EARLY "MENTAL TESTS"

An especially prominent position in the development of psychological testing is occupied by the American psychologist James McKeen Cattell. The newly

[2] For a fascinating account of the early development of major statistical concepts and the persons responsible for them, see Cowles (1989).

established science of experimental psychology and the still newer testing movement merged in Cattell's work. For his doctorate at Leipzig, he completed a dissertation on reaction time, under Wundt's direction. While lecturing at Cambridge in 1888, Cattell's interest in the measurement of individual differences was reinforced by contact with Galton. On his return to America, Cattell was active both in the establishment of laboratories for experimental psychology and in the spread of the testing movement.

In an article written by Cattell in 1890, the term "mental test" was used for the first time in the psychological literature. This article described a series of tests that were being administered annually to college students in the effort to determine their intellectual level. The tests, which had to be administered individually, included measures of muscular strength, speed of movement, sensitivity to pain, keenness of vision and of hearing, weight discrimination, reaction time, memory, and the like. In his choice of tests, Cattell shared Galton's view that a measure of intellectual functions could be obtained through tests of sensory discrimination and reaction time. Cattell's preference for such tests was also bolstered by the fact that simple functions could be measured with precision and accuracy, whereas the development of objective measures for the more complex functions seemed at that time a well-nigh hopeless task.

Cattell's tests were typical of those to be found in a number of test series developed during the last decade of the nineteenth century. Such test series were administered to schoolchildren, college students, and miscellaneous adults. At the Columbian Exposition held in Chicago in 1893, Jastrow set up an exhibit at which visitors were invited to take tests of sensory, motor, and simple perceptual processes and to compare their skill with the norms (J. Peterson, 1926; Philippe, 1894). A few attempts to evaluate such early tests yielded very discouraging results. The individual's performance showed little correspondence from one test to another (Sharp, 1898–1899; Wissler, 1901), and it exhibited little or no relation to independent estimates of intellectual level based on teachers' ratings (T. L. Bolton, 1891–1892; J. A. Gilbert, 1894) or academic grades (Wissler, 1901).

A number of test series assembled by European psychologists of the period tended to cover somewhat more complex functions. Kraepelin (1895), who was interested primarily in the clinical examination of psychiatric patients, prepared a long series of tests to measure what he regarded as basic factors in the characterization of an individual. The tests, employing chiefly simple arithmetic operations, were designed to measure practice effects, memory, and susceptibility to fatigue and to distraction. Another German psychologist, Ebbinghaus (1897), administered tests of arithmetic computation, memory span, and sentence completion to schoolchildren. The most complex of the three tests, sentence completion, was the only one that showed a clear correspondence with the children's scholastic achievement.

In an article published in France in 1895, Binet and Henri criticized most of the available test series as being too largely sensory and as concentrating unduly on simple, specialized abilities. They argued further that, in the measurement of the more complex functions, great precision is not necessary, since individual differences are larger in these functions. An extensive and varied list of tests was proposed, covering such functions as memory, imagination, attention, comprehension, suggestibility, aesthetic appreciation, and many others. In these tests, we can recognize the trends that were eventually to lead to the development of the famous Binet intelligence scales.

BINET AND THE RISE OF INTELLIGENCE TESTS

Binet and his co-workers devoted many years to active and ingenious research on ways of measuring intelligence. Many approaches were tried, including even the measurement of cranial, facial, and hand form and the analysis of handwriting. The results, however, led to a growing conviction that the direct, even though crude, measurement of complex intellectual functions offered the greatest promise. Then a specific situation arose that brought Binet's efforts to immediate practical fruition. In 1904, the Minister of Public Instruction appointed Binet to the previously cited commission to study procedures for the education of retarded children. It was in connection with the objectives of this commission that Binet, in collaboration with Simon, prepared the first Binet-Simon Scale (Binet & Simon, 1905).

This scale, known as the 1905 scale, consisted of 30 problems or tests arranged in ascending order of difficulty. The difficulty level was determined empirically by administering the tests to 50 normal children aged 3 to 11 years, and to some mentally retarded children and adults. The tests were designed to cover a wide variety of functions, with special emphasis on judgment, comprehension, and reasoning, which Binet regarded as essential components of intelligence. Although sensory and perceptual tests were included, a much greater proportion of verbal content was found in this scale than in most test series of the time. The 1905 scale was presented as a preliminary and tentative instrument, and no precise objective method for arriving at a total score was formulated.

In the second, or 1908, scale, the number of tests was increased, some unsatisfactory tests from the earlier scale were eliminated, and all tests were grouped into age levels on the basis of the performance of about 300 normal children between the ages of 3 and 13 years. Thus, in the 3-year level were placed all tests passed by 80 to 90% of normal 3-year-olds; in the 4-year level, all tests similarly passed by normal 4-year-olds; and so on to age 13. The child's score on the entire test could then be expressed as a *mental level* corresponding to the age of normal children whose performance he or she equaled. In the various translations and adaptations of the Binet scales, the term "mental age" was commonly substituted for "mental level." Since mental age is such a simple concept to grasp, the introduction of this term undoubtedly did much to popularize intelligence testing.[3] Binet himself, however, avoided the term "mental age" because of its unverified

[3] F. L. Goodenough (1949, pp. 50–51) noted that in 1887, 21 years before the appearance of the 1908 Binet-Simon Scale, S. E. Chaille published in the *New Orleans Medical and Surgical Journal* a series of tests for infants arranged according to the age at which the tests are commonly passed. Partly because of the limited circulation of the journal and partly, perhaps, because the scientific community was not ready for it, the significance of this age-scale concept passed unnoticed at the time. Binet's own scale was influenced by the work of some of his contemporaries, notably Blin and Damaye, who prepared a set of oral questions from which they derived a single global score for each child (T. H. Wolf, 1973).

developmental implications and preferred the more neutral term "mental level" (T. H. Wolf, 1973).

A third revision of the Binet-Simon Scale appeared in 1911, the year of Binet's untimely death. In this scale, no fundamental changes were introduced. Minor revisions and relocations of specific tests were instituted. More tests were added at several year levels, and the scale was extended to the adult level.

Even prior to the 1908 revision, the Binet-Simon tests attracted wide attention among psychologists throughout the world. Translations and adaptations appeared in many countries, including several in the United States. The first was by H. H. Goddard, then research psychologist at the Vineland Training School (for mentally retarded children). The Goddard revision was influential in the acceptance of intelligence testing by the medical profession (Zenderland, 1987). It arrived at a propitious moment to meet the urgent need for a standardized measure to diagnose and classify mentally retarded persons. As a testing instrument, however, it was soon outdistanced by the more extensive and psychometrically refined Stanford-Binet, developed by L. M. Terman and his associates at Stanford University (Terman, 1916). It was in this test that the intelligence quotient (IQ), or ratio between mental age and chronological age, was first used. The later revisions of this test have been widely employed and will be more fully considered in chapter 8. Of special interest, too, is the first Kuhlmann-Binet revision, which extended the scale downward to the age of 3 months (Kuhlmann, 1912). This scale represents one of the earliest efforts to develop preschool and infant tests of intelligence.

GROUP TESTING

The Binet tests, as well as all their revisions, are *individual scales* in the sense that they can be administered to only one person at a time. Many of the tests in these scales require oral responses from the examinee or necessitate the manipulation of materials. Some call for individual timing of responses. For these and other reasons, such tests are not adapted to group administration. Another characteristic of the Binet type of test is that it requires a highly trained examiner. Such tests are essentially clinical instruments, suited to the intensive study of individual cases.

Group testing like the first Binet scale, was developed to meet a pressing practical need. When the United States entered World War I in 1917, a committee was appointed by the American Psychological Association to consider ways in which psychology might assist in the conduct of the war. This committee, under the direction of Robert M. Yerkes, recognized the need for the rapid classification of the million and a half recruits with respect to general intellectual level. Such information was relevant to many administrative decisions, including rejection or discharge from military service, assignment to different types of service, or admission to officer-training camps. It was in this setting that the first group intelligence test was developed. In this task, the army psychologists drew on all available test materials, and especially on an unpublished group intelligence test prepared by Arthur S. Otis, which he turned over to the army. A major contribution of Otis's test, which he designed while a student in one of Terman's graduate courses, was the introduction of multiple-choice and other "objective" item types.

The tests finally developed by the army psychologists came to be known as the Army Alpha and the Army Beta. The former was designed for general routine testing; the latter was a nonlanguage scale employed with illiterates and with foreign-born recruits who were unable to take a test in English. Both tests were suitable for administration to large groups.

Shortly after the end of World War I, the army tests were released for civilian use. Not only did the Army Alpha and Army Beta themselves pass through many revisions, but they also served as models for most group intelligence tests. The testing movement underwent a tremendous spurt of growth. Soon group intelligence tests were being devised for all ages and types of persons, from preschool children to graduate students. Large-scale testing programs, previously impossible, were now being launched with zestful optimism. Because group tests were designed as mass testing instruments, they not only permitted the simultaneous examination of large groups but they also used simplified instructions and administration procedures, thereby requiring a minimum of training on the part of the examiner. Schoolteachers began to give intelligence tests to their classes. College students were routinely examined prior to admission. Extensive studies of special adult groups, such as prisoners, were undertaken. And soon the general public became IQ-conscious.

The application of such group intelligence tests far outran their technical improvement. That the tests were still technically crude was often forgotten in the rush of gathering scores and drawing practical conclusions from the results. When the tests failed to meet unwarranted expectations, skepticism and hostility toward all testing often resulted. Thus, the testing boom of the 1920s, based on the indiscriminate use of tests, may have done as much to retard as to advance the progress of psychological testing.

APTITUDE TESTING

Although intelligence tests were originally designed to sample a wide variety of functions in order to estimate the individual's general intellectual level, it soon became apparent that such tests were quite limited in their coverage. Not all important functions were represented. In fact, most intelligence tests were primarily measures of verbal ability and, to a lesser extent, of the ability to handle numerical and other abstract and symbolic relations. Gradually, psychologists came to recognize that the term "intelligence test" was a misnomer, since only certain aspects of intelligence were measured by such tests.

To be sure, the tests covered abilities that are of prime importance in the culture for which they were designed. But it was realized that more precise designations, in terms of the type of information these tests were able to yield, would be preferable. For example, a number of tests that would probably have been called intelligence tests during the 1920s later came to be known as scholastic aptitude tests. This shift in terminology was made in recognition of the fact that many so called intelligence tests measure that combination of abilities demanded and fostered by academic work.

Even prior to World War I, psychologists had begun to recognize the need for tests of special aptitudes to supplement the global intelligence tests. These *special aptitude tests* were developed particularly for use in vocational counseling and in the selection and classification of industrial and military personnel. Among the most widely used are tests of mechanical, clerical, musical, and artistic aptitudes.

The critical evaluation of intelligence tests that followed their widespread and indiscriminate use during the 1920s also revealed another noteworthy fact: An individual's performance on different parts of such a test often showed marked variation. This was especially apparent on group tests, in which the items are commonly segregated into subtests of relatively homogeneous content. For example, a person might score relatively high on a verbal subtest and low on a numerical subtest, or vice versa. To some extent, such internal variability is also discernible on a test like the Stanford-Binet, in which, for example, all items involving words might prove difficult for a particular individual, whereas items employing pictures or geometric diagrams may place her or him at an advantage.

Test users, and especially clinicians, frequently utilized such intercomparisons in order to obtain more insight into the individual's psychological makeup. Thus, not only the IQ or other global score but also performance on item clusters or subtests would be examined in the evaluation of the individual case. Such a practice is not to be generally recommended, however, because intelligence tests were not designed for the purpose of differential aptitude analysis. Often the subtests being compared contain too few items to yield a stable or reliable estimate of a specific ability. As a result, the obtained difference between subtest scores might be reversed if the individual were retested on a different day or with another form of the same test. If such intra-individual comparisons are to be made, tests are needed that are specially designed to reveal differences in performance in various functions.

While the practical application of tests demonstrated the need for multiple aptitude tests, a parallel development in the study of trait organization was gradually providing the means for constructing such tests. Statistical studies on the nature of intelligence had been exploring the interrelations among scores obtained by many persons on a wide variety of different tests. Such investigations were begun by the English psychologist Charles Spearman (1904, 1927) during the first decade of the twentieth century. Subsequent methodological developments, based on the work of such American psychologists as T. L. Kelley (1928) and L. L. Thurstone (1938, 1947b), as well as on that of other American and English investigators, have come to be known as *factor analysis*.

The contributions that the methods of factor analysis have made to test construction will be more fully examined and illustrated in chapter 11. For the present, it will suffice to note that the data gathered by such procedures have indicated the presence of a number of relatively independent factors, or traits. Some of these traits were represented, in varying proportions, in the traditional intelligence tests. Verbal comprehension and numerical reasoning are examples of this type of trait. Others, such as spatial, perceptual, and mechanical aptitudes, were found more often in special aptitude tests than in intelligence tests.

One of the chief practical outcomes of factor analysis was the development of *multiple aptitude batteries*. These batteries are designed to provide a measure of the individual's standing in each of a number of traits. In place of a total score or IQ, a separate score is obtained for such traits as verbal comprehension, numerical aptitude, spatial visualization, arithmetic reasoning, and perceptual speed. Such batteries thus provide a suitable instrument for making the kind of intra-individual analysis, or differential diagnosis, that test users had been trying for many years to obtain, with crude and often erroneous results, from intelligence tests. These batteries also incorporate into a comprehensive and systematic testing program much of the information formerly obtained from special aptitude tests, since the multiple aptitude batteries cover some of the traits not ordinarily included in intelligence tests.

Multiple aptitude batteries represent a relatively late development in the testing field. Nearly all appeared since 1945. In this connection, the work of the military psychologists during World War II should be noted. Much of the test research conducted in the armed services was based on factor analysis and was directed toward the construction of multiple aptitude batteries. In the Air Force, for example, special batteries were constructed for pilots, bombardiers, radio operators, range finders, and many other military specialists. A report of the batteries prepared in the Air Force alone occupies at least 9 of the 19 volumes devoted to the aviation psychology program during World War II (*Army Air Forces,* 1947–1948). Research along these lines is still in progress under the sponsorship of various branches of the armed services. A number of multiple aptitude batteries have likewise been developed for civilian use and are widely applied in educational and vocational counseling and in personnel selection and classification. Examples of such batteries will be discussed in chapters 10 and 17.

A more recent development, emerging in the late 1980s and early 1990s, provides a fundamental integration of two previously contrasting approaches to mental measurement, represented by traditional intelligence tests and by multiple aptitude batteries (Anastasi, 1994). It is coming to be recognized that human ability can be properly assessed at different levels of breadth, from the narrowly defined aptitudes of specific tests (or even individual items), through increasingly broader trait levels, to an overall score such as the traditional IQ. For different testing purposes, a different level of breadth is most appropriate. Accordingly, recently developed intelligence tests, such as the Differential Ability Scales, or recent revisions of earlier tests, such as the fourth edition of the Stanford-Binet (both described in chapter 8), combine comprehensive coverage of multiple aptitudes with flexible multilevel scoring for specific testing purposes. Although both of these examples are individually administered intelligence tests, the same comprehensive and flexible approach to test construction and use is having an impact on group administered batteries, such as those discussed in chapter 10. The theoretical basis and practical implications of this ability-testing merger are discussed in chapter 11, in connection with current developments regarding the nature of intelligence.

STANDARDIZED ACHIEVEMENT TESTS

While psychologists were busy developing intelligence and aptitude tests, traditional school examinations were undergoing a number of technical improvements (O. W. Caldwell & Courtis, 1923; Ebel & Damrin, 1960). An important step in this direction was taken by the Boston public schools in 1845, when written examinations were substituted for the oral interrogation of students by visiting examiners. Among the arguments offered at the time in support of this innovation were that written examinations put all students in a uniform situation, permitted a wider coverage of content, reduced the element of chance in question choice, and eliminated the possibility of favoritism on the examiner's part. All these arguments have a familiar ring: They were used much later to justify the replacement of essay questions by objective multiple-choice items.

After the turn of the century, the first standardized tests for measuring the outcomes of school instruction began to appear. Spearheaded by the work of E. L. Thorndike, these tests utilized measurement principles developed in the psychological laboratory. Examples include scales for rating the quality of handwriting and written compositions, as well as tests in spelling, arithmetic computation, and arithmetic reasoning. Still later came the achievement batteries, initiated by the publication of the first edition of the Stanford Achievement Test in 1923. Its authors were three early leaders in test development: Truman L. Kelley, Giles M. Ruch, and Lewis M. Terman. Foreshadowing many characteristics of modern testing, this battery provided comparable measures of performance in different school subjects, evaluated in terms of a single normative group.

At the same time, evidence was accumulating regarding the lack of agreement among teachers in grading essay tests. By 1930, it was widely recognized that essay tests not only were more time consuming for examiners and examinees but also yielded less reliable results than the "new type" of objective items.[4] As the latter came into increasing use in standardized achievement tests, there was a growing emphasis on the design of items to test the understanding and application of knowledge and other broad educational objectives. The decade of the 1930s also witnessed the introduction of test-scoring machines, for which the new objective tests could be readily adapted.

The establishment of statewide, regional, and national testing programs was another noteworthy parallel development. Probably the best known of these programs is that of the College Entrance Examination Board (CEEB). Established at the turn of the century to reduce duplication in the examining of entering college freshmen, this program has undergone profound changes in its testing procedures and in the number and nature of participating colleges—changes that reflect intervening developments in both testing and education. In 1947, the testing functions of the CEEB were merged with those of the Carnegie Corporation and the American Council on Education to form Educational Testing Service (ETS). In subsequent years, ETS has assumed responsibility for a growing number of testing programs on behalf of universities, professional schools, government agencies, and other institutions. Mention should also be made of the American College Testing Program established in 1959 to screen applicants to colleges not included in the CEEB program, and of several national testing programs for the selection of highly talented students for scholarship awards.

Achievement tests are used not only for educational purposes but also in the selection of applicants for industrial and government jobs. Mention has already been made of the systematic use of civil service examinations in the Chinese

[4] Research bearing on the relative effectiveness of essay and objective item types will be cited in chapter 17 in connection with the educational use of tests.

empire, dating from about 150 B.C. (Bowman, 1989). In modern times, selection of government employees by examination was introduced in European countries in the late eighteenth and early nineteenth centuries. The U.S. Civil Service Commission installed competitive examinations as a regular procedure in 1883 (Kavruck, 1956). Test construction techniques developed during and prior to World War I were introduced into the examination program of the U.S. Civil Service with the appointment of L. J. O'Rourke as director of the newly established research division in 1922. Today this work is conducted by a large and technically sophisticated research staff within the unit designated as the U.S. Office of Personnel Management.

As more and more psychologists trained in psychometrics participated in the construction of standardized achievement tests, the technical aspects of achievement tests increasingly came to resemble those of intelligence and aptitude tests. Procedures for constructing and evaluating all these tests have much in common. The increasing efforts to prepare achievement tests that would measure the attainment of broad educational goals, as contrasted to the recall of factual minutiae, also made the content of achievement tests resemble more closely that of intelligence tests. Today the difference between these two types of tests is chiefly one of degree of specificity of content and extent to which the test presupposes a designated course of prior instruction.

ASSESSMENT OF PERSONALITY

Another area of psychological testing is concerned with the affective or nonintellectual aspects of behavior, to be discussed in chapters 13–16. Tests designed for this purpose are commonly known as personality tests, although many psychologists prefer to use the term "personality" in a broader sense, to refer to the entire individual. Intellectual as well as nonintellectual traits would thus he included under this heading. In the terminology of psychological testing, however, the designation "personality test" most often refers to measures of such characteristics as emotional states, interpersonal relations, motivation, interests, and attitudes.

An early precursor of personality testing is illustrated by Kraepelin's use of the free association test with psychiatric patients. In this test, the examinee is given specially selected stimulus words and is required to respond to each with the first word that comes to mind. Kraepelin (1892) also employed this technique to study the psychological effects of fatigue, hunger, and drugs; he concluded that all these agents increase the relative frequency of superficial associations. Sommer (1894), also writing during the last decade of the nineteenth century, suggested that the free association test might he used to differentiate between the various forms of mental disorder. The free association technique has subsequently been utilized for a variety of testing purposes and is still currently employed. Mention should also be made of the work of Galton, Pearson, and Cattell in the development of standardized questionnaire and rating-scale techniques. Although originally devised for other purposes, these procedures were eventually employed by others in constructing some of the most common types of current personality tests.

The prototype of the personality questionnaire, or *self-report inventory* (chap. 13), is the Personal Data Sheet developed by Woodworth during World

War I (DuBois, 1970; Franz, 1919, pp. 171–176; L. R. Goldberg, 1971; Symonds, 1931, chap. 5). This test was designed as a rough screening device for identifying seriously disturbed men who would be disqualified for military service. The inventory consisted of a number of questions dealing with common symptoms of psychopathology, which respondents answered about themselves. A total score was obtained by counting the number of symptoms reported. The development of the Personal Data Sheet was not completed early enough to permit its operational use before the war ended. Immediately after the war, however, civilian forms were prepared, including a special form for use with children. The Woodworth Personal Data Sheet, moreover, served as a model for most subsequent emotional adjustment inventories. In some of these questionnaires, an attempt was made to subdivide emotional adjustment into more specific forms, such as home adjustment, school adjustment, and vocational adjustment. Other tests concentrated more intensively on a narrower area of behavior or were concerned with more distinctly social responses, such as dominance–submission in interpersonal contacts. A later development was the construction of tests for quantifying the expression of attitudes and interests (chap. 14). These tests, too, were based essentially on questionnaire techniques.

Another approach to the measurement of personality is through the application of *performance* or *situational tests* (chap. 16). In such tests, the examinee has a task to perform whose purpose is often disguised. Most of these tests simulate everyday-life situations quite closely. The first extensive application of such techniques is to be found in the tests developed in the late 1920s and early 1930s by Hartshorne, May, and their associates (1928, 1929, 1930). This series, standardized on schoolchildren, was concerned with such behavior as cheating, lying, stealing, cooperativeness, and persistence. Objective, quantitative scores could be obtained on each of a large number of specific tests. Another illustration, for the adult level, is provided by the series of situational tests developed during World War II in the Assessment Program of the Office of Strategic Services (OSS, 1948). These tests were concerned with relatively complex and subtle social and emotional behavior and required rather elaborate facilities and trained personnel for their administration. The interpretation of the individual's responses, moreover, was relatively subjective.

Projective techniques (chap. 15) represent a third approach to the study of personality and one that has shown phenomenal growth, especially among clinicians. In such tests, the client is given a relatively unstructured task that permits wide latitude in its solution. The assumption underlying such methods is that the individual will project her or his characteristic modes of response into such a task. Like the performance and situational tests, projective techniques are more or less disguised in their purpose, thereby reducing the chances that the respondent can deliberately create a desired impression. The previously cited free association test represents one of the earliest types of projective techniques. Sentence-completion tests have also been used in this manner. Other tasks commonly employed in projective techniques include drawing, arranging toys to create a scene, extemporaneous dramatic play, and interpreting pictures or inkblots.

All available types of personality tests present certain difficulties, both practical and theoretical. Each approach has its own special advantages and disadvantages. On the whole, personality testing has lagged behind ability testing in its practical accomplishments. But such lack of progress cannot be attributed to insufficient effort. Research on the measurement of personality has attained impressive proportions since 1950, and many ingenious devices and technical improvements are under investigation. It is rather the special difficulties encountered in the measurement of personality that account for the slow advances in this area.

Two significant unifying trends are emerging from current research with personality tests (see Anastasi, 1985b, 1992a, 1993; Digman, 1990; L. R. Goldberg, 1993; Simon, 1994). First, there is increasing evidence of mutual influence between affective ("personality") and cognitive ("ability") traits, in both task performance and behavior development. The traditional distinction between the two types of traits is coming to be recognized as artificially imposed for convenience in describing and measuring different aspects of behavior. Second, theoretical analyses of the nature and composition of personality support the reintegration of cognitive and affective traits into a comprehensive model of human activity that subsumes all forms of behavior. This comprehensive model relates to basic research on both intellectual traits (chap. 11) and affective traits (chap. 13).

EMERGENCE OF MODERN TESTING IN INDIA

In India, the concept of using psychological tests has gained momentum in the last few years. Although, psychological tests were widely used in clinical and educational assessment and intervention, its deployment in other domains of psychology is limited. With the advent of international tests in the Indian market, the awareness and inclination to use such tests in an organizational context has increased manifold. Across an employee's work life, psychological tests are deployed to assess an individual's general cognitive ability, personality, motivations, job-fit, etc. in order to take an informed decision about an individual's selection or development. Today, psychological tests are preferred by business and human resource professionals to minimize the biases in their selection, promotion, and career advancement decisions. Therefore, there is a need to focus on scientifically developed and validated indigenous tests that can cater to the diverse audience in India. While most of the international tests have their Indian adaptations, they seem relevant only for multinational companies or large corporations catering to the highly educated urban population. Although the indigenous tests bridge this gap, the general neglect in establishing the predictive validity of these tests and their lack of online availability hampers their deployment in clinical, educational, and occupational setups. More often than not, Indian tests are either used for research purposes or in scenarios where paper-pencil administration is required or where a test's predictive validity is not a real concern.

Psychology as a field of study was imported lock, stock, and barrel from the West, and in 1916, it was first implanted at the Calcutta University, followed by Mysore and Patna universities. In Mysore University, M. V. Gopalaswami, after obtaining his Ph.D. in London under Charles Spearman, established this department in 1924. He developed Indian adaptations of Western intelligence tests and applied psychological principles in the field of education. Gopalaswami was also the first to set up an animal laboratory in India. The Department of Psychology at the Mysore University offered masters degree in psychology. Following the legacy of Gopalaswami, in 1998, the department revised most of the syllabi in line with the tenets of science with a greater emphasis on practicum. This is the second oldest department in the country.

The psychology department at the Patna University was established in 1946 in collaboration with the Institute of Psychological Research and Services, Patna, with emphasis on psychoanalytic and clinical assessments and interventions. Within a short period of time, the department emerged as a major center for teaching, research, and counseling services.

These early establishments in the field of psychology and psychological testing inspired the establishment of psychology departments in other universities. Work in the early stages of this area dealt with the construction and standardization of achievement and intelligence tests, aptitude scales, and personality inventories. Many popular western tests were adapted into Indian languages. Despite these efforts, there exist some challenges in conducting majority of these tests. First, most of these tests demanded certain proficiency in language skills from the test takers, thus limiting its applicability for a larger population. Second, classical psychometric theories guided the construction of almost all these tests which, owing to sub-cultural and language differences now require a fresh perspective on their usefulness. Lastly, there has been a general neglect in establishing the validity of these tests. Most of the information available on these tests provide no or scarce information regarding test validity. Though a large number of tests have been developed in India, their ability to predict performance or any other construct is left much to be desired.

The good news is that considerable improvements have been made in the last few years and test developers are focusing on developing high quality psychological tests. Also, capitalizing on the gap in the market, many technology companies in collaboration with psychologists and psychometricians have started to develop indigenous tests that are empirically strong, accessible, and affordable and can cater to the diverse audience.

PART 2

Technical and Methodological Principles

Norms and the Meaning of Test Scores

Part Two, which consists of chapters 3 to 7, provides an introduction to basic concepts and methodology needed for an understanding of psychological tests and for the proper interpretation of test results. The successive chapters deal with norms, reliability, validity, and item analysis and test design. The present chapter is concerned with the development and use of norms and with other procedures that facilitate the test user's interpretation of test scores. In the absence of additional interpretive data, a raw score on any psychological test is meaningless. To say that an individual has correctly solved 15 problems on a mathematical reasoning test, or identified 34 words in a vocabulary test, or successfully assembled a mechanical object in 57 seconds conveys little or no information about her or his standing in any of these functions. Nor do the familiar percentage scores provide a satisfactory solution to the problem of interpreting test scores. A score of 65% correct on one vocabulary test, for example, might be equivalent to 30% correct on another, and to 80% correct on a third. The difficulty level of the items making up each test will, of course, determine the meaning of the score. Like all raw scores, percentage scores can be interpreted only in terms of a clearly defined and uniform frame of reference.

Scores on psychological tests are most commonly interpreted by reference to *norms* that represent the test performance of the standardization sample. The norms are thus empirically established by determining what persons in a representative group actually do on the test. Any individual's raw score is then referred to the distribution of scores obtained by the standardization sample, to discover where he or she falls in that distribution. Does the score coincide with the average performance of the standardization group? Is it slightly below average? Or does it fall near the upper end of the distribution?

In order to ascertain more precisely the individual's exact position with reference to the standardization sample, the raw score is converted into some relative measure. These derived scores are designed to serve a dual purpose. First, they indicate the individual's relative standing in the normative sample and thus permit an evaluation of her or his performance in reference to other persons. Second, they provide comparable measures that permit a direct comparison of the individual's performance on different tests. For example, if a girl has a raw score of 40 on a vocabulary test and a raw score of 22 on an arithmetic reasoning test, we obviously know nothing about her relative performance on the two tests. Is she better in vocabulary or in arithmetic, or equally good in both? Since raw scores on different tests are usually expressed in different units, a direct comparison of such scores is impossible. The difficulty level of the particular test would also affect such a comparison between raw scores. Derived scores, on the other hand, can be expressed in the same units and referred to the same or to closely similar normative samples for different tests. The individual's relative performance in many different functions can thus be compared.

There are various ways in which raw scores may be converted to fulfill the two objectives stated above. Fundamentally, however, derived scores are expressed in one of two major ways: (1) developmental level attained, or (2) relative position within a specified group. Both these types of scores *and* some of their common variants are considered in separate sections of this chapter. But first it will be necessary to examine a few elementary statistical concepts that underlie the development and utilization of norms. The following section is included simply to clarify the meaning of certain common statistical measures. Simplified computational examples are given only for this purpose and not to provide training in statistical methods. For computational details and specific procedures to be followed in the practical application of these techniques, the reader is referred to any recent textbook on psychological statistics (e.g., D. C. Howell, 1997; Runyon & Haber, 1991; West, 1991). There is growing recognition of the need for basic knowledge of statistical methodology, not only for test users but also for anyone who wants to read with understanding the published research reports in any area of psychology (L. S. Aiken, West, Sechrest, & Reno, 1990; Anastasi, 1991; Lambert, 1991; S.T. Meier, 1993).

STATISTICAL CONCEPTS

A major object of statistical method is to organize and summarize quantitative data in order to facilitate their understanding. A list of 1,000 test scores can be an overwhelming sight. In that form, it conveys little meaning. A first step in bringing order into such a chaos of raw data is to tabulate the scores into a *frequency distribution*, as illustrated in Table 3–1. Such a distribution is prepared by grouping the scores into convenient class intervals and tallying each score in the appropriate interval. When all scores have been entered, the tallies are counted to find the frequency, or number of cases, in each class interval. The sums of these frequencies will equal N, the total number of cases in the group. Table 3–1 shows the scores of 1,000 college students in a code-learning test in which one set of

Table 3-1

Frequency Distribution of Scores of 1,000 College Students on a Code-Learning Test

Class Interval	Frequency
52–55	1
48–51	1
44–47	20
40–43	73
36–39	156
32–35	328
28–31	244
24–27	136
20–23	28
16–19	8
12–15	3
8–11	2
	N = 1,000

(Data from Anastasi, 1934, p. 34.)

artificial words, or nonsense syllables, was to be substituted for another. The raw scores, giving number of correct syllables substituted during a two-minute trial, ranged from 8 to 52. They have been grouped into class intervals of 4 points, from 52–55 at the top of the distribution down to 8–11. The frequency column reveals that two persons scored between 8 and 11, three between 12 and 15, eight between 16 and 19, and so on.

The information provided by a frequency distribution can also be presented graphically in the form of a distribution curve. Figure 3–1 shows the data of Table 3–1 in graphic form. On the baseline, or horizontal axis, are the scores grouped into class intervals; on the vertical axis are the frequencies, or number of cases falling within each class interval. The graph has been plotted in two ways, both forms being in common use. In the *histogram,* the height of the column erected over each class interval corresponds to the number of persons scoring in that interval. We can think of each individual standing on another's shoulders to form the column. In the *frequency polygon,* the number of persons in each interval is indicated by a point in the center of the class interval and across from the appropriate frequency. The successive points are then joined by straight lines.

Except for minor irregularities, the distribution shown in Figure 3–1 resembles the bell-shaped *normal curve.* A mathematically determined perfect normal curve appears in Figure 3–2. This type of curve has important mathematical properties and provides the basis for many kinds of statistical analyses. For the present purpose, however, only a few features will be noted. Essentially, the curve indicates that the largest number of cases cluster in the center of the range and that the number drops off gradually in both directions as the extremes are approached.

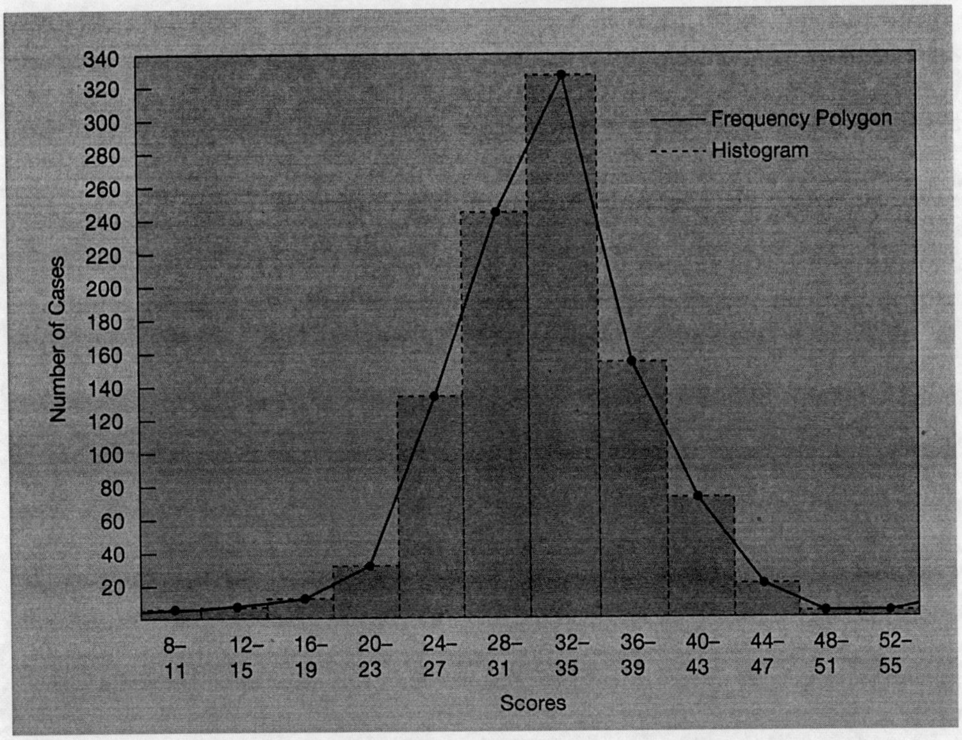

Figure 3-1. Distribution Curves: Frequency Polygon and Histogram.
(Data from Table 3–1.)

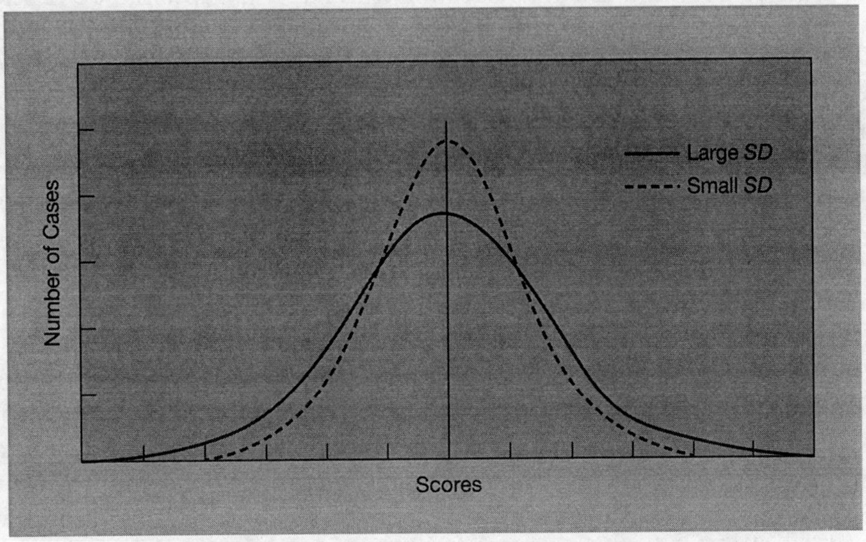

Figure 3-2. Frequency Distributions with the Same Mean but Different Variability.

The curve is bilaterally symmetrical, with a single peak in the center. Most distributions of human traits, from height and weight to aptitudes and personality characteristics, approximate the normal curve. In general, the larger the group, the more closely will the distribution resemble the theoretical normal curve.

A group of scores can also be described in terms of some measure of *central tendency.* Such a measure provides a single, most typical or representative score to characterize the performance of the entire group. The most familiar of these measures is the average, more technically known as the *mean* (*M*), and it is found by adding all scores and dividing the sum by the number of cases (*N*). Another measure of central tendency is the *mode,* or most frequent score. In a frequency distribution, the mode is the midpoint of the class interval with the highest frequency. Thus, in Table 3–1, the mode falls midway between 32 and 35, being 33.5. It will be noted that this score corresponds to the highest point on the distribution curve in Figure 3–1. A third measure of central tendency is the *median,* or middlemost score when all scores have been arranged in order of size. The median is the point that bisects the distribution, half the cases falling above it and half below.

Further description of a set of test scores is given by measures of *variability,* or the extent of individual differences around the central tendency. The most obvious and familiar way for reporting variability is in terms of the *range* between the highest and lowest score. The range, however, is extremely crude and unstable, for it is determined by only two scores. A single unusually high or low score would thus markedly affect its size. A more precise method of measuring variability is based on the difference between each individual's score and the mean of the group.

At this point, it will be helpful to look at the example in Table 3–2, in which the various measures under consideration have been computed on 10 cases. Such a small group was chosen in order to simplify the demonstration, although in actual practice we would usually be dealing with larger groups. Table 3–2 serves also to introduce certain standard statistical symbols that should be noted for future reference. Original raw scores are conventionally designated by a capital X, and a small x is used to refer to deviations of each score from the group mean. The symbol Σ means "sum of." It will be seen that the first column in Table 3–2 gives the data for the computation of mean and median. The mean is 40; the median is 40.5, falling midway between 40 and 41—five cases (50%) are above the median and five below. There is little point in finding a mode in such a small group, since the cases do not show clear-cut clustering on any one score. Technically, however, 41 would represent the mode, because two persons obtained this score, while all other scores occur only once.

The second column shows how far each score deviates above or below the mean of 40. The sum of these deviations will always equal zero, because the positive and negative deviations around the mean necessarily balance, or cancel each other out ($+ 20 - 20 = 0$). If we ignored signs, of course, we could average the absolute deviations, thus obtaining a measure of the average amount by which each person deviates from the group mean. Although of some descriptive value, such an "average deviation" is not suitable for use in further mathematical analyses because of the arbitrary discarding of signs and is therefore not employed in practice.

A much more serviceable measure of variability is the *standard deviation* (symbolized by either *SD* or σ), in which the negative signs are legitimately eliminated by squaring each deviation. This procedure has been followed in the last

Table 3–2

Illustration of Central Tendency and Variability

	Score (X)	Deviation ($x = X - M$)		Dev. Squared (x^2)
50% of cases	48	+8	+20	64
	47	+7		49
	43	+3		9
	41	+1		1
	41	+1		1
Median = 40.5 →	40	0	−20	0
50% of cases	38	−2		4
	36	−4		16
	34	−6		36
	32	−8		64
	$\sum X = 400$			$\sum x^2 = 244$

$$M = \frac{\sum X}{N} = \frac{400}{10} = 40$$

$$\text{Variance} = \sigma^2 = \frac{\sum x^2}{N} = \frac{244}{10} = 24.40$$

$$SD \text{ or } \sigma = \sqrt{\frac{\sum x^2}{N}} = \sqrt{24.40} = 4.9$$

Note. The symbols Σ and σ given in this table are the capital and lowercase of the same Greek letter, pronounced "sigma." In many statistical writings, *SD* (or simply *S*) refers to the standard deviation of the sample on which the data were actually obtained, while σ refers to the estimated value of the standard deviation in the population from which the sample was drawn.

column of Table 3–2. The sum of this column divided by the number of cases[1] $\left(\frac{\sum x^2}{N}\right)$ is known as the *variance*, or *mean square deviation*. The variance has proved extremely useful in sorting out the contributions of different factors to individual differences in test performance. For the present purposes, however, our chief concern is with the *SD*, which is the square root of the variance, as shown in Table 3–2. This measure is commonly employed in comparing the variability of different groups. In Figure 3–2, for example, are two distributions having the same mean but differing in variability. The distribution with wider individual difference yields a larger *SD* than the one with narrower individual differences. When assessing the relative performance of two groups, we should compare both *SDs* and means. If the two groups differ in variability, it may indicate group differences in the proportion of high scorers, low scorers, or both, regardless of

[1] The computations illustrated in this chapter deal with *descriptive statistics,* which refers to the sample actually measured; in *inferential statistics,* the N is replaced by N-1 in order to estimate corresponding population values from sample data. The smaller the sample, the greater will be the difference between sample and population values. For explanation, see any current statistics text (e.g., Comrey & Lee, 1992).

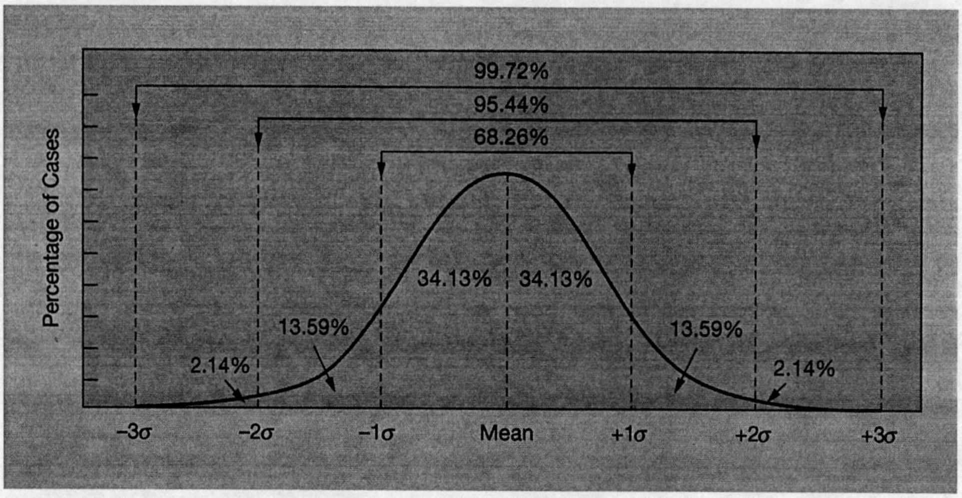

Figure 3-3. Percentage Distribution of Cases in a Normal Curve.

mean differences. Comprehensive procedures for combining the effects of mean differences and *SD* differences are available (see, e.g., Feingold, 1995).

The *SD* also provides the basis for expressing an individual's scores on different tests in terms of norms, as will be shown in the section on standard scores. The interpretation of the *SD* is especially clear-cut when applied to a normal or approximately normal distribution curve. In such a distribution, there is an exact relationship between the *SD* and the proportion of cases, as shown in Figure 3–3. On the baseline of this normal curve have been marked distances representing one, two, and three standard deviations above and below the mean. For instance, in the example given in Table 3–2, the mean would correspond to a score of 40; $+1\sigma$ would correspond to 44.9 (i.e., 40 + 4.9); $+2\sigma$, to 49.8 (i.e., $40 + 2 \times 4.9$); and so on. The percentage of cases that fall between the mean and $+1\sigma$ in a normal curve is 34.13. Because the curve is symmetrical, 34.13% of the cases are likewise found between the mean and -1σ, so that between $+1\sigma$ and -1σ on both sides of the mean there are 68.26% of the cases. Nearly all the cases (99.72%) fall within $\pm 3\sigma$ from the mean. These relationships are particularly relevant in the interpretation of standard scores and percentiles, discussed in later sections.

DEVELOPMENTAL NORMS

One way in which meaning can be attached to test scores is to indicate how far along the normal developmental path the individual has progressed. Thus an 8-year-old who performs as well as the average 10-year-old on an intelligence test may be described as having a mental age of 10; a mentally retarded adult who performs at the same level would likewise be assigned an MA of 10. In a different context, a fourth-grade child may be characterized as reaching the sixth-grade norm in a reading test and the third-grade norm in an arithmetic test. Other developmental systems utilize more highly qualitative descriptions of behavior in specific functions, such as sensorimotor activities or concept formation. However expressed, scores based on developmental norms tend to be psychometrically crude and do not lend themselves well to precise statistical treatment.

Nevertheless, they have considerable appeal for descriptive purposes, especially in the intensive clinical study of individuals and for certain research purposes.

Mental Age. In chapter 2 it was noted that the term "mental age" was widely popularized through the various translations and adaptations of the Binet-Simon scales, although Binet himself had employed the more neutral term "mental level." In age scales such as the Binet and its revisions (prior to 1986), items were grouped into year levels. For example, those items passed by the majority of 7-year-olds in the standardization sample were placed in the 7-year level, those passed by the majority of 8-year-olds were assigned to the 8-year level, and so forth. A child's score on the test would then correspond to the highest year level that he or she could successfully complete. In actual practice, the individual's performance showed a certain amount of *scatter.* In other words, examinees failed some tests below their mental age and passed some above it. For this reason, it was customary to compute the *basal age,* that is, the highest age at and below which all tests were passed. Partial credits, in months, were then added to this basal age for all tests passed at higher year levels. The child's mental age on the test was the sum of the basal age and the additional months of credit earned at higher age levels.

Mental age norms have also been employed with tests that are not divided into year levels. In such a case, the child's raw score is first determined. Such a score may be the total number of correct items on the whole test; or it may be based on time, on number of errors, or on some combination of such measures. The mean raw scores obtained by the children in each year group within the standardization sample constitute the age norms for such a test. The mean raw score of the 8-year-old children, for example, would represent the 8-year norm. If an individual's raw score is equal to the mean 8-year-old raw score, then her or his mental age on the test is 8 years. All raw scores on such a test can be transformed in a similar manner by reference to the age norms.

It should be noted that the mental age unit does not remain constant with age but tends to shrink with advancing years. For example, a child who is one year retarded at age 4 will be approximately three years retarded at age 12. One year of mental growth from ages 3 to 4 is equivalent to three years of growth from ages 9 to 12. Since intellectual development progresses more rapidly at the earlier ages and gradually decreases as the individual approaches her or his mature limit, the mental age unit shrinks correspondingly with age. This relationship may be more readily visualized if we think of the individual's height as being expressed in terms of "height age." The difference, in inches, between a height age of 3 and 4 years would be greater than that between a height age of 10 and 11. Owing to the progressive shrinkage of the MA unit, one year of acceleration or retardation at, let us say, age 5 represents a larger deviation from the norm than does one year of acceleration or retardation at age 10.

Grade Equivalents. A grade norm (or grade equivalent) is defined as the mean score obtained by students in a given grade level. For instance, if the average number of problems solved correctly in an arithmetic test by the students of fourth grade is 23, then a score of 23 corresponds to a grade equivalent of 4.0. Intermediate grade equivalents, representing fractions of a grade, are usually calculated by interpolation, although they can also be obtained directly by testing students at different times within an academic year. Assuming that the academic year covers ten months, successive months can be expressed as decimals. For example, 4.0 refers to an average performance at the beginning of the fourth grade (let's say April testing), and 4.5 in the middle of the grade (let's say September testing), and so forth.

Grade equivalents depict the level of test performance for each grade in the normative sample. These scores indicate that a student of a certain grade has attained the same scores (or number of correct answers) as the average student in the test's norm group. A grade norm is rarely used with ability tests. For example, if a student obtains a grade equivalent score of 4.5 on a test of basic reading skills, it means that the student has obtained the same score as the average student of the fourth grade in the test's norm group. It does not mean the student acquired or demonstrated the same level of proficiency consistent with curricular expectations as the average student of the fourth grade at the student's school. Hence, grade equivalents are used in school settings to report the levels of achievement of students.

Despite their sudden popularity in India, grade norms have several shortcomings. First, the content of instruction varies from grade to grade. Hence, grade norms are appropriate only for subjects taught throughout the grade levels, which are covered by the test. They are not generally applicable at a high school level, where many subjects may be studied for only one or two years. Even with the subjects taught in each grade, the emphasis given on different subjects may vary from grade to grade; therefore, the progress may be better in one subject than in the other during the course of a particular grade. In other words, grade units are noticeably unequal, and these inequalities occur unevenly in different subjects.

Ordinal Scales. Ordinal scales approach is based on the identification of some invariant neurodevelopmental sequence of development in a child such as crawling, standing, walking, and running. In ordinal scales, successful performance at one level implies successful performance at the other preceding levels. The scales developed within this framework are based on the sequential patterning and uniformity of developmental sequences. An example of the application of ordinal scales is the work of Gesell and associates in which the sequential patterning of early behavior development is emphasized.

The well-known ordinal scales are Piaget's stages of development. The broad stages, which span the period from infancy through adolescence, are sensorimotor, pre-operational, concrete operational, and formal operational stages. Piaget's research focused on the development of cognitive processes from infancy to the mid-teens. He was concerned with the specific concepts rather than the broad abilities. An example of such a concept, or schema, is object permanence, whereby the child is aware of the identity and continuing existence of objects when they are seen from different angles or when they are out of sight. Another widely studied concept is conservation or the recognition that an attribute remains constant over changes in perceptual appearance, as when the same quantity of liquid is poured into differently shaped containers or when rods of the same length are placed in different spatial arrangements.

Such Piagetian tasks have been used widely in research by developmental psychologists and have been organized into standardized assessment instruments such as Bayley Scales of Infant Development (BSID). The assessment instruments use ordinal scales and the attainment of one stage is contingent upon completion of the earlier stages in the development of the concept. Tasks in these assessments are designed to reveal the dominant aspects of each developmental stage. The empirical data are gathered to assess the level of each stage. In this respect, the procedure differs from that followed in the constructing age scales, in which items are selected in the first place based on their differentiation between successive ages. Due to the intuitively appealing concepts, the Piagetian approach is readily understandable by laypersons, thereby increasing the interest in the contributions of this approach. However, it comes with its own limitations. For example, it tends to be psychometrically crude on a few occasions, difficult to work with statistically, and may be misleading because a person can earn a high developmental level by excelling at lower developmental level tasks.

In a nutshell, ordinal scales are designed to identify the stage reached by a child in the development of specific behavior functions. Although scores may be reported in terms of approximate age levels, such scores are secondary to a qualitative description of the child's characteristic behavior. The ordinality of such scales refers to the uniform progression of development through successive stages. So far, these scales typically provide information about what a child is actually able to do.

WITHIN-GROUP NORMS

Nearly all standardized tests now provide some form of within-group norms. With such norms, the individual's performance is evaluated in terms of the performance of the most nearly comparable standardization group, as when comparing a child's raw score with that of children of the same chronological age or in the same school grade. Within-group scores have a uniform and clearly defined quantitative meaning and can be appropriately employed in most types of statistical analyses.

Percentiles. Percentile scores are expressed in terms of the percentage of persons in the standardization sample who fall below a given raw score. For example, if 28% of the persons obtain fewer than 15 problems correct on an arithmetic reasoning test, then a raw score of 15 corresponds to the 28th percentile (P_{28}). A percentile indicates the individual's relative position in the standardization sample. Percentiles can also be regarded as ranks in a group of 100, except that in ranking it is customary to start counting at the top, the best person in the group receiving a rank of one. With percentiles, on the other hand, we begin counting at the bottom, so that the lower the percentile, the poorer the individual's standing.

The 50th percentile (P_{50}) corresponds to the median, already discussed as a measure of central tendency. Percentiles above 50 represent above-average performance; those below 50 signify inferior performance. The 25th and 75th percentiles are known as the first and third quartile points (Q_1 and $Q3$), because they cut off the lowest and highest quarters of the distribution. Like the median, they provide convenient landmarks for describing a distribution of scores and comparing it with other distributions.

Percentiles should not be confused with the familiar percentage scores. The latter are raw scores, expressed in terms of the percentage of correct items; percentiles are derived scores, expressed in terms of percentage of persons. A raw score lower than any obtained in the standardization sample would have a percentile rank of zero (P_0); one higher than any score in the standardization sample would have a percentile rank of 100 (P_{100}). These percentiles, however, do not imply a zero raw score and a perfect raw score.

Percentile scores have several advantages. They are easy to compute and can be readily understood, even by technically untrained persons. Moreover, percentiles are universally applicable. They can be used equally well with adults and children and are suitable for any type of test, whether it measures aptitude or personality variables.

A few of the widely followed or practiced aptitude and personality tests in India, such as Watson Glaser Critical Thinking Appraisal (WGCTA), Raven's Progressive Matrices (RPM), Core Abilities Assessment, SOSIE personality assessment, Hogan Personality Inventory (HPI), and Hogan Development Survey (HDS), use percentile scores for presenting the insights about an individual.

The chief drawback of percentile scores arises from the marked inequality of their units, especially at the extremes of the distribution. If the distribution of raw scores approximates the normal curve, as is true of most test scores, then raw score differences near the median or center of the distribution are exaggerated in the percentile transformation, whereas raw score differences near the ends of the distribution are greatly shrunk. This distortion of distances between scores can be seen in Figure 3–4. In a normal curve, it will be recalled, cases cluster closely at the center and scatter more widely as the extremes are approached. Consequently, any given percentage of cases near the center covers a shorter distance on the baseline than does the same percentage near the ends of the distribution. In Figure 3–4, this discrepancy in the gaps between percentile ranks (*PR*)

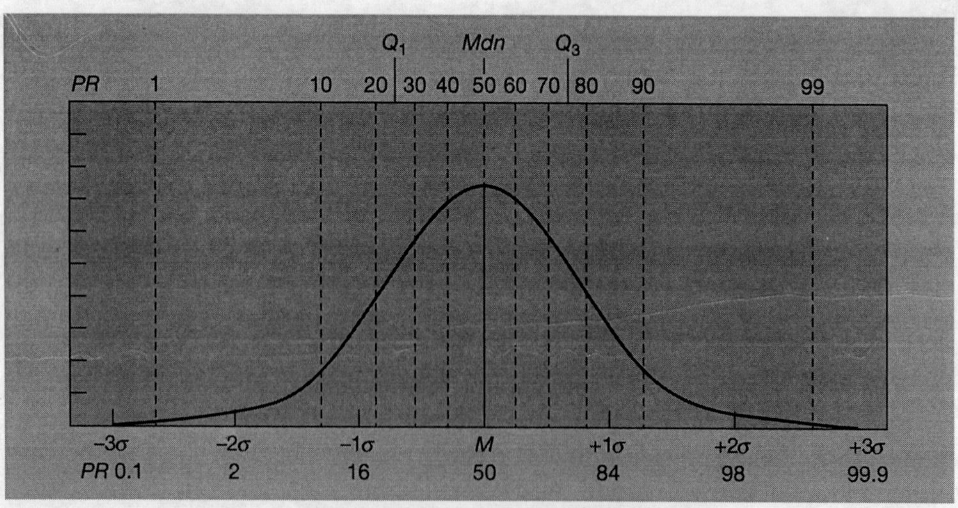

Figure 3–4. Percentile Ranks in a Normal Distribution.

can readily be seen if we compare the distance between a *PR* of 40 and a *PR* of 50 with that between a *PR* of 10 and a *PR* of 20. Even more striking is the discrepancy between these distances and that between a *PR* of 10 and *PR* of 1. (In a mathematically derived normal curve, zero percentile is not reached until infinity and hence cannot be shown on the graph.)

The same relationship can be seen from the opposite direction if we examine the percentile ranks corresponding to equal σ-distances from the mean of a normal curve. These percentile ranks are given under the graph in Figure 3–4. Thus, the percentile difference between the mean and $+1\sigma$ is 34 (84 − 50). That between $+1\sigma$ and $+2\sigma$ is only 14 (98 − 84).

It is apparent that percentiles show each individual's relative position in the normative sample but not the amount of difference between scores. If plotted on arithmetic probability paper, however, percentile scores can also provide a correct visual picture of the differences between scores. Arithmetic probability paper is a cross-section paper in which the vertical lines are spaced in the same way as the percentile points in a normal distribution (as in Fig. 3–4), whereas the horizontal lines are uniformly spaced, or vice versa (as in Fig.3–5). Such *normal percentile charts* can be used to plot the scores of different persons on the same test or the scores of the same person on different tests. In either case, the actual interscore difference will be correctly represented. Many aptitude and achievement

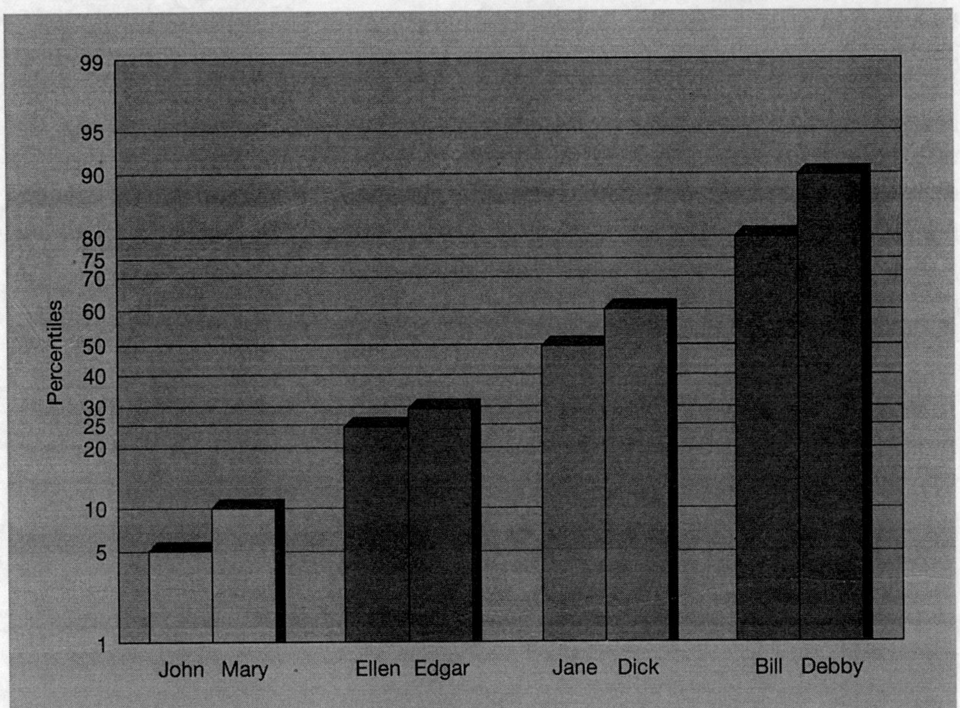

Figure 3–5. A Normal Percentile Chart: Percentiles are spaced so as to correspond to equal distances in a normal distribution. Compare the score distance between John and Mary with that between Ellen and Edgar; within both pairs, the percentile difference is 5 points. Jane and Dick differ by 10 percentile points, as do Bill and Debby.

batteries now utilize this technique in their score profiles, which show the individual's performance in each test.

Standard Scores. Current tests such as 16 Personality Factors (16PF), 15 Factor Questionnaire (15FQ), and Personality and Preference Inventory (PAPI) are making increasing use of the standard scores, which are the most satisfactory type of derived scores from most of the viewpoints. Standard scores express the individual's distance from the mean in terms of the standard deviation of the distribution.

Standard scores may be obtained by either linear or nonlinear transformations of the original raw scores. When found by a *linear transformation,* they retain the exact numerical relations of the original raw scores, because they are computed by subtracting a constant from each raw score and then dividing the result by another constant. The relative magnitude of differences between standard scores derived by such a linear transformation corresponds exactly to that between the raw scores. All properties of the original distribution of raw scores are duplicated in the distribution of these standard scores. For this reason, any computations that can be carried out with the original raw scores can also be carried out with linear standard scores, without any distortion of results.

Linearly derived standard scores are often designated simply as "standard scores" or "*z* scores." To compute a *z* score, we find the difference between the individual's raw score and the mean of the normative group and then divide this difference by the *SD* of the normative group. Table 3–3 shows the computation of *z* scores for two individuals; one falls 1 *SD* above the group mean, the other .40 *SD* below the mean. Any raw score that is exactly equal to the mean is equivalent to a *z* score of zero. It is apparent that such a procedure will yield derived scores that have a negative sign for all persons falling below the mean. Moreover, because the total range of most groups extends no further than about 3 *SDs* above and below the mean, such standard scores will have to be reported to at least one decimal place in order to provide sufficient differentiation among individuals.

Both the above conditions—that is, the occurrence of negative values and of decimals—tend to produce awkward numbers that are confusing and difficult to

Table 3-3

Computation of Standard Scores

$$z = \frac{X - M}{SD} \qquad M = 60 \qquad SD = 5$$

HELEN'S SCORE	*BILL'S SCORE*
$X_1 = 65$	$X_2 = 58$
$z_1 = \frac{65-60}{5}$	$z_2 = \frac{58-60}{5}$
$= +1.00$	$= -0.40$

use for both computational and reporting purposes. For this reason, some further linear transformation is usually applied, simply to put the scores into a more convenient form. For example, the scores on the Scholastic Assessment Tests (SAT) of the College Board are standard scores adjusted to a mean of 500 and an *SD* of 100. Thus a standard score of −1 on this test would be expressed as 400 (500 − 100 = 400). Similarly, a standard score of +1.5 would correspond to 650 (500 + 1.5 × 100 = 650). To convert an original standard score to the new scale, it is simply necessary to multiply the standard score by the desired *SD* (100) and add it to or subtract it from the desired mean (500). Any other convenient values can be arbitrarily chosen for the new mean and *SD*. Scores on the separate subtests of the Wechsler Intelligence Scales, for instance, are converted to a distribution with a mean of 10 and an *SD* of 3. All such measures are examples of linearly transformed standard scores.

It will be recalled that one of the reasons for transforming raw scores into any derived scale is to render scores on different tests comparable. The linearly derived standard scores discussed in the preceding section will be comparable only when found from distributions that have approximately the same form. Under such conditions, a score corresponding to 1 *SD* above the mean, for example, signifies that the individual occupies the same position in relation to both groups. The score exceeds approximately the same percentage of persons in both distributions, and this percentage can be determined if the form of the distribution is known. If, however, one distribution is markedly skewed and the other normal, a z score of +1.00 might exceed only 50% of the cases in one group but would exceed 84% in the other.

In order to achieve comparability of scores from dissimilarly shaped distributions, nonlinear transformations may be employed to fit the scores to any specified type of distribution curve. The mental age and percentile scores described in earlier sections represent nonlinear transformations, but they are subject to other limitations already discussed. Although under certain circumstances another type of distribution may be more appropriate, the normal curve is usually employed for this purpose. One of the chief reasons for this choice is that most raw score distributions approximate the normal curve more closely than they do any other type of curve. Moreover, physical measures such as height and weight, which use equal-unit scales derived through physical operations, generally yield normal distributions. Another important advantage of the normal curve is that it has many useful mathematical properties, which facilitate further computations.

Normalized standard scores are standard scores expressed in terms of a distribution that has been transformed to fit a normal curve. Such scores can be computed by reference to tables giving the percentage of cases falling at different *SD* distances from the mean of a normal curve. First, the percentage of persons in the standardization sample falling at or above each raw score is found. This percentage is then located in the normal curve frequency table, and the corresponding normalized standard score is obtained. Normalized standard scores are expressed in the same form as linearly derived standard scores, that is, with a mean of zero and an *SD* of 1. Thus, a normalized score of zero indicates that the individual falls at the mean of a normal curve, excelling 50% of the group. A score of −1 means that he or she surpasses approximately 16% of the group; and a score of +1, that he or she surpasses 84%. These percentages correspond to a distance of 1 *SD* below and 1 *SD* above the mean of a normal curve, respectively, as can be seen by reference to the bottom line of Figure 3–4.

Like linearly derived standard scores, normalized standard scores can be put into any convenient form. If the normalized standard score is multiplied by 10 and added to or subtracted from 50, it is converted into a *T score,* a type of score first proposed by W. A. McCall (1922). On this scale, a score of 50 corresponds to the mean, a score of 60 to 1 *SD* above the mean, and so forth. Another well-known transformation is represented by the *stanine* scale, developed by the United States Air Force during World War II. This scale provides a single-digit system of scores with a mean of 5 and an *SD* of approximately 2.[2] The name "stanine" (a contraction of "*standard nine*") is based on the fact that the scores run from 1 to 9. The restriction of scores to single-digit numbers has certain computational advantages, since each score requires only a single column on a computer.

Table 3-4

Normal Curve Percentages for Use in Stanine Conversion

Percentage	4	7	12	17	20	17	12	7	4
Stanine	1	2	3	4	5	6	7	8	9

Raw scores can readily be converted to stanines by arranging the original scores in order of size and then assigning stanines in accordance with the normal curve percentages reproduced in Table 3–4. For example, if the group consists of exactly 100 persons, the 4 lowest-scoring persons receive a stanine score of 1, the next 7 a score of 2, the next 12 a score of 3, and so on. When the group contains more or fewer than 100 cases, the number corresponding to each designated percentage is first computed, and these numbers of cases are then given the appropriate stanines. Thus, out of 200 cases, 8 would be assigned a stanine of 1 (4% of 200 = 8). With 150 cases, 6 would receive a stanine of 1 (4% of 150 = 6). For any group containing from 10 to 100 cases, Bartlett and Edgerton (1966) prepared a table whereby ranks can be directly converted to stanines. Because of their practical as well as theoretical advantages, stanines have been used widely, especially with aptitude and achievement tests.

Although normalized standard scores are the most satisfactory type of score for the majority of purposes, there are nevertheless certain technical objections to normalizing all distributions routinely. Such a transformation should be carried out only when the sample is large and representative and when there is reason to believe that the deviation from normality results from defects in the test rather than from characteristics of the sample and from other factors affecting the behavior under consideration. It should also be noted that when the original distribution of raw scores approximates normality, the linearly derived standard scores and the normalized standard scores will be very similar. Although the methods

[2] Kaiser (1958)proposed a modification of the stanine scale that involves slight changes in the percentages and yields an *SD* of exactly 2, thus being easier to handle quantitatively. Other variants are the C scale (Guilford & Fruchter, 1978, pp.484–487), consisting of 11 units and also yielding an *SD* of 2, and the 10-unit *sten* scale, with 5 units above and 5 below the mean (Canfield, 1951).

Table 3-5

Widely Employed Tests in India Using Normalized Standard Scores

Type of Normalized Standard Scores	Examples of the Test(s)
Sten Scores	16 Personality Factors (16 PF), 15 Factor Questionnaire (15FQ), Occupational Personality Questionnaire (OPQ), Personality and Preferençe Inventory (PAPI)
Stanine Scores	Orpheus Personality Questionnaire, Watson Glaser Critical Thinking Appraisal (only sub-scale scores)
T- Scores	Neo–Personality Inventory (Neo–PI), Minnesota Multiphasic Personality Inventory (MMPI)

of deriving these two types of scores are quite different, the resulting scores will be nearly identical under such conditions. Obviously, the process of normalizing a distribution that is already virtually normal will produce little or no change. Whenever feasible, it is generally more desirable to obtain a normal distribution of raw scores by proper adjustment of the difficulty level of test items rather than by subsequently normalizing a markedly nonnormal distribution. With an approximately normal distribution of raw scores, the linearly derived standard scores will serve the same purposes as normalized standard scores.

The Deviation IQ. In an effort to convert MA scores into a uniform index of the individual's relative status, the ratio IQ (Intelligence Quotient) was introduced in early intelligence tests. Such an IQ was simply the ratio of mental age to chronological age, multiplied by 100 to eliminate decimals (IQ = 100 × MA/CA). Obviously if a child's MA equaled her or his CA, that child's IQ was exactly 100. An IQ of 100 thus represented normal or average performance. IQs below 100 indicated "retardation"; those above 100, "acceleration."

The apparent logical simplicity of the traditional ratio IQ, however, soon proved deceptive. A major technical difficulty is that, unless the *SD* of the IQ distribution remains approximately constant with age, IQs will not be comparable at different age levels. An IQ of 115 at age 10, for example, may indicate the same degree of superiority as an IQ of 125 at age 12, since both may fall at a distance of 1 *SD* from the means of their respective age distributions. In actual practice, it proved very difficult to construct tests that met the psychometric requirements for comparability of ratio IQs throughout their age range. Chiefly for this reason, the ratio IQ has been largely replaced by the so-called deviation IQ, which is actually another variant of the familiar standard score. The deviation IQ is a standard score with a mean of 100 and an *SD* that approximates the *SD* of the Stanford-Binet IQ distribution. Although the *SD* of the Stanford-Binet ratio IQ (last used in the 1937 edition) was not exactly constant at all ages, it fluctuated around a median value slightly greater than 16. Hence, if an *SD* close to 16 is chosen in reporting standard scores on a newly developed test, the resulting scores can be interpreted in the same way as Stanford-Binet ratio IQs. Since Stanford-Binet IQs have been in use for many years, testers and clinicians have become accustomed to interpreting and classifying test performance in terms of such IQ levels. They have learned what to expect from individuals with IQs of 40, 70, 90, 130, and so forth. There are therefore certain practical advantages in the use of a derived scale that corresponds to the familiar distribution of Stanford-Binet IQs. Such a correspondence of score units can be achieved by the selection of numerical values for the mean and *SD* that agree closely with those in the Stanford-Binet distribution.

The most commonly followed or practised intelligence tests in India and abroad that deploy the Deviation IQ approach are Wechsler Adult Intelligence Scale (WAIS), Wechsler Intelligence Scale for Children (WISC), Cognitive Assessment System (CAS), Kaufman Brief Intelligence Test (KBIT), and Detroit Tests of Learning Aptitude.

It should be added that the use of the term "IQ" to designate such standard scores may be somewhat misleading. Such IQs are not derived by the same methods employed in finding traditional ratio IQs. They are *not* ratios of mental ages and chronological ages. The justification lies in the general familiarity of the term "IQ," and in the fact that such scores *can* be interpreted as IQs provided that their SD is approximately equal to that of previously known IQs. Among the first tests to express scores in terms of deviation IQs were the Wechsler Intelligence Scales. In these tests, the mean is 100 and the *SD* 15. Deviation IQs are also used in a number of current group tests of intelligence and in the third (1960) revision of the Stanford-Binet itself.

With the increasing use of deviation IQs, it is important to remember that deviation IQs from different tests are comparable only when they employ the same or closely similar values for the *SD*. This value should always be reported in the manual and carefully noted by the test user. If a test maker chooses a different value for the *SD* in making up the deviation IQ scale, the meaning of any given IQ on that test will be quite different from its meaning on other tests. These discrepancies are illustrated in Table 3–6, which shows the percentage of cases in normal distributions with *SDs* from 12 to 18 who would obtain IQs at different levels. These *SD* values have actually been employed in the IQ scales of published tests. Table 3–6 shows, for example, that an IQ of 70 cuts off the lowest 3.1% when the *SD* is 16 (as in the Stanford-Binet); but it may cut off as few as 0.7% (*SD* = 12) or as many as 5.1% (*SD* = 18). An IQ of 70 has been used traditionally as a cutoff point for identifying clinically significant mental retardation. The same discrepancies, of course, apply to IQs of 130 and above, which might be used in selecting children for special programs for the intellectually gifted. The IQ range between 90 and 110, generally described as normal, may include as few as 42% or as many as 59.6% of the population, depending on the test chosen. To be sure, test publishers are making efforts to adopt the uniform *SD* of 16 in new tests and in new editions of earlier tests. There are still enough variations among currently available tests, however, to make the checking of the *SD* imperative.

Interrelationships of Within-Group Scores. At this stage in our discussion of derived scores, the reader may have become aware of a approchement among the various types of scores. Percentiles have gradually been taking on at least a graphic resemblance to normalized standard scores. Linear standard scores are indistinguishable from normalized standard scores if the original distribution of

Table 3-6

Percentage of Cases of Each IQ Interval in Normal Distributions with Mean of 100 and Different Standard Deviations

IQ Interval	Percentage Frequency			
	SD = 12	*SD* = 14	*SD* = 16	*SD* = 18
130 and above	0.7	1.6	3.1	5.1
120–129	4.3	6.3	7.5	8.5
110–119	15.2	16.0	15.8	15.4
100–109	29.8 } 59.6	26.1 } 52.2	23.6 } 47.2	21.0 } 42.0
90–99	29.8	26.1	23.6	21.0
80–89	15.2	16.0	15.8	15.4
70–79	4.3	6.3	7.5	8.5
Below 70	0.7	1.6	3.1	5.1
Total	100.0	100.0	100.0	100.0

(Courtesy of The Psychological Corporation.)

raw scores closely approximates the normal curve. Finally, standard scores have become IQs and vice versa. In connection with the last point, a reexamination of the meaning of a ratio IQ on such a test as the Stanford-Binet will show that these early ratio IQs can themselves be interpreted as standard scores. If we know that the distribution of Stanford-Binet ratio IQs had a mean of 100 and an *SD* of approximately 16, we can conclude that an IQ of 116 falls at a distance of 1 *SD* above the mean and represents a standard score of +1.00. Similarly, an IQ of 132 corresponds to a standard score of+2.00, an IQ of 76 to a standard score of–1.50, and so forth. Moreover, a Stanford-Binet ratio IQ of 116 corresponds to a percentile rank of approximately 84, because in a normal curve 84% of the cases fall below+1.00 *SD* (Fig. 3–4).

Figure 3–6 summarizes the relationships that exist in a normal distribution among the types of scores so far discussed in this chapter. These include *z* scores, College Entrance Examination Board (CEEB) scores, Wechsler deviation IQs (*SD* = 15), T scores, stanines, and percentiles. Ratio IQs on any test will coincide with the given deviation IQ scale if they are normally distributed and have an *SD* of 15. Any other normally distributed IQ could be added to the chart, provided we know its *SD*. If the *SD* is 20, for instance, then an IQ of 120 corresponds to +1 *SD*, an IQ of 80 to–1 *SD*, and so on.

In conclusion, the exact form in which scores are reported is dictated largely by convenience, familiarity, and ease of developing norms. Standard scores in any form (including the deviation IQ) have generally replaced other types of scores because of certain advantages they offer with regard to test construction and statistical treatment of data. Most types of within-group derived scores, however, are fundamentally similar if carefully derived and properly interpreted. When certain statistical conditions are met, each of these scores can be readily translated into any of the others.

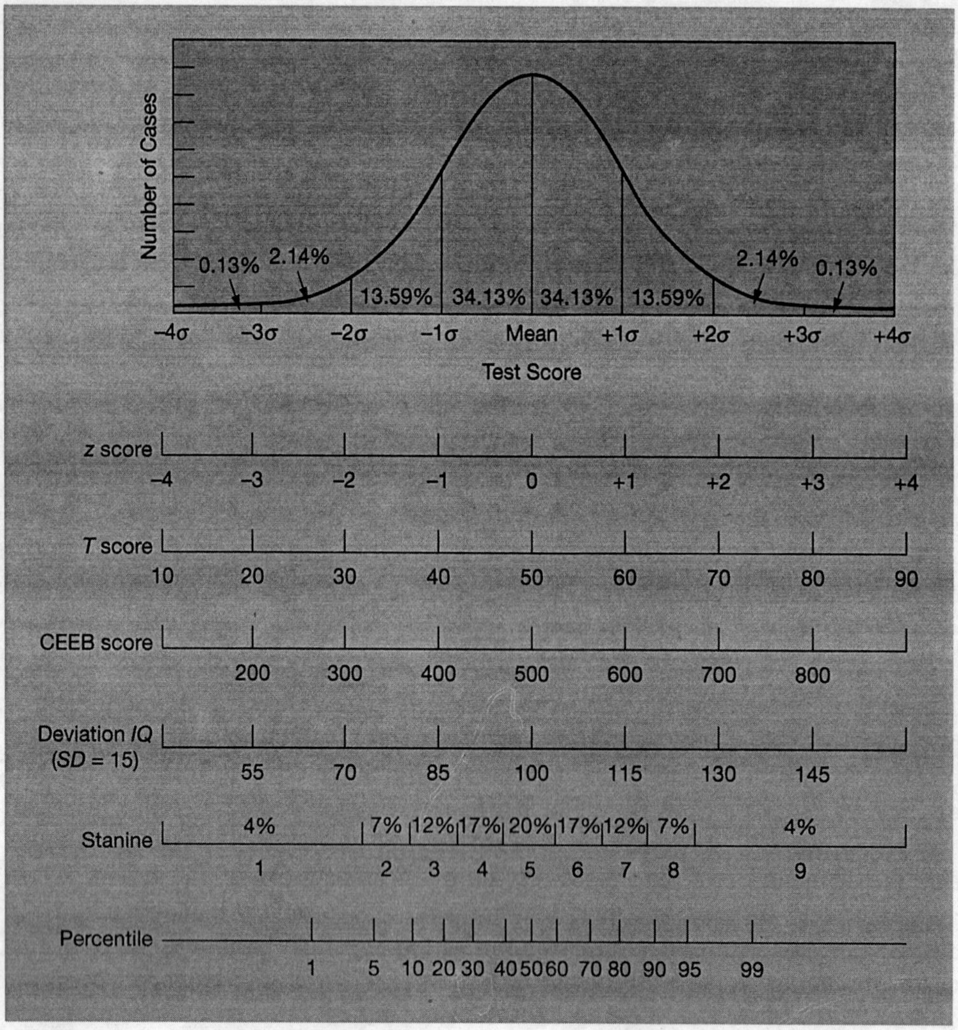

Figure 3-6. Relationships among Different Types of Test Scores in a Normal Distribution.

RELATIVITY OF NORMS

Intertest Comparisons. An IQ, or any other score, should always be accompanied by the name of the test on which it was obtained. Test scores cannot be properly interpreted in the abstract; they must be referred to particular tests. If the school records show that Bill Jones received an IQ of 94 and Terry Brown an IQ of 110, such IQs cannot be accepted at face value without further information. The positions of these two students might have been reversed by exchanging the particular tests that each was given in her or his respective school.

Similarly, an individual's relative standing in different functions may be grossly misrepresented through lack of comparability of test norms. Let us suppose that a student has been given a verbal comprehension test and a spatial aptitude test to determine her relative standing in the two fields. If the verbal ability test was standardized on a random sample of high school students, while the spatial test was standardized on a selected group of students attending elective shop courses, the examiner might erroneously conclude that the individual is much more able along verbal than along spatial lines, when the reverse may actually be the case.

Still another example involves longitudinal comparisons of a single individual's test performance over time. If a schoolchild's cumulative record shows IQs of 118, 115, and 101 at the fourth, fifth, and sixth grades, the first question to ask before interpreting these changes is, "What tests did the child take on these three occasions?" The apparent decline may reflect no more than the differences among the tests. In that case, the child would have obtained these scores even if the three tests had been administered within a week of one another.

There are three principal reasons to account for systematic variations among the scores obtained by the same individual on different tests. First, tests may differ in *content* despite their similar labels. So-called intelligence tests provide many illustrations of this confusion. Although commonly described by the same blanket term, one of these tests may include only verbal content, another may tap predominantly spatial aptitudes, and still another may cover verbal, numerical, and spatial content in about equal proportions. Second, the *scale units* may not be comparable. As explained earlier in this chapter, if IQs on one test have an *SD* of 12 and IQs on another have an *SD* of 18, then an individual who received an IQ of 112 on the first test is most likely to receive an IQ of 118 on the second. Third, the composition of the *standardization samples* used in establishing norms for different tests may vary. Obviously, the same individual will appear to have performed better when compared with a less able group than when compared with a more able group.

Lack of comparability of either test content or scale units can usually be detected by reference to the test itself or to the test manual. Differences in the respective normative samples, however, are more likely to be overlooked. Such differences probably account for many otherwise unexplained discrepancies in test results.

The Normative Sample. Any norm, however, expressed, is restricted to the particular normative population from which it was derived. The test user should never lose sight of the way in which norms are established. Psychological test norms are in no sense absolute, universal, or permanent. They merely represent the test performance of the persons constituting the standardization sample. In choosing such a sample, an effort is usually made to obtain a representative cross-section of the population for which the test is designed.

In statistical terminology, a distinction is made between *sample* and *population*. The sample refers to the group of persons actually tested. The population designates the larger, but similarly constituted, group from which the sample is drawn. For example, if we wish to establish norms of test performance for the population of 10-year-old, urban, public school boys, we might test a carefully chosen sample of 500 10-year-old boys attending public schools in several American cities. The sample would be checked with reference to geographical distribution, socioeconomic level, ethnic composition, and other relevant characteristics to ensure that it was truly representative of the defined population.

In the development and application of test norms, considerable attention should be given to the standardization sample. It is apparent that the sample on which the norms are based should be large enough to provide stable values. Another, similarly chosen sample of the same population should not yield norms that diverge appreciably from those obtained. Norms with a large sampling error would obviously be of little value in the interpretation of test scores.

Equally important is the requirement that the sample be representative of the population under consideration. Subtle selective factors that might make the sample unrepresentative should be carefully investigated. A number of such selective factors are illustrated in institutional samples. Because such samples are usually large and readily available for testing purposes, they offer an alluring field for the accumulation of normative data. The special limitations of these samples, however, should be carefully analyzed. Testing persons in school, for example, will yield an increasingly superior selection of cases in the successive grades, owing to the progressive dropping out of the less able students. Nor does such elimination affect different subgroups equally. For example, the rate of selective elimination from school is greater for boys than for girls, and it is greater at lower than at higher socioeconomic levels.

Selective factors likewise operate in other institutional samples, such as prisoners, patients in mental hospitals, or institutionalized mentally retarded persons. Because of the many special factors that determine institutionalization itself, such groups are not representative of the entire population of law breakers, mentally disturbed persons, or mentally retarded persons. For example, mentally retarded individuals with physical handicaps are more likely to be institutionalized than are the physically fit. Similarly, the relative proportion of severely retarded persons will be much greater in institutional samples than in the total population.

Closely related to the question of sample representativeness is the need for defining the specific population to which the norms can be generalized. Obviously, one way of ensuring that a sample is representative is to restrict the population to fit the specifications of the available sample. For example, if the population is defined to include only 14-year-old schoolchildren rather than all 14-year-old children, then a school sample would be representative. Ideally, of course, the desired population should be defined in advance in terms of the objectives of the test. Then a suitable sample should be assembled. Practical obstacles in obtaining participants, however, may make this goal unattainable. In such a case, it is far better to redefine the population more narrowly than to report norms on an ideal population that is not adequately represented by the standardization sample. In actual practice, very few tests are standardized on such broad populations as is popularly assumed. No test provides norms for the human species! And it is doubtful whether many tests give truly adequate norms for such broadly defined populations as "adult American men," "10-year-old American children," and the like. Consequently, the samples obtained by different test constructors may be unrepresentative of their alleged populations and biased in different ways. Hence, the resulting norms may not be comparable.

When interpreting test scores, the test user should take into account the specific influences that may have acted upon the normative sample employed in standardizing the particular test. Such influences would include special selective factors, as well as societal conditions prevailing at the time the normative data were collected (Anastasi, 1985d).

National Anchor Norms. One solution for the lack of comparability of norms is to use an anchor test to work out equivalency tables for scores on different tests. Such tables are designed to show what score in Test A is equivalent to each score in Test B. This can be done by the *equipercentile method,* in which scores are considered equivalent when they have equal percentiles in a given group. For example, if the 80th percentile in the same group corresponds to an IQ of 115 on Test A and to an IQ of 120 on Test B, then Test-A-IQ 115 is considered equivalent to Test B-IQ-120. This approach has been followed to a limited extent by some test publishers, who have prepared equivalency tables for a few of their own tests (e.g., Lennon, 1966a).

More ambitious proposals have been made from time to time for calibrating each new test against a single anchor test, which has itself been administered to a highly representative, national normative sample (Lennon, 1966b). An example of this procedure is provided by the Anchor Test Study conducted by Educational Testing Service under the auspices of the U. S. Office of Education (Jaeger, 1973). This study represents a systematic effort to provide comparable and truly representative national norms for seven of the most widely used reading achievement tests for elementary schoolchildren. Through a well-controlled experimental design, more than 300,000 fourth-, fifth-, and sixth-grade schoolchildren were examined in 50 states. The anchor test consisted of the reading comprehension and vocabulary subtests of the Metropolitan Achievement Test, for which new norms were established in one phase of the project. In the calibrating phase of the study, each child took the reading comprehension and vocabulary subtests from two of the seven batteries, each battery being paired in turn with every other battery. Some groups took parallel forms of the two subtests from the same battery. In still other groups, all the pairings were duplicated in reverse sequence, in order to control for order of administration. From statistical analyses of all these data, score equivalency tables for the seven tests were prepared by the equipercentile method. A manual for interpreting scores was prepared for use by school systems and other interested persons (Loret, Seder, Bianchini, & Vale, 1974).

The data from the calibrating phase of the Anchor Test Study were subsequently used to develop a single score scale, designated as the National Reference Scale (Rentz & Bashaw, 1977). The conversion table thus developed permits the transformation of a score from any form of the seven tests at any of the grade levels into a three-place score on a uniform, continuous scale. This scale was constructed by using the item analysis and scaling methods of the Rasch model, one of the simplest of the item analysis models discussed in a later section of this chapter and described more fully in chapter 7.

For many testing purposes, it is useful to have comparable scores from different tests that are expressed on a uniform scale of measurement and referred to a single normative sample. It should be noted, however, that there are different degrees and kinds of score comparability. The comparability obtained in particular situations depends upon the similarity of the tests in content and in such psychometric properties as reliability and difficulty level, as well as on the statistical procedures used to achieve comparability (Angoff, 1984; Angoff & Cowell, 1986; P. W. Holland & Rubin, 1982). Tests should not be described as equated or fully equivalent unless they are truly interchangeable. Nevertheless, different kinds and degrees of comparability *can* facilitate the interpretation of test results, provided that the comparable scores are used appropriately and with full knowledge of how they were derived.

Specific Norms. Another approach to the nonequivalence of existing norms—and probably a more realistic one for most tests—is to standardize tests on more narrowly defined populations, so chosen as to suit the specific purposes of each test. In such cases, the limits of the normative population should be clearly reported with the norms. Thus, the norms might be said to apply to "employed clerical workers in large business organizations" or to "first-year engineering students." For many testing purposes, highly specific norms are desirable. Even when representative norms are available for a broadly defined population, it is often helpful to have separately reported *subgroup norms*. This is true whenever recognizable subgroups yield appreciably different scores on a particular test. The subgroups may be formed with respect to age, grade, type of curriculum, sex, geographical region, urban or rural environment, socioeconomic level, and many other variables. The use to be made of the test determines the type of differentiation that is most relevant, as well as whether general or specific norms are more appropriate.

Mention should also be made of *local norms*, often developed by the test users themselves within a particular setting. The groups employed in deriving such norms are even more narrowly defined than the subgroups considered previously. Thus, an employer may accumulate norms on applicants for a given type of job within a particular company. A college admissions office may develop norms on its own student population. Or a single elementary school may evaluate the performance of individual pupils in terms of its own score distribution. These local norms are more appropriate than broad national norms for many testing purposes, such as the prediction of subsequent job performance or college achievement, the comparison of a child's relative achievement in different subjects, or the measurement of an individual's progress over time.

Fixed Reference Group. Although the way most derived scores are computed provides an immediate normative interpretation of test performance, there are some notable exceptions. One type of nonnormative scale utilizes a fixed reference group in order to ensure *comparability and continuity* of scores, without providing normative evaluation of performance. With such a scale, normative interpretation requires reference to independently collected norms from a suitable population. Local or other specific norms are often used for this purpose.

One of the earliest examples of scaling in terms of a fixed reference group is provided by the score scale of the College Board Scholastic Aptitude Test[3] (Donlon, 1984). Between 1926 (when this test was first administered) and 1941, SAT scores were expressed on a normative scale, in terms of the mean and *SD* of

[3] This test was later renamed *the Scholastic Assessment Test*, in order to reflect the altered orientation toward the nature of test scores, which emerged toward the end of the twentieth century. (See especially chap. 12 for the effect of individual differences in experiential history on test performance.)

the candidates taking the test at each administration. As the number and variety of College Board member colleges increased and the composition of the candidate population changed, it was concluded that scale continuity should be maintained. Otherwise, an individual's score would depend on the characteristics of the group tested during a particular year. An even more urgent reason for scale continuity stemmed from the observation that students taking the SAT at certain times of the year performed less well than those taking it at other times, owing to the differential operation of selective factors. After 1941, therefore, all SAT scores were expressed in terms of the mean and *SD* of the approximately 11,000 candidates who took the test in 1941. These candidates constituted the fixed reference group employed in scaling subsequent forms of the test. Thus, a score of 500 on any form of the SAT corresponded to the mean of the 1941 sample; a score of 600 fell 1 *SD* above that mean, and so forth.

To permit translation of raw scores on any form of the SAT into these fixed-reference-group scores, a short anchor test (or set of common items) was included in each form. Each new form was thereby linked to one or two earlier forms, which in turn were linked with other forms by a chain of items extending back to the 1941 form. These nonnormative SAT scores could then be interpreted by comparison with any appropriate distribution of scores, such as that of a particular college, a type of college, a region, and so on. These specific norms are more useful in making college admission decisions than would be annual norms based on the entire candidate population. Any changes in the candidate population over time, moreover, can be detected only with a fixed score scale. More recently, the SAT scale has been "recentered" on the performance of over a million students who graduated from high school in 1990 and took the test as juniors or seniors. Scores for students completing the SAT after April 1, 1995, are reported on the "recentered" scale derived from the 1990 reference group. Interpretive materials and aids have been developed to assist test users in converting individual and aggregate scores from the former scale and vice versa (see chap. 17). A full and diversified interpretation of individual performance is thus permitted for specific testing purposes.[4]

Scales built from a fixed reference group are analogous in one respect to scales employed in physical measurement. In this connection, Angoff (1962, pp. 32–33) commented:

> There is hardly a person here who knows the precise original definition of the length of the foot used in the measurement of height or distance, or which king it was whose foot was originally agreed upon as the standard; on the other hand, there is no one here who does not know how to evaluate lengths and distances in terms of this unit. Our ignorance of the precise original meaning or derivation of the foot does not lessen its usefulness to us in any way. Its usefulness derives from the fact that it remains the same over time and allows us to familiarize ourselves with it. Needless to say, precisely the same considerations apply to other units of measurement—the inch, the mile, the degree of Fahrenheit, and so on. In the field of psychological measurement it is similarly reasonable to say that the original definition of the scale is or should be of no consequence. What is of consequence

[4] We acknowledge the assistance of Wayne Camera of the College Board in obtaining the information reported herein.

is the maintenance of a constant scale—which, in the case of a multiple-form testing program, is achieved by rigorous form-to-form equating—and the provision of supplementary normative data to aid in interpretation and in the formation of specific decisions, data which would be revised from time to time as conditions warrant.

Item Response Theory. Since the 1970s, there has been a sharp upsurge of interest in a class of mathematically sophisticated procedures for scaling the difficulty of test items (Hambleton, 1989; Hambleton, Swaminathan, & Rogers, 1991; Jaeger, 1977). Because of the extensive computations required, these procedures became practicable only with the increasing availability of highspeed computers. Although differing in complexity and in specific mathematical procedures, these approaches were originally grouped under the general title of *latent trait models*. The basic measure they used is the probability that a person of specified ability (the so-called latent trait) succeeds on an item of specified difficulty. There is no implication, however, that such latent traits or underlying abilities exist in any physical or physiological sense, nor that they cause behavior. The latent traits are statistical constructs that are derived mathematically from empirically observed relations among test responses. A rough, initial estimate of an examinee's latent trait is the total score he or she obtains on the test. In order to avoid the false impression created by the term "latent trait," some of the leading exponents of these procedures have substituted the more precisely descriptive term "item response theory," or IRT (Lord, 1980; D. J. Weiss & Davison, 1981). This designation has achieved general usage within psychology.

Essentially, IRT models are used to establish a uniform "sample-free" scale of measurement that is applicable to individuals and groups of widely varying ability levels and to test content of widely varying difficulty levels. Like the use of a fixed reference group described in the preceding section, IRT models need anchor items or a common test as a bridge across examinee samples and across tests or sets of items. However, rather than using the mean and *SD* of a specific reference group to define the origin and the unit size of the scale, IRT models set origin and unit size in terms of data representing a wide range of ability and item difficulty, which may come from several samples. Usually the origin is set near the center of this range. The common scale unit is derived mathematically from the item data; it has several advantages, both theoretical and practical, over the earlier item analysis procedures. The specific methodology will be discussed further in chapter 7, in connection with techniques of item analysis. IRT is gradually being incorporated in large-scale testing programs. For example, beginning in 1982, this procedure was adopted for equating total scores on the new forms of the SAT, so as to express them on the continuing, uniform scale (Camara, Freeman, & Everson, 1996; Donlon, 1984).

The general problem of *test equating*, whereby scores from different forms of a test are expressed on a uniform score scale, has received increasing attention. The technical problems of the diverse approaches that are being explored for this purpose are beyond the scope of this text. For a comprehensive survey and critical evaluation of such methodology, the reader is referred to P. W. Holland and Rubin (1982) and to Petersen, Kolen, and Hoover (1989).

COMPUTERS AND INTERPRETATION OF TEST SCORES

The technology has proved to be beneficial in achieving a faster turnaround time in conducting psychological tests, administering these tests on large populations simultaneously, and generating quick results and reports. Apart from the core clinical settings where a face-to-face testing becomes essential, most of the psychological tests in other domains use technology to administer tests and obtain results. Moreover, the increasing rate of computerization of aspects such as scoring, test design, reliability, and validity estimation has led to significant improvement in the dependability and predictability of testing.

The impact of computers and technology is evident in several levels of psychological testing and psychometrics. The first major development was the computerized statistical packages. Complex calculations based on the principles of mathematics have been simplified by these statistical packages. In India, Microsoft Excel is the most preferred software for conducting psychological analysis, while IBM SPSS (Statistical Package for the Social Sciences) has gained momentum recently to run the test analysis. There are other advanced computerized statistical packages such as MPlus and STATA that are widely used in other countries. In India, a challenge that has been observed is, people use readily available statistical packages without fully understanding them. Thus, many novice users find that computers can produce almost endless alternative analyses while their knowledge is limited on the important aspects of the analysis. Teaching, training, and guiding students on such statistical software would change this situation. Books and reading materials that are available on using the statistical packages and interpreting analyses could widen the knowledge of the users.

Computerization has also impacted the development and administration of item banks. Computerized item banks based on the item response theory (IRT) and Rasch (R) models are widely prevalent in Western countries. Internationally, IRT-based item banks have reached their pinnacle; however, this is a fairly new concept in India and many testing companies are exploring opportunities to build their in-house capabilities in this field.

Computerization has greatly affected test administration field. Computerized administration of tests is preferred over paper-pencil testing due to reasons mentioned earlier. Individual test administrations, in particular, are time consuming; whereas, computerization potentially saves time. Further, computer programs are written to allow the testing platform to adapt its questioning to the initial responses of the respondent. In a paper-pencil test, there is no way of knowing how a test taker would respond and, thus, all eventualities have to be covered. However, after knowing some initial information, any irrelevant question can be eliminated in a computerized adaptive test. In addition, the difficulty level of the test can also be tailored as per the ability of an applicant. If a test taker encounters difficulty, the test can be made slightly easier as per his or her ability and vice versa. Such adaptive testing techniques have their own advantages and few organizations in India are focusing on adaptive testing. However, it is still at its nascent stage due to lack of several elements, such as knowledge, software, and sophistication which are needed to interpret the IRT models. The lack of awareness and faith of educational, psychological, and business professionals in models they have difficulties in understanding, also contribute to the nascence of adaptive testing.

Lastly, the role of computerization is being extended in the generation of test reports. No longer do the psychological test reports present mere numbers. With the help of technology, narrative reports are generated in a form that is suitable for the test taker or other end user. However, narrative reports should not be treated as a final analysis of an individual and a substitute for professional advice and consultancy. For instance, most of the Indian organizations arrange either one-on-one or group feedback sessions for the participants with a trained professional or a psychologist, to enable the respondents to understand their narrative reports in their own occupational and personal contexts.

DOMAIN-REFERENCED TEST INTERPRETATION

An approach to testing that aroused a surge of activities in the 1970s was the criterion-referenced testing. Until then, emphasis was always laid on the norm-referenced testing in which the psychometric tests were selected in such a way that the test scores would have a normal distribution, if administered to a large sample and that they could be easily standardized. The objective of doing so was to arrive at the maximum discrimination between individuals and to use the performance of the entire group of people in the normative population as the standard against which each individual was compared. The responses of an individual on a test were interpreted in terms of his or her relationship to the average. Although comparisons against the norm are very useful and are widely used in tests used for Indian organizations, there are some situations in which such comparisons may not seem appropriate and where the performance of the respondent would be more appropriately measured against an outside criterion. Such tests are developed with particular reference to performance of an objectively defined criterion and are called criterion-referenced testing, popularly known as domain-referenced, content-referenced and objective-referenced.

A domain-referenced test provides a basis for determining an individual's level of knowledge and skills in relation to a well-defined domain of the content. Often, one or more performance standards are set on the test score scale to aid in-test score interpretation. Domain-referenced tests, introduced by Glaser (1962) and Popham (1969), are also known as competency tests, basic skills tests, mastery tests, performance tests or assessments, etc. Such tests attempt to determine an individual's level of performance in relation to a well-defined domain of the content. On the contrary, norm-referenced tests (discussed in the previous paragraph) determine an individual's level of performance on the constructs measured by a test in relation to a well-defined reference group of candidates, referred to as the norm group. In a nutshell, one can say that domain-referenced tests are content-centered, and norm-referenced tests are respondent-centered.

Domain-referenced testing gained importance after McClelland's article appeared in the *American Psychologist* in 1973. Following a review of the literature, he surmised that ability testing based on norm-referenced test principles was ineffective as a selection tool in employment settings. His perspective was that such tests may prove unfair to minorities or to people who do not belong to economically and socially advantaged backgrounds. McClelland emphasized on the deploying criterion-referenced competencies to predict important behaviors. This emphasis on competencies rather than abilities is central to the models that underlie the National Vocational Qualification (NVQ) assessment system, and Occupational Information Network (O*NET) in the Western countries.

Many experts across organizations feel that domain-referenced testing is the most suitable mechanism for a competency-oriented approach to measure job performance. This is because the interpretation of test performance has something to do with what the respondent knows or can do and not how he or she is compared with other examinees (Brennan, 1981). If the test adequately represents the domain of interest, it can be scored by the examinees to indicate how much of the content domain has been mastered. For example, a student scoring 60 on a domain-referenced final examination in intermediate English vocabulary can be assumed to know about 60 percent of the words in the specified domain of English vocabulary, as defined by the content of the course (Lennon, 1956). Today, domain-referenced testing is widely used in Indian organizations where an individual's performance is mapped against specific criteria defined by organizations in their competency frameworks. Moreover, these models also underpin the popularity of the assessment and development centers, and interventions by organizations where candidates are asked to perform a number of short, pre-specified practical tasks (work-sample tests) that reflect the nature of the job or the applied role.

MINIMUM QUALIFICATIONS AND CUTOFF SCORES

Practical Needs and Pitfalls. The concept of mastery in domain-referenced testing is only one example of the practical use of cutoff scores in decision making. Minimum qualifications must be specified and implemented for a multitude of purposes in everyday life. In many situations, safety considerations require the setting of cutoff points in performance, as in granting a driver's license, selecting airline pilots, or employing workers in a nuclear plant. In education, passing a course or graduating from a school presents other situations that demand all-or-none classifications of persons (Jaeger, 1989). In clinical and counseling practice, decisions regarding treatment or action recommendations may call for similar judgments.

A particularly strong argument for the use of cutoff scores pertains to the presence of critical variables required for the performance of certain functions. These are variables in which a deficiency could not be compensated by outstanding ability in other variables. In such cases, a high score on a comprehensive selection battery could mask a deficiency on a critical skill. Yet individuals falling below the required minimum on the essential skill would fail, regardless of their other abilities. For example, operators of sonar equipment must have good auditory discrimination. During World War II, U.S. Navy recruits were initially selected for training as sonar operators on the basis of their combined scores on tests of auditory discrimination and mechanical comprehension. As a result, a number of college-trained men who excelled in mechanical comprehension but happened to be deficient in the essential auditory skills were assigned to such training, with subsequent failure. Standard Navy procedure required that those failing in their first training assignment be transferred to general sea duty as apprentice seamen—thereby losing their potential specialized services. Further analysis of the situation led in time to the substitution of a cutoff screening procedure for this selection purpose. For most job-related variables, however, the relation to job performance tends to be linear, so that the higher the test score the better the performance (Coward & Sackett, 1990). In such cases, a person's actual score is a better predictor than her or his position relative to a cutoff point.

Insofar as the use of cutoff scores cannot be avoided in many practical decisions, it is essential to be aware of the pitfalls in such evaluations and to utilize procedures to reduce judgment errors. For example, efforts should be made to mitigate the limitations of a single test score. When feasible, the cutoff should be a band of scores, rather than a single score obtained in one administration of a particular test. Moreover, decisions about individuals should depend on multiple sources of information about each person, wherein test scores are supplemented by other relevant performance data, both past and present. If cutoff points on tests are set by a panel of judges, the panel should include adequate representation of experts on both the relevant area of task performance and the principles of test construction and use. Above all, cutoff scores should whenever possible be established or verified on the basis of empirical data. Specifically, this implies that test scores be obtained from groups that clearly differ on the relevant criterion behavior, such as the actual performance of a given type of job. It is this performance, of course, that the test is designed to predict and in which the cutoff is designed to ensure a safe, or acceptable, or desirable minimum. A clear illustration of an empirical method for setting cutoff scores on a personnel selection test is provided by the expectancy tables discussed in the following section.

Expectancy Tables. One of the ways of interpreting the meaning of a test score is in terms of the person's expected criterion performance, as in a training program or on a job. This usage of the term "criterion" follows standard psychometric practice, as when a test is said to be validated against a particular criterion (see chap. 1). Strictly speaking, the term "criterion-referenced testing" should refer to this type of performance interpretation, while the other approaches discussed in the preceding section can be more precisely described as content-referenced or domain-referenced.

An expectancy table gives the probability of different criterion outcomes for persons who obtain each test score. For example, if a student obtained a score of 530 on the College Board Scholastic Assessment Test (SAT), what are the chances that her or his freshman grade-point average in a specific college will fall in the A, B, C, D, or F category? This type of information can be obtained by examining the bivariate distribution of predictor scores (from SAT) plotted against criterion status (freshman grade-point average). If the number of cases in each cell of such a bivariate distribution is changed to a percentage, the result is an expectancy table, such as the one illustrated in Table 3–7. The data for this table were obtained from 211 seventh-grade students enrolled in mathematics courses.

The predictor was the Numerical Reasoning test of the Differential Aptitude Tests, administered at end of first semester. The criterion was final, second-semester course grades. The correlation between test scores and criterion was .60.

The first column of Table 3–7 shows the test scores, divided into four class intervals; the number of students whose scores fell into each interval is given in the second column. The remaining entries in each row of the table indicate the

Table 3–7

Expectancy Table Showing Relation between DAT Numerical Reasoning Test and Course Grades in Mathematics for 211 Students in Grade 7

Test Score	Number of cases	Percentage Receiving Each Grade			
		D & below	C	*B*	*A*
30 & above	22	5	0	36	59
20–29	104	9	21	43	27
10–19	71	37	37	24	3
Below 10	14	43	36	14	7

(Adapted from *Technical Manual for Differential Aptitude Tests,* 5th ed., p. 152. Reproduced by permission.

percentage of cases within each test-score interval who received each grade at the end of the course. Thus, of the 22 students with scores of 30 or above on the Numerical Reasoning test, 5% received grades of D or below, none received C, 36% received B, and 59% A. At the other extreme, of the 14 students scoring below 10 on the test, 43% received grades of D or below, 36% C, and 14% B. The anomalous 7% receiving A, representing only one case, is virtually useless information for purposes of generalizability, as is the 5% with test-score of 30 or above who received a grade of D or lower, again represented by one case. Nevertheless, within the limitations of the available data, the percentages in Table 3–7 provide estimates of the probability that an individual will receive a given criterion grade. For example, if a new student receives a DAT Numerical Reasoning score of 24 (i.e., in the 20–29 interval), we would conclude that the probability of her or his obtaining a course grade of A is 27 out of 100; the probability of her or his obtaining a grade of B is 43 out of 100, and so on.

In many practical situations, criteria can be dichotomized into "success" and "failure" in a job, a course of study, or other undertaking. Under these conditions, an *expectancy chart* can be prepared, showing the probability of success or failure corresponding to each score interval. Figure 3–7 is an example of such an expectancy chart. Based on a pilot selection battery developed by the U.S. Air Force, this expectancy chart shows the percentage of pilot cadets scoring within each stanine on the battery who failed to complete primary flight training. It can be seen that 77% of the cadets receiving a stanine of 1 were eliminated in the course of training, while only 4% of those at stanine 9 failed to complete the training satisfactorily. Between these extremes, the percentage of failures decreases consistently over the successive stanines. On the basis of this expectancy chart, it could be predicted, for example, that approximately 40% of pilot cadets who obtain a stanine score of 4 will fail and approximately 60% will satisfactorily complete primary flight training. Similar statements regarding the probability of success and failure could be made about individuals who receive each stanine. Thus, an individual with a stanine score of 4 has a 60:40 or 3:2

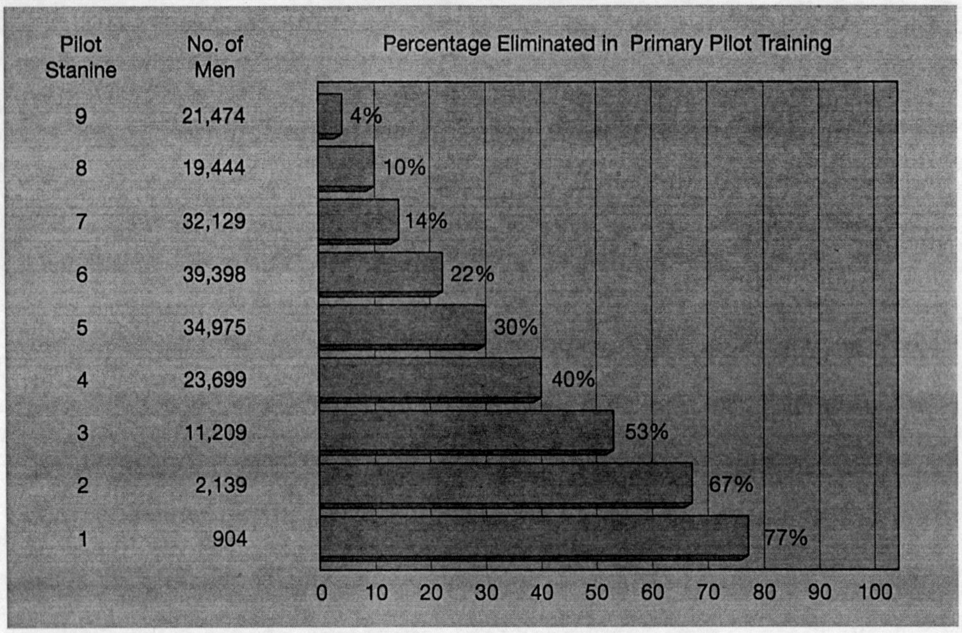

Figure 3-7. Expectancy Chart Showing Relation between Performance on Pilot Selection Battery and Elimination from Primary Flight Training.
(From J.C. Flanagan, 1947, p. 58.)

chance of completing primary flight training. Besides providing a criterion-referenced interpretation of test scores, it can be seen that both expectancy tables and expectancy charts give a general idea of the validity of a test in predicting a given criterion. For this reason, a more detailed discussion of empirical procedures for setting cutoff scores is given at the end of chapter 6, in a section on decision models for fair use of tests. Also included in that section are references to mathematical procedures for setting optimal cutoff scores under various conditions. Specific applications of cutoff scores in major areas of psychological practice may also be found in chapter 17.

Chapter Four

Reliability

"Reliability" refers to the consistency of scores obtained by the same persons when they are reexamined with the same test on different occasions, or with different sets of equivalent items, or under other variable examining conditions. This concept of reliability underlies the computation of the *error of measurement* of a single score, whereby we can predict the range of fluctuation likely to occur in a single individual's score as a result of irrelevant or unknown chance factors.

The concept of reliability has been used to cover several aspects of score consistency. In its broadest sense, test reliability indicates the extent to which individual differences in test scores are attributable to "true" differences in the characteristics under consideration and the extent to which they are attributable to chance errors. To put it in more technical terms, measures of test reliability make it possible to estimate what proportion of the total variance of test scores is *error variance*. These are not "errors" in the sense that they could be avoided or corrected through improved methodology. The error terminology has been inherited from an earlier era in psychology when interest centered on finding general laws of behavior and assessing individuals on what were assumed to be rigidly fixed underlying traits. Today, psychologists recognize variability as an intrinsic property of all behavior and seek to investigate and sort out the many sources of such variability.

With regard to score reliability, the crux of the matter lies in the definition of error variance. Factors that might be considered error variance for one purpose would be classified under true variance for another. For example, if we are interested in measuring fluctuations of mood, then the day-by-day changes in scores on a test of cheerfulness-depression would be relevant to the purpose of the test and would hence be part of the true variance of the scores. If, on the other hand, the test is designed to measure more permanent personality characteristics, the same daily fluctuations would fall under the heading of error variance.

Essentially, any condition that is irrelevant to the purpose of the test represents error variance. Thus, when examiners try to maintain uniform testing conditions by controlling the testing environment, instructions, time limits, rapport, and other similar factors, they are reducing error variance and making the test scores more reliable. Despite optimum testing conditions, however, no test is a perfectly reliable instrument. Hence, every test should be accompanied by a statement of its reliability. Such a measure of reliability characterizes the test when it is administered under standard conditions and given to persons similar to those constituting the normative sample. The characteristics of this sample should therefore be specified, together with the type of reliability that was measured.

There could, of course, be as many varieties of test reliability as there are conditions affecting test scores, since any such conditions might be irrelevant for a certain purpose and would thus be classified as error variance. The types of reliability computed in actual practice, however, are relatively few. In this chapter, the principal techniques for measuring the reliability of test scores will be examined, together with the sources of error variance identified by each.[1]

Since all types of reliability are concerned with the degree of consistency or agreement between two independently derived sets of scores, they can all be expressed in terms of a *correlation coefficient*. Accordingly, the next section will consider some of the basic characteristics of correlation coefficients, in order to clarify their use and interpretation. More technical discussion of correlation, as well as more detailed specifications of computing procedures, can be found in any elementary textbook of educational or psychological statistics, such as Runyon and Haber (1991) or D. C. Howell (1997).

THE CORRELATION COEFFICIENT

Meaning of Correlation. Essentially, a correlation coefficient (r) expresses the degree of correspondence, or *relationship*, between two sets of scores. Thus, if the top-scoring individual in variable 1 also obtains the top score in variable 2, the second-best individual in variable 1 is second best in variable 2, and so on down to the poorest individual in the group, then there would be a perfect correlation between variables 1 and 2. Such a correlation would have a value of +1.00.

A hypothetical illustration of a perfect positive correlation is shown in Figure 4–1. This figure presents a scatter diagram, or bivariate distribution. Each tally mark in this diagram indicates the score of one person in both variable 1 (horizontal axis) and variable 2 (vertical axis). It will be noted that all of the 100 cases in the group are distributed along the diagonal running from the lower left-to the upper right-hand corner of the diagram. Such a distribution indicates

[1] This approach to score reliability has sometimes been called a generalizability theory of reliability (see Brennan, 1994; Crick & Brennan, 1982; Cronbach, Gleser, Nanda, & Rajaratnam, 1972; Feldt & Brennan, 1989; Shavelson & Webb, 1991). This is not a sufficiently specific designation, however, because generalizability applies to all aspects of a test score and, in fact, to all scientific data. A more precise description of this reliability procedure is based on its identification of variance components as relevant or irrelevant.

a perfect positive correlation (+1.00), since it shows that each person occupies the same relative position in both variables. The closer the bivariate distribution of scores approaches this diagonal, the higher will be the positive correlation.

Figure 4–2 illustrates a perfect negative correlation (−1.00). In this case, there is a complete reversal of scores from one variable to the other. The best individual in variable 1 is the poorest in variable 2 and vice versa, this reversal being consistently maintained throughout the distribution. It will be noted that, in this scatter diagram, all persons fall on the diagonal extending from the upper left-to the lower right-hand corner. This diagonal runs in the reverse direction from that in Figure 4–1.

A zero correlation indicates complete absence of relationship, such as might occur by chance. If each person's name were pulled at random out of a box to determine her or his position in variable 1, and if the process were repeated for variable 2, a zero or near-zero correlation would result. Under these conditions, it would be impossible to predict an individual's relative standing in variable 2 from a knowledge of her or his score in variable 1. The top-scoring person in variable 1 might score high, low, or average in variable 2. By chance, some persons might score above average in both variables, or below average in both; others might fall above average in one variable and below in the other; still others might be above the average in one and at the average in the second, and so forth. There would be no regularity in the relationship from one individual to another.

The coefficients found in actual practice generally fall between these extremes, having some value higher than zero but lower than 1.00. Correlations between measures of abilities are nearly always positive, although frequently low. When a negative correlation is obtained between two such variables, it usually results

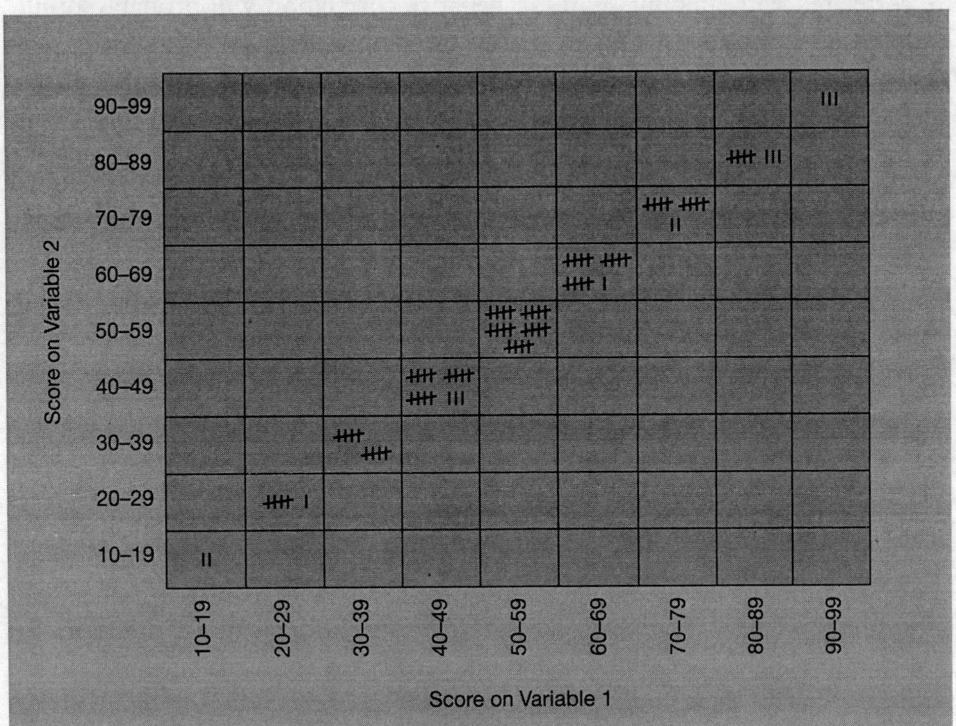

Figure 4-1. Bivariate Distribution for a Hypothetical Correlation of +1.00.

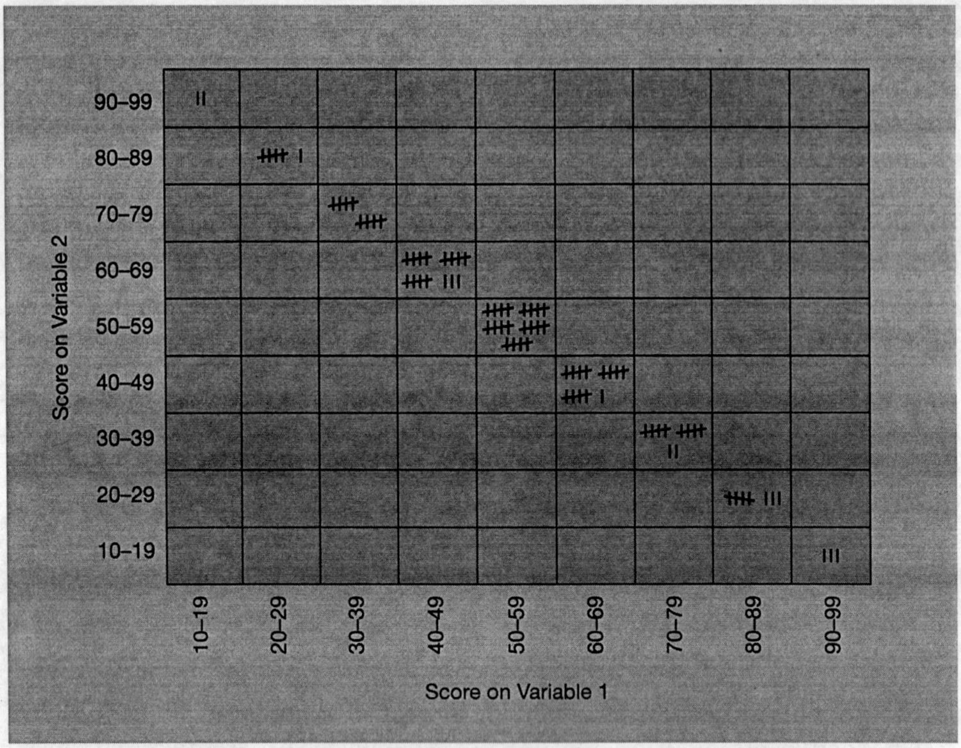

Figure 4-2. Bivariate Distribution for a Hypothetical Correlation of −1.00.

from the way in which the scores are expressed. For example, if time scores are correlated with amount scores, a negative correlation will probably result. Thus, if each person's score on an arithmetic computation test is recorded as the number of minutes required to complete all items, while the score on an arithmetic reasoning test represents the number of problems correctly solved, a negative correlation can be expected. In such a case, the poorest (i.e., slowest) individual will have the numerically highest score on the first test, while the best individual will have the highest score on the second.

Correlation coefficients may be computed in various ways, depending on the nature of the data. The most common is the *Pearson Product-Moment Correlation Coefficient*. This correlation coefficient takes into account not only the person's position in the group but also the amount of her or his deviation above or below the group mean. It will be recalled that when each person's standing is expressed in terms of standard scores, persons falling above the average receive positive standard scores, while those below the average receive negative scores. Thus, an individual who is superior in both variables to be correlated would have two positive standard scores; one inferior in both would have two negative standard scores. If, now, we multiply each individual's standard score in variable 1 by her or his standard score in variable 2, all of these products will be positive, provided that each person falls on the same side of the mean on both variables. The Pearson correlation coefficient is simply the mean of these products. It will have a high positive value when corresponding standard scores are of equal sign and of approximately equal amount in the two variables. When persons above the average in one variable are below the average in the other, the corresponding cross-products will be negative. If the sum of the cross-products is negative, the correlation will be negative. When some products are positive and some negative, the correlation will be close to zero.

In actual practice, it is not necessary to convert each raw score to a standard score before finding the cross-products, since this conversion can be made once for all after the cross-products have been added. There are many shortcuts for computing the Pearson correlation coefficient. The method demonstrated in Table 4–1 is not the quickest, but it illustrates the meaning of the correlation coefficient more clearly than other methods that utilize computational shortcuts. Table 4–1 shows the computation of a Pearson *r* between the mathematics and reading scores of 10 children. Next to each child's name are her or his scores in the mathematics test (*X*) and the reading test (*Y*). The sums and means of the 10 scores are given under the respective columns. The third column shows the deviation (*x*) of each mathematics score from the mathematics mean; and the fourth column shows the deviation (*y*) of each reading score from the reading mean. These deviations are squared in the next two columns, and the sums of the squares are used in computing the standard deviations of the mathematics and reading scores by the method described in chapter 3. Rather than dividing each *x* and *y* by its corresponding *SD* to find standard scores, we perform this division only once at the end, as shown in the correlation formula in Table 4–1. The cross-products in the last column (*xy*) have been found by multiplying the corresponding deviations in the *x* and *y* columns. To compute the correlation (*r*), the sum of these cross-products is divided by the number of cases (*N*) and by the product of the two standard deviations ($SD_x SD_y$).

Statistical Significance. The correlation of .40 found in Table 4–1 indicates a moderate degree of positive relationship between the mathematics and reading scores. There is some tendency for those children doing well in mathematics also to perform well on the reading test and vice versa, although the relation is not close. If we are concerned only with the performance of these 10 children, we can accept this correlation as an adequate description of the degree of relation existing between the two variables in this group. In psychological research, however, we are usually interested in generalizing beyond the particular *sample* of individuals tested to the larger *population* they represent. For example, we might want to know whether mathematics and reading ability are correlated among American schoolchildren of the same age as those we tested. Obviously, the 10 cases actually examined would constitute a very inadequate sample of such a population. Another comparable sample of the same size might yield a much lower or a much higher correlation.

There are statistical procedures for estimating the probable fluctuation to be expected from sample to sample in the size of correlations, means, standard deviations, and any other group measures. The question usually asked about correlations, however, is simply whether the correlation is significantly greater than zero. In other words, if the correlation in the population is zero, could a correlation as high as that obtained in our sample have resulted from sampling error alone? When we say that a correlation is "significant at the 1% (.01) level," we mean the chances are no greater than one out of 100 that the population correlation is zero. Hence, we conclude that the two variables are truly correlated.

Table 4–1

Computation of Pearson Product-Moment Correlation Coefficient

Pupil	Mathematics X	Reading Y	x	y	x^2	y^2	xy
Bill	41	17	+1	−4	1	16	−4
Carol	38	28	−2	+7	4	49	−14
Geoffrey	48	22	+8	+1	64	1	8
Ann	32	16	−8	−5	64	25	40
Bob	34	18	−6	−3	36	9	18
Jane	36	15	−4	−6	16	36	24
Ellen	41	24	+1	+3	1	9	3
Ruth	43	20	+3	−1	9	1	−3
Dick	47	23	+7	+2	49	4	14
Mary	40	27	0	+6	0	36	0
Σ	400	210	0	0	244	186	86
M	40	21					

$$SD_x = \sqrt{\frac{244}{10}} = \sqrt{24.40} = 4.94 \qquad SD_y = \sqrt{\frac{186}{10}} = \sqrt{18.60} = 4.31$$

$$r_{xy} = \frac{\Sigma xy}{(N)(SD_x)(SD_y)} = \frac{86}{(10)(4.94)(4.31)} = \frac{86}{212.91} = .40$$

Significance levels refer to the risk of error we are willing to take in drawing conclusions from our data. If a correlation is said to be significant at the .05 level, the probability of error is 5 out of 100. Most psychological research applies either the .01 or the .05 levels, although other significance levels may be employed for special reasons.

The correlation of .40 found in Table 4–1 fails to reach significance even at the .05 level. As might have been anticipated, with only 10 cases it is difficult to establish a general relationship conclusively. With this size of sample, the smallest correlation significant at the .05 level is .63. Any correlation below that value simply leaves unanswered the question of whether the two variables are correlated in the population from which the sample was drawn. The minimum correlations significant at the .01 and .05 levels for groups of different sizes can be found by consulting tables of the significance of correlations in any statistics textbook. For interpretive purposes in this book, however, only an understanding of the general concept is required.

For many years, significance levels have been the traditional way of evaluating correlations. Nevertheless, there is now a growing awareness of the inadequacy and defects of this procedure. To show that a reliability coefficient (or any correlation) is significantly greater than zero provides little knowledge for either theoretical or practical purposes. Especially when obtained on a small sample, even a high correlation fails to meet the "significance test." A substitute approach that has been receiving increasing attention considers the actual magnitude of the obtained correlation and estimates a *confidence interval* within which the population correlation is likely to fall at a specified confidence level (see, e.g., Carver, 1993; J. Cohen, 1994; Hunter & Schmidt, 1990; Olkin & Finn, 1995; Schmidt, 1996; W. W. Tryon, 1996). This trend toward confidence intervals, as a supplement to if not a substitute for significance testing, foreshadows an important shift in the analysis of correlation coefficients in the years ahead.

A confidence interval estimates the probability such that the true population mean lies within a range around a sample mean. Confidence intervals are used when one wants to describe the amount of uncertainty associated with a sample estimate of a population parameter. Often, researchers and statisticians choose 90%, 95%, or 99% confidence levels.

The Reliability Coefficient. Correlation coefficients have many uses in the analysis of psychometric data. The measurement of test reliability represents one application of such coefficients. An example of a reliability coefficient, computed by the Pearson Product-Moment method, is given in Figure 4–3. In this

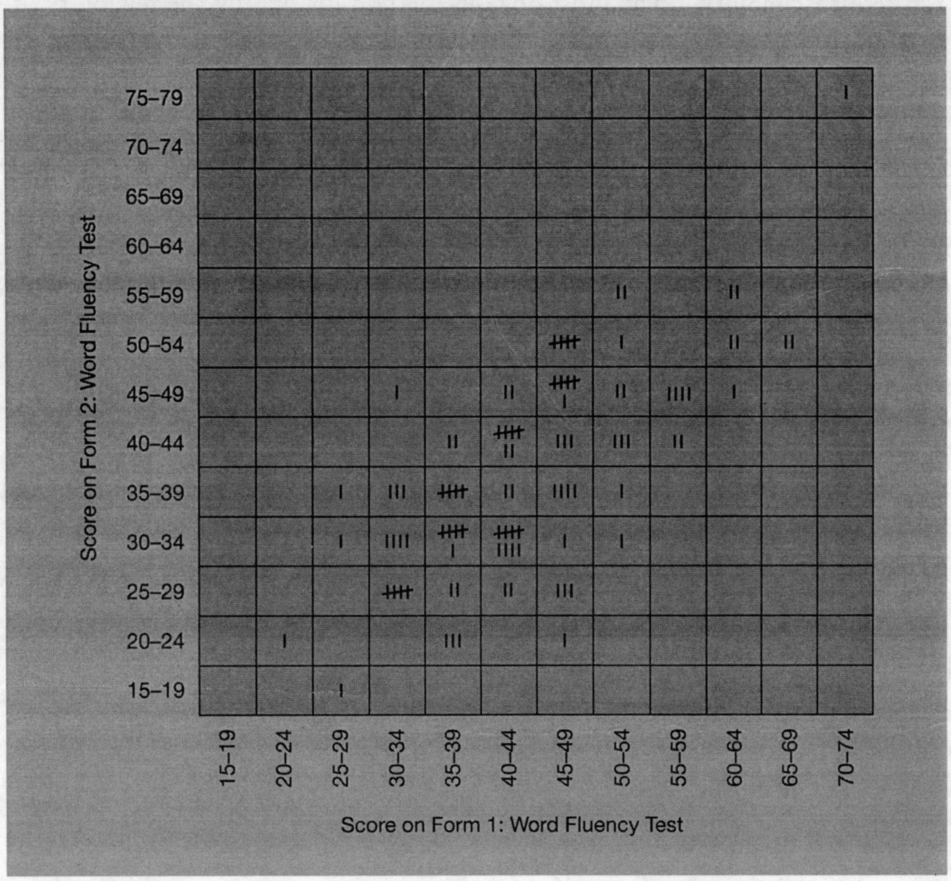

Figure 4–3. A Reliability Coefficient of .72.
(Data from Anastasi & Drake, 1954.)

case, the scores of 104 persons on two equivalent forms of a Word Fluency test[2] were correlated. In one form, the test takers were given five minutes to write as many words as they could that began with a given letter. The second form was identical, except that a different letter was employed. The two letters were chosen by the test authors as being approximately equal in difficulty for this purpose.

The correlation between the number of words written in the two forms of this test was found to be .72. This correlation is high and significant at the .01 level. With 104 cases, any correlation of .25 or higher is significant at this level. Nevertheless, the obtained correlation is somewhat lower than is desirable for reliability coefficients, which usually fall in the .80s or .90s. An examination of the scatter diagram in Figure 4–3 shows a typical bivariate distribution of scores corresponding to a high positive correlation. It will be noted that the tallies cluster close to the diagonal extending from the lower left-to the upper right-hand corner; the trend is definitely in this direction, although there is a certain amount of scatter of individual entries. In the following section, the use of the correlation coefficient in computing different measures of test reliability will be considered.

TYPES OF RELIABILITY

Test-Retest Reliability. The most obvious method for finding the reliability of test scores is by repeating the identical test on a second occasion. The reliability coefficient (r_{tt}) in this case is simply the correlation between the scores obtained by the same persons on the two administrations of the test. The error variance corresponds to the random fluctuations of performance from one test session to the other. These variations may result in part from uncontrolled testing conditions, such as extreme changes in weather, sudden noises and other distractions, or a broken pencil point. To some extent, however, they arise from changes in the condition of the test takers themselves, as illustrated by illness, fatigue, emotional strain, worry, recent experiences of a pleasant or unpleasant nature, and the like. Retest reliability shows the extent to which scores on a test can be generalized over different occasions; the higher the reliability, the less susceptible the scores are to the random daily changes in the condition of the test takers or of the testing environment.

When retest reliability is reported in a test manual, the interval over which it was measured should always be specified. Since retest correlations decrease progressively as this interval lengthens, there is not one but an infinite number of retest reliability coefficients for any test. It is also desirable to give some indication of relevant intervening experiences of the persons on whom reliability was measured, such as educational or job experiences, counseling, psychotherapy, and so forth.

Apart from the desirability of reporting length of interval, what considerations should guide the choice of interval? Illustrations could readily be cited of tests showing high reliability over periods of a few days or weeks, but whose scores reveal an almost complete lack of correspondence when the interval is

[2] One of the subtests of the SRA Tests of Primary Mental Abilities for Ages 11 to 17. The data were obtained in an investigation by Anastasi and Drake (1954).

extended to as long as ten or fifteen years. Many preschool intelligence tests, for example, yield moderately stable measures within the preschool period but are virtually useless as predictors of late childhood or adult IQs. In actual practice, however, a simple distinction can usually be made. Short-range, random fluctuations that occur during intervals ranging from a few hours to a few months are generally included under the error variance of the test score. Thus, in checking this type of test reliability, an effort is made to keep the interval short. In testing young children, the period should be even shorter than for older persons, since at early ages progressive developmental changes are discernible over a period of a month or even less. For any type of person, the interval between retests should rarely exceed six months.

Any additional changes in the relative test performance of individuals that occur over longer periods of time are apt to be cumulative and progressive rather than entirely random. Moreover, they are likely to characterize a broader area of behavior than that covered by the test performance itself. Thus, one's general level of scholastic aptitude, mechanical comprehension, or artistic judgment may have altered appreciably over a ten-year period, owing to unusual intervening experiences. The individual's status may have either risen or dropped appreciably in relation to others of her or his own age, because of circumstances peculiar to the individual's own home, school, or community environment, or for other reasons such as illness or emotional disturbance.

The extent to which such factors can affect an individual's psychological development provides an important problem for investigation. This question, however, should not be confused with that of the reliability of a particular test. When we measure the reliability of the Stanford-Binet, for example, we do not ordinarily correlate retest scores over a period of ten years, or even one year, but over a few weeks. To be sure, long-range retests have been conducted with such tests, but the results are generally discussed in terms of the predictability of adult intelligence from childhood performance, rather than in terms of the reliability of a particular test. The concept of reliability is generally restricted to short-range, random changes that characterize the test performance itself rather than the entire behavior domain that is being tested.

It should be noted that different behavior functions may themselves vary in the extent of daily fluctuation they exhibit. For example, steadiness of delicate finger movements is undoubtedly more susceptible to slight changes in the person's condition than is verbal comprehension. If we wish to obtain an overall estimate of the individual's habitual finger steadiness, we would probably require repeated tests on several days, whereas a single test session would suffice for verbal comprehension. Again we must fall back on an analysis of the purposes of the test and on a thorough understanding of the behavior the test is designed to predict.

Although apparently simple and straightforward, the test-retest technique presents difficulties when applied to most psychological tests. Practice will probably produce varying amounts of improvement in the retest scores of different individuals. Moreover, if the interval between retests is fairly short, the test takers may recall many of their former responses. In other words, the same pattern of right and wrong responses is likely to recur through sheer memory. Thus, the scores on the two administrations of the test are not independently obtained, and the correlation between them will be spuriously high. The nature of the test itself may also change with repetition. This is especially true of problems involving reasoning or ingenuity. Once the test taker has grasped the principle involved in the problem or has worked out a solution, he or she can reproduce the correct response in the future without going through the intervening steps. Only tests that are not appreciably affected by repetition lend themselves to the retest technique. A number of sensory discrimination and motor tests would fall into this category. For the large majority of psychological tests, however, retesting with the identical test is not an appropriate technique for finding a reliability coefficient.

Alternate-Form Reliability. One way of avoiding the difficulties encountered in test-retest reliability is through the use of alternate forms of the test. The same persons can thus be tested with one form on the first occasion and with another, equivalent form on the second. The correlation between the scores obtained on the two forms represents the reliability coefficient of the test. It will be noted that such a reliability coefficient is a measure of both temporal stability and consistency of response to different item samples (or test forms). This coefficient thus combines two types of reliability. Since both types are important for most testing purposes, however, alternate-form reliability provides a useful measure for evaluating many tests.

The concept of item sampling, or *content sampling*, underlies not only alternate-form reliability hut also other types of reliability to be discussed shortly. It is therefore appropriate to examine it more closely. Most students have probably had the experience of taking a course examination in which they felt they had a "lucky break" because many of the items covered the very topics they happened to have studied most carefully. On another occasion, they may have had the opposite experience, finding an unusually large number of items on areas they had failed to review. This familiar situation illustrates error variance resulting from content sampling. To what extent do scores on this test depend on factors *specific* to the particular selection of items? If a different investigator, working independently, were to prepare another test in accordance with the same specifications, how much would an individual's score differ on the two tests?

Let us suppose that a 40-item vocabulary test has been constructed as a measure of general verbal comprehension. Now suppose that a second list of 40 different words is assembled for the same purpose, and that the items are constructed with equal care to cover the same range of difficulty as the first test. The differences in the scores obtained by the same individuals on these two tests illustrate the type of error variance under consideration. Owing to fortuitous factors in the past experience of different individuals, the relative difficulty of the two lists will vary somewhat from person to person. Thus, the first list might contain a larger number of words unfamiliar to individual A than does the second list. The second list, on the other hand, might contain a disproportionately large number of words unfamiliar to individual B. If the two individuals are approximately equal in their overall word knowledge (i.e, in their "true scores"), B will nevertheless excel A on the first list, while A will excel B on the second. The relative standing of these two persons will therefore be reversed on the two lists, owing to chance differences in the selection of items.

Like test-retest reliability, alternate-form reliability should always be accompanied by a statement of the length of the interval between test administrations, as well as a description of relevant intervening experiences. If the two forms are administered *in immediate succession*, the resulting correlation shows reliability across forms only, not across occasions. The error variance in this case represents fluctuations in performance from one set of items to another, but not fluctuations over time.

In the development of alternate forms, care should, of course, be exercised to ensure that they are truly parallel. Fundamentally, parallel forms of a test should be independently constructed tests designed to meet the same specifications. The tests should contain the same number of items, and the items should be expressed in the same form and should cover the same type of content. The range and level of difficulty of the items should also be equal. Instructions, time limits, illustrative examples, format, and all other aspects of the test must likewise be checked for equivalence.

It should be added that the availability of parallel test forms is desirable for other reasons besides the determination of test reliability. Alternate forms are useful in follow-up studies or in investigations of the effects of some intervening experimental factor on test performance. The use of several alternate forms also provides a means of reducing the possibility of coaching or cheating.

Although much more widely applicable than test-retest reliability, alternate-form reliability also has certain limitations. In the first place, if the behavior functions under consideration are subject to a large practice effect, the use of alternate forms will reduce but not eliminate such an effect. To be sure, if all test takers were to show the same improvement with repetition, the correlation between their scores would remain unaffected, since adding a constant amount to each score does not alter the correlation coefficient. It is much more likely, however, that individuals will differ in amount of improvement, owing to extent of previous practice with similar material, motivation in taking the test, and other factors. Under these conditions, the practice effect represents another source of variance that will tend to reduce the correlation between the two test forms. If the practice effect is small, reduction will be negligible.

Another related question concerns the degree to which the nature of the test will change with repetition. In certain types of ingenuity problems, for example, any item involving the same principle can be readily solved by most persons once they have worked out the solution to the first. In such a case, changing the specific content of the items in the second form would not suffice to eliminate this carry-over from the first form. Finally, it should be added that alternate forms are unavailable for many tests, because of the practical difficulties of constructing truly equivalent forms. For all these reasons, other techniques for estimating test reliability are often required.

Split-Half Reliability. From a single administration of one form of a test it is possible to arrive at a measure of reliability by various split-half procedures. In such a way, two scores are obtained for each person by dividing the test into equivalent halves. It is apparent that split-half reliability provides a measure of consistency with regard to content sampling. Temporal stability of the scores does not enter into such reliability, because only one test session is involved. This type of reliability coefficient is sometimes called a coefficient of internal consistency, since only a single administration of a single form is required.

To find split-half reliability, the first problem is how to split the test in order to obtain the most nearly equivalent halves. Any test can be divided in many different ways. In most tests, the first half and the second half would not be equivalent, owing to differences in nature and difficulty level of items, as well as to the cumulative effects of warming up, practice, fatigue, boredom, and any other factors varying progressively from the beginning to the end of the test. A procedure that is adequate for most purposes is to find the scores on the odd and even items of the test. If the items were originally arranged in an approximate order of difficulty, such a division yields very nearly equivalent half-scores. One precaution to be observed in making such an odd-even split pertains to groups of items dealing with a single problem, such as questions referring to a particular mechanical diagram or to a given passage in a reading test. In this case, a whole group of items should be assigned intact to one or the other half. Were the items in such a group to be placed in different halves of the test, the similarity of the half-scores would be spuriously inflated, since any single error in understanding the problem might affect items in both halves.[3]

Once the two half-scores have been obtained for each person, they may be correlated by the usual method. It should be noted, however, that this correlation actually gives the reliability of only a half-test. For example, if the entire test consists of 100 items, the correlation is computed between two sets of scores each of which is based on only 50 items. In both test-retest and alternate-form reliability, on the other hand, each score is based on the full number of items in the test.

Other things being equal, the longer a test, the more reliable it will be.[4] It is reasonable to expect that, with a larger sample of behavior, we can arrive at a more adequate and consistent measure. The effect that lengthening or shortening a test will have on its coefficient can be estimated by means of the Spearman-Brown formula, given below:

$$r_{nn} = \frac{nr_{tt}}{1+(n-1)r_{tt}}$$

in which r_{nn} is the estimated coefficient, r_{tt} is the obtained coefficient, and n is the number of times the test is lengthened or shortened. Thus, if the number of test items is increased from 25 to 100, n is 4; if it is decreased from 60 to 30, n is 1/2. The Spearman-Brown formula is widely used in determining reliability by the split-half method, many test manuals reporting reliability in this form. When applied to split-half reliability, the formula always involves doubling the length of the test. Under these conditions, it can be simplified as follows:

$$r_{tt} = \frac{2r_{hh}}{1+r_{hh}}$$

in which r_{hh} is the correlation of the half-tests.

---

[3] There is now good empirical evidence to support this expectation, and considerable research has accumulated on the statistical treatment of such integrated item groupings, or "testlets" (Sireci, Thissen, & Wainer, 1991).

[4] Lengthening a test, however, will increase only its consistency in terms of content sampling, not its stability over time (see Cureton, 1965; Cureton et al., 1973).

An alternate method for finding split-half reliability was developed by Rulon (1939). It requires only the variance of the *differences* between each person's scores on the two half-tests (SD_d^2) and the variance of total scores (SD_x^2); these two values are substituted in the following formula, which yields the reliability of the whole test directly:

$$r_{tt} = 1 - \frac{SD_d^2}{SD_x^2}$$

It is interesting to note the relationship of this formula to the definition of error variance. Any difference between a person's scores on the two half-tests represents irrelevant or error variance. The variance of these differences, divided by the variance of total scores, gives the proportion of error variance in the scores. When this error variance is subtracted from 1.00, it gives the proportion of "true" variance for a specified test use, which is equal to the reliability coefficient.

Kuder-Richardson Reliability and Coefficient Alpha. A fourth method for finding reliability, also utilizing a single administration of a single form, is based on the consistency of responses to all items in the test. This *interitem consistency* is influenced by two sources of error variance: (1) content sampling (as in alternate-form and split-half reliability); and (2) heterogeneity of the behavior domain sampled. The more homogeneous the domain, the higher the interitem consistency. For example, if one test includes only multiplication items while another comprises addition, subtraction, multiplication, and division items, the former test will probably show more interitem consistency than the latter. In the latter, more heterogeneous test, one test taker may perform better in subtraction than in any of the other arithmetic operations; another may score relatively well on the division items, but less well in addition, subtraction, and multiplication; and so on. A more extreme example would be represented by a test consisting of 40 vocabulary items, in contrast to one containing 10 vocabulary, 10 spatial relations, 10 arithmetic reasoning, and 10 perceptual speed items. In the latter test, there might be little or no relationship between an individual's performance on the different types of items.

It is apparent that test scores will be less ambiguous when derived from relatively homogeneous tests. Suppose that in the highly heterogeneous 40-item test cited previously, Smith and Jones both obtain a score of 20. Can we conclude that the performances of the two on this test were equal? Not at all. Smith may have correctly completed 10 vocabulary items, 10 perceptual speed items, and none of the arithmetic reasoning and spatial relations items. In contrast, Jones may have received a score of 20 by the successful completion of 5 perceptual speed, 5 spatial relations, 10 arithmetic reasoning, and no vocabulary items.

Many other combinations could obviously produce the same total score of 20. This score would have a very different meaning when obtained through such dissimilar combinations of items. In the relatively homogeneous vocabulary test, on the other hand, a score of 20 would probably mean that the test taker had succeeded with approximately the first 20 words, if the items were arranged in ascending order of difficulty. He or she might have failed two or three easier words and correctly responded to two or three more difficult items beyond the 20th, but such individual variations are slight in comparison with those found in a more heterogeneous test.

A highly relevant question in this connection is whether the criterion that the test is trying to predict is itself relatively homogeneous or heterogeneous. Although homogeneous tests are to be preferred because their scores permit fairly unambiguous interpretation, a single homogeneous test is obviously not an adequate predictor of a highly heterogeneous criterion. Moreover, in the prediction of a heterogeneous criterion, the heterogeneity of test items would not necessarily represent error variance. Traditional intelligence tests provide a good example of heterogeneous tests designed to predict heterogeneous criteria. In such a case, however, it may be desirable to construct several relatively homogeneous tests, each measuring a different phase of the heterogeneous criterion. Thus, unambiguous interpretation of test scores could be combined with adequate criterion coverage.

The most common procedure for finding interitem consistency is that developed by Kuder and Richardson (1937). As in the split-half methods, interitem consistency is found from a single administration of a single test. Rather than requiring two half-scores, however, this technique is based on an examination of performance on each item. Of the various formulas derived in the original article, the most widely applicable, commonly known as "Kuder-Richardson formula 20," is the following:

$$r_{tt} = \left(\frac{n}{n-1}\right)\frac{SD_t^2 - \Sigma pq}{SD_t^2}$$

In this formula, r_{tt} is the reliability coefficient of the whole test, n is the number of items in the test, and SD_t is the standard deviation of total scores on the test. The only new term in this formula, Σpq, is found by tabulating the proportion of persons who pass (p) and the proportion who do not pass (q) each item. The product of p and q is computed for each item, and these products are then added for all items, to give Σpq. Since in the process of test construction p is often routinely recorded in order to find the difficulty level of each item, this method of determining reliability involves little additional computation.

It can be shown mathematically that the Kuder-Richardson reliability coefficient is actually the mean of all split-half coefficients resulting from different splittings of a test (Cronbach, 1951).[5] The ordinary split-half coefficient, on the other hand, is based on a planned split designed to yield equivalent sets of items. Hence, unless the test items are highly homogeneous, the Kuder-Richardson coefficient will be lower than the split-half reliability. An extreme example will serve to highlight the difference. Suppose we construct a 50-item test out of 25 different kinds of items such that items 1 and 2 are vocabulary items, items 3 and 4 arithmetic reasoning, items 5 and 6 spatial orientation, and so on. The odd and even scores on this test could theoretically agree quite closely, thus yielding a high split-half reliability coefficient. The homogeneity of this test, however, would be very low, since there would be little consistency of performance among the entire set of 50 items. In this example, we would expect the Kuder-Richardson reliability to be much lower than the split-half reliability. In fact, the difference

[5] This is strictly true only when the split-half coefficients are found by the Rulon formula (based on the variance of the differences between the two half-scores), not when they are found by correlation of halves and Spearman-Brown formula (Novick & Lewis, 1967).

between Kuder-Richardson and split-half reliability coefficients may serve as a rough index of the heterogeneity of a test.

The Kuder-Richardson formula is applicable to tests whose items are scored as right or wrong, or according to some other all-or-none system. Some tests, however, may have multiple-scored items. On a personality inventory, for example, the respondent may receive a different numerical score on an item, depending on whether he or she checks "usually," "sometimes," "rarely," or "never." For such tests, a generalized formula has been derived, known as coefficient alpha (Cronbach, 1951; Kaiser & Michael, 1975; Novick & Lewis, 1967). In this formula, the value Σpq is replaced by $\Sigma(SD_i^2)$, the sum of the variances of item scores. The procedure is to find the variance of all individuals' scores for each item and then to add these variances across all items. The complete formula for coefficient alpha is given as follows:

$$r_{tt} = \left(\frac{n}{n-1}\right)\frac{SD_t^2 - \Sigma(SD_i^2)}{SD_t^2}$$

Scorer Reliability. It should now be apparent that the different types of reliability vary in the factors they subsume under error variance. In one case, error variance covers temporal fluctuations; in another, it refers to differences between sets of parallel items; and in still another, it includes any interitem inconsistency. On the other hand, the factors *excluded* from measures of error variance are broadly of two types: (a) those factors whose variance should remain in the scores, since they are part of the true differences under consideration; and (b) those irrelevant factors that can be experimentally controlled. For example, it is not customary to report the error of measurement resulting when a test is administered under distracting conditions or with a longer or shorter time limit than that specified in the manual. Timing errors and serious distractions can be empirically eliminated from the testing situation. Hence, it is not necessary to report special reliability coefficients corresponding to "distraction variance" or "timing variance."

Similarly, most tests provide such highly standardized procedures for administration and scoring that error variance attributable to these factors is negligible. This is particularly true of group tests designed for mass testing and computer scoring. With such instruments, we need only to make certain that the prescribed procedures are carefully followed and adequately checked. With clinical instruments employed in intensive individual examinations, on the other hand, there is evidence of considerable *examiner variance.* Through special experimental designs, it is possible to separate this variance from that attributable to temporal fluctuations in the test taker's condition or to the use of alternate test forms.

One source of error variance that can be checked quite simply is *scorer variance.* Certain types of tests—notably tests of creativity and projective tests of personality—leave a good deal to the judgment of the scorer. With such tests, there is as much need for a measure of scorer reliability as there is for the more usual reliability coefficients. Scorer reliability can be found by having a sample of test papers independently scored by two examiners. The two scores thus obtained by each test taker are then correlated in the usual way, and the resulting correlation coefficient is a measure of scorer reliability. This type of reliability is commonly computed when subjectively scored instruments are employed in research. Test manuals should also report it when appropriate.

Overview. The different types of reliability coefficients discussed in this section are summarized in Tables 4–2 and 4–3. In Table 4–2, the operations followed in obtaining each type of reliability are classified with regard to number of test forms and number of testing sessions required. Table 4–3 shows the sources of variance treated as error variance by each procedure.

Any reliability coefficient may be interpreted directly in terms of the *percentage of score variance* attributable to different sources. Thus, a reliability coefficient of .85 signifies that 85% of the variance in test scores depends on true variance in the trait measured, and 15% depends on error variance (as operationally defined by the specific procedure followed). The statistically sophisticated reader may recall that it is the *square* of a correlation coefficient that represents proportion of common variance. Actually, the proportion of true variance in test scores is the square of the correlation between scores on a single form of the test and true scores, which are free from chance errors. This correlation, known as the index of reliability,[6] is equal to the square root of the reliability coefficient $\left(\sqrt{r_{tt}}\right)$. When the index of reliability is itself squared, the result is the original reliability coefficient (r_{tt}), which can therefore be interpreted directly as the percentage of true variance for a designated test use.

Experimental designs that yield more than one type of reliability coefficient for the same group permit the analysis of total score variance into different components. Let us consider the following hypothetical example. Forms A and B of a creativity test have been administered with a two-month interval to 100 sixth-grade children. The resulting alternate-form reliability is .70. From the responses on either form, a split-half reliability coefficient can also be computed.[7] This coefficient, stepped up by the Spearman-Brown formula, is .80. Finally, a second scorer has rescored a random sample of 50 papers, from which a scorer reliability of .92 is obtained. The three reliability coefficients can now be analyzed to yield the error variances shown in Table 4–4 and Figure 4–4 It will be noted that by subtracting the error variance attributable to content sampling alone (split-half

Table 4-2

Techniques for Measuring Reliability, in Relation to Test Form and Testing Session

	Test Forms Required	
Testing Sessions Required	*One*	*Two*
One	Split-Half Kuder-Richardson	Alternate-Form (Immediate)
Two	Test-Retest	Alternate-Form (Delayed)

[6] Derivations of the index of reliability, based on two different sets of assumptions, are given by Gulliksen (1950, chaps. 2 and 3).

[7] For a better estimate of the coefficient of internal consistency, split-half correlations could be computed for each form and the two coefficients averaged by the appropriate statistical procedures (e.g., Fishery z–transformation).

Table 4–3

Sources of Error Variance in Relation to Reliability Coefficients

Type of Reliability Coefficient	Error Variance
Test-Retest	Time sampling
Alternate-Form (Immediate)	Content sampling
Alternate-Form (Delayed)	Time sampling and content sampling
Split-Half	Content sampling
Kuder-Richardson and Coefficient Alpha	Content sampling and content heterogeneity
Scorer	Interscorer differences

Table 4–4

Analysis of Sources of Error Variance in a Hypothetical Test

From delayed alternate-form reliability:	1–.70 = .30	(time sampling plus content sampling)
From split-half, Spearman-Brown reliability:	1–.80 = .20*	(content sampling)
Difference	.10*	(time sampling)
From scorer reliability:	1–.92 = .08*	(interscorer difference)
Total Measured Error Variance* = .20 + .10 + .08 = .38*		
True Variance = 1 – .38 = .62		

* Error Variance

reliability) from the error variance attributable to both content and time sampling (alternate-form reliability), we find that .10 of the variance can be attributed to time sampling alone. Adding the error variances attributable to content sampling (.20), time sampling (.10), and interscorer difference (.08) gives a total error variance of .38 and hence a true variance of .62. These proportions, expressed in the more familiar percentage terms, are shown graphically in Figure 4–4. This sorting out of sources of variance is the essence of the so-called generalizability theory of reliability. Complex experimental designs permitting simultaneous assessment of more sources of score variance and the interactions among them can be found in detailed topical treatments, such as Brennan (1984), Cronbach et al. (1972), Feldt and Brennan (1989), and Shavelson and Webb (1991).

RELIABILITY OF SPEEDED TESTS

Both in test construction and in the interpretation of test scores, an important distinction is that between the measurement of speed and of power. A pure *speed test* is one in which individual differences depend entirely on speed of performance. Such a test is constructed from items of uniformly low difficulty, all of which are well within the ability level of the persons for whom the test is designed. The time limit is made so short that no one can finish all the items. Under these conditions, each person's score reflects only the speed with which he or she worked. A pure *power test*, on the other hand, has a time limit long enough to permit everyone to attempt all items. The difficulty of the items is steeply graded, and the test includes some items too difficult for anyone to solve, so that no one can get a perfect score.

Speed tests are suitable for testing visual perception, numerical facility, and other abilities related to vocational success. Tests of psychomotor abilities such as eye–hand coordination can be examples of a speed test. For those who are competent in English, a task of quickly writing a set of spellings would be a speed test. A test where a participant is asked to press a button as many times as possible in 30 seconds would be another example of a speed test. Power tests tend to be more relevant to the purposes such as academic or professional evaluation for which the highest level of difficulty at which an individual can succeed is of greater interest than his or her speed on easy tasks. Most of the tests, such as the Watson Glaser Critical Thinking Appraisal (WGCTA) and Raven's Progressive Matrices (RPM), which assess cognitive ability, are power tests. In practice, a definite but ample time is set for power tests.

It will be noted that both speed and power tests are designed to prevent the achievement of perfect scores. The reason for such a precaution is that perfect scores are indeterminate, since it is impossible to know how much higher the individual's score would have been if more items, or more difficult items, had been included. To enable each individual to show fully what he or she is able to accomplish, the test must provide adequate ceiling, either in number of items or in difficulty level. An exception to this rule is found in mastery testing, as illustrated by the domain-referenced tests discussed in chapter 3. The purpose of such testing is not to establish the limits of what the individual can do but to determine whether a preestablished performance level has or has not been reached.

In actual practice, the distinction between speed and power tests is one of degree, most tests depending on both power and speed in varying proportions.

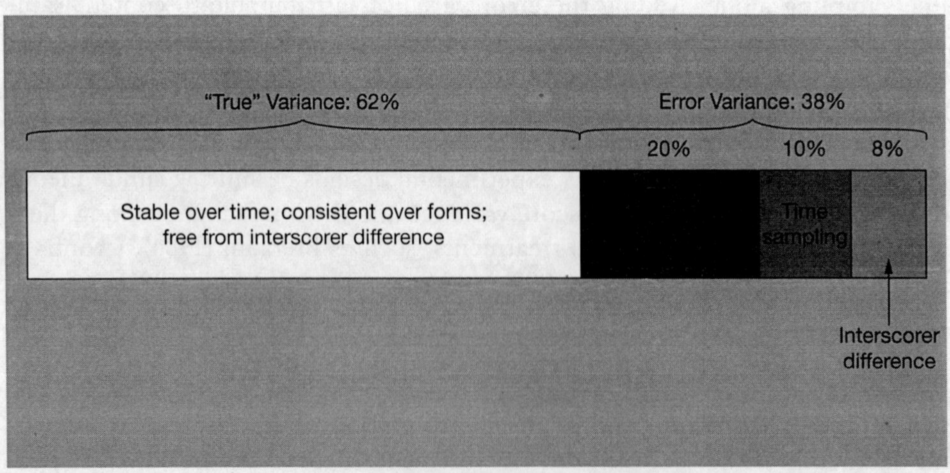

Figure 4-4. Percentage Distribution of Score Variance in a Hypothetical Test.

Information about these proportions is needed for each test in order not only to understand what the test measures but also to choose the proper procedures for evaluating its reliability. Single-trial reliability coefficients, such as those found by odd-even or Kuder-Richardson techniques, are inapplicable to speeded tests. To the extent that individual differences in test scores depend on speed of performance, reliability coefficients found by these methods will be spuriously high. An extreme example will help to clarify this point. Let us suppose that a 50-item test depends entirely on speed, so that individual differences in score are based wholly on number of items attempted, rather than on errors. Then, if individual A obtains a score of 44, he or she will obviously have 22 correct odd items and 22 correct even items. Similarly, individual B, with a score of 34, will have odd and even scores of 17 and 17, respectively. Consequently, except for accidental careless errors on a few items, the correlation between odd and even scores would be perfect, or +1.00. Such a correlation, however, is entirely spurious and provides no information about the reliability of the test.

An examination of the procedures followed in finding both split-half and Kuder-Richardson reliability will show that both are based on the consistency in *number of errors* made by the examinee. If, now, individual differences in test scores depend, not on errors, but on speed, the measure of reliability must obviously be based on consistency in *speed of work*. When test performance depends on a combination of speed and power, the single-trial reliability coefficient will fall below 1.00, but it will still be spuriously high. As long as individual differences in test scores are appreciably affected by speed, single-trial reliability coefficients cannot be properly interpreted.

What alternative procedures are available to determine the reliability of significantly speeded tests? If the test-retest technique is applicable, it would be appropriate. Similarly, equivalent-form reliability may be properly employed with speed tests. Split-half techniques may also be used, provided that the split is made in terms of time rather than in terms of items. In other words, the half-scores must be based on separately timed parts of the test. One way of effecting such a split is to administer two equivalent halves of the test with separate time limits. For example, the odd and even items may be separately printed on different pages, and each set of items given with one-half the time limit of the entire test. Such a procedure is tantamount to administering two equivalent forms of the test in immediate succession. Each form, however, is half as long as the test proper, while the test takers' scores are normally based on the whole test. For this reason, either the Spearman-Brown or some other appropriate formula should be used to find the reliability of the whole test.

If it is not feasible to administer the two half-tests separately, an alternative procedure is to divide the total time into quarters and to find a score for each of the four quarters. This can easily be done by having the test takers mark the item on which they are working whenever the examiner gives a prearranged signal. The number of items correctly completed within the first and fourth quarters can then be combined to represent one half-score, while those in the second and third quarters can be combined to yield the other half-score. Such a combination of quarters tends to balance out the cumulative effects of practice, fatigue, and other factors. This method is especially satisfactory when the items are not steeply graded in difficulty level.

When is a test appreciably speeded? Under what conditions must the special precautions discussed in this section be observed? Obviously, the mere employment of a time limit does not signify a speed test. If all test takers finish within the given time limit, speed of work plays no part in determining the scores. Percentage of persons who fail to complete the test might be taken as a crude index of speed versus power. Even when no one finishes the test, however, the role of speed may be negligible. For example, if everyone completes exactly 40 items of a 50-item test, individual differences with regard to speed are entirely absent, although no one had time to attempt all the items.

The essential question, of course, is: "To what extent are individual differences in test scores attributable to speed?" In more technical terms, we want to know what proportion of the total variance in test scores is speed variance. This proportion can be estimated roughly by finding the variance of number of items completed by different persons and dividing it by the variance of total test scores (SD_c^2/SD_t^2). In the example cited in the preceding paragraph, in which every individual finishes 40 items, the numerator of this fraction would be zero, since there are no individual differences in number of items completed ($SD_c^2 = 0$). The entire index would thus equal zero in a pure power test. On the other hand, if the total test variance (SD_t^2) is attributable to individual differences in speed, the two variances will be equal and the ratio will be 1.00. Several more refined procedures have been developed for determining this proportion, but their detailed consideration falls beyond the scope of this book.

An example of the effect of speed on single-trial reliability coefficients is provided by data collected in an investigation of the first edition of the SRA Tests of Primary Mental Abilities for Ages 11 to 17 (Anastasi & Drake, 1954). In this study, the reliability of each test was first determined by the usual odd-even procedure. These coefficients are given in the first row of Table 4–5. Reliability coefficients were then computed by correlating scores on separately timed halves. These coefficients are shown in the second row of Table 4–5. Calculation of speed indexes showed that the Verbal Meaning test was primarily a power test, while the Reasoning test was somewhat more dependent on speed. The Space and Number tests proved to be highly speeded. It will be noted in Table 4–5 that, when it is properly computed, the reliability of the Space test is .75, in contrast to a spuriously high odd-even coefficient of .90. Similarly, the reliability of the Reasoning test drops from .96 to .87, and that of the Number test drops from .92 to .83. The reliability of the relatively unspeeded Verbal Meaning test, on the other hand, shows a negligible difference when computed by the two methods.

Table 4–5

Reliability Coefficients of Four of the SRA Tests of Primary Mental Abilities for Ages 11 to 17 (1st Edition)

Reliability Coefficient Found by:	Verbal Meaning	Reasoning	Space	Number
Single-trial odd-even method	.94	.96	.90	.92
Separately timed halves	.90	.87	.75	.83

(Data from Anastasi & Drake, 1954.)

DEPENDENCE OF RELIABILITY COEFFICIENTS ON THE SAMPLE TESTED

Variability. An important condition influencing the size of a reliability coefficient is the nature of the group on which reliability is measured. In the first place, any correlation coefficient is affected by the range of individual differences in the group. If every member of a group were nearly alike in spelling ability, then the correlation of spelling with any other ability would be close to zero in that group. It would obviously be impossible, within such a group, to predict an individual's standing in any other ability from a knowledge of her or his spelling score.

Another, less extreme, example is provided by the correlation between two aptitude tests, such as a verbal comprehension and an arithmetic reasoning test. If these tests were administered to a highly homogeneous sample, such as a group of 300 college sophomores, the correlation between the two would probably be very low. Because of restriction of range, there is little relationship, within such a selected sample of college students, between any individual's verbal ability and her or his numerical reasoning ability. On the other hand, were the tests to be given to a heterogeneous sample of 300 persons, ranging from mentally retarded persons to college graduates, a high correlation would undoubtedly be obtained between the two tests. The mentally retarded examinees would obtain poorer scores than the college graduates on *both* tests, and similar relationships would hold for other subgroups within this highly heterogeneous sample.

Examination of the hypothetical scatter diagram given in Figure 4–5 will further illustrate the dependence of correlation coefficients on the variability, or extent of individual differences, within the group. This scatter diagram shows a high positive correlation in the entire, heterogeneous group, since the entries are closely clustered about the diagonal extending from lower left- to upper right-hand corners. If, now, we consider only the subgroup falling within the small rectangle in the upper right-hand portion of the diagram, it is apparent that the correlation between the two variables is close to zero. Individuals falling within this restricted range in both variables represent a highly homogeneous group, as did the college sophomores mentioned previously.

Like all correlation coefficients, reliability coefficients depend on the variability of the sample within which they are found. Thus, if the reliability coefficient reported in a test manual was calculated for a group ranging from fourth-grade children to high school students, it cannot be assumed that the reliability would be equally high within, let us say, an eighth-grade sample. When a test is to be used to discriminate individual differences within a more homogeneous sample than the standardization group, the reliability coefficient should be redetermined on such a sample. Formulas for estimating the reliability coefficient to be expected when the standard deviation of the group is increased or decreased are available in elementary statistics textbooks. It is preferable, however, to recompute the reliability coefficient empirically on a group comparable to that on which the test is to be used. For tests designed to cover a wide range of age or ability, the test manual should report separate reliability coefficients for relatively homogeneous subgroups within the standardization sample.

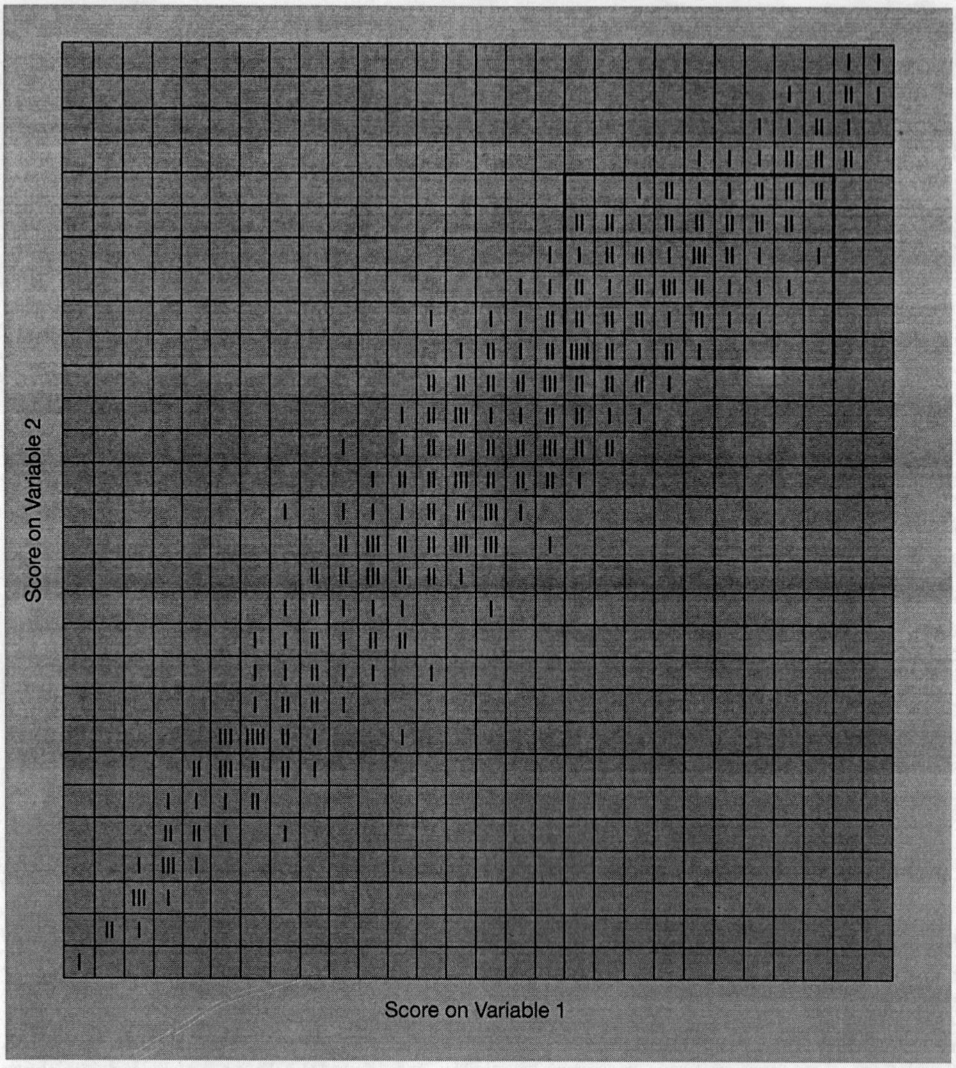

Figure 4-5. The Effect of Restricted Range upon a Correlation Coefficient.

Ability Level. Not only does the reliability coefficient vary with the extent of individual differences in the sample, but it may also vary between groups differing in average ability level. These differences, moreover, cannot usually be predicted or estimated by any statistical formula but can be discovered only by empirical tryout of the test on groups differing in age or ability level. Such differences in the reliability of a single test may arise in part from the fact that a slightly different combination of abilities is measured at different difficulty levels of the test. Or the length of the test may vary at different age levels. Even when the number of available items is the same, the upper and lower extremes may not provide enough items at the appropriate difficulty level to permit individuals to demonstrate adequately what they are able to do (ceiling or floor effects). Ceiling effect usually happens when the test given is too easy and all the testers score very high. In contrast, floor effect occurs when the test is too difficult and most of the test takers score very low. In other tests, reliability may be relatively low for the younger and less able groups, since their scores are unduly influenced by guessing.

It is apparent that every reliability coefficient should be accompanied by a full description of the type of group on which it was determined. Special attention should be given to the variability and the ability level of the sample. The reported reliability coefficient is applicable only to samples similar to that on which it was computed. A desirable and growing practice in test construction is to fractionate the standardization sample into more homogeneous subgroups, with regard to age, sex, grade level, occupation, and the like, and to report separate reliability coefficients for each subgroup. Under these conditions, the reliability coefficients are more likely to be applicable to the samples with which the test is to be used in actual practice.

STANDARD ERROR OF MEASUREMENT

Interpretation of Individual Scores. The reliability of a test may be expressed in terms of the standard error of measurement (SEM), also called the standard error of a score. This measure is particularly well suited to the interpretation of individual scores. For many testing purposes, it is therefore more useful than the reliability coefficient. The standard error of measurement can be easily computed from the reliability coefficient of the test, by the following formula:

$$\text{SEM} = SD_t\sqrt{1-r_{tt}}$$

in which SD_t is the standard deviation of the test scores and r_{tt} is the reliability coefficient, both computed on the same group. For example, if deviation IQs on a particular intelligence test have a standard deviation of 15 and a reliability coefficient of .89, the SEM of an IQ on this test is: $15\sqrt{1-.89} = 15\sqrt{.11} = 15(.33) = 5$.

To understand what the SEM tells us about a score, let us suppose that we had a set of 100 IQs obtained with the above test by a single child, Janet. Because of the types of chance errors discussed in this chapter, these scores vary, falling into a normal distribution around Janet's true score. The mean of this distribution of 100 scores can be taken as the "true score" for a specified test use, and the standard deviation of the distribution can be taken as the SEM. Like any standard deviation, this standard error can be interpreted in terms of the normal curve frequencies discussed in chapter 3 (see Fig. 3–3). It will be recalled that between the mean and $\pm 1\sigma$, there are approximately 68% of the cases in a normal curve. Thus, we can conclude that the chances are roughly 2:1 (or 68:32) that Janet's IQ on this test will fluctuate between ±1 SEM or 5 points on either side of her true IQ. If her true IQ is 110, we would expect her to score between 105 and 115 about two thirds (68%) of the time.

If we want to be more certain of our prediction, we can choose higher odds than 2:1. Reference to Figure 3–3 (chap. 3) shows that $\pm 3\sigma$ covers 99.7% of the cases. It can be ascertained from normal curve frequency tables that a distance of 2.58σ on either side of the mean includes exactly 99% of the cases. Hence, the chances are 99:1 that Janet's IQ will fall within 2.58 SEM, or (2.58) (5) = 13 points, on either side of her true IQ. We can thus state at the 99% confidence level (with only one chance of error out of 100) that Janet's IQ on any single administration of the test will lie between 97 and 123 (110 – 13 and 110 + 13). If Janet were given 100 equivalent tests, her IQ would fall outside this band of values only once.

In actual practice, of course, we do not have the true scores, but only the scores obtained in a single test administration. Under these circumstances, we can apply the above reasoning in the reverse direction. If an individual's obtained score is unlikely to deviate by more than 2.58 SEM from her true score, we could argue that her *true* score must lie within 2.58 SEM of her *obtained* score. Although we cannot assign a probability to this statement for any given obtained score, we *can* say that the statement would be correct for 99% of all the cases. On the basis of this reasoning Gulliksen (1950, pp. 17–20) proposed that the standard error of measurement be used as illustrated above, in order to estimate the reasonable limits of the true score for persons with any given obtained score. It is in terms of such "reasonable limits" that the error of measurement is customarily interpreted in psychological testing, and it will be so interpreted in this book.[8]

The standard error of measurement and the reliability coefficient are obviously alternative ways of expressing test reliability. Unlike the reliability coefficient, the error of measurement is independent of the variability of the group on which it is computed. Expressed in terms of individual scores, it remains unchanged when found in a homogeneous or a heterogeneous group. On the other hand, being reported in score units, the error of measurement will not be directly comparable from test to test. The usual problems of comparability of units would thus arise when errors of measurement are reported in terms of arithmetic problems, words in a vocabulary test, and the like. Hence, if we want to compare the reliability of *different tests*, the reliability coefficient is the better measure. To interpret *individual scores,* the standard error of measurement is more appropriate.

Neither reliability coefficients nor errors of measurement, however, can be assumed to remain constant when *ability level* varies widely. The differences in reliability coefficients discussed in the preceding section remain when errors of measurement are computed at different levels of the same test. A comprehensive solution for this problem is provided by the IRT techniques of item analysis cited in chapter 3. Spanning a wide ability range, these techniques offer a means of expressing the measurement accuracy of a test as a function of the level of ability. The procedure yields a *test information curve* that depends only on the items included in the test and permits an estimation of the error of measurement at each ability level. Further discussion of these techniques is given in chapter 7.

The SEM (or some other index of measurement accuracy) provides a safeguard against placing undue emphasis on a single numerical score. So important is this application of the SEM that an increasing number of published tests now report scores, not as a single number, but as a score band within which the individual's true score is likely to fall. The College Board provides data on the SEM and an explanation of its use, not only in materials distributed to high school and college counselors, but also in the individual score reports on the SAT sent to test takers. The SEM is likewise covered in instructional materials for use in orienting students regarding the meaning of their test scores. Information on SEMs is also provided for use in interpreting scores on the Graduate Record Examinations (*GRE 1995–96 guide*).

---

[8] Other procedures have been proposed that use an estimated "true" score as the center of the confidence interval (Dudek, 1979; Glutting, McDermott, & Stanley, 1987). If the reliability coefficient, is high, this procedure has little effect; if it is low, both true score and size of confidence interval are computed from the same fallible reliability coefficient. Moreover, the optimal procedure varies with the particular purpose for which the test scores are to be used (e.g., for long-term prediction or current performance assessment).

Interpretation of Score Differences. It is particularly important to consider test reliability and errors of measurement when evaluating the *differences* between two scores. Thinking in terms of the range within which each score may fluctuate serves as a check against overemphasizing small differences between scores. Such caution is desirable both when comparing test scores of different persons and when comparing the scores of the same individual in different abilities. Similarly, changes in scores following instruction or other experimental variables need to be interpreted in the light of errors of measurement.

A frequent question about test scores concerns the individual's relative standing in different areas. Is Doris more able along verbal than along numerical lines? Does Tom have more aptitude for mechanical than for verbal activities? If Doris scored higher on the verbal than on the numerical subtests on an aptitude battery and Tom scored higher on the mechanical than on the verbal, how sure can we be that they would still do so on a retest with another form of the battery? In other words, could the score differences have resulted merely from the chance selection of specific items in the particular verbal, numerical, and mechanical tests employed? These questions are especially relevant to the proper interpretation of scores on multiscore batteries in both abilities and personality traits (Anastasi, 1985a). Examples and further discussion of the problems to be considered in interpreting a person's score profile on such batteries can be found in chapters 8 and 10 (for ability tests) and chapter 13 (for personality tests).

Because of the growing interest in the interpretation of score profiles, test publishers have been developing report forms that permit the evaluation of scores in terms of their errors of measurement. An example is the individual report form for use with the Differential Aptitude Tests, which includes the sort of information illustrated in Figure 4–6. On this form, percentile scores on each subtest of

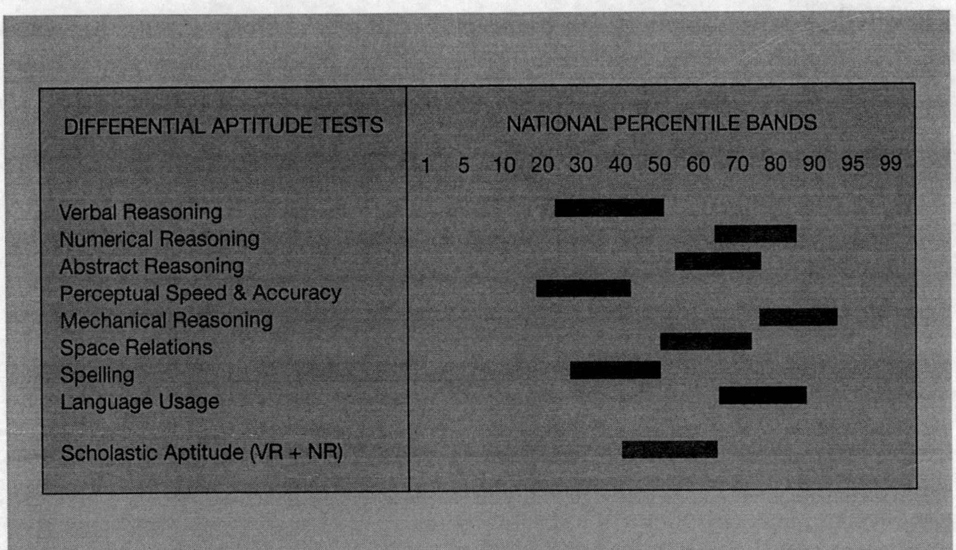

Figure 4–6. Score Profile on the Differential Aptitude Tests, Illustrating Use of Percentile Bands.

(Data from *Individual Report, Differential Aptitude Tests,* 5th ed. Copyright © 1990 by The Psychological Corporation. Reproduced by permission.)

the battery are plotted as percentile bands, with the obtained percentile at the center. Each percentile bar corresponds to a distance of 1 SEM on either side of the obtained score—hence the probability that the individual's "true" score falls within the bar is approximately 2 to 1 (.68 to .32). In interpreting the profiles, test users are advised not to attach importance to differences between scores whose percentile bars overlap, especially if they overlap by more than halt their length. In the profile illustrated in Figure 4–6, for example, the difference between the Verbal Reasoning and Numerical Reasoning scores probably reflects a genuine difference in ability level; that between Numerical Reasoning and Abstract Reasoning probably does not; the difference between Abstract Reasoning and Mechanical Reasoning is in the doubtful range.

It is good to bear in mind that the standard error of the difference between two scores is larger than the error of measurement of either of the two scores. This follows from the fact that this difference is affected by the chance errors present in *both* scores. The standard error of the difference between two scores can be found from the standard errors of measurement of the two scores by the following formula:[9]

$$SE_{\text{diff.}} = \sqrt{(SEM_1)^2 + (SEM_2)^2}$$

in which $SE_{\text{diff.}}$ is the standard error of the difference between the two scores, and SEM_1 and SEM_2 are standard errors of measurement of the separate scores. By substituting $SD\sqrt{1-r_{11}}$ for SEM_1 and $SD\sqrt{1-r_{22}}$ for SEM_2, we may rewrite the formula directly in terms of reliability coefficients, as follows:

$$SE_{\text{diff.}} = SD\sqrt{2-r_{11}-r_{22}}$$

In this substitution, the same *SD* was used for tests 1 and 2, since their scores would have to be expressed in terms of the same scale before they could be compared.

We may illustrate the above procedure with the Verbal and Performance IQs on the Wechsler Adult Intelligence Scale–Revised (WAIS-R). The split-half reliabilities of these scores are .97 and .93, respectively. WAIS-R deviation IQs are expressed on a scale with a mean of 100 and an *SD* of 15. Hence the standard error of the difference between these two scores can be found as follows:

$$SE_{\text{diff.}} = 15\sqrt{2-.97-.93} = 4.74$$

To determine how large a score difference could be obtained by chance at the .05 level, we multiply the standard error of the difference (4.74) by 1.96. The result is 9.29, or approximately 10 points. Thus, the difference between an individual's WAIS-R Verbal and Performance IQ should be at least 10 points to be significant at the .05 level.[10]

---

[9] This formula should not be confused with the formula for the standard error of a difference between two *group means*, which includes a correlation term when the two variables to be compared are correlated. *Errors of measurement* in two variables are random errors and hence are assumed to be uncorrelated.

[10] More precise estimate can be obtained by using the actual reliabilities and *SDs* found within each group. When thus computed, the minimum significant Verbal–Performance difference at the .05 level, as reported in the test manul, ranges from 8.83 to 12.04. Most of the values, however, are close to 10.

RELIABILITY APPLIED TO MASTERY TESTING AND CUTOFF SCORES

It will be recalled from chapter 3 that domain-referenced tests usually (but not necessarily) evaluate performance in terms of mastery rather than degree of achievement. A major statistical implication of mastery testing is a reduction in variability of scores among persons. Theoretically, if everyone continues training until the skill is mastered, variability is reduced to zero. In an earlier section of this chapter, we saw that *any* correlation, including reliability coefficients, is affected by the variability of the group in which it is computed. As the variability of the sample decreases, so does the correlation coefficient. Obviously, then, it would be inappropriate to assess the reliability of most domain-referenced tests by applying the usual procedures to a group of persons after they have reached the preestablished mastery level. Under these conditions, even a highly stable and internally consistent test could yield a reliability coefficient near zero.

This apparent difficulty in the assessment of reliability arises from a failure to consider what the domain-referenced tests are designed to measure. In actual practice, these tests are used essentially to differentiate between those persons who have and those who have not acquired the skills and knowledge required for a designated activity. The specific purpose for which the test is administered may vary widely, from obtaining a driver's license or assignment to an occupational specialty to advancing to the next unit in an individualized instructional program or admission to a particular course of study. Nevertheless, in all such situations, the fact that a test is used at all implies the expectation of variability in performance among individuals. A major portion of this variability reflects individual differences in amount of prior training in the relevant functions.

More than a dozen different techniques have been specifically designed to evaluate the reliability of domain-referenced tests (Berk, 1984b; Brennan, 1984; Subkoviak, 1984). Some of these techniques are appropriate for simple mastery–nonmastery decisions, in which all classification errors are considered equally serious regardless of their distance from the cutoff score. In such cases, test and retest with parallel forms can be used to find the percentage of persons for whom the same decision is reached on both occasions. These data can be further analyzed by computing appropriate indexes of agreement and significance values. Other procedures take into account the actual scores obtained on the two occasions and provide indexes that reflect each person's deviation above or below any given cutoff score. The choice of a particular procedure should take into account the nature and uses of the test, the position of cutoff scores, and other psychometric features of the test. Relevant considerations have been extensively discussed in the technical literature (see Berk, 1984a; Feldt & Brennan, 1989).

Chapter Five

Validity: Basic Concepts

The validity of a test concerns *what* the test measures and *how well* it does so. It tells us what can be inferred from test scores. In this connection, we should guard against accepting the test name as an index of what the test measures. Test names provide short, convenient labels for identification purposes. Most test names are far too broad and vague to furnish meaningful clues to the behavior area covered, although increasing efforts are being made to use more specific and empirically definable test names. The trait measured by a given test can be defined only through an examination of the objective sources of information and empirical operations utilized in establishing its validity. Moreover, the validity of a test cannot be reported in general terms. No test can be said to have "high" or "low" validity in the abstract. Its validity must be established with reference to the particular use for which the test is being considered.

Fundamentally, all procedures for determining test validity are concerned with the relationships between performance on the test and other independently observable facts about the behavior characteristics under consideration. The specific methods employed for investigating these relationships are numerous and have been described by various names. These traditional labels focus on different aspects of validity, of special interest for different test uses. As the applications of tests developed and expanded, concepts of validity altered accordingly (Anastasi, 1986a; Messick, 1988, 1989).

EVOLVING CONCEPTS OF TEST VALIDITY

Among the earliest uses of tests was in the assessment of what individuals had learned in specified content areas. Today, that use is represented by end-of-course examinations in school and by licensing tests for driving a car or qualifying for a specified occupation. This type of test, commonly designated as an achievement test, is typically evaluated by comparing its content with the content domain it is designed to assess. Such a descriptive approach is still relevant in validating tests for certain applications, and it will be considered in one section of this chapter.

As testing moved into its second stage over time, the emphasis shifted to prediction. How will different persons respond in a given situation, now or at some future time? How will this individual react in different specified situations? Performance in the situation for which behavior was to be predicted came to be designated as the criterion. For this purpose, test validity was usually reported as a correlation co efficient between test scores and a direct and independent measure of that criterion. This procedure is especially appropriate for the use of tests in the selection or placement of individuals for educational programs, for jobs, or for particular treatment programs. Thus, for a mechanical aptitude test, the criterion might be subsequent job performance as a machinist; for a scholastic aptitude test, it might be college grades; and for a neuroticism test, it might be associates' ratings or other available information regarding the individual's behavior in various life situations.

The current stage in the history of testing reflects two major trends: (1) a strengthened theoretical orientation and (2) a close linkage between psychological theory and verification through empirical and experimental hypothesis testing. These trends are evident in test construction and validation, as they are in other areas of psychology as a whole (Anastasi, 1992a, 1992b, 1995). One result of these trends is a growing recognition of the value of constructs in describing and understanding human behavior. Constructs are broad categories, derived from the common features shared by directly observable behavioral variables. They are theoretical entities, not themselves directly observable. Interest in constructs led to the introduction of what was first considered to be a third kind of test validity, namely construct validity (AERA, APA, NCME, 1985; APA, AERA, NCME, 1974; Cronbach & Meehl, 1955). Eventually, construct validity came to be recognized as the fundamental and all-inclusive validity concept, insofar as it specifies what the test measures. Content and predictive validation procedures are among the many sources of information that contribute to the definition and the understanding of the constructs assessed by a test. At the same time, they provide valuable information in their own right and are preeminent in the evaluation of tests for certain uses. Hence the concepts (and terms) have survived, despite their integration into the comprehensive concept of construct validity.

CONTENT-DESCRIPTION PROCEDURES

Nature. Content-description validation procedures involve essentially the systematic examination of the test content to determine whether it covers a representative sample of the behavior domain to be measured. Such a validation procedure is commonly used in tests designed to measure how well the individual has mastered a specific skill or course of study. It might seem that mere inspection of the content of the test should suffice to establish its validity for such a purpose. A test of multiplication, spelling, or bookkeeping would seem to be valid by definition if it consists of multiplication, spelling, or bookkeeping items, respectively.

The solution, however, is not so simple as it appears to be. One difficulty is that of adequately sampling the item universe. The behavior domain to be tested must be systematically analyzed to make certain that all major aspects are covered by the test items, and in the correct proportions. For example, a test can easily become overloaded with those aspects of the field that lend themselves more readily to the preparation of objective items. The domain under consideration should be fully described in advance, rather than being defined after the test has been prepared. A well-constructed educational test, for example, should cover the objectives of instruction, not just its subject matter. Content must therefore be broadly defined to include major objectives, such as the application of principles and the interpretation of data, as well as factual knowledge. Moreover, validity depends on the relevance of the individual's test responses to the behavior area under consideration, rather than on the apparent relevance of item content. Mere inspection of the test may fail to reveal the processes actually used by examinees in taking the test.

It is also important to guard against any tendency to overgeneralize regarding the domain sampled by the test. For instance, a multiple-choice spelling test may measure the ability to recognize correctly and incorrectly spelled words. But it cannot be assumed that such a test also measures ability to spell correctly from dictation, frequency of misspellings in written compositions, and other aspects of spelling ability (Ahlström, 1964; Knoell & Harris, 1952). Still another difficulty arises from the possible inclusion of irrelevant factors in the test scores. For example, a test designed to measure proficiency in mathematics or mechanics may be unduly influenced by the ability to understand verbal directions or by speed of performing simple, routine tasks.

Specific Procedures. Content validity is built into a test from the outset through the choice of appropriate items. For educational tests, the preparation of items is preceded by a thorough and systematic examination of relevant course syllabi and textbooks, as well as by consultation with subject-matter experts. On the basis of the information thus gathered, *test specifications* are drawn up for the item writers. These specifications should show the content areas or topics to be covered, the instructional objectives or processes to be tested, and the relative importance of individual topics and processes. The final specifications should indicate the number of items of each kind to be prepared for each topic. For example, assessment of reading ability may include understanding vocabulary in context, literal comprehension of content, and drawing correct inferences from the given information. It may also sample material from different sources, such as essays, poems, newspaper articles, or instructions for operating equipment. A mathematics test may cover computational skills, the solution of verbally presented problems, and the application of learned processes to new and unfamiliar contexts.

The discussion of content validation in the manual of an educational achievement test should include a description of the procedures followed in ensuring that the test content is appropriate and representative. If subject-matter experts participated in the test-construction process, their number and professional qualifications should be stated. If they served as judges in classifying items, the directions they were given should be reported, as well as the extent of agreement among judges. Because curricula and course content change over time, it is particularly desirable to give the dates when subject-matter experts were consulted. Information should likewise be provided about number and nature of course syllabi and textbooks surveyed, including publication dates.

A number of empirical procedures are also commonly followed in order to supplement the content validation of an educational achievement test. Both total scores and performance on individual items can be checked for grade progress. In general, those items are retained that show the largest gains in the percentages of children passing them from the lower to the upper grades. Other supplementary procedures that may be employed, when appropriate, include analyses of types of errors commonly made on a test and observation of the work methods employed by test takers. The latter could be done by testing students individually with instructions to "think aloud" while solving each problem. The contribution of speed can be checked by noting how many persons fail to finish the test or by one of the more refined methods discussed in chapter 4. To detect the possible irrelevant influence of ability to read instructions on test performance, scores on the test may be correlated with scores on a reading comprehension test. On the other hand, if the test is designed to measure reading comprehension, giving the questions without the reading passage on which they are based will show how many could be answered simply from the test takers' prior information or other irrelevant cues (Scherich & Hanna, 1977).

Applications. Especially when bolstered by such empirical checks as those already illustrated, content validation provides an adequate technique for evaluating achievement tests. It permits us to answer two questions that are basic to the validity of educational and occupational achievement tests: (1) Does the test cover a representative sample of the specified skills and knowledge? (2) Is test performance reasonably free from the influence of irrelevant variables? Content validation is particularly appropriate for the domain-referenced tests described in chapter 3. Because performance on those tests is interpreted in terms of content meaning, it is obvious that content validation is a prime requirement for their effective use. Nevertheless, other types of validity evidence are also relevant to a full evaluation of the effectiveness of such tests (see Hambleton, 1984b).

Content validation is also applicable to certain occupational tests designed for employee selection and classification, discussed in chapter 17. This type of validation evidence is suitable when the test is an actual job sample or otherwise calls for the same skills and knowledge required on the job. In such cases, a thorough job analysis should be carried out in order to demonstrate the close resemblance between the job activities and the test. A clear, step-by-step account of the application of these validation procedures to the development of an industrial reading test is illustrated by Schoenfeldt, Schoenfeldt, Acker, and Perlson (1976). Working closely with job incumbents and supervisors, the investigators surveyed the reading requirements of entry-level jobs in a large manufacturing company in terms of both subject matter and comprehension skills. Test items were then constructed to match these requirements. This approach is used widely in developing tests for government employees at federal and state levels (Hardt, Eyde, Primoff, & Tordy, 1981; Menne, McCarthy, & Menne, 1976; Primoff & Eyde, 1988; Tordy, Eyde, Primoff, & Hardt, 1976).

For aptitude and personality tests, on the other hand, content validation is usually inappropriate and may, in fact, be misleading. Although considerations of relevance and representativeness of content must obviously enter into the initial stages of constructing any test, eventual validation of aptitude or personality tests requires empirical verification by the procedures to be described in the following sections. These tests bear less intrinsic resemblance to the behavior domain they are trying to sample than do achievement tests. Consequently, the content of aptitude and personality tests can do little more than reveal the hypotheses that led the test constructor to choose a certain type of content for measuring a specified trait. Such hypotheses need to be empirically confirmed to establish the validity of the test.

Unlike achievement tests, aptitude and personality tests are not based on a specified course of instruction or uniform set of prior experiences from which test content can be drawn. Hence, in the latter tests, individuals are likely to vary more in the work methods or psychological processes employed in responding to the same test items. The identical test might thus measure different functions in different persons. Under these conditions, it would be virtually impossible to determine the psychological functions measured by the test from an inspection of its content. For example, college graduates might solve a problem in verbal or mathematical terms, while a mechanic would arrive at the same solution in terms of spatial visualization. Or a test measuring arithmetic reasoning among high school freshmen might measure only individual differences in speed of computation when given to college students.

Face Validity. Content validity should not be confused with face validity. The latter is not validity in the technical sense; it refers, not to what the test actually measures, but to what it appears superficially to measure. Face validity pertains to whether the test "looks valid" to the examinees who take it, the administrative personnel who decide on its use, and other technically untrained observers. Fundamentally, the question of face validity concerns rapport and public relations. Although common usage of the term "validity" in this connection may make for confusion, face validity itself is a desirable feature of tests. For example, when tests originally designed for children and developed within a classroom setting were first extended for adult use, they frequently met with resistance and criticism because of their lack of face validity. Certainly if test content appears irrelevant, inappropriate, silly, or childish, the result will be poor cooperation, regardless of the actual validity of the test. Especially in adult testing, it is not sufficient for a test to be objectively valid. It also needs face validity to function effectively in practical situations. Face validity also affects the acceptability of a test in legislative and judicial decisions, as well as its evaluation by the general public.

In a direct and innovative research program on testing as viewed by the test taker (cited in chap. 1), Baruch Nevo and his associates included the investigation of face validity (B. Nevo, 1985, 1992; B. Nevo & Sfez, 1985). First, they called attention to the paucity of available research on face validity, despite its probable contribution to prevalent attitudes toward tests. They then proposed a quantitative assessment of face validity by having test takers and other psychometrically unsophisticated interested persons rate the suitability of a test for its intended use; the same procedures may be employed in rating individual test items or a battery of tests. Illustrative data were reported from an analysis of the responses on an Examinee Feedback Questionnaire completed by 1,385 Israeli students who had taken a six-test university entrance examination. The results showed promising interrater agreement, retest reliability, and differentiation among tests and among subgroups of respondents planning to major in different fields. It was recommended that both qualitative and quantitative data about face validity be regularly reported in test manuals.

Face validity can often be improved by merely reformulating test items in terms that appear relevant and plausible in the particular setting in which they will be used. For example, if a test of simple arithmetic reasoning is constructed for use with machinists, the items should be worded in terms of machine operations rather than in terms of "how many oranges can be purchased for 86 cents" or other traditional schoolbook problems. Similarly, an arithmetic test for naval personnel can be expressed in naval terminology, without necessarily altering the functions measured. To be sure, face validity should never be regarded as a substitute for objectively determined validity. It cannot be assumed that improving the face validity of a test will improve its objective validity. Nor can it be assumed that when a test is modified so as to increase its face validity, its objective validity remains unaltered. The validity of the test in its final form should always be directly checked.

CRITERION-PREDICTION PROCEDURES

Concurrent and Predictive Validation. Criterion prediction validation procedures indicate the effectiveness of a test in predicting an individual's performance in specified activities. In India, one of the primary reasons for using tests is to predict a respondent's potential for future success. Criterion related validity evidence occurs when a statistical relationship exists between scores of the tests and one or more criteria, or between scores of the tests and measures of performance. For example, by collecting test scores and criterion scores (e.g. job performance ratings, grades in a training course, supervisor ratings etc.), one can determine the level of confidence that may be placed on using test scores to predict job success in an organization. There are two types of criterion prediction validation procedures: concurrent and predictive. Whenever a criterion measure is available at the time of testing, the concurrent validity of the test can be determined. When scores on the criterion are not available at the time of testing, but are available after the test has been administered, the focus is on the predictive validity of the test.

Predictive validity is represented as a correlation between the test scores itself and a score of the degree of success in the selected field. For instance, a test will have a high predictive validity if the scores on the test of a cognitive ability are highly correlated with various jobs, academic success criteria, job performance capabilities related to thinking, problem solving, decision making, etc. Cronbach (1970) characterized validity coefficients of 0.30 or better as having "definite practical value". The US Department of Labor (1999) has provided the following guidelines for interpreting validity coefficients:

- Above 0.35 are considered "very beneficial"
- 0.21–0.35 are considered "likely to be useful"
- 0.11–0.20 "depends on the circumstances"
- Below 0.11 are "unlikely to be useful"

In the Indian business environment, it is important to point out that relatively lower validities, for example .20, may justify the use of tests in a selection program. In this context, the practical value of the test depends not only on the validity coefficient, but also on other factors. For instance, seeing a huge gap in the skills that make young graduates employable for high-stake jobs and roles, it may be fair to assume that the base rate for success (i.e. the proportion of people who would be successful in the absence of any selection procedure) will be low (i.e. a few people would be successful on the job), and hence tests of low validity can have considerate utility or value.

In a number of instances, concurrent validation is employed merely as a substitute for predictive validation. It is usually impracticable to extend validation procedures over the time required for predictive validation or to obtain a suitable preselection sample for testing purposes. As a compromise solution, therefore, tests are administered to a group on whom criterion data are already available. Thus, the test scores of college students may be compared with their cumulative grade-point average at the time of testing, or those of employees compared with their current job success.

For certain uses of psychological tests, concurrent validation is the most appropriate type and can be justified in its own right. Concurrent validity typically is done with the gold standard test of the construct (e.g. if a new test of intelligence is proposed, it should be compared to an IQ test or any test which is the test of that trait), and would be done simultaneously. Essentially, the new test must measure the trait as efficiently as the established one, and should be either easy to administer or of a shorter duration. Concurrent validity describes the correlation of a new test with existing tests that purport to measure the same construct. Thus, a new intelligence test ought to correlate with existing intelligence tests. A few statisticians, however, feel that this is a rather weak procedure for establishing validity on its own as both the old and the new tests may correlate well and yet neither may measure intelligence. Therefore, this has been one of the major criticisms directed against the concurrent validation procedures. However, concurrent validity, although never sufficient on its own, is important. If old tests and new tests measuring the same construct are not correlated with each other, then it is a serious cause of concern.

Because the criterion for concurrent validation is always available at the time of testing, we might ask what function is served by the test in such situations. Basically, such tests provide a simpler, quicker, or less expensive substitute for the criterion data. For example, if the criterion consists of continuous observation of a patient during a two-week hospitalization period, a test that could sort out normals from disturbed and doubtful cases would appreciably reduce the number of persons requiring such extensive observation.

Criterion Contamination. An essential precaution in finding the validity of a test is to make certain that the test scores do not themselves influence any individual's criterion status. For example, if a college instructor or a supervisor in an industrial plant knows that a particular individual scored very poorly on an aptitude test, such knowledge might influence the grade given to the student or the rating assigned to the worker. Or a high-scoring person might be given the benefit of the doubt when academic grades or on-the-job ratings are being prepared. Such influences would obviously raise the correlation between test scores and criterion in a manner that is entirely spurious or artificial.

This possible source of error in test validation is known as criterion contamination, since the criterion ratings become "contaminated" by the rater's knowledge of the test scores. To prevent the operation of such an error, it is absolutely essential that no person who participates in the assignment of criterion ratings have any knowledge of the examinees' test scores. For this reason, test scores employed in "testing the test" must be kept strictly confidential. It is sometimes difficult to convince teachers, employers, military officers, and other line personnel that such a precaution is essential. In their urgency to utilize all available information for practical decisions, such persons may fail to realize that the test scores must be put aside until the criterion data mature and validity can be checked.

Criterion Measures. A test may be validated against as many criteria as there are specific uses for it. Any method for assessing behavior in any situation could provide a criterion measure for some particular purpose. The criteria employed in finding the validities reported in test manuals, however, fall into a few common categories. Some of the criteria are as follows:

- **Academic Achievement:** This is the most frequently employed criterion in validating intelligence tests. The specific indices used as criterion measures include school grades, achievement test scores, promotion and graduation records, special honors and awards, and teachers' or instructors' ratings for intelligence. The various indices of academic achievement have provided criterion data at all educational levels, from primary grades to college and post-graduate institutions. Although employed principally in the validation of general intelligence tests, they have also served as criteria for certain multiple-aptitude and personality tests.
- **Performance in Specialized Training:** In the development of special aptitude tests, a frequent type of criterion is based on the performance in specialized training. For example, mechanical aptitude tests may be validated against final achievement in shop courses. Various business school courses such as MS Office or accounting software provide criteria for aptitude tests in these areas. Similarly, performance in music or art schools has been employed in validating music or art aptitude tests. Several professional aptitude tests have been validated in terms of achievement in schools of law, medicine, dentistry, engineering, and other areas. In the case of custom-made tests, designed for use within a specific testing program, training records are a frequent source of criteria data. An outstanding illustration is the validation of air force pilot selection tests against performance in basic flight training. Performance in training programs is commonly used as a criterion for test validation in other military occupational specialties and in some industrial validation studies.

Among the specific indices of training performance employed for criterion purposes, it may be mentioned that achievement tests are administered on completion of training, formally assigned grades, instructors' ratings, and successful completion of the training program. Multiple aptitude batteries have often been checked against grades in specific high school or college courses, in order to determine their validity as differential predictors. For example, scores on a verbal comprehension test may be compared with grades in English courses, spatial visualization scores may be compared with geometry grades and so forth.

- **Job Performance:** For many purposes, the most satisfactory type of criterion measure is based on the follow-up records of actual job performance. This criterion has been used to some extent in the validation of general intelligence as well as personality tests, and to a larger extent in the validation of special aptitude tests. It is a common criterion in the validation of custom-made tests for specific jobs. The jobs in question may vary widely in both level and kind, including work in businesses, industries, professions, and defense services. Most measures of job performance, although probably not representing the ultimate criteria, at least provide good intermediate criteria for many testing purposes. In this respect, they are to be preferred over training records. On the other hand, the measurement of job performance does not permit as much uniformity of conditions as is possible during training. Moreover, since it usually involves a longer follow-up, the criterion of job performance is likely to entail a loss in the number of available participants. Because of the variation in the nature of nominally similar jobs in different organizations, test manuals reporting validity data against the job criteria should describe not only the specific criterion measures employed but also the job duties performed by the workers.
- **Contrasted Groups:** Validation by the method of contrasted groups generally involves a composite criterion that reflects the cumulative and uncontrolled selective influences of everyday life. This method is used quite commonly in the validation of personality tests. Thus, in validating a test of social traits, the test performance of sales persons or executives, may be compared with that of clerks or engineers. The assumption underlying such a procedure is that, with reference to many social traits, individuals who have entered and remained in such occupations such as selling or executive work will excel persons in such fields, as clerical work or engineering. Similarly, college students who engage in many extracurricular activities may be compared with those who have participated in none during a comparable period of college attendance. Occupational groups have frequently been used in the development and validation of interest tests, such as, Strong Vocational Interest Blank (SVIB), as well as in the preparation of attitude scales.
- **Psychiatric Diagnosis:** In the development of certain personality tests, psychiatric diagnosis is used both as a basis for the selection of items and as an evidence of test validity. Psychiatric diagnosis may serve as a satisfactory criterion provided it is based on a prolonged observation and detailed case history, rather than on a cursory psychiatric interview or examination. In the latter case, there is no reason to expect the psychiatric diagnosis to be superior to the test score itself, as an indication of the individual's emotional condition. Such a psychiatric diagnosis could not be regarded as a criterion measure, but rather as an indicator or predictor whose own validity would have to be determined.

- **Ratings:** The ratings discussed earlier merely represented a subsidiary technique for obtaining information regarding such criteria as academic achievement, performance in specialized training, or job success. The use of ratings is now considered as the very core of the criterion measure. Under these circumstances, the ratings themselves define the criterion. Moreover, such ratings are not restricted to the evaluation of specific achievement, but involve a personal judgment by an observer regarding any of the variety of traits that psychological tests attempt to measure. Thus, the participants in the validation sample might be rated on characteristics such as dominance, mechanical ingenuity, originality, leadership, and honesty. Ratings have been employed in the validation of almost every type of test. They are particularly useful in providing criteria for personality tests, since objective criteria are much more difficult to find in this area. This is especially true of distinctly social traits, in which ratings based on personal contact may constitute the most logically defensible criterion. Although ratings, when obtained under carefully controlled conditions, may be subject to many judgmental errors, they represent a valuable source of criterion data.
- **Previously available tests:** Correlations between a new test and previously available tests are frequently cited as evidence of validity, and it has been discussed in detail in previous sections. When the new test is an abbreviated or simplified form of a currently available test, the latter can be regarded as a proper criterion measure.

Validity Generalization. Criterion-prediction validity is often used in local validation studies, in which the effectiveness of a test for a specific program is to be assessed. This is the approach followed, for example, when a given company wishes to evaluate a test for selecting applicants for one of its jobs or when a given college wishes to determine how well an academic aptitude test can predict the course performance of its students. Criterion-prediction validity can be best characterized as the practical validity of a test for a specified purpose.

When standardized aptitude tests were first correlated with performance on presumably similar jobs in industrial validation studies, the validity coefficients were found to vary widely (Ghiselli, 1959, 1966). Similar variability among validity coefficients was observed when the criteria were grades in various school courses (G. K. Bennett, Seashore, & Wesman, 1984). Such findings led to widespread pessimism regarding the generalizability of test validity to different situations. Until the mid-1970s, "situational specificity" of psychological requirements was generally regarded as a serious limitation in the usefulness of standardized tests in personnel selection. In a sophisticated statistical analysis of the problem, however, Schmidt, Hunter, and their associates demonstrated that much of the variance among obtained validity coefficients may be a statistical artifact resulting from small sample size, criterion unreliability, and restriction of range in employee samples.[1]

[1] This work was part of a continuing research program reported in many articles and monographs. The publications most relevant to the present topic include (but are not limited to) Pearlman, Schmidt, and Hunter (1980), Schmidt, Gast-Rosenberg, and Hunter (1980), Schmidt, and Hunter (1977), Schmidt, Hunter, and Pearlman (1981), and Schmidt, Hunter, Pearlman, and Shane (1979).

The industrial samples available for test validation are generally too small to yield a stable estimate of the correlation between predictor and criterion. For the same reason, the obtained coefficients may be too low to reach statistical significance in the sample employed and may thus fail to provide evidence of the test's validity. It has been estimated that about half of the validation samples used in industrial studies include no more than 40 or 50 cases (Schmidt, Hunter, & Urry, 1976). With such small samples, the application of criterion-prediction validation is not technically feasible.

Applying their newly developed techniques to data from many samples drawn from a large number of occupational specialties, Schmidt, Hunter, and their co-workers were able to show that the validity of tests of verbal, numerical, and reasoning aptitudes can be generalized far more widely across occupations than had previously been recognized. The variance of validity coefficients typically found in earlier industrial studies proved to be no greater than would be expected by chance. This was true even when the particular job functions appeared to be quite dissimilar across jobs. Evidently, the successful performance of a wide variety of occupational tasks depends to a significant degree on a common core of cognitive skills. The tests included in these studies covered chiefly the type of content and skills sampled in traditional intelligence and scholastic aptitude tests. It would seem that this cluster of cognitive skills and knowledge is broadly predictive of performance in both academic and occupational activities demanded in advanced technological societies. Nevertheless, more precise selection decisions can generally be reached by considering scores on two or three broad cognitive clusters, preferably supplemented by measures of technical task-specific skills for particular jobs (Hartigan & Wigdor, 1989; L. L. Wise, McHenry, & Campbell, 1990; Zeidner & Johnson, 1991).

Meta-Analysis. Typically, the task of combining data from multiple studies had primarily been the purview of the narrative review. An expert in a given field would read the studies that addressed a question, summarize the findings, and then arrive at a conclusion – for example, that the treatment in question was, or was not, effective. However, this approach suffers from some limitations such as the inherent subjectivity coupled with the lack of transparency and the less usefulness of narrative reviews due to the availability of information. Due to these limitations, beginning in the mid 1980s and taking root in the 1990s, researchers in many fields have been moving away from the narrative review and adopting systematic reviews or meta-analysis. Meta-analysis refers to the analysis of analyses. T is defined as the statistical analysis of a large collection of analyses resulting from individual studies for the purpose of integrating the findings (Glass, 1976).[2] Unlike the narrative review, where reviewers implicitly assign some level of importance to each study, the weights assigned to each study in meta-analysis are based on some mathematical and logical criteria that are specified in advance. By combining the published findings of several studies and weighting them insofar as possible on the basis of mathematical criteria and substantive features of each study, meta-analysis may reveal substantial positive findings. Furthermore, meta-analysis

[2] Glass, G. V., "Primary, Secondary, and Meta-analysis of Research", *Educational Researcher*, Vol. 5(10), 1976, p. 3–8.

permits the computation of effect sizes. For both theoretical and practical purposes, the estimated magnitude of a difference or a correlation is more useful than is the simple demonstration that it is significantly greater than zero. Interest in meta-analysis is steadily increasing and procedural refinements are constantly being developed at a global level. In India, it is yet to reach its potential.

CONSTRUCT-IDENTIFICATION PROCEDURES

The term "construct validity" was officially introduced into the psychometrist's lexicon in 1954 in the *Technical Recommendations for Psychological Tests and Diagnostic Techniques* (APA, 1954), which constituted the first edition of the current *Testing Standards.* The first detailed exposition of construct validity appeared the following year in an article by Cronbach and Meehl (1955). The discussions of construct validation that followed—and that are continuing with undiminished vigor—have served to make the implications of its procedures more explicit and to provide a systematic rationale for their use. Construct validation has focused attention on the role of psychological theory in test construction and on the need to formulate hypotheses that can be proved or disproved in the validation process. Construct validation has also stimulated the search for novel ways of gathering validity data. Although several of the techniques employed in investigating construct validity had long been familiar, the field of operation has been expanded to admit a wider variety of procedures.

The construct validity of a test is the extent to which the test may be said to measure a theoretical construct or trait. Examples of such constructs are scholastic aptitude, mechanical comprehension, verbal fluency, speed of walking, neuroticism, and anxiety. Each construct is developed to explain and organize observed response consistencies. It derives from established interrelationships among behavioral measures. Construct validation requires the gradual accumulation of information from a variety of sources. Any data throwing light on the nature of the trait under consideration and the conditions affecting its development and manifestations represent appropriate evidence for this validation. Illustrations of specific techniques that contribute to construct identification are considered in the following sections.

Developmental Changes. A major criterion employed in the validation of a number of traditional intelligence tests is *age differentiation.* Such tests as the Stanford-Binet and most preschool tests are checked against chronological age to determine whether the scores show a progressive increase with advancing age. Since abilities are expected to increase with age during childhood, it is argued that the test scores should likewise show such an increase, if the test is valid. The very concept of an age scale of intelligence, as initiated by Binet, is based on the assumption that "intelligence" increases with age, at least until maturity.

The criterion of age differentiation, of course, is inapplicable to any functions that do not exhibit clear-cut and consistent age changes. In the area of personality measurement, for example, it has found limited use. Moreover, it should be noted that, even when applicable, age differentiation is a necessary but not a sufficient condition for validity. Thus, if the test scores fail to improve with age, such a finding probably indicates that the test is not a valid measure of the abilities it was designed to sample. On the other hand, to prove that a test measures something that increases with age does not define the area covered by the test very precisely. A measure of height or weight would also show regular age increments, although it would obviously not be designated an intelligence test.

A final point should be emphasized regarding the interpretation of the age criterion. A psychological test validated against such a criterion measures behavior characteristics that increase with age under the conditions existing in the type of environment in which the test was standardized. Because different cultures may stimulate and foster the development of dissimilar behavior characteristics, it cannot be assumed that the criterion of age differentiation is a universal one. Like all other criteria, it is circumscribed by the particular cultural context in which it is derived.

Developmental analyses are also basic to the construct validation of the Piagetian ordinal scales cited in chapters 3 and 9. A fundamental assumption of such scales is the *sequential patterning* of development, such that the attainment of earlier stages in concept development is prerequisite to the acquisition of later conceptual skills. There is thus an intrinsic hierarchy in the content of these scales. The construct validation of ordinal scales should therefore include empirical data on the sequential invariance of the successive steps. This involves checking the performance of children at different levels in the development of any tested concept, such as conservation or object permanence. Do children who demonstrate mastery of the concept at a given level also exhibit mastery at the lower levels?

Correlations with Other Tests. Correlations between a new test and similar earlier tests are sometimes cited as evidence that the new test measures approximately the same general area of behavior as other tests designated by the same name, such as "intelligence tests" or "mechanical aptitude tests." Unlike the correlations found in criterion-prediction validity, these correlations should be moderately high, but not too high. If the new test correlates too highly with an already available test, without such added advantages as brevity or ease of administration, then the new test represents needless duplication.

Correlations with other tests are employed in still another way to demonstrate that the new test is relatively free from the influence of certain irrelevant factors. For example, a special aptitude test or a personality test should not have a high correlation with tests of general intelligence or scholastic aptitude. Similarly, reading comprehension should not appreciably affect performance on such tests. Accordingly, correlations with tests of general intelligence, reading, or verbal comprehension are sometimes reported as indirect or negative evidence of validity. In these cases, high correlations would make the test suspect. Low correlations, however, would not in themselves ensure validity. It will be noted that this use of correlations with other tests is similar to one of the supplementary techniques described under content-description procedures.

Factor Analysis. Developed as a means of identifying psychological traits, factor analysis is particularly relevant to construct-validation procedures. Essentially, factor analysis is a refined statistical technique for analyzing the interrelationships of behavior data. For example, if 20 tests have been given to 300 persons, the first step is to compute the correlations of each test with every other. An inspection of the resulting table of 190 correlations may itself reveal certain clusters among the tests, suggesting the location of common traits. Thus, if such tests as vocabulary, analogies, opposites, and sentence completion have high correlations with one another and low correlations with all other tests, we could tentatively infer the presence of a verbal comprehension factor. Because such an inspectional analysis of a correlation table is difficult and uncertain, more precise statistical techniques have been developed to locate the common factors required to account for the obtained correlations. These techniques of factor analysis are examined further in chapter 11, in connection with their use in research on the nature of intelligence, where they originated.

In the process of factor analysis, the number of variables or categories in terms of which each individual's performance can be described is reduced from the number of original tests to a relatively small number of factors, or common traits. In the example cited above, five or six factors might suffice to account for the intercorrelations among the 20 tests. Each individual might thus be described in terms of her or his scores in the five or six factors, rather than in terms of the original 20 scores. A major purpose of factor analysis is to simplify the description of behavior by reducing the number of categories from an initial multiplicity of test variables to a few common factors, or traits.

After the factors have been identified, they can be utilized in describing the factorial composition of a test. Each test can thus be characterized in terms of the major factors determining its scores, together with the weight or loading of each factor and the correlation of the test with each factor. Such a correlation is sometimes reported as the *factorial validity* of the test. Thus, if the verbal comprehension factor correlates .66 with a vocabulary test, the factorial validity of this vocabulary test as a measure of the trait of verbal comprehension is .66. It should be noted that factorial validity is essentially the correlation of the test with whatever is common to a group of tests or other indices of behavior. The set of variables analyzed can, of course, include both test and nontest data. Ratings and other criterion measures can thus be utilized, along with other tests, to explore the factorial composition of a particular test and to define the common traits it measures.

Internal Consistency. In the published description of certain tests, especially in the personality domain, the statement is made that the test has been validated by the method of internal consistency. The essential characteristic of this method is that the criterion is none other than the total score on the test itself. Sometimes an adaptation of the contrasted group method is used, extreme groups being selected on the basis of the total test score. The performance of the upper criterion group on each test item is then compared with that of the lower criterion group. Items that fail to show a significantly greater proportion of "passes" (or keyed responses) in the upper than in the lower criterion group are considered invalid, and are either eliminated or revised. Correlational procedures may also be employed for this purpose. For example, the biserial correlation between "pass-fail" on each item and total test score can be computed. Only those items yielding significant item-test correlations would be retained. A test whose items were selected by this method can be said to show internal consistency, since each item differentiates among respondents in the same direction as does the entire test.

Another application of the criterion of internal consistency involves the correlation of subtest scores with total score. Many intelligence tests, for instance, consist of separately administered subtests (such as vocabulary, arithmetic, picture completion, etc.) whose scores are combined in finding the total test score. In the construction of these tests, the scores on each subtest are often correlated with total score, and any subtest whose correlation with total score is too low is eliminated. The correlations of the remaining subtests with total score are then reported as evidence of the internal consistency of the entire instrument.

It is apparent that internal consistency correlations, whether based on items or subtests, are essentially measures of homogeneity. Because it helps to characterize the behavior domain or trait sampled by the test, the degree of homogeneity of a test has some relevance to its construct validity. Nevertheless, the contribution of internal consistency data to test validation is limited. In the absence of data external to the test itself, little can be learned about what a test measures.

Convergent and Discriminant Validation. In a thoughtful analysis of construct validation, D. T. Campbell (1960) pointed out that, in order to demonstrate construct validity, we must show not only that a test correlates highly with other variables with which it should theoretically correlate but also that it does *not* correlate significantly with variables from which it should differ. In an earlier article, D. T. Campbell and Fiske (1959) described the former process as convergent validation and the latter as discriminant validation. Correlation of a quantitative reasoning test with subsequent grades in a math course would be an example of convergent validation. For the same test, discriminant validity would be evidenced by a low and insignificant correlation with scores on a reading comprehension test, since reading ability is an irrelevant variable in a test designed to measure quantitative reasoning.

It will be recalled that the requirement of low correlation with irrelevant variables was discussed in connection with supplementary and precautionary procedures followed in content validation. Discriminant validation is also especially relevant to the validation of personality tests, in which irrelevant variables may affect scores in a variety of ways.

Campbell and Fiske (1959) proposed systematic experimental design for the dual approach of convergent and discriminant validation, which they called the *multitrait-multimethod matrix*. Essentially, this procedure requires the assessment of two or more traits by two or more methods. A hypothetical example provided by Campbell and Fiske will serve to illustrate the procedure. Table 5–1 shows all possible correlations among the scores obtained when three traits are each measured by three methods. The three traits could represent three personality characteristics, such as (A) dominance, (B) sociability, and (C) achievement motivation. The three methods could be (1) a self-report inventory, (2) a projective technique, and (3) peer ratings. Thus, A_1 would indicate dominance scores on the self-report inventory, A_2 dominance scores on the projective test; C_3 would represent peer ratings on achievement motivation.

The hypothetical correlations given in Table 5–1 include reliability coefficients (in parentheses, along principal diagonal) and validity coefficients (in boldface, along three shorter diagonals). In these validity coefficients, the scores obtained for the same trait by different methods are correlated; each measure is thus being checked against other, independent measures of the same trait, as in the familiar validation procedure. The table also includes correlations between *different* traits measured by the *same* method (in solid triangles) and correlations between *different* traits measured by *different* methods (in broken triangles). For satisfactory construct validity, the validity coefficients should obviously be higher than the correlations between different traits measured by different methods; they should also be higher than the correlations between different traits measured by the same method. For example, the correlation between dominance scores from a self-report inventory and dominance scores from a projective test should be higher than the correlation between dominance and sociability scores from a self- report inventory. If the latter correlation, representing common method variance, were high, it might indicate, for example, that a person's scores on this inventory are unduly affected by some irrelevant common factor such as ability to understand the questions or desire to make oneself appear in a favorable light on all traits.

Experimental Interventions. A further source of data for construct validation is provided by experiments on the effect of selected variables on test scores. In checking the validity of a test for use in an individualized instructional program, for example, one approach is through a comparison of pretest and posttest scores. The rationale of such a test calls for low scores on the pretest, administered before the relevant instruction, and high scores on the posttest. This relationship can also be checked for individual items in the test. Ideally, the largest proportion of examinees should fail an item on the pretest and pass it on the posttest. Items that are commonly failed on both tests are too difficult, and those passed on both

Table 5-1

Hypothetical Multitrait-Multimethod Matrix

		Method 1			Method 2			Method 3		
	Traits	A_1	B_1	C_1	A_2	B_2	C_2	A_3	B_3	C_3
Method 1	A_1	(.89)								
	B_1	.51	(.89)							
	C_1	.38	.37	(.76)						
Method 2	A_2	.57	.22	.09	(.93)					
	B_2	.22	.57	.10	.68	(.94)				
	C_2	.11	.11	.46	.59	.58	(.84)			
Method 3	A_3	.56	.22	.11	.67	.42	.33	(.94)		
	B_3	.23	.58	.12	.43	.66	.34	.67	(.92)	
	C_3	.11	.11	.45	.34	.32	.58	.58	.60	(.85)

Note. Letters A, B, C refer to traits, subscripts 1, 2, 3 to methods. Validity coefficients (monotrait-heteromethod) are the three diagonal sets of boldface numbers; reliability coefficients (monotrait-monomethod) are the numbers in parentheses along principal diagonal. Solid triangles enclose heterotrait-monomethod correlations; broken triangles enclose heterotrait-heteromethod correlations.

(From Campbell & Fiske, 1959, p. 82. Copyright 1959 by the American Psychological Association. Reprinted by permission.)

tests too easy, for the purposes of such a test. If a sizable proportion of examinees pass an item on the pretest and fail it on the posttest, there is obviously something wrong with the item, or the instruction, or both.

A test designed to measure anxiety-proneness can be administered to persons who are subsequently put through a situation designed to arouse anxiety, such as taking an examination under distracting and stressful conditions. The initial anxiety test scores can then be correlated with physiological and other indices of anxiety expression during and after the examination. A different hypothesis regarding an anxiety test could be evaluated by administering the test before and after an anxiety-arousing experience and seeing whether test scores rise significantly on the retest. Positive findings from such an experiment would indicate that the test scores reflect current anxiety level. In a similar way, experiments can be designed to test other hypotheses regarding the trait measured by a given test.

Structural Equation Modeling. In addition to the identification of constructs in both test scores and criterion performance, an important advance in test validation was the consideration of relations among constructs and of the path whereby a construct affects criterion performance (J. P. Campbell, 1990a; Messick, 1989; Schmidt, Hunter, & Outerbridge, 1986). For example, a person's interest in a particular area may influence job performance through increasing her or his learning of relevant factual knowledge, through acquisition of required procedural skills, or through the development of the motivation needed to exert and sustain maximal effort in carrying out the necessary activities. Investigating *how* an identified construct or personal trait leads to good or poor performance contributes substantially to understanding why a test has high or low validity in a given situation. Such an analysis is facilitated by a statistical procedure known as structural equation modeling, whose use has increased impressively in the 1980s and 1990s. See, for example, the establishment of the journal, *Structural Equation Modeling* (1994). This procedure is closely related to several versions of path analysis, and both are often informally designated as "causal modeling."[3]

What, specifically, is structural equation modeling designed to accomplish, and how did it originate? In elementary statistics, one soon learns that correlation does not indicate causation. A familiar example is spurious age correlation. Among schoolchildren ranging in age form 6 to 14 years, the correlation between height and proficiency in arithmetic is likely to be high; but we cannot conclude that either variable affects the other. The correlation results largely from age, which is in turn associated with amount of schooling. In an effort to investigate causal relations, researchers in the 1960s and 1970s began to use cross-lagged experimental designs (D. T. Campbell & Stanley, 1966; Cook & Campbell, 1976, pp. 284–293). For example, to analyze the reciprocal causal influence between a student's attitude toward math and her or his math performance, measures of attitude toward math and performance in math could be obtained at two points in time. The cross-lagged correlation could then be found between math attitude

[3] In order to avoid philosophical implications about ultimate or complete causation of any event, psychologists have preferred more neutral expressions, such as the statements that A determines, influences, or affects B. Nevertheless, the term "causal" is sometimes used to refer to all these relations, with the assumption that its limitations are understood (see, e.g., L. R. James, Mulaik, & Brett, 1982, chap. 1; P. A. White, 1990).

at Time 1 and math performance at Time 2, and between math performance at Time 1 and math attitude at Time 2. The size of the two correlations would indicate the relative strength of the influence in each direction. For a few years, this seemed a promising way to assess the effect of two variables on each other.

Before long, however, both logical and statistical analyses revealed serious weaknesses in the use of cross-lagged correlations. Although the basic cross-lagged design was excellent, the use of simple, zero-order correlations was likely to distort results and lead to incorrect conclusions about causal relations (Rogosa, 1980). Among the sources of error in this procedure are the failure to take into account, first, correlations between the initial variables and between the subsequent variables; second, the reliability of the variables and their stability over time; and third, the possible contribution of unmeasured variables, such as age and schooling in the classical example cited above. Structural equation modeling provides ways of avoiding such difficulties. Essentially, it does so by using regression equations to predict the dependent from the independent variables in cross-lagged or other causal models. In this procedure, partial correlations are used in finding the regression coefficients, thereby incorporating all correlations among the variables; both measurement and sampling errors are taken into account; and some provision is made at least to recognize the possibility of additional, unmeasured causal variables (Bentler, 1988; L. R. James et al., 1982; Loehlin, 1992; Rogosa, 1979).

The first step in structural equation modeling is to design a model of the hypothesized causal relations to be tested. It is important that this model be based on thorough familiarity with existing knowledge about the variables and the situation under investigation. The hypothesized relations should have a sound theoretical rationale. The actual testing of the model is done by solving a set of simultaneous linear regression equations.[4] In causal modeling, there are usually more equations than unknowns, which permits solutions for several alternative models. Each model is compared with the original, empirical correlation matrix for goodness of fit. However, several causal models may fit the data about equally well (MacCallum, Wegener, Uchino, & Fabrigar, 1993). These statistically equivalent models may represent different causal paths and hence provide alternative explanations for the empirically observed effects. On the basis of the investigator's knowledge of the situation, he or she must then evaluate the alternative models for their plausibility and substantive meaningfulness.

Another feature of structural equation modeling is that causal relations are typically computed between constructs, rather than between isolated measured variables. For instance, to assess a student's attitude toward math, several indicators could be used, such as measures of interest, goal orientation, self-concept of one's math aptitude, and other relevant affective variables. The common variance among these indicators would then define a construct of the individual's attitude toward math, which can itself be related to subsequent math performance. This use of constructs provides more stable and reliable estimates, in which the error and specific variances of the separate indicators cancel out.

[4] For an introduction to detailed procedure, see Bollen (1989) and Loehlin (1992). The actual computations can be carried out by available computer programs, such as LISREL (Hayduk, 1988; Jöreskog & Sörbom, 1986, 1989) and EQS (Bentler, 1985).

There are currently several methodological approaches to structural equation modeling, as well as individual modifications and procedural refinements under consideration (see, e.g., Anderson & Gerbing, 1988; Bentler, 1990; Bollen & Long, 1993; Breckler, 1990; Cole, Maxwell, Arvey, & Salas, 1993; James, 1980; Mulaik et al., 1989). While still in a state of development, however, structural equation modeling is a promising procedure for combining theoretical, experimental, and statistical approaches. It has already been widely applied to problems in such areas as developmental, personality and social, industrial, and educational psychology (e.g., Graves & Powell, 1988; L. A. James & L. R. James, 1989; MacCallum & Browne, 1993; McCardle, 1989; Parkerson, Lomax, Schiller, & Walberg, 1984; Shavelson & Bolus, 1982). Efforts at unification and simplification of procedure are also under way (e.g., Jöreskog & Sörbom, 1993).

Contributions from Cognitive Psychology. The 1970s witnessed a rapprochement of experimental psychology and psychometrics, which is beginning to yield significant contributions to an understanding of the constructs assessed by tests of intelligence and other broadly defined aptitudes (Ronning, Glover, Conoley, & Witt, 1987; R. E. Snow & Lohman, 1989). As early as the 1950s, cognitive psychologists had begun to apply the concepts of information processing to the study of human problem-solving. Some investigators designed computer programs that carry out these processes and thereby simulate human thought. Programs can be written to simulate the performance of persons at different levels of skill, and with such programs it is possible to predict the number and kinds of errors made and the time required for different responses. In designing a program, the investigator usually begins with a task analysis that may include introspecting about one's own method of solving the problem, having subjects think aloud, or using more refined observational procedures. By comparing the performance of the computer with that of children and adults, or that of experts and novices, in solving the same problem, investigators can test their hypotheses regarding what persons do in carrying out the tasks. Examples of the tasks investigated by these methods include conventional puzzles, problems in logic, chess games, algebra word problems, physics problems, and diagnostic problems in medical practice (Chi, Glaser, & Farr, 1988; J. H. Larkin, McDermott, Simon, & Simon, 1980a, 1980b; Newell & Simon, 1972; Simon, 1976).

The variables identified by these investigations include processes (procedural skills) and declarative knowledge (facts and information). The cognitive models specify the intellectual processes used to perform the task, the way the processes are organized, the relevant knowledge store, and how this knowledge is represented in memory and retrieved when needed. Increasing attention is also being given to what has been called an executive process or metacognition, which refers to the control the individual exercises over her or his own choice of processes, representations, and strategies for carrying out the task. In the 1970s, some cognitive psychologists began to apply these task-analysis and computer-simulation techniques to an exploration of what intelligence tests measure. Individual investigators approached this problem from several different angles (see Resnick, 1976; Sternberg, 1981, 1984, 1985b). The resulting research is gradually contributing to significant advances in test construction and use.

The implications of cognitive research for construct validation are especially well demonstrated in the work of Embretson (1983, 1986, 1995a). Observing that traditional construct validation has been too limited in its approach, Embretson proposed two principal aspects of test validation: (1) construct representation and (2) nomothetic span. It is on the second, nomothetic span, that traditional construct-related validation has focused. This is concerned with the relations of test performance within a "nomothetic network" of other variables. Such relations are generally investigated through correlations of test scores with other measures, which may include criterion performance and other real-life data.

The object of construct representation, on the other hand, is to identify specific information-processing components and knowledge stores needed to perform the tasks set by the test items. *Task decomposition*[5] can be applied experimentally to conduct such analyses. Examples of possible procedures include the manipulation of task complexity, the presentation of partial tasks, or the provision of cues that alter the task demands. Mathematical models have been developed to measure the contribution of different response components to item performance. Another widely used procedure for cognitive task analysis is *protocol analysis* (Ericsson, 1987; Ericsson & Simon, 1993; van Someren, Barnard, & Sandberg, 1994). In this procedure, individuals are instructed to "think aloud" as they perform a task or solve a problem. The tasks could range from mentally multiplying two given numbers, recalling details of a past event, or locating the cause of an equipment malfunction to answering successive items on an ability test. A byproduct of this procedure is the possible discovery that the same test item may evoke quite different cognitive processes in respondents who vary in their experiential backgrounds.

What can we conclude regarding the contribution that cognitive psychology has made thus far to construct-related validation? While still in an exploratory stage, information-processing approaches have contributed heuristic concepts to guide further research. They have clearly focused attention on *response processes*, in contrast to the traditional concentration on the end products of thought in psychometric research. Analyzing test performance in terms of specific cognitive processes should certainly strengthen and expand our understanding of what the tests measure. Moreover, analyzing individuals' performance at the level of elementary component processes should eventually make it possible to pinpoint each person's sources of weakness and strength and thereby enhance the diagnostic use of tests (Embretson, 1987, 1994; Estes, 1974; Pellegrino & Glaser, 1979; Sternberg & Weil, 1980). This, in turn, should facilitate the tailoring of training programs to the individual's needs. In summary, the relation between the psychometric and cognitive approaches can be characterized, first, from the standpoint of applied research and practice as *complementary*. Here, each is the preferred approach for different assessment purposes. Second, from the standpoint of basic research and theory, their relation can be characterized as *reciprocal*. Here, each helps to clarify and enrich the other; in combination, they enhance our understanding of intelligent behavior.

[5] For details, see Butterfield, Nielsen, Tangen, and Richardson (1985), Embretson (1985b), and Sternberg (1977, 1980).

OVERVIEW AND INTEGRATION

Comparison of Validation Procedures. We have considered several ways of asking, "How valid is this test?" To point up the distinctive features of the different validation procedures, let us apply each in turn to a test consisting of 50 assorted arithmetic problems. Four ways in which this test might be employed, together with the type of validation procedure appropriate to each, are illustrated in Table 5–2. This example highlights the fact that the choice of validation procedure depends on the use to be made of test scores. The same test, when employed for different purposes, should be validated in different ways. If an achievement test is used to predict subsequent performance at a higher educational level, as when selecting high school students for college admission, it needs to be evaluated against the criterion of subsequent college performance rather than in terms of its content validity.

Inclusiveness of Construct Validation. The examples given in Table 5–2 focus on the differences among the various types of validation procedures. Further consideration of these procedures, however, shows that content-, criterion-, and construct-related validities do not correspond to distinct or logically coordinate categories. On the contrary, construct-related validity is a comprehensive concept, that includes the other types. All the specific techniques for content analysis and for measuring criterion relations, which were discussed in earlier sections of this chapter, could have been listed again under construct identification. For example, the correlations of a mechanical aptitude test with performance in shop courses and in a wide variety of jobs contribute to our understanding of the construct measured by the test. The construct identification would be further strengthened by comparing the scores of contrasted groups of successful and unsuccessful workers.

Table 5-2

Validation of a Single Arithmetic Test for Different Purposes

Testing Purpose	Illustrative Question	Evidence of Validity
Achievement test in elementary school arithmetic	How much has Dick learned in the past?	Content description
Aptitude test to predict performance to high school mathematics	How well will Jane in the future?	Criterion prediction: temporal
Technique for diagnosing learning disabilities	Does Bill's performance indicate specific disabilities?	Criterion prediction: concurrent
Measure of quantitative reasoning	How does Helen's score relate to other indicators of her reasoning ability?	Construct identification

Validity against various practical criteria is commonly reported in test manuals to aid the potential user in understanding what a test measures. Although he or she may not be directly concerned with the prediction of any of the specific criteria employed, by examining such criteria the test user is able to build up a concept of the behavior domain sampled by the test. If we follow this thinking a bit further, we can see that all test use and all interpretation of test scores imply construct validity, a fact that is being increasingly recognized (J. P. Campbell, 1990a; Guion, 1991; Messick, 1980b, 1988, 1989; Tenopyr, 1986). Since tests are rarely, if ever, used under conditions that are identical with those under which validity data were gathered, some degree of generalizability of results is inevitably involved. The interpretive meaning of test scores is always based on constructs, which may vary widely in breadth or generalizability with regard to behavior domains, populations, and contexts.

Messick (1980b, 1989) argued convincingly that the term "validity," insofar as it designates the interpretive meaningfulness of a test, should be reserved for construct validity. Other procedures with which the term "validity" has been traditionally associated should, be maintained, be designated by more specifically descriptive labels. Thus, content validity can be labeled "content relevance" and "content coverage," to refer to domain specifications and domain representativeness, respectively. Criterion-related validity can be labeled "predictive utility" and "diagnostic utility," to correspond to predictive and concurrent validation. These more clearly descriptive labels undoubtedly contribute to a better understanding of what the various procedures actually accomplish. Nevertheless, the distinctions among different types of validation procedures are useful in identifying tests for particular purposes. They should therefore be reported in test manuals in a clearly identifiable form.

From another angle, even when the immediate practical application focuses on content description (as in educational assessment) or criterion prediction (as in job selection), the use of constructs of appropriate breadth is more effective than are measures of specific test performance. Criterion research makes it increasingly clear that both criterion measures and test scores can be more effectively expressed as matching constructs. Furthermore, the investigation of causal relations among constructs, as in structural equation modeling, is coming to be accepted as a significant contribution to the understanding of how and why tests work.[6]

Validation in the Test Construction Process. It is being increasingly recognized that the development of a valid test requires multiple procedures, which are employed sequentially, at different stages of test construction (Anastasi, 1986a; Guion, 1991; Jackson, 1970, 1973; N. G. Peterson et al., 1990). Validity is thus built into the test from the outset, rather than being limited to the last stages of test development, as in traditional, criterion-related validation. The validation process begins with the formulation of detailed trait or construct definitions,

---

[6] An example of the possible application of these more sophisticated test validation procedures can be found in L. A. King and D. W. King (1990).

derived from psychological theory, prior research, or systematic observation and analyses of the relevant behavior domain. Test items are then prepared to fit the construct definitions. Empirical item analyses follow, with the selection of the most effective, or valid, items from the initial item pools. Other appropriate internal analyses may then be carried out, including statistical analyses of item clusters or subtests. The final stage includes validation of various scores and interpretive combinations of scores through statistical analyses against external, real-life criteria.

Almost any information gathered in the process of developing or using a test is relevant to its validity. Certainly, data on internal consistency and on retest reliability help to define the homogeneity of the construct and its temporal stability. Norms may well provide additional construct specification, especially if they include separate normative data for subgroups classified by age, sex, or other demographic variables that affect the individual's experiential history and thereby her or his test performance. Moreover, after a test is released for operational use, the interpretive meaning of its scores may continue to be clarified and enriched through the gradual accumulation of clinical observations and through special research projects.[7]

Individual and Social Consequences of Testing. Some psychometricians recommend that an additional feature be included in the concept of test validity, namely, the *consequences* of testing on individuals and on society. A notable exponent of this broadening of the validity concept is Messick (1980b, 1988, 1989, 1995). Special emphasis is placed on the unintended consequences of specific uses of tests that may be detrimental to individuals or to members of certain ethnic or other populations with diverse experiential backgrounds. An excellent analysis of the problems of balancing different goals and values in the assessment of job applicants is illustrated by the report of a committee of experts convened by the National Research Council, which studied the situation with unusual thoroughness (Hartigan & Wigdor, 1989—see especially chaps. 13 and 14).

The ethical and social implications of test use certainly demand widespread concern. Some introduction to these problems will be given in chapter 18. More technical aspects are treated in chapter 6, in connection with the question of "test bias." However, as noted by other psychometricians (e.g., Cole & Moss, 1989), to incorporate these questions in the concept of validity does not appear to be the most effective way to meet them. They cannot be answered by means of empirical data and statistical analysis alone. Nor should the desired values be concealed in statistical manipulations. They need to be explicitly stated and discussed as an independent goal, to be considered in addition to the strictly empirical and statistically demonstrated validity of the particular test use. A wise decision regarding the balancing of conflicting goals is reached by methods appropriate to the handling of value systems (Mullen & Roth, 1991; Zeichmeister & Johnson, 1992).[8] Such methods require human judgment, systematic debate, compromises, and conflict resolution, in which the exponents of different value systems are adequately

---

[7] For a successful application of this comprehensive model of test validation, see Elliott (1990b, chap. 9).

[8] See also Arkes (1993) for a broader view, with additional references.

represented. To combine the empirical, statistically supported procedures of determining validity with an evaluation of the social and ethical consequences of particular test uses only confuses and obfuscates the solution.

One conclusion that emerges from a consideration of this difficult and important problem is to reaffirm the major role of the test user, already suggested in chapter 1. When value judgments are required, especially in individual cases, one more serious responsibility is placed on the test user. In the choice of appropriate tests, as well as in the interpretation of results, the test user can control the consequences of testing. The broad value orientation and social sensitivity of such a test user can contribute significantly to the proper use of tests, not only from the scientific but also from the ethical standpoint.[9]

[9] It might be noted parenthetically that a novel approach to psychology as a whole proposes "discursive psychology," whereby problems are investigated both through discourse among persons in the everyday life world and through traditional experimental methods (see e.g., Harré & Stearns, 1995; J. Smith, Harré, & Van Langenhove, 1995).

Chapter Six

Validity: Measurement and Interpretation

Chapter 5 was concerned with concepts of validity and sources of validation data; this chapter deals with quantitative expressions of validity and their interpretation. Test users are concerned with validity at either or both of two stages. First, when considering the suitability of a test for their purposes, they examine available validity data reported in the test manual or other published reports. Through such information, they arrive at a tentative concept of what psychological functions the test actually measures, and they judge the relevance of such functions to their proposed use of the test. In effect, when test users rely on published validation data, they are dealing with construct validity, regardless of the specific procedures used in gathering the data. As we have seen in chapter 5, the criteria employed in published studies cannot be assumed to be identical with those the test user wants to predict. Jobs bearing the same title in two different companies are rarely identical. Two courses in freshman English taught in different colleges may be quite dissimilar. Hence, some degree of validity generalization is required in test selection.

Because of the diversity of testing needs and of the inferences to be drawn from test scores, some test users may wish to check the validity of any chosen test against local criteria. Although published data may strongly suggest that a given test should have high validity in a particular situation, direct corroboration is desirable when technically feasible. The determination of validity against specific local criteria represents the second stage in the test users' evaluation of validity. The techniques to be discussed in this chapter are especially relevant to the analysis of validity data obtained by test users themselves. Most of them are also useful, however, in understanding and interpreting the validity data reported in test manuals.

VALIDITY COEFFICIENT AND ERROR OF ESTIMATE

Measurement of Relationship. A validity coefficient is a correlation between test score and criterion measure. Because it provides a single numerical index of test validity, it is commonly used in test manuals to report the validity of a test against each criterion for which data are available. The data used in computing any validity coefficient can also be expressed in the form of an expectancy table or expectancy chart, illustrated in chapter 3. In fact, such tables and charts provide a convenient way to show what a validity coefficient means for the person tested. It will be recalled that expectancy charts give the probability that an individual who obtains a certain score on the test will attain a specified level of criterion performance. For example, with Table 3–6, if we know a student's score on the Numerical Reasoning test of the Differential Aptitude Tests (DAT), we can look up the chances that he or she will earn a particular grade in a seventh grade mathematics course. The same data yield a validity coefficient of .60. When both test and criterion variables are continuous, the familiar Pearson Product-Moment Correlation Coefficient is applicable. Other types of correlation coefficients can be computed when the data are expressed in different forms, as when a twofold pass-fail criterion is employed (e.g., Fig. 3–7). The specific procedures for computing these different kinds of correlations can be found in any standard statistics text.

Conditions Affecting Validity Coefficients. As in the case of reliability, it is essential to specify the *nature of the group* on which a validity coefficient is found. The same test may measure different functions when given to individuals who differ in age, sex, educational level, occupation, or any other relevant characteristic. Persons with different experiential backgrounds, for example, may utilize different work methods to solve the same test problem. Consequently, a test could have high validity in predicting a particular criterion in one population and little or no validity in another. Or it might be a valid measure of different functions in the two populations. Tests designed for use with diverse populations should cite appropriate data on population generalizability in their technical manuals. Moreover, within a population that varies widely in test scores, the validity coefficient may differ appreciably in different parts of the score range and should be checked in appropriate subgroups (R. Lee & Foley, 1986).

The question of *sample heterogeneity is* relevant to the measurement of validity, as it is to the measurement of reliability, since both characteristics are commonly reported in terms of correlation coefficients. It will be recalled that, other things being equal, the wider the range of scores, the higher will be the correlation. This fact should be kept in mind when interpreting the validity coefficients given in test manuals.

A special difficulty encountered in many validation samples arises from *preselection*. For example, a new test that is being validated for job selection may be administered to a group of newly hired employees on whom criterion measures of job performance will eventually be available. It is likely, however, that such employees represent a superior selection of all those who applied for the job. Hence, the range of such a group in both test scores and criterion measures will be curtailed at the lower end of the distribution. The effect of such preselection will therefore be to lower the validity coefficient. In the subsequent use of the test, when it is administered to all applicants for selection purposes, the validity can be expected to be somewhat higher.

Validity coefficients may also change over time because of changing selection standards. An example is provided by a comparison of validity coefficients computed over a 30-year interval with Yale students (Burnham, 1965). Correlations were found between a predictive index based on College Board tests and high school records, on the one hand, and average freshman grades, on the other. This correlation dropped from .71 to .52 over the 30 years. An examination of the bivariate distributions clearly revealed the reason for this drop. Because of higher admission standards, the later class was more homogeneous than the earlier class in both predictor and criterion performance. Consequently, the correlation was lower in the later group, although the accuracy with which individuals' grades were predicted showed little change. In other words, the observed drop in correlation did *not* indicate that the predictors were less valid than they had been 30 years earlier. Had the differences in group homogeneity been ignored, it might have been wrongly concluded that this was the case.

For the proper interpretation of a validity coefficient, attention should also be given to the *form of the relationship* between test and criterion. The computation of a Pearson correlation coefficient assumes that the relationship is linear and uniform throughout the range. Research on the relationship of test scores to job performance has shown that these conditions are generally met (Coward & Sackett, 1990; Hawk, 1970). Nevertheless, special circumstances may alter this relationship, and the test user should be alert to such possibilities. For example, a particular job may require a minimum level of reading comprehension, to enable employees to read instruction manuals, labels, and the like. Once this minimum is exceeded, however, further increments in reading ability may be unrelated to degree of job success. This would be an example of a nonlinear relation between test and job performance. An examination of the bivariate distribution or scatter diagram obtained by plotting reading comprehension scores against criterion measures would show a rise in job performance up to the minimal required reading ability and a leveling off beyond that point. Hence, the entries would cluster around a curve rather than a straight line.

In other situations, the line of best fit may be a straight line, but the individual entries may deviate further around this line at the upper than at the lower end of the scale. Suppose that performance on a scholastic aptitude test is a necessary but not a sufficient condition for successful achievement in a course. That is, the low-scoring students will perform poorly in the course; but among the high- scoring students, some will perform well in the course and others will perform poorly because of low motivation, lack of interest, or other adverse conditions. In this situation, there will be wider variability of criterion performance among the high-scoring than among the low-scoring students. This condition in a bivariate distribution is known as heteroscedasticity. The Pearson correlation assumes homoscedasticity or equal variability throughout the range of the bivariate distribution. In the present example, the bivariate distribution would be fan-shaped—wide at the upper end and narrow at the lower end. An examination of the bivariate distribution itself will usually give a good indication of the nature of the relationship between test and criterion. Expectancy tables and expectancy charts also correctly reveal the relative effectiveness of the test at different levels.

Magnitude of a Validity Coefficient. How high should a validity coefficient be? No general answer to this question is possible, since the interpretation of a validity coefficient must take into account a number of concomitant circumstances. The obtained correlation, of course, should be high enough to be *statistically significant* at some acceptable level, such as the .01 or .05 levels discussed in chapter 4. In other words, before drawing any conclusions about the validity of a test, we should be reasonably certain that the obtained validity coefficient could not have arisen through chance fluctuations of sampling from a population correlation of zero.

Having established a significant correlation between test scores and criterion, however, we need to evaluate the size of the correlation in the light of the uses to be made of the test. If we wish to predict an individual's exact criterion score, such as the grade-point average a student will receive in college, the validity coefficient may be interpreted in terms of the *standard error of estimate* (SE_{est}), which is analogous to the error of measurement discussed in connection with reliability. It will be recalled that the error of measurement indicates the margin of error to be expected in an individual's score as a result of the unreliability of the test. Similarly, the error of estimate shows the margin of error to be expected in the individual's predicted criterion score, as a result of the imperfect validity of the test.

The error of estimate is found by the following formula:

$$SE_{est} = SD_y\sqrt{1 - r_{xy}^2}$$

in which r_{xy}^2 is the square of the validity coefficient and SD_y is the standard deviation of the criterion scores. It will be noted that if the validity were perfect ($r_{xy} = 1.00$), the error of estimate would be zero. On the other hand, with a test having zero validity, the error of estimate is as large as the standard deviation of the criterion distribution $\left(SE_{est} = SD_y\sqrt{1-0} = SD_y\right)$. Under these conditions, the prediction is no better than a guess; and the range of prediction error is as wide as the entire distribution of criterion scores. Between these two extremes are to be found the errors of estimate corresponding to tests of varying validity.

Reference to the formula for SE_{est} will show that term $\sqrt{1 - r_{xy}^2}$ serves to indicate the size of the error *relative to the error that would result from a mere guess* (i.e., with zero validity). In other words, if $\sqrt{1 - r_{xy}^2}$ is equal to 1.00, the error of estimate is as large as it would be if we were to guess the individual's criterion score. The predictive improvement attributable to the use of the test would thus be nil.

If the validity coefficient is .80, then $\sqrt{1 - r_{xy}^2}$ is equal to .60, and the error is 60% as large as it would be by chance. To put it differently, the use of such a test enables us to predict the individual's criterion performance with a margin of error that is 40% smaller than it would be if we were to guess.

It would thus appear that even with a validity of .80, which is unusually high, the error of predicted scores is considerable. If the primary function of psychological tests were to predict each individual's exact position in the criterion distribution, the outlook would be quite discouraging. When examined in the light of the error of estimate, most tests do not appear very efficient. In most testing situations, however, it is not necessary to predict the specific criterion performance of individual cases, but rather to determine which individuals will exceed a certain minimum standard of performance, or cutoff point, in the criterion. What are the chances that Mary Greene will graduate from medical school, that Tom Higgins will pass a course in calculus, or that Beverly Bruce will succeed as an astronaut? Which applicants are likely to be satisfactory clerks, insurance agents, or machine operators? Such information is useful not only for group selection but also for individual career planning. For example, it is advantageous for a student to know that she has a good chance of passing all courses in law school, even if we are unable to estimate with certainty whether her grade average will be 74 or 81.

A test may appreciably improve predictive efficiency if it shows *any* significant correlation with the criterion, however low. Under certain circumstances, even validities as low as .20 or .30 may justify inclusion of the test in a selection program. For many testing purposes, evaluation of tests in terms of the error of estimate is unrealistically stringent. Consideration must be given to other ways of evaluating the contribution of a test, ways that take into account the types of decisions to be made from the scores. Some of these procedures will be illustrated in the following section.

TEST VALIDITY AND DECISION THEORY

Proponents of decision theory emphasize that the purpose of psychological testing is not purely measurement, but measurement in the context of decision making. For many years, people were getting selected, classified, and placed in jobs through procedures that were haphazard and unsystematic. No scientific basis existed for selection and people got employed based on their subjective perceptions and interpretations, such as physical features, social status, social connections, and many more. With the advent of application of decision theory to psychological tests, many such processes are following sound logic to take a decision. For instance, personnel selection has been concerned with identifying, from a pool of applicants, the right or the most fit applicant for a job or role. Here, the principles of decision theory prove beneficial. Psychological test serves as a supporting tool to the selection process in sorting applicants who are ready for the job, who are not-so-ready, and those who require a few training interventions. In these situations, test results are used to determine who are likely to succeed or fail on the criterion task; so that in future, test takers with poor scores on the predictor test can be filtered out of the selection process. This is the rationale by which employers require applicants to obtain a certain minimum score on the relevant employment test. Applicants who obtain the specified minimum score (cut-off score) or higher on the test are accepted, and those who score below the cut-off score are rejected. This procedure is often viewed by candidates as impersonal and unkind; however, the main objective is the initial screening that aims to increase the probabilities of the eventual selection of candidates, best qualified for the job.

This initial screening process is usually followed by classification. Such decisions may involve grouping of employees on the basis of their scores on more than one psychological test. This process usually consists of a sequence of stages entailing a series of pass-fail (yes-no) decisions based on information from various other selection methods such as application blanks, letters of reference, telephonic interviews, face-to-face interviews, and psychological tests. This process enables the employer to make better predictions of future behavior on the basis of the past and the present behavior. The more reliable and valid the information is, the greater the likelihood of making accurate decisions and predictions about an individual's ability to perform on the job.

One of the approaches for linking tests and decision making is mentioned below.

Basic Approach. Let us suppose that 100 applicants were given an aptitude test and were followed up until each could be evaluated for success on a certain job. Figure 6–1 shows the bivariate distribution of test scores and measures of job success for the 100 employees. The correlation between these two variables is slightly below .70. The minimum acceptable job performance, or criterion cutoff point, is indicated in the diagram by a heavy horizontal line. The 40 cases falling below this line would represent job failures; the 60 above the line, job successes. If all 100 applicants are hired, therefore, 60% will succeed on the job. Similarly, if a smaller number were hired at random, without reference to test scores, the proportion of successes would probably be close to 60%. Suppose, however, that the test scores are used to select the 45 most promising applicants out of the 100 (selection ratio = .45). In such a case, the 45 individuals falling to the right of the heavy vertical line would be chosen. Within this group of 45, it can be seen that there are 7 job failures, or *false acceptances,* falling below the heavy horizontal line, and 38 job successes. Hence, the percentage of job successes is now 84 rather than 60 (i.e., 38/45 = .84). This increase is attributable to the use of the test as a screening instrument. It will be noted that errors in predicted criterion score that do not affect the decision can be ignored. Only those prediction errors that cross the cutoff line and hence place the individual in the wrong category will reduce the selective effectiveness of the test.

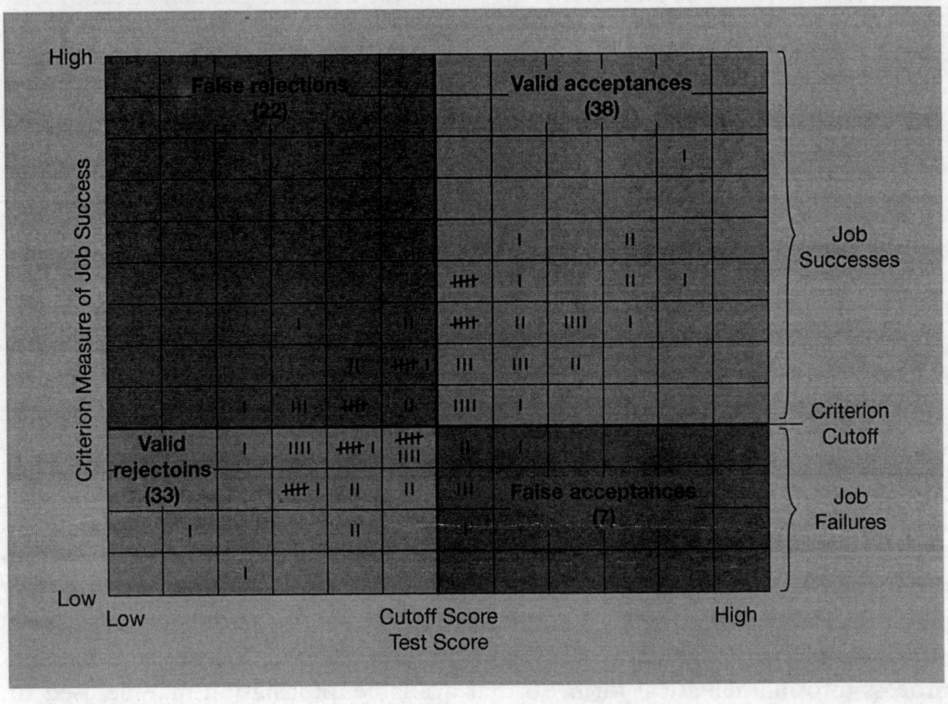

Figure 6–1. Increase in the Proportion of "Successes" Resulting from the Use of a Selection Test.

For a complete evaluation of the effectiveness of the test as a screening instrument, another category of cases in Figure 6–1 must also be examined. This is the category of *false rejections,* comprising the 22 persons who score below the cutoff point on the test but above the criterion cutoff. From these data, we would estimate that 22% of the total applicant sample are potential job successes who will be lost if the test is used as a screening device with the present cutoff point. In setting a cutoff score on a test, attention should be given to the percentage of false rejects, as well as to the percentages of successes and failures within the selected group. In certain situations, the cutoff point should be set sufficiently high to exclude all but a few possible failures. This would be the case when the job is of such a nature that a poorly qualified worker could cause serious loss or damage. An example would be a commercial airplane pilot. Under other circumstances, it may be more important to admit as many qualified persons as possible, at the risk of including more failures. In the latter case, the number of false rejects can be reduced by the choice of a lower cutoff score. Other factors that normally determine the position of the cutoff score include the available personnel supply, the number of job openings, and the urgency or speed with which the openings must be filled.[1]

In many personnel decisions, the selection ratio is determined by the practical demands of the situation. Because of supply and demand in filling job openings, for example, it may be necessary to hire the top 40% of applicants in one case and the top 75% in another. When the selection ratio is not externally imposed, the cutting score on a test can be set at that point giving the maximum differentiation between criterion groups. This can be done roughly by comparing the distribution of test scores in the two criterion groups. More precise mathematical procedures for setting optimal cutting scores have also been worked out (Darlington & Stauffer, 1966; I. Guttman & Raju, 1965; Jaeger, 1989; Livingston & Zieky, 1982; Martin & Raju, 1992; Rorer, Hoffman, & Hsieh, 1966). These procedures make it possible to take into account other relevant parameters, such as the relative seriousness of false rejections and false acceptances. Insofar as such evaluations are incorporated in the process, however, human judgment needs to be involved at some point.

In the terminology of decision theory, the example given in Figure 6–1 illustrates a simple *strategy,* or plan for deciding which applicants to accept and which to reject. In more general terms, a strategy is a technique for utilizing information in order to reach a decision about individuals. In this case, the strategy was to accept the 45 persons with the highest test scores. The increase in percentage of successful employees from 60 to 84 could be used as a basis for estimating the net benefit resulting from the use of the test.

Statistical decision theory was developed by Wald (1950) with special reference to the decisions required in the inspection and quality control of industrial products. Many of its implications for the construction and interpretation of psychological tests have been systematically worked out by Cronbach and Gleser (1965). Essentially, decision theory is an attempt to put the decision-making process into mathematical form, so that available information may be used to

[1] Similar points were made from a different angle in the introductory discussion of cutoff scores in chapter 3.

arrive at the most effective decision under specified circumstances. Some of the basic concepts of decision theory are proving helpful in the reformulation and clarification of certain questions about tests. A few of these ideas were introduced into testing before the formal development of statistical decision theory and were later recognized as fitting into that framework.

Prediction of Outcomes. A precursor of decision theory in psychological testing is to be found in the Taylor-Russell tables (1939), which permit a determination of the net gain in the selection accuracy attributable to the use of a test. The information required includes the validity coefficient of the test, the proportion of applicants who must be accepted (selection ratio), and the proportion of successful applicants selected without the use of a test (base rate). A change in any of these three conditions can alter the predictive efficiency of the test.

For purposes of illustration, one of the Taylor-Russell tables has been reproduced in Table 6–1. This table is designed for use when the base rate, or percentage of successful applicants selected prior to the use of the test, is 60. Other tables are provided by Taylor and Russell for other base rates. Across the top of the table are given different values of the selection ratio, and along the side are the test validities. The entries in the body of the table indicate the proportion of successful persons selected after the use of the test. Thus, the difference between .60 and any one table entry shows the increase in proportion of successful selections attributable to the test.

Obviously if the selection ratio were 100%—that is, if all applicants had to be accepted—no test, however valid, could improve the selection process. Reference to Table 6–1 shows that, when as many as 95% of applicants must be admitted, even a test with perfect validity ($r = 1.00$) would raise the proportion of successful persons by only 3% (.60 to .63). On the other hand, when only 5% of applicants need to be chosen, a test with a validity coefficient of only .30 can raise the percentage of successful applicants selected from 60 to 82. The rise from 60 to 82 represents the *incremental validity* of the test (Sechrest, 1963), or the increase in predictive validity attributable to the test. It indicates the contribution the test makes to the selection of individuals who will meet the minimum standards in criterion performance. In applying the Taylor-Russell tables, of course, test validity should be computed on the same sort of group used to estimate percentage of prior successes. In other words, the contribution of the test is not evaluated against chance success unless applicants were previously selected by chance—a most unlikely circumstance. If applicants had been selected on the basis of previous job history, letters of recommendation, and interviews, the contribution of the test should be evaluated on the basis of what the test adds to these previous selection procedures.

The incremental validity resulting from the use of a test depends not only on the selection ratio but also on the base rate. In the previously illustrated job selection situation, the base rate refers to the proportion of successful employees prior to the introduction of the test for selection purposes. Table 6–1 shows the anticipated outcomes when the base rate is .60. For other base rates, we need to consult the other appropriate tables in the cited reference (H. C. Taylor & Russell, 1939). Let us consider an example in which test validity is .60 and the selection ratio is 40%. Under these conditions, what would be the contribution

Table 6-1

Proportion of "Successes" Expected Through the Use of Test of Given Validity and Given Selection Ratio, for Base Rate .60.

	Selection Ratio										
Validity	.05	.10	.20	.30	.40	.50	.60	.70	.80	.90	.95
.00	.60	.60	.60	.60	.60	.60	.60	.60	.60	.60	.60
.05	.64	.63	.63	.62	.62	.62	.61	.61	.61	.60	.60
.10	.68	.67	.65	.64	.64	.63	.63	.62	.61	.61	.60
.15	.71	.70	.68	.67	.66	.65	.64	.63	.62	.61	.61
.20	.75	.73	.71	.69	.67	.66	.65	.64	.63	.62	.61
.25	.78	.76	.73	.71	.69	.68	.66	.65	.63	.62	.61
.30	.82	.79	.76	.73	.71	.69	.68	.66	.64	.62	.61
.35	.85	.82	.78	.75	.73	.71	.69	.67	.65	.63	.62
.40	.88	.85	.81	.78	.75	.73	.70	.68	.66	.63	.62
.45	.90	.87	.83	.80	.77	.74	.72	.69	.66	.64	.62
.50	.93	.90	.86	.82	.79	.76	.73	.70	.67	.64	.62
.55	.95	.92	.88	.84	.81	.78	.75	.71	.68	.64	.62
.60	.96	.94	.90	.87	.83	.80	.76	.73	.69	.65	.63
.65	.98	.96	.92	.89	.85	.82	.78	.74	.70	.65	.63
.70	.99	.97	.94	.91	.87	.84	.80	.75	.71	.66	.63
.75	.99	.99	.96	.93	.90	.86	.81	.77	.71	.66	.63
.80	1.00	.99	.98	.95	.92	.88	.83	.78	.72	.66	.63
.85	1.00	1.00	.99	.97	.95	.91	.86	.80	.73	.66	.63
.90	1.00	1.00	1.00	.99	.97	.94	.88	.82	.74	.67	.63
.95	1.00	1.00	1.00	1.00	.99	.97	.92	.84	.75	.67	.63
1.00	1.00	1.00	1.00	1.00	1.00	1.00	1.00	.86	.75	.67	.63

Note. A full set of tables can be found in H. C. Taylor and Russell (1939) and in McCormick and Ilgen (1980, Appendix B).

(From H. C. Taylor & Russell, 1939, p. 576.)

of incremental validity of the test if we begin with a base rate of 50% ? And what would be the contribution if we begin with more extreme base rates of 10% and 90% ? Reference to the appropriate Taylor-Russell tables for these base rates shows that the percentage of successful employees would rise from 50 to 75 in the first case; from 10 to 21 in the second; and from 90 to 99 in the third. Thus, the improvement in percentage of successful employees attributable to the use of the test is 25 when the base rate was 50, but only 11 and 9 when the base rates were more extreme.

The implications of extreme base rates are of special interest in clinical psychology, where the base rate refers to the frequency of the pathological condition to be diagnosed in the population tested (Buchwald, 1965; Cureton, 1957a; Meehl &. Rosen, 1955; J. S. Wiggins, 1973/1988). For example, if 5% of the intake population of a clinic has organic brain damage, then 5% is the base rate of brain damage in this population. Although the introduction of any valid test will improve predictive or diagnostic accuracy, the improvement is greatest when the base rates are closest to 50%. With the extreme base rates found with rare pathological conditions, however, the improvement may be negligible. Under these conditions, the use of a test may prove to be unjustified when the cost of its administration and scoring is taken into account. In a clinical situation, this cost would include the time of professional personnel that might otherwise be spent on the treatment of additional cases (Buchwald, 1965). The number of false positives, or normal individuals incorrectly classified as pathological, would of course increase this overall cost in a clinical situation.

When the seriousness of a rare condition makes its diagnosis urgent, tests of moderate validity may be employed in an early stage of sequential decisions. For example, all cases might first be screened with an easily administered test of moderate validity. If the cutoff score is set high enough (high scores being favorable), there will be few false negatives but many false positives, or normals diagnosed as pathological. The latter can then be detected through a more intensive individual examination given to all cases diagnosed as positive by the test. This solution would be appropriate, for instance, when available facilities make the intensive individual examination of all cases impracticable.

Relation of Validity to Productivity. In many practical situations, what is required is an estimate of the effect of the selection test, which is not on the percentage of persons exceeding the minimum performance, but on the overall productivity of the selected persons–how does the actual level of job proficiency or criterion achievement of the workers, hired on the basis of the test, compare with that of the total applicant sample that would have been hired without the test? Following H.C. Taylor and J.T. Russell's work in 1939 of finding relationship of validity coefficients to the practical effectiveness of tests in selection, several investigators addressed this question.[2] Brogden (1946) first demonstrated that the expected increase in output is directly proportional to the validity of the test. Thus, the improvement resulting from the use of a test with validity of 0.50 is 50% as great as the improvement expected from a test of perfect validity.

The relation between test validity and expected rise in criterion achievement can be readily seen in Table 6–2.[3] Expressing criterion scores as standard scores with a mean of zero and an SD of 1.00, this table gives the expected mean criterion score of workers selected with a test of given validity and with a given selection ratio. In this context, the base output mean, corresponding to the performance of applicants selected without use of the test, is given in the column for

---

[2] Taylor, H. C., & Russell, J. T. (1939), "The Relationship of Validity Coefficients to the Practical Effectiveness of Tests in Selection: Discussion and Tables", *Journal of Applied Psychology*, Vol. 23(5), p. 565.

[3] A table including more values for both selection ratios and validity coefficients was prepared by Naylor and Shine (1965).

Table 6–2

Mean Standard Criterion Score of Accepted Cases in Relation to Test Validity and Selection Ratio

Selection Ration	Validity Coefficient																				
	.00	.05	.10	.15	.20	.25	.30	.35	.40	.45	.50	.55	.60	.65	.70	.75	.80	.85	.90	.95	1.00
.05	.00	.10	.21	.31	.42	.52	.62	.73	.83	.94	1.04	1.14	1.25	1.35	1.46	1.56	1.66	1.77	1.87	1.98	2.08
.10	.00	.09	.18	.26	.35	.44	.53	.62	.70	.79	.88	.97	1.05	1.14	1.23	1.32	1.41	1.49	1.58	1.67	1.76
.15	.00	.08	.15	.23	.31	.39	.46	.54	.62	.70	.77	.85	.93	1.01	1.08	1.16	1.24	1.32	1.39	1.47	1.55
.20	.00	.07	.14	.21	.28	.35	.42	.49	.56	.63	.70	.77	.84	.91	.98	1.05	1.12	1.19	1.26	1.33	1.40
.25	.00	.06	.13	.19	.25	.32	.38	.44	.51	.57	.63	.70	.76	.82	.89	.95	1.01	1.08	1.14	1.20	1.27
.30	.00	.06	.12	.17	.23	.29	.35	.40	.46	.52	.58	.64	.69	.75	.81	.87	.92	.98	1.04	1.10	1.16
.35	.00	.05	.11	.16	.21	.26	.32	.37	.42	.48	.53	.58	.63	.69	.74	.79	.84	.90	.95	1.00	1.06
.40	.00	.05	.10	.15	.19	.24	.29	.34	.39	.44	.48	.53	.58	.63	.68	.73	.77	.82	.87	.92	.97
.45	.00	.04	.09	.13	.18	.22	.26	.31	.35	.40	.44	.48	.53	.57	.62	.66	.70	.75	.79	.84	.88
.50	.00	.04	.08	.12	.16	.20	.24	.28	.32	.36	.40	.44	.48	.52	.56	.60	.64	.68	.72	.76	.80
.55	.00	.04	.07	.11	.14	.18	.22	.25	.29	.32	.36	.40	.43	.47	.50	.54	.58	.61	.65	.68	.72
.60	.00	.03	.06	.10	.13	.16	.19	.23	.26	.29	.32	.35	.39	.42	.45	.48	.52	.55	.58	.61	.64
.65	.00	.03	.06	.09	.11	.14	.17	.20	.23	.26	.28	.31	.34	.37	.40	.43	.46	.48	.51	.54	.57
.70	.00	.02	.05	.07	.10	.12	.15	.17	.20	.22	.25	.27	.30	.32	.35	.37	.40	.42	.45	.47	.50
.75	.00	.02	.04	.06	.08	.11	.13	.15	.17	.19	.21	.23	.25	.27	.30	.32	.33	.36	.38	.40	.42
.80	.00	.02	.04	.05	.07	.09	.11	.12	.14	.16	.18	.19	.21	.22	.25	.26	.28	.30	.32	.33	.35
.85	.00	.01	.03	.04	.05	.07	.08	.10	.11	.12	.14	.15	.16	.18	.19	.20	.22	.23	.25	.26	.27
.90	.00	.01	.02	.03	.04	.05	.06	.07	.08	.09	.10	.11	.12	.13	.14	.15	.16	.17	.18	.19	.20
.95	.00	.01	.01	.02	.02	.03	.03	.04	.04	.05	.05	.06	.07	.07	.08	.08	.09	.09	.10	.10	.11

(From Brown & Ghiselli, 1953, p. 342.)

zero validity. Using a test with zero validity is equivalent to using no test at all. To illustrate the use of the table, let us assume that the highest-scoring 20% of the applicants are hired (selection ratio = .20) by means of a test whose validity coefficient is .50. Reference to Table 6–2 shows that the mean criterion performance of this group is .70 *SD* above the expected base mean of an untested sample. With the same 20% selection ratio and a perfect test (validity coefficient = 1.00), the mean criterion score of the accepted applicants would be 1.40, just twice what it would be with the test of validity .50. Similar direct linear relations will be found if other mean criterion performances are compared within any row of Table 6–2. For instance, with a selection ratio of 60%, a validity of .25 yields a mean criterion score of .16, while a validity of .50 yields a mean of .32. Again, doubling the validity doubles the output rise.

The analysis of productivity in relation to test validity was carried further by Schmidt and his associates (Schmidt, Hunter, McKenzie, & Muldrow, 1979). Using the job of computer programmer in the federal government as an illustration, these investigators estimated the dollar value of the productivity increase resulting from one year's use of a computer aptitude test (validity = .76) in selecting new hires. They arrived at their estimates through the application of decision-theoretic techniques to data available in the U.S. Office of Personnel Management. Expected gains were computed for nine selection ratios ranging from .05 to .80, and for five validity coefficients of prior selection procedures ranging from zero (random selection) to .50.

The results indicated impressive gains in productivity from the use of the test under all these conditions. When use of the test was compared with random selection, the dollar gain ranged from $97.2 million for a selection ratio of .05 to $16.5 million for a selection ratio of .80. With prior selection validity of .50, the corresponding gains ranged from $33.3 million to $5.6 million. These gains would be spread over the expected tenure of the newly hired employees, which for computer programmers in the federal government averaged slightly under 10 years. It should also be noted that the estimates are based on the assumption that selection proceeds from the top-scoring applicants downward, until the specified selection ratio is reached. In other words, the procedure assumes optimum use of the selection process.

Using census data to assess the number of persons employed as computer programmers in the entire population of the United States, the investigators also worked out corresponding estimates of the effect of using the given test on the national level. In a still broader subsequent study, Hunter and Schmidt (1981) explored the possible application of the same statistical techniques to the entire national work force, across all occupations. These preliminary estimates are admittedly crude and tentative, and alternative procedures for such analyses tend to yield lower estimates (Burke & Frederick, 1984; U.S. Department of Labor, 1983b; Weekley, Frank, O'Connor, & Peters, 1985). Nevertheless, available results strongly suggest that effective methods for allocating people to jobs can contribute substantially to national productivity. The nature of work productivity, as well as the individual and organizational conditions that affect it, are receiving increasing attention. This is a growing area of criterion research in test validation, which is showing noticeable theoretical and methodological advances (J. P. Campbell, Campbell, & Associates, 1988; Hunter, Schmidt, & Judiesch, 1990; Raju, Burke, &Normand, 1990).

The Concept of Utility in Decision Theory. It is characteristic of decision theory that tests are evaluated in terms of their effectiveness in a particular situation. Such evaluation takes into account not only the validity of the test in predicting a particular criterion, but also a number of other parameters including base rate and selection ratio. Another important parameter is the relative utility of expected outcomes, the judged favorableness or unfavorableness of each outcome. As noted by Wood, et al. (2007), test utility can be summed by the question: "Does the use of this test results in better patient outcomes or more efficient delivery of services?" For example, an experiment might be envisioned in which individual career counseling agents are randomly assigned to two groups. One group is tested with the career guidance inventory and the results were provided to the counselors, while the other group is not tested, but proceeds directly for counseling. If the tested group showed more clarity about their career choices or required fewer sessions to achieve clarity about career choices, then it can be concluded that the utility of the test has been demonstrated.

However, research on the utility of psychological tests is scanty, and the lack of adequate systems for assigning values to outcomes, in terms of a uniform utility scale, has been one of the chief obstacle in the application of decision theory. Nonetheless, there is a need to assess the utility of many instruments and tests in a systematic matter, and psychologists and statisticians are experimenting with several methods to achieve the same.

Sequential Strategies and Adaptive Treatments. In some situations, the effectiveness of a test may be increased through the use of more complex decision strategies that take still more parameters into account. Two examples will serve to illustrate these possibilities. First, tests may be used to make *sequential* rather than terminal decisions. With the simple decision strategy illustrated in Figure 6–1, all decisions to accept or reject are treated as terminal. Figure 6–2, on the other hand, shows a two-stage sequential decision. Test A could be a short and easily administered screening test. On the basis of performance on this test, individuals would be sorted into three categories, including those clearly accepted or rejected, as well as an intermediate "uncertain" group to be examined further with more intensive techniques, represented by Test B. On the basis of the second-stage testing, this group would be sorted into accepted and rejected categories.

Another strategy, suitable for the diagnosis of psychological disorders, is to use only two categories, but to test further *all* cases classified as positives (i.e., possibly pathological) by the preliminary screening test. This is the strategy cited earlier in this section, in connection with the use of tests to diagnose pathological conditions with very low base rates.

It should also be noted that many personnel decisions are in effect sequential, although they may not be so perceived. Incompetent employees hired because of prediction errors can usually be discharged after a probationary period; failing students can be dropped from college at several stages. In such situations, it is only adverse selection decisions that are terminal. To be sure, incorrect selection decisions that are later rectified may be costly in terms of several value systems. But they are often less costly than terminal wrong decisions.

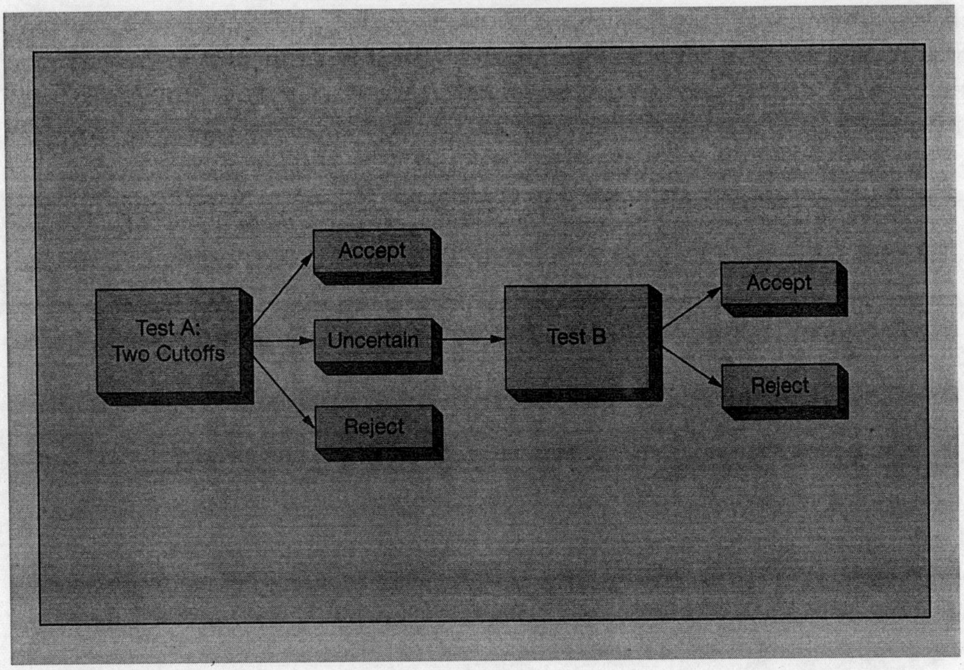

Figure 6-2. A Sequential Decision Strategy

A second condition that may alter the effectiveness of a psychological test is the availability of alternative treatments and the possibility of *adapting treatments* to individual characteristics. An example would be the utilization of different training procedures for workers at different aptitude levels, or the introduction of remedial instruction programs for students with certain educational disabilities. Under these conditions, the decision strategy followed in individual cases should take into account available data on the interaction of initial test score and differential treatment. When adaptive treatments are utilized, the success rate is likely to be substantially improved. Because the assignment of individuals to alternative treatments is essentially a classification rather than a selection problem, more will be said about the required methodology in a later section on classification decisions.

The examples cited illustrate a few of the ways in which the concepts and rationale of decision theory can assist in the evaluation of psychological tests for specific testing purposes. Essentially, decision theory has served to focus attention on the complexity of factors that determine the contribution a given test can make in a particular situation. The validity coefficient alone cannot indicate whether or not a test should be used, since it is only one of the factors to be considered in evaluating the impact of the test on the efficacy of the total decision process.[4]

Moderator Variables. The validity of a test for a given criterion may vary among subgroups differing in personal characteristics. The classic psychometric model assumes that prediction errors are characteristic of the test rather than of

[4] For a fuller discussion of the implications of decision theory for test use, see J. S. Wiggins (1973/1988, chap. 6) and, at a more technical level, Cronbach and Gleser (1965).

the person and that these errors are randomly distributed among persons. The flexibility of approach ushered in by decision theory stimulated some exploration of prediction models involving interaction between persons and tests. Such interaction would imply that the same test may be a better predictor for certain classes or subsets of persons than it is for others. For example, a given test may be a better predictor of criterion performance for men than for women, or a better predictor for applicants from a lower than for applicants from a higher socioeconomic level. In these examples, sex and socioeconomic level are known as *moderator variables,* since they moderate the validity of the test (Saunders, 1956).

Interests and motivation may function as moderator variables. Thus, if applicants have little interest in a job, they will probably perform poorly regardless of their scores on relevant aptitude tests. Among such persons, the correlation between aptitude test scores and job performance would be low. For individuals who are interested and highly motivated, on the other hand, the correlation between aptitude test score and job success may be quite high. The 1950s and 1960s witnessed a flurry of research on a wide variety of possible moderator variables. A series of studies by Ghiselli (1956, 1960, 1963, 1968) were concerned with the prediction of job performance. Other investigators tested hypotheses regarding the role of personality variables, particularly in the prediction of college achievement (N. Frederiksen & Gilbert, 1960; N. Frederiksen & Melville, 1954; Grooms & Endler, 1960; L. J. Strieker, 1966).

One relatively consistent finding was a sex difference in the predictability of academic grades. Surveys covering several hundred correlation coefficients from many sources reported higher correlations for women than for men between aptitude test scores and grades (Gross, Faggen, & McCarthy, 1974; Schmitt, Mellon, & Bylenga, 1978; Seashore, 1962). The same trend was found in high school and college, although the trend was more pronounced at the college level. The data do not indicate the reason for this sex difference in the predictability of academic achievement, but it may be interesting to speculate about it in the light of other known sex differences. If women students in general tend to be more conforming and more inclined to accept the values and standards of the school situation, their class achievement will probably depend largely on their abilities. If, on the other hand, men students tend to concentrate their efforts on those activities (in or out of school) that arouse their individual interests, these interest differences would introduce additional variance in their course achievement and would make it more difficult to predict achievement from aptitude test scores. It should be noted, however, that the sex differences in these validity coefficients, although fairly consistent, were generally small. Moreover, there is some indication that the differences tended to be smaller in the later studies, a finding that could reflect changing attitudes of women in the late 1960s and the 1970s.

In general, early expectations about the contribution of moderator variables were not fulfilled (Abrahams & Alf, 1972; Pinder, 1973; Zedeck, 1971). Methodological analyses revealed many pitfalls. Cross-validation in new samples frequently failed to corroborate initial findings. And it did not appear likely that the use of moderators would substantially improve the prediction that could be achieved through other means. In the light of present knowledge, no variable can be *assumed* to moderate validities in the absence of explicit evidence for such an effect. The concept of moderator variables may nevertheless have heuristic value in furthering the understanding of individual behavior, as in clinical case studies, and in suggesting fresh hypotheses that should be investigated with proper methodological controls. In fact, the 1980s and 1990s witnessed a revival of interest in moderator variables. Although undetected by earlier procedures, some moderator variables can now be identified through more sophisticated statistical analyses (Morris, Sherman, & Mansfield, 1986; E. F. Stone &. Hollenbeck, 1989).

COMBINING INFORMATION FROM DIFFERENT TESTS

For the prediction of practical criteria, not one but several tests may often be required. Most criteria are complex, the criterion measure depending on a number of different traits. A single test designed to measure such a criterion would thus have to be highly heterogeneous. It has already been pointed out, however, that a relatively homogeneous test, measuring largely a single trait, is more satisfactory because it yields less ambiguous scores (chap. 5). Hence, it is often preferable to use a combination of several relatively homogeneous tests, each covering a different aspect of the criterion, rather than a single test consisting of a hodgepodge of many different kinds of items.

When a number of specially selected tests are employed together to predict a single criterion, they are known as a *test battery.* The chief problem arising in the use of such batteries concerns the way in which scores on the different tests are to be combined in arriving at a decision regarding each individual. The procedures followed for this purpose are of two major types, namely, multiple regression equation and profile analysis. When tests are administered in the intensive study of individual cases, as in clinical diagnosis, counseling, or the evaluation of high-level executives, it is a common practice for the examiner to utilize test scores without further statistical analysis. In preparing a case report and in making recommendations, the examiner relies on judgment, past experience, and theoretical rationale to interpret score patterns and integrate findings from different tests.

Multiple Regression Equation. The multiple regression equation yields a predicted criterion score for each individual on the basis of her or his scores on all tests in the battery. The following regression equation illustrates the application of this technique to predicting a student's achievement in high school mathematics courses from her or his scores on verbal (V), numerical (N), and reasoning (R) tests:

$$\text{Mathematics Achievement} = .21V + .21N + .32R + 1.35$$

In this example, the test scores and the criterion score are expressed as stanines. Any other score scale could be used for this purpose. In the above equation, the student's stanine score on each of the three tests is multiplied by the corresponding weight given in the equation. The sum of these products, plus a constant (1.35), gives the student's predicted stanine position in mathematics courses. Suppose that Betty Jones receives the following stanine scores:

Verbal	6
Numerical	4
Reasoning	8

The estimated mathematics achievement of this student is found as follows:

$$\text{Math. Achieve.} = (.21)(6) + (.21)(4) + (.32)(8) + 1.35 = 6.01$$

Betty's predicted stanine is approximately 6. It will be recalled (chap. 3) that a stanine of 5 represents average performance. Betty would thus be expected to do somewhat better than average in mathematics courses. Her very superior performance in the reasoning test ($R = 8$) and her above-average score on the verbal test ($V = 6$) compensate for her poor score in speed and accuracy of computation ($N = 4$).

Specific techniques for the computation of regression equations can be found in texts on psychological statistics (e.g., D. C. Howell, 1997; Runyon & Haber, 1991). Essentially, such an equation is based on the correlation of each test with the criterion, as well as on the inter correlations among the tests. Obviously, those tests that correlate higher with the criterion should receive more weight. It is equally important, however, to take into account the correlation of each test with the other tests in the battery. Tests correlating highly with one another represent needless duplication, since they cover to a large extent the same aspects of the criterion. The inclusion of two such tests will not appreciably increase the validity of the entire battery, even though both tests may correlate highly with the criterion. In such a case, one of the tests would serve about as effectively as the pair; only one would therefore be retained in the battery.

Even after the most serious instances of duplication have been eliminated, however, the tests remaining in the battery will correlate with one another to varying degrees. For maximum predictive value, tests that make a more nearly unique contribution to the total battery should receive greater weight than those that partly duplicate the functions of other tests. In the computation of a multiple regression equation, each test is weighted in direct proportion to its correlation with the criterion and in inverse proportion to its correlations with the other tests. Thus, the highest weight will be assigned to the test with the highest validity and the least amount of overlap with the rest of the battery.

The validity of the entire battery can be found by computing the multiple correlation (R) between the criterion and the battery. This correlation indicates the highest predictive value that can be obtained from the given battery, when each test is given optimum weight for predicting the criterion in question. The optimum weights are those determined by the regression equation.

It should be noted that these weights are optimum only for the particular sample in which they were found. Because of chance errors in the correlation coefficients used in deriving them, the regression weights may vary from sample to sample. Hence, the battery should be cross-validated by correlating the predicted criterion scores with the actual criterion scores in a new sample. Formulas are available for estimating the amount of *shrinkage* in a multiple correlation to be expected when the regression equation is applied to a second sample, but empirical verification is preferable whenever possible. The larger the sample on which regression weights were derived, the smaller the shrinkage will be.[5]

[5] Under certain conditions, unit weights or other alternatives may be preferable to the regression weights. For a brief overview of research on various weighting schemes, see Dunnette and Borman (1979).

In certain situations, the predictive validity of a battery may be improved by including in the regression equation a test having a zero correlation with the criterion but a high correlation with another test in the battery. This curious situation arises when the test that is uncorrelated with the criterion acts as a *suppressor variable* to eliminate or suppress the irrelevant variance in the other test (Conger & Jackson, 1972). For example, reading comprehension might correlate highly with scores on a mathematical or a mechanical aptitude test, because the test problems require the understanding of complicated written instructions. If reading comprehension is irrelevant to the job behavior to be predicted, the reading comprehension required by the tests introduces error variance and lowers the predictive validity of the tests. Administering a reading comprehension test and including scores on this test in the regression equation will eliminate this error variance and raise the validity of the battery. The suppressor variable appears in the regression equation with a negative weight. Thus, the higher an individual's score on reading comprehension, the more is deducted from his or her score on the mathematical or mechanical test. In any situation, however, the more direct procedure of revising a test to eliminate the irrelevant variance is preferable to the indirect statistical elimination of such variance through a suppressor variable. When changes in the test are not feasible, the investigation of suppressor variables should be considered. In such cases, the effect of the suppressor variable should always be checked in a new sample.

Profile Analysis and Cutoff Scores. In addition to the individualized profile analyses employed in clinical assessment, the pattern of test scores obtained with a personnel selection battery can be evaluated in terms of multiple cutoff scores. Briefly, this procedure involves the establishment of a minimum cutoff score on each test. When this method is applied strictly, every person who falls below the minimum score an *any one* of the appropriate tests is rejected. In choosing appropriate tests and establishing cutoff scores for a given occupation, it is customary to consider more than test validities. If only tests yielding significant validity coefficients were taken into account, one or more essential abilities in which all workers in the occupation excel might be overlooked—hence the need for considering also those aptitudes in which workers excel as a group, even when individual differences beyond a certain minimum are unrelated to degree of job success. In some jobs, moreover, workers may be so homogeneous in a key trait that the range of individual differences is too narrow to yield a significant correlation between test scores and criterion.

This use of the multiple cutoff method is most fully illustrated with the General Aptitude Test Battery (GATB)[6] developed by the United States Employment Service for use in the occupational counseling and referral program of its state employment service offices (U.S. Department of Labor, 1970). Of the nine aptitude scores yielded by this battery, those to be considered for each occupation were chosen on the basis of criterion correlations, as well as means and standard deviations of workers in that occupation and the qualitative observations of job analysts.

[6] This widely used test battery is discussed further in chapter 17, in connection with the industrial and organizational use of tests.

The strongest argument for the use of multiple cutoffs rather than a regression equation is based on the possibility of compensatory scores. In other words, a serious deficiency in one skill may remain undetected in the person's total battery score because of a high score on another test. If the deficiency occurs in a skill that is critical for performance of the particular job, the chosen applicant will fail. This situation, however, can be avoided by identifying one or more critical skills that may be required in a particular job and applying a cutoff only on the corresponding tests. For the majority of tests, it is usually preferable to retain the actual score, because the higher the test score the better will be the individual's job performance. In most jobs, there is a linear relation between predictor score and criterion performance. It should be added that extensive research with the GATB has provided strong evidence for such linearity of relation (Coward & Sackett, 1990; Hartigan & Wigdor, 1989; Hawk, 1970). Under these conditions, selecting individuals on the basis of the actual magnitude of their test scores yields better job performance than does accepting all those who exceed minimum cutoff scores.

USE OF TESTS FOR CLASSIFICATION DECISIONS

The Nature of Classification. Psychological tests may be used for purposes of selection, placement, or classification. In *selection,* each individual is either accepted or rejected. Deciding whether or not to admit a student to college, to hire a job applicant, or to accept an army recruit for officer training are examples of selection decisions. When selection is done sequentially, the earlier stages are often called "screening," the term "selection" being reserved for the more intensive final stages. "Screening" may also be used to designate any rapid, rough selection process even when not followed by further selection procedures.

Both placement and classification differ from selection in that no one is rejected, or eliminated from the program. All individuals are assigned to appropriate "treatments" so as to maximize the effectiveness of outcomes. In *placement,* the assignments are based on a single score. This score may be derived from a single test, such as a mathematics achievement test. If a battery of tests has been administered, a composite score computed from a single regression equation would be employed. Examples of placement decisions include the sectioning of college freshmen into different mathematics classes on the basis of their achievement test scores, assigning applicants to clerical jobs requiring different levels of skill and responsibility, and identifying psychiatric patients as "more disturbed" and "less disturbed" for purposes of therapy. It is evident that in each of these decisions only one criterion is employed and that placement is determined by the individual's position along a single predictor scale.

Classification, on the other hand, always involves two or more criteria. In a military situation, for example, classification is a major problem, since each individual in an available personnel pool must be assigned to the military specialty where he or she can serve most effectively. Classification decisions are likewise required in industry, when new employees are assigned to training programs for different kinds of jobs. Other examples include the counseling of students regarding choice of college curriculum (science, liberal arts, etc.), as well as field of concentration. Counseling is based essentially on classification, since the client is told her or his chances of succeeding in different academic programs or occupations. Clinical diagnosis is likewise a classification problem, the major purposes of each diagnosis being a decision regarding the most appropriate type of therapy.

Although placement can be done with either one or more predictors, classification requires multiple predictors whose validity is individually determined against each criterion. A classification battery requires a different regression equation for each criterion. Some of the tests may have weights in all the equations, although of different values; others may be included in only one or two equations, having zero or negligible weights for some of the criteria. Thus, the combination of tests employed out of the total battery, as well as the specific weights, differs with the particular criterion. An early example of such a classification battery is that developed by the U.S. Air Force for assignment of personnel to different training programs. This battery, consisting of both paper-and-pencil and apparatus tests, provided stanine scores for pilots, navigators, bombardiers, and a few other aircrew specialties. By finding an individual's estimated criterion scores from the different regression equations, it was possible to predict whether, for example, he or she was better qualified as a pilot than as a navigator. A far more extensive and later example is Project A, the U.S. Army Selection and Classification Project (J. P. Campbell, 1990b).

Differential Validity. In the evaluation of a classification battery, the major consideration is its differential validity against the separate criteria. The object of such a battery is to predict the *difference* in each person's performance in two or more jobs, training programs, or other criterion situations. Tests chosen for such a battery should yield very different validity coefficients for the separate criteria. In a two-criterion classification problem, for example, the ideal test would have a high correlation with one criterion and a zero correlation (or preferably a negative correlation) with the other criterion. General intelligence tests are relatively poor for classification purposes, since they predict success about equally well in most areas. Hence, their correlations with the criteria to be differentiated would be too similar. An individual scoring high on such a test would be classified as successful for either assignment, and it would be impossible to predict in which he or she would be better. In a classification battery, we need some tests that are good predictors of criterion A and poor predictors of criterion B, and other tests that are poor predictors of A and good predictors of B.

Statistical procedures have been developed for selecting tests so as to maximize the differential validity of a classification battery (Brogden, 1946a, 1951, 1954; Horst, 1954; Mollenkopf, 1950b; Zeidner & Johnson, 1991). When the number of criteria is greater than two, however, the problem becomes quite complex. In practice, various empirical approaches have been followed to approximate the desired goals. A thorough analysis of the complexities of the classification problem is provided by J. P. Campbell (1990a, pp. 715–721).

Multiple Discriminant Functions. An alternative way of handling classification decisions is by means of the multiple discriminant function (French, 1966). Essentially, this is a mathematical procedure for determining how closely the individual's scores on a whole set of tests approximate the scores typical of persons in a given occupation, curriculum, psychiatric syndrome, or other category. A person would then be assigned to the particular group he or she resembles most closely. Although the regression equation permits the prediction of degree of success in each field, the multiple discriminant function treats all persons in one category as of equal status. Group membership is the only criterion data utilized by this method. The discriminant function is useful when criterion scores are unavailable and only group membership can be ascertained. Some tests, for instance, are validated by administering them to persons in different occupations, although no measure of degree of job success is available for individuals within each field.

The discriminant function is also appropriate when there is a nonlinear relation between the criterion and one or more predictors. For example, in certain personality traits there may be an optimum range for a given occupation. Individuals having either more or less of the trait in question would thus be at a disadvantage. It seems reasonable to expect, for instance, that salespersons showing a moderately high amount of social dominance would be most likely to succeed, and that the chances of success would decline as scores move in either direction from this region. With the discriminant functions, we would tend to select individuals falling within this optimum range. With the regression equation, on the other hand, the more dominant the score, the more favorable would be the predicted outcome. If the correlation between predictor and criterion were negative, of course, the regression equation would yield more favorable predictions for the low scorers. But there is no direct way whereby an intermediate score would receive maximum credit. Although in many instances the two techniques would lead to the same choices, there are situations in which persons would be differently classified by regression equations and discriminant functions. For most psychological testing purposes, regression equations provide a more effective technique. Under certain circumstances, however, the discriminant function is better suited to yield the required information.

Maximizing the Utilization of Talent. Differential prediction of criteria with a battery of tests permits a fuller utilization of available human resources than is possible with a single general test or with a composite score from a single regression equation. As we saw in the Taylor-Russell tables and elsewhere in this chapter, the effectiveness of any test in selecting personnel for a given job depends on the selection ratio. In classification decisions, we work with a smaller selection ratio and are thus able to assign better-qualified persons to each job. If out of 100 applicants, 10 are needed to fill each of two different jobs, the selection ratio is 10% for each job, when separate predictors are employed for each. If a single predictor (such as a general intelligence test) were used to select applicants for both jobs, the selection ratio would be 20%, since we could do no better than take the top 20 applicants.

Even when predictors for the two jobs are highly correlated, so that some of the same applicants will qualify for both jobs, there is considerable gain from the use of separate predictors. This situation is illustrated in Table 6–3, which shows the mean standard criterion score of workers selected for each of two jobs by a selection strategy (single predictor) and by a classification strategy involving

Table 6–3

Mean Standard Criterion Score of Persons Placed on Two Jobs by Selection or Classification Strategies

Selection Ratio for each job	Selection: Single predictor	Classification: Two predictors whose intercorrelation is				
		0	.20	.40	.60	.80
5%	.88	1.03	1.02	1.01	1.00	.96
10	.70	.87	.86	.84	.82	.79
20	.48	.68	.67	.65	.62	.59
30	.32	.55	.53	.50	.46	.43
40	.18	.42	.41	.37	.34	.29
50	.00	.31	.28	.25	.22	.17

(Adapted from Brogden, 1951, p. 182.)

two different predictors, each validated against its own job criterion. If workers were assigned by chance, with no selection, the mean standard score in this scale would be zero. This would be the case if the selection ratio were 50% for each job, so that 100% of the applicants would have to be hired. Note that even under these conditions, job performance would be improved by the use of two predictors, as shown in the last row of the table. With two uncorrelated predictors, mean job performance would be .31 (approximately 1/3 of a standard deviation above the chance value). As the correlation between the predictors increases, the job effectiveness of the selected employees decreases; but it remains better than chance even when the correlation is .80. With lower selection ratios, we can of course obtain better-qualified personnel. As can be seen in Table 6–3 however, for each selection ratio, mean job performance is better when applicants are chosen through classification than through selection strategies.

A practical illustration of the advantages of classification strategies is provided by the use of Aptitude Areas scores in the assignment of personnel to military occupational specialties in the U.S. Army (Maier & Fuchs, 1973). In this research, each Aptitude Area corresponded to a group of Army jobs requiring a similar pattern of aptitudes, knowledge, and interests. From a 13-test classification battery, combinations of three to five tests were used to find the individual's score in each Aptitude Area. Figure 6–3 shows the results of an investigation of 7,500 applicants for enlistment in which the use of Aptitude Area scores was compared with the use of a global screening test, the Armed Forces Qualification Test (AFQT). It will be noted that only 56% of this group reached or exceeded the 50th percentile on the AFQT, while 80% reached or exceeded the average standard score of 100 on their best Aptitude Area. Thus, when individuals are allocated to specific jobs on the basis of the aptitudes required for each job, a very large majority are able to perform as well as the average of the entire sample or better. This apparent impossibility, in which nearly everyone could be above average, can be attained by capitalizing on the fact that nearly everyone excels in *some* aptitude.

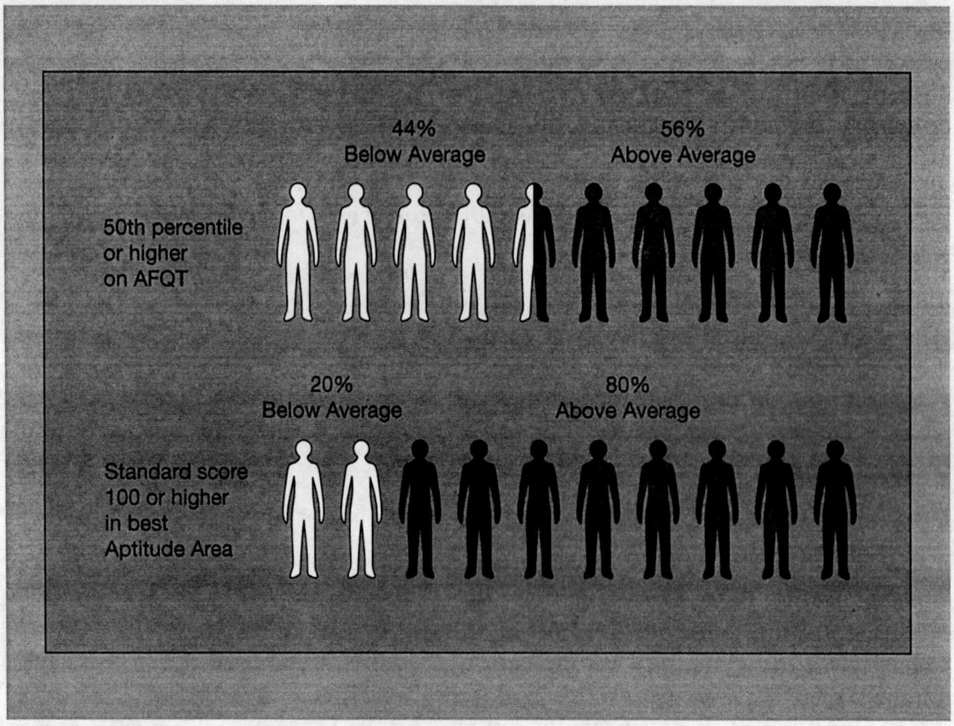

Figure 6-3. Percentages Scoring Above Average on AFQT and on Best Aptitude Area of Army Classification Battery in a Sample of 7,500 Applicants for Enlistment.
(Data from U.S. Army Research Institute for the Behavioral and Social Sciences. Courtesy of J. E. Uhlaner.)

The same point was illustrated with a quite different population in a study of gifted children by Feldman and Bratton (1972). For demonstration purposes, 49 children in two fifth-grade classes were evaluated on each of 19 measures, all of which had previously been used to select students for special programs for the gifted. Among these measures were global scores on a group intelligence test and on an educational achievement battery, tests of separate aptitudes and separate academic areas such as reading and arithmetic, a test of creative thinking, grades in music and art, and teachers' nominations of the most "gifted" and the most "creative" children in each class. When the five highest-ranking children selected by each criterion were identified, they included 92% of the group. Thus, it was again shown that nearly all members of a group will excel when multivariate criteria are employed.

STATISTICAL ANALYSES OF TEST BIAS

The Problem. If we want to use tests to predict outcomes in some future situation, such as an applicant's performance in college or on a job, we need tests with high predictive validity against the particular criterion. This requirement is commonly overlooked in the development of so-called culture-fair tests (discussed further in chaps. 9 and 12). In the effort to include in such tests only functions common to different cultures or subcultures, we may choose content that has little relevance to any criterion we wish to predict. A better solution is to choose criterion-relevant content and then investigate possible population differences in the effectiveness of the test for its intended purpose. Validity coefficients, regression weights, and cutoff scores may vary as a function of differences in the test takers' experiential backgrounds. These values should therefore be checked within subgroups for which there is reason to expect such effects. These possible subgroup differences will be recognized as a special case of the role of moderator variables discussed in a preceding section. And it will be recalled that the search for significant and stable moderator effects has proved disappointing. In the present section, we shall examine specific applications of this type of analysis to minority populations in the United States.

It should be noted that the predictive characteristics of test scores are less likely to vary among cultural groups when the test is intrinsically relevant to criterion performance. If a verbal test is employed to predict nonverbal job performance, a fortuitous validity may be found in one cultural group because of traditional associations of past experiences within that culture. In a group with a different experiential background, however, the validity of the test may disappear. On the other hand, a test that directly samples criterion behavior, or one that measures essential prerequisite skills, is likely to retain its validity in different groups.

Since the mid-1960s, there has been a rapid accumulation of research on possible ethnic differences in the predictive meaning of test scores.[7] The large majority of studies conducted thus far have dealt with African-Americans, although a few have included other ethnic minorities. The problems investigated are generally subsumed under the heading of *test bias*. In this context, the term "bias" is employed in its well-established statistical sense, to designate constant or systematic error as opposed to chance error. This is the same sense in which we speak of a biased sample, in contrast to a random sample. The principal questions that have been raised regarding test bias pertain to validity coefficients (slope bias) and to the relationship between group means on the test and on the criterion (intercept bias). These questions will be examined in the next two sections.

Slope Bias. To facilitate an understanding of the technical aspects of test bias, let us begin with a scatter diagram, or bivariate distribution, such as those illustrated in chapter 4 (especially Fig. 4–3). For the present purpose, the horizontal axis (X) represents scores on a test and the vertical axis (Y) represents criterion scores, such as college grade-point average or an index of job performance. It will be recalled that the tally marks, showing the position of each individual on both test and criterion, indicate the direction and general magnitude of the correlation between the two variables. The line of best fit drawn through these tally marks is known as the regression line, and its equation is the regression equation. In this example, the regression equation would have only one predictor. The multiple regression equations discussed earlier in this chapter have several predictors, but the principle is the same.

---

[7] Only a few representative studies can be cited from this voluminous literature. For an overview of the problem and an analysis of its many facets, we recommend N. S. Cole and Moss (1989), Hunter, Schmidt, and Rauschem berger (1977), and C. R. Reynolds and Brown (1984).

When both test and criterion scores are expressed as standard scores ($SD = 1.00$), the *slope* of the regression line equals the correlation coefficient. For this reason, if a test yields a significantly different validity coefficient in the two groups, this difference is described as slope bias. This type of group difference is often designated as "differential validity." Several investigators have also employed the term "single-group validity" to refer to a test whose validity coefficient reached statistical significance in one group but failed to do so in another.

Figure 6–4 provides schematic illustrations of regression lines for several bivariate distributions.[8] The ellipses represent the region within which the tally

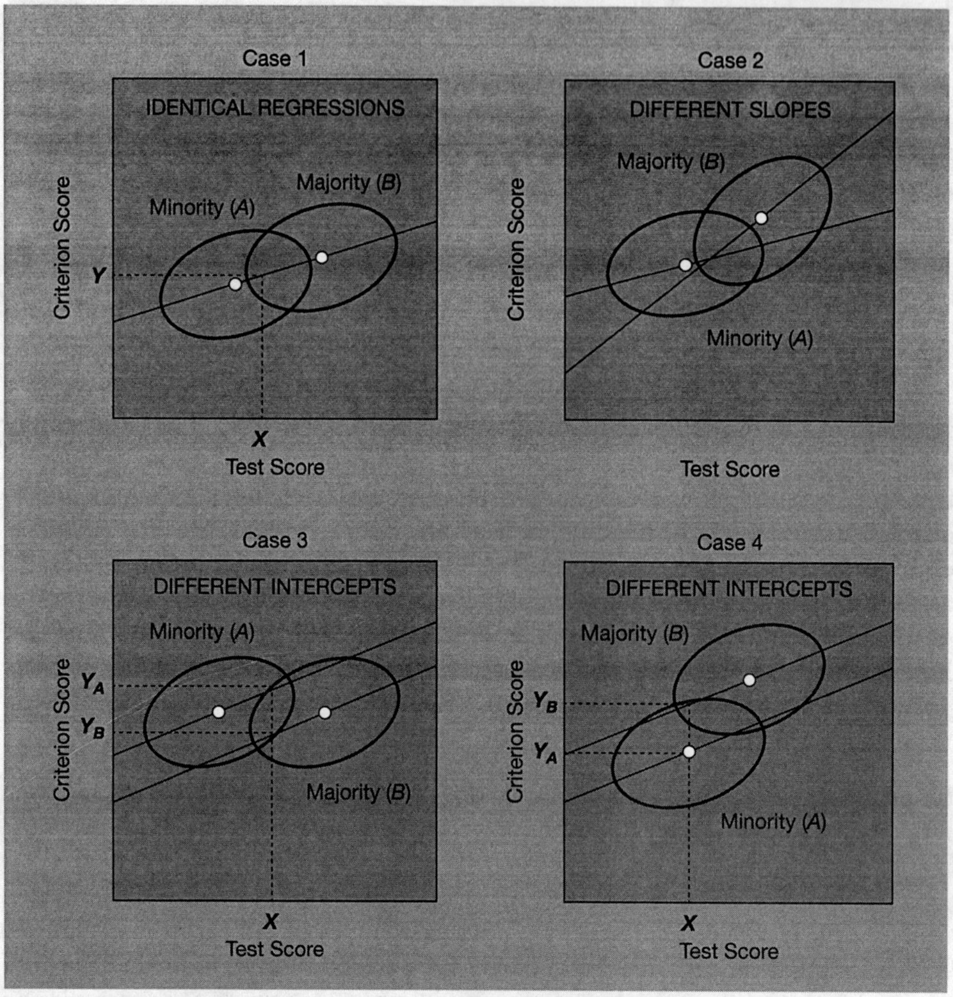

Figure 6–4. Slope and Intercept Bias in Predicting Criterion Scores. The ellipses show the regions within which members of each group fall when their scores are plotted against their criterion performance.

(Cases 1, 2, and 4 adapted from M. A. Gordon, 1953, p. 3.)

[8] The type of analysis of test bias illustrated in Figure 6–4 has come to be known as the "Cleary model" because it was used by Cleary (1968) in a widely cited study of College Board Scholastic Aptitude Test scores of minority students. The mathematical procedures were developed by Gulliksen and Wilks (1950), and their application to ethnic and sex comparisons was suggested by Humphreys (1952). The diagrams in Figure 6–4 were adapted from a study by M. A. Gordon (1953) conducted in the U.S. Air Force under Humphreys' direction.

marks of each sample would fall. Case 1 shows the bivariate distribution of two groups with different means in the predictor, but with identical regression lines between predictor and criterion. In this case, there is no test bias, since any given test score (X) corresponds to the identical criterion score (Y) in both groups. Case 2 illustrates slope bias, with a lower validity coefficient in the minority group.

In differential validity studies, a common difficulty arises from the fact that the number of cases in the minority sample is often much smaller than in the majority sample. Under these conditions, the same validity coefficient could be statistically significant in the majority sample and not significant in the minority sample (so-called single-group validity). With 100 cases, for example, a correlation of .27 is clearly significant at the .01 level; with 30 cases, the same correlation falls far short of the minimum value required for significance even at the .05 level. For this reason, the proper procedure to follow in such differential validation studies is to evaluate the difference between the two validity coefficients, rather than to test each separately for significance (Humphreys, 1973). By the latter procedure, one could easily "demonstrate" that a test is valid for, let us say, Whites and not valid for Blacks. All that would be needed for this purpose is a large enough group of Whites and a small enough group of Blacks!

A sophisticated statistical analysis of the results of 19 published studies reporting validity coefficients for Black and White employment samples casts serious doubt on the conclusions reached in some of the earlier studies (Schmidt, Berner, & Hunter, 1973). Taking into account the obtained validities and the size of samples in each study, the investigators demonstrated that the discrepancies in validity coefficients found between Blacks and Whites did not differ from chance expectancy. This conclusion was corroborated in a later, more comprehensive analysis covering 39 studies (Hunter, Schmidt, & Hunter, 1979). The topic of differential validity for minority and nonminority job applicants elicited continuing discussion over more than a decade. Some investigators observed that, because of methodological limitations, the results were merely inconclusive. It is noteworthy, however, that no evidence of differential validity was found in well-designed, large-scale studies on industrial samples (J. T. Campbell, Crooks, Mahoney, & Rock, 1973) and Army personnel (Maier & Fuchs, 1973). In general, the methodologically sounder studies proved to be those less likely to find differential validity.

Similar results have been obtained in numerous investigations of Black and White college students (Breland, 1979). Validity coefficients of the College Board Scholastic Aptitude Test and other college admission tests for Black students were generally as high as those obtained for White students, or higher. These relationships were found when the Black and White samples were attending the same colleges, as well as when they were attending separate colleges. Working at a very different level, B. C. Mitchell (1967) studied the validities of two educational readiness tests against end-of-the-year achievement test scores of first-grade schoolchildren. In the large samples of Black and White children tested, validities of total scores and of subtests were very similar for the two ethnic groups, although tending to run somewhat higher for the Blacks. In summary, comprehensive surveys and critical analyses of available studies have failed to support the hypothesis that ability tests are less valid for Blacks than for Whites in predicting occupational or educational performance (Hunter, Schmidt, & Rauschenberger, 1984; Linn, 1978).

Although comparable studies with other minorities are much fewer, similar results have been obtained with Hispanic Americans for both educational and employment testing (Breland, 1979; Duran, 1983, 1989; Pennock-Román, 1990; Schmidt, Pearlman, & Hunter, 1980). For Hispanic Americans, however, the interpretation of test scores is complicated by varying degrees of bilingualism and by attitudinal and cultural variables in the home that affect not only test performance but also academic and occupational achievement; under these conditions, we would not expect predictive validity to be affected. In a well-designed survey of published research on the use of tests for college admission, Duran (1983) observed that altering the tests does not offer a promising solution for these problems among Hispanic-American students; rather, the problems need to be investigated and resolved directly. Nevertheless, test scores should be interpreted with full knowledge of the moderating background variables in individual cases. Furthermore, any generalization regarding Hispanic Americans should take into account possible differences among subgroups, such as Puerto Ricans, Mexican Americans, and others.

Intercept Bias. Even when a test yields the same validity coefficients for two groups, it may still show intercept bias. The intercept of a regression line refers to the point at which the line intersects the axis. A test exhibits intercept bias if it systematically underpredicts or overpredicts criterion performance for a particular group. Let us look again at Case 1 in Figure 6–4, in which majority and minority samples show identical regressions. Under these conditions, there is neither slope nor intercept bias. Although the groups differ significantly in mean test scores, they show a corresponding difference in criterion performance. In Case 3, on the other hand, the two groups have regression lines with the same slope but different intercepts. In this case, the minority group (A) has a higher intercept than the majority group (B); that is, the minority regression line intersects the Y axis at a higher point than does the majority regression line. Although the validity coefficients computed within each group are equal, any test score (X) will correspond to different criterion scores in the two groups, as shown by points Y_A and Y_B The same test score thus has a different predictive meaning for the two groups.

Psychologists who are concerned about the possible unfairness of tests for minority group members visualize a situation illustrated in Case 3. Note that, in this case, the majority excels on the test, but majority and minority perform equally well on the criterion. Selecting all applicants in terms of a test cutoff established for the majority group would thus discriminate unfairly against the minority. Under these conditions, use of the majority regression line for both groups *under predicts* the criterion performance of minority group members. This situation is likely to occur when a large proportion of test variance is irrelevant to criterion performance and measures functions in which the majority excels the minority. A thorough job analysis and satisfactory test validity provide safeguards against the choice of such a test.

The problem of intercept bias relates most closely to what has popularly been designated "test fairness." Although the terms "test fairness" and "test bias" are sometimes used broadly and interchangeably to cover all aspects of test use with cultural minorities, it has become customary to identify test fairness (or unfairness) with intercept bias. This usage was followed in the *Uniform Guidelines on Employee Selection Procedures* (1978). In the section on *Fairness* (14B), the defining statement reads:

> When members of one race, sex, or ethnic group characteristically obtain lower scores on a selection procedure than members of another group, and the differences in scores are not reflected in differences in a measure of job performance, use of the selection procedure may unfairly deny opportunities to members of the group that obtains the lower scores.

Empirical investigations of actual test use, however, have shown either no significant intercept bias or, more often, a slight tendency in the *opposite* direction, as illustrated in Case 4, Figure 6–4. Here the majority group (B) has a higher intercept than the minority group (A). Under these conditions, use of the majority regression line and cutoff score for both groups over predicts the criterion performance of minority group members and hence discriminates *in favor* of the minority group. Such results have been obtained in the prediction of college grades (Breland, 1979; Duran, 1983; Zeidner, 1987), law school grades (Linn, 1975), performance in Army and Air Force training programs (M. A. Gordon, 1953; Maier & Fuchs, 1973; C. W. Shore & Marion, 1972), and a wide variety of industrial criteria (see Hunter et al., 1984, for survey).

It has been demonstrated mathematically that Case 4 (Fig. 6–4) occurs if two groups differ in one or more *additional variables* that correlate positively with both test and criterion (Linn & Werts, 1971; Reilly, 1973). The small over prediction is a statistical artifact of considering one predictor at a time. As more predictors are added to the battery, the over prediction decreases, a fact that has been empirically verified with several populations, ranging from law school students and office clerks to kindergarten children (see Hunter et al., 1984).

It is interesting to note that the same results have been obtained when comparisons were made between groups classified according to educational or socioeconomic level. The Army Classification Battery tended to over predict the performance of high school dropouts and under predict the performance of college graduates in training programs for military occupational specialties (Maier, 1972). Similarly, the college grades of students whose fathers were in the professions were under predicted from various academic aptitude tests, while the grades of students from lower occupational levels tended to be overpredicted (Hewer, 1965). In all these studies, comparisons of higher-scoring and lower-scoring groups revealed either no significant difference in intercepts or a slight bias in favor of the groups scoring lower on the tests.

Decision Models for Fair Use of Tests. Gradually, the focus of research began to shift from the evaluation of test bias to the design of selection strategies for fair test use with cultural minorities. If a selection strategy follows the regression (see Cleary) model illustrated in Figure 6–4, individuals will be chosen (for college admission, employment, etc.) solely on the basis of their predicted criterion scores. This strategy will maximize overall criterion performance, without regard to other goals of the selection process. According to this strategy, a fair use of tests in selection is one that is based only on the best estimate of criterion performance for each individual.

Several other decision models were proposed that have the effect of selecting larger proportions of persons from the lower-scoring group. This effect is in line with the goal that is generally designated by such terms as "affirmative action" or the reduction of "adverse impact" in the selection process. When first introduced, these alternative models appeared to follow procedures quite different from those of the regression model.[9] It was later demonstrated, however, that they could all be expressed as variants of one comprehensive model (Darlington, 1971; Gross & Su, 1975; Petersen & Novick, 1976). The differences among the various models can be explained in terms of the value judgments implicit in each model. The role of values in decision strategies was illustrated earlier in this chapter (see Fig. 6–2). It will be recalled that the assignment of a relative *utility* to each outcome requires a judgment of the degree of favorableness or unfavorableness of that outcome. These value judgments, together with the probability of each outcome, are used in computing the total expected utility (*EU*) of the decision strategy.

The decision-theoretic analyses of fair test use demonstrated that the proposed models differ in their definition of fairness, insofar as they implicitly assign different values to acceptance and rejection of potential successes and failures within minority and nonminority populations. The expected utility model makes the underlying social values explicit. This approach calls for an overt statement of utilities, which cannot be reached through statistical means but requires open discussion and successive approximations to balance conflicting goals (N. S. Cole & Moss, 1989; Darlington, 1976; Messick, 1989). Among the goals to be reconciled are those of providing equality of opportunity for all individuals, maximizing success rate and productivity, increasing the demographic mix and representativeness of the work force (at least in certain occupations), and extending preferential treatment to groups disadvantaged by past inequities.

Finally, it should he emphasized that statistical adjustments in test scores, cutoffs, and prediction formulas hold little promise as a means of correcting social inequities. The use of statistical manipulations that conceal score differences through separate subgroup-or race-norming[10] is likely to harm individuals by assigning them to jobs or educational programs for which they lack the necessary prerequisite skills or knowledge. The result is likely to be poor performance, which will not only affect the individual adversely in self-concept and attitude toward work but may also contribute to the perpetuation of a stereotype that persons from some cultural or ethnic category are poor performers. More constructive solutions are suggested by other approaches earlier in this chapter. One is illustrated by multiple-aptitude testing and classification strategies that permit the fullest utilization of the diverse aptitude patterns fostered by different

---

[9] The literature on the various decision models for fair test use is extensive, and much of it is quite technical. For simple summaries of the distinguishing features and implications of different models, see Bond (1981), Dunnette and Borman (1979, pp. 497–500), Gross and Su (1975, pp. 350–351), and C. R. Reynolds (1982). Fuller explanations can be found in Hunter and Schmidt (1976) and Hunter et al. (1977).

[10] See, e.g., D. C. Brown (1994), L. S. Gottfredson (1994), and Sackett and Wilk (1994).

cultural backgrounds. A broader consideration of relevant personality traits, motivation, and attitudes also contributes to the prediction of job or educational performance. Another approach is through adaptive treatments, such as individualized training programs. In order to maximize the tit of such programs to individual characteristics, it is essential that tests reveal as fully and accurately as possible the person's present level of development in the requisite abilities. Comprehensive decision models provide a framework for combining a diversity of approaches and value systems and assessing the overall effectiveness of each solution.

Chapter seven

Item Analysis

Familiarity with the basic concepts and techniques of item analysis, like knowledge about other phases of test construction, can help test users in their evaluation of published tests. In addition, item analysis is particularly relevant to the construction of informal, local tests, such as the quizzes and examinations prepared by teachers for classroom use. Some of the general guidelines for effective item writing, as well as the simpler statistical techniques of item analysis, can materially improve classroom tests and are worth using even with small groups.

Items can be analyzed qualitatively, in terms of their content and form, and quantitatively, in terms of their statistical properties. Qualitative analysis includes the consideration of content validity, discussed in chapter 5, as well as the evaluation of items in terms of effective item-writing procedures. Quantitative analysis includes principally the measurement of item difficulty and item discrimination. Both the validity and the reliability of any test depend ultimately on the characteristics of its items. High reliability and validity can be built into a test in advance through item analysis. Tests can be improved through the selection, substitution, or revision of items.

Item analysis makes it possible to shorten a test and at the same time to increase its validity and reliability. Other things being equal, a longer test is more valid and reliable than a shorter one. The effect of lengthening or shortening a test on the reliability coefficient was discussed in chapter 4, where the Spearman-Brown formula for estimating this effect was also introduced. These estimated changes in reliability occur when the discarded items are equivalent to those that remain, or when equivalent new items are added to the test. Similar changes in validity will result from the deletion or addition of items of equivalent validity. All such estimates of change in reliability or validity refers to the lengthening or shortening of tests through a *random* selection of items, without item analysis. When a test is shortened by eliminating the least satisfactory items, however, the short test may be more valid and reliable than the original longer instrument.

ITEM DIFFICULTY

For most testing purposes, the difficulty of an item is defined in terms of the percentage (or proportion) of persons who answer it correctly. Item difficulty is obtained by calculating the ratio of the number of respondents who respond correctly to the total number of respondents. For any individual item, the index of item difficulty (p) varies from 0 to 1. Note that easier the item, larger would be the index. A word that is correctly defined by 70% of the standardization sample ($p = 0.70$) is regarded as easier than the one that is correctly defined by 15% of the standardization sample ($p = 0.15$). It is customary to arrange items in order of difficulty, so that the test takers begin with relatively easy items and proceed to items of increasing difficulty. This arrangement gives confidence to the test takers in approaching the test and reduces the likelihood of their time being wasted on items beyond their ability and also to avoid negligence of the easier items that they can answer correctly.

Furthermore, the item-difficulty index serves as a useful tool in identifying items that should be altered or discarded in a psychological test. When an item has a difficulty index near 0, it implies that almost everyone has answered it incorrectly. Such items are psychometrically unproductive because it does not provide information about differences between the test takers. The same can be said about an item with a difficulty index near 1.0, where almost all the test takers provide a correct answer. For all testing purposes, such items should be either rewritten or removed from the test. Conversely, the items can make more differentiations as the difficulty level inches closer to 0.50. Suppose, out of 100 people, 50 pass an item and 50 fail it ($p = 50$). Then this item enables one to differentiate between each of those who have passed and each of those who have failed. For maximum differentiation, then, it would seem that one should choose all items at the 0.50 item difficulty level. However, determining the optimal level of item difficulty is a complicated process. Typically, item difficulties that float around 0.5, ranging between 0.3 and 0.7, maximize the information provided by the test, about the differences between the abilities of test takers.

However, this rule of thumb varies from situation to situation. For example, for multiple-choice items, the optimal level of item difficulty needs to be adjusted for the effects of guessing. In general, the optimal level of item difficulty can be computed from the formula $(1.0 + g)/2$, where g is the chance success level (Gregory, 2015). Thus, for a four option multiple choice item, the chance success level is 0.25 and the optimal level of difficulty would be $(1.0 + .25)/2$, or about 0.63. Similarly, for a three option multiple choice item, the chance success level is 0.33 and the optimal level of difficulty would be $(1.0 + .33)/2$, or about 0.67.

Moreover, it depends on the purpose of the test. If the test is to be used for identification of high potential candidates by means of a cutting score, it may be desirable to select items with difficulty levels outside the 0.3 to 0.7 range. Similarly, if a test is used to select graduate students for a university that admits only a select few of its many applicants, then it should contain many difficult items. A test to identify children with learning disability, in a class for remedial education program, should contain many easy items. In all these cases, there will be a useful discrimination among test takers near the cutting score – a very high score for the graduate admissions and a very low score for students eligible for remedial programs – but little discrimination among the remaining test takers (Allen & Yen, 1979). It is apparent from these examples that the appropriate difficulty level of items depends upon the purpose of the test. Although, in most testing situations, items clustering around a medium difficulty (0.50) yield the maximum information about each individual's performance level; decisions about the item difficulty cannot be made routinely, without knowing how the test scores will be used.

Thurstone Absolute Scaling. Indices of item difficulty expressed as percentages or normal curve units are limited to the ability range covered by the sample from which they were obtained. For several purposes, however, there is a need for a measure of item difficulty applicable across different samples varying in the ability level. In educational achievement tests, for example, it is advantageous to be able to compare a child's score over several successive grades on a uniform scale. Yet, it would obviously be impracticable to scale the items appropriate for all grades by administering them to a single group, since some items would be too difficult and some too easy for almost everyone in the group.

To address such challenges, Louis Leon Thurstone (1925) developed the method of absolute scaling. This method is for obtaining a measure of absolute item difficulty based on the results of different age groups of test takers. The methodology for determining individual item difficulty on an absolute scale is quite complex, but the underlying rationale is not too difficult to understand. A set of common test items is administered to two or more age groups. The relative difficulty of these items between any two age groups serves as the basis for making a series of interlocking comparisons for all items and all age groups. One age group serves as the standard or reference or anchor group (Gregory, 2015).

Essentially, this procedure involves two steps. First, the scale values of items are to be found separately within each group by converting the percentage of passing of each item into normal curve – standard deviation distances or z values. Second, all these scale values need to be translated into corresponding values for one of the groups, chosen as a standard or anchor group. Any group can be chosen as a reference group, such as the first group tested, the youngest group, a group in the middle of the range, or some other convenient group. What is required is a set of common, anchor items administered to two or more groups and scaled within each group. The scale values of the same items in two (or more) groups serve to define the relation between the groups and permit the transmutation of all item difficulty values from one group to another. This method of absolute scaling is widely used in cognitive ability testing and aptitude testing.

ITEM DISCRIMINATION

Choice of Criterion. Item discrimination refers to the degree to which an item differentiates correctly among test takers in the behavior that the test is designed to measure. When the test as a whole is to be evaluated by means of criterion-related validation, the items may themselves be evaluated and selected on the basis of their relationship to the same external criterion. This procedure has been followed especially in the development of certain personality and interest tests, discussed in chapters 13 and 14. It is also the method generally followed in choosing items for inclusion in biographical inventories, which typically cover a heterogeneous collection of background facts about the individual. In these types of instruments, there is no a priori basis for grading a response as right or wrong, or assigning it a scoring weight, except by comparison with the criterion status of persons who give that response. From an initial pool of items, those items are retained that best differentiate among persons classified in different criterion categories, such as various occupations or psychiatric syndromes. Frequently, the criterion groups consist of successes and failures in an academic course, a training program, or a type of job.

In the domain-referenced mastery testing described in chapter 3, items can be evaluated by comparing the item performance of individuals who have had varying amounts of instruction in the relevant functions (Panell & Laabs, 1979; L. A. Shepard, 1984). Usually the comparison is between the proportion of persons who give the correct item response in a pre-instruction and a post-instruction group. Because these tests are used to determine whether individuals have reached a specified level of mastery, individual differences in overall performance on a single occasion are minimized. Hence, internal item analyses will not be meaningful, and an external criterion, such as amount of relevant instruction, is needed.

In other types of achievement tests, as in many aptitude tests, item discrimination is usually investigated against total score on the test itself.[1] For educational achievement tests, an external criterion is not typically available. For aptitude tests, the increasing emphasis on construct validation makes total score an appropriate criterion for item selection. In the initial stages of test development, the total score provides a first approximation to a measure of the ability, trait, or construct under investigation.

Let us examine further the implications of choosing items on the basis of an external criterion and on the basis of total test score. The former tends to maximize the validity of the test against the external criterion, the latter to maximize the internal consistency or homogeneity of the test. Under certain conditions, the two approaches may lead to opposite results, the items chosen on the basis of external validity being the very ones rejected on the basis of internal consistency. Let us suppose that the preliminary form of a scholastic aptitude test consists of 100 arithmetic items and 50 vocabulary items. In order to select items from this initial pool by the method of internal consistency, some index of agreement

---

[1] Item-test correlations will be somewhat inflated by the common specific and error variance in the item and the test of which it is a part. Formulas are available to correct for this part-whole effect (Guilford & Fruchter, 1978, pp. 165–167).

between performance on each item and total score on the 150 items will be computed. It is apparent that such an index would tend to be higher for the arithmetic than for the vocabulary items, since the total score is based on twice as many arithmetic items. If it is desired to retain the 75 "best" items in the final form of the test, it is likely that most of these items will prove to be arithmetic problems. In terms of the external criterion of scholastic achievement, however, the vocabulary items might have been more valid predictors than the arithmetic items. If such is the case, the item analysis will have served to lower rather than raise the validity of the test.

The practice of rejecting items that have low correlations with total score provides a means of purifying or homogenizing the test. By such a procedure, the items with the highest average intercorrelations will be retained. This method of selecting items will increase test validity only when the original pool of items measures a single trait and when this trait is present in the criterion or construct to be assessed. Some types of tests, however, measure a combination of traits required by a complex criterion. Purifying the test in such a case may reduce its criterion coverage and thus lower validity.

The selection of items to maximize criterion-related test validity may be likened to the selection of tests that will yield the highest validity for a battery. It will be recalled (chap. 6) that the test contributing most toward battery validity is one having the highest correlation with the criterion and the lowest correlation with the other tests in the battery. If this principle is applied to the selection of items, it means that the most satisfactory items are those with the highest external validities and the lowest coefficients of internal consistency. Thus, an item that has a high correlation with the external criterion but a relatively low correlation with total score would be preferred to one correlating highly with both criterion and test score, since the first item presumably measures an aspect of the criterion not adequately covered by the rest of the test.

It might seem that items could be selected by the same methods used in choosing tests for inclusion in a battery. Thus, each item could be correlated with the external criterion and with every other item. The best items chosen by this method could then be weighted by means of a regression equation. Such a procedure, however, is neither feasible nor theoretically defensible. Not only would the computation labor be excessive, but interitem correlations are also subject to wide sampling fluctuation, and the resulting regression weights would be too unstable to provide a satisfactory basis for item selection. An even more serious objection, however, is that the resulting test would be so heterogeneous in content as to preclude meaningful interpretation of the test score.

External validation and internal consistency are both desirable objectives of test construction. The relative emphasis to be placed on each varies with the nature and purpose of the test. For many testing purposes, a satisfactory compromise is to sort the relatively homogeneous items into separate tests or subtests, each of which covers a different aspect of the external criterion. Thus, breadth of coverage is achieved through a variety of tests, each yielding a relatively unambiguous score, rather than through heterogeneity of items within a single test. By such a procedure, items with low indices of internal consistency would not be discarded but would be segregated. As a result, fairly high internal consistency would be attained within each subtest or item group.

Statistical Indices of Item Discrimination. Since item responses are generally recorded as right or wrong, the measurement of item discrimination usually involves a dichotomous variable (the item) and a continuous variable (the criterion). In certain situations, the criterion, too, may be dichotomous, as in graduation versus nongraduation from college, or success versus failure on a job. Moreover, a continuous criterion may be dichotomized for purposes of analysis.

Over fifty different indices of item discrimination have been developed and used in test construction. One difference among them pertains to their applicability to dichotomous or continuous measures. Among those applicable to dichotomous variables, moreover, some assume a continuous and normal distribution of the underlying trait on which the dichotomy has been artificially imposed; others assume a true dichotomy. Another difference concerns the relation of item difficulty to discrimination. Certain indices measure item discrimination independently of item difficulty. Others yield higher discrimination values for items close to the .50 difficulty level than for those at the extremes of difficulty.

Despite differences in procedure and assumptions, most item discrimination indices provide closely similar results (Oosterhof, 1976). Although the numerical values of the indices may differ, the items that are retained and those that are rejected on the basis of different discrimination indices are largely the same. In fact, the variation in item discrimination data from sample to sample is generally greater than that among different methods.

Use of Extreme Groups. A common practice in item analysis is to compare the proportion of cases that pass an item in contrasting criterion groups. When the criterion is measured along a continuous scale, as in the case of course grades, job ratings, output records, or total scores on the test, upper (U) and lower (L) criterion groups are selected from the extremes of the distribution. Obviously, the more extreme the groups the sharper will be the differentiation. But the use of very extreme groups, such as upper and lower 10%, would reduce the reliability of the results because of the small number of cases utilized. In a normal distribution, the optimum point at which these two conditions balance is reached with the upper and lower 27% (T. L. Kelley, 1939). When the distribution is flatter than the normal curve, the optimum percentage is slightly greater than 27 and approaches 33 (Cureton, 1957b). With small groups, as in an ordinary classroom, the sampling error of item statistics is so large that only rough results can be obtained. Under these conditions, therefore, we need not he too concerned about the exact percentage of cases in the two contrasted groups. Any convenient number between 25% and 33% will serve satisfactorily.

With the large and normally distributed samples employed in the development of standardized tests, it has been customary to work with the upper and lower 27% of the criterion distribution.

Simple Analysis with Small Groups. Because item analysis is frequently conducted with small groups, such as the students who have taken a classroom quiz, we shall consider first a simple procedure especially suitable for this situation. Let us suppose that in a class of 60 students we have chosen the 20 students (33%) with the highest and the 20 with the lowest test scores. We now have three groups of papers which we may call the Upper (U), Middle (M), and Lower (L) groups. First, we need to tally the correct responses to each item given by students in the three groups. This can be done most readily if we list the item numbers in one column and prepare three other columns headed U, M, and L. As we come to each student's paper, we simply place a tally next to each item he or she answered correctly. This is done for each of the 20 papers in the U group, then for each of the 20 in the M group, and finally for each of the 20 in the L group. We are now ready to count up the tallies and record totals for each group as shown in Table 7–1. For illustrative purposes, the first seven items have been entered. A rough index of the discriminative value of each item can be found by subtracting the number of persons answering it correctly in the L group from the number answering it correctly in the U group. These U – L differences are given in the last column of Table 7–1. A measure of item difficulty can be obtained with the same data by adding the number passing each item in all three criterion groups (U + M + L).

Examination of Table 7–1 reveals four questionable items that have been identified for further consideration or for class discussion. Two items, 2 and 7, have been singled out because one seems to be too easy, having been passed by 56 out of 60 students, and the other too difficult, having been passed by only 5. Items 4 and 5, while satisfactory with regard to difficulty level, show a negative and a zero discriminative value, respectively. We would also consider in this category any items with a very small positive U - L difference, of roughly three or less when groups of approximately this size are being compared. With larger groups, we would expect larger differences to occur by chance in a non-discriminating item.

Table 7–1

Simple Item Analysis Procedure: Number of Persons Giving Correct Response in Each Criterion Group

Item	U (20)	M (20)	L (20)	Difficulty (U + M + L)	Discrimination (U – L)
1	15	9	7	31	8
2	20	20	16	56[a]	4
3	19	18	9	46	10
4	10	11	16	37	–6[a]
5	11	13	11	35	0[a]
6	16	14	9	39	7
7	5	0	0	5[a]	5
•					
•					
•					
•					
75					

[a]Items chosen for discussion.

The purpose of item analysis in a teacher-made test is to identify deficiencies either in the test or in the teaching. Discussing questionable items with the class is often sufficient to diagnose the problem. If the wording of the item was at fault, the item can be revised or discarded in subsequent testing. Discussion may show, however, that the item was satisfactory, but the point being tested had not been properly understood. In that case, the topic may be reviewed and clarified. In narrowing down the source of the difficulty, it is often helpful to carry out a supplementary analysis, as shown in Table 7–2, with at least some of the items chosen for discussion. This tabulation gives the number of students in the U and L groups who chose each option in answering the particular items.

Although Item 2 has been included in Table 7–2, there is little more we can learn about it by tabulating the frequency of each wrong option, since only 4 persons in the L group and none in the U group chose wrong answers. Discussion of the item with the students, however, may help to determine whether the item as a whole was too easy and therefore of little intrinsic value, whether some defect in its construction served to give away the right answer, or whether it is a good item dealing with a point that happened to have been effectively taught and well remembered. In the first case, the item would probably be discarded, in the second it would be revised, and in the third it would be retained unchanged.

The data on Item 4 suggest that the third option had some unsuspected implications that led 9 of the better students to prefer it to the correct alternative. The point could easily be settled by asking those students to explain why they chose it. In Item 5, the fault seems to lie in the wording either of the stem or of the correct alternative, because the students who missed the item were uniformly distributed over the four wrong options. Item 7 is an unusually difficult one that was answered incorrectly by 15 of the U and all of the L group. The slight clustering of responses on incorrect option 3 suggests a superficial attractiveness of

Table 7–2

Response Analysis of Individual Items

Item	Group	Response Options				
		1	2	3	4	5
2	Upper	0	0	0	20	0
	Lower	2	0	1	16	1
4	Upper	0	10	9	0	1
	Lower	2	16	2	0	0
5	Upper	2	3	3	11	2
	Lower	1	3	3	11	2
7	Upper	5	3	5	4	3
	Lower	0	5	8	3	4
•						
•						
•						

Note: Correct options are in bold type.

this option, especially for the more easily misled L group. Similarly, the lack of choices of the correct response (option 1) by any of the L group suggests that this alternative was so worded that superficially, or to the uninformed, it seemed wrong. Both of these features, of course, are desiderata of good test items. Class discussion might show that Item 7 is a good item dealing with a point that few class members had actually learned.

The Index of Discrimination. If the numbers of persons passing each item in U and L criterion groups are expressed as percentages, the difference between these two percentages provides an index of item discrimination that can be interpreted independently of the size of the particular sample in which it was obtained. This index has been repeatedly described in the psychometric literature (see, e.g., Ebel, 1979; A. P. Johnson, 1951; Oosterhof, 1976) and has been variously designed as *U – L, ULI, ULD,* or simply D. Despite its simplicity, it has been shown to agree quite closely with other, more elaborate measures of item discrimination (Engelhart, 1965; Oosterhof, 1976). The computation of D can be illustrated by reference to the data previously reported in Table 7–1. First, the numbers of persons passing each item in the U and L groups are changed to percentages. The difference between the two percentages is the Index of Discrimination (*D*), shown in Table 7–3. This index can have any value between +100 and −100. If all members of the U group and none of the L group pass an item, *D* equals 100. Conversely, if all members of the L group and none of the U group pass it, *D* equals −100. If the percentages of both groups passing an item are equal, *D* will be zero.

As is true of several indices of item discrimination, the values of *D* are not independent of item difficulty but are biased in favor of intermediate difficulty levels. Table 7–4 shows the maximum possible value of *D* for items with different percentages of correct responses. If either 100% or 0% of the total sample pass an item, there can be no difference in percentage passing in U and L groups; hence *D* is zero. At the other extreme, if 50% pass an item, it would be possible for all the U cases and none of the L cases to pass it, thus yielding a *D* of 100 (100 – 0 = 100). If 70% pass, the maximum value that *D* could take can be illustrated as

Table 7–3

Computation of Index of Discrimination

Item	Percentage Passing		Index of Descrimination (*D*)
	Upper Group	*Lower Group*	
1	75	35	40
2	100	80	20
3	95	45	50
4	50	80	–30
5	55	55	0
6	80	45	35
7	25	0	25

Note: Data from Table 7–1.

Table 7-4

Relation of Maximum Value of *D* to Item Difficulty

Percentage Passing item	Maximum value of *D*
100	0
90	20
70	60
50	100
30	60
10	20
0	0

follows: (U) $\frac{50}{50} = 100\%$; (L) $\frac{20}{50} = 40\%$; D = 100 - 40 = 60. It will be recalled that, for most testing purposes, items closer to the 50% difficulty level are preferable. Hence, item discrimination indices that favor this difficulty level are often appropriate for item selection.

Phi Coefficient. Many indices of item discrimination report the relationship between item and criterion in the form of a correlation coefficient. One of these is the phi coefficient (ϕ). Computed from a fourfold table, ϕ is based on the proportions of cases passing and failing an item in U and L criterion groups. Like all correlation coefficients, it yields values between +1.00 and −1.00. The ϕ coefficient assumes a genuine dichotomy in both item response and criterion variable. Consequently, it is strictly applicable only to the dichotomous conditions under which it was obtained and cannot be generalized to any underlying relationship between the traits measured by item and criterion. Like the D index, ϕ is biased toward the middle difficulty levels—that is, it yields the highest possible correlations for dichotomies closest to a 50–50 split.

The significance level of a ϕ coefficient can be readily computed through the relation of ϕ to both chi square and the normal curve ratio. Applying the latter, we can identify the minimum value of ϕ that would reach statistical significance at the .05 or .01 levels with the following formulas:

$$\phi_{.05} = \frac{1.96}{\sqrt{N}}$$

$$\phi_{.01} = \frac{2.58}{\sqrt{N}}$$

In these formulas, N represents the total number of cases in both criterion groups combined. Thus, if there were 50 cases in U and 50 in L groups, N would be 100 and the minimum ϕ significant at the .05 level would be $1.96 \div \sqrt{100} = .196$. Any item whose ϕ reached or exceeded .196 would thus correlate with the criterion at the .05 level of significance.

Point-Biserial Correlation. As a final example of a commonly used measure of item discrimination, the biserial correlation may be considered. Typically, the biserial correlation coefficient is used when a test developer may desire a test with high level of internal consistency in which the items are reasonably homogenous. In a test where individual items are typically dichotomous in nature (right or wrong, yes or no) often scored 1 or 0, and total scores constitute a continuous variable, point- biserial correlation coefficient is computed. As a rule of thumb, the higher the point-biserial correlation between an individual item and the total score, the more useful is the item from the standpoint of internal consistency. Furthermore, the relevance of an individual dichotomous item is also determined by the extent to which scores on it are distributed between the two outcomes of 0 and 1. Although it may seem strange, it is possible to compute the standard deviation for dichotomous items. "If an individual item has a standard deviation of 0, then everyone obtains the same score (all right or all wrong). The closer the item approaches a 50-50 split of right and wrong scores, the greater is its standard deviation. In general, the greater the standard deviation of an item, the more useful is the item to the overall scale" (Gregory, 2015). By computing this correlation, the test developer will be able to determine the "outliers" and eliminate the items that have the lowest index. Items with the lowest index will have poor internal consistency or weak dispersion of scores and will therefore not solve the objective of measuring an attribute on a psychological test that differentiates between groups.

Item Response Theory (IRT): Basic Features.[2] The mathematical approach under consideration, item response theory, has also been designated latent trait theory and item characteristic curve (ICC) theory. A fundamental feature of this approach is that item performance is related to the estimated amount of the respondent's "latent trait," symbolized by the Greek letter θ (theta). As used in this context, a "latent trait" refers to a statistical construct; there is no implication that it is a psychological or physiological entity with an independent existence. In cognitive tests, the latent trait is generally called the ability measured by the test. Total score on the test is often taken as an initial estimate of that ability.

Item characteristic curves are plotted from mathematically derived functions, rather than from the empirical data used in item-test regression curves. Different IRT models utilize different mathematical functions, based on diverse sets of assumptions. Some models use normal give functions (i.e., cumulative normal distributions); others use logistic functions, which take advantage of some mathematically convenient properties of logarithmic relations. In general, the results obtained with the various models are substantially similar, provided their assumptions are met in the particular situations. Figure 7–1 shows item characteristic curves for three hypothetical items. The horizontal axis gives the ability scale (θ), estimated from total test score and other information available about test responses in a particular sample. The vertical axis gives $P_i(\theta)$, the probability of a correct response to Item i as a function of the person's position on the ability scale (θ). This probability is derived from data on the proportion of persons at different ability levels who passed the item.

---

[2] For a clear overview of IRT methodology and its applications, see Hambleton et al. (1991). More technical surveys and critical evaluations can be found in Hambleton (1989) and Drasgow and Hulin (1990). For the introduction of IRT into psychometrics, see Lord (1980), D. J. Weiss (1983), and D. J. Weiss and Davidson (1981).

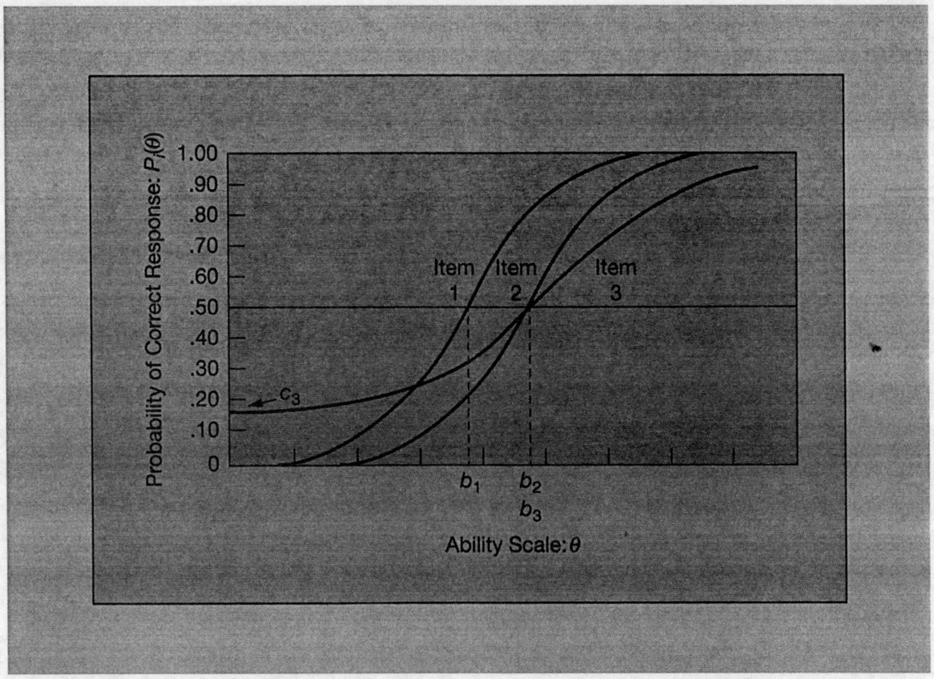

Figure 7–1. Hypothetical Item Characteristic Curves for Three Items

In the complete, three-parameter model, each ICC is described by three parameters derived mathematically from the empirical data. The item discrimination parameter (a_i) indicates the slope of the curve. It is inversely related to the distance one must travel along the ability continuum (θ) in order to increase $P_i(\theta)$.

The higher the value of a_i the steeper the slope. In Figure 7–1, Items 1 and 2 have the same a_i or discriminative value; Item 3 has a lower a_i, since its curve rises more slowly. The item difficulty parameter (b_i) corresponds to the location on the ability axis at which the probability of a correct response, $P_i(\theta)$, is 0.50. It will be seen that Items 2 and 3 have the same b_i while Item 1 is easier, requiring less ability for a 0.50 probability of correct response. IRT models designed to deal with multiple-choice items often include a third parameter, the so-called guessing parameter (c_i).[3] It represents the probability that a correct response occurs by chance. In a multiple-choice item, even examinees at very low ability levels have a higher than zero probability of giving a correct response. This is illustrated by Item 3 in Figure 7–1, whose lower asymptote is considerably above zero.

Estimates of both item parameters and ability are typically computed by iterative or successive-approximation procedures; the approximations are repeated until the values stabilize. In addition to yielding mathematically refined indices of item difficulty and item discrimination, IRT techniques provide several other benefits. An important feature of this approach is its treatment of reliability and error of measurement through *item information functions.* These functions, which are computed for each item, provide a sound basis for choosing items in test construction. The item information function takes all item parameters into account and shows the measurement efficiency of the item at different ability levels.

[3] Some investigators recommend that c_i be called simply a lower-asymptote or chance parameter for the ICC, because three-parameter models treat c_i as independent of ability, whereas guessing is a function of ability.

The most widely publicized contribution of IRT models pertains to the sample- free nature of their results, technically described as *invariance of item parameters.* It is a basic concept of IRT theory that item parameters should be invariant when computed in groups differing in ability. This means that a uniform scale of measurement can be provided for use in different groups. It also means that groups as well as individuals can be tested with a different set of items, appropriate to their ability levels, and their scores will be directly comparable. Each person's test score is based not only on the number but also on the preestablished difficulty levels, of items answered correctly.

When many different samples are to be tested, one procedure is to work with a large item pool or item bank that has been pre-calibrated on a large random sample. When the ability range is very wide, as in achievement test series overlapping many school grades, it is necessary to use common items (variously called anchor, linkage, or calibration items), in order to bridge the gaps across groups. Once the items in the pool are calibrated, any subset of items can be administered to any group or individual, and the resulting scores will be comparable.

Other IRT Models. In the preceding section, we examined a three-parameter model. Two-parameter models, which omit the chance-response parameter (c_i), are appropriate when the effects of guessing on test performance can be regarded as negligible. A one-parameter model, based only on the difficulty (b_i) of a set of items, was developed by Rasch (1966; see also Andersen, 1983) and has been adapted and strongly championed by some investigators (e.g., Wright, 1977; Wright & Stone, 1979). This model is based on the assumption that both guessing and item differences in discrimination are negligible. In constructing tests, the proponents of the Rasch model frequently discard those items that do not meet these assumptions. As discussed earlier, there are three basic models of IRT known as one, two, and three parameter models, depending on how many of the three variables are needed to describe the item characteristic curve (item difficulty, item discrimination, and the probability of getting the answer right with zero ability, i.e. the guessing effects are considered). Rasch demonstrated that as long as all the items had equal discrimination, it was possible to produce a single-item parameter that was independent of the respondents who used to pilot it, and of the other items included in the pilot. It generated a single statistic for each item which enabled that item to be used in a wide variety of different testing situations, regardless of other items which were included in the test and of the particular respondents involved. This approach is widely used in the calibration of item banks. Moreover, many ready-to-use test-developing platforms outside India such as Concerto and Tao Testing are based on the principles of Rasch-model (R-model) of IRT. It has been argued, too, that IRT models are quite "robust," in the statistical sense, meaning that various assumptions may be violated within limits, without distortion of results. This, of course, is a matter for empirical verification.

The models considered thus far assume *unidimensionality* of the test; that is, it is assumed that item responses can be attributed to a single trait. In general, the unidimensionality assumption can be adequately met if test performance depends on a single predominant trait, even though other traits may affect performance in minor ways. More general models, applicable to multidimensional tests, have also been designed, but the computational procedures are more laborious.

Still other variants have been developed to handle graded (rather than dichotomous or right–wrong) item responses (Samejima, 1969), or to analyze the different response options in multiple-choice items (Bock, 1972).

Current Status. The relative merits of alternative models of IRT are still widely debated. There is need for much more checking of mathematically derived values, not only with artificial data and computer simulation but also with live data. The invariance of item parameters needs especially to be widely investigated in realistic situations. For example, the same items may involve a different mix of abilities when performed by persons with different experiential backgrounds or by the same person at different stages of learning. From another angle, an impressive number and variety of computer programs are already available for IRT data (see, e.g., Hambleton, 1989, pp. 171–172); but the programs are in a constant state of flux through reevaluation, revisions, and replacements.[4]

While the theoretical and methodological diversities are being worked out, there is nevertheless an increasing use of IRT procedures in practical test development. The techniques of IRT are rapidly being incorporated in newly constructed tests and in revised editions of widely used test batteries developed by commercial test publishers. Examples include the California Achievement Tests and the Comprehensive Tests of Basic Skills, as well as the Differential Ability Scales described in chapter 8. IRT is particularly appropriate for certain newly emerging types of testing, such as computerized adaptive testing (CAT), discussed in chapter 10. In such testing, each test taker may respond to a different set of items, but all are scored on a uniform scale (Wainer et al., 1990). A major application of IRT is in the long-term project to develop a CAT version of the Armed Services Vocational Aptitude Battery (Wiskoff & Schratz, 1989).

Future of Item Response Theory (IRT) Models. With the advancements in computer programming, the programs for carrying out analyses for the Rasch one parameter, two parameter, and three parameter models have gained considerable momentum in the international market. The technique has proved to be particularly useful within the computerized testing, where the items to be presented can be chosen on the basis of the responses already given, enabling dependable results from the administration of 50% fewer items (Haladyna & Roid, 1983). Furthermore, the use of item response theory models have proved beneficial when one needs to compare the scores of respondents who have taken tests at different levels of difficulty (Rust & Golombok, 2009). This might apply, for instance, when an easy and a difficult version of the same examination system needs to be combined to generate a common set of marks. In a nutshell, IRT approaches have revolutionized the field of psychometrics, especially the domain of test construction and item-bank generation. However, this field is yet to find its importance in India. It is felt that introduction of courses on IRT model and training workshops at college and university levels will resolve this problem. There is a need to make practitioners more aware about the concepts and applications of such computer programs and languages.

[4] An outstanding current example is the ASCAL program for two-and three-parameter logistic IRT calibration, distributed by Assessment Systems Corporation (address in Appendix B). Also relevant is the recent development of a generalized linear item-response theory (GLIRT), from which different IRT models can be derived and which can accommodate different item formats (Mellenbergh, 1994).

ITEM BIAS

Item bias describes a situation where a bias exists within the individual items of a test. For instance, items developed in the US has money in dollars and cents would not be appropriate for use in India. Linguistic forms of item bias are the most common, especially where usage of English language is involved. Since English is a widely used language, some words, phrases or idioms used in tests may be more familiar and easy to comprehend by people who have English as a first language as opposed to those who have English as a second language. It is for this reason that when international tests are introduced in India, their items are first reviewed and corrected for item bias and only then, the adapted test versions are launched.

There are many ways to identify and eliminate item bias. The easiest way to check is to carry out an item analysis separately for the groups involved such as speakers of English as a first versus second language, graduates versus post graduates, etc. Once the comparison groups are identified, the item difficulty values of each item are compared between the groups in the item analysis. This can easily be achieved if the items are placed in the order of difficulty in one of the groups, so that the deviations can be recognized in the other. For example, items 1, 2, and 3 have item difficulty index of 0.80, 0.75, and 0.68, respectively, in group 1, whereas in group 2, the item difficulty index for these items may be 0.82, 0.45, and 0.65, respectively. From this, one can notice that item number 2 is distinctive or peculiar due to a large difference and it can be deleted or changed. It is unlikely that the items will have exactly the same difficulty index for the two groups and one can have a rough idea of what to expect. The larger the difference is in the difficulty index between the two groups, the more problematic it can become. A simple inspection like this often suffices. Furthermore, one can also carry out statistical tests to check for the existence of item bias. This can be achieved, for example, by conducting a two-way (group by item) analysis of variance with the difficulty value as the dependent variable, comparing the point-biserial correlation coefficients between the items and the total score for the two groups, by comparing factor analyses for the two groups (Rust & Golombok, 2009). There are many other approaches such as the chi-square approach (Scheuneman, 1980) and item characteristic curve approach. The underlying principle is that where an item is clearly biased, it should show up irrespective of the approach being used, since the various techniques mentioned above are more likely to disagree only in borderline cases. When eliminating biased items, pragmatic considerations are usually more important than issues of the exact statistical process being followed or not. It may be fair to say that one must use the easiest or the most straightforward approach, even where their conclusions may not be exact.

CROSS-VALIDATION

Meaning of Cross-Validation. It is essential that test validity be computed on a different sample of persons from that on which the items were selected. This independent determination of the validity of the entire test is known as cross-validation. Any validity coefficient computed on the same sample that was used for item-selection purposes will capitalize on random sampling errors within that particular sample and will consequently be spuriously high. In fact, a high validity coefficient could result under such circumstances even when the test has no validity at all in predicting the particular criterion.

Let us suppose that out of a sample of 100 medical students, the 30 with the highest and the 30 with the lowest medical school grades have been chosen to represent contrasted criterion groups. If, now, these two groups are compared in a number of traits actually irrelevant to success in medical school, certain chance differences will undoubtedly be found. Thus, there might be an excess of private-school graduates and of red-haired persons within the upper criterion group. If we were to assign each individual a score by crediting her or him with one point for private-school graduation and one point for red hair, the means of such scores would undoubtedly be higher in the upper than in the lower criterion group. This is not evidence for the validity of the predictors, however, since such a validation process is based on a circular argument. The two predictors were chosen in the first place on the basis of the chance variations that characterized this particular sample. And the *same* chance differences are operating to produce the mean differences in total score. When tested in another sample, however, the chance differences in frequency of private-school graduation and red hair are likely to disappear or be reversed. Consequently, the validity of the scores will collapse.

An Empirical Example. A classic demonstration of the need for cross-validation is provided by an early investigation conducted with the Rorschach inkblot test (Kurtz, 1948). In an attempt to determine whether the Rorschach could be of any help in selecting sales managers for life insurance agencies, this test was administered to 80 such managers. These managers had been carefully chosen from several hundred employed by eight life insurance companies, so as to represent an upper criterion group of 42 considered very satisfactory by their respective companies, and a lower criterion group of 38 considered unsatisfactory. The 80 test records were studied by a Rorschach expert, who selected a set of 32 signs, or response characteristics, occurring more frequently in one criterion group than in the other. Signs found more often in the upper criterion group were scored +1 if present and 0 if absent; those more common in the lower group were scored −1 or 0. Since there were 16 signs of each type, total scores could range theoretically from −16 to +16.

When the scoring key based on these 32 signs was reapplied to the original group of 80 persons, 79 of the 80 were correctly classified as being in the upper or lower group. The correlation between test score and criterion would thus have been close to 1.00. However, when the test was cross-validated on a second comparable sample of 41 managers, 21 in the upper and 20 in the lower group, the validity coefficient dropped to a negligible .02. It was thus apparent that the key developed in the first sample had no validity for selecting such personnel.

An Example with Chance Data. That the use of a single sample for item selection and test validation can produce a completely spurious validity coefficient under pure chance conditions was vividly demonstrated in a classic study by Cureton (1950). The criterion to be predicted was the grade-point average of each of 29 students registered in a psychology course. This criterion was dichotomized into grades of B or better and grades below B. The "items" consisted of 85 tags, numbered from 1 to 85 on one side. To obtain a test score for each student, the 85 tags were shaken in a container and dropped on the table. All tags that fell with numbered side up were recorded as indicating the presence of that particular item in the student's performance. A complete record for each student was thus obtained from 29 throws of the 85 tags, showing the presence or absence of each item or response sign in that student's performance. Because of the procedure followed in generating these chance scores, Cureton facetiously named the test the "B-Projective Psychokinesis Test."

An item analysis was then conducted, with each student's grade-point average as the criterion. On this basis, 24 "items" were selected out of the 85. Of these, 9 occurred more frequently among the students with an average grade of B or better and received a weight of +1; 15 occurred more frequently among the students with an average grade below B and received a weight of −1. The sum of these item weights constituted the total score for each student. Despite the known chance derivation of these "test scores," their correlation with the grade criterion in the original group of 29 students proved to be .82. Such a finding is similar to that obtained with the Rorschach scores in the previously cited study. In both instances, the apparent correspondence between test score and criterion resulted from the utilization of the same chance differences both in selecting items and in determining validity of total test scores.

Conditions Affecting Validity Shrinkage. The amount of shrinkage of a validity coefficient in cross-validation depends in part on the size of the original item pool and the proportion of items retained. When the number of original items is large and the proportion retained is small, there is more opportunity to capitalize on chance differences and thus obtain a spuriously high validity coefficient. Another condition affecting amount of shrinkage in cross-validation is size of sample. Since spuriously high validity in the initial sample results from an accumulation of sampling errors, smaller groups (which yield larger sampling errors) exhibit greater validity shrinkage.

If items are chosen on the basis of previously formulated hypotheses, derived from psychological theory or from past experience with the criterion, validity shrinkage in cross-validation will be minimized. For example, if a particular hypothesis required that the answer "Yes" be more frequent among successful students, then the item would *not* be retained if a significantly larger number of "Yes" answers were given by the *unsuccessful* students. The opposite, blindly empirical approach would be illustrated by assembling a miscellaneous set of questions with little regard to their relevance to the criterion behavior, and then retaining all items yielding significant positive or negative correlations with the criterion. Under the latter circumstances, we would expect much more shrinkage than under the former. A well-designed demonstration of the differences in validity shrinkage that actually occur when items are chosen by rational or by empirical strategies is provided by T. W. Mitchell and Klimoski (1986). In summary, shrinkage of test validity in cross-validation will be greatest when samples are small, the initial item pool is large, the proportion of items retained is small, and items are assembled without previously formulated rationale.

DIFFERENTIAL ITEM FUNCTIONING

Statistical Procedures. As one aspect of the investigation of test bias for minority groups, the analysis of "item bias" has received increasing attention. Such analysis is concerned essentially with the *relative difficulty* of individual test items for groups with dissimilar cultural or experiential backgrounds. In psychometric terminology, this area of item analysis is known as differential item functioning (DIF). It seeks to identify items for which equally able persons from different cultural groups have different probabilities of success. For this purpose, equal ability means equal with regard to the construct that the test is designed to assess, or the criterion behavior it is designed to predict. Many methods have been developed for identifying such differentially functioning items, including both statistical and judgmental procedures (Berk, 1982; Camilli & Shepard, 1994; Hambleton & Rogers, 1989; P. W. Holland & Thayer, 1988; P. W. Holland & Wainer, 1993; Osterlind, 1983; C. R. Reynolds & Brown, 1984).

A major problem is that demographic (or other experiential) group differences in item difficulty are closely associated with mean differences in performance level on the test as a whole. Consequently, items that have good discriminative value in terms of total score are likely to appear as "biased" items and be discarded. Several procedures have been employed to control for such differences in total score. With increasing access to computers, one of the most promising methods is based on item response theory (IRT). These procedures are especially appropriate when large samples are available. As shown earlier in this chapter, the item characteristic curves (ICC) for each item indicate the probability of correct response in relation to the ability scale for the test (Fig. 7–1). By comparing the ICC for the same item in any two groups, we can identify those items with substantial differential functioning relative to the overall test performance of the groups, which is expressed on a uniform scale. This comparison is illustrated by the two items in Figure 7–2. It can be seen that, for Item 1, the ICCs for Groups A and B are quite dissimilar, while for Item 2 they are closely similar. For each item, the area between the two ICCs may be used to identify the range of tested ability within which there is evidence of DIF. Once DIF items are identified, by whatever procedure is employed, the next step is to inquire into the nature and source of the difference. The answer to this question determines the disposition of the item. For this purpose, judgmental procedures may be needed, possibly in combination with further statistical analysis.

Judgmental Procedures. There is no single "best method" of item-bias analysis for all purposes. Because different methods provide somewhat different kinds of information, it is desirable to employ a combination of methods. The appropriate combination depends upon the anticipated uses of the test and upon the type of inferences to be drawn from the scores. Generally, the best combination includes some statistical and some judgmental procedures.

When properly applied, judgmental procedures can provide useful information not otherwise obtainable (Scheuneman, 1982; Tittle, 1982). Judgmental analysis is especially appropriate at the initial and final stages of test construction, to precede and follow statistical analyses. It is commonly introduced early in the development of a test to screen out content that is potentially offensive or

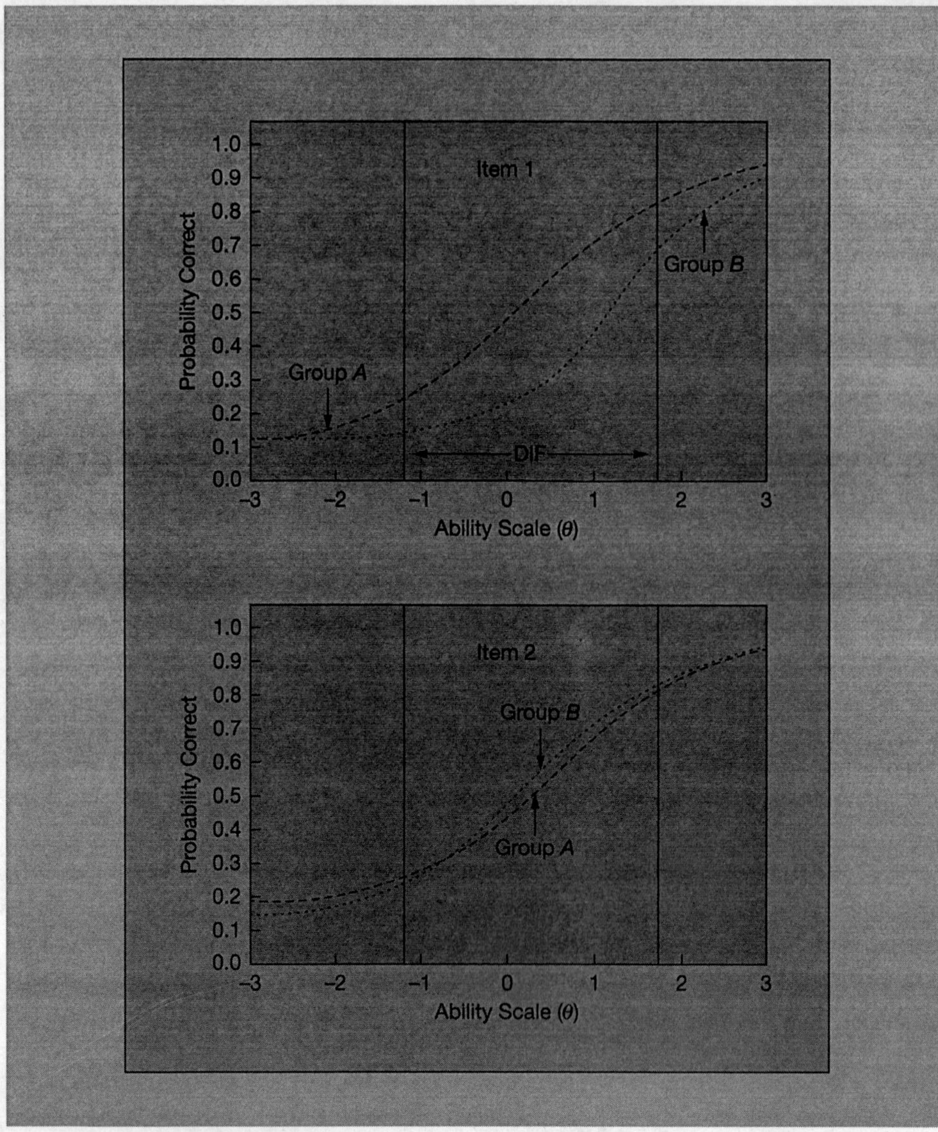

Figure 7-2. Item Characteristic Curves (ICC) for Two Items, Illustrating Large and Small Amounts of Differential Item Functioning (DIF).

(Graphs adapted from Pashley, 1992, by permission.)

demeaning to minorities, or content that perpetuates cultural stereotypes with regard to occupational or other societal roles. For this purpose, major test publishers regularly use preliminary item reviews by their own staff and by representative outside consultants (Berk, 1982, chap. 9). Such reviews also help to identify test content that may be culturally restricted and hence unfamiliar to particular populations of test takers. It should be noted, however, that judgmental reviews have *not* generally proved successful in predicting the relative difficulty or discriminative power of items for different populations (Plake, 1980; Sandoval & Miille, 1980; Scheune-man, 1982). Statistical analyses of empirical results are needed for this purpose.

On the other hand, not all deviant items identified by statistical procedures can be assumed to be biased. The results need to be interpreted through a second and different kind of judgmental review. At this stage, the items are examined for possible sources of deviancy. The statistical outliers do not usually reveal any common feature or any obvious reason for deviancy; each item needs to be considered individually. A few outliers may simply reflect statistical artifacts arising from the particular procedure. In other cases, the deviant performance may result from any of a wide variety of conditions that have different implications for test interpretation. The proper evaluation of such deviant items calls for familiarity with both the content domain of the test and the experiential differences among test-taker populations.

A possible reason for deviancy is that an item does not measure the same construct in different groups. For example, an analogies term may measure verbal reasoning in one group but vocabulary knowledge in another, because it contains a key word unfamiliar to many members of a particular minority. Similarly, an arithmetic problem may measure mathematical ability in one group but ability to understand complex verbal statements in another. In these two examples, the missing knowledge was not relevant to the construct measured by the test as a whole. Suppose, however, that mathematical items involving decimals are found to be relatively more difficult for members of a particular group. This difference is relevant to the construct of mathematical ability. Hence, such outliers are not, in this sense, biased items.

When deviant items are identified statistically, the source of the deviancy may be in part clarified through further statistical procedures, such as an analysis of wrong options chosen in a multiple-choice item. These supplementary analyses, in combination with judgmental reviews, should provide the basis for appropriate action. The deviant item may be discarded, revised as a whole, or altered in any flawed portion; the test instructions may be expanded or clarified; or the original item may be retained, after reconsideration in the light of the test specifications. The item analysis may even suggest a reevaluation of the test specifications themselves. The result could be either a change in the test specifications or a clarification regarding the particular inferences than can be drawn from the test scores.

A Notorious Case of Misuse of DIF. Considerable publicity was given to what was probably the first case considered by a court of law that was based primarily on item analysis in the evaluation of "test bias." This case became widely known as the "Golden Rule case," because it related to the use of a licensing examination in the hiring of employees by the Golden Rule Insurance Company. The similarity between the name of the company and the common use of the same two words in a very different sense probably added to the general confusion. The final settlement of the case was based on a comparison of group differences in sheer percentage of persons passing an item, with no effort to equate groups in any measure of the ability the test was designed to assess, nor any consideration of the validity of the items for the intended purpose of the test. The decision was clearly in complete violation of the concept of differential item functioning and would be likely to eliminate the very items that were the best predictors of job performance.

Because of its wide misunderstanding and its possible precedence-setting influence on both occupational and educational use of tests, the fallacy in the "Golden Rule" decision was examined from several angles in critical evaluations (e.g., Lim & Drasgow, 1990), including an official statement by the American Psychological Association.[5] The decision was also the subject of a symposium at an APA annual convention, most of whose papers were subsequently published in a special journal issue of *Educational and Psychological Measurement: Issues and Practices* (Bond, 1987; Faggen, 1987; Linn & Drasgow, 1987). A consideration of this notorious case highlights the potential practical hazards in efforts to assess "test bias" through superficial and incomplete indicators.

EXPLORATIONS IN ITEM DEVELOPMENT

In recent times, the awareness about adaptive or tailored testing has increased. In adaptive testing, the specific items administered to a test taker depend on the test taker's responses to previous items. Depending on the person's ability, items are automatically selected and administered. Item banks or pools for such adaptive tests are assembled by computer programs to follow one of the item response methodologies. The concept of online tests has gained momentum over the traditional testing procedure in India, especially in occupational setting. The administration of the test, it's scoring, and report generation are done online. Most of the test publishers have their own test taking platforms through which they can generate test links for the test takers who can take the test from anywhere in the world. And the reports of these tests are generated instantly. A lot of time and effort goes into the preparation of programs and logics by software developers and psychologists to make it extremely convenient for the end-user to administer a test and interpret its results. Moreover, the ability of the online test taking environment to simulate the physical test taking environment (proctored conditions) by detecting cheating and copying has made the computerized psychological tests even more lucrative for the respondents. However, prior to giving a test, the examiner must ensure that the candidate who is taking the test must be given a detailed set of instructions about the purpose of the test and expectations. Prior to giving the test, the examiner should help test takers to be prepared, motivated, and relatively free from stress and other disruptive conditions. This can be done either over an e-mail, a phone call, or a video-conferencing. While technology has made the development, administration, and interpretation of psychological tests a little less tedious and more scientific, the importance of human involvement in each of these aspects must not be overlooked. Technology serves as a support tool for individuals and must not be treated as a substitute for human interface and expertise.

[5] Prepared by the APA Committee on Psychological Tests and Assessment, the statement was approved by relevant APA Boards and by the Council of Representatives.

PART 3

Ability Testing

Chapter Eight

Individual Tests

In Part Two, we were concerned with the major principles of psychological testing. We are now ready to apply these principles to the evaluation of specific tests. We now know what questions to ask about each test and where to look for the answers. The test manuals and the *Mental Measurements Year books* are among the principal sources that may be consulted to obtain information regarding any of the tests cited.[1]

The purpose of the remaining parts of the book is twofold. One objective is to afford an opportunity to observe the application of testing principles to a wide variety of tests. Another is to acquaint the reader with a few outstanding tests in each of the major areas. No attempt will be made to provide a comprehensive survey of available tests within any area. Such a survey would be outside the scope of this book. Moreover, it would probably be outdated before publication, because of the rapidity with which new or revised tests appear. For these reasons, the discussion will concentrate on a few representative tests in each category, chosen either because of their widespread use or because they illustrate important developments in testing procedure. We consider ability testing in Part Three, personality testing in Part Four, and the applications of testing to a variety of contexts in Part Five. Unless otherwise indicated, all data about tests discussed in the text are taken from the test manual or technical supplements supplied by the test publishers. Readers who want to review a particular test themselves may consult a suggested outline for test

[1] The ten-volume *Test Critiques* series (Kyser & Sweetland, 1984–1994) provides another useful source of information and reviews on hundreds of tests.

evaluation in the *Study Guide* for this text (Urbina, 1997). The *Testing Standards* (AERA, APA, NCME, 1985) provide more detailed guidelines for this purpose.

Traditionally called "intelligence tests," the types of tests to be discussed in this and the next chapter are the direct descendants of the original Binet scales. Such tests are designed for use in a wide variety of situations and are validated against relatively broad criteria (see L. R. Aiken, 1996). They characteristically provide a single summary score, such as the traditional IQ, as an index of the examinee's general level of performance. Usually, they also yield scores on subtests or groups of subtests assessing more narrowly defined aptitudes. Because so many intelligence tests are validated against measures of academic achievement, they are often designated tests of scholastic aptitude or academic intelligence. Intelligence tests are frequently employed as preliminary screening instruments, to be followed by tests of special aptitudes. This practice is especially prevalent in the testing of normal adolescents or adults for educational and occupational counseling, personnel selection, and similar purposes. Another common use of general intelligence tests is to be found in clinical testing, especially in the identification and classification of mentally retarded persons. For clinical purposes, individually administered tests are generally employed. Among the most widely used individual (as contrasted to group) intelligence tests are the Stanford-Binet and Wechsler scales discussed in this chapter. Because the Stanford-Binet is the first test to be covered in this text, it is discussed more fully than are other tests throughout the book. This is done in order to illustrate at the outset the kinds of information to be considered in evaluating a test. It should be noted, however, that the discussions of particular tests throughout this book are not to be regarded as test reviews, such as are provided in sources like the *Mental Measurements Yearbooks*. For the purposes of this text, attention is usually focused on special contributions of a particular test or on the features that distinguish it from other tests.[2]

STANFORD-BINET INTELLIGENCE SCALE

Evolution of the Scales. The original Binet-Simon Scales, briefly described in chapter 2, were published in France in 1905, 1908, and 1911. Since then, it has been through a series of translations and adaptations. It is now in its fifth edition, which was released in 2003. (See Table 8–1)

Stanford-Binet Intelligence Scales, Fifth Edition (SB5): General Description. In the earlier editions of the Stanford-Binet scales, only a composite IQ score was obtained. Although the pattern of right and wrong answers could be analyzed qualitatively, the earlier versions of the test (prior to the fourth edition) did not provide a basis for quantitative analysis of the subcomponents of the entire scale. This shortcoming was corrected in the subsequent fourth and fifth edition.

The development of SB5 was guided by modern cognitive theories that see intelligence as a combination of five factors, namely fluid reasoning, knowledge, quantitative, visual-spatial, and working memory. Each of these five factors of intelligence can be assessed in two distinct categories – nonverbal and verbal – resulting in an instrument with 10 subtests (see Table 8–2).

---

[2] See Flanagan, Genshaft, and Harrison's (1997) edited volume on *Contemporary Intellectual Assessment* for an excellent overview of many of the topics discussed in Part Three of this text.

Table 8-1

Evolution of Stanford-Binet Intelligence Scale

Year	Test Name	Description
1905	Binet and Simon	Simple 30 item test. Clinically useful, but poorly standardized
1908	Binet and Simon	Longer than the 1905 version. Introduced a form of scoring with the concept of mental age. Still, poorly standardized.
1911	Binet and Simon	Version to include adults, but still a limited scale.
1916	Stanford-Binet (1st ed): Terman and Merrill	Introduction to the concept of IQ. Better standardization (*N* = 1,000 children and 400 adults). Emphasis upon verbal materials.
1937	Stanford-Binet (2nd ed): Terman and Merrill	First use of parallel forms – L&M. Better standardization; test contained 129 items.
1960	Stanford-Binet (3rd ed): Terman and Merrill	Parallel forms combined into a single form (L&M); modern item analysis methods deployed, extensive checks on item difficulty (*N* = 4,500 children). Still, more emphasis given on verbal items.
1972	Stanford-Binet (3rd ed): Terman and Merrill, Thorndike	Re-standardization of the Stanford-Binet (3rd Ed) on 2,100 subjects.
1986	Stanford-Binet (4th ed): Thorndike, Hagen, and Sattler	Complete restructuring of the test into 15 subtests; excellent standardization (*N* = 5,013 persons ages 0-2 to 11-23).
2003	Stanford-Binet (5th ed): Roid	Five factors of intelligence. Measures intelligence of ages 2 to 85+.

The SB5 provides a number of different perspectives on the intellectual and cognitive abilities of an individual: 10 subtest scores (mean of 10, SD of 3), three IQ scores (the Full Scale IQ, Verbal IQ, and Non-Verbal IQ), as well as five factor scores (fluid reasoning, knowledge, quantitative, visual-spatial, and working memory). The IQ and factor scores are normed to a mean of 100 and an SD of 15.

Routing Procedure. The Stanford-Binet Scale is one of the first examples of an adaptive test (Reckase, 1989), and the SB5 retains its historical tradition of adaptive testing by using a routing procedure to estimate the general cognitive ability of an individual before proceeding to the remainder of the test. The objective of the routing procedure is to identify the appropriate starting points for subsequent subtests. SB5 includes a nonverbal routing test in addition to vocabulary test, and it uses performance on these subtests to route to the nonverbal and verbal age scales. These routing items also provide the abbreviated IQ score, often used for screening purposes. The purpose of the routing procedure is two folds: a) it reduces the number of test items administered, and, therefore, it saves time; and b) it reduces the number of test items without the loss of measurement precision because it was constructed on the elements of item response theory.

Table 8-2

Organization of Stanford-Binet Intelligence Scale, Fifth Edition

Factors/ Domains	Fluid Reasoning	Knowledge	Quantitative Reasoning	Visual-Spatial Processing	Working Memory
Non-Verbal	Activities: Object Series or Matrices (Routing)	Activities: Procedural Knowledge (2–3) Picture Absurdities (4–6)	Activities: Quantitative Reasoning (2–6)	Activities: Form Board (1–2) Form Patterns (3–6)	Activities: Delayed Response (1) Block Span (2–6)
Verbal	Activities: Early Reasoning (2–3), Verbal Absurdities (4), Verbal Analogies (4)	Activities: Vocabulary (Routing)	Activities: Quantitative Reasoning (2–6)	Activities: Position and Direction (2–6)	Activities: Memory for Sentences (2–3) Last Word (4–6)

N.B: The numbers appearing along with activities are the levels of test item difficulty at which they appear (in item books 2 and 3). Please note that the levels don't refer to age. (Reference: *http://www.emporia.edu/~persingj/IQ20.htm)*

Administration and Scoring. The standard material to administer SB5 are designed like games with colorful artwork, toys, and manipulatives that engage the attention of children. Three easel-style booklets present items on one side of each page and examiner directions and scoring guidelines on the other. Each item has spoken directions that the examiners read in boldface type, along with other directions for using manipulative scoring guidelines and correct answers. Item Book 1 includes two subtests—Matrices and Vocabulary—that function as an Abbreviated Battery, producing a Brief IQ score that determines the starting point for the remaining subtests. Item Book 2 presents (in order of difficulty) nonverbal subtests, which are especially useful in assessing individuals with limited English proficiency, hearing impairments, learning disabilities, traumatic brain injury, and autism spectrum disorders. Item Book 3 presents verbal subtests (again in order of difficulty). So, examiners do not need a separate manual to read while arranging stimuli and manipulatives.

The test can be scored either manually or automatically via computer. The scoring program provides raw score conversion, an extended score report, a graphical report, and a brief narrative summary with interpretive guidelines and suggestions.

Standardization and Norms. The standardization consisted of 4,800 subjects in the age group 2 to above 85 years. Care was taken to assure that the sample was representative of the population census of the US in 2001. Bias reviews were conducted on all items for these variables: gender, ethnicity, cultural, religion, region, and socio-economic status. Additionally, the SB5 was co-normed with the Bender Visual Motor Gestalt Test (second edition) and linked to the Woodcock-Johnson Tests of Cognitive Abilities.

Reliability. Using the split-half method and correcting with the Spearman-Brown prediction formula, reliability coefficients were extremely high for the Full Scale Score (0.98). The Nonverbal IQ (0.95) and Verbal IQ (0.96) showed excellent stability, and the Abbreviated Battery (0.91) was also considered excellent as it contained only two subtests. Reliabilities for the Factor Indexes ranged from 0.90 to 0.92. For the ten subtests, reliabilities ranged from 0.84 to 0.89.

Validity. Extensive validity studies were conducted, including clinical-group differences, correlations with other tests, age trends, factor structure, and consequential validity. The first such studies explored the relationship between the fifth (SB5) and the fourth edition (SB: FE) and the Form L-M. There was a high correlation of 0.90 between the SB5 Full Scale and the SB: FE Composite Scale. The difference in the Full Scale Score of the SB5 and the one score of the Form L-M was found to be correlated, but not as great as predicted. Differences in scoring and nonverbal aspects of the tests were observed, as the Full Scale and Verbal Score correlations were high at 0.85 and 0.88, respectively. Comparisons were also made with other intelligence tests. The extensive validity studies revealed a high correlation between the composite IQ scores of the SB5 and the composite scores of previous SB edition and all of the major IQ batteries used for all populations. Many of these studies are presented in the Technical Manual and others in the Supplemental Interpretive Manual.

Other Technical Features. The SB5 provides an option of providing Change-Sensitive Scores (CSSs) that use modern item response theory scaling to convert the raw scores into criterion-referenced scores—anchored to age levels and the complexity of the items at each score level. These scores, as with norm-referenced scores, have excellent measurement properties. Because the CSSs measure absolute levels of ability across age, they provide a means to compare changes in an individual's scores over time. It enables the individuals to see the relatively small gains or losses in intellectual ability across time with students in special education. It helps to overcome the barriers associated with norm-referenced scores such as percentiles with students in special education. When normative scores such as percentiles are used alone instead of CSSs, changes across years are often hidden because the individual with special needs often lags behind peers and doesn't appear to improve with time.

In a nutshell, the SB5 is a very promising tool of measuring intelligence which is especially useful at both ends of the cognitive spectrum, allowing earlier identification of individuals with delays or cognitive difficulties and measuring gifted adolescents and adults. Due to this, it finds its wide applicability in the clinical, educational, and neuropsychological assessment. It helps to diagnose a wide variety of developmental disabilities and exceptionalities. Based on the care with which the instrument was constructed, SB5 is likely to be a mainstay of individual intelligence testing in myriad settings. In the Indian context, however, one needs to use this assessment with caution and tact as the Indian norm groups are not available yet.

THE WECHSLER SCALES

The intelligence scales developed by David Wechsler include several successive editions of three scales designed for adults, school-age children, and preschool children. Besides their use as measures of intelligence, the Wechsler scales have been investigated as a possible aid in psychiatric diagnosis. Beginning with the observation that brain damage, psychotic deterioration, and emotional difficulties may affect some intellectual functions more than others, Wechsler and other clinical psychologists argued that an analysis of an individual's relative performance on different subtests should reveal specific psychiatric disorders.

Evolution of the Wechsler Intelligence Scales. The first form of the Wechsler scales, also known as the Wechsler-Bellevue Intelligence Scale, was published in 1939. One of the primary objectives of its preparation was to provide an intelligence test suitable for adults. While presenting this scale for the first time, Wechsler (1939) pointed out that previously available intelligence tests had been designed primarily for school children and had been adapted for adult use by adding more difficult items of the same kind. Since then, it has been through a series of translations and adaptations (see Table 8–3).

Table 8–3

Evolution of Wechsler Intelligence Scales

Year	Authors/Test Name	Description
1939	Wechsler-Bellevue	Developed at Bellevue Hospital in New York with the objective of identifying psychotic and clinical disabilities. The test consisted of six verbal and five performance subtests.
1946	Wechsler-Bellevue II	Designed to be an equivalent and alternate form of the Wechsler-Bellevue. The major limitation of this test was that it never got adequately standardized.
1949	Wechsler Intelligence Scale for Children (WISC)	A downward extension of the Wechsler-Bellevue II, for children between the ages of 5 years and 15 years 11 months. Unfortunately, the standardization sample contained white population only.
1955	Wechsler Adult Intelligence Scale (WAIS)	A restandardization of the Wechsler-Bellevue scale with some item revisions, for adults aged 16 years and above.
1967	Wechsler Preschool and Primary Scale of Intelligence (WPPSI)	For children between the ages of 4 years and 6 years 6 months, the WPPSI was the first test to adequately sample racial minorities for the norms.
1974	Wechsler Intelligence Scale for Children-Revised (WISC-R)	A revision of the WISC, with updated items especially on Information, Vocabulary and Picture Completion. The new norms included black and other minorities in appropriate proportion. For children between the ages 6 years and 16 years 11 months.
1981	Wechsler Adult Intelligence Scale-Revised (WAIS-R)	Revised version of the WAIS, with 80 percent of the original items retained, norms updated, verbal and performance subtests alternated.
1989	Wechsler Preschool and Primary Scale of Intelligence-Revised (WPPSI-R)	Revised version of the first WPPSI scale with dated and biased items eliminated, for children between the ages 3 years and 7 years 3 months. Object Assembly was added and the norms updated.
1991	Wechsler Intelligence Scale for Children-III (WISC-III)	Revised and renormed version of the WISC-R.

(Countinued)

Table 8-3 (*Countinued*)

1997	Wechsler Adult Intelligence Scale-III (WAIS-III)	Revised and renormed version of the WAIS and the WAIS-R. Provided scores for Verbal IQ, Performance IQ, and Full Scale IQ, along with four secondary indices (Verbal Comprehension, Working Memory, Perceptual Organization, and Processing Speed).
1999	Wechsler Abbreviated Scale of Intelligence (WASI)	Designed to meet the demand for a quick, reliable measure of intelligence in clinical, educational, and research settings. Provides scores for Verbal IQ, Performance IQ, and Full Scale IQ.

The most recent editions of the Wechsler Intelligence scales are the WPPSI-IV, WISC-IV, and WAIS-IV. All these three scales possess some common features as discussed below:

- There are 13 to 15 subtests. The multiple subtests approach allows the evaluator to analyze intra-individual differences with respect to the different aspects of intelligence rather than just considering a single global score. Furthermore, it enables both the evaluator and the test taker to understand their strengths and development areas.
- All these recent editions have empirically broken down the test into composite scores and a full-scale IQ. The original Wechsler Intelligence Scales provided only two composite scores—Verbal IQ and Performance IQ—the revisions of which are progressing towards a more sophisticated partitioning into composite scores yielding from factor-analytic research. The WISC-IV and WAIS-IV provide the composite or index scores for four domains, namely Verbal Comprehension (VCI), Perceptual Reasoning (PRI), Working Memory (WMI), and Processing Speed (PSI). The WPPSI-IV provides all these scores along with one additional score on fluid reasoning.
- A common metric exists for IQ and Index Scores. The mean is 100 for IQ and Index Scores, and the standard deviation (SD) is 15 for all tests and age groups. The scaled scores on each subtest have a mean of 10 and an SD of approximately 3, which allows the evaluator and the test taker to analyze the sub-test scores to understand relative strengths and development areas.

For a better understanding, a closer look at the latest editions of Wechsler Intelligence Scale for Children (WISC) and Wechsler Adult Intelligence Scale (WAIS) is required.

Wechsler Intelligence Scale for Children-IV (WISC-IV). WISC-IV was developed in 2003 and was designed for children between the ages of 6 years and 16 years 11 months. It consists of 10 core and 5 subtests grouped into 4 index scores, namely VCI, PRI, WMI, and PSI. Recent research works (Sattler& Dumont, 2004; Wechsler, 2003) have indicated that speed, working memory, and attention are the optimal means of measuring intelligence; and hence, part of the rationale for the development of WISC-IV lies on this finding and is reflected in the Working Memory and Processing Speed indexes. Furthermore, these indexes help in diagnosing learning disabilities, attention disorders, and cognitive

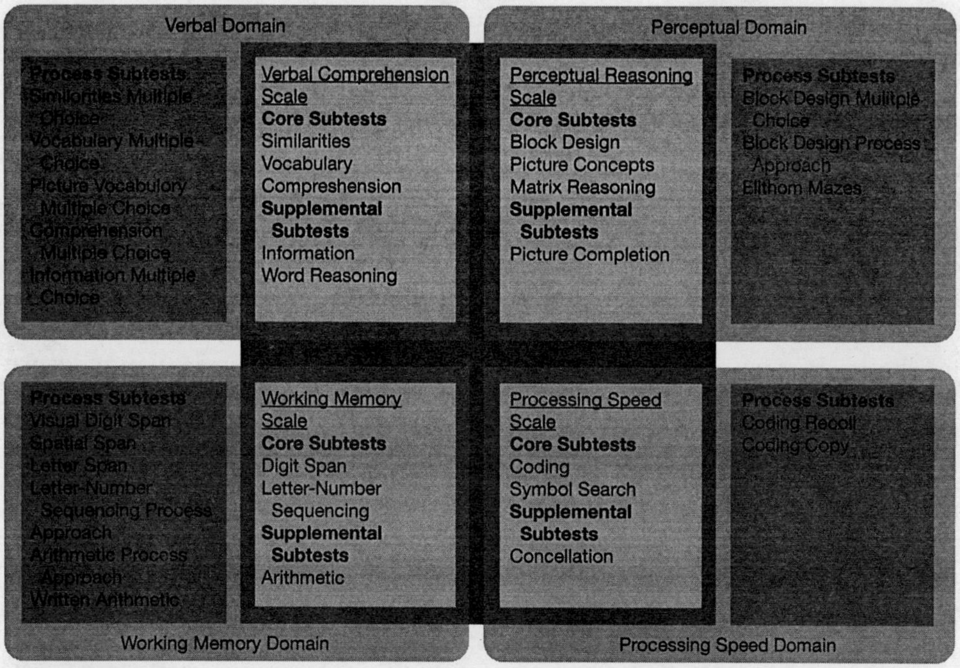

Figure 8-1. Test Composition of Wechsler Intelligence Scale for Children-IV (WISC-IV) (Reference: *https://www.pearsonclinical.ca/en/products/product-master.html/item-86*

impairments. The key feature of the WISC-IV is that it consists of downward extensions and revisions of subtests found on WISC-III and WAIS-III. (Please refer to Figure 8–1).

The standardization group consisted of 2,200 children who were stratified on the basis of age, gender, race, ethnicity, geographical region, and parental education. The sample closely paralleled the census data of the US from the year 2000. Internal consistency for the Full Scale and the Index Scores ranged from 0.79 to 0.89. To establish validity, an inter-correlation study was conducted on all subtests. It was found that all inter-subtest correlations were significant. The Verbal Comprehension scale correlated highly with each other and with the Arithmetic and Picture Completion subtests (Wechsler, 2004). The correlation is 0.87 between WISC-III VIQ and WISC-IV VCI . It is 0.74 between WISC-III PIQ and WISC-IV PRI. Various other studies were conducted to determine the validity of internal structure such as the factor analysis of subtests and test items, and confirmatory factor analysis for goodness of fit of items.

Wechsler Adult Intelligence Scale, Fourth Edition (WAIS-IV). WAIS-IV provides an individually administered test of intelligence for individuals between 16 and 90 years of age. It provides a composite of intellectual functioning using 15 separate subtests that are combined into four cognitive skill categories, including Verbal Comprehension (4 subtests), Perceptual Reasoning (5 subtests), Working Memory (3 subtests), and Processing Speed (3 subtests). The strength of these four cognitive skill categories was emphasized in several construct validity studies. For instance, a variety of confirmatory factor analyses are reported that compared the six different structural models, including the four hypothesized factors described above, a one-factor model, and several multifactor combinations. Results typically supported the four-factor model based on Verbal Comprehension, Perceptual Reasoning, Working Memory, and Processing Speed subscores. The total composite scale based on all subtests is interpreted as a measure of general intellectual ability. The 15 subtests are administered in a prescribed order, which requires a maximum of 2 hours of completion time for most examinees. Administration guidelines and discontinuation rules are stated clearly in the 258-page administration and scoring manual. Detailed scoring rules are provided as well. [3]

The WAIS-IV is the most recent version of the most frequently administered intelligence test for older adolescents and adults, to measure general intelligence by administrating numerous subtests, each of which is an indicator and estimator of intelligence. The WAIS-IV is a major and an important revision of its predecessor. For instance, in WAIS-IV, the earlier subtests of Object Assembly and Picture Arrangement, Digit Symbol-Incidental Learning, and Digit Symbol-Copy were dropped, thus, reducing the number of subtests with manipulative objects to one (Block Design). New subtests were added such as Visual Puzzles, Figure Weights, and Cancellation. Verbal IQ (VIQ) and Performance IQ (PIQ) are no longer provided with the WISC-IV. The current Verbal Comprehension Index (VCI) is similar to the notion of VIQ; however, from a psychometric standpoint, to measure verbal comprehension for adolescent and adult population VCI is a clear, more relevant, and direct method than VIQ. VCI is now the preferred index. Likewise, the Perceptual Reasoning Index (PRI) is similar to the former notion of PIQ. Yet, as a more refined measure of perceptual reasoning, PRI is the preferred index. To put it simply, VCI and PRI fit the factor analytic data better. The Working Memory Index (WMI) consists of subtests—Digit Span and Arithmetic—that are sensitive to attention and immediate memory. A low score on this index may suggest that the test taker may possess an attention or memory problem, especially with orally presented materials. The Processing Speed Index (PSI) comprises subtests—Symbol Search and Coding—that require the high speed process of visual information. It may help in detection of various neurological and neuropsychological conditions.

The standardization of the WAIS-IV was undertaken with great care and precision, and it was based on the data gathered by the US Bureau of the Census in 2005. The total sample of 2,200 adults (ages 16–91) was carefully stratified on the basis of demographic variables such as age, gender, race, ethnicity, geographical region, and education. The standardized sample was divided into 13 age bands: 16–17, 18–19, 20–24, 25–29, 30–34, 35–44, 45–54, 55–64, 65–69, 70–74, 75–79, 80–84, 85–90. Detailed information about the sampling and the standardization plan, including a wide variety of demographic variables at 13 age bands for the nationally representative sample, is included in the technical manual. These percentages closely match the national census data of the US. The Technical Manual also provides extensive validity and reliability data for individual subtests and

[3] Plake, B. S., & Impara, J. C., "The Fourteenth Mental Measurements yearbook," *Buros Institute of Mental Measurements* (2001), University of Nebraska-Lincoln (pp. 684–688); Retrived from http://www.ux1.eiu.edu/~cfglc/Adobe%20pdf/Publications-Papers/Canivez%20(2010)%20Buros%20MMY%20WAIS-IV%20Review.pdf on August 1, 2016.

composite scores across 13 age bands using coefficient alpha. Coefficients are good to excellent in all cases, ranging from the lower side of 0.80s to the upper side of 0.90s. Stability coefficients, using test-retest reliabilities, are presented for each subtest and composites for four different age bands. Coefficients are good to excellent in all cases, ranging from mid 0.70s to upper 0.80s. To arrive at a criterion-related validity, the WAIS-IV subscales and composites were correlated with a variety of other tests, including the WAIS-III, WISC-IV, and Brown Attention Deficit Disorder Test (Brown ADD). Correlations between the scores were in the 0.80 range with tests that measure similar constructs, providing convergent validity evidence. In contrast, WAIS-IV scores were negatively correlated with the Brown ADD scales, providing discriminant validity evidence. A complement of studies was also reported for special and gifted populations[4].

In summary, the WAIS-IV test is seen as one of the best measures of general intellectual functioning available. This test is ideally suited for high-stakes decision making related to assessment of intellectual ability, because it is a labor-intensive and expensive test to administer. It assesses four important dimensions of cognitive ability, including Verbal, Perceptual, Working Memory, and Processing Speed. Experts believe that each of these four dimensions is a strong correlate of learning, school achievement, and cognitive development.

The most recent editions of the Wechsler Intelligence scales that are adapted for India are Wechsler Adult Intelligence Scale–Fourth Edition, India (WAIS-IV INDIA), Wechsler Abbreviated Scale of Intelligence–Second Edition, India (WASI–II INDIA), and Wechsler Memory Scale–Third Edition, India (WMS-III INDIA). In the ensuing section, a closer look at the Indian version of the Wechsler Adult Intelligence Scale (WAIS) has been taken.

WAIS-IV INDIA. This is adapted and standardized for India in response to the shifting demographic and clinical landscape in the country. This was done in order to provide a comprehensive and advanced measure of cognitive ability in adolescents and adults. It provides subtests and composite scores that represent intellectual functioning in specific cognitive domains as well as composite scores that represent general intellectual ability (i.e., Full Scale IQ). WAIS-IV INDIA is the updated version of WAIS-III. Some of the advantages of WAIS-IV INDIA are: a) it is culturally adapted and includes the culturally appropriate test items; b) it identifies development needs by making the administration process more efficient, adding teaching items to ensure that the task is well understood, reducing the vocabulary level as per Indian English proficiency levels for verbatim instructions, and reducing emphasis on motor demands and timed performance, and providing enlarged visual stimuli; c) it has improved the psychometric properties for Indian population by providing Indian norms with enhanced clinical utility along with norms for older adults, improving floor and ceiling effects, providing expanded range for Full Scale IQ (FSIQ), improving reliability for subtest and composite scores, and reducing the item bias; d) it has updated structural foundations such as provision of Index Score Structure rather than Dual IQ scores, requirement of fewer subtests to generate Full Scale IQ score and four Index Scores (VCI, PRI, WMI, & PSI) along with a new measure of fluid intelligence

---

[4] *Ibid.*, p.190

(visual puzzles), enhanced measures of working memory (Revised Arithmetic and Digit Span to emphasize Working Memory), and improved measures of processing speed to reduce fine motor demands; and e) it is more user-friendly due to reduced testing time, revised instructions for clarity and consistency, redesigned record form, and increased portability.

To summarize, WAIS-IV India serves as a brilliant psycho-educational tool to obtain a comprehensive assessment of general cognitive functioning, learning difficulties, and giftedness. It tends to provide information for clinical and neuropsychological evaluation, thereby enabling the users to identify cognitive strengths and weaknesses in a variety of neurological conditions and accordingly prescribe treatment planning and placement decisions. Experts feel that WAIS-IV India is a highly reliable and valid tool for academic, educational, and research purposes as it keeps in mind the cultural nuances prevailing in India.

THE KAUFMAN SCALES

The Kaufman scales are individually administered clinical instruments designed for many uses for which tests such as the Stanford Binet and Wechsler Scales, were developed and have been traditionally employed (Kaufman & Kaufman, 1983a, 1983b, 1990, 1993). Developed in the 1980s and early 1990s, the Kaufman scales incorporate the recent advances in test construction. The Kaufman Assessment Battery for Children (K-ABC – Kaufman & Kaufman, 1983a, 1983b) and the Kaufman Adolescent and Adult Intelligence Test (KAIT – Kaufman and Kaufman, 1993), in particular, represent attempts on the part of their authors, both of whom were involved in the development of WISC-R. They sought to create instruments that, by design, would be anchored in evolving theories of intelligence, would include developmentally appropriate tasks, and would provide useful information for a variety of assessment situations.

Kaufman Assessment Battery for Children (KABC). The KABC was developed by A.S. Kaufman and N.L. Kaufman to assess the problem-solving abilities of 2.5–12.5 year-old children requiring Simultaneous Processing (seven subtests) and Sequential Mental Processing (three subtests). The Simultaneous Processing subtests require synthesis and organization of spatial and visuoperceptual content that can be surveyed as a whole. The Sequential Mental Processing subsets require serial or temporal arrangement, and they utilize verbal, numerical, and visuoperceptual content, as well as short-term memory. The battery also includes an Achievement Scale to measure acquired skills in reading and arithmetic. Based on extensive research in neuropsychology and cognitive psychology, the KABC was designed especially for preschool, minority, and exceptional children (Aiken & Groth-Marnat, 2006). In this assessment test, 13 of the 16 game like subtests can be administered in 35 to 85 minutes. The battery yields four global scores: Sequential Processing, Simultaneous Processing, Mental Processing Composite (combing the first two), and Achievement. Each of these is a standard score with a mean of 100 and an SD of 15.

Published in 2004, KABC-II, a revision of the KABC, is meant for children between ages 3 and 18 years (Kaufman & Kaufman, 2004). KABC-II is based on a dual theoretical foundation, using the Luria's neuropsychological model of simultaneous and successive reasoning process, and the Cattell-Horn-Carroll (CHC) model of fluid and crystallized abilities that help users to obtain the data required for each individual. Following Luria's model, the subtests comprise each of the four scales – Simultaneous Processing, Sequential Processing, Planning Ability, and Learning Ability – and require a total of 25 to 55 minutes administration time. The subtests comprising the five scales (Visual Processing, Short Term Memory, Fluid Reasoning, Long-Term Storage and Retrieval, and Crystallized Ability) of core battery, following the CHC model, take a total of 35 to 70 minutes. The overall composite scores obtained from the four to five scales are a Mental Processing Index and a Non-Verbal Index, following the Luria model, and a Fluid Crystallized Index and a Non-Verbal Index, following the CHC model. This dual theoretical model gives options to the user. With the KABC-II, one can choose the CHC model for children from a mainstream cultural and language background. If Crystallized Ability would not be a fair indicator of the child's cognitive ability, then the Luria model may be chosen that excludes verbal ability. Either of the approaches gives a global score that is highly valid and that shows small differences between ethnic groups. Moreover, a nonverbal option allows assessing a child whose verbal skills are significantly limited. In addition to these core subtests, a number of supplemental subtests can be administered for further exploration of hypotheses concerning a child's cognitive abilities.

Kaufman Adolescent and Adult Intelligence Test (KAIT). The KAIT (Kaufman & Kaufman, 1993) was designed as a measure of intelligence for individuals aged 11 to 85 years or older. It represents an attempt to integrate the theory of crystallized and fluid intelligence articulated by Horn and Cattell (1996). The battery is composed of a Crystallized Scale with subtests—Auditory Comprehension, Double Meanings and Definitions—that measure concepts acquired from schooling and acculturation, and a Fluid Scale with subtests—Rebus Learning, Mystery Codes, and Logical Steps—that tap the ability to solve new problems. An expanded battery, intended for use with individuals suspected of neurological damage, can also be employed by adding any of the four specified subtests, namely Memory for Block Designs, Famous Faces, Rebus Recall, and Auditory Recall. The KAIT test also includes a brief Mental Status test to assess the attention and orientation in test takers who are too cognitively impaired to take the full battery.

In terms of its technical qualities, KAIT appears to meet psychometric standards as well as many current generations of major intelligence scales. Its normative sampling is adequate, and the reliability and validity data reported in the technical manual appears promising. The battery is relatively easy to administer. Moreover, the manual includes information that is quite helpful in the administration and scoring of a test (e.g. what to do when someone responds in a language other than English).

Kaufman Brief Intelligence Test-Second Edition (KBIT-2). The KBIT-2 is a brief, individually administered measure of verbal and nonverbal intelligence that can be administered to test takers aged 4 to 90 years. Published in 2004, KBIT-2 is a revised version of the original Kaufman Brief Intelligence Test (KBIT) which was published in 1990.

It was designed as a quick screening instrument to estimate the level of intellectual functioning. Furthermore, it can be used in a variety of clinical, educational, vocational, and research settings. Some of the uses quoted for it are 'screening to identify high-risk children who require subsequent in-depth evaluation', 'testing adolescent or adult job applicants to facilitate hiring or placement decisions', and 'measuring the intelligence of groups for research purposes[5]'. Administration of KBIT-2 takes about 15 to 30 minutes. As it is relatively easy to administer KBIT-2 and since all items are scored objectively, the test may be administered by suitably trained technicians and professionals, including qualified teachers.

The test comprises three subtests, two verbal, and one nonverbal. The two verbal subtests—Verbal Knowledge and Riddles—measure verbal, school-related skills by assessing a person's word knowledge, range of general information, verbal concept formation, and reasoning ability. The nonverbal subtest matrices measure the person's ability to perceive relationships and complete visual analogies. Theoretically, the verbal subtests measure crystallized ability and the nonverbal subtests measure an amalgam of fluid reasoning and visual processing. Three global scores are obtained—verbal, nonverbal and the overall score, also called the IQ Composite. Age-based standard scores having a mean of 100 and an SD of 15 are provided for the verbal and nonverbal domains and the IQ Composite. The normative sample comprises 2,120 children and adults from the US. So far, neither any Indian sample has been used nor are there any Indian adaptation.

The manual provides a good range of information to support the construct and concurrent validity of the test. Through the studies, it is suggested that KBIT-2 verbal scores are valid measures of crystallized ability, nonverbal scores are a measure of fluid or visual abilities, and the IQ composite is a measure of general intelligence(g). The predictive validity of KBIT-2 has not been assessed and no factor-analytic studies have been conducted. Furthermore, there is good evidence that KBIT-2 is a reliable instrument when used with a US sample. Although no equivalency data is provided to show the US norms equate to an Indian sample, there is no evidence to suggest that this same pattern of reliability data would emerge in an Indian sample. Internal consistency was assessed by correlating split-halves based on Rasch calibration of item difficulties, and adjustment using the Spearman-Brown formula. Internal consistency reliability values reported for verbal (mean = 0.91, range = 0.86−0.96), nonverbal (mean = 0.88, range = 0.78−0.93), and IQ composite (mean = 0.93, range = 0.89−0.96) are excellent. Test-retest reliabilities and correlations for the verbal, nonverbal, and IQ composite scores were 0.80 or higher (means of 0.91, 0.83 and 0.90, respectively), with the single exception of the nonverbal score for children aged 4 to 12 years, where the correlation was 0.76.

In a nutshell, KBIT-2 is a potentially useful measure of intelligence that is quick and easy to administer. However, the absence of any local standardization suggests that its use in India is not to be recommended without the guidance of a professional, educational, clinical counselor, or practitioner. The lack of India

[5] Kaufman Brief Intelligence Test, Second Edition (KBIT-2), Test Review - Reviewers: Stephen Fisher & Kari Carstairs. The British Psychological Society. Psychological Testing Centre. *http://ptc.bps.org.uk/test-registration-test-reviews/search-test-reviews*

standardization goes beyond the provision of norms and extends to the items used in the test itself, several of which are culturally specific to the US.

Two other noteworthy intelligence tests designed by Alan Kaufman and Nadeen Kaufman are the Kaufman Test of Educational Achievement (KTEA-II) and Kaufman Survey of Early Academic and Language Skills (K-SEALS).

DIFFERENTIAL ABILITY SCALES

The Differential Ability Scales (DAS) by C.D. Elliot (1990a, 1990b) is a revision and extension of the British Ability Scales (BAS) developed in Great Britain in the 1970s (Elliott, Murray, & Pearson, 1979). The uniqueness of DAS is that the terms "intelligence" and "IQ" are not part of the DAS vocabulary (Elliott, 1990a, p.vi). Rather, the organization, scoring, and interpretation of the scale focus on the precisely defined behaviors that are actually being assessed. This is mentioned in the preface to the DAS handbook. Such an explicit statement, appearing for the first time in the handbook of a general ability scale, should help to dispel the stereotypes and misconceptions associated with the popular use of such terms.

DAS was primarily designed to measure specific abilities with adequate reliability, so as to aid the achieving of more complex goals of individual assessment, namely differential diagnosis and treatment planning. The choice of tasks included in the battery was guided by a theoretical as well as an empirical rationale. The theoretical underpinning is eclectic and flexible. It uses a hierarchical approach to mental abilities that can accommodate different levels of generality and provide a broad base of information from which hypotheses about individual test takers can be derived. This structure is quite compatible with empirical findings about the development of cognitive abilities.

The latest edition–Differential Ability Scales, Second Edition (DAS-II)–comes out of a vision to provide the psychologist with an insight into how a child processes information to devise appropriate interventions and/or recommendations for the classroom and at home. It is a comprehensive, individually administered, clinical instrument for assessing the cognitive abilities that are important for learning. The test may be administered to children aged 2 years 6 months (2:6) through 17 years 11 months (17:11). DAS-II provides a composite score reflecting conceptual and reasoning abilities, cluster scores measuring more specific ability areas (verbal comprehension, nonverbal, and spatial reasoning), and individual subtest scores representing a range of diverse abilities. The subtests are grouped into the Early Years and School-Age cognitive batteries with subtests that are common to both batteries and those that are unique to each battery. The Early Years core battery contains subtests for two age levels: children aged 2:6 through 3:5 take four core subtests to obtain the General Conceptual Ability (GCA) score, and children aged 3:6 through 6:11 take six core subtests which contribute to the GCA composite score. The School-Age core battery contains subtests to assess children aged 7:0 through 17:11.

These 20 subtests measure a variety of cognitive abilities including verbal and visual working memory, immediate and delayed recall, visual recognition and matching, processing and naming speed, phonological processing, and understanding of basic number concepts. These subtests involve tasks and activities that are appropriate to the developmental level of every child.

Subtests include Copying, Early Number Concepts, Matching Letter-like Forms, Matrices, Naming Vocabulary, Pattern Construction, Phonological Processing, Picture Similarities, Rapid Naming, Recall of Designs, Recall of Digits, Recall of Objects, Recall of Sequential Order, Recognition of Pictures, Sequential and Quantitative Reasoning, Verbal Similarities, Speed of Information Processing, Verbal Comprehension, and Word Definitions. Seventeen subtests have been retained from the original DAS, though the majority of these subtests now contain new or revised items. The Block Building subtest has been combined with the Pattern Construction subtest, and the Matrices subtest now contains a set of new or revised items for young children. Four new subtests have been added namely Recall of Sequential Order, Rapid Naming, Phonological Processing, and Recall of Digits-Backward.

Through these subtests, DAS-II helps in identifying people who may have speech or language impairments, or who may be deaf or hard-of-hearing. It allows for quick administration and engaging materials that make it appealing especially to young children. Users may find the scoring procedures to be tedious; however, the computerized scoring assistant tends to help with this issue. Overall, DAS-II may provide a user-friendly, time-efficient measure of general cognitive ability that proves useful in the context of a full psycho-educational battery of assessment measures.

DAS-NAGLIERI COGNITIVE ASSESSMENT SYSTEM

Das-Naglieri Cognitive Assessment System (CAS) (Naglieri & Das, 1997) is based on the Planning, Attention, Simultaneous, and Successive (PASS) model of intelligence proposed by its authors. In turn, the model is grounded in the theory of cognition and brain organization espoused by the Russian neuropsychologist, A.R. Luria. Its most recent edition, the Cognitive Assessment System, Second Edition (CAS2), was designed to measure cognitive processing abilities important for a broad range of differential diagnoses and instructional planning in individuals aged 5:0 through 18:11. It provides practitioners with a valid and reliable tool to evaluate children's strengths and weaknesses in important areas of cognitive processing.

The CAS2 Extended Battery has three subtests in each of the four PASS scales – Planned Codes, Planned Connections, and Planned Number Matching (Planning Scale); Expressive Attention, Number Detection, and Receptive Attention (Attention Scale); Matrices, Verbal-Spatial Relations, Figure Memory (Simultaneous processing Scale); and Word Series, Sentence Repetition (ages 5-7) or Sentence Questions (ages 8-18), and Visual Digit Span (Successive processing Scale). The Core Battery includes two subtests from each of the four PASS scales. Each PASS scale as well as the CAS2 Full Scale yields a standard score with a mean of 100 and an SD of 15. Furthermore, it yields five supplemental composite scores: Executive Function without Working Memory, Executive Function with Working Memory, Working Memory, Verbal Content, and Nonverbal Content. A visual versus auditory comparison is also provided.

The standardization sample was a representative group of 2,200 children and adolescents aged 5:0 through 17:11 years. A stratified random sampling plan was used to obtain a sample that closely matched the US population. Extensive reliability and validity information is reported in the Interpretive Handbook or Technical Manual that accompanies the test. Full Scale reliability is 0.96 with the PASS Scale reliabilities ranging from 0.83 to 0.93. Details on various validity studies that establish construct, concurrent, predictive, and discriminant validity are available in the Interpretive Handbook. For example, validity studies with special populations (including people who are mentally retarded those who have learning disabilities, or are gifted, have attention deficits, or traumatic brain injuries) indicate the differences in PASS Scales' performance for these groups, thereby supporting the discriminant validity of CAS2. Furthermore, validity evidence reported in the Interpretive and Technical Manual demonstrates the test's value for assessment of diverse groups of children.

It is noteworthy that the results may be particularly helpful when assessing special populations. The Interpretive Handbook contains additional resources for users, such as implications for intervention based on the test results, descriptions of several research-based instructional programs directly linked to PASS theory, and an illustrative report presenting a written interpretation of CAS2 results. In a nutshell, it may be fair to say that this test will become an important, as well as an innovative tool for the assessment of cognitive status.

OTHER TESTS

There are several indigenous intelligent tests that one can use for a variety of purposes. One could refer to the catalog available in the National Library of Educational and Psychological Tests (NLEPT), located in the Department of Educational Psychology and Foundations of Education, NCERT, New Delhi. Most of these tests can be purchased from Prasad Psycho Corporation, New Delhi. Also, the well-established foreign tests, that were discussed in this chapter, are also readily available online on their respective test publishers' and test distributors' websites.

Chapter Nine

Tests for Special Populations

The tests discussed in this chapter include both individual and group scales. They were developed primarily for use with persons who cannot be properly or adequately examined with traditional instruments, such as the individual scales described in the preceding chapter or the typical group tests to be considered in the next chapter. Historically, the kinds of tests surveyed in this chapter were designated as performance, nonlanguage, or nonverbal tests.

Performance tests, on the whole, involve the manipulation of objects, with a minimal use of paper and pencil. *Nonlanguage tests* require no language on the part of either the examiner or examinee. The instructions for these tests can be given by demonstration, gesture, and pantomime, without the use of oral or written language. A prototype of nonlanguage group tests was the Army Examination Beta, which was developed for testing foreign-speaking and illiterate recruits during World War I (Yerkes, 1921). Revisions of this test were subsequently prepared for civilian use. For most testing purposes, it is not necessary to eliminate all language from the test administration, since test takers usually have some knowledge of a common language. Moreover, short, simple instructions can usually be translated or given successively in two languages without appreciably altering the nature or difficulty of the test. None of these tests, however, requires the test takers themselves to use either written or spoken language.

Still another related category is that of *nonverbal tests,* more properly designated as nonreading tests. Most tests for primary school and preschool children fall into this category, as do tests for illiterates and nonreaders at any age level. While requiring no reading or writing, these tests make extensive use of oral instructions and communication on the part of the examiner. Moreover, they frequently measure verbal comprehension—such as vocabulary recognition and the understanding of sentences and short paragraphs—through the use of pictorial items which are supplemented with and accompanied by oral instructions. Unlike the nonlanguage tests, they would thus be unsuited for individuals who have hearing impairments or who do not speak English.

Although the traditional distinctions between performance, nonlanguage, and nonverbal tests contribute to an understanding of the purposes that different tests may serve, these distinctions have become somewhat blurred as more and more test batteries have been developed that cut across these three categories. The combination of verbal and performance tests in the Wechsler scales is a classic example.

In the present chapter, tests have been classified, not in terms of their content or administrative procedures, but with reference to their principal uses. Four major categories can be recognized from this viewpoint: tests for the infant and preschool level; tests employed for a comprehensive assessment of mentally retarded persons; tests for persons with diverse sensory and motor handicaps; and tests designed for use across cultures or subcultures. Such a classification schema must remain flexible, however, since several of the tests have proved useful in more than one context. This is especially true of some of the instruments originally designed for cross-cultural testing, which are now more commonly used in clinical examinations.[1]

Finally, although some of the tests covered in this chapter were designed as group tests, they are frequently administered individually. A few are widely used in clinical testing to supplement the usual type of intelligence tests and thus provide a fuller picture of the individual's intellectual functioning. Several permit the kind of qualitative observations associated with individual testing and may require considerable clinical sophistication to make a detailed interpretation of test performance possible. On the whole, they are closer to the individual tests illustrated in chapter 8 than to the group tests surveyed in chapter 10.

INFANT AND PRESCHOOL TESTING

All tests designed for infants and preschool children require individual administration. Some kindergarten children can be tested in small groups with the types of tests constructed for the primary grades. In general, however, group tests are not applicable until the child has reached school age. Most tests for children below the age of six are either performance or oral tests. A few involve rudimentary manipulation of paper and pencil.

It is customary to subdivide the first five years of life into the infant period and the preschool period. The first extends from birth to the age of approximately 18 months; the second from 18 to 60 months. From the viewpoint of test administration, it should be noted that the infant must be tested while lying down, supported on a person's lap, or otherwise held, as illustrated later in this

---

[1] For further information, evaluation, and references pertaining to many of the types of tests illustrated in this chapter, see Sattler (1988, chaps. 12, 14, and 15).

chapter. Speech is of little use in giving test instructions, although the child's own language development provides relevant data. Many of the tests deal with sensorimotor development, as demonstrated by the infant's ability to lift her or his head, turn over, reach for and grasp objects, and follow a moving object with the eyes. The preschool child, on the other hand, can walk, sit at a table, use her or his hands in manipulating test objects, and communicate by language. At the preschool level, the child is also much more responsive to the examiner as a person, whereas for the infant the examiner serves primarily as a means of providing stimulus objects. Preschool testing is a more highly interpersonal process—a feature that augments both the opportunities and the difficulties presented by the test situation.

The proper psychological examination of young children requires coverage of a broad spectrum of behavior, including social and emotional traits as well as motor, language, and other cognitive abilities. In addition, there has been an increasing recognition of the need to take into account the nature of the child's environment in the assessment of children (Vazquez Nuttall, Romero, & Kalesnik, 1992). This ecological orientation is reflected in some of the instruments discussed in this chapter. Typical scales, designed for infancy and early childhood and representing a diversity of approaches, are considered in this section. The Wechsler Preschool and Primary Scale of Intelligence Revised also belongs in this category but was covered in chapter 8 in order to maintain the continuity of the Wechsler series. The Stanford-Binet, Kaufman Assessment Battery for Children, and Differential Ability Scales, all of which were discussed in chapter 8, are utilized in the assessment of preschool children as well, since they encompass the 2- to 6-year-old period in addition to older ages.

Historical Background of Infant and Preschool Testing. One of the earliest systematic attempts to understand the development of normal infants and preschoolers was made in a series of longitudinal studies by Arnold Gesell and his associates at Yale (Ames, 1989). These studies, which spanned a total of four decades, led to the preparation of the Gesell Developmental Schedules which, when first published (Gesell et al., 1940), represented a pioneering attempt to provide a systematic, empirically based method of assessing the behavior development of young children. Most of the data for the schedules are obtained through the direct observation of the child's responses to standard toys and other stimulus objects and are supplemented by information provided by the parent or principal caretaker. Over the years, the Gesell schedules were used widely by psychologists and pediatricians in both research and practice and, as revised and updated by other investigators, they are still used by some to supplement medical examinations, especially for the identification of neurological defects and organically caused behavioral abnormalities in early life.[2] Although the schedules have been superseded by newer, more psychometrically sophisticated instruments in most clinical settings, the items and procedures pioneered by Gesell and his associates have been incorporated into most other developmental scales designed for the infant level.

---

[2] For the most recent manual for the revised version of the original Gesell schedules, see Knobloch, Stevens, and Malone (1980). There are several other tests that have used the name of Gesell in their title, but none of them cover the period of infancy. (See TIP-IV for a list of those that are currently available and the 9th MMY for reviews of some of them).

The decades of the 1960s to the 1990s witnessed an upsurge of interest in tests for infants and preschool children. One early contributing factor for this increased interest was the rapid expansion of educational programs for mentally retarded children; another was the widespread development of preschool programs of compensatory education for culturally disadvantaged children. More recently, there have been a series of legislative mandates aimed at the early identification and remediation of all types of physical and mental disabilities in both preschoolers and infants. Several of these laws (e.g., P.L. 99–457) are amendments or extensions of the Education for All Handicapped Children Act (P.L. 94–142), which is discussed in more detail later in this chapter. At any rate, in order to meet these pressing practical needs, new tests and publications have appeared at a very fast pace, and considerable research has been conducted on innovative approaches to assessment.[3]

STANDARDISED TESTS OF EARLY CHILDHOOD DEVELOPMENT

Bayley Scales of Infant Development. The Bayley Scales of Infant and Toddler Development, Third Edition (Bayley-III; Bayley, 2006) measures cognitive, language, motor, social-emotional, and adaptive development. It is a revision of its predecessor, the Bayley Scales of Infant Development, Second Edition (BSID-II; Bayley, 1993). The Bayley-III examines all the facets of a young child's development. It is meant for children within the age range of 1 to 42 months. With this tool, it is possible to obtain detailed information, even from non-verbal children, about their ways of functioning.

It consists of five scales. The first three scales, that is, the Cognitive Scale, the Language Scale, and the Motor Scale, are administered by the clinician. The other two scales, the Social-Emotional Scale and the Adaptive Behavior Scale (from the Social-Emotional and Adaptive Behavior Questionnaire), are completed by the parents or the primary caregiver.

The Cognitive Scale has 91 items and it assesses play skills, information processing (attention to novelty, habituation, memory, and problem-solving), counting, and number skills. It does not contain separate subtests. The Language Scale has 48 items, and it contains receptive and expressive language subtests to assess communication skills including language and gestures. The Motor Scale has 138 items and yields separate scores on Fine Motor, Gross Motor along with a composite Motor Scale. The Social-Emotional Scale consists of 35 items and assesses emotional and social functioning as well as sensory processing. It does not contain separate subtests. The Adaptive Behavior Scale assesses the attainment of practical skills – "communication, community use, health and safety, leisure, self-care, self-direction, functional, pre-academics, home living, social and motor (Gregory, 2015)" – necessary for a child to function independently and meet the environmental demands. This scale provides separate scores for each of these practical skills along with a composite score on general adaptive behavior.

[3] A brief but informative history of preschool assessment can be found in M. F. Kelley and Surbeck (1991). For other relevant material on infant and preschool testing see Aylward (1994), Bracken (1991b), Culbertson and Willis (1993), Kamphaus (1993), C. R. Reynolds and Kamphaus (1990a), and Vazquez Nutall, Romero, and Kalesnik (1992).

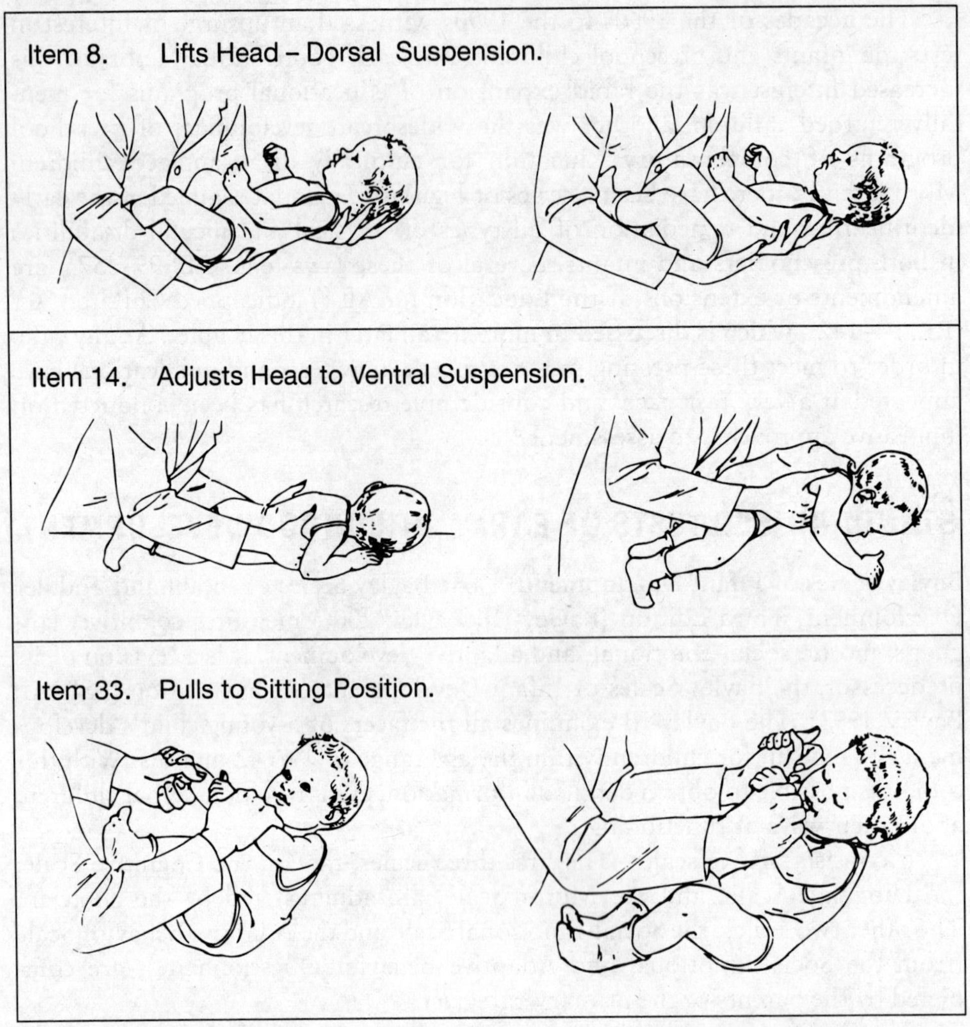

Figure 9–1. Infant Testing as Illustrated in the Manual for the Bayley Scales of Infant Development—Second Edition.

(Adapted from Bayley, 1993, pp. 143, 145, and 150. Copyright © 1993 by The Psychological Corporation. Reproduced by permission.)

According to the technical manual, because of the nature of the test and the chances of its results getting misused, Bayley-III may only be administered by trained professionals who have experience in the administration and interpretation of comprehensive developmental assessments and should have completed some formal graduation or professional training in administering and interpreting such assessments. This assessment must not be used to diagnose a specific disorder in any one area.

McCarthy Scales of Children's Abilities. At the preschool level, a well-constructed instrument is the McCarthy Scales of Children's Abilities (MSCA—McCarthy, 1972), suitable for children between the ages of 2½ and 8½ years. It consists of 18 tests, giving the examiner multiple opportunities to observe the child's approach to a variety of problems and stimuli. The tests are grouped into six overlapping scales: Verbal, Perceptual-Performance, Quantitative, General Cognitive, Memory, and Motor. The General Cognitive score, based on 15 of the 18 tests in the battery, comes closest to the traditional global measure of intellectual development. This General Cognitive Index (GCI) is a normalized standard score, reported in the same units as traditional IQs (with a mean of 100 and an SD of 16) and found within each 3-month age group. In the development of the MSCA, the term IQ was deliberately avoided because of its many misleading connotations. The GCI is described as an index of the child's functioning at the time of testing, with no implications of immutability or etiology. Scores on the 5 additional scales are based on the same age groups and have a mean of 50 and an SD of 10.

Over two decades of extensive research with the McCarthy scales have accumulated since this instrument, designed to be uniquely suited to the cognitive assessment of young children, was published. Of particular use are the many studies conducted with children of ethnic minorities and detailed by Valencia (1990), as well as the wealth of validity data summarized by him and by Bracken (1991a). With regard to the clinical use of the McCarthy scales, the guide prepared by Kaufman and Kaufman (1977) is still an indispensable aid. The prevailing view among the many reviewers is that despite some weaknesses, these scales are both effective and useful. The psychometric properties of the scales are adequate for the most part, especially for the middle range of their target population.

Piagetian Scales. Although applicable well beyond the preschool level, the scales modeled on the developmental theories of Jean Piaget have thus far found their major applications in early childhood. All such scales are in an experimental form; few are commercially available. Most have been developed for use in the authors' own research programs, although some of these scales are available to other research workers. The major contribution of Piagetian scales to the psychological testing of children consists in their ability to provide both a theoretical framework that focuses on developmental sequences in thinking processes and an assessment procedure characterized by flexibility and qualitative interpretation.

Some of the features of Piagetian scales, with special reference to normative interpretation of performance, were discussed in chapter 3. Basically, Piagetian scales are ordinal in the sense that they presuppose a uniform sequence of development through successive stages. These stages, spanning the period from infancy to adolescence and beyond, are designated as the sensorimotor, the preoperational, the concrete operational, and the formal operational stages. The scales also follow a "criterion-referenced" approach, insofar as they provide qualitative descriptions of what the child is actually able to do. Piagetian tasks focus on the long-term development of specific concepts or cognitive schemata[4] rather than on broad traits. With regard to administration, the major object of Piagetian

[4] "Schemata" is the plural of "schema," a term commonly encountered in Piagetian writings and signifying essentially a framework into which the individual fits incoming sensory data.

scales is to elicit the child's explanation for an observed event and the reasons that underlie her or his explanation. Scoring is characteristically based on the quality of the responses to a relatively small number of problem situations presented to the child rather than on the number or difficulty of successfully completed items. For this purpose, the child's misconceptions revealed by the incorrect responses are of primary interest. The examiner concentrates more on the process of problem solving than on the product.

Because of its highly individualized procedures, Piagetian testing is well suited for clinical work. It has also attracted the attention of educators because it permits the integration of testing and teaching. Its most frequent use, however, is still in research on developmental psychology. The tests themselves can be classified into two categories: (1) ordinal scales for infancy; and (2) tasks designed to assess the attainment of the preoperational, concrete operational, and formal operational stages. Several examples of each exist and their use in a variety of research contexts has been recently reviewed by D. Sexton, Kelley, and Surbeck (1990). One test of each type, selected partly because of availability, is described below.

The Ordinal Scales of Psychological Development were prepared by Uzgiris and Hunt (1975) and are also known as the Infant Psychological Development Scales. They are designed to assess the acquisition of cognitive competencies between the ages of 2 weeks and 2 years. These ages encompass approximately what Piaget characterized as the sensorimotor period and within which he recognized six levels. In order to increase the sensitivity of their instruments, Uzgiris and Hunt classified the responses into more than six levels, the number varying from 7 to 14 in the different scales. The series includes six scales, designated as follows:

1. *Object Permanence*—the child's emerging notion of independently existing objects is indicated by the visual following of an object and by her or his searching for an object after it is hidden with increasing degrees of concealment.
2. *Development of Means for achieving desired environmental ends*—the child uses her or his own hands and other means, such as strings, stick, support, etc., in reaching for objects.
3. *Imitation*—including both gestural and vocal imitation.
4. *Operational Causality*—the child recognizes and adapts to objective causality, as shown by responses ranging from visually observing her or his own hands to eliciting desired behavior from a human agent and activating a mechanical toy.
5. *Object Relations in Space*—the child coordinates schemata of looking and listening to localize objects in space and understands such relations as container, equilibrium, gravity.
6. *Development of Schemata for relating to objects*—the child responds to objects by looking, feeling, manipulating, dropping, throwing, etc., and by socially instigated schemata appropriate to particular objects (e.g., "driving" a toy car, building with blocks, wearing beads, naming objects).

No norms are provided, but the authors collected data on the psychometric properties of their scales by administering them to 84 infants who were the children of graduate students and of staff members at the University of Illinois. Both observer agreement and test-retest agreement after a 48–hour interval are reported. In general, the tests appear quite satisfactory in both respects. Indices of ordinality, computed for each scale from the scores of the same 84 children, are also reported as highly satisfactory.[5]

Although the Ordinal Scales developed by Užgiris and Hunt were meant to be only provisional, they have been used extensively for research purposes.[6] The scales were originally designed to measure the effects of specific environmental conditions on the rate and course of development in infants. Studies of infants reared under different conditions and of infants participating in intervention programs have thus far indicated significant effects of these environmental variables on the mean age at which children attain different steps in the developmental scales. These and other studies describing the use of the Ordinal Scales for mapping cognitive development in both normal and exceptional infants are reviewed in a book edited by the authors of the scales (Užgiris & Hunt, 1987). The sequence of acquisitions traced by the scales pertain primarily to the infant's interactions with inanimate objects, interactions which, in turn, are seen as precursors to the development of communicative behavior and other adaptive skills (Dunst & Gallagher, 1983; Kahn, 1987).

The second example of a Piagetian instrument to be discussed is the Concept Assessment Kit—Conservation (CAK), a test distributed by a regular test publishing company on the same basis as other psychological tests. Designed for children aged from 4 to 7 years, it provides a measure of one of the best-known Piagetian concepts. Conservation refers to the child's realization that such properties of objects as weight, volume, and number remain unchanged when the objects undergo transformations in shape, position, form, or other attributes. The authors (Goldschmid & Bentler, 1968b) focused on conservation as an indicator of the child's transition from the preoperational to the concrete operational stage of thinking, which Piaget places roughly at the age of 7 or 8 years.

Throughout the test, the procedure is essentially the same. The child is shown two identical objects; then the examiner makes certain transformations in one of them and interrogates the child about their similarity or difference. After answering, the child is asked to explain her or his answer. In each item, one point is scored for the correct judgment of equivalence and one point for an acceptable explanation. For example, the examiner begins with two standard glasses containing equal amounts of water (continuous quantity) or grains of corn (discontinuous quantity) and pours the contents into a flat dish or into several small glasses. In another task, the examiner shows the child two equal balls of Playdoh and then flattens one into a pancake and asks whether the ball is as heavy as the pancake.

---

[5] Procedures for the measurement of ordinality and the application of scalogram analysis to Piagetian scales are controversial, a fact that should be borne in mind in interpreting any reported indices of ordinality (see F. H. Hooper, 1973; A, C. Rosenthal, 1985).

[6] The potential value of the scales in clinical assessment is also widely recognized; one significant step toward realizing this potential was the publication of a manual and scoring forms specifically designed for the clinical and educational use of the scales (Dunst, 1980).

Three forms of the test are available. Forms A and B are parallel, each providing six conservation tasks: Two-Dimensional Space, Number, Substance, Continuous Quantity, Discontinuous Quantity, and Weight. The correlation between the scores on these two forms is .95. Form C includes two different tasks—Area and Length—and correlates .76 and .74 with Forms A and B, respectively.

Norms were established on a standardization sample of 560 boys and girls between the ages of 4 and 8, obtained from schools, day-care centers, and Head Start centers in the area of Los Angeles, California. These norms must be regarded as tentative in view of the small number of cases in each age group and because of the limitations in representativeness of the sample. Mean scores for each age group show a systematic rise with age, with a sharp rise between 6 and 8 years, as anticipated from Piagetian theory.

The authors carried out various statistical analyses to assess: scorer reliability; Kuder-Richardson, parallel-form, and retest reliability; scalability, or ordinality; and factorial composition (see also Goldschmid & Bender, 1968a). Although based on rather small samples, the results indicate generally satisfactory reliability and good evidence of ordinality and of the presence of a large common factor of conservation throughout the tasks.

Comparative studies in seven countries suggest that the test is applicable in widely diverse cultures, yielding high reliabilities and showing approximately similar age trends (Goldschmid et al., 1973). Differences among cultures and subcultures, however, have been found in the mean ages at which concepts are acquired—i.e., the age curves may be displaced horizontally by one or two years (see also Figurelli & Keller, 1972; Wasik & Wasik, 1971). Training in conservation tasks has been found to improve scores significantly (see also Goldschmid, 1968; B. J. Zimmerman & Rosenthal, 1974a, 1974b). The manual cites suggestive data about the construct validity of the test, as does a recent study by F. A. Campbell and Ramey (1990).

Evaluation of the Piagetian Approach. There is still controversy, on both theoretical and empirical grounds, regarding the Piagetian approach to cognitive development (see, e.g., Inhelder, de Caprona, & Cornu-Wells, 1987; Liben, 1983; Sugarman, 1987). There are questions about the implications of training effects and about whether or not cross-cultural differences affect the interpretation of Piagetian developmental stages. A major obstacle encountered in identifying stages through ordinal scales is what Piagetian researchers call "*decalage*,"[7] or inconsistencies in the anticipated sequences. There is a growing body of data that casts doubt on the implied continuities and regularities of intellectual development. Too often the stage corresponding to a given individual's performance varies with the task, not only when different processes are required for its solution, but also when the same process is applied to different contents (Dasen, 1977; Goodnow, 1976; Horn, 1976; J. McV. Hunt, 1976).

It should also be noted that Piagetian scales have been found to correlate substantially with standardized intelligence tests (Gottfried & Brody, 1975; Kaufman, 1971; M. E. Sexton, 1987) and to correlate about as much with school

7 Literally, an "unwedging" of the theoretically expected response pattern.

achievement of first-grade children as did a group intelligence test (Kaufman & Kaufman, 1972). Such overlap has been strongly corroborated by independent investigators with different instruments (Humphreys, Rich, & Davey, 1985). What these findings suggest is that despite pronounced differences in methodology, Piagetian scales, standardized intelligence tests, and school achievement measures have much in common. In addition, they each contribute unique and valuable elements to the overall assessment of children. The Piagetian scales are more difficult to administer and much more time consuming but, especially when integrated with norm- and domain-referenced measures, they yield a much richer picture of what the child can do and how he or she does it (D. Sexton et al., 1990).

Current research on the mental activities of young children is progressing apace. The empirical findings both revise and expand the early Piagetian concepts (see, e.g., Butterworth, Harris, Leslie, & Wellman, 1991; Whiten, 1991). In fact, there now exist a number of innovative approaches, collectively labelled as "neo-Piagetian," that address issues regarding cognitive development from a perspective influenced to different degrees by Piaget's theory and by the point of view of information processing (Beilin & Pufall, 1992; Demetriou, 1988). In the realm of assessment, some neo-Piagetian investigators are combining various dynamic approaches and using mediated learning in a formalized manner to try to evaluate mental capacity with minimal reliance on an individual's previous knowledge base (Pascual-Leone & Ijaz, 1991). These techniques, which are still quite experimental, aim to be applicable to children as young as two or three years old as well as to individuals from various cultural, social, and linguistic backgrounds.

CURRENT TRENDS IN INFANT AND EARLY CHILDHOOD ASSESSMENT

Historically, the validity of intelligence tests has been linked primarily to the criteria of age differentiation and correlations with academic performance. For infants, adequate progress has been gauged almost exclusively by comparing their results to same-age norms on the wide range of tasks included in developmental scales such as Bayley's. Recent societal efforts at early identification and remediation of deficits, however, require that tools which are designed to assess cognitive functioning in infants have predictive power. Thus, in spite of the difficulties posed by trying to track the developmental changes in intellectual competence at various age levels, there have been renewed attempts to generate instruments and procedures that will prove to be of sufficient predictive value for practical use.

One of the more intriguing new approaches consists of measures of information processing skills, such as the Fagan Test of Infant Intelligence or FTII (Fagan, 1992; Fagan & Detterman, 1992). This approach is based on the well-established finding of infants' preference for novelty, which makes the study of their ability to abstract and retain information possible. The Fagan Test, designed to differentiate normal children from those with cognitive deficits, assesses selective visual attention to novelty in 3 to 12 month-old infants. The stimuli are pictures of faces and the score is based on the amount of time devoted to novel, as opposed to familiar pictures. Figure 9–2 shows the portable stage version of this

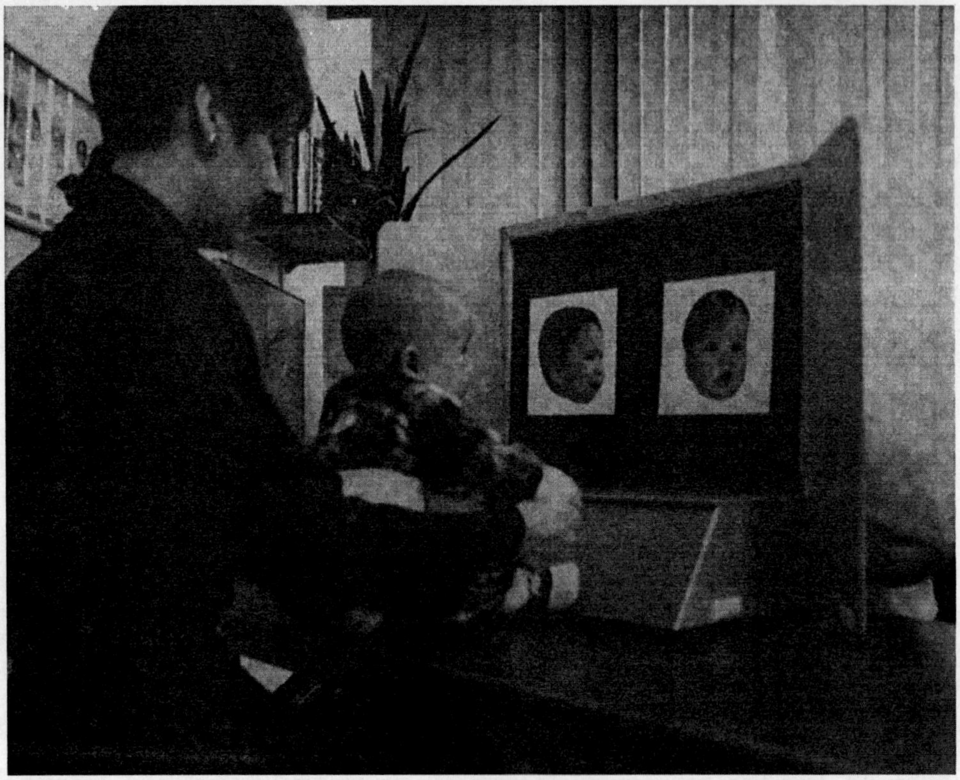

Figure 9-2. Portable Stage Version of the Fagan Test of Infant Intelligence.
(From Fagan & Detterman, 1992, p. 189. Copyright © 1992 by Ablex Publishing. Reproduced by permission.)

instrument which has been found to predict performance on intelligence tests. Correlations between Fagan test scores and IQ at the age of 3 years range from mid 0.40 to approximately 0.60. In contrast, one of the studies (Tasbihsazan, Nettelbeck, Kirby, 2003) indicated poor correlation between Fagan test scores and IQ, thereby suggesting that FTII may not be a sound instrument to measure intelligence. Therefore, it may be fair to say that FTII may be used as a screening tool rather than be treated as a general predictor of intelligence among children. However, the validation studies are scant for FTII and more research data needs to be gathered before the traditional measures of infant intelligence are disregarded in favor of the FTII and the likes.

There is also increasing recognition of the fact that, in order for interventions to be effective, the assessment of young children has to be comprehensive as well as accurate and valid. Reliance on a single global score, whether it is called an IQ or a developmental index, is inadequate for most practical purposes. Such scores may serve to classify children into categories, but they do not inform their users about the strengths and weaknesses of the child. Individualized assessment of infants and children, as well as of older persons, needs to include multiple methods and multiple sources of information across pertinent domains, such as language, motor, and social skills. In response to these requirements, new systems for assessment are being developed, involving procedures and professionals from various disciplines.

The Infant-Toddler Developmental Assessment (IDA), which is based on the work done by a multidisciplinary group of early childhood specialists (Provence,

Erikson, Vater, & Palmeri, 1995a, 1995b, 1995c), exemplifies this trend. The IDA is essentially a framework that guides the team process of identifying children, from birth to 3 years, who are at risk of developmental delays. Materials provided with the IDA facilitate the gathering, recording, interpretation, and synthesis of data from referral through to the development of a plan. The procedures include parental involvement through each phase, a health review, and a developmental assessment based on observation and interviews with parents and other caregivers. The portion of the IDA that most resembles traditional measures of infant development is the Provence Birth to Three Developmental Profile. Although the profile uses standard administration and scoring procedures in assessing eight developmental domains and sequences, its scores are age-referenced in terms of well-documented developmental milestones rather than through standard scores, percentile ranks, or other within-group comparisons. In this regard Sally Provence, the pediatrician who authored the profile, followed the tradition established by Gesell in his developmental schedules. The effectiveness of the IDA, like that of any other tool, is obviously linked to the training and experience of the professionals who use it and needs to be evaluated further through both research and clinical use. Nevertheless, it and other systems like it have been designed to meet the criticisms levelled against the practice of excessive reliance on intelligence tests (see, e.g., Goodman, 1990) and, if properly implemented, could prove to be of great practical value. It should be noted that use of the IDA does not preclude the administration of traditional measures of cognitive functioning or any other instruments for those purposes, such as gauging a child's relative standing among her or his age peers, where they might be needed.

Besides the move toward more comprehensive and integrated assessment, two other trends that are having significant impact on the testing of young children, and in the testing of most of the other special populations discussed in this chapter, should be mentioned. The first is the influence of the ecological perspective in the assessment process, a perspective that calls for taking into account the various aspects of the child's environment.[8] The second concerns an increased emphasis on the link between assessment and intervention, which has long been recognized in clinical work, where diagnosis is inextricably tied to treatment. The need to produce prescriptive guidelines for teachers, based on the individual's unique profile of abilities and disabilities, is now seen as essential in the context of early intervention and education as well (Bagnato & Neisworth, 1991; Witt, Elliott, Gresham, & Kramer, 1988).

COMPREHENSIVE ASSESSMENT OF MENTALLY RETARDED[9] PERSONS

The testing of children with either mental or physical disabilities underwent a conspicuous spurt of growth in the United States following the passage of the Education for All Handicapped Children Act of 1975 (P.L. 94–142)—now amended to be referred to as the Individuals with Disabilities Education Act

[8] The assessment of environments is discussed in a later section of this chapter.

[9] Nowadays most commonly used words for mentally retarded is mentally challenged or mentally disabled to increase sensitization and remove the taboo around people suffering from this condition.

(IDEA)—and related statutes.[10] The implementation of this legislation requires four basic procedures: (1) all children with disabilities must be identified through preliminary screening instruments; (2) the children thus identified are to be evaluated by a team of specialists to determine each child's educational needs; (3) the school must develop an individualized educational program to meet these needs; and (4) each child is to be reevaluated periodically in the course of the program. Tests suitable for use in educational programs that meet the requirements of the law are discussed in several portions of this book, including chapters 8 and 17, as well as in this and the two adjoining sections of the present chapter (also see Jacobson & Mulick, 1996).

In its manual on definition and classification, the American Association on Mental Retardation (AAMR, 1992) states that "mental retardation refers to substantial limitations in present functioning. It is characterized by significantly subaverage intellectual functioning, existing concurrently with related limitations in two or more of the following applicable adaptive skill areas: communication, self-care, home living, social skills, community use, self-direction, health and safety, functional academics, leisure, and work" (p. 1). The manual also stipulates that the condition is manifested before the age of 18. This definition does not differ substantially from the previous one (Grossman, 1983, p. 11). However, the associated system of classification has changed dramatically to accommodate the view that mental retardation is not a trait but a disability that stems from the interaction between the limitations of an individual and the demands of the environment. Whereas the previous system specified levels of mental retardation from mild to profound, based on intelligence test performance, the current one classifies the intensities of supports needed by the individual across four dimensions (intellectual functioning and adaptive skills, psychological/emotional considerations, physical health/etiology considerations, and environmental considerations). The definition of the intensities of supports, along with examples, are listed in Table 9–1.[11]

The current definition reaffirms the notion that intellectual limitation is a necessary but not a sufficient condition for mental retardation. In order for the latter to exist, intellectual limitation must have an impact on adaptive or coping skills. The threshold level of intelligence test performance used to demarcate mental retardation is a score of 70 to 75 on a scale with a mean of 100 and an *SD* of 15, or *approximately* 2 or more standard deviations below the mean; this allows for error of measurement and accentuates the fact that there are no sharp dividing lines between the "mentally retarded" and the "normal." The elimination of the levels of retardation and the increased emphasis on adaptive skills and environmental considerations are aimed at focusing on the unique pattern of strengths and weaknesses present in an individual and on the possibility of growth. The AAMR's revisions have proved to be somewhat controversial. Some critics have charged that the new specifications are imprecise, cannot be assessed reliably, and will increase the proportion of the population eligible for special services in

---

[10] The major ones of these are P.L. 99–457 and P.L. 101–476, passed in 1986 and 1990, respectively. For discussions of the implications of federal legislation and court cases on the testing and assessment of children, see Ayers, Day, and Rotatori (1990), DeMers, Fiorello, and Langer (1992). M. P. Kelly and Melton (1993), and Sattler (1988, pp. 767–784).

[11] The American Psychiatric Association's current *Diagnostic and Statistical Manual of Mental Disorders* (DSM–IV—1994) still specifies four degrees of severity of mental retardation based on levels of IQ, namely, Mild, Moderate, Severe, and Profound.

Table 9-1

Definition and Examples of Intensities of Supports

Intermittent
Supports on an "as needed basis."Characterized by episodic nature, person not always needing the support(s), or short-term supports needed during life-span transitions (e.g., job loss or an acute medical crisis). Intermittent supports may be high or low intensity when provided.

Limited
An intensity of supports characterized by consistency over time, time-limited but not of an intermittent nature, may require fewer staff members and less cost than more intense levels of support(e.g., time-limited employement training or transitional supports during the school-to-adult period).

Extensive
Supports characterized by regular involvement(e.g., daily) in at least environments(such as work or home) and not time-limited(e.g., long-term support and long-term home living support).

Pervasive
Supports characterized by their constancy, high intensity; provided across environment; potential ;life-sustaining nature. Pervasive supports typically involve more staff members and intrusiveness than do extensive or time-limited supports.

(From AAMR, 1992, p. 26. Copyright © 1992 by the American Association on Mental Retardation. Reproduced by permission.)

the schools (Gresham, MacMillan, & Siperstein, 1995; MacMillan, Gresham, & Siperstein, 1993; Matson, 1995). Others contend that these objections lack empirical grounding (Reiss, 1994). In any case, both the manner in which evaluations are conducted as well as the results of the evaluations themselves are likely to change as a result of the adoption of different standards; however, it is probably too soon to assess the full effects of the revisions.

Besides individual tests of intelligence, such as those described in chapter 8, assessment programs for mentally retarded persons typically include measures of adaptive behavior in everyday life situations.[12] The prototype of scales designed to assess adaptive behavior is the Vineland Social Maturity Scale, developed in the 1930s by the director of the Vineland Training School, Edgar Doll (1935/1965). As a result of his observations of the differences among mentally retarded patients, Doll created a standardized record form designed to assess an individual's developmental level both in looking after her or his practical needs and in taking responsibility in daily living. Its latest revision, the Vineland Adaptive Behavior Scales (VABS—P. L. Harrison, 1985; Sparrow, Balia, & Cicchetti, 1984a, 1984b), is available in three versions, which may be used independently or in combination. Two of the scales are Interview Editions, whereby information is obtained through a semistructured interview with a parent or other caregiver. One of these versions is the 297-item Survey Form, which is most similar to the earlier Vineland. The other is the 577-item Expanded Form, which also provides a systematic basis

[12] It should he noted that not all of the major individual intelligence scales work equally well when applied to mentally retarded persons (see, e.g., Spruill, 1991).

for preparing individualized educational or treatment programs. Both versions are applicable from birth through 18 years and to low-functioning adults. The third version is the Classroom Edition, comprising a 244-item questionnaire to be filled out by a classroom teacher; it covers ages 3 through 12 years. The correlations between the Classroom Edition and the Survey Form scores range from .31 to .54, which indicates that the two should not be used interchangeably.

All versions of the Vineland focus on what the individual usually and habitually *does*, not on what he or she *can* do. The items are classified under four major adaptive domains; these are shown in Table 9–2, together with their subdomains and brief descriptions of the behavior covered. Both Interview Editions also include an optional set of 32 items dealing with maladaptive or undesirable behaviors that may interfere with the individual's functioning. All versions provide well-designed forms for reporting results to parents.

Table 9-2

Content of the Vineland Adaptive Behavior Scales

Domains and subdomains	Description
Communication	
Receptive	What the individual understands
Expressive	What the individual says
Written	What the individual reads and writes
Daily Living Skills	
Personal	How the individual eats, dresses, and practices
Domestic	Personal hygiene.
Community	What household tasks the individual performs
	How the individual uses time, money, the telephone, and job skills
Socialization	
Interpersonal Relationship	How the individual interacts with others
Play and Leisure Time	How the individual plays and uses leisure time
Coping skills	How the individual demonstrates responsibility and sensitivity to others.
Motor Skills	
Gross	How the individual users arms and legs for movement and coordination.
Fine	How the individuals uses hands and fingers to manipulate objects.
Adaptive Behavior composite	Composite of the four domains listed above
Maladaptive Behavior[a]	Undesirable behaviors that may interfere with adaptive functioning.

[a]Included for optional use in Survey Form and Expanded Form, but not in Classroom Edition.

(Adapted from Sparrow, Balia, & Cicchetti, 1984a, p. 3.)

The two Interview Editions were standardized on a representative national sample of 3,000 individuals, who ranged in age from birth to 18 years 11 months and who were stratified according to the 1980 U.S. Census on the basis of sex, ethnic group, community size, region, and parents' educational level. Supplementary norms were also established on special groups, including residential and non residential samples of mentally retarded adults and residential samples of emotionally disturbed, visually impaired, and hearing-impaired children. The Classroom Edition was standardized on nearly 3,000 children who ranged in age from 3 years to 12 years 11 months; who were drawn from schools in 38 states; and who were stratified on the same basis used for the other editions.

Standard scores with mean of 100 and SD of 15 are provided for the four domain scores and for the Adaptive Behavior Composite on all three forms. Error bands (based on SEM) are given for five different confidence levels (from 68% to 99%). Also available for the same summary scores are percentile ranks, stanines, age equivalents, and adaptive levels (i.e., qualitative descriptive categories). For subdomain scores, the results can be expressed as adaptive levels and as age equivalents; for maladaptive behavior, results are reported as qualitative (maladaptive) levels only. The supplementary norms can be used to find percentile ranks and adaptive levels within each appropriate special group. Software is available for converting raw scores to derived scores and for profile analysis.

For all editions, the median internal consistency reliability coefficients for the domain and composite scores are mostly in the high .90s. Understandably, the reliabilities run lower for the subdomains, and they vary widely with age level and content area. The median subdomain reliabilities, however, are mostly in the .70s and .80s. Data on retest and interrater reliabilities suggest good stability over short time intervals and satisfactory agreement between two different interviewers administering the scale to the same respondents.

Several types of data summarized in the manuals for the three forms contribute to construct validation. To some extent, validity was built into the instrument through the initial formulation of adaptive behavior constructs that guided the preparation and selection of items. Empirical validation data are provided in analyses of the standardization samples, as well as in studies by independent investigators. They include data on developmental trends in performance domains and subdomains; factor analyses of domain and subdomain scores; comparisons of score profiles obtained from samples of mentally retarded and disabled individuals included in the supplementary norms; and correlations with other adaptive behavior inventories and with such ability tests as the WISC-R, K-ABC, and Peabody Picture Vocabulary Test.

In general, the procedures employed in developing and evaluating the Vineland were of high technical quality and are fully and clearly described in the manuals. They reflect advances that occurred since the publication of the earlier edition. However, the practical effectiveness of the instrument depends on a thorough knowledge of its psychometric characteristics as described in the manual and in the literature that has accumulated on it.[13]

---

[13] See, for example, Middleton, Keene, and Brown (1990), Both and Barnett (1988), Raggio and Massingale (1990), Schatz and Hamdan-Allen (1995), and Silverstein (1986). For further description and independent evaluations of the three forms of the Vineland, see I.A. Campbell (1985) and C.R. Reynolds (1986).

There has been widespread interest in the use of assessment results as a basis for designing and choosing appropriate training programs for mentally retarded persons. This interest, in turn, has led to the development of an increasing number of scales for measuring adaptive behavior.[14] One example is the Adaptive Behavior Scales (ABS), which were developed by the AAMR and designed with the same general objectives as the Vineland. The AAMR Adaptive Behavior Scale—Residential and Community, Second Edition (ABS-RC:2—Nihira, Leland, & Lambert, 1993)—was standardized on over 4,000 adults with developmental disabilities living in community or residential settings; it has scores on 18 domains, of which 10 are concerned with coping skills and 8 with social behavior, including various types of maladaptive patterns. On the other hand, the AAMR Adaptive Behavior Scale—School, Second Edition (ABS-S:2— Lambert, Nihira, & Leland, 1993)—was normed on both mentally retarded and non-retarded students, ranging in age from 3 to 18 years.

Another area that needs to be assessed in mentally retarded individuals is motor development (also examined in infant scales). The prototype of instruments for that purpose is the Oseretsky Tests of Motor Proficiency, originally published in Russia in 1923. Other applications of the Oseretsky tests are found in the testing of children with motor handicaps, minimal brain dysfunction, or learning disabilities, particularly in connection with the administration of individualized training programs. The current revision of the Oseretsky scales is the Bruininks-Oseretsky Test of Motor Proficiency (Bruininks,1978). Requiring 45 to 60 minutes, the complete battery comprises 46 items grouped into 8 subtests. It yields 3 scores: a Gross Motor Composite measuring performance of the large muscles of shoulders, trunk, and legs; a Fine Motor Composite measuring performance of the small muscles of the fingers, hands, and forearm; and a Total Battery Composite. There is also a 14-item Short Form, requiring 15 to 20 minutes and providing a single index of general motor proficiency. Performance can be expressed in terms of age-based standard scores, percentile ranks, and stanines. Age equivalents are also available for each subtest. The battery was standardized on a sample of 765 children between the ages of 4½ and 4½, chosen so as to be representative of the U.S. population. Test-retest reliability of the composite scores, over intervals of 7 to 12 days, cluster in the .80s. Validity was investigated in several ways, including factor analysis of items, age differentiation, and comparisons between children with and without mental retardation and learning disabilities.

One of the main challenges in the assessment of mental retardation lies in distinguishing between this condition and developmental delays, especially during infancy and early childhood. Not only is cognitive assessment in this period less reliable than at other ages, as we have seen, but there is also the possibility that what manifests as impaired cognitive functioning may be the result of various other conditions (Hodapp, Burack, & Zigler, 1990). Chief among the factors that can affect a child's level of intellectual performance and adaptive skills in a negative direction are sensory and motor disabilities and an adverse

[14] For surveys of many of these scales, see Fox and Meyer (1990), Knoff (1992), and Sattler (1988, chap. 15).

home environment. The remainder of this chapter includes discussions of issues related to both of these factors which may, of course, be present either singly or in combination.

TESTING PERSONS WITH PHYSICAL DISABILITIES

Although the problems presented by the testing of disabled persons have received some attention over several decades, special efforts to meet these problems were stimulated by legislation enacted since the 1970s. The provision of suitable education for all physically disabled children is covered by the previously cited Individuals with Disabilities Education Act. At a much broader level, the general Civil Rights provisions mandated for other minorities were largely extended to cover physically disabled persons, first through Section 504 of the Rehabilitation Act of 1973 and, more recently, by the Americans with Disabilities Act of 1990 (ADA—P L. 101–336).[15] These laws prohibit discrimination in the areas of: (1) employment practices; (2) accessibility of physical facilities; (3) preschool, elementary, and secondary education; (4) postsecondary education; and (5) health, welfare, and social services. The ADA strengthens earlier mandates and extends them to organizations in the private sector. In India, the universal guidelines for assessment and certification of the disabilities, such as visual impairment, locomotor disability, speech and hearing, mental retardation, and multiple disabilities, were finalized by a group of experts and were notified by the Ministry of Social Justice and Empowerment, government of India, in June 2001.[16]

The testing of physically disabled children at an early age is especially important in order to provide appropriate educational experiences from the outset. Such an approach helps to prevent the cumulative learning deficits that would magnify the effects of the disability on intellectual development.[17] At any age, the testing of physically disabled persons presents special problems with reference to test administration and the proper interpretation of test performance. Thus far, the principal ways of handling such testing include: (1) modification of the testing medium, time limits, and content of existing tests; and (2) individualized, clinical assessment that combines test scores with other sources of data from biographical history, interviewing, and the judgment of adequately informed everyday-life observers, such as teachers (AERA, APA, NCME, 1985, chap. 13; Bailey & Wolery, 1989; Barnett, 1983; Culbertson & Willis, 1993; Eyde, Nester, Eleaton, & Nelson, 1994; Scarpati, 1991; Sherman & Robinson, 1982).

Efforts to establish separate norms for persons with specific physical disabilities or to design tests specially for such groups are usually hampered by the small number of available cases. This limitation applies especially to low incidence and multiple disabilities and to the use of tests in contexts—such as graduate

---

[15] For a review of the implications of the ADA for psychological testing, see Nester (1994). The psychometric and assessment issues raised by this act are thoroughly discussed in a statement of the American Psychological Association Division of Evaluation, Measurement and Statistics, which was published in the January 1993 issue of *The Score*, the division's newsletter.

[16] Ministry of Social Justice and Empowerment, "Guidelines for other Disabilities", June 1, 2001, accessed on July 21, 2016 (http://www.ccdisabilities.nic.in/page.php?s=&p=guide_others&t=pb)

[17] Further information about patterns of development in young disabled children and procedural considerations in their assessment can be found in Wachs and Sheehan (1988).

and professional school admissions—that involve specially selected samples. Nevertheless, research has been continuing on the performance of persons with different physical disabilities who have taken either standard or specially adapted versions of various tests.

One of the most ambitious series of studies was carried out at the Educational Testing Service using standard and nonstandard versions of the College Board SAT and the GRE General Test with four classes of disabled applicants—namely, hearing impaired, visually impaired, learning disabled, and physically impaired (Willingham et al., 1988). The psychometric characteristics investigated included reliability, differential item functioning, factor structure, and other indices of validity related to performance levels and predictive power; test content, timing, and accommodations were also studied. In general, the results show that the procedural adaptations are comparable to standard testing in most respects, including the meaning of scores. However, prediction of academic performance from scores, or prior grades, is not as accurate for persons with disabilities as it is for others; and there are questions concerning the factor structure and item functioning of some of the test adaptations (R. E. Bennett, Rock, &. Novatkoski, 1989; Rock, Bennett, & Jirele, 1988; Willingham, 1988). In addition, the time limits in the nonstandard versions have been found to be relatively more lenient, a finding that supports the controversial practice of "flagging" scores obtained using these versions. Thus, the need to develop empirically-based comparable time limits has emerged as a critical one (see, e.g., Wainer, 1993a, pp. 9–10).

There are still many unresolved psychometric and ethical issues concerning the testing of persons with disabilities. Although more research is needed, it is also necessary to recognize that some of the problems may be insoluble because they derive from the fact that *every* person presents a unique configuration of types and degrees of abilities, disabilities, and personal characteristics. Nevertheless, for practical purposes, there is now a greater level of awareness of and sensitivity toward the needs of disabled persons than ever before—as well as improved guidance on how to conduct testing with them. In addition, new advances in instrumentation, such as voice synthesizers that simulate speech and other computer-controlled electronic devices, offer the possibility of a wide range of promising testing innovations, including many that would be of value in this area (see, e.g., Educational Testing Service, 1992; Wilson, 1991).

The following sections consider special testing problems and procedures with reference to three major categories of physical disability—namely, hearing, visual, and motor impairments.

Hearing Impairments.[18] Owing to their general retardation in language development, hearing-impaired children are usually handicapped by verbal tests, even when the verbal content is presented visually. The earlier the onset of deafness in young children, the more severe is this handicap. Fortunately, recent advances in the assessment of auditory functioning have made it possible to diagnose hearing loss accurately—and start habilitation procedures—within the first few months of life (Shah & Boyden, 1991).

[18] For reviews of the issues and considerations pertinent to the assessment of hearing-impaired children, see Bradley-Johnson and Evans (1991), Y. Mullen (1992), and Sullivan and Burley (1990).

The testing of deaf children was the primary object in the development of some of the earliest performance scales, such as the Printner-Paterson Performance Scale and the Arthur Performance Scale. Special adaptations of the Wechsler scales are often employed in testing deaf persons. Most of the verbal tests can be administered if the oral questions are typed on cards. Various procedures for communicating the instructions for the performance tests have been worked out (see, e.g., Sattler, 1988, 1992); in fact, the WISC-R Performance Scale has been the most widely used test of intelligence for hearing-impaired children in the United States. With such modifications of standard testing procedures, however, one cannot assume that reliability, validity, and norms remain unchanged. Given the extensive use of the Wechsler scales with the hearing impaired, however, there is a copious literature on their psychometric properties when applied to samples of hearing-impaired individuals (see, e.g., Braden, 1985; Mailer & Braden, 1993; Sullivan & Schulte, 1992). In general, these studies indicate that there are substantial similarities in the factor structure of the scales and in the predictive and construct validity of the Performance Scale for hearing-impaired and non-impaired children.

The tests mentioned thus far were standardized on hearing persons. Many investigators have concluded that when levels of performance are comparable to those of hearing persons, as is the case for the Wechsler Performance scales, there is no need for separate norms for hearing-impaired individuals. At the same time, norms obtained on deaf children are useful in a number of situations pertaining to their educational development. To meet this need, some efforts have been made to establish special norms for existing tests, as illustrated by the standardization of the WISC-R Performance Scale for Deaf Children (R. J. Anderson & Cisco, 1977).

At a more basic level, the Hiskey-Nebraska Test of Learning Aptitude (Hiskey, 1966) was developed and standardized on deaf and hard-of-hearing children. This is an individual test suitable for ages 3 to 17. Speed was eliminated, since it is difficult to convey the idea of speed to deaf children. An attempt was also made to sample a wider array of intellectual functions than those covered by most performance tests. Pantomime and practice exercises that communicate the instructions, as well as intrinsically interesting items that establish rapport, are used in the test. Items were chosen with special reference to the limitations of deaf children, with final selection being based chiefly on the criterion of age differentiation. Norms were derived separately from 1,079 deaf and 1,074 hearing children; parallel instructions for testing both types of children are provided in the manual, which contains a discussion of desirable practices to be followed in testing deaf children. Although the norms for it are dated, the Hiskey-Nebraska has adequate reliability and validity evidence and is still considered one of the best tests for use with hearing-impaired children (Sullivan & Burley, 1990).

Over the past five decades the evolution of knowledge about the intellectual consequences of deafness has been astonishing. Much of this history is discussed by Braden (1994) in a comprehensive review of over 200 studies of deaf people involving more than 170,000 research participants. This work describes many of the intriguing findings in this literature, including the fact that deaf children who have deaf parents score above the norms for non-impaired children on performance tests. Although the reasons for these findings are not yet fully understood, there is no question that deafness is a far more complex variable than was previously thought. Etiology, extent, ages of onset and detection of hearing loss, as well as mode of communication, educational placement, parental hearing status, and presence of additional disabilities are all factors that interact and contribute to the differential cognitive performance of hearing-impaired individuals.

Visual Impairments.[19] Testing the blind presents a very different set of problems from those encountered with the deaf. Oral tests can be most readily adapted for blind persons, while performance tests are least likely to be applicable. In addition to the usual oral presentation by the examiner, other suitable testing techniques have been utilized, such as tape recordings. Some tests, such as the College Board Scholastic Assessment Test (SAT), are also available in large-type formats or in braille. The latter technique is somewhat limited in its applicability, however, because of: the greater bulkiness of materials printed in braille compared to those provided in ink; the slower reading rate for braille; and the number of blind persons who are not facile braille readers. The test taker's responses may likewise be recorded in braille or on a keyboard. Specially prepared embossed answer sheets or cards are also available for use with true-false, multiple-choice, and other selected-response items. In many individually administered tests, of course, oral or gestural responses can be obtained.

Among the earliest examples of general intelligence tests that have been adapted for blind persons is the Binet. The first Hayes-Binet revision for testing the blind was based on the 1916 Stanford-Binet. In 1942, the Interim Hayes-Binet[20] was prepared from the 1937 Stanford-Binet (Hayes, 1942, 1943). The most recent adaptation—comparable to the Stanford-Binet Form L-M—is the Perkins-Binet Tests of Intelligence for the Blind. This instrument was standardized on and has separate forms for partially sighted and blind children (C. J. Davis, 1980).

The Wechsler scales have also been adapted for blind test takers. These adaptations consist essentially in using the verbal tests and omitting the performance tests. A few items inappropriate for the blind are replaced by alternates. In general, the studies of children who have poor vision or blindness suggest that these conditions may have a negative impact on their cognitive development, even in the verbal area, because of the limitations such conditions impose on the range and variety of their experiences. The Wechsler profiles of visually impaired children have shown a similar pattern across various studies; the results suggest that the factorial composition of the tasks is different for them than it is for normally sighted children. Although global IQs cannot be considered accurate measures of the overall cognitive functioning of visually impaired children, in the hands of informed examiners, the Wechsler scales can provide useful diagnostic information regarding the strengths and weaknesses of these children (Groenveld & Jan, 1992).

---

19 For reviews of issues and procedures in the assessment of visually impaired children, see Bradley-Johnson (1994), Fewell (1991), M. S. Moore and McLaughlin (1992), and Orlansky (1988).

20 Originally designated as an interim edition because of the tentative nature of its standardization, this revision has come to be known by this name in the literature.

Very few instruments have been developed specifically for use with visually impaired persons. Possibly the best known example of these is the Blind Learning Aptitude Test (BLAT—Newland, 1979). The BLAT is an individually administered test that incorporates items adapted from other tests, such as Raven's Progressive Matrices, and other nonverbal items, and presents them in an embossed format. Emphasis is placed on the learning process rather than on the products of past learning, which might handicap the blind child. Normative data, though dated, compare favorably with those usually available for instruments designed for special populations. Information regarding reliability and validity is scant and requires further research. Nevertheless, the BLAT can be a useful component, along with verbal tests, in the evaluation of blind children of elementary school age.

A more recent example, still in the developmental stages, has derived from the attempt of a group of investigators in the Netherlands to provide a comprehensive measure of intelligence for children with visual impairments. The Intelligence Test for Visually Impaired Children (ITVIC—Dekker, Drenth, Zaal, & Koole, 1990) incorporates haptic or tactile versions of tasks such as Block Design into a battery that includes several nonverbal and verbal subtests.[21] Additional research on the ITVIC, with a wider range of subjects, is needed; however, the initial studies show promising results in terms of the validity of the instrument (Dekker, 1993; Dekker, Drenth, & Zaal, 1991; Dekker & Koole, 1992).

As is the case with all the other special conditions discussed in this chapter, visual impairments occur in a wide range of gradations and quite often in combination with other problems. Thus, the decision of whether to use standard tests, adaptations of them, or specially designed tests for the blind depends on the objectives of the assessment and the unique characteristics of the person in question. In general, test users should always remember that modifications of tests, such as tactile presentations of visual designs or extended time limits, cannot be assumed to measure the same constructs as the original versions.

Motor Impairments.[22] Although usually able to receive auditory and visual stimulation, persons with orthopedic disabilities may have such severe motor disorders as to make oral or written responses impracticable. The attempt to manipulate form boards or other performance materials would likewise meet difficulties. Working against a time limit or in strange surroundings often increases the motor disturbance in the orthopedically impaired. Their greater susceptibility to fatigue makes short testing sessions necessary.

Some of the severest motor disabilities are found among persons with cerebral palsy. Yet surveys of these cases have often employed common intelligence tests such as the Stanford-Binet. In such studies, the most severely disabled were usually excluded as untestable. Frequently, informal adjustments in testing

[21] The Haptic Intelligence Scale is a similar measure developed and normed on blind adults during the 1950s and early 1960s (Shurrager & Shurrager, 1964). It consists of six performance subtests patterned after the Wechsler Bellevue Intelligence Scale—namely, Digit Symbol, Object Assembly, Block Design, Object Completion, Pattern Board, and Bead Arithmetic.

[22] A review of measures useful in the assessment of gross motor functions in young children can be found in H. G. Williams (1991). C. Robinson and Fiber (1988) describe a process-oriented approach to the assessment of young children using Piagetian sensorimotor and preoperational tasks.

procedure were made to adapt the test to the child's response capacities. Both of these procedures, of course, are makeshifts.

A more satisfactory approach lies in the development of testing instruments suitable for even the most severely impaired individuals. A number of specially designed tests or adaptations of existing tests are now available for this purpose, although their normative and validity data are often meager. Several of the tests to be discussed in the next section, originally designed for use in cross-cultural testing, have also proved applicable to disabled persons. Adaptations of the Leiter International Performance Scale and the Porteus Mazes, suitable for administration to children with cerebral palsy, have been prepared (Allen & Collins, 1955; Arnold, 1951). In both adapted tests, the examiner manipulates the test materials while the test taker responds only by appropriate head movements. Raven's Progressive Matrices provide a useful tool for this purpose as well. Since this test is given with no time limit, and since the response may be indicated orally, in writing, or by pointing or nodding, it appears to be especially appropriate for orthopedically disabled individuals. Despite the flexibility and simplicity of its response indicator, this test—in its various forms—covers a wide range of difficulty and provides a fairly high test ceiling. Successful use of this test has been reported in studies of individuals with cerebral palsy and other motor disorders (see, e.g., Capitani, Sala, & Marchitti, 1994).

Another type of test that permits the utilization of a simple pointing response is *picture vocabulary tests.* These tests provide a rapid measure of "use" vocabulary, which makes them especially applicable to persons unable to vocalize well (such as those with cerebral palsy) and to those who are deaf. Since they are easy to administer and can be completed in about 15 minutes, picture vocabulary tests are also useful as a rapid screening device in situations where administration of a comprehensive individual intelligence test is not feasible.

The Peabody Picture Vocabulary Test, Fourth Edition (PPVT-4), is typical of these instruments. It is a test of receptive vocabulary and offers several enhancements to its previous test editions. It comes in two equivalent forms, each consisting of four practice plates and 228 testing plates. Each plate contains four line drawings of objects or everyday scenes (Gregory, 2015). The examiner presents a series of pictures to each examinee, says a word describing one of the pictures, and asks the individual to point to the one picture that best describes the stated word. Although it is an untimed test, the total administration time should not take more than 15 minutes. Raw scores are converted to standard scores with a mean of 100 and a standard deviation of 15. The PPVT-4 test was standardized on a national sample of individuals aged 2 years and 6 months to over and above 90 years. Data from approximately 3,500 subjects was used to arrive at the normative scores. Reliability and validity data for this edition is exceptionally strong with all coefficients in the 0.90 range (Dunn and Dunn, 2015).

The beauty of the PPVT-4 is that it takes care to minimize and balance cultural influences in the test items. Independent consultants and reviewers from various countries and ethnicities have reviewed the content and the artwork during the test development phase; and several adjustments and changes were made following their feedback and reviews (Dunn & Dunn, 2015). The test items are presented in the form of attractive artwork that is balanced for racial and gender differences, including people with physical disabilities (Gregory, 2015, p. 295). Since the test is treated as a culturally fair assessment, it finds its applicability across several countries including India.

MULTICULTURAL TESTING

The testing of people with highly dissimilar cultural backgrounds always plays a pivotal role in India because of the diversity. Tests are needed for maximum utilization of human resources. With the rapid expansion of educational facilities, emerging economies like India require testing for various purposes such as admission, counseling, and employment. With increasing globalization, there is a mounting demand for tests to aid the job selection and placement of personnel, particularly in the new and upcoming professional and non-traditional career choices, apart from medical and engineering.

Traditionally, cross-cultural tests have tried to rule out one or more parameters along which cultures vary. A well-known example of such a parameter is *language*. If the cultural groups to be tested spoke different languages, tests were developed that required no language on the part of either examiner or test takers. When educational backgrounds differed widely and illiteracy was prevalent, *reading* was ruled out. Oral language was not eliminated from these tests because they were designed for persons speaking a common language. Another parameter in which cultures or subcultures differ is that of *speed*. Not only the tempo of daily life, but also the motivation to hurry and the value attached to rapid performance vary widely among national cultures, among ethnic minority groups within a single nation, and between urban and rural subcultures (see, e.g., Klineberg, 1928; R.R. Knapp, 1960; M. Womer, 1972). Accordingly, cross-cultural tests have often— though not always—tried to eliminate the influence of speed by allowing long time limits and giving no premium for faster performance.

Still other parameters along which cultures differ pertain to *test content*. Several nonlanguage and nonreading tests, for example, call for items of information that are specific to certain cultures. Thus, they may require the test taker to understand the function of such objects as violin, postage stamp, gun, pocketknife, telephone, piano, or mirror. Persons reared in certain cultures may lack the experiential background to respond correctly to such items. It was chiefly to control this type of cultural parameter that the classic "culture-free" tests were first developed. Following a brief examination of typical tests designed to eliminate one or more of the above parameters, we shall turn to an analysis of alternative approaches to cross-cultural testing.

Typical Traditional Instruments.[23] In their efforts to construct tests applicable across cultures, psychometricians followed a variety of procedures, some of which are illustrated by the tests considered in this section. The Leiter International Performance Scale–Revised (Roid & Miller, 1997) is an individually administered performance test, originally published in 1940. It was developed through several years of use with different ethnic groups in Hawaii. The scale was subsequently applied to several African groups by Porteus and to a few other national groups

[23] Reviews of several of the nonverbal measures discussed in this and the preceding sections, as well as other such tests, can be found in Naglieri and Prewett (1990).

by other investigators. A revision issued in 1948 was based on further testing of U.S. children, high school students, and Army recruits during World War II. The 1997 edition is based on samples of over 2,000 normal and atypical individuals from the U.S. between the ages of 2 and 20 years. A distinctive feature of the Leiter, since adopted by other instruments, is the almost complete elimination of verbal instructions. Each test begins with a very easy task of the type to be encountered throughout that test. The comprehension of the tasks—which are administered individually and with no time limit—is treated as part of the test. All of the graphic stimulus materials are presented on easels; the test taker responds by selecting the cards with the most appropriate pictures and placing them on a response tray, as seen in Figure 9–3.

The Leiter scale was designed to cover a wide range of functions, similar to those found in verbal scales. In its current form, the coverage has been expanded significantly and now encompasses four domains, namely, Reasoning, Visualization, Attention, and Memory. Among the tasks included at the various ages in the Reasoning and Visualization domains are: design analogies, form completion, matching, sequential ordering (illustrated in Fig. 9–3), classification, paper folding, and figural rotation. The Attention and Memory domain tests include sustained and divided attention measures and a variety of immediate and delayed memory tasks. As might be expected, the revised Leiter scale has been updated considerably and is more sophisticated than earlier versions with regard to its psychometric characteristics. For example, item response theory was

Figure 9–3. Typical Materials for Use in the Leiter International Performance Scale—Revised. The partially completed task that is illustrated belongs in the Sequential Order Test and requires the examinee to select five out of the six response cards and place them correctly on the tray.

(Courtesy of the Stoelting Company.)

used to calibrate difficulty levels, and scores are no longer expressed as ratio IQs. In addition, the availability of representative contemporary norms and the expanded content should enhance the usefulness of the scale. The new manual includes information on various types of reliability and validity evidence.

Raven's Progressive Matrices (RPM) was designed primarily as a measure of Spearman's *g* factor or general intelligence (J. Raven, 1983; Raven, Raven, & Court, 1995). In keeping with Spearman's theoretical analysis of *g*, this test requires chiefly the education of relations among abstract items. The items consist of a set of matrices, or arrangements of design elements into rows and columns, from each of which a part has been removed. The task is to choose the missing insert from given alternatives. The easier items require accuracy of discrimination; the more difficult items involve analogies, permutations and alternations of patterns, and other logical relations. Two typical items from the Standard Progressive Matrices are illustrated in Figure 9–4. The test is usually administered with no time limits and can be given individually or in groups. Very simple oral instructions are required.

The RPM is available in three forms, differing in level of difficulty. The Standard Progressive Matrices (SPM—1996 Edition) is the form suitable for average individuals between the ages of 6 and 80 years. An easier form, the Coloured Progressive Matrices (CPM—1990 Edition), is available for younger children and for special groups who cannot be adequately tested with the SPM for various reasons. Norms for the CPM are available for children from 5½ to 11½ and for samples of nonretarded persons aged 60 to 89 years and of mentally retarded adults. A third form, the Advanced Progressive Matrices (APM—1994 Edition) was developed for above-average adolescents and adults.

Raven's Advanced Progressive Matrices (APM) test is widely used in organizations to make all types of selection decisions. It is a culturally fair test and the instructions of the test are available in multiple languages including Chinese, Japanese, French, German, Spanish, Swedish, and Portuguese. It is a timed test

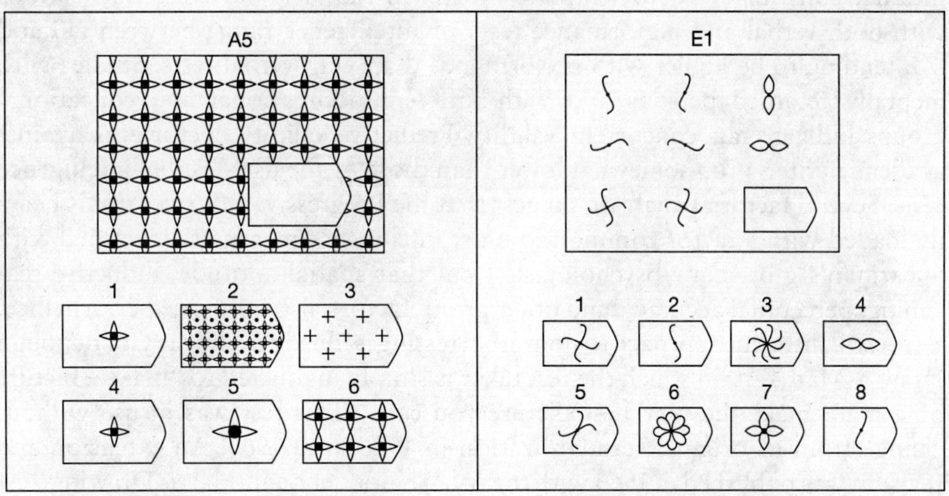

Figure 9–4. Typical Items from the Standard Progressive Matrices (SPM). One easy item (A5) and one difficult item (El) are shown.

(Reproduced by permission of J. C. Raven Ltd.)

containing 23 test items and lasts up to 45 minutes. Raven's APM test is extensively used to assess an individual's problem-solving and decision-making ability in an unfamiliar and ambiguous environment. This test of changing environment aids employers to know the extent to which their existing and future employees are comfortable with unfamiliar and changing situations. As Raven's test is a non-verbal measure of mental ability, it tends to offer insights about an individual's capacity for analyzing and solving problems, abstract reasoning, and learning potential.

The manual for all levels of the RPM is available in sections that can be purchased separately or in any desired combination and can be assembled in a single binder. Section 1 gives a general overview and was last updated in 1995; the publication dates of the other sections range from 1990 to 1996. They include the specific manuals for each of the three levels of the RPM. The manuals for two vocabulary tests standardized for use in combination with the RPM are also part of the Raven's package. The last section of the manual summarizes additional research on reliability, validity, and supplementary norms obtained in various countries and on special populations (Court & Raven, 1995). Several research supplements with British standardization data and normative information gathered in North America, Ireland, and Germany, as well as an annotated bibliography of over 2,000 studies are also available.[24]

Although there is a large accumulation of published research on the RPM, the studies are scattered and heterogeneous, having been designed for a variety of different purposes. The test authors recommend that potential users identify those studies and populations most relevant to their own interests; but they caution that the studies vary widely in methodology, size of samples, and technical quality.

In general, retest reliability in groups of older children and adults that were moderately homogeneous in age ranges approximately from .70 to .90. At the lower score ranges, however, reliability falls considerably below these values. Internal consistency coefficients are mostly in the .80s and .90s. Correlations with both verbal and performance tests of intelligence range between .40 and .75, tending to be higher with performance than with verbal tests. Studies with mentally retarded persons and with different occupational and educational groups indicate fair concurrent validity. Predictive validity coefficients against academic criteria run somewhat lower than those of the usual verbal intelligence tests. Several factorial analyses suggest that the Progressive Matrices test is heavily loaded with a factor common to most intelligence measures (identified with Spearman's g by many psychologists), but that spatial aptitude, inductive reasoning, perceptual accuracy, and other group factors also influence performance.

A still different approach to nonverbal testing is illustrated by the Goodenough Draw-a-Man Test, in which the test taker is simply instructed to "make a picture of a man; make the very best picture you can." This test was in use without change from its original standardization in 1926 until 1963. An extension and revision was published in 1963 with the title of Goodenough-Harris Drawing Test (D. B. Harris, 1963). In the revision, as in the original test, emphasis is placed

[24] The latter can be obtained on disk and in hard copy from J. H. Court, at an address on record with the publisher of the RPM.

different cultures. This is the basic approach of the culture-fair tests, although their repeated validation in different cultures has often been either neglected altogether or inadequately executed. Without such a step, however, we cannot be sure that the test is relatively free from culturally restricted elements. Moreover, it is unlikely that any single test could be designed that would fully meet these requirements across a wide range of cultures.

Nevertheless, multicultural assessment techniques are needed for basic research on some fundamental questions. One of these questions pertains to the generality of psychological principles and constructs derived within a single culture (Anastasi, 1958, chap. 18; Berry et al., 1992; Irvine, 1983; Irvine &. Carroll, 1980). Another question concerns the role of environmental conditions in the development of individual differences in behavior—a problem that can be more effectively studied within the wide range of environmental variation provided by highly dissimilar cultures. Research of this sort calls for instruments that can be administered under at least moderately comparable conditions in different cultures. Safeguards against incorrect interpretations of results obtained with such instruments should be sought in appropriate experimental designs and in the investigators' thorough familiarity with the cultures or subcultures under investigation. What is required is the identification of particular experiential variables within any given culture that may be related to socially significant differences in behavioral development characterizing that culture (J. W. Berry, 1983; Brislin, 1993; Segall, 1983; Whiting, 1976). An outstanding example—from the realm of personality testing—of how such research efforts may be carried out can be found in the Cross-Cultural Anxiety Series of publications. This series addresses itself exclusively to the measurement of anxiety across different cultures and has been extraordinarily fruitful in expanding the knowledge base about this construct and about how anxiety is experienced by people from around the world (see, e.g., Spielberger & Diaz-Guerrero, 1990).

A second major approach is to develop a test within one culture and administer it to persons with different cultural backgrounds. In this case, we should avoid the mistake of regarding any test developed within a single cultural framework as a universal yardstick for measuring "intelligence" or other constructs. Nor should we assume that a low score on such a test has the same causal explanation for both a member of the test culture and for a member of another culture. What *can* be ascertained by such an approach is the cultural distance between groups, as well as the individual's degree of acculturation and her or his readiness for educational and vocational activities that are culture-specific. Some investigators have sought to dramatize the fact that the cultural milieu in which an individual is reared affects the cognitive skills and knowledge he or she acquires. Early examples include a footprint recognition test standardized on aboriginal Australians (Porteus, 1931) and a Draw-a-Horse Test standardized on Pueblo Indian children (DuBois, 1939). In both cases, the cultural group on which the test was developed excelled in comparisons with other groups.

As a third approach, different tests (or substantial adaptations of existing tests) may be developed within each culture, validated against local criteria, and used only within the appropriate culture. This approach is illustrated by the development of tests for industrial and military personnel within particular cultures. One example is provided by the test-development program conducted in several developing nations of Africa, Asia, and Latin America under the sponsorship of the United States Agency for International Development (Schwarz & Krug, 1972). In such instances, the tests are validated against the specific educational and vocational criteria they are designed to predict, and performance is evaluated in terms of local norms. Each test is applied only within the culture in which it was developed, and no cross-cultural comparisons are attempted. If the criteria to be predicted are technological, however, "Western-type intelligence" is likely to be needed, and the tests will reflect the direction in which the particular culture is evolving rather than its prevalent cultural characteristics at the time.

An extensive literature has accumulated on the psychological testing of cultural minorities within pluralistic societies such as the United States, Israel, and the Netherlands (see, e.g., Bleichrodt &. Drenth, 1991; Duran, 1989; Figueroa, 1990; Hessel & Hamers, 1993; Samuda, Kong, Cummins, Lewis, & Pascual-Leone, 1991; Zeidner, 1988). In the present book, this material is treated wherever it can be most clearly presented. Thus, in chapter 18, the focus is on ethical and social concerns and responsibilities in the use of tests with cultural minorities. The technical psychometric problems of test bias and item-group interactions were considered in chapters 6 and 7. In the present chapter, the focus was on instruments developed for cross-cultural ability testing. Problems in the interpretation of the results of cross-cultural testing, together with current trends, will be considered in chapter 12.

Today, multicultural testing is moving away from the construction of special tests and is focusing more and more on the role of the examiner during the testing process. Basically, it is the responsibility of the examiner to: (1) obtain information about the examinee's cultural background; (2) choose a test that is best suited for the purpose for which it is being used; (3) present and administer the test effectively for the particular individual; and (4) interpret the test results in the light of both the individual's experiential background and the context (occupational, educational, community, etc.) for which the examinee's qualifications are being assessed. These features of the examiner's role will be discussed further in chapter 12.

Chapter Ten

Group Testing

While individual tests such as the Stanford-Binet and the Wechsler scales find their principal application in the clinic, group tests are used primarily in the educational system, government service, industry, and the military services. It will be recalled that mass testing began during World War I with the development of the Army Alpha and the Army Beta for use in the United States Army. The former was a verbal test designed for general screening and placement purposes. The latter was a nonlanguage test for use with persons who could not properly be tested with the Alpha owing to foreign-language background or illiteracy. The pattern established by these tests was closely followed in the subsequent development of a large number of group tests for civilian application.

Revisions of the civilian forms of both original Army tests continued in use for several decades. In the armed services, the Armed Forces Qualification Test (AFQT) was subsequently developed as a preliminary screening instrument, followed by multiple-aptitude classification batteries for assignment to occupational specialties. The AFQT provided a single score based on an equal number of vocabulary, arithmetic, spatial relations, and mechanical ability items. Still later, the Armed Services Vocational Aptitude Battery (ASVAB) was developed for use in all the armed services as a composite selection and classification battery. Some of the subtests of ASVAB serve as the common qualification component. For personnel classification, each service selects and combines subtests to fit its specific occupational specialty needs.

In this chapter, we shall consider first the principal differences between group and individual tests. This will be followed by an overview of emerging procedures for individually tailored group testing and computer utilization in testing programs. Then we shall introduce some current examples of broad-range group tests for general use. Finally, we shall consider a major current trend in test development and use that is discernible in group tests, as well as in the individual tests discussed in chapter 8. This trend is toward a merging of tests originally designed as overall measures of a single comprehensive ability (e.g., intelligence, academic aptitude) with multiple aptitude batteries. More and more ability tests are being adapted to facilitate flexibility of use, whereby a single instrument can yield scores of varying breadth, from general to specific, to suit the wide diversity of testing purposes and situations.

GROUP TESTS VERSUS INDIVIDUAL TESTS

Typical Differences in Test Design. Group tests necessarily differ from individual tests in form and arrangement of items. Although open-ended questions calling for free responses could be used—and were used in the early group tests—today the typical group test employs *multiple-choice items.* This change was obviously required for uniformity and objectivity of scoring. Another major difference between traditional individual and group tests is in the control of item difficulty. In individually administered tests, the examiner follows entry rules, as well as basal and ceiling rules, to ensure that each test taker is examined with items that are appropriate for her or his ability level. In group tests, items of similar content are arranged in increasing order of difficulty within *separately timed subtests.* This item organization provides each test taker with an opportunity to try each type of item, such as vocabulary, arithmetic, and spatial, and to complete the easier items of each type before trying the more difficult ones on which he or she might otherwise waste a good deal of time.

A practical difficulty encountered with separate subtests, however, is that the less experienced or less careful examiners may make timing errors. Such errors are more likely to occur and are relatively more serious with several short time limits than with a single long time limit for the whole test. To reconcile the use of a single time limit with an arrangement permitting all test takers to try all types of items at successively increasing difficulty levels, some tests utilize the *spiral-omnibus format.* One of the earliest tests to introduce this format was the Otis Self-Administering Tests of Mental Ability, which, as its name implies, endeavored to reduce the examiner's role to a minimum. In a spiral-omnibus test, the easiest items of each type are presented first, followed by the next easiest type, and so on in a rising spiral of difficulty level, as illustrated below:

Answer

1. The opposite of hate is:
   1. enemy, 2. fear, 3. love, 4. friend, 5. joy .... ( )
2. If 3 pencils cost 25 cents, how many pencils can be bought for 75 cents? .... ( )
3. A bird does not always have:
   1. wings, 2. eyes, 3. feet, 4. a nest, 5. a bill .... ( )
4. The opposite of honor is:
   1. glory, 2. disgrace, 3. cowardice, 4. fear, 5. defeat.......... ( )

In order to avoid the necessity of repeating instructions in each item and to reduce the number of shifts in instructional set required of the test takers, some tests apply the spiral-omnibus arrangement not to single items but to blocks of 5 to 10 items.

Advantages of Group Testing. Group tests are designed primarily as instruments for mass testing. In comparison with individual tests, they have both advantages and disadvantages. On the positive side, group tests can be administered simultaneously to as many persons as can be fitted comfortably into the available space and reached through a microphone. Large-scale testing programs were made possible by the development of group testing techniques. By utilizing only printed items and simple responses that can be recorded on a test booklet or answer sheet—or on a computer—the need for a one-to-one relationship between examiner and examinee was eliminated.

A second way in which group tests facilitated mass testing was by greatly simplifying the examiner's role. In contrast to the extensive training and experience required to administer the Stanford-Binet, for example, most group tests require only the ability to read simple instructions to the test takers and to keep accurate time. Some preliminary training sessions are desirable, of course, since inexperienced examiners are likely to deviate inadvertently from the standardized procedure in ways that may affect test results. Because the examiner's role is minimized, however, group testing can provide more uniform conditions than does individual testing. The use of tape-recorded instructions, as well as computer administration, offers further opportunities for standardizing procedure and eliminating examiner variance in large-scale testing. Scoring is typically more objective in group testing and can be done by a clerk. Most group tests can now be scored by computers.

From another angle, group tests characteristically provide better established norms than do individual tests. Because of the relative ease and rapidity of gathering data with group tests, it is customary to test large, representative samples in the standardization process. In the most recently standardized group tests, it is not unusual for the normative samples to number between 100,000 and 200,000, in contrast to the 1,000 to 8,000 cases laboriously accumulated in standardizing the most carefully developed individual intelligence scales.

Disadvantages of Group Testing. Although group tests have several desirable features and serve a well-nigh indispensable function in present-day testing, their limitations should also be noted. In group testing, the examiner has much less opportunity to establish rapport, obtain cooperation, and maintain the interest of the examinees. Any temporary condition of the examinee, such as illness, fatigue, worry, or anxiety, that may interfere with test performance is less readily detected in group than in individual testing. In general, persons unaccustomed to testing may be somewhat more handicapped on group than on individual testing. There is also some evidence suggesting that emotionally disturbed children may perform better on individual than on group tests (Bower, 1969; Willis, 1970).

From another angle, group tests have been attacked because of the restrictions imposed on the examinee's responses. Criticisms have been directed particularly against multiple-choice items and against such standard item types as analogies, similarities, and classification (Hoffman, 1962; LaFave, 1966). Some of the arguments are ingenious and provocative. One contention is that such items may penalize a brilliant and original thinker who sees unusual implications in the answers. It should be noted parenthetically that if this happens, it must be a rare occurrence, in view of the item analysis and validity data. If it does occur in one or two items in an individual's test, moreover, it would hardly have an appreciable effect on that examinee's total score. Some critics have focused on the importance of analyzing errors and inquiring into the reasons why an individual chooses a particular answer, as in the typical Piagetian approach (Sigel, 1963). It is undoubtedly true that group tests provide little or no opportunity for direct observations of the examinee's behavior or for identifying the causes of atypical performance. For this and other reasons, when important decisions about individuals are to be made, it is desirable to supplement group tests either with individual examination of doubtful cases or with additional information from other sources.

Still another limitation of traditional group testing is its lack of flexibility, insofar as every examinee is ordinarily tested on all items. Available testing time could be more effectively utilized if each examinee concentrated on items appropriate to her or his ability level. Moreover, such a procedure would avoid boredom from working on too-easy items, at one extreme, and mounting frustration and anxiety from attempting items beyond the individual's present ability level, at the other. Individual tests typically provide for the examiner to choose items on the basis of the test taker's own prior responses. This distinction between individual and group tests is especially important when the test is designed to cover a wide ability range.

ADAPTIVE TESTING AND COMPUTER-BASED ADMINISTRATION

Individually Tailored Tests. In the effort to combine some of the advantages of individual and group testing, several techniques are being explored. Major interest thus far has centered on ways of adjusting item coverage to the response characteristics of individual test takers. In the rapidly growing literature on the topic, this approach has been variously designated as adaptive, sequential, branched, tailored, individualized, programmed, dynamic, or response-contingent testing. Although it is possible to design paper-and-pencil group tests that incorporate such adaptive procedures (Cleary, Linn, & Rock, 1968; Lord 1971a), these techniques lend themselves best to computerized test administration.

Adaptive testing can follow a wide variety of procedural models (DeWitt & Weiss, 1974; Larkin & Weiss, 1974; Weiss, 1974; Weiss & Betz, 1973). A simple example involving two-stage testing is illustrated in Figure 10–1. In this hypothetical test, all examinees take a 10–item routing test, whose items cover a wide difficulty range. Depending on her or his performance on the routing test, each examinee is directed to one of the three 20–item measurement tests at different levels of difficulty. Thus, each person takes only 30 items, although the entire test comprises 70 items. A different arrangement is illustrated in the pyramidal test shown in Figure 10–2. In this case, all examinees begin with an item of intermediate difficulty. If an individual's response to this item is correct, she or he is routed

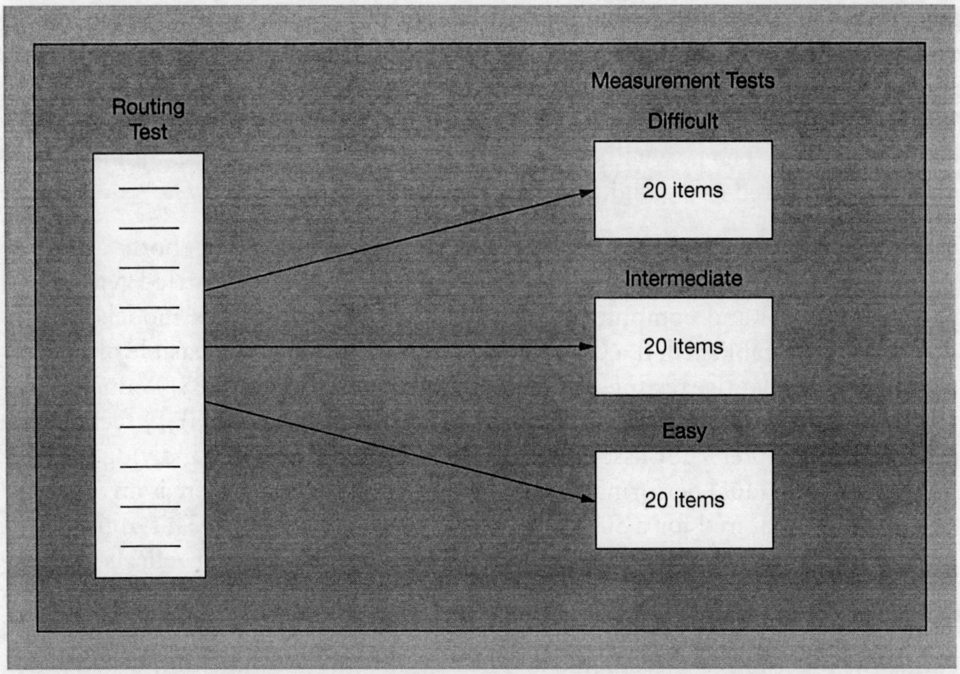

Figure 10-1. Two-Stage Adaptive Testing with Three Measurement Levels. Each examinee takes routing test and one measurement test.

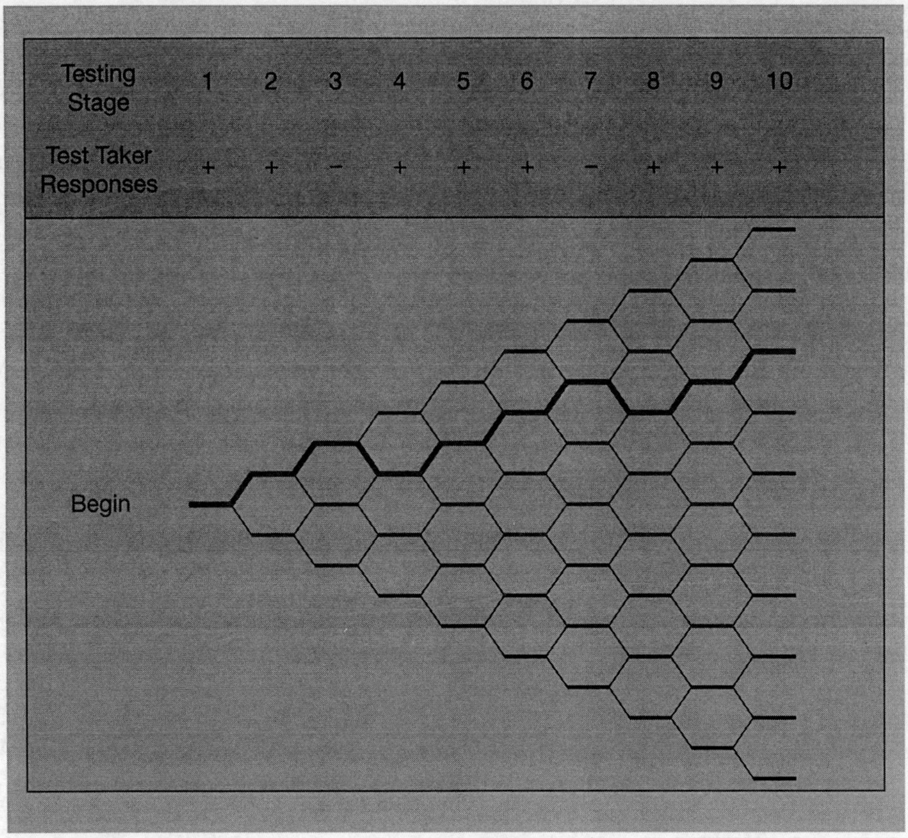

Figure 10-2. Pyramidal Testing Model. Heavy line shows route of test taker whose item responses are listed across the top.

upward to the next more difficult item; if the response is wrong, he or she moves downward to the next easier item. This procedure is repeated after each item response, until the individual has given 10 responses. The illustration shows a 10–stage test, in which each examinee is given 10 items out of the total pool of 55 items in the test. The heavy line shows the route followed by one examine whose responses are listed as + (Right) or–(Wrong) along the top.

Computerized Adaptive Testing (CAT). Several variants of both adaptive testing models illustrated in Figures 10–1 and 10–2 have been tried with both paper-and-pencil and computer forms. However, more complex models, which do not use preestablished, fixed patterns of item sequences, are feasible only with computerized adaptive testing (Embretson, 1992; B. F. Green, 1983; Wainer et al., 1990). These CAT procedures utilize the item-response theory (IRT) techniques described in chapter 7 for assembling the item pool, for testing individuals, and for scoring individual performance. For each item in the pool, there is an estimate of the ability required for a 50–50 chance of passing that item. This ability estimate is the score the individual receives for passing that item. It reflects the difficulty level, discriminative value, and probability of guessing correctly that are associated with that item. Also available is the item information function, indicating the precision of measurement. The test information function, which is the sum of the item information functions, serves the same purpose as the traditional standard error of measurement (SEM). Following each item response, the computer selects the next item on the basis of the individual's total response history up to that point. Testing continues with the addition of new items until the test information function reaches a preestablished standard. Thus all individuals are measured to the same level of precision.

The individual's score is based not on the number of items answered correctly, but on the difficulty level and other psychometric characteristics of those items. The total test score is derived from the ability estimates corresponding to each item passed. This ability estimate is readjusted and refined as each new item is added, until the predetermined measurement precision is reached. Such scores will be comparable for all persons examined with the item pool, regardless of the particular set of items given to each individual. The actual procedures for constructing a CAT instrument can be facilitated through the use of several available computer programs, such as MicroCAT, distributed by Assessment Systems Corporation.[1]

In general, research by various methods indicates that individualized adaptive testing can achieve the same reliability and validity as conventional tests, with a much smaller number of items and less testing time. It also provides greater precision of measurement for individuals at the upper and lower extremes of the ability range covered by the test (Lord, 1970, 1971a, 1971b, 1971c; Weiss, 1982). There has also been considerable research showing that the correlations between properly constructed CAT forms of tests and their paper-and-pencil forms are about as high as the reliability coefficients of most tests. Such findings suggest that essentially the same constructs can be measured by both modalities (Mead & Drasgow, 1993). At the same time, there are testing situations for which CAT is not suitable, such as speed tests and screening tests that sort persons in terms

[1] Address given in Appendix B. See also Quan, Park, Sandahl, and Wolfe (1984) and Weiss and Vale (1987).

of a cutoff score (Wainer, 1993b). Special attention has been given to the development of technical guidelines for assessing CAT instruments (Green, Bock, Humphreys, Linn, &Reckase, 1984).

Adaptive testing is especially appropriate for use in the individualized instructional programs cited in chapter 3, in which students proceed at their own pace and may therefore require test items at widely different difficulty levels. Computerized testing makes it possible to stop testing as soon as the individual's responses provide enough information for a decision about her or his content mastery. Other uses of computerized adaptive testing are being actively investigated and developed in several settings. One application is illustrated by a computerized adaptive test developed jointly by Educational Testing Service and the College Board for assigning entering college freshmen to appropriate English and mathematics courses (Smittle, 1990; Ward, Kline, & Flaugher, 1986). Because of its individualized item selection, this test requires little testing time and provides immediate scoring. Hence, it can be administered at registration time and permits immediate placement of students in courses or sections best suited to their present performance level.

Another major application of CAT is in large-scale personnel selection and classification programs in industry, government, and the military services. CAT is especially appropriate for these purposes, for at least three reasons: (1) the steady flow of applicants to be tested, thereby precluding the testing of very large groups at any one time and place; (2) the wide range of ability levels to be covered; and (3) the greater test security, since each applicant receives a different set of items from a large pool stored in the computer. Explanatory research toward the development of a CAT version of the Armed Services Vocational Aptitude Battery (ASVAB) has been in progress for some time (McBride & Martin, 1983; Moreno, Wetzel, McBride, & Weiss, 1984; Wiskoff & Schratz, 1989). Gradually, CAT editions are being developed for major existing group tests, such as the Differential Aptitude Tests,[2] described in the last section of this chapter. For many practical applications, as well as for substantive research on the nature and sources of individual differences, CAT offers undoubted advantages. A clear and effective presentation of its promise for the future of testing can be found in Embretson (1992).

GROUP TESTS FOR ABILITY TESTING

Unlike major individual scales and computerized adaptive tests, traditional group tests present the same test items to all the test takers, regardless of their individual responses. For this reason, any given group test must cover a relatively restricted range of difficulty suitable for that particular age, grade, or ability level for which it is designed. To provide comparable measures of intellectual development over a broader range, a typical group intelligence test consists of a series of multiple-choice questions arranged in a spiral-omnibus format or as a series of separately timed tests (Aiken & Groth-Marnat, 2006, p.135). As per practitioners, while scoring group intelligence tests, it is important to interpret them with caution. The background of a candidate's school grades, interview, observation data, and other relevant information must be considered while interpreting the raw scores, percentile ranks, standard scores, or any other numerical measure.

[2] DAT-Adaptive (1987), corresponding to paper-and-pcncil DAT-Form V (1981).

If available, interpretative reports should be used and people with low scores should ideally be given additional individual tests before a selective or diagnostic decision is made. It is noteworthy that, in recent times, the group intelligence tests have been renamed differently and are preferably called multilevel batteries. This change reflects the growing recognition that the term intelligence has acquired too many excess meanings, which may lead to misinterpretations of test scores. Some of the representative multilevel batteries are Otis-Lennon School Ability Test (OLSAT), cognitive ability test (CogAT), and test of cognitive skills (TCS) (see Table 10–1). These three tests will be referred to, throughout the text of this chapter. However, out of these tests, one of the most popular multilevel batteries is the CogAT.

CogAT is designed to assess a test taker's ability to reason and solve problems by using verbal, quantitative, and spatial (non-verbal) test items. It includes two levels for covering Grade K (pre-primary or kindergarten) through Grade 3 and eight levels for covering Grade 3 through Grade 12. Each level is printed in a separate booklet. Test takers, taking different levels, start and stop with different sets of items. The test is designed such that most test takers will be tested with items that are at an intermediate level of difficulty for them and discrimination will be most effective. Levels A through H contain the same nine subtests, grouped into three batteries as follows:

a. Verbal Battery: Verbal Classification, Sentence Completion, Verbal Analogies
b. Quantitative Battery: Quantitative Relations, Number Series, Equation Building
c. Nonverbal Battery: Figure Classification, Figure Analogies, Figure Analysis.

These subtests use no words or numbers, but only geometric or figural elements, and the items bear little relation to formal school instructions. Each subtest is preceded by practice exercises with detailed explanations. Practice tests

Table 10-1

Representative Multilevel Batteries

Battery	Grade Range	Number of Levels	Jointly Normed with
Otis-Lennon School Ability Test (OLSAT, 7th ed.)	K–12	1	Stanford Achievement Test Series (9th ed.)
Cognitive Abilities Test (CogAT, Form 5)	K–3 3–12	2 8	Iowa Tests of Basic Skills (Grades K–9) Tests of Achievement and Proficiency (tirades 9–12) Iowa Tests of Educational Development (Grades 9–12)
Test of Cognitive Skills (2nd ed., TCS/2)	2–12[a]	6	California Achievement Tests (5th ed.) Comprehensive Tests of Basic Skills (4th ed.)

[a]There is also a separate Primary Test of Cognitive Skills (PTCS), with a different set of tests appropriate to the kindergarten and first-grade levels.

that can be given in advance of the actual administration are also available. Figure 10–3 shows a typical item from six of the nine subtests, with condensed and slightly reworded instructions. In the level of difficulty, these items correspond

Verbal Classification: Think how the words in dark type are alike. Then find the wod in the line below that goes with them.

Kind **Friendly** **Helpful**

A capable **B** active **C** generous **D** pretty **E** strong

Verbal Analogies: Figure out how the first two words go together. Then find the word that completes the second pair in the same way.

Ship → **Harbor** : **Truck** →

A drive **B** highway **C** garage **D** gasoline **E** freight

Number Series: Figure out the rule used to arrange the number series below. Then choose the number that should come next.

3 2 1 3 2 1 →

A 0 **B** 1 **C** 2 **D** 3 **E** 4

Equation Building: The numbers and signs at the top can be put together so as to give one of the answers at the bottom. Mark that answer.

2 4 8 – –

J 0 **K** 2 **L** 4 **M** 6 **N** 10

Figure Classification: The first three figures are alike in some way. Find the figure at the right that is like the first three.

J K L M N

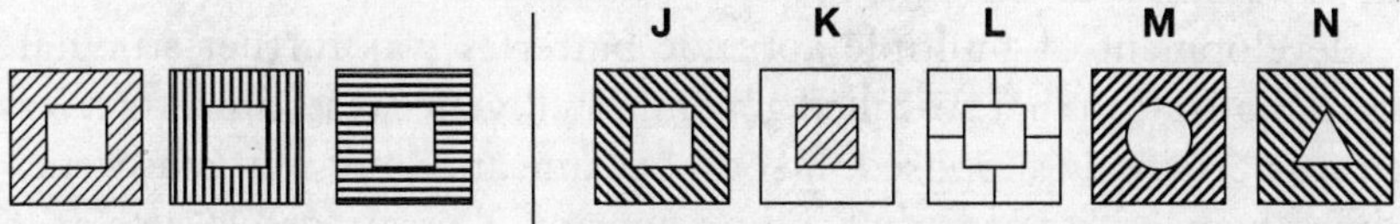

Figure Analogies: Decide how then first two figures are related to each other. Then find the one figure at the right that completed the second pair in the same way.

J K L M N

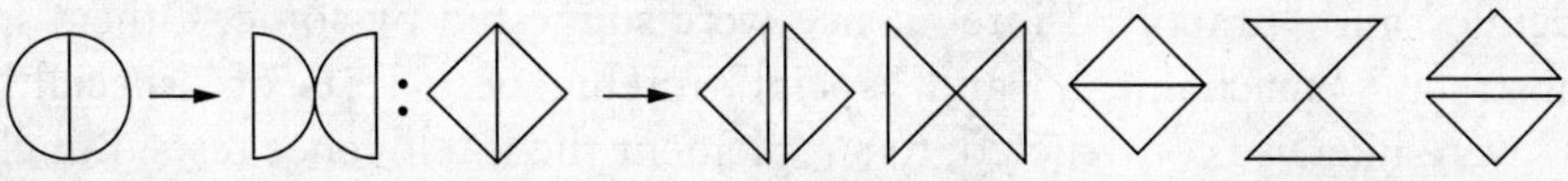

Figure 10–3. Some Item Types from Cognitive Abilities Test. Responses marked on separate answer sheet. Correct answers: C, C, D, K, J, K.

(From CogAT, Form 5, Practice Test for Levels A–H. Copyright © 1993 by The Riverside Publishing Company. Reproduced by permission.)

roughly to items given for Grades 4 to 6. The manual recommends that all three batteries be given to each child, in three testing sessions. For most children, the Non-verbal Battery does not predict school achievement as accurately as the Verbal and Quantitative batteries. Nonetheless, a comparison of performance on the three batteries may provide useful information regarding special abilities or disabilities.

MEASURING MULTIPLE APTITUDES

Traditional intelligence tests, whether administered individually or to groups, were designed primarily to yield a single, global measure of the individual's general level of cognitive development, such as an IQ. Both practical and theoretical developments, however, soon drew attention to certain differentiable aptitudes within the loose conglomerate represented by early intelligence tests. These developments led to the construction of separate tests for the measurement of a few widely applicable aptitudes. At the same time, they led to a refined definition and a fuller understanding of what the intelligence tests themselves measured.

A number of events contributed to the growing interest in the measurement of different aptitudes. First, there was an increasing recognition of intraindividual variation in performance on intelligence tests. Crude attempts to compare the individual's relative standing on different subtests or item groups antedated the development of multiple aptitude batteries by many years. Intelligence tests, however, were not designed for this purpose. The subtests or item groups were often too unreliable to justify intraindividual comparisons. In the construction of intelligence tests, moreover, items or subtests were generally chosen to provide a unitary and internally consistent measure. In such a selection, an effort was therefore made to minimize, rather than maximize, intraindividual variation. Subtests or items that correlated very low with the rest of the scale would, in general, be excluded. Yet these are the very parts that would probably have been retained if the emphasis had been on the differentiation of abilities. Because of the way in which most intelligence tests were constructed, it is unlikely that performance on these tests can be significantly differentiated into more than two categories, such as verbal and nonverbal, or linguistic and quantitative.

The development of multiple aptitude batteries was further stimulated by the gradual realization that so-called general intelligence tests are in fact less general than was originally supposed. It soon became apparent that many such tests were primarily measures of verbal comprehension. Certain areas, such as that of mechanical abilities, were usually untouched, except in some of the performance and nonlanguage scales. As these limitations of intelligence tests became evident, psychologists began to qualify the term "intelligence." Distinctions between "academic" and "practical" intelligence were suggested by some. Others spoke of "abstract," "mechanical," and "social" intelligence. Tests of "special aptitudes" were likewise constructed, to supplement the intelligence tests. But closer analysis showed that the intelligence tests themselves could be said to measure a certain combination of special aptitudes, such as verbal and numerical abilities.

A strong impetus to differential aptitude testing was also provided by the growing activities of psychologists in career counseling, as well as in the selection and classification of industrial and military personnel. The early development of spe-cialized tests in clerical, mechanical, and other vocational areas is a reflection of such interests. The assembling of test batteries for the selection of applicants for admission to schools of medicine, law, engineering, dentistry, and other professional fields represents a similar development which had been in progress for many years. Moreover, a number of differential aptitude batteries, such as those prepared by the armed services and by the U.S. Employment Service, were the direct result of occupational selection or classification work.

Finally, the study of trait organization through the techniques of *factor analysis*[3] provided the theoretical basis for the construction of multiple aptitude batteries. Through such factor-analytic research, the different abilities loosely grouped under "intelligence" could be more systematically identified, sorted, and defined. Tests could then be selected so that each represented the best available measure of one of the factors or traits identified by factor analysis.

Differential Aptitude Tests. One of the most widely used multiple aptitude batteries is the Differential Aptitude Tests (DAT). First published in 1947, the DAT has been periodically revised (5th ed., Form C, 1992). The battery was designed principally for use in educational and career counseling of students in grades 8 to 12. The 5th–edition DAT is available in two levels: Fevel 1, designed primarily for students in Grades 7 to 9 and adults who have completed these years of schooling; and Fevel 2, for students in Grades 10 to 12 and adults with more than 9 years of schooling but who may not have graduated from high school.

The DAT comprises the following eight tests: Verbal Reasoning, Numerical Reasoning, Abstract Reasoning, Perceptual Speed and Accuracy, Mechanical Reasoning, Space Relations, Spelling, and Language Usage. Sample items from four of these tests are shown in Figure 10–4. A Practice Test covering all eight areas is available for advance use with examinees. There is also a special form, the Differential Aptitude Tests for Personnel and Career Assessment, in which each of the eight tests has been shortened and printed in a separate booklet. With this form, particular tests may be chosen for relevance to specific occupations and used singly.[4]

Like most major current tests, the DAT can be completely administered in a computerized version. A more recent development that is now being explored is a computerized adaptive testing (CAT) form (DAT Adaptive), available since 1987. As in all adaptive testing, the examinee takes only those items that are appropriate for her or his performance level. For this CAT version, the items used were from an earlier DAT (Form V) and were analyzed by the Rasch model, a simplified, one parameter model of item response theory (see chap. 7).

An extensive collection of DAT validity data has been assembled over the years, both by the test publisher and by independent investigators who applied the battery in different occupational settings or included it in research projects. Most of these data are concerned with predictive validity in terms of high school achievement in both academic and vocational programs. Many of the coefficients are high, even with intervals as long as three years between test and criterion data. The results are somewhat less encouraging with regard to differential predic-tion.

[3] This topic will be discussed in chapter 11.

[4] A Career Interest Inventory was standardized jointly with the 5th edition DAT. It can be administered, scored, and interpreted in combination with the DAT for educational and career counseling.

Verbal Reasoning

Choose the correct pair of words to fill the blanks. The first word of the pair goes in the blank space at the beginning of the sentence; the second word of the pair goes at the end of the sentence.

...... is to fin as bird is to ......

A water — feather C fish — wing
B shark — nest D flipper — fly
E fish — sky

The correct answer is C

Numerical Reasoning

What number should replace R in this addition problem?

	F	G	H	J	K
7R +R 88	9	6	4	3	None of these

The correct answer is F

Mechanical Reasoning

Which load will be easier to pull through soft sand?

The correct answer is C

Space Reasoning

Which of the following figures could be made by folding the pattern at the left?

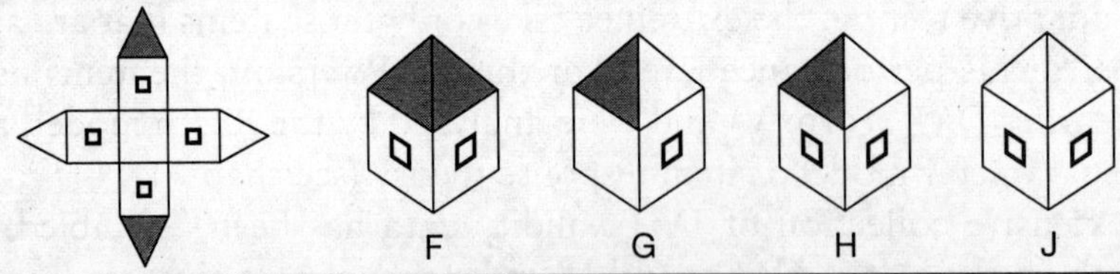

The correct answer is H

Figure 10-4. Sample Items from Differential Aptitude Tests, 5th ed.

Although, in general, verbal tests correlate more highly with English courses and numerical tests with mathematics courses, there is evidence of a large general factor underlying performance in all academic work. Verbal Reasoning, for example, gives high correlations with most courses. It is chiefly for this reason that the VR + NR score was introduced as an index of scholastic aptitude. Being the sum of the scores on the Verbal Reasoning and Numerical Reasoning subtests, this index correlates in the .70s and .80s with composite criteria of academic achieve- ment. Norms are provided for this index, which is one of the scores regularly included in the DAT profile (see Fig. 4–6). There is also a *Partial Battery,* containing only the VR and NR subtests, which can be used only if a general index of scholastic aptitude is wanted.

From another angle, there is growing evidence that traditional tests of "general intelligence" or "scholastic aptitude"— whether designed for individual or group administration—yield substantial validity coefficients against a wide variety of educational and occupational criteria (L. S. Gottfredson, 1986a; Guion & Gibson, 1988; Pearlman, et al., 1980; Schmidt, Hunter, Pearlman, &. Shane, 1979). Such tests include essentially the same cluster of cognitive skills and knowledge assessed by the VR + NR score from the DAT. Thus it can be seen that the early gap between intelligence and multiple aptitude tests is being bridged from both ends. Tests like the DAT have been placing more emphasis on the use and interpretation of broad scores, such as VR + NR. At the same time, the initially general tests were putting more emphasis on the use and interpretation of separate subtest scores and profile analysis. For reviews of the DAT, see Hattrup (1995) and N. Schmitt (1995).

Multidimensional Aptitude Battery, Second Edition (MAB-II). An even closer approximation to the emerging pattern for ability testing is exemplified in the recently developed MAB-II, released in 1998. The first edition of this ability testing (MAB) was launched in 1984 and this group test was designed to assess the same aptitudes as the Wechsler Adult Intelligence Scale (WAIS-R). It includes five subtests in the Verbal Scale—Information, Comprehension, Arithmetic, Similarities and Vocabulary—and five in Performance—Scale Digit Symbol, Picture Completion, Spatial, Picture Arrangement, and Object Assembly—and it yields Verbal, Performance, and Full Scale Deviation IQ scores. This test is suitable for adolescents and adults, but is not recommended for use with mentally challenged individuals whose condition could interfere with their understanding of or following the test instructions. While the test is similar to WAIS-R, two differences emerge out clearly. Firstly, the WAIS-R Digit Span subtest has no parallel in the MAB. This subtest would be difficult to present in paper-and-pencil format; also, it is tended to correlate lowest with Full Scale Wechsler scores. Secondly, the Block Design subtest of the WAIS-R has been replaced by the Spatial subtest in MAB-II. Considerable ingenuity was displayed in designing paper-and-pencil items to measure the same functions covered by the individually administered WAIS-R; and this was especially true of the performance subtests. Figure 10–5 shows a simple, demonstration item for the Picture Completion subtest and one for the Spatial subtest.

MAB-II is a relatively minor revision of the first edition and the technical features of the two versions are nearly identical. Detailed psychometric information is available for the original version in the test technical document.

Picture Completion – Choose the letter that begins the word describing the missing part of the picture.

A. L
B. E
C. B
D. W
E. F

The answer is **Light**, so **A** should be marked.

Spatial – Choose one figure to the right of the vertical line which is the same as the figure on the left. One figure can be turned to look like the figure on the left; the others would have to be flipped over.

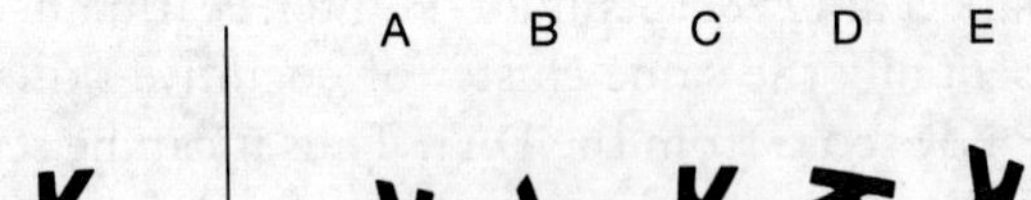

The corrcet answer is **A,** so **A** should be marked. The others **BCDE** would have to be flipped over.

Figure 10-5. Demonstration Items from Two Performance Tests of the Multidimensional Aptitude Battery (MAB).

Strong reliabilities and validity coefficients have been reported in making this assessment a great tool for research, career counseling, selection, and screening in clinical settings. As indicated earlier, the key is to view low scores as a basis for follow-up testing with an individual cognitive test prior to making any decision. The practitioners must keep in mind that MAB and MAB II are group tests and must not be misused in individual cases. These tests should be not be used in isolation for diagnostic decisions or for placement into programs such as classes for intellectually-gifted or intellectually-challenged individuals (Gregory, 2015).

Chapter Eleven

Nature of Intelligence

All psychological tests are designed to measure behavior. Hence the selection of proper tests and the interpretation of test results require knowledge about human behavior. Familiarity with relevant behavioral research is needed not only by the test constructor but also by the test user. In this and the following chapter, we examine some accumulated knowledge about the behavior that tests of intellectual skills are designed to assess. What can psychological research contribute to the understanding of: (1) the behavior measured by tests of cognitive abilities or "intelligence," (2) the sources of individual differences in such behavior and (3) the predictability of such behavior at a subsequent time and in other contexts.

To begin with, it should be noted that the unqualified term "intelligence" is used with a wide diversity of meanings, not only by the general public but also by members of different disciplines, such as biology, philosophy, or education (see Sternberg, 1990), and by psychologists who specialize in different areas or identify with different theoretical orientations (e.g., H. Gardner, 1983, 1993; Sternberg, 1985a, 1989—see also Brody, 1992; Lubinski & Benbow, 1995; Messick, 1992; H. Rowe, 1991). An early display of this diversity of meanings was provided in 1921, when the editor of the *Journal of Educational Psychology* invited 17 leading investigators to contribute their definitions and concepts of intelligence ("Intelligence. . . ," 1921). A similar survey was undertaken 65 years later (Sternberg & Detterman, 1986). An examination of these publications should be of considerable theoretical interest and should provide a basis for lively discussion and possibly some convergence among conflicting views. For the present purpose, however, our goal is more narrowly limited: What should we know about that particular segment of human intelligence assessed by traditional intelligence tests and symbolized by the IQ? It is in this more circumscribed sense that the term "intelligence" is used in the present discussion (see Anastasi, 1983c).

MEANING OF AN IQ

For the general public, IQ is not identified with a particular type of score on a particular test but is often a shorthand designation for intelligence.[1] So prevalent has this usage become that it cannot be merely ignored or deplored as a popular misconception. To be sure, when considering the numerical value of a given IQ, we should always specify the test from which it was derived. Different intelligence tests that yield an IQ do in fact differ in content and in other ways that affect the interpretation of their scores. Some of these differences among tests sharing the common label of "intelligence test" were apparent in the examples considered in the preceding chapters. Nonetheless, there is a need to reexamine the general connotations of the construct "intelligence," as symbolized by the IQ.

First, tested intelligence should be regarded as a descriptive rather than an explanatory concept. An IQ is an expression of an individual's ability level at a given point in time, in relation to the available age norms. No intelligence test can indicate the reasons for one's performance. To attribute inadequate performance on a test or in everyday life activities to "inadequate intelligence" is a tautology and in no way advances our understanding of the individual's handicap. In fact, it may serve to delay efforts to explore the actual causes of the handicap in the individual's personal history.

Intelligence tests, as well as any other kind of tests, should be used not to label individuals but to help in understanding them. This point has been emphasized for many years in many sources, ranging from the writings of individual psychologists to the formal reports of national committees (Hobbs, 1975a, 1975b; National Commission. . . , 1990). A widely publicized book (Herrnstein & Murray, 1994), entitled *The Bell Curve,* has served to perpetuate various stereotypes and misconceptions about ethnic and gender differences in intelligence test performance and has added confusion and controversy to an already complex problem. An objective and factual treatment of the relevant points is provided in a report by the American Psychological Association Task Force on Intelligence (Neisser et al., 1996). A symposium at the 1995 convention of the American Psychological Association was also devoted to clarifying relevant issues (Steele, Chair, August 1995). To bring persons to their maximum functioning level we need to start where they are at the time; we need to assess their strengths and weaknesses and plan accordingly. If a reading test indicates that a child is retarded in reading, we do not label the child as a nonreader and stop; nor do we administer a nonverbal test to conceal the handicap. Instead, we concentrate on teaching the child to read. An important goal of contemporary testing, moreover, is to contribute to self-understanding and personal development. The information provided by tests is being used increasingly to assist individuals in educational and career planning

[1] When first introduced, the IQ (Intelligence Quotient) did refer to a type of score—i.e., the ratio of mental age to chronological age (see chap. 3).

and in making decisions about their own lives. The attention being given to effective ways of communicating test results to the individual attests to the growing recognition of this application of testing.

A second major point to bear in mind is that intelligence is not a single, unitary ability, but a composite of several functions. The term is commonly used to cover that combination of abilities required for survival and advancement within a particular culture (Anastasi, 1986c). It follows that the specific abilities included in this composite, as well as their relative weights, vary with time and place. In different cultures and at different historical periods within the same culture, the qualifications for successful achievement differ. The changing composition of intelligence can also be recognized within the life of the individual, from infancy to adulthood. One's relative ability tends to increase with age in those functions whose value is emphasized by one's culture or subculture; and one's relative ability tends to decrease in those functions whose value is deemphasized.

Typical intelligence tests designed for use with school-age children or adults measure largely verbal abilities; to a lesser degree, they also cover abilities to deal with numerical and other abstract symbols. These are the abilities that predominate in school learning. Most intelligence tests can therefore be regarded as measures of scholastic aptitude or academic intelligence. The IQ is both a reflection of prior educational achievement and a predictor of subsequent educational performance. Because the functions taught in the educational system are of basic importance in modern, technologically advanced cultures, the score on a test of academic intelligence is also an effective predictor of performance in many occupations and other activities of daily life in such cultures.

It should be noted, of course, that there are many important psychological functions that intelligence tests have never undertaken to measure. Mechanical, motor, musical, and artistic aptitudes are obvious examples. Motivational, emotional, and attitudinal variables are important determiners of achievement in all areas. In fact, some psychologists include personality components in their definition of intelligence (e.g., H. Gardner, 1983). Similarly, creativity research is identifying both cognitive and personality variables that are associated with creative productivity. All this implies, of course, that both individual and institutional decisions should be based on as much relevant data as can reasonably be gathered. To base decisions on tests alone, and especially on one or two tests alone, is clearly a misuse of tests. Decisions must be made by persons. Tests represent one source of data utilized in making decisions; they are not themselves decision making instruments.

Much of our information about what intelligence tests measure comes from practical studies of the validity of the tests in predicting educational and vocational achievement. At a more theoretical level, the late 1970s witnessed a strong upsurge of interest in the construct of intelligence, as measured by intelligence tests (Humphreys, 1979; Resnick, 1976; Sternberg & Detterman, 1979). This interest has continued with undiminished vigor, spanning different fields of psychology and pursued through diverse methodological approaches and from varied theoretical orientations. It is reflected in continuing series of volumes (Detterman, 1985–1993; Sternberg, 1982–1989), as well as in a complete encyclopedia devoted to the topic (*Encyclopedia of Human Intelligence,* 1994).

Efforts to understand what intelligence tests measure have included not only the standard statistical procedures of construct validation, such as factor analysis, but also the application of information-processing techniques to the tasks presented in intelligence tests (see chap. 5). The latter approach focuses on the elementary processes whereby a test taker arrives at the answer to a test question, rather than considering only the correctness of the answer. This type of analysis should contribute substantially to the diagnostic use of tests and to the development of training programs to meet specific individual needs.

HERITABILITY AND MODIFIABILITY[2]

Much confusion and controversy have resulted from the application of heritability estimates to intelligence test scores. A well-known example is an article by Jensen (1969) that engendered great furor and led to many heated arguments, some of which are continuing in the 1990s. Although there are several aspects to this controversy and the issues are complicated, a major substantive source of controversy pertains to the interpretation of heritability estimates. Specifically, a heritability index shows the proportional contribution of genetic or hereditary factors to the total variance of a particular trait in a given population under existing conditions. For example, the statement that the heritability of Stanford-Binet IQ among urban American high school students is .70 would mean that 70% of the variance found in these scores is attributable to hereditary differences and 30% is attributable to environment.

Heritability indexes have been computed by various formulas (see, e.g., Jensen, 1969; Loehlin, Lindzey, & Spuhler, 1975), but their basic data are measures of familial resemblance in the trait under consideration. A frequent procedure is to utilize intelligence test correlations of monozygotic (identical) and dizygotic (fraternal) twins. Correlations between monozygotic twins reared together and between monozygotic twins reared apart in foster homes have also been used.

Several points should be noted in interpreting heritability estimates. First, the empirical data in familial resemblances are subject to some distortion because of the unassessed contributions of environmental factors. For instance, there is evidence that monozygotic twins share a more closely similar environment than do dizygotic twins (Anastasi, 1958, pp. 287–288; Koch, 1966). And the environments of siblings reared together may be psychologically quite dissimilar (Daniels & Plomin, 1985). Another difficulty is that twin pairs reared apart are not assigned at random to different foster homes, as they would be in an ideal experiment; it is well known that foster home placements are selective with regard to characteristics of the child and the foster family. Hence, the foster home environments of the twins within each pair are likely to show sufficient resemblance to account for some of the correlation between their test scores. There is also evidence that twin data regarding heritability may not be generalizable to the population at large because of the greater susceptibility of twins to prenatal trauma leading to severe

[2] The question discussed in this section relates to a small part of an extensive area of research on the operation of heredity and environment in behavior development. A comprehensive view of the general topic, which includes critical evaluations of heritability indexes, can be found in Brauth, Hall, and Dooling (1991), Bronfenbrenner and Ceci (1994), Horowitz (1994), Plomin and McClcarn (1993), and Plomin and Reade (1991).

mental retardation. The inclusion of such severely retarded cases in a sample may greatly increase the twin correlation in intelligence test scores (Nichols & Broman, 1974).

Apart from questionable data, heritability indexes have other intrinsic limitations (see Anastasi, 1971; Hebb, 1970). It is noteworthy that in the early part of the previously cited article, Jensen (1969, pp. 33–46) clearly listed these limitations among others. First, the concept of heritability is applicable to populations, not individuals. For example, in trying to establish the etiology of a particular child's mental retardation, the heritability index would be of no help. Regardless of the size of the heritability index in the population, the child's mental retardation could have resulted from a defective gene, as in phenylketonuria (PKU), from prenatal brain damage, or from extreme experiential deprivation.

Second, heritability indexes refer to the population on which they were found at the time. Any change in either hereditary or environmental conditions would alter the heritability index. For instance, an increase in inbreeding, as on an isolated island, would reduce the variance attributable to heredity and hence lower the heritability index; increasing environmental homogeneity, on the other hand, would reduce the variance attributable to environment and hence raise the heritability index. Furthermore, a heritability index computed within one population is not applicable to an analysis of the differences in test performance between two populations, such as different ethnic groups.

Third, heritability does not indicate the degree of modifiability of a trait. Even if the heritability index of a trait in a given population is 100%, it does not follow that the contribution of environment to that trait is unimportant. An extreme example may help to clarify the point. Suppose in a hypothetical adult community everyone has the identical diet. All receive the same food in identical quantities. In this population, the contribution of food to the total variance of health and physical condition would be zero, since food variance accounts for none of the individual differences in health and physique. Nevertheless, if the food supply were suddenly cut off, the entire community would die of starvation. Conversely, improving the quality of the diet could well result in a general rise in the health of the community.

Regardless of the magnitude of heritability indexes found for IQs in various populations, one empirical fact is well established: The IQ is not fixed and unchanging; and it is amenable to modification by environmental interventions. Some evidence for this conclusion is examined in the next chapter, in connection with longitudinal studies. There has been some progress in identifying characteristics of accelerating and decelerating environments. Rises and drops in IQ may also result from both fortuitous environmental changes occurring in a child's life and planned environmental interventions. Major changes in family structure, sharp rises or drops in family income level, or adoption into a foster home may produce conspicuous increases or decreases in IQ.

Worldwide interest in systematic programs for the development of intelligence spread rapidly in the late 1970s and the 1980s, and continues to the present. This is illustrated by the publication the *Human Intelligence International Newsletter* from 1980 to 1987. With an international editorial board, this newsletter provided a quarterly report on cognitive research and its educational applications. Another major example is the 10-year program established and systematically implemented in Venezuela under government sponsorship. Covering many specific projects for the development of "thinking skills" from infancy to old age, this program has stimulated the initiation of similar projects in several other countries (Collins and Mangieri, 1992; Greenwald, 1982, 1984; Herrnstein, Nickerson, Sánchez, & Swets, 1986; Nickerson, 1988; Spitz, 1986; Sternberg, 1986).

Research on the effects of planned interventions at the infant and preschool levels will be examined in chapter 12. Also noteworthy, however, is the growing body of evidence demonstrating the effectiveness of such interventions at later life stages. Although on a smaller scale than those directed at the preschool level, programs for school-age children have yielded encouraging results (Bloom, 1976; Brown & Campione, 1986; Campione & Brown, 1987; Jacobs & Vandeventer, 1971; Olton & Crutchfield, 1969; Resnick & Glaser, 1976). Some investigators have focused on still older age levels, working with college and professional-school students; and they, too, report significant improvement in both academic achievement and scholastic aptitude test performance (Bloom & Broder, 1950; Whimbey, 1975, 1977, 1980). Research on elderly persons has also yielded evidence of learning and transfer effects following training interventions (Willis, Blieszner, & Bakes, 1981). Still other investigators have concentrated on educable mentally retarded children and adolescents, again with significant improvements (Babad & Budoff, 1974; Budoff & Corman, 1974; Feuerstein, 1980; Feuerstein et al, 1987; Hamilton & Budoff, 1974; Rand, Tannenbaum, & Feuerstein, 1979).[3]

These programs provide training in widely applicable cognitive skills, problemsolving strategies, and efficient learning habits. Of special interest is the emphasis on self-monitoring or autocriticism as a condition for effective performance (Flavell, 1979; Owings, Petersen, Bransford, Morris, & Stein, 1980; Whimbey, 1975). The evaluation of one's own performance and the recognition of what one understands and what one does not understand represent an important first step toward improving performance. All too often, the unsuccessful learner is unable to differentiate between true understanding and inaccurate or superficial understanding. There is evidence that children with learning disabilities are especially deficient in autocriticism and in monitoring their own cognition (Kot-sonis & Patterson, 1980).

Other examples of the type of cognitive skills taught in these intellectual development programs were cited in chapter 1. In that chapter, such training in widely applicable intellectual skills was contrasted with narrowly limited coaching on test items. As was observed in that connection, a crucial question to investigate in evaluating intellectual development programs is the extent of transfer or generalizability of the effects of training beyond the types of content and settings in which the training occurred. A related question pertains to the durability of the improvement.

A further consideration is the time required by the older child or the adult to accumulate the content knowledge that is also a part of intelligence and contributes to the person's readiness to learn more advanced material. There is increasing evidence that, except at very elementary levels, problem-solving schemas

[3] For critical evaluations of Feuerstein's approach, see Anastasi (1980) and Blagg (1991).

and concepts are domain-specific, that is, they are associated with particular subject-matter areas. Problem-solving skills are closely linked with the organized content store accumulated by the individual within a specific field of knowledge (Bransford, Sherwood, Vye, & Rieser, 1986; Brown & Campione, 1986; Glaser, 1984; Larkin, McDermott, Simon, & Simon, 1980a; Neimark, 1987; Resnick & Neches, 1984; Richardson, Angle, Hasher, Logie, & Stoltus, 1996). Although the older person, armed with efficient learning techniques, can build up this content store more quickly than he or she would have as a child, it is unrealistic to expect this to occur during a short training program. The older the person, the larger the knowledge gap to be filled. Failure to recognize this point may lead to disappointment and weaken confidence in the efficacy of all such training programs.

MOTIVATION AND INTELLIGENCE

Although it is customary and convenient to classify tests into separate categories, it should be recognized that all such distinctions are superficial. In interpreting test scores, personality and aptitudes cannot be kept apart. An individual's performance on an aptitude test, as well as her or his performance in school, on the job, or in any other context, is influenced by her or his achievement drive, persistence, value system, freedom from handicapping emotional problems, and other characteristics traditionally classified under the heading of "personality."

There is increasing recognition of the role of students' motivation in school learning (Bloom, 1976, chap. 4; Budoff, 1987; Feuerstein et al, 1987; J. G. Nichols, 1979; Renninger, Hidi, & Krapp, 1992; R. E. Snow, 1989). The individual's interests, attitudes, and self-concept as a learner influence her or his openness to a learning task, the desire to learn it well, the attention given to the teacher, and the time devoted to the task. And there is evidence that these individual reactions are significantly related to educational achievement (Baron, 1982; Dreger, 1968; J. McV. Hunt, 1981).

At a more basic level, there is a growing consensus that aptitudes can no longer be investigated independently of affective variables (Anastasi, 1985b, 1994; Izard, Kagan, & Zajonc, 1989; Kanfer, Ackerman, & Cudeck, 1989, Part IV; Moore & Isen, 1990; Saklofske & Zeidner, 1995; Salovey & Sluyter, 1997; R. E. Snow, 1992; Spaulding, 1994; Sternberg &Ruzgis, 1994).

The effects of transitory affective states on the individual's current performance are well established. Even more important is the cumulative effect of personality traits on the direction and extent of the individual's intellectual development. Relevant data come from several types of research, including long-term longitudinal studies (Eichorn, Clausen, Haan, Honzik, & Mussen, 1981) and, more recently, the application of structural equation modeling to the analysis of causal relations (Shavelson & Bolus, 1982). Such studies provide evidence that the prediction of a person's subsequent intellectual development can be substantially improved by combining information about motivation and attitudes with scores on aptitude tests.

One of the ways whereby motivation and other affective variables may contribute to the development of aptitudes is through the amount of time the individual spends on a particular activity relative to other activities competing for attention. On the basis of some 25 years of research on achievement motivation, J. W. Atkinson and his co-workers (Atkinson, 1974; Atkinson, O'Malley, & Lens, 1976) formulated a comprehensive schema representing the interrelationships of abilities, motivation, and environmental variables. A key concept in this schema is time-on-task, namely, the time an individual devotes to one kind of activity, such as studying or carrying out a job-related function. Motivation influences both the efficiency with which a task is performed and the time spent on it relative to other activities. Level of performance depends upon the individual's relevant abilities and the efficiency with which he or she applies those abilities to the current task. The final achievement or product reflects the combined influence of level of performance and time spent at work.

Another major component of the Atkinson schema pertains to the lasting, cumulative effect of task performance on the individual's own cognitive and motivational development. This step represents a feedback loop to the individual's own traits. Its influence should be manifested in that person's future performance, both on tests and in real-life activities. The predictive value of the Atkinson schema was demonstrated with both computer simulations and empirical analyses of longitudinal data on high school students (Atkinson, 1974; Atkinson et al., 1976; Lens, Atkinson, & Yip, 1979).

The effect of sheer time-on-task is enhanced by attention control. What one attends to, how deeply attention is focused, and how long attention is sustained contribute to one's cognitive growth. The selectivity of attention leads to selective learning—and this selection will differ among persons exposed to the same immediate situation. Such selective learning, moreover, may influence the relative development of different aptitudes and thereby contribute to the formation of diverse trait patterns (Anastasi, 1970, 1983a, 1986b). Basically, the several aspects of attention control serve to intensify the effect of time devoted to relevant activities and hence increase its influence on aptitude development.

The relation between personality and intellect is reciprocal. Not only do personality characteristics affect intellectual development, but intellectual level may also affect personality development. Suggestive data in support of this relation were provided in a study by Plant and Minium (1967). Drawing upon the data gathered in five available longitudinal investigations of college-bound young adults, the authors selected the upper and lower 25% of each sample in terms of intelligence test scores. These contrasted groups were then compared on a series of personality tests that had been administered to one or more of the samples. The personality tests include measures of attitudes, values, motivation, and interpersonal and other noncognitive traits. The results of this analysis revealed a strong tendency for the high-aptitude groups to undergo substantially more "psychologically positive" personality changes than did the low-aptitude groups.

The success an individual attains in the development and use of her or his aptitudes is bound to influence that person's emotional adjustment, interpersonal relations, and self-concept. In the self-concept, we can see most clearly the mutual influence of aptitudes and personality traits. The child's achievement in school, on the playground, and in other situations helps to shape her or his self-concept; and this self-concept at any given stage influences her or his subsequent performance, in a continuing spiral. In this regard, the self-concept operates as a sort of private self-fulfilling prophecy.

In recent years, there has been an increasing interest in the study of affective factors in infant development. Several investigations have found substantial correlations between ratings of infant behavior on personality variables and subsequent cognitive development assessed by such instruments as the WISC-R and the Stanford-Binet (Birns & Golden, 1972; R. B. McCall, 1976; Palisin, 1986; Yarrow & Pedersen, 1976). In general, infants who exhibit positive affect, active interest, and responsiveness in a test situation are likely to learn more and to advance faster in cognitive development as a result of their early experiences. They are also likely to respond favorably in later, academic activities that involve interaction with adults in goal-oriented tasks. A further advantage stems from the influence such infant behavior exerts on the social behavior of adult caretakers, which will in turn enhance the child's opportunities for learning (Haviland, 1976; Wilson & Matheny, 1983).

More specifically, studies of the environmental-mastery motive in infants have revealed some promising relations to subsequent measures of intellectual competence. The infant's environmental-mastery behavior includes the observation, exploration, and manipulation of her or his environment. By its very nature, this motive should be a prime contributor to cognitive development. And there is increasing evidence in the experimental literature that it does so contribute (Hrncir, Speller, & West, 1985; White, 1978; Yarrow et al., 1984; Yarrow et al., 1983). In fact, some of the findings suggest that early indicators of a child's environmental-mastery motivation may be a better predictor of later intellectual competence than are earlier measures of competence. Research on infancy is leading toward a rapprochement between the study of affective and cognitive development. It may help to bring about a more integrated utilization of affective and cognitive data in the interpretation of test results at any age level.

FACTOR ANALYSIS OF INTELLIGENCE

Psychological research on the identification of mental traits grew out of an interest in the nature and composition of human intelligence.[4] Such research begins with the intercorrelations of the scores obtained by a sample of persons on a wide variety of ability tests. The correlation table is then subjected to further mathematical analyses, in order to identify common factors or traits among the tests. The various procedures currently available for this purpose are designated by the generic name of *factor analysis*.

The Factor Matrix. The principal object of factor analysis is to simplify the description of data by reducing the number of necessary variables, or dimensions. Thus, if we find that five factors are sufficient to account for all the common variance in a battery of 20 tests, we can for most purposes substitute 5 scores for the original 20 without sacrificing essential information. The usual practice is to retain from among the original tests those providing the best measures of each of the factors.

[4] For some historical perspective, see Anastasi (1984b).

All techniques of factor analysis begin with a complete table of intercorrelations among a set of tests. Such a table is known as a correlation matrix. Every factor analysis ends with a factor matrix, that is, a table showing the weight or loading of each of the factors in each test. A hypothetical factor matrix involving only two factors is shown in Table 11–1. The factors are listed across the top and their weights in each of the 10 tests are given in the appropriate rows.

Several different methods for analyzing a set of variables into common factors have been derived. As early as 1901, Pearson pointed the way for this type of analysis; and Spearman (1904, 1927) developed a precursor of modern factor analysis. T. L. Kelley (1935) and Thurstone (1947b) in America and Burt (1941) in England did much to advance the method. Alternative procedures, modifications, and refinements have been developed by many others. The availability of high-speed computers is leading to the adoption of more refined and laborious techniques. Although differing in their initial postulates, most of these methods yield similar results. For an introduction to the specific procedures of factor analysis, the reader is referred to such texts as Comrey and Lee (1992) or Loehlin (1992). For a brief and simple overview of the basic concepts and procedures, see Kim and Mueller (1978a, 1978b) and P. Kline (1993).

It is beyond the scope of this book to cover the mathematical basis or the computational procedures of factor analysis. An understanding of the results of factor analysis, however, need not be limited to those who have mastered its specialized methodology. Even without knowing how the factor loadings were computed, it is possible to see how a factor matrix is utilized in the identification and interpretation of factors. For an effective reading of reports of factor-analytic research, however, familiarity with a few other concepts and terms is helpful.

The References Axes. It is customary to represent factors geometrically as references axes in terms of which each test can be plotted. Figure 11–1 illustrates this procedure. In this graph, each of the 10 tests from Table 11–1 has been plotted against the two factors, which correspond to axes I and II. Thus, the

Table 11-1

A Hypothetical Factor Matrix

Test	Factor I	Factor II
1. Vocabulary	0.74	0.54
2. Analogies	0.64	0.39
3. Sentence Completion	0.68	0.43
4. Disarranged Sentences	0.32	0.23
5. Reading Comprehension	0.70	0.50
6. Addition	0.22	–0.51
7. Multiplication	0.40	–0.50
8. Arithmetic Problems	0.52	–0.48
9. Equations Relations	0.43	–0.37
10. Number Series Completion	0.32	–0.25

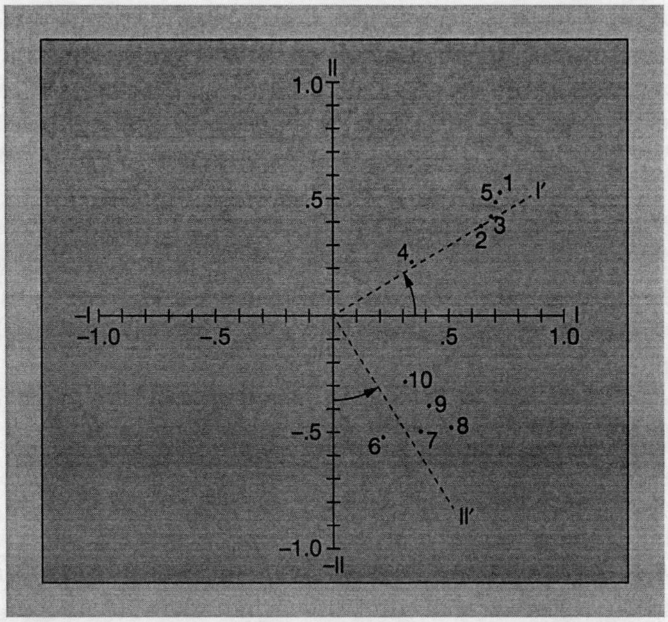

Figure 11-1. A Hypothetical Factor Pattern, Showing Weights of Two Group Factors in Each of 10 Tests.

point representing Test 1 is located by moving .74 of the distance along axis I and .54 of the distance along axis II. The points corresponding to the remaining 9 tests are plotted in the same way, using the weights given in Table 11–1. Although all the weights on Factor I are positive, it will be noted that on Factor II some of the weights are positive and some negative. This can also be seen in Figure 11–1, where Tests 1 to 5 cluster in one part of the graph and Tests 6 to 10 in another.

In this connection it should be noted that the position of the reference axes is not fixed by the data. The original correlation table determines only the position of the tests (i.e., points in Fig. 11–1) *in relation to each other.* The same points can be plotted with the reference axes in any position. For this reason, factor analysts usually rotate axes until they obtain the most satisfactory and easily interpretable pattern. This is a legitimate procedure, somewhat analogous to measuring longitude from, let us say, Chicago rather than Greenwich.

The reference axes in Figure 11–1 were rotated to position I and II, shown by the broken lines.[5] This rotation was carried out in accordance with Thurstone's criteria of *positive manifold* and *simple structure.* The former requires the rotation of axes to such a position as to eliminate all significant negative weights. Most psychologists regard negative factor loadings as logically inapplicable to aptitude tests, since such a loading implies that the higher the individual rates in the particular factor, the poorer will be her or his performance on the test. The criterion of simple structure means essentially that each test shall have

[5] The reader may feel that rotated Axis II should have been labeled – II′, to correspond to the unrotated–II. Which pole of the axis is labeled plus and which minus, however, is an arbitrary matter. In the present example, the rotated axis II′ has been "reflected" in order to eliminate negative weights.

loadings on as few factors as possible.[6] Both of these criteria are designed to yield factors that can be most readily and unambiguously interpreted. If a test has a high loading on a single factor and no significant loading on any other, we can learn something about the nature of the factor by examining the content of the test. If instead the test has moderate to low loadings on six factors, it can tell us little about the nature of any of these factors.

It will be seen that on the rotated axes in Figure 11–1 all the verbal tests (Test 1 to 5) fall along or very close to axis I′. Similarly, the numerical tests (Test 6 to 10) cluster closely around axis II′. The new factor loadings, measured along the rotated axes, are given in Table 11–2. The reader may easily verify these factor loadings by preparing a paper "ruler" with a scale of units corresponding to that in Figure 11–1. With this ruler, distances can be measured along the rotated axes. The factor loadings in Table 11–2 include no negative values except for very low, negligible amounts attributable to sampling errors. All of the verbal tests have high loadings on Factor I′ and practically zero loadings on Factor II′. The numerical tests, on the other hand, have high loadings on Factor II′ and low, negligible loadings on Factor I′. The identification and naming of the two factors and the description of the factorial composition of each test have thus been simplified by the rotation of reference axes. In actual practice, the number of factors is often greater than two—a condition that complicates the geometrical representation and the statistical analysis but does not alter the basic procedure.

Table 11-2

Rotated Factor Matrix

Test	Factor I′	Factor II′
1. Vocabulary	.91	–.06
2. Analogies	.75	.02
3. Sentence Completion	.80	.00
4. Disarranged Sentences	.39	–.02
5. Reading Comprehension	.86	–.04
6. Addition	–.09	.55
7. Multiplication	.07	.64
8. Arithmetic Problems	.18	.68
9. Equation Relations	.16	.54
10. Number Series Completion	.13	.38

(Data from Figure 11–1)

[6] This criterion requires that tests have loadings on some factors that do not differ significantly from zero. Such a requirement can now be tested empirically through available statistical procedures for finding the standard error of factor loadings (Cudeck & O'Dell, 1994).

Some factor analysts use a theoretical model as a guide in the rotation of axes. Invariance, or the corroboration of the same factors in independent but comparable investigations, is also taken into account. There is currently an increasing use of factor analysis in a confirmatory rather than an exploratory role. It is often combined with structural equation modeling (see chap. 5) in evaluating a theoretically formulated model of the operation of different variables in task performance (see, e.g., Loehlin, 1992).

Interpretation of Factors. Once the rotated factor matrix has been computed, we can proceed with the interpretation and naming of factors. This step calls for psychological insight rather than statistical training. To learn the nature of a particular factor, we simply examine the tests having high loadings on that factor and try to discover what psychological processes they have in common. The more tests there are with high loadings on a given factor, the more clearly we can define the nature of the factor. In Table 11–2, for example, it is apparent that Factor I′ is verbal and Factor II′ is numerical.

The factor loadings given in Table 11–2 also represent the correlation of each test with the factor.[7] It will be recalled that this correlation is the factorial validity of the test (chap. 5). From Table 11–2 we can say, for instance, that the factorial validity of the Vocabulary test as a measure of the verbal factor is .91. The factorial validity of the Addition test, in terms of the numerical factor, is .55. Obviously, the first five tests have negligible validity as measures of the numerical factor, and the last five have practically no validity as measures of the verbal factor.

Factorial Composition of a Test. One of the basic theorems of factor analysis states that the total variance of a test is the sum of the variances contributed by the common factors (shared with other tests) and the specific factors (occurring in that test alone), plus the error variance. We have already encountered error variance in the analysis of test scores (chap. 4). If, for instance, the reliability coefficient of a test is .83, we conclude that 17% of the variance of scores on this test is error variance (1.00 – .83 = .17). Through factor analysis, we can further subdivide the sources of variance contributing toward performance on any test.

Let us consider two hypothetical tests listed in Table 11–3. For each test, the table gives its factor loading in Verbal (V), Numerical (N), and Reasoning (R) factors, as well as its reliability coefficient. Since factor loading also represents the correlation between the test and the factor, the square of the factor loading gives us the proportion of common variance between the test and that factor. In the last section of the table, each factor loading has been squared to show the proportional contribution of that factor to the total variance of test scores. Thus, we find that in the Arithmetic Reasoning test 16% of the variance is attributable to the Verbal factor, 30% to the Numerical factor, and 36% to the Reasoning factor. The error variance in the last column is found by simply subtracting the reliability coefficient from the total variance (1.00 – .90 = .10). Whatever is left represents the specificity of this test, that is, that portion of its "true" variance

[7] This is true only when an orthogonal rotation of axes is applied. With oblique rotation, to he defined in a later section of this chapter, factor loadings and factor correlations bear a simple relation to each other and each can be found from the other by appropriate computations.

Table 11–3

Source of Variance of Test Scores

Test	Common Factor Loadings V	N	R	Reliability Coefficient	Proportional Contribution V	N	R	Specific	Error
1. Arithmetic Reasoning	.40	.55	.60	.90	.16	.30	.36	.08	.10
2. Multiplication	.10	.70	.30	.85	.01	.49	.09.	.26	.15

it does not share with any other test with which it was factor analyzed. For the Arithmetic Reasoning test, we have:

$$.16 + .30 + .36 + .10 = .92$$
$$1.00 - .92 = .08$$

Figure 11–2 provides a pictorial breakdown of the sources of variance for the two tests on Table 11–3.

Any individual's performance on these two tests depends on the amounts of each of the relevant abilities or factors he or she possesses, as well as the relative weights of these factors in the particular test. Thus, if we had the individual's score in the V, N, and R factors, expressed in the same units, we could weight each score by multiplying it by the corresponding factor loading. The sum of these products would provide an estimate of the individual's score on the test. The smaller the contribution of specific and error factors to the test, the more accurate this estimate would be.

In the example given in Table 11–3, if an individual rates very high in V, this would help her or him much more on the Arithmetic Reasoning than on the Multiplication test. In fact, it would help four times as much, since the weight of

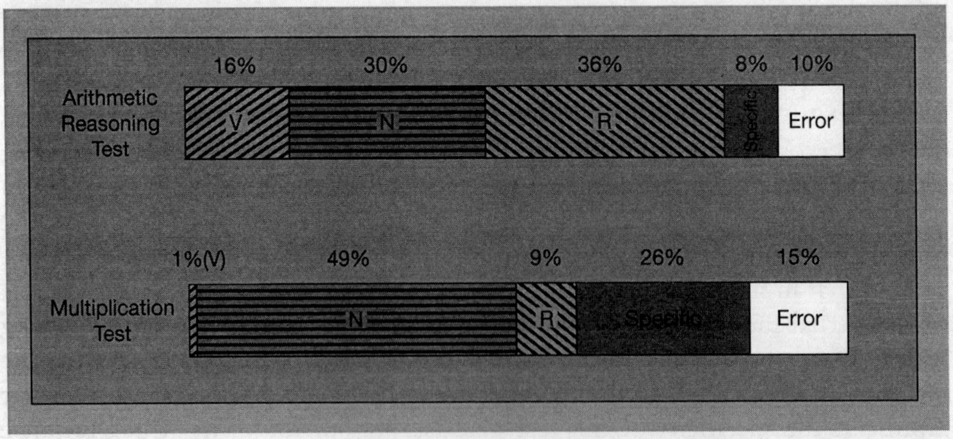

Figure 11–2. Percentage of Common, Specific, and Error Variance in Two Hypothetical Tests.
(Data from Table 11–3.)

the V factor is four times as great in Arithmetic Reasoning as in Multiplication (.40 vs. .10). Of the three common factors, N would have the greatest effect on Multiplication (loading = .70) and R would have the greatest effect on Arithmetic Reasoning (loading = .60).

Factor Loadings and Correlation. A second basic theorem of factor analysis concerns the relationship between factor loadings and the correlations among variables. The correlation between any two variables is equal to the sum of the cross-products of their common-factor loadings. Since specific and error factors are unique to each variable, they cannot contribute to the correlation between variables. The correlation between any two variables depends only on the factors that these two variables share. The larger the weights of these common factors in the two variables, the higher will be the correlation between the variables. The correlation between the two tests given in Table 11–3 can be found by multiplying the loadings of each of the three common factors in the two tests and adding the products as shown below:

$$r_{12} = (40)\ (.10) + (.55)(.70) + (.60)(.30) = .60$$

Oblique Axes and Second-Order Factors. The axes employed in Figure 11–1 are known as *orthogonal axes,* since they are at right angles to each other. Occasionally, the test clusters are so situated that a better fit can be obtained with *oblique axes.* In such a case, the factors would themselves be correlated. Some investigators have maintained that orthogonal, or uncorrelated, factors should always be employed, since they provide a simpler and clearer picture of trait relationships. Others insist that oblique axes should be used when they fit the data better, since the most meaningful categories need not be uncorrelated. An obvious example is that of height and weight. Although it is well known that height and weight are highly correlated, they have proved to be useful categories in the measurement of physique.

When the factors are themselves correlated, it is possible to subject the intercorrelations among the factors to the same statistical analysis we employ with intercorrelations among tests. In other words, we can "factorize the factors" and derive *second-order factors.* This process has been followed in a number of studies with both aptitude and personality variables. Certain investigations with aptitude tests have yielded a single second-order general factor. As a rule, American factor analysts have proceeded by accounting for as much of the common variance as possible through group factors and then identifying a general factor as a second-order factor if the data justified it. British psychologists, on the other hand, have usually begun with a general factor, to which they attributed the major portion of the common variance, and then turned to group factors to account for any remaining correlation. These procedural differences reflect differences in theoretical orientation to be discussed in the following section.

THEORIES OF TRAIT ORGANIZATION

For more than half a century, the statistical techniques of factor analysis have been applied widely in an effort to understand the nature and organization of abilities involved in a diversity of human activities. Nevertheless, these techniques are still most closely associated with research on cognitive abilities or "intelligence," where factor analysis originated. A recently completed survey of all available factor-analytic studies of cognitive abilities provides an impressive summary of such research (Carroll, 1993). Covering over 70 years of studies, this enterprise represents much more than a literature survey; it also includes the re-analysis of more than 450 data sets from the original studies. In the same source, different theoretical models of intelligence are described and evaluated within their historical framework. In the present section, we shall consider only a few widely known theories of intelligence, selected because of their impact on the construction and use of tests.

The Two-Factor Theory. The first theory of trait organization based on a statistical analysis of test scores was the two-factor theory developed by the British psychologist Charles Spearman (1904, 1927). In its original formulation, this theory maintained that all intellectual activities share a single common factor, called the *general factor,* or g. In addition, the theory postulated numerous *specifics,* or *s* factors, each being strictly specific to a single activity. Positive correlation between any two functions was thus attributed to the g factor. The more highly the two functions were "saturated" with g, the higher the correlation between them would be. The presence of specifics, on the other hand, tended to lower the correlation between functions.

Although two types of factors, general and specific, are posited by this theory, it is only the single factor g that accounts for correlation. In contrast to other theories of trait relations, therefore, it could be more precisely characterized as a single-factor theory, although the original designation has persisted. Figure 11–3 illustrates the basis for correlation among tests according to this theory. In this illustration, tests 1 and 2 would correlate highly with each other since each is highly saturated with g, as shown by the shaded areas. The white area in each test

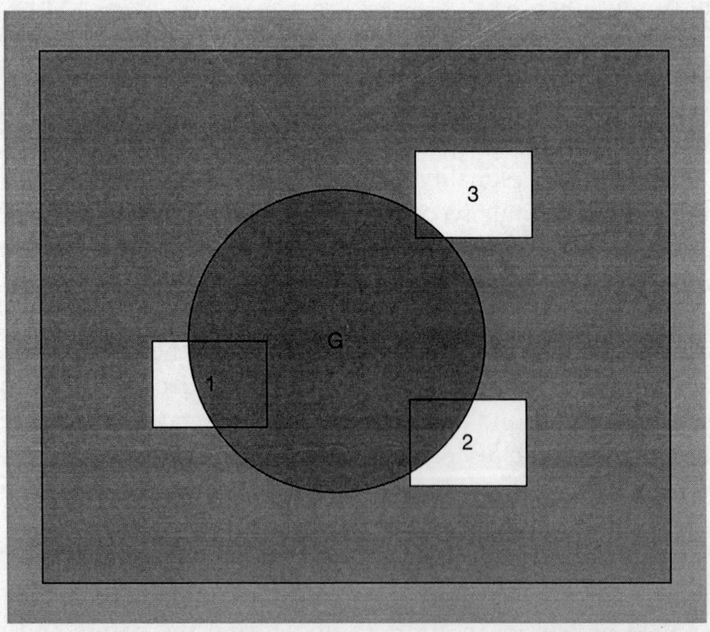

Figure 11–3. Correlation Model Underlying Two-Factor Theory.

represents specific and error variance. Test 3 would have low correlations with each of the other two tests, since it contains very little *g*.

It follows from the two-factor theory that the aim of psychological testing should be to measure the amount of each individual's *g*. If this factor runs through all abilities, it furnishes the only basis for prediction of the individual's performance from one situation to another. It would be futile to measure specific factors, since each by definition operates in only a single activity. Accordingly, Spearman proposed that a single test, highly saturated with *g*, be substituted for the heterogeneous collection of items found in intelligence tests. He suggested that tests dealing with abstract relations are probably the best measures of *g* and could be used for this purpose. Examples of tests constructed as measures of *g* include Raven's Progressive Matrices and Cattell's Culture Fair Intelligence Test.

From the outset, Spearman realized that the two-factor theory must be qualified. When the activities compared are similar, a certain degree of correlation may result over and above that attributable to the *g* factor. Thus, in addition to general and specific factors, there might be another, intermediate class of factors, not so universal as *g* nor so strictly specific as the *s* factors. Such a factor, common to a group of activities but not to all, was designated a *group factor.* In the early formulation of his theory, Spearman admitted the possibility of very narrow and negligibly small group factors. Following later investigations by several of his students, he included much broader group factors such as arithmetic, mechanical, and linguistic abilities.

Multiple-Factor Theories. The prevalent American view of trait organization, based on early factor-analytic research, recognized a number of moderately broad group factors, each of which could enter with different weights into different tests. For example, a verbal factor could have a large weight in a vocabulary test, a smaller weight in a verbal analogies test, and a still smaller weight in an arithmetic reasoning test. Figure 11–4 illustrates the intercorrelations among five tests in terms of a multiple-factor model. The correlations of Tests 1, 2, and 3 with each other result from their common loadings with the verbal factor (V). Similarly, the correlation between Tests 3 and 5 results from the Spatial factor (S), and that between Tests 4 and 5 from the Number factor (N). Tests 3 and 5 are factorially complex, each having appreciable loadings in more than one factor: V and S in Test 3, N and S in Test 5. From the second basic theorem of factor analysis, discussed in the preceding section, we can also tell something about the relative magnitude of the intercorrelations. For example, Test 3 will correlate higher with Test 5 than with Test 2 because the weights of the S factor in Tests 3 and 5 (diagonally striped areas) are larger than the weights of the V factor in Tests 2 and 3 (horizontally striped areas).

The publication of T. F. Kelley's *Crossroads in the Mind of Man* (1928) paved the way for a large number of studies in quest of particular group factors. Chief among the factors proposed by Kelley were manipulation of spatial relationships, facility with numbers, facility with verbal material, memory, and speed. This list has been modified and extended by subsequent investigators employing the more modern methods of factor analysis discussed in the preceding section.

One of the leading exponents of multiple-factor theory was Thurstone. On the basis of extensive research by himself and his students, Thurstone proposed

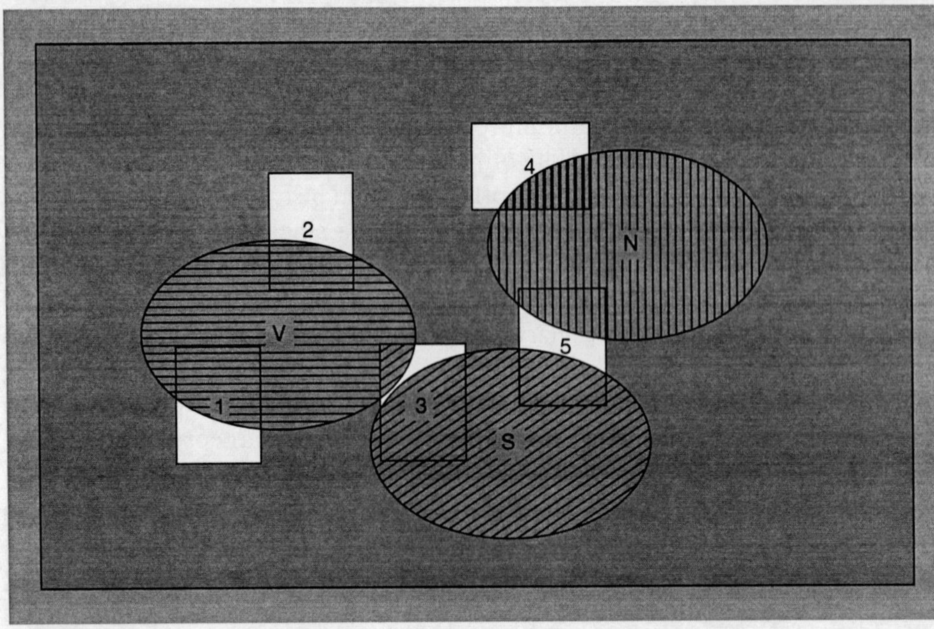

Figure 11-4. Correlation Model Underlying Multiple-Factor Theories.

about a dozen group factors which he designated "primary mental abilities." Those most frequently corroborated in the work of Thurstone and of other independent investigators (French, 1951; Harman, 1975; Thurstone, 1938; Thurstone & Thurstone, 1941) include the following:

V. *Verbal Comprehension:* The principal factor in such tests as reading comprehension, verbal analogies, disarranged sentences, verbal reasoning, and proverb matching. It is most adequately measured by vocabulary tests.

W. *Word Fluency:* Found in such tests as anagrams, rhyming, or naming words in a given category (e.g., boys' names, words beginning with the letter T).

N. *Number:* Most closely identified with speed and accuracy of simple arithmetic computations.

S. *Space:* This factor may represent two distinct factors, one covering perception of fixed spatial or geometric relations, the other manipulatory visualizations, in which changed positions or transformations must be visualized (McGee, 1979; Portegal, 1982).

M. *Associative Memory:* Found principally in tests demanding rote memory for paired associates. There is some evidence to suggest that this factor may reflect the extent to which memory crutches are utilized (Christal, 1958). The evidence is against the presence of a broader factor through all memory tests. Other restricted memory factors, such as memory for temporal sequences and for spatial position, have been suggested by some investigations.

P. *Perceptual Speed:* Quick and accurate grasping of visual details, similarities, and differences. This factor may be the same as the speed factor identified by Kelley and other early investigators. This is one of several factors subsequently identified in perceptual tasks (Thurstone, 1944).

I. (or R). Induction (or *General Reasoning):* The identification of this factor was least clear. Thurstone originally proposed an inductive and a deductive factor. The latter was best measured by tests of syllogistic reasoning and the former by tests requiring the respondent to find a rule, as in a number series completion test. Evidence for the deductive factor, however, was much weaker than for the inductive. Moreover, other investigators suggested a general reasoning factor, best measured by arithmetic reasoning tests.

It should be noted that the distinction between general, group, and specific factors is not so basic as may at first appear. If the number or variety of tests in a battery is small, a single general factor may account for all the correlations among them. But when the same tests are included in a larger battery with a more heterogeneous collection of tests, the original general factor may emerge as a group factor, common to some but not all tests. Similarly, a certain factor may be represented by only one test in the original battery, but may be shared by several tests in the larger battery. Such a factor would have been identified as a specific in the original battery, but would become a group factor in the more comprehensive battery. In the light of these considerations, it is not surprising to find that intensive factorial investigations of special areas have yielded many factors in place of the one or two primary mental abilities originally identified in each area. Such has been the case in studies of verbal, perceptual, memory, and reasoning tests.

Factorial research seems to have produced a bewildering multiplication of factors. The number of cognitive factors reported to date by different investigators is considerably over 100. A certain amount of order was achieved by cross-identification of factors reported by different investigators and often given different names (Ekstrom, French, & Harman, 1979; French, 1951; Harman, 1975). Such cross-identification can be accomplished when there are several tests common to the investigations being compared. To facilitate this process, a group of factor analysts assembled a kit of "reference tests" measuring the principal aptitude factors identified at that time. This kit, distributed by Educational Testing Service (Ekstrom, French, Harman, & Dermen, 1976; *ETS kit,* 1976), made it easier for different investigators planning factorial research to include some common tests in their batteries.

It is apparent that even after these efforts at simplification and coordination, the number of factors remains large. Human behavior is varied and complex, and it is unrealistic to expect a dozen or so factors to provide an adequate description of it. For specific purposes, however, we can choose appropriate factors with regard to both nature and breadth. For example, if we were selecting applicants for a difficult and highly specialized mechanical job, we would probably want to measure fairly narrow perceptual and spatial factors that closely match the job requirements. In selecting college students, on the other hand, a few broad factors such as verbal comprehension, numerical facility, and general reasoning would be most relevant.

Structure-of-Intellect Model. Some factor analysts have tried to simplify the picture of trait relationships by organizing the traits into a systematic schema. On the basis of more than two decades of factor-analytic research, Guilford (1967, 1988; Guilford & Hoepfner, 1971) proposed a boxlike model, which he called the structure-of-intellect (SI) model. Illustrated in Figure 11–5, this model[8] classifies intellectual traits along three dimensions:

Operations—what the respondent does. These include cognition, memory recording, memory retention, divergent production (prominent in creative activity), convergent production, and evaluation.

Contents—the nature of the materials or information on which operations are performed. These include visual, auditory, symbolic (e.g., letters, numbers), semantic (e.g., words), and behavioral (information about other persons' behavior, attitudes, needs, etc.).

Products—the form in which information is processed by the respondent. Products are classified into units, classes, relations, systems, transformations, and implications.

Since this classification includes 6 x 5 x 6 categories, there are 180 cells in the model. In each cell, at least one factor or ability is expected; some cells may contain more than one factor. Each factor is described in terms of all three dimensions. Upon the completion of the Aptitudes Research Project—a 20-year coordinated program of research on the SI model—Guilford and his associates had identified 98 of the anticipated factors (Guilford & Hoepfner, 1971). An alphabetical list and brief description of the many tests developed in the course of this 20-year project can be found in the book by Guilford and Hoepfner (1971, Appendix B).

Although at least one test has been directly designed on the SI model, namely the Structure of Intellect Learning Abilities Test (Meeker, Meeker, & Roid, 1985), the model itself has had little impact on the development and application of tests for general use.[9] It should be borne in mind that the SI model, like all models of trait organization, provides one schema for representing the obtained correlations among variables. Because of the method employed in the rotation of axes, the empirical corroboration of the SI model does not preclude other models (Carroll, 1972; Horn & Knapp, 1973). Different rotations of the same data could be found to fit other models equally closely. Re-analyses of Guilford's original factor-analytic data have, in fact, found that other models fitted the data better than the SI model and were also more consistent with theoretical and practical interpretations (Bachelor, 1989; Carroll, 1993).

On the other hand, a favorable indirect effect of the SI project is the focusing of attention on the distinction between operation and content in the identification of factors. This distinction has helped to clarify both the factors identified through factor analysis and the processes investigated through cognitive psychology, as well as the relation between the two. More will be said about this point

[8] As a result of Guilford's later research, this model differs from the earlier model (Guilford, 1967) by the separation of the figural. content facet into visual and auditory components, and the memory operation facet into recording and retention (Guilford, 1988).

[9] For relevant references, see Carroll (1993), especially pp. 57–60.

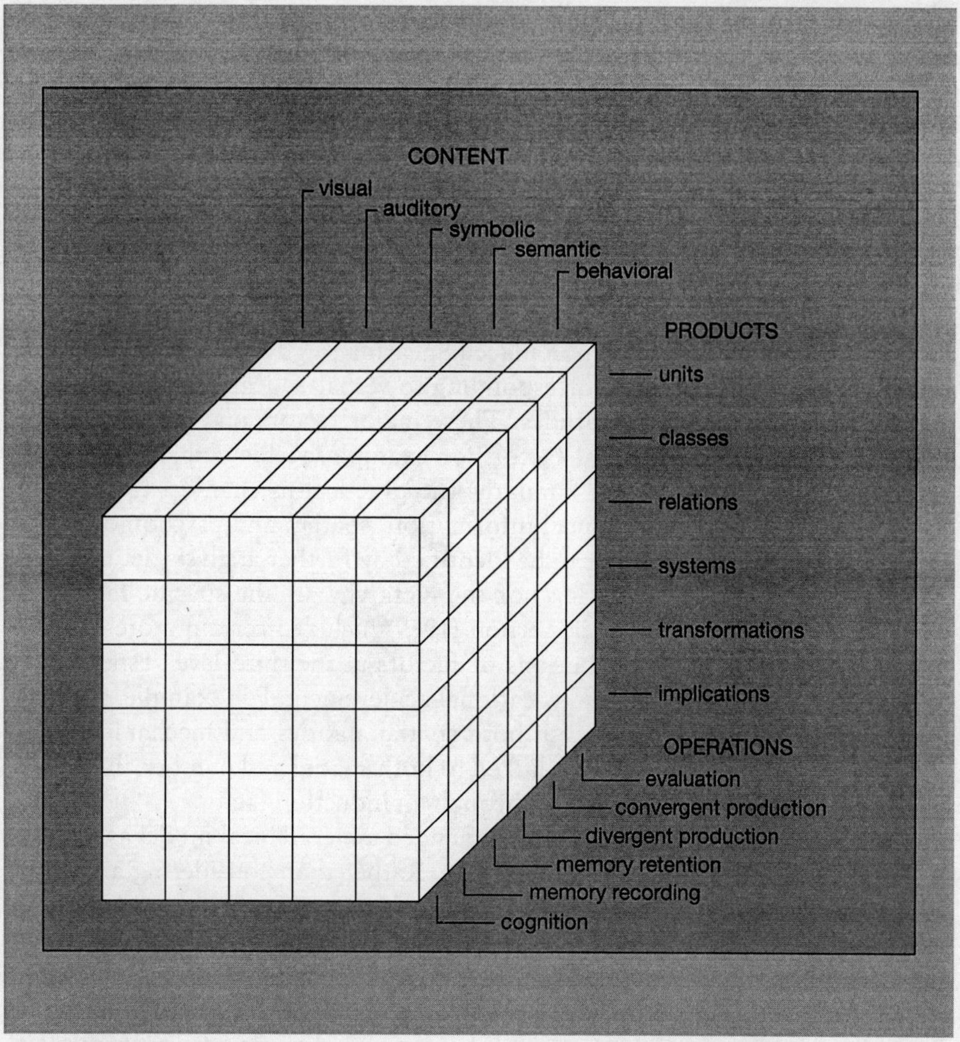

Figure 11-5. Three-Dimensional Model of the Structure of Intellect.

(As revised by Guilford, 1988, p. 3. Copyright © 1988 by *Educational and Psychological Measurement*. Reproduced by permission.)

in the final section of this chapter, dealing with the nature and development of traits. Another indirect effect of the SI model is its differentiation between convergent and divergent thinking. The latter concept, with its implication of atypical behavior, has been widely adopted in analyses of creativity. Efforts to develop tests of divergent thinking, independent of the content domain, however, have generally proved unsuccessful. Divergent thinking and creative productivity have proved to be specific to the field or subject-matter to which they are applied, such as a particular science (e.g., biology or physics) or a particular art form (e.g., music or sculpture). Moreover, a creative idea or product must be meaningful or useful within its particular culture; mere divergence, without qualitative advancement, does not constitute creativity. Research on the broad topic of creativity itself, in whatever context and form manifested, has been progressing apace.

The growing interest in this field is illustrated by the series of volumes on creativity research published in the 1990s, under the editorship of R. S. Albert (1991–1994). The individual books included in this series provide a wide coverage of the topic, from the varied manifestations of creativity to ways of fostering and developing creative behavior.

Hierarchical Theories. An alternative schema for the organization of factors was proposed by a number of British psychologists, including Burt (1949) and Vernon (1960), and by Humphreys (1962) in the United States. A diagram illustrating Vernon's application of this system is reproduced in Figure 11–6. At the top of the hierarchy, Vernon placed Spearman's g factor. At the next level are two broad group factors, corresponding to verbal-educational *(v:ed)* and to practical-mechanical *(k:m)* aptitudes. These major factors may be further subdivided. The verbal-educational factor, for example, yields verbal and numerical subfactors, among others. Similarly, the practical-mechanical factor splits into such subfactors as mechanical-information, spatial, and psychomotor abilities. Still narrower subfactors can be identified by further analysis, let us say, of the verbal tasks. At the lowest level of the hierarchy are the specific factors. In a later elaboration of the model, Vernon (1969) included certain more complex interrelations and cross-contributions of factors at the third level, especially in connection with educational and vocational achievement. For example, scientific and technical abilities are linked to both spatial abilities and mechanical information; mathematical abilities are linked to both spatial and number abilities, as well as more directly to the g factor through an induction factor.

Humphreys (1962, 1970) also recommended a hierarchical model as a means of coping with the proliferation of factors. Rather than considering any single level of factors as primary, however, he suggested that each test constructor or user choose that level of the hierarchy that is most appropriate for her or his purposes. Humphreys recognized, moreover, that a single test may be classified into more than one hierarchy, with reference to content, process, and other facets. To measure any one facet, he proposed that the test be made *heterogeneous* with

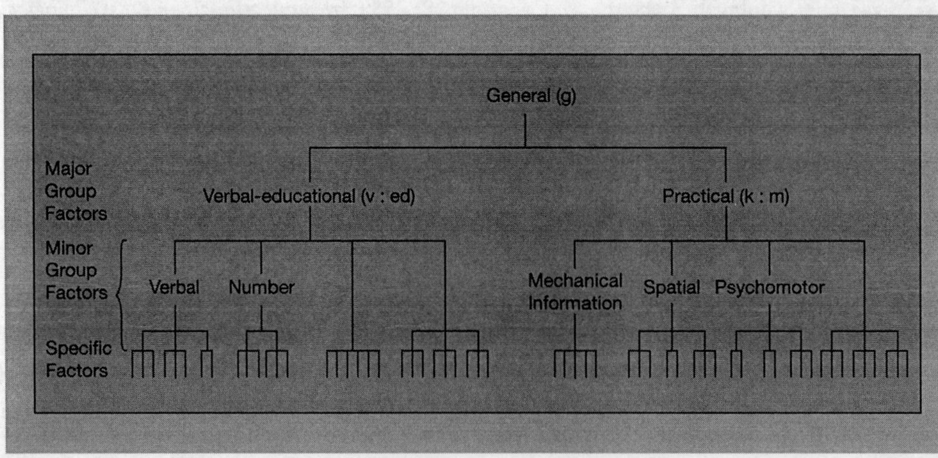

Figure 11–6. Model of a Hierarchical Organization of Abilities.
(Adapted from. P. E. Vernon, 1960, p. 22. Copyright © 1960, Methuen & Co., Ltd. Reproduced by permission.)

regard to all other facets. For example, if we are interested in the person's ability to solve analogies problems, we should use a test that includes verbal, numerical, pictorial, and spatial analogies. If we wish to measure verbal ability, we should do so with a variety of item types, such as vocabulary, analogies, and series completion. This procedure contrasts with that employed by Guilford, who sought separate factors (and tests) for each homogeneous cell in his three-way classification. In his later work, however, Guilford (1981) followed a partial hierarchical organization in identifying higher-order factors among some of the factors in his original structure-of-intellect model.

The hierarchical model of intelligence is being accepted more and more widely for both theoretical and practical purposes (see Anastasi, 1992a, 1994; Carroll, 1993; Gustafsson, 1984, 1989; Lubinski & Dawis, 1992). As a theoretical model of trait relations, it reconciles the single general factor (Spearman's *g)* with multiple-factor patterns. Methodologically, it has been shown that the multiple-factor and the hierarchical solutions are mathematically equivalent and transposable from one to the other (Harman, 1976, chap. 15; Schmid & Leiman, 1957). The oblique-axis solution (with correlated factors) that leads to the hierarchical model can be transposed into an orthogonal-axis solution (with uncorrelated factors). In the latter solution, the second-order factors emerge as first-order factors of different breadth. The broader factors have loadings on more variables than do the narrower factors.

From a practical standpoint, a major advantage of tests developed from a hierarchical pattern is that such tests combine comprehensive aptitude coverage with flexibility of use. To fit different testing purposes, the test user can choose a single overall battery score, or one or more scores on clusters of tests measuring more narrowly defined factors. Under certain circumstances, scores on individual subtests may be useful in identifying either weakness or strength in specialized skills.

The increasing impact of the hierarchical model on the construction and use of ability tests was cited in chapter 2, as a historical development that unified traditional intelligence tests with multiple aptitude batteries. Examples of such hierarchical approach were given in chapter 8 for individual tests and in chapter 10 for group tests. Among the clearest examples of the combination of comprehensive coverage and flexible use are the Differential Ability Scales (Elliott, 1990b), for individual testing, and the Multidimensional Aptitude Battery (Jack-son, 1994b), for group testing. A noteworthy feature of the effective flexibility of scoring levels in such tests is the provision of norms for the interpretation of scores at the chosen level. Without such separate-level norms, a proper evaluation of the test taker's performance at different levels of the hierarchy would be unavailable.

NATURE AND DEVELOPMENT OF TRAITS

That different investigators may arrive at dissimilar models of trait organization becomes less perplexing when we recognize that the traits identified through factor analysis are simply an expression of correlation among behavior measures. They are not underlying entities or casual factors, but descriptive categories. Hence, it is conceivable that different principles of classification may be applicable to the same data. The concept of factors as descriptive categories was explicit in the early writings of Thomson (1948), Burt (1941, 1944), and Vernon (1960) in England, and those of R. C. Tryon (1935) in America. All these writers called attention to the vast multiplicity of behavioral elements, which may become organized into clusters through either hereditary or experiential linkages.

Experiential History. There has been an increasing recognition of the role of the individual's experiential history in the development of intelligence and the formation of group factors (Anastasi, 1986b; Greeno, 1989). It is not only the level of performance in different abilities but also the way in which performance is organized into distinct traits that is influenced by experiential background. Differences in factor patterns have been found to be associated with different cultures or subcultures, socioeconomic levels, and types of school curricula (see Anastasi, 1970, 1983a, 1986b, 1994; Vernon, 1969). Changes in factor patterns over time are also relevant. These include long-term changes—which may reflect the cumulative effect of everyday life experiences—as well as short-term changes resulting from practice and other experimentally controlled learning experiences (Baltes, Cornelius, Spiro, Nesselroade, & Willis, 1980; Birren, Cunningham, & Yamamoto, 1983; Fleishman, 1972; Fleishman & Mumford, 1989; Khan, 1970, 1972; Reinert, 1970). Research on animals has also yielded suggestive evidence regarding the experimental production of factors by the control of early experiences (Whimbey & Denenberg, 1966).

The factorial composition of the same objective task may differ among individuals with diverse experiential backgrounds. One reason for these individual differences may be found in the use of different methods to carry out the same task. Individuals with highly developed verbal abilities, for example, will tend to utilize verbal mediators to solve a mechanical or spatial problem; those whose experiences have been predominantly mechanical, on the other hand, will tend to follow a perceptual or spatial approach in solving the same problem. Relevant evidence was provided by French (1965), who found that the factorial composition of the same tests differed between groups of persons classified according to their typical problem-solving styles. Suggestive evidence can also be found in a study by C. H. Frederiksen (1969) on the cognitive strategies subjects use in memorizing words. In the course of learning, individuals may change their choice of strategy and thereby alter the factorial composition of the task as performed by them. Similar shifts in aptitude requirements have been shown to occur over longer periods of time in the course of instruction (R. B. Burns, 1980).

Mechanisms of Trait Formation. A mechanism for the emergence of factors is provided by the familiar concepts of learning set and transfer of training (Carroll, 1966; G. A. Ferguson, 1954, 1956; Simon, 1990; Whiteman, 1964). The establishment of learning sets enables the individual to learn more efficiently when presented with a new problem of the same kind. In Harlow's (1949, 1960) classic experiments with monkeys, after the animal had solved problems requiring the differentiation between certain shapes (like triangle and circle), it learned to discriminate between *other* shapes much more rapidly than did animals without such experience. The animal had established a learning set for differentiating shapes; it knew what to look for when faced with a new problem. The animal had thus "learned how to learn" this type of problem.

Similarly, many of the skills developed through formal schooling, as in reading and arithmetic computation, are applicable to a wide variety of subsequent learning situations. Efficient and systematic problem-solving techniques can likewise be applied to the solution of new problems. Individual differences in the extent to which these skills have been acquired will be reflected in the performance of a large number of different tasks; and in a factor analysis of these tasks, these widely applicable skills would emerge as broad group factors. The breadth of the transfer effect, or the variety of tasks to which a skill is applicable, would thus determine the breadth of the resulting group factor.

Another major source of trait formation is the contiguity or co-occurrence of learning experiences. For example, persons in educationally advanced cultures are likely to develop a broad verbal-educational factor running though all activities learned in school. A narrower factor of numerical aptitude may result from the fact that all arithmetic processes are taught together by the same teacher in the same classroom. Hence, the child who is discouraged, antagonized, or bored during the arithmetic period will tend to fall behind in learning *all* these processes; the one who is stimulated and gratified in the arithmetic class will tend to learn well all that is taught in that class period and to develop attitudes that will advance his or her subsequent numerical learning.

However developed, the factors or abilities identified through factor analysis are descriptive categories, reflecting the changing interrelationships of performance in a variety of situations. These factors are not static entities but are themselves the product of the individual's cumulative experiential history. Insofar as the interrelationships of experiences vary among individuals and groups, different factor patterns may be expected among them. As the individual's experiences change—through formal education, occupational functions, and other continuing activities—new traits may become differentiated or previously existing traits may merge into broader composites.

Factor Analysis and Cognitive Task Analysis. The more recently developed information-processing procedures of cognitive psychology are making significant contributions, not only to an understanding of what intelligence tests measure (see chap. 5) but also to an understanding of the formation and development of factors. Protocol analysis, whereby the individual is directed to "think aloud" as he or she solves a problem or performs an intellectual task, provides a promising approach to the analysis of human thinking (Ericsson & Simon, 1993). As research on cognitive processes continued, however, there was increasing evidence of the *domain specificity* of thinking processes. Except at the most elementary levels, processing skills tend to be specific to the type of content processed; and they are acquired as the content knowledge is mastered and organized for ready retrieval.

On the other hand, the traits most commonly identified through factor analysis deal chiefly with content domains, such as verbal, numerical, and spatial. Those less common factors that are defined by processes, such as associative memory, general reasoning, or divergent thinking, are themselves found to be domain-specific when assessed through specially developed tests. Whether a test is derived from factor analysis or from cognitive analysis, the fundamental distinction is that between a process and the domain in which it is applied. The relevant domain may refer to the *content* that is processed (e.g., linguistic, mathematical, mechanical, etc.)

or to the *context* in which it is performed, as identified by cultural, social, geographical, occupational, or other environmental categories.

The development of cognitive psychology, from its early efforts to identify *the processes* of human intelligence to its rapidly advancing exploration of the domain specificity of all cognitive processes, is reflected in the impressive growth of publications that highlight domain specificity.[10] It is also noteworthy that tests developed to assess the content-defined traits derived by factor analysis have proved to be good predictors of everyday life performance. It is likely that such factors may be indirectly identifying clusters of processing skills appropriate for the given content domain. Thus the person who obtains a high score on a verbal aptitude test may excel not only in the extent and organization of verbal knowledge but also on the use of specialized processing skills required in the verbal domain.

General Intelligence. Factor-analytic research on intelligence has been concerned not only with what intelligence tests measure but also with the nature of intelligence, wherever manifested. When considered from this broader viewpoint, human intelligence comprises that combination of cognitive skills and knowledge demanded, fostered, and rewarded by the experiential context within which the individual functions (Anastasi, 1986c). In this generalized construct of intelligence, domain specificity is even more basic than it is in the narrower processes identified by protocol analysis or factor analysis. Many aspects of intelligence develop while the individual is learning factual knowledge and processing skills within a single domain, such as a particular cultural context or a specific occupation.

Early efforts to identify a single, universally applicable intelligence produced the traditional "intelligence tests." Soon such tests came to be known as measures of academic intelligence or scholastic aptitude, which was the particular intelligence they were actually assessing. The term "practical intelligence" was then proposed as a different kind of intelligence, not covered by traditional tests (see Anastasi, 1986b; Neisser, 1976; Sternberg & Wagner, 1986). Such practical intelligence, however, is not a single intelligence but rather a multiplicity of intelligences, applicable in different practical domains (Lave, 1988; Rogoff & Lave, 1984). There are not two types of intelligence, academic and practical; intelligence is a multifaceted construct.

A weakness of traditional factor analysis arises from the inadequate attention given to the choice of variables to be factor analyzed (Anastasi, 1988a). Obviously, the factors identified by such an analysis are derived from the intercorrela-tions among the chosen variables. Most investigations of intelligence began with a set of scores on tests designed to measure school-taught performance. Hence the factors that emerged represented academic intelligence. In educationally advanced cultures, such factors prove to be good predictors of school achievement; they also yield moderately high correlations with performance on many jobs for which schooling itself is relevant. If we want to assess intelligence in broader contexts, however, we need to start with people's performance in real-life, culturally valued activities. Although students in school are readily accessible participants in testing research, it is becoming evident that adults in various occupations are available. Research can be so organized as to benefit the

[10] See, for example, Greeno (1989), E. Hunt (1987), Schneider and Weinert (1990), Simon (1990), and Sternberg and Frensch (1991).

participants and also yield well-controlled scientific data. There are increasing examples of such collaborative research effectively conducted in industrial and farming contexts (e.g., Fleishman & Reilly, 1992b; Lubinski & Dawis, 1992; Whyte, 1991).

Some of the procedures developed in cognitive psychology have themselves highlighted the domain specificity of intelligence. One approach to the investigation of cognitive processes is through the protocol analysis of contrasted groups, such as experts and novices in a particular activity (e.g., chess players, typists, computer programmers). It has been repeatedly established that the individual's performance level and employment of cognitive skills is strictly specific to the particular domain. A special advantage of this procedure of cognitive psychology is that the research has been conducted on a wide variety of activities from real-life contexts. Such activities range from waiters' memory for restaurant orders to medical diagnosis and judicial court decisions (Chi et al., 1988; Ericsson & Smith, 1991).

The concept of domain specificity has been having an increasing effect on the psychological study of several topics. For example, it is clearly reflected in the current definitions of genius and giftedness. The identification of gifted children has shifted from a specified IQ level (Terman et al., 1925) to superior talent in any of a multitude of socially desirable fields (Csikszentmihalyi, Rathunde, & Whalen, 1993; Feldman & Bratton, 1972; Horowitz & O'Brien, 1985; Subotnik & Arnold, 1994). Similarly, early efforts to design general process tests of creativity or diver-gent thinking have clearly encountered domain specificity (Baer, 1993; Runco, 1991, 1994; Subotnik & Arnold, 1994). Some progress has now been made in integrating domain in tests of creativity. For instance, one of the researches demonstrated that training in relevant skills increases the creative performance on tasks directly related to the training. In this study, the researcher taught poetry that was related to divergent thinking skills to 79 seventh-grade students over several weeks. These 79 students and a matched group of 78 other students later wrote both poems and stories that were rated for creativity by experts. The results highlighted that the experimental group wrote more creative poems than stories. At first, this seems to contradict the reported success of many general creativity training programs. However, the success of these programs can be attributed to the fact that such programs typically employ a wide variety of content and thus teach a wide variety of domain-specific skills in creativity, even if their goal is to teach a general, all-purpose creative-thinking skill (Baer, 1998). It appears that the union of cognitive psychology with psychometric factor analysis has not only enriched the understanding of intellectual functioning but has also brought both types of research closer to the world of daily living.

Chapter Twelve

Psychological Issues in Ability Testing

An inevitable consequence of the expansion and growing complexity of any scientific endeavor is an increasing specialization of interests and functions among its practitioners. Such specialization is clearly apparent in the relationship of psychological testing to the mainstream of contemporary psychology (Anastasi, 1967, 1991). Specialists in psychometrics have raised techniques of test construction to truly impressive pinnacles of quality. While providing technically superior instruments, however, they have given relatively little attention to ensuring that test users had the psychological information needed for the proper use of such instruments. As a result, outdated interpretations of test performance all too often survived without reference to the results of pertinent behavioral research. This partial isolation of psychological testing from other fields of psychology—with its consequent misuses and misinterpretations of tests—accounts in part for the public discontent with psychological testing that began in the 1950s, rose to a strident crescendo in the 1970s, and lingers in various contexts today. The topics chosen for discussion in this chapter illustrate ways in which the findings of psychological research can contribute to the effective use of ability tests and help to correct popular misconceptions about "the IQ" and similar scores.

LONGITUDINAL STUDIES OF CHILDREN'S INTELLIGENCE

An important approach to the understanding of the construct "intelligence" is through longitudinal studies of the same individuals over long periods of time. Although such investigations may be regarded as contributing to the long-term predictive validation of specific tests, they have broader implications for the nature of intelligence and the meaning of intelligence test scores. When intelligence was believed to be largely an expression of hereditary potential, each individual's "IQ" was expected to remain very nearly constant throughout life. Any observed variation on retesting was attributed to weaknesses in the measuring instrument—either inadequate reliability or poor selection of functions tested. With increasing research on the nature of intelligence, however, has come the realization that intelligence itself is both complex and dynamic. In the following sections, we shall examine typical findings of longitudinal studies of intelligence and shall inquire into the conditions making for both stability and instability of tested abilities.

Stability of Intelligence Test Performance. An extensive body of data has accumulated showing that, over the elementary, high school, and college period, intelligence test performance is quite stable (see Anastasi, 1958, pp. 232–238; Bornstein & Krasnegor, 1989; McCall, Appelbaum, & Hogarty, 1973). In an early Swedish study of a relatively unselected population, for example, Husén (1951) found a correlation of .72 between the test scores of 613 third-grade schoolboys and the scores obtained by the same persons 10 years later, on their induction into military service. In a later Swedish study, Härnqvist (1968) reported a correlation of .78 between tests administered at 13 and 18 years of age to over 4,500 young men. Even preschool tests show remarkably high correlations with later retests. In a longitudinal study of 140 children conducted at Fels Research Institute (Sontag, Baker, & Nelson, 1958), Stanford-Binet scores obtained at 3 and at 4 years of age correlated .83. The correlation with the 3-year tests decreased as the interval between retests increased, but by age 12 it was still as high as .46. Of special relevance to the Stanford-Binet is the follow-up conducted by Bradway, Thompson, and Cravens (1958) on children originally tested between the ages of 2 and 5½ as part of the 1937 Stanford-Binet standardization sample. Initial IQs correlated .65 with 10-year retests and .59 with 25-year retests. The correlation between the 10-year retest (mean age = 14 years) and 25-year retest (mean age = 29 years) was .85.

As would be expected, retest correlations are higher, the shorter the interval between tests. With a constant interval between tests, moreover, retest correlations tend to be higher the older the children. The effects of age and retest interval on retest correlations exhibit considerable regularity and are themselves highly predictable (R. L. Thorndike, 1933, 1940). One explanation for the increasing stability of intelligence test scores with age is provided by the *cumulative nature of intellectual development*. The individual's intellectual skills and knowledge at each age include all her or his earlier skills and knowledge plus an increment of new acquisitions. Even if the annual increments bear no relation to each other, a growing consistency of performance level would emerge, simply because earlier acquisitions constitute an increasing proportion of total skills and knowledge as age increases.

Although such overlapping of skills and knowledge at successive ages may account for some of the increasing stability of test scores in the developing individual, two additional conditions merit consideration. The first is the *environmental stability* characterizing the developmental years of the most persons. Hence, whatever advantages or disadvantages they had at one stage of their development tend to persist in the interval between retests. Children tend to remain in the same family, the same socioeconomic level, and the same cultural milieu as they grow up. They are not typically shifted at random from intellectually stimulating to intellectually retarding environments.

At the same time, it should be noted that the psychological environments of siblings in the same family are far from identical. There is a growing amount of carefully gathered data showing the various ways whereby the experiential history of siblings reared together may differ (Boer & Dunn, 1992; Dunn & Plomin, 1990; Hetherington, Reiss, & Plomin, 1993). Having a younger or an older sibling is itself a significantly different psychological experience from that of being an only child. Nature of parental child-rearing practices, as well as parents' own response to the child's behavior, may also vary for siblings bom at different times. Moreover, major events affecting family life—such as divorce, large shifts in family income, or moving from a rural to an urban environment—may differently affect children who are themselves at different developmental stages. To all these potential differences must be added the cumulative experiences that different siblings may have outside the family. Hence, although familial continuity may contribute to stability of an individual child's test performance, it does not necessarily lead to sibling resemblance.

A second condition contributing to the general stability of the individual's intelligence test performance pertains to the role of *prerequisite learning skills* on subsequent learning. Not only does the individual retain prior learning, but much of her or his prior learning provides tools for subsequent learning. Hence, the more progress a child has made in the acquisition of intellectual skills and knowledge at any one point in time, the better able he or she is to profit from subsequent learning experiences. The concept of readiness in education is an expression of this general principle. The sequential nature of learning is also implied in the previously discussed Piagetian approach to mental development, as well as in various individualized instructional programs.

Instability of Intelligence Test Performance. Correlation studies of test scores provide actuarial data, applicable to group predictions. Hence, scores tend to be quite stable in this actuarial sense. Studies of individuals, on the other hand, may reveal large upward or downward shifts in test scores. Sharp rises or drops may occur as a result of major environmental changes in a child's life. Drastic changes in family structure or home conditions, severe or prolonged illness, and therapeutic or remedial programs are examples of the type of events that may alter the child's subsequent intellectual development. Children who remain in the same environment, however, may show a large increase or decrease in test scores, on retesting. These changes, of course, mean that the child is developing at a faster or at a slower rate than the normative population on which the test was standardized. In general, children in educationally disadvantaged environments tend to lose and those in favorable environments tend to gain in score with age. One of the studies indicated that intelligence is not just a factor of genetic influences, but is shaped by social environments (Turkheimer, Haley, Waldron, D'Onofrio and Gottesman, 2003). It is neither genes nor the environmental factors that shape an individual's IQ in isolation, but it is the interaction between the genes and the environment that impacts intellectual development. Turkheimer et al. (2003)

examined intelligence of twin pairs raised in very different socioeconomic backgrounds. The researchers hypothesized that if the socioeconomic environment does not affect intelligence, then the impact of genetic differences between the twins, coming from different socioeconomic backgrounds, on intelligence measures should be small. It was found that when twins were reared in environments of high socioeconomic status, their genes accounted for approximately 72 percent of variance in intelligence scores between them. When twins were reared in environments of low socioeconomic status, their genes accounted for only about 8 percent of variance in intelligence within them.[1] This confirmed the researchers' initial hypothesis that socioeconomic background has a major impact on genetic influences on intelligence. They reasoned that environment of high socioeconomic status is enriching and inspiring, and provides people with the intellectual stimulation necessary to unlock their genetic potential. In contrast, environment of low socioeconomic status is impoverished and lack the necessary stimuli and resources to unlock a person's genetic potential.[2]

Furthermore, research on the factors associated with increases and decreases in intelligence test scores throws light on the conditions determining the intellectual development in general. It also suggests that prediction of subsequent intellectual status can be improved if measures of the individual's emotional and motivational characteristics, and of his/her environment are combined with the initial test scores. From still another viewpoint, such research findings point the way to intervention programs that can effectively alter the course of intellectual development in desired directions.

INTELLIGENCE IN EARLY CHILDHOOD

The assessment of intelligence at the two extremes of the age range presents special theoretical and interpretive problems. One of these problems pertains to the functions that should be tested. What constitutes intelligence for the infant and the preschool child? What constitutes intelligence for the older adult? The second problem is not entirely independent of the first. Unlike the schoolchild, the infant and preschooler have not been exposed to the standardized series of experiences represented by the school curriculum. In developing tests for the elementary, high school, and college levels, test constructors have a large fund of common experiential material from which they can draw test items. Prior to school entrance, on the other hand, the child's experiences are far less standardized, despite certain broad cultural uniformities in child-rearing practices. Under these conditions, both the construction of tests and the interpretation of test results are much more difficult. To some extent, the same difficulty is encountered in testing older adults, whose schooling was completed many years earlier and who have since been engaged in highly diversified activities. In this and the

---

[1] Turkheimer, E., Haley, A., Waldron, M., D'Onofrio, B., & Gottesman, I. I. (2003). Socioeconomic status modifies heritability of IQ in young children. Psychological Science, 14(6), 623–628. Retrieved June 7, 2016, from https://www.researchgate.net/profile/Andreana_Haley/publication/8997472_Socioeconomic_status_modifies_heritability_of_IQ_in_young_children/links/0deec516b9271c1c48000000.pdf

[2] *Ibid.*

next section, we shall examine some of the implications of these problems for early childhood and adult testing, respectively.

Predictive Validity of Infant and Preschool Tests. The conclusion that emerges from longitudinal studies is that preschool tests (especially when administered after the age of 2 years) have moderate validity in predicting subsequent intelligence test performance, but that infant tests have virtually none (Bayley, 1970; Lewis, 1973; McCall, Hogarty, & Hurlburt, 1972). Combining the results reported in eight studies, McCall and his associates (1972) computed the median correlations between tests administered during the first 30 months of life and childhood IQ obtained between 3 and 18 years. Several trends are apparent in their findings. First, tests given during the first year of life have little or no long-term predictive value. Second, infant tests show some validity in predicting IQ at preschool ages (3–4 years), but the correlations exhibit a sharp drop beyond that point, after children reach school age. Third, after the age of 18 months, predictive validities are moderate and stable, being mostly in the '40s and '50s. When predictions are made from these ages, the correlations seem to be of the same order of magnitude, whether the retest occurred at any time from age 3 to age 18.

The lack of long-term predictive validity of infant tests needs to be evaluated further with regard to other related findings. First, predictions may be improved by considering developmental trends through repeated testing. Second, several investigators have found that infant tests have much higher predictive validity within nonnormal, clinical populations than within normal populations. Significant validity coefficients in the .60s and .70s have been reported for children with initial IQs below 80, as well as for groups having known or suspected neurological abnormalities (Ireton, Thwing, & Gravem, 1970; Knobloch & Pasamanick, 1963, 1966; Werner, Honzik, & Smith, 1968). Infant tests appear to be most useful as aids in the diagnosis of defective development resulting from organic pathology of either hereditary or environmental origin.

In the absence of organic pathology, the child's subsequent development is determined largely by the environment in which he or she is reared. This the test cannot be expected to predict. In fact, parental education and other, more specific characteristics of the home environment are better predictors of subsequent intellectual level than are infant test scores; and beyond 18 months, prediction is appreciably improved if test scores are combined with indices of familial socioeconomic status (Bayley, 1955; McCall et al., 1972; Pinneau, 1961; Werner et al., 1968). It has also been proposed that individual differences in infancy may be relatively minor and transitory, since normal development is essentially species-general at this early stage (R. B. McCall, 1981). In subsequent years, individual differences widen, become increasingly more stable across age, and yield higher correlations with both genetic and environmental factors (Plomin, De Fries, & Fulker, 1988). Nevertheless, it should be noted that the 1990s have yielded increasing research activity on the predictive value of infant cognitive behavior, with promising results (Colombo, 1993).

Nature of Early Childhood Intelligence. The validity of infant intelligence tests and the meaning of early performance measures can be understood more fully when viewed against research on the nature of early childhood intelligence.

The findings of such research fail to support the conception of a developmentally constant and unitary intellectual ability in infancy (Lewis, 1973, 1976; McCall et al., 1972). Negligible correlations may be found over intervals even as short as three months; and correlations with performance on the same or different scales at the age of two years and beyond are usually insignificant. Moreover, there is little correlation among different scales administered at the same age. These results have been obtained with both standardized instruments such as the Bayley Scales of Infant Development and with ordinal scales of the Piagetian type (Gottfried & Brody, 1975; King & Seegmiller, 1973; Lewis, 1976; Lewis & McGurk, 1972).

Several investigators have concluded that, while lacking predictive validity, infant intelligence tests are valid indicators of the child's cognitive abilities at the time (Bayley, 1970; Stott & Ball, 1965; Thomas, 1970). According to this view, a major reason for the negligible correlations between infant tests and subsequent performance is to be found in the changing nature and composition of intelligence with age. Intelligence in infancy is qualitatively different from intelligence at school age; it consists of a different combination of abilities.

In a series of intensive studies, McCall and his co-workers explored the changing nature of infant intelligence at six-month intervals during the first two years of life (R. B. McCall, 1976; McCall, Eichorn, & Hogarty, 1977; McCall et al., 1972). Through statistical analyses of intercorrelations of different skills within each six-month level, as well as correlations across age between the same skills and between different skills, these researchers looked for precursors of later developments in infant behavior. One conclusion that emerges from this research is that the predominant behavior at different ages exhibits qualitative changes that represent orderly and reasonable transitions. When the responses of infants to Gesell items were factor-analyzed separately at successive six-month age levels, the first-factor scores at each level correlated significantly across ages. Yet the behavioral composition of these first factors varied from age to age. In other words, the specific manifestations of mental competence differed across age levels, although competence at one age predicted competence at later ages when each was assessed through age-appropriate behaviors.

The concept of *developmental transformations* has been introduced to describe the changes in age-appropriate manifestations of intellectual competence. Further evidence of such qualitative changes in competence behavior is provided by the research of Yarrow and his associates on the infant's mastery of her or his environment (Messer et al., 1986; Morgan & Harmon, 1984; Yarrow et al., 1983; Yarrow et al., 1984; Yarrow & Messer, 1983). The results showed a temporal progression in both the tasks that elicited this behavior and the specific kind of behavior elicited, such as visual regard, manipulation, and persistence in problem solving. For example, the infant first discovers that he or she can affect the environment, as in dropping a block to see it fall and hear it hit the floor, or waving a bell to make it ring. Later, environmental mastery is manifested in more complex goal-directed activities, such as using detours or means–end relationships to obtain a toy. Through the identification of such specific age-appropriate behaviors, both the construct validity and the predictive validity of early childhood assessments of intelligence can be more effectively investigated. It is also important to consider the role of content knowledge in the exercise of intellectual processes and cognitive strategies (Reese, 1987), a fact that is being increasingly recognized in research on cognitive psychology as a whole.

PROBLEMS IN THE TESTING OF ADULT INTELLIGENCE

Age Decrement. A distinctive feature introduced by the Wechsler scales for measuring adult intelligence (chap. 8) was the use of a declining norm to compute deviation IQs. Raw scores on the WAIS (and WAIS-R) subtests are first transmuted into standard scores with a mean of 10 and an *SD* of 3. These scaled scores are expressed in terms of fixed reference groups consisting of 500 persons between the ages of 20 and 34 years included in the standardization samples. The sum of the scaled scores on the 11 subtests is used in finding the deviation IQ in the appropriate age table. If we examine the sums of the scaled scores directly, however, we can compare the performance of different age groups in terms of a single, continuous scale. Figure 12–1 shows the means of these total scaled scores for the age levels included in the national standardization sample.

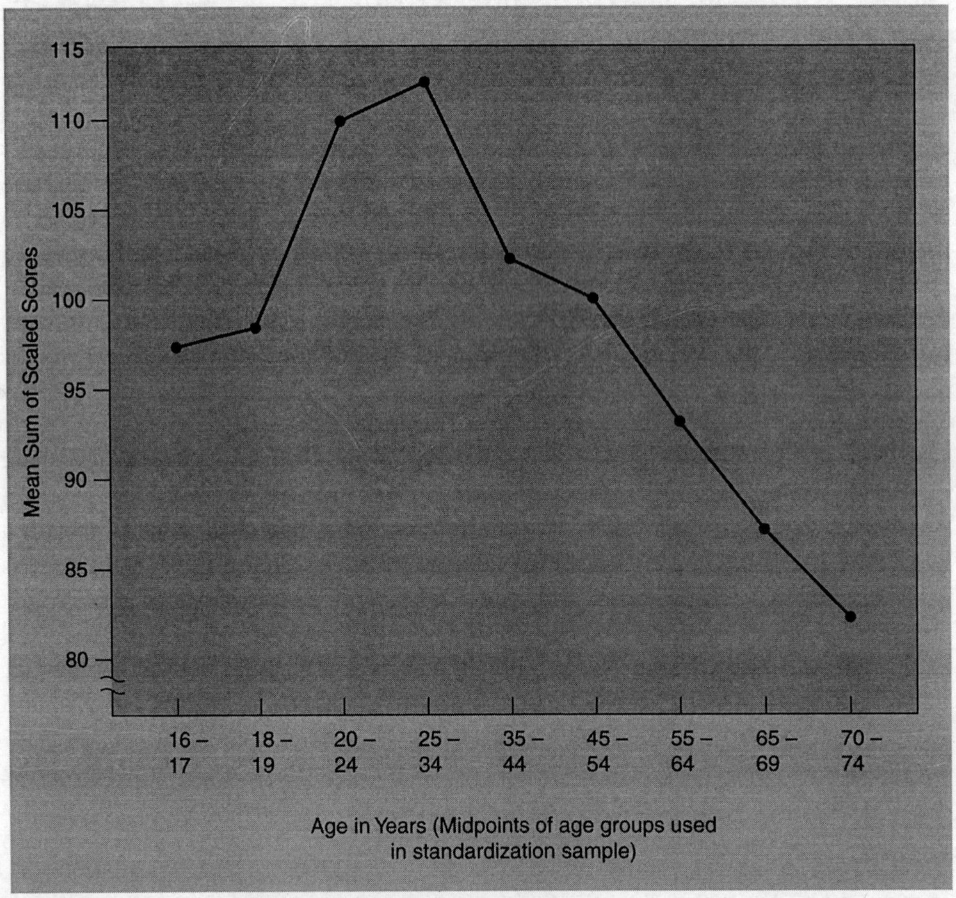

Figure 12–1. Decline in WAIS–R Full Scale Scaled Scores Across Age Cohorts.
(Data from Wechsler, 1981, p. 26.)

As can be seen in Figure 12–1, the scores reach a peak between the ages of 20 and 34 and then decline steadily in all older age groups. The deviation IQ is found by referring an individual's total scaled score to the norm for her or his own age group. Thus, if the test taker shows the same decline in performance with age as does the normative sample, her or his IQ should remain constant. Wechsler's original rationale for this procedure was that it is "normal" for a person's tested ability to decline with age beyond the 30s.

In the interpretation of the age decline illustrated in Figure 12–1, however, we must consider an essential feature of the samples employed in test standardization. Because every standardization sample is a *normative* sample, it should reflect existing population characteristics at each age level (Anastasi, 1956). It follows that, when the educational level of the general population has been rising over several decades, older groups at any one point in time will have received less education than have younger groups. This educational difference is clearly reflected in the standardization samples of both the WAIS (tested between 1953 and 1954) and the WAIS-R (tested between 1976 and 1980). In both samples, the maximum years of schooling are found in the 20-to 34-year levels, and educational level drops consistently in the older groups. Although the later, WAIS-R sample received much more education as a group than did the WAIS sample, the age decline in years of schooling is just as pronounced within the later as it is within the earlier standardization sample. And the corresponding age decline in WAIS-R–scaled scores closely parallels that found with the earlier WAIS.

Age differences in amount of education are inevitable if a test standardization sample is to be truly representative of the population of the country at the time the norms are established. Nevertheless, the educational differences complicate the interpretation of the observed score decrements. The older groups in the standardization sample may have performed more poorly on the test not because they were growing old but because they had received less education than the younger groups.

The results obtained with the standardization samples of the Wechsler scales are typical of the findings of traditional cross-sectional studies of adult intelligence. Cross-sectional comparisons, in which persons of different ages are examined at the same time, are likely to show an apparent age decrement because cultural changes are confounded with the effects of aging. Amount of formal education is only one of many variables in which age groups may differ. Other cultural changes have occurred in human societies during the past half century that make the experiential backgrounds of 20-year-olds and 70-year-olds quite dissimilar. Certainly changes in communication media, such as radio, television, and internet, and in transportation facilities have greatly increased the range of information available to the developing individual. Improvements in nutrition and medical care would also indirectly influence behavior development.

Longitudinal studies, based on retests of the same persons over periods of 5 to 40 years, have generally revealed the opposite trend, the scores tending to improve with age. Several of these longitudinal investigations have been conducted with intellectually superior groups, such as college graduates or individuals initially chosen because of high IQs (Bayley & Oden, 1955; R. B. Burns, 1966; D. P. Campbell, 1965; Nisbet, 1957; Owens, 1953, 1966). For this reason, some writers have argued that the findings may be restricted to persons in the higher intellectual or educational levels and do not apply to the general population. However, similar results have been obtained in other longitudinal studies with intermediate samples (Charles & James, 1964; Eisdorfer, 1963; Tuddenham, Blumenkrantz, & Wilkin, 1968), as well as with mentally retarded adults outside of institutions (Baller, Charles, & Miller, 1967; Bell & Zubek, 1960; Charles, 1953).

Neither cross-sectional nor longitudinal studies alone can provide a conclusive interpretation of observed age changes. On the one hand, age differences in educational level can produce a spurious age decrement in test performance in cross-sectional studies. On the other hand, as persons grow older, they are themselves exposed to cultural changes that may improve their performance on intelligence tests. Several excellent analyses of the methodological difficulties inherent in each procedure, together with the required experimental designs, have been published.[3] Basically, what is needed is the combination of several procedures, as in the *cross-sequential design* (K. W. Schaie, 1965, 1994; Shock et al., 1984). This design combines data from traditional cross-sectional and longitudinal testing with *time-lag comparisons.* The latter requires the testing of same-age cohorts[4] at different time periods. For instance, 20-year-olds tested in 1940 are compared with 20-year-olds tested in 1970.

A few studies provide data that permit at least a partial analysis of the contributing factors. Owens (1966) in his 40-year retest of Iowa State University students and D. P. Campbell (1965) in his 25-year retest of University of Minnesota students also tested *present* freshmen in the respective colleges. Thus, multiple comparisons could be made between the performance of the two groups tested at the same age 25 to 40 years apart, and the performance of a single group tested before and after the same time intervals. In both studies, the initial group improved over its own earlier performance but performed about on a par with the younger group tested at the later date. Such findings suggest that it is cultural changes and other experiential factors, rather than age per se, that produce both the rises and declines in scores obtained with the more limited experimental designs. The increasing interest in research on learning by older adults is evident in the comprehensive survey by Kausler (1994). The book certainly helps to dispel stereotypes about the effects of aging on learning. Although based on well-established scientific findings, the book provides many linkages to everyday life experience.

The Seattle Longitudinal Study (SLS). A particularly well-planned, long-term research program using the cross-sequential design is the Seattle Longitudinal Study (K. W. Schaie, 1994; Schaie & Hertzog, 1986). Beginning in 1956, the investigators administered a battery of ability tests[5] to a stratified random sample

[3] See, for example, Baltes (1968), Botwinik (1984, chaps. 20, 21), Buss (1973), Nesselroade and Reese (1973), Nesselroade and Von Eye (1985), K. W. Schaie (1973, 1988a), and Schaie and Hertzog (1986).

[4] As used in this context, a cohort is a group of persons of the same age, that is, born in the same year or other specified period.

[5] Initially, the tests included the Primary Mental Abilities battery developed by Thurstone through factor analysis of generally recognized aspects of intelligence (see chap. 11). A later version, the Schaie-Thurstone Adult Mental Abilities Test, was developed for use in this project. (K. W. Schaie, 1988b). Eventually scores were reported for constructs rather than for single tests, in order to provide more stable and generalizable results.

of 500 persons, drawn from a population of approximately 18,000 members of a prepaid medical plan. This population is described as fairly representative of the census figures for a large metropolitan area. The sample included 25 men and 25 women at each five-year interval from 21 to 70. In successive stages of the SLS, the tests were administered over six cycles (from 1956 to 1991). Included in each cycle were available survivors of the original sample, as well as new samples introduced in each period.

The basic experimental design of the SLS included repeated longitudinal retests of the same persons, cross-sectional comparisons of different age cohorts tested at the same time (e.g., 30-year-olds compared with 50-year-olds tested in 1977), and comparisons of specific age cohorts tested at different times (e.g., 30-year-olds in 1963 and 30-year-olds in 1984). Through appropriate statistical analyses of data from the various types of comparisons, it was possible to identify performance changes associated with age, those associated with cultural changes in the particular society, and those associated with individual practice and experience. As illustrated in Figure 12–2, the results showed that, in most functions, age decline begins later and tends to be less steep than suggested by the traditional cross-sectional comparisons.

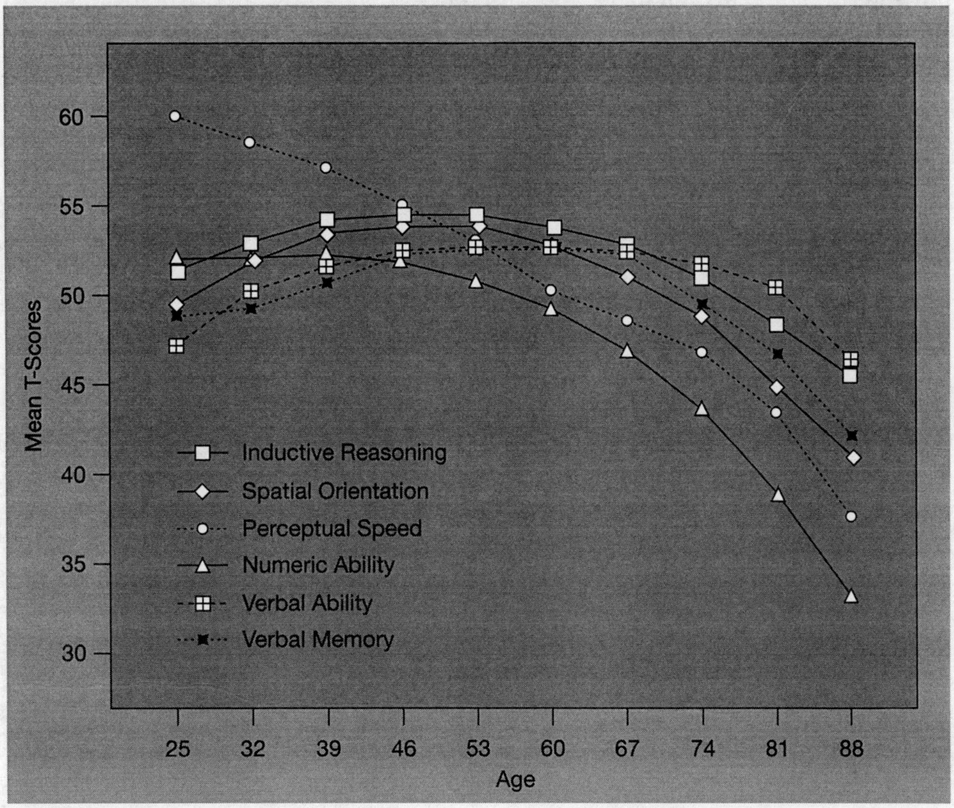

Figure 12–2. Longitudinal Estimates of Mean Factor Scores for Ability Constructs. (From K. W. Schaie, 1994, p. 308.) Note: Data accumulated from 7-year within-person retests.

In addition to a comprehensive and systematic approach to the long-disputed effect of age on performance, the SLS investigated several other related questions. For instance, it was found that age changes vary with the intellectual function assessed, such as verbal ability, numerical ability, and perceptual speed (see Figure 12–2). Hence, an overall measure of intelligence (such as an IQ) would have confused and obscured both rises and declines in ability. Considerable research was also concerned with the causes of change, especially the performance declines found for the more elderly persons. Among the principal variables associated with declining performance were poor health status, specific diseases, inactivity, lack of continued practice in particular functions, and such personality conditions as lowered motivation and decreased flexibility. As a result of such findings, intervention procedures were developed in an effort to halt or reverse the observed ability declines with age. Current SLS research is especially directed to the development of such remedial programs (see K. W. Schaie, 1994; Schaie & Hertzog, 1986).

Furthermore, recent findings of the SLS focused upon finding the relationship between adult cognition and personality. In one of the studies, the researchers reasoned that the study of cognition and aging might be advanced by introducing personality constructs as possible influencing factors that might explain some proportion of age-related changes and differences in cognitive performance (Schaie, Willis, and Caskie, 2004). It was found that there was a modest but significant concurrent relationship between personality trait measures and ability constructs, and that personality dimensions were found to be related to high performance on cognitive abilities. The major contribution of this study was that even though the SLS did not originally focus on the assessment of personality traits, Schaie et al. demonstrated that it is possible to utilize suitable research methods that permit longitudinal analyses' bearing upon the contributions of personality constructs in understanding adult cognition.

Individual Differences and Age. In addition to the basic findings that age decrements are smaller and occur later in life than was formerly supposed, current research generally reveals wide individual differences in ability at all age levels. Any generalization, whether pertaining to age decrement or cohort differences, must be qualified by a recognition of the wide individual variability found in all situations. Individual differences within any one age level are much greater than the average difference between age levels. As a result, the distributions of scores obtained by persons of different ages overlap extensively. This simply means that large numbers of older persons can be found whose performance equals that of younger persons. Moreover, the best performers within the older groups excel the poorest performers within the younger groups. Nor is such overlapping limited to adjacent age levels; the ranges of performance still overlap when extreme groups are compared. Thus some 80-year-olds will do better than some 20-year-olds.

What is even more relevant to the present topic, however, is that the *changes* that occur with aging vary with the individual. Thus, between the ages of 50 and 60, for example, some persons may show a decrease, some no appreciable change, and some an increase in test performance. The amount of change, whether it be a drop or a rise, will also vary widely among individuals. Moreover, intensive studies of persons of advanced age, extending into the seventh, eighth, and ninth decades of life, indicate that intellectual functioning is more closely related to the individual's health status than to chronological age (Birren et al., 1983; Palmore, 1970; Schaie & Gribbin, 1975). Other contributing factors are a favorable environment, with varied opportunities for intellectual stimulation, and the maintenance of a flexible lifestyle (K. W. Schaie, 1994; Schaie & Hertzog, 1986).

Nature of Adult Intelligence. Within the life span, traditional intelligence testing has been oriented chiefly toward the schoolchild and the college student. At these levels, the test constructor can draw on the large common pool of experiences that have been organized into academic curricula. Most intelligence tests measure how well the individual has acquired the intellectual skills taught in the schools; and they can in turn predict how well the student is prepared for the next level in the educational ladder. Tests for adults, including the Wechsler scales, as well as the PMA tests used in the Seattle Longitudinal Study, draw largely on this identifiable common fund of experience. As the individual grows older and her or his own formal educational experiences recede farther into the past, this fund of common experience may become increasingly less appropriate to assess her or his intellectual functioning. Adult occupations are more diversified than childhood schooling. The cumulative experiences of adulthood may thus stimulate a differential development of abilities in different persons.

Because intelligence tests are closely linked to academic abilities, it is not surprising to find that even the earliest studies of adults have shown larger age increments in score among those individuals who have continued their education longer (D. P. Campbell, 1965; Härnqvist, 1968; Husén, 1951; Lorge, 1945; Owens, 1953). Similarly, persons whose occupations are more "academic" in content, calling into play verbal and numerical abilities, are likely to maintain their performance level or show improvement in intelligence test scores over the years, while those engaged in occupations emphasizing mechanical activities or interpersonal relations may show a loss. Some suggestive data in support of this hypothesis are reported by M. Williams (1960), who compared the performance of 100 persons, ranging in age from 65 to over 90, on a series of verbal and nonverbal tests. Rather striking correspondences were found between the individual's occupation and her or his relative performance on the two types of tasks. Longitudinal investigations of adults have also found suggestive relationships between total IQ changes and certain biographical inventory items (Charles & James, 1964; Owens, 1966).

Each time and place fosters the development of skills appropriate to its characteristic demands. Within the life span, these demands differ for the infant, the schoolchild, the adult in different occupations, and the retired septuagenarian (Bakes, Reese, & Lipsitt, 1980). An early demonstration of the implications of this fact for intelligence testing was provided by Demming and Pressey (1957). These investigators began with a task analysis of typical adult functions, conducted through informal surveys of reading matter and of reported daily activities and problems. On this basis, they prepared preliminary forms of some 20 tests "indigenous" to the older years. The tests emphasized practical information, judgment, and social perception. Results with three of these tests, administered together with standard verbal and nonverbal tests to samples of different ages, showed that the older persons excelled the younger on the new tests while the reverse relationship held for the traditional tests. All these types of research suggest that whether intelligence test scores rise or decline with increasing age in adulthood depends largely on what experiences the individual undergoes during those years and on the relationship between these experiences and the functions covered by the tests. At a broader level, all test results can be best understood within a contextual framework. Task analyses of behavior in a diversity of adult settings, including occupational and other areas of socially significant activity, should both improve test construction and clarify the meaning of test scores (Anastasi,1986b).

GENERATIONAL CHANGES IN INTELLIGENCE TEST PERFORMANCE–A PERSPECTIVE

What happens to the performance on intelligence tests of a population over long time periods? For example, how does the intelligence of people in the year 2010 compare to the intelligence of their family in the early 1990s? Since the US is a highly developed nation, it might be expected that intelligence differences there will be small. It may be fair to assume that their human gene pool has remained constant for centuries now. Moreover, only a small fraction of any generation may be exposed to the extremities of environmental deprivation or enrichment that might inhibit or enhance intelligence drastically. This attributes to a hypothesis that any generational change in population intelligence would be minimal.

On this issue, James Flynn (Flynn, 1987; Dickens and Flynn, 2001) drew attention to the large rises in intelligence (i.e. IQ scores) throughout the twentieth century and, thus, refuted this hypothesis. His observation was based on an extensive research of successive editions of intelligence tests such as Stanford-Binet and Wechsler tests from 1932 to 1981. Flynn administered successive editions of these intelligence tests to people from various generations and conclusively indicated that on an average, there has been a linear and uninterrupted increase in the human intellectual abilities. The IQ scores on these tests were normalized for each study being conducted. Normalization process yields the average score for a particular group of people. The same test was administered to the next generation and the normalizedd results were compared with the previous test edition. The results confirmed higher IQ scores across generations (Flynn, 2007). He observed that almost all test editions established a higher standard than its predecessor. This apparent rise in IQ over generations is known as the Flynn effect in honor of the psychologist, James Flynn, who first identified the occurrence (Flynn, 2007). Flynn effect is described as massive IQ gains at about 3 points per decade and in some cases more. In the US, the average IQ increased about 22 points between 1932 and 2002. This brings us to a critical question, "What does the Flynn effect tell us about the nature of measures of intelligence?"

The subsequent paragraphs will discuss the role of environment in explaining the rise in IQ, and in the process, it will shed some light upon the nature versus nurture argument in the growth and development of intelligence.

A substantial amount of evidence has accumulated on the role of genes explaining the individual differences in intelligence. These are based on the findings of studies of identical twins that have been reared separately. The rationale behind these investigations is that if identical twins possess same level of intelligence in spite of growing up in different environments, then that cannot happen as a result of the similarities in their environments or experiences, but it must be attributed to the twins' identical genes. Furthermore, if identical twins who are reared apart are more similar in their intelligence levels than non-identical twins who are reared apart, it gives further support to the genetic endowment of intelligence. The results of the investigations have supported the above-mentioned arguments, thus providing evidence that differences in cognitive ability are inherited. However, due to the practical constraints faced by researchers in studying identical twins, one should be careful in generalizing these findings. Likewise, the high heritability of cognitive ability in group studies has led some researchers to conclude that people's environment play a small role in shaping their intellectual abilities (Jensen, 1973; Herrnstein and Murray, 1994).[6] A heritability ratio is an estimate of the proportion of trait variability in a population living in a particular environment that is determined by variations in genetic inheritance (Alland, 1996).[7] Estimates on heritability of intelligence have varied from 0.4 or less to as much as 0.7 in different studies. A heritability of 0.4, for example, suggests that on an average, about 40 percent of the individual differences that are observed in intelligence are in some way attributable to genetic individual differences and about 60 percent of the differences are attributable to individual differences in the environment. It should be noted that heritability is not a measure of the extent to which intelligence is genetic. An attribute can be the outcome of exclusively genetic causes and yet have zero heritability, as in the case with eye color within a population where everyone has blue eyes. Since heritability depends on the range of typical environments in the population that is studied, high heritability in intelligence implies favorable environmental circumstances. If everyone is treated same environmentally and given good opportunities to learn, then any difference that is observed will largely be due to genes and heritability. However, if environment treats people differently, then heritability will be lower. For instance, some studies have found that the heritability of intelligence among people living in affluent white American suburbs to be considerably higher than among the inhabitants of urban ghettos (Brace, 1996). This suggests a possibility that within the intelligence theory and psychometric tradition, the researchers may have taken for granted the role of genetic sources of variability as a cause of differences in intelligence.

The Flynn effect suggests the importance of environment on IQ, with culture being a critical component of one's environment. One must note that intelligence is defined culturally as well. For example, most western theorists define intelligence in terms of disposition, ability or attribute of a person that is manifested in physiological, verbal, and behavioral terms. In contrast, the Indian conception of intelligence stands for adaptive potentiality of a person in different domains of life. It is not restricted to the cognitive domain alone. This adaptive potentiality

---

[6] Retrieved from http://www.brookings.edu/~/media/Files/rc/papers/2007/05education_dickens/05education_dickens.pdf

[7] Howe, M., Chapter 7: Genetics and Intelligence, *IQ in Question: The Truth about Intelligence* (1997), London: SAGE Publications Ltd.

consists of a range of skills that help one to overcome the life problems, to grow, and become what one wants to be (Srivastava and Mishra, 1999).

The Flynn effect has not been studied in India. Limited yet useful IQ data on India[8] (some more is available in psychologist Richard Lynn and political scientist Tatu Vanhanen's books *IQ* and *Global Inequality* (2006) and *IQ* and the *Wealth of Nations* (2002)), point towards low average IQ scores. The causes underlying such low average intelligence scores could be attributed to the diversity and versatility of the Indian population, which made it extremely complicated and difficult for the researchers to come up with a nationally representative sample. Furthermore, India has been severely burdened by malnutrition, disease, and illiteracy in its earlier decades, which may have led to lower average intelligence scores among the general population. When another study compared Africans (average IQ around 70) to African-Americans (average IQs around 85), it was found that tropical poverty can prevent people from reaching their genetic potential in IQ.[9] This study reinforces the belief that lower average intelligence scores in the Indian sample could be due to the environmental differences rather than the genetic differences.

In the earlier decades, it may be fair to hypothesize that unlike the developed nations, the people in India may have been exposed to the extremities of environmental deprivation or enrichment that inhibited the improvement of intelligence. Knowing this, common sense dictates that any generational change in intelligence due to environmental factors would be noticeable. For instance, India's economy, health facilities, exposure to new facets of development, and various such parameters have increased at a much faster pace in the past decade, thereby providing better exposure to the current and future generations to broaden their intellectual horizon.

Thus, these diversities have to be considered and an appropriate measure of intelligence is to be chosen. Srivastava et al. (1996) mentioned in their report that school counselors use only four tests, namely Raven's Standard Progressive Matrices (SPM) (96 percent), the test of general mental ability by Jalota (27 percent), Bhatia's Performance Battery (22 percent), and an Indian adaptation of the Stanford-Binet test by Kulshrestha (4 percent). The overall satisfaction with the tests was found to be inadequate. The counselor made additional efforts to assess the intelligence and deployed more than one mode of assessment such as intelligence test (42 percent), scholastic achievement (27 percent), teacher's rating (11 percent), student's interview (9 percent), observation of student's behavior (7 percent), and parental interview (7 percent) (Baral and Das, 2004). The need for using multiple tools to assess intelligence could be attributed to the difference in definitions of intelligence. About one-third of school counselor conceptualized intelligence as the ability of an individual to adjust to the environment. Another group of practitioners defined intelligence as a global capacity (15 percent) and others defined intelligence as a composite of different mental abilities (15 percent) (Baral and Das, 2004). Probably, this was the the reason why Wechsler scales proved to be inadequate as a measure of general ability (IQ) in

---

8 Retrieved from http://isteve.blogspot.com/2008/05/indian-iq-part-1-diaspora-demographics.html; accessed on August 17, 2016.

9 *Ibid*. 284.

this context. One study examined the Wechsler Adult Intelligence Scale-Revised (WAIS-R) as it relates to the course in arithmetic and concluded that arithmetic subtests in WAIS-R should not be timed for Indian subjects. The researchers argued that particularly in the case of subjects aged 50 years or above, power rather than speed was an important consideration, as older subjects performed better than younger subjects when speed was not taken into account (Pershad, 1987). Thus, the traditional models of intelligence that emphasize excessively on cognitive ability may not suffice in an Indian context. Probably, Sternberg's triarchic theory or Gardner's theory of multiple intelligences may serve the purpose due to the theory's broad application.

All the above arguments suggest that nurture argument of intelligence holds significance in the development of human intelligence, and environment can impact the growth and development of intelligence.

Like all studies of intelligence, the Flynn effect has also been a point of debate. Researchers have questioned the Flynn effect on several fronts such as erroneous assumptions on intelligence tests and sparse research dedication to uncovering individual differences.

Erroneous Assumptions on Intelligence Tests. For example, Flynn's arguments are grounded in the unproven assumption that similarly named Wechsler scores measure the same constructs across editions (Kaufman, 2010; Zhou, Zhu, and Weiss, 2010) and Flynn's interpretations of select Wechsler measures (similarities and performance tests), as measures of the novel abstract problem solving that characterizes fluid intelligence (McGrew, 2010), may not be highly accurate.

Sparse Research Dedication to Uncovering Individual Differences. Dickens and Flynn (2001) proposed the idea of the individual multiplier that explains how "a small genetic advantage on the part of an individual captures powerful environmental forces (Flynn, 2007, p. 88)". However, the study of individual differences within the Flynn effect was unable to determine which characteristics served as individual multipliers and which did not (Ceci and Kanaya, 2010).

Regardless of these criticisms, the Flynn effect has surely sensitized psychologists to the dangers of rendering conclusions based on intelligence tests. It suggests that conceptualization of intelligence in traditional theories may be inadequate and intellectual ability is not an immutable and an unchanging characteristic. Furthermore, it points towards a piece of information that says, intelligence may not purely be inherited and environment tends to play a role in its development. In the end, a quote from Lewis Terman (1921) succinctly captures the essence of the current state of IQ:

> "We must guard against defining intelligence solely in terms of ability to pass the tests of a given intelligence scale. It should go without saying that no existing scale is capable of adequately measuring the ability to deal with all possible kinds of material on all intelligence levels."

CULTURAL DIVERSITY IN ABILITY TESTING

Experts feel that people in non-western cultures often have ideas about intelligence that differ fundamentally from those that have shaped western intelligence tests. People in western cultures are more likely to view intelligence as a means for individuals to be objective and engage in rational debate; while people in eastern cultures, such as India, may see intelligence as an ability to adapt to the social roles effectively. "A major challenge is to balance the need to compare people from various cultures according to a standard measure with the need to assess people in the light of their own values and concepts".[10] When psychologists began to develop instruments for cross-cultural testing, they hoped that it would be at least theoretically possible to measure hereditary intellectual potential independently of the impact of cultural experiences. The individual's behavior was thought to be overlaid with a sort of cultural veneer whose penetration became the objective of what were called culture-free tests. It is now recognized that hereditary and environmental factors operate jointly at all the stages in an individual's intellectual development and their effects are inextricably intertwined in the resulting behavior. It is, therefore, futile to try to devise a test that is free from cultural influences. Hence, the objective is to construct tests that presuppose only experiences that are common to different cultures. For this reason, terms such as culture-common, culture-fair and cross-cultural, replaced the earlier culture-free label.

Nevertheless, no single test can be universally applicable or equally fair to all cultures. There are as many varieties of culture-fair tests as there are parameters in which cultures differ. A non-reading test may be culture-fair in one situation, a non-language test in another, performance test in a third, and a translated adaptation of a verbal test in a fourth. While reducing cultural differentials in test performance, cross-cultural tests cannot completely eliminate such differentials. Every test tends to favor persons from the culture in which it was developed. The mere use of paper and pencil or the presentation of abstract tasks having no immediate practical significance will favor some cultural groups and limit others. Emotional and motivational factors likewise influence test performance. Among the many relevant conditions differing from culture to culture that may be mentioned are the intrinsic interest of the test content, rapport with the examiner, drive to do well on a test, desire to excel others, and past habits of solving problems individually or cooperatively.

Most traditional cross-cultural tests utilized non-verbal content in the hope of obtaining a more nearly culture-fair measure of the same intellectual functions measured by verbal intelligence tests. Both assumptions underlying this approach are questionable. First, it cannot be assumed that non-verbal tests measure the same functions as verbal tests, no matter how similar they may appear. A spatial analogies test is not merely a non-verbal version of a verbal analogies test. Even tests like Raven's Progressive Matrices and other non-language tests are deliberately designed to tap reasoning and abstract conceptualization, where factorial analyses have revealed a large contribution of non-verbal factors to the variance of test scores (e.g. R.S. Das, 1963). Such findings are corroborated by more recent research in cognitive psychology, which has repeatedly demonstrated the content specificity of thinking process. Problem-solving strategies and skills are developed while responding to a particular content domains and in particular contexts.

---

[10] Etienne, B. Intelligence across cultures. *Monitor on Psychology.* Retrieved on June 8, 2016, from http://www.apastyle.org/learn/faqs/cite-newspaper.aspx

From a different angle, a growing body of evidence suggests that non-language tests may be more culturally loaded than language tests. Investigations with a wide variety of cultural groups in many countries found larger group differences in performance and other non-verbal tests than in verbal tests (Irvine, 1969a, 1969b; Jensen, 1968; Ortar, 1963, 1972; Trimble, Lonner, & Boucher, 1983; Vernon, 1969). There is also evidence that figural tests may be more subject to training effects than verbal and numerical tests are (Irvine, 1983). The use of pictorial representation itself may be unsuitable in cultures unaccustomed to representative drawing. A two-dimensional reproduction of an object is not an exact replica of the original; it simply presents certain cues which, as a result of past experience, lead to the perception of the object. If the cues are highly reduced, as in a picture of a head to represent a whole person, and if the necessary past experience is absent, the correct perception may not follow. There is now a considerable body of empirical data indicating marked differences in the perception of pictures by persons in different cultures (R. J. Miller, 1973; Segall, Campbell, & Herskovits, 1966).

From still another angle, non-verbal, spatial-perceptual tests frequently require relatively abstract thinking processes and analytic cognitive styles characteristic of middle-class Western cultures (J. W. Berry, 1972; R. A. Cohen, 1969). Persons reared in other cultural contexts may be much less accustomed to such problem-solving approaches. Cultures differ in the value they place on generalization and on the search for common features in disparate experiences. In some cultures, behavior is typically linked to contexts and situations. The response to a question may depend on who asks the question and on what type of content is involved (Cole & Bruner, 1971; Goodnow, 1976; Neisser, 1976, 1979).

There is, of course, no procedural difficulty in administering a verbal test across cultures speaking a common language. When language differences necessitate a translation of a test, problems arise regarding the comparability of norms and the equivalence of scores. It should also be noted that a simple translation rarely suffices. Some adaptation and revision is generally required. There may be item content that is more familiar in one culture than in the other. It should be borne in mind that cultural factors that affect test responses are likely to influence the broader behavior domain that the test is designed to sample. For example, in India, it is a multi-language speaking culture, but most of the Indian schools, colleges, and jobs require proficiency in English language. In such situations, inadequate mastery of English may limit a child not only on an intelligence test but also in school work, contacts with fellow students, and play activities; and thus, this limitation might interfere with the subsequent emotional and intellectual development. In an adult, it could seriously restrict job performance, interpersonal relations, and other significant life activities. Many other similar examples of such cultural differentials can be cited. Some are cognitive differentials, such as reading disabilities or ineffective strategies for solving abstract problems; whereas, some are attitudinal or motivational differentials, such as lack of interest in intellectual activities, hostility towards authority figures, low achievement drive, or poor self-concept. All such conditions can be ameliorated by several means, ranging from language instruction and functional literacy training to personal counseling and psychotherapy. All such means are likely to affect both test performance and daily activities of children and adults.

The importance of language in both test performance and everyday activities has led to the development of language proficiency tests in the original and adopted languages. Most of the currently available tests in India deal with English and Hindi, and in some cases, they are translated in regional languages.

PART 4

Personality Testing

Chapter Thirteen

Self-Report Personality Inventories

Although the term "personality" is sometimes employed in a broader sense, in conventional psychometric terminology "personality tests" are instruments for the measurement of emotional, motivational, interpersonal, and attitudinal characteristics, as distinguished from abilities.[1] In the next four chapters, we examine the major varieties of personality tests. For the present purpose, the available instruments are classified according to method of obtaining data from individuals. This chapter deals with self-report personality inventories. In chapter 14 we consider techniques for the measurement of interests and attitudes. The tests covered in both of these chapters are predominantly paper-and-pencil, self-report questionnaires suitable for group administration, although many of them can, of course, be employed in individual assessment. The use of projective techniques for the assessment of personality characteristics is discussed in chapter 15. In chapter 16, a number of miscellaneous approaches for assessing personality are surveyed, among which several have been widely accepted and gained popularity across the globe.

The number of available personality tests runs into several hundred. Especially numerous are the personality inventories and the projective techniques. In this book we shall be concerned primarily with the types of approaches that have been explored in the assessment of personality. A few of the most widely known tests of each type will be briefly described for illustrative purposes. Several books have been written exclusively about personality assessment through tests as well as through other techniques.

[1] For more background on current approaches to personality theory and research, see L. R. Aiken (1993), Burger (1993), and Maddi (1989).

For more detailed treatment of the topic, the reader is referred to these specialized books (e.g., Angleitner & Wiggins, 1986; Butcher, 1995; Lanyon & Goodstein, 1997; and J. S. Wiggins, 1973/1988).

In the development of personality inventories, several approaches have been followed in formulating, assembling, selecting, and grouping items. Among the major procedures in current use are those based on content relevance, empirical criterion keying, factor analysis, and personality theory. Each of these approaches will be discussed and illustrated in the following sections. It should be noted, however, that they are not alternative or mutually exclusive techniques. Theoretically, all can be combined in the development of a single personality inventory. In actual practice, most inventories now use two or more of these procedures.

Although some personality tests are used as group screening instruments, the majority find their principal application in clinical and counseling settings. For this reason, the next four chapters need to be considered in conjunction with the perspectives of those specialized contexts presented in chapter 17. In their present state of development, most personality tests should be regarded either as aids in individual assessment or as research instruments.

CONTENT-RELATED PROCEDURES

The prototype of self-report personality inventories was the Woodworth Personal Data Sheet, developed for use during World War I (see references in chap. 2). This inventory was essentially an attempt to standardize a psychiatric interview and to adapt the procedure for mass testing. Accordingly, Woodworth gathered information regarding common neurotic and preneurotic symptoms from the psychiatric literature as well as through conferences with psychiatrists. It was in reference to these symptoms that the inventory questions were originally formulated. The questions dealt with such deviant behaviors as abnormal fears or phobias, obsessions and compulsions, nightmares and other sleep disturbances, excessive fatigue and other psychosomatic symptoms, feelings of unreality, and motor disturbances such as tics and tremors. In the final selection of items, Woodworth applied certain statistical checks, to be discussed in the next section. Nevertheless, it is apparent that the primary emphasis in the construction and use of this inventory was placed on the content relevance of its items, as indicated in the sources from which they were drawn as well as in the common recognition of certain kinds of behavior as maladaptive. The legacy of Woodworth to modern personality inventory construction is apparent in the fact that when pools of new items are developed, the instructions to item writers are still generally based on a content analysis of the behavior area to be assessed.

A modern example of the content-related approach to self-report inventory development is the Symptom Checklist-90-Revised (SCL-90-R—Derogatis, 1994). The SCL-90-R was designed to screen for psychological problems and symptoms of psychopathology. It consists of 90 symptoms, described briefly (e.g., Poor appetite, Faintness or dizziness). Respondents are asked to indicate, using a 5-point scale, how much they have been distressed by each of the problems during the past seven days. The SCL-90-R provides separate norms for male and female adult and adolescent nonpatients, as well as for psychiatric inpatients and outpatients. However, some of the norms are not sufficiently representative; for example, the psychiatric inpatient normative group was predominantly of lower socioeconomic status, and the adolescent group was mostly middle class and almost totally White.

The SCL-90-R items resemble those of earlier checklist-type instruments not only in that they were selected on the basis of content relevance and clinical utility, but also in that some of them can be traced back to the Woodworth Personal Data Sheet through intermediate scales like the Hopkins Symptom Checklist and the Cornell Medical Index (Derogatis & Lazarus, 1994). The items are organized into nine dimensions of psychopathology, namely, Somatization, Depression, Anxiety, Hostility, Psychoticism, Interpersonal Sensitivity, Phobic Anxiety, Paranoid Ideation, and Obsessive-Compulsive symptoms. Factor analytic studies of these scales suggest that they are intercorrelated and thus not very useful in differential diagnosis; nevertheless, the global indices derived from the Checklist have proved to be reliable indicators of the presence and severity of psychopathology (Payne, 1985). The SCL-90-R and related instruments, such as the Brief Symptom Inventory, can be used most appropriately as part of a battery, in the evaluation of change through a course of therapy, and in research on the outcome of various treatments.

The principal advantage of the content-related approach to personality inventory development lies in the simplicity and directness of the method. While these features make it possible to have relatively brief and economical instruments, their transparency also affords examinees a greater opportunity for conscious attempts at manipulation of the results than do other methods. Content-based instruments typically do not have the features designed to prevent or detect response biases that are discussed later in this chapter (Bornstein, Rossner, Hill, & Stepanian, 1994). For this reason, exclusive reliance on their results as a basis for any decision is not recommended.

EMPIRICAL CRITERION KEYING

Basic Approach. *Empirical criterion keying* refers to the development of a scoring key in terms of some external criterion. The procedure involves the selection of items to be retained and the assignment of scoring weights to each response. In the construction of the previously cited Woodworth Personal Data Sheet, some of the statistical checks applied in the final selection of items pointed the way for criterion keying. Thus, no item was retained in this inventory if 25% or more of a normal sample answered it in the unfavorable direction. The rationale underlying this procedure was that a behavior characteristic that occurs with such frequency in an essentially normal sample cannot be indicative of abnormality. The method of contrasted groups was likewise employed in the selection of items. Only symptoms reported at least twice as often in a previously diagnosed psychoneurotic group than in a normal group were retained.

Despite some use of such empirical checks, however, content-related approaches rely essentially on a literal or veridical interpretation of questionnaire items. The response to each question is regarded as an index of the actual presence or absence of the specific problem, belief, or behavior described by the question. In empirical criterion keying, on the other hand, the responses are treated as diagnostic or symptomatic of the criterion behavior with which they were found to be associated. In an early description of this approach, Meehl (1945) wrote:

> . . . the verbal type of personality inventory is *not* most fruitfully seen as a "self-rating" or self-description whose value requires the assumption of accuracy on the part of the testee in his observations of self. Rather is the response to a test item taken as an intrinsically interesting segment of verbal behavior, knowledge regarding which may be of more value than any knowledge of the "factual" material about which the item superficially purports to inquire. Thus if a hypochondriac says that he had "many headaches" the fact of interest is that he *says* this. (p. 9)

A self-report inventory is indubitably a series of standardized verbal stimuli. When criterion-keying procedures have been followed, the responses elicited by these stimuli are scored in terms of their empirically established behavior correlates. They are thus treated like any other psychological test responses. That questionnaire responses may correspond to the person's *perception* of reality does not alter this situation. It merely provides one hypothesis to account for the empirically established validity of certain items.

The Minnesota Multiphasic Personality Inventories

The outstanding example of empirical criterion keying in personality test construction is the Minnesota Multiphasic Personality Inventory (MMPI). In recent years, the MMPI has been revised and reconstituted into two separate versions, the MMPI-2 (Butcher, Dahlstrom, Graham, Tellegen, & Kaemmer, 1989) and the MMPI-Adolescent (MMPI-A—Butcher et al, 1992). In spite of the existence of these newer versions, no discussion of either can proceed without reference to the original MMPI and the role it played in the history of personality assessment. Although a thorough description of it is beyond the scope of this text, it must be noted that for a period of almost half a century, the MMPI was the most widely used and the most thoroughly researched personality test.[2]

In many ways the MMPI, as an instrument, was a victim of its own success. Conceived in the 1930s by Starke R. Hathaway, a clinical psychologist, and J. Charnley McKinley, a neuropsychiatrist, it was initially published through a series of articles in the 1940s to serve as an aid in the process of psychiatric diagnosis.[3] Thereafter, its effectiveness in detecting psychopathology and differentiating between the then rather crude nosological categories led to its being used for an ever-expanding set of purposes, beyond its original aim. By the 1960s, the MMPI was firmly entrenched as *the* leading personality test and used as frequently, or more, with normal subjects in counseling, employment, medical, military, and forensic settings, as with psychiatric patients. By the 1980s, the MMPI literature numbered several thousand references documenting, among many other things,

---

[2] For a fairly concise description of the original MMPI, see earlier editions of this text (e.g., Anastasi, 1988b). More extensive treatments of this instrument can be found in the classic volumes by Dahlstrom, Welsh, and Dahlstrom (1972, 1975).

[3] The original articles have been reproduced in Dahlstrom and Dahlstrom (1980).

the use of its 13 basic scales with a large variety of populations, the development of hundreds of special scales based on its items, and a vast array of empirical correlates of scale elevations and profile patterns. However, by that time, its well-documented conceptual and psychometric problems appeared more troublesome in light of advances in the fields of psychopathology and personality theory, as well as in test construction. Furthermore, by then it had also been clearly demonstrated that the narrowly based and outdated norms of the test were inappropriate for contemporary examinees, so that the very basis for determining abnormality rested on a uncertain foundation (Colligan, Osborne, Swenson, & Offord, 1983, 1989). In effect, the original standardization sample had become something akin to a nonnormative reference group, in terms of which the score scale was defined. The much more extensive data subsequently collected with reference to profile codes then provided the basis for normative interpretation.

Thus, the committee charged with restandardizing the MMPI faced the difficult task of modernizing the instrument while trying to save the wealth of interpretive material relevant to the assessment of personality and, especially, of psychopathology embedded within the MMPI's basic structure. For the sake of continuity, the committee chose to retain the vast majority of the items, all of the original clinical and validity scales, and many of the supplementary scales, along with their built-in weaknesses. The major changes were: a complete renorming of the inventory; the development of uniform T scores for the eight original clinical scales and all of the content scales; the revision and deletion of outdated or otherwise objectionable items, as well as the addition of new ones; the creation of several new validity, supplementary, and content scales; and the separation of the inventory into two versions, suitable for different age groups.

The Minnesota Multiphasic Personality Inventory-2. The MMPI-2 items consist of 567 affirmative statements to which the test taker gives the responses "True" or "False." The first 370 items, which are virtually identical to those in the MMPI except for editorial changes and reordering, provide all the responses needed to score the original 10 "clinical" and three "validity" scales. The remaining 197 items (107 of which are new) are needed to score the full complement of 104 new, revised, and retained validity, content, and supplementary scales and subscales that make up the complete inventory. The items range widely in content, covering such areas as general health; affective, neurological, and motor symptoms; sexual, political, and social attitudes; educational, occupational, family, and marital questions; and many well-known neurotic or psychotic behavior manifestations, such as obsessive and compulsive states, delusions, hallucinations, ideas of reference, phobias, and sadistic and masochistic trends. Dahlstrom (1993a) has prepared a manual supplement that provides all the information necessary to compare the items of the MMPI-2 with the original ones. A few illustrative items, followed by the numbers they bear in the current form of the test, are shown below:[4]

My sleep is fitful and disturbed. (39)
I believe I am being plotted against. (138)

[4] From Minnesota Multiphasic Personality Inventory-2.

I am worried about sex. (166)
When I get bored I like to stir up some excitement. (169)
Most people inwardly dislike putting themselves out to help other people. (286)

The MMPI-2 provides scores on 10 basic "clinical scales," which are the same as those in the original MMPI and are listed below:

1. Hs: Hypochondriasis
2. D: Depression
3. Hy: Hysteria
4. Pd: Psychopathic deviate
5. Mf: Masculinity-femininity
6. Pa: Paranoia
7. Pt: Psychasthenia
8. Sc: Schizophrenia
9. Ma: Mania
10. Si: Social introversion

Eight of these scales were developed empirically, in the 1940s, by criterion keying of items that differentiated between small clinical samples, mostly of about 50 persons each, representing the traditional psychiatric diagnosis in use at the time, and a normal control group of 724 visitors and relatives of patients in the University of Minnesota hospitals (Hathaway & McKinley, 1940, 1943). The Masculinity-femininity scale, originally intended to distinguish between homosexual and heterosexual men, was developed from the differences between male soldiers and female airline employees in item-endorsement frequency. Scores on this scale indicate the extent to which a person's interests and attitudes match the stereotype of her or his sex group. The Social introversion scale, added later, was derived from the responses of two contrasted groups of college students selected on the basis of extreme scores on a test of introversion-extraversion.

In retaining the basic scales of the MMPI intact (except for nine deleted items, a number of editorial changes, and a reordering of the items), the MMPI-2 developers sought to preserve the wealth of clinically useful information associated with the interpretation of profile codes based on patterns of scores on those scales (Graham, 1993; Greene, 1991). However, also retained were the obsolete notions of psychopathology implicit in those scales and the consequences of the naive and flawed application of the empirical method of contrasted criterion group keying. Other problems, such as the multidimensionality and overlap of the basic scales, were kept as well (Helmes & Reddon, 1993).

An outstanding feature of the original MMPI was its use of three so-called validity scales, which have also been retained in the MMPI-2.[5] These scales are not concerned with validity in the technical sense. In effect, they represent checks on carelessness, misunderstanding, malingering, and the operation of special response sets and test-taking attitudes. The validity scores include:

Lie Score (L): based on a group of items that make the respondent appear in a favorable light but are unlikely to be truthfully answered in the favorable direction (e.g., I do not like everyone I know).

Infrequency Score (F): determined from a set of 60 (out of the original 64) items answered in the scored direction by no more than 10% of the MMPI

[5] There is also a Cannot Say (?) score representing the number of items that were double-marked or omitted. If this count exceeds 30 items, the test record is considered highly suspect and probably invalid.

standardization group. Although representing undesirable behavior, these items do not fit any particular pattern of abnormality. Hence, it is unlikely that any one person will actually show all or most of these symptoms. A high F score may indicate scoring errors, carelessness in responding, gross eccentricity, psychotic processes, or deliberate malingering.

Correction Score (K): using still another combination of specially chosen items, this score provides a measure of test-taking attitude believed to be more subtle. A high K score may indicate defensiveness or an attempt to "fake good." A low K score may represent excessive frankness and self-criticism or a deliberate attempt to "fake bad."

The first two scores (L, F) are ordinarily used for an overall evaluation of the test record. If either of these scores exceeds a specified value, the record is considered invalid. The K score, on the other hand, was designed to function as a suppressor variable. It is employed to compute a correction factor that is added to the scores on some clinical scales to obtain adjusted totals. The effectiveness of this use of the K score is questionable; therefore, scores on the affected scales can be reported with and without this correction. Although an unusually high K score would in itself make a record suspect and call for further scrutiny, moderate elevations of the K scale may in fact reflect ego strength and a positive adjustment. It is particularly important to evaluate elevations in light of the individual's history and life circumstances.

Among the 21 supplementary scales of the MMPI-2 are three new "validity" indicators that can help to assess the care and veracity with which the test takers respond to the inventory. They are the Back F (F_b) scale, the Variable Response Inconsistency Scale (VRIN), and the True Response Inconsistency Scale (TRIN). Whereas the F_b scale is basically an extension of the original F scale for items that appear in the second half of the inventory, VRIN and TRIN are new scales that consist of pairs of items with similar or opposite meanings and are aimed at detecting inconsistent or contradictory responses.

The basic profile form for the MMPI-2 (Fig. 13–1) includes the 13 validity and clinical scales carried over from the original version. There are also separate profile forms for 15 content scales, 27 content component scales, 21 supplementary scales, and 28 Harris-Lingoes subscales.[6] Some of these scales and subscales are new, and some have been retained from the original; all of them, however, are scored by using the MMPI-2 normative sample of 2,600 adults, aged 16 to 84. This sample is far more representative of the current population of the United States than the original Minnesota normative group, having been collected in seven different states in an attempt to reflect the U.S. population in terms of significant demographic variables, including gender, age, and ethnicity (Dahlstrom & Tellegen, 1993). Nevertheless, the representativeness of the sample has been questioned, primarily because of its high levels of occupational and educational attainment and underrepresentation of Hispanics and Asian Americans, compared with the 1980 census figures (Duckworth, 1991).

---

[6] As of 1996, the 10 Wiener-Harmon Subtle-Obvious subscales are no longer available from the MMPI-2 publisher.

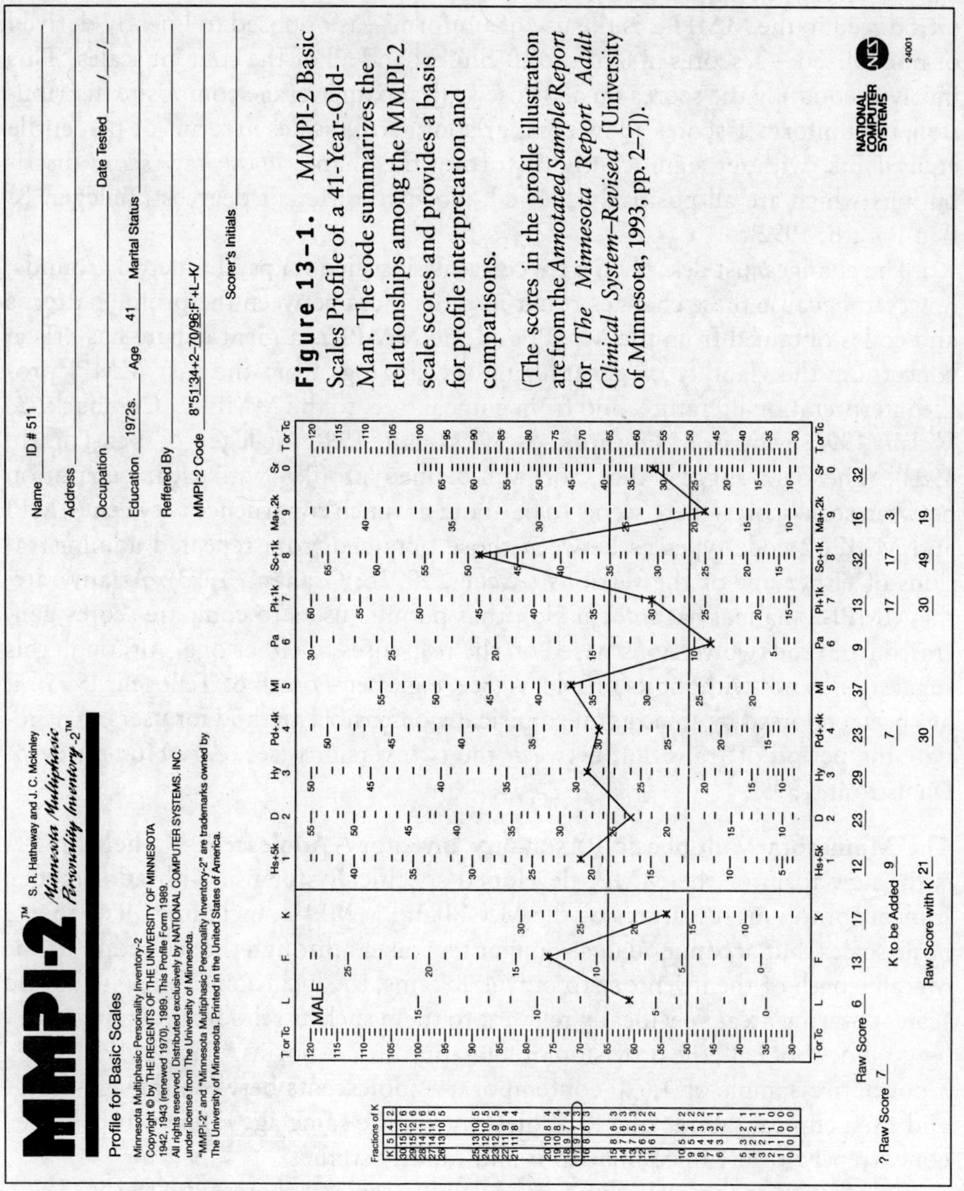

Figure 13-1. MMPI-2 Basic Scales Profile of a 41-Year-Old-Man. The code summarizes the relationships among the MMPI-2 scale scores and provides a basis for profile interpretation and comparisons.

(The scores in the profile illustration are from the *Annotated Sample Report* for *The Minnesota Report Adult Clinical System–Revised* [University of Minnesota, 1993, pp. 2–7]).

The main result of the renorming of the MMPI was a lowering in the score elevation of clinical profiles. This change, which had been widely anticipated, is probably due to generational differences, as well as to special factors unique to the original Minnesota sample and to the way in which it was used in the development of the MMPI (D. S. Nichols, 1992). At any rate, the cutoff T score necessary for considering a scale elevation to be of clinical interest is now 65, or approximately 1.5 *SDs* above the mean, as opposed to 70. Another innovation introduced in the MMPI-2 is the use of uniform—as opposed to linearly derived or nomialized—T scores in 8 of the 10 clinical and all of the content scales. This involved equating the scores on all those scales to an average composite distribution; the uniform T scores allow comparisons across scales in terms of percentile equivalents, without significantly distorting the shape of the raw score distributions which are all positively skewed, albeit to different degrees (Tellegen & Ben-Porath, 1992).

The changes just described were certainly justified on psychometric grounds; however, because these changes result in differences between the profile patterns and codes obtained from the MMPI and the MMPI-2, a great debate has arisen concerning the viability of generalizing the findings from the vast MMPI profile interpretation literature, and from clinical lore, to the MMPI-2 (Chojnacki & Walsh, 1992; Morrison, Edwards, & Weissman, 1994; Tellegen & Ben-Porath, 1993). The data suggest that, for well-defined profiles with clear separation between scale scores, there seems to be about as much congruence between MMPI and MMPI-2 code types as between those obtained from repeated administrations of either one of the versions (Archer, 1992b; Graham, 1993). At any rate, the MMPI-2 manual has information that permits users to compare scores generated from the two versions based on the responses to either one. Although this suggestion is not without its problems (see, e.g., Ben-Porath & Tellegen, 1995), it has been endorsed by some as an empirically defensible method for users to negotiate the period of transition between the two versions (see, e.g., Humphrey & Dahlstrom, 1995).

The Minnesota Multiphasic Personality Inventory–Adolescent. TheMMPI-A is the new form of the MMPI developed specifically for use with adolescents. It incorporates most features of the MMPI and MMPI-2, including all of the 13 basic scales, but accommodates younger test takers through the reduction of the overall length of the inventory to only 478 items, the inclusion of new items and scales covering areas specifically relevant to them such as school and family problems, and, above all, the provision of age-appropriate norms. The MMPI-A used a normative sample of 1,620 contemporary adolescents between the ages of 14 and 18; a clinical sample of 713 adolescents in the same age range was collected concurrently for use in comparisons and validity studies.

In addition to the basic clinical and validity scales it shares with the MMPI-2, the MMPI-A has its own validity scales (FI and F2), as well as some content and supplementary scales and subscales that are unique to it and some that are common to both instruments. Although a great deal of research, including norms and conversion tables published by Dahlstrom et al., (1972) and Marks, Seeman, and Haller (1974), supported the use of the MMPI with adolescents, that research does not necessarily apply to the MMPI-A, which is more of a brand new instrument than a revision. As such, its usefulness will have to be determined through the accumulation of research and interpretive materials that started concurrently with its publication (Archer, 1992a; Butcher & Williams, 1992; Williams, Butcher, Ben-Porath, & Graham, 1992).

Minnesota Multiphasic Personality Inventory-2-Restructured Form (MMPI-2-RF) The newer version of Minnesota Multiphasic Personality Inventory, MMPI-2-RF, was published in 2008 and contains only 338 true-false items with Restructured Clinical (RC) Scales at its core. This version of the test provides a valuable alternative to the MMPI-2 test. The MMPI-2 test continues to be published and fully supported by the University of Minnesota Press and distributed exclusively by Pearson (Ben-Porath and Tellegen, 2016). While the MMPI-2-RF is a new measure and takes about half the time to complete (usually 30 to 50 minutes), it is seen by practitioners that MMPI-2 is still a widely used test because of its existing large research base and familiarity with psychologists.

Concluding Comments on the Minnesota Multiphasic Personality Inventories (MMPI). In spite of its origin as a prototypical product of naively applied empiricism, and of repeated rumors about its imminent demise, the MMPI has managed to survive. In fact, although its original purpose was to aid in the process of psychiatric classification, and the procedures followed in its development made it unsuitable for personality assessment, the MMPI has been widely used with normal as well as psychiatric patients. In India, it is mostly used in clinical or psychiatric settings. The MMPI and its revised versions have incorporated a number of additional procedures and interpretative strategies into the original, empirically derived framework of inventories. In India, a Hindi translated version of the MMPI and its short form was used in a number of research studies (Mathur and Paliwal, 1986; Trivedi and Raghavan, 1991). However, information on the translation, adaptation, or cross-cultural equivalence is scanty. An Indian adaptation of the MMPI, the Multi-phasic Questionnaire, has also been developed and standardized on the Indian population (Chattopadhyay, Som, & Biswas, 1993). However, it seems that the information on its psychometric properties is not readily available in the global literature.

California Psychological Inventory

Over the years of its existence, the MMPI has served as a basis for the development of other widely used inventories. An outstanding example is the California Psychological Inventory (CPI). While drawing nearly half of its items from the MMPI, the CPI was developed specifically for use with normal adult populations. In its latest revision, the CPI—Third Edition—consists of 434 items to be answered "True" or "False" and yields scores on 20 scales (Gough & Bradley, 1996). Three are "validity" scales designed to assess test-taking attitudes. These scales are designated as: Well-being (Wb), based on responses by normals asked to "fake bad"; Good impression (Gi), based on responses by normals asked to "fake good"; and Communality (Cm), based on a frequency count of highly popular responses. The remaining 17 scales provide scores in such personality dimensions as Dominance, Sociability, Self-acceptance, Responsibility, Socialization,

Self-control, Achievement-via-conformance, Achievement-via-independence, Empathy, and Independence. The last two scales were added in the 1987 revision.

For 13 of these 17 scales, items were selected on the basis of contrasted group responses, against such criteria as course grades, social class membership, participation in extracurricular activities, and ratings. The ratings were obtained through peer nominations, which have been found to constitute an effective assessment technique for many interpersonal traits (see chap. 16). For the remaining 4 scales, items were originally grouped subjectively and then checked for internal consistency. Cross-validation of all scales on sizable samples has yielded significant group differences, although the overlapping of contrasted criterion groups is considerable and criterion correlations are often low.

As in the MMPI-2, all CPI scores are reported in terms of a standard score scale with a mean of 50 and an *SD* of 10; at present, this scale is based on a normative sample of 3,000 females and 3,000 males drawn from the CPI archives so as to represent the general population of the United States in terms of age, socioeconomic level, and geographic area. Norms are provided separately for females, males, and both genders combined. In addition, means and *SDs* of scores on each scale are given for many special groups.

The CPI, originally published in 1956, was conceptualized as an "open system" from which elements could be removed and to which elements could be added as the need arose (Gough, 1987, p. 1). Accordingly, through the revisions it has undergone, the inventory has been shortened from its original length of 480 items— down to 462 in the 1987 revision and most recently to 434 items—to delete those that might be objectionable to some respondents or legally questionable in light of the Americans with Disabilities Act of 1990 (P.F. 101-336), especially in personnel selection settings. Using the extensive archival data available for more than 13,000 subjects on all of the CPI items, Gough and Bradley have striven to maintain the reliability and validity of the basic scales by keeping their length constant through substitution of deleted items with others that are functionally equivalent in terms of the extent of their correlation with the criteria for scale membership.

Research with the CPI has provided a great deal of information that is helpful in analyzing profiles based on both individual scale elevations and configurations or patterns of scores on two or more scales, in a manner akin to the MMPI's code type interpretation tradition (McAllister, 1996). Cross-cultural studies suggest that the CPI is useful in exploring personality differences between ethnic groups (see Dana, 1993; Davis, Hoffman, & Nelson, 1990). In addition to the basic scales, several others have been developed by various methods. Examples include a Managerial Potential Scale and a Work Orientation Scale (Gough, 1984, 1985). An applications guide has been prepared as an aid to the professional user, with special reference to the use of the CPI in personnel selection and career development (Meyer &. Davis, 1992).

Since its 1987 revision, the CPI has also included a three-dimensional typological model for classifying high-scoring and low-scoring individuals on three structural or vector scales identified by factor and item analyses. The structural scales measure the higher-order dimensions of Internality vs. Externality, Norm-acceptance vs. Norm-rejection, and Self-realization. Scores on the first two of these scales are used to categorize respondents into four personality types (Alpha, Beta, Gamma, and Delta) while scores on the third vector scale purportedly gauge level of integration or realization of the positive potential associated with one's type. The typological model is apparently an appealing feature for organizational users of the inventory but it has been criticized for the vague description of the procedures used to derive it (Engelhard, 1992). In addition, it shares the conceptual and psychometric weaknesses inherent in the classification of people into types based on arbitrarily dichotomizing one or more continuous dimensions.[7]

In its latest version, the CPI offers a 260-item omnibus assessment of normal personality. It is essentially a short form of the California Psychological Inventory™ (CPI™) instrument which has been available for almost 50 years and has an established research base of nearly 2,000 citations (Gough, 2002). The latest version of CPI was developed in order to make the instrument available to more people and to a greater range of applications. The test items were carefully selected to meet the demands of business professionals such as human resources managers, organizational development consultants, training and development professionals, and executive coaches (CPP, Inc., 2002). The real benefit is that it delivers 29 CPI scales, including 20 folk scales and 3 vector scales, in an assessment that requires 40 percent less time to complete. The primary application of the CPI 260 instrument is intended to be in the domain of work and organizational life. The updated language, revised scale names, and new interpretive materials will encourage its use in today's organizations. Some practitioners may find the instrument to be useful in broader applications of personal development; however, it should be noted that it is not intended for clinical assessment (CPP, Inc., 2002).

Personality Inventory for Children

Although not utilizing MMPI items or data, the Personality Inventory for Children (PIC) was constructed with the same general methodology as the MMPI and the CPI (Wirt & Lachar, 1981; Wirt, Lachar, Klinedinst, & Seat, 1991). The PIC was developed through some 20 years of research by a group of investigators at the University of Minnesota who had been thoroughly exposed to the rationale and clinical use of the MMPI. It is designed for children and adolescents between the ages of 3 and 16. A major difference between the PIC and the MMPI pertains to the way the information is obtained; the true–false questionnaire items are answered not by the child but by a knowledgeable adult, usually the mother. This procedure is consistent with the common practice in children's clinics of interviewing parents as the principal source of information about the child's presenting problems and case history. This inventory, in effect, provides a systematic way of gathering such information and of interpreting it in terms of normative and diagnostic data.

The original PIC comprised a total of 600 items, grouped into three "validity scales," a general screening scale, and 12 clinical scales. The validity scales include: the Lie scale, consisting of items that make the child appear in an unrealistically favorable light; the Frequency scale, comprising rarely endorsed items; and the

[7] See the discussion of the Myers-Briggs Type Indicator in chapter 16.

Defensiveness scale, designed to assess parental defensiveness about the child's behavior. The screening scale, namely, Adjustment, is used to identify children in need of psychological evaluation. The 12 clinical scales were designed to assess the child's cognitive development and academic achievement, several well-established types ot emotional and interpersonal problems (e.g., Depression, Anxiety, Withdrawal, and Hyperactivity), and the psychological climate of the family.

PIC was developed because most children have a low reading comprehension, and the self-report inventories become less reliable and less valid when used with children (Aiken, & Groth-Marnat, 2006, p. 414).[8] Therefore, this instrument was designed where adults rate children. This test, in its second edition (PIC-2), consists of 275 true-false items concerning child behavior and can be completed by a parent in approximately 40 minutes. PIC-2 has three response validity scales—inconsistency, dissimulation and defensiveness—and nine adjustment scales—cognitive impairment, delinquency, family dysfunction, impulsivity, distractibility, psychological discomfort, reality distortion, social skills deficits, social withdrawal, and somatic concern.[9] Each adjustment scale consists of two or three subscales. PIC-2 also has a shorter version, Behavioral Summary, which can be used for screening, research, and monitoring behavior change. It consists of the first 96 items of PIC-2 and provides scores on eight adjustment scales.[10]

It is noteworthy that the PIC-2 is not a self-report type inventory but an inventory of observed behavior. However, parental reporting does have limitations that have been generally recognized and noted by the authors of PIC-2. As they point out, responses may partially reflect the motivation, attitudes, and personal or cultural standards of a parent. Thus, some inconsistencies among reports of different observers, such as two parents, and between parental reports and self-reports of their children can be expected and are, in fact, found. One way to deal with this unavoidable problem of differing perspectives is to assess special response tendencies that may have distorted the data through the "validity scales". A second alternative is to gather and compare reports from more than one observer. A third avenue is to gather and compare data of self-report and observers' report.

Another version, the Personality Inventory for Youth (PIY), has been developed as a self-report measure. Although the PIY can be used by itself, ideally, it provides the basis for a more comprehensive assessment using the profiles from parents and children conjointly (Lachar & Gruber, 1995a, 1995b). The authors of the PIY used the first 280 items of the PIC-R as a point of departure for the item pool; most items were transformed from the third-to the first-person format with little change (e.g., "My child often brings friends home" became "I often bring friends home"). Some items had to be edited more substantially to conform to their intended meaning; others had to be discarded as inappropriate for self-report at the target age level (which was set at 9 to 18 years of age) due to the problems with self-reporting at younger ages. A few items are altogether

---

[8] Aiken, L. R., & Groth-Marnat, G. (2006). Psychological Testing and Assessment. Boston, IL: Pearson Education Group.

[9] *Ibid.*

[10] *Ibid.*

new. The final version of the PIY consists of 270 items comprising nine nonoverlapping clinical scales, 24 nonoverlapping subscales, and four "validity scales." The first 80 items can be used as an Abbreviated Form for screening purposes. The PIY was developed and standardized using a sample of 2,337 students in regular education classes and a clinical sample of 1,178 children and adolescents (Lachar & Gruber, 1993). In a nutshell, both of these instruments share an impressive empirical foundation and offer an advantage by providing an integrated set of multidimensional tools specially designed for use with children and adolescents.

Much work remains to be done with both the PIC-R and the PIY. The norms of the PIC, gathered in the late 1950s and early 1960s, should be updated, and its research base for the preschool age range needs to be expanded (Knoff, 1989). However, these two instruments share an impressive empirical foundation and the advantage of providing an integrated set of multidimensional tools specifically designed for use with children and adolescents.

FACTOR ANALYSIS IN TEST DEVELOPMENT

In an effort to arrive at a systematic classification of personality traits, a number of psychologists turned to factor analysis. This technique, already discussed in connection with the organization of cognitive abilities, is ideally suited to the task of reducing the number of categories necessary to account for behavioral phenomena by looking for consistent patterns in their occurrence. It will be recalled that an element of subjectivity is likely to enter into the identification of factors, since the process depends on an examination of measures or items having the highest loading on each factor (see chap. 11). Hence, the cross-identification of factors from separate investigations using different measures is difficult and has been a source of discrepancies in the labels applied to traits as well as in their number. In addition, there are a variety of ways in which factor analysis can be applied to the study of personality traits. Of these, two major traditions of research have coexisted for several decades and have, to some extent, coalesced in recent years.

One of the traditions, centering on the use of personality questionnaire data, is exemplified by a series of studies by Guilford and his co-workers (see Guilford, 1959, chap. 16; Guilford & Zimmerman, 1956). Rather than correlating total scores on existing inventories, these investigators computed the intercorrelations among individual items from many personality inventories. As a by-product of this research, three personality inventories were developed and eventually combined into the Guilford-Zimmerman Temperament Survey. This inventory yields separate scores for ten traits, each score based on 30 different items. Examples of these traits include Restraint, Ascendance, Emotional Stability, and Friendliness.

Another of the pioneering applications of factorial methods to the development of personality inventories, sometimes referred to as the "lexical" tradition, is to be found in the work that R. B. Cattell started in the 1940s (John, Angleitner, & Ostendorf, 1988). In an attempt to obtain a comprehensive description of personality, Cattell began by assembling all personality trait names occurring either in the dictionary (as compiled by Allport and Odbert, 1936) or in the psychiatric and psychological literature. This list of almost 18,000 terms was first reduced by combining obvious synonyms. The smaller trait list was then employed in obtaining associates' ratings of a heterogeneous group of adults. Intercorrelations and factor analyses of these ratings and of self-report questionnaire data led to the identification of what Cattell described as "the primary source traits of personality," a designation that seems to imply more universality and stability of results than appear justified by the antecedent research. It is characteristic of Cattell's approach that he regards factor analysis not as a data-reduction technique, but as a method for discovering underlying, causal traits (Cattell, 1979).

The Sixteen Personality Factor Questionnaire (16 PF). On the basis of their factorial research, Cattell and his co-workers have developed a number of personality inventories, of which the best known is the Sixteen Personality Factor Questionnaire, currently in its fifth edition (Cattell, Cattell, & Cattell, 1993; Conn & Rieke, 1994; Russell & Karol, 1994). Originally published in 1949, the 16 PF is designed for ages 16 and over and yields 16 scores in such traits as Social Boldness, Dominance, Vigilance, Emotional Stability, and Rule Consciousness. The 16 factors, identified by the same letters across the various editions of the 16 PF, have been refined over the years and renamed, as the esoteric terminology that Cattell originally used to designate the traits has been largely discarded. For example, the extremes anchoring the dimension now called Social Boldness were first labeled "Threctia" and "Parmia," at the shy and bold ends, respectively. The second-order factors of the 16 PF, which previously ranged between four and eight in number, are now designated as "global factors" and limited to 5, a number that conforms to the popular five-factor model to be discussed in the next section.

The fifth edition of the 16 PF is available in only one form and contains 185 items, most of which were selected from previous forms of the questionnaire on the basis of their content and the quality of their psychometric properties. The 16 PF has been renormed on a sample of 2,500 individuals selected to represent approximately the U.S. population as of the 1990 census in terms of gender, race, age distribution, and education. One of the unique features of the 16 PF is the inclusion of 15 items presented contiguously at the end of the inventory under the title "Problem Solving Questions"; these items comprise the Reasoning scale, which is intended as a quick measure of mental ability. In addition, the questionnaire now has three indices of response styles designed to assess acquiescence, random responding, and attempts to present oneself unrealistically as having either socially desirable or undesirable qualities.

Internal consistency and test-retest reliability for the 16 primary factor scales of the 16 PF are better in the fifth edition than they were in earlier ones. Similarly, the Technical Manual for this edition contains a great deal more information on validity than did earlier manuals. However, the problem of lack of factorial independence of the 16 primary scales, evident in earlier editions, seems to persist in this one. This difficulty is underscored by the uniform inability of other investigators who have used Cattell's original variables to replicate anywhere near as many as 16 factors. Instead, most studies using the data on which Cattell based his system have found only between 4 and 7 factors (Dig-man, 1990; L. R. Goldberg, 1993). The first attempts to replicate Cattell's primary factors were made by D. W. Fiske (1949) and resulted in a five-factor solution; this work is now widely cited as the earliest version of the contemporary model discussed next.

The "Five-Factor Model" and Why it Works. Current writings on personality assessment have given increasing attention to the so-called Five-Factor Model (FFM), which represents an unusual level of consensus among personality researchers from the various factor analytic traditions (Costa & Widiger, 1994; Digman, 1990; McCrae & John, 1992; Wiggins & Pincus, 1992). At the same time, the particular way in which the model has been presented has led to considerable criticism and controversy (Block, 1995; Carlson, 1992; Goldberg, 1993; Kroger & Wood, 1993; Loevinger, 1994).[11] Essentially, the Five-Factor Model is an attempt to use a hierarchical pattern of analysis in order to simplify the vast collection of available data about the affective behavior of individuals. It thereby renders the information more manageable in assessing individuals and predicting their behavior in given situations. The factors are descriptive rather than explanatory; and they are no more basic than the individual items or specific tests from which they were derived.

The Five-Factor Model is similar to the hierarchical structure obtained by factor analysis of ability tests discussed in chapter 11. Although several investigators over the past four decades have coincided in arriving at five factors as the number needed to account for most of the correlations among a vast amount of personality description data, the appropriate number of factors for particular purposes could actually be better characterized as 5 ± 2; and the names given to each factor are also controversial (see, e.g., Digman, 1990, p. 423; Loevinger, 1994; Paunonen, 1993). This is to be expected, since the factors reflect different selections of inventories, scales, response formats, and samples from which they were derived.

Some confusion and misunderstanding have resulted from the way the procedure for the Five-Factor Model was reported. There is an implication that *the* basic factors of personality have been "discovered" through some new approach. Actually, the factors correspond to the second level of a hierarchy resulting from factor analyses of personality test and rating scale data. It is noteworthy that the second level of the hierarchy, yielding factors of medium breadth, has proved most practicable, and replicable, in both cognitive and affective assessment. Because they aggregate or combine measures from the lower levels of behavioral descriptors and of more narrowly defined traits, these factors yield more reliable scores—and the resulting validities are correspondingly higher. If a test battery has been constructed with a hierarchical model, and if norms are provided for different levels, as is done in such cognitive batteries as the Differential Ability Scales described in chapter 8, the battery can be applied with maximum flexibility to suit specific purposes. For example, after identifying the midlevel factor that is most characteristic of an individual, the analysis can be supplemented by examining that person's scores on the narrower, more detailed tests on the lower level.

---

[11] See also other articles following Kroger and Wood in the same Comment section of the *American Psychologist*, 1993, pp. 1298-4304.

The two investigators most closely associated with the Five Factor Model have developed a test that fits their version of the model. In its current edition, the NEO-PI-3 (McCrae, Costa, Jr., and Martin, 2005)[12] provides scores on the five major domains of personality (Neuroticism, Extraversion, Openness, Agreeableness, and Conscientiousness) and the six facets that define each domain to provide a comprehensive and detailed assessment of general personality. Table 13.1 provides a snapshot of the NEO PI-R Domains and Facets. Although, it is an earlier version of NEO-PI-3, but the domains and facets are similar in both these versions. NEO-PI-3 is also appropriate for use with adolescents as young as 12 years. The NEO-PI-3 retains the reliability and validity of the NEO-PI-R and features new normative data. To lower the reading level 38 test items from the NEO-PI-R have been revised or edited, thereby making the instrument more appropriate for younger examinees or adults with lower educational levels.[13] The abbreviated version, the NEO-Five Factor Inventory (NEO-FFI), consists of 60 items and takes only 10-15 minutes to complete. The NEO Five-Factor Inventory-3 (NEO-FFI-3) is the updated version of the NEO-FFI and is a 60-item version of the NEO-PI-3. Fifteen of the 60 NEO-FFI items have been replaced to improve readability and psychometric properties. It provides a quick, reliable, and accurate measure of the five domains of personality and is particularly useful when time is limited and when global information on personality is needed.[14]

Table 13-1

Domains and Facets of the Revised NEO Personality Inventory (NEO PI-R)

NEUROTICISM	EXTRAVERSION	OPENNESS TO EXPERIENCE
Anxiety (N1)	Warmth (El)	Fantasy (Ol)
Angry Hostility (N2)	Gregariousness (E2)	Aesthetics (O2)
Depression (N3)	Assertiveness (E3)	Feelings (O3)
Self-Consciousness (N4)	Activity (E4)	Actions (O4)
Impulsiveness (N5)	Excitement-Seeking (E5)	Ideas (O5)
Vulnerability (N6)	Positive Emotions (E6)	Values (O6)

AGREEABLENESS	CONSCIENTIOUSNESS
Trust (A1)	Competence (C1)
Straightforwardness (A2)	Order (C2)
Altruism (A3)	Dutifulness (C3)
Compliance (A4)	Achievement (C4)
Modesty (A5)	Self-Discipline (C5)
Tender-Mindedness (A6)	Deliberation (C6)

(Adapted from Costa & McCrae, 1992b, p. 2. Copyright © 1992 by Psychological Assessment Resources, Inc. Reproduced by permission.)

[12] Robert R. McCrae, Paul T. Costa, Jr. & Thomas A. Martin (2005) The NEO–PI–3: A More Readable Revised NEO Personality Inventory, Journal of Personality Assessment, 84:3, 261-270, DOI: 10.1207/s15327752jpa8403_05. Retrieved June 8, 2016 from the World Wide Web: http://dx.doi.org/10.1207/s15327752jpa8403_05

[13] Ibid.

[14] Authors of the tests-Paul T. Costa, Jr., Ph.D., & Robert R. McCrae, Ph.D. © 1989, 1992, 2010

The Five-Factor (or "Big Five") Model as postulated by McCrae and Costa has been widely, though by no means universally, accepted as a useful framework for the exploration of personality traits. Differences exist even among factor analytically oriented investigators both in the number of intermediate-level factors they propose and in their definitions (L. R. Goldberg, 1993; Zuckerman, Kuhlman, Joireman, Teta, & Kraft, 1993). Nevertheless, in its various versions, the model has spurred a flurry of research activity aimed at the cross-identification of factors and integration of various perspectives, such as the significant aspects of the normal and pathological personalities (see, e.g., Hofstee, de Raad, & Goldberg, 1992). Related work in test development and refinement of existing scales is also proceeding apace (Costa & McCrae, 1994, 1995; Costa & Widiger, 1994; Harkness, McNulty, & Ben-Porath, 1995; Hogan & Hogan, 1992).

In evaluating the results of this activity, one should keep in mind that factor analysis merely provides a technique for grouping items into relatively homogeneous and independent clusters. Such groupings facilitate the investigation of validity against empirical criteria, permit a more efficient combination of scores for the prediction of specific criteria, and contribute toward construct definition. Homogeneity and factorial purity are desirable goals in test construction. But they are not substitutes for empirical validation or sound theoretical grounding.

PERSONALITY THEORY IN TEST DEVELOPMENT

Personality theories have usually originated in clinical settings. The amount of experimental verification to which they have subsequently been subjected varies tremendously from one theoretical system to another. Regardless of the extent of such objective verification, a number of personality tests have been constructed within the framework of one or another personality theory. Clinically formulated hypotheses have been especially prominent in the development of projective techniques, considered in chapter 15. While this approach to test construction has been followed less often for self-report inventories, a few outstanding examples are available.

Millon Clinical Multiaxial Inventory. Although following the MMPI tradition in several ways and designed for the same purposes, the Millon Clinical Multiaxial Inventory–Ill (MCMI-III—Millon, Millon, & Davis, 1994), originally published in 1977, introduces significant methodological innovations. In fact, its development was deliberately undertaken to meet the criticisms of the MMPI and to utilize intervening advances in the diagnosis of psychopathology and test construction.

The MCMI-III is grounded in Millon's biopsychosocial views of personality functioning and psychopathology (Millon, 1969, 1981, 1990; Millon et al, 1996). His theory encompasses a matrix of personality styles derived from combining types along two dimensions, namely, source of reinforcement (i.e., detached, discordant, dependent, independent, and ambivalent) and pattern of coping behavior (i.e., active or passive). Millon's theory of personality styles served as one of the conceptual bases in the original formulation of the Axis II personality disorders categories of the *Diagnostic and Statistical Manual of Mental Disorders–III* (DSM-III–1980) prepared by the American Psychiatric Association, now in its fourth edition (DSM-IV—1994). In turn, the clinical scales of the MCMI-III are consistent with, though not identical to, the classificatory system followed in the DSM-IV. Efforts to coordinate the inventory as closely as possible with the evolving framework of the DSMs have, in fact, prompted the frequent revisions that the MCMI has undergone.

The MCMI-III contains 175 brief, self-descriptive statements to be marked "true" or "false" by the respondent. The score profile includes 24 clinical scales, each based on 12 to 24 overlapping items that often appear in as many as three different scales, albeit with different weights; items that meet all of the validation criteria for their "home" scale are given a weight of 2, whereas subsidiary items receive a weight of 1. As can be seen in Table 13–2, the clinical scales are grouped into four major categories, namely, Clinical Personality Patterns, Severe Personality Pathology, Clinical Syndromes, and Severe Syndromes. The first two of these categories contain scales designed to assess the enduring Axis II personality pattern disorders of the DSM, at different levels of severity. The other two encompass some of the Axis I syndromes of the DSM. There are also three modifying indices and a validity check designed to detect atypical response patterns and test-taking biases. The MCMI originally could be scored only by computer; currently, in addition to mail-in scoring services and software for generating profiles and interpretive reports, hand scoring is available, although it is quite laborious because of the need to incorporate score transformations and several adjustments.

One of the most significant innovations introduced by the MCMI is the use of standard scores called Base Rate (BR) scores which, instead of being normalized, are anchored to the prevalence rates of the characteristics being measured.

Table 13-2

Scales of the Millon Clinical Multiaxial Inventory-III

Clinical Personality Patterns	Clinical Syndromes
Schizoid	Anxiety
Avoidant	Somatoform
Depressive	Bipolar: Manic
Dependent	Dysthymia
Histrionic	Alcohol Dependence
Narcissistic	Drug Dependence
Antisocial	Post-Traumatic Stress Disorder
Aggressive (Sadistic)	
Compulsive	**Severe Syndromes**
Passive-Aggressive (Negativistic)	Thought Disorder
Self-Defeating	Major Depression
	Delusional Disorder

Severe Personality Pathology	Modifying Indices	Validity Index
Schizotypal	Disclosure	
Borderline	Desirability	
Paranoid	Debasement	

(Adapted from Millon et al, 1994, p. 2.)

The cutoff BR scores of the MCMI scales are set to reflect actuarial base rate data within psychiatric populations for the particular conditions the scales assess and thus enhance differential diagnosis. Because prevalence rates may vary in different clinical populations and settings, the BR scores of some of the MCMI-III scales can be adjusted for setting, chronicity, and scores on anxiety and depression, as well as certain response patterns.

Item development for the MCMI followed the multifaceted approach characteristic of recent practice in the construction and validation of personality inventories. In this regard, the MCMI cuts across the methodology described in several sections of this chapter. The procedure included a sequence of three major steps: (1) theoretical-substantive (i.e., writing and selecting items to fit clinically relevant constructs), (2) internal-structural (e.g., item-scale correlations and endorsement frequencies), and (3) external-criterion (e.g., differentiation of diagnostic groups from reference group and cross-validation on new samples).

The reference groups employed for the item analyses of the MCMI-III and its predecessors consisted of undifferentiated psychiatric patients, rather than normal samples. It is primarily because of the exclusive use of clinical samples in the derivation of norms and transformed scores that the author clearly states: "The MCMI-III is not a general personality instrument to be used for normal populations or for any purpose other than diagnostic screening or clinical assessment" (Millon et al., 1994, p. 5). Furthermore, scale cutoff scores and profile interpretations are geared to those displaying psychopathology in the midranges of severity rather than those whose problems are either close to normal or extremely severe. Some of the MCMI studies using normal subjects have found them scoring higher than psychiatric patients—but at subclinical levels—whereas others show some normals scoring at pathological levels on certain scales (e.g., Histrionic and Narcissistic). These findings confirm the inadvisability of administering the inventory to normals and suggest that, at midlevel elevations, these scales may even measure healthy personality attributes (Wetzler, 1990).

One of the major purposes of the MCMI is to be of help in the process of differential diagnosis. This task is complicated by the fact that psychiatric conditions can coexist within the same individual at the same time. The relatively frequent revisions and refinements the MCMI has undergone since its initial publication are commendable, but they also make the task of evaluating the extent to which it has met its objectives more difficult. However, a great deal of research has been accumulated on the earlier versions of the instrument, and a number of related publications that will help its users are starting to emerge. Research findings indicate that the overlap of items across scales can detract from their discriminating power, especially when test takers are in the midst of anxiety and depressive states; and more data about the diagnostic efficiency of the clinical syndrome scales are needed. Nevertheless, the MCMI is a potentially valuable tool for diagnosing personality disorders and evaluating their treatment (Choca, Shanley, & Van Denburg, 1992; Craig, 1993; Goncalves, Woodward, & Millon, 1994; Retzlaff, 1995; C. R. Reynolds, 1992a).[15]

---

[15] The Schedule for Nonadaptive and Adaptive Personality (SNAP) is an interesting new measure that is also designed to evaluate personality pathology. In contrast to the MCMI, the SNAP uses scales derived through factor analyses (see, e.g., Clark, McEwen, Collard, & Hickok, 1993).

Recently, Millon has developed two new instruments that extend his approach to the assessment of personality and psychopathology. One is the Millon Adolescent Clinical Inventory (MACI—Millon, Millon, & Davis, 1993), intended to be the tool of choice for use in the assessment of adolescents between the ages of 13 and 19 in clinical settings. The MACI evolved from the Millon Adolescent Personality Inventory (MAPI—Millon, Green, & Meagher, 1982), an older instrument originally designed for use in both clinical assessment as well as vocational counseling and academic advising, with scales that assess the basic personality styles, expressed concerns, and behavioral tendencies of adolescents.[16] The Millon Index of Personality Styles (MIPS—Millon, 1994), on the other hand, is intended as a measure of personality for normal adults who seek assistance for work, family, or social problems in various counseling settings. The MIPS was standardized on adult and college samples and combines elements of Millon's personality theory with those of Freud and Jung.

Edwards Personal Preference Schedule. Among the personality theories that have stimulated test development, one of the most prolific has been the manifest need system proposed by Murray and his associates at the Harvard Psychological Clinic (Murray et al., 1938). One of the first inventories designed to assess the strength of such needs was the Edwards Personal Preference Schedule (EPPS—Edwards, 1959). Beginning with 15 needs drawn from Murray's list, Edwards prepared sets of items whose content appeared to fit each of these needs. Examples include the need for Achievement (to do one's best and accomplish something difficult), Deference (to conform to what is expected of one), Exhibition (to be the center of attention), Interception (to analyze the motives and feelings of oneself and others), Dominance (to influence others and to be regarded as a leader), and Nurturance (to help others in trouble).

The inventory consists of 210 pairs of statements in which items from each of the 15 scales are paired with items from the other 14.[17] Within each pair, the test takers choose one statement as more characteristic of themselves. It is important to bear in mind that, due to this forced choice, the EPPS results in *ipsative* scores—that is, the strength of each need is expressed not in absolute terms, but in relation to the strength of the individual's other needs. The frame of reference in ipsative scoring is the individual rather than the normative sample. Because the sum of all the subscale scores is a constant for all test takers, if a person's score on one subscale moves one point up, another subscale score must move one point down. Under these conditions, two individuals with identical scores on the EPPS may differ markedly in the absolute strength of their needs. Although the EPPS provides norms for conversion of its scores to percentiles, the advisability of conversion may be questioned because of the ipsative nature of the scores. While the ipsative frame of reference may be the most suitable for *intraindividual* comparisons, such as those needed in the assessment of interests and other preferences, normative reference data are necessary for the sort of *interindividual*

[16] The MAPI is now recommended as a tool for use in nonclinical assessments of personality in normal adolescents only.

[17] This item form, which represents an important feature of the EPPS, will he discussed further in the next section, as an example of the forced-choice technique.

comparisons used, for example, in the assessment of abnormality (Fedorak & Coles, 1979).

However, the combination of both frames of reference makes the interpretation of scores confusing and less meaningful than would be the case with a consistently ipsative *or* consistently normative approach.

Although the validity data reported in the EPPS manual are meager, a large number of independent validation studies have been published. The results of these validation studies, however, are often difficult to interpret because most of them have failed to take into account the ipsative nature of the scores. With ip-sative scores, the mean intercorrelation of individual scales tends to be negative and the mean correlation of all the scales with any outside variable will approach zero (Hicks, 1970). Owing to these artificial constraints, ipsative scores cannot be properly analyzed by the usual correlational procedures. It is not surprising, therefore, that the published validation studies have yielded conflicting and inconclusive results (see, e.g., Piedmont, McCrae, & Costa, 1992). In spite of its simplicity and noteworthy features, the EPPS is in need of revision to eliminate technical weaknesses related to item form and score interpretation.

Personality Research Form and Other Jackson Inventories. The Personality Research Form (PRF) reflects many technical advances in test construction, including some item-selection procedures that would have been virtually impossible before the availability of high-speed computers. The PRF exemplifies Douglas N. Jackson's approach to personality test development, which begins with explicit, detailed descriptions of the constructs to be measured. These descriptions form the basis for item writing as well as for defining the traits to be rated by judges in the validation studies (Jackson, 1970, 1989b).

The PRF is available in five different options, including two sets of parallel forms (A,B and AA,BB) of 300 and 440 items, respectively. The longer forms provide 22 scale scores each based on 20 items, including two validity scores, Infrequency and Desirability; the shorter forms have only fifteen 20-item scales. An additional version (Form E), developed later through the use of more sophisticated item analytic techniques, consists of 352 of the best items from the longer forms and provides scores on all 22 scales, although each contains only 16 items. Form E, which is now the most frequently used, also has an easier vocabulary level than the others. The Infrequency score, designed as an index of carelessness, failure to understand directions, and other nonpurposeful responding, is based on the number of highly unlikely responses chosen by the test taker; examples include "I try to get at least some sleep every night" and "I make all my own clothes and shoes." Although desirability bias was substantially reduced in advance by the procedures employed in item development and selection, a Desirability scale is also provided. The manual correctly observes that unusually high or low scores on that scale may indicate not only atypical test-taking attitudes (e.g., deliberate attempt to create a favorable impression vs. malingering) but also important personality characteristics in their own right (e.g., high self-regard or high degree of conventional socialization vs. low self-regard).

Like several other personality instruments, the PRF took Murray's personality theory as its starting point. Drawing upon the extensive research and theoretical literature that had accumulated during three decades, Jackson formulated behaviorally oriented and mutually exclusive definitions of 20 personality constructs or traits. Of these, 12 have the same names as those in the EPPS. For each of the 20 bipolar personality scales, the manual provides a description of high scorers and a set of defining trait adjectives. Two illustrative scale definitions are shown in Table 13–3.

Through carefully controlled procedures, pools of more than 100 items were generated for each scale. Twenty items were then selected for each scale based on high hiserial correlation with total scale score and low correlation with scores on other trait scales and on the Desirability scale. Items yielding extreme endorsement proportions were eliminated. Through a specially developed computer program, items were assigned to the parallel forms in terms of biserial correlation with their own scale, as well as endorsement frequency. The procedures used in the construction of Form E included the calculation of an item efficiency index for each item. Based on weights derived from various statistical item parameters, the index allows each item to be ranked within its scale on the basis of its efficiency.

The construct validity of the PRF depends to a large extent on the procedures followed in the development and selection of items for each scale. Subsequent factorial analyses corroborated the grouping of items into the 20 scales. Correlations with comparable scales in the California Psychological Inventory, Guilford-Zimmerman Temperament Survey, and NEO-PI, among others, provide additional support for the identification of traits. Although studies of the correlations between various instruments designed to measure Murray's needs—such as the PRF, EPPS, TAT (chap. 15), and ACL (chap. 16)—have yielded inconsistent results,

Table 13–3

Examples of Scale Definitions from Personality Research Form

Scale	Description of High Scorer	Defining Trait Adjectives
Cognitive Structure	Does not like ambiguity or uncertainty in information; wants all questions answered completely; desires to make decisions based upon definite knowledge, rather than upon guesses or probabilities.	precise, exacting, definite, seeks certainty, meticulous, perfectionistic, clarifying, explicit, accurate, rigorous, literal, avoids ambiguity, defining, rigid, needs structure.
Sentience	Notices smells, sounds, sights, tastes, and the way things feel; remembers these sensations and believes that they are an important part of life; is sensitive to many forms of experience; may maintain an essentially hedonistic or aesthetic view of life.	aesthetic, enjoys physical sensations, observant, earthy, aware, notices environment, feeling, sensitive, sensuous, open to experience, perceptive, noticing, discriminating, alive to impressions.

(From Jackson, 1989b, pp. 6-7.)

there seems to be more support for the construct validity of the PRF than for some of the other tools; this would not be surprising in light of the careful attention given to the formulation of traits in the development of the PRF (Costa & Mc-Crae, 1988; D. W. Fiske, 1973; Rezmovic & Rezmovic, 1980). Data on the empirical validity of the PRF against pooled peer ratings and self-ratings have also yielded promising results. It is noteworthy that the PRF has proven to be applicable across several cultures, even in non-Western ones (Jackson, Guthrie, Astilla, & Elwood, 1983; Paunonen, Jackson, Trzebinski, & Forsterling, 1992). On the whole, as the extensive annotated bibliography compiled by MacLennan (1992) attests, the PRF is an excellent research instrument, but more information is still needed to determine its effectiveness in practical situations.[18]

The Jackson Personality Inventory–Revised (JPI-R), developed after the PRF through similar though more refined scale construction procedures, has a more practical orientation (Jackson, 1976, 1994a). The trait scales were chosen from the personality and social psychological literature partly because of their relevance to the prediction of behavior of normal subjects in a variety of contexts. Among the traits covered by the 15 scales are anxiety, cooperativeness, responsibility, social astuteness, and tolerance. Validity data were gathered not only through correlations with peer ratings and self-ratings, using the multitrait-multimethod matrix model, but also through studies of particular groups for whom relevant behavioral data in real-life contexts were available. In the recent revision of this inventory, the norms for college students were updated and new norms for blue-and white-collar workers were developed to support its use in academic counseling and employment settings. In addition, a number of technical modifications and minor changes were made on the scales, which are now grouped into five higher-order clusters that are largely compatible with the Five Factor Model (FFM) categories discussed in an earlier section. Specifically, the JPI-R's Extroverted, Dependable, and Analytical clusters are substantially similar to the Extraversion, Conscientiousness, and Openness to Experience dimensions of the FFM, respectively. In addition, the Emotional cluster of the JPI-R seems to represent a combination of the FFM's Neuroticism and Agreeableness. However, the Opportunistic cluster of the JPI-R, which draws from its Social Astuteness and Risk Taking scales, has no direct link to the FFM and is thus seen as a unique factor.

Turning to the assessment of psychopathology, Jackson has employed the same stringent standards applied in the PRF and JPI to the construction of the Basic Personality Inventory (BPI—Jackson, 1989a). The BPI, which was developed over a period of about 15 years, aims to recreate the diagnostic efficiency associated with the MMPI, using scales that are more substantial in terms of content, psychometric purity, and range of applicability. Although the BPI is in need of more representative norms, especially for adults, it has already shown promise for clinical use in the area of juvenile delinquency (Holden & Jackson, 1992; for review, see Urbina, 1995).

In this overview of self-report inventories, the reader has probably noticed an increasing tendency to combine different approaches. This is particularly true of the Jackson inventories, and of other new inventories developed in the

---

[18] This instrument has been extensively reviewed in the Mental Measurements Yearbooks: 7th MMY, #123; 8th MMY, #643; 10th MMY, #282; see also TIP-IV for an updated reference list.

past decade, which employ all strategies except the empirical criterion keying of items. In addition, even the Minnesota inventories, which are the preeminent examples of empirical criterion keying, now contain scales based on content and factor analysis. There is some evidence suggesting that personality inventory scales constructed by any of the four major methods outlined in this chapter can all be effective, at least with regard to convergent and predictive validity (Burisch, 1986). However, the content-and theory-based procedures are easier to construct, more efficient to use, and more likely to show discriminant validity than the empirical criterion keying approach, which in turn is the one that is least compatible with the rest. Furthermore, there is ample agreement to the effect that: (a) the development of inventories should start with an explicit definition of the trait or construct to be measured; and (b) the organizational structure outlined by Campbell and Fiske in their multitrait-multimethod matrix (see chap. 5) provides an optimal strategy for the examination of the construct validity of personality inventories (Angleitner, John, & Löhr, 1986; Hogan & Nicholson, 1988; Ozer & Reise, 1994).

TEST-TAKING ATTITUDES AND RESPONSE BIASES

Faking and Social Desirability. Self-report inventories are especially subject to the possibility of deliberate misrepresentation. Despite introductory remarks to the contrary, most items on such inventories have one answer that is recognizable as socially more desirable or acceptable than the others. On such tests, respondents may be motivated to "fake good," or choose answers that create a favorable impression, as when applying for a job or seeking admission to an educational institution. Under other circumstances, respondents may be motivated to "fake bad," thus making themselves appear more psychologically disturbed than they are. This may occur, for example, in the testing of persons on trial for a criminal offense.

Evidence of the success with which respondents can dissemble on personality inventories is plentiful (see, e.g., Jacobs & Barron, 1968; Radcliffe, 1966; Strieker, 1969; J. S. Wiggins, 1966). A common classroom demonstration consists in asking different groups to assume specified roles. For example, one section of the class is directed to answer each question as it would be answered by a happy and well-adjusted college student; another section is told to respond in the manner of a severely maladjusted person; and in the last section, respondents are instructed to answer the items truthfully with reference to their own behavior. Or the same persons may take the test twice, first with instructions to simulate in a specified way and later under ordinary conditions. The results of such studies clearly demonstrate the facility with which the desired impression can be deliberately created. It is interesting to note that even specific simulation for a particular vocational objective can also be successfully carried out (Wesman, 1952). Current research indicates that, especially on self-report inventories, the "face validity"[19] of an item increases its susceptibility to faking, under both realistic and controlled laboratory conditions. The more readily respondents can identify the trait

[19] See chapter 5.

being assessed from the item wording, the more frequently they give the desirable response (Bornstein et al., 1994).

The tendency to choose socially desirable responses on a self-report inventory need not indicate deliberate deception on the part of the respondent. A. L. Edwards (1957), who first investigated the social desirability variable, conceptualized it primarily as a façade effect, or tendency to "put up a good front," of which the respondent is largely unaware. This tendency may indicate lack of insight into one's characteristics, self-deception, or an unwillingness to face up to one's limitations. Other investigators (Crowne & Marlowe, 1964; N. Frederiksen, 1965) have presented evidence to suggest that the strength of the social desirability response set is related to the individual's more general need for self-protection, avoidance of criticism, social conformity, and social approval. On the other hand, the individual who chooses unfavorable items in a self-description may be motivated by a need for attention, sympathy, or help in meeting personal problems. Persons seeking psychotherapy, for example, are likely to make themselves appear more maladjusted on a personality inventory than they actually are.

Furthermore, it cannot be assumed that basic research is free from the effects of response sets. In the context of studies on attitude change, for example, investigators have shown that results may be influenced by such conditions as the participant's perception of what the experimenter expects, the desire to protect one's own image, and the wish to please or frustrate the experimenter (Silverman & Shulman, 1970). Unsuspected differences in these response sets may account in part for failures to replicate results when the experiments are repeated.

Some investigators (Paulhus 1984, 1986; Paulhus & Reid, 1991) have underscored the difference between the notions of impression management[20] and self-deception as explanations for socially desirable—or undesirable—responding. *Impression management* refers to conscious dissembling designed to create a specific effect desired by the respondent. It is seen as a contaminant of self-report data and as something that must in itself be assessed and, whenever possible, minimized or contained. On the other hand, self-deception, which consists of usually positively biased responding that the test taker actually believes to be true, is a great deal more complex. Self-deception is linked to other concepts pertaining to the self, such as self-image and self-esteem, as well as to the psychoanalytic notion of defense mechanisms. Thus, it is a variable worth studying in its own right as possibly indicative of good adjustment, up to a point, and predictive of other independent criteria. It has, for example, been noted that some self-report scales may give results that show "illusory mental health" on the part of defensive deniers who strive to maintain a belief in their own adjustment (see, e.g., Shedler, Mayman, & Manis, 1993). Therefore, the relationship between self-deception and adjustment seems to be neither simple nor direct. To complicate things even further, it appears that certain linguistic characteristics of items interact with respondent variables to produce biased responses (Helfrich, 1986).

Several procedures have been followed in the effort to meet the problem of faking and related response sets in personality inventories. The construction of relatively "subtle" or socially neutral items may reduce the operation of these factors in some inventories; however, as Jackson (1971) pointed out, often those

[20] "Manipulation" and "other-deception" are sometimes used instead of "impression management."

items also have low validity for the dimension under consideration. Ideally, and in fact in a number of situations, the test instructions and the establishment of rapport should motivate test takers to respond frankly, if they are convinced that it is to their advantage to do so. This approach is ineffective in certain situations, however; and it probably does not have much effect on social desirability response sets of which the individual is unaware.

Another approach to the evaluation of socially desirable responding and other forms of impression management is to construct special scales—which can either be embedded in an inventory or administered by themselves in a battery of tests—for that purpose. One of the earliest such scales was Edwards' (1957) social desirability (SD) scale, developed by selecting items on the basis of the agreement of judges regarding their extremely high or low social desirability values. Others, such as the CPI's Good Impression scale and J. S. Wiggins' (1959) SD scale, have selected items on the basis of differences in endorsement frequencies by subjects responding under "fake good" conditions and those responding under normal conditions. A third method is exemplified by the MMPI's Lie scale, which contains items written so that they will be answered in the socially desirable direction only by respondents who exhibit an unrealistic positive bias. Other measures aimed specifically at the detection of malingering and of careless or random responding, such as the F scale of the MMPI, have been devised.[21] Still another procedure, directed not to the detection but to the prevention of dissimulation, is the use of forced-choice items.

Forced-Choice Technique. Essentially, the forced-choice technique requires the respondent to choose between two descriptive terms or phrases that appear equally acceptable but differ in validity. The paired phrases may both be desirable or both undesirable. Forced-choice items may also contain three, four, or five terms. In such cases, respondents must indicate which phrase is most characteristic and which is least characteristic of themselves. Still another variant requires a choice between two contrasting responses within the same trait, scored for a single scale. Although rarely employed in personality inventories, this item form has the advantage of yielding normative rather than ipsative scores and hence imposing no artificial constraints on the interrelationships among different scales. An example is provided by the Myers-Briggs Type Indicator, discussed in chapter 16.

Use of the forced-choice technique to control social desirability requires two types of information regarding each response alternative—namely, its social desirability or "preference index" and its validity or "discriminative index." The latter may be determined on the basis of any specific criterion the inventory is designed to predict, such as academic achievement or success on a particular kind of job; or it may be based on the factor loading of items or their theoretical relevance to different traits. Social desirability can be found by having the items rated for this variable by a representative group, or by ascertaining the frequency with which the item is endorsed in self-descriptions. It has been shown that frequency of choice and judged social desirability correlate very highly (Edwards, 1957).

[21] For a thorough review of scales for the assessment of malingering, see Berny, Wetter, and Baer (1995).

In other words, the *average* self-description of a population agrees closely with its average description of a desirable personality.

Although the influence of social desirability may be reduced in forced-choice items, it cannot be assumed that it is completely eliminated. When items of the EPPS were presented in a free-choice format, the scores correlated quite highly with those obtained on the forced-choice format of the same test (Lanyon, 1966). Furthermore, the judged social desirability of particular items is not constant for all purposes but may differ for different occupations. Thus, a forced-choice test whose items were equated in general social desirability could still be faked when taken by job applicants, candidates for admission to professional schools, and other specifically oriented groups. From another angle, it has been found that when items are paired on the basis of average *group* judgments of general social desirability, they may be far from equated for *individuals* (N. Wiggins, 1966).

In conclusion, it appears that the forced-choice technique has not proved as effective as had been anticipated in controlling faking or social desirability response sets. At the same time, the forced-choice item format, particularly when it yields ipsative scores, introduces other technical difficulties and eliminates information about absolute strength of individual characteristics that may be of prime importance in some testing situations.

Response Sets and Response Styles. The tendency to choose response alternatives on the basis of social desirability is only one of several response sets that have been identified in self-report inventory responding (Lanyon & Goodstein, 1982, pp. 158–169). Although the voluminous literature on the operation of response sets in personality inventories dates largely from the 1950s, the influence of response sets in both ability and personality tests was observed by earlier investigators (see Block, 1965, chap. 2). One of the response sets that attracted early attention was *acquiescence,* or the tendency to answer "True" or "Yes." Acquiescence is conceptualized as a continuous variable; at one end of the scale are the consistent "Yeasayers" and at the other end the consistent "Naysayers" (Couch & Keniston, 1960). The implications of this response set for the construction of personality inventories is that the number of items in which a "Yes" or "True" response is keyed positively in any trait scale should equal the number of items in which a "No" or "False" response is keyed positively. This balance can be achieved by the proper selection or rewording of items, as was done in the PRF and is now being done with most new inventories.[22]

Another response set is *deviation,* or the tendency to give unusual or uncommon responses. Berg (1967) proposed this hypothesis and demonstrated its operation with nonverbal content in a specially developed test requiring an expression of preference for geometric figures. Scales made up of items likely to be answered in one direction by almost all test takers, such as the Infrequency scale of Jackson's PRF, were intended to identify such deviant response patterns. However, Jackson himself, among others, has pointed out that these scales tend to lack conceptual relevance to external criteria and, therefore, pose a problem especially in contexts like employment settings where the relevance of questionnaire items

[22] Helmes and Reddon (1993) have also pointed out that, if a scale is bipolar and its item keying is unbalanced, the amount of information conveyed by low scores is substantially reduced.

is considered important. Because of this, the Infrequency scale of the JPI was removed when that inventory was revised (Jackson, 1994a). The tendency to use the extreme choices on a rating scale (e.g., 1s and 7s on a seven-point scale) has also been identified as a possible response bias (Paulhus, 1991).

Research on response sets such as social desirability, acquiescence, and deviation has passed through several stages. When first identified, response sets were regarded as a source of irrelevant or error variance to be eliminated from test scores. Later, these response sets came to be regarded as indicators of broad and durable personality characteristics that were worth measuring in their own right (Jackson & Messick, 1958, 1962; J. S. Wiggins, 1962). At this stage, they were commonly described as *response styles* and an elaborate edifice of empirical data was built around them. Eventually, these data were challenged from many directions (Block, 1965; Heilbrun, 1964; Rorer, 1965). Block (1965), for example, presented strong evidence supporting a content-oriented interpretation of the two major factors generally found to account for most of the common variance in the MMPI scales, which exponents of response sets and response styles had interpreted as social desirability and acquiescence.

The controversy over response sets and content-versus-style in personality assessment has never been fully settled (Edwards, 1990; Hogan & Nicholson, 1988; Jackson & Paunonen, 1980).[23] The majority of test developers and investigators seem to agree that personality inventory scores are likely to reflect a combination of self-deception, impression management, and realistic self-portrayal and that the weight of each of these components will vary with the individual and the occasion. Some, however, view attempts to improve the trustworthiness of self-report data through special scales and items as possibly counterproductive in that they may reduce the validity of scales especially for normal, as opposed to pathological, samples. Such authors advocate the use of clinical skills in eliciting a patient's cooperation and in interpreting scores, as well as the inclusion of ratings from knowledgeable informants whenever there is reason to suspect serious distortion (see, e.g., Costa & McCrae, 1992a).

Most other workers, especially those involved in the assessment of psychopathology, continue to use so-called "validity" scales, with the awareness that they may also reflect personality styles and characteristics. In fact, some of the newest and technically more advanced instruments for the assessment of psychopathology, such as Jackson's BPI and Morey's PAI, use balanced keying of items *and* special scales for detecting invalidating response sets. There is also a new variety of such scales, exemplified by the VRIN and TRIN scales of the MMPI-2 and MMPI-A, that make use of specially selected item pairs that are either similar or opposite in content to detect inconsistent or contradictory responding. Because of the way they are constituted, the VRIN and TRIN scales, which are similar to Greene's (1978) Carelessness scale for the original MMPI, are not likely to be confounded by valid personality trait variance (Ozer & Reise, 1994).

At any rate, the argument about response sets and styles has stimulated extensive research and has produced several hundred publications. Like many scientific controversies, its net effect has been to sharpen our understanding of

[23] See also other articles following Edwards in the same Comment section of the *American Psychologist*, 1990, pp.289–295.

methodological problems and thereby improve the construction of personality inventories and their use in both research and applied settings.

TRAITS, STATES, PERSONS, AND SITUATIONS

Interactions of Persons and Situations. A long-standing controversy regarding the generalizability of psychological traits versus the situational specificity of behavior reached a peak in the late 1960s and the 1970s. Several developments in the 1960s focused attention on narrowly defined "behaviors of interest" and away from broadly defined traits. In the area of abilities, this focus is illustrated by individualized instructional programs and domain-referenced testing (chap. 3) and by the diagnosis and treatment of learning disabilities (chap. 17). In the personality realm, the strongest impetus toward behavioral specificity in testing came from the social learning and social cognitive theories that underlie behavior modification and behavior therapy (Bandura, 1969, 1986; Goldfried & Kent, 1972; Mischel, 1968, 1969, 1973). Criticism was directed especially toward the early view of traits as fixed, unchanging, underlying causal entities. This kind of criticism had been anticipated in the earlier research and writing of several psychologists, with regard to all traits—cognitive as well as noncognitive (see chap. 11). Although few psychologists had really argued for this extreme view of traits, during the heyday of the situational specificity argument it was hard to find any who would identify herself or himself as a "trait theorist" (Jackson & Paunonen, 1980).

Situational specificity in particular is much more characteristic of personality traits than it is of abilities. For example, a person might be quite sociable and outgoing at the office, but shy and reserved at social gatherings. Or a student who cheats on examinations might be scrupulously honest in money matters. An extensive body of empirical evidence was assembled by Mischel (1968) and D. Peterson (1968) showing that individuals do exhibit considerable situational specificity in many nonintellective dimensions, such as aggression, social conformity, dependency, rigidity, honesty, and attitudes toward authority. Part of the explanation for the higher cross-situational consistency of cognitive than of noncognitive functions may be found in the greater standardization of the individual's reactional biography in the intellectual than in the personality domain (Anastasi, 1958, chap. 11; 1970, 1983a). The formal school curriculum, for example, contributes to the development of broadly applicable cognitive skills in the verbal and numerical areas. Personality development, on the other hand, occurs under far less uniform conditions. In the personality domain, moreover, the same response may lead to social consequences that are positively reinforcing in one situation and negatively reinforcing in another. The individual may thus learn to respond in quite different ways in different contexts. Such dissimilarities in experiential history, across individuals as well as across situations and cultures, also lead to greater ambiguity in personality test items than is found in cognitive test items. Thus, the same response to a given question on a personality inventory—which can in itself be construed as a "situation"—may have different significance from one person to another.

It should be noted that the trait-situation question is also related to the familiar heredity-environment question (D. C. Rowe, 1987). Hereditary influences are likely to be manifested through relatively enduring individual traits, which may nevertheless include a trait of adaptability to situational demands. Environmental influences may contribute to situational variance (or specificity) as well as to trait stability, because the individual's environment may itself exhibit major consistencies over time and situations. Appropriate experimental designs with repeated measurements obtained longitudinally and cross-situationally should enhance our understanding of both the heredity-environment and the trait-situation questions.

Both the theoretical discussions and the research on person-by-situation interaction have undoubtedly enriched our understanding of the many conditions that determine individual behavior, and they have contributed to the development of sophisticated research designs. Concurrently, there has been a growing consensus among the adherents of contrasting views to the effect that trait and situational explanations of behavior can coexist and that, in fact, behavior is determined through the interaction of trait and situational variables. The rapprochement was especially evident in a number of well-balanced and thoughtful discussions of the problem published from the late 1970s to the late 1980s.[24] Several noteworthy points emerged from these discussions. Behavior exhibits considerable temporal stability when measured reliably, that is, by summing repeated observations preferably made by multiple observers who are knowledgeable about the person being evaluated. When random samples of persons and situations are studied, individual differences contribute more to total behavior variance than do situational differences. Interaction between persons and situations contributes as much as do individual differences, or slightly more. To identify broad personality traits, we need to measure the individual across many situations, using dimensions that are publicly observable and behaviors that are relevant to the dimensions in question, and aggregate the results (Epstein, 1980; Kenrick & Funder, 1988). In spite of the relative consensus achieved on many of these matters, and of what has been learned already, there are still more questions and new questions about both sides of the person-situation debate (see, e.g., Funder, 1991).

The Person. The degree of behavioral specificity across situations itself varies from person to person. Individuals differ in the extent to which they alter their behavior to meet the demands of each situation. In this respect, moderate inconsistency indicates effective and adaptive flexibility, while excessive consistency indicates maladaptive rigidity. Moreover, the particular situations across which behavior is consistent may vary among persons. This intersituational consistency is influenced by the way in which individuals perceive and categorize situations. And such grouping of situations, in turn, depends on the individual's goals, motives, and feelings as well as on her or his prior experience with similar situations.[25]

---

[24] Amelang and Borkenau (1986), Bern and Funder (1978), Endler and Magnusson (1976), Epstein (1979, 1980), Epstein and O'Brien (1985), Hogan, DeSoto, and Solano (1977), Kenrick and Funder (1988), Mischel (1977, 1979), and Mischel and Peake (1982). See also Anastasi (1983b) for overview.

[25] This conception of behavioral consistencies derives from the early idiographic approach to personality assessment formulated by Allport (1937) and G. A. Kelly (1963), among others.

Individual differences in consistency are of great interest to psychologists in general for obvious reasons. To the extent that such differences can be reliably assessed, they could be used as a moderator variable in the prediction of behavior. In addition, from the psychometric standpoint, intrapersonal and interpersonal differences in consistency are considered crucial in moderating the validity—and reliability—of all psychological measures. It is therefore not surprising that efforts are under way, from a variety of directions, to devise ways to assess these differences. One method is based on ratings people assign to themselves on different trait dimensions; scores are derived from each person's variance across ratings. Low interitem scale variances represent the quality of *traitedness,* which has, in fact, been linked to higher validity coefficients (Amelang & Borkenau, 1986; Baumeister & Tice, 1988). A different approach is represented by Lanning's (1991) notion of "scalability," defined as the degree to which a person maintains a normative ordering of behavioral items across situations as assessed by self-report.

An intriguing proposal that links the concepts of person-situation interaction and social desirability, in terms of the process underlying responses to personality questionnaire items, is Jackson's "threshold theory" of responding (see, e.g., Helmes & Jackson, 1989; Jackson, 1986b). This model is based on the premise that inventory items represent a microcosm of behavior in the real world. It uses item response theory methods to scale personality item content (see chap. 7). Jackson suggests that, just as the responses of many individuals to a single item can be used to derive an item characteristic curve, a single subject's responses to many items can be used similarly to plot a subject characteristic curve. Such a curve would predict a person's likelihood of endorsing items and would be based on the salience of the desirability dimension for the subject in question, her or his threshold or willingness to respond positively to items in terms of social desirability, and the desirability of the items themselves.

The Situation. Situations also differ in the behavioral constraints they impose. Thus we could predict with a high level of confidence that readers will remain silent in a library and that motorists will stop at a red light. Similarly, persons—whatever their trait structure—are likely to swim at the beach and to read in the library. Nevertheless, certain individuals may spend their time reading while at the beach, and others may spend all too much time daydreaming about swimming while in the library. One way to better understand the constraints that situations impose on behavior is by studying the characteristics of various behavior settings. Roger Barker's recently updated work on ecological psychology provides a promising set of tools for classifying behavior settings and for describing various facets of the environment (Schoggen, 1989).

Cross-cultural differences can be seen as a special, and more pervasive, instance of situational variability. As such, they afford a unique opportunity to study the consistencies and inconsistencies in the behavior of persons. To this end, the approaches to cross-cultural testing discussed in chapters 9 and 12 in the context of ability measures can also be used to investigate other psychological traits.

When applied to cultures other than the one in which they were developed, personality tests show large differences. Any explanation of such cultural and subcultural differences requires specific knowledge of the conditions and circumstances prevailing within each group. This has been increasingly recognized in the assessment of psychopathology in culturally diverse groups within the United States (Malgady, Rogler, & Costantino, 1987; Paniagua, 1994). Group differences on tests such as the MMPI, for example, can reflect nothing more than differences in interpretation of individual items or instructions. Cultural differences in the type of behavior considered socially desirable may likewise influence scores; elevated scores on a scale assessing depression in some groups could result from strong traditions of self-deprecation and modesty. In still other groups, high scores may indicate the prevalence of genuine emotional problems arising from child-rearing practices, conflicts of social roles, minority group frustrations, and other broad cultural differences.

The issue of personality assessment across cultures is broader than the transportability of tests; rather, it involves the transportability of conceptual systems, such as traits and trait hierarchies, that are applied to behavior (Guthrie, Jackson, Astilla, & Elwood, 1983). Furthermore, just as was earlier discovered in the assessment of the ability domain, there is now a growing recognition that some important personality dimensions are not universal. Accordingly, in addition to the ongoing efforts to adapt and translate traditional Anglo-American instruments for use with different populations, some personality measures designed to assess specific dimensions indigenous to cultural and subcultural groups are now being developed (see, e.g., Dana, 1993; Lonner & Berry, 1986). However, whereas some specific items and inventories may not be transportable across cultures, there is reason to believe that the hierarchical trait model may be useful in integrating cross-cultural findings. That is, provided one begins by measuring behaviors identified as significant within each culture with instruments appropriate to each, it may be possible to identify some higher-level psychological constructs that may be universal or at least broadly generalizable across cultures (Anastasi, 1992c; Diaz-Guerrero & Diaz-Loving, 1990).

Traits and Situations. That traits and situations are not incompatible ways of categorizing behavior is illustrated by self-report inventories for assessing *test anxiety* (I. G. Sarason, 1980). An example is the Test Anxiety Inventory[26] (TAI) developed by Spielberger and his associates (Spielberger et al., 1980). This instrument is essentially a trait measure. The trait, however, is defined in terms of a specified class of situations, those centering on tests and examinations. Persons high in test anxiety tend to perceive evaluative situations as personally threatening. The inventory comprises 20 statements describing reactions before, during, or after tests or examinations. Respondents are asked to indicate how they *generally* feel by marking how frequently they experience each reaction (almost never, sometimes, often, almost always). Typical examples include "I freeze up on important exams" and "While taking examinations, I have an uneasy, upset feeling." The TAI yields a total score on anxiety proneness in test situations, as well as subscores on two major components identified through factor analysis—namely, worry and emotionality. In this context, worry is defined as "cognitive concerns about the consequences of failure" and emotionality as "reactions of

[26] Labeled "Test Attitude Inventory" on the test taker's form and so listed in the 9th MMY and TIP-IV.

the autonomic nervous system that are evoked by evaluative stress" (Spielberger et al, 1980, p. 1).

Still further degrees of situational specification are provided in the Test Anxiety Profile (Oetting & Deffenbacher, 1980).[27] On this instrument, respondents rate their reactions on items covering feelings of anxiety and thought interference. Both types of anxiety scores are obtained for each of six testing situations in which respondents are instructed to imagine themselves, ranging from "multiple-choice test" and "unannounced 'pop' quiz" to "giving a talk."

Perhaps because of the prevalence of test anxiety, and the relative ease of investigating it within the academic setting, research and theorizing on the topic continue with undiminished vigor both in the United States and in other countries (Hagtvet & Johnsen, 1992). At any rate, this construct provides a good model of how trait and situational concepts can be useful in categorizing behavior, especially in the personality domain. Depending upon the purpose of the test, trait constructs may be defined with different degrees of breadth or narrowness and may be linked to specified types of situations.

Traits and States. Another way to conceptualize the behavior domain assessed by personality tests involves a differentiation between traits and states. This differentiation is most clearly exemplified in the State-Trait Anxiety Inventory (STAI) developed by Spielberger and his co-workers (Spielberger, 1985; Spielberger et al., 1983). In the construction of this instrument, state anxiety (S-Anxiety) was defined as a transitory emotional condition characterized by subjective feelings of tension and apprehension. Such states vary in intensity and fluctuate over time. S-Anxiety is measured by 20 short descriptive statements which the individual answers in reference to how he or she feels *at the moment* (e.g., "I feel calm"; "I am jittery"). The answers are recorded by indicating the intensity of the feeling (not at all, somewhat, moderately so, very much so).

Trait anxiety (T-Anxiety) refers to relatively stable anxiety-proneness, that is, the individual's tendency to respond to situations perceived as threatening with elevated S-Anxiety intensity. Respondents are instructed to indicate how they *generally* feel by marking the frequency with which each of the 20 statements applies to them (almost never, sometimes, often, almost always). Examples of the statements are "I am inclined to take things hard" and "I am a steady person." Individuals high in T-Anxiety tend to exhibit S-Anxiety elevations more often than do individuals low in T-Anxiety, because they react to a wider range of situations as threatening or dangerous. They are especially responsive to interpersonal situations posing some threat to their self-esteem, such as performance evaluation or the experience of failure. Whether or not S-Anxiety increases in a given situation, however, depends upon the extent to which the individual perceives the situation as threatening or dangerous on the basis of her or his past experience. The STAI and its companion version for children, the State-Trait Anxiety Inventory for Children (STAIC), have been translated into 43 languages and dialects and have accumulated a bibliography of more than 6,000 studies (Spielberger, 1989; Spielberger & Sydeman, 1994).

[27] The Test Anxiety Profile is no longer in print. However, license to reproduce it for research purposes may be obtained by writing to Eugene Oetting at the Department of Psychology, Colorado State University, Fort Collins, CO 80523.

The state-trait differentiation was applied by Spielberger and his associates in another subsequently developed inventory, the State-Trait Anger Expression Inventory (STAXI) (Spielberger, 1988; Spielberger, Johnson, Russell, Crane, Jacobs, and Worden, 1985). Its latest version, STAXI-2 (Spielberger,1999), is a 57-item inventory, which measures the intensity of anger as an emotional state (State Anger) and the disposition to experience angry feelings as a personality trait (Trait Anger). The instrument consists of six scales that measure the intensity of anger and the disposition to experience angry feelings. The respondents have to respond to the test items on a 4-point scale that assesses the intensity of anger at a particular moment and the frequency of anger experience, expression, and control.

CURRENT STATUS OF PERSONALITY INVENTORIES

Until a few years ago, personality inventories were widely used in the clinical setting in India. Recently, deployment of personality inventories in the educational and occupational settings has gained momentum. For instance, in the occupational setting, several personality instruments are used to assess a person's job fitness and to understand the personality as a whole to design and deploy developmental interventions. For example, the Myers-Briggs Type Indicator or MBTI is a popular and widely used personality assessment tool for individual development, team building and development, development of managers and leaders, assessment of leadership and creative potential, education, and career counselling. Other personality assessments such as SOSIE Personality Assessment, Hogan Personality Inventory, Hogan Development Survey, Caliper Profile, and Talent Q are widely used by organizations across an employee's lifecycle. Details of all listed and other personality assessments are available on the Internet. In addition to this, indigenous personality instruments are also gaining attention for assessing blue-collar workers and other non-traditional roles that require custom assessments. Since the number of qualified practitioners is considerably less in India, the needs and demands for training in the use of personality tests are considerable. Workshops and certifications are offered in association with regional conferences. Indian psychometric assessment firms also provide opportunities to address these issues with Indian psychologists. Furthermore, it may be a good idea that international associations could explore closer collaboration with independent practitioners to increase the awareness and test competence issues in using and interpreting personality assessments, in an effort to raise the standards governing the development and usage of tests at the local level in India.

Chapter Fourteen

Measuring Interests and Attitudes

The nature and strength of one's interests and attitudes represent an important aspect of personality. These characteristics materially affect educational and occupational achievement, interpersonal relations, the enjoyment one derives from leisure activities, and other major phases of daily living. Although tests typically are directed toward the measurement of one or the other of these variables, the available instruments cannot rigidly be classified according to such discrete categories as interests and attitudes. Overlapping is the rule. Thus, a questionnaire designed to assess the relative strength of interests in investigative, artistic, or conventional occupations also might be said to gauge the individual's attitudes toward pure science, art for art's sake, practical tasks, and the like.

Values are also clearly related to life choices and are often discussed in conjunction with interests, attitudes, and preferences. A great deal of research has been, and continues to be, done by personality and social psychologists on the topic of values, including some interesting and wide-ranging investigations of the generality of values across cultures (S. H. Schwartz, 1992, 1994; S. H. Schwartz & Sagiv, 1995; Super & Šverko, 1995). In recent years, however, relatively few developments have occurred in the area of standardized, commercially available instruments aimed exclusively at the assessment of values. This is related to several problems specific to the measurement of values, such as the difficulties of sampling systematically, and at the appropriate level of abstraction, from value domains. In addition, some of the early and most widely used value measures proved to be incompatible with the way values eventually came to be conceptualized in the field (Braithwaite & Scott, 19911).[1] While some "stand-alone" tests, such as the Life Values Inventory (Brown & Crace, 1996) and The Values Scale (Nevill & Super, 1989) are still being published or revised, much of the formal assessment of values is now incorporated within instruments designed to facilitate career decision making and to assess work-related attitudes and motives.[2]

The study of *interests* received its strongest impetus from educational and career counseling, which will be discussed in chapter 17. To a slightly lesser extent, the development of tests in this area was also stimulated by occupational selection and classification. From the viewpoint of both the worker and the employer, a consideration of the individual's interests is of practical significance. The assessment of *opinions and attitudes* originated largely as a problem in social psychology. Attitudes toward different groups, for example, have obvious implications for intergroup relations. Similarly, the gauging and prediction of public opinion regarding a wide variety of issues, institutions, or practices are of deep concern to the social psychologist, as well as to the worker in business, politics, and other applied fields. The measurement of opinions and attitudes has also made rapid strides in the areas of consumer research and employee relations.

All instruments surveyed in this chapter are self-report inventories developed by one or more of the methods described in chapter 13. It should be noted, however, that in this area, as in the measurement of all personality constructs, other procedures are being continually explored. Examples of these other procedures are discussed in chapters 15 and 16.

INTEREST INVENTORIES: CURRENT SETTING

The large majority of interest inventories[3] are designed to assess the individual's interests in different fields of work. Some also provide an analysis of interests in educational curricula or fields of study, which in turn are usually related to career decisions. Although the frequency of test use in counseling has remained fairly stable since the 1950s, the use of interest tests has increased relative to that of ability tests (Zytowski & Warman, 1982). The more recently developed or revised inventories reflect certain major changes in career counseling. One of these changes pertains to the increasing emphasis on *self-exploration*. More and more instruments provide opportunities for the individual to study the detailed test results and relate them to occupational information and other data about personal qualifications and experience. Training in career decision making has itself received increasing attention. The occupational interest inventories to be

---

1 For example, the Study of Values (Allport, Vernon, & Lindzey, 1960), one of the first values inventories, consisted mostly of items related to preferences, beliefs, and interests, rather than values; at present, it is no longer in print.

2 Descriptions of many instruments mostly or exclusively concerned with values can be found in Anastasi (1988b, pp. 580–583), Braithwaite and Scott (1991), and Dawis (1991, pp. 845–850).

3 A comprehensive guide to interest inventories and other career assessment instruments, now in its third edition, is published by the National Career Development Association (Kapes, Mastie, & Whitfield, 1994). For overviews of important theoretical and methodological issues in the field, as well as examples of some of the major instruments, see Borgen (1986) and Hansen (1990).

discussed in this chapter should be considered against the background provided on career assessment in chapter 17.

A second and related change concerns the goal of interest measurement. Today, there is more and more emphasis on *expanding the career options* open to the individual. In fact, the term "exploration validity" is used to designate the effect that interest inventories can have in terms of increasing behaviors instrumental to career exploration (see, e.g., Randahl, Hansen, & Haverkamp, 1993). Thus, the interest inventory, as well as the more comprehensive career orientation programs cited in chapter 17, are being used to acquaint the individual with suitable occupations that he or she might not otherwise have considered.

The third significant change is itself associated with this expansion of career options. It relates to a concern about the *sex fairness* of interest inventories. In general, interest inventories compare an individual's expressed interests with those typical of persons engaged in different occupations. This is done either in the scoring of individual item responses, or in the interpretation of scores in broad interest areas, or both. While this approach certainly represents an objective, empirical procedure for evaluating one's interests, it tends to perpetuate existing group differences among occupations. If there are large discrepancies in the proportion of men and women in some occupations, such as engineering or nursing, these differences tend, in one way or another, to influence the interpretation of results obtained by males and females on interest inventories. For this reason, considerable discussion and intensive research efforts have been devoted to ways of reducing possible sex bias in interest inventories (Tittle & Zytowski, 1978; Zytowski & Borgen, 1983). A set of guidelines for the assessment of sex bias and sex fairness in career inventories has also been prepared and widely distributed.[4] Nearly every newly developed or revised inventory shows the influence of these guidelines and makes some provision for dealing with the issue of sex fairness. One of the steps taken has been the elimination of sex bias in the wording of inventory items. In addition, other common solutions have involved balancing the content of items evenly in terms of typical differences in sex role socialization and providing the most appropriate norms possible for each sex group on inventory scales. These measures have improved the quality of technical data available to career counselors and other users of interest inventories. However, because of lingering sex differences in interest patterns and in occupational group membership, there are still social policy issues concerning the interpretation and use of interest inventory data that need to be carefully considered in the career assessment of women (Hackett & Lonborg, 1994).

A related development has come to the fore even more recently, largely in response to legislation aimed at providing vocational guidance to disabled and disadvantaged populations[5] (L. S. Gottfredson, 1986b; Reed, Rotatori, & Day, 1990; Szymula, 1990). Among other things, the special requirements of persons with disabilities in terms of vocational assessment have prompted the development

---

[4] Prepared as part of a study conducted by the National Institute of Education. A copy is reproduced in Tittle and Zytowski (1978, pp. 151–153).

[5] Two specific instances of such legislation are the Carl D. Perkins Vocational Education Act of 1984 (P.L. 98–524) and the Carl D. Perkins Vocational and Applied Technology Education Act Amendments of 1990 (P.L. 101–392).

of several picture interest inventories that use drawings or audiovisual stimuli such as slide-tape and videocassette formats (Elksnin & Elksnin, 1993; Kapes et al., 1994, pp. 307–345). The first generation of these instruments, designed to bypass the reading demands of traditional paper-and-pencil interest inventories, is inadequate from the psychometric standpoint, especially in the realm of validity. However, picture interest inventories represent an innovative way of administering test stimuli that is likely to develop further as technology improves and the need to provide alternative measures for special populations expands. Modifications of traditional instruments, such as the ones described in chapter 9 in connection with ability tests for special populations, can, of course, be used in the assessment of interests as well. The impetus provided by the Americans with Disabilities Act of 1990 (P.L. 101–336) is certain to stimulate further interest and work in the area (Bruyère & O'Keeffe, 1994).

THE STRONG INTEREST INVENTORY™ (SII)

Origins and Development of the SII. This interest inventory, whose latest edition was published in 1994, has a long history. The general approach followed in its construction was first formulated by E. K. Strong, Jr., while attending a 1919–1920 graduate seminar on interest measurement at the Carnegie Institute of Technology (D. P. Campbell, 1971, chap. 11; Fryer, 1931, chap. 3). When first published in 1927, the Strong Vocational Interest Blank® (SVIB) introduced two principal procedures in the measurement of occupational interests. First, the items dealt with the respondent's like or dislike for a wide variety of specific activities, objects, or types of persons that he or she commonly encountered in daily living. Second, the responses were empirically keyed for different occupations. These interest inventories were thus among the first tests to employ criterion keying of items, subsequently followed in the development of such personality inventories as the MMPI and CPI (chap. 13). It was found that persons engaged in different occupations were characterized by common interests that differentiated them from persons in other occupations. These differences in interests extended not only to matters pertaining directly to job activities, but also to school subjects, hobbies, sports, types of plays or books the individual enjoyed, social relations, and many other facets of everyday life. It thus proved feasible to prepare an inventory that explored an individual's interests in familiar things and thereby to determine how closely her or his interests resembled those of persons successfully engaged in particular occupations.

Beginning in the 1970s, extensive innovations have been introduced and implemented in successive revisions of the SII (D. P. Campbell, 1974; D. P. Campbell & Hansen, 1981; Hansen & D. P. Campbell, 1985; Harmon, Hansen, Borgen, & Hammer, 1994). The principal changes include (1) the introduction of a theoretical framework to guide the organization and interpretation of scores, (2) the merging of the earlier men's and women's forms and the renorming of all occupational scales on new male and female samples, and (3) a substantial increase in the number of scales for vocational/technical occupations requiring less than a college degree for entry—a category that had been underrepresented in earlier editions.

Strong Interest Inventory (SII): SII is the latest revision of the SVIB. This revision was developed with the objective of shortening the instrument, adding current occupations, increasing the level of business, technology, and teamwork measures and broadening the assessment of work and leisure activities (as cited in Gregory, 2015, p. 488). The SII consisted of 291 items that had to be responded to on a 5-point Likert scale. The standardization sample comprised 2,250 people

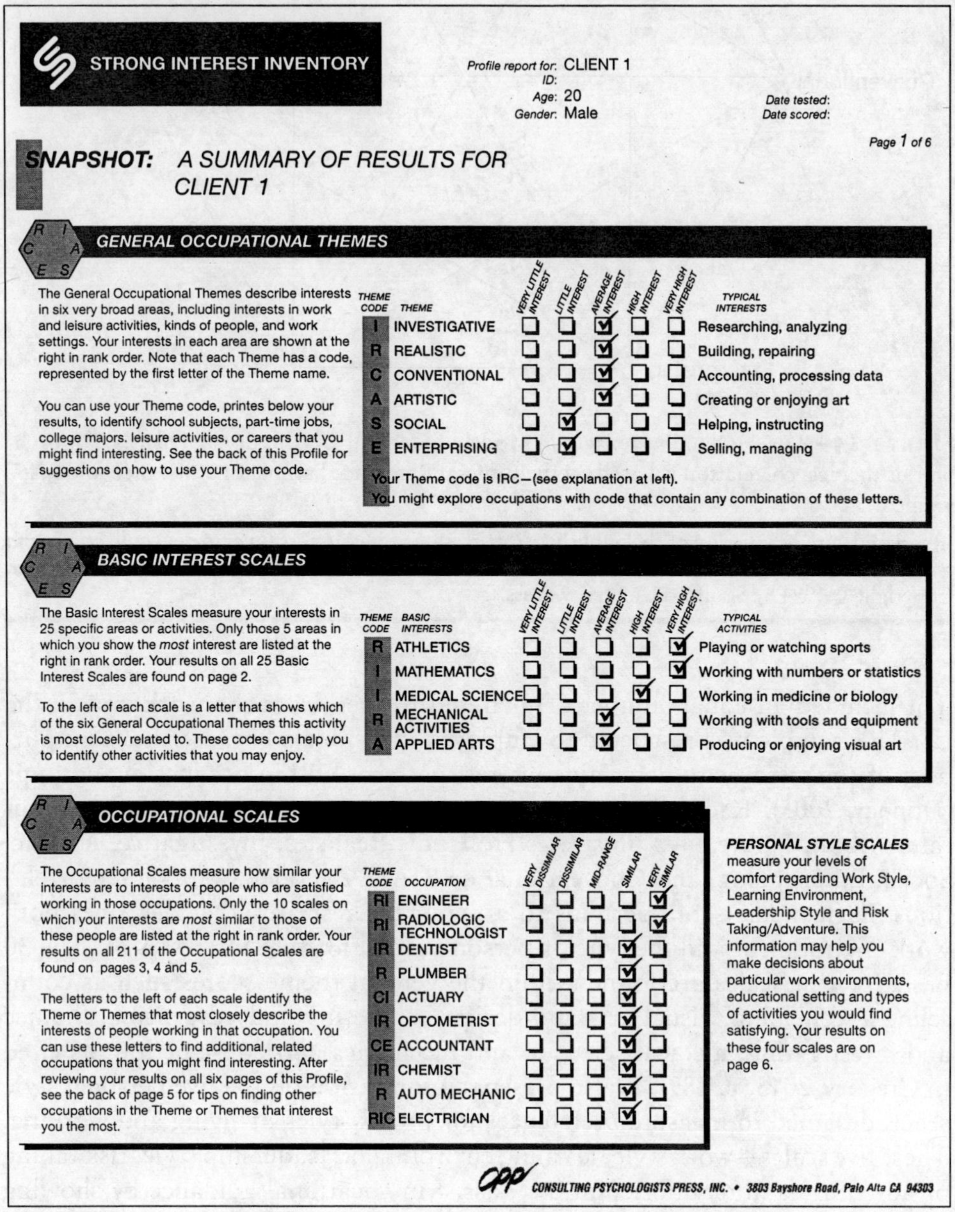

STRONG INTEREST INVENTORY

Profile report for: CLIENT 1
ID:
Age: 20
Gender: Male

Date tested:
Date scored:

Page 1 of 6

SNAPSHOT: A SUMMARY OF RESULTS FOR CLIENT 1

GENERAL OCCUPATIONAL THEMES

The General Occupational Themes describe interests in six very broad areas, including interests in work and leisure activities, kinds of people, and work settings. Your interests in each area are shown at the right in rank order. Note that each Theme has a code, represented by the first letter of the Theme name.

You can use your Theme code, printes below your results, to identify school subjects, part-time jobs, college majors. leisure activities, or careers that you might find interesting. See the back of this Profile for suggestions on how to use your Theme code.

THEME CODE	THEME	VERY LITTLE INTEREST	LITTLE INTEREST	AVERAGE INTEREST	HIGH INTEREST	VERY HIGH INTEREST	TYPICAL INTERESTS
I	INVESTIGATIVE			✓			Researching, analyzing
R	REALISTIC			✓			Building, repairing
C	CONVENTIONAL			✓			Accounting, processing data
A	ARTISTIC			✓			Creating or enjoying art
S	SOCIAL		✓				Helping, instructing
E	ENTERPRISING		✓				Selling, managing

Your Theme code is IRC—(see explanation at left).
You might explore occupations with code that contain any combination of these letters.

BASIC INTEREST SCALES

The Basic Interest Scales measure your interests in 25 specific areas or activities. Only those 5 areas in which you show the *most* interest are listed at the right in rank order. Your results on all 25 Basic Interest Scales are found on page 2.

To the left of each scale is a letter that shows which of the six General Occupational Themes this activity is most closely related to. These codes can help you to identify other activities that you may enjoy.

THEME CODE	BASIC INTERESTS	VERY LITTLE INTEREST	LITTLE INTEREST	AVERAGE INTEREST	HIGH INTEREST	VERY HIGH INTEREST	TYPICAL ACTIVITIES
R	ATHLETICS					✓	Playing or watching sports
I	MATHEMATICS					✓	Working with numbers or statistics
I	MEDICAL SCIENCE				✓		Working in medicine or biology
R	MECHANICAL ACTIVITIES			✓			Working with tools and equipment
A	APPLIED ARTS			✓			Producing or enjoying visual art

OCCUPATIONAL SCALES

The Occupational Scales measure how similar your interests are to interests of people who are satisfied working in those occupations. Only the 10 scales on which your interests are *most* similar to those of these people are listed at the right in rank order. Your results on all 211 of the Occupational Scales are found on pages 3, 4 and 5.

The letters to the left of each scale identify the Theme or Themes that most closely describe the interests of people working in that occupation. You can use these letters to find additional, related occupations that you might find interesting. After reviewing your results on all six pages of this Profile, see the back of page 5 for tips on finding other occupations in the Theme or Themes that interest you the most.

THEME CODE	OCCUPATION	VERY DISSIMILAR	DISSIMILAR	MID-RANGE	SIMILAR	VERY SIMILAR
RI	ENGINEER					✓
RI	RADIOLOGIC TECHNOLOGIST					✓
IR	DENTIST				✓	
R	PLUMBER				✓	
CI	ACTUARY				✓	
IR	OPTOMETRIST				✓	
CE	ACCOUNTANT				✓	
IR	CHEMIST				✓	
R	AUTO MECHANIC				✓	
RIC	ELECTRICIAN				✓	

PERSONAL STYLE SCALES measure your levels of comfort regarding Work Style, Learning Environment, Leadership Style and Risk Taking/Adventure. This information may help you make decisions about particular work environments, educational setting and types of activities you would find satisfying. Your results on these four scales are on page 6.

CPP CONSULTING PSYCHOLOGISTS PRESS, INC. • 3803 Bayshore Road, Palo Alta CA 94303

Figure 14-1. Summary of Results on the Strong Interest Inventory. Page 1 of the profile provides a "snapshot" of the scores obtained by a 20-year-old male college student choosing a major.

(Form reprinted with permission of the publisher from p. 236, *Strong Interest Inventory: Applications and technical guide,* by Lenore W. Harmon, Jo-Ida C. Hansen, Fred H. Borgen, and Allen L. Hammer. Copyright © 1994 by Stanford University Press.)

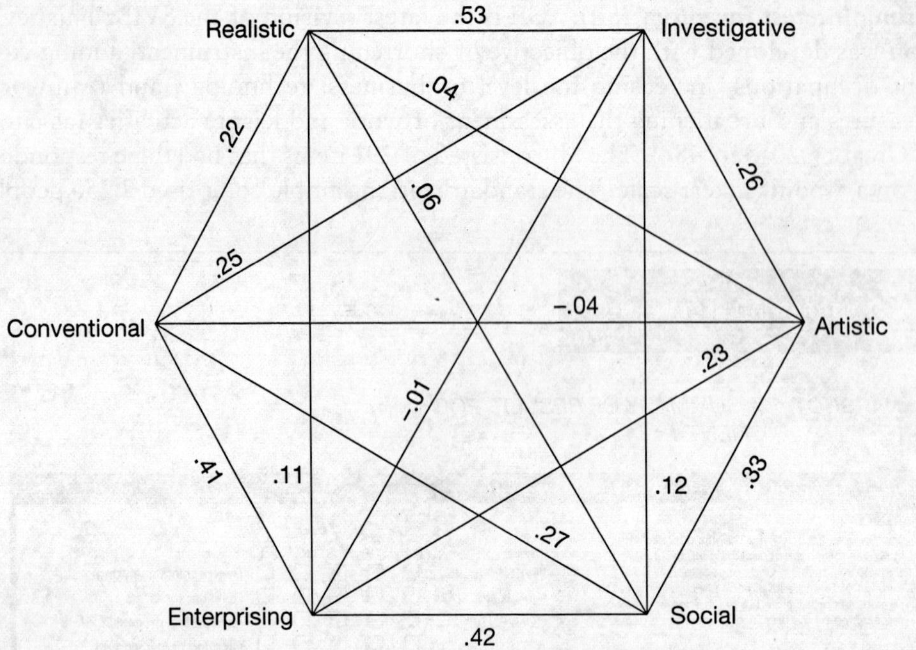

Figure 14–2. Holland's Hexagonal Model of General Occupational Themes. For each pair of themes, correlation is based on the General Reference Sample of 9,484 men and 9,467 women.

(Reprinted with permission of the publisher from p. 51, *Strong Interest Inventory: Applications and technical guide,* by Lenore W. Harmon, Jo-Ida C. Hansen, Fred H. Borgen, and Allen L. Hammer. Copyright © 1994 by Stanford University Press.)

that included an equal number of men and women from the workforce in the US. This sample was restricted to employed individuals because the main purpose of the test was to determine interest patterns within occupational groups (Donnay, 2005). Racial and ethnic groups represent the US population accurately (Ibid). Figure 14–2 illustrates Holland's Realistic, Investigative, Artistic, Social, Enterprising, and Conventional or RIASEC model and its intercorrelations. Each theme score pertains to a major interest area that describes both work environment and the type of person needed for that interest area. The 30 basic interest scales are found within the general theme scores such as counseling and helping, visual arts and design, marketing and advertising, finance and investigating, medical sciences, and mechanics and construction (as cited in Gregory, 2015, p. 489). It also presents information on the five personal style scales designed to measure preferences for broad styles of living and working. These five scales – work style, learning environment, leadership style, risk taking or adventure and team orientation – assist in vocational guidance by showing the level of comfort with distinctive styles. Figure 14–1 provides a snapshot of SII report. Each of these personal style scales and all test scores are expressed as standard scores with a mean of 50 and an SD of 10.

In India, SII is widely used. It enables individuals to identify rich and fulfilling career paths and gives different perspectives on careers, from general areas of interest to specific occupations. It is applicable to both educational and professional environments and is highly useful for coaching, career development and outplacement. However, in the Indian context, one needs to use this assessment under the guidance of either a qualified career counselor or a qualified practitioner or psychologist in order to interpret and understand the results as the Indian norm groups and occupations have not been updated yet.

Scoring and Interpretation. All scores on the Strong inventory are reported as standard scores with a mean of 50 and an *SD* of 10. For both General Occupational Themes and Basic Interest Scales, the normative sample—from which standard scores are computed—is the combined-sex GRS (N = 18,951). Both the interpretive labels and graphic representations of scores on the profiles, however, are based on the same-sex norms. Comparisons with other-sex norms can also be made by reference to the graphs presented on the profile forms. On the Occupational Scales, each respondent actually receives two standard scores—one derived from the female occupational sample, the other from the male occupational sample. These reporting procedures, while directed primarily to same-sex comparisons, provide the necessary data for counselors and respondents to make cross-sex comparisons for fuller and more effective interpretation of response patterns in individual cases.

The SII *Applications and Technical Guide* (Harmon et al., 1994) is of outstanding quality and contains much information to aid the counselor in interpreting results and discussing their possible implications with the client. For instance, profiles yielding internally consistent results tend to have higher predictability. On the other hand, certain inconsistencies, as between Basic Interest Scales and Occupational Scales, provide useful insight into the nature and sources of the respondent's expressed preferences. From another angle, the results obtained with the inventory can be generalized to other, related occupations through linkages that have been established with the occupations listed in the *Dictionary of Occupational Titles* (DOT) developed by the U.S. Department of Labor (1991) and other similar reference materials (Gottfredson & Holland, 1989; Harmon et al., 1994, Appendixes A & B). The *Applications and Technical Guide* also has several chapters devoted to the use of the Strong with special populations, such as culturally diverse groups and people with disabilities. In addition, several other publications designed to help both clients and counselors understand and use the results of the Strong are available (see, e.g., Borgen & Grutter, 1995; Hirsh, 1995; Prince, 1995).

Psychometric Evaluation. The Strong has undergone a continuing research program that has yielded extensive data about its reliability and validity (D. P. Campbell, 1971, 1977; Hansen & Campbell, 1985; Harmon et al., 1994). For the Occupational Scales, the median retest reliability for a sample of 191 employed adults, after intervals of between three and six months, was .90; for the Basic Interest Scales, the corresponding reliability was .86; and for the General Occupational Themes, it was .89. Long-term stability of the Occupational Scales for previous editions of the Strong is also high. The correlations for periods extending up to 20 years fall mostly in the .60s and .70s for individuals under the age of 25 and in the .80s for those over 25.

Concurrent validation data are provided by the degree of differentiation among various occupational samples, and between occupational samples and the reference samples. For the 211 occupational samples included in the 1994 revision, the median overlap was 36 percent; this reflects an average separation of slightly under two standard deviations between the occupational scales and the GRSs. Predictive validity has been checked in several samples over long intervals for previous versions of the Strong. The evidence indicates substantial correspondence between initial occupational profile and the occupation eventually pursued. A specific example is provided by a 40-year follow-up of a sample of psychologists whose professional careers revealed some suggestive relations between the flatness versus distinctness of their original profiles and such occurrences as frequency of job changes and shifting from teaching or research to administrative or applied work (Vinitsky, 1973). Another investigation found strikingly high cross-cultural profile similarities among samples of psychologists tested in nine Western nations (Lonner & Adams, 1972). In spite of the extensive research base that the Strong inventories have accumulated over the years and of their apparent solidity as indicators of occupational choice and tenure, new studies using the latest revision need to be undertaken in order to investigate its predictive validity directly.

With regard to construct validation, the relations of the Occupational Scales to the General Occupational Themes, as well as the interrelations of the themes portrayed in Figure 14–2 among themselves, are of special relevance. The R-I-A-S-E-C model developed by Holland (1966, 1985/1992) has been of enormous heuristic value in the study of vocational interests and the Strong inventories have in turn been an integral part of that research tradition, along with the other interest measures that utilize the same scheme. Research findings using the Strong, as well as other inventories, generally have been quite consistent with the predictions of the model.

The structure and organization of the SII have allowed it to be modified and expanded in a number of ways through its continuing revisions. The Strong inventory is not only a pioneer in the field of interest measurement; it is also the most widely used among counseling psychologists in the United States (Watkins, Campbell, & Nieberding, 1994). A few other instruments have been in use nearly as long and almost as widely. The period since the 1960s, however, has witnessed a rapid growth in the development of new instruments in this area. In part, this development reflects the growing attention to career exploration and the recognition that interests play a key role in such exploration.

The comprehensive programs for career exploration discussed in chapter 17 typically include measures of occupational interests, which are used in combination with multiple-aptitude test scores and job information. For example, interest data elicited with the Career Interest Inventory (CII) can be used in conjunction with the Differential Aptitude Tests, with which it was standardized (Psychological Corporation, 1991a). Similarly, the Occupational Aptitude Survey and Interest Schedule–2 (OASIS-2—Parker, 1991a, 1991b) was designed to assist high school students in vocational exploration and career development by providing scores on 6 aptitude and 12 interest factors. Another variation in the area of career planning is exemplified by the Harrington-O'Shea Career Decision-Making

System–Revised (CDM-R—Harrington & O'Shea, 1993), which attempts to integrate self-reported data on interests, values, and abilities with job information. The Campbell Interest and Skill Survey (CISS—Campbell, Hyne, & Nilsen, 1992) also measures self-reported interests and skills and is organized in a way reminiscent of the Strong inventory, with which David P. Campbell—author of the CISS—was involved for quite some time. The addition of data on skills allows comparisons of high and low patterns of scores on the interests and skills scales; this, in turn, expands the basis for career exploration and decision making provided by the survey. Reviews of the CII, OASIS-2, CDM-R, and CISS can be found in Kapes et al. (1994).

INTEREST INVENTORIES: OVERVIEW AND SOME HIGHLIGHTS

Among the many currently available interest inventories, four have been chosen for individual mention because each illustrates some noteworthy feature in its theoretical orientation, its methodology, or the type of population for which it was designed. No attempt will be made to describe or evaluate these instruments in detail; all have been reviewed recently in the *Mental Measurements Yearbooks,* either in their current or former versions.

Jackson Vocational Interest Survey (JVIS). The JVIS (Jackson, 1977) is selected for special attention—first, because it exemplifies sophisticated test construction procedures, and second, because in several respects its approach contrasts sharply with that followed in the SII. The original publication dates of the Strong and the Jackson inventories are 50 years apart. The Strong focuses on specific occupations, both in item selection and normative interpretations; the Jackson uses broad interest areas in both item development and scoring system. The Strong occupational scales represent an extreme example of empirical criterion keying and criterion-related validation; the Jackson exemplifies construct validation at every stage in its development. In the Strong, the large majority of items are independently marked Like, Indifferent, or Dislike by the respondent; in the Jackson, all items are of the forced-choice type.

As in the development of the Personality Research Form and the Jackson Personality Inventory described in chapter 13, the first step in the development of the JVIS was to define the constructs or dimensions to be measured. These dimensions, chosen on the bases of published research on the psychology of work and of factor-analytic and rational classifications of vocational interest items, were of two types. One was defined in terms of work roles, the other in terms of work styles. *Work roles* pertain to what a person does on the job. Some of these roles are closely associated with a particular occupation or type of occupation, such as engineering, law, or elementary education. Others, such as human-relations management and professional advising, cut across many occupations. *Work styles* refer not to job-related activities, but to preferences for working environments or situations in which a certain kind of behavior is expected. Work style dimensions are typically related to a person's values either directly or indirectly. Examples of work styles include planfulness, independence, and dominant leadership.

Development of the inventory followed several steps, including successive tryouts and statistical analyses of items that had been prepared to fit detailed specifications for each of the work roles and work styles. Starting with an initial pool of over 3,000 items, originally presented singly for a like–dislike response, the procedure included factor analyses of subsets of the items prepared for each scale. The presence of response bias, reflected in a large general factor, was removed statistically before proceeding with further item analyses. Items were selected if they showed high correlations with total factor scores on their own scale and low correlations with other scales. Pairs of items that represented different work roles or work styles and had shown similar endorsement frequencies when they were presented singly were assembled for the forced-choice format.[6]

The final form of the JVIS contains 34 basic interest scales, covering 26 work roles and 8 work styles. The inventory was designed to be equally applicable to both sexes, although separate percentile norms for female and male subgroups are also available. Norms were derived from large samples of college and high school students in the United States and Canada. A high score on any of the 34 JVIS basic interest scales indicates an interest in the things people do in a particular field of work, as well as in the way people in that work context are expected to act.

The JVIS can be hand-scored quickly and conveniently for the 34 scales. However, the computer-based scoring options available utilize more recent norms and provide several additional score analyses either in a short report or in a newly revised extended narrative report. The latter gives individualized descriptive and interpretive material as well as a good deal of information to aid in career exploration. For example, the computer-generated reports include scores derived from a factor analysis of the 34 basic interest scales. These scores, modeled after Holland's six themes, include the following 10 General Occupational Themes: Expressive, Logical, Inquiring, Practical, Assertive, Socialized, Helping, Conventional, Enterprising, and Communicative. A measure of Academic Satisfaction and indices of Response Consistency and Infrequency, as well as a tally of Unscorable Responses, is also provided. Other available score analyses involve comparisons of the respondent's profile as a whole with modal profiles obtained by college students in 17 clusters of academic major fields and by persons engaged in 32 occupational clusters. The occupational profiles were derived from joint administrations of the JVIS and Strong inventories which, through statistical analyses, established a linkage between the two inventories. This linkage provided a means of using the extensive occupational database of the Strong in interpreting JVIS scores.[7]

Some reviewers have suggested that the wording of the JVIS items may be too sophisticated for many high school students (D. T. Brown, 1989; J. W. Shepard, 1989). The survey item booklet has recently undergone a few minor changes in wording, but these are related to updating the terminology used rather than to simplifying it. A revision of the manual, incorporating norms gathered in the

---

[6] However, in contrast to other forced-choice instruments, the pairing of the JVIS items was accomplished in such a way that the resulting scores are *not* ipsative in nature.

[7] For a full description of the procedures that were followed, see Jackson (1977, chap. 4) and Jackson and Williams (1975),

mid-1990s, is also forthcoming shortly. In the meantime, a handbook on applications of the JVIS to career counseling (Verhoeve, 1993) and an occupations guide (Jackson, 1995) are available from the publisher.

The Kuder Occupational Interest Survey and Its Predecessors. The interest inventories developed by Frederic Kuder have been in use almost as long as the Strong series. The earliest was the Kuder Preference Record–Vocational, whose approach to the measurement of interests differed from the Strong's in two major ways. First, Kuder used forced-choice triad items, in which the respondents indicated which of the three activities they would like most and which least. Second, scores were obtained not for specific occupations, but for 10 broad interest areas—namely, Outdoor, Mechanical, Computational, Scientific, Persuasive, Artistic, Literary, Musical, Social Service, and Clerical. Items for each scale were formulated and tentatively grouped on the basis of content validity; final item selection was based on internal consistency and low correlations with other scales. The Kuder General Interest Survey (KGIS) was developed later as a revision and downward extension of the Kuder Preference Record–Vocational. Designed for Grades 6 to 12, this form uses simpler language and easier vocabulary, requiring only a sixth-grade reading level. Reviews of the KGIS (M. Pope, 1995; D. Thompson, 1995) can be found in the 12th MMY.

A still later version, the Kuder Occupational Interest Survey (KOIS), provides scores with reference to specific occupational groups, as does the Strong inventory (Kuder, 1966; Kuder & Diamond, 1979; Kuder & Zytowski, 1991). Unlike the Strong, however, the KOIS does not employ a general reference group. Instead, the respondent's score on each occupational scale is expressed as a correlation between her or his interest pattern and the interest pattern of the particular occupational group.[8] This interest survey can be scored on site or through the publisher by means of optical scanning, and it can also be administered and scored on a computer. Scores are currently available for 109 specific occupational groups and 40 college majors. Some scales have been developed only on men, some only on women, and some on both. Scores on all scales, however, are reported for both female and male respondents. The occupations covered by this inventory vary widely in level, ranging from beautician and truck driver to chemist and lawyer.

Through intensive statistical analysis of the scores of 3,000 persons (100 in each of 30 core groups representative of the occupations and college-major fields covered by the inventory), Kuder demonstrated that better differentiation between occupational groups can be achieved with the scoring system employed in this survey than with the occupational scales derived through the use of a general reference group. Research on other occupational scales is continuing (Zytowski, 1992).

The KOIS now provides *both* occupational scores and 10 broad, homogeneous basic interest scores, labeled Vocational Interest Estimates (VIE). The VIE are percentile scores derived from short scales equivalent to the 10 interest area

[8] The correlation employed is the lambda coefficient developed by Clemans (1958). This is essentially a point-biserial correlation adjusted for differences in homogeneity of different criterion groups. The dichotomous variable consists of the marked versus unmarked responses on the individual's answer sheet; the continuous variable is the proportion of persons in the criterion group marking each response.

scores of the early Kuder Preference Record. They can also be converted to the Holland R-I-A-S-E-C theme codes by direct correspondence for some scales and by averaging percentiles on two or three Kuder scales for others (e.g., average of Kuder Artistic, Literary, and Musical for Holland Artistic). Reviewers have generally praised the technical characteristics of the KOIS while pointing to the dearth of predictive validity data on this instrument. The failure to address the effects of its forced-choice format on scores has also been criticized (see Herr, 1989; Tenopyr, 1989).

Career Assessment Inventory—The Vocational Version (CAI-VV).[9] First released in 1975, the CAI (Johansson, 1984) is patterned closely on the Strong inventory. In contrast to most interest inventories, however, it was designed specifically for persons seeking a career that does *not* require a four-year college degree or advanced professional training. It concentrates on skilled trades, technical work, and service occupations. Examples of the currently available occupational scales are aircraft mechanic, dental hygienist, cafeteria worker, computer programmer, and registered nurse. The 305 inventory items are grouped under three content categories: Activities, School Subjects, and Occupations. Each item provides five response options, from "like very much" to "dislike very much." Written at a sixth-grade reading level, the CAI can also be used with adults who have poor reading skills. Like the Strong, the CAI provides scores on three major types of scales, including the 6 Holland General Theme scales, 22 homogeneous Basic Interest Area scales, and 91 Occupational scales. Administrative Indices and four Nonoccupational scales are also included.

Although the procedures followed in developing the CAI were closely similar to those used in the Strong, all data gathering and statistical analyses were carried out independently for this inventory. Except for the General Theme scales, the particular scales developed in each category are thus specific to the CAI. For reviews of the CAI-VV, see Kehoe (1992) and Vacc (1992).

Self-Directed Search (SDS). Another approach to the assessment of occupational interests is illustrated by the Self-Directed Search (SDS). This instrument was developed by Holland, whose hexagonal model of general occupational themes (discussed earlier in this chapter) has attracted wide attention and has been incorporated in several current inventories (Holland, 1985/1992; Holland, Fritzsche, & Powell, 1994; Holland & Gottfredson, 1976; Holland, Powell, & Fritzsche, 1994).

As its title implies, the SDS was designed as a self-administered, self-scored, and self-interpreted vocational counseling instrument. Although organized around interests, the procedure also calls for self-ratings of abilities and reported competencies. The individual fills out the Self-Assessment Booklet, scores the responses, and calculates six summary scores corresponding to the themes of the Holland model (Realistic, Investigative, Artistic, Social, Enterprising, and

[9] Two versions of the CAI are currently available, namely, The Vocational Version (VV) and The Enhanced Version (EV). The description in this section deals only with the VV. The EV, although very similar in structure, is a completely separate instrument (Johansson, 1986) that is applicable to a greater number and range of occupations, including many that require postsecondary education.

Conventional). The three highest summary scores are used to find a three-letter code.[10] An accompanying booklet, the Occupations Finder, is employed to locate, among 1,335 occupations, those whose codes resemble the respondent's summary code.

These occupations were chosen so as to represent nearly all of the workers in the United States; with a conversion code, the user can also explore all occupations in the *Dictionary of Occupational Titles.* Additional instructions, procedures, and sources of information are provided to facilitate the individual's career decisions.

The SDS is widely used in a variety of settings and has generated considerable research, both by the author and by independent investigators. In the years since its publication, it has undergone repeated revisions to simplify procedure and reduce sex bias in career decisions. Its chief practical appeal stems from its brevity and simplicity, its do-it-yourself feature, and its role in expanding the individual's career options. In addition to the regular form of the inventory (Form R), three other versions of the instrument are available: (1) Form E (Easy), developed for individuals with limited reading skills; (2) Form CP (Career Planning), designed for adults who are in the midst of career transitions; and (3) the Career Explorer version, aimed at middle school and junior high school students.

With regard to the psychometric properties of the SDS, indices of reliability are generally satisfactory for the summary scores. Construct validation of the basic six themes relies principally on the research that led to the formulation of the themes and on subsequent confirmatory factor analytic studies that are mostly supportive (see, e.g., Oosterveld, 1994). The concurrent validity and predictive efficiency of the SDS fluctuate depending on the makeup of samples in terms of age, sex, educational level, and distribution of types (Holland, Fritzsche, & Powell, 1994). Criticisms of the SDS center around some of its scoring and interpretive procedures (M. H. Daniels, 1989; Manuele-Adkins, 1989). Nevertheless, the consensus of reviewers' opinions is that this instrument provides a simple, inexpensive, and relatively accurate way to explore vocations. A bibliography for the SDS and several informative booklets for use in conjunction with it are available from the publisher.

J. L. Holland (1966, 1985/1992) aligns himself clearly with those who regard occupational preferences as the choice of a way of life—a choice that reflects the individual's self-concept and major personality characteristics. Each of Holland's occupational themes corresponds to a "type" or cluster of personality attributes. A given individual may be described in terms of one or more predominant types. The themes also correspond to model environments in terms of which different occupational settings may be characterized. These environments comprise not only physical features and work demands but also the kinds of persons with whom the individual works (co-workers, supervisors, customers, clients, students). According to Holland, individuals seek environments that are congruent

[10] Although the SDS is designed to be self-scoring, the manual recommends some supervision and checking of scores. A study of 107 randomly selected individuals of various ages who took the current edition of the SDS showed that 7.5% had derived codes containing incorrect letters or transpositions (Holland, Powell, & Fritzsche, 1994, p. 16).

with their personality types; and such congruence enhances work satisfaction, job stability, and achievement.

From a different perspective, Holland's general approach to the assessment of vocational interests is in line with certain developments in the psychology of career decisions. Super (1953, 1957, 1990) has repeatedly maintained that vocational choices are the implementations of self-concepts. There is a fairly lengthy research tradition dealing with personality differences among occupational groups (see, e.g., Borgen, 1986; Costa, McCrae, & Holland, 1984; Osipow, 1973, chap. 6; Pietrofesa & Splete, 1975, chap. 4; Super & Bohn, 1970, chap. 5). Occupational choice often reflects the individual's basic emotional needs. And occupational adjustment is a major component of general life adjustment (Tait, Padgett, & Baldwin, 1989). The assessment of vocational interests—and more specifically the identification of those occupational groups whose interests and attitudes an individual shares most closely—thus becomes a focal point in the understanding of different personalities.[11]

SOME SIGNIFICANT TRENDS

Inventory Development and Use. Among the clearest developments apparent in current interest measures are the merging of the two major theoretical positions in vocational psychology, as well as of the different approaches to inventory construction, and the cross-utilization of empirical data banks for interpretive purposes. More and more instruments are providing scores on *both* homogeneous, broad interest scales and specific occupational scales. The six occupational themes of Holland's model have surfaced in an increasing number of recently developed or revised inventories.

From a different angle, linkages are being established with empirical occupational data available on large populations. This was illustrated by the use of Strong occupational data in the interpretation of results on the Jackson Vocational Interest Survey. It is also illustrated in the linkage of many current inventories, such as the Holland SDS and the SII, with the data provided in the *Dictionary of Occupational Titles* (U.S. Department of Labor Employment and Training Administration, 1991). These are promising developments which strengthen and enhance the usefulness of any single instrument. The effects should be beneficial, provided that linkages are established by sound psychometric procedures and that steps are taken to guard against possible overgeneralization in score interpretation.

Another characteristic of newly developed or recently revised interest inventories is the expansion of the occupational levels they cover. At the outset, interest inventories focused on professional careers, with a smattering of occupations requiring less than a college or professional school education. Although some early efforts were made to expand coverage downward (e.g., Clark, 1961), the

[11] Waller, Lykken, and Tellegen (1995) report some pertinent findings concerning the interrelationships between occupational interests, leisure time interests, and personality traits in a large sample of participants in the Minnesota Twin Registry. Their studies suggest that while personality traits clearly mediate the person-occupation fit, the three sets of characteristics can be conceptualized as distinct domains.

resulting inventories were not widely used. In contrast, we now find the latest revision of the Strong offering a substantial number of scales for vocational/technical occupations that do not require a college degree for entry. Furthermore, some more recently developed tools, such as the vocational version of the Career Assessment Inventory (Johansson, 1984) and the Career Directions Inventory (Jackson, 1986), were designed principally for persons whose education does not extend beyond secondary or technical schools. Such developments probably reflect, at least in part, a growing recognition of the importance of effective career choices at all occupational levels, as well as the crucial role of interests in successful and personally satisfying work experience in all types of jobs.

Still another discernible trend has implications that extend beyond interest inventories to other kinds of testing. In a provocative look into the future of interest inventories, J. L. Holland (1986) referred to the growing recognition of such inventories as intervention techniques. What *effects* does the inventory have on the test taker? For example, it can support and strengthen existing vocational aspirations in one person. In another, it can stimulate a comprehensive exploration of the world of work, with attention to hitherto unconsidered options. In still another, it can provide increased self-understanding. Such diversity of possible effects may be reflected not only in individualized score interpretations, but also in the administration and construction of interest inventories. This may represent another likely application of computerized adaptive testing.

In the 1990s, the psychology of vocational choice and career development has been enriched by the application of paradigms from the field of cognitive psychology (see, e.g., Peterson, Sampson, & Reardon, 1991). Viewing vocational decision making as a problem-solving activity, likely to recur through the lifespan, has underscored the need to provide individuals with the knowledge and information processing skills required for arriving at optimal solutions. Many new instruments are embedded within comprehensive programs for career exploration that are a logical extension of Super's views on career development and of Holland's approach to vocational choice. It has become increasingly clear that the area of vocational behavior offers unparalleled opportunities for engaging individuals actively and directly in the use of the insights and tools of psychology (Borgen, 1991).

In India, most of the interest inventories are based on the theoretical model of Holland's occupational themes and RIASEC scales such as the Career Decision-Making System (CDM). It enables an individual to align their interests, abilities and values to the global occupations. It is primarily used by school students in order to determine their career paths. Qualified practitioners such as School Counselors, Career Counselors, Classroom Teachers and School Psychologists can make the students undertake this assessment under their guidance and help them interpret the test results in light of the Indian context. The major advantages of CDM are that it helps secondary and higher secondary students to explore career paths, enables college students to obtain clarity about their career direction and make informed decisions in selecting coursework, and facilitates the career changers to obtain clarity in their future career paths and to understand if they have the desired abilities and work values that will support their new career paths (Harrington and O'Shea, 1982). More information and details on Career Decision-Making System (CDM) is available on the Internet with Pearson being its sole distributor in India. Like SII, this assessment should ideally be used under the guidance of either a qualified career counselor or a qualified practitioner/psychologist in order to interpret and understand the results in the Indian context as the Indian norm groups and occupations have not been updated yet.

OPINION SURVEYS AND ATTITUDE SCALES

Nature of Instruments. An attitude is often defined as a tendency to react favorably or unfavorably toward a designated class of stimuli, such as a national or ethnic group, a custom, or an institution. It is evident that, when so defined, attitudes cannot be directly observed but must be inferred from overt behavior, both verbal and nonverbal. In more objective terms, the concept of attitude may be said to connote *response consistency* with regard to certain categories of stimuli. In actual practice, the term "attitude" has been most frequently associated with social stimuli and with emotionally toned responses. It also often involves value judgments.

Opinion is sometimes differentiated from attitude, but the proposed distinctions are neither consistent nor logically defensible. More often the two terms are used interchangeably, and they will be so employed in this discussion. With regard to assessment methodology, however, opinion surveys are traditionally distinguished from attitude scales. *Opinion surveys* are characteristically concerned with replies to specific questions, which need not be related. The answers to such questions are kept separate rather than combined into a total score. An employee opinion survey, for example, might include questions about work schedules, rate of pay, fringe benefits, company cafeteria, and relations to supervisors; each of these items is included because of its intrinsic relevance to the improvement of employee relations. The replies to each question are separately tabulated in the effort to identify sources of employee satisfaction and dissatisfaction.[12]

Attitude scales, on the other hand, typically yield a total score indicating the direction and intensity of the individual's attitude toward a company, group of people, policy, or other stimulus category. In the construction of an attitude scale, the different questions are designed to measure a single attitude or unidimensional variable, and some objective procedures are usually followed in the effort to approach this goal. An employee attitude scale, for example, yields a single score showing the individual's degree of job satisfaction or overall attitude toward the company.

Major Types of Attitude Scales. In all attitude scales, respondents indicate their agreement or disagreement with a series of statements about the object of the attitude. Special procedures have been devised in the effort to achieve unidimensionality or homogeneity of items, equality of distances between scale units, and comparability of scores from scale to scale. The technical problems involved in constructing attitude scales have received extensive attention, and the

[12] A multivolume series edited by Fink (1995) provides a comprehensive guide specifically devoted to the planning, preparation, implementation, and analysis of surveys.

methodology has made notable theoretical and statistical advances. It is beyond the scope of this text to discuss specialized scaling techniques, which now constitute a growing area of statistical method (Jones & Koehly, 1993; D. J. Mueller, 1986; Ostrom, Bond, Krosnick, & Sedikides, 1994; Procter, 1993; Reckase, 1990; Young, 1984). Nevertheless, we can briefly examine three major approaches to attitude scale construction that are commonly encountered in the psychological testing literature. These approaches are represented by the Thurstone, Guttman, and Likert types of scales.

Thurstone's adaptation of psychophysical methods to the quantification of judgment data represented an important milestone in attitude scale construction (Thurstone, 1959; Thurstone & Chave, 1929). By these procedures, Thurstone and his co-workers prepared about 20 scales for measuring attitudes toward war, capital punishment, the church, patriotism, censorship, and many other institutions, practices, issues, and national or ethnic groups. The development of a *Thurstone-type scale* begins with the assembling of many statements expressing a wide range of attitudes toward the object under consideration. A large number of judges are asked individually to sort the statements into piles (usually 11) for degree of favorableness. The judges do not indicate their own attitudes; they only classify the statements. The median position assigned to each statement by the judges is the scale value of that statement. The variability of the judgments is taken as an index of its ambiguity, insofar as different judges assign the statement to different categories. Items are chosen so as to exhibit minimum variability and a wide spread of scale values, approximating equal spacing across the 11-point range. In the final attitude scale, the statements are presented in random order, with no indication of their scale values. The respondent's score is the median scale value of all the statements he or she endorses.

The *Guttman-type scale* was originally developed as a technique for determining whether a set of attitude statements is unidimensional (L. Guttman, 1944, 1947). In Guttman's sense, a perfect scale exists if a respondent who agrees with a certain statement of a particular attitude also agrees with milder statements of that attitude. In other words, such attitude scale items can be ordered along a continuum of intensity or difficulty of acceptance. Each person's position on the scale would thus completely determine her or his responses. If we know the most extreme statement an individual will accept, we should be able to reproduce all her or his responses. In actual practice, such reproducibility cannot be fully attained, because of errors of measurement in each response; it can only be approximated within certain limits. The essential procedure in the development of a Guttman scale is to identify a set of items that fall into an ordered sequence in terms of their endorsement by respondents. Items that do not fit this requirement are discarded. A person's score on a Guttman scale is found by examining the patterns of items that he or she endorses. It may be recalled that the same concept of ordinality, or uniform progression of performance, underlies the Piagetian scales discussed in chapters 3 and 9.

Because the construction of a Thurstone scale requires rather elaborate procedures, and the conditions of a Guttman scale are difficult to meet in practice, Likert (1932) developed a type of scale that is easier to construct while yielding equally satisfactory reliability. The *Likert-type scale* begins with a series of statements, each of which expresses an attitude that is either clearly favorable or clearly unfavorable. Items are selected on the basis of the responses of persons to whom they are administered in the process of test construction. The principal basis for item selection is internal consistency, although external criteria are also employed when available. Likert scales call for a graded response to each statement. The response is usually expressed in terms of the following five categories: strongly agree (SA), agree (A), undecided (U), disagree (D), and strongly disagree (SD). To score the scale, the response options are credited 5, 4, 3, 2, or 1 from the favorable to the unfavorable end. For example, "strongly agree" with a favorable statement would receive a score of 5, as would "strongly disagree" with an unfavorable statement. The sum of the item credits represents the individual's total score, which must be interpreted in terms of empirically established norms.

Most attitude scales have been developed for use in particular research projects. Some were designed for the investigation of employee attitudes and morale. Others have been used to assess the outcome of educational and training programs. Attitude scales may contribute to the evaluation of different instructional procedures designed to modify particular attitudes. Or they may be employed in measuring the changes in student attitudes toward literature, art, different ethnic and cultural groups, or social and economic problems following a given educational program. One of the most extensive applications of attitude measurement is to be found in research in social psychology. Practically every textbook on social psychology contains sections on attitudes and their measurement. Among the many problems investigated through attitude measurement may be mentioned group differences in attitudes, the role of attitudes in intergroup relations, background factors associated with the development of attitudes, the interrelation of attitudes (including factor analyses and other multivariate analysis methods), trends and temporal shifts in attitudes, and the experimental alteration of attitudes through interpolated experiences.[13] Relatively few attitude scales have been published, although most are fully described in the research literature. An extensive collection of early attitude scales constructed for a variety of purposes was assembled in a book by M. E. Shaw and Wright (1967). Information about more recently developed measures of certain attitudes and values, such as alienation and anomie, self-esteem, and locus of control, can be found in *Measures of Personality and Social Psychological Attitudes,* edited by Robinson, Shaver, and Wrightsman (1991).

In India, several opinion surveys and attitude scales are developed across various domains of educational psychology, social psychology, and organizational psychology. The details of these surveys and attitude scales are presented in a catalog that serves as a reference guide, and it is available in the National Library of Educational and Psychological Tests (NLEPT), located in the Department of Educational Psychology and Foundations of Education, NCERT, New Delhi.

A Note on Gender-Related Variables and Measures. Previous editions of this book have included sections covering measures of sex roles and related concepts, such as masculinity, femininity, and androgyny, at some length, whereas the present one does not. Although research and instruments aimed at assessing these

[13] An excellent overview of the vast subspecialty of social psychology that deals with attitudes can be found in Eagly and Chaiken (1993). For a briefer review of the literature on attitudes and attitude change, see Olson and Zanna (1993).

phenomena have continued to proliferate (see, e.g., Lenney, 1991), many investigators in the field agree that it is in a state of conceptual disarray. From the broader perspective of individual differences in gender-related variables, Betz (1995) has prepared an excellent update on the current state of knowledge regarding such variables. She concludes that the lack of a theoretical framework—and of substantive conceptual definitions—has caused progress in the study of gender-related phenomena to be limited. To this, it undoubtedly should be added that the past two decades have also witnessed unprecedented changes in the cultural views of gender in the United States and elsewhere around the world. At any rate, as Betz points out, global explanatory concepts for gender-related differences, such as sex roles or masculinity-femininity, have largely remained unsupported by empirical findings. According to her, in order for further progress to occur, more work needs to be done on careful conceptualization and definition of constructs that can be placed within a meaningful and coherent theoretical framework.

LOCUS OF CONTROL

The construct described as "locus of control" first came into prominence with the publication of a monograph by Rotter (1966). In this publication, Rotter presented the scale he had developed to assess the individual's generalized expectancies for internal versus external control of reinforcement (I-E Scale). This instrument was constructed within the context of social-learning theory. In explaining its use, Rotter wrote, "The effect of reinforcement following some behavior. . . is not a simple stamping-in process but depends upon whether or not the person perceives a causal relationship between his own behavior and the reward" (1966, p. 1). Internal control refers to the perception of an event as contingent upon one's behavior or one's relatively permanent characteristics. External control, on the other hand, indicates that a positive or negative reinforcement following some action of the individual is perceived as not being entirely contingent upon her or his own action but the result of chance, fate, or luck; or it may be perceived as under the control of powerful others and unpredictable because of the complexity of forces surrounding the individual.

The I-E Scale is a forced-choice self-report inventory. Two illustrative items are given in Table 14–1. The complete list of items, together with standard instructions for administering them, can be found in Rotter's monograph (1966). Considerable information regarding the I-E Scale is presented in the original publication, including percentile norms on several hundred male and female students from a single university, together with means and *SDs* of some dozen other samples comprising mostly college groups. Data on many other groups have subsequently accumulated from independent research projects. A substantial body of data on construct validity is also available. Factorial analyses initially indicated that a single general factor could account for most of the response variance. Other factor analyses, however, subsequently suggested that the construct may be subdivided into several distinguishable factors, as illustrated by a belief in a difficult world, an unjust world, an unpredictable world, and a politically unresponsive world (B. E. Collins, 1974). Several later studies likewise found multifactorial structures.

Table 14-1

Two Illustrative Items from the Internal-External (I-E) Scale

(a) In the long run, people get the respect they deserve in this world.
(b) Unfortunately, an individual's worth often passes unrecognized no matter how hard he tries.

(a) Becoming a success is a matter of hard work; luck has little or nothing to do with it.
(b) Getting a good job depends mainly on being in the right place at the right time.

Instructions state: "This is a questionnaire to find out the way in which certain important events in our society affect different people. . . . Please select the one statement of each pair *(and only* one) which you more strongly *believe* to be the case as far as you're concerned."

(From Rotter, 1966, p. 11. Reprinted by permission.)

By the mid-to late 1970s, it had been well established that control expectancies of the kind tapped by the I-E Scale could play a meaningful role in helping to predict certain behaviors. However, investigators in the field also recognized that in order to maximize predictive accuracy, measures of control expectancies needed to be targeted to the specific populations and areas of behavior under study. Since then, several diverse locus of control scales have been developed. Some are tailored for use with different populations, including school-age and preschool children (see, e.g., Connell, 1985; Herzberger, Linney, Seidman, & Rappaport, 1979; Nowicki & Duke, 1983). Others are aimed at assessing control beliefs with regard to specific realms, such as marital satisfaction or mental health status (D. J. Hill & Bale, 1980; P.C. Miller, Lefcourt, & Ware, 1983). Still others encompass causal beliefs concerning different areas (e.g., achievement and affiliation) or different spheres of control, such as personal efficacy, interpersonal control, and sociopolitical control (Lefcourt, von Baeyer, Ware, & Cox, 1979; Paulhus, 1983). Reproductions of several available scales, with basic psychometric data, can be found in Lefcourt (1991).

The number and range of available instruments to assess the locus of control construct attest to its continued vitality. More than 5,000 entries are listed under this topic in the psychological literature PsycINFO database for the years 1984 to 1995. Investigations of the role of control expectancies in health-related practices are especially numerous. In addition, locus of control is an important aspect of motivation in general and is closely related to other key areas of personality research, including attribution theory, learned helplessness, and self-efficacy, among many others (Skinner, 1995).

Chapter Fifteen

Projective Techniques

The available supply of projective techniques is large and diversified. In this chapter, we consider the major varieties of such techniques, together with some well-known examples. Except for special points peculiar to particular techniques, no critical evaluation of individual instruments will be undertaken. Instead, a summary evaluation of projective techniques will be given in a separate section, with emphasis on common methodological problems. Projective techniques present a curious discrepancy between research and practice. When evaluated as psychometric instruments, the large majority make a poor showing. Yet their popularity in clinical use continues unabated (Bellak, 1992; Lubin, Larsen, & Matarazzo, 1984; Piotrowski, 1984; Piotrowski, Sherry, & Keller, 1985; Piotrowski & Zalewski, 1993; Watkins, 1991). The nature and implications of this inconsistency will be examined in the last section.

The literature on projective techniques is vast, running to over 6,000 references on a single instrument. For a broader coverage of available projective techniques, the reader is referred to Klopfer and Taulbee (1976), Rabin (1981, 1986), and Reynolds and Kamphaus (1990b, chaps. 3–8). The *Mental Measurements Yearbooks* contain reviews of most current instruments. The *Journal of Personality Assessment*,[1] while open to articles on all types of tests, publishes a wealth of material on various aspects of the use of projective techniques.

[1] This publication has undergone several title changes since it was started by Bruno Klopfer in 1936 as the *Rorschach Research Exchange* newsletter; from 1950 to 1963 it was called the *Journal of Projective Techniques*.

NATURE OF PROJECTIVE TECHNIQUES

A major distinguishing feature of projective techniques is to be found in their assignment of a relatively *unstructured* task, that is, a task that permits an almost unlimited variety of possible responses. In order to allow free play to the individual's fantasy, only brief, general instructions are provided. For the same reason, the test stimuli are usually vague or ambiguous. The underlying hypothesis is that the way in which the individual perceives and interprets the test material or "structures" the situation will reflect fundamental aspects of her or his psychological functioning. In other words, it is expected that the test materials will serve as a sort of screen on which respondents "project" their characteristic thought processes, needs, anxieties, and conflicts.

Typically, projective instruments also represent *disguised* testing procedures, insofar as test takers are rarely aware of the type of psychological interpretation that will be made of their responses. Projective techniques are likewise characterized by a *global* approach to the appraisal of personality. Attention is focused on a composite picture of the whole personality, rather than on the measurement of separate traits. Finally, projective techniques are usually regarded by their exponents as especially effective in revealing *covert, latent,* or *unconscious* aspects of personality. Moreover, the more unstructured the test, it is argued, the more sensitive it is to such covert material. This follows from the assumption that the more unstructured or ambiguous the stimuli, the less likely they are to evoke defensive reactions on the part of the respondent.

Projective methods originated within a clinical setting and have remained predominantly a tool for the clinician. Some have evolved from therapeutic procedures (such as art therapy) employed with psychiatric patients. In their theoretical framework, most projective techniques reflect the influence of traditional and modern psychoanalytic concepts. There have also been scattered attempts to lay a foundation for projective techniques in stimulus-response theory and in perceptual theories of personality (see, e.g., Lindzey, 1961/1977). It should be noted, of course, that the specific techniques need *not* be evaluated in the light of their particular theoretical slants or historical origins. A procedure may prove to be practically useful or empirically valid for reasons other than those initially cited to justify its introduction.

INKBLOT TECHNIQUES

The Rorschach. One of the most popular projective techniques is that employing the Rorschach inkblots (Aronow & Reznikoff, 1983; Aronow, Reznikoff, & Moreland, 1994; Erdberg & Exner, 1984; Exner, 1993). Developed by the Swiss psychiatrist Hermann Rorschach (1921/1942), this technique was first described in 1921. Although standardized series of inkblots had previously been used by psychologists in studies of imagination and other functions, Rorschach was the first to apply inkblots to the diagnostic investigation of the personality as a whole. In the development of this technique, Rorschach experimented with a large number of inkblots, which he administered to different psychiatric groups. As a result of such clinical observations, those response characteristics that differentiated between the various psychiatric syndromes were gradually incorporated into a scoring system. The scoring procedures were further sharpened by supplementary testing of mentally retarded and normal persons, as well as artists, scholars, and other distinct groups of people. Rorschach's methodology thus represented an early, informal, and relatively subjective application of criterion keying.

Due to Rorschach's untimely death, in 1922, the development of what was in effect a test in progress was pursued by his colleagues and students. In the ensuing decades, the use of Rorschach's technique expanded greatly both in Europe and in the United States. However, in the absence of a single systematizer, the procedures for administering, scoring, and interpreting "*the* Rorschach" proliferated and evolved into several methods or systems.[2] By the 1960s, to speak of it as a single, standardized test was, in fact, inaccurate. The various systems and users shared only the 10 original stimulus cards and some basic interpretive postulates derived from Rorschach's original work.

Each of the Rorschach cards has printed on it a bilaterally symmetrical inkblot similar to the one illustrated in Figure 15–1. Five of the blots are executed in shades of gray and black only; two contain additional touches of bright red; and the remaining three combine several pastel shades. Typically, during administration of the Rorchach, the respondent is shown each inkblot, one at a time, and asked to tell what the blot could represent. Besides keeping a verbatim record of the responses to each card, examiners usually note reaction time and duration of responses, position or positions in which the cards are held, spontaneous remarks, emotional expressions, and other incidental behavior of the respondent during the test session. At some point following the presentation of the 10 cards, most examiners question the individual systematically regarding the parts and aspects of each blot to which the associations were given. During this inquiry, the respondents also have an opportunity to elaborate and clarify on their earlier responses.

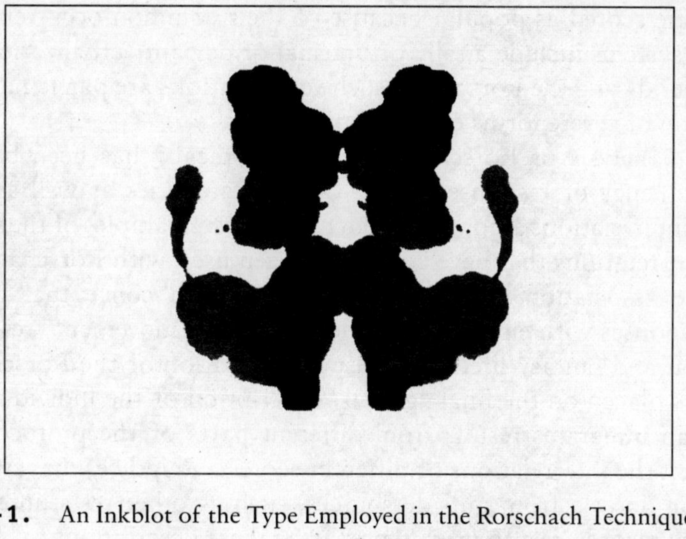

Figure 15-1. An Inkblot of the Type Employed in the Rorschach Technique.

[2] For a more thorough history of the Rorschach and its evolution, see Exner (1969, 1993).

The major differences among the various Rorschach systems that flourished from the 1930s to the 1960s were in their scoring methods and, consequently, on interpretive matters. Basically, the focus of concern for Rorschach interpretation may be placed either on the content of the responses or on their formal characteristics, such as location, determinants, form quality, and the various quantitative summaries derived from the responses. Although the Rorschach systems differed a great deal in the details of scoring and interpreting responses to the cards, many of them did share the basic classification of scoring categories. *Location* refers to the part of the blot with which the respondent associates each response. Does he or she use the whole blot, a common detail, an unusual detail, white space, or some combination of these areas? The *determinants* of the response include form, color, shading, and "movement." Although there is of course no movement in the blot itself, the respondent's perception of the blot as a representation of a moving object is scored in this category. Further differentiations are made within these categories. For example, human movement, animal movement, and abstract or inanimate movement are separately scored. Similarly, shading may be perceived as representing depth, texture, hazy forms such as clouds, or achromatic reproductions of colors as in a photograph. The *form quality* or *form level* of responses may refer to the precision with which they match the location used, to their originality, or to both. In addition, the cognitive complexity of responses and other qualitative aspects of the percepts may also be scored in some systems.

The treatment of *content* also has varied from one Rorschach system to another, although certain major categories are regularly employed. Chief among these are human figures, human details (or parts of human figures), animal figures, and animal details. Other broad scoring categories may include art objects, plants, maps, clouds, blood, X-rays, clothing, sexual percepts, and landscapes. A popularity score is often found on the basis of the relative frequency of different responses among people in general. For each of the 10 cards, certain specific responses are scored as popular because of their common occurrence. In addition, most systems include a tally of unusual or deviant verbalizations made by the test taker during the Rorschach; such verbalizations are particularly useful in the detection of severe forms of psychopathology.

Further analysis of Rorschach responses typically has been based on the relative frequency of responses in the various categories as well as on certain ratios and interrelations among different categories. Examples of the sort of qualitative interpretations that have commonly been used with Rorschach responses include the association of "whole" responses with conceptual thinking, of "color" responses with emotionality, and of "human movement" responses with imagination and fantasy life. In the usual application of the Rorschach, major emphasis is placed on the final "global" description of the individual, in which the clinician integrates results from different parts of the protocol and takes into account the interrelations of different scores and indices. In actual practice, information derived from outside sources, such as other tests, interviews, and case history records, is also used in preparing these descriptions.

Exner's Comprehensive System. By the 1960s, the Rorschach had fallen into disrepute as a psychometric instrument. Researchers found themselves stymied by the difficulties inherent in the method itself, such as the variability in the total number of responses, the influence of examiner effects, and the interdependence of scores, as well as by the proliferation of scoring systems. These circumstances made the investigation of the reliability and validity of the Rorschach a piecemeal enterprise, fraught with methological flaws, and ultimately disappointing in terms of results. Many clinical psychologists continued to use the Rorschach regularly, but the majority of them admitted that they did not follow a single system faithfully. Instead, they tended to use the Rorschach data in their own preferred way, which could range from totally impressionistic, qualitative interpretation to adherence to one or more of the systems, more or less stringently, as they saw fit.

The vast differences that had developed among the five major Rorschach systems in use in the United States were documented by John E. Exner, Jr. (1969) who had worked with Samuel Beck and Bruno Klopfer, two of the most diverse Rorschach systematizes.[3] Through his extensive investigations of the clinical use of the Rorschach and of its research literature, Exner became intrigued by the possibility of distilling into a single system all of the empirically defensible and useful features that the method might possess. For the past quarter century, he has led the most ambitious and fruitful effort ever mounted to put the Rorschach on a psychometrically sound basis (Exner, 1974, 1991, 1993, 1995; Exner & Weiner, 1995).

First, Exner developed a comprehensive Rorschach system that integrated elements culled from the five major approaches. In this Comprehensive System, Exner provides standardized administration, scoring, and interpretative procedures selected on the basis of empirical comparisons among various practices. The emphasis is on structural rather than on content variables. In fact, according to Exner, the object of scoring responses is the derivation of the *structural summary* which is at the core of his system and provides the basis for most interpretive postulates. Each response is coded on several different scoring categories, including location, determinants, form quality, contents, organizational activity, and popularity, among others. The coded responses are listed and the frequencies of the codes are tallied; these elements are then used in the calculation of the ratios, percentages, and indices that complete the structural summary. Interpretative statements can be derived, in light of the entire Rorschach record, from variables at various levels of complexity. Some hypotheses are linked to simple frequencies, like the extent to which a single determinant (e.g., shading) is used; others are based on the combined occurrence of two or more variables, such as the number of human and animal contents. The most complex level of analysis involves constellations of several variables and empirically derived cutoff scores. These variables are grouped into indices (e.g., Schizophrenia Index, Depression Index, and Coping Deficit Index) which presumably reflect the likelihood that certain disorders or conditions are present.[4]

Using this uniform system, which has evolved and been refined over the past two decades, Exner and his associates have collected a considerable body of

---

[3] The other three major systems were those of Marguerite Hertz, Zygmunt Piotrowski, and David Rapaport with Roy Schafer.

[4] Computer-based scoring and interpretation assistance programs for the Comprehensive System are available and require only the initial coding of responses.

psychometric data, including norms on adults, children, and adolescents as well as various psychiatric reference samples. Studies of retest reliability over several time intervals, ranging from a few days to three years, indicate considerable temporal stability for most of the scored variables. The careful delineation of scoring guidelines for the Comprehensive System has made it possible for trained examiners to obtain fairly high rates of interscorer agreement. In fact, one of the major contributions of Exner's work is the provision of a uniform Rorschach system that permits comparability among the research findings of different investigators.[5] It is therefore not surprising that the Comprehensive System has become the most frequently taught approach to scoring and interpreting the Rorschach and has proved to be of value in increasing the statistical power of Rorschach research (see, e.g., Acklin, McDowell, & Orndoff, 1992; Ritzler & Alter, 1986).

In spite of the clear methodological improvements that Exner's system has brought to the Rorschach, several important questions remain. The chief and most complicated of these is the issue of validity. The literature bearing on this question is enormous and still full of contradictory findings. The Rorschach, like the MMPI, has been used for a wide array of purposes, many of which go well beyond the original intent of its author; and this multiplicity of uses adds to the complexity of investigating its validity. In general, meta-analytic research has shown that indices of convergent validity for the Rorschach are comparable to those obtained with the MMPI (Atkinson, Quarrington, Alp, & Cyr, 1986; K. C. H. Parker, Hanson, & Hunsley, 1988). In addition, Exner's own extensive work with the Rorschach lends substantial support to the validity of many constructs assessed through his system, and to its usefulness in describing certain aspects of personality functioning. However, when it comes to diagnosing complex current conditions or predicting future behavior, the research results have been mixed (Exner, 1996; Weiner, 1994a; Wood, Nezworski, & Stejskal, 1996a, 1996b).

A major complicating factor in the interpretation of Rorschach scores is the total number of responses—known as response productivity, or R. When large differences in R occur between individuals or groups, differences in other scoring categories are likely to follow. Thus, the differences found in certain categories may be only an artifact resulting from variations in R. To this intrinsic characteristic of Rorschach scores may be added the fact that response productivity appears to be related to other variables, such as intellectual level and amount of education.[6] Characteristically, Rorschach investigators differ in their views of the significance and extent of the problems presented by variations in response productivity. G. J. Meyer (1992, 1993), for example, has called for further investigation of the psychological meaning of R and of the merits versus disadvantages of controlling or adjusting for this variable. Others consider that its impact has already been shown to be insignificant in most circumstances (Exner, 1992; Weiner, 1995b). Still others maintain that the problems posed by R need to be

[5] However, the issue of how best to quantify interrater agreement on the Rorschach is not yet settled. For a discussion of this problem and a comparison of three different methods of estimating scorer reliability for Rorschach data, see McDowell and Acklin (1996).

[6] An interesting finding—related to R—from the research literature on the Rorschach's susceptibility to malingering, is that when subjects are asked to fake psychosis on the Rorschach, there is a reduction in response productivity (G. G. Perry & Kinder, 1990).

handled in different ways depending on the use that is to be made of the data and, in the case of research data, depending on how much the distributions depart from normality (Kinder, 1992; Lipgar, 1992).

The Comprehensive System developed by Exner is not without its critics. Many Rorschach users have objected to the atheoretical nature of Exner's approach and to its underutilization of content data—which, they contend, seriously reduces its clinical utility. Critics have also noted that the system is exceedingly complex, as well as occasionally vague and contradictory. Moreover, Exner's own research has been faulted for its small sample sizes, large numbers of variables, dearth of cross-validation studies, and inaccesibility to public scrutiny.[7] Be that as it may, the fact remains that the availability of Exner's system, together with the research data he and his associates have compiled, has injected new life into the Rorschach as a psychometric instrument.

Alternative Approaches. In spite of the wide acceptance that Exner's Comprehensive System has achieved, there are still a number of contrasting approaches to the Rorschach that coexist with it. In fact, many have credited Exner's work with reviving interest in the Rorschach from these other perspectives as well as from his own. One alternative, more strongly clinical in its orientation, is described by Aronow and his colleagues (Aronow & Reznikoff, 1976, 1983; Aronow et al., 1994, 1995). This approach treats the Rorschach essentially as a standardized clinical interview that samples a person's perceptual operations. It focuses on the interpretation of content, rather than on structural variables or perceptual determinants of responses. Nevertheless, available content scales and scoring systems are not considered sufficiently dependable as psychometric instruments for use in individual diagnosis. Rather, these authors recommend a strictly clinical application of the Rorschach as a means of enhancing the idio-graphic understanding of the individual case—and they observe that most experienced clinicians gravitate toward this approach because of its usefulness in the process of psychotherapy. Their interpretations rely principally on the content of responses, supplemented by verbal and nonverbal behavior. On the basis of available research and clinical experience, Aronow and his coworkers have prepared a set of guideliness for more effective and dependable idiographic interpretations. For example, they suggest that responses which depart from the commonplace and those less closely bound to the stimulus properties of particular blots are more likely to be significant in the individual case. Similarly, the authors caution against rigid systems of symbol interpretation that attach fixed meanings to content categories or assign invariant evocative qualities to the Rorschach blots. Instead, they offer procedures for investigating the meaning of responses in a conservative fashion that is compatible with general psychodynamic principles and makes use of the individual's own experiential history.

Another alternative current approach to the Rorschach is the one espoused by Paul Lerner (1991). This work stands in sharp contrast to Exner's atheoretical stance in that it is steeped in modern psychoanalytic theory, as it has evolved since the 1970s. Whereas Exner (1989) contends that the Rorschach is a test in which

[7] For a sampling of these and other criticisms of Exner's work, see Aronow, Reznikoff, and Moreland (1995), Kleiger (1992), P. M. Lerner (1994), W. Perry (1993), Viglione (1989), Vincent and Harman (1991), and Wood, Nezworski, and Stejskal (1996a, 1996b).

projection rarely comes into play, Lerner considers it to be fundamentally a projective method for accessing the internal world of the individual.[8] Lerner's text provides a guide to the clinical uses of the Rorschach and to its research applications in the assessment of object representations, defensive maneuvers, and other concepts that are central to modern psychodynamic theories.

A special clinical application of the Rorschach is illustrated by the consensus Rorschach (Aronow et al., 1994, chap. 13; Blanchard, 1968; Cutter & Farberow, 1970). In this adaptation, the inkblots are presented for joint interpretation by married couples or other family members, coworkers, juvenile gang members, or other natural groups. Through discussion and negotiation, the participants must reach agreement on a single, common set of responses. The technique has been used, with apparent success, as a basis for exploring interpersonal relationships and various other kinds of social behavior.

The Rorschach has been described, accurately, as "a test that has repeatedly outlived its obituaries" (Peterson, 1994, p. 396). Its demise has been predicted many times because, like all of the most frequently used psychological tests, the Rorschach has been among the most misused as well. Currently, the technique is experiencing a tremendous resurgence both in terms of research activity and theorizing; although different ways of approaching the Rorschach persist, users of all types appear convinced that it has special value in studying perceptual, cognitive, and affective aspects of personality functioning. Some are satisfied viewing the Rorschach simply as a method for generating data that can be used from various perspectives, while others are engaged in efforts to link the empirical and theoretical traditions as well as different theoretical approaches to the Rorschach into a totally integrated system (see, e.g., Acklin, 1995; Blatt, 1990; P. M. Lerner, 1994; Meloy & Singer, 1991; Weiner, 1994b; Willock, 1992).

The Rorschach Inkblot Test may prove to be an effective way to determine emotional and intellectual functioning (that is, diagnosing underlying thought disorder) and integration, and differentiating psychotic from non-psychotic thinking in individuals. Although it might seem to adopt a subjective approach in its method of analyzing, it still takes into consideration the emotional characteristics of an individual and gives complete freedom to contribute his or her answer rather than select one out of a predetermined set of answers. In order to use this assessment properly, professionals need to be appropriately qualified and rigorously certified in administering, scoring, and interpreting the test. Review of literature indicates that the Rorschach Inkblot Test is psychometrically sound and provides valid assessments of personality characteristics and can facilitate differential diagnosis, treatment planning, and evaluation. In India, it is widely used by both clinicians and researchers. Many practitioners feel that Rorschach's norms cannot be used universally across countries and differences within the same cultural group are also seen. In their view, the Rorschach norms established in India differ considerably and face the lack of reliable norms. Mental health professionals and practitioners in India are left with no alternative but to interpret Rorschach norms on the basis of their own experience, which results in subjective bias. To make this tool more effective and valid in India, norms should be developed keeping

[8] The reasons for this apparent contradiction are rooted in the divergent views of these authors concerning the nature of projection and of the examinee's task on the Rorschach.

in mind the Indian sensibilities rather than creating it on biased interpretations which would render the test unreliable, unscientific, and invalid.

The Holtzman Inkblot Technique. Even before Exner began to work on his comprehensive Rorschach system, a serious effort to apply a psychometric orientation to the inkblot technique was undertaken by Wayne H. Holtzman. Modeled after the Rorschach, the Holtzman Inkblot Technique (HIT) was so designed as to eliminate the principal technical deficiencies of the earlier instrument (Holtzman, 1961, 1986; Holtzman, Thorpe, Swartz, & Herron, 1961). The changes in stimulus materials and procedures are sufficiently extensive, however, to require that the Holtzman be regarded as a different test and evaluated without reference to the Rorschach. The Holtzman technique provides two parallel series of 45 cards each; the blots were selected from a large preliminary pool on the basis of empirical criteria aimed at maximizing their effectiveness. Only one response per card is obtained. Both achromatic and colored cards are included; a few inkblots are markedly asymmetric.

Administration and scoring of the HIT were well standardized and clearly described from the outset. Scores are obtained in 22 response variables, including many that parallel those of the Rorschach and some additional variables, such as anxiety and hostility. For each variable, percentile scores are available for normal samples of children and adults and for a number of deviant groups (E. F. Hill, 1972; Holtzman, 1975). Scorer reliability appears to be highly satisfactory. Split-half, alternate-form, and test-retest reliability investigations have shown differences across the response variables, though most of the results are encouraging. A group form of the test, using slides, yields scores on most variables that are comparable to those obtained through individual administration (Holtzman, Moseley, Reinehr, & Abbott, 1963; Swartz & Holtzman, 1963). The HIT 25, a short version that consists of the first 25 cards from Form A of the HIT with 2 responses per card, has been proposed recently by Holtzman (1988) and is in the process of being normed (Swartz, 1992).

Considerable validity data on the HIT have been accumulated, mostly with quite promising results (Gamble, 1972; Holtzman, 1975, 1986, 1988; Leichsenring, 1991; Sacchi & Richaud de Minzi, 1989; Swartz, 1973). The validation research has followed a variety of approaches, including the study of developmental trends, cross-cultural comparisons, correlations with other tests and with behavioral indicators of personality characteristics, and contrasted group comparisons with both normal respondents and psychiatric patients. A handbook prepared by E. F. Hill (1972) is directed particularly to the clinical use of the HIT.

It is apparent that the HIT has some psychometric advantages over the Rorschach. The availability of parallel forms permits not only the measurement of retest reliability but also adequate follow-up studies. The restriction of responses to one per card holds response productivity (R) constant for each respondent, thus avoiding many of the pitfalls of Rorschach scoring. It should be noted, however, that response length (number of words) is still uncontrolled and, as in the Rorschach, has proved to be significantly related to several HIT scores (Megargee, 1966). In spite of its advantages, however, there is a relative paucity of information on the HIT compared to the Rorschach, and more data are needed to establish the diagnostic significance of the various scores and the construct validity of the personality variables assessed by this technique (for reviews, see Cundick, 1985; Dush, 1985).

PICTORIAL TECHNIQUES

Thematic Apperception Test. In contrast to inkblot techniques, the Thematic Apperception Test (TAT) presents more highly structured stimuli and requires more complex and meaningfully organized verbal responses. Interpretation of responses by the examiner is usually based on content analysis of a rather qualitative nature. First developed by Henry Murray and his staff at the Harvard Psychological Clinic (Murray et al., 1938), the TAT has not only been widely used in clinical practice and research, but it has also served as a model for the development of many other instruments (J. W. Atkinson, 1958; Bellak, 1993; Dana, 1996b; R. Harrison, 1965; Holmstrom, Silber, & Karp, 1990; Klopfer & Taulbee, 1976, pp. 554–558; Obrzut & Boliek, 1986).

The TAT materials consist of 19 cards containing vague pictures in black and white and one blank card.[9] The respondent is asked to make up a story to fit each picture, telling what led up to the event shown in the picture, describing what is happening at the moment and what the characters are feeling and thinking, and giving the outcome. In the case of the blank card, the respondent is instructed to imagine some picture on the card, describe it, and then tell a story about it. The original procedure outlined by Murray in the test manual requires two one-hour sessions, 10 cards being employed during each session. The cards reserved for the second session were deliberately chosen to be more unusual, dramatic, and bizarre, and the accompanying instructions urge respondents to give free play to their imagination. Four overlapping sets of 20 cards are available—for boys, girls, males over 14, and females over 14. Most clinicians use abridged sets of specially selected cards, seldom giving more than 10 cards to a single respondent.

In the original method of interpreting TAT stories (Murray et al., 1943), the examiner first determines who is the "hero," the character of either sex with whom the respondent has presumably identified herself or himself. The content of the stories is then analyzed principally in reference to Murray's list of "needs" and "press." Some of the proposed needs were described in chapter 13, in connection with the Edwards Personal Preference Schedule. Examples include achievement, affiliation, and aggression. *Press* refers to environmental forces that may facilitate or interfere with the satisfaction of needs. Being attacked or criticized, receiving affection, being comforted, and exposure to physical danger are illustrations of press. In assessing the importance or strength of a particular need or press for the individual, special attention is given to the intensity, duration, and frequency of its occurrence in different stories, as well as to the uniqueness of its association with a given picture. The assumption is made that unusual material, which departs from the common responses to each picture, is more likely to have significance for the individual.

A fair amount of normative information has been published regarding the most frequent response characteristics for each card, including the way each card is perceived, the themes developed, the roles ascribed to the characters, emotional

[9] For an intriguing historical account of the origin of the TAT images, see W. G. Morgan (1995).

tones expressed, speed of responses, length of stories, and the like (J. W. Atkinson, 1958; W. E. Henry, 1956; Murstein, 1972). Although these normative data provide a general framework for interpreting individual responses, most clinicians rely heavily on "subjective norms" built up through their own experience with the test and on the knowledge they have acquired about the examinee through other means. A number of quantitative scoring schemes and rating scales have been developed that yield good scorer reliability. Since their application is rather time-consuming, however, such scoring procedures are seldom used in clinical practice. Although typically given as an individual oral test in the clinical situation, the TAT may also be administered in writing and as a group test.

The TAT has been used extensively in personality research. Unfortunately, the wide diversity of administration and scoring procedures, and even of stimulus materials, associated with the TAT rubric has extended to research uses as well as clinical practice (Keiser & Prather, 1990). This diversity has made it very difficult to investigate the psychometric properties of "the TAT" as a distinct psychological test because the method lacks the basic requirement of uniformity. In addition, a considerable body of experimental data is available to show that such conditions as hunger, sleep deprivation, and social frustration significantly affect TAT responses (J. W. Atkinson, 1958). While supporting the projective hypothesis, the sensitivity of the TAT to such temporary conditions may complicate the meaning of responses. The question of internal consistency of TAT responses has also received attention (J. W. Atkinson, 1981; Entwisle, 1972). And some control should be applied for length of stories, or productivity—a problem that the TAT shares with the Rorschach (J. W. Atkinson & Raynor, 1974, chap. 3).

Nevertheless, the value of thematic apperception techniques, in general, and of the TAT, in particular, is not in question. Recent investigations confirm the clinical utility of various versions of the TAT both for traditional applications, such as assessing extent of psychopathology and use of defense mechanisms, and for novel uses, such as the evaluation of problem-solving skills (Cramer & Blatt, 1990; Hibbard et al., 1994; Ronan, Colavito, & Hammontree, 1993; Ronan, Date, & Weisbrod, 1995). One of the most promising applications of the TAT is with newly developed scales for the clinical assessment of object relations (Alvarado, 1994; Barends, Westen, Leigh, Silbert, & Byers, 1990; Freedenfeld, Ornduff, & Kelsey, 1995; Westen, 1991; Westen, Lohr, Silk, Gold, & Kerber 1990). Nor is the usefulness of the TAT confined to the thematic analysis of responses; formal characteristics of both the structure and content of TAT stories may also be fruitfully employed in the study of individuals and groups (see, e.g., Cramer, 1996; McGrew & Teglasi, 1990; Teglasi, 1993)..

TAT in India. In 1960, Uma Choudhary, a lecturer in Kolkata, developed an Indian adaptation of the Thematic Apperception Test (TAT). The images of the original test were modified for the Indian population and the test kit consisted of a set of 14 cards, one manual, and 50 record and analysis blank. From the available limited literature on the Internet, it seems that TAT, along with other psychological tests, was used in Service Selection Board (SSB) interview for commission into the Indian Armed Forces. Furthermore, a few practitioners may use it as a research tool in the areas of psychology such as dream analysis, interpretation, and occupation selection. Its applicability is also seen in forensic psychology

Figure 15–2. One of the Pictures Used in the Roberts Apperception Test for Children. (Copyright © 1982 by Western Psychological Services. Reproduced by permission.)

to evaluate crime suspects or to screen candidates for high-stress and security occupations. TAT may prove to be beneficial in hiring people for high risk occupations such as aircraft piloting and flight engineering, security, chemical manufacturing, engineering, construction, ground maintenance, electrical, mining, truck driving, police or traffic and other patrolling, taxi driving, and other public safety positions in order to understand their underlying dispositions and assess whether or not they are experiencing any psychological or emotional disorders.

The Rosenzweig Picture-Frustration Study. The TAT and related techniques we have just considered use pictures to stimulate the free play of fantasy and to evoke elaborate verbal responses. In contrast, the Rosenzweig Picture-Frustration Study (P-F Study), described in this section, is more circumscribed in coverage and calls for simpler responses. This instrument is available in separate forms for adults, aged 14 and over (Rosenzweig, 1950, 1978a, 1978d); for adolescents, aged 12 to 18 (Rosenzweig, 1970, 1976b, 1981a); and for children, aged 4 to 13 (Rosenzweig, 1960, 1977, 1981b, 1988). Derived from the author's theory of frustration and aggression, the P-F Study presents a series of cartoons in which one person frustrates another or calls attention to a frustrating condition. Two of these cartoons, taken from the children's form, are shown in Figure 15–3. In the blank space provided, the respondent writes what the frustrated person would reply.

Responses on the P-F Study are classified with reference to type and direction of aggression. Types of aggression include: obstacle-dominance, emphasizing the frustrating object; ego-defense, focusing attention on the protection of the frustrated person; and need-persistence, concentrating on the constructive solution of the frustrating problem. Direction of aggression is scored as: extraggressive, or turned outward onto the environment; intraggressive, or turned inward

Figure 15–3. Typical Items from the Rosenzweig Picture-Frustration Study, Children's Form.
(Copyright © 1976 by Saul Rosenzweig. Reproduced by permission.)

upon oneself; and imaggressive, or turned off in an attempt to gloss over or evade the situation. In scoring the test, the percentage of responses falling into each of these categories is compared with the corresponding normative percentages. A group conformity rating (GCR), showing the individual's tendency to give responses that agree with the modal responses of the standardization sample, may also be obtained.

Being more limited in coverage, more highly structured, and relatively objective in its scoring procedures, the P-F Study lends itself better to statistical analysis than do most other projective techniques. Systematic efforts have been made from the outset to gather norms and to check its reliability and validity. Over some fifty years, considerable research has been conducted with the P-F Study by both the test author and other investigators. This research literature deals with the psychometric properties of the instrument and with such topics as clinical diagnosis, developmental changes, sex differences, cultural differences, and the relationship between humor and aggression (Graybill, 1990, 1993; Nevo & Nevo, 1983; Rosenzweig, 1976a, 1978b, 1978c; Rosenzweig & Adelman, 1977—for reviews, see Viglione, 1985; Wagner, 1985).

The Rosenzweig Picture Frustration Study has been adapted for both the children and adult population in India. It is widely used for research purposes and understanding aggressive behaviors and its relationships with other variables in children. Scores are interpreted in terms of the frustration theory and available norms on the instrument.

VERBAL TECHNIQUES

Although all projective instruments discussed thus far require verbal responses, certain projective techniques are wholly verbal, utilizing only words in both stimulus materials and responses. Some of these verbal techniques can be administered in either oral or written form, but all are suitable for written group administration. When so administered, of course, they presuppose a minimum reading level and thorough familiarity with the language in which the test was developed. These requirements thus preclude the use of such techniques with young children or with persons who are illiterate or who do not speak English.

A technique that antedated the flood of projective tests by more than half a century is the *word association test*. Originally known as the "free association test," this technique was first systematically described by Galton (1879). Wundt and J. McK. Cattell subsequently introduced it into the psychological laboratory, where it was adapted to many uses. The procedure involves simply the presentation of a series of disconnected words, to each of which the individual is told to respond by giving the first word that comes to mind. The early experimental psychologists, as well as the first mental testers, saw in such association tests a tool for the exploration of thinking processes.

The clinical application of word association methods was stimulated largely by the psychoanalytic movement, although other psychiatrists, such as Kraepelin, had previously investigated such techniques. Among the psychoanalysts, Jung's contribution to the systematic development of the word association test is most conspicuous. Jung (1910) selected stimulus words to represent common "emotional complexes" and analyzed the responses with reference to reaction time, content, and physical expressions of emotional tension. Over thirty years later, a similar word association technique was developed at the Menninger Clinic by Rappaport and his associates (1946/1968). According to its authors, the test had a dual aim: to aid in detecting impairment of thought processes and to suggest significant areas of conflict. Mention may also be made of the use of the word association technique as a "lie detector."[10] This application was likewise initiated by Jung and was subsequently subjected to extensive research—both in the laboratory and in practical situations (Burtt, 1931; Lindsley, 1955). The rationale offered to justify the employment of word association in the detection of lying or guilt was similar to that applied in using it to uncover areas of emotional conflict.

A different approach to the word association test is illustrated by the early work of Kent and Rosanoff (1910). Designed principally as a psychiatric screening instrument, the Kent-Rosanoff Free Association Test utilized completely objective scoring. The stimulus words consisted of 100 common, neutral words, chosen because they tend to evoke the same associations from people in general. For example, to the word *table,* most people respond "chair"; to *dark,* they say "light." A set of frequency tables was prepared—one for each stimulus word—showing the number of times each response was given in a sample of 1,000 normal adults. In scoring the test, an "index of commonality" was derived from the frequency values of the responses of each examinee. Comparisons of psychotic individuals with normals suggested that psychotics obtain a lower index of commonality than normals.

The diagnostic use of word association techniques declined, however, with the gradual realization that response frequency also varies widely with age,

[10] The word association technique is no longer used in this manner. For a discussion of more recent applications of the "lie detector" or polygraph method in industrial/organizational settings, see chapter 17.

socioeconomic and educational level, regional and cultural background, creativity, and other factors. Hence, proper interpretation of results requires gathering norms on many subgroups and updating them periodically, as word usage evolves. In addition, the popularity of the traditional psychoanalytic concepts that stimulated the development of these techniques has also diminished (Rabin & Zlotogorski, 1981). The Kent-Rosanoff test has nevertheless retained its position as a standard laboratory tool. Additional norms have been gathered in several countries, and the technique has been extensively employed in research on verbal behavior and personality (Goldfarb & Halpern, 1984; Isaacs & Chen, 1990; Jenkins & Russell, 1960; Palermo & Jenkins, 1963; Postman & Keppel, 1970; Van der Made-Van Bekkum, 1971).

Another verbal projective technique, *sentence completion,* has been widely employed in both research and clinical practice (P. A. Goldberg, 1965; Haak, 1990; D. H. Hart, 1986; Lah, 1989). In terms of length of responses, amount of structure, and other respects, sentence completion tests occupy the middle ground between word association and thematic techniques. Generally, the opening words, or sentence stems, permit an almost unlimited variety of possible completions. Examples might be: My ambition . . .; Women . . .; What worries me . . .; My mother. . . . The sentence stems are frequently formulated so as to elicit responses relevant to the personality domain under investigation. This flexibility of the sentence completion technique represents one of its advantages for clinical and research purposes. Nevertheless, some standardized forms have been published for more general application.

A widely used example is the Rotter Incomplete Sentences Blank (RISB—Rotter & Rafferty, 1950), consisting of 40 sentence stems. The directions to the test taker read: "Complete these sentences to express *your real feelings.* Try to do every one. Be sure to make a complete sentence." Each completion is rated on a 7-point scale according to the degree of adjustment or maladjustment indicated. Illustrative completions corresponding to each rating are given in the manual. With the aid of these specimen responses, fairly objective scoring is possible. The sum of the individual ratings provides a total adjustment score that can be used for screening purposes. The response content can also be examined clinically for more specific diagnostic clues. The newly revised manual of the RISB includes updated normative information and a review of research studies conducted since 1950 (Rotter, Lah, & Rafferty, 1992).

Many other sentence completion tests have been developed for the assessment of different target populations and for a variety of research and psychodiagnostic uses[11] (for descriptions of several traditional instruments, see D. H. Hart, 1986; Lah, 1989; Rabin & Zlotogorski, 1981). Some interesting recent additions to this field include instruments designed to detect malingering during disability examinations, to predict managerial effectiveness, and to assess constructs, such as defense mechanisms, that may be relevant in the assessment of personality (Carson & Gilliard, 1993; N. L. Johnson & Gold, 1995; Timmons, Lanyon, Almer, & Curran, 1993).

[11] An instrument that has been widely used in research is the Washington University Sentence Completion Test. Designed especially for assessing stages in the development of self-conceptualization, it is discussed in chapter 16 together with other measures of self-concept.

AUTOBIOGRAPHICAL MEMORIES

One of the most recent and promising developments in the area of projective verbal techniques is the resurgence of interest in the use of *autobiographical memories* for personality assessment. Analyzing memories, especially those of early life, in order to understand recurrent or intractable conflicts in later life has, of course, been a staple in psychodynamic psychotherapy since the time of Freud.[12] In addition, Alfred Adler, one of Freud's original followers who went on to found his own school of individual psychology, considered that the very first memory, specifically, holds the key to understanding the individual's "style of life." As a result, Adlerian psychologists have used early memories as clinical tools, and occasionally in research, since the 1930s (see, e.g., Hafner, Fakouri, & Labrentz, 1982; Slavik, 1991). Other theorists have also acknowledged the central role that autobiographical memories—usually viewed as constructions or projections rather than as true historical accounts—can play in the evolution of personality. By and large, however, after a flurry of interest in the early part of the twentieth century, this seemingly vital source of information concerning personality has not been consistently or systematically explored until recently.

Since the early 1980s, as a result of the influence of the cognitive point of view in psychology, there has been a renewal of interest in autobiographical memory, in general, and in its special function in personality organization, in particular (Bruhn & Last, 1982; Ross, 1991; Rubin, 1986; Singer & Salovey, 1993). The work of Arnold R. Bruhn has been outstanding in this area (Bruhn, 1984, 1985, 1990a, 1990b). After reviewing the models previously applied by Freudians, Adlerians, and ego psychologists to the interpretation of early memories, he has proposed a new conceptual framework for them, as well as a more systematic way of employing them. In Bruhn's cognitive-perceptual theory, autobiographical memories (EMs) are central to the understanding of personality. Thus, the development of a standardized method for gathering and interpreting them has been one of Bruhn's priorities. The Early Memories Procedure (EMP—Bruhn, 1989, 1992a, 1992b) is a self-administered paper-and-pencil instrument that samples 21 autobiographical memories from the entire lifespan, not just childhood. The first part calls for six general or "spontaneous" memories, delimited primarily by specific timeframes (i.e., the five earliest memories and a particularly important lifetime memory); the second part comprises 15 specific or "directed" memories that explore a diverse set of events and areas that may be clinically relevant (e.g., a traumatic memory, one's first punishment memory, or one's happiest memory).[13] In addition to narrative descriptions of each memory, the EMP includes various probes regarding the clarity, affective tone, significance, and various other elements of the memories. Bruhn considers EMs of specific events to be stories—or metaphors—that reflect what people have consciously learned or intuited from their life experiences. He also believes that these stories are often

---

[12] See Bruhn (1995a) for a brief history of the use of autobiographical memories in personality assessment.

[13] The EMP directions also solicit memories of "an inappropriate sexual experience" and of "being physically or emotionally abused"; however, respondents may check boxes indicating they have had no such experiences. This option, as well as the paper-and-pencil format of the EMP, reduces the possibility of obtaining the kind of "suggested" memories of abuse that have concerned both mental health professionals and the general public (see, e.g., Loftus, 1993).

inaccurate or distorted but maintains that their veracity is immaterial for clinical purposes because, as is the case for other projective productions, the value of EMs lies in their power to reveal current concerns, attitudes, beliefs, and affective states.

Although Bruhn and his associates have devised, and revised, a Comprehensive Early Memories Scoring System (CEMSS-R—Last & Bruhn, 1991), Bruhn's approach to the scoring and interpretation of autobiographical memories is quite flexible.[14] He views EMs as complex psychological phenomena whose explanation may require different theoretical models and, consequently, different scoring systems. In fact, he has advocated the development of customized scoring systems, or "boutique" systems, based on empirically observed aspects of the EMs of criterion groups, for the purposes of making specific predictions. Bruhn and his collaborators have obtained promising data with scoring systems designed to predict proneness to delinquency and to violence (Davidow & Bruhn, 1990; Tobey & Bruhn, 1992).

The EMP is clearly a technique still in the process of development. No normative work has yet been undertaken. Although adequate levels of interjudge agreement have been obtained with several of the scoring categories that Bruhn and his associates have devised, there is not much empirical evidence of other types of reliability for EMs. Undoubtedly, obtaining these and other psychometric data on the EMP may be problematic. As is the case with other projective material, the very act of categorizing and quantifying autobiographical memories entails a consequent loss of information that may be uniquely valuable and appropriate for understanding the person in question. Nevertheless, the procedure has the potential to become a very useful tool for personality assessment, especially within the context of psychotherapy (see, e.g., Ritzler, 1993b). Furthermore, systematic samples of autobiographical memories are more likely to be clinically significant than other kinds of verbal material—such as dream reports, free speech samples, or stories—that have been used for similar purposes and in similar ways.[15]

PERFORMANCE TECHNIQUES

A large and amorphous category of projective techniques comprises many forms of relatively free self-expression. It is characteristic of all these techniques that they have been employed as therapeutic as well as diagnostic procedures. Through the opportunities for self-expression that these activities afford, it is believed, the individual not only reveals her or his emotional difficulties but also relieves them. The methods most frequently employed in this category are drawing and play techniques of various types, including the dramatic use of toys. Not surprisingly, the majority of these methods were specifically designed for the assessment of children, though in many cases they may also be used with adults.

---

[14] One of the interpretive techniques that Bruhn strongly recommends is the use of a precis—or concise summary—of the EM, a procedure often used with the TAT and related instruments.

[15] For some intriguing anecdotal examples of the clinical value of early memories, including a comparison of EMs taken from the autobiographical writings of Nixon and Freud, see Bruhn (1995b).

Drawing Techniques. Although almost every art medium, technique, and type of subject matter has been investigated in the search for significant diagnostic clues in the evaluation of personality, special attention has centered on drawings of the human figure.[16] A well-known early example is the Machover Draw-a-Person Test (D-A-P—Machover, 1949). In this test, the individual is provided with paper and pencil and is told to "draw a person." Upon completion of the first drawing, he or she is asked to draw a person of the opposite sex—or of a different gender—from that of the first figure. While the respondent draws, the examiner notes her or his comments, the sequence in which differents parts are drawn, and other procedural details. The drawing is usually followed by a series of questions to elicit specific information about the age, schooling, occupation, and other facts associated with the characters portrayed. The inquiry may include a request for the respondent to make up a story about each person drawn.

The interpretation of the D-A-P as proposed by Machover is essentially qualitative and abounds in sweeping generalizations based on single indicators, such as "Disproportionately large heads will often be given by individuals suffering from organic brain disease." Although reference is made to "thousands of drawings" examined in clinical contexts, and a few selected cases are cited for illustrative purposes, no systematic presentation of data accompanies the original published report of the test. In addition, subsequent validation studies by other investigators generally have failed to lend support to Machover's diagnostic interpretations (see, e.g., Klopfer & Taulbee, 1976, pp. 558–561).

Another method for the utilization of human figure drawings (HFDs) of children and young adolescents—one that is grounded on a more solid empirical foundation— has been devised by Koppitz (1968, 1984). As a result of her abiding belief in the clinical usefulness of HFDs in the assessment of children, Koppitz developed and standardized two objective scoring systems using drawings produced by 1,856 public school children between the ages of 5 and 12. One of the systems, based primarily on the Goodenough-Harris Drawing Test (see chap. 9) and on Koppitz's own clinical experience, uses HFDs as a developmental test of mental maturity. The second, derived from the work of Machover and others, is a projective test of children's interpersonal attitudes and concerns. It consists of 30 "emotional indicators" that differentiated between the drawings of children with and without emotional problems. These indicators rarely occurred among the normal children in the sample and, unlike the developmental set, are presumably unrelated to age and maturation level. They include: (a) *quality signs,* such as transparencies and shading of the face; (b) *special features,* such as tiny heads or grotesque figures; and (c) *omissions* of some expected items, such as the neck or the eyes.

Some of the aggregate features of HFDs, such as bizarreness or total number of "emotional indicators," appear to discriminate between children who show problems and those who are well adjusted (D. T. Marsh, Linberg, & Smeltzer,

---

16 The use of human figure drawings as a nonverbal measure of cognitive functioning is discussed in chapter 9.

1991; Naglieri & Pfeiffer, 1992; Yama, 1990). However, both Koppitz and other investigators have warned against the use of single indicators or "signs" for diagnostic purposes. The consensus regarding HFDs seems to be that they can provide only a very general idea of the level of emotional adjustment of children. Furthermore, as far as diagnostic applications are concerned, most experts agree that drawings should be used only to generate hypotheses and that they must be interpreted in the context of other information about the individual (M. V. Cox, 1993; Knoff, 1993; Tharinger &. Stark, 1990).

In spite of these cautions and restrictions, not only has the popularity of human figure drawings continued unabated but, in fact, several additional drawing tasks have been devised. One of the most widely used test is the House-Tree-Person (H-T-P) which requires the respondent to complete separate drawings of a house, a tree, and a person and is also given the opportunity to describe, define, and interpret these drawings (Buck, 1948, 1992). The characteristics and features of the drawings themselves, along with a fairly extensive inquiry following the drawing tasks, are typically used as a source of hypotheses about general areas of conflict and concern. The respondent or applicant's responses are analyzed and interpreted by a trained professional using the guidelines in the H-T-P interpretive manual. H-T-P test provides broad insight on anti-social and psychopathologic personality, sexual abuse, and drug and alcohol abuse through data yielding individuals' efficiency, sensitivity, maturity, flexibility, personality integration, level of interaction with environment, conscious and unconscious mental processes, suppressed or repressed dispositions, and conflicts. The design of H-T-P serves as an advantage in assessing individuals who are culturally different, educationally deprived, developmentally disabled, or non English-speaking. H-T-P is easy to use and time effective as it takes approximately 10 minutes to administer; and individuals in the age range of 3–99 years can undertake this assessment. Like other projective techniques, this test is widely used by organizational psychologists to assess the moral, ethical, and deviant behaviors of an individual for the purpose of hiring and selecting blue-collar workers.

A newer technique that seems to have unusual potential as a clinical instrument is the Kinetic Family Drawing (KFD—R. C. Burns, 1982; R. C. Burns & Kaufman, 1970, 1972). This test asks children to draw a picture of everyone in their family, including themselves, "doing something." The KFD has generated a very large number of investigations; in a recent review of the literature, Handler and Habenicht (1994) state that in spite of methodological problems in the research done on this technique, there are a number of promising findings that warrant further pursuit with more sophisticated analyses, such as multiple regression. The distance and degree of interaction between the figures in the KFD, for example, appear to he among the most psychologically meaningful features of the drawings.

Ever more imaginative tasks continue to be devised. For example, the collaborative drawing technique literally requires a whole family, or a couple, to complete a single drawing cooperatively while in the presence of one or more therapists who observe closely the behavior of all participants (G. Smith, 1991).

This interactive technique took its inspiration from the KFD and is used primarily in the context of family therapy.[17]

Play Techniques and Toy Tests.[18] Various kinds of play techniques and toy tests, involving such objects as puppets, dolls, and miniatures, have been widely used in projective testing. Originating in play therapy with children, these materials have subsequently been adapted for the diagnostic testing of both adults and children. The objects are usually selected because of their associative value. Among the articles most frequently employed for these purposes, for example, are dolls representing adults and children of both sexes, animals, furniture, bathroom and kitchen figures, and other household furnishings. The Scenotest, pictured in Figure 15–4, consists of a standardized set of equipment of this type and an accompanying handbook. It was published in Switzerland in the 1960s and has recently become available in the United States (Staabs, 1991). Play with such articles is expected to reveal the child's attitude toward her or his own family, as well as sibling rivalries, fears, aggressiveness, conflicts, and the like. The examiner notes what items the child chooses and what he or she does with them, as well as the child's verbalizations, emotional expressions, and other overt behavior.

With children, the examiner simply makes available the collection of toys for free play. With adults, the materials are presented with general instructions to carry out some task of a highly unstructured nature. These instructions may, of course, also be employed with children. Frequently, the task has dramatic features, as in the arrangement of figures on a miniature stage set. The materials for the Scenotest, for example, come in a flat, portable case that has a lid which can actually be used as a "stage" with the various figures and accessories (see Fig. 15–4).

Play techniques for the diagnosis and assessment of children have been catalogued in a comprehensive volume edited by Schaefer, Gitlin, and Sandgrund (1991). In addition to projective tools, such as puppet techniques, this work describes a wide assortment of play scales for the assessment of specific problems—ranging from autism to hyperactivity—and for the developmental evaluation of such areas as competence, mastery motivation, and infant temperament. Also included are scales for use in play therapy and for assessing parent–child and peer interaction. As Schaefer and his collaborators acknowledge, many of the techniques they present are still in the initial stages of development. Nevertheless, the diverse collection of approaches they have gathered includes some ingenious measures and offers both highly structured formal observation methods that might be best suited for research as well as many clinically oriented instruments.

---

[17] Further discussion of the use of projective drawings, and reviews of several of the techniques mentioned in this section, can be found in Cummings (1986), Hammer (1986), Handler (1996), and Knoff (1990).

[18] For a general discussion of procedures and interpretation of projective play, from a viewpoint that emphasizes psychoanalytic theory and developmental perspectives, see Krall (1986).

Figure 15–4. Standardized Materials from the Scenotest.

(Courtesy of Hogrefe & Huber Publishers. Copyright © 1994 by Hogrefe & Huber Publishers. Reproduced by permission.)

EVALUATION OF PROJECTIVE TECHNIQUES

It is evident that projective techniques differ widely among themselves. Some appear more promising than others because of more favorable empirical findings, sounder theoretical orientation, or both. Regarding some techniques, such as the Rorschach, voluminous data have been gathered, although their interpretation is still often uncertain. About others, little is known, either because of their recent origin, or because objective verification is hindered by the intrinsic nature of the instruments or by the attitudes of their exponents.

A related observation is that the differences between projective techniques and standardized tests are not as large or as fundamental as may appear at first sight. Not only in their psychometric properties, but also in the nature of the task presented to test takers and the ways in which the results are interpreted, it has been argued convincingly that projective techniques and self-report inventories differ in degree rather than in kind (Levy, 1963). Individual instruments fall into a continuum; although at the extremes the differences are easily recognizable, overlapping in several features is evident at the center.

To evaluate each projective instrument individually and to attempt to summarize the extensive pertinent literature would require a separate volume. Within this chapter, critical comments have been interjected only in the cases of instruments that presented unique features—whether of a favorable or unfavorable nature. Several general questions, however, can be raised to some extent about most projective techniques. These questions can be conveniently considered in summary form.

Rapport and Applicability. Most projective techniques represent an effective means for "breaking the ice" during the initial contacts between clinician and client. The task is usually intrinsically interesting and often entertaining. It tends to divert the individual's attention away from herself or himself and thus reduces embarassment and defensiveness. And it offers little or no threat to the respondent's prestige, since any response one gives is "right."

Certain projective techniques may be especially useful with young children, illiterates, and persons with language difficulties or speech defects. Nonverbal media would be readily applicable to all these groups. And oral responses to pictorial and other nonlanguage stimuli could be secured from the first two. With all these verbally limited groups, projective techniques may help the test taker to communicate with the examiner. These techniques may also aid individuals in clarifying for themselves some aspects of their own behavior that they had not previously verbalized.

Faking. In general, projective instruments are less susceptible to faking than are self-report inventories. The purpose of projective techniques is usually disguised.[19] Even if an individual has some psychological sophistication and is familiar with the general nature of a particular instrument, such as the Rorschach or TAT, it is still unlikely that he or she can predict the intricate ways in which the responses will be scored and interpreted. As the results of a recent series of studies comparing an objective and a projective measure of dependency suggest, there seems to be a clearcut relationship between the face validity of a test and its susceptibility to faking (Bornstein, Rossner, Hill, & Stepanian, 1994). Moreover, the respondent soon becomes absorbed in the task and hence is less likely to resort to the customary disguises and restraints of interpersonal communication.

On the other hand, it cannot be assumed that projective tests are completely immune to faking. Several experiments with the Rorschach, TAT, and other projective instruments have shown that significant differences do occur when respondents are instructed to alter their responses so as to create favorable or unfavorable impressions, or when they are given statements suggesting that certain types of responses are more desirable (Masling, 1960). There is considerable experimental evidence that responses to projective tests can in fact be successfully altered in both a "fake good" and a "fake bad" direction, although the latter may be easier to accomplish. Such results have been obtained with several projective instruments, including the Rorschach, TAT, Rosenzweig P-F Study, and sentence completion tests (Albert, Fox, & Kahn, 1980; Exner, 1991; Kaplan & Eron, 1965; Meltzoff, 1951; Netter & Viglione, 1994; Perry & Kinder, 1990; Schwartz, Cohen, & Pavlik, 1964). The skilled examiner is alert to signs of faking, both in

[19] To the extent that the examinee is unaware of the nature and purpose of the assessment within which these techniques are used, their disguised nature presents an ethical problem (see chap. 18).

the nature of individual responses and response patterns and in inconsistencies with other sources of data about the respondent.

Examiner and Situational Variables. It is obvious that most projective techniques are inadequately standardized with respect to both administration and scoring, or are not used in a standardized fashion in clinical practice. Yet there is evidence that even subtle differences in the phrasing of verbal instructions and in examiner–examinee relationships can appreciably alter performance on these tests (Baughman, 1951; Exner, 1993; Hamilton & Robertson, 1966; Herron, 1964; Klinger, 1966; Klopfer & Taulbee, 1976). Even when employing identical instructions, some examiners may be more encouraging or reassuring, others more threatening, owing to their general manner and appearance. Such differences may affect response productivity, defensiveness, stereotypy, imaginativeness, and other basic performance characteristics. In the light of these findings, problems of administration and testing conditions assume even greater importance than in other psychological tests.

Equally serious is the lack of objectivity in scoring and interpretation. Even when objective scoring systems have been developed and followed, the final steps in the evaluation and integration of the raw data usually depend on the skill and clinical experience of the examiner. The most disturbing implication of this situation is that the interpretation of scores is often as projective for the examiner as the test stimuli are for the examinee. In other words, the final interpretation of projective test responses may reveal more about the theoretical orientation, favorite hypotheses, and personal idiosyncrasies of the examiner than it does about the examinee's personality dynamics.

Norms. Another conspicuous deficiency common to many projective instruments pertains to normative data. Such data may be completely lacking, grossly inadequate, or based on vaguely described populations. In the absence of adequate objective norms, the clinician falls back on her or his "general clinical experience" to interpret projective test performance. But such a frame of reference is subject to all the distortions of memory that are themselves reflections of theoretical bias, preconceptions, and other idiosyncrasies of the clinician. Moreover, any one clinician's contacts may have been limited largely to persons who are atypical in education, socioeconomic level, sex ratio, age distribution, or other relevant characteristics. In at least one respect the clinician's experience is almost certain to produce a misleading picture, since he or she deals predominantly with disturbed or pathological individuals. The clinician may thus lack enough firsthand familiarity with the characteristic reactions of normal people on the tests. The Rorschach norms gathered by Exner represent efforts to correct some of the more obvious lacks in this regard.

Interpretation of projective test performance often involves subgroup norms, of either a subjective or an objective nature. Such norms may lead to faulty interpretations unless the subgroups were equated in other respects. For example, if the schizophrenics and normals on whom the norms were derived differed also in educational level, the observed disparities between schizophrenic and normal performance may have resulted from educational inequality rather than from schizophrenia. Systematic or constant errors may also operate in the comparison of various psychiatric syndromes. For instance, there is some evidence that clinicians have a tendency to overdiagnose schizophrenia, instead of bipolar disorder, in some ethnic groups and in younger individuals; similarly, conversion disorder has been reported to be more common in individuals of lower socioeconomic status (American Psychiatric Association, 1994).

Reliability. Although projective techniques continue to be widely used in clinical and forensic settings, their scientific status remains highly controversial. In view of the special nature of scoring procedures and the inadequacies of normative data in projective testing, scorer reliability becomes an important consideration.[20] For projective techniques, a proper measure of scorer reliability should not only include the objective and preliminary scoring, but also the final integrative and interpretive stages. For instance, the interscorer reliabilities of TAT techniques have typically been in the .80 to .90 range (Fineman, 1977), while their internal consistency and test-retest reliability have been concerning. In an influential critique of the TAT, Entwisle (1972) concluded, on the basis of numerous published studies, that the internal consistency of the scoring scheme for TAT rarely exceeded .30 to .40. There has been little subsequent data to challenge Entwisle's conclusion; although, some authors have questioned the relevance of internal consistency statistics for evaluating the TAT's reliability (e.g. Cramer, 1999).

Retest reliability also presents special problems. With long intervals, the test should detect genuine personality changes that may occur. With short intervals, a retest may show no more than recall of original responses. When investigators instructed respondents to write different TAT stories on a retest, in order to determine whether the same themes would recur, most of the scored variables yielded insignificant retest correlations (Lindzey and Herman, 1955). It is also relevant to note that many scores derived from projective techniques are based on very inadequate response samples. In the case of the Rorschach, for instance, the number of responses within a given individual's protocol that falls under such categories as animal movement, human movement, shading, color, unusual detail, and the like may be so few as to yield extremely unreliable indices. Large chance variations are expected under such circumstances. Ratios and percentages computed with such unreliable measures are even more stable than the individual measures themselves (Cronbach, 1949).

Validity. For any test, the most fundamental question is that of validity. Many validation studies of projective tests have been concerned with concurrent criterion-related validation. Most of these have compared the performance of contrasted groups, such as occupational or diagnostic groups. As was pointed out in connection with norms, however, these groups often differ in other respects, such as age or education. Other investigations of concurrent validity have used essentially a matching technique, in which personality descriptions derived from test records are compared with descriptions or data about the same persons taken

---

[20] In recognition of the importance of ensuring an adequate level of objectivity in scoring practices, the Journal of Personality Assessment, since 1991, has required authors of articles that report Rorschach research to submit evidence of at least 80% agreement between two or more scorers for all major scoring categories.

from case histories, psychiatric interviews, or long-range behavioral records. A few studies have investigated predictive validity against such criteria as success in specialized training, job performance, or response to psychotherapy. There has been an increasing trend to investigate the construct validity of projective instruments by testing specific hypotheses that underlie the use and interpretation of each test.

The large majority of published validation studies on projective techniques are inconclusive because of procedural deficiencies in either experimental controls or statistical analysis, or both. Some methodological deficiencies may have the effect of producing *spurious evidence of validity* where none exists. An example is the contamination of either criterion or test data. Thus, the criterion judges may have had some knowledge of the respondent's test performance. Similarly, the examiner may have obtained cues about the respondent's characteristics from conversation with her or him in the course of test administration, or from case history material and other nontest sources. The customary control for the latter type of contamination in validation studies is to utilize blind analysis, in which the test record is interpreted by a scorer who has had no contact with the respondent and who has no information about her or him other than that contained in the test protocol. Clinicians have argued, however, that blind analysis is an unnatural way to interpret projective test responses and does not correspond to the way these instruments are used in clinical practice.

Another common source of spurious validity data is failure to cross-validate (Kinslinger, 1966). Because of the large number of potential diagnostic signs or scorable elements that can be derived from most projective tests, it is very easy by chance alone to find a set of such signs that differentiate significantly between criterion groups. The validity of such a scoring key, however, will collapse to zero when applied to new samples.

A more subtle form of error is illustrated by stereotype accuracy. Certain descriptive statements, such as might occur in a Rorschach protocol, may apply widely to persons in general, or to young men, or to hospitalized patients, or to whatever category of persons is sampled by the particular investigation.[21] Agreement between criterion and test data with regard to such statements would therefore yield a spurious impression of validity. Some check on this error is needed, such as a measure of the agreement between the test evaluation of one respondent and the criterion evaluation of another respondent in the same category. This measure would indicate the amount of spurious agreement resulting from stereotype accuracy under the conditions of the particular investigation (see, e.g., L. H. Silverman, 1959).

Still another common source of error, arising from reliance on clinical experience in the validation of diagnostic signs, is what Chapman (1967) labeled "illusory validation." This phenomenon may account in part for the continued use of instruments and systems of diagnostic signs for which empirical validity findings are predominantly negative. In a classic series of experiments to test this phenomenon, Chapman and Chapman (1967) presented college students

---

[21] The use of such generally applicable statements is an example of the "Barnum effect" cited in chapter 17 (Dunnette, 1957; Meehl, 1956). For a well-balanced survey on the extensive research on this effect., see Klopfer (1983, pp. 510–514).

with a set of human figure drawings similar to those obtained in the Machover Draw-a-Person Test (D-A-P). The results showed that participants responded in terms of preestablished popular stereotypes even though these associations were not supported by the data that had been presented to them during their experimental "learning experience." For example, they listed atypical eyes as being associated with suspiciousness; a large head with worry about intelligence; and broad shoulders with concern about manliness. Not only were the interpretations unrelated to the empirical associations which the participants had "studied," but in other experiments these stereotyped cultural associations also proved to be resistant to change under intensive training conditions designed to establish counter associations. In other words, persons retained their a priori expectations even when exposed to contradictory observations.

Illusory validation is a special example of the mechanism that underlies the survival of superstitions. We tend to notice and recall whatever fits our expectations; and we tend to ignore and forget whatever is contrary to our expectations. This mechanism may actually interfere with the discovery and use of valid diagnostic signs in the course of clinical observation by clinicians who are strongly wedded to a particular diagnostic system. The original research of Chapman and Chapman with the D-A-P has been corroborated by similar studies with the Rorschach and with the Incomplete Sentences Blank (Chapman & Chapman, 1969; Golding & Rorer, 1972; Starr & Katkin, 1969).

Moreover, it is suggested that projective tests reveal something about the unconscious through the use of ambiguous stimuli. However, research has shown little evidence supporting the ideas that they can actually do this (Merrell, 2003). Most projective techniques have low validity coefficients. Also, it is seen by the practitioners that most of the manuals for the tests only mention the research that is in support of the test, and not the research against it, which is inappropriate. (Kline, 2000). Furthermore, a few researchers have found a number of contextual factors to have an effect such as the race and gender of the tester, the mood of the tester while administering the test, and what the subject thinks the test is measuring (Kline, 2000). Another question emerges on the wide range of aspects that projective tests measure. Since it is accepted that these tests measure nearly all aspects of the personality, as opposed to other techniques that focus on one or a couple of aspects, it may be fair to say that a test that claims to measure such a wide range could be questioned on its validity and effectiveness (Kline, 2000).

The Projective Hypothesis. The traditional assumption regarding projective techniques has been that the individual's responses to the ambiguous stimuli presented to her or him reflect significant and relatively enduring personality attributes. Although it is clear that projective test responses can and do reflect the response styles and abiding traits of individuals, a large and growing body of research indicates that many other factors can affect those responses. To the extent that retest reliability has been measured, marked temporal shifts have frequently been observed, indicating the operation of considerable chance error. More direct evidence regarding the susceptibility of projective test responses to temporary states is provided by several experimental studies demonstrating the effect on such responses of factors such as hunger, sleep deprivation, drugs, anxiety, and frustration. Significant response differences have likewise been found in relation to instructional sets, examiner characteristics, and the respondent's perception of the testing situation. Ability factors—and particularly verbal ability—clearly affect scores on most projective tests. In the light of all these findings, projective test responses can be meaningfully interpreted only when the examiner has extensive information about the circumstances under which they were obtained and the aptitudes and experiential background of the respondent.

From another angle, the advantages of using unstructured or ambiguous stimuli have been questioned (Epstein, 1966). Such stimuli are ambiguous for the examiner as well as for the examinee; thus they tend to increase ambiguity in the interpretation of the examinee's responses. With structured stimuli, on the other hand, it is possible to select stimuli relevant to the personality characteristics to be assessed and to vary the nature of the stimuli to explore fully a given personality dimension. Such a procedure makes for clearer interpretation of test performance than is possible with the shotgun approach of unstructured stimuli. There is also evidence against the common assumption that the less structured the stimuli, the more likely they are to elicit projection and to tap "deep" layers of personality (Klopfer & Taulbee, 1976; Murstein, 1963). Actually, the relation between ambiguity and projection appears to be nonlinear, with an intermediate degree of ambiguity representing an optimum for purposes of projection.

The assumption that fantasy, as elicited by such projective techniques as the TAT, reveals covert motivational dispositions has also been called into question. For example, in a 20-year longitudinal study of TAT fantasy and relevant overt behavior, adolescent activities predicted adult TAT imagery much better than adolescent TAT imagery predicted adult activities (McClelland, 1966; Skolnick, 1966). In one instance, individuals who had shown upward social mobility obtained higher scores on achievement needs as adults; but those who obtained higher achievement need scores in adolescence were not among the ones who subsequently showed upward social mobility.

Findings such as these reverse the relationship implied by the traditional rationale of projective techniques. They can be explained if we regard TAT responses not as direct projective expressions of motives, but as samples of the individual's thoughts, which may in turn have been influenced by her or his previous actions. Individuals who have achieved more and those who were more often exposed to achievement-oriented models in the developmental history tend to perceive more achievement themes in ambiguous pictures.

In summary, many types of research have tended to cast doubt about various aspects of the projective hypothesis. There is ample evidence that a variety of alternative explanations may account for the individual's responses to unstructured or ambiguous test stimuli.

Projective Techniques as Psychometric Instruments. Many projective techniques are clearly found wanting when evaluated in accordance with test standards. This is evident from the data summarized in the preceding sections with regard to standardization of administration and scoring procedures, adequacy of norms, reliability, and validity. Yet, after several decades of contradictory results, the use of projective techniques remains substantially unchanged and may, in fact, be undergoing a growth spurt. Projective tests are used considerably in clinical use, though the scientific evidence is often debated. The criticism of lack of scientific evidence to support them and their continued popularity has been referred to as the "projective paradox" (Cordón, 2005). In response to the statistical criticism of the projective tests, one of the test authors said that his test actually discovers "fate and existential possibilities hidden in the inherited familial unconscious and the personal unconscious, even those hidden because never lived through or because have been rejected. Is any statistical method able to span, understand and integrate mathematically all these possibilities? I deny this categorically" (Spiteri, n.d.). However, there is a need for much more validity data to specify the nature of the constructs measured by their scores, as well as for more normative data on clearly defined populations. Thus, while coming closer to meeting test standards than having other projective techniques, most of these instruments are not ready for routine operational use in helping to make decisions and predictions about people.

Projective Techniques as Clinical Tools. Rather than being regarded and evaluated as psychometric instruments or *tests* in the strict sense of the term, most projective instruments are regarded as clinical tools. Thus, they may serve as supplementary qualitative interviewing aids in the hands of a skilled clinician. Their value as clinical tools is proportional to the skill of the clinician and hence cannot be assessed independently of the individual clinician using them. Attempts to evaluate them in terms of the usual psychometric procedures may thus be inappropriate. But by the same token, the use of elaborate scoring systems that yield quantitative scores is not only wasteful but also misleading. Such scoring procedures lend the results an illusory semblance of objectivity and may create the unwarranted impression that the given technique can be treated as a test. The special value of projective techniques is more likely to emerge when they are interpreted by qualitative, clinical procedures than when they are quantitatively scored and interpreted, as if they were objective psychometric instruments.

In India, projective techniques are widely used as clinical tools. Clinical psychologists use this tool along with interviews, case interviews or historical data. Such processes are helpful, provided they are not accepted as final, but are constantly tested against information elicited through subsequent inquiry, test responses, reaction to therapy, or other behavior on the part of the client. It follows from the nature of interviewing and projective techniques that decisions should not be based on any single datum or score obtained from such sources. These techniques serve best in sequential decisions, by suggesting leads for further exploration or hypotheses about the individual for subsequent verification.

Borrowing a concept from information theory, Cronbach and Gleser (1965) characterized interviewing and projective techniques as "wideband" procedures. Bandwidth, or breadth of coverage, is achieved at the cost of lowered fidelity or dependability of information. Objective psychometric tests characteristically yield a narrow band of information at a high level of dependability. In contrast, projective and interviewing techniques provide a much wider range of information of lower dependability. Moreover, the kinds of data furnished by any one projective technique may vary from individual to individual. One person's TAT responses, for example, may tell us a good deal about her or his aggression and little or nothing about creativity or achievement need; another person's record may permit a thorough assessment of the degree of creativity and of the strength of achievement need, while revealing little about her or his aggression. Such a lack of uniformity in the kinds of information provided in individual cases helps to explain the low validities found when projective test responses are analyzed for any single trait across a group of persons.

It is interesting to note that a similar unevenness characterizes clinicians' interpretations of individual records. Thus, in an early study of the validity of the TAT, Henry and Farley (1959, p. 22) concluded:

> There is no single correct way of employing the TAT interpretation. There was little item agreement between judges, but each judge made enough "correct" decisions to yield a highly significant agreement figure. Judges may arrive at essentially the same interpretive implications of the test report, by quite different routes; or judges may differ individually in their ability to utilize TAT predictions in different areas ... or for different subjects.

The nature of clinical judgment through which projective and interviewing data may be used in reaching decisions about individual clients is receiving increasing attention from psychologists (see chap. 17). In this process, the very constructs or categories in terms of which the data are organized are built up inductively through an examination of the particular combination of data available in each case. The special function of the clinician is to make predictions from unique or rare combinations of events about which it is impracticable to prepare any statistical table or equation. By creating new constructs to lit the individual, the clinician can predict from combinations of events he or she has never encountered before. In making these predictions, the clinician can also take into account the varied significance of similar events for different individuals. Such clinical predictions are helpful, provided they are not accepted as final but are constantly tested against information elicited through subsequent inquiry, test responses, reaction to therapy, or other behavior on the part of the client. It follows from the nature of interviewing and projective techniques that decisions should not be based on any single datum or score obtained from such sources. These techniques serve best in sequential decisions, by suggesting leads for further exploration or hypotheses about the individual for subsequent verification.

Chapter Sixteen

Other Assessment Techniques

The self-report inventories and projective techniques surveyed in the preceding chapters represent the best-known and most widely used instruments for personality appraisal. Nevertheless, there still remains a rich supply of other devices that are being explored for this purpose. Out of this diversity of approaches may come techniques that will eventually stimulate progress in new directions. The procedures considered in this chapter are principally research techniques, although some may also serve as supplementary assessment tools in applied contexts, such as counseling or organizational psychology work. A wide variety of approaches is represented by the specific techniques cited. Several of them are hard to classify because they assess constructs that span the realms of abilities and personality. Three major categories include measures of cognitive styles and personality types; situational tests; and techniques designed to assess self-concepts and personal constructs. To add further perspective to this survey, some attention is given to the use of nontest techniques in personality assessment, including naturalistic observations, interviewing, ratings, and the analysis of life-history data.

MEASURES OF STYLES AND TYPES

Even though, in this book and elsewhere, ability and personality testing are discussed separately, in actual test use and particularly in test score interpretation the cognitive and affective realms cannot be kept apart.[1] The behavior samples that make up psychological tests are cross-sections of a person's behavioral repertoire; as such, they contain information about all aspects of the person at once. In chapter 11, for example, we reviewed evidence of the growing consensus that aptitudes cannot be investigated independently of affective variables because performance on ability tests is clearly dependent on achievement drive, persistence, values, and the like. Similarly, in chapter 13, we discussed the idea that individuals differ in the consistency of their behavior across situations as a function of how they perceive and categorize situations, which, in turn, depends on their prior experience and learning. Moreover, throughout the chapters in Parts Three and Four, we have considered measures purportedly aimed at assessing either ability or personality that also include aspects pertinent to affective or cognitive functioning, respectively.

There are a number of ways of dealing with the multiplicity of factors inherent in human behavior. We can, for instance, simply examine the correlation between measures of traits like anxiety and problem-solving ability (see, e.g., Zeidner, 1995). We can also use multivariate techniques, such as factor analysis and multidimensional scaling, to separate the components within a set of behavioral data (Jones & Sabers, 1992). Structural schemes that accommodate several variables and represent their interrelationships topographically can be devised as well. The hierarchical model of the organization of abilities developed by Vernon (see chap. 11), Holland's hexagonal representation of occupational themes (see chap. 14), and the interpersonal circumplex model (see, e.g., Hofstee et al., 1992) are examples of this type of arrangement within single realms of behavior.[2] Yet another approach is to use categories that are in themselves complex and that encompass both cognitive and affective elements. Emotional intelligence (Salovey & Mayer, 1990; Mayer & Salovey, 1993) is one such construct that has recently garnered a good deal of attention (see, e.g., Goleman, 1995). Cognitive styles and personality types, discussed in the next two sections, also exemplify this kind of approach. They represent attempts to capture qualitative differences in the patterns or configurations of human behavior.

Cognitive Styles. *Cognitive styles* refer essentially to one's preferred and typical modes of perceiving, remembering, thinking, and problem solving (Messick et al., 1976). They are regarded as broad stylistic behavioral characteristics that cut across abilities and personality and are manifested in many activities and media. An extensive research literature has accumulated on various cognitive styles and related concepts, such as learning and thinking styles (Brodzinsky, 1982; Furnham, 1995; Globerson & Zelniker, 1989; Goldstein & Blackman, 1978a, 1978b; Grigorenko & Sternberg, 1995; Jonassen & Grabowski, 1993; Kogan, 1976; Messer, 1976; Sternberg, 1994; Witkin &Goodenough, 1981).

---

[1] The need to integrate these domains in general psychological theory and research, as well as in practice, is being increasingly recognized. See, for example, the two recent volumes devoted to the interface between personality and intelligence edited by Saklofske and Zeidner (1995) and Sternberg and Ruzgis (1994).

[2] The spherical representation of vocational interests proposed by Tracey and Rounds (1996), mentioned in chapter 14, is an example of a more complex scheme involving multiple dimensions.

One of the principal sources of differentiation of cognitive styles can be found in the area of perceptual functions. A large body of experimental literature has demonstrated significant relationships between the individual's attitudinal, motivational, or emotional characteristics and her or his performance on perceptual or cognitive tasks. It should also be recognized that a number of projective techniques—notably the Rorschach—may be regarded as essentially perceptual tests (see, e.g., Blatt, 1990).

Of the factors identified in early factorial analyses of perception, one that has proved particularly fruitful in personality research is flexibility of closure (Pemberton, 1952; Thurstone, 1944). A common type of test for this factor requires the identification of a figure amid distracting and confusing details. Two items from a test with a high loading in this factor (Gottschaldt Figures) are shown in Figure 16–1. Several early studies reported suggestive data indicating possible relationships between this perceptual factor and personality traits. In one investigation, for example, persons who excelled in flexibility of closure had high self-ratings on trait descriptions such as socially retiring, independent of the opinion of others, analytical, interested in theoretical and scientific problems, and disliking systematization and routine (Pemberton, 1952). Over the intervening years, investigators have employed adaptations of the Gottschaldt Figures in research on both cognitive and noncognitive behavior.

Approaching the problem from a different angle, Witkin and his associates (Witkin et al., 1954/1972) identified the ability to resist the disruptive influence of conflicting contextual cues as an important variable in the long-term study of perceptual space orientation. Through various tests utilizing a rod and frame that could be independently moved, a tilting chair, and a tilting room, these investigators were able to show that individuals differ widely in their "field dependence," or the extent to which their perception of the upright is influenced by the surrounding visual field. Odd–even and retest reliabilities were high, and most of the intercorrelations among the different spatial orientation tests were significant.

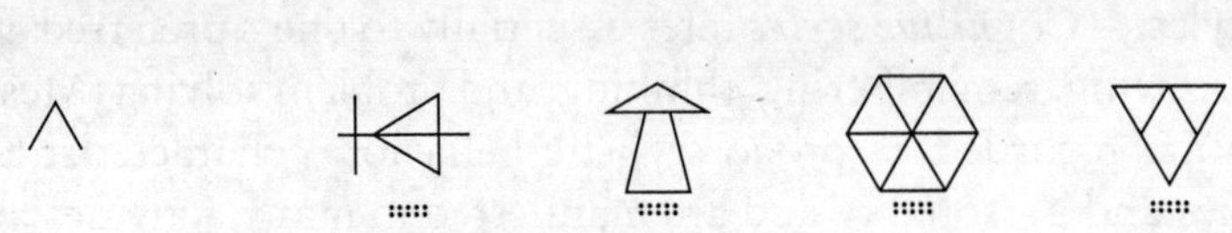

Flexibility of Closure (Gottschaldt Figures): Which of the four drawings at the right contain the design at the left?

Figure 16–1. Items Illustrating Perceptual Tasks Employed in Personality Assessment. (From Thurstone, 1950, p. 7.)

Thus, a substantial body of data was amassed to indicate that field dependence is a relatively stable, consistent trait, having a certain amount of generality.

Of even more interest are the significant correlations between these orientation tests and the Embedded Figures Test (similar to the Gottschaldt Figures illustrated in Fig. 16–1), which has been considered as a measure of field dependence in a purely visual, paper-and-pencil situation. As more research accumulated, field dependence–independence came to be regarded as the perceptual component of a broader personality dimension, designated as global versus articulated cognitive style, or psychological differentiation (Witkin, Dyk, Faterson, Goodenough, & Karp, 1962/1974). There is evidence that this cognitive style exhibits considerable stability through childhood and early adulthood and is related to a number of personality variables, such as leadership (Weissenberg & Gruenfeld, 1966), social conformity (Witkin et al., 1974), and many others (see, e.g., Jonassen & Grabowski, 1993, chap. 7).

The scope and diversity of research on field dependence are truly impressive, ranging from interpersonal relations (Witkin & Goodenough, 1977) to learning and memory (D. R. Goodenough, 1976), mathematics achievement (Vaidya & Chansky, 1980), choice of field of study in college and graduate school (Raskin, 1985), cross-cultural differences (J. W. Berry, 1976), and work environment preferences (Wooten, Barner, & Silver, 1994). An example of the intriguing relationships that emerge from surveys of many studies is the finding that field-independent persons tend to follow active, "participant" approaches to learning, whereas field-dependent persons more often use "spectator" approaches. One recent investigation comparing the outcomes of multiple-choice tests and performance-based assessments, for instance, suggests that the latter favor field-independent students (Lu & Suen, 1995). In interpersonal situations, on the other hand, the field-dependent tend to have certain advantages in getting along with others. They tend to be more attentive to social cues, more responsive to other persons' behavior, and more emotionally open than are the field-independent persons. It appears that neither end of the field dependent–independent continuum is necessarily or uniformly favorable or unfavorable; rather, the value of deviations in either direction depends on the demands of particular situations.

Much of this research has used the Embedded Figures Test, which is relatively easy to administer. Published forms of this test are available for the adult, child, and preschool levels, as well as for group administration (Coates, 1972; Witkin, Oltman, Raskin, & Karp, 1971). Two demonstration items from the Group Embedded Figures Test are shown in Figure 16–2. In both the children's and the preschool forms, the complex figures are recognizable, familiar objects, and the tests are administered individually. The original adult form is also individually administered.

Although there has been a continuous stream of research on the subject (see, e.g., Bertini, Pizzamiglio, & Wapner, 1985), much remains to be done to clear up inconsistencies found in studies of field independence and its relationship to a wide diversity of behavioral variables. One problem pertains tea nomenclature and, in turn, reflects differences in how field independence is regarded. Some investigators have concluded, based on its correlation with measures of g, that the field independence construct is a cognitive ability after all; others have classified

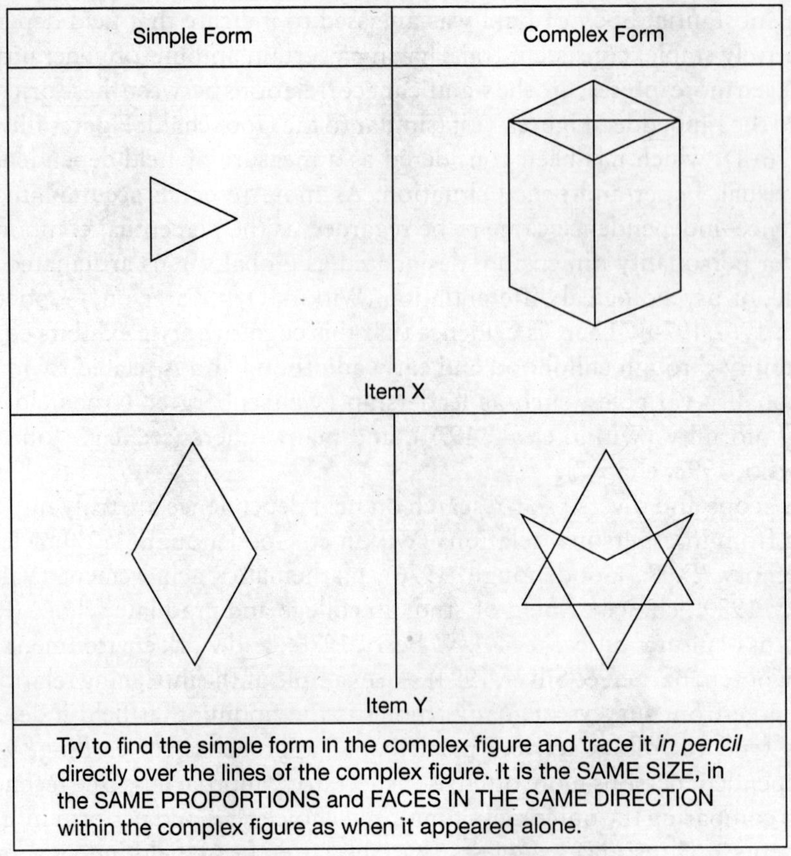

Figure 16–2. Demonstration Items from the Group Embedded Figures Test. (Copyright © 1972 by Consulting Psychologists Press. Reproduced by permission.)

it as a cognitive "control" and have placed it at an intermediate position, between cognitive abilities and cognitive styles (McKenna, 1984; Jonasson & Grabowski, 1993). A related obstacle to generalization is presented by lack of uniformity among studies with regard to participant characteristics and methodology. For instance, findings suggest that whereas the results on paper-and-pencil measure ded Figures Test, are heavily influenced by general intelligence, scores on performance tests, like the Portable Rod-and-Frame, are more purely a reflection of field independence as a value-free stylistic variable (Arthur & Day, 1991).

In spite of the conceptual and methodological obstacles their study may present, cognitive styles are of great theoretical and practical interest.[3] Because they lie at the intersection between abilities and personality, these styles can influence and modulate behavior in both the affective and intellectual realms. Thus, questions about their nature and characteristics, such as the extent to which they are fixed or flexible, acquire considerable importance (see, e.g., Niaz, 1987). Furthermore,

[3] It should be noted that cognitive styles vary in complexity. Some styles pertain to relatively simple differences; for example, the reflective-versus-impulsive style, or cognitive tempo, is defined only by the speed with which individuals respond to problem situations, especially those involving a high degree of uncertainty (Kagan,. 1965; S. B. Messer, 1976). Others, such as Sternberg's thinking styles (1988, 1994b), encompass more complex patterns of dispositions.

in endeavors where learning is a primary goal, there has been increasing recognition that the efficiency of both instruction and assessment may be considerably improved by taking stylistic factors into account (Furnham, 1995; Jonassen & Grabowski, 1993; Lu & Suen, 1995; Sternberg, 1988, 1994b; Zelniker, 1989).

Personality Types. Like cognitive styles, *personality types* also refer to constructs that have been used to explain similarities and differences in preferred modes of thinking, perceiving, and behaving within and across individuals. Fundamentally, personality types are categories defined by certain configurations of two or more traits or attributes. As explanations for human behavior, typologies have a long history that dates back to the ancient Greek theory of body humors— blood, black bile, yellow bile, and phlegm—and the temperament types associated with them, namely, sanguine, melancholic, choleric, and phlegmatic. Typological systems often have enormous popular appeal because they offer relatively simple, seemingly firm bases for understanding and possibly explaining one's behavior and that of others. Such systems vary a good deal in the number and kind of dimensions that can be used to generate types.

Within psychology, a number of different typologies have been devised over the years. Some, like Sheldon's system for classifying personality types on the basis of physique (Sheldon & Stevens, 1942/1970), were based mostly on speculation and have been discarded for lack of corroborating evidence. Others, like the MMPI code types described in chapter 13, arose from empirical observations, continued to evolve, and are still in use (Graham, 1993). Most typological systems encompass distinctions within a single area, such as occupations or temperaments. A few pertain to more than one domain. Among the latter, Alan Miller's efforts to synthesize existing typologies across the cognitive, affective, and motivational dimensions stand out. Miller's (1991a, 1991b) conceptual linkages across systems are based on a review and analysis of a large number of typologies within the three areas and should prove to be of considerable heuristic value.

Myers-Briggs Type Indicator. One of the most enduring typological classifications was devised by Jung (1921/1971) and has served as the foundation for the Myers-Briggs Type Indicator (MBTI—Myers, 1962; Myers & McCaulley, 1985), which is a widely used instrument for the assessment of personality in normal individuals.[4] The MBTI uses Jung's well-known dichotomy of extraverted and introverted attitudes (E and I), and his classifications of opposing ways of perceiving (sensation versus intuition—S vs. N) and of contrasting approaches to judgment (thinking versus feeling—T vs. F). It also includes a polarity of preferences in orientation toward the outer world (judgment or perception—J or P) that was not explicit in Jung's work. The scores on these four—presumably independent—dimensions result in sixteen possible "type formulas" that give combinations of the letters of the preferred direction within each of the four dimensions. For example, the combination "INTP" represents the "introverted, intuitive, thinking, and perceptive" type.[5] Each preferred direction also has a

[4] The MBTI was mentioned briefly in chapter 13 in connection with the use of the forced-choice technique in self-report personality inventories.

[5] According to the MBTI manual, such a person would, among other things, (a) be quiet and reserved, (b) enjoy solving problems with logic and analysis, (c) be interested mainly in ideas, and (d) tend to have sharply defined interests (Myers & McCaulley, 1985).

numerical score that indicates the strength of the preference and is calculated from the difference in points between the poles of each dimension.

The results of the MBTI, unlike those of most other personality inventories, are intended primarily for use by the respondent and are presented in a non-judgmental fashion. Two of the most fundamental premises used in interpreting the results of the MBTI are (a) that all types are valuable and necessary and have special strengths and vulnerabilities and (b) that individuals are more skilled within their preferred functions, processes, and attitudes. These characteristics have contributed to the popularity of the MBTI and to its application for a variety of purposes, including career guidance, counseling, and team selection and development. The psychometric difficulties posed by the MBTI scores have been well documented (for reviews, see DeVito, 1985; J. S. Wiggins, 1989). In particular, reviewers have objected to the forced dichotomies of the Myers-Briggs, whereby identical profile type letters are assigned on the basis of difference scores that may vary considerably in magnitude. Nevertheless, a substantial amount of research with the instrument continues to be carried out. In addition to investigations addressing the validity of the MBTI, a number of studies have also explored alternative ways of scoring it (see, e.g., Davis, Grove, & Knowles, 1990; Girelli & Stake, 1993; Harvey & Murry, 1994). Moreover, variations of the Myers-Briggs and adaptations of its constructs for various uses have also been devised. One noteworthy variation is the recently developed Student Styles Questionnaire (Oakland, Glutting, & Horton, 1996), which is aimed at evaluating styles of learning, working, and relating in students between the ages of 8 and 17 years.

Notwithstanding the popularity of the Myers-Briggs and of a few other typologies, historically, most psychologists who study personality have conceived of it as a psychic entity made up of components, or traits, on which people differ quantitatively, rather than as a taxonomy based on qualitative differences. Furthermore, within scientific psychology there has been a general reluctance to use types as explanatory concepts. This reluctance has stemmed primarily from three sources: (a) the emphasis that many personality theorists have placed on the need to understand and value the uniqueness of individuals, (b) the implicit link between types and stereotypes and the inherent dangers associated with the latter, and (c) the paucity of adequate quantitative methods for identifying and analyzing categorical data.

In a series of recent developments, however, some of the traditional objections to typological constructs appear to have been challenged. For instance, Paul Meehl believes that it is time to explore empirically the possible existence of naturally occurring, nonarbitrary classes—or taxa—within the nonpathological range of individual differences in personality. Fie and his associates have proposed new taxometric methods that can be used to identify such classes (Meehl, 1992, 1995; Meehl & Golden, 1982; Meehl & Yonce, 1994).[6] Similarly, after reviewing a number of geometric trait models of personality, ranging from unidimensional bipolar traits to multidimensional circumplexes, Dahlstrom (1995) concludes that such models are inadequate to the task of organizing personality constructs

[6] Although there is little evidence concerning their transportability from one situation to another, the subgroups generated through cluster analyses of biodata—discussed later in this chapter—also offer interesting possibilities from the point of view of typological classification.

and research. According to him, the inherently configural nature of personality structure and functioning requires "a schema of pigeon-holes to summarize in a faithful and accurate way how we differ and how we resemble each other" (p. 14). Finally, even the deeply entrenched notion that stereotypes are usually inaccurate and destructive has recently been questioned (Lee, Jussim, & McCauley, 1995).

These and other developments portend a renewed interest in, and a more sophisticated approach to, the use of multidimensional categories, such as types and styles, as part of the conceptual arsenal available to study and explain individual differences in behavior. Nevertheless, regardless of how useful or popular such constructs may be, they will undoubtedly coexist with—not replace—approaches that emphasize the unique aspects of individuals and of their behavior. In the assessment of people, the dangers of reifying types and using them simplistically or overinclusively as explanatory concepts always need to be kept in mind.

SITUATIONAL TESTS

Although the term "situational test" was popularized during and following World War II, tests fitting this description had been developed prior to that time. Essentially, a situational test is one that places the test taker in a situation closely resembling or simulating a "real life" criterion situation. Such tests thus show certain basic similarities to the job-sample techniques employed in constructing occupational achievement tests and to the performance-based assessments of educational achievement, both of which are described in chapter 17. In the present tests, however, the criterion behavior that is sampled is usually more varied and complex. Moreover, performance is evaluated primarily in terms of emotional, interpersonal, attitudinal, and other personality variables, rather than in terms of abilities and knowledge.

Tests of the Character Education Inquiry. Among the earliest situational tests—although they were not so labeled at the time—were those constructed by Hartshorne, May, and their associates (1928, 1929, 1930) for the Character Education Inquiry (CEI). These tests were designed principally as research instruments for use in an extensive project on the nature and development of character in children. Nevertheless, the techniques can be adapted to other testing purposes, and a number have been so utilized.

In general, the CEI techniques made use of familiar, natural situations within the schoolchild's daily routine. The tests were administered in the form of regular classroom examinations, as part of the pupil's homework, in the course of athletic contests, or as party games. Moreover, the children were not aware that they were being tested, except insofar as ordinary school examinations might be involved in the procedure. At the same time, all of the Hartshorne-May tests represented carefully standardized instruments which yielded objective, quantitative scores.

The CEI tests were designed, in novel and ingenious ways, to measure such behavior characteristics as honesty, self-control, and altruism. The largest number were concerned with honesty and involved situations in which the children were made to believe that they could cheat without being detected. In the

Circles Puzzle, for example, the child was instructed to make a mark in each of 10 small, irregularly arranged circles, while keeping her or his eyes shut. Control tests under conditions that precluded peeking indicated that a score of more than 13 correctly placed marks in a total of three trials was highly improbable. A score above 13 was therefore recorded as evidence of peeking.

Most of the CEI tests proved to have good discriminative power, yielding a wide range of individual differences in scores. Reliability also appeared to be fairly satisfactory. The children's responses, however, showed considerable situational specificity. The intercorrelations of different tests within each category (e.g., honesty tests or persistence tests) proved to be very low. This specificity is understandable when we consider the operations of the child's interests, values, and motives in different situations. For example, the child who is motivated to excel in schoolwork is not necessarily concerned about achievement in athletic contests or party games. These motivational differences would in turn be reflected in the child's behavior on honesty tests administered in these different contexts. Both in their findings and in their interpretations, the CEI investigators anticipated the emphasis on situational specificity by four decades. However, subsequent reanalyses of the CEI data have suggested that a more appropriate model includes both a general factor of honesty and a situational component and that there is even some evidence for a general factor of moral character (Burton, 1963; Rushton, 1984).[7]

Situational Tests in Assessment Centers and Roleplaying Techniques. Situational tests constituted a major part of the assessment-center program introduced by the United States Office of Strategic Services (OSS) during World War II. The assessment-center technique involves essentially a "living-in" period of several days, during which candidates are observed and examined in a variety of ways. It represented the principal procedure in the selection of military personnel for critical overseas assignments (Murray & MacKinnon, 1946; OSS Assessment Staff, 1948). Similar procedures were subsequently incorporated in the Institute for Personality Assessment and Research at the University of California, as well as in a number of large-scale assessment projects for both military and civilian personnel.[8] Still later, the assessment-center technique, together with some situational tests, was adopted by large industrial corporations for the evaluation of high-level executives.

One type of test developed by the OSS was the *situational stress* test, designed to sample the individual's behavior under stressful, frustrating, or emotionally disruptive conditions. For example, the examinee was assigned a task to perform with two "helpers" who were obstructive and uncooperative. Another type of situational test employed a *leaderless group* as a device for appraising such characteristics as teamwork, resourcefulness, initiative, and leadership. In such tests, the assigned task requires the cooperative efforts of a group of examinees, none of whom is designated as leader or given specific responsibilities. Examples from the OSS program include the Brook Situation, involving the transfer of personnel

[7] For an interesting analysis of the role that the Hartshorne and May studies have played in the debate concerning the teaching of virtues and character development, see Vitz (1990).

[8] An account of these milestone assessment studies, beginning with the OSS program, can be found in J. S. Wiggins (1973/1988, chap. 11).

and equipment across a brook with maximum speed and safety; and the Wall Situation, in which people and materials had to be conveyed over a double wall separated by an imaginary canyon.

A variant of this technique is the Leaderless Group Discussion (LCD). Requiring a minimum of equipment and time, the LCD has been used widely in the selection of such groups as military officers, civil service supervisors and administrators, industrial executives and management trainees, sales trainees, teachers, and social workers. Essentially, the group is assigned a topic for discussion during a specified period. Examiners observe and rate each person's performance but do not participate in the discussion. Although often used under informal and unstandardized conditions, the LGD has been subjected to considerable research. Studies with this technique suggest that, especially when raters are properly trained, it can be an effective tool for predicting performance in jobs requiring verbal communication, verbal problem solving, and acceptance by peers (Bass, 1954; Greenwood & McNamara, 1967; Guilford, 1959; Thornton & Zorich, 1980).

Some situational tests employ *roleplaying* or improvisation to elicit the behavior of interest. In fact, the previously cited leaderless group discussions, as well as certain other situational tests, may be regarded as variants or elaborations of roleplaying. Although roleplaying was one of the techniques used in the OSS assessment program, it has earlier origins and wider applications. A comprehensive survey of the history, rationale, and varieties of the roleplaying or improvisation technique can be found in McReynolds and DeVoge (1978). In this technique, the individual is explicitly instructed to play a part, either overtly (with or without other persons) or by reporting verbally what he or she would do or say. The situation may be presented realistically, as on a stage, or through audiotape, videotape, or printed description.[9]

The improvisation technique continues to enjoy great popularity, although much of its use is informal and tailored to specific settings and local conditions. One major application is in the occupational assessment of personnel, especially when interpersonal behavior is important in job functions (Stricker, 1982; Stricker & Rock, 1990). A special example pertains to the evaluation of counselor effectiveness. In this situation, the prospective counselor is observed—or videotaped—while conducting a counseling session with a "coached client," that is, a staff member or fellow student in the role of a client who presents a preselected and standardized problem (see, e.g., Connor, 1994, pp.72–75; Kelz, 1966; Neufeldt, Iversen, & Juntunen, 1995; A. Williams, 1995). When videotaping is used, a trainee can monitor and evaluate her or his own performances, in addition to being rated by assessors and peers.[10]

[9] Multimedia and interactive computer technologies allow entirely new ways of presenting realistic stimulus situations and response options to test takers. For a discussion of possibilities and problems in developing multimedia tests and a description of an interactive video instrument measuring conflict resolution skills, see Drasgow, Olson-Buchanan, and Moberg (1996) and Olson-Buchanan, Drasgow, Moberg, Mead, and Keenan (1996).

[10] In clinical psychology, roleplaying has undergone extensive and systematic development within several different theoretical orientations, particularly in behavior modification programs, family therapy, and marriage counseling.

Assessment-center techniques have repeatedly proved to be effective predictors of a variety of criteria (see, e.g., Coulton & Feild, 1995; Howard & Bray, 1988; Ritchie, 1994; Tziner, Ronen, & Hacohen, 1993). They have been extensively used in fields in which selection criteria are complex, such as law enforcement work (J. L. Coleman, 1987; Moore & Unsinger, 1987). Some work has even been done on adapting these techniques for use with deaf job applicants (Berkay, 1993). Because of the breadth of their applicability, we cannot generalize about the validity of *the* assessment-center technique; the results differ from one center to another, depending upon the specific procedures employed, the nature of the criterion, and the qualifications of the assessors. In general, validity coefficients tend to be highest when methodologies are soundest—such as in studies that use several devices, including peer evaluations—and focus on relevant and directly observable behavioral dimensions (Gaugler, Rosenthal, Thornton, & Bentson, 1987; Shore, Shore, & Thornton, 1992; Thornton & Byham, 1982). In spite of extensive research, a number of questions about assessment-center techniques remain unanswered. Probably the most vexing question of all pertains to the inability of several investigations to demonstrate convergent validity across different methods of assessing particular dimensions of performance.[11]

SELF-CONCEPTS AND PERSONAL CONSTRUCTS

The 1980s and 1990s have witnessed a resurgence of interest in the self-concept and related constructs (Byrne, 1996; Harter, 1990; Hattie, 1992; Markus & Wurf, 1987; Oosterwegel & Oppenheimer, 1993; Wylie, 1989).[12] Several current approaches to personality assessment concentrate on the way individuals view themselves and others. Such techniques often reflect the influence of phenomenological psychology, which focuses on how events are *perceived* by the individual. The individual's self-description thus becomes of primary importance in its own right, rather than being regarded as a second-best substitute for other behavioral observations. Interest also centers on the extent of self-acceptance shown by the individual.

The procedures considered in this section all have as their primary focus individuals' perceptions of themselves and others. Although a few instruments are published tests, many were developed for use in specific research projects and are available in the published reports of these projects. Some are of interest chiefly because of their association with particular theories of personality or with an active area of ongoing research. Others are widely applicable techniques used in studying a variety of problems.

Washington University Sentence Completion Test. It might be argued that self-concept tests do not differ essentially from the self-report inventories discussed in chapter 13. True, but it would be more accurate to say that self-report inventories are actually measures of self-concept. The interpretation of inventory responses in terms of self-conceptualization forms the basis of the theoretical

[11] For brief but informative reviews of assessment-center research, see Landy, Shankster, and Kohler (1994, pp. 277–278), and Schmidt, Ones, and Hunter (1992, pp. 635–637).

[12] An overview of the philosophical and psychological approaches to the self and self-related processes, from the 17th through the 20th centuries, can be found in Levin (1992).

approach to personality development formulated by Loevinger (1966a, 1966b, 1976, 1987, 1993; Loevinger & Ossorio, 1958). Bringing together many disparate findings from her own research and that of others, Loevinger proposed a personality trait that she defined as the capacity to conceptualize oneself, or to "assume distance" from oneself and one's impulses. According to Loevinger, it is the manifestations of this trait in personality inventories that have been described in such terms as facade, test-taking defensiveness, response set, social desirability, acquiescence, and personal style. In common with a number of other psychologists, Loevinger regards such test-taking attitudes not as instrumental errors to be ruled out but as the major source of valid variance in personality inventories.

On the basis of data from many sources, Loevinger suggested that ability to form a self-concept increases with age, intelligence, education, and socioeconomic level. At the lowest point, illustrated by the infant, the individual is incapable of self-conceptualization. As the ability develops, the child gradually forms a stereotyped, conventional, and socially acceptable concept of herself or himself. This stage Loevinger considers typical of adolescence. With increasing maturity, the individual progresses beyond such a stereotyped concept to a differentiated and realistic self-concept. At this point, individuals are fully aware of their idiosyncrasies and accept themselves for what they are.

It is this trait of self-conceptualization, designated as ego development or ego level, that Loevinger and her associates undertook to measure in the Washington University Sentence Completion Test (WUSCT—Loevinger, 1985, 1987; Loevinger & Wessler, 1970; Loevinger, Wessler, & Redmore, 1970). The authors' theoretical framework postulates nine levels of ego development, as follows: Pre-social, Impulsive, Self-Protective, Conformist, Self-Aware, Conscientious, Individualistic, Autonomous, and Integrated. All but the first level, which precedes the emergence of verbal skills, can be assessed through the WUSCT. Each sentence completion is assigned an ego level rating, and a composite score on the entire test is computed from these values. The WUSCT was based on research conducted with women and adolescent girls and was later adapted for use with men and boys. The test has since been revised and now provides comparable forms for men and women (Loevinger, 1985; Novy, 1992). A new scoring manual presents data for both females and males (Hy & Loevinger, 1996).

Continuing research with the WUSCT has provided evidence supporting its reliability (Novy & Francis, 1992; Weiss, Zillberg, & Genevro, 1989) and its validity as a measure of the construct of ego development among various samples (Bushe & Gibbs, 1990; Novy, Gaa, Frankiewicz, Liberman, & Amerikaner, 1992; Westenberg & Block, 1993). A particularly fruitful application of the instrument has been in the study of sex differences in ego development (Cohn, 1991). One of the few problematic aspects of the WUSCT, shared by other sentence completion tests and techniques that allow for open-ended verbal responses, is that its scores tend to correlate with, and may in some cases be influenced by, verbal fluency and vocabulary level (see, e.g., Vaillant & McCullough, 1987; Westenberg & Block, 1993). Although this possibility needs to be taken into account in designing research with the WUSCT, as well as in other uses of the test, it is consonant with its theoretical underpinnings and need not invalidate results.

Self-Esteem Inventories and Related Measures. In an ever-expanding body of research, the construct of self-concept merges with certain related constructs designated as self-esteem (Baumeister, 1993; Bednar & Peterson, 1995) and perceived self-efficacy (Bandura, 1982, 1995; Maddux, 1995; Schwarzer, 1992). A major thrust of this research relates to the effect of the individual's self-evaluation on her or his performance. Self-esteem is, in fact, typically described as the evaluative component of the self-concept. On a long-tenn, cumulative basis, such self-evaluations may influence the development of cognitive and affective traits. In particular, there is widespread agreement that self-esteem is a crucial determinant of such psychologically important variables as coping ability and sense of well-being.

The construct of self-esteem is, at first glance, deceptively simple. It is often assumed to be a general evaluative attitude toward oneself, ranging from extremely positive to extremely negative, that is stable and entirely subjective in nature. The measurement of self-esteem for research and applied purposes has traditionally proceeded on the basis of these assumptions. So much so, in fact, that Blascovich and Tomaka (1991) in their comprehensive review of measures of self-esteem and self-concept identified Rosenberg's (1965) Self-Esteem Scale (SES)—a ten-item, face valid, self-report scale—as the most frequently used measure of its kind.

Simple and obvious measures of global self-esteem, like the SES, do appear to be relatively stable over time and may be useful as a gauge of general self-regard for some purposes. Nevertheless, many investigators have found that the relation between self-concept and behavior can be more clearly demonstrated if the former is viewed as a hierarchical, multidimensional construct and is assessed accordingly (Fleming & Courtney, 1984; Marsh, Byrne, & Shavelson, 1992; Marsh & Shavelson, 1985; Shavelson & Bolus, 1982; Shavelson, Hubner, & Stanton, 1976; Uguroglu & Walberg, 1979). Under certain circumstances, the use of a single, global self-esteem measure may yield inconsistent results or fail to reveal significant correlations with other variables, whereas a more narrowly defined construct, such as academic self-concept, will yield consistent and significant results. This is especially true with those persons for whom academic achievement may not rank high in the personal value system. In such cases, a high global self-concept, slanted to reflect the respondent's own value system, may not correlate significantly with academic achievement or intellectual functioning. Furthermore, research indicates that measures of "experienced self-esteem," based on self-reports, and measures of "presented self-esteem," based on the reports of others, do not always correlate (Demo, 1985).

As a result of these findings, research in recent years, has shifted away from unidimensional conceptualizations of self-esteem and toward studies of its specific facets, and it has proliferated rapidly. Especially numerous are investigations of the relationship between academic self-concept and academic achievement in children and adolescents. In this particular area, studies using sophisticated methodologies—such as structural equation modeling and longitudinal designs that allow for the analysis of the direction of causal relations—have supported the notion that academic self-concepts are linked to specific fields of study. More importantly, they have shown that these concepts correlate with, predict, and influence subsequent academic achievement (Fortier, Vallerand, & Guay, 1995; House, 1995; Lyon & MacDonald, 1990; H. W. Marsh, 1990a, 1990b).

The newest measures of self-concept make use of the extensive theoretical and empirical literature that has accumulated in this area. The Student Self-Concept Scale (SSCS—Gresham, Elliott, & Evans-Fernandez, 1993), for example, is a commercially available measure that uses Bandura's (1982, 1986) theory of self efficacy as a starting point and draws from other theories and research findings as well. It assesses three major domains of self-concept, namely, academic, social, and self-image. Within each of these domains, respondents indicate not only how confident they are that they are able to do what the items state but also how important the items are to them and how confident they are that having certain attributes or doing certain things will lead to certain outcomes. The SSCS produces both subscale and composite scores that are norm-referenced, separately, for female and male students at the elementary and high school levels.

A similar, albeit not commercially available, measure—the Personal and Academic Self-Concept Inventory (PASCI—Fleming & Whalen, 1990)—was developed using high school and college students. This measure attempts to operationalize and further investigate the hierarchical, multifaceted model of self-concept developed by Shavelson and his colleagues. The PASCI is the fourth revision and expansion of an experimental scale originally developed in the 1950s to assess feelings of inadequacy.[13] The current version consists of a global self-esteem scale and six additional facet scales. Of these, two deal with social aspects of the self-concept (Social Acceptance and Social Anxiety), two pertain to its physical aspects (Physical Appearance and Physical Ability), and the two remaining are academic (Math Ability and Verbal Ability). The SSCS and the PASCI are, of course, subject to the response biases inherent in all self-report measures and discussed in chapter 13. Moreover, they both still need to document their effectiveness further, within the contexts for which they were developed. However, from the point of view of construct differentiation and content specification, they are representative of the advances that have been made in the conceptualization and measurement of self-esteem.

The Adjective Check List. Several broadly oriented techniques have been developed specifically for assessing self-concepts. A widely applicable instrument that is commercially available is the Adjective Check List (ACL). Originally constructed for use in the research program of the Institute for Personality Assessment and Research (IPAR), this instrument provides a list of 300 adjectives arranged alphabetically from "absentminded" to "zany" (Gough, 1960; Gough & Heilbrun, 1983). Respondents mark all the adjectives they consider descriptive of themselves.

In its current form, the ACL can be scored for 37 scales, four of which assess response sets. A major cluster of scales was originally prepared on a rational or content basis, by assigning adjectives to each of the 15 Murray needs covered by

---

[13] Blascovich and Tomaka (1991) provide a summary of the evolution of this instrument, as well as reviews of many other self-esteem, measures. Shavelson's model has been one of the most influential in the field and was also used in the conceptualization of the SSCS. For information on the model, see Marsh et al., (1992), Marsh and Shavelson (1985), Shavelson and Bolus (1982), and Shavelson et al., (1976).

the EPPS (see chap. 13). An additional set of nine "topical scales" was developed principally through empirical criterion keying of items to measure various traits considered important in interpersonal behavior. The two remaining clusters of scales were designed to fit specialized personality theories, namely, Berne's (1961, 1966) Transactional Analysis theory and Welsh's (1975b) theory of creativity and intelligence. For all 37 scales, a principal source of empirical validation data, employed at some stage in the development of each scale, was the direct observation of participants in assessment-center programs at IPAR and the resulting trait ratings. On the basis of these IPAR assessments as well as other supplementary research, the manual provides personality descriptions of persons scoring high and low on each scale.

As a research instrument, the ACL has been applied to a staggering variety of problems, drawn from such areas as psychopathology, occupational choice, creativity, political and economic behavior, and even patients' reactions to orthodontia and to contact lenses. It has also been employed in rating historical personages from their biographies and published works (Welsh, 1975a) and in characterizing inanimate objects, such as cities and automobiles. More recently, the ACL has been used in studies of the developmental changes in women at midlife (Helson & Wink, 1992; Wink & Helson, 1993; York & John, 1992), and in investigations of narcissism (Wink, 1991, 1992), among others (for reviews, see Teeter, 1985; Zarske, 1985).[14]

Q Sort. Another special technique suitable for investigating self-concepts is the Q sort, originally developed by Stephenson (1953) to implement an approach to research known as Q methodology (see, e.g., Kerlinger, 1986, chap. 32; McKeown & Thomas, 1988). In the Q sort technique, the respondent is given a set of cards containing statements or trait names to be sorted into piles ranging from "most characteristic" to "least characteristic" of herself or himself. The items may come from a standard list, but more often they are designed to fit the individual case. To ensure uniform distribution of ratings, a "forced normal" distribution is used, the respondent being instructed to place a specified number of cards in each pile. Such a distribution can be prepared for any size of item sample by reference to a normal curve table. It should be noted that, like the forced-choice technique discussed in chapter 13, the Q sort yields ipsative rather than normative data. In other words, respondents tell us which they consider their strong and which their weak traits, but not how strong they believe themselves to be in comparison with other persons or with some outside norm.

Q sorts have been employed to study a variety of psychological problems (Bem & Funder, 1978; Block, 1961/1978; Kogan & Block, 1991; Ozer, 1993; Rogers & Dymond, 1954). In intensive investigations of individual personality, the respondent is often asked to re-sort the same set of items within different frames of reference. For example, the items may be sorted as they apply to oneself and to other persons, such as one's father, mother, husband, or wife. Or they may be sorted as they apply to oneself in different settings, such as job, home, or social situations. Q sorts can likewise be obtained for individuals as they believe

[14] A complete bibliography of the ACL through 1980 is available from the test publisher (Gough & Heilbrun, 1980).

they actually are (real self), as they believe others see them (social self), and as they would like to be (ideal self). To observe change, Q sorts may be obtained successively at different stages during psychotherapy, a procedure that has been followed especially by client-centered therapists. With therapy, the self-concept tends to become more favorable and to resemble more closely the individual's ideal self-concept (Rogers & Dymond, 1954, chap. 4).[15]

The Semantic Differential. This technique was first developed by Osgood and his associates (Osgood, Suci, & Tannenbaum, 1957) as a tool for research on the psychology of meaning, although its possibilities for personality assessment were soon recognized. The Semantic Differential represents a standardized and quantified procedure for measuring the connotations of any given concept for the individual. Each concept is rated on a 7-point graphic scale as being more closely related to one or the other of a pair of opposites, as illustrated in Figure 16–3. For every concept, a series of these bipolar adjectival scales is employed; usually 15 or more scales are included. Intercorrelations and factorial analyses of the original set of 50 scales developed by Osgood revealed three major factors: *Evaluative,* with high loadings in such scales as goodbad, valuable–worthless, and clean-dirty; *Potency,* found in such scales as strong-weak, large–small, and heavy–light; and *Activity,* identified in such scales as active–passive, fast–slow, and sharp–dull. The evaluative factor is the most conspicuous, accounting for the largest percentage of total variance.

Responses on the Semantic Differential can be analyzed in several ways. For quantitative treatment, the ratings on each scale can be assigned numerical values from 1 to 7, or from –3 to +3. The overall similarity of any two concepts

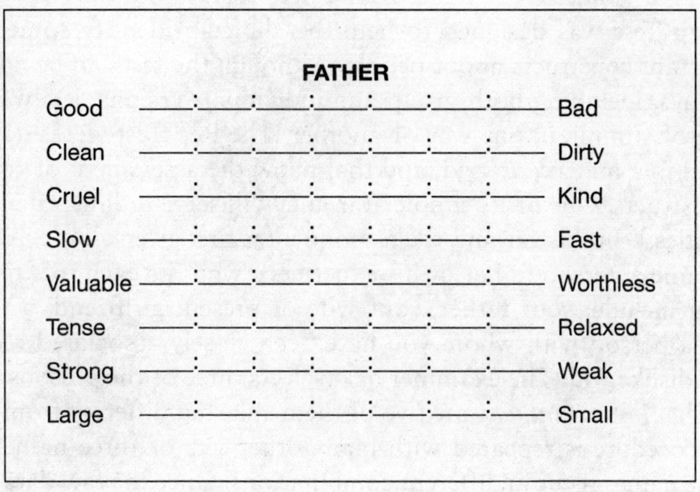

Figure 16–3. Illustration of the Semantic Differential Technique. In rating the concept "Father," the respondent places a check mark on the appropriate segment of each scale. Usually a much larger number of scales is employed.

[15] All these procedures can, of course, he followed also with the previously described Adjective Check List or with any other techniques for assessing self-concepts. In addition, Q sorts and checklists can he used to report observers' evaluation as discussed later in this chapter.

for an individual or a group can then be measured in terms of their positions on all scales. The connotations of all concepts rated by a single individual can be investigated by computing the "score" of each concept in the three principal factors described above. Thus, on a scale extending from –3 to +3, a given individual's concept of "My Brother" may rate –2 in the evaluative factor, 0.1 in potency, and 2.7 in activity.

The concepts to be rated can be chosen to fit whatever problem is being investigated. Respondents can, for example, be asked to rate themselves, members of their family, friends, employers, teachers, or public figures; members of different ethnic or cultural groups; persons engaged in different occupations; activities, such as studying or outdoor sports; abstract ideas, such as confusion, hatred, sickness, peace, or love; product names or brand names; and radio or television programs. The Semantic Differential has been applied in many different contexts, in research on such varied problems as clinical diagnosis and therapy, vocational choices, cultural differences, and consumers' reactions to products and brand names (Snider & Osgood, 1969). Moreover, further refinements of the technique itself continue to be made as well (see, e.g., Cogliser & Schriesheim, 1994). The bibliography on the Semantic Differential includes more than 2,000 references.

Role Construct Repertory Test. A technique devised specifically as an aid in clinical practice is the Role Construct Repertory Test (Rep Test) developed by G. A. Kelly (1955, 1963, 1970). The development of the Rep Test is intimately related to Kelly's personality theory. A basic proposition in this theory is that the concepts or constructs an individual uses to perceive objects or events influence her or his behavior. In the course of psychotherapy, it is frequently necessary to build new constructs and to discard some old constructs before progress can be made.

The Rep Test was designed to help the clinician identify some of the client's important constructs about people. Although the test can be administered in many ways, including both group and individual versions, it always involves the sorting of stimuli, in one way or another. The Rep Test yields data that can be arranged in a matrix, or grid, and that allow the assessment of relationships among constructs. One of its simpler variants will serve to illustrate its essential characteristics.[16] In this variant, the respondent is first given a Role Title List and asked to name a person in her or his experience who fits each role title. Typical roles might include: your father, your wife or present girlfriend, a teacher you liked, and a person with whom you have been closely associated recently who appears to dislike you. The examiner next selects three of the persons named and asks, "In what *important way* are two of them alike but different from the third?"

This procedure is repeated with many other sets of three names, in which some of the names recur in different combinations. Once the raw data of relevant constructs have been generated in this fashion and organized in grid form, their implications can be analyzed. Although the Rep Test yields a wealth of qualitative data, many quantitative procedures also have been developed to establish how important the elicited constructs are to the individual. These procedures range from simple descriptive statistics to highly complex structural analyses.

[16] For descriptions of other procedural variants, see Bannister and Mair (1968), Beail (1985), Landfield and Epting (1987), G. J. Neimeyer (1989), and Winter (1992).

Software programs are available to aid in both the content and structural analyses of protocols (see, e.g., Winter, 1992).

The Rep Test, in its various modifications, has been used in a considerable amount of research on problems relating to, among other things, personality theory, social cognition, education, and communication, as well as to psychotherapy and assessment. Among the indices derived from the respondent's classifications of familiar persons is one designated as *cognitive complexity.* This index is based on the number of different constructs employed by an individual and is regarded as a measure of cognitive style. A higher degree of cognitive complexity means that the individual employs more dimensions, and hence a more differentiated cognitive system, in organizing or representing the environment (Bieri, 1971; Bieri et al., 1966; Goldstein & Blackman, 1978a, pp. 483–487; 1978b). However, cognitive complexity itself is a multifaceted construct, and its degree of correlation with other variables depends to a large extent on how it is conceptualized and measured (see, e.g., Goldsmith & Nugent, 1984).

After a period of relative dormancy, the 1980s witnessed a resurgence of interest in Kelly's personal construct theory, and research within its framework has continued at an increasing pace since then (Bannister, 1985; Burr & Butt, 1992; Epting & Landfield, 1985; Fransella & Thomas, 1988; G. J. Neimeyer & R. A. Neimeyer, 1990; R. A. Neimeyer & G. J. Neimeyer, 1992). Kelly's theory also has been used as one of the pillars of constructivism.[17] Because it is ideally suited to investigating the unique ways in which the individual derives and organizes meaning, the Rep Test itself has undergone extensive use in recent years. Investigators are now applying more sophisticated statistical techniques, such as hierarchical cluster analysis and multidimensional scaling, in analyzing repertory grid data (see, e.g., Merluzzi, 1991; Ogilvie & Ashmore, 1991). The technique, however, is subject to so many variations that generalizations about its effectiveness and psychometric properties cannot be made.

Perceived Environment and Social Climate. The concept of the environment enters into psychology in many ways.[18] We have already considered the significant role that observers' assessment of the environment can play in the context of testing special populations (chap. 9), as well as the impact that cultural and situational variables have on the expression of cognitive and affective traits (chaps. 9, 11, 12, & 13). From a phenomenological perspective, the assessment of environments and social climates through the reported perceptions of the persons within each milieu can also contribute significantly to the understanding of individuals and groups.

A number of measures have been devised to describe and evaluate physical and social aspects of the environment (for reviews of several of these, see Walsh &. Betz, 1995, chap. 11). The ten Social Climate Scales, developed by Rudolph H.

[17] Constructivism is a lively and rather controversial movement within psychology that sees human beings as proactive agents whose major endeavor is to make meaning out of experience and calls for multiple perspectives on knowledge—beyond positivism (Gergen, 1985; Mahoney, 1991; G. J. Neimeyer, 1993; R. A. Neimeyer & Mahoney, 1995).

[18] In fact, after three decades of activity, the study of environment and behavior is a multidisciplinary field that is flourishing not only in the United States but also around the world (see, e.g., Bonnes & Secchiaroli, 1995; Groat, 1995; McAndrew, 1993; Stokols, 1995; Stokols & Altman, 1987).

Moos (1974, 1993a, 1993b, 1993c, 1994a; Moos & Spinrad, 1984) at Stanford University, are among the most frequently used and versatile instruments of this type. The Social Climate Scales are applicable in the following contexts: hospital-based and community psychiatric treatment programs, sheltered care and correctional facilities, military settings, university student residences, high school classrooms, work milieus, and families; there is also a more general group environment scale for task-oriented, social, and mutual support groups. Most of the scales consist of 90 or 100 true–false items with which the respondent describes her or his perception of the given environment. Items were originally prepared to tap theoretically chosen environmental dimensions, such as press toward involvement, autonomy, or order; final items were empirically selected on the basis of their ability to discriminate among contexts, as well as their internal consistency within sub-scales. Each of the ten scales has been revised and updated one or more times (Moos, 1994b; Moos & Moos, 1994; Trickett & Moos, 1995). The Social Climate Scales can be administered in three different forms which measure (a) actual perceptions of the real environment, (b) perceptions of an ideal environment, and (c) expectations about an unknown environment of a certain type.

Each environmental context is described in terms of 7 to 10 subscale scores that assess various dimensions of the environment. Several of these dimensions recur in the scales for different contexts. In fact, despite the wide diversity of contexts covered by the Social Climate Scales, the subscales in each context all fit into the same tripartite classification, including (1) Relationship Dimensions (e.g., Involvement, Support, Peer Cohesion); (2) Personal Growth Dimensions (e.g., Autonomy, Task Orientation, Competition); and (3) System Maintenance and Change Dimensions (e.g., Order & Organization, Clarity, Innovation). It is also noteworthy that the Social Climate Scales were designed for relatively small units within complex and heterogeneous institutions—for example, a classroom rather than a whole school, a treatment program rather than a whole hospital, a university residence center rather than a whole university. In this respect, these scales yield more readily interpretable and less ambiguous data than would be obtained from a composite assessment of an entire organization. Although the *User's Guide* for the Social Climate Scales (Moos, 1994a) indicates that they may be applied in clinical assessment, organizational consulting, and program evaluation, several reviewers believe that the scales are more suitable for research on the determinants and consequences of perceptions about the environment (Allison, 1995; Loyd, 1995; R. O. Mueller, 1995; Saudargas, 1989; Sheehan, 1995; C. R. Smith, 1989).

OBSERVER REPORTS

The tests considered thus far give ample evidence of the variety of approaches that have been followed in the assessment of personality. Yet the best that can be said about most of them is that they are promising experimental techniques suitable for research purposes or useful instruments when interpreted by a skilled clinician in conjunction with other information about the person. It is apparent that for the assessment of personality one cannot rely entirely on standardized tests. Other sources of information are needed to follow up or supplement the leads provided by test scores, to assess traits for which no adequate tests are available, and to obtain criterion data for developing and validating personality tests.

Direct observations of behavior play an essential part in personality appraisal, whether in the clinic, counseling center, classroom, personnel office, or any other context calling for individual evaluations. To place such behavioral observations in the proper perspective, we must remember that all tests are themselves evaluations of small samples of behavior. To be sure, these behavior samples are obtained and evaluated under standardized conditions. But against the obvious advantages of such standardized procedures, we must balance the advantages of a much more extensive sampling of behavior available through observational techniques in natural settings. To take an extreme example, if we had a detailed biography of a person extending from birth to age 30, we could probably predict her or his subsequent behavior more accurately than could be done with any test or battery of tests. Such a record of all the minutiae and circumstances of a person's life would be hard to come by; but if we had it, we could make predictions from a 30-year behavior sample rather than from the one-or two-hour samples provided by tests.

In all the techniques to be considered in this section, what the individual does in natural contexts over relatively long periods of time is transmitted through the medium of one or more observers. Much can be done to improve the accuracy and communicability of such observations.

Naturalistic Observation. Techniques for the direct observation of spontaneous behavior in natural settings have been employed most widely by child psychologists, particularly with preschool children. Although such procedures can be followed with persons of any age, the younger the individual the less likely it is that the behavior of interest will be affected by the presence of the observer or that the individual will have developed the social fapades that complicate the interpretation of behavior. These observational techniques have also proved useful in the classroom, especially if the observer is the teacher or someone else who fits readily into the normal school setting. A major application of such assessment techniques is to be found in behavior modification programs conducted in schools, homes, child care centers, clinics, hospitals, or any other context (Hartmann & Wood, 1990; Kent & Foster, 1977; Lalli & Goh, 1993). Several ingenious applications of naturalistic observation have also been devised for social psychology (Webb, Campbell, Schwartz, Sechrest, & Grove, 1981) and cross-cultural research (Bochner, 1986).

Naturalistic observation covers a wide variety of procedures (Adler & Adler, 1994; Jones, Reid, & Patterson, 1975; Sattler, 1988, chap. 17). They range from comprehensive long-term techniques, as illustrated by the diary method, to more narrowly circumscribed, shorter, and more highly controlled observations, as illustrated by time sampling. The latter comprises a representative distribution of short observation periods. Depending on the nature and purpose of the observations, such periods may vary in length from less than a minute to several hours; periods of five minutes or less are the most common. The observations may be concentrated in one day or spaced over several months. They may cover all behavior occurring during the specified period; but more often they are limited to a particular kind of behavior, such as language, locomotion, interpersonal behavior, or aggression. Checklists of what to look for are a useful observational aid. Other procedural aids include observational schedules, record forms, coding systems, and mechanical recording devices (W. W. Tryon, 1985, chaps. 7 & 8). When practicable, recordings can be made on audiotape, film, or videotape.[19] Portable microcomputer systems that allow enhancements in the collection and analysis of observation data are available as well (Kratochwill, Doll, & Dickson, 1991, pp. 137–141; Repp & Felce, 1990).

It might be noted that naturalistic observations have much in common with the previously discussed situational tests. They differ principally in two respects: In naturalistic observations, no control is exerted over the stimulus situation, and— at least in most observational methods—a more extensive behavior sample is observed. Interest in research on naturalistic observation techniques is on the rise, especially in reference to their ecological validity and their usefulness in assessing changes over time (see, e.g., Barkley, 1991; Kaminer, Feinstein, & Seifer, 1995).

The Interview. Mention should also be made of the time-honored source of information provided by interviewing techniques. Interviewing serves many purposes in clinical psychology, counseling, personnel psychology, and education. Discussions of the methods, applications, and effectiveness of interviewing, and of research on the interviewing process, can be found in many sources.[20] In form, interviews may vary from the highly structured (representing little more than an orally administered questionnaire), through patterned or guided interviews covering certain predetermined areas, to nondirective and depth interviews in which the interviewer merely sets the stage and encourages the interviewee to talk as freely as possible. The use of structured interviews for both clinical and research purposes in the area of psychiatric diagnosis is now commonplace. These instruments are standardized and typically provide quantitative scores in addition to diagnostic classifications; thus, they have to be evaluated by the same psychometric standards of reliability and validity that apply to all tests. For reviews of various structured interview protocols, see Hodges and Zeman (1993), Kamphaus and Frick (1996, chap. 12), and Rogers (1995).

Interviews provide chiefly two kinds of information. First, they afford an opportunity for direct observation of a rather limited sample of behavior manifested during the interview situation itself. For example, the individual's speech, language usage, poise, and manner in meeting a stranger can be noted. A second—and perhaps more important—function of interviewing, however, is to elicit life-history data. What the individual has done in the past is a good indicator of what he or she may do in the future, especially when interpreted in light

---

[19] An unusually comprehensive example of an assessment system based largely on observational data, is the one devised by Gottman (1994, 1996) for the analysis of marital relationship processes. The system, which includes elements reminiscent of the assessment-center methodology, was developed and tested through a long-term program of research aimed at isolating the factors that predict the eventual outcome of a marriage.

[20] The extensive literature on interviewing includes periodic surveys of relevant research (Eder, Kacmar, & Ferris, 1989; Graves, 1993; Groth-Marnat, 1990, chap. 3; Landy et al, 1994; McDaniel, Whetzel, Schmidt, & Maurer, 1994), as well as interviewing guides and recommendations for improving interviewing procedures, especially in clinical practice (Bierman, 1990; Lukas, 1993; Morrison, 1995; Rogers, 1995; Shea, 1988) and in personnel selection (Fear & Chiron, 1990; Webster, 1982). A model for teaching and learning the basic skills that are applicable across most interview settings can be found in Gorden (1992).

of concomitant circumstances and of the person's own comments regarding her or his actions. The interview should concern itself not only with what has happened to the individual but also with her or his perceptions of these events and current evaluations of them.

On the interviewer's part, the interview requires skill in gathering and in interpreting data. An interview may lead to wrong decisions because important information was not elicited or because given data were inadequately or incorrectly interpreted. A critical qualification of the successful interviewer is sensitivity in identifying clues in the interviewee's behavior or in facts he or she reports. Such clues then lead to further probing for other facts that may either support or contradict the original hypothesis.

Ratings. Although ratings may be obtained in many contexts and for diverse purposes, the present section is concerned with the use of ratings as an evaluation of the individual by the rater on the basis of cumulative, uncontrolled observations of daily life. Such ratings differ from naturalistic observations in that the data are accumulated casually and informally; they also involve interpretation and judgment, rather than simple recording of observations. In contrast to both naturalistic observation and interviews, however, they typically cover a longer observation period, and the information is obtained under more realistic conditions. Ratings are used extensively in assessing individuals in educational and industrial settings, in obtaining criterion data for test validation, and for many research purposes. Since the 1970s, there has been a significant upsurge of research on rating techniques, with emphasis on comprehensive, systematic investigations and sufficient standardization of definitions and procedures to facilitate comparison of findings across studies (Borman, 1991; Landy & Farr, 1983; Ozer & Reise, 1994, pp. 370–371; Saal, Downey, & Lahey, 1980; Sulsky & Balzer, 1988).

Much can be done to improve the accuracy of ratings. A common difficulty arises from ambiguity in either trait names, scale units, or both. To meet this problem, each trait should be defined in specific terms, and the ratings should be expressed in a form that will be uniformly interpreted by all raters. Rather than using numbers or general descriptive adjectives that convey different meanings to different raters, degrees of a trait may be more clearly identified in terms of carefully formulated behavioral anchors (Dickinson & Zellinger, 1980). There is also evidence that the relative accuracy of different scale formats may vary with the nature of the job or the performance function to be rated (Borman, 1979; J. M. Feldman, 1986).

One of the conditions that affect the validity of ratings is the extent of the rater's *relevant contact* with the person to be rated (Freeberg, 1969; Landy & Farr, 1980; Paulhus & Bruce, 1992; Wiggins & Pincus, 1992, pp. 493–496). It is not enough to have known the person for a long time; the rater should have had an opportunity to observe her or him in situations in which the behavior in question could be manifested. For example, if an employee has never had an opportunity to make decisions on the job, her or his ability to do so cannot be evaluated by the supervisor. In many rating situations, it is desirable to include a space to be checked in lieu of a rating if the rater has had no opportunity to observe the particular trait in a given individual.

Ratings are subject to a number of errors.[21] A well-known example is the *halo effect*. Traditionally, this phenomenon has been defined as a tendency on the part of raters to be unduly influenced by a single favorable or unfavorable trait which colors their judgment of the individual's other traits. The presence of a halo effect is usually inferred from the observed intercorrelations among ratings assigned across different performance dimensions. Although the halo effect is still viewed in the traditional way—and as a unitary construct—by some investigators, several other possible ways of conceptualizing it and of defining it operationally have come to the fore (Balzer & Sulsky, 1992; Kozlowski, Kirsch, & Chao, 1986; Murphy & Anhalt, 1992; Nathan, 1986).[22]

Another error that can affect ratings data is the *error of central tendency,* or the tendency to place persons in the middle of the scale and to avoid extreme positions. Still another is the *leniency error,* referring to the reluctance of many raters to assign unfavorable ratings. The former causes a bunching of ratings in the center of the scale, the latter at the upper end. Both errors reduce the effective width of the scale and make ratings less discriminative. One way to eliminate these errors is to employ ranking or other *order-of-merit procedures* that force discrimination among individuals and hence maximize the information yielded by the ratings. Naturally, though, techniques that are applicable when comparisons are made within a single group do not permit direct comparisons across groups evaluated by different raters.

An unexpected finding of the cumulative research on rating errors has been that the relationship between measures of such errors as halo or leniency and other more direct indicators of the accuracy of ratings is far from simple and is often counterintuitive. Several investigators who have conducted meta-analytic research and reviewed the literature on rating errors have concluded that the conceptual and methodological problems inherent in appraisal of performance through ratings preclude the use of measures of such errors as a gauge of the accuracy of ratings (Balzer & Sulsky, 1992; Borman, 1991; Murphy & Anhalt, 1992; Murphy & Balzer, 1989).

Nevertheless, the rating process can usually be improved by training the raters. Research in various settings has demonstrated the effectiveness of training in increasing reliability and validity of ratings and in reducing common judgment errors (Bernardin & Buckley, 1981; McIntyre, Smith, & Hassett, 1984; Pulakos, 1986; Stamoulis & Hauenstein, 1993; Sulsky & Day, 1992, 1994). It should be noted, however, that many different types of training have been included in rater training programs, and their effects vary in kind, amount, and duration. Training may involve providing raters with a uniform reference standard by which to evaluate performance, analyzing common rating errors and ways of minimizing their influence, or improving observational skills. Any one or some combination of these and other types of training could be most appropriate for particular rating contexts and purposes. In most situations, however, enhancing the raters' observational skills is likely to yield favorable results.

[21] Much of the research on rating errors is reported in the *Journal of Applied Psychology.*

[22] Some of these other conceptualizations view halo error, at least partly, as a function of the ratee, and even of the specific context of the evaluation, as well as of the rater.

Clinical assessment often requires the collection of data from informants who are acquainted with the behavior patterns of the individual who is being assessed. Rating scales provide an efficient way of gathering such data and are particularly useful in the assessment of children and adolescents. A number of standardized scales for obtaining ratings from parents and teachers have been published in recent years and are now commercially available.[23] One particularly comprehensive example is the Behavior Assessment System for Children (BASC—Reynolds & Kamphaus, 1992). This system includes components for self-report and observer data in addition to the Teacher Rating Scales and Parent Rating Scales which are available in three forms, ranging from the preschool to the adolescent age levels (for a review, see R. B. Kline, 1994).

Nominating Technique. A rating procedure that is especially useful in obtaining peer assessments is the nominating technique. Originally developed in sociometry (J. L. Moreno, 1953) for investigating group structure, this technique may be used within any group of persons who have been together long enough to be acquainted with one another, as in a class, factory, club, or military unit. Each individual is asked to choose one or more group members with whom he or she would like to study, work, eat lunch, play, or carry out any other designated function. Respondents may be asked to nominate as many group members as they wish, or a specified number (such as first, second, and third choice), or only one person for each function.

When used for individual assessment, the nominations received by any one person can serve to identify potential leaders (who receive many choices) as well as isolates (who are rarely or never mentioned). In addition, several indices can be computed for a more precise assessment of each individual. The simplest is a count of the number of times an individual was nominated for a specific function, which can be treated as her or his peer rating. The nominating technique may be employed with reference to any behavior of interest. For example, respondents can be asked to name the person who has the most original ideas, who can be counted on to get the job done, or who is the best sport. They may be asked to designate not only the person who is most like the given description but also the one who is least like it. In that case, positive nominations would be weighted +1 and negative nominations −1 in totaling each person's score.[24] It should be added that peer assessments can also be obtained through other procedures such as ranking or rating; but the nominating technique seems to have proved most successful and has been used most often.

However obtained, peer assessments have generally emerged as one of the most dependable of rating techniques in such diverse groups as military personnel, industrial supervisors, Peace Corps volunteers, schoolchildren, and college students (Cole & White, 1993; Gresham & Little, 1993; Hughes, 1990; Kamphaus & Frick, 1996, chap. 10; Kane & Lawler, 1978; J. S. Wiggins, 1973/1988,

---

[23] Discussions of this type of instrument and reviews of several of them can be found in Kamphaus and Frick (1996), Piacentini (1993), and Witt, Heffer, and Pfeiffer (1990).

[24] When negative nominations are obtained, examiners should be particularly careful to prevent any potentially deleterious effects of the procedure. For a discussion of the ethics of peer-referenced assessment with children and adolescents, see Gresham and Little (1993, pp. 174–175) and Kamphaus and Frick (1996, pp. 201–203).

pp. 356–363). When checked against a variety of practical criteria dependent on interpersonal relations, such ratings usually have been found to have good concurrent and predictive validity. These findings are understandable when we consider some of the features of peer ratings. First, the number of raters is generally large, including all group members. Second, an individual's peers are often in a particularly favorable position to observe her or his typical behavior. They may thus be better judges of certain interpersonal traits than teachers, supervisors, and other outside observers. Third, and probably most important, is the fact that the opinions of group members—right or wrong— influence their actions and hence partly determine the nature of the individual's subsequent interactions with the group. Other comparable groups may be expected to react toward the individual in a similar fashion. Sociometric ratings may thus be said to have content validity in the same sense as work samples.

Checklists and Q Sorts. Any self-report instrument, such as the personality and interest inventories discussed in chapters 13 and 14, may also be employed by an observer in describing another person.[25] Measures designed to assess selfconcept are especially well suited to this purpose. The Adjective Check List (ACL) has been used extensively to obtain observers' evaluations in the IPAR research program (Gough & Heilbrun, 1983). Trained psychologists who have observed the participant closely over a two-or three-day assessment period record their evaluations by checking the appropriate adjectives on the list.

The Q sort has also been widely used for observer evaluations. Block (1961/1978) originally developed the California Q-Sort Deck to provide a standard language for comprehensive personality evaluations by professionally trained observers. The deck was subsequently published for more general distribution and revised to make its language appropriate for lay users as well as professionals. An adaptation for use at younger ages, the California Child Q-Set, is also available (for review, see Heilbrun, 1985). For all forms, the materials consist of 100 statements to be sorted into a 9-point forced distribution. The statements are sorted with regard to their "salience" for the individual—that is, their importance in specifying the unique and essential characteristics of the person who is being evaluated. Thus, the ipsative frame of reference typical of Q sorts is retained; the individual is not compared with outside normative standards.

The availability of such uniform sets of Q-sort items facilitates communication and assures comparability of data from different observers. The standard Q sort can also be used for a number of other research purposes (see, e.g., Caspi et al., 1992; Reise & Oliver, 1994; Wink, 1992). Another application involves the use of this technique in individual assessments. In this connection, Block (1961/1978) provides examples of three "defining Q sorts," representing a consensus evaluation of an optimally normal individual and two psychiatric syndromes, with which a given individual's Q sort can be compared. Similar defining Q sorts may be developed for any desired category of persons.

---

[25] The Personality Inventory for Children (PIC) and the Personality Inventory for Youth (PIY)—described in chapter 13—are, in fact, parallel instruments in (a) self-report form (PIY) and (b) in the form of an inventory of observed behavior (PIC).

BIODATA

In the discussion of interviewing techniques earlier in this chapter, reference was made to the importance of life-history data. Information about a person's past behavior and experiences is of interest both to theoreticians trying to understand patterns of personality and cognitive development and to applied psychologists trying to assess individuals and predict behavior. This is so primarily because the way an individual has responded in particular situations in the past is a promising source of information on how that individual will respond to similar situations in the future.

Life-history data can be obtained through several methods, of which interviewing and questionnaires are probably the most ubiquitious, especially in clinical and counseling psychology. Diaries and autobiographical writings also provide a rich source of information for psychobiographers and others interested in the study of individual lives (see, e.g., J. S. Wiggins & Pincus, 1992, pp. 487–493).[26]

And investigators who conduct longitudinal studies not only collect but also create records of life-history data through repeated observation and measurement of their subjects over time (Funder, Parke, Tomlinson-Keasey, & Widaman, 1993).

The most structured method of gathering and using life-history data, however, is through the biographical inventories or scales—now collectively referred to as biodata measures—devised for the prediction of performance in industrial and educational settings. Like the personality and interest inventories surveyed in chapters 13 and 14, the biographical inventory is a standardized self-report instrument in which responses to items are selected from among two or more options rather than constructed by the respondent. Although most of their questions generally pertain to relatively objective and readily verifiable facts, when they are scored and used for assessment or prediction, biographical scales—like structured interviews—must meet the same psychometric standards of reliability and validity as any other test. Typical items deal with amount and nature of education, job experiences, special skills, hobbies, and recreational activities. Frequently the individual's reaction to prior experiences is sought, as when respondents are asked about the courses they liked best and least in school, or what they liked or disliked in their job experiences.[27]

Historically, biographical scale items have been selected and weighted by criterion keying, as in the construction of such inventories as the MMPI and the Strong, discussed in chapters 13 and 14. The resulting inventory is then cross-validated against the same criterion in a new sample. When these procedures are followed, biodata inventories have proved to be consistently good predictors of performance in a wide variety of contexts. Inventories have been developed against such varied criteria as amount of insurance sold by life insurance agents, job turnover of bank clerks, productivity of research scientists, artistic creativity of high school students, and performance of naval personnel in diver training. Such measures have proved valid as predictors of job performance in groups ranging from unskilled and blue-collar workers to professionals and high-level

26 The use of autobiographical memories as a projective tool is discussed in chapter 15.

27 A thorough presentation of the domain and attributes of biodata items can be found in Mael (1991).

executives (Anastasi, 1979, pp. 79–80; Owens, 1983). At the same time, a limitation of many biographical inventories developed for specific jobs by empirical methods has been that they are not transportable or generalizable. Their applicability tends to be limited to the particular settings and criteria employed in their development (Baird, 1985; Hunter & Hunter, 1984).

Biographical measures continue to be the subject of extensive research. There has been considerable exploration of rational and factor analytic approaches to the development of biodata scales (Hough & Paullin, 1994; Schoenfeldt & Mendoza, 1994). In contrast to the empirical selection and criterion-keying of items, the rational approach usually begins with the identification of major relevant constructs through job analyses and surveys of published sources in both the empirical and theoretical literature. This is followed by factor analyses of the preliminary item pool, from which final items are chosen for the resulting factor scales. The relative merits of the various approaches to the construction of biodata scales are a subject of continued debate, although it is clear that each approach has strengths as well as weaknesses. The ideal approach is a construct validation strategy that incorporates as many varied elements as possible (Hough & Paullin, 1994).

In addition to the traditional approaches to inventory development, new methods of generating, selecting, and keying biodata items are being tried in an effort to make the resulting instruments more generalizable and transportable (see, e.g., Rothstein, Schmidt, Erwin, Owens, & Sparks, 1990; Russell, Mattson, Devlin, & Atwater, 1990). William A. Owens pioneered one of the most productive avenues of research which uses clustering techniques to identify subgroups of individuals who share modal patterns of life-history experiences (Mumford, Stokes, & Owens, 1990; Mumford & Stokes, 1992; Owens & Schoenfeldt, 1979). Such findings can then be applied to the prediction of multiple criteria. More importantly, the study of subgroups identified through these methods can lead to a level of understanding of the developmental patterns in the lives of individuals that combines elements of the idiographic and nomothetic approaches (Hein & Wesley, 1994).

Today, after years of carefully controlled research, biodata measures are among the most dependable and effective means of assessment and selection in education, industry, government, and other contexts. Furthermore, the history of biodata research highlights, in an unusually clear fashion, the mutual interdependence of basic and applied science. To wit, the methods and results of studies conducted to solve pragmatic problems of personnel selection are contributing to the formulation of a theoretical framework for understanding the development of behavior patterns across a lifetime.

Nevertheless, the implementation of biodata measures is not without its problems, which are practical and political, as well as technical. Chief among these problems are concerns about (a) legal issues, such as invasion of privacy, and equal employment opportunity matters (Sharf, 1994), and (b) the susceptibility of biodata measures and retrospective reports to faking and other sources of inaccuracy (Henry, Moffitt, Caspi, Langley, & Silva, 1994; Lautenschlager, 1994; Trent & Laurence, 1993). Much of the available research on all aspects of the development and use of biographical instruments has been summarized in the *Biodata Handbook* (Stokes, Mumford, & Owens, 1994).

PART 5

Applications of Testing

Chapter Seventeen

Major Contexts of Current Test Use

Psychological tests are used for a wide variety of purposes, and their areas of application are continually expanding. Having reviewed representative examples of various types of tests in some detail, we now turn to a consideration of issues that pertain to their application. In this chapter, we consider three major areas within which tests serve a multiplicity of functions; these areas of test use can be broadly designated as the educational, occupational, and clinical/counseling contexts. In the next, and final, chapter we discuss ethical and social issues that relate to testing practices across all areas.

EDUCATIONAL TESTING

Nearly every type of available test is used in the schools. Intelligence, special aptitude, multiple aptitude, and personality tests can all he found in the repertoire of the educational counselor and the school psychologist. Teachers and educational administrators frequently have to act on the results obtained with several different kinds of tests. Certain types of tests, however, have been specifically developed for use in educational contexts.[1] It is with such tests that this section is concerned. They include instruments designed for prediction and classification within specific educational settings and many varieties of educational achievement tests.

Achievement Tests: Their Nature and Uses. Surpassing all other types of standardized tests in sheer numbers, *achievement* tests are designed to

[1] Both the 1985 *Testing Standards* (AERA, APA, NCME) and their proposed revision (see chap. 1) have a chapter devoted to the use of tests in education.

measure the effects of a specific program of instruction or training. It has been customary to contrast achievement tests with aptitude tests, the latter including general intelligence tests, multiple aptitude batteries, and special aptitude tests. From one point of view, the difference between achievement and aptitude testing is a difference in the degree of uniformity of relevant antecedent experience. Thus, achievement tests measure the effects of relatively standardized sets of experiences, such as a course in elementary French, trigonometry, or computer programming. In contrast, *aptitude* test performance reflects the cumulative influence of a multiplicity of experiences in daily living. We might say that aptitude tests measure the effect of learning under relatively uncontrolled and unknown conditions, whereas achievement tests measure the effects ofleaming that occurred under partially known and controlled conditions.

A second distinction between aptitude and achievement tests pertains to their respective uses. Aptitude tests serve to predict subsequent performance. They are employed to estimate the extent to which the individual will profit from a specified course of training, or to forecast the quality of her or his achievement in a new situation. Achievement tests, on the other hand, generally represent a terminal evaluation of the individual's status on the completion of training. The emphasis in such tests is on what the individual can do at the time.

It should be recognized, however, that no distinction between aptitude and achievement tests can be applied rigidly. Some aptitude tests may depend on fairly specific and uniform prior learning, and some achievement tests cover relatively broad and unstandardized educational experiences. Similarly, an achievement test may be used as a predictor of future learning. As such, it serves the same function as an aptitude test. For example, achievement tests on premedical courses can serve as predictors of performance in medical school.

In an effort to avoid the excess meanings that have become associated with the terms "aptitude" and "achievement," the more neutral term "ability" is being substituted more and more to designate measures of cognitive behavior.[2] Any cognitive test, regardless of what it has been called traditionally, provides a sample of what the individual knows at the time he or she is tested and measures the level of development attained in one or more abilities. No test reveals how or why the individual reached that level. To answer the latter questions, one must delve into other concomitant variables, and especially into the person's experiential background. In this sense, every test score has a past that needs to be explored for proper understanding of the individual who obtained it. The same test score also has a future, insofar as it permits some prediction of what that individual will do in other, nontest situations, as well as at some future time.

Tests of developed abilities—whether designed as general intelligence tests, multiple aptitude batteries, special aptitude tests, or achievement tests—may be ordered along a continuum in terms of the specificity of experiential background that they presuppose. This continuum is illustrated in Figure 17–1.

---

[2] One distinct example of the changes taking place with regard to test labels is provided by the new names for the College Board examinations, which became effective in 1994. The widely known SAT abbreviation now stands for Scholastic Assessment Test, rather than Scholastic Aptitude Test. The new SAT has been regrouped into two components—the SAT-I: Reasoning Test, which replaces the former Scholastic Aptitude Test, and the SAT-II: Subject Tests, which replace the former Achievement Tests. These changes were accompanied by other, more substantial innovations in the tests that will be discussed in a later section of this chapter.

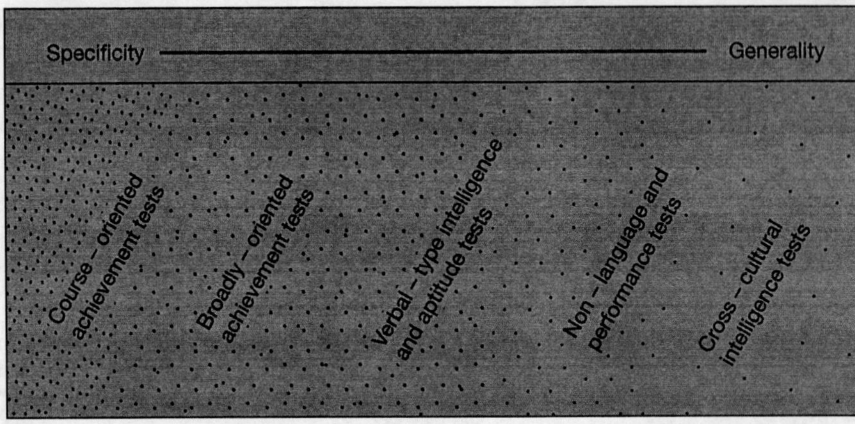

Figure 17–1. Tests of Developed Abilities: Continuum of Experiential Specificity.

At one extreme are the course-oriented achievement tests covering narrowly defined technical skills or factual information. A test in Russian vocabulary or television maintenance would fall at this end of the continuum. Next come the broadly oriented achievement tests commonly used today to assess the attainment of major, long-term educational goals. Here we find tests focusing on the understanding and application of scientific principles, the interpretation of literature, or the appreciation of art. Still somewhat broader in orientation are tests of basic cognitive skills—such as reading comprehension, arithmetic computation, and logical reasoning—that affect the individual's performance in a wide variety of activities. It is apparent that here achievement tests fuse imperceptibly with traditional intelligence and aptitude tests.[3] The predominantly verbal cognitive batteries, traditionally designated as intelligence tests, are close to the broadest achievement tests. Next come nonlanguage and performance tests, usually requiring no reading or writing. At the extreme generality end are the cross-cultural tests designed for use with persons of widely varied experiential backgrounds.

Labeling some instruments as "aptitude tests" and others as "achievement tests" has led to certain misuses of test results. A common example is the practice of identifying as underachievers those children whose achievement test scores are lower than their scholastic aptitude or intelligence test scores. Actually, such intraindividual differences in test scores reflect the fact that no two tests (or other performance indicators such as course grades) correlate perfectly with each other. The question of under- or overachievement can be more accurately formulated as overprediction or underprediction from the first to the second test. Among the reasons for the prediction errors in individual cases are the unreliability of the measuring instruments, differences in content coverage, the varied effects of attitudinal and motivational factors on the two measures, and the impact of such intervening experiences as remedial instruction or a long illness (R. L. Thorndike, 1963).

The many roles that achievement tests can play in the educational process have long been recognized. As an aid in the assignment of grades—or in any

[3] This overlapping can be demonstrated empirically through an examination of the close similarity of content, and the degree of correlation, between tests with such labels (see, e.g., W. Coleman & Cureton, 1954; Cooley & Lohnes, 1976).

other assessment of achieved competence—standardized achievement tests have the advantages of objectivity, uniformity, and efficiency. If properly constructed, they have other merits, such as adequacy of content coverage and reduction of the operation of irrelevant and chance factors in scoring procedures. Achievement tests also constitute an important feature of remedial teaching programs. In this connection, they can be useful both in the identification of students with special educational disabilities and in the measurement of progress in the course of remedial work.

For all types of learners, the periodic administration of well-constructed and properly chosen achievement tests may serve to facilitate learning. Such tests can reveal weaknesses in past learning, give direction to subsequent learning, and motivate the learner. The incentive value of "knowledge of results" has been repeatedly demonstrated by psychological experiments in many types of learning situations, with learners of widely varying age and education. The effectiveness of such self-checking is generally heightened by immediacy.

From another angle, achievement tests provide a means of adapting instruction to individual needs. Teaching can be most fruitful when it meets the learner at whatever stage he or she happens to be. Ascertaining what individuals are already able to do and what they already know about a subject is thus a necessary first step for effective teaching. By giving tests at the beginning of the school year, educators can take constructive steps to fill the major gaps in knowledge revealed by test results. Further examples of the role of achievement tests in the teaching process can be found in connection with domain-referenced testing and the individually tailored instructional systems discussed in chapter 3.

Finally, achievement tests may be employed as aids in the evaluation and improvement of teaching and in the formulation of educational goals. Achievement tests can provide information on the adequacy with which essential content and skills are actually being taught. By focusing attention on such issues and by providing concrete facts, achievement tests stimulate an analysis of educational objectives and encourage a critical examination of the content and methods of instruction.[4] Since public demands for accountability have risen, in the past few decades, there has been an unprecedented amount of testing, at educational institutions of all levels. Much of this testing is mandated by states and local school districts, as well as by the federal government (B. Gifford, 1989b; Hartle & Battaglia, 1993; National Council on Education Standards and Testing, 1992). The National Assessment of Educational Progress, known informally as "the nation's report card," is one of the best known examples of an ongoing government' mandated testing program (see, e.g., Alexander & James, 1987; Gentile, Martin-Rehrmann, & Kennedy, 1995; E. G. Johnson, 1992; Messick, Beaton, & Lord, 1983; NAEP, 1985; F. B. Womer, 1970). Because of the pervasiveness of standardized tests and the wide-ranging economic consequences that may be linked to their results, the tests themselves have been subjected to intense scrutiny and criticism. The methods used to assess educational progress, once the exclusive province of test specialists,

[4] Recent publications in the areas of mathematics and science education (see, e.g., Penner, Batsche, Knoff, & Nelson, 1993) and in the enhancement, of thinking skills (see, e.g., Mulcahy, Short, & Andrews, 1991) exernplify the kind of sound, solution-oriented work that can result from such critical examination.

have thus become the focus of a highly politicized debate that has received the attention of legislators and industrial leaders, as well as the general public (R. E. Bennett & Ward, 1993; Courts & Mclnemey, 1993; Gifford & O'Connor, 1992; S. P. Robinson, 1993; G. P. Wiggins, 1993). For a discussion of the issues and trends involved in school testing and assessment programs that are mandated by external sources, see Linn and Gronlund (1995, chap. 18).

Construction versus Choice. Historically, the traditional school examinations consisted of a set of questions to be answered orally or in writing. In either case, the examinee composed and formulated the response. The term "essay question" came to be used broadly to cover all free-response questions, including not only those demanding a lengthy essay but also those requiring the examinee to produce a short answer or to work out the solution for a mathematical problem. "Objective questions," by contrast, were those that called for the choice of a correct answer out of the alternatives provided for each question. Although there are several kinds of items that require examinees to select a response, such as true-false and matching, the multiple-choice question has been, by far, the most widely used, the most thoroughly studied, and, also, the most frequently criticized type of test item.

Critics of the multiple-choice format argue that it promotes rote memorization and learning of isolated facts rather than development of problem-solving skills and conceptual understanding. In addition, many uninformed people within the educational and political establishments equate multiple-choice items with standardized testing and disparage both of these elements of assessment methodology at once.[5] In an ironic turn of events, the same standardized testing programs used to chart educational progress often have been seen as contributing to the educational deficits they have uncovered (Courts & Mclnerney, 1993; H. Gardner, 1992; Resnick & Resnick, 1992). Unfortunately, the criticisms about excessive and inappropriate use of standardized tests have been thoroughly justified in some cases. At any rate, charges that testing drives the curriculum and that both are in urgent need of reform have emanated from educators at all levels and have grown increasingly stronger in the past two decades. Advocates of educational reform believe that a major overhaul is needed in curricular goals and instructional methods, as well as in the tools of assessment, and they perceive all of these areas as inextricably tied.

Since the philosophical, political, and practical aspects of educational reform are beyond the scope of this book, we shall confine ourselves to discussing some of the proposed alternatives in assessment methodology. These alternatives are described by various rubrics, such as "performance-based" assessment, "authentic" assessment, and "direct" assessment (see, e.g., E. L. Baker, O'Neil, & Linn, 1993; Linn & Gronlund, 1995, chap. 10). Although each of these represents somewhat different emphases, one of the central features they all share is a marked preference for tasks that—like the former "essay questions"—require the examinee to generate an answer. These items are now described as *constructed-response or open-ended tasks.* They are contrasted with *selected-response tasks,* which is the term applied to items that require the examinee only to choose a response

[5] It should be noted that the instruments used in many large-scale educational testing programs—such as the SAT, the NAEP tests, and other standardized achievement measures—have been using essay questions and other open-ended item formats for some time.

from among the options presented, such as multiple-choice items and the other types of questions that used to be called "objective." Constructed-response items may involve simple completions (such as "fill-in-the-blanks"), problem solving, and essays, as well as a variety of presentations or performances like playing an instrument, giving a speech, or repairing a machine.[6]

The method known as *portfolio assessment* provides another set of alternatives. This type of evaluation tool is aimed primarily at making the process of educational assessment as meaningful and realistic as possible. Although there are a wide range of procedures to which the term is applied, a portfolio usually consists of a cumulative record—collected over an extended period of time—of samples of students' work in specific areas, such as writing or any other endeavor that involves a process in which progress can be documented (Camp, 1993; Gitomer, 1993; D. P. Wolf, 1993). The portfolio method of assessment offers a great deal of flexibility and can be implemented more or less formally and with various degrees of collaboration between the student and the teacher (see Karlsen, 1992, for an example of a published instrument of this type).

The reader will have gathered even from this brief overview that a great deal of attention is being paid to the means by which evaluations of learning and of students' work are conducted. This concern extends not only to what different items measure and how well they measure it, but also to other psychological aspects of test items. For example, Zeidner (1993) has investigated students' attitudes toward item formats and found that they prefer multiple-choice items rather than essays. Lu and Suen's (1995) research indicates that performance-based assessment tends to favor field-independent over field-dependent students (see chap. 16). Other investigators have looked into the relationship between test anxiety and item types and found that scores on constructed-response tests seem to be more affected by anxiety than those of selected-response tests (Crocker & Schmitt, 1987). A discussion of variables that may impinge on the motivation of test takers and affect their responsiveness and performance—for example, the purpose of an assessment procedure—as well as several other factors that may have a bearing on the interpretation of constructed-response and multiple-choice tests can be found in R. E. Snow (1993).

At the same time, the empirical literature concerning the strictly psychometric properties of performance-based tasks used in academic settings has been accumulating gradually.[7] Both the pace of the research and the direction of the results differ widely depending on the specific types of items in question. A fairly large number of studies have investigated the reliability of the scoring procedures used for constructed-response tasks, which—like those applied to the situational tests discussed in chapter 16—often consist of ratings (E. L. Baker et al., 1993; Linn & Gronlund, 1995, chap. 10). Interrater reliabilities are generally quite favorable when the scoring rules are clear and well developed and when the raters are properly trained. On the other hand, the generalizability of results across topics and tasks is typically low, which suggests that constructed-response items

---

[6] Test items can, of course, be classified along various other dimensions besides whether they involve construction or selection of responses. Examples of two different taxonomies of item types can be found in R. E. Bennett (1993) and R. E. Snow (1993).

[7] See, especially, R. E. Bennett and Ward (1993).

have a relatively high degree of task specificity. This finding is not surprising, considering that such items are typically more complex and allow a wider range of responses than do selected-response items.

With regard to the issue of validity, the research base is still rather limited, at least for the least restrictive and most innovative types of constructed-response tasks. One of the most crucial preliminary questions is the extent to which constructed-response and selected-response items measure equivalent traits or skills. Although the evidence on this issue is not yet extensive, Traub's (1993) review of studies on the subject suggests that the degree of equivalence varies across domains. For instance, when different item formats are used in tests of reading comprehension or mathematical knowledge, they tend to yield equivalent results—whereas, in the writing domain, it appears that the type of item employed does have a significant effect on scores.

Meanwhile, the use of multiple-choice items is still pervasive. In fact, the introduction of different item formats into educational tests, coupled with the severe criticism to which multiple-choice items have been subjected, appears to have stimulated efforts to improve them. Guidance on how to develop, review, and evaluate multiple-choice items is readily available (see, e.g., Haladyna, 1994), and research on specific aspects of this format, such as the optimum number of options to use, continues (Trevisan, Sax, & Michael, 1991, 1994). Furthermore, a number of variations and refinements of the genre of selected-response tasks are also being explored and disseminated (see, e.g., Linn & Gronlund, 1995, chap. 8; Sax, 1991; Sired, Thissen, & Wainer, 1991; Wainer & Kiely, 1987; Wainer & Lewis, 1990).

Direct comparisons between constructed-response and selected-response items have been carried out as well (e.g., Lukhele, Thissen, & Wainer, 1994). Much of the time, such comparisons seem to favor multiple-choice items with regard to criteria such as economy, efficiency, and predictive validity, especially when they are compared with the traditional essay questions (Anastasi, 1988b, pp. 416–418; R. E. Bennett, 1993). It must be noted, however, that the problem of evaluating and comparing different assessment formats at a time when both the goals and the methods of assessment are in a state of flux is anything but straightforward. Moreover, it is important to keep in mind that item format is only one among many variables that interact with one another to determine the fairness, accuracy, and overall quality of an assessment procedure. The purpose of the assessment and the content domain in question, as well as the characteristics of the individuals who are assessed, all need to be considered (E. L. Baker et al., 1993; R. E. Bennett, 1993; Dwyer, 1993; Mislevy, 1993). For instance, issues such as the differential effects of failure on the subsequent motivation of test takers may be placed ahead of other criteria for evaluating items, especially for students who have handicapping conditions or are otherwise disadvantaged. However, it is worth noting that, at present, there is no reason to believe that performance-based assessment results in narrowing the gap that has existed between the scores of Whites and those of some ethnic minorities on standardized tests of the multiple-choice variety; in fact, some research indicates that this type of score disparity may be greater with constructed-response than with selected-response tests (Hartle & Battaglia, 1993). Current issues in the educational assessment of culturally and linguistically diverse students are discussed further by Cancelli and Arena (1996), K. W. Howell and Rueda (1996), and Shinn and Baker (1996).

TYPES OF EDUCATIONAL TESTS

In the 1990 Annual Report of the Educational Testing Service, the Board of Trustees of that organization predicted that educational testing would change more in the succeeding 10 years than it had in the previous 50 (ETS, 1990). It now appears that this prediction was accurate and could be reiterated easily for the coming decade. Tests of all kinds are undergoing significant revisions and new assessment tools are being devised at a rapid pace. The following review, therefore, centers on the types of instruments used traditionally in educational contexts—along with some ongoing innovations within each type—rather than on detailed descriptions of individual tests.

General Achievement Batteries. Several batteries are available for measuring general educational achievement in the areas most commonly covered by academic curricula. This type of test can be used from the primary grades to the adult level, although its major application has been in the elementary school. Typically, these batteries provide profiles of scores on individual subtests or in major academic areas. An advantage of such batteries, as against independently constructed achievement tests, is that they may permit horizontal or vertical comparisons, or both. Thus, an individual's relative standing in different subject-matter areas or educational skills can be evaluated in terms of a uniform normative sample. Or the student's progress from grade to grade can be reported in terms of a single score scale. The test user should check whether a particular battery was so standardized as to yield either or both kinds of comparability.

Although some general achievement batteries are designed exclusively for the elementary grades or for high school, most span a broad range extending into both levels and occasionally even into the first year of college. A few provide a single battery for the grade range covered, but the large majority have several overlapping batteries in separate test booklets for use at different levels. Some batteries actually form a coordinated series, permitting comparable measurement from Grades K through 12. One such combination is the Iowa Tests of Basic Skills, the Tests of Achievement and Proficiency, and the Iowa Tests of Educational Development; another is the Stanford Achievement Test Series.

A noteworthy feature of some achievement batteries is that they were concurrently normed with tests of academic intelligence or scholastic abilities. Major examples include achievement batteries that were paired with three multilevel tests illustrated in chapter 10, namely, the Stanford Achievement Test Series with the Otis-Lennon School Ability Test; the Iowa Tests series and Tests of Achievement and Proficiency with the Cognitive Abilities Test; and the California Achievement Tests and Comprehensive Tests of Basic Skills with the Test of Cognitive Skills (see Table 10–1). The use of the same standardization sample in these cases permits direct comparisons of the scores any student obtains on the two types of tests. Usually, the two tests correlate highly, and individuals will obtain closely similar scores on them. For students who score substantially higher on either type of test, it is desirable to explore possible reasons for the discrepancy.

The achievement battery measures largely what the individual has learned in basic school courses; the cognitive skills test assesses a broader range of abilities and knowledge learned both in and out of school. Any significant performance discrepancy could reflect the influence of specific abilities or disabilities, or of such noncognitive factors as motivation, interests, and attitudes. The individual's experiential background often provides clues to the conditions leading to unusual discrepancies in test performance.

Achievement batteries obviously differ in the technical level of their test construction procedures. Nevertheless, as a group, they meet high standards of test development, especially with regard to size and representativeness of normative samples, reliability, and content validation. Detailed test specifications for item writing are generally followed by thorough item analyses, including the application of item response theory methods. Special procedures are commonly employed for avoiding gender and ethnic bias. All batteries typically include an assessment of basic skills in reading, language, and mathematics, in combination with varying amounts of content knowledge in science and social studies. Several include subtests designed to measure study skills or ability to use various information sources. Moreover, in response to demands for more flexible and informative assessment tools, publishers of the major standardized achievement batteries now offer a greater variety of items and options. Open-ended items and a wider range of selected-response items—designed to measure higher order thinking skills and set within more meaningful contexts—are currently being used. Publishers provide increased flexibility in adapting assessment packages to the requirements of local curricula, using various mixes of item content and formats as well as scoring options. They also offer more linkages between tests and instructional materials.[8]

Tests of Minimum Competency in Basic Skills. The past two decades witnessed a mounting concern about the low competence level of many high school graduates in reading, writing, and arithmetic skills. This concern led to popular demands for competency tests in basic skills as a means of certifying the attainment of minimum competency and as a basis for awarding a high school diploma. Such demands aroused a storm of controversy; most of the objections centered on the likelihood of misuses and misinterpretations of minimum-competency tests, and on the educational rigidities and bureaucratic controls that might ensue.[9] While most states have established policies regarding minimum-competency testing, their policies and procedures vary widely in the time and grade level at which the tests are administered, the particular use made of results, and the nature and degree of local autonomy in the development or

[8] An example of this trend is the TerraNova series, recently published by CTB/McGraw-Hill. The components of this series include: the new Comprehensive Tests of Basic Skills (CTBS); a Multiple Assessments edition, which combines selected-response and constructed-response items; a Performance Assessments edition, which provides longer open-ended tasks scored locally or by the publisher; and a Custom Component, which offers supplemental items designed to assess specialized curriculum objectives.

[9] For a comprehensive discussion of the minimum-competency testing movement, and the technical psychometric problems involved therein, see Berk (1986). Another thorough review of the issues and problems involved in the use of tests to certify student competence can be found in Jaeger (1989).

choice of tests. Furthermore, tests that are used to make decisions about granting or withholding diplomas must reflect the specific curricula they cover. Because of all these reasons, appropriate tests are now usually developed by schools, school systems, or state agencies themselves, often with the assistance of test publishers who can provide technically trained personnel, large item banks, and reporting services that can be adapted especially to meet local objectives. Such tests may include some components of the standardized achievement batteries discussed earlier or they may be custom-made for a specific locality.

In recent years the focus of interest in ascertaining mastery of basic skills has extended to the adult population.[10] The cumulative effects of large school dropout rates and low levels of competence among high school graduates, as well as the great rise in the number of non-English-speaking immigrants, have fostered concerns about the competitiveness of the U.S. labor force in the world market. The findings of the National Adult Literacy Survey, conducted in 1992 by ETS under the auspices of the Department of Education, have reinforced this concern. The survey revealed that almost one half of the U.S. population placed at the lowest two (out of five) possible levels of literacy (Kirsch, Jungeblut, Jenkins, & Kolstad, 1993).

Tests of competency in basic skills designed especially for adults are typically developed in connection with adult education classes, educational programs conducted in penal institutions, and job training programs. An outstanding example is the Tests of Adult Basic Education (TABE, Forms 7 & 8, 1994). The TATE battery encompasses five graduated levels of difficulty across five different content areas that include reading, language, and applied mathematics. The results are reported as norm-referenced scores and also in terms of competency-based information that can be used diagnostically. In addition to its regular forms, the TABE is available in a special version suitable for use in a work environment and in a Spanish edition (TABE Español) designed to measure the basic skills of Spanish-speaking adults in their primary language.

Teacher-Made Classroom Tests. Undoubtedly the largest number of tests covering the content of specific courses or parts of courses are prepared by instructors for use in their own classrooms. The vast diversity among courses on the same subject and with identical titles—especially at the high school level and beyond—is well known. Under these conditions, no external standardized test could suffice. The preparation of local classroom tests, however, can be substantially improved by an application of the techniques and accumulated experience of professional test constructors. The development of classroom tests can be divided into three major steps: (1) planning the test, (2) item writing, and (3) item analysis. Some simple techniques of item analysis, suitable for use with small

[10] The concept of "functional literacy" (Sticht, 1975)—which has been extended to mean competence in the use of language in speaking and writing, as well as in understanding and using various documents, and in arithmetic computation—underlies this discussion. Functional competence is defined in terms of the demands of practical situations, such as the difficulty level and amount of reading required to perform particular jobs or, more broadly, the basic educational skills required to manage one's own life in a modern society.

groups, were described in chapter 7. A brief overview of the other two steps is given in the following paragraphs.[11]

The test constructor who plunges directly into item writing is likely to produce a lopsided test. Without an advance plan, some areas will be overrepresented, whereas others may remain untouched. It is generally easier to prepare objective items on some topics than on others. And it is easier to prepare items that require the recall of simple facts than to devise items calling for critical evaluation, integration of different facts, or application of principles to new situations. Thus, the test constructed without a blueprint is likely to be overloaded with relatively impermanent and less important material. Many of the popular criticisms of selected-response tests stem from the common overemphasis on rote memory and trivial details in poorly constructed tests.

To guard against these fortuitous imbalances of item coverage, *test specifications* should be drawn up before any items are prepared. For classroom examinations, such specifications should be based on outlines of instructional objectives and content areas to be covered and should reflect decisions about the relative importance of each of these aspects through the number of items allotted to each topic and objective.[12] The test constructor must also decide on the most appropriate *item form* for the material. The relative merits of objective and open-ended items, discussed in an earlier section of this chapter with special reference to their use in large-scale, standardized testing programs, also need to be considered in the construction of classroom tests. Finally, many practical rules for effective *item writing* have been formulated on the basis of years of experience in preparing items and empirical evaluation of responses. Anyone planning to prepare a classroom test would do well to consult one of the sources summarizing these suggestions (e.g., Ebel, 1979, chaps. 4–9; Haladyna, 1994, chaps. 4–6; Linn & Gronlund, 1995, chaps. 6–9; Millman & Green, 1989).

Tests for the College Level. A number of tests and testing programs have been developed for use in the admission, placement, and counseling of college students. One that is outstanding is the Scholastic Assessment Tests (SAT) Program of the College Board, presently composed of two elements, namely, the SAT I: Reasoning Test, which has replaced the Scholastic Aptitude Test's Verbal and Mathematical sections, and the SAT II: Subject Tests, which have replaced the former SAT Achievement Tests.[13] The SAT I consists primarily of multiple-choice questions measuring verbal and mathematical abilities. It is meant for use—as a supplement to high school grades and other information—in the assessment of a student's readiness to perform college-level work. The SAT II tests, on the other hand, are designed to assess knowledge in specific subject areas (e.g., literature, chemistry, and world history) and can be used for placement as well as for admissions.

---

[11] For further guidance on the preparation of classroom tests and other assessment procedures, see Linn and Gronlund (1995, chaps. 5–13).

[12] Examples of test specification tables can be found in Anastasi (1988b, p. 431) and Linn and Gronlund (1996, p. 122).

[13] For further historical background on the SAT program, see Anastasi (1988b, pp. 328–331) and Donlon (1984).

The SAT Program tests have changed in content and format, as well as in name. For instance, in the Verbal section of the SAT I, there is increased emphasis on critical reading and reasoning. Similarly, the Math section now requires students to produce, rather than merely to select, some of their answers, and—in keeping with current standards—the use of calculators is permitted throughout the Math section. The SAT II tests have also changed and presently include more direct assessment of skills through the use of listening components and writing samples.

As of April 1995, the SAT Program test scores are no longer reported in terms of a fixed reference group dating back to 1941 (see chap. 3). Instead, the SAT score scale has been "recentered," using a new reference group from the 1990s, so that average performance is once again represented by a score of approximately 500.[14] The recentering has made the SAT scores more precise and reliable, especially at the highest and lowest ends of the scale. In addition, the interpretation of scores is easier; for example, verbal and math scores can now be compared directly with one another without reference to percentile rankings, because both have been realigned. Moreover, since a score of 500 is the midpoint of the 200 to 800 range, the "intuitive" average and the actual average will be the same. The College Board has disseminated tables and other tools that simplify the conver- sion of original scale scores to recentered scale scores in order to help maintain the continuity between the two scales. Information about the reliability, difficulty levels, and completion rates of the revised SAT examinations is currently available in handbooks prepared especially for counselors and admission officers as well as in other ETS and College Board research reports and publications (College Board, 1995a, 1995b).[15] A preliminary study comparing the traditional SAT with a prototype version of the SAT I found the newer test to be a slightly better predictor of freshman GPA than the former (Hale, Bridgeman, Lewis, Pollack, & Wang, 1992). Additional evidence on the validity of the revised SAT examinations will be included in a forthcoming technical supplement that should be available in the late 1990s.

Another nationwide program, launched in 1959, is the American College Testing Program (ACT, 1995–1996). Originally limited largely to state university systems, this program grew rapidly and is now used in many colleges throughout the country. The current ACT Assessment includes four tests: English, Mathematics, Reading, and Science Reasoning. Reflecting the point of view of its founder, E. F. Lindquist, this examination program provides a set of samples of college work. It overlaps traditional aptitude and achievement tests, focusing on the basic intellectual skills required for satisfactory performance in college. The noncognitive components of the ACT Assessment include: a High School Course/Grade Information questionnaire, the ACT Interest Inventory, and a

[14] By the early 1990s, average SAT scores had drifted down from 500 in both areas to 424 in the Verbal area and 478 in Math.

[15] Because of their function in the selection of college students, the SAT exams are frequently subject to critical scrutiny. Recently, for instance, it was reported that test takers can correctly answer many multiple-choice questions based on the SAT reading tasks without referring to the passages that accompany the questions. This finding has reignited the controversy concerning the extent to which extraneous background knowledge affects SAT scores (see, e.g., S. Katz & Lautenschlager, 1995).

Student Profile Section with questions about students' aspirations, plans, accomplishments, and other background information. Historically, the ACT has not come up to the technical standards set by the SAT. However, validity data compare favorably with those found for other instruments in similar settings.

It should be noted that tests such as the SAT and the ACT are not intended as substitutes for high school grades in the prediction of college achievement. High school grades can predict college grades as well as or slightly better than most tests. When test scores are combined with high school grades, however, the prediction of college performance is improved. In part, this improvement stems from the fact that a uniform, objective test serves as a corrective for the variability in grading standards among different high schools. Furthermore, such tests are not subject to the possible personal biases or to other arbitrary factors that may enter into the assignment of course grades.

There is also increasing use of specialized achievement tests as college equivalency examinations. High school students with additional preparation in certain areas may take tests in the College Board's Advanced Placement Program (APP) to gain admission to college with advanced standing in one or more subjects. A related development is to be found in the College Level Examination Program (CLEP), also administered by the College Board. The general purpose of this program is to facilitate the granting of college credit by examination and to provide a national system for evaluating college-level education acquired through independent study and other nontraditional procedures. A similar test series, the ACT Proficiency Examination Program, is administered by the American College Testing Program. Although it includes some academic subjects, such as Anatomy and Physiology and Abnormal Psychology, this program covers mostly occupational areas, such as Nursing and Accounting.

Graduate School Admission. The practice of testing applicants for admission extends to graduate and professional schools. Most of the tests designed for this purpose represent a combination of general intelligence and achievement tests. A well-known example is the Graduate Record Examinations (GRE). This series of tests originated in 1936 in a joint project of the Carnegie Foundation for the Advancement of Teaching and the graduate schools of four universities. Now greatly expanded, the program is conducted by Educational Testing Service, under the general direction of the Graduate Record Examinations Board. Students are tested at designated centers—in well over 100 countries around the world—prior to their admission to graduate school. The test results are used by the universities to aid in making admission and placement decisions and in selecting recipients for scholarships, fellowships, and special appointments. The GRE include a General Test and Subject Tests in various fields of specialization.[16] The current General Test yields separate scores for verbal, quantitative, and analytical abilities. The Subject Tests are now available in 16 areas, including biology, computer science, French, mathematics, music, political science, and psychology. The psychometric characteristics of the GRE are reported in the latest edition of the guide to their use *(GRE 1995–96 Guide)*. In general, the Subject Test scores are

[16] Prior to 1982, the General Test was called the Aptitude Test and the Subject Tests were called Advanced Tests. As with the SAT, the names were changed to avoid potential misunderstanding about the purpose of the tests.

better predictors of first-year graduate grade point average (GPA) than either the General Test score composites or undergraduate GPA, but the combination of all three measures provides the highest predictive validities. These multiple correlations fall between the mid .40s and the low .60s for various fields.

In October 1992, the GRE Program started administering a computerized version of the traditional form of the General Test, and in November 1993 a computer-adaptive General Test was introduced. Despite some initial difficulties concerning potential security risks with the computerized GRE General Test, the advantages of computerization are such that the GRE Board may eliminate all paper-and-pencil testing by as early as 1999. The General Test is also being revised to include a Writing Test and a Mathematical Reasoning Test, and some constructed-response questions ("Update on the New GRE," 1995).

Diagnostic and Prognostic Testing. In contrast to the general achievement batteries and other achievement tests discussed earlier, the tests discussed in this section are designed to analyze a person's particular strengths and weaknesses within a subject-matter domain and to suggest causes for her or his difficulties. The majority of these diagnostic instruments are individually administered and, therefore, most often considered to be clinical tools. Some of them, however, are separate components of the major achievement batteries previously discussed and are intended for group administration. Most of the published diagnostic group tests deal with reading, mathematics, and language skills and offer both normative and content-referenced information. Examples of this approach are provided by the Stanford Diagnostic Mathematics Test and the Stanford Diagnostic Reading Test, and by the California Diagnostic Reading and Mathematics Tests. The publishers of these two series have also produced separate instruments for the assessment and diagnosis of writing skills. Both the Stanford Writing Assessment Program and the CTB Writing Assessment System use direct samples of writing in various modes—such as descriptive or narrative writing—and offer several scoring options.

In connection with the use of all diagnostic tests, one point deserves special emphasis. The diagnosis of learning disabilities and the subsequent program of remedial teaching are the proper functions of a trained specialist. No battery of diagnostic tests can suffice for this purpose. The diagnosis and treatment of severe learning disabilities require an intensive clinical case study, preferably interdisciplinary, including supplementary information on sensory capacities and motor development, medical and health history, complete educational history, data on home and family background, and a thorough investigation of possible emotional difficulties. Although survey and group diagnostic tests may serve to identify individuals in need of further attention, the diagnosis and treatment of learning disabilities require specialized techniques. Some of these procedures were discussed in chapter 9, and the topic will be considered further in this chapter in connection with clinical testing.

Certain types of tests designed for use in educational contexts are essentially prognostic instruments. As such, they function as aptitude rather than as achievement tests. At the same time, they frequently resemble achievement tests in content, because what they undertake to predict is usually performance in a specific course of study. Typical of this approach is the Orleans-Hanna Algebra

Prognosis Test (Hanna, Sonnenschein, & Lenke, 1983). In this test, students are provided with a set of short, simple "lessons" in algebra and are immediately tested on what they have learned. The test thus consists of work samples in which the students' later course learning is predicted from their performance in the sample learning tasks. A more unusual, and experimental, example of prognostic testing is provided by the artifical language tests devised by the U.S. Office of Personnel Management and by the Department of Defense in order to predict ability to learn a new language (Diane, Brogan, & McCauley, 1991).

Another method of assessment, although with a completely individualized orientation, has received increasing attention since the 1980s. Essentially, this approach follows a test-teach-test procedure, generally described as dynamic or guided assessment, and is associated with remedial instruction. The individual's learning potential is evaluated by observing how well he or she can leam in a one-to-one relation with a professional who functions in the triple role of examiner, instructor, and clinician. A major exponent of this method is Feuerstein (1979); several related approaches are discussed by A. L. Brown, Campione, Webber, and McGilly (1992) and by Lidz (1987, 1997). Because of its distinctly clinical nature, dynamic assessment is considered more fully in a later section of this chapter.

Curriculum-based measurement represents yet another set of techniques devised in order to link assessment and intervention (Deno, 1992; L. S. Fuchs, 1993; Fuchs & Deno, 1991; Shinn, 1989). Although some curriculum-based assessment approaches can be quite informal, others involve standardized measures of student performance in basic skills, such as reading, spelling, and arithmetical computation; for a comparison of models, see Shinn, Rosenfield, and Knutson (1989). The common denominator of these techniques is a strongly behavioral orientation and a direct relationship to the tasks that make up the curriculum common to elementary education, as opposed to the inferential and norm-referenced approach of traditional psychometric instruments. Curriculum-based assessment has been used primarily in special education settings.

Assessment in Early Childhood Education. Many new instruments for measuring the educational development of young children have been published in the past three decades. Several influences contributed to the amount and nature of this activity (see chaps. 9 and 12). Research in early cognitive development, the burgeoning of programs for preschool education, and the widespread concern about the effects of cultural handicaps on the child's ability to profit from school instruction have all played major roles.[17] Some of the tests were designed principally to measure the outcomes of early childhood education and thus function as achievement tests. Others are presented as predictive instruments to assess the child's readiness for first-grade instruction. The two types of instruments merge imperceptibly, however, and each can usually serve either purpose.

School readiness refers essentially to the attainment of prerequisite skills, knowledge, attitudes, motivations, and other appropriate behavioral traits that enable the learner to profit maximally from school instruction. These prerequisites are what J. McV. Flunt and Kirk (1974) called the "entry skills" that the child

[17] The last of these has culminated in the articulation of a national, educational goal stating that, by the year 2000, all children in the United States should start school ready to leam (National Council on Education Standards and Testing, 1992).

needs to cope with the teaching-learning situation encountered in the first grade. Readiness entails certain minimum levels of physical and sensorimotor development, achieved through maturation, as well as prior learning. Increasingly, emphasis is being placed on the hierarchical development of knowledge and skills, whereby the acquisition of simple concepts equips the child for the learning of more complex concepts at any age.

Readiness tests are generally administered upon school entrance. While they have much in common with intelligence tests for the primary grades, readiness tests place more emphasis on the abilities found to be important in learning to read. Some attention is also given to the prerequisites of numerical thinking and to the sensorimotor control required in learning to write. Among the specific functions frequently covered are visual and auditory discrimination, motor control, aural comprehension, vocabulary, quantitative concepts, and general information. A widely used readiness battery is the Metropolitan Readiness Tests, Sixth Edition (MRT6—for reviews of an earlier edition of the MRT, see Mabry, 1995 and Stoner, 1995). A different approach to school readiness is illustrated by tests that focus on the child's understanding of common relational concepts, such as the Boehm Test of Basic Concepts—Revised and the Bracken Basic Concept Scale (for reviews, see Fitzmaurice & Witt, 1989; Linn, 1989; Turco, 1989; and Ysseldyke, 1989). A discussion of the concept of school readiness, along with issues concerning its assessment, can be found in Gredler (1992).

Concluding Comments. The field of education is in a state of flux, and educational testing reflects it, both in the United States and around the world. Change is likely to persist and intensify for the foreseable future.[18] Many observers agree that there is a need to integrate assessment and instruction further and in such a way that these aspects of the educational enterprise complement each other better, to the advantage of the learner[19] (H. Gardner, 1992; Nitko, 1989). Most also recognize that,both testing and teaching always will be subject to amelioration through theoretical and empirical advances. No single assessment or instructional tool will ever suffice; each has its limitations. Moreover, different students require different approaches. Thus, the search for improvements must, and will, go on.

OCCUPATIONAL TESTING

Psychological tests are commonly employed as aids in occupational decisions, including both individual counseling and institutional decisions concerning the selection and classification of personnel. In this section we discuss applications of testing that pertain to the assessment of the individual's occupational

---

[18] See, for example, E. L. Baker and O'Neils (1994) volume assessing technological innovations in education and training, R. E. Snow and Lohman's (1989) discussion of the implications of cognitive psychology for educational measurement, and Oakland and Hambleton's (1995) work on current international developments in academic assessment.

[19] In fact, new computer-based systems incorporating instructional, assessment, and management features that can be individually tailored are rapidly appearing. The Learning Plus program developed by ETS for adult learners who need to improve their basic academic skills and IBM's SchoolVista software for K–12 are two state-of-the-art examples of this kind of tools.

qualifications as viewed by the institutions responsible for the selection, assignment, and evaluation of personnel.

Organizations in the business and industrial sectors, in the federal, state, and local levels of government, and in the different branches of the armed services use almost every type of available test in personnel decision making. Multiple aptitude batteries and special aptitude tests have often been developed for occupational purposes, as have the situational tests described in chapter 16. Personality inventories (chap. 13) and biodata (chap. 16) are being used increasingly as well. A brief overview of the use of tests and other instruments in the selection and classification of personnel is provided by Landy et al. (1994); comprehensive treatments of the topic can be found in three recent books edited by Rumsey, Walker, and Harris (1994), Schmitt, Borman, et al. (1993), and Schuler, Farr, and Smith (1993). Major aspects of industrial/organizational use of tests are examined intensively in several chapters of the handbook edited by Dunnette and Hough (1990–1992).[20] The Society for Industrial and Organizational Psychology (SIOP, 1987) has prepared and adopted a set of principles for the validation and use of personnel selection procedures. While concerned with good practice in the choice, development, and evaluation of all personnel selection procedures, these principles are highly relevant to standardized tests. In addition, both the current *Testing Standards* (AERA, APA, NOME, 1985) and their proposed revision (see chap. 1) have a chapter on the topic of testing in employment settings. Another major application of occupational testing—also covered in both versions of the *Testing Standards*—is in the licensing and certification of persons deemed qualified to practice in any of a large number of trades and professions.[21]

As in our treatment of educational tests, in this section we shall concentrate on those tests specially designed for occupational purposes, over and above the more widely applicable instruments discussed in other chapters. We shall also ex-amine briefly some of the procedures and issues involved in assembling and validating tests in employment settings.

Validation of Employment Tests

From the standpoint of both employee and employer, it is obviously of prime importance that individuals be placed in jobs for which they have appropriate qualifications. Effective placement also implies that traits irrelevant to the requirements of the particular job should not affect selection decisions, either favorably or unfavorably. If a mechanical ability test requires a much higher level of reading comprehension than does the job, its use would not lead to the most effective utilization of personnel for that job. The simple psychometric fact that test validity must be ascertained for particular uses of the test has long been familiar. It has acquired new urgency because of the widespread concern about the job placement of culturally and educationally disadvantaged minorities (see

[20] The latest volume of the handbook—edited by Triandis, Dunnette, and Hough (1994)—deals with industrial/organizational psychology issues in various cultures from around the world.

[21] Testing in the professions, including testing for certification and licensure of psychologists, is discussed by Anastasi (1988b, pp. 468–474). For a more recent examination of issues pertaining to the validation and use of licensure and certification exams in general, see the special issue of *Evaluation & the Health Professions* edited by LaDuca (1994) on that subject.

chap. 18). An invalid test or one that includes elements not related to the job under consideration may unfairly exclude minority group members who could perform the job satisfactorily.

Another relevant concern, both for organizations and for society at large, stems from the demonstrated relationship between job productivity and the validity of selection instruments. Procedures for assessing this relation and typical results were cited in chapter 6. The estimated gains and losses in productivity associated with rises and drops in the validity of personnel selection procedures are substantial. In organizations hiring many employees, such as government agencies, the cumulative value of such gains and losses is so large that it deserves close attention.

For several decades, the prevalent opinion in personnel psychology was that selection tests should undergo full-scale validation against local criteria of job performance. Specific procedures for such criterion-prediction validation were discussed in chapters 5 and 6. However, a full-scale longitudinal validation study is unrealistic in the large majority of situations. Even under unusually favorable conditions, with access to large employee samples, several practical limitations become apparent (see, e.g., Anastasi, 1972; J. T. Campbell, Crooks, Mahoney, & Rock, 1973). In view of the practical difficulties in conducting full-scale local criterion-prediction validation, a number of alternative procedures have been explored.

Global Procedures for the Assessment of Performance. One approach to personnel selection uses assessment procedures that resemble the total job situation as closely as possible. This resemblance, however, can never be complete. A *probationary appointment* comes closest to being a true replica of the job. But even in this case, the shortness of the period and the knowledge that the appointment is probationary may influence worker behavior in a number of ways. *Job samples* represent another attempt to approximate actual job performance. In the job sample, the task is actually a part of the work to be performed on the job, but the task and working conditions are uniform for all applicants. Some job-sample tests are custom-made to fit specific jobs. The representativeness of the work sample and the closeness with which the task duplicates job conditions are essential considerations. Familiar examples are driving tests, as well as standardized tests for office skills, such as typing and operating various business machines.

Some tests employ *simulation* to reproduce the functions performed on the job. Simulations merge imperceptibly with job samples. Examples range from the operation of a miniature punch press to simulators for locomotive engineers and for airplane pilots. Simulators have been used for both training and testing purposes in the United States space program administered by NASA, as well as in a number of military specialties.

To this list may be added *assessment center techniques* (see chap. 16), which have been used largely in evaluating managerial or administrative personnel (Bray, 1982; Finkle, 1983; Moses, 1985; Thornton & Byham, 1982). A distinctive feature of this approach is the inclusion of situational tests, such as the *in-basket,* a technique adapted for testing executives in many contexts (N. Frederiksen, 1962, 1966; Shapira & Dunbar, 1980). Simulating the familiar "in-basket" found on the administrator's desk, this test provides a carefully prepared set of incoming letters, memoranda, reports, papers to be signed, and similar items. Before taking the test, the examinee has an opportunity to study background materials for orientation and information regarding the hypothetical job. During the test proper, the task is to handle all the matters in the in-basket as the examinee would on the job. All actions must be recorded in writing but may include letters, memos, decisions, plans, directives, information to be obtained or transmitted, agenda for meetings, or any other notes. Other assessment center techniques may employ roleplaying, group problem-solving, and business games. A common feature is the use of multiple assessors and peer ratings. Many of the traits evaluated pertain to motivation, interpersonal skills, and other personality variables.

Although depending at least in part on job resemblance as evidence of their "job relatedness," these global performance assessment procedures have also been evaluated, both singly and in various combinations, against a variety of criteria (see Landy et al., 1994; Schmidt, Ones, & Hunter, 1992).

Job Analysis and the Job Element Method. There is a growing interest in the application of content validation to personnel selection tests. In all its forms, this validation depends on a thorough and systematic job analysis (McCormick, 1979). To be effective, a job analysis must identify the requirements that differentiate a particular job from other jobs. A description in terms of vague generalities that would be equally applicable to most jobs is of little use for this purpose. To obtain a well rounded picture of job activities, the job analyst may draw upon several sources of information. Published training and operating manuals, performance records, and, especially, subject-matter experts—such as supervisors, instructors, or experienced workers in a field—are frequently consulted.

An effective job analysis also should concentrate on those aspects of performance that differentiate most sharply between the better and the poorer workers. In his classic book on *Aptitude Testing,* Hull (1928) stressed the importance of these differentiating aspects of job performance. Later, this concept was reemphasized by J. C. Flanagan (1949, 1954), who proposed the critical incident technique. Essentially, this technique calls for factual descriptions of specific instances of job behavior that are characteristic of either satisfactory or unsatisfactory workers.

The focus on critical job requirements led to the development of the job element method for constructing tests and demonstrating their content validity (McCormick, 1979, 1983; McCormick, Jeanneret, & Mecham, 1972; Primoff, 1975; Primoff & Eyde, 1988). This method was fully developed and widely employed by Primoff and his associates at the U.S. Office of Personnel Management (formerly the U.S. Civil Service Commission). Essentially, job elements are the units describing critical work requirements. Although various adaptations of the job element method differ in the details of procedure, all provide for the descrip-tion of job activities in terms of specific behavioral requirements, from which test items can be directly formulated. The specific behavioral statements can, in turn, be grouped under broader categories, or constructs—such as computational accuracy, dexterity of hands and arms, visual discrimination, or ability to work under pressure. There is a growing body of research aimed at the development of a general taxonomy of job performance in terms of broad behavioral constructs (Fleishman, 1975; Fleishman & Quaintance, 1984; Fleishman & Reilly, 1992b).

Job analysis methods can contribute to facilitating the effective use of tests across many superficially different jobs. This is illustrated by instruments such as the Fleishman Job Analysis Survey (F-JAS) and the Work Keys system. The F-JAS is a job analysis tool designed to describe jobs in terms of the knowledge, skills, and abilities required to perform them. Fifty-two out of its 72 scales cover carefully defined abilities in the cognitive, psychomotor, physical, and sensory/ perceptual domains, and most of these have been linked to existing tests (Fleishman & Mumford, 1991; Fleishman & Reilly, 1992a, 1992b). The remaining 20 scales deal with the Interpersonal/Social and Knowledge/Skills domains and are still under development. On the other hand, the Work Keys system—recently devised by the American College Testing Program (ACT, 1995; Scruggs, 1994)— concentrates on a much smaller set of generic workplace skills, such as "Locating Information," that can be taught in a reasonable period of time. Within this framework, however, the system provides a coordinated package of tools for: (1) job analysis and profiling; (2) assessment of skill levels; (3) feedback to individuals, educators, and employers; and (4) instructional support in the implementation of training or educational curricula.

Job analysis is one of the oldest and most viable methods developed in industrial psychology. Its application in validating employment tests has kept expanding as advances in computer technology have made the collection and analysis of job data more economical.[22] In addition, information gathered through careful job analyses can be put to many other uses, such as establishing the value of a job in the marketplace or designing jobs (see, e.g., Campion, 1994; I. L. Goldstein, Zedeck, & Schneider, 1993).

The Prediction of Job Performance. Practical difficulties inherent in the conduct of local criterion-prediction validation (see chaps. 5 and 6) have led to a relative dearth of such studies. Still, the fact remains that many organizations require forecasts of future job performance in order to make personnel selection and placement decisions.[23] For these purposes, the techniques of synthetic validation and validity generalization increasingly have become the alternatives of choice. Both allow estimates of the validity of a test for a particular job to be made in the absence of local validation. And, as empirical data accumulate, both methods should provide convergent evidence about the nature of the constructs assessed (J. P. Campbell, 1990a).

The concept of *synthetic validation* is based on the job element method premise that it is possible to identify skills, knowledge, and other performance requirements common to many different jobs. Synthetic validity has been defined as "the inferring of validity in a specific situation from a systematic analysis of job elements, a determination of test validity for these elements, and a combination of elemental validities into a whole" (Balma, 1959, p. 395). Essentially, this

---

[22] An overview of advances and problems in job analysis methodology can be found in Harvey (1991). Knapp, Russell, and Campbell (1993) describe specific applications of job analysis in the context of selection and classification of armed services personnel.

[23] For a provocative discussion about the limitations of prediction as a paradigm in personnel selection, see de Wolff (1993).

technique involves three steps: (1) detailed job analysis to identify the job elements and their relative weights in a particular job; (2) analysis and empirical study of each test to determine the extent to which it measures proficiency in performing each of these job elements; and (3) finding the validity of each test for the given job synthetically from the weights of these elements in the job and in the test. A statistical procedure for computing this validity was developed by Primoff (1959; Primoff & Eyde, 1988). Designated as the J-coefficient (for job coefficient), this procedure is essentially an adaptation of multiple regression equations, discussed in chapter 6. Other approaches to synthetic validation have been described by J. P. Hollenbeck and Whitemer (1988) and by Mossholder and Arvey (1984).

Validity generalization procedures—originally developed by Schmidt and Hunter (1977) and described in chapter 5—provide another avenue for validating personnel selection tests. Basically, this approach permits the application of prior validity findings to a new situation through meta-analytic techniques (Schmidt, Hunter, Pearlman, & Hirsh, 1985). The actual extent to which findings obtained through meta-analyses are generalizable has been called into question by some. Critics have underscored the differences that exist across job situations as well as methodological problems in estimating parameters. This, in turn, has led to refinements in meta-analytic methods and, subsequently, to their increased acceptance and application. Although some controversial points remain, and there is still room for further improvements, it is undeniable that validity generalization methods have contributed greatly to the vitality of theory, research, and practice in occupational testing (see, e.g., L. R. James et al., 1992; Landy et al., 1994; Schmidt et al., 1993).

The Criterion of Job Performance. Some of the most promising work in the field of personnel selection and classification stems from the renewed attention that is being given to criteria. It may be recalled, from chapter 5, that there is a vast array of indices that can be viewed as criterion measures, depending on how the criterion is defined. Nevertheless, within each validation study, a single convenient measure of job performance typically has been used to represent "the" criterion, regardless of the purpose of the prediction process. Until recently, in spite of repeated calls for more careful consideration of criteria, extending over several decades (see, e.g., L. R. James, 1973; Tenopyr, 1986; Wallace, 1965), little was done about this crucial problem. However, in the past few years, several investigators have been working toward a clearer conceptualization of job performance and a better understanding of its determinants (Borman, 1991; Campbell, McCloy, Oppler, & Sager, 1993; B. F. Green & Wigdor, 1991; Schmidt & Hunter, 1992).

One new model of job performance which promises to play an important heuristic role is the multiple factor theory that John P. Campbell and his coworkers have been developing in conjunction with the U.S. Army Selection and Classification Project (Project A—J. P. Campbell 1990a, 1990b, 1994; Campbell, McHenry, & Wise, 1990). Campbell's model takes into account the multifaceted nature of job performance and separates the various elements subsumed under that rubric. Initially, the model makes some fundamental distinctions between those aspects of work evaluation that are under the control of the worker—for example, the behaviors involved in job performance itself—and those that are not—for example, the consequences of job performance (effectiveness), its relative costs (productivity), and the value placed on each of these aspects by the organization (utility). With regard to job performance itself, the theory postulates that any job entails multiple performance components (tasks) and that the determinants of each component consist of various combinations of knowledge, skill, and motivational elements within the worker. Furthermore, each determinant of job performance has certain more or less specifiable antecedents—such as training, reinforcement contingencies, and individual traits—that can influence the performance indirectly through their effects on the level of knowledge, skills, and motivation of the individual. In addition, these determinants of job performance interact with one another, with a consequent impact on performance.

Although the multiple factor theory of job performance is still evolving (J. P. Campbell, 1990a, 1994; D. J. Knapp & Campbell, 1993), its design is quite compatible with other major conceptual and methodological advances in the evaluation of job behavior (Borman, 1991). The model presently identifies eight general factors of job performance, including such characteristics as consistency of effort, personal discipline, leadership, job-specific task proficiency, and other kinds of task proficiencies. These factors are presumed to be broad enough to encompass the main elements needed to describe all the jobs listed in the *Dictionary of* Occupational *Tides.* In addition, the model specifies three kinds of determinants of individual differences in job performance—namely, declarative knowledge, procedural knowledge and skill, and motivation—as well as their antecedents. This comprehensive and clearly articulated theoretical structure should prove to be applicable in a wide range of research on job performance constructs.

Occupational Use of Tests

As the preceding discussion suggests, the appropriateness of test use in personnel decisions cannot be considered apart from the specific purposes, situations, and populations involved in a given context.[24] It also should be noted that—whereas we may categorize tests by types for the sake of discussion—in practice, the demarcation lines between knowledge, abilities, skills, and personality traits are not always clear. Thus, it may be more fruitful to think about work behavior as determined by *response capabilities,* as some have suggested (Lubinski & Dawis, 1992). Moreover, although the validity of a test is often reviewed in isolation, tests are hardly ever used by themselves. Most test-based personnel decisions employ a combination of one or more measures as well as some other kind of assessment tool—such as an interview or background data.[25] Keeping all of these caveats in mind, we now turn to consider the use of tests in occupational settings.

The Role of Academic Intelligence. "Intelligence" is a broad term, with many definitions. What constitutes intelligence undoubtedly varies in different

[24] For a brief look at the multiplicity of variables that impinge on the success of the person-context interaction, see Sternberg (1994a).

[25] See Guion (1991) for an excellent overview of the process of personnel assessment, selection, and placement, including findings concerning the validity and fairness of various tests and other types of predictors.

cultures, during different historical epochs, and at different life stages (see chaps. 11 and 12). Traditional intelligence tests, in contrast, cover a more narrowly limited, identifiable cluster of cognitive skills and knowledge which, nevertheless, has proved to be widely predictive of performance in both academic and occupational activities demanded in modern technological societies. Because it deals largely with knowledge and skills developed in the course of formal schooling in such societies, this ability cluster is frequently described as academic intelligence or scholastic ability. Its content includes principally verbal comprehension, quantitative reasoning, and other aspects of abstract thinking.

It is well known that performance on tests of academic intelligence correlates substantially with amount of education. It would thus seem that educational requirements could be established to cover the applicant's qualifications in this important cluster of cognitive skills and knowledge. There are difficulties, however, in the way of this solution. Amount of education is an indirect index of the individual's cognitive developmental status, and the correlation between the two is far from perfect. Mere exposure to formal schooling does not ensure equal learning of what has been taught; moreover, the knowledge and skills normally developed through schooling *can* be acquired in other ways. It is therefore fairer to the individual to test her or his knowledge and cognitive skills rather than to accept or reject applicants on the basis of amount of formal education.

Among commercially published instruments, several short tests of academic intelligence have been specially developed for use in industry. An example is the Wonderlic Personnel Test (Wonderlic Personnel Test, Inc., 1992). Begun as a revision of an early group intelligence test (the Otis Self-Administering Tests of Mental Ability), the Wonderlic is a 50-item, 12-minute test. It includes a variety of item types with verbal, numerical, and some spatial content—presented in a spiral-omnibus format—and yields a single score. Available in many forms, this test has accumulated extensive norms on various occupational groups over its several decades of use, and its predictive value for training and job success is well documented (for reviews, see Belcher, 1992; Schmidt, 1985; Schoenfeldt, 1985).

Interest in the potential usefulness of general academic intelligence tests for personnel selection has been reawakened by research on validity generalization (see, e.g., Hunter, 1986). Of particular relevance are the findings that tests of verbal and numerical reasoning have some predictive validity for a wide variety and range of jobs. In addition, the validity rises for jobs with more extensive demands for decision making and information processing. However, although tests of general cognitive ability contribute substantially to the prediction of job performance, especially for complex jobs, predictive accuracy may be enhanced by the assessment of additional variables. Chief among these are the more specialized skills and knowledge required by particular jobs—including psychomotor skills and tacit or procedural knowledge—as well as noncognitive variables, such as temperamental and attitudinal characteristics (see, e.g., Ackerman, 1992; J. P. Campbell, 1990b; Carroll, 1992; Kanfer, Ackerman, Murtha, & Goff, 1995; Sternberg, Wagner, Williams, & Horvath, 1995). Many of these relationships have been demonstrated in large-scale research projects with the classification batteries employed in the armed services and in certain civilian government agencies.

Aptitude Batteries for Special Programs.[26] The General Aptitude Test Battery (GATB) was developed by the United States Employment Service (USES) for use by employment counselors in state employment service offices (U.S. Department of Labor, 1970). In addition, the battery may be obtained by nonprofit organizations such as secondary schools, colleges, and prisons. At present, the GATB includes 12 tests; 4 of the tests require simple apparatus, while the other 8 are paper-and-pencil tests. The entire battery can be administered in approximately 2½ hours. It yields scores on nine factors and on three major composite measures derived from the factors, all of which are listed in Table 17–1.

GATB score utilization can proceed through two distinct approaches. The first makes use of multiple-cutoff scores on the most significant aptitudes required for relatively homogeneous groups of jobs. One mechanism used with this approach is the Occupational Aptitude Pattern (OAP) structure developed in the 1970s (U.S. Department of Labor, 1979, 1980). OAPs for more than 60 job families, covering thousands of occupations, have been prepared. For each job group, cutoff scores denoting high, medium, and low levels of qualification on the pertinent aptitudes have been calculated and can be employed to counsel individuals about suitable careers.[27] A second approach to the use of the GATB was derived through the application of validity generalization (VG) techniques to data from more than 500 prior USES validity studies. This procedure, which came to be known as the VG-GATB, uses validity estimates based on appropriate combinations of scores for all jobs within each job family (U.S. Department of Labor, 1983a, 1983c, 1983d). Predictions are based on three composite measures— cognitive, perceptual, and psychomotor—derived from the original factor scores. Of the three, the cognitive composite yields the highest validity coefficients for most jobs, but the psychomotor composite can enhance prediction as jobs decrease in complexity (Hunter & Hunter, 1984).

Through the facilities of the USES, an extensive body of data has been accumulated on the GATB, much of which attests to its exceptional reliability and substantial predictive validity (for reviews, see B. Bolton, 1994; Kirnan &

Table 17–1

General Aptitude Test Battery (GATB) Factors and Composites

Factors		
G. *General Learning Ability*	S. *Spatial Aptitude*	K. *Motor Coordination*
V. *Verbal Aptitude*	P. *Form Perception*	F. *Finger Dexterity*
N. *Numerical Aptitude*	Q. *Clerical Perception*	M. *Manual Dexterity*
Composites		
Cognitive = G + V + N	Perceptual = S + P + Q	Psychomotor = K + F + M

[26] See chapters 10 and 11 for background pertinent to this section.

[27] The Special Aptitude Test Battery (SATB) groups provide an alternative mechanism for the use of cutoff scores with the GATB. The multiple-cutoff strategy is more fully discussed in chapter 6. In the realm of selection, as opposed to counseling, the most appropriate use of cutoff scores is for a preliminary screening of applicants in one or more critical skills.

Geisinger, 1986). However, the practice of subgroup norming—implemented in the 1980s with the VG-GATB in order to ensure comparable rates of referrals for White, Black, and Hispanic applicants—led to a heated political debate about fairness in preemployment testing (Hartigan & Wigdor, 1989). The debate culminated with the passage of the Civil Rights Act of 1991 (P.L. 102-166), which prohibited subgroup norming. This legislation has affected the use of the battery and has made its future uncertain (L. S. Gottfredson, 1994; Wigdor & Sackett, 1993—also see chap. 18). Nevertheless, a research program that includes the development of two new forms and an experimental computerized adaptive version of the GATB is still in progress.

Another major selection and classification tool is the Armed Services Vocational Aptitude Battery (ASVAB), developed jointly for use in all the U.S. armed services (Bayroff & Fuchs, 1970). The battery is administered to high school students interested in military occupations and to individuals who have applied to enter the military. Current forms of the ASVAB include ten subtests listed in Table 17–2.[28] The Armed Forces Qualification Test (AFQT) is a composite score used by all the services as a gauge of general trainability in screening potential recruits. In addition, each of the services combines subtests to form composites for its own personnel selection and classification needs. For example, the Army's Combat composite consists of the AR + CS + AS + MC component subtests.

Standard scores for the ASVAB are based on norms obtained from a representative sample of American youths (U.S. Department of Defense, 1982). The factor structure of the battery has been examined at some length. Findings typically show a general factor that accounts for about 60 percent of the total ASVAB variance and four group factors that have been repeatedly replicated (J. R. Welsh, Watson, & Ree, 1990). The four factors, along with the subtests on which they have the highest loadings, are: (1) Verbal (WK and PC); (2) Speed (NO and CS); (3) Quantitative (AR and MK); and (4) Technical (AS, MC, and El).

Table 17–2

Armed Services Vocational Aptitude Battery (ASVAB)

ASVAB Subtests	
General Science (GS)	Arithmetic Reasoning (AR)[a]
Word Knowledge (WK)[a]	Mathematics Knowledge (MK)[a]
Paragraph Comprehension (PC)[a]	Mechanical Comprehension (MC)
Electronics Information (EI)	Auto and Shop Information (AS)
Coding Speed (CS)[b]	Numerical Operations (NO)[b]

[a]AFQT composite [b]Speeded

[28] There is also a Computerized Adaptive Testing version of the ASVAB (CAT-ASVAB), which has been under development since 1979 and now is being used operationally for some military entrance processing (T. L. Russell, Reynolds, & Campbell, 1994). For a description of the CAT-ASVAB and its development, see Wiskoff & Schratz (1989).

The validities of the ASVAB subtests and composites have been investigated against a variety of job and educational performance criteria. As might be imagined, validity coefficients differ substantially depending on the type and number of criteria employed. In general, validities are higher for "can-do" criteria—such as general soldiering and technical proficiency—than for "will-do" criteria—such as effort, leadership, and personal discipline. As might be expected, the former are assessed through job knowledge and "hands-on" measures, whereas the latter typically are assessed through supervisor, peer, and self ratings (McHenry, Hough, Toquam, Hanson, & Ashworth, 1990; T. L. Russell et al., 1994).

The most extensive examination of the ASVAB was initiated by the U.S. Department of Defense in 1980, as a part of the Joint-Service Job Performance Measurement/Enlistment Standards (JPM) Project (Wigdor & Green, 1991a, 1991b). This massive project is aimed at developing robust measures of performance for entry level military jobs so that meaningful and valid enlistment standards can be set for the all-volunteer armed forces. The first phase of the JPM established that the ASVAB is a good predictor of high-fidelity, performance-based indicators of job proficiency.[29] It also provided support for the differential validity of the ASVAB composite scores for different jobs. However, the magnitude of the average score differences between Black and nonminority examinees was considerably greater on the AFQT and on paper-and-pencil tests of job knowledge than on the hands-on job sample tests. This suggests the possibility that some of the ASVAB measures may overestimate the size of the actual group differences in job performance. If corroborated, this situation would parallel some of the findings obtained with the GATB (Hartigan & Wigdor, 1989). Furthermore, the validity coefficients of the ASVAB against various criteria were modest enough to justify a search for additional predictors. The second phase of the JPM project is exploring models for enlistment standards that will enhance the overall utility of selection and classification decisions, both in terms of costs and levels of performance.

The U.S. Army's Selection and Classification Project (Project A) encompasses another important segment of the research on the ASVAB and on new predictors of military job performance. Project A originated as the Army's own extensive response to the mandate of the JPM project and is arguably the largest and most expensive personnel selection research project ever (Schmidt et al., 1992). In addition to its contribution to building a theory of job performance—discussed in an earlier section of this chapter—the work of Project A has involved development and evaluation of many new predictors that go beyond the traditional cognitive functions of the ASVAB. The evolving battery includes computer-administered perceptual and psychomotor tests; it also involves specially constmcted inventories designed to assess personality, temperamental, and background variables as well as interests (McHenry et al., 1990; N. G. Peterson et al., 1990). Moreover, the large scale and longitudinal nature of Project A have also made it possible to study validity changes over time to an unprecedented extent (J. P. Campbell, 1990b).[30]

[29] The conceptual and methodological work that went into developing performance-based measures is a valuable contribution of the JPM project which should prove applicable in the field of educational assessment and elsewhere.

[30] A final report on Project A research, in the form of a volume co-edited by J. P. Campbell and D. Knapp, is scheduled for publication in the late 1990s.

Special Aptitude Tests. Even prior to the development of multiple aptitude batteries, many people recognized that intelligence tests were limited in their coverage of abilities. Efforts were soon made to fill the major gaps by means of special aptitude tests covering the more concrete and practical abilities, such as mechanical aptitude. The demands of occupational selection and counseling likewise stimulated the development of measures of spatial, clerical, musical, and artistic aptitudes. Tests of vision, hearing, muscular performance, and motor dexterity have also been widely used in selecting and classifying personnel for industrial and military purposes.[31]

A word should be added about the concept of *special aptitudes.* The term originated at a time when the major emphasis in testing was placed on general intelligence. Mechanical, musical, and other special aptitudes were thus regarded as supplementary to the "IQ" in the description of the individual. With the advent of factor analysis, however, it was gradually recognized that intelligence itself comprises a number of relatively independent aptitudes, such as verbal comprehension, numerical reasoning, spatial visualization, and the like. Moreover, several of the traditional special aptitudes, such as mechanical and clerical, are now incorporated in some of the multiple aptitude batteries.

What, then, is the role of special aptitude tests? First, there are certain areas, such as vision, hearing, motor dexterity, and artistic talents, that are rarely included in multiple aptitude batteries. The situations requiring tests in these areas are too specialized to justify the inclusion of such tests in standard batteries. Special aptitude tests are also employed, however, in areas that are covered in multiple aptitude batteries, such as clerical and mechanical aptitudes. In several testing programs, tests of academic intelligence are combined with specially selected tests of other relevant aptitudes. One reason for this practice is to be found in the extensive normative and validation data available for some widely used tests of special aptitudes. Another reason, undoubtedly, is the flexibility that this procedure provides, not only in the choice of relevant aptitudes but also in the fullness with which each aptitude is measured for specific purposes.

Many tests have been devised to measure speed, coordination, and other *psychomotor skills.* Most are concerned with manual dexterity, but a few involve leg or foot movements that may be required in performing specific jobs. Some measure a combination of motor and perceptual, spatial, or mechanical aptitudes. The principal application of these tests has been in the selection of industrial and military personnel. Psychomotor tests are characteristically apparatus tests, although several paper-and-pencil adaptations have been designed for group administration. An example of a published instrument requiring several simple manipulative skills is the Crawford Small Parts Dexterity Test (Crawford & Crawford, 1981), shown in Figure 17–2. In Part I of this test, the examinee uses tweezers to insert pins into close-fitting holes and then places a small collar over each pin. In Part II, small screws are placed in threaded holes and screwed down with a screwdriver. The score is the time required to complete each part.

What can be said about the effectiveness of psychomotor tests as a whole? The most important point to note in evaluating such tests is the high degree of

[31] An overview of personnel selection procedures specifically for jobs that are physically demanding is presented by J.C. Hogan (1992).

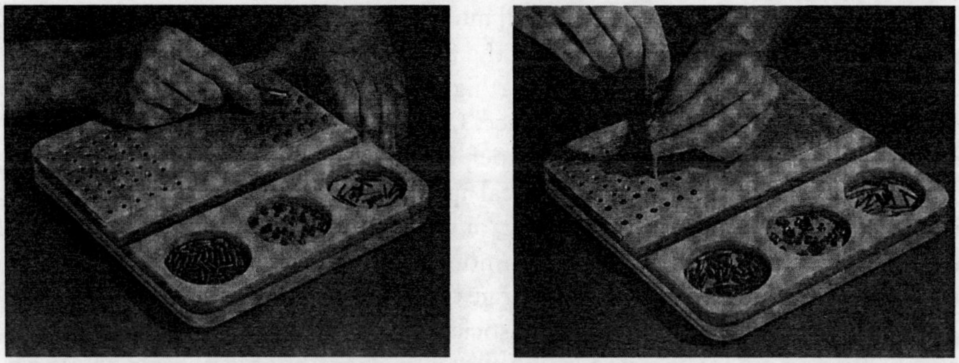

Figure 17-2. Crawford Small Parts Dexterity Test.
(Courtesy of The Psychological Corporation.)

specificity of motor functions. Intercorrelations and factor analyses of large numbers of motor tests have failed to reveal broad group factors such as those found for intellectual functions (Fleishman, 1975; Fleishman & Quaintance, 1984, chap. 12). In considering the validity of psychomotor tests, we need to differentiate between complex motor tests that closely resemble the particular criterion performance they are trying to predict and tests of simple motor functions designed for more general use. The former are custom-made tests—now typically computerized— that reproduce the combination of motor aptitudes required by the criterion and have shown fair validity. Some Air Force tests, for example, have been shown to improve prediction of flying performance (see, e.g., R. H. Cox, 1989; Kantor & Carretta, 1988). For most purposes, however, the use of such tests is not practicable, since a very large number of tests would have to be devised to match different criteria. With regard to commercially available motor tests, the functions they measure are very simple, and their validities against most criteria are not high. For this reason, such tests can serve best as part of a selection battery, rather than as single predictors.

Mechanical aptitude tests cover a variety of functions. Psychomotor factors enter into some of the tests in this category, either because the rapid manipulation of materials is required in the performance of the test or because special subtests designed to measure motor dexterity are included in a paper-and-pencil test. Perceptual and spatial aptitudes also play an important part in many of these tests. Finally, mechanical reasoning and sheer mechanical information predominate in a number of mechanical aptitude tests.

It is important to recognize the diversity of functions subsumed under the heading of mechanical aptitude, since each function may be differently related to other variables. For example, mechanical information tests are much more dependent on past experience with mechanical objects than are abstract spatial or perceptual tests. Similarly, gender differences may be reversed from one of these functions to another. Thus, in manual dexterity and in perceptual discrimination tests, women generally excel; in abstract spatial tests, a small but significant average difference in favor of males is usually found; while in mechanical reasoning or information tests, men are markedly superior (Anastasi, 1981c; Hedges & Nowell, 1995).

Among the aptitudes included in all multiple aptitude batteries is spatial aptitude. This is the ability measured by the Space Relations test of the DAT (see chap. 10); it has been found to have a high loading in many performance and nonlanguage tests of general intelligence. One of the best single measures of this aptitude is the Revised Minnesota Paper Foma Board Test (Likert & Quasha, 1995). Another major type of mechanical aptitude test is concerned with mechanical information, mechanical reasoning, or mechanical comprehension. Although they require some familiarity with common tools and mechanical relations, these tests assume no more technical knowledge than can be acquired through everyday experience in a modem industrialized society. Some of the early tests in this field required the examinee to assemble common mechanical objects from the given parts. For general testing purposes, paper-and-pencil group tests are now widely employed. A well-known example of this type of test is the Bennett Mechanical Comprehension Test (G. K. Bennett, 1994). Utilizing pictures about which short questions are to be answered—such as those illustrated in Figure 17–3—this test emphasizes the understanding of mechanical principles as applied to a wide variety of everyday life situations.

Tests designed to measure *clerical aptitudes* are characterized by a common emphasis on perceptual speed and accuracy. A typical example is the Minnesota Clerical Test (MCT—Andrew, Paterson, & Longstaff, 1979), which consists of two separately timed subtests, Number Comparison and Name Comparison. In the first, the test taker is given 200 pairs of numbers, each containing from 3 to 12 digits. If the two numbers in the pair are identical, a check mark is placed between them. The task is similar in the second subtest, proper names being substituted for numbers.

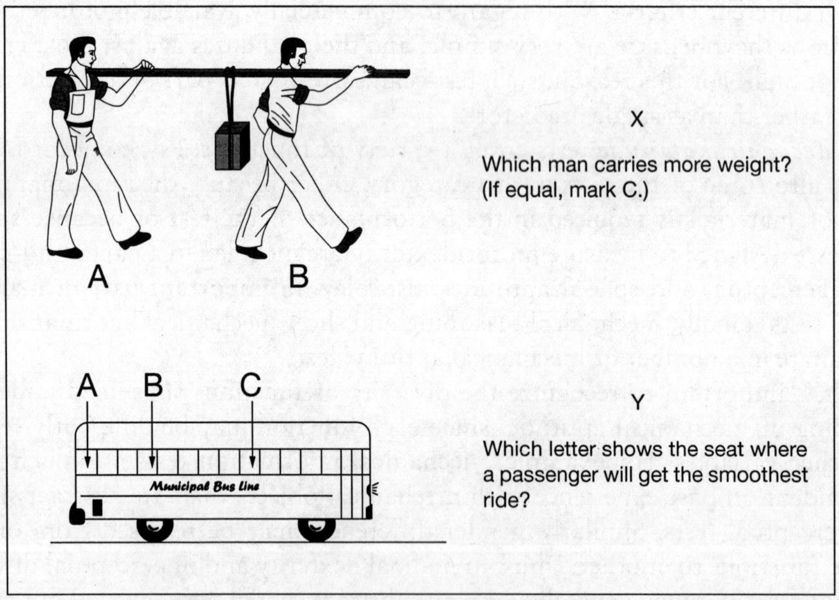

Figure 17–3. Sample Items from the Bennett Mechanical Comprehension Test. Answers are recorded on a separate answer sheet.

Such relatively homogeneous tests as the MCT measure only one aspect of clerical work. Clerical jobs cover a multiplicity of functions. Moreover, the number and particular combination of duties vary tremendously with the type and level of job. Despite such a diversity of activities, however, job analyses of clerical work generally indicate that a relatively large proportion of time is spent in tasks requiring speed and accuracy in perceiving details. To be sure, many types of jobs besides that of clerk require perceptual speed and accuracy. Inspectors, checkers, packers, and a host of other factory workers obviously need this ability, though many of these jobs are being replaced by electronic scanning devices.

Several tests of clerical aptitude combine perceptual speed and accuracy with other functions required for clerical work. Among the tools used are job-sample tests for such activities as alphabetizing, classifying, coding, and the like. In addition, some measure of verbal and numerical ability may be included, to serve in lieu of a general intelligence test. Other clerical aptitude tests include such office skills as business vocabulary, business information, spelling, and language usage. Some clerical tests are more properly classified as achievement or job sample tests, since they measure skills acquired after the completion of specialized training. Examples include stenographic and typing skills tests, as well as tests on data entry and data retrieval skills like the CRT Skills Test by Science Research Associates (SRA, 1990).

The rapid growth in the use of computers for office work led to the publication of several tests for *computer-related aptitudes.* Many of these were designed for the counseling or selection of potential trainees. Examples include the Computer Literacy and Computer Science Tests and the Computer Programmer Aptitude Battery (for reviews of these instruments, see Mahurin, 1992; Marco, 1992; Schafer, 1992). Although these tests represented timely applications of psychometrics to personnel assessment at the time they were developed—between the 1960s and the early 1980s—the pace of technological change is so fast that some of them already have become obsolete. Gradually, newer instruments are becoming available, both for instruction and for competency testing in the use of specific software programs, such as dBASE, WordPerfect, and Lotus 1-2-3.[32]

Recent strides in recognizing the significance of the cognitive dimensions of interpersonal and intrapersonal functioning (see, e.g., H. Gardner, 1983; Salovey & Mayer, 1990) are likely to stimulate the development of standardized objective instruments aimed at assessing the *social and emotional aspects of intelligence* in the context of work. Such instruments have been heretofore practically nonexistent, as the adequacy of interpersonal and intrapersonal functioning in employment settings has traditionally been gauged either through personality tests or through interviews and assessment center techniques. The Teamwork-KSA Test, a recently published paper-and-pencil measure designed to predict effective teamwork, is one of the first instruments within this new category. Based on a review of the literature of work groups in organizations, the test attempts to measure the knowledge, skills, and abilities of examinees in the interpersonal and self-management domains. The multiple-choice items present hypothetical questions dealing with conflict resolution, communication, and collaborative problem

[32] These tests, and several other computer-related instruments, are available from the SRA Product Group of McGraw-Hill/London House (see Appendix B).

solving, as well as with goal setting, planning, and other self-management skills (M. J. Stevens & Campion, 1994). Further work and experimentation with this and other similar instruments are sure to follow.

Personality Testing in the Workplace

In the mid-1980s, Bernardin and Bownas (1985) noted that the use of personality evaluation techniques—including such unscientific methods as handwriting analysis—was flourishing in industrial settings, while the academic community had largely neglected the subject for almost two decades.[33] Since then, a tremendous resurgence of work in the area has occurred, prompted by methodological and theoretical developments. From a methodological viewpoint, the application of meta-analysis and the use of causal modeling techniques (see chap. 5) have stimulated research on the noncognitive traits that can affect job performance. Meta-analyses have been employed primarily to investigate the validity and utility of personality constructs across settings. Path analysis and structural equation modeling techniques (see chap. 5) are used to study the interrelationships among predictors and to explore the attributes and conditions leading to differing levels of job performance. The extent to which some critical variables, like ability level and job autonomy, moderate the relationship between personality and performance is also under study. In general, the goals of these investigations go beyond prediction, toward an understanding of the constructs and processes that determine the large variations that exist in job performance (Barrick & Mount, 1991, 1993; Hough, Eaton, Dunnette, Kamp, &. McCloy, 1990; Matthews, Jones, & Chamberlain, 1992; McHenry et al., 1990; Schmidt & Hunter, 1992; Tett, Jackson, & Rothstein, 1991).

The more methodologically sophisticated research of the past decade or two has provided considerable support for the use of carefully constructed personality tests in employment decisions across a variety of settings. An important issue that still bears further investigation is that of determining the most relevant personality dimensions relative to performance in particular jobs, or job families. For example, whereas a high degree of sociability might be required for some jobs, the opposite may be the case for others. Even a characteristic like conscientiousness, which may appear at first glance to be desirable for all jobs, might upon further investigation prove to involve attributes that may be counterproductive for certain endeavors—such as creative pursuits—at least in some respects. As a result of considerations such as this, some attention is now starting to be directed toward establishing the temperamental and interpersonal requirements of jobs (R. Hogan, Hogan, & Roberts, 1996; Landy et al., 1994).

A great deal of recent research activity has centered on exploring the usefulness of the Five-Factor Model of personality structure, in its various forms, to the prediction of job performance criteria (see chap. 13 and R. Hogan, 1991). The popularity of the Five-Factor Model in personnel selection research is not coincidental. After all, the five (± 2) factors were distilled from vast arrays of

---

[33] See Anastasi (1985e) for an historical overview of personality testing in industry and for a discussion of several basic methodological and practical problems connected with it. Kanfer et al. (1995) provide a review of progress in the application of concepts from personality and intelligence theories to the field of industrial and organizational psychology.

personality description data and represent a model for describing normal personalities upon which there is a fair amount of agreement. Each of the domains subsumed by the model is widely applicable to all sorts of everyday behavior, including the performance of job duties. The dimension of Emotional Stability, for instance, is essential in jobs that require quick decision-making under stressful conditions, such as law enforcement, airplane piloting, truck driving, and medical emergency work. Agreeableness, on the other hand, is an indispensable quality for any job that involves extensive interpersonal contact. Not surprisingly, however, the Conscientiousness factor is the one that has emerged from several meta-analytic investigations as the most ubiquitious and substantial personality predictor of job performance (Barrick & Mount, 1991, 1993; Schmidt & Hunter, 1992). Even so, agreement is still far from universal either with regard to the definition of the construct of Conscientiousness or to the question of its primacy (see, e.g., Loevinger, 1994; Tett et al., 1991).

Integrity Tests. The application of integrity or honesty tests in hiring decisions came into special prominence after the passage of the Employee Polygraph Protection Act of 1988 (P. L. 100-347), which prohibited the use of polygraphs in screening personnel, except in special settings such as government agencies.[34] As a result of this legislation, paper-and-pencil measures of trustworthiness—widely known as "integrity tests"—proliferated. These measures, which typically inquire about an applicant's attitudes toward and history of involvement in theft and other illicit behaviors, quickly came under scrutiny both from within and outside psychology.[35] In one of the most comprehensive investigations of integrity tests, Ones, Viswesvaran, and Schmidt (1993) conducted a meta-analysis based on 665 validity coefficients. Their study estimated that the average operational validity of integrity tests for predicting supervisory ratings of job performance is .41 and indicated that these tests can also be of value in the prediction of disruptive behavior on the job.

In spite of a fairly substantial degree of support gathered for the use of integrity tests, within certain parameters, their application in preemployment selection decisions remains problematic. Current concerns center on the tests' possible susceptibility to coaching and faking and on their relative ineffectiveness in predicting specific forms of job misbehavior, such as theft (see, e.g., Alliger, Lilienfeld, & Mitchell, 1996; Camara & Schneider, 1995).

Leadership. The selection of effective leaders poses another significant challenge in the field of personnel decisions. Leadership is one of the most sought-after qualities in the workplace because it encompasses the ability to persuade others to work toward a common cause. Effective leadership can have powerful

[34] One of the earliest critical reviews of the topic of lie detection and polygraphy written by a psychologist is Lykken's (1981) hook. Briefer and more recent reviews and discussions can be found in DePaulo (1994), Honts (1994), Kircher and Raskin (1992), Lykken (1992), and Saxe (1994).

[35] See, for example, the report of a task force that the American Psychological Association formed to look into this issue (L. R. Goldberg, Grenier, Guion, Sechrest, Wing, 1991). Further information is available in K. R. Murphy's (1993) comprehensive volume on the general topic of honesty in the workplace. For brief but informative discussions of integrity testing in personnel selection, see Camara and Schneider (1994), Sackett (1994), and the Comment section of the June 1995 *American Psychologist*.

consequences in enhancing organizational functioning; ineffective leadership can be disastrous. Thus, it is not surprising that many types of cognitive and personality measures, as well as assessment center techniques, interviews, simulations, and biodata questionnaires, are applied to the selection of top management. Often, the assessment process involved in selecting high-level executives includes multiple methods and extends over a period of several hours or days. Such procedures are very similar to clinical testing and are typically quite costly.

For the most part, apparently, the resources devoted to the careful selection of individuals who go from the regular workforce into leadership positions are relatively meager compared to the potential impact of these decisions. Possibly as a consequence of this situation, managerial incompetence seems to be exceedingly high (R. Hogan, Curphy, & Hogan, 1994). Although interest in studying leadership behavior has a long history in applied psychology, and has resulted in an extensive literature on the subject, much remains to be done in terms of identifying and clarifying the empirical correlates of effective leadership. For further information on leadership measures and on theoretical and methodological advances in the study of leadership in organizations, see Bass (1990), Clark and Clark (1990), and Yukl and Van Fleet (1992).

Instruments. With the exception of the intensive assessment procedures used in the selection of top-level executives and some specialized personnel—such as intelligence agents, astronauts, and the like—the vast majority of job applicants who take personality tests simply are given a self-report inventory of the type described in chapter 13. Inventories aimed at the detection of psychopathology, such as the MMPI, are still employed for screening purposes in some sensitive occupations, but concerns over invasion of privacy and the misuse of results have led to the predominant use of measures designed to assess personality in normal subjects (see chap. 18). In fact, several of the older multidimensional self-report inventories that originally were meant for normal subjects—for example, the CPI—have been recently revised in ways that will make them more appropriate for use in the workplace. In the meantime, some newer measures, like the Hogan Personality Inventory (HPI—R. Hogan & Hogan, 1992), have been designed primarily for occupational settings in the first place. Other tests are being developed for a much narrower range of applications; examples include the PDI Customer Service Inventory and the PDI Employment Inventory, which is an instrument designed to screen applicants who will be dependable and stable hourly employees (see Paajanen, Hansen, & McLellan, 1993).

Concluding Comments. Technological developments are currently transforming the nature of work in ways that will far exceed the changes brought about by the industrial revolution. The rapid pace of change poses a tremendous challenge for personnel psychologists, while the methodological advances made possible by new technologies offer immense opportunities.[36] Just when it has become feasible to do the type of large-scale and highly sophisticated research that allows investigators to arrive at some fairly definitive answers to questions that have been around for a long time, the questions themselves are beginning to

[36] For a discussion of the transformations that are occurring in the workplace and the consequences they are likely to have for personnel work, see Landy, Shanksten-Cawley, and Kohler Moran (1995).

change. Meanwhile, the impact of computer technologies on personnel testing, while visible, is still only starting (Bartram, 1993; Burke, 1993; Schoenfeldt & Mendoza, 1991). Some of the more exciting applications of technology to testing—such as interactive multimedia tests—are just in the preliminary stages of development (Desmarais, Masi, Olson, Barbera, & Dyer, 1994; Drasgow et al., 1996). Many more can be foreseen but have not yet been realized. Altogether, though, there seems to be more ample room than ever for the thoughtful application of psychological principles and methods to improving the utilization of human resources (Bray et al., 1991; Gatewood & Feild, 1993).

TEST USE IN CLINICAL AND COUNSELING PSYCHOLOGY

Clinical and counseling psychologists employ a wide variety of tests, including most of the types already discussed. Periodic surveys have been conducted regarding the use of tests by samples of clinical and counseling psychologists who differ in their theoretical orientations and work settings (Archer, Maruish, Imhof, & Piotrowski, 1991; Lubin, Larsen, & Matarazzo, 1984; Piotrowski & Keller, 1992; Watkins et al., 1994; Watkins, Campbell, Nieberding, & Hallmark, 1995). High in frequency of use are such individual intelligence tests as the Wechsler scales, as well as multiple aptitude batteries like the DAT (see chap. 10). Many of the personality tests considered in chapters 13 through 16 are especially prominent in the repertory of clinicians and counselors (Butcher & Rouse, 1996). Certain diagnostic educational tests are appropriate in cases of learning disabilities and other school-related problems. In addition, clinicians and counselors use many brief questionnaires and rating scales for a quick evaluation of the multiplicity of problems encountered in practice. Many of these measures are described in a source-book by J. Fischer and Corcoran (1994).

The present section of this chapter focuses primarily on areas that require the application of multiple tests and other tools in the assessment of individuals, as opposed to the use of a single instrument in isolation. Psychological assessments of this sort are conducted by psychologists from various fields, although many have been trained in clinical and counseling psychology and their subspecialties. Clinical psychologists traditionally have conducted assessments aimed at diagnostic, prognostic, and therapeutic decisions in mental health settings (Butcher, 1995; Hersen, Kazdin, & Bellack, 1991; Hurt, Reznikoff, & Clarkin, 1991; Maruish, 1994), whereas counseling psychologists originally specialized exclusively in vocational assessment and guidance (S. D. Brown & Lent, 1992; Drummond, 1996; Gelso & Fretz, 1992). Other major fields in which psychological assessment is practiced, such as school psychology and forensic psychology,[37] derive their identification from the settings where professionals work (Shapiro, 1991; Vance, 1993; Weiner & Hess, 1987). Additional specialties utilizing psychological assessment techniques are defined by the types of problems they study, such as health psychology (N. Adler & Matthews, 1994; Streiner & Norman, 1995; S. E. Taylor, 1990) and neuropsychology, a field which is concerned with brain-behavior relationships (Benton, 1994; Maruish & Moses, 1997). Still others

[37] Forensic psychology is the practice of psychology in courts of law, in relation to legal matters, or with adjudicated or incarcerated individuals.

are identified by the kinds of patients or clients they serve—for example, children, couples, or families (Conoley & Werth, 1995; Fruzzetti & Jacobson, 1992; Kamphaus & Frick, 1996). Many practitioners work in even more highly specialized areas, like pediatric neuropsychology (Batchelor & Dean, 1996) or medical rehabilitation (Cushman & Scherer, 1995). All of these fields and subspecialties are evolving constantly. In addition, the boundaries between some specialties have become less clear and, in some cases, almost disappeared.

A notable instance of this overlap is the growing rapprochement between clinical and counseling psychology (see, e.g., Anastasi, 1979, 1990a; May, 1990).[38] Counseling psychologists increasingly can be found working in private practice, clinics, and hospital settings. At the same time, some clinical psychologists are now applying their skills in career assessment and personnel selection (Lowman, 1989, 1991, 1993). In a visible sign of the changes that are taking place, the proposed new *Testing Standards* address the use of tests for diagnosis and individual evaluation in clinical, counseling, and school settings within a single chapter entitled "Psychological Testing and Assessment," whereas the 1985 *Standards* dealt with clinical testing and test use in counseling separately (see chap. 1).

Psychological Assessment. What, then, does psychological assessment entail as it is practiced across specialties, settings, problem areas, and populations? One of its main characteristics is a focus on the intensive study of one or more individuals (e.g., a couple or a family) through multiple sources of data. By establishing and maintaining rapport, the clinician may elicit from the client pertinent facts about her or his life history not readily accessible in other ways. Such life-history data provide a particularly sound basis for understanding an individual and predicting subsequent behavior. Furthermore, the clinician contributes to the fact-finding process by serving as a stimulus in an interpersonal situation. In this regard, the clinical interview functions as a situational test or simulation, providing a sample of the client's interpersonal behavior under more-or-less controlled conditions.

Information derived from observation, interviewing, and the case history is combined with test scores to provide an integrated picture of the individual (Beutler & Berren, 1995). The clinician thus has available certain safeguards against overgeneralizing from test scores. This fact probably accounts at least in part for the continued use of some tests whose psychometric properties are either weak or unproved. As long as such instruments serve primarily to suggest leads for the skilled clinician to follow up, their retention can be justified. There is a danger, of course, that a relatively inexperienced and overzealous clinician, unmindful of the limitations of an instrument, may place more confidence in scores than is justified.

Another defining attribute of psychological assessment is its aim, which generally is to help in making informed decisions pertaining to differential diagnosis, career selection, treatment recommendations, educational planning, child

[38] Because of this circumstance, as well as for the sake of convenience, in this section the term "clinician" will be used to denote any professional involved in the practice of psychological assessment. Nevertheless, it is useful to bear in mind that the educational backgrounds of these professionals may be in any one of several specialties and, thus, their orientations and areas of expertise do vary. For information about test use by clinical, counseling, industrial/organizational, and school psychologists in their traditional settings, see P. S. Wise (1989).

custody determinations, culpability, and many more such matters of practical significance to one or more persons. Decision-making proceeds by means of the collection, analysis, integration, and thoughtful reporting of relevant behavioral data. At the center of the process of psychological assessment is a continuing sequence of hypothesis generation and hypothesis testing about the individual case. Each item of information—whether it be an event recorded in the case history, a comment by the client, or a test score—suggests a hypothesis about the individual that will be confirmed or refuted as other facts are gathered. In this respect as well, it should be kept in mind that any single source of data, no matter how seemingly reliable, may yield inaccurate information at times.[39]

Fundamentally, all the activities connected with a psychological assessment—from the clear elucidation of its primary purpose to the communication of results—involve professional *judgment* based on knowledge about the specific problems and populations at hand. Moreover, the application of individual tests and other assessment tools requires specialized skills in their use and a careful consideration of their characteristics, in light of the purpose and context of the assessment (Drummond, 1996; C. T. Fischer, 1985; Groth-Marnat, 1990; G. Goldstein & Hersen, 1990; Hood & Johnson, 1997; Maloney & Ward, 1976; Tallent, 1992; Walsh & Betz, 1995). In this respect, the clinical method has been contrasted with the administration of objective, standardized tests and the use of statistical or actuarial procedures for combining data through regression equations, multiple cutoffs, and other "mechanical formulas" (chap. 6; also see Dawes, Faust, & Meehl, 1993; L. R. Goldberg, 1991; Kleinmuntz, 1990; Wedding & Faust, 1989).

The ecological viewpoint, which emphasizes the need to take the context of a person's life into account, has had a significant influence in assessment work, as it has in developmental psychology and related fields (see, e.g., Moen, Elder, & Lüscher, 1995). Similarly, heightened awareness of the role of culture in all behavior—including the problems that lead people to seek help from mental health professionals—has stimulated a great deal of interest in information about and guidelines for culturally competent assessment practice (see, e.g., American Psychiatric Association, 1994, pp. xxiv and 843–849; Dana, 1993, 1996; Prediger, 1993; Suzuki et al., 1996).

Intelligence Tests in the Context of Individual Assessment. Tests such as the Wechsler scales and the Stanford-Binet (see chap. 8) are fundamentally individual, clinical instruments. When an alert and trained clinician is in active contact with an examinee during the hour or so required to administer a test, he or she can hardly fail to learn more about that person than is conveyed by an IQ or some other single score. This is still true if a test is administered by a technician, provided that a complete record of the test taker's responses is retained.

Besides using intelligence tests to assess an individual's general level of intellectual functioning, clinicians also customarily explore the pattern, or profile, of test scores for significant strengths and weaknesses. Profile analysis provides data that may be of help in the diagnosis of brain damage and various forms of psychopathology that affect intellectual functioning differently. The Wechsler

[39] A representative sample of current methodological issues in psychological assessment research can be found in a special issue of *Psychological Assessment* (September 1995, Vol. 7, #3).

scales have lent themselves especially well to such profile analysis, since all subtest scores are expressed in directly comparable standard scores. From the outset, Wechsler described a number of diagnostic uses of his scales. Since then, several clinicians have recommended additional techniques, and profile analysis has been applied with other instruments as well (Delaney & Hopkins, 1987; Elliott, 1990b; Kaufman, 1990, 1994; Matarazzo, 1972; Sattler, 1988, 1992). Most profile analysis techniques employ variations of three major procedures. The first involves an evaluation of the amount of *scatter,* or extent of variation among the individual's various scores, including: Verbal and Performance IQ differences; overall subtest scatter; and comparisons of individual subtest scaled scores with the means of various groupings of subtest scores, such as verbal or speeded subtests. The second procedure consists of analyzing the salient features of an individual's profile in light of *base rate data* about the frequency or rarity of such features within the normative group. The third approach is based on *score patterns* associated with particular clinical syndromes such as Alzheimer's disease, learning disabilities, or anxiety states. Wechsler and other investigators have described patterns of high and low subtest scores as well as subtest combinations characterizing these and other disorders (see, e.g., Kaufman, 1990; Matarazzo, 1972).

Several decades of research on the various forms of pattern analysis with the Wechsler scales have provided little statistical support for their diagnostic value.[40] In fact, critics of this approach have attacked almost every aspect of it at one point or another (F. C. Goldstein & Levin, 1985; Kavale & Forness, 1984; Macmann & Barnett, 1994a, 1994b; McDermott, Fantuzzo, & Glutting, 1990). Nevertheless, judging from the continued popularity of the Wechsler scales in clinical practice as well as from the enormous literature designed to systematize, facilitate, and improve the utilization of score pattern analysis, it is clear that this is still the preferred approach to interpreting intelligence test data.

At a purely qualitative level, any irregularity of performance may also suggest avenues for further exploration. Significant leads can emerge from the form as well as from the content of test responses. Bizarreness, overelaboration, or excessive self-reference, for example, may indicate personality disorders. A qualitative analysis of both errors and correct responses may provide useful clues about problem-solving approaches, conceptual development, or cognitive styles. Atypical content of test responses is a further source of leads. Still another source of qualitative data available during the administration of an individual intelligence test is the general behavior of the examinee in the testing situation. Examples include motor activities, speech, emotional responses, and attitude toward the examiner, as well as approach to the test materials and the testing environment. As a rule, because of their idiosyncratic nature, such qualitative cues cannot be validated by quantitative methods adapted to the measurement of group trends. Nevertheless, in recognition of the critical role that behavioral observations can play, some instruments designed to systematize and quantify the recording and the interpretation of some test session behavior have been appearing (see, e.g., the Guide to the Assessment of Test Session Behavior for the WISC-III and the WIAT by Glutting and Oakland, 1992).

---

[40] See Anastasi (1985a) for a discussion of some of the methodological requirements that must be considered in evaluating this research.

A clear illustration of the sophisticated clinical use of intelligence tests—combining psychometric data with qualitative observations—is provided by Alan S. Kaufman. In his books on "intelligent"—and intelligence—testing, Kaufman (1979, 1990, 1994) demonstrates in detail how the clinician can integrate statistical information about test scores with knowledge about human development, personality theory, and other areas of psychological research. Kaufman emphasizes the importance of considering both the skills and the extraneous conditions that can influence subtest performance as well as the need for supplementary information—from other tests, case history, and clinical observation of test behavior— against which to intepret score patterns. Test scores, along with other data sources, lead to the formulation of hypotheses about the individual, which can be tested as more information is gathered to round out the picture. The most important feature of the Kaufman method is that it calls for individualized interpretations of test performance, rather than uniform application of any one type of pattern analysis. The same score pattern may lead to quite different interpretations for different individuals.

The basic approach described by Kaufman undoubtedly represents a major contribution to the clinical use of intelligence tests (see, e.g., Roecker, 1995). Even its critics acknowledge that it has become the method of choice for teaching intelligence testing and has guided the creation of much of the software available to aid in the interpretation of intelligence tests (McDermott, Fantuzzo, Glutting, Watkins, & Baggaley, 1992).[41] The guidelines provided by Sattler (1988, 1992) are also excellent illustrations of the combined psychometric and clinical use of individual intelligence tests. It should be recognized, however, that the implementation of these approaches requires a sophisticated clinician who is well in-formed in several fields of psychology and not pressed for time. Moreover, the availability of computer-based interpretive programs—while in some ways facilitating the application of these methods—can easily lead the hurried or less knowledgeable examiner to overinterpret the data the programs provide.

In the meantime, new procedures for the utilization of intelligence test profiles are being developed, some of which combine elements from both the psychometric and clinical perspectives. One interesting innovation being explored is the "core profile" approach. McDermott, Glutting, and their coworkers (Glutting, McDermott, Prifitera, & McGrath, 1994, 1995; McDermott, Glutting, Jones, & Noonan, 1989), as well as Donders (1996), have applied cluster analyses—of various types—to the standardization data from the Wechsler scales. The goal of these analyses is to generate basic profile types that might help in classifying test results and in testing hypotheses about their clinical significance. A complementary line of investigation uses multidimensional scaling to identify prototypical ability profiles in the population (Davison, Gasser, & Ding, 1996). This research is aimed at eventually quantifying the degree of correspondence between an individual's

[41] For information about various criticisms of Kaufman's method, as well as for his counterarguments, see Kaufman (1994, chap.1). One problem with several of the negative reviews of Kaufman's approach is that they seem to assume that clinicians will use it to make decisions based solely on the magnitude of scores and score differences. While it is true that the mechanical application of profile analysis techniques can be very misleading, this assumption is quite contrary to what Kaufman recommends, as well as to the principles of sound assessment practice (Moreland et al., 1995).

observed profile and the prototypical profiles that emerge from a given test battery. Although these investigations are intriguing, as of now, they are still exploratory and do not yet have clinical utility (see, e.g., Ryan & Bohac, 1994).

Neuropsychological Assessment

Methodological Problems in the Diagnosis of Brain Damage. Knowledge about the behavioral effects of brain damage dates largely from the writings of Kurt Goldstein and his associates in the early 1920s (Goldstein & Scheerer, 1941). Following extensive observations of soldiers who had sustained brain injuries during World War I, Goldstein formulated his classic description of the intellectual impairment associated with brain damage. Among the principal symptoms were a diminution in the ability for abstract thought and a tendency to respond to extraneous stimuli that may disrupt normal perception.

Widespread concern with brain injury in children arose in the late 1930s and in the 1940s, following the research of Alfred Strauss and his associates (Strauss & Lehtinen, 1947; H. Werner & Strauss, 1941, 1943). These investigators identified a group of mentally retarded children whose case histories showed evidence of brain injury due to trauma or infection occurring before, during, or shortly after birth. The behavioral description of these children represented an extension and elaboration of the adult syndrome formulated by Goldstein. It delineated a distinctive pattern of both intellectual and emotional disorders that was widely accepted as characteristic of "the" brain-injured child. Included in this pattern were specific perceptual and conceptual disorders combined with relatively high verbal ability, as well as overactivity, distractibility, and aggressiveness. For many years, both research and practice with brain-injured children was dominated by a uni-dimensional concept of "organicity." This approach led to a search for diagnostic tests of organic involvement as such and an attempt to devise remedial or educational programs suitable for brain-injured children as a whole.

Since the 1950s, psychologists have increasingly recognized that brain damage may lead to a wide variety of behavioral patterns, a recognition that has spurred the development of clinical neuropsychology, a field that aims to apply what is known about brain-behavior relationships in the diagnosis and rehabilitation of brain-damaged individuals. No one symptom or set of symptoms need be common to all brain-injury cases. In fact, brain damage may produce the opposite behavior pattern in two individuals. Such findings are consistent with the wide diversity of the underlying organic pathology itself. A significant advance in the analysis of brain-behavior relationships was made by the research of Ralph Reitan and his co-workers at the Indiana University Medical Center (see Matarazzo, 1972, chap. 13; Reitan, 1955, 1966). These investigations showed that left-hemisphere lesions tend to be associated with lower Verbal than Performance IQ on the Wechsler scales (V < P). The opposite pattern (V > P) predominates in groups with lesions in the right hemisphere and with diffuse brain damage.

Neuropsychological research has continued to sort out the complex interactions of other variables with the behavioral effects of brain pathology (see, e.g., Kolb & Whishaw, 1990). There is a good deal of evidence indicating that *age* affects the behavioral symptoms resulting from brain damage. The behavioral effects will also depend upon the amount of learning and intellectual development that has occurred prior to the injury. Research on preschool children, for example, indicates that at this age level brain lesions tend to affect intellectual functions more massively than they do later on.

Chronicity has also been found to affect test performance and to interact with age effects. Available data suggest that the amount of time elapsed since the injury may be related not only to progressive physiological changes but also to the extent of behavioral recovery through learning or compensatory readjustments. Finally, it should be noted that in some cases intellectual impairment may be the *indirect result* of brain damage. Throughout the individual's development, organic and experiential factors interact. Some of the behavioral difficulties included in the classic picture of brain-injured children, for example, may be an indirect effect of the frustrations and interpersonal problems experienced by a child with an organically caused intellectual deficiency. Whether or not these behavioral difficulties persist may therefore depend on the attitudes and the degree of understanding exhibited by parents, teachers, and other significant persons in the child's environment.

It is abundantly evident that brain damage covers a wide variety of organic disorders, with correspondingly diverse behavioral manifestations. The test performance of brain-injured persons can be expected to vary with the source, extent, and locus of the cerebral damage; the age at which the damage occurred; the age when the individual's behavior is being assessed; the duration of the pathological condition; and the extent and types of intervention the individual has received. To expect behavioral homogeneity among those affected by brain pathologies would thus be highly unrealistic.

From another angle, the same intellectual or behavioral disorder—and the same diagnostic sign in test performance—may result from organic, emotional, or mixed etiologies. A conspicuous example is persistent forgetfulness. Memory difficulties of various sorts can be a symptom of one of many types of dementias, with known organic causes, or of depressive disorders of emotional origin; in addition, the onset of an organic memory disorder is frequently accompanied by depression, presenting a mixed picture. The assessment of memory problems and the differentiation between dementia and depression in older adults, in particular, are among the most common referral questions in clinical neuropsychology (Butters, Delis, & Lucas, 1995; Poon, 1986; Reeves & Wedding, 1994; Storandt & VandenBos, 1994). Experiential factors, which may be unrelated to the brain damage in some cases and may be related to it—more or less directly—in others, can complicate the diagnostic picture even further. Thus, the interpretation of any specific diagnostic sign in test performance requires additional information about the individual's experiential background and personal history. For instance, one important piece of information needed in order to gauge the magnitude of cognitive deficits—as well as the extent of recovery of intellectual functions—is the person's premorbid level of ability (see, e.g., Matarazzo, 1990). Educational attainment is frequently used as a rough indicator of premorbid functioning, but additional estimation methods based on historical data and post-traumatic test performance have also been devised (Vanderploeg, 1994b).

Altogether, the practice of neuropsychological assessment is one of the most demanding clinical tasks, requiring—as it does—the application of knowledge about cognitive, personality, neurological, and general physiological functioning in both the normal and pathological ranges. It is, therefore, not surprising that the research literature in this field and practical handbooks designed to guide students and practitioners continue to accumulate at a prodigious rate. One extensive compendium of research and clinical information is in the multivolume *Handbook of Neuropsychology,* edited by Boiler and Grafman (1988–1995). Additional reference works on the general practice of neuropsychological assessment and intervention have been prepared recently by Adams, Parsons, Culbertson, and Nixon (1996), Golden, Zillmer, and Spiers (1992), Lezak (1995), Touyz, Byrne, and Gilandas (1994), Vanderploeg (1994a), and R. F. White (1992). More specialized treatises on such topics as forensic neuropsychology (Valciukas, 1995), neuropsychological assessment of occupational neurotoxic exposure (Agnew & Masten, 1994), and neuropsychological evaluation of Spanish speakers (Ardila, Rosselli, & Puente, 1994), among many others, continue to appear at a rapid pace.

Neuropsychological Instruments. A large number of tests have been specially designed as clinical instruments for assessing neuropsychological impairment[42] (see, e.g., Lezak, 1995; Spreen & Strauss, 1991). These tests are often designated as indicators of "organicity" or brain damage. Chief among the functions assessed by these instruments are those considered most sensitive to pathological processes, such as perception of spatial relations and memory for newly learned material. The Bender Visual Motor Gestalt Test, commonly known as the Bender-Gestalt Test (BGT—Bender, 1938; Canter, 1996; Heaton, Baade, & Johnson, 1978; Koppitz, 1964, 1975; Pascal & Suttell, 1951), and the Benton Visual Retention Test—Fifth Edition (BVRT—Sivan, 1991) exemplify these types of instruments and have been used as screening tests for many decades. Because of the wide diversity of organic brain dysfunctions and accompanying behavioral deficits, however, no one test is adequate for screening for brain damage in general; single tests like the BGT and BVRT are even less suited for differential diagnosis.

Clinical neuropsychologists frequently use a combination of available tests assessing different skills and deficits, in a fashion that has been labeled as the "flexible battery" approach (see, e.g., Bauer, 1994; Goodglass, 1986). This procedure has the advantage of providing combinations of tests that are tailored to the presenting problems in individual cases. But it also has several limitations. There is likely to be some unnecessary duplication of functions among tests, and some critical areas may be overlooked. The advance selection of tests appropriate for each case puts a heavy burden on the clinician's expertise and judgment. Moreover, independently developed tests are not likely to be comparable with regard to norms and score scales. Empirical data on the interrelations of different tests are also likely to be meager. Consequently, it is difficult to interpret results in terms of score patterns.

[42] Tests in this category are regularly reviewed in the Mental Measurements Yearbooks (see TIP-IV, p. 1116, for a current listing).

For these reasons, systematic efforts have been made to assemble comprehensive standardized batteries that provide measures of all significant neuropsychological skills. Such a battery can serve several functions. It can detect brain damage with a high degree of success. It can also help to identify and localize the impaired brain areas. It can differentiate among particular syndromes associated with cerebral pathology. And it can help in planning rehabilitation training by revealing the specific type and extent of behavioral deficits. Two major examples of comprehensive neuropsychological batteries are the Halstead-Reitan Neuropsychological Test Battery (HRB—Reitan & Wolfson, 1993) and the Luna-Nebraska Neuropsychological Battery (LNNB—Golden, Purisch, & Hammeke, 1985). Both of these batteries have versions for use with children and share a common purpose, but they differ in several important ways. The HRB, which is the older of the two, was developed by Reitan from the work of Halstead (1947) and offers examiners some flexibility in the number and selection of tests to be administered (for reviews, see Dean, 1985; M. J. Meier, 1985).[43] The LNNB incorporates some of Luria's theories and diagnostic procedures (Christensen, 1975; Luria, 1973, 1980); it is more highly standardized in content, materials, administration, and scoring and requires considerably less time to administer than the HRB (for reviews, see J. H. Snow, 1992; Van Gorp, 1992).

Recent developments in the direct assessment of brain impairment through electroencephalography and neuroimaging techniques, such as magnetic resonance imaging (MRI) and positron emission tomography (PET), are having a profound impact on basic and clinical neuropsychology. Although available technologies are continually being improved, no diagnostic technique is 100% dependable. In most cases, neuropsychologists work with neurologists and other specialists to obtain corroborative information from various sources. In the clinical context, carefully standardized behavioral measures serve an important function in assessment and in the planning and monitoring of rehabilitation programs, along with other procedures. And, in the realm of basic science, the integration of neuropsychological and neuroimaging methodologies offers some of the greatest promise in advancing knowledge about brain-behavior relationships (see, e.g., Gur & Gur, 1991, 1994).

Identifying Specific Learning Disabilities

Since the 1970s, there has been a continuous wave of programs for the diagnosis and remediation of learning disabilities (LD). Educators have become increasingly aware of the high frequency of this type of handicap among schoolchildren, and even among college students and other adults (see, e.g., Gregg, Hoy, & Gay, 1996; Kravets & Wax, 1992; Wang, Reynolds, & Walberg, 1991), although the large number of individuals placed in this category may reflect in part misclassification resulting from the looseness with which the term has been applied. The varied terminology applied to these cases reflects both changing approaches over time

[43] An integrated computer-based system for compiling raw scores from many of the tests in the HRB (as well as other instruments) and transforming them into a uniform scale, corrected for age and education, was developed by Russell and Starkey (1993). The program also profiles and summarizes the results to facilitate interpretation. A similar system was prepared by Heaton, Grant, and Matthews (1991) in printed form and has recently been computerized.

and differences between the medical, educational, and psychological orientations to LD (see, e.g., American Psychiatric Association, 1980, 1994). According to the definition set forth by the federal government in Public Law 94-142, the legislation which provides for the education of children with various disabilities (see chap. 9), a *specific learning disability* is described as

> ... a disorder in one or more of the basic psychological processes involved in understanding or in using language, spoken or written, which may manifest itself in an imperfect ability to listen, think, speak, read, write, spell, or do mathematical calculations. The term includes such conditions as perceptual handicaps, brain injury, minimal brain dysfunction, dyslexia, and developmental aphasia. The term does not include children who have learning problems which are primarily the result of visual, hearing, or motor handicaps, of mental retardation, of emotional disturbance, or of environmental, cultural, or economic disadvantage. *(Federal Register,* 1977, p. 65083)

P.L. 94-142 further specifies that the diagnosis of learning disability should be applied only to children who (1) show a "severe discrepancy" between intellectual ability and achievement in various communication and mathematical skills and (2) are not achieving in a manner commensurate with their age and ability levels, even when provided with appropriate education.[44] It follows from this definition that the designation of learning disability should not be employed until several other conditions have been eliminated as possible causes of the child's educational or psychological difficulties. Over the years, it has been recognized increasingly that the heterogeneous LD population comprises subgroups that can be differentiated in terms of symptom clusters (Rourke, 1990; Feagans, Short, & Meltzer, 1991; Geary, 1993; S. R. Hooper & Willis, 1989; Pennington, 1991; Shankweiler et al., 1995; H. L. Swanson & Keogh, 1990). Nevertheless, there are still wide differences in theoretical orientation even among specialists on LD. These differences are reflected in both testing instalments and remedial programs.

Typically, children with learning disabilities show normal or above-normal intelligence, in combination with pronounced difficulties in learning one or more basic educational skills (most often, reading). It should be noted, however, that specific learning disabilities may occur at any intellectual level, even though mentally retarded children with LD do not meet the legal definition of learning disabled. LD children also manifest various combinations of associated behavioral symptoms. Chief among such symptoms are difficulties in perceiving and encoding information, poor integration of input from different sense modalities, and disruption of sensorimotor coordination. Disturbances of language development typically occur in LD children. Deficiencies in memory, attention control, and conceptual skills are common, as are certain emotional and motivational symptoms. In particular, aggression and other affective and interpersonal problems may develop, often as a direct result of the academic failures and frustrations engendered by the child's learning disabilities. In evaluating the child's behavior, one should bear in mind that many specific difficulties that are normal at an early age (e.g., in a three-year-old) represent a dysfunction if they persist

[44] For further discussion of P.L. 94–142 and its ramifications in diagnosing LD, see C. R. Reynolds (1990, 1992b). Sattler (1988, pp. 598–617) offers a brief but highly informative overview of learning disabilities and their assessment.

to an older age. A developmental frame of reference is therefore needed, with qualitative if not quantitative norms.

Assessment Techniques. Regardless of theoretical orientation, there is general agreement that the identification of learning disabilities requires a wide assortment of tests and supplementary observational procedures. This follows from at least three features of the diagnostic problem: (1) the variety of behavioral disorders associated with this condition, (2) individual differences in the particular combination of symptoms, and (3) the need for highly specific information regarding the nature and extent of the disabilities in each case.

Usually, the assessment of children with learning disabilities is a cooperative effort by a professional team. The classroom teacher can administer group tests and employ other screening or wide-band instruments. Regular achievement batteries may also serve in this connection, particularly those designed for primary and preschool levels and permitting "criterion-referenced" (i.e., content-referenced) analyses of specific strengths and weaknesses. Several instruments cited in the educational testing section of this chapter are appropriate for this purpose.

Individually administered, wide-range achievement tests are especially useful for the assessment of learning disabilities. These tests may be given by teachers, although the supplementary qualitative observations and score interpretations can be handled more effectively by a clinician. One of the instruments in this category is the Kaufman Test of Educational Achievement (K-TEA—Kaufman & Kaufman, 1985). The administration of this test, with the pervasive easel-type kit, is shown in Figure 17–4. A few batteries include some subtests classified as

Figure 17–4. Administration of the Kaufman Test of Educational Achievement (K-TEA), Showing Use of an Easel Kit. The cards on their ring binder form a freestanding easel that simultaneously displays each test item to the test taker and the corresponding directions to the examiner.
(Courtesy of American Guidance Service.)

measures of aptitudes or cognitive ability and some classified as measures of achievement. Among the most comprehensive of these is the Woodcock-Johnson Psycho-Educational Battery—Revised (WJ-R—McGrew, 1994; McGrew, Werder, & Woodcock, 1991). Such tests as the Stanford-Binet, the K-ABC, and the Wechsler scales not only provide a global index, such as an IQ, to help differentiate between mental retardation and specific learning disabilities, but they also yield much qualitative information regarding specific deficiencies (Kaufman, 1990, 1994; Sattler, 1988, 1992). For example, these tests can reveal possible deficiencies in the perception and recall of visual patterns, motor difficulties, limitations of short-term memory, inability to handle abstract concepts, and many types of language disorders. The publishers of the Wechsler scales have also developed the Wechsler Individual Achievement Test (WIAT—Psychological Corporation, 1992), a comprehensive battery that is linked to the intelligence scales and intended to complement them in the assessment of learning disabilities.

Although existing tests can be helpful in the implementation of current guidelines for the assessment of learning disabilities, many investigators have repeatedly called for a new and more informative approach to the diagnosis and evaluation of LD children. These calls center primarily on the need for a clear theoretical rationale to guide assessment practice and for a deeper understanding of the specific processes involved in each case, in order to improve both assessment and remediation efforts (see, e.g., Das, Naglieri, & Kirby, 1994; R. B. Kline, Snyder, & Castellanos, 1996; C. R. Reynolds, 1992b).

Dynamic Assessment. The term "dynamic assessment" covers a variety of clinical procedures that involve essentially the deliberate departure from standardized or uniform test administration in order to elicit additional qualitative data about an individual. Although skilled clinicians have been employing such procedures for some time, this approach has gained in popularity since the 1970s (Lidz, 1981, 1987, 1991, 1995). It has been used as a supplementary source of data, not only in cases of specific learning disabilities but also with other children who have been experiencing difficulties with their schooling, such as those with mild or moderate mental retardation. The utility of this approach for the assessment of giftedness—especially in economically disadvantaged children—has also been tentatively explored (see, e.g., Bolig & Day, 1993).

One of the earliest of these qualitative adaptations of testing procedure is known as "testing the limits." In this procedure, additional cues may be provided by the examiner; the more cues are needed for a satisfactory performance, the greater the learning disability. The alterations of standard procedure used in testing the limits are similar to some of the special adaptations introduced in testing persons with physical disabilities, and the same interpretive cautions and limitations apply to the resulting performance (see chap. 9).

A more recently developed approach has been designated as *learning-potential assessment* (Babad & Budoff, 1974; Campione & Brown, 1979; Feuerstein, 1979; Glutting & McDermott, 1990; Hlamers, Sijtsma, & Ruijssenaars, 1993; Lidz, 1991). The term "potential" in this name may carry an unwarranted implication that the ability in question was always present and needed only to be "uncovered." In effect, however, these procedures involve a test-teach-test format in which the student is taught by various means to perform a task that he or she was initially unable to carry out. Superficially, this technique is similar to that followed in some of the prognostic educational tests in which test takers are given a sample task requiring the sort of learning they will encounter in a particular course of study. The present application differs from that of prognostic tests in at least two ways: (1) the test taker is given instructions or special suggestions, and (2) the tasks usually involve more broadly applicable learning or problem-solving skills.

The dynamic assessment techniques pioneered by Feuerstein and others offer promise in several directions. By linking assessment and instruction, they promote research on the modifiability of scholastic aptitude and on the development of optimal remediation programs. In addition, they provide the qualified clinician an assessment tool that can produce more illuminating descriptions of cognitive performance and of its responsiveness to remedial interventions than standardized intelligence tests. In spite of these advantages, dynamic techniques have not escaped criticism. One question concerns their *transportability,* or the extent to which they can be used effectively by different clinicians. Another pertains to the *generalizability* of the remedial effects achieved with these very broad tasks (usually nonverbal reasoning problems similar to the Raven's Progressive Matrices or to the Weschler Performance scale items) to real-life school performance. Furthermore, although most proponents of dynamic assessment techniques would like to get away from the reliance on scores that is typical of "static" cognitive measures (such as intelligence tests), the problem of how to document change without using numbers—in some fashion—has proven to be intractable (A. L. Brown et al., 1992; R. E. Snow, 1990). Nevertheless, the exploration of the potential usefulness of dynamic assessment techniques continues apace. Some of the promising work recently reported involves a clarification of the role of different instructional strategies in the comprehension of mathematical concepts, and the development of a computer-based dynamic assessment system for performance on multidigit multiplication problems (Gerber, Semmel, & Semmel, 1994; Jitendra, Kameenui, & Carnine, 1994).

From another angle, the multidimensional latent trait model for change developed by Embretson (1987, 1990, 1992) circumvents many of the nearly insurmountable technical difficulties for measuring performance change or learning inherent in traditional test use (see, e.g., Cronbach & Furby, 1970). Embretson's approach uses item response theory (IRT, discussed in chap. 7) and computerized adaptive testing (CAT, discussed in chap. 10) to bypass these problems by testing each individual with items close to her or his threshold level, where learning effects are largest; items at this level also yield the most reliable estimate of each individual's performance. Moreover, by applying the task-decomposition procedures developed in cognitive psychology, Embretson is able to vary systematically the specific cognitive processes required to perform the task presented by each test item. This can be done, for example, by using subtasks that demand only certain steps of the complete solution; or by presenting cues or specific knowledge required for one or more steps in the solution; or by providing instruction that influences particular aspects of task performance. It is apparent that Embretson's ongoing contribution represents a significant achievement in psychometrics which brings together developments from such diverse fields as clinical psychology, cognitive research, mathematical statistics, and computer technology (Embretson, 1993, 1995).

Behavioral Assessment

The various techniques subsumed under the general concept of behavior modification represent a direct utilization of major learning principles in the practical management of behavior change. Basically, these techniques involve the application of conditioning principles to the acquisition and strengthening of wanted behavior and the elimination of unwanted behavior. Behavior therapy has gradually broadened to comprise an expanding variety of psychological problems, an everexpanding repertoire of intervention techniques, and the consideration of cognitive and affective—along with overt motor—responses (Bandura, 1969, 1986; Hersen et al., 1991; Lazarus, 1981).

Assessment Techniques. In the early applications of behavior therapy, assessment received little attention. Since the mid-1970s, however, the importance of assessment procedures has been increasingly recognized (Barrios, 1988; A. S. Bellack & Hersen, 1988; Haynes, 1991; Mash & Terdal, 1988; Nelson & Hayes, 1986; O'Brien & Haynes, 1993; Ollendick & Hersen, 1993).[45] The principal functions to be served by assessment procedures in behavior therapy can be subsumed under three headings. First, assessment techniques help in *defining the individual's problem* through a functional analysis of relevant behavior. Essentially, such an analysis involves a full specification of the treatment objective—such as overcoming a phobia or obsessive thoughts—and includes a description of the stimuli that elicit the target behavior, the situations in which such behavior occurs, and the nature, magnitude, and frequencies of particular responses. A second way in which assessment procedures can guide the behavior therapist is in *selecting appropriate treatments.* Third, there is a need for *assessing the behavior change* that results from treatment. Such assessments should include techniques for monitoring change—so as to permit evaluation of treatment effectiveness and the introduction of procedural alterations if necessary—as well as terminal measures to establish attainment of a satisfactory status and to plan for follow-up procedures as needed.

In considering specific assessment procedures, we should note, first, that the same procedure can often provide information relevant to all three functions. Second, the choice of procedures depends on the nature of the problem, the characteristics of the client—including the environment in which he or she must operate—and the facilities available at the particular clinic. Third, a combination of several assessment procedures is desirable in most cases.

Available assessment procedures can themselves be classified under three major types: self-report by the client, direct observation of behavior, and physiological measures. Although not every center can afford the facilities required for *physiological measures,* these measures provide supplementary objective data in the assessment of certain conditions, such as anxiety, sexual arousal disorders, and sleep disorders (Sturgis & Gramling, 1988). Examples include measures of electrodermal, muscular, and electro-ocular activity, as well as of cardiovascular, sexual, and cerebral functioning.

---

[45] Instruments in this category are regularly reviewed in the *Mental Measurements Yearbooks* (see TIP-IV, pp. 1095–1096, for a current listing. For information about the use of computer technology in various types of behavioral assessment procedures, see Kratchowill et al. (1991).

Direct observation of the target behavior can be conducted in naturalistic situations by parents, teachers, institutional personnel, or special observers. Observational aids such as checklists, rating scales, and daily schedules may be employed. Such observations are subject to several weaknesses (Barrios, 1993; also see chap. 16). For this reason, analogue situations are often employed in clinics. There is also increasing exploration of the use of mechanical sensors or monitors that can provide a continuous, objective record of behavior in both real-life and contrived situations (W. W. Tryon, 1985, 1991).

Self-report by the client comprises a diversity of techniques. They include clinical interviews by the therapist, self-monitoring records of target behavior and associated conditions kept by the client, and a variety of written checklists and inventories. Some standardized self-report inventories are used, in either the original or adapted versions, for preliminary screening and identification, as well as for monitoring of target behaviors. Among the simplest and most widely used of these is the revised Beck Depression Inventory (BDI—Beck & Steer, 1993), a 21-item instrument designed to assess the severity of depression through self-ratings.[46] One of the newest standardized measures is the Alcohol Use Inventory (Horn, Wanberg, & Foster, 1990), a 228-item self-report inventory that assesses involvement with the use of alcohol in a conceptually and psychometrically sophisticated fashion, involving multiple scales at different levels of generality (for reviews, see Drummond, 1995; McNeely, 1995). Many other instruments have been prepared for use in specific research projects or treatment programs, and, although some of them have not themselves been published, they are usually fully described and reproduced in journal articles or books (see, e.g., A. S. Bellack & Hersen, 1988).

Recently, other instruments have been developed which comprise objective rating scales to be completed by multiple informants. One of the most comprehensive of these is the Behavior Assessment System for Children (BASC) by Cecil Reynolds and Randy Kamphaus (1992), already mentioned in chapter 16. This system includes behavior rating scales for parents and teachers and a form for coding and recording direct observations of classroom behavior; in addition, the BASC provides a self-report questionnaire for the children themselves and a structured interview schedule through which parents can provide a developmental history. The Social Skills Rating System (SSRS—Gresham & Elliott, 1990) also provides forms for parents, teachers, and students themselves to evaluate the positive and problematic behaviors of students in educational and family settings. One of the particularly helpful features of the SSRS, according to reviewers, is that it provides a component that permits the linkage of the assessment results with the planning of intervention strategies (for reviews, see Benes, 1995; Furlong & Karno, 1995).

Career Assessment

The practice of career assessment involves helping an individual discern the most appropriate career choice, in light of the person's abilities, interests, goals, values, and temperament, as well as the requirements of a given occupation. Few areas of

[46] For an extensive bibliography on the BDI and reviews of an earlier edition, see the 11th MMY.

life are as important to people as their occupations, not only because of the great amount of time most persons spend at work but also because work can usually provide opportunities for many intrinsic and extrinsic rewards (Šuper & Sverko, 1995). In addition, the current climate of rapid changes in the nature and conditions of employment is prompting many more people to consider their career choices not just once but often several times within their lifetimes. Thus, it is not surprising that theorizing in the field of career choice and career development is proceeding at a very lively pace. Already in the 1990s, the number of major new theoretical formulations in the area has equaled or exceeded those produced since the 1950s when both Donald Super (1953) and John Holland (1959) made their first significant contributions to the field.[47]

From the point of view of testing, we have already considered the instruments that are most directly applicable in the career counseling of individuals, namely—the interest inventories discussed in chapter 14 and the multiple' aptitude batteries described in chapter 10, as well as in the occupational testing section of this chapter. Choosing a career often implies the choice of a general lifestyle, with its characteristic set of values. Because interest inventories essentially assess the individual's value system, they are coming more and more to be regarded as focal in effective career planning. In this section, we examine two more specialized kinds of instruments that have been particularly designed for career counseling: comprehensive programs for career exploration and measures of career maturity. Many more instruments are described and reviewed in the indispensable guide to career assessment instruments of all types prepared by Kapes, Mastie, and Whitfield (1994), now in its third edition.

Comprehensive Programs for Career Exploration. Several multiple aptitude batteries have been incorporated into career guidance systems. An example is provided by the Differential Aptitude Tests (DAT), described in chapter 10, which can be used in combination with the Career Interest Inventory (CII—Psychological Corporation, 1991a, 1991b). These two instruments were developed jointly in order to facilitate comparisons between their results in the process of career guidance.

Another example is the program developed by the U.S. Employment Service, whose General Aptitude Test Battery (GATB) was discussed in the occupational testing section of this chapter. Among the most useful tools that resulted from the USES career counseling program are the *Complete Guide for Occupational Exploration* (CGOE—Farr, 1992) and the *Enhanced Guide for Occupational Exploration* (EGOE—Maze & Mayall, 1995). Intended for use by counselors as well as by students and job seekers themselves, these guides group thousands of occupations in the world of work by major interest areas and by ability patterns and other requirements for successful performance. The individual can use the guides for preliminary career exploration by identifying those work groups in which he or she has a strong interest and then checking the training and skills

---

[47] See Brown, Brooks, et al. (1996) for a useful overview of these and other well-established theories about career choice, as well as some provocative emerging contributions. Savickas and Lent's *Convergence in Career Development Theories* (1994) is another valuable source of information on the theories and on how they resemble, differ from, and complement one another. Many of the chapters in these two edited books are written by the original theorists themselves.

they require. The CGOE lists all 12,741 occupations listed in the *Dictionary of Occupational Titles* (U.S. Department of Labor, 1991), whereas the EGOE lists only 2,800—comprising 95 percent of the workforce—but provides more information on each.

A newer approach to career counseling provides a procedure for integrating available information from many sources into a comprehensive career exploration program. The information may include scores from a variety of tests (each with its own normative and interpretive data), biographical data (including education and job experience), and the individual's expressed interests, preferences, and value system. This approach is illustrated in varying degrees by several available instruments, such as the Harrington-O'Shea Career Decision-Making System—Revised (Harrington & O'Shea, 1993) and the American College Testing (ACT) Career Planning Program (ACT, 1994).

An outstanding example of such integrative career-exploration programs is the revised version of the System for Interactive Guidance Information (SIGI-PLUS), cited in chapter 3. Using an interactive program, SIGI-PLUS enables the individual to conduct two-way communication with the computer—asking and answering questions, providing data, and soliciting information. An extensive database on job characteristics and requirements is included in the program, with provision for incorporating additional local data. Originally designed for use with college and university students, SIGI-PLUS has been updated for use with adults wishing to make career changes or enter the job market at different life stages. The program is so designed as to guide the individual in examining relevant facts and proceeding along a systematic route toward effective decision making (M. R. Katz, 1993; Norris, Schott, Shatkin, & Bennett, 1986). Even such a well-designed computer-administration system, however, cannot perform the whole career-decision function for the individual. The intervention of a trained counselor may be needed to encourage the individual to think through her or his particular needs and traits at different stages of career development (see, e.g., Tiedeman, 1994).

Assessment of Career Maturity. Another type of instrument specifically developed for use in career counseling is concerned with the individual's level of career maturity. This concept emerged from a long-term research project on career development conducted by Super and his associates (Super et al., 1957; Super & Overstreet, 1960). *Career maturity* refers to individuals' mastery of the vocational tasks appropriate to their age level, and their effectiveness in coping with such tasks. The research itself comprised a 20-year longitudinal investigation of approximately 100 ninth-grade boys. The findings suggested that the major career development task at the junior high school level is that of preparing to make career choices. Other research on career development, by both crosssectional and longitudinal approaches, has been contributing data that help fill out the picture (see, e.g., Crites, 1969; Gribbons & Lohnes, 1982; Super, 1980, 1985). A major finding of the more recent research is that all types of career behavior may occur throughout most of the life span, even though one type predominates at each life stage. Increasing attention is being given to career changes in adult life; these changes stem from a variety of factors both in one's own personal life and in the nature of occupations (Kummerow, 1991; Lowman, 1991, 1993; Pickman, 1994; Walsh & Osipow, 1993).

One of the by-products of the research on career development has been the construction of standardized measures of career maturity (Kapes et al., 1994, pp. 241–272). An example is the Career Development Inventory prepared by Super and designed to assess readiness to decide on a career and to highlight any aspects of career orientation in which individuals need assistance (A. S. Thompson & Lindeman, 1981, 1984). A related type of instrument is the Career Beliefs Inventory (Krumboltz, 1991), which was developed as an aid to career counseling with the specific goal of identifying any beliefs that may be blocking an individual's attainment of career goals.

Clinical Judgment

What the clinician does in assessing a client may be regarded as a special case of person cognition or interpersonal perception—the process through which anyone comes to know and understand another person (Kruglanski, 1989). In the clinical situation, however, judgmental accuracy differs from ordinary social circumstances in several significant ways. Much has been written about the data-processing, synthesizing, or interpretive role of the clinician. Research on the process of clinical judgment has thrown considerable light on some of the possible sources of error in this process, such as the influence of cultural stereotypes and reliance on fallacious prediction principles. Examples of the latter include failure to consider base rates or regression effects, and the assumption that more highly intercorrelated predictors yield higher validity (see, e.g., L. R. Goldberg, 1991).

Given the same set of facts, such as test scores or life-history data, will clinical judgment provide more accurate predictions of subsequent behavior than would be obtained by the routine application of a regression equation or other empirically derived formula? The question has practical as well as theoretical importance, because once a statistical strategy—or algorithm—has been developed, it can be applied by a clerk or a computer, thus freeing the clinician for other functions. In a classic book entitled *Clinical Versus Statistical Prediction,* Meehl (1954) discussed the process of clinical judgment and surveyed investigations comparing the two types of prediction. Meehl showed that, with only one questionable exception, the routine application of statistical procedures yielded at least as many correct predictions as did clinical analysis, and frequently more. The publication of Meehl's book, and subsequent reaffirmations of his conclusion, stimulated a lively controversy that is still active (see, e.g., Anastasi, 1988b, pp. 511–515; Dawes, Faust, & Meehl, 1993; Kleinmuntz, 1990).

In spite of the apparent superiority of the actuarial approach, when clinical and statistical procedures are applied to the same data, it is important to bear in mind that the clinical process offers certain advantages. A major contribution of the clinical method, for example, is that data are obtained in areas where satisfactory tests are unavailable, through careful interviewing and observations of behavior. The clinical method is also better suited than the statistical method to the processing of rare and idiosyncratic events whose frequency is too low to permit the development of statistical strategies.

In summary, the most effective procedure in our present state of knowledge combines clinical and statistical approaches (Matarazzo, 1990). The clinician should use all the objective test data and actuarial strategies applicable to the particular situation, while supplementing this information with facts and inferences attainable only through clinical methods. The validity of clinical predictions against actual outcomes should be investigated systematically whenever feasible.[48] More data are also needed on the consistency of predictions about the same persons made by different clinicians and by the same clinicians at different times. Insofar as possible, the process and cues on which clinical predictions are based should be made explicit in the clinical records. Such a practice would not only facilitate research and training but would also serve to encourage reliance on sound data and defensible interpretations. Finally, the "clinician as instrument" is an important concept. This is illustrated in ongoing research on characteristics that moderate clinical judgment accuracy. Through a series of ongoing investigations, Spengler and his colleagues have concluded that psychologists with lower levels of cognitive complexity are more likely to form biased clinical judgments than those with higher cognitive complexity (Spengler &. Strohmer, 1994; Walker & Spengler, 1995).

The Assessment Report: A Final Synthesis. In chapter 18 we will examine some of the broad issues involved in the communication of test results, with particular reference to ethical and social implications. For the clinician, such communication usually includes the preparation of a written test report or case report that is often followed by discussion or consultation with the client, parents, teachers, or other professionals. Even in those situations that do not require a written report, it is a good idea to prepare one as a record for future reference. The preparation of a report also helps to organize and clarify the clinician's own thinking about the case and to sharpen her or his interpretations. Report writing represents the final stage in the clinician's synthesizing function. In its content, the report should draw upon all the data sources (test and nontest) available to the clinician.

Several books provide guidelines for report writing.[49] Without duplicating the many lists of suggestions that can be found in such sources, we shall focus on some of the major points. First, there is no one standard form or outline for all reports. Both content and style should and do vary with the purpose of the assessment, the context in which it is conducted, the persons to whom the report is addressed, and the theoretical orientation and professional background of the clinician. It is especially important to adapt the report to the needs, interests, and background of those who will receive it. For example, a report addressed to a lawyer needs to be quite different from one addressed to a psychotherapist.

---

[48] Some large-scale projects of this nature, aimed at evaluating the validity of decisions or predictions based on assessment procedures, are currently being planned. One such investigation, already in progress under the auspices of the Society for Personality Assessment, is a complete literature review—to be followed by meta analyses—of studies that have used personality assessment procedures or instruments to make predictions about aspects of therapy or about medical, legal, or life outcomes (Handler & Meyer, 1996, Spring/Summer).

[49] Sattler (1988, chap. 23) gives a comprehensive view of problems and pitfalls, with many practical suggestions, and summarizes pertinent research on report writing. Other sources, with illustrative case reports, include Ownby (1991) and Tallent (1993).

Nevertheless, for both of them, the clinician should select what is relevant to answering the questions raised at the outset from the mass of data he or she has gathered.

The report also should concentrate on each individual's differentiating characteristics—the high and low points—rather than on traits in which the individual's standing is close to the average. A test of the effectiveness of a report is to see whether it is unique to the individual or whether it applies equally well to other persons. It is a relatively easy task to prepare a pseudo-report from general, stereotyped statements that apply to most people. A considerable body of research has demonstrated that such reports are readily accepted as "remarkably accurate" self-descriptions by a large majority of persons (Goodyear, 1990; Klopfer, 1983; Snyder & Larson, 1972; Tallent, 1992, pp. 236–238). This pseudo-validation has been called the "Barnum effect," after Phineas T. Barnum, the famous showman who is credited with the remark that "there's a sucker born every minute." Reliance on such generally applicable personality descriptions is a favorite device of fortune tellers and other charlatans.

The primary focus of the report should be on interpretations and conclusions, although test records and other detailed data may be separately appended in some cases.[50] Specific data, such as individual responses and subtest scores, should ordinarily be cited only to illustrate or clarify a point. Reports should be carefully organized and integrated. They should be written simply so as to communicate and not to obfuscate. Books on the preparation of assessment reports usually contain helpful hints for good writing, as well as references to standard manuals of style. One particularly entertaining little book that should make writing less painful for both writer and reader is *The Elements of Style* by Strunk and White (1979).

The Role of Computers in Psychological Assessment

Computer scoring of many kinds of tests, including self-report personality inventories, has been available for several decades. Most of the computer programs also carry out routine statistical analyses, providing such further information as various types of derived scores, score intervals in terms of the SEM, and score profiles. Narrative consultative reports constitute a more sophisticated application of computer technology to the reporting and utilization of test data (Butcher, 1987; Moreland, 1992). Essentially, these programs use a large database of qualitative interpretive statements that are attached to particular levels or patterns of quantitative scores. Apart from saving the clinician's time, this procedure has other advantages. The computer is able to search, systematically and consistently, through a far more extensive database than would be feasible for an individual clinician; it can also reliably apply more complex rules to the actuarial data in selecting appropriate statements; and it can insert into the process

[50] See the June 1996 *American Psychologist* for a "Statement on the Disclosure of Test Data" prepared by the Committee on Psychological Tests and Assessment of the American Psychological Association.

many other related variables, such as demographic data from different normative populations.[51]

Unquestionably, the potential contribution of computers to psychological assessment is impressive (Butcher, 1987; Eyde, 1987; Gutkin & Wise, 1991; Moreland, 1992). Much of this potential, however, is only beginning to be explored (Embretson, 1992). For example, the application of branching techniques and adaptive testing, whose advantages are now widely recognized in ability testing, is just beginning to find its way into personality testing (Ben-Porath & Butcher, 1986; Jackson, 1985, 1991) and has not yet produced any instruments suitable for clinical use.

On the other hand, computer technologies have led to the development and rapid proliferation of many new instruments for the assessment of cognitive functioning which are already being used in clinical neuropsychology, as well as in the assessment of learning disabilities and attention disorders (see, e.g., Krug, 1988, 1993; Stoloff & Couch, 1992). For the foreseeable future, it is unlikely that adequate assessment of neurocognitive functioning will be accomplished solely by means of computerized test administration (Golden, 1987). Nevertheless, computers do make it possible to vary task presentation conditions more precisely so as to assess performance on different task components. They also allow the recording and evaluation of response parameters—such as timing—in ways that are not possible with paper-and-pencil or even individual tests. The MicroCog: Assessment of Cognitive Functioning (MicroCog—Powell et al., 1993; Powell & Whitla, 1994a, 1994b) is an example of a recently developed computer-administered battery designed to screen for possible signs of cognitive impairment in adults. MicroCog consists of 18 subtests—in the areas of attention and mental control, memory, reasoning and calculation, spatial processing, and reaction time—that make use of the unique capabilities of computer technology. Potential uses of this relatively quick and inexpensive battery include the assessment of mild to moderate levels of cognitive deterioration in older adults and monitoring cognitive performance among employees who might be exposed to noxious stimuli, as well as other instances requiring the precise evaluation of neurocognitive changes.

Many other new instruments for the assessment of specific functions have also been developed and will undoubtedly continue to appear in years to come. Among the earliest measures of this nature are several continuous performance tests, such as the Test of Variables of Attention (TOVA—Leark, Dupuy, Greenberg, Corman, &. Kindschi, 1996), which is available in an auditory as well as a visual version. Additional examples include the Vigil Continuous Performance Test (Cegalis, Cegalis, & Bowlin, 1993) and the Paced Auditory Serial Addition Test (PASAT—Cegalis & Birdsall, 1995), both of which involve multimedia software packages that allow for the assessment of attention in the visual and auditory modalities. Figure 17–5 shows a child taking the visual version of the TOVA.

---

[51] Most publishers and distributors of software for test profile reports, narrative reports, and other computer-assisted test interpretation options provide sample reports and demonstration disks to potential users. In addition, the *Psychware Sourcebook* (Krug, 1993), which is one of the most complete sources of information currently available on computer-based assessment products, contains reproductions of many sample reports.

Figure 17–5. A Child Taking the Test of Variables of Attention (TOVA) Responds by Pressing an External Microswitch Mechanism Attached to One of the Computer's Ports. (Courtesy of American Guidance Service.)

From another angle, computers also have the potential to integrate data from many sources, including all kinds of available tests, case history, and direct behavioral observations (see, e.g., Watkins & McDermott, 1991). Although the computer could thereby assume the clinician's synthesizing function for the individual case, the computerized database necessary for developing and maintaining such integrative programs is still not available.

Among current applications, there are also serious pitfalls to be considered (Moreland, 1992). Most available systems of computer-assisted test interpretation combine clinical and statistical procedures. The specific mix of quantitative data and clinical judgment varies among the systems, as do also the technical quality of the database and the clinical expertise of the judgments. Moreover, the information needed to evaluate a particular system is often unavailable because of proprietary concerns.

It is largely because of the absence of the necessary technical information that the potential misuses of computerized test interpretation programs have aroused widespread concern (Eyde & Kowal, 1987; Fowler & Butcher, 1986; Matarazzo, 1986a, 1986b; Moreland, 1987). Some programs already meet adequate scientific and professional standards or are being revised to meet that goal; several are of unknown quality and have never been reviewed by qualified professionals; far too many are being oversold through unverified claims in their promotional literature. The first guidelines for the evaluation and use of computerized interpretive services were promulgated by the American Psychological Association in 1986; additions and revisions to these guidelines are being incorporated into the new

Testing Standards, currently under preparation. Some additional guidance on the use of computerized psychological testing tools is available in a few other publications (see, e.g., Bersoff & Hofer, 1991; Moreland, 1992).

Concluding Comments. Altogether, the field of psychological assessment as practiced by various specialists is undergoing change as rapidly as the other areas considered in this chapter. In addition to the multitude of computer-based developments that are continually taking place, and to the other trends that have already been singled out throughout this last section of the chapter, there is a renewed emphasis on the need for assessment tools that are oriented toward positive mental health rather than psychopathology. One recent example is the Quality of Life Inventory (QOLI—Frisch, 1994), which is a measure of life satisfaction that can be used in treatment planning as well as in the evaluation of treatment outcomes. Several other measures of this type are currently in various stages of development. Another interesting new, and unique, kind of instrument is the Cross-Cultural Adaptability Inventory (CCAI—C. Kelley & Meyers, 1993), which as its name implies is a self-assessment tool intended to help individuals decide on their readiness to adapt to other cultures. The Student Adaptation to College Questionnaire (SACQ—R. W. Baker & Siryk, 1989) is yet another tool which, like the CCAI, typifies the application of psychological testing to individual self-understanding and self-enhancement, an application that is a direct outgrowth of the influence of counseling psychology and that is likely to expand greatly in the future.

Chapter Eighteen

Ethical and Social Considerations in Testing

In this chapter, we will look at the ethical and social considerations in testing that is practiced globally (like APA, BPS etc.) by sharing certain codes that are devised by National Academy of Psychology (NAOP) and followed in the Indian Psychological Community.

In both their research and the practical applications of their procedures, psychologists have long been concerned with questions of professsional ethics. A concrete example of this concern is the systematic empirical program followed in the early 1950s to develop the first formal code of ethics for the profession. This extensive undertaking resulted in the preparation of a set of standards that was officially adopted by the American Psychological Association (APA) and first published in 1953. These standards undergo continual review and refinement, leading to the periodic publication of revised editions. The current version, *Ethical Principles of Psychologists and Code of Conduct* (APA, 1992),[1] comprises a preamble and six general principles designed to guide psychologists toward the *highest ideals* of the profession. It also provides eight ethical standards with *enforceable rules* for psychologists functioning within diverse contexts.

The *Ethics Code* is implemented by the APA Ethics Committee, which investigates and adjudicates complaints against members of the association. The rules and procedures for the operation of this committee as well as its yearly reports are published in the *American Psychologist,* the official journal of the American Psychological Association (see, e.g., APA, Ethics

[1] In an effort to disseminate the *Ethical Principles of Psychologists and Code of Conduct*—hereinafter referred to as the *Ethics Code*—as widely as possible, the APA will send a single copy of this publication, free of charge, to anyone who requests it.

Committee, 1995, 1996). An indispensable guidebook offering commentary and illustrations on the application of the ethical standards has been prepared by former Ethics Committee members who were involved in the latest revision of the Ethics Code (Canter, Bennett, Jones, & Nagy, 1994). Another useful collection of historical and contemporary readings on ethics in psychology, including discussions of ethical dilemmas in a variety of settings, has been recently compiled by Bersoff (1995). Pope and Vasquez's (1991) volume on *Ethics in Psychotherapy and Counseling* includes a chapter on assessment issues which provides some good practical advice. Weiner (1995a) has recently written a helpful chapter on how to anticipate ethical and legal challenges in personality assessment.

The 1990s have witnessed a rapid proliferation of legislative actions at the federal and state levels, court decisions, and professional guidelines from a diversity of viewpoints, many of which impinge on the practice of psychology in general and on the use of psychological tests in particular. Several of these developments have already been discussed in earlier chapters in the context of specific types of testing issues and practices. All too often, the combined effect of these injunctions has involved confusion, inconsistencies, and conflicts for the practitioner.

Increasingly, attention has focused on providers of psychological services who need to balance the ethical principles of their profession with legal and regulatory mandates, as well as with the institutional policies of the organizations where they work. Accordingly, the American Psychological Association, through its various offices and committees, has striven to provide guidance and information to members by monitoring pertinent developments and by promulgating standards, guidelines, and statements on issues likely to present problems for practicing psychologists. The *General Guidelines for Providers of Psychological Services* (APA, 1987a) and the *Specialty Guidelines for the Delivery of Services* (APA, 1981—currently under revision) were promulgated to aid those involved in the professional practice of psychology within several contexts. Additional guidance on specific issues is provided in other documents, such as the *Guidelines for Child Custody Evaluations in Divorce Proceedings,* drafted by the Committee on Professional Practice and Standards (APA, COPPS, 1994), and several others mentioned throughout this chapter. In addition, since the late 1980s, the APA has been preparing a series of volumes that summarize and analyze the laws affecting mental health professionals in each state; as of this writing, about a dozen of these volumes have been published and, in some cases, have been updated already (see, e.g., Caudill & Pope, 1995; Petrila & Otto, 1995; Shuman, 1990, 1993; Wulach, 1991).

The APA Committee on Psychological Tests and Assessment (CPTA) is specifically devoted to considering problems regarding sound testing and assessment practices, and to providing technical advice concerning those practices to other APA groups. It has produced several documents, which will be mentioned later in this chapter, with guidance on test-related problems and practices. The CPTA also reviews the work of the Joint Committee on Testing Practices (JCTP), a group established by the APA and other professional organizations concerned with testing. In turn, the Joint Committee has developed a *Code of Fair Testing Practices in Education* (JCTP, 1988) and other products aimed at improving the manner in which tests are applied and at preventing their misuse (see, e.g., Eyde et al., 1988, 1993). Currently, the JCTP is preparing a statement on the "Rights and Responsibilities of Test Takers."

Ethical Issues in Psychological Testing and Assessment. Psychologists often work with individuals in sensitive situations. An important step in becoming a qualified professional or consumer of psychological services is to be aware of the ethical issues faced by psychologists. If you are providing psychological services you are obligated to remain informed regarding current ethical standards or issues. If you are a consumer of psychological services, the professional should keep you informed regarding your rights. If you find yourself in a situation where ethical standards are being violated or have doubts regarding the correct course of action, consult a colleague. There are certain key ethical issues with which a reader should be familiar with.

User Qualifications and Professional Competence. Generally, competence is established through training, experience, supervised practice, or a combination of these activities. Any practitioner should be willing to discuss their competencies with consumers about services and be ready to make referrals to others when an administration of tests requires understanding of the intricacies of both administration and interpretation. Graduate course work and many hours of supervised practice are needed to acquire the necessary skills. The practitioner is also obligated to update skills with formal course work, reading, or other professional development activities. National Academy of Psychology (NAOP) is the apex professional body responsible for guarding and driving the professional standards and ethics related to psychological testing in India. In 2009, National Academy of Psychology (NAOP) constituted the Committee on Accreditation and Psychological Testing (CAPT), in order to move towards establishing national levels of standards, certifications, and accreditations related to psychological testing. CAPT is a committee of NAOP and seeks approvals from the executive committee of NAOP for making any major decisions. NAOP conducts Level 1 and Level 2 Qualifications in Occupational Testing and Assessment through CAPT. Their mission is to design, deliver, and maintain a practical, efficient, and cost-effective model of certifications and accreditations for promoting competent and ethical use of psychological tests and for enforcing professional standards in psychological testing and allied activities in India (http://www.naopindia.org/psychological-testing).

Protection of Privacy. In most circumstances, private information must be kept confidential and not revealed to others. However, there are important exceptions to this rule. These exceptions may be taken in situations in which confidential information can be used to prevent harm being caused to another person. In times of testing effectiveness, it may be necessary to keep the examinee ignorant of the specific ways in which the responses to any one test are to be interpreted. Nevertheless, a person should not be subjected to any testing program under false pretences. Of primary importance in this connection is the obligation to have a clear understanding with the test taker regarding the utilization of the test results. Although concerns about the invasion of privacy have been most commonly expressed about personality tests, they logically apply to any type of test. Certainly, any intelligence, aptitude, and achievement test may reveal limitations in skills and knowledge that an individual would rather not disclose. Moreover, any observation of an individual's behavior – as in an interview, a casual conversation, or other personal encounter – may yield information that the individual would prefer to conceal and that he or she may reveal unwittingly. The fact that psychological tests have often been singled out in discussions of invasions of privacy probably reflects prevalent misconceptions about tests as well as their frequent misuse as a sole basis for assessing individuals. If all tests were recognized as measures of behavior samples, with no mysterious powers to penetrate beyond behavior, popular fears, and suspicion would be lessened. Similarly, if tests were interpreted only within the context of comprehensive assessments, whenever decisions of importance to the individual are at stake, the undue amount of weight often placed upon any given test result would diminish. Psychologists, consultants, and qualified practitioners have to offer a variety of services in their roles. Informed consent is a central principle in these actions. This means that the end users of psychological services have the right to know precisely what services are being offered, what benefits can be expected, and what risks are involved. After being so informed, these end users and test takers then have the right to refuse the services or terminate participation. However, the legalities around informed consent and protection of privacy are not strict. Therefore, it is the responsibility of the practitioner to ensure that the information is not misused and people are made aware of their rights when undertaking a psychological assessment and allied services.

Test Related Factors. In a country like India, where there is a diverse population, it is important to differentiate between factors that affect both test and criterion behavior, and factors whose influence is restricted to the test. The test-related factors reduce validity. Examples of such factors include previous experience in taking tests, motivation to perform well in tests, rapport with the examiner, undue emphasis on speed, and any other variables that affect performance on the particular test, but irrelevant to the broad behavior domain under consideration. Special efforts should be made to reduce the operation of these test-related factors when testing persons with dissimilar cultural backgrounds or persons with disabilities. Adequate test taking orientation procedures, preliminary practice, and other such steps devised for this purpose are highly desirable.

Specific test content may also influence test scores in ways that are unrelated to the assessing ability of the test. In a test of arithmetic reasoning, for example, the use of names or pictures of objects unfamiliar in a particular group, religion, or culture would represent a test-restricted handicap. Another more subtle way in which specific test content may spuriously affect performance is through the test takers' emotional and attitudinal responses. Stories or pictures portraying typical urban middle-class family scenes, for example, may alienate a child reared in a low income group. The perpetuation of gender stereotypes in test content, such as in the portrayal of male doctors or pilots and female nurses or flight attendants, may also have detrimental effect. In light of these considerations, most test publishers now make special efforts to eliminate inappropriate test content. In fact, the review of test content with reference to positive or negative implications for minority test takers is a common step in the test construction process.

Responsible Use and Protection of the Intellectual Property of Tests. Psychologists should protect the security of standardized and controlled tests wherever possible. This includes respecting copyright restraints and preventing unauthorized access to psychometric instruments. If the necessity arises, psychologists may need to educate colleagues and the public about the appropriate use of tests and the need to safeguard the confidentiality of the test content. In a multidisciplinary team context, other professional colleagues, who are not trained in psychometrics, may request the right to access or use the tests. While non-standardized checklists or systematic observations may be not be used by psychologists, any test relying on standardized administration and interpretation which have been validated against normative groups should not be made available.

Interpretation and Use of Test Scores. Psychologists, consultants, and qualified practitioners should interpret test scores in conjunction with other collateral information, such as information from interview, information given by relatives and friends, observational data and previous assessment reports. Far reaching conclusions or diagnoses which have high impact on the test taker's life should be avoided on the basis of a psychometric test or a one-off assessment. Test takers' environment and reasonable alternative explanations for the test results should be considered. Barriers such as test taker's emotional, psychological, and physical-mental state, side effects of medication, language or cultural barriers, educational limitations of understanding, the testing environment, the interaction with the tester, fatigue, and the client's recent and historic background tend to impact the test performance and must be considered during the interpretation of test results and taking decisions based on them. At times, one needs to differentiate between impairment of functioning which is either transient and short term or more enduring. Constraints on interpretation may also include the lack of normative data for a test taker's ethnic, cultural, or social group. Identified constraints should be recorded and allowed for in the interpretation of results. If the same psychometric instrument has been undertaken on an individual previously, the assessing psychologist should be mindful of any practice effects and allow for that in the interpretation of results. Comparison of scores on repeat assessments may give useful information. A computer-interpreted test result or a computer-generated report is not adequate as an assessment report. The psychologist has a responsibility to evaluate and provide feedback on the computer-based interpretation of test performance or the computer-generated report in the light of additional information, observations, and other known data. Lastly, over-generalizing of test results must be avoided. The extrapolation of that result to predict success in real-life situations, such as academic success, current, and future employment status, performance of daily living tasks, etc. should only be done if the test's predictive validity in all different spheres of life has been established.

Objectivity of Tests. When social stereotypes and prejudices may distort interpersonal evaluations, tests provide a safeguard against favoritism and arbitrary decisions. When properly used, tests serve an important function in preventing irrelevant and unfair discrimination.

Responsibilities of Test Publishers. Test publishers must ensure that tests are purchased in accordance with the competency levels set by some test producers and that specific training be undertaken for using the specific test in a competent and useful way. For instance, many psychometric instruments (particularly those used in human development and employment selection) are now available for purchase online. This may degrade the usefulness of some tests. While psychologists and test publishers are bound by their professional obligations to maintain ethical conduct, others may not be so responsible. It behoves test publishers to lead by example and to demonstrate that there is an added value in having a disciplined, scientifically-sound approach to an assessment which integrates information (often complex) to enable useful interpretations and application to the issue of interest. There may also be a need to educate stakeholders of the potential risks that may arise from the misuse of psychometrics.

To summarize, the issues outlined here are not exhaustive and there are many other important ethical considerations. An attempt has been made to provide a broad outline of ethical practice in psychological testing as examples. Specific courses elaborate on these issues and help to identify situations in which they apply. However, each individual needs to be aware of the role that ethical guidelines play in directing the application of psychological testing to the problems of the real world.

Appendix A

Alphabetical Listing of Tests and Other Assessment Tools

This table lists all tests discussed or mentioned in the text, except for: (a) out-of-print tests cited for historical reasons only; (b) tests that are not yet published; and (c) tests described in the literature and available only from their authors. For further information, see the *Mental Measurements Yearbooks* and other publications from the Buros Institute of Mental Measurements, *Test Critiques* (Keyser & Sweetland, 1984–1994), as well as other sources cited in chapter 1.

TEST NAME (ABBREVIATION)/PUBUSHER'S CODE[1]

AAMR Adaptive Behavior Scale (ABS) / PRO-ED
ACT Assessment / ACT
Adjective Check List (ACL) / CPP
Alcohol Use Inventory (AUI) / NCS
Armed Forces Qualification Test (AFQT) / U.S. Military
Armed Services Vocational Aptitude Battery (ASVAB) / U.S. Military
Basic Personality Inventory (BPI) / Sigma
Bayley Infant Neurodevelopmental Screener (BINS) / TPC
Bayley Scales of Infant Development—Second Edition (Bayley-II) / TPC
Beck Depression Inventory (BDI) / TPC
Behavior Assessment System for Children (BASC) / AGS
Bender Visual Motor Gestalt Test (Bender-Gestalt) / WPS
Bennett Mechanical Comprehension Test (BMCT) / TPC
Benton Visual Retention Test, Fifth Edition (BVRT) / TPC

[1] Appendix B contains the complete names and addresses of the test publishers listed here, arranged in alphabetical order according to the Publishers' codes used in this Appendix.

Boehm Test of Basic Concepts—Revised (Boehm-R) / TPC
Bracken Basic Concept Scale (BBCS) / TPC
Brief Symptom Inventory (BSI) / NCS
British Ability Scales (BAS) / NFER-Nelson
Bruininks-Oseretsky Test of Motor Proficiency / AGS
California Achievement Tests—Fifth Edition (CAT) / CTB
California Child Q-Set / CPP
California Diagnostic Mathematics Tests (CDMT) / CTB
California Diagnostic Reading Tests (CDRT) / CTB
California Psychological Inventory—Third Edition (CPI-3) / CPP
California Q-Sort Deck / CPP
Campbell Interest and Skill Survey (CISS) / NCS
Career Assessment Inventory—The Enhanced Version (CAI-EV) / NCS
Career Assessment Inventory—The Vocational Version (CAI-VV) / NCS
Career Beliefs Inventory (CBI) / CPP
Career Development Inventory (CDI) / CPP
Career Directions Inventory (CDI) / Sigma
Career Interest Inventory (CII) / TPC
Career Planning Program (CPP) / ACT
Children's Apperception Test (C.A.T.) / CPS
Cognitive Abilities Test (CogAT, Form 5) / Riverside
College Level Examination Program (CLEP) / ETS
Columbia Mental Maturity Scale (CMMS) / TPC
Comprehensive Tests of Basic Skills—Fourth Edition (CTBS/4) / CTB
Computer Programmer Aptitude Battery (CPAB) / SRA
Concept Assessment Kit—Conservation (CAK) / EdITS
Crawford Small Parts Dexterity Test (CSPDT) / TPC
Cross-Cultural Adaptability Inventory (CCAI) / NCS
CRT Skills Test / SRA
Culture Fair Intelligence Test/IPAT
Das-Naglieri Cognitive Assessment System (CAS) / Riverside
Differential Ability Scales (DAS) / TPC
Differential Aptitude Tests—Computerized Adaptive Edition (DAT Adaptive) / TPC
Differential Aptitude Tests—Fifth Edition (DAT) / TPC Draw-a-Man Test (see Goodenough-Flarris Drawing Test)
Edwards Personal Preference Schedule (EPPS) / TPC
Embedded Figures Test (EFT) / CPP
Fagan Test of Infant Intelligence / Infantest
Fleishman Job Analysis Survey (F-JAS) / MRI
General Aptitude Test Battery (GATB) / USES
Goodenough-Harris Drawing Test / TPC
Graduate Record Examinations (GRE) / ETS
Group Embedded Figures Test / CPP
Guide to the Assessment of Test Session Behavior for the WISC-III and the WIAT / TPC
Guilford-Zimmerman Temperament Survey (GZTS) / CPP
Halstead-Reitan Neuropsychological Test Battery (HIRB) / RNL
Haptic Intelligence Scale / Stoelting
Harrington-O'Shea Career Decision-Making System—Revised (CDM-R) / AGS

Hogan Personality Inventory—Second Edition (HPI) / HAS
House-Tree-Person (H-T-P) / WPS
Infant-Toddler Developmental Assessment (IDA) / Riverside
Iowa Tests of Basic Skills / Riverside
Iowa Tests of Educational Development / Riverside
Jackson Personality Inventory—Revised (JPI-R) / Sigma
Jackson Vocational Interest Survey (JVIS) / Sigma
Kaufman Adolescent and Adult Intelligence Test (KAIT) / AGS
Kaufman Assessment Battery for Children (K-ABC) / AGS
Kaufman Brief Intelligence Test (K-BIT) / AGS
Kaufman Test of Educational Achievement (K-TEA) / AGS
Kuder General Interest Survey (KGIS) / CTB
Kuder Occupational Interest Survey (KOIS) / CTB
Kuder Preference Record—Vocational (KPR-V) / CTB
Leiter International Performance Scale—Revised (LIPS-R) / Stoelting
Luria-Nebraska Neuropsychological Battery (LNNB) / WPS
Machover Draw-a-Person Test (D-A-P) / Thomas
McCarthy Scales of Children's Abilities (MSCA) / TPC
Metropolitan Achievement Test—Seventh Edition (MAT) / TPC
Metropolitan Readiness Tests—Sixth Edition (MRT) / TPC
MicroCog: Assessment of Cognitive Functioning / TPC
Millon Adolescent Clinical Inventory (MACI) / NCS
Millon Adolescent Personality Inventory (MAPI) / NCS
Millon Clinical Multiaxial Inventory-Ill (MCMI-III) / NCS
Millon Index of Personality Styles (MIPS) / TPC
Minnesota Clerical Test (MCT) / TPC
Minnesota Multiphasic Personality Inventory—Adolescent (MMPI-A) / UMP
Minnesota Multiphasic Personality Inventory—2 (MMPI-2) / UMP
Multidimensional Aptitude Battery (MAB) / Sigma
Myers-Briggs Type Indicator (MBTI) / CPP
Occupational Aptitude Survey and Interest Schedule—Second Ed. (OASIS-2) / PRO-ED
Ordinal Scales of Psychological Development / UIP
Orleans-Hanna Algebra Prognosis Test / TPC
Otis-Lennon School Ability Test—Seventh Edition (OLSAT7) / TPC
Paced Auditory Serial Addition Test (PASAT) / ForThought
PDI Customer Service Inventory / PDI PDI Employment Inventory / PDI
Peabody Picture Vocabulary Test—Revised (PPVT-R) / AGS
Personality Assessment Inventory (PAI) / PAR
Personality Inventory for Children—Revised (PIC-R) / WPS
Personality Inventory for Youth (PIY) / WPS
Personality Research Form (PRF) / Sigma
Porteus Mazes / TPC
Quality of Life Inventory (QOLI) / NCS
Raven's Progressive Matrices (RPM) / Oxford (U.S. Distributor: TPC)
Revised Minnesota Paper Form Board Test (RMPFBT) / TPC
Revised NEO Personality Inventory (NEO PI-R) / PAR
Roberts Apperception Test for Children (RATC) / WPS
Rorschach / H & H

Rotter Incomplete Sentences Blank (ISB) / TPC
Schaie-Thurstone Adult Mental Abilities Test / CPP
Schedule for Nonadaptive and Adaptive Personality (SNAP) / UMP
Scholastic Assessment Test (SAT) / ETS Self-Directed Search (SDS) / PAR
Senior Apperception Test (S.A.T.) / CPS
Sixteen Personality Factor Questionnaire—Fifth Edition (16PF) / IPAT
Social Climate Scales / CPP
Social Skills Rating System (SSRS) / AGS
Stanford Achievement Test—Eighth Edition / TPC
Stanford'Binet Intelligence Scale—Fourth Edition (SB-IV) / Riverside
Stanford Diagnostic Mathematics Test—Third Edition (SDMT) / TPC
Stanford Diagnostic Reading Test—Third Edition (SDRT) / TPC
Stanford Writing Assessment Program / TPC
State-Trait Anger Expression Inventory (STAXI) / PAR
State-Trait Anxiety Inventory (STAI) / CPP
State-Trait Anxiety Inventory for Children (STAIC) / CPP
Strong Interest Inventory (SII) / CPP
Structure of Intellect Learning Abilities Test / WPS
Student Adaptation to College Questionnaire (SACQ) / WPS
Student Self-Concept Scale (SSCS) / AGS
Student Styles Questionnaire / TPC
Symptom Checklist-90—Revised (SCL-90-R) / NCS
System for Interactive Guidance Information—Revised (SIGI-PLUS) / ETS
Teamwork-KSA / SRA
Tell-Me-A-Story (TEMAS) / WPS
TerraNova series / CTB
Test Anxiety Inventory (TAI) / CPP
Test of Cognitive Skills—Second Edition (TCS/2) / CTB
Test of Nonverbal Intelligence—Second Edition (TONI-2) / PRO-ED
Test of Variables of Attention (T.O.V.A) / UAD
Tests of Achievement and Proficiency / Riverside
Tests of Adult Basic Education (TABE) / CTB
The Holtzman Inkblot Technique (HIT) / TPC
Thematic Apperception Test (TAT) / Harvard
The Rosenzweig Picture-Frustration Study (P-F Study) / PAR
The Scenotest / H & H
The Values Scale / CPP
Vigil Continuous Performance Test (VIGIL) / ForThought
Vineland Adaptive Behavior Scales (VABS) / AGS
Washington University Sentence Completion Test (WUSCT) / Erlbaum
Wechsler Adult Intelligence Scale—Revised (WAIS-R) / TPC
Wechsler Individual Achievement Test (WIAT) / TPC
Wechsler Intelligence Scale for Children—Third Edition (WISC-III) / TPC
Wechsler Preschool and Primary Scale of Intelligence—Revised (WPPSI-R) / TPC
Wonderlic Personnel Test / Wonderlic
Woodcock-Johnson Psycho-Educational Battery—Revised (WJ-R) / Riverside
Woodcock Reading Mastery Tests—Revised / AGS Work Keys / ACT

Appendix B

Addresses of Test Publishers, Distributors, and Test-Related Organizations

AAMR	•	American Association on Mental Retardation 444 North Capitol Street, N.W., Suite 846 Washington, DC 20001-1512
ABPP	•	American Board of Professional Psychology 2100 East Broadway, Suite 313 Columbia, MO 65201-6082
ACA	•	American Counseling Association 5999 Stevenson Avenue Alexandria, VA 22304-3300
ACT	•	American College Testing Program ACT National Office 2201 North Dodge Street P.O. Box 168 Iowa City, IA 52243-0168
AERA	•	American Educational Research Association 1230 Seventeenth Street, N.W. Washington, DC 20036-3078
AGS	•	American Guidance Service, Inc. 4201 Woodland Road Circle Pines, MN 55014-1796

APA	•	American Psychological Association 750 First Street, N.E. Washington, DC 20002-4242
ASC	•	Assessment Systems Corporation 2233 University Avenue, Suite 200 St. Paul, MN 55114
ATP	•	Association of Test Publishers 655 Fifteenth Street, N.W., Suite 320 Washington, DC 20005
BoTA	•	Board on Testing and Assessment National Research Council 2101 Constitution Avenue, N.W. Washington, DC 20418
Buros	•	Buros Institute of Mental Measurements P.O. Box 880348 135 Bancroft Hall Lincoln, NE 68588-0348
CEEB	•	College Entrance Examination Board 45 Columbus Avenue New York, NY 10023-6992
CPP	•	Consulting Psychologists Press, Inc. 3803 East Bayshore Road P.O. Box 10096 Palo Alto, CA 94303
CPS	•	C.P.S., Inc. P.O. Box 83 Larchmont, NY 10538
CTB	•	CTB/McGraw-Hill 20 Ryan Ranch Road Monterey, CA 93940
EdITS	•	Educational and Industrial Testing Service P.O. Box 7234 San Diego, CA 92167
EEOC	•	Equal Employment Opportunity Commission 1801 L Street Washington, DC 20507

Erlbaum	•	Lawrence Erlbaum Associates, Inc. 10 Industrial Avenue Mahwah, NJ 07430-2262
ETS	•	Educational Testing Service Publications Order Services PO. Box 6736 Princeton, NJ 08541-6736
	•	ETS Test Collection Mailstop 30-B Rosedale Road Princeton, NJ 08541-0001
ForThought	•	ForThought, Ltd. Nine Trafalgar Square Nashua, NH 03063
GRE	•	Graduate Record Examinations Educational Testing Service P.O. Box 6000 Princeton, NJ 08541-6000
Harcourt Brace	•	Harcourt Brace Educational Measurement Educational Testing Division of TPC 555 Academic Court San Antonio, TX 78204-2498
Harvard	•	Harvard University Press 79 Garden Street Cambridge, MA 02138
HAS	•	Hogan Assessment Systems, Inc. P.O. Box 521176 Tulsa, OK 74152
H&H	•	Hogrefe & Huber Publishers United States Office: P.O. Box 2487 Kirkland, WA 98083 Swiss Office: Verlag Hans Huber Langgass-Strasse 76 CH-3000 Bern 9 Switzerland

IBM	•	IBM K-12 Education 4111 Northside Parkway Atlanta, GA 30327
Infantest	•	Infantest Corporation P.O. Box 18765 Cleveland Heights, OH 44118-0765
IPAT	•	Institute for Personality and Ability Testing, Inc. P.O. Box 1188 Champaign, IL 61824-1188
MRI	•	Management Research Institute, Inc. 6701 Democracy Blvd., Suite 300 Bethesda, MD 20817
NCME	•	National Council on Measurement in Education 1230 Seventeenth Street, N.W. Washington, DC 20036
NCS	•	National Computer Systems, Inc. P.O. Box 1416 Minneapolis, MN 55440
NFER-Nelson	•	NFER-Nelson Publishing Company, Ltd. Darville House, 2 Oxford Road East Windsor-Berkshire, SL4 IDF United Kingdom
Oxford	•	Oxford Psychologists Press, Ltd. Lambourne House 311 321 Banbury Road Oxford OX2 7JH England
PAR	•	Psychological Assessment Resources, Inc. P.O. Box 998 Odessa, FL 33556-0998
PDI	•	Personnel Decisions International 2000 Plaza VII 45 South Seventh Street Minneapolis, MN 55402-1608
PRO-ED	•	PRO-ED 8700 Shoal Creek Boulevard Austin, TX 78757-6897

Riverside	•	The Riverside Publishing Company 425 Spring Lake Drive Itasca, IL 60143
RNL	•	Reitan Neuropsychological Laboratory 2920 South Fourth Avenue Tucson, AZ 85713-4819
The Score	•	Newsletter for Division 5 of the American Psychological Association 4201 Woodland Road Circle Pines, MN 55014
Sigma	•	Sigma Assessment Systems, Inc. United States Office: 1110 Military Street P.O. Box 610984 Port Huron, MI 48061-0984 Canadian Office: Research Psychologists Press, Inc. 650 Waterloo Street, Suite 100 P.O. Box 3292, Station B London, ON N6A 4K3
SilverPlatter	•	SilverPlatter Information 100 River Ridge Drive Norwood, MA 02062-5043
SIOP	•	Society for Industrial and Organizational Psychology, Inc. P.O. Box 87 Bowling Green, OH 43402
SPA	•	Society for Personality Assessment 750 First Street, N.E. Washington, DC 20002-4242
SRA	•	McGraw-Hill/London House SRA Business and Industry Assessments 9701 West Higgins Road Rosemont, IL 60018-4720
Stoelting	•	Stoelting Company 620 Wheat Lane Wood Dale, IL 60191

Swets	•	Swets Test Services Heereweg 347b 2161 CA Lisse Nederland
Thomas	•	Charles C Thomas Publisher 2600 South First Street Springfield, IL 62794-9265
TPC	•	The Psychological Corporation 555 Academic Court San Antonio, TX 78204-2498
UAD	•	Universal Attention Disorders, Inc. 4281 Katella #215 Los Alamitos, CA 90720
UIP	•	University of Illinois Press 1325 South Oak Street Champaign, IL 61820
UMP	•	University of Minnesota Press Test Division 111 Third Avenue South, Suite 290 Minneapolis, MN 55401
USES	•	United States Employment Service Western Assessment Research and Development Center 140 East 300 South Salt Lake City, UT 84111
U.S. Military	•	United States Military Entrance Processing Command Attn.: Technical Directorate 2500 Green Bay Road North Chicago, IL 60064-3094
Wonderlic	•	Wonderlic Personnel Test, Inc. 1509 North Milwaukee Avenue Libertyville, IL 60048-1380
WPS	•	Western Psychological Services 12031 Wilshire Boulevard Los Angeles, CA 90025-1251

References

Abrahams, N. M., & Alf, E., Jr. (1972). Pratfalls in moderator research. *Journal of Applied Psychology, 56,* 245–251.

Ackerman, P. L. (1992). Predicting individual differences in complex skills acquisition: Dynamics of ability determinants. *Journal of Applied Psychology, 77,* 598–614.

Acklin, M. W. (1995). Integrative Rorschach interpretation. *Journal of Personality Assessment, 64,* 235–238.

Acklfn, M. W., McDowell, C. J., & Orndoff, S. (1992). Statistical power and the Rorschach: 1975–1991. *Journal of Personality Assessment, 59,* 366–379.

ACT ASSESSMENT: USER HANDBOOK. (1995–1996). Iowa City, IA: ACT Publications.

Adams, R. L., Parsons, O. A., Culbertson, J. L., & Nixon, S. J. (Eds.). *(1996). Neuropsychology for clinical practice: Etiology, assessment, and treatment of common neurological disorders.* Washington, DC: American Psychological Association.

Adcock, C. J. (1965). Review of Thematic Apperception Test. *Sixth Mental Measurements Yearbook,* 533–535.

Adler, L. L., & Gielen, U. P. (Eds.). (1994). *Cross-cultural topics in psychology.* New York: Praeger.

Adler, N., & Matthews, K. (1994). Health psychology: Why do some people get sick and some stay well? *Annual Review of Psychology, 45,* 229–259.

Adler, P. A., & Adler, P. (1994). Observational techniques. In N. K. Denzin & Y. S. Lincoln (Eds.), *Handbook of qualitative research* (pp. 377–392). Thousand Oaks, CA: Sage.

Agnew, J., & Masten, V. L. (1994). Neuropsychological assessment of occupational neurotoxic exposure. In M. L. Bleecker & J. A. Hansen (Eds.), *Occupational neurology and* clinical *neurotoxicology* (pp. 113–131). Baltimore: Williams & Wilkins.

Ahlstrom, K. G. (1964). *Studies in spelling: I. Analysis of three different aspects of spelling ability* (Rep. No. 20). Uppsala, Sweden: Uppsala University, Institute of Education.

Aiken, L. R. (1993). *Personality: Theories, research, and applications.* Englewood Cliffs, NJ: Prentice Hall.

Aiken, L. R. (1996). Assessment *of intellectual functioning* (2nd ed.). New York: Plenum.

Aiken, L. R., & Groth-Marnat, G. (2006). *Psychological Testing and Assessment.* Boston, IL: Pearson Education Group.

Aiken, L. R., & Groth-Marnat, G. (2006). *Psychological Testing* and *Assessment.* Boston, IL: Pearson Education Group.

AIKEN, L. R., & GROTH-MARNAT, G. (2006). Psychological Testing and Assessment. Boston, IL: Pearson Education Group.

AIKEN, L. R., & GROTH-MARNAT, G. (2006). *Psychological Testing and Assessment*. Boston, IL: Pearson Education Group.

AIKEN, L. R., & GROTH-MARNAT, G. (2006). *Psychological Testing and Assessment*. Boston, IL: Pearson Education Group.

AIKEN, L. R., & GROTH-MARNAT, G. (2006). *Psychological Testing and Assessment*. Boston, IL: Pearson Education Group.

AIKEN, L. R., AND GROTH-MARNAT, G. (2006). *Psychological testing and assessment*. Boston, IL: Pearson Education Group.

AIKEN, L. S., WEST, S. G., SECHREST, L., & RENO, R. R. (1990). Graduate training in statistics, methodology, and measurement in psychology. *American Psychologist, 45*, 721–734.

ALBERT, R. S. (Series Ed.). (1991–1994). *Creativity Research Series*. Norwood, NJ: Ablex.

ALBERT, S., FOX, H. M., & KAHN, M. W. (1980). Faking psychosis on the Rorschach: Can expert judges detect malingering? *Journal of Personality* Assessment, *44*, 115–119.

ALEXANDER, L., & JAMES, H. T. (1987). *The nation's report card: Improving the assessment of student achievement*. Boston: Harvard Graduate School of Education, National Academy of Education.

ALLEN, R. M., & COLLINS, M. G. (1955). Suggestions for the adaptive administration of intelligence tests for those with cerebral palsy. *Cerebral Palsy Review, 16*, 11–14.

ALLIGER, G. M., LILIENFELD, S. O., &. MITCHELL, K. E. (1996). The susceptibility of overt and covert integrity tests to coaching and faking. *Psychological Science, 7*, 32–39.

ALLISON, J. A. (1995). Review of the Family Environment Scale, Second Edition. *Twelfth Mental Measurements Yearbook,* 384–385.

ALLPORT, G. W. *(1937). Personality: A psychological interpretation*. New York: Holt.

ALLPORT, G. W., & ODBERT, H. S. (1936). Trait names, a psycholexical study. *Psychological Monographs, 47(1,* Whole No. 211).

ALLPORT, G. W., VERNON, P. E., & LINDZEY, G. (1960). *Study of Values* (3rd ed.): *Manual*. Chicago: Riverside.

ALVARADO, N. (1994). Empirical validity of the Thematic Apperception Test. *Journal of Personality Assessment, 63*, 59–79.

AMELANG, M., &. BORKENAU, P. (1986). The trait concept: Current theoretical considerations, empirical facts, and implications for personality inventory construction. In Angleitner & J. S. Wiggins (Eds.), *Personality assessment via questionnaires: Current issues in theory and measurement* (pp. 7–34). Berlin: Springer-Verlag.

AMERICAN ASSOCIATION ON MENTAL RETARDATION. (1992). *Mental retardation: Definition, classification, and systems of supports* (9th ed.). Washington, DC: Author.

AMERICAN COLLEGE TESTING PROGRAM. (1994). *Counselor's manual for the ACT Career Planning Program, 3rd ed. Iowa City,* IA: Author.

AMERICAN COLLEGE TESTING PROGRAM. (1995). *Work Keys* [Brochure]. Iowa City, IA: Author.

AMERICAN COUNSELING ASSOCIATION (ACA). (1989). *Responsibilities of users of standardized tests*. Alexandria, VA: Author.

AMERICAN EDUCATIONAL RESEARCH ASSOCIATION, AMERICAN PSYCHOLOGICAL ASSOCIATION, & NATIONAL COUNCIL ON MEASUREMENT IN EDUCATION. (1985).

Standards for educational and psychological testing. Washington, DC: American Psychological Association.

AMERICAN EDUCATIONAL RESEARCH ASSOCIATION, AMERICAN PSYCHOLOGICAL ASSOCIATION, & NATIONAL COUNCIL ON MEASUREMENT IN EDUCATION (1996). *Standards for educational and psychological testing.* Manuscript in preparation.

AMERICAN PSYCHIATRIC ASSOCIATION. (1980). *Diagnostic and statistical manual of mental disorders* (3rd ed.). Washington, DC: Author.

AMERICAN PSYCHIATRIC ASSOCIATION. (1994). *Diagnostic and statistical manual of mental disorders* (4th ed.). Washington, DC: Author.

AMERICAN PSYCHOLOGICAL ASSOCIATION (1954). *Technical recommendations for psychological tests and diagnostic techniques.* Washington, DC: American Psychological Association (Also in *Psychological Bulletin, 51* [2, Pt. 2].)

AMERICAN PSYCHOLOGICAL ASSOCIATION. (1982). *Ethical principles in the conduct of research with human participants.* Washington, DC: Author.

AMERICAN PSYCHOLOGICAL ASSOCIATION. (1987a). General guidelines for providers of psychological services. *American Psychologist, 42,* 712–723.

AMERICAN PSYCHOLOGICAL ASSOCIATION. (1987b). Model act for state licensure of psychologists. *American Psychologist, 42,* 696–703.

AMERICAN PSYCHOLOGICAL ASSOCIATION (1991). The *PsycLIT Database* (January, 1983-September, 1991). Washington, DC: Author.

AMERICAN PSYCHOLOGICAL ASSOCIATION. (1992). Ethical principles of psychologists and code of conduct. *American Psychologist, 47,* 1597–1611.

AMERICAN PSYCHOLOGICAL ASSOCIATION. (1993). *Directory of the American Psychological Association.* Washington, DC: Author.

AMERICAN PSYCHOLOGICAL ASSOCIATION (1994). *Program: 102nd annual convention.* Washington, DC: Author.

AMERICAN PSYCHOLOGICAL ASSOCIATION, AMERICAN EDUCATIONAL RESEARCH ASSOCIATION, NATIONAL COUNCIL ON MEASUREMENT IN EDUCATION. (1974). *Standards for Educational and Psychological Tests.* Washington, DC: American Psychological Association.

AMERICAN PSYCHOLOGICAL ASSOCIATION, BOARD OF ETHNIC MINORITY AFFAIRS. (1990). *Guidelines for providers of psychological services to ethnic, linguistic, and culturally diverse populations.* Washington, DC: Author.

AMERICAN PSYCHOLOGICAL ASSOCIATION, COMMITTEE ON LEGAL ISSUES. (1996). Strategies for private practitioners coping with subpoenas or compelled testimony for client records or test data. *Professional Psychology: Research and Practice, 27,* 245–251.

AMERICAN PSYCHOLOGICAL ASSOCIATION, COMMITTEE ON PROFESSIONAL PRACTICE AND STANDARDS. (1993). Record keeping guidelines. *American Psychologist, 48,* 984–986.

AMERICAN PSYCHOLOGICAL ASSOCIATION, COMMITTEE ON PROFESSIONAL PRACTICE AND STANDARDS. (1994). Guidelines for child custody evaluations in divorce proceedings. *American Psychologist, 49,* 677–680.

AMERICAN PSYCHOLOGICAL ASSOCIATION, COMMITTEE ON PROFESSIONAL STANDARDS. (1981). Specialty guidelines for the delivery of services. *American Psychologist, 36,* 639–681.

AMERICAN PSYCHOLOGICAL ASSOCIATION, COMMITTEE ON PSYCHOLOGICAL TESTS AND ASSESSMENT. (1988). *Implications for test fairness of the "Golden Rule" Company settlement.* Washington, DC: Author.

AMERICAN PSYCHOLOGICAL ASSOCIATION, COMMITTEE ON PSYCHOLOGICAL TESTS AND ASSESSMENT. (1995). *Statement on the use of secure psychological tests in the education of graduate and undergraduate psychology students.* Washington, DC: Author.

American Psychological Association, Committee on Psychological Tests and Assessment. (1996). Statement on the disclosure of test data. *American Psychologist, 51,* 644–648.

American Psychological Association, Division of Evaluation, Measurement, and Statistics. (1993, January). Psychometric and assessment issues raised by the Americans with Disabilities Act (ADA). *The Score Newsletter, 15, 1–2, 7–15.*

American Psychological Association, Ethics Committee. (1994). Report of the Ethics Committee. *American Psychologist, 49, 659–666.*

American Psychological Association, Ethics Committee. (1995). Report of the Ethics Committee, 1994. American *Psychologist, 50,* 706–713.

American Psychological Association, Ethics Committee. (1996). Rules and procedures. *American Psychologist, 51, 529–548.*

American Psychological Association, Joint Interim Committee for the Identification and Recognition of Specialties and Proficiencies. (1995a). *Principles for the recognition of proficiencies in psychology.* Washington, DC: Author.

American Psychological Association, Joint Interim Committee for the Identification and Recognition of Specialties and Proficiencies. (1995b). *Principles for the recognition of specialties in professional psychology. Washington,* DC: Author.

American Psychological Association, Task Force on Intelligence (1995). *Intelligence: knowns and unknowns.* Washington, DC: APA Science Directorate.

Ames, L. B. (1937). The sequential patterning of prone progression in the human infant. *Genetic Psychology Monographs, 19,* 409–460.

Ames, L. B. (1989). *Arnold Gesell—Themes of his work*. New York: Human Sciences Press.

Anastasi, A. (1934). Practice and variability. *Psychological Monographs, 45* (5, Whole No. 204).

Anastasi, A. (1954). *Psychological testing.* New York: Macmillan.

Anastasi, A. (1956). Age changes in adult test performance. *Psychological Reports, 2, 509.*

Anastasi, A. (1958). *Differential psychology* (3rd ed.). New York: Macmillan.

Anastasi, A. (Ed.). (1965). *Individual differences.* New York: Wiley.

Anastasi, A. (1967). Psychology, psychologists, and psychological testing. *American Psychologist, 22,* 297–306.

Anastasi, A. (1970). On the formation of psychological traits. *American Psychologist, 25,* 899–910.

Anastasi, A. (1971). More on heritability: Addendum to the Hebb and Jensen interchange. *American Psychologist, 26,* 1036–1037.

Anastasi, A. *(1972).* Technical critique. In L. A. Crooks (Ed.), *Proceedings of Invitational Conference on "An investigation of sources of bias in the prediction of job performance: A six-year study"* (pp. 79–88). Princeton, NJ: Educational Testing Service.

Anastasi, A. (1979). *Fields of applied psychology* (2nd ed.) New York: McGraw-Hill.

Anastasi, A. (1980). Review of R. Feuerstein et al., *The dynamic assessment of retarded performers: The Learning Potential Assessment Device, theory, instruments, and techniques. Rehabilitation Literature, 41* (1–2), 28–30.

Anastasi, A. (1981a). Coaching, test sophistication, and developed abilities. *American Psychologist, 36,* 1086–1093.

ANASTASI, A. (1981b). Diverse effects of training on tests of academic intelligence. In F. Green (Ed.), *Issues in testing: Coaching, disclosure, and ethnic bias* (pp. 5–20). San Francisco: Jossey-Bass.

ANASTASI, A. (1981c). Sex differences: Historical perspectives and methodological implications. *Developmental Review, 1,* 187–206.

ANASTASI, A. (1983a). Evolving trait concepts. *American Psychologist, 38,* 175–184.

ANASTASI, A. (1983b). Traits, states, and situations: A comprehensive view. In H. Wainer &. S. Messick (Eds.), *Principals of modern psychological measurement: A Festschrift for Frederic M. Lord* (pp. 345–356). Hillsdale, NJ: Erlbaum.

ANASTASI, A. (1983c). What do intelligence tests measure? In S. B. Anderson & J. S. Helmick (Eds.), On *educational testing* (pp. 5–28). San Francisco: Jossey-Bass.

ANASTASI, A. (1984a). The K-ABC in historical and contemporary perspective. *Journal of Special Education, 18,* 357–366.

ANASTASI, A. (1984b). Traits revisited—with some current implications. In D. P. Rogers (Ed.), *Foundations of psychology: Some personal views* (pp. 185–206). New York: Praeger.

ANASTASI, A. (1985a). Interpreting results from multiscore batteries. *Journal of Counseling and Development, 64,* 84–86.

ANASTASI, A. (1985b). Reciprocal relations between cognitive and affective development: With implications for sex differences. In T. B. Sonderegger (Ed.), *Psychology and gender* (Nebraska Symposium on Motivation, Vol. 32, pp. 1–35). Lincoln, NE: University of Nebraska Press.

ANASTASI, A. (1985c). Review of Kaufman Assessment Battery for Children. *Ninth Mental Measurements Yearbook,* Vol. 1, 769–771.

ANASTASI, A. (1985d). Some emerging trends in psychological measurement: A fifty-year perspective. *Applied Psychological Measurement,* 9, 121–138.

ANASTASI, A. (1985e). The use of personality assessment in industry: Methodological and interpretive problems. In H. J. Bernardin &. D. A. Bownas (Eds.), *Personality assessment in organizations* (pp. 1–20). New York: Praeger.

ANASTASI, A. (1986a). Evolving concepts of test validation. *Annual Review of Psychology, 37,* 1–15.

ANASTASI, A. (1986b). Experiential structuring of psychological traits. *Developmental Review,* 6, 181–202.

ANASTASI, A. (1986c). Intelligence as a quality of behavior. In R. J. Sternberg & D. K. Detterman (Eds.), *What is intelligence? Contemporary viewpoints on its nature and definition* (pp. 19–21). Norwood, NJ: Ablex.

ANASTASI, A. (1988a). Explorations inhuman intelligence: Some uncharted routes. *Applied Measurement in Education, 1* (3), 207–213.

ANASTASI, A. (1988b). *Psychological testing* (6th ed.). New York: Macmillan.

ANASTASI, A. (1990a). Diversity and flexibility. *The Counseling Psychologist, 18,* 258–261.

ANASTASI, A. (1990b). What is test misuse? Perspectives of a measurement expert. *Proceedings of the 1989 ETS Invitational Conference* (pp. 15–25). Princeton, NJ: Educational Testing Service.

ANASTASI, A. (1991). The gap between experimental and psychometric orientations. *Journal of the Washington Academy of Sciences, 81,* 61–73.

ANASTASI, A. (1992a). Are there unifying trends in the psychologies of the 1990s? In M. E. Donnelly (Ed.), *Reinterpreting the legacy of William James* (pp. 29–48). Washington, DC: American Psychological Association.

ANASTASI, A. (1992b). A century of psychological science. *American Psychologist, 47,* 842–843.

ANASTASI, A. (1992c). Introductory remarks. In K. F. Geisinger (Ed.), *Psychological testing of Hispanics* (pp. 1–7). Washington, DC: American Psychological Association.

ANASTASI, A. (1993). A century of psychological testing: Origins, problems, and progress. In T. K. Fagan & G. R. VandenBos (Eds.). *Exploring applied psychology: Origins and critical analysis* (pp. 13–36). Washington, DC: American Psychological Association.

ANASTASI, A. (1994). Aptitude testing. *Encyclopedia of human behavior* (Vol. 1, pp. 211–221). San Diego, CA: Academic Press.

ANASTASI, A. (1995). Psychology evolving: Linkages, hierarchies, and dimensions. In F. Kessel (Ed.), *Psychology, science and human affairs: Essays in honor of William Bevan* (pp. 245–260). Boulder, CO: Westview Press.

ANASTASI, A., &. DRAKE, J. (1954). An empirical comparison of certain techniques for estimating the reliability of speeded tests. *Educational and Psychological Measurement, 14,* 529–540.

ANDERSEN, E B. (1983). Analyzing data using the Rasch model. In S. B. Anderson &. J. S. Helmick (Eds.), *On educational testing* (pp. 193–223). San Francisco: Jossey-Bass.

ANDERSON, J. C., & GERBING, D. W. (1988). Structural equation modeling in practice: A review and recommended two-step approach. *Psychological Bulletin, 103,* 411–423.

ANDERSON, R. J., & SISCO, F. HL. (1977). *Standardization of WISC-R Performance Scale for Deaf Children.* Washington, DC: Gallaudet College, Office of Demographic Studies.

ANDREW, D. M., PATERSON, D. G., & LONGSTAFF, H. P. (1979). *Manual: Minnesota Clerical Test.* Cleveland, OH: Psychological Corporation.

ANGLEITNER, A., JOHN, O. P., & LÖHR, F. J. (1986). It's *what* you ask and *how* you ask it: An item metric analysis of personality questionnaires. In A. Angleitner & J. S. Wiggins (Eds.), *Personality assessment via questionnaires: Current issues in theory and measurement* (pp. 61–107). Berlin: Springer-Verlag.

ANGLEITNER, A., & WIGGINS, J. S. (eds.). (1986). *Personality assessment via questionnaires: Current issues in theory and measurement.* Berlin: Springer-Verlag.

ANGOFF, W. H. (1962). Scales with non meaningful origins and units of measurement. *Educational and Psychological Measurement,* 22, 27–34.

ANGOFF, W. H. (1974). Criterion-referencing, norm-referencing, and the SAT. *College Board Review,* 92, 3–5, 21.

ANGOFF, W. H. (1984). *Scales, norms, and equivalent scores.* Princeton, NJ: Educational Testing Service.

ANGOFF, W. H., & COWELL, W. R. (1986). An examination of the assumption that the equating of parallel forms is population-independent. *Journal of Educational Measurement, 23,* 327–345.

ARCHER, R. P. (1992a). MMP1-A: *Assessing adolescent psychopathology.* Hillsdale, NJ: Erlbaum.

ARCHER, R. P. (1992b). Review of the Minnesota Multiphasic Personality Inventory-2. *Eleventh Mental Measurements Yearbook,* 558–562.

ARCHER, R. P. &. KRISHNAMURTHY, R. (1994). A structural summary approach for the MMPI-A: Development and empirical correlates. *Journal of Personality Assessment,* 63, 554–573.

ARCHER, R. P., KRISHNAMURTHY, R., & JACOBSON, J. M. (1994). *MMPI-A casebook.* Odessa, FL: Psychological Assessment Resources.

ARCHER, R. R, MARUISH, M., IMHOF, E. A., & PLOTROWSKI, C. (1991). Psychological test usage with adolescent clients: 1990 survey findings. *Professional Psychology: Research and Practice, 22,* 247–252.

ARDILA, A., ROSSELLI, M., & PUENTE, A. E. (1994). *Neuropsychological evaluation of the Spanish speaker.* New York: Plenum Press.

ARKES, H. R. (1993). A practical guide to decision making [Review of the book *Decision making: Its logic and practice*]. *Contemporary Psychology, 38,* 926–927.

ARMY AIR FORCES AVIATION PSYCHOLOGY PROGRAM, RESEARCH REPORTS. (1947–1948). (Nos. 1–19). Washington, DC: U.S. Government Printing Office.

ARNOLD, G. F. (1951). A technique for measuring the mental ability of the cerebral palsied. *Psychological Service Center Journal, 3,* 171–180.

ARONOW, E., & REZNIKOFF, M. (1976). *Rorschach* content *interpretation.* Orlando, FL: Grune & Stratton.

ARONOW, E., & REZNIKOFF, M. (1983). *A Rorschach introduction: Content and perceptual approaches.* Orlando, FL: Grune & Stratton.

ARONOW, E., REZNIKOFF, M., & MORELAND, K. (1994). *The Rorschach technique: Perceptual basics, content interpretation, and applications.* Boston: Allyn & Bacon.

ARONOW, E., REZNIKOFF, M., & MORELAND, K. (1995). The Rorschach: Projective technique or psychometric test? *Journal of Personality Assessment, 64,* 213–228.

ARTHUR, W., JR., & DAY, D. V. (1991). Examination of the construct validity of alternative measures of field dependence/independence. *Perceptual and Motor Skills, 72,* 851–859.

ASSOCIATION OF TEST PUBLISHERS. (1996). *Model guidelines for preemployment integrity testing (*2nd ed.*).* Washington, DC: Author.

ATKINSON, D. R., MORTEN, G., & SUE, D. W. (1993). *Counseling American minorities: A cross-cultural perspective* (4th ed.). Madison, WI: Brown & Benchman/Wm. C. Brown.

ATKINSON, J. W. (ed.). (1958). *Motives in fantasy, action, and society.* New York: Van Nostrand.

ATKINSON, J. W. (1974). Motivational determinants of intellective performance and cumulative achievement. In J. W. Atkinson &. J. O. Raynor (Eds.), *Motivation and achievement* (pp. 389–410). Washington, DC: Winston.

ATKINSON, J. W. (1981). Studying personality in the context of an advanced motivational psychology. *American Psychologist, 36,* 117–128.

ATKINSON, J. W., & BIRCH, G. (1978). An *introduction to motivation* (2nd ed.). New York: Van Nostrand.

ATKINSON, J. W., & FEATHER, N. T. (Eds.). (1966). A *theory of achievement motivation.* New York: Wiley.

ATKINSON, J. W., O'MALLEY, R M., & LENS, W. (1976). Motivation and ability: Interactive psychological determinants of intellective performance, educational achievement, and each other. In W. H. Sewell, R. M. Hauser, & D. L. Featherman (Eds.), *Schooling and achievement in American society* (pp. 29–60). New York: Academic Press.

ATKINSON, J. W., & RAYNOR, J. O. (Eds.). (1974). *Motivation arid achievement.* Washington, DC: Winston.

ATKINSON, L., QUARRINGTON, B., ALP, I. E., & CYR, J. J. (1986). Rorschach validity: An empirical approach to the literature. *Journal of Clinical Psychology, 42,* 360–362.

AYERS, W., DAY, G. F, & ROTATORI A. F. (1990). Legal, judicial, and IEP parameters of testing. In A. F. Rotatori, R. A. Fox, D. Sexton, & J. Miller (Eds.)., *Comprehensive assessment in special education: Approaches, procedures, and concerns* (pp. 124–144). Springfield, IL: Charles C Thomas.

AYLWARD, G. P. (1992). Review of Differential Ability Scales. *Eleventh Mental Measurements Yearbook*, 281–282.

AYLWARD, G. P. (1994). *Practitioner's guide to developmental and psychological testing.* New York: Plenum Press.

AYLWARD, G. P. (1995). *Bayley Infant Neurodevelopmental Screener: Manual.* San Antonio, TX: The Psychological Corporation.

BABAD, E. Y., & BUDOFF, M. (1974). Sensitivity and validity of learning-potential measurement in three levels of ability. *Journal of Educational Psychology, 66,* 439–447.

BACHELOR, P. A. (1989). Maximum likelihood confirmatory factor-analytic investigation of factors within Guilford's structure of intellect model. *Journal of Applied Psychology, 74,* 797–804.

BAER, J. (1993). *Creativity and divergent thinking: A task-specific approach.* Hillsdale, NJ: Erlbaum.

BAER, J. (1998). The case for domain specificity of creativity. *Creativity Research Journal, 11*(2), 173–177.

BAGNATO, S. J., & NEISWORTH, J. T. (1991). *Assessment for early intervention: Best practices for professionals.* New York: Guilford Press.

BAILEY, D. B., JR., & WOLERY, M. (1989). *Assessing infants and preschoolers with handicaps.* Columbus, OH: Merrill.

BAIRD, L. L. (1985). *Field trial of a user-oriented adaptation of the inventory of documented accomplishments as a tool in graduate admissions* (ETS Res. Rep. 85–13). Princeton, NJ: Educational Testing Service.

BAKER, E. L., & O'NEIL, H. E, JR. (Eds.). (1994). Technology *assessment in education and training.* Hillsdale, NJ: Erlbaum.

BAKER, E. L., O'NEIL, H. E, & LINN, R. L. (1993). Policy and validity prospects for performance-based assessment. *American Psychologist, 48,* 1210–1218.

BAKER, F. B. (1989). Computer technology in test construction and processing. In R. L. Linn (Ed.), *Educational measurement* (3rd ed., pp. 409–428). New York: American Council on Education/Macmillan.

BAKER, R. W., &. SIRYK, B. (1989). SACQ—*Student Adaptation to College Questionnaire: Manual.* Los Angeles: Western Psychological Services.

BALLER, W. R., CHARLES, D. C., & MILLER, E. L. (1967). Mid-life attainment of the mentally retarded: A longitudinal study. *Genetic Psychology Monographs*, 75, 235–329.

BALMA, M. J. (1959). The concept of synthetic validity. *Personnel Psychology, 12,* 395–396.

BALTES, P. B. (1968). Longitudinal and cross-sectional sequences in the study of age and generation effects. *Human Development, 11,* 145–171.

BALTES, P. B., CORNELIUS, S. W., SPIRO, A. ILL, NESSELROADE, J. R., & WILLIS, S. L. (1980). Integration vs. differentiation of fluid-crystallized intelligence in old age. *Developmental Psychology,* 16, 625–635.

BALTES, P. B., REESE, H. W., & LIPSITT, L. P. (1980). Life-span developmental psychology. *Annual Review of Psychology, 31, 65*–110.

BALZER, W. K., & SULSKY, L. M. (1992). Halo and performance appraisal research: A critical examination. *Journal of Applied Psychology,* 77, 975–985.

BANDURA, A. (1969). *Principles of behavior modification.* New York: Holt, Rinehart & Winston.

BANDURA, A. (1982). Self-efficacy mechanism in human agency. *American Psychologist, 37,* 720–725.

BANDURA, A. (1986). *Social foundations of thought and action: A social cognitive theory.* Englewood Cliffs, NJ: Prentice Hall.

BANDURA, A. (Ed.). (1995). *Self-efficacy in changing societies.* New York: Cambridge University Press.

BANNISTER, D. (Ed.). (1985). *Issues and approaches in personal construct theory.* Orlando, FL: Academic Press.

BANNISTER, D., & MAIR, J. M. M. (1968). *The evaluation of personal constructs.* Orlando, FL: Academic Press.

BARENDS, A., WESTEN, D., LEIGH, J., SILBERT, D., & BYERS, S. (1990). Assessing affect-tone of relationship paradigms from TAT and interview data. *Psychological Assessment, 2,* 329–332.

BARKLEY, R. A. (1991). The ecological validity of laboratory and analogue assessment methods of ADHD symptoms. *Journal of Abnormal and Child Psychology, 19,* 149–178.

BARNETT, D. W. (1983). *Nondiscriminatory multifactored assessment: A sourcebook.* New York: Human Sciences Press.

BARON, J. (1982). Personality and intelligence. In R. J. Sternberg (Ed.), *Handbook of human intelligence* (pp. 308–351). New York: Cambridge University Press.

BARRICK, M. R., & MOUNT, M. K. (1991). The Big Five personality dimensions and job performance: A meta-analysis. *Personnel Psychology, 44, 1–26.*

BARRICK, M. R., & MOUNT, M. K. (1993). Autonomy as a moderator of the relationships between the Big Five personality dimensions and job performance. *Journal of Applied Psychology,* 78, 111–118.

BARRIOS, B. A. (1988). On the changing nature of behavioral assessment. In A. S. Bellack & M. Hersen (Eds.), *Behavioral assessment: A practical handbook* (3rd ed., pp. 3–41). New York: Pergamon Press.

BARRIOS, B. A. (1993). Direct observation. In T. H. Ollendick & M. Hersen (Eds.), *Handbook of child and adolescent assessment* (pp. 140–164). Boston: Allyn & Bacon.

BART, W. M., &. ALRASIAN, P. W. (1974). Determination of the ordering among seven Piagetian tasks by an ordering-theoretic method. *Journal of Educational Psychology, 66,* 277–284.

BARTLETT, C. J., & EDGERTON, H. A. (1966). Stanine values for ranks for different numbers of things ranked. *Educational and Psychological Measurement, 26,* 287–289.

BARTRAM, D. (1993). Emerging trends in computer-assisted assessment. In H. Schuler, J. L. Farr, & M. Smith (Eds.), *Personnel selection and assessment: Individual and organizational perspectives* (pp. 267–288). Hillsdale, NJ: Erlbaum.

BASS, B. M. (1954). The leaderless group discussion. *Psychological Bulletin, 51,* 465–492.

BASS, B. M. (1990). *Bass and Stodgill's handbook of leadership* (3rd ed.). New York: Free Press.

BATCHELOR, E. S., JR., & DEAN, R. S. (Eds.). (1996). *Pediatric neuro-psychology: Interfacing assessment and treatment for rehabilitation.* Boston: Allyn & Bacon.

BAUER, R. M. (1994). The flexible battery approach to neuropsychological assessment. In R. D. Vanderploeg (Ed.), *Clinician's guide to neuropsychological assessment* (pp. 259–290). Hillsdale, NJ: Erlbaum.

BAUGHMAN, E. E. (1951). Rorschach scores as a function of examiner difference. *Journal of Projective Techniques, 15,* 243–249.

BAUMEISTER, R. F. (Ed). (1993). *Self-esteem: The puzzle of low self-regard.* New York: Plenum Press.

BAUMEISTER, R. F., & TICE, D. M. (1988). Metatraits. *Journal of Personality, 56,* 571–598.

BAYLEY, N. (1955). On the growth of intelligence. *American Psychologist, 10,* 805–818.

BAYLEY, N. (1970). Development of mental abilities. In P. H. Mussen (Ed.), *Carmichael's manual of child psychology* (Vol. 1, pp. 1163–1209). New York: Wiley.

BAYLEY, N. (1993). *Bayley Scales of Infant Development Second Edition: Manual.* San Antonio, TX: Psychological Corporation.

BAYLEY, N., & ODEN, M. H. (1955). The maintenance of intellectual ability in gifted adults. *Journal of Gerontology, 10,* 91–107.

BAYROFF, A. G., & FUCHS, E. F. (1970). *Armed Services Vocational Aptitude Battery* (Tech. Res. Rep. 1161). Arlington, VA: U.S. Army Research Institute for the Behavioral and Social Sciences.

BEAIL, N. (Ed.). *(1985). Repertory grid technique and personal constructs: Applications in clinical and educational settings.* Cambridge, MA: Brookline Books.

BECK, A. T., & STEER, R. A. (1993). *Beck Depression Inventory: Manual.* San Antonio, TX: Psychological Corporation.

BECKER, K. A. (2003). History of the Stanford-Binet Intelligence Scales: Content and Psychometrics. (Stanford-Binet Intelligence Scales, Fifth Edition Assessment Service Bulletin No. 1). Itasca, IL: Riverside Publishing.

BEDNAR, R. L., & PETERSON, S. R. (1995). *Self-esteem: Paradoxes and innovations in clinical theory and practice* (2nd ed.). Washington, DC: American Psychological Association.

BEILIN, H., & PUFALL, P. (Eds.). (1992). *Piaget's theory: Prospects and possibilities.* Hillsdale, NJ: Erlbaum.

BEJAR, I. I. (1980). Biased assessment of program impact due to psychometric artifacts. *Psychological Bulletin, 87,* 513–524.

BEJAR, I. I. (1985). Speculations on the future of test design. In S. E. Embretson (Ed.), *Test design: Developments in psychology and psychometrics* (pp. 279–294). Orlando, FL: Academic Press.

BEJAR, I. I. (1991). A *generative approach to psychological and educational measurement.* (Res. Rep. No. 91–20). Princeton, NJ: Educational Testing Service.

BEJAR, I. I., STABLER, E. P, & CAMP, R. (1987). *Syntactic complexity and psychometric difficulty: A preliminary investigation.* (Res. Rep. No. 87–25). Princeton, NJ: Educational Testing Service.

BELCHER, M. J. (1992). Review of the Wonderlic Personnel Test. *Eleventh Mental Measurements Yearbook,* 1044–1046.

BELL, A., & ZUBEK, J. (1960). The effect of age on the intellectual performance of mental defectives. *Journal of Gerontology, 15,* 285–295.

BELL, F O., HOFF, A. L., & HOYT, K. B. (1964). Answer sheets do make a difference. *Personnel Psychology, 17,* 65–71.

BELLACK, A. S., &. HERSEN, M. (Eds.). (1988). *Behavioral assessment: A practical handbook* (3rd ed.). New York: Pergamon Press.

BELLAK, L. (1992). Projective techniques in the computer age. *Journal of Personality Assessment, 58,* 445–453.

BELLAK, L. (1993). *The Thematic Apperception Test, the Children's Apperception Test, and the Senior Apperception Test in clinical use* (5th ed.). Boston: Allyn & Bacon.

BELLAK, L., & BELLAK, S. S. (1973). *Manual: Senior Apperception Technique.* Larchmont, NY: C. P. S.

BELLAK, L., & HURVICH, M. S. (1966). A human modification of the Children's Apperception Test (CAT-H). *Journal of Projective Techniques and Personality Assessment, 30*, 228–242.

BELMONT, J. M., & BUTTERFIELD, E. C. (1977). The instructional approach to developmental cognitive research. In R. V. Kail, Jr., & J. W. Hagen (Eds.), *Perspectives on the development of memory and cognition* (pp. 437–481). Hillsdale, NJ: Erlbaum.

BEM, D. J., & FUNDER, D. C. (1978). Predicting more of the people more of the time: Assessing the personality of situations. *Psychological Review, 85*, 485–501.

BENASICH, A. A., & BEJAR, I. I. (1992). The Fagan Test of Infant Intelligence: A critical review. *Journal of Applied Developmental Psychology, 13*, 153–171.

BENDER, L. (1938). A visual motor Gestalt test and its clinical use. *American Orthopsychiatric Association, Research Monographs*, No. 3.

BENES, K. M. (1995). Review of the Social Skills Rating System. *Twelfth Mental Measurements Yearbook*, 965–967.

BENGTSON, V. L., & SCHAIE, K. W. (Eds.). (1989). *The course of later life: Research and reflections*. New York: Springer.

BENNETT, G. K. (1994). *Manual: BMCT-Bennett Mechanical Comprehension Test* (2nd ed.). San Antonio, TX: Psychological Corporation.

BENNETT, G. K., SEASHORE, H. G., & WESMAN, A. G. (1984). *Differential Aptitude Tests: Technical Supplement*. San Antonio, TX: Psychological Corporation.

BENNETT, R. E. (1993). On the meanings of constructed response. In R. E. Bennett & W. Ward (Eds.), *Construction versus choice in cognitive measurement: Issues in constructed response, performance testing, and portfolio assessment* (pp. 1–27). Hillsdale, NJ: Erlbaum.

BENNETT, R. E., ROCK, D. A., & NOVATKOSKI, I. (1989). Differential item functioning on the SAT-M Braille Edition. *Journal of Educational Measurement, 26*, 67–79.

BENNETT, R. E., & WARD, W. C. (Eds.). (1993). *Construction versus choice in cognitive measurement: Issues in constructed response, performance testing, and portfolio assessment*. Hillsdale, NJ: Erlbaum.

BEN-PORATH, Y. S., &. BUTCHER, J. N. (1986). Computers in personality assessment: A brief past, an ebullient present, and an expanding future. *Computers in Human Behavior, 2*, 163–182.

BEN-PORATH, Y. S., & TELLEGEN, A. (1995). How (not) to evaluate the comparability of MMPI and MMPI-2 profile configurations: A reply to Humphrey and Dahlstrom. *Journal of Personality* Assessment, 65, 52–58.

BEN-PORATH, Y.S., TELLEGEN, A. (2016). Minnesota Multiphasic Personality Inventory-2-Restructured Form® (MMPI-2-RF®). Retrieved June 1, 2016, from *http://www.pearsonclinical.com/psychology/products/100000631/minnesota-multiphasic-personality-inventory-2-rf-mmpi-2-rf.html#tab-details*.

BENTLER, P M. (1985). Theory and implementation of EQS: A structural equations program. Los Angeles: BMDP Statistical Software.

BENTLER, P. M. (1988). Causal modeling via structural equation modeling. In J. R. Nesselroade & R. B. Cattell (Eds.), *Handbook of multivariate experimental psychology* (2nd ed., pp. 317–335). New York: Plenum Press.

BENTLER, P. M. (1990). Comparative fit indexes in structural models. *Psychological Bulletin, 107*, 238–246.

BENTON, A. L. (1994). Neuropsychological assessment. *Annual Review of Psychology, 45*, 1–23.

BERG, I. A. (1967). The deviation hypothesis: A broad statement of its assumptions and postulates. In I. A. Berg (Ed.), *Response set in personality assessment* (pp. 146–190). Chicago: Aldine.

BERK, R. A. (Ed.). (1982). *Handbook of methods for detecting test bias.* Baltimore: Johns Hopkins University Press.

BERK, R. A. (Ed.). (1984a). A *guide to* criterion-referenced *test construction.* Baltimore: Johns Hopkins University Press.

BERK, R. A. (1984b). Selecting the index of reliability. In R. A. Berk (Ed.), A *guide to criterion-referenced test construction* (pip. 231–266). Baltimore: Johns Hopkins University Press.

BERK, R. A. (1986). Minimum competency testing: Status and potential. In B. S. Plake & J. C. Witt (Eds.), *The future of testing* (pp. 89–144). Hillsdale, NJ: Erlbaum.

BERKAY, P. J. (1993). The adaptation of assessment center group exercises for deaf job applicants. *Journal of the American Deafness and Rehabilitation Association, 27,* 16–24.

BERMAN, J. J. (Ed.). (1990). *Cross-cultural perspectives* (Nebraska Symposium on Motivation, 1989). Lincoln: University of Nebraska Press.

BERNARDIN, H. J., & BOWNAS, D. A. (Eds.). (1985). *Personality assessment in organizations.* New York: Praeger.

BERNARDIN, H. J., & BUCKLEY, M. R. (1981). Strategies in rater training. *Academy of Management Review, 6,* 205–212.

BERNE, E. (1961). *Transactional analysis in psychotherapy.* New York: Grove Press.

BERNE, E. (1966). *Principles of group treatment.* New York: Oxford University Press.

BERNSTEIN, L. (1956). The examiner as an inhibiting factor in clinical testing. *Journal of Consulting Psychology, 20,* 287–290.

BERRY, D. T., WETTER, M. W., & BAER, R. A. (1995). Assessment of malingering. In J. N. Butcher (Ed.), *Clinical personality assessment: Practical approaches* (pp. 236–248). New York: Oxford University Press.

BERRY, J. W. (1972). Radical cultural relativism and the concept of intelligence. In L. J. Cronbach &. P. J. D. Drenth (Eds.), *Mental tests and cultural adaptations* (pp. 77–88). The Hague: Mouton.

BERRY, J. W. (1976). *Human ecology and cognitive style: Comparative studies in cultural and psychological adaptation.* Beverly Hills, CA: Sage.

BERRY, J. W. (1983). Textured contexts: Systems and situations in cross-cultural psychology. In S. H. Irvine & J. W. Berry (Eds.), *Human assessment and cultural factors* (pp. 117–125). New York: Plenum Press.

BERRY, J. W., POORTINGA, Y. H., SEGALL, M. H., & DASEN, P. R. (1992). *Cross-cultural psychology: Research and applications.* New York: Cambridge University Press.

BERSOFF, D. N. (1981). Testing and the law. *American Psychologist, 36,* 1047–1056.

BERSOFF, D. N. (1983). Regarding psychologists testily: The legal regulation of psychological assessment. In C. J. Scheirer & B. L. Hammonds (Eds.), *Psychology and law* (pp. 37–88). Washington, DC: American Psychological Association.

BERSOFF, D. N. (1984). Social and legal influences on test development and usage. In B. S. plake (Ed.), *Social and technical issues in testing: Implications for test construction and usage* (pp. 87–109). Hillsdale, NJ: Erlbaum.

BERSOFF, D. N. (1995). *Ethical conflicts in psychology.* Washington, DC: American Psychological Association.

BERSOFF, D. N., & HOFER, P. J. (1991). Legal issues in computerized psychological testing. In T. B. Gutkin & S. L. Wise (Eds.), *The computer and the decision-making process* (pp. 225–243). Hillsdale, NJ: Erlbaum.

BERTINI, M., PIZZAMIGLIO, L., & WAPNER, S. (1985). *Field dependence in psychological theory, research, and application: Two symposia in memory of Herman A. Withín.* Hillsdale, NJ: Erlbaum.

BETZ, N. E. (1995). Gender-related individual differences variables: New concepts, methods, and measures. In D. Lubinski & R. V. Dawis (Eds.), *Assessing individual differences in human behavior* (pp. 119–143). Palo Alto, CA: Davies-Black.

BEUTLER, L. E., & BERREN, M. R. (1995). *Integrative* assessment *of adult personality.* New York: Guilford Press.

BIERI, J. (1971). Cognitive structures in personality. In H. M. Schroder & P. Suedfeld (Eds.), *Personality theory and information processing* (pp. 178–208). New York: Ronald Press.

BIERI, J., ATKINS, A. L., BRIAR, S., LEAMAN, R. L., MILLER, H., & TRIPODI, T. (1966). *Clinical and social judgment: The discrimination of behavioral information.* New York: Wiley.

BIERMAN, K. L. (1990). Using the clinical interview to assess children's interpersonal reasoning and emotional understanding. In C. R. Reynolds & R. W. Kamphaus (Eds.), *Handbook of psychological and educational assessment of children: Personality, behavior, and context* (pp. 204–219). New York: Guilford Press.

BINET, A., & HENRI, V. (1895). La psychologie individuelle. *Année Psychologique, 2,* 411–463.

BINET, A., & SIMON, TH. (1905). Methodes nouvelles pour le diagnostic du niveau intellectuel des anormaux. *Année Psychologique, 11,* 191–244.

BIRNS, B., & GOLDEN, M. (1972). Prediction of intellectual performance at 3 years from infant test and personality measures. *Merrill-Palmer Quarterly, 18,* 53–58.

BIRREN, J. E., & BENGTSON, V. L. (1988). *Emergent theories of aging.* New York: Springer.

BIRREN, J. E., CUNNINGHAM, W. R., &. YAMAMOTO, K. (1983). Psychology of adult development and aging. *Annual Review of Psychology, 34,* 543–575.

BIRREN J. E., &. SCHAIE, K. W. (1991). Handbook of the psychology of aging (3rd ed.). San Diego, CA: Academic Press.

BISKIN, B. H. (1992). Review of the State-Trait Anger Expression Inventory, Research Edition. *Eleventh Mental Measurements Yearbook,* 868–869.

BLACK, A. M., FEUER, M. J., GUIDROZ, K., & LESGOLD, A. M. (Eds.). (1996). *Transitions in work and learning: Implications for assessment.* Washington, DC: National Academy Press.

BLAGG, N. (1991). *Can we teach intelligence? A comprehensive evaluation of Feuerstein's Instrumental Enrichment Program.* Hillsdale, NJ: Erlbaum.

BLAHA, J., & WALLBROWN, F. H. (1991). Hierarchical factor structure of the Wechsler Preschool and Primary Scale of Intelligence-Revised. *Psychological Assessment, 3,* 455–463.

BLANCHARD, W. H. (1968). The consensus Rorschach: Background and development. *Journal of Projective Techniques and Personality Assessment, 32,* 327–330.

BLASCOVICH, J., & TOMAKA, J. (1991). Measures of self-esteem. In J. P. Robinson, P. R. Shaver, &. L. S. Wrightsman (Eds.), *Measures of personality and social psychological attitudes.* San Diego, CA: Academic Press.

BLATT, S. J. (1990). The Rorschach: A test of perception or an evaluation of representation. *Journal of Personality Assessment, 55,* 394–416.

BLEICHRODT, N., & DRENTH, P. J. D. (Eds.). (1991). *Contemporary issues in cross-cultural psychology.* Amsterdam: Swets & Zeitlinger.

BLOCK, J. (1965). *The challenge of response sets: Unconfounding meaning, acquiescence, and social desirability in the MMP1.* New York: Irvington.

BLOCK, J. (1978). *The Q sort method in personality assessment and psychiatric research.* Palo Alto, CA: Consulting Psychologists Press. (Original work published 1961)

BLOCK, J. (1995). A contrarian view of the five-factor approach to personality description. *Psychological Bulletin, 117,* 187–215.

BLOOM, B. S. (1976). *Human characteristics and school learning.* New York: McGraw-Hill.

BLOOM, B. S., & BRODER, L. (1950). *Problem-solving processes of college students.* Chicago: University of Chicago Press.

BOARD ON TESTING AND ASSESSMENT. (1995). *Evaluation of the U.S. Employment Service work plan for the GATB improvement project.* Washington, DC: National Academy Press.

BOCHNER, S. (1986). Observational methods. In W. J. Lonner & J. W. Berry (Eds.), *Field methods in cross-cultural research* (pp. 165–201). Beverly Hills, CA: Sage.

BOCK, R. D. (1972). Estimating item parameters and latent ability when responses are scored in two or more nominal categories. *Psychometrika, 37,* 29–51.

BOEHM, A. E. (1985). Review of Home Observation for Measurement of the Environment. *Ninth Mental Measurements Yearbook,* Vol. 1, 663–665.

BOER, F., &. DUNN, J. (Eds.). (1992). *Children's sibling relationships: Developmental and clinical issues.* Hillsdale, NJ: Erlbaum.

BOLIG, E. E., & DAY, J. D. (1993). Dynamic assessment and giftedness: The promise of assessing training responsiveness. *Roeper Review, 16,* 110–113.

BOLLEN, K. A. (1989). *Structural equations with latent variables.* New York: Wiley.

BOLLEN, K. A., & LONG, J. S. (Eds.). (1993). *Testing structural equation models.* Newbury Park, CA: Sage.

BOLLER, F., & GRAFMAN, J. (Series Eds.). (1988–1995). *Handbook of neuropsychology.* Amsterdam: Elsevier.

BOLTON, B. (1994). [Review of the General Aptitude Test Battery]. In J. T. Kapes, M. M. Mastie, & E. A. Whitfield (Eds.), *A counselor's guide to career assessment instruments* (3rd ed., pp. 117–123). Alexandria, VA: National Career Development Association.

BOLTON, T. L. (1891–1892). The growth of memory in school children. *American Journal of Psychology, 4,* 362–380.

BOND, L. (1981). Bias in mental tests. In B. F. Green (Ed.), *Issues in testing: Coaching, disclosure, and ethnic bias* (pp. 55–77). San Francisco: Jossey-Bass.

BOND, L. (1987). The Golden Rule settlement: A minority perspective, *Educational Measurement: Issues & Practice, 6,* 18–20.

BOND, L. (1989). The effects of special preparation on measures of scholastic ability. In R. L. Linn (Ed.), *Educational measurement* (3rd ed., pp. 429–444). New York: American Council on Education/Macmillan.

BONJEAN, C. M., HILL, R. J. & MCLEMORE, S. D. (1967). *Sociological measurement:* An *inventory of scales and indices.* San Francisco: Chandler.

BONNES, M., & SECCHIAROLI, G. (1995). *Environmental psychology: A psychosocial introduction.* Thousand Oaks, CA: Sage.

BORENSTEIN, M. H., HIGGINS, L. V., & ROTHSTEIN, J. P. T. (2009). HR (2009). *Introduction to Meta-analysis.* Chichester, England: Wiley. doi, 10, 9780470743386.

BORENSTEIN, M. H., HIGGINS, L. V., & ROTHSTEIN, J. P. T. (2009). HR (2009). Introduction to meta-analysis. Chichester, England: Wiley. doi, *10,* 9780470743386.

BORENSTEIN, M. H., HIGGINS, L. V., AND ROTHSTEIN, J. P. T. (2009). HR (2009). *Introduction to meta-analysis.* Chichester, England: Wiley. doi, 10, 9780470743386.

BORENSTEIN, M. H., HIGGINS, L. V., AND ROTHSTEIN, J. P. T. (2009). HR (2009). *Introduction to meta-analysis. Chichester, England: Wiley.* doi, 10, 9780470743386.

BORGEN, F. H. (1986). New approaches to the assessment of interests. In W. B. Walsh & S. H. Osipow (Eds.), *Advances in vocational psychology, Vol. 1. The assessment of interests* (pp. 83–125). Hillsdale, NJ: Erlbaum.

BORGEN, F. H. (1991). Megatrends and milestones in vocational behavior: A 20-year counseling psychology retrospective. *Journal of Vocational Behavior, 39*, 263–290.

BORGEN, F. H., & DONNAY, D. A. C. (1996). Slicing the vocational interest pie one more time: Comment on Tracey and Rounds (1996). *Journal of Vocational Behavior, 48*, 42–52.

BORGEN, E, & GRUTTER, J. (1995). *Where do I go next? Using your Strong results to manage your career.* Palo Alto, CA: Consulting Psychologists Press.

BORING, E. G. (1950). A *history of experimental psychology* (Rev. ed.). New York: Appleton-Century Crofts.

BORMAN, W. C. (1979). Format and training effects on rating accuracy and rating errors. *Journal of Applied Psychology, 64*, 410–421.

BORMAN, W. C. (1991). Job behavior, performance, and effectiveness. In M. D. Dunnette &. L. M. Hough (Eds.), *Handbook of industrial and organizational psychology* (2nd ed., Vol. 2, pp. 271–326). Palo Alto, CA: Consulting Psychologists Press.

BORNSTEIN, M. H. (Ed). (1991). *Cultural approaches to parenting.* Hillsdale, NJ: Erlbaum.

BORNSTEIN, M. H., & KRASNEGOR, N. A. (Eds.). (1989). *Stability and continuity in mental development: Behavioral and biological perspectives.* Hillsdale, NJ: Erlbaum.

BORNSTEIN, R. F., ROSSNER, S. C., HILL, E. L., & STEPANIAN, M. L. (1994). Face validity and fakability of objective and projective measures of dependency. *Journal of Personality Assessment, 63*, 363–386.

BOTWINICK, J. (1984). *Aging and behavior: A comprehensive integration of research findings* (3rd ed.). New York: Springer.

BOUDREAU, J. W. (1991). Utility analysis for decisions in human resource management. In M. D. Dunnette & L. M. Hough (Eds.), *Handbook of industrial and organizational psychology* (2nd ed., Vol. 2, pp. 621–745). Palo Alto, CA: Consulting Psychologists Press.

BOWER, E. M. (1969). *Early identification of emotionally handicapped children in school* (2nd ed.). Springfield, IL: Charles C Thomas.

BOWMAN, M. L. (1989). Testing individual differences in ancient China. *American Psychologist, 44*, 576–578.

BRACE, C. L. (1996). A four-letter word called "Race". *Race and other misadventures: Essays in honor of Ashley Montagu in his Ninetieth year*, 106–141.

BRACKEN, B. A. (Ed.). (1991a). The assessment of preschool children with the McCarthy Scales of Children Abilities. In B.A. Bracken (Ed.), *The psychoeducational assessment of preschool children* (2nd ed., pp. 53–85). Boston: Allyn & Bacon.

BRACKEN, B. A. (1991b). *The psychoeducational assessment of preschool children (2nd ed.).* Boston: Allyn & Bacon.

BRADEN, J. P. (1985). The structure of nonverbal intelligence in deaf and hearing subjects. *American Annals of the Deaf, 130*, 496–501.

BRADEN, J. P. (1994). *Deafness, deprivation, and* IQ. New York: Plenum Press.

BRADLEY, R. H., & BRISBY, J. A. (1993). Assessment of the home environment. In J. L. Culbertson & D. J. Willis (Eds.), *Testing young children: A reference guide for developmental, psychoeducational, and psychosocial assessments* (pp. 128–166). Austin, TX: PRO-ED.

BRADLEY, R. H., &. CALDWELL, B. M. (1984). The HOME inventory and family demographics. *Developmental Psychology, 20,* 315–320.

BRADLEY-JOHNSON, S. (1994). *Psychoeducational assessment of students who are visually impaired or Blind: Infancy Through High School* (2nd ed.). *Austin, TX: PRO-ED.*

BRADLEY-JOHNSON, S., &. EVANS, L. D. (1991). *Psychoeducational assessment of hearing' impaired students: Infancy through high school. Austin,* TX: PRO-ED.

BRADWAY, R, THOMPSON, W., & CRAVENS, R. B. (1958). Preschool IQ's after twenty-five years. *Journal of Educational Psychology, 49,* 278–281.

BRAITHWAITE, V. A., & SCOTT, W. A. (1991). Values. In J. P. Robinson, P. R. Shaver, &. L. S. Wrightsman, (Eds.), *Measures of personality and social psychological attitudes* (pp. 661–753). San Diego, CA: Academic Press.

BRANSFORD, J., SHERWOOD, R., VYE, N., & RIESER, J. (1986). Teaching thinking and problem solving: Research foundations. *American Psychologist, 41,* 1078–1089.

BRAUTH, S. E., HALL, W. S., & DOOLING, R. J. (Eds.). (1991). *Plasticity of development.* Cambridge, MA: MIT Press.

BRAY, D. W. (1982). The assessment center and the study of lives. *American Psychologist, 37,* 180–189.

BRAY, D. W. et al. (1991). *Working with organizations and their people: A guide to human resources practice.* New York: Guilford Press.

BRECKLER, S. J. (1990). Applications of covariance structure modeling in psychology: Cause for concern? *Psychological Bulletin, 107,* 260–273.

BRELAND, H. M. (1979). *Population validity and college entrance measures* (College Board Res. Monog. No. 8). New York: College Entrance Examination Board.

BRENNAN, R. L. (1981). Some Statistical Procedures for Domain-Referenced Testing: A Handbook for Practitioners. *ACT Technical Bulletin,* 38, Iowa City, Iowa: American College Testing Program.

BRENNAN, R. L. (1984). Estimating the dependability of the scores. In R. A. Berk (Ed.), A *guide to criterion-referenced test construction* (pp. 292–334). Baltimore: Johns Hopkins University Press.

BRENNAN, R. L. (1994). Variance components in generalizability theory. In C. R. Reynolds (Ed.), *Cognitive assessment: A multidisciplinary perspective* (pp. 175–207). New York: Plenum Press.

BRIDGEMAN, B. (1974). Effects of test score feedback on immediately subsequent test performance. *Journal of Educational Psychology, 66,* 62–66.

BRISLIN, R. W. (1993). *Understanding culture's influence on behavior.* Fort Worth, TX: Harcourt Brace Jovanovich.

BRODY, N. (1992). Intelligence (2nd ed.). New York: Basic Books.

BRODZINSKY, D. M. (1982). Relationship between cognitive style and cognitive development*: A 2-year longitudinal study.* Developmental Psychology, 18, 617–626.

BROGDEN, H. E. (1946a). An approach to the problem of differential prediction. *Psychometrika, 11,* 139–154.

BROGDEN, H. E. (1946b). On the interpretation of the correlation coefficient as a measure of predictive efficiency. *Journal of Educational Psychology, 37,* 65–76.

BROGDEN, H. E. (1951). Increased efficiency of selection resulting from replacement of a single predictor with several differential predictors. *Educational and Psychological Measurement, 11,* 173–196.

BROGDEN, H. E. (1954). A simple proof of a personnel classification theorem. *Psychometrika, 19,* 205–208.

BRONFENBRENNER, U., & CECI, S. (1994). Nature-nurture reconceptualized in developmental perspective: A bioecological model. *Psychological Review, 101,* 568–586.

Broughton, R. (1990). The prototype concept in personality assessment. *Canadian Psychology, 31*, 26–37.

Broughton, R., Boyes, M. C., &. Mitchell, J. (1993). Distance-from-the-Prototype (DISPRO) personality assessment for children. *Journal of Personality Assessment*, 60, 32–47.

Brown, A. L. (1974). The role of strategic behavior in retardate memory. In N. R. Ellis (Ed.), *International Review of Research in Mental Retardation* (Vol. 7, pp. 55–111). New York: Academic Press.

Brown, A. L., &. Campione, J. C. (1986). Psychological theory and the study of learning disabilities. *American Psychologist, 41*, 1059–1068.

Brown, A. L., Campione, J. C., Webber, L. S., & Mcgilly, K. (1992). Interactive learning environments: A new look at assessment and instruction. In B. R. Gifford & M. C. O'Connor (Eds.), *Changing assessments: Alternative views of aptitude, achievement and instruction* (pp. 121–211). Boston: Kluwer.

Brown, C. W., & Ghiselli, E. E. (1953). Percent increase in proficiency resulting from use of selective devices. *Journal of Applied Psychology*, 37, 341–345.

Brown, D., Brooks, L., & Associates. (1996). *Career choice and development* (3rd ed.). San Francisco: Jossey-Bass.

Brown, D., & Crace R. K. (1996). *Life Values Inventory: Manual and user's guide.* Chapel Hill, NC: Life Values Resources.

Brown, D. C. (1994). Subgroup norming: Legitimate testing practice or reverse discrimination? *American Psychologist, 49*, 927–928.

Brown, D. C. (1995, April). Test user qualifications. *The Score Newsletter, 18*, 8–9.

Brown, D. C. (1996, January). When personality matters on the job. *The Score Newsletter, 19*, 4–5.

Brown, D. T. (1989). Review of the Jackson Vocational Interest Survey. *Tenth Mental Measurements Yearbook*, 401–403.

Brown, L., Sherbenou, R. J., & Johnsen, S. K. (1990). *Test of Nonverbal Intelligence: A language-free measure of cognitive ability* (2nd ed.). Austin, TX: PRO-ED.

Brown, L., Sherbenou, R. J., & Johnsen, S. K. (2010). *TONI–4, Test of Nonverbal Intelligence*. Pro-Ed.

Brown, S. D., & Lent, R. W. (Eds.). (1992). *Handbook of counseling psychology* (2nd ed.). New York: Wiley.

Bruhn, A. R. (1984). Use of early memories as a projective technique. In P. Mc-Reynolcls & C. J. Chelune (Eds.), *Advances in psychological assessment* (Vol. 6, pp. 109–150). San Francisco: Jossey-Bass.

Bruhn, A. R. (1985). Using early memories as a projective technique—The Cognitive Perceptual method. *Journal of Personality Assessment, 49*, 587–597.

Bruhn, A. R. (1989). *The Early Memories Procedure*. Bethesda, MD: Author.

Bruhn, A. R. (1990a). Cognitive-perceptual theory and the projective use of autobiographical memory. *Journal of Personality* Assessment, 55, 95–114.

Bruhn, A. R. (1990b). *Earliest childhood memories: Vol. 1. Theory and application to clinical practice.* New York: Praeger.

Bruhn, A. R. (1992a). The Early Memories Procedure: A projective test of autobiographical memory, Part 1. *Journal of Personality Assessment, 58*, 1–15.

Bruhn, A. R. (1992b). The Early Memories Procedure: A projective test of autobiographical memory, Part 2. *Journal of Personality Assessment, 58*, 326–346.

Bruhn, A. R. (1995a). Early memories in personality assessment. In J. N. Butcher (Ed.), *Clinical personality assessment: Practical approaches* (pp. 278–301). New York: Oxford University Press.

Bruhn, A. R. (1995b). Ideographic aspects of injury memories: Applying contextual theory to the Comprehensive Early Memories Scoring System—Revised. *Journal of Personality Assessment*, 65, 195–236.

BRUHN, A. R., & LAST, J. (1982). Earliest childhood memories: Four theoretical perspectives. *Journal of Personality Assessment, 46,* 119–127.

BRUININKS, R. H. (1978). *Bruininks-Oseretsky Test of Motor Proficiency: Examiner's manual*. Circle Pines, MN: American Guidance Service.

BRUYÈRE, S. M., & O'KEEFE, J. (Eds.). (1994). *Implications of the Americans with Disabilities Act for psychology.* Washington, DC: American Psychological Association.

BUCHWALD, A. M. (1965). Values and the use of tests. *Journal of Consulting Psychology, 29,* 49–54.

BUCK, J. N. (1948). The H-T-P technique, a qualitative and quantitative method. *Journal of Clinical Psychology, 4,* 317–396.

BUCK, J. N. (1992). *House-Tree-Person projective drawing technique* (H-T-P): *Manual and interpretative guide* (Revised by W. L. Warren). Los Angeles, CA: Western Psychological Services.

BUDOFF, M. (1987). A learning potential assessment battery. In C. S. Lidz (Ed.), *Dynamic assessment:* An *interactive approach to evaluating learning potential* (pp. 167–193). New York: Guilford Press.

BUDOFF, M., & CORMAN, L. (1974). Demographic and psychometric factors related to improved performance on the Kohs learning potential procedure. *American Journal of Mental Deficiency,* 78, 578–585.

BURGEMEISTER, B. B., BLUM, L. H., &. LORGE, I. (1972). *Columbia Mental Maturity Scale: Guide for administering and interpreting* (3rd ed.). New York: Harcourt Brace Jovanovich.

BURGER, J. M. (1993). *Personality* (3rd ed.). Pacific Grove, CA: Brooks/Cole.

BURISCH, M. (1986). Methods of personality inventory development—A comparative analysis. In A. Angleitner & J. S. Wiggins (Eds.), *Personality assessment via questionnaires: Current issues in theory and measurement* (pp. 109–120). Berlin: Springer-Verlag.

BURKE, M. J. (1993). Computerized psychological testing: Impacts on measuring predictor constructs and future job behavior. In N. Schmitt, W. C. Borman et. al. (Eds.). *Personnel selection in organizations* (pp. 203–239). San Francisco: Jossey-Bass.

BURKE, M. J. & FREDERICK, J. T. (1984). Two modified procedures for estimating standard deviations in utility analyses. *Journal of Applied Psychology, 69,* 482–489.

BURNHAM, P. S. (1965). Prediction and performance. In *From high school to college: Readings for counselors* (pp. 65–71). New York: College Entrance Examination Board.

BURNS, R. B. (1966). Age and mental ability: Retesting with thirty-three years' interval. *British Journal of Educational Psychology,* 36, 116.

BURNS, R. B. (1980). Relation of aptitudes to learning at different points in time during instruction. *Journal of Educational Psychology, 72,* 785–795.

BURNS, R. C. (1982). *Self-growth in families: Kinetic Family Drawings (K-F-D) research and applications.* New York: Brunner/Mazel.

BURNS, R. C., & KAUFMAN, S. H. (1970). *Kinetic Family Drawings (K-F-D): An introduction to understanding children through kinetic drawings.* New York: Brunner/Mazel.

BURNS, R. C., & KAUFMAN, S. H. (1972). *Actions, styles, and symbols in Kinetic Family Drawings (K-F-D): An interpretative manual*. New York: Brunner/Mazel.

BUROS, O. (Ed.). (1974). *Tests in print II*. Lincoln, NE: Buros Institute of Mental Measurements.

BUROS, O. K. (Ed.). (1975). *Vocational tests and reviews.* Highland Park, NJ: Gryphon Press.

BURR, V., & BUTT, T. (1992). *Invitation to personal construct psychology.* London: Whurr.

BURT, C. (1941). *The factors of the mind: An introduction to factor-analysis in psychology.* New York: Macmillan.

BURT, C. (1944). Mental abilities and mental factors. *British Journal of Educational Psychology, 14, 85–89.*

BURT, C. (1949). The structure of the mind; a review of the results of factor analysis. *British Journal of Educational Psychology, 19,* 110–111; 176–199.

BURTON, R. V. (1963). Generality of honesty reconsidered. *Psychological Review, 70,* 481–499.

BURTT, H. E. (1931). *Legal psychology.* Englewood Cliffs, NJ: Prentice Hall.

BUSHE, G. R., & GIBBS, B. W. (1990). Predicting organization development consulting competence from the Myers-Briggs Type Indicator and stage of ego development. *Journal of Applied Behavioral Science, 26,* 337–357.

BUSS, A. R. (1973). An extension of developmental models that separate ontogenetic changes and cohort differences. *Psychological Bulletin,* 80, 466–479.

BUTCHER, J. N. (Ed.) (1985). Perspectives on computerized psychological assessment [Special issue]. *Journal of Consulting and Clinical Psychology,* 53(6).

BUTCHER, J. N. (Ed.). (1987). *Computerized psychological assessment: A practitioner's guide.* New York: Basic Books.

BUTCHER, J. N. (1990). MMPI-2 *in psychological treatment.* New York: Oxford University Press.

BUTCHER, J. N. (Ed.). (1995). *Clinical personality assessment: Practical approaches.* New York: Oxford University Press.

BUTCHER, J. N. (Ed.). (1996). *International adaptations of the* MMPI-2: *Research and clinical applications.* Minneapolis: University of Minnesota Press.

BUTCHER, J. N., DAHLSTROM, W. G., GRAHAM, J. R., TELLEGEN, A., & KAEMMER, B. (1989). *Minnesota Multiphasic Personality Inventory-2* (MMPI-2*): Manual for administration and scoring.* Minneapolis: University of Minnesota Press.

BUTCHER, J. N., GRAHAM, J. R., & BEN-PORATH, Y. S. (1995). Methodological problems and issues in MMPI, MMPI-2, and MMPI-A Research. *Psychological Assessment,* 7, 320–329.

BUTCHER, J. N., GRAHAM, J. R., WILLIAMS, C. L., & BEN-PORATH, Y. S. (1990). *Development and use of the MMPI-2 content scales.* Minneapolis: University of Minnesota Press.

BUTCHER, J. N., & ROUSE, S. V. (1996). Personality: Individual differences and clinical assessment. *Annual Review of Psychology, 47,* 87–111.

BUTCHER, J. N., & WILLIAMS, C. L. (1992). *Essentials of MMPI-2 and MMPI-A interpretation.* Minneapolis: University of Minnesota Press.

BUTCHER, J. N., WILLIAMS, C. L., GRAHAM, J. R., ARCHER, R. R, TELLEGEN, A., BEN-PORATH, Y. S., & KAEMMER, B. (1992). *Minnesota Multiphasic Personality Inventory-Adolescent (MMPI-A): Manual for administration, scoring, and interpretation.* Minneapolis: University of Minnesota Press.

BUTTERFIELD, E. C., NIELSEN, D., TANGEN, K. L., & RICHARDSON, M. B. (1985). Theoretically based psychometric measures of inductive reasoning. In S. E. Embretson (Ed.), *Test design: Developments in psychology and psychometrics* (pp. 77–147). Orlando, FL: Academic Press.

BUTTERS, N., DELIS, D. C., & LUCAS, J. A. (1995). Clinical assessment of memory disorders in amnesia and dementia. *Annual Review of Psychology, 46,* 493–523.

BUTTERWORTH, G. E., HARRIS, P. L., LESLIE, A. M., & WELLMAN, H. M. (Eds.). (1991). *Perspectives on the child's theory of mind.* Oxford, England: British Psychological Society and Oxford University Press.

Byrne, B. M. (1996). *Measuring self-concept across the life span: Issues and instrumentation*. Washington, DC: American Psychological Association.

Caldwell, B. M., & Bradley, R, H. (1978). *Home Observation for Measurement of the Environment*. Little Rock, AR: Authors.

Caldwell, B. M., &. Bradley, R. H. (1984). *Home Observation for Measurement of the Environment*. Little Rock: University of Arkansas.

Caldwell, O. W., & Courtis, S. A. (1923). *Then and now in education, 1845–1923*. Yonkers, NY: World Book.

Camara, W., Freeman, J., & Everson, H. (1996). *Using the SAT: Technical supplement*. New York: College Entrance Examination Board. Manuscript in preparation.

Camara, W. J., &. Schneider, D. L. (1994). Integrity tests: Facts and unresolved issues. *American Psychologist, 49*, 112–119.

Camara, W. J., & Schneider, D. L. (1995). Questions of construct breadth and openness of research in integrity testing. *American Psychologist, 50*, 459–460.

Camilli, G., & Shepard, L. A. (1994). *Methods for identifying biased test items*. Newbury Park, CA: Sage.

Camp, R. (1993). The place of portfolios in our changing views of writing assessment. In R. E. Bennett & W. C. Ward (Eds.), *Construction versus choice in cognitive measurement: Issues in constructed response, performance testing, portfolio assessment* (pp. 183–212). Hillsdale, NJ: Erlbaum.

Campbell, D. P. (1965). A cross-sectional and longitudinal study of scholastic abilities over twenty-five years. *Journal of Counseling Psychology, 12*, 55–61.

Campbell, D. P. (1971). *Handbook for the Strong Vocational Interest Blank*. Stanford, CA: Stanford University Press.

Campbell, D. P. (1974). *Manual for the Strong-Campbell Interest Inventory*. Stanford, CA: Stanford University Press.

Campbell, D. P. (1977). *Manual for the Strong-Campbell Interest Inventory* (rev. ed.). Stanford, CA: Stanford University Press.

Campbell, D. P, & Hansen, J. C. (1981). *Manual for the SVIB-SCII* (3rd ed.). Stanford, CA: Stanford University Press.

Campbell, D. R, Hyne, S. A., & Nilsen, D. L. (1992). *Manual for the Campbell Interest and Skill Survey (CISS)*. Minneapolis, MN: National Computer Systems.

Campbell, D. T. (1950). The indirect assessment of social attitudes. *Psychological Bulletin, 47*, 15–38.

Campbell, D. T. (1960). Recommendations for APA test standards regarding construct, trait, and discriminant validity. *American Psychologist, 15*, 546–553.

Campbell, D. T., & Fiske, D. W. (1959). Convergent and discriminant validation by the multitrait-multimethod matrix. *Psychological Bulletin, 56*, 81–105.

Campbell, D. T., & Stanley, J. C. (1966). *Experimental and quasi-experimental designs for research*. Chicago: Rand McNally.

Campbell, F. A., & Ramey, C. T. (1990). The relationship between Piagetian cognitive development, mental test performance, and academic achievement in high risk students with and without early educational experience. *Intelligence, 14*, 293–308.

Campbell, I. A. (1985). Review of the Vineland Adaptive Behavior Scales. *Ninth Mental Measurements Yearbook*, Vol. 2, 1660–1662.

Campbell, J. P. (1990a). Modeling the performance prediction problem in industrial and organizational psychology. In M. D. Dunnette & L. M. Hough (Eds.), *Handbook of industrial and organizational psychology* (2nd ed., Vol. 1, pp. 687–732). Palo Alto, CA: Consulting Psychologists Press.

CAMPBELL, J. P (1990b). An overview of the Army Selection and Classification Project (Project A). *Personnel Psychology,* 43, 231–239.

CAMPBELL, J. P. (1994). Alternative models of job performance and their implications for selection and classification. In M. G. Rumsey, C. B. Walker, & J. H. Harris (Eds.), *Personnel selection and classification* (pp. 33–51). Hillsdale, NJ: Erlbaum.

CAMPBELL, J. P., CAMPBELL, R. J., & ASSOCIATES (1988). *Productivity in organizations: New perspectives from industrial and organizational psychology.* San Francisco: Jossey-Bass.

CAMPBELL, J. P., MCCLOY, R. A., OPPLER, S. H., & SAGER, C. E. (1993). A theory of performance. In N. Schmitt, W. C. Borman, et al. (Eds.), *Personnel selection in organizations* (pp. 35–70). San Francisco: Jossey-Bass.

CAMPBELL, J. P., MCHENRY, J. J., &. WISE, L. L. (1990). Modeling job performance in a population of jobs. *Personnel Psychology, 43,* 313–333.

CAMPBELL, J. T., CROOKS, L. A., MAHONEY, M. H., & ROCK, D. A. (1973). *AN investigation of sources of bias in the prediction of job performance: A six-year study.* Princeton, NJ: Educational Testing Service.

CAMPION, M. A. (1994). Job analysis for the future. In M. G. Rumsey, C. B. Walker, &. J. H. Harris (Eds.), *Personnel selection and classification* (pp. 1–12). Hillsdale, NJ: Erlbaum.

CAMPIONE, J. C., & BROWN, A. L. (1979). Toward a theory of intelligence: Contributions from research with retarded children. In R. J. Sternberg & D. K. Detterman (Eds.), *Human intelligence: Perspectives on its theory and measurement* (pp. 139–163). Norwood, NJ: Ablex.

CAMPIONE, J. C., & BROWN, A. L. (1987). Linking dynamic assessment with school achievement. In C. S. Lidz (Ed.), *Dynamic assessment: An interactive approach to evaluating learning potential* (pp. 76–109). New York: Guilford Press.

CANCELLI, A. A., & ARENA, S. T. (1996). Multicultural implications of performance-based assessment. In L. A. Suzuki, P. J. Meller, & J. G. Ponterotto (Eds.), *Handbook of multicultural assessment: Clinical, psychological, and educational applications* (pp. 319–347). San Francisco: Jossey-Bass.

CANFIELD, A. A. (1951). *THE* "sten" scale—A modified C-scale. *Educational and Psychological Measurement, 11,* 295–297.

CANTER, A. (1996). The Bender-Gestalt Test (BGT). In C. S. Newmark (Ed.), *Major psychological assessment instruments* (2nd ed., pp. 400–432). Boston: Allyn & Bacon.

CANTER, M. B., BENNETT, B. E., JONES, S. E., & NAGY, T. F. (1994). *Ethics for psychologists: A commentary on the APA ethics code.* Washington, DC: American Psychological Association.

CAPITANI, E., SALA, S. D., & MARCHITTI, C. (1994). Is there a cognitive impairment in MND? A survey with longitudinal data. *Schweizer Archiv für Neurologie und Psychiatrie, 145,* 11–13.

CARLSON, R. (1992). Shrinking personality: One cheer for the Big Five [Review of R. R. McCrae and P. T. Costa, Jr., *Personality in adulthood*]. *Contemporary Psychology, 37,* 644–645.

CARROLL, J. B. (1963). A model of school learning. *Teachers College Record, 64,* 723–733.

CARROLL, J. B. (1966). Factors of verbal achievement. In A. Anastasi (Ed.), *Testing problems in perspective* (pp. 406–413). Washington, DC: American Council on Education.

CARROLL, J. B. (1970). Problems of measurement related to the concept of learning for mastery. *Educational Horizons, 48,* 71–80.

CARROLL, J. B. (1972). Stalking the wayward factors [Review of *The analysis of intelligence* by J. P Guilford & R. Hoepfner]. *Contemporary Psychology, 17,* 321–324.

CARROLL, J. B. (1987). New perspectives in the analysis of abilities. In R. R. Ronning, J. A. Glover, J. C. Conoley, & J. C. Witt (Eds.), *The influence of cognitive psychology* on *testing* (pp. 267–284). Hillsdale, NJ: Erlbaum.

CARROLL, J. B. (1992). Cognitive abilities: The state of the art. *Psychological Science,* 3, 266–270.

CARROLL, J. B. (1993). *Human cognitive abilities: A survey of factor-analytic studies.* New York: Cambridge University Press.

CARSON, K. R, & GILLIARD, D. J. (1993). Construct validity of the Miner Sentence Completion Scale. *Journal of Occupational and Organizational Psychology,* 66, 171–175.

CARVER, R. P. (1993). The case against statistical significance testing, revisited. *Journal of Experimental Education, 61,* 287–292.

CASCIO, W. E, & MORRIS, J. R. (1990). A critical analysis of Hunter, Schmidt, and Coggins (1988) "Problems and pitfalls in using capital budgeting and financial accounting techniques in assessing the utility of personnel programs." *Journal of Applied Psychology, 75,* 410–417.

CASHEN, V. M., & RAMSEYER, G. C. (1969). The use of separate answer sheets by primary age children. *Journal of Educational Measurement, 6,* 155–158.

CASPI, A., BLOCK, J., BLOCK, J. H., KLOPP, B., LYNAM, D., MOFFITT, T. E., & STOUTHAMER-LOEBER, M. (1992). A "common language" version of the California Child Q-Set for personality assessment. *Psychological Assessment, 4,* 512–523.

CATTELL, R. B. (1979). *Personality and learning theory: Vol. I The structure of personality and its environment*. New York: Springer.

CATTELL, R. B., CATTELL, A. K., & CATTELL, H. E. (1993). *Sixteen Personality Factor Questionnaire, Fifth Edition*. Champaign, IL: Institute for Personality and Ability Testing.

CAUDILL, O.B., JR., & POPE, K. S. (1995). *Law and mental health professionals: California*. Washington, DC: American Psychological Association.

CEGALIS, J. A., & BIRDSALL, W. (1995). *Paced Auditory Serial Attention Task*. Nashua, NH: ForThought.

CEGALIS, J. A., CEGALIS, S., & BOWLIN, J. (1993). *Vigil/W: Continuous Performance Test*. Nashua, NH: ForThought.

CHAPMAN, L. J. (1967). Illusory correlation in observational report. *Journal of Verbal Learning and Verbal Behavior,* 6, 151–155.

CHAPMAN, L. J., & CHAPMAN, J. P. (1967). Genesis of popular but erroneous psychodiagnostic observations. *Journal of Abnormal Psychology, 72,* 193–204.

CHAPMAN, L. J., & CHAPMAN, J. P. (1969). Illusory correlation as an obstacle to the use of valid psychodiagnostic signs. *Journal of Abnormal Psychology, 74,* 271–280.

CHARLES, D. C. (1953). Ability and accomplishment of persons earlier judged mental deficient. *Genetic Psychology Monographs, 47,* 3–71.

CHARLES, D. C., & JAMES, S. T. (1964). Stability of average intelligence. *Journal of Genetic Psychology, 105,* 105–111.

CHATTOPADHYAY, P.K., SOM, B., & BISWAS, D. (1993). Air Pollution and Health Hazards: An Exploratory Study. *Indian Journal of Clinical Psychology, 20,* 25–30.

CHI, M. T. H., GLASER, R., & FARR, M. J. (Eds.). (1988). *The nature of expertise.* Hillsdale, NJ: Erlbaum.

CHOCA, J. P, SHANLEY, L. A., & VAN DENBURG, E. (1992). *Interpretive guide to the Milion Clinical Multiaxial Inventory (MCMI)* . Washington, DC: American Psychological Association.

CHOJNACKI, J. T., & WALSH, W. B. (1992). The consistency of scores and configural patterns between the MMPI and MMPI-2. *Journal of Personality Assessment,* 59, 276–289.

CHRISTAL, R. E. (1958). Factor analytic study of visual memory. *Psychological Monographs, 72* (13, Whole No. 466).

CHRISTENSEN, A. L. (1975). *Luria's neuropsychological investigation.* New York: Spectrum.

CLARK, K. E. (1961). *Vocational interests of non-professional men.* Minneapolis: University of Minnesota Press.

CLARK, K. E., & CLARK, M. B. (Eds.). (1990). *Measures of leadership.* West Orange, NJ: Leadership Library of America.

CLARK, L. A., MCEWEN, J. L., COLLARD, L. M., & HICKOK, L. G. (1993). Symptoms and traits of personality disorder: Two new methods for their assessment. *Psychological Assessment*, 5, 81–91.

CLEARY, T. A. (1968). Test bias: Prediction of grades of Negro and white students in integrated colleges. *Journal of Educational Measurement, 5,* 115–124.

CLEARY, T. A., LINN, R. L., & ROCK, D. A. (1968). An exploratory study of programmed tests. *Educational and Psychological Measurement, 28,* 347–349.

CLEMANS, W. V. (1958). An index of item-criterion relationship. *Educational and Psychological Measurement, 18,* 167–172.

COATES, S. (1972). *Preschool Embedded Figures Test.* Palo Alto, CA: Consulting Psychologists Press.

COFFMAN, W. E. (1985). Review of Kaufman Assessment Battery for Children. *Ninth Mental Measurements Yearbook,* Vol. 1, 771–773.

COGLISER, C. C., & SCHRIESHEIM, C. A. (1994). Development and application of a new approach to testing the bipolarity of semantic differential items. *Educational and Psychological Measurement, 54, 594–605.*

COHEN, J. (1994). The earth is round (p. 05). *American Psychologist, 49,* 997–1003.

COHEN, R. A. (1969). Conceptual styles, culture conflict, and nonverbal tests. *American Anthropologist, 71,* 828–856.

COHN, L. D. (1991). Sex differences in the course of personality development: A metaanalysis. *Psychological Bulletin,* 109, 252–266.

COLBERG, M. (1985). Logic-based measurement of verbal reasoning: A key to increased validity and economy. *Personnel Psychology, 38,* 347–359.

COLBERG, M., NESTER, M. A., & TRATTNER, M. H. (1985). Convergence of the inductive and deductive models in the measurement of reasoning abilities. *Journal of Applied Psychology, 70,* 681–694.

COLE, D. A., MAXWELL, S. E., ARVEY, R., & SALAS, E. (1993). Multivariate group comparisons of variable systems: MANOVA and structural equation modeling. *Psychological Bulletin, 114,* 174–184.

COLE, D. A., & WHITE, K. (1993). Structure of peer impressions of children's competence: Validation of the Peer Nomination of Multiple Competencies. *Psychological Assessment*, 5, 449–456.

COLE, M., & BRUNER, J. S. (1971). Cultural differences and inferences about psychological processes. *American Psychologist,* 26, 867–876.

COLE, N. S., & MOSS, P. A. (1989). Bias in test use. In R. L. Linn (Ed.), *Educational measurement* (3rd ed., pp. 201–219). New York: American Council on Education/ Macmillan.

COLEMAN, J. L. (1987). *Police assessment testing: An assessment center handbook for law enforcement personnel.* Springfield, IL: Charles C Thomas.

COLEMAN, W., & CURETON, E. E. (1954). Intelligence and achievement: "The jangle fallacy" again. *Educational and Psychological Measurement,* 14, 347–351.

COLLEGE BOARD. (1995a). *Admission officer's handbook for the SAT Program.* New York: College Entrance Examination Board.

COLLEGE BOARD. (1995b). *Counselor's handbook for the SAT Program*. New York: College Entrance Examination Board.

COLLIGAN, R. C., OSBORNE, D., SWENSON, W. M., & OFFORD, K. P. (1983). *The MMPI: A contemporary nonnative study.* New York: Praeger.

COLLIGAN, R. C., OSBORNE, D., SWENSON, W. M„ & OFFORD, K. P. (1989). *The MMPI: A contemporary normative study of adults* (2nd ed.). Odessa, FL: Psychological Assessment Resources.

COLLINS, B. E. (1974). Four components of the Rotter Internal-External Scale: Belief in a difficult world, a just world, a predictable world, and a politically responsive world. *Journal of Personality and Social Psychology, 29*, 381–391.

COLLINS, C., & MANGIERI, J. N. (Eds.). (1992). *Teaching thinking: An agenda for the 21st century.* Hillsdale, NJ: Erlbaum.

COLLINS, L. M., & HORN, J. L. (Eds). (1991). Best *methods for the analysis of change:* Recent *advances, unanswered questions, future directions.* Washington, DC: American Psychological Association.

COLLINS, R. C. (1993). Head Start: Steps toward a two-generation program strategy. *Young Children, 48 (2)*, 25–73.

COLOMBO, J. (1993). *Infant cognition: Predicting later intellectual functioning.* Newbury Park, CA: Sage.

COMREY, A. L., & LEE, H. B. (1992). *A first course in factor analysis* (2nd ed.). Hillsdale, NJ: Erlbaum.

CONGER, A. J., & JACKSON, D. N. (1972). Suppressor variables, prediction, and the interpretation of psychological relationships. *Educational and Psychological Measurement, 32, 579–599.*

CONN, S. R., & RIEKE, M. L. (Eds.). (1994). *The 16 PF Fifth* Edition *technical manual.* Champaign, IL: Institute for Personality and Ability Testing.

CONNELL, J. P. (1985). A new multidimensional measure of children's perceptions of control. *Child Development*, 56, 1018–1041.

CONNOR, M. (1994). *Training the counselor: An integrative model*. London: Routledge.

CONOLEY, J. C., & WERTH, E. B.(Eds.). (1995). *Family assessment*. Lincoln, NE: Buros Institute of Mental Measurements.

CONSORTIUM FOR LONGITUDINAL STUDIES. (1983). *As the twig is bent...: Lasting effects of preschool programs.* Hillsdale, NJ: Erlbaum.

COOK, T. D., & CAMPBELL, D. T. (1976). The design and conduct of quasi-experiments and true experiments in field settings. In M. D. Dunnette (Ed.), *Handbook of industrial and organizational psychology* (pp. 223–326). Chicago: Rand-McNally.

COOK, T. D., COOPER, H., CORDRAY, D. S., HARTMAN, H., HEDGES, L. V., LIGHT, R. J., LOUIS, T. A., & MOSTELLER, F. (1992). *Meta-analysis for explanation: A casebook*. New York: Russell Sage Foundation.

COOLEY, W. W., & GLASER, R. (1969). The computer and individualized instruction. *Science, 166*, 574–582.

COOLEY, W. W., & LOHNES, P. (1976). *Evaluation research in education*. New York: Wiley.

COOPER, H., & HEDGES, L. V. (Eds.). (1994). *The handbook of research synthesis.* New York: Russell Sage Foundation.

CORDÓN, LUIS A. (2005). Popular psychology: An encyclopaedia. Westport, Conn: Greenwood Press. pp. 201–204. Retrieved June 11, 2016, from https://en.wikipedia.org/wiki/Projective_test.

COSDEN, M. (1992). Review of the Draw A Person: A quantitative scoring system. *Eleventh Mental Measurements Yearbook*, 287–289.

COSTA, R T., JR., & MCCRAE, R. R. (1988). From catalogue to classification: Murray's needs and the five-factor model. *Journal of Personality and Social Psychology, 55*, 258–265.

COSTA, P. T., JR., & MCCRAE, R. R. (1992a). Normal personality assessment in clinical practice: The NEO *Personality inventory. Psychological Assessment, 4*, 5–13.

COSTA, P. T., JR., & MCCRAE, R. R. (1992b). Revised NEO *Personality Inventory (NEO PIR) and NEO Five-Factor Inventory (NEO-FFI) professional manual.* Odessa, FL: Psychological Assessment Resources.

COSTA, P. T., JR., & MCCRAE, R. R. (1994). *Bibliography for the Revised NEO Personality Inventory and NEO Five-Factor Inventory (NEO-FFI).* Odessa, FL: Psychological Assessment Resources.

COSTA, P. T., JR., & MCCRAE, R. R. (1995). Domains and Facets: Hierarchical personality assessment using the Revised NEO Personality Inventory. *Journal of Personality Assessment, 64*, 21–50.

COSTA, P. T., JR., MCCRAE, R. R., &. HOLLAND, J. L. (1984). Personality and vocational interests in an adult sample. *Journal of Applied Psychology, 69*, 390–400.

COSTA, P. T., JR., & WIDIGER, T. A. (Eds.). (1994). *Personality disorders and the Five-Factor Model of personality.* Washington, DC: American Psychological Association.

COSTANTINO, G., MALGADY, R. G., & ROGLER, L. H. (1988). *TEMAS (Tell-Me-A-Story): Manual*. Los Angeles, CA: Western Psychological Services.

COUCH, A., &. KENISTON, K. (1960). Yea sayers and naysayers: Agreeing response set as a personality variable. *Journal of Abnormal and Social Psychology, 60*, 151–174.

COULTON, G. F., & FEILD, H. S. (1995). Using assessment centers in selecting entry-level police officers: Extravagance or justified expense? *Public Personnel Management, 24*, 223–254.

COURT, J. H., & RAVEN, J. (1995). *Manual for Raven's Progressive Matrices and vocabulary scales: Sect. 7. Research and references.* Oxford, England: Oxford Psychologists Press.

COURTS, P. L., & MCINERNEY, K. H. (1993). *Assessment in higher education: Politics, pedagogy, and portfolios. Westport,* CT: Praeger.

COWARD, W. M., & SACKETT, P. R. (1990). Linearity of ability-performance relationships: A reconfirmation. *Journal of Applied Psychology, 73*, 297–300.

COWLES, M. (1989). *Statistics in psychology: An historical perspective.* Hillsdale, NJ: Erlbaum.

COX, M. V. (1993). *Children's drawings of the human figure.* Hove, UK: Erlbaum.

COX, R. H. (1989). Psychomotor screening for USAF pilot candidates: Selecting a valid criterion. *Aviation, Space, and Environmental Medicine, 60*, 1153–1156.

CPP, INC. (2002, February). Brief Technical Report on the CPI 260® Instrument (Tech. Rep. No. 2002-3). Mountain View, CA: Author. Retrieved June 10, 2016, from *https://www.cpp.com/products/cpi260/CPI260_Technical_Brief.pdf.*

CRAIG, R. J. (Ed.). (1993). *The Millon Clinical Multiaxial Inventory: A clinical research information synthesis.* Hillsdale, NJ: Erlbaum.

CRAIK, F. I. M., & SALTHOUSE, T. A. (Eds.). (1992). *The handbook of aging and cognition*. Hillsdale, NJ: Erlbaum.

CRAMER, P. (1996). *Storytelling, narrative, and the Thematic Apperception Test*. New York: Guilford Press.

CRAMER, P. (1999). Future Directions for the Thematic Apperception Test. *Journal of Personality Assessment, 72*, 74–92

CRAMER, R, & BLATT, S. J. (1990). Use of the TAT to measure change in the defense mechanisms following intensive psychotherapy. *Journal of Personality* Assessment, *54*, 236–251.

CRAWFORD, J. E., & CRAWFORD, D. M. (1981). *Crawford Small Parts Dexterity Test: Manual*. San Antonio, TX: Psychological Corporation.

CRICK, G. E., & BRENNAN, R. L. (1982). GENOVA. *A generalized analysis of variance system* [Computer program and manual]. Dorchester: University of Massachusetts at Boston, Computer Facilities.

CRITES, J. O. (1969). *The maturity of vocational attitudes in adolescence.* Iowa City: University of Iowa.

CROCKER, L., & SCHMITT, A. (1987). Improving multiple-choice test performance for examinees with different levels of test anxiety. *Journal of Experimental Education, 55,* 201–205.

CRONBACH, L. J. (1949). Statistical methods applied to Rorschach scores: A review. *Psychological Bulletin, 46,* 393–429.

CRONBACH, L. J. (1951). Coefficient alpha and the internal structure of tests. *Psychometrika, 16,* 297–334.

CRONBACH, L. J., &. DRENTH, R J. D. (Eds.). (1972). *Mental tests and cultural adaptation.* The Hague: Mouton.

CRONBACH, L. J., & FURBY, L. (1970). How we should measure change—or should we? *Psychological Bulletin, 74,* 68–80.

CRONBACH, L. J., & GLESER, G. C. (1965). *Psychological tests and personnel decisions* (2nd ed.). Champaign: University of Illinois Press.

CRONBACH, L. J., GLESER, G. C., NANDA, H., &. RAJARATNAM, N. (1972). *The dependability of behavioral measurements: Theory of generalizability for scores and profiles.* New York: Wiley.

CRONBACH, L. J., & MEEHL, P. E. (1955). Construct validity in psychological tests. *Psychological Bulletin, 52,* 281–302.

CROWNE, D. P, & MARLOWE, D. (1964). *The approval motive: Studies in evaluative dependence.* New York: Wiley.

CSIKSZENTMIHALYI, M., RATHUNDE, K., & WHALEN, S. (1993). *Talented teenagers: The roots of success and failure.* New York: Cambridge University Press.

CUDECK, R., &. O'DELL, L. L. (1994). Applications of standard error estimates in unrestricted factor analysis: Significance tests for factor loading and correlations. *Psychological Bulletin, 115,* 475–487.

CULBERTSON, J. L., & WILLIS, D. J. (Eds.). (1993). *Testing young children: a reference guide for developmental, psychoeducational, and psychosocial assessments.* Austin, TX: PRO-ED.

CULLER, R. E., & HOLAHAN, C. J. (1980). Test anxiety and academic performance: The effects of study-related behavior. *Journal of Educational Psychology, 72,* 16–20.

Culture and psychology. (1995). Vol. 1, No. 1. Newbury Park, CA: Sage.

CUMMINGS, J. A. (1986). Projective drawings. In H. M. Knoff (Ed.), *The assessment of child and adolescent personality* (pp. 199–244). New York: Guilford Press.

CUNDICK, B. P. (1985). Review of the Holtzman Inkblot Technique. *Ninth Mental Measurements Yearbook,* Vol. 1, 661–662.

CURETON, E. E. (1950). Validity, reliability, and baloney. *Educational and Psychological Measurement, 10,* 94–96.

CURETON, E. E. (1957a). Recipe for a cookbook. *Psychological Bulletin, 54,* 494–497.

CURETON, E. E. (1957b). The upper and lower twenty-seven percent rule. *Psychometrika, 22,* 293–296.

CURETON, E. E. (1965). Reliability and validity: Basic assumptions and experimental designs. *Educational and Psychological Measurement, 25,* 327–346.

CURETON, E. E., COOK, J. A., FISCHER, R. T., LASER, S. A., ROCKWELL, N. J., & SIMMONS, J. W. (1973). Length of test and standard error of measurement. *Educational and Psychological Measurement, 33,* 63–68.

CUSHMAN, L. A., & SCHERER, M. J. (Eds.). (1995). *Psychological assessment in medical rehabilitation*. Washington, DC: American Psychological Association.

CUTTER, F., & FARBEROW, N. L. (1970). The consensus Rorschach. In B. Klopfer, M. M. Mayer, F. B. Brawer, & W. G. Klopfer (Eds.), *Developments in the Rorschach technique* (Vol. 3, pp. 209–261). San Diego, CA: Harcourt Brace Jovanovich.

DAHLSTROM, W. G. (1993a). *The items in the MMPl-2: Alterations in wording, patterns of interrelationships, and changes in endorsements, Supplement to the MMPI-2 manual for administration and scoring.* Minneapolis: University of Minnesota Press.

DAHLSTROM, W. G. (1993b). Tests: Small samples, large consequences. American Psychologist, 48, 393–399.

DAHLSTROM, W. G. (1995). Pigeons, people, and pigeon holes. *Journal of Personality Assessment, 64,* 2–20.

DAHLSTROM, W. G., & DAHLSTROM, L. E. (Eds.). (1980). *Basic readings* on *the* MMP1: *A new selection on personality measurement*. Minneapolis: University of Minnesota Press.

DAHLSTROM, W. G., & TELLEGEN, A. (1993). *Socioeconomic status and the MMPI-2: The relation of MMPI-2 patterns to levels of education and occupation, Supplement to the MMP1–2 manual for administration and scoring.* Minneapolis: University of Minnesota Press.

DAHLSTROM, W. G., WELSH, G. S., & DAHLSTROM, L. E. (1972). *An MMPI handbook: Vol. 1. Clinical interpretation*. Minneapolis: University of Minnesota Press.

DAHLSTROM, W. G., WELSH, G. S., & DAHLSTROM, L. E. (1975). *An MMPI handbook: Vol. 2. Research applications.* Minneapolis: University of Minnesota Press.

DALAI, A. K. (2011). A Journey Back to the Roots: Psychology in India. *Foundations of Indian Psychology,* 1: Theories and Concepts, 27.

DANA, R. H. (1984). Intelligence testing of American Indian children: Sidesteps in quest of ethical practice. *White Cloud Journal,* 3 (3), 35–43.

DANA, R. H. (1993). *Multicultural assessment perspectives for professional psychology.* Boston: Allyn & Bacon.

DANA, R. H. (1996a). Culturally competent assessment practice in the United States. *Journal of Personality Assessment,* 66, 472–487.

DANA, R. FH. (1996b). The Thematic Apperception Test (TAT). In C. S. Newmark (Ed.), *Major psychological assessment instruments* (2nd ed., pp. 166–205). Boston: Allyn & Bacon.

DANIELS, D., & PLOMIN, R. (1985). Differential experience of siblings in the same family. *Developmental Psychology, 21,* 747–760.

DANIELS, M. H. (1989). Review of the Self-Directed Search: A guide to educational and vocational planning—1985 Revision. *Tenth Mental Measurements Yearbook,* 735–738.

DARLINGTON, R. B. (1971). Another look at "culture fairness." *Journal of Educational Measurement, 8,* 71–82.

DARLINGTON, R. B. (1976). A defense of "rational" personnel selection, and two new methods. *Journal of Educational Measurement, 13,* 43–52.

DARLINGTON, R. B., &. STAUFFER, G. F. (1966). A method for choosing a cutting point on a test. *Journal of Applied Psychology, 50,* 229–231.

DAS, J. P. (1984). Simultaneous and successive processes and K-ABC. *Journal of Special Education, 18,* 229–238.

DAS, J. P., KIRBY, J. R., & JARMAN, R. F. (1975). Simultaneous and successive syntheses: An alternative model for cognitive abilities. *Psychological Bulletin, 82,* 87–103.

DAS, J. P., KIRBY, J. R., &. JARMAN, R. F. (1979). *Simultaneous and successive cognitive processes.* New York: Academic Press.

DAS, J. P., & MOLLOY, G. N. (1975). Varieties of simultaneous and successive processing in children. *Journal of Educational Psychology, 67,* 213–220.

DAS, J. P., NAGLIERI, J. A., & KIRBY, J. R. (1994). *Assessment of cognitive processes: The PASS theory of intelligence.* Boston: Allyn & Bacon.

DAS, R. S. (1963). Analysis of the components of reasoning in nonverbal tests and the structure of reasoning in a bilingual population. *Archiv für die Gesamte Psychologic, 115* (3), 217–229.

DASEN, P. K. (Ed.). (1977). *Piagetian psychology: Cross-cultural contributions.* New York: Halsted Press.

DAVIDOW, S., & BRUHN, A. R. (1990). Earliest memories and the dynamics of delinquency: A replication study. *Journal of Personality Assessment, 54,* 601–616.

DAVIS, C. J. (1980). *Perkins-Binet Tests of Intelligence for the Blind.* Watertown, MA: Perkins School for the Blind.

DAVIS, D. L., GROVE, S, J., &. KNOWLES, P. A. (1990). An experimental application of personality type as an analogue for decision-making style. *Psychological Reports, 66,* 167–175.

DAVIS, F. B. (1959). Interpretation of differences among averages and individual test scores. *Journal of Educational Psychology, 50,* 162–170.

DAVIS, G. L., HOFFMAN, R. G., & NELSON, K. S. (1990). Differences between Native Americans and Whites on the California Psychological Inventory. *Psychological Assessment, 2,* 238–242.

DAVIS, W. E. (1969a). Effect of prior failure on subjects' WA1S Arithmetic subtest scores. *Journal of Clinical Psychology, 25,* 72–73.

DAVIS, W. E. (1969b). Examiner differences, prior failure, and subjects' arithmetic scores. *Journal of Clinical Psychology, 25,* 178–180.

DAVISON, M. L., GASSER, M., &. DING, S. (1996). Identifying major profile patterns in a population: An exploratory study of WAIS and GATB patterns. *Psychological Assessment, 8,* 26–31.

DAWES, R. M., FAUST, D., &. MEEHL, P E. (1993). Statistical prediction versus clinical prediction: Improving what works. In G. Keren & C. Lewis (Eds.), A *handbook for data analysis in the behavioral sciences: Methodological issues* (pp. 351–367). Hillsdale, NJ: Erlbaum.

DAWIS, R. V. (1991). Vocational interests, values, and preferences. In M. D. Dunnette & L. M. Hough (Eds.), *Handbook of industrial and organizational psychology* (2nd ed., Vol. 2, pp. 833–871). Palo Alto, CA: Consulting Psychologists Press.

DAWIS, R. V. (1992). The structure(s) of occupations: Beyond R1ASEC. *Journal of Vocational Behavior, 40,* 171–178.

DEAN, R. S. (1977). Reliability of the WISC-R with Mexican-American children. *Journal of School Psychology, 15,* 267–268.

DEAN, R. S. (1979). Predictive validity of the WISC-R with Mexican-American children. *Journal of School Psychology, 17,* 55–58.

DEAN, R. S. (1980). Factor structure of the WISC-R with Anglos and Mexican-Americans. *Journal of School Psychology, 18,* 234–239.

DEAN, R. S. (1985). Review of Halstead-Reitan Neuropsychological Test Battery. *Ninth Mental Measurements Yearbook,* Vol. 1, 644–646.

DE GROOT, A. M. B., & BARRY, C. (Eds.). (1993). The multilingual community: Bilingualism. *European Journal of Cognitive Psychology,* 4(4). Hove, England: Erlbaum.

DEB, S. (2001, October). A study on the Negative Effects of Academic Stress. Paper presented at the International Seminar on Learning and Motivation, Kedah Darul Aman, Malaysia

DEKKER, R. (1993). Visually impaired children and haptic intelligence test scores: Intelligence Test for Visually Impaired Children (ITVIC). *Developmental Medicine and Child Neurology, 35*, 478–489.

DEKKER, R., DRENTH, P. J. D., & ZAAL, J. N. (1991). Results of the Intelligence Test for Visually Impaired Children (ITVIC). *Journal of Visual Impairment and Blindness, 85*, 261–267.

DEKKER, R., DRENTH, P. J. D., ZAAL, J. N., & KOOLE, F. D. (1990). An intelligence test series for blind and low vision children. *Journal of Visual Impairment and Blindness, 84*, 71–76.

DEKKER, R., & KOOLE, F. D. (1992). Visually impaired children's visual characteristics and intelligence. *Developmental Medicine* and *Child Neurology, 34*, 123–133.

DELANEY, E. & HOPKINS, T. (1987). *Stanford-Binet Intelligence Scale—Examiner's handbook: An expanded guide for fourth edition users*. Chicago: Riverside.

DEMERS, S. T., FIORELLO, C., & LANGER, K. L. (1992). Legal and ethical issues in preschool assessment. In E. Vazquez Nutall, I. Romero, & J. Kalesnik (Eds.), *Assessing and screening preschoolers: Psychological and educational dimensions* (pp. 43–54). Boston: Allyn & Bacon.

DEMETRIOU, A. (1988). *The Neo-Piagetian theories of cognitive development: Toward an integration*. Amsterdam: North-holland.

DEMMING, J. A., & PRESSEY, S. L. (1957). Tests "indigenous to the adult and older years. *Journal of Counseling Psychology, 4*, 144–148.

DEMO, D. H. (1985). The measurement of self-esteem: Refining our methods. *Journal of Personality and Social Psychology, 48*, 1490–1502.

DENNIS, W. (1966). Goodenough scores, art experience, and modernization. *Journal of Social Psychology, 68*, 211–228.

DENNY, J. P. (1966). Effects of anxiety and intelligence on concept formation. *Journal of Experimental Psychology, 72, 596–602.*

DENO, S. L. (1992). The nature and development of curriculum-based measurement. *Preventing School Failure, 36*, 5–10.

DEPAULO, B. M. (1994). Spotting lies: Can humans learn to do better? *Current Directions in Psychological Science, 3*, 83–86.

DEROGATIS, L. R. (1994). *SCL-90-R: Symptom Checklist-90-R: Administration, scoring, and procedures manual* (3rd ed.). Minneapolis, MN: National Computer Systems.

DEROGATIS, L. R., &. LAZARUS, L. (1994). SCL-90-R, Brief Symptom Inventory, and matching clinical rating scales. In M. E. Maruish (Ed.), *The use of psychological testing for treatment planning and outcome assessment* (pp. 217–248). Hillsdale, NJ: Erlbaum.

DESMARAIS, L. B., MASI, D. L., OLSON, M. J., BARRERA, K. M., & DYER, P. J. (1994, April). *Scoring a multimedia situational judgment test: IBM's experience*. Paper presented at the annual conference of the Society for Industrial and Organizational Psychology, Nashville, TN.

DETTERMAN, D. K. (Ed.). (1985–1993). *Current topics in human intelligence* (Vols. 1–3). Norwood, NJ: Ablex.

DETTERMAN, D. K., & STERNBERG, R. J. (Eds.). (1982). *How and how much can intelligence be increased*. Norwood, NJ: Ablex.

DEVITO, A. J. (1985). Review of Myers-Briggs Type Indicator. *Ninth Mental Measurements Yearbook*, Vol. 2, 1030–1032.

DEWITT, L. J., & WEISS, D. J. (1974). *Computer software* system *for adaptive ability measurement* (Res. Rep. 74–1). Minneapolis: Department of Psychology, University of Minnesota, Psychometric Methods Program.

DEWOLFF, C. J. (1993). *The prediction paradigm*. In H. Schuler, J. L. Farr, &. M. Smith (Eds.), *Personnel selection and assessment: Individual and organizational perspectives* (pp. 253–265). Hillsdale, NJ: Erlbaum.

DIANE, C. C., BROGAN, F. S., & MCCAULEY, D. E., JR. (1991). A *validation study of artificial language tests for border patrol guards*. Washington, DC: Office of Personnel Research and Development.

DIAZ-GUERRERO, R. (1990). The need for ethnopsychology of cognition and personality. In I. Ayman & Y. Tanaka (Organizers) *Symposium: Appropriate Psychology for developing countries* Kyoto, Japan: International Association of Applied Psychology for Developing Countries.

DIAZ-GUERRERO, R., & DIAZ-LOVING, R. (1990). Interpretation in cross-cultural personality assessment. In C. R. Reynolds & R. W. Kamphaus (Eds.), *Handbook of psychological and educational assessment of children: Personality, behavior and context* (pp. 491–523). New York: Guilford Press.

DIAZ-GUERRERO, R., & SZALAY, L. B. (1991). *Understanding Mexicans and Americans*. New York: Plenum Press.

DICKENS, W. T., & FLYNN, J. R. (2001). Heritability estimates versus large environmental effects: the IQ paradox resolved. *Psychological Review*, *108*(2), 346.

DICKINSON, T. L., & ZELLINGER, P. M. (1980). A comparison of behaviorally anchored rating and mixed standard scale formats. *Journal of Applied Psychology*, *65*, 147–154.

DIENER, E., & CRANDALL, R. (1978). *Ethics in social and behavioral research*. Chicago: University of Chicago Press.

DIFFERENTIAL APTITUDE TESTS, FIFTH EDITION: COUNSELOR'S MANUAL. (1991). San Antonio, TX: Psychological Corporation.

DIFFERENTIAL APTITUDE TESTS, FIFTH EDITION: TECHNICAL MANUAL. (1992). San Antonio, TX: Psychological Corporation.

DIGMAN, J. M. (1990). Personality structure: Emergence of the Five-Factor Model. *Annual Review of Psychology*, *41*, 417–440.

DOBBIN, J. (1984). *How to take a test: Doing your best*. Princeton, NJ: Educational Testing Service.

DOLL, E. A. (1965). *Vineland Social Maturity Scale: Manual of directions* (rev. ed.). Circle Pines, MN: American Guidance Service. (1st ed., 1935)

DONDERS, J. (1996). Cluster subtypes in the WISC-III standardization sample: Analysis of factor index scores. *Psychological Assessment, 8, 312–318*.

DONLON, T. F. (Ed.). (1984). *The College Board Technical Handbook for the Scholastic Aptitude Test and Achievement Tests*. New York: College Board Publications.

DONLON, T. F. (1984). *The College Board Technical Handbook for the Scholastic Aptitude Test and Achievement Tests*. New York: College Entrance Examination Board.

DONNAY, D. A. (2005). *Strong Interest Inventory Manual: Research, Development, and Strategies for Interpretation*. CPP.

DOYLE, K. O., JR. (1974). Theory and practice of ability testing in ancient Greece. *Journal of the History of the Behavioral Sciences, 10*, 202–212.

DRASGOW, F., & HULIN, C. L. (1990). Item response theory. In M. D. Dunnette & L. M. Hough (Eds.), *Handbook of industrial and organizational psychology* (2nd ed., Vol. 1, pp. 577–636). Palo Alto, CA: Consulting Psychologists Press.

DRASGOW, E, OLSON-BUCHANAN, J. B., &. MOBERG, P. J. (1996). *Development of interactive video assessments.* Manuscript submitted for publication.

DREGER, R. M. (1968). General temperament and personality factors related to intellectual performances. *Journal of Genetic Psychology, 113,* 275–293.

DROEGE, R. C. (1966), Effects of practice on aptitude scores. *Journal of Applied Psychology, 50,* 306–310.

DRUMMOND, R. J. (1995). Review of the Alcohol Use Inventory. *Twelfth Mental Measurements Yearbook,* 65–66.

DRUMMOND, R. J. (1996). *Appraisal procedures for counselors and helping professionals* (3rd ed.). Englewood Cliffs, NJ: Merrill.

DUBOIS, P. H. (1939). A test standardized on Pueblo Indian children. *Psychological Bulletin, 36, 523.*

DUBOIS, P. H. (1970). *A history of psychological testing.* Boston: Allyn & Bacon.

DUCKWORTH, J C. (1991). The Minnesota Multiphasic Personality Inventory-2: A review. *Journal of Counseling and Development, 69,* 564–567.

DUDEK, F. J. (1979). The continuing misinterpretation of the standard error of measurement. *Psychological Bulletin, 86,* 335–337.

DUNCAN, O. D. (1961). A socioeconomic index for all occupations. In A. J. Reiss, Jr. (Ed.), *Occupations and social status* (pp. 109–138). New York: Free Press of Glencoe.

DUNN, J. A. (1967). Inter- and intra-rater reliability of the new Harris-Goodenough Draw-a-Man Test. *Perceptual and Motor Skills, 24,* 269–270.

DUNN, J., & PLOMIN, R. (1990). *Separate lives: Why siblings are so different.* New York: Basic Books.

DUNN, L(loyd), M., & Dunn, L(Eota), M. (1981). *Peabody Picture Vocabulary Test—Revised: Manual for Forms L and M.* Circle Pines, MN: American Guidance Service.

DUNN, L. M., & DUNN, D. M. (2015). *Peabody Picture Vocabulary Test: PPVT 4.* Pearson.

DUNNETTE, M. D. (1957). Use of the sugar pill by industrial psychologists. *American Psychologist, 12,* 223–225.

DUNNETTE, M. D., & BORMAN, W. C. (1979). Personnel selection and classification systems. *Annual Review of Psychology, 30,* 477–525.

DUNNETTE, M. D., & HOUGH, L. M. (Eds.). (1990–1992). *Handbook of industrial and organizational psychology* (2nd ed., Vols. 1–3). Palo Alto, CA: Consulting Psychologists Press.

DUNST, C. J. (1980). *A clinical and educational manual for use with the Užgiris and Hunt Scales of Infant Psychological Development.* Austin, TX: PRO-ED.

DUNST, C. J., & GALLAGHER, J. L. (1983). Piagetian approaches to infant assessment. *Topics in Early Childhood Special Education,* 3, 44–62.

DURAN, R. P. (1983). *Hispanics' education and background: Predictors of college achievement.* New York: College Entrance Examination Board.

DURAN, R. P. (1989). Testing of linguistic minorities. In R. L. Linn (Ed.), *Educational measurement* (3rd ed., pp. 573–587). New York: American Council on Education/Macmillan.

DUSH, D. M. (1985). Review of the Holtzman Inkblot Technique. *Ninth Mental Measurements Yearbook,* Vol. 1, 602–603.

DWYER, C. A. (1993). Innovation and reform: Examples from teacher assessment. In R. E. Bennett & W. C. Ward (Eds.), *Construction versus choice in cognitive measurement: Issues in constructed response, performance testing, and portfolio assessment* (pp. 265–289). Hillsdale, NJ: Erlbaum.

DYER, H. S. (1973). Recycling the problems of testing. *Proceedings of the 1972 Invitational Conference on Testing Problems, Educational Testing Service, 85–95.*

EAGLY, A. H., & CHAIKEN, S. (1993). *The psychology of attitudes.* Fort Worth, TX: Harcourt Brace Jovanovich.

EBBINGHAUS, H. (1897). Über eine neue Methode zur Prüfung geistiger Fähigkeiten und ihre Anwendung bei Schulkindern. *Zeitschrift für Angewandte Psychologie,* 13, 401–459.

EBEL, R. L. (1962). Content standard test scores. *Educational and Psychological Measurement, 22,* 15–25.

EBEL, R. L. (1972). Some limitations of criterion-referenced measurement. In G. H. Bracht, K. D. Hopkins, & J. C. Stanley (Eds.), *Perspective in educational and psychological measurement* (pp. 144–149). Englewood Cliffs, NJ: Prentice Hall.

EBEL, R. L. (1979). *Essentials of educational measurement* (3rd ed.). Englewood Cliffs, NJ: Prentice Hall.

EBEL, R. L., &. DAMRIN, D. E. (1960). Tests and examinations. *Encyclopedia of educational research* (3rd ed., pp. 1502–1517). New York: Macmillan.

EDER, R. W., KACMAR, K. M., & FERRIS, G. R. (1989). Employment interview research: History and synthesis. In R. W. Eder & G. R. Ferris (Eds.), *The employment interview: Theory, research, and practice* (pp. 17–31). Newbury Park, CA: Sage.

EDUCATIONAL TESTING SERVICE. (1990). *Annual report.* Princeton, NJ: Author.

EDUCATIONAL TESTING SERVICE. (1992). ETS conference examines the technology of computer-based testing for people with disabilities. *ETS Developments,* 38(1), 6–7.

EDWARDS, A. L. (1957). *The social desirability variable in personality assessment and research.* New York: Dryden.

EDWARDS, A. L. (1959). *Edwards Personal Preference Schedule: Manual.* New York: Psychological Corporation.

EDWARDS, A. L. (1990). Construct validity and social desirability. *American Psychologist, 45,* 287–289.

EICHORN, D. H., CLAUSEN, J. A., HAAN, N., HONZIK, M. R, & MUSSEN, P. H. (Eds.). (1981). *Present and past in middle life.* New York: Academic Press.

The Eighth Mental Measurements Yearbook. (1978). Highland Park, NJ: Gryphon Press.

EISDORFER, C. (1963). The WAIS performance of the aged: A retest evaluation. *Journal of Gerontology, 18,* 169–172.

EKSTROM, R. B., FRENCH, J. W., & HARMAN, H. H. (1979). Cognitive factors: Their identification and replication. *Multivariate Behavioral Research Monographs,* No. 79–2.

EKSTROM, R. B., FRENCH, J. W., HARMAN, H. H., & DERMEN, D. (1976). *Manual for kit of factor-referenced cognitive tests* (3rd ed.). Princeton, NJ: Educational Testing Service.

The Eleventh Mental Measurements Yearbook. (1992). Lincoln, NE: Buros Institute of Mental Measurements.

ELKSNIN, L. K., & ELKSNIN, N. (1993). A review of picture interest inventories: Implications for vocational assessment of students with disabilities. *Journal of Psychoeducational Assessment, 11,* 323–336.

ELLIOTT, C. D. (1990a). *Differential Ability Scales: Administration and scoring manual.* San Antonio, TX: Psychological Corporation.

ELLIOTT, C. D. (1990b). *Differential Ability Scales: Introductory and technical handbook.* San Antonio, TX: Psychological Corporation.

ELLIOTT, C. D., MURRAY, D. J., & PEARSON, L. S. (1979). *British Ability Scales.* Windsor, England: National Foundation for Educational Research.

EMBRETSON, S. E. (1983). Construct validity: Construct representation versus nomothetic span. *Psychological Bulletin, 93,* 179–197.

EMBRETSON, S. E. (Ed.). (1985a). *Test design: Developments in psychology and psychometrics.* Orlando, FL: Academic Press.

EMBRETSON, S. E. (1985b). Multicomponent latent trait models for test design. In S. E. Embretson (Ed.), *Test design: Developments in psychology and psychometrics* (pp. 195–218). Orlando, FL: Academic Press.

EMBRETSON, S. E. (1986). Intelligence and its measurement: Extending contemporary theory to existing tests. In R. J. Sternberg (Ed.), *Advances in the psychology of human intelligence* (Vol. 3, pp. 335–368). Hillsdale, NJ: Erlbaum.

EMBRETSON, S. E. (1987). Toward development of a psychometric approach. In C. S. Lidz (Ed.), *Dynamic assessment: An interactive approach to evaluating learning potential* (pp. 135–164). New York: Guilford Press.

EMBRETSON, S. (1990). Diagnostic testing by measuring learning processes: Psychometric considerations for dynamic testing. In N. Frederiksen, R. Glaser, A. Lesgold, & M. G. Shafto (Eds.), *Diagnostic monitoring of skill and knowledge acquisition* (pp. 407–432). Hillsdale, NJ: Erlbaum.

EMBRETSON, S. E. (1991). A multidimensional latent trait model for measuring learning and change. *Psychometrika, 56,* 495–515.

EMBRETSON, S. E. (1992). Computerized adaptive testing: Its potential substantive contributions to psychological research and assessment. *Current Directions in Psychological Science, 1,* 129–131.

EMBRETSON, S. (1993). Psychometric models for learning and cognitive processes. In N. Frederiksen, R. J. Mislevy, & I. I. Bejar (Eds.), *Test theory for a new generation of tests* (pp. 125–150). Hillsdale, NJ: Erlbaum.

EMBRETSON, S. (1994). Applications of cognitive design systems to test development. In C. R. Reynolds (Ed.), *Cognitive assessment: A multidisciplinary perspective* (pp. 107–135). New York: Plenum Press.

EMBRETSON, S. E.(1995a). Developments toward a cognitive design system for psychological tests. In D. Lubinsky & R. V. Dawis (Eds.), *Assessing individual differences in human behavior: New methods, concepts, and findings* (pp. 17–46). Palo Alto, CA: Consulting Psychologists Press.

EMBRETSON, S. E. (1995b). A measurement model for linking individual learning to processes and knowledge: Application to mathematical reasoning. *Journal of Educational Measurement,* 32, 277–294.

Encyclopedia of human intelligence. (1994). New York: Macmillan.

ENDLER, N. S., & MAGNUSSON, D. (1976). Toward an interactional psychology of personality. *Psychological Bulletin, 83,* 956–974.

ENGELHARD, G. (1992). Review of the California Psychological Inventory, Revised Edition. *Eleventh Mental Measurements Yearbook,* 139–141.

ENGELHART, M. D. (1965). A comparison of several item discrimination indices. *Journal of Educational Measurement, 2,* 69–76.

ENTWISLE, D. R. (1972). To dispel fantasies about fantasy-based measures of achievement motivation. *Psychological Bulletin,* 77, 377–391.

EPSTEIN, S. (1966). Some theoretical considerations on the nature of ambiguity and the use of stimulus dimensions in projective techniques. *Journal of Counseling Psychology,* 30, 183–192.

EPSTEIN, S. (1979). The stability of behavior: I. On predicting most of the people much of the time. *Journal of Personality and Social Psychology, 27,* 1097–1121.

EPSTEIN, S. (1980). The stability of behavior; II. Implications for psychological research. *American Psychologist,* 35, 790–806.

EPSTEIN, S., & O'BRIEN, E. J. (1985). The person-situation debate in historical and current perspective. *Psychological Bulletin, 98,* 513–537.

EPTING, F., &. LANDFIELD, A. W. (Eds.). (1985). *Anticipating personal construct psychology.* Lincoln: University of Nebraska Press.

EQUAL EMPLOYMENT OPPORTUNITY COMMISSION. (EEOC). (1994, May). *Enforcement guidance: Preemployment disability-related inquiries and medical examinations under the Americans with Disabilities Act of 1990 (EEOC Notice, 915.002).* Washington, DC: Author.

EQUAL EMPLOYMENT OPPORTUNITY COMMISSION (EEOC). (1995, October). *ADA enforcement guidance: Preemployment disability-related questions and medical examinations.* Washington, DC: Author.

ERDBERG, P., & EXNER, J. E., JR. (1984). Rorschach assessment. In G. Goldstein & M. Hersen (Eds.), *Handbook of psychological assessment* (pp. 332–347). New York: Pergamon.

ERGENE, T. (2003). Effective interventions on test anxiety reduction a meta-analysis. *School Psychology International,* 24(3), 313–328.

ERICSSON, K. A. (1987). Theoretical implications from protocol analysis on testing and measurement. In R. R. Ronning, J. A. Glover, J. C. Conoley, &. J. C. Witt (Eds.), *The influence of cognitive psychology on testing* (pp. 191–226). Hillsdale, NJ: Erlbaum.

ERICSSON, K. A., & SIMON, H. A. (1993). *Protocol analysis: Verbal reports as data* (rev. ed.). Cambridge, MA: MIT Press.

ERICSSON, K. A., & SMITH, J. (Eds.). (1991). *Toward a general theory of expertise: Prospects and limits.* New York: Cambridge University Press.

ESQUIROL, J. E. D. (1838). *Des maladies mentales considérées sous les rapports medical, hygiénique, et médico-légal* (2 vols.). Paris: Bailliére.

ESTES, W. K. (1974). Learning theory and intelligence. *American Psychologist, 29,* 740–749.

ETS kit of factor-referenced cognitive tests. (1976). Princeton, NJ: Educational Testing Service.

ETS Standards for quality and fairness. (1987). Princeton, NJ: Educational Testing Service. (Original edition published 1981)

EVANS, F. R., & PIKE, L. W. (1973). The effects of instruction for three mathematics item formats. *Journal of Educational Measurement, 10,* 257–272.

EXNER, J. E., JR. (1966). Variations in WISC performances as influenced by differences in pretest rapport. *Journal of General Psychology, 74,* 299–306.

EXNER, J. E., JR. (1969). *The Rorschach systems.* New York: Grune & Stratton.

EXNER, J. E., JR. (1974). *The Rorschach: A comprehensive system.* New York: Wiley.

EXNER, J. E., JR. (1989). Searching for projection in the Rorschach. *Journal of Personality Assessment,* 53, 520–536.

EXNER, J. E., JR. (1991). *The Rorschach: A comprehensive system: Vol. 2. Interpretation (2nd ed.).* New York: Wiley.

EXNER, J. E., JR. (1992). R in Rorschach research: A ghost revisited. *Journal of Personality Assessment, 58,* 245–251.

EXNER, J. E., JR. (1993). *The Rorschach: A comprehensive system: Vol. 1. Basic foundations* (3rd ed.). New York: Wiley.

EXNER, J. E., JR. (Ed.). (1995). *Issues and methods in Rorschach research.* Mahwah, NJ: Erlbaum.

EXNER, J. E., JR. (1996). A comment on "The Comprehensive System for the Rorschach: A critical examination." *Psychological Science, 7,* 11–13.

EXNER, J. E., JR., & WEINER, I. B. (1995). *The Rorschach: A comprehensive system: Vol.* 3. Assessment *of children and adolescents* (2nd ed.). New York: Wiley.

EYDE, L. D. (1987). Computerized psychological testing: An introduction. *Applied Psychology: An International Review,* 36(3/4), 223–235.

EYDE, L. D., & KOWAL, D. M. (1987). Computerized test interpretation services: Ethical and professional concerns regarding U.S. producers and users. *Applied Psychology: An International Review,* 36(3/4), 401–417.

EYDE, L. D., MORELAND, K. L., ROBERTSON, G. J., PRIMOFF, E. S., & MOST, R. B. (1988). Test User Qualifications: A data-based approach to promoting good test use. *Issues in scientific psychology.* Washington, DC: American Psychological Association, Science Directorate.

EYDE, L. D., NESTER, M. A., HEATON, S. M., & NELSON, A. V. (1994). *Guide for administering written employment examinations to persons with disabilities.* Washington, DC: U. S. Office of Personnel Management.

EYDE, L. D., & QUAINTANCE, M. K. (1988). Ethical issues and cases in the practice of personnel psychology. *Professional Psychology: Research and Practice, 19*(2), 148–154.

EYDE, L. D., ROBERTSON, G. J., KRUG, S. E,, MORELAND, K. L., ROBERTSON, A. G., SHEWAN, C. M., HARRISON, P. L., PORCH, B. E., HAMMER, A. L., & PRIMOFF, E. S. (1993). *Responsible test use: Case studies for assessing human behavior.* Washington, DC: American Psychological Association.

FAGAN, J. F. (1992). Intelligence: A Theoretical Viewpoint. *Current Directions in Psychological Science, 1,* 82–86.

FAGAN, J. F. (1992). Intelligence: A theoretical viewpoint. *Current Directions in Psychological Science, 1*(3), 82–86.

FAGAN, J. F., & DETTERMAN, D. K. (1992). The Fagan Test of Infant Intelligence: A technical summary. *Journal of Applied Developmental Psychology, 13,* 173–193.

FAGGEN, J. (1987). Golden Rule revisited: Introduction. *Educational Measurement: Issues and Practice,* 6, 5–8

FANTUZZO, J. W., BLAKEY, W. A., & GORSUCH, R. L. (1989). *WAIS-R: Administration and scoring training manual.* San Antonio, TX: Psychological Corporation.

FARR, J. M. (Ed.). (1992). *The complete guide for occupational exploration.* Indianapolis, IN: JIST.

FEAGANS, L. V., SHORT, E. J., & MELTZER, L. J. (Eds.). (1991). *Subtypes of learning disabilities: Theoretical perspectives and research.* Hillsdale, NJ: Erlbaum.

FEAR, R. A., &. CHIRON, R. J. (1990). *The evaluation interview* (4th ed.). New York: McGraw-Hill.

FEDERAL REGISTER. (1977). *Handicapped Children Rule,* 42(250). Washington, DC: U.S. Government Printing Office.

FEDORAK, S., & COLES, E. M. (1979). Ipsative vs. normative interpretation of test scores: A comment on Allen and Forman's (1976) norms on Edwards Personal Preference Schedule for female Australian therapy students. *Perceptual and Motor Skills, 48,* 919–922.

FEINGOLD, A. (1995). The additive effects of differences in central tendency and variability are important in comparisons between groups. *American Psychologist, 50,* 5–13.

FELDHUSEN, J. F, & KLAUSMEIER, H. J. (1962). Anxiety, intelligence, and achievement in children of low, average, and high intelligence. *Child Development,* 33, 403–409.

FELDMAN, D. H., & BRATTON, J. C. (1972). Relativity and giftedness: Implications for equality of educational opportunity. *Exceptional Children, 38,* 491–492.

FELDMAN, J. M. (1986). Instrumentation and training for performance appraisal: A perceptual-cognitive viewpoint. In K. M. Rowland & G. Ferris (Eds.), *Research in personnel and human resources management* (Vol. 4). Greenwich, CT: JAI Press.

Feldt, L. S., &. Brennan, R. L. (1989). Reliability. In R. L. Linn (Ed.), *Educational measurement* (3rd ed., pp. 105–146). New York: American Council on Education/ Macmillan.

Ferguson, G. A. (1954). On learning and human ability. *Canadian Journal of Psychology, 8,* 95–112.

Ferguson, G. A. (1956). On transfer and the abilities of man. *Canadian Journal of Psychology, 10,* 121–131.

Ferguson, R. L., & Novick, M. R. (1973). *Implementation of a Bayesian system for decision analysis in a program of individually prescribed instruction* (ACT Res. Rep. No. 60). Iowa City: American College Testing Program.

Feuer, M. J., & Kober, N. (Eds.). (1995). *Anticipating Goals 2000: Standards, assessment, and public policy.* Washington, DC: National Academy Press.

Feuerstein, R. (1979). *The dynamic assessment of retarded performers: The Learning Potential Assessment Device, theory, instruments, and techniques.* Baltimore: University Park Press.

Feuerstein, R. (1980). *Instrumental enrichment: An intervention program for cognitive modifiability.* Baltimore: University Park Press.

Feuerstein, R. (1991). Cultural difference and cultural deprivation: Differential patterns of adaptability. In N. Bleichrodt &. P. J. D. Drenth (Eds.), *Contemporary issues in cross-cultural psychology* (pp. 21–33). Amsterdam: Swets & Zeitlinger.

Feuerstein, R., & Feuerstein, S. (1991). Mediated learning experience: A theoretical review. In R. Feuerstein, P. S. Klein, & A. J. Tannenbaum (Eds.), *Mediated learning experience (MLE): Theoretical, psychosocial, and learning implications* (pp. 3–51). London: Freund.

Feuerstein, R., Rand, Y., Jensen, M. R., Kaniel, S., & Tzuriel, D. (1987). Prerequisites for assessment of learning potential: The LPAD model. In C. S. Lidz (Ed.), *Dynamic* assessment: *An interactive approach to evaluating learning potential* (pp. 35–51). New York: Guilford Press.

Fewell, R. R. (1991). Assessment of visual functioning. In B. A. Bracken (Ed.), *The psychoeducational assessment of preschool children* (2nd ed., pp. 317–340). Boston: Allyn & Bacon.

Figueroa, R. A. (1990). Assessment of linguistic minority group children. In C. R. Reynolds & R. W. Kamphaus (Eds.), *Handbook of psychological and educational assessment of children: Intelligence and achievement* (pp. 671–696). New York: Guilford Press.

Figurelli, J. C., & Keller, H. R. (1972). The effects of training and socioeconomic class upon the acquisition of conservation concepts. *Child Development, 43,* 293–298.

Finding information about psychological tests. (1995). Washington, DC: American Psychological Association, Science Directorate.

Fineman, S. (1977). The achievement motive and its measurement. Where are we now? *British Journal of Psychology,* 68, 1–22.

Fink, A. (Ed.). (1995). *The survey kit* (Vols. 1–9). Thousand Oaks, CA: Sage.

Finkle, R. B. (1983). Managerial assessment centers. In M. D. Dunnette (Ed.), *Handbook of industrial and organizational psychology* (pp. 861–888). New York: Wiley.

Fischer, C. T. (1985). *Individualizing psychological assessment*. Monterey, CA: Brooks/Cole.

Fischer, J., &. Corcoran, K. (1994). *Measures for clinical practice: A sourcebook* (2nd ed., vols. 1–2). New York: Free Press.

Fiske, D. W. (1949). Consistency of the factorial structures of personality ratings from different sources. *Journal of Abnormal and Social Psychology, 44,* 329–344.

FISKE, D. W. (1973). Can a personality construct be validated empirically? *Psychological Bulletin, 80,* 89–92.

FISKE, M., & CHIRIBOGA, D. A. (1990). *Change mid continuity in adult life.* San Francisco: Jossey-Bass.

FITZGERALD, B. J., PASEWARK, R. A., & FLEISHER, S. (1974). Responses of an aged population on the Gerontological and Thematic Apperception Tests. *Journal of Personality Assessment, 38,* 234–235.

FLTZMAURICE, C., & WITT, J. C. (1989). Review of the Boehm Test of Basic Concepts—Revised. *Tenth Mental Measurements Yearbook,* 101–102.

FLANAGAN, D. P., & ALFONSO, V. C. (1995). A critical review of the technical characteristics of new and recently revised intelligence tests for preschool children. *Journal of Psychoeducational Assessment, 13,* 66–90.

FLANAGAN, D. P., GENSHAFT, J. L., & HARRISON, P. L. (Eds.). (1997). *Contemporary intellectual assessment: Theories, tests, and issues. New York: Guilford Press.*

FLANAGAN, J. C. (1947). Scientific development of the use of human resources: Progress in the Army Air Forces. *Science, 105,* 57–60.

FLANAGAN, J. C. (1949). Critical requirements: A new approach to employee evaluation. *Personnel Psychology, 2,* 419–425.

FLANAGAN, J. C. (1954). The critical incident technique. *Psychological Bulletin, 51,* 327–358.

FLANAGAN, J. C. (1962). Symposium: Standard scores for aptitude and achievement tests: Discussion. *Educational and Psychological* Measurement, 22, 35–39.

FLAVELL, J. H. (1963). *The developmental psychology of Jean Piaget.* New York: Van Nostrand-Reinhold.

FLAVELL, J. H. (1979). Metacognition and cognitive monitoring: A new area of cognitive-developmental inquiry. *American Psychologist, 34,* 906–911.

FLEISHMAN, E. A. (1972). On the relation between abilities, learning, and human performance. *American Psychologist,* 27, 1018–1032.

FLEISHMAN, E. A. (1975). Toward a taxonomy of human performance. *American* Psychologist, 30, 1127–1149.

FLEISHMAN, E. A., &. MUMFORD, M. D. (1989). Abilities as causes of individual differences in skill acquisition. *Human Performance,* 2 (3), 201–223.

FLEISHMAN, E. A., & MUMFORD, M. D. (1991). Evaluating classifications of job behavior: A construct validation of the ability requirement scales. *Personnel Psychology, 44,* 523–575.

FLEISHMAN, E. A., & QUAINTANCE, M. K. (1984). *Taxonomies of human performance: The description of human tasks.* Orlando, FL: Academic Press.

FLEISHMAN, E. A., & REILLY, M. E. (1992a). *Administrator's guide* F-JAS: *Fleishman Job Analysis Survey.* Bethesda, MD: Management Research Institute.

FLEISHMAN, E. A., & REILLY, M. E. (1992b). *Handbook of human abilities: Definitions, measurements, and job task requirements.* Bethesda, MD: Management Research Institute.

FLEMING, J. S., & COURTNEY, B. E. (1984). The dimensionality of self-esteem. II. Hierarchical facet model for revised measurement scales. *Journal of Personality and Social Psychology, 46,* 404–421.

FLEMING, J. S., & WHALEN, D. J. (1990). The Personal and Academic Self-Concept Inventory: Factor structure and gender differences in high school and college samples. *Educational and Psychological Measurement, 50, 951–961.*

FLYNN, J. R. (1984). The mean IQ of Americans: Massive gains 1932 to 1978. *Psychological Bulletin,* 95, 29–51.

FLYNN, J. R. (1987). Massive IQ Gains in 14 Nations: What IQ Tests Really Measure. *Psychological Bulletin,* *101*(2), 171.

Ibid., 171–191.

FLYNN, J. R. (2007). *What is intelligence?: Beyond the Flynn effect.* Cambridge University Press.

FOOTE, J., & KAHN, M. W. (1979). Discriminative effectiveness of the Senior Apperception Test with impaired and nonimpaired elderly persons. *Journal* of *Personality Assessment, 43,* 360–364.

FORSTER, A. A., & MATARAZZO, J. D. (1990). Assessing the intelligence of adolescents with the Wechsler Adult Intelligence Scale-Revised (WAIS-R). In C. R. Reynolds & R. W. Kamphaus (Eds.), *Handbook of psychological and educational assessment of children* (pp. 166–182). New York: Guilford Press.

FORTIER, M. S., VALLERAND, R. J., & GUAY, F. (1995). Academic motivation and school performance: Toward a structural model. *Contemporary Educational Psychology, 20,* 257–274.

FOUAD, N. A., & DANCER, L. S. (1992). Cross-cultural structure of interests: Mexico and the United States. *Journal of Vocational Behavior, 40,* 129–143.

FOWLER, R. D., &. BUTCHER, J. N. (1986). Critique of Matarazzo's views on computerized testing: All sigma and no meaning. *American Psychologist, 41,* 94–96.

FOX, R. A., & MEYER, D. J. (1990). Assessment of adaptive behavior. In A. F. Rotatori, R. A. Fox, D. Sexton, & J. Miller (Eds.), *Comprehensive assessment in special education: Approaches, procedures, and concerns* (pp. 309–338). Springfield, IL: Charles C Thomas.

FRANSELLA, E, & THOMAS, L. (1988). Experimenting *with* personal *construct psychology.* London: Routledge, Chapman & Hall.

FRANZ, S. I. (1919). *Handbook of mental examination methods* (2nd ed.). New York: Macmillan.

FREDERIKSEN, C. H. (1969). Abilities, transfer, and information retrieval in verbal learning. *Multivariate Behavioral Research Monographs,* No. 69–2.

FREDERIKSEN, N. (1962). Factors in in-basket performance. *Psychological Monographs,* 76(22, Whole No. 541).

FREDERIKSEN, N. (1965). Response set scores as predictors of performance. *Personnel Psychology, 18,* 225–244.

FREDERIKSEN, N. (1966). In-basket tests and factors in administrative performance. In A. Anastasi (Ed.), *Testing problems in perspective* (pp. 208–221). Washington, DC: American Council on Education.

FREDERIKSEN, N., &. GILBERT, A. C. F. (1960). Replication of a study of differential predictability. *Educational and Psychological Measurement, 20,* 759–767.

FREDERIKSEN, N., & MELVILLE, S. D. (1954). Differential predictability in the use of test scores. *Educational and Psychological Measurement, 14,* 647–656.

FREEBERG, N. E. (1969). Relevance of rater-ratee acquaintance in the validity and reliability of ratings. *Journal of Applied Psychology,* 53, 518–524.

FREEDENFELD, R. N., ORNDUFF, S. R., & KELSEY, R. M. (1995). Object relations and physical abuse: A TAT analysis. *Journal of Personality Assessment, 64,* 552–568.

FREEDLE, R. (Ed.). (1990). *Artificial intelligence and the future of testing.* Hillsdale, NJ: Erlbaum.

FREILICH, M., RAYBECK, D., & SAVISHINSKY, J. (Eds.). (1991). *Deviance:* Anthropological *perspectives.* Westport, CT: Greenwood.

FRENCH, J. W. (1951). The description of aptitude and achievement tests in terms of rotated factors. *Psychometric Monographs,* No. 5.

FRENCH, J. W. (1962). Effect of anxiety on verbal and mathematical examination scores. *Educational and Psychological Measurement, 22,* 553–564.

FRENCH, J. W. (1965). The relationship of problem-solving styles to the factor composition of tests. *Educational and Psychological Measurement, 25, 9–28.*

FRENCH, J. W. (1966). The logic of and assumptions underlying differential testing. In A. Anastasi (Ed.), *Testing problems in perspective* (pp. 321–330). Washington, DC: American Council on Education.

FRISCH, M. B. (1994). *QOL1—Quality of Life Inventory: Manual and treatment guide.* Minneapolis, MN: National Computer Systems.

FRUZZETTI, A. E., & JACOBSON, N. S. (1992). Assessment of couples. In J. C. Rosen & P. McReynolds (Eds.), *Advances in psychological assessment* (Vol. 8, pp. 201–224). New York: Plenum Press.

FRYER, D. (1931). *Measurement of interests.* New York: Holt.

FUCHS, L. S. (1993). Enhancing instructional programming and student achievement with curriculum-based measurement. In J. Kramer (Ed.), *Curriculum-based measurement* (pp. 65–104). Lincoln, NE: Buros Institute of Mental Measurements.

FUCHS, L. S., &. DENO, S. L. (1991). Paradigmatic distinctions between instructionally relevant measurement models. *Exceptional Children, 57,* 488–500.

FUNDER, D. C. (1991). Explorations in behavioral consistency: Properties of persons, situations, and behaviors. *Journal of Personality and Social Psychology, 60,* 773–794.

FUNDER, D. C., PARKE, R. D., TOMLINSON-KEASEY, C., & WIDAMAN, K. (Eds.). (1993). *Studying lives through time: Personality and development.* Washington, DC: American Psychological Association.

FURLONG, M., &. KARNO, M. (1995). Review of the Social Skills Rating System. *Twelfth Mental Measurements Yearbook,* 967–969.

FURNHAM, A. (1995). The relationship of personality and intelligence to cognitive learning style and achievement. In D. H. Saklofske & M. Zeidner (Eds.), *International handbook of personality and intelligence* (pp. 397–413). New York: Plenum Press.

GAGNÉ, R. (1965). *The conditions of learning.* New York: Holt, Rinehart & Winston.

GALTON, F. (1879). Psychometric experiments. *Brain, 2,* 149–162.

GALTON, F. (1883). *Inquiries into human faculty and its development. London:* Macmillan.

GAMBLE, K. R. (1972). The Holtzman Inkblot Technique: A review. *Psychological Bulletin,* 77, 172–194.

GARDNER, H. (1983). *Frames of mind: The theory of multiple intelligences.* New York: Basic Books.

GARDNER, H. (1992). Assessment in context: The alternative to standardized testing. In B. R. Gifford & M. C. O'Connor (Eds.), *Changing assessments: Alternative views of aptitude, achievement and instruction* (pp. 77–119). Boston: Kluwer.

GARDNER, H. (1993). *Multiple intelligences: The theory in practice.* New York: Basic Books.

GARDNER, J. W. (1961). *Excellence.* New York: Harper.

GATEWOOD, R. D., & FEILD, H. S. (1993). *Human resource selection* (3rd ed.). Chicago: Dryden Press.

GAUDRY, E., & SPIELBERGER, C. D. (1974). *Anxiety and educational achievement.* New York: Wiley.

GAUGLER, B. B., ROSENTHAL, D. B., THORNTON, G. C., III, & BENTSON, C. (1987). Meta-analysis of assessment center validity. *Journal of Applied Psychology, 72,* 493–511.

GDOWSKI, C. L., LACHAR, D., & KLINE, R. B. (1985). A PIC profile typology of children and adolescents: I. Empirically-derived alternative to traditional diagnosis. *Journal of Abnormal Psychology, 94,* 346–361.

GEARY, D. C. (1993). Mathematical disabilities: Cognitive, neuropsychological, and genetic components. *Psychological Bulletin, 114,* 345–362.

GEISINGER, K. F. (Ed.). (1992). *Psychological testing of Hispanics.* Washington, DC: American Psychological Association.

GEISINGER, K. F. (1994). Cross-cultural normative assessment: Translation and adaptation issues influencing the normative interpretation of assessment instruments. *Psychological Assessment, 6,* 304–312.

GELSO, C. J., & FRETZ, B. R. (1992). *Counseling psychology.* San Diego, CA: Harcourt Brace Jovanovich.

GENTILE, C. A., MARTIN-REHRMANN, J., & KENNEDY, J. H. (1995). *Windows into the classroom: NAEP's 1992 writing portfolio study.* Washington, DC: U.S. Department of Education, Office of Educational Research and Improvement.

GERBER, M. M., SEMMEL, D. S., & SEMMEL, M. I. (1994). Computer-based dynamic assessment of multidigit multiplication. *Exceptional Children, 61,* 114–125.

GERGEN, K. J. (1985). The social constructionist movement in modern psychology. *American Psychologist, 40,* 266–275.

GESELL, A., et al. (1940). *The first five years of life.* New York: Harper.

GESELL, A., & AMATRUDA, C. S. (1947). *Developmental diagnosis* (2nd ed.). New York: Hoeber-Harper.

GHISELLI, E. E. (1956). Differentiation of individuals in terms of their predictability. *Journal of Applied Psychology, 40,* 374–377.

GHISELLI, E. E. (1959). The generalization of validity. *Personnel Psychology, 12,* 397–402.

GHISELLI, E. E. (1960). The prediction of predictability. *Educational and Psychological Measurement, 20,* 3–8.

GHISELLI, E. E. (1963). Moderating effects and differential reliability and validity. *Journal of Applied Psychology, 47,* 81–86.

GHISELLI, E. E. (1966). *The validity of occupational aptitude tests.* New York: Wiley.

GHISELLI, E. E. (1968). Interaction of traits and motivational factors in the determination of the success of managers. *Journal of Applied Psychology, 52,* 480–483.

GIFFORD, B. R. (Ed.). (1989a). *Test policy and test performance: Education, language, and culture.* Boston: Kluwer.

GIFFORD, B. R. (Ed.). (1989b). *Test policy and the politics of opportunity allocation: The workplace and the law.* Boston: Kluwer.

GIFFORD, B. R., & O'CONNOR, M. C. (Eds.). (1992). *Changing assessments: Alternative views of aptitude, achievement, and instruction.* Boston: Kluwer.

GILBERT, J. A. (1894). Researches on the mental and physical development of school children. *Studies from the Yale Psychological Laboratory, 2,* 40–100.

GLASS, G. V. (1976). *Primary, secondary, and meta-analysis of research.* Educational Researcher, 5(10), 3–8.

GLNSBURG, H., & OPPER, S. (1969). *Piaget's theory of intellectual development: An introduction.* Englewood Cliffs, NJ: Prentice Hall.

GLRELLLI, S. A., & STAKE, J. E. (1993). Bipolarity in Jungian type theory and the Myers-Briggs Type Indicator. *Journal of Personality Assessment, 60,* 290–301.

GITOMER, D. H. (1993). Performance assessment and educational measurement. In R. E. Bennett & W. C. Ward (Eds.), *Construction versus choice in cognitive measurement: Issues in constructed response, performance testing, and portfolio assessment* (pp. 241–263). Hillsdale, NJ: Erlbaum.

GLASER, R. (1963). Instructional technology and the measurement of learning outcomes. *American Psychologist, 18,* 519–522.

GLASER, R. (1984). Education and thinking: The role of knowledge. *American Psychologist,* 39, 93–104.

GLASS, G. V. (1976). Primary, secondary, and meta-analysis of research. Educational Researcher, *5,* 3–8.

GLOBERSON, T., & ZELNIKER, T. (Eds.). (1989). *Cognitive style and cognitive development*. Norwood, NJ: Ablex.

GLUTTING, J. J., &. KAPLAN, D. (1990). Stanford-Binet Intelligence Scale: Fourth Edition: Making the case for reasonable interpretations. In C. R. Reynolds & R. W. Kamphaus (Eds.), *Handbook of psychological and educational assessment of children: Intelligence and Achievement* (pp. 277–295). New York: Guilford Press.

GLUTTING, J. J., & MCDERMOTT, P. A. (1990). Principles and problems in learning potential. In C. R. Reynolds & R. W. Kamphaus (Eds.), *Handbook of psychological and educational* assessment *of children: Intelligence and achievement* (pp. 296–347). New York: Guilford Press.

GLUTTING, J. J., MCDERMOTT, P. A., PRIFITERA, A., & MCGRATH, E. A. (1994). Core profile types for the WISC-III and WIAT: Their development and application in identifying multivariate IQ-achievement discrepancies. *School Psychology Review, 23,* 619–639.

GLUTTING, J. J., MCDERMOTT, P. A., PRIFITERA, A., & MCGRATH, E. A. (1995). "Core profile types for the *WISC-III* and WIAT: Their development and application in identifying multivariate IQ-achievement discrepancies": Errata. *School Psychology Revieiv, 24,* 123–124.

GLUTTING, J. J., MCDERMOTT, P. A., & STANLEY, J. C. (1987). Resolving differences among methods of establishing confidence limits for test scores. *Educational and Psychological Measurement, 47,* 607–614.

GLUTTING, J. J., & OAKLAND, T. (1992). *Guide to the Assessment of Test Session Behavior for the* WISC-III *and the W1AT* (GATSB). San Antonio, TX: Psychological Corporation.

GOETZ, E. T., & HALL, R. J. (1984). Evaluation of the Kaufman Assessment Battery for Children from an information-processing perspective. *Journal of Special Education, 18,* 281–296.

GOLDBERG, L. R. (1971). A historical survey of personality scales and inventories. In P. McReynolds (Ed.), *Advances in psychological assessment* (vol. 2, pp. 293–336). Palo Alto, CA: Science and Behavior Books.

GOLDBERG, L. R. (1991). Human mind versus regression equation: Five contrasts. In D. Cicchetti &. W. M. Grove (Eds.), *Thinking clearly about psychology: Essays in honor of Paul E. Meehl* (Vol. 1, pp. 173–184). Minneapolis: University of Minnesota Press.

GOLDBERG, L. R. (1993). The structure of phenotypic personality traits. *American Psychologist, 48,* 26–34.

GOLDBERG, L. R., GRENIER, J. R., GUION, R. M., SECHREST, L. B., & WING, H. *(1991). Questionnaires used in the prediction of trustworthiness in pre-employment selection decisions: An APA task force report*. Washington, DC: American Psychological Association.

GOLDBERG, P. A. (1965). A review of sentence completion methods in personality assessment. *Journal of Projective Techniques and Personality Assessment, 29,* 12–45.

GOLDEN, C. J. (1981). The Luria-Nebraska Children's Battery: Theory and formulation. In G. W. Hynd & J. E. Obrzut (Eds.), *Neuropsychological assessment and the school-age child: Issues and procedures* (pp. 277–302). New York: Grune & Stratton.

GOLDEN, C. J. (1987). Computers in neuropsychology. In J. N. Butcher (Ed.), *Computerized psychological assessment: A practitioner's guide* (pp. 344–354). New York: Basic Books.

GOLDEN, C. J., PURISCH, A. D., & HAMMEKE, T. A. (1985). *Luria-Nebraska Neuropsychological Battery: Forms I and II Manual.* Los Angeles: Western Psychological Services.

GOLDEN, C. J., ZLLLMER, E. A., & SPIERS, M. V. (1992). *Neuropsychological* assessment *and intervention.* Springfield, IL: Charles C Thomas.

GOLDFARB, R., & HALPERN, H. (1984). Word association responses in normal adult subjects. *Journal of Psycholinguistic Research, 13,* 37–55.

GOLDFRIED, M. R., &. KENT, R. N. (1972). Traditional versus behavioral personality assessment: A comparison of methodological and theoretical assumptions. *Psychological Bulletin,* 77, 409–420.

GOLDING, S. L., & RORER, L. G. (1972). Illusory correlation and subjective judgment. *Journal of Abnormal Psychology, 80,* 249–260.

GOLDMAN, B. A., & MITCHELL, D. F. (1995). *Directory of unpublished experimental mental measures* (Vol. 6). Washington, DC: American Psychological Association.

GOLDSCHMID, M. L. (1968). Role of experience in the acquisition of conservation. *Proceedings of the 76th Annual Convention of the American Psychological Association,* 361–362.

GOLDSCHMID, M. L., & BENTLER, P. M. (1968a). Dimensions and measurements of conservation. *Child Development, 39,* 787–802.

GOLDSCHMID, M. L., &. BENTLER, P. M. *(1968b). Manual: Concept Assessment Kit—Conservation.* San Diego, CA: Educational and Industrial Testing Service.

GOLDSCHMID, M. L., BENTLER, P. M., DEBUS, R. L., RAWLINSON, R., KOHNSTAMM, MODGIL, S., NICHOLLS, J. G., REYKOWSKI, J., STRUPCZEWSKA, B., WARREN, N. (1973). A cross-cultural investigation of conservation. *Journal of Cross-Cultural Psychology, 4,* 75–88.

GOLDSMITH, R. E., & NUGENT, N. (1984). Innovativeness and cognitive complexity: A second look. *Psychological Reports, 55,* 431–438.

GOLDSTEIN, F. C., & LEVIN, H. S. (1985). Intellectual and academic outcome following closed head injury in children and adolescents: Research strategies and empirical findings. *Developmental Neuropsychology, 1,* 195–214.

GOLDSTEIN, G., & HERSEN, M. (Eds.) (1990). *Handbook of psychological assessment* (2nd ed.). New York: Pergamon Press.

GOLDSTEIN, I. L., ZEDECK, S., & SCHNEIDER, B. (1993). An exploration of the job analysis-content validity process. In N. Schmitt, W. C. Borman, et al. (Eds.), *Personnel selection in organizations* (pp. 3–34). San Francisco: Jossey-Bass.

GOLDSTEIN, K., & SCHEERER, M. (1941). Abstract and concrete behavior: An experimental study with special tests. *Psychological Monographs,* 53(2, Whole No. 230).

GOLDSTEIN, K. M., & BLACKMAN, S. (1978a). Assessment of cognitive style. In P. McReynolds (Ed.), *Advances in psychological* assessment (Vol. 4, pp. 462–525). San Francisco: Jossey-Bass.

GOLDSTEIN, K. M., & BLACKMAN, S. (1978b). *Cognitive style: Five approaches and relevant research.* New York: Wiley-Interscience.

GOLEMAN, D. (1995). *Emotional intelligence.* New York: Bantam Books.

GONCALVES, A. A., WOODWARD, M. J„ & MLLLON, T. (1994). Millon Clinical Multiaxial Inventory-II. In M. E. Maruish (Ed.), *The use of psychological testing for treatment planning and outcome assessment* (pp. 161–184). Hillsdale, NJ: Erlbaum.

GONZALEZ, R. (1996). Circles and squares, spheres and cubes: What's the deal with circumplex models? *Journal of Vocational Behavior, 48,* 77–84.

GOODENOUCH, D. R. (1976). The role of individual differences in field dependence as a factor in learning and memory. *Psychological Bulletin, 83,* 675–694.

GOODENOUCH, F. L. (1949). *Mental testing: Its history, principles, and applications.* New York: Rinehart.

GOODGLASS, H. (1986). The flexible battery in neuropsychological assessment. In T. Incagnoli, G. Goldstein, & C. J. Golden (Eds.), *Clinical application of neuropsychological test batteries* (pp. 121–134). New York: Plenum Press.

GOODMAN, J. F. (1990). Infant intelligence: Do we, can we, should we assess it? In C. R. Reynolds & R. W. Kamphaus (Eds.), *Handbook of psychological and educational assessment of children: Intelligence and achievement* (pp. 183–208). New York: Guilford Press.

GOODNOW, J. J. (1976). The nature of intelligent behavior: Questions raised by cross-cultural studies. In L. B. Resnick (Ed.), *The nature of intelligence* (pp. 169–188). Hillsdale, NJ: Erlbaum.

GOODYEAR, R. K. (1990). Research on the effects of test interpretation: A review. *Counseling Psychologist, 18,* 240–257.

GORDEN, R. L. (1992). *Basic interviewing skills.* Itasca, IL: F. E. Peacock.

GORDON, L. V., & ALF, E. F. (1960). Acclimatization and aptitude test performance. *Educational and Psychological Measurement, 20,* 333–337.

GORDON, M. A. (1953). *A study of the applicability of the same minimum qualifying scores for technical schools to White males, WAF, and Negro males* (Tech. Rep. No. 53–34). Lackland Air Force Base, TX: Personnel Research Laboratory.

GORMLY, A. V., & BRODZINSKY, D. M. (1993). *Life-span human development* (5th ed.). San Diego, CA: Harcourt Brace Jovanovich.

GOTTFREDSON, G. D. (1996). Prestige in vocational interests. *Journal of Vocational Behavior, 48,* 68–72.

GOTTFREDSON, G. D., &. HOLLAND, J. L. (1989). *Dictionary of Holland occupational codes (DHOC)* (2nd ed.). Odessa, FL: Psychological Assessment Resources.

GOTTFREDSON, L. S. (Ed.). (1986a). The g factor in employment. *Journal of Vocational Behavior, 29,* 293–450.

GOTTFREDSON, L. S. (1986b). Special groups and the beneficial use of vocational interest inventories. In W. B. Walsh & S. H. Osipow (Eds.), *Advances in vocational psychology: Vol. 1. The assessment of interests* (pp. 127–198). Hillsdale, NJ: Erlbaum.

GOTTFREDSON, L. S. (1994). The science and politics of race-norming. *American* Psychologist, 49, 955–963.

GOTTFRIED, A. W., & BRODY, N. (1975). Interrelationships between and correlates of psychometric and Piagetian scales of sensorimotor intelligence. *Developmental Psychology, 11,* 379–387.

GOTTMAN, J. M. (1994). *What predicts divorce! The relationship between marital processes and marital outcomes.* Hillsdale, NJ: Erlbaum.

GOTTMAN, J. M. (Ed.). (1995). *The analysis of change.* Hillsdale, NJ: Erlbaum.

GOTTMAN, J. M. (Ed.). (1996). *What predicts divorce?: The measures.* Mahwah, NJ: Erlbaum.

GOUGH, H. G. (1960). The Adjective Check List as a personality assessment research technique. *Psychological Reports, 6,* 107–122.

GOUGH, H. G. (1984). A managerial potential scale for the California Psychological Inventory. *Journal of Applied Psychology, 69,* 233–240.

GOUGH, H. G. (1985). A work orientation scale for the California Psychological Inventory. *Journal of Applied Psychology, 70,* 505–513.

GOUGH, H. G. (1987). *California Psychological Inventory Administrator's guide.* Palo Alto, CA: Consulting Psychologists Press.

GOUGH, H. G., (2002). CPI™ Bibliography. Mountain View, CA: CPP, Inc.

GOUGH, H. G., & BRADLEY, P. (1996). *CPI manual* (3rd ed.). Palo Alto, CA: Consulting Psychologists Press.

GOUGH, H. G., & BRADLEY, P. (1996). CPI™ manual (3rd ed.). Mountain View, CA: CPP, Inc.

GOUGH, H. G., & HEILBRUN, A. B., JR. (1980). *The Adjective Check List bibliography.* Palo Alto, CA: Consulting Psychologists Press.

GOUGH, H. G., & HEILBRUN, A. B., JR. (1983). *The Adjective Check List manual* (rev. ed.). Palo Alto, CA: Consulting Psychologists Press.

GRAHAM, J. R. (1993). MMPI-2: *Assessing personality and psychopathology* (2nd ed.). New York: Oxford University Press.

GRAVES, L. M. (1993). Sources of individual differences in interviewer effectiveness: A model and implications for future research. *Journal of Organizational Behavior, 14,* 349–370.

GRAVES, L. M., & POWELL, G. N. (1988). An investigation of sex discrimination in recruiters' evaluations of actual applications. *Journal of Applied Psychology, 73,* 20–29.

GRAYBILL, D. (1990). Developmental changes in the response types versus aggression categories on the Rosenzweig Picture-Frustration Study, Children's Form. *Journal of Personality Assessment, 55,* 603–609.

GRAYBILL, D. (1993). A longitudinal study of changes in children's thought content in response to frustration on the Children's Picture-Frustration Study. *Journal of Personality Assessment, 61,* 531–535.

GRE 1995–96 *guide to the use of the Graduate Record Examinations Program.* (1995). Princeton, NJ: Educational Testing Service.

GREDLER, G. R. (1992). *School readiness:* Assessment *and educational issues.* Brandon, VT: Clinical Psychology.

GREEN, B. F. (1983). The promise of tailored tests. In H. Wainer & S. Messick (Eds.), *Principals of modern psychological measurement* (pp. 69–80). Hillsdale, NJ: Erlbaum.

GREEN, B. F., BOCK, R. D., HUMPHREYS, L. G., LINN, R. L., &. RECKASE, M. D. (1984). Technical guidelines for assessing computerized adaptive tests. *Journal of Educational Measurement, 21,* 347–360.

GREEN, B. F., JR., &. WIGDOR, A. K. (1991). Measuring job competency. In A. K. Wigdor & B. F. Green, Jr. (Eds.), *Performance assessment in the workplace: Vol. 2. Technical issues* (pp. 53–74). Washington, DC: National Academy Press.

GREEN, D. R., FORD, M. R, &. FLAMER, G. B. (Eds.) (1971). *Measurement and Piaget: Proceedings of the CTB/McGraw-Hill Conference on Ordinal Scales of Cognitive Development.* New York: McGraw-Hill.

GREENE, R. L. (1978). An empirically derived MMPI carelessness scale. *Journal of Clinical Psychology, 34,* 407–410.

GREENE, R. L. (1991). *The MMP1–2/MMPI: An interpretive manual.* Boston: Allyn & Bacon.

GREENO, J. G. (1989). A perspective on thinking. *American Psychologist, 44,* 134–141.

GREENWALD, G. (1982). Intelligence for peace: First international symposium on Venezuelan project for development of intelligence. *Human Intelligence International Newsletter,* 3 (6), pp. 1, 3.

GREENWALD, G. (1984). Venezuelan ministry ends—Intelligence projects continue. *Human Intelligence International Newsletter,* 5(1), p. 1.

GREENWOOD, J. M., & MCNAMARA, W. J. (1967). Interrater reliability in situational tests. *Journal of Applied Psychology, 51,* 101–106.

GREGG, N., HOY, C., & GAY, A. F. (Eds.). (1996). *Adults with learning disabilities: Theoretical and practical perspectives.* New York: Guilford Press.

GREGORY, R. J. (2015). *Psychological Testing: History, Principles, and Applications.* Harlow: Pearson.

GRESHAM, F. M., & ELLIOTT, S. N. (1990). *Social Skills Rating System: Manual.* Circle Pines, MN: American Guidance Service.

GRESHAM, F. M., ELLIOTT, S. N., &. EVANS-FERNANDEZ, S. E. (1993). *Student Self-Concept Scale: Manual.* Circle Pines, MN: American Guidance Service.

GRESHAM, F. M., &. LITTLE, S. G. (1993). Peer-referenced assessment strategies. In T. H. Ollendick & M. Hersen (Eds.), *Handbook of child and adolescent assessment* (pp. 165–179). Boston: Allyn & Bacon.

GRESHAM, F. M., MACMILLAN, D. L., SIPERSTEIN, G. N. (1995). Critical analysis of the 1992 AAMR definition: Implications for school psychology. *School Psychology Quarterly,* 10, 1–19.

GRIBBONS, W. D., &. LOHNES, P. R. (1982). *Careers in theory and experience.* Albany: State University of New York Press.

GRIGORENKO, E. L., & STERNBERG, R. J. (1995). Thinking styles. In D. H. Saklofske & M. Zeidner (Eds.), *International handbook of personality and intelligence* (pp. 205–229). New York: Plenum Press.

GROAT, L. (ed.). (1995). *Giving places meaning.* San Diego, CA: Academic Press.

GROENVELD, M., & JAN, J. E. (1992). Intelligence profiles of low vision and blind children. *Journal of Visual Impairment and Blindness, 86,* 68–71.

GROOMS, R. R., &. ENDLER, N. S. (1960). The effect of anxiety on academic achievement. *Journal of Educational Psychology,* 51, 299–304.

GROSS, A. L., FAGGEN, J., & MCCARTHY, K. (1974). The differential predictability of the college performance of males and females. *Educational and Psychological Measurement, 34,* 363–365.

GROSS, A. L., & SU, W. H. (1975). Defining a "fair" or "unbiased" selection model: A question of utilities. *Journal of Applied Psychology, 60,* 345–351.

GROSSMAN, H. J. (ed.). (1983). *Classification in mental retardation.* Washington, DC: American Association on Mental Retardation.

GROTH-MARNAT, G. (1990). *Handbook of psychological* assessment (2nd ed.). New York: Wiley.

GUERTIN, W. H., FRANK, G. H., & RABIN, A. I. (1956). Research with the Wechsler-Bellevue Intelligence Scale: 1950–1955. *Psychological Bulletin, 53,* 235–257.

GUERTIN, W. H., LADD, C. E., FRANK, G. H., RABIN, A. I., & HIESTER, D. S. (1966). Research with the Wechsler Intelligence Scale for Adults: 1960–1965. *Psychological Bulletin,* 66, 385–409.

GUERTIN, W. H., LADD, C. E., FRANK, G. H., RABIN, A. I., & HIESTER, D. S. (1971). Research with the Wechsler Intelligence Scale for Adults: 1965–1970. *Psychological Record, 21,* 289–339.

GUERTIN, W. H., RABIN, A. I., FRANK, G. H., & LADD, C. E. (1962). Research with the Wechsler Intelligence Scale for Adults: 1955–1960. *Psychological Bulletin, 59,* 1–26.

Guidelines for providers of psychological services to ethnic, linguistic, and culturally diverse populations. (1993). *American Psychologist, 48,* 45–48.

GUILFORD, J. P. (1959). *Personality.* New York: McGraw-Hill.

GUILFORD, J. P. (1967). *The nature of human intelligence.* New York: McGraw-Hill.

GUILFORD, J. P. (1981). Higher-order structure-of-intellect abilities. *Multivariate Behavioral Research, 16,* 411–435.

GUILFORD, J. P. (1988). Some changes in the Structure-of-Intellect Model. *Educational and Psychological Measurement, 48,* 1–4.

GUILFORD, J. P., & FRUCHTER, B. (1978). *Fundamental statistics in psychology and education* (6th ed.). New York: McGraw-Hill.

GUILFORD, J. P., & HOEPFNER, R. (1971). *The analysis of* intelligence. New York: McGraw-Hill.

GUILFORD, J. P. & ZIMMERMAN, W. S. (1956). Fourteen dimensions of temperament. *Psychological Monographs,* 70 (10, Whole No. 417).

GUION, R. M. (1991). Personnel assessment, selection, and placement. In M. D. Dunnette &. L. M. Hough (Eds.), *Handbook of industrial and organizational psychology* (2nd ed., Vol. 2, pp. 327–397). Palo Alto, CA: Consulting Psychologists Press.

GUION, R. M., &. GIBSON, W. M. (1988). Personnel selection and placement. *Annual Review of Psychology, 39,* 349–374.

GULLIKSEN, H. (1950). *Theory of mental tests.* New York: Wiley.

GULLIKSEN, H., &. WILKS, S. S. (1950). Regression tests tor several samples. *Psychometrika, 15,* 91–114.

GUR, R. C., & GUR, R. E. (1991). The impact of neuroimaging on human neuropsychology. In R. G. Lister & H. J. Weingartner (Eds.), *Perspectives in cognitive neuroscience* (pp. 417–435). New York: Oxford University Press.

GUR, R. C., & GUR, R. E. (1994). Methods for the study of brain-behavior relationships. In A. Frazer, P. B. Molinoff, & A. Winokur (Eds.), *Biological bases of brain function and disease* (pp. 261–279). New York: Raven Press.

GUSTAFSSON, J. E. (1984). A unifying model for the structure of intellectual abilities. *Intelligence*, 8, 179–203.

GUSTAFSSON, J. E. (1989). Broad and narrow abilities in research on learning and instruction. In R. Kanfer, R L. Ackerman, & R. Cudeck (Eds.), *Abilities, motivation, and methodology* (pp. 203–237). Hillsdale, NJ: Erlbaum.

GUTHRIE, G. M., JACKSON, D. N., ASTILLA, E., & ELWOOD, B. (1983). Personality measurement: Do the scales have similar meanings in another culture? In S. H. Irvine & J. W. Berry (Eds.), *Human assessment and cultural factors* (pp. 377–382). New York: Plenum Press.

GUTKIN, T. B., & REYNOLDS, C. R. (1981). Factorial similarity of the WISC-R for white and black children from the standardization sample. *Journal of Educational Psychology,* 73, 227–231.

GUTKIN, T. B., & WISE, S. (Eds.). (1991). *The computer and the decision-making process.* Hillsdale, NJ: Erlbaum.

GUTTMAN, I., & RAJU, N. S. (1965). A minimum loss function as determiner of optimal cutting scores. *Personnel Psychology, 18,* 179–185.

GUTTMAN, L. (1944). A basis for scaling qualitative data. *American Sociological Review, 9,* 139–150.

GUTTMAN, L. (1947). The Cornell technique for scale and intensity analysis. *Educational and Psychological Measurement*, 7, 247–280.

GYURKE, J. S. (1991). The assessment of preschool children with the Wechsler Preschool and Primary Scale of Intelligence—Revised. In B. A. Bracken (Ed.), *The psychoeducational assessment of preschool children* (2nd ed., pp. 86–106). Boston: Allyn & Bacon.

HAAK, R. A. (1990). Using the sentence completion to assess emotional disturbance. In C. R. Reynolds & R. W. Kamphaus (Eds.), *Handbook of psychological and educational* assessment *of children: Personality, behavior, and context* (pp. 147–167). New York: Guilford Press.

HACKETT, G., & LONBORG, S. D. (1994). Career assessment and counseling for women. In W. B. Walsh & S. H. Osipow (Eds.), *Career counseling for women* (pp. 43–85). Hillsdale, NJ: Erlbaum.

HAFNER, J. L., FAKOURI, M. E., & LABRENTZ, H. L. (1982). First memories of "normal" and alcoholic individuals. *Individual Psychology: Journal of Adlerian Theory, Research, and Practice, 38,* 238–244.

HAGTVET, K. A., & JOHNSEN, T. B. (Eds.). (1992). *Advances in test anxiety research* (Vol. 7). Amsterdam: Swets & Zeitlinger.

HALADYNA, T. M. (1994). *Developing and validating multiple-choice test items.* Hillsdale, NJ: Erlbaum.

HALADYNA, T.M. AND ROID, G.H. (1983). A comparison of two approaches to criterion referenced test construction. *Journal of Educational Measurement*, 20, 271–282.

HALE, G. A., BRIDGEMAN, B., LEWIS, C., POLLACK, J. M., &. WANG, M. (1992). *A comparison of the predictive validity of the current SAT and an experimental prototype* (ETS Res. Rep. 92–32). Princeton, NJ: Educational Testing Service.

HALSTEAD, W. C. (1947). *Brain and intelligence.* Chicago: University of Chicago Press.

HALVERSON, H. M. (1933). The acquisition of skill in infancy. *Journal of Genetic Psychology, 43,* 3–48.

HAMBLETON, R. K. (1984a). Determining test length. In R. A. Berk (Ed.), A *guide to criterion-referenced test construction* (pp. 144–168). Baltimore: Johns Hopkins University Press.

HAMBLETON, R. K. (1984b). Validating the test score. In R. A. Berk (Ed.), A *guide to criterion-referenced test construction* (pp. 199–230). Baltimore: Johns Hopkins University Press.

HAMBLETON, R. K. (1989). Principles and selected applications of item responses theory. In R. L. Linn (Ed.), *Educational measurement* (3rd ed., pp. 147–200). New York: American Council on Education/Macmillan.

HAMBLETON, R. K. (1994). Guidelines for adapting educational and psychological tests: A progress report. *European Journal of Psychological Assessment, 10,* 229–244.

HAMBLETON, R. K. (1996). *Guidelines for adapting tests (Final Report).* Washington, DC: National Center for Education Statistics.

HAMBLETON, R. K., & NOVICK, M. R. (1973). Toward an integration of theory and method for criterion-referenced tests .*Journal of Educational Measurement, 10,* 159–170.

HAMBLETON, R. K., & ROGERS, H. J. (1989). Detecting potentially biased test items: Comparison of IRT area and the Mantel-Haenszel methods. *Applied Measurement in Education,* 2, 313–334.

HAMBLETON, R. K., SWAMINATHAN, H. S., & ROGERS, H. J. (1991). *Fundamentals of item response theory.* Newbury Park, CA: Sage.

HAMERS, J. H. M., SIJTSMA, K., & RUIJSSENAARS, A. J. J. M. (Eds.). (1993). *Learning potential assessment: Theoretical, methodological, and practical issues.* Amsterdam: Swets & Zeitlinger.

HAMILTON, J. L., & BIJDOFF, M. (1974). Learning potential among the moderately and severely mentally retarded. *Mental Retardation, 12,* 33–36.

HAMILTON, R. G., & ROBERTSON, M. H. (1966). Examiner influence on the Holtzman Inkblot Technique. *Journal of Projective Techniques and Personality Assessment, 30,* 553–558.

HAMMER, E. F. (1986). Graphic techniques with children and adolescents. In A. I. Rabin (Ed.), *Projective techniques for adolescents and children* (pp. 239–263). New York: Springer.

HANDLER, L. (1996). The clinical use of drawings: Draw-A-Person, House-Tree-Person, and Kinetic Family drawings. In C. S. Newmark (Ed.), *Major psychological assessment instruments* (2nd ed., pp. 206–293). Boston: Allyn &. Bacon.

HANDLER, L., & HABENICHT, D. (1994). The Kinetic Family Drawing technique: A review of the literature. *Journal of Personality Assessment*, 62, 440–464.

HANDLER, L., & MEYER, G. J. (1996, Spring/Summer). Put your money where your mouth is! Mary Cerney's legacy. SPA *Exchange, 6*, 6–7.

HANNA, G.S., SONNENSCHEIN, J. L., & LENKE, J. M. (1983). The contribution of work-sample test items, student reported past grades, and student predicted grades in forecasting achievement in first-year algebra. *Educational and Psychological Measurements, 43*, 243–249.

HANSEN, J. C. (1987). Cross-cultural research on vocational interests. Measurement *and Evaluation in Counseling and Development, 19*, 163–176.

HANSEN, J. C. (1990). Interest inventories. In G. Goldstein & M. Hersen (Eds.), *Handbook of psychological assessment* (2nd ed., pp. 173–194). New York: Pergamon Press.

HANSEN, J. C. (1996). What goes around, comes around. *Journal of Vocational Behavior, 48*, 73–76.

HANSEN, J. C., & CAMPBELL, D. P. (1985). *Manual for the SVIB-SCII* (4th ed.). Stanford, CA: Stanford University Press.

HANSON, F. A. (1993). *Testing testing: Social consequences of the examined life. Berkeley:* University of California Press.

HAPLIP, B., JR., & PANEK, P, E. (1993). *Adult development and aging* (2nd ed.). New York: Harper-Collins College.

HARDT, R. H, EYDE, L. D., PRIMOFF, E. S., & TORDY, G. R. (1981). *The New York State Trooper job element examination: Final technical report.* Albany: New York State Police. (National Technical Information Service, Springfield, VA 22161)

HARKNESS, A. R., MCNULTY, J. L., & BEN-PORATH, Y. S. (1995). The Personality Psychopathology Five (PSY-5): Constructs and MMPI-2 scales. *Psychological Assessment, 7*, 104–114.

HARLOW, H. F. (1949). The formation of learning sets. *Psychological Revieiv, 56*, 51–65.

HARLOW, H. F. (1960). Learning set and error factor theory. In S. Koch (Ed.), *Psychology:* A *study of a science* (Vol. 2, pp. 492–537). New York: McGraw-Hill.

HARMAN, H. H. (1975). *Final report of research on assessing human abilities* (ONR Contract N00014-71-C-0117 Project NR 150 329). Princeton, NJ: Educational Testing Service.

HARMAN, H. H. (1976). *Modern factor analysis* (3rd ed.). Chicago: University of Chicago Press.

HARMON, L. W. (1996). Lost in space: A response to "The spherical representation of vocational interests" by Tracey and Rounds. *Journal of Vocational Behavior, 48*, 53–58.

HARMON, L. W., HANSEN, J. C., BORGEN, F. H., & HAMMER, A. L. (1994). *Strong Interest Inventory: Applications and technical guide.* Palo Alto, CA: Consulting Psychologists Press.

HÄRNQVIST, K. (1968). Relative changes in intelligence from 13 to 18. *Scandinavian Journal of Psychology, 9*, 50–82.

HARRÉ, R., &. STEARNS, P. (Eds.).(1995). *Discursive psychology in practice.* Thousand Oaks, CA: Sage.

HARRINGTON, T. F., & O'SHEA, A. J. (1982). *The Harrington-O'Shea Career Decision-making System: Manual for Use with Self-scored and Machine-scored Editions.* American Guidance Service.

HARRINGTON, T. F., & O'SHEA, A. J. (1993). *The Harrington-O'Shea Career Decision-Making System Revised: Manual.* Circle Pines, MN: American Guidance Service.

HARRIS, D. B. (1963). *Children's drawings as measures of intellectual maturity: A revision and extension of the Goodenough Draw-a-Man Test.* San Diego, CA: Harcourt Brace Jovanovich.

HARRIS, J. A. (1973). The computer: Guidance tool of the future. In W. E. Coffman (Ed.), *Frontiers of educational measurement and information systems—1973* (pp. 121–142). Boston: Houghton Mifflin.

HARRIS, M. J., & ROSENTHAL, R. (1985). Mediation of interpersonal expectancy effects: 31 meta-analyses. *Psychological Bulletin, 97*, 363–386.

HARRISON, P. L. (1985). *Vineland Adaptive Behavior Scales: Classroom Edition manual*. Circle Pines, MN: American Guidance Service.

HARRISON, R. (1965). Thematic apperception methods. In B. B. Wolman (Ed.), *Handbook of clinical psychology* (pp. 562–620). New York: McGraw-Hill.

HART, B., & RLSLEY, T. R. (1995). *Meaningful differences in the everyday experience of young American children*. Baltimore: Brookes.

HART, D. H. (1986). The sentence completion techniques. In H. M. Knoff (Ed.), *The assessment of child and adolescent personality* (pp. 245–272). New York: Guilford Press.

HARTER, S. (1990). Issues in the assessment of the self-concept of children and adolescents. In A. M. La Greca (Ed.), *Through the eyes of the child: Obtaining self-reports from children and adolescents* (pp. 292–325). Boston: Allyn & Bacon.

HARTIGAN, J. A., & WIGDOR, A. K. (Eds.). (1989). *Fairness in employment testing: Validity generalization minority issues, and the General Aptitude Test Battery.* Washington, DC: National Academy Press.

HARTLE, T. W., & BATTAGLIA, P. A. (1993). The federal role in standardized testing. In R. E. Bennett & W. C. Ward (Eds.), *Construction versus choice in cognitive measurement: Issues in constructed response, performance testing, and portfolio assessment* (pp. 291–311). Hillsdale, NJ: Erlbaum.

HARTMANN, D. P, & WOOD, D. D. (1990). Observational methods. In A. S. Bellack, M. Hersen, & A. E. Kazdin (Eds.), *International handbook of behavior modification and therapy* (2nd ed., pp. 107–138). New York: Plenum Press.

HARTSHORNE, H., & MAY, M. A. (1928). *Studies in deceit*. New York: Macmillan.

HARTSHORNE, H., MAY, M. A., & MALLER, J. B. (1929). *Studies in service and self-control*. New York: Macmillan.

HARTSHORNE, H., MAY, M. A., & SHUTTLEWORTH, F. K. (1930). *Studies in the organization of character.* New York: Macmillan.

HARVEY, R. J. (1991). Job Analysis. in M. D. Dunnette & L. M. Hough (Eds.), *Handbook of industrial and organizational psychology* (2nd ed., Vol. 2, pp. 71–163). Palo Alto, CA: Consulting Psychologists Press.

HARVEY, R. J., &. MURRY, W. D. (1994). Scoring the Myers-Briggs Type Indicator: Empirical comparison of preference score versus latent-trait methods. *Journal of Personality Assessment, 62*, 116–129.

HASKINS, R. (1989). Beyond metaphor: The efficacy of early childhood education. *American Psychologist, 44*, 274–282.

HASSELBLAD, V., & HEDGES, L. V. (1995). Meta-analysis of screening and diagnostic tests. *Psychological Bulletin, 117*, 167–178.

HATHAWAY, S. R., & MCKINLEY, J. C. (1940). A Multiphasic Personality Schedule (Minnesota): I. Construction of the schedule. *Journal of Psychology, 10*, 249–254.

HATHAWAY, S. R., & MCKINLEY, J. C. (1943). *The Minnesota Multiphasic Personality Inventory* (rev. ed.). Minneapolis: University of Minnesota Press.

HATT, C. V. (1985). Review of Children's Apperception Test. *Ninth Mental Measurements Yearbook*, Vol. 1, 315–316.

HATTIE, J. (1992). Self-concept. Hillsdale, NJ: Erlbaum.

HATTRUP, K. (1995). Review of the Differential Aptitude Tests, Fifth Edition. *Twelfth Mental Measurements Yearbook*, 302–304.

HAVILAND, J. (1976). Looking smart: The relationship between affect and intelligence in infancy. In M. Lewis (Ed.), *Origins of intelligence: Infancy* and *early childhood* (pp. 353–377). New York: Plenum Press.

HAWK, J. A. (1970). Linearity of criterion-GATB aptitude relationships. *Measurement and Evaluation in Guidance, 2*, 249–251.

HAYDUK, L. A. (1988). *Structural equation modeling with LISREL: Essentials and advances.* Baltimore: Johns Hopkins University Press.

HAYES, S. P. (1942). Alternative scales for the mental measurement of the visually handicapped. *Outlook for the Blind, 36*, 225–230.

HAYES, S. P. (1943). A second test scale for the mental measurement of the visually handicapped. *Outlook for the Blind, 37*, 37–41.

HAYNES, S. N. (1991). Behavioral assessment. In M. Hersen, A. E. Kazdin, & A. S. Bellack (Eds.), *The clinical psychology handbook* (2nd ed., pp. 430–464). New York: Pergamon Press.

HEATON, R. K., BAADE, L. E., &. JOHNSON, K. L. (1978). Neuropsychological test results associated with psychiatric disorders in adults. *Psychological Bulletin, 85*, 141–162.

HEATON, R. K., GRANT, I., & MATTHEWS, C. G. (1991). *Comprehensive norms for an expanded Halstead-Reitan battery.* Odessa, FL: Psychological Assessment Resources.

HEBB, D. O. (1970). A return to Jensen and his social science critics. *American Psychologist, 25*, 568.

HEDGES, L. V. (1988). The meta-analysis of test validity studies: Some new approaches. In R. Wainer & H. I. Braun (Eds.), *Test validity* (pp. 191–212). Hillsdale, NJ: Erlbaum.

HEDGES, L. V., & NOWELL, A. (1995). Sex differences in mental test scores, variability, and numbers of high-scoring individuals. Science, 269, 41–45.

HEILBRUN, A. B., JR. (1964). Social-learning theory, social desirability, and the MMPI. *Psychological Bulletin, 61*, 377–387.

HEILBRUN, A. B., JR. (1985). Review of the California Child Q-Set. *Ninth Mental* Measurements *Yearbook*, Vol. 1, 248–249.

HEIN, M., & WESLEY, S. (1994). Scaling biodata through subgrouping. In G. S. Stokes, M. D. Mumford, & W. A. Owens (Eds.), *Biodata handbook: Theory, research, and use of biographical information in selection and performance prediction* (pp. 171–196). Palo Alto, CA: Consulting Psychologists Press.

HELFRICH, H. (1986). On linguistic variables influencing the understanding of questionnaire items. In A. Angleitner & J. S. Wiggins (Eds.), *Personality assessment via questionnaires: Current issues in theory and measurement* (pp. 178–188). Berlin: Springer Verlag.

HELMES, E., & JACKSON, D. N. (1989). Prediction models of personality item responding. *Multivariate Behavioral Research, 24*, 71–91.

HELMES, E., & REDDON, J. R. (1993). A perspective on developments in assessing psychopathology: A critical review of the MMPI and MMPI-2. *Psychological Bulletin, 113*, 453–471.

HELSON, R., & WINK, P. (1992). Personality change in women from the early 40s to the early 50s. *Psychology and Aging*, 7, 46–55.

HENRY, B., MOFFITT, T. E., CASPI, A., LANGLEY, J., & SILVA, P. A. (1994). On the "Remembrance of things past": A longitudinal evaluation of the retrospective method. *Psychological Assessment*, 6, 92–101.

HENRY, W. E. (1956). *The analysis of fantasy: The thematic apperception technique in the study of personality.* New York: Wiley.

HENRY, W. E., & FARLEY, J. (1959). The validity of the Thematic Apperception Test in the study of adolescent personality. *Psychological Monographs, 73* (17, Whole No. 487).

HERMAN, S. J. (1994). *Hiring right: A practical guide.* Thousand Oaks, CA: Sage.

HERR, E. L. (1989). Review of the Kuder Occupational Interest Survey, Revised (Form DD). *Tenth Mental Measurements Yearbook,* 425–427.

HERRNSTEIN, R. J., & MURRAY, C. (1994). *The Bell Curve: Intelligence and Class Structure in American life.* New York: Free Press.

HERRNSTEIN, R. J., NICKERSON, R. S., SÁNCHEZ, M., & SWETS, J. A. (1986). Teaching thinking skills. *American Psychologist, 41,* 1279–1289.

HERRON, E. W. (1964). Changes in inkblot perception with presentation of the Holtzman inkblot technique as an "intelligence test." *Journal of Projective Techniques and Personality Assessment, 28,* 442–447.

HERSEN, M., KAZDIN, A. E., & BELLACK, A. S. (Eds.). (1991). *The clinical psychology handbook* (2nd ed.). Elmsford, NY: Pergamon Press.

HERZBERGER, S. D., LLNNEY, J. A., SEIDMAN, E., & RAPPAPORT, J. (1979). Preschool and primary locus of control scale: Is it ready for use? *Developmental Psychology, 15,* 320–324.

HESSEL, M. G. P., & HAMERS, J. H. M. (1993). The Learning Potential Test for Ethnic Minorities. In J. H. M. Hamers, K. Sijtsma, &. A. J. J. M. Ruijssenaars (Eds.), *Learning potential* assessment: *Theoretical, methodological, and practical issues.* Amsterdam: Swets & Zeitlinger.

HETHERINGTON, E. M., REISS, D., & PLOMIN, R. (Eds.). (1993). *The separate social worlds of siblings: The impact of nonshared environment on development.* HILLSDALE, *NJ:* Erlbaum.

HEWER, V. H. (1965). Are tests fair to college students from homes with low socioeconomic status? *Personnel and Guidance Journal, 43,* 764–769.

HIBBARD, S., FARMER, L., WELLS, C., DIFILLIPO, E., BARRY, W., KORMAN, R., & SLOAN, R (1994). Validation of Cramer's defense mechanism manual for the TAT. *Journal of Personality Assessment,* 63, 197–210.

HICKS, L. E. (1970). Some properties of ipsative, normative, and forced normative measures. *Psychological Bulletin, 74,* 167–184.

HILL, D. J., & BALE, R. M. (1980). Development of the Mental Health Locus of Control and Mental Health Locus of Origin Scales. *Journal of Personality Assessment, 44,* 148–156.

HILL, E. F. (1972). *Holtztnan Inkblot Technique: A handbook for clinical application.* San Francisco: Jossey-Bass.

HILL, K. T., & SARASON, S. B. (1966). The relation of test anxiety and defensiveness to test and school performance over the elementary school years. *Monographs of the Society for Research in Child Development, 31,* (2, Serial No. 104).

HILL, T. D., REDDON, J. R., & JACKSON, D. N. (1985). The factor structure of the Wechsler Scales: A brief review. *Clinical Psychology Review,* 5, 287–306.

HIRSH, S. K. (1995). *Strong Interest Inventory resource: Strategies for group and individual interpretations in business and organizational settings.* Palo Alto, CA: Consulting Psychologists Press.

HLSKEY, M. S. (1966). *The Hiskey-Nebraska Test of Learning Aptitude.* Lincoln, NE: Union College Press.

HOBBS, N. (1975a). *The futures of children.* San Francisco: Jossey-Bass.

HOBBS, N. (Ed.). (1975b). *Issues in the classification of children* (Vols. 1 & 2). San Francisco: Jossey-Bass.

HODAPP, R. M., BURACK, J. A., & ZLGLER, E. (Eds.). (1990). *Issues in the developmental approach to mental retardation.* New York: Cambridge University Press.

HODGES, K., & ZEMAN, J. (1993). Interviewing. In T. H. Ollendick & M. Hersen (Eds.), *Handbook of child and adolescent assessment* (pp. 65–81). Boston: Allyn & Bacon.

HOFER, P. J., &. GREEN, B. F. (1985). The challenge of competence and creativity in computerized psychological testing. *Journal of Consulting and Clinical Psychology, 53,* 826–838.

HOFFMAN, B. (1962). *The tyranny of testing.* New York: Crowell-Collier.

HOFSTEE, W. K. B., DE RAAD, B. & GOLDBERG, L. R. (1992). Integration of the Big Five and circumplex approaches to trait structure. *Journal of Personality and Social Psychology,* 63, 146–163.

HOGAN, J. C. (1992). Physical Abilities. in M. D. Dunnette & L. M. Hough (Eds.), *Handbook of industrial and organizational psychology* (2nd ed., Vol. 2, pp. 753–831). Palo Alto, CA: Consulting Psychologists Press.

HOGAN, R. T. (1991). Personality and personality measurement. In M. D. Dunnette & L. M. Hough (Eds.), *Handbook of industrial and organizational psychology* (2nd ed., Vol. 2, pp. 873–919). Palo Alto, CA: Consulting Psychologists Press.

HOGAN, R., CURPHY, G. J., & HOGAN, J. (1994). What we know about leadership: Effectiveness and personality. *American Psychologist, 49,* 493–504.

HOGAN, R., DESOTO, S. B., & SOLANO, C. (1977). Traits, tests, and personality research. *American Psychologist, 32,* 255–264.

HOGAN, R., & HOGAN, J. (1992). *Hogan Personality Inventory manual* (2nd ed.). Tulsa, OK: Hogan Assessment Systems.

HOGAN, R., HOGAN, J., &. ROBERTS, B. W. (1996). Personality measurement and employment decisions: Questions and answers. *American Psychologist, 51,* 469–477.

HOGAN, R., & NICHOLSON, R. A. (1988). The meaning of personality test scores. *American Psychologist,* 43, 621–626.

HOLDEN, R. R., & JACKSON, D. N. (1992). Assessing psychopathology using the Basic Personality Inventory: Rationale and applications. In J. C. Rosen & P. McReynolds (Eds.), *Advances in psychological assessment* (Vol. 8, pp. 165–199). New York: Plenum Press.

HOLLAND, J. L. (1959). A theory of vocational choice. *Journal of Counseling Psychology, 59,* 35–45.

HOLLAND, J. L. (1966). *The psychology of vocational choice.* Waltham, MA: Blaisdell.

HOLLAND, J. L. (1985). *The self directed search: Specimen set.* Psychological Assessment Resources.

HOLLAND, J. L. (1986). New directions for interest testing. In B. S. Plake & J. C. Witt (Eds.), *The future of testing* (pp. 245–267). Hillsdale, NJ: Erlbaum.

HOLLAND, J. L. (1992). *Making vocational choices: A theory of vocational personalities and work environments* (2nd ed.). Odessa, FL: Psychological Assessment Resources. (Original work published 1985)

HOLLAND, J. L., FRITZSCHE, B. A., & POWELL, A. B. (1994). *The Self Directed Search* (SDS) *Technical manual—1994 edition.* Odessa, FL: Psychological Assessment Resources.

HOLLAND, J. L., & GOTTFREDSON, G. D. (1976). Using a typology of persons and environments to explain careers; some extensions and clarification. *Counseling Psychologist,* 6, 20–29.

HOLLAND, J. L., & GOTTFREDSON, G. D. (1992). Studies of the hexagonal model: An evaluation (or, The perils of stalking the perfect hexagon). *Journal of Vocational Behavior, 40,* 158–170.

HOLLAND, J. L., POWELL, A. B., & FRITZSCHE, B. A. (1994). *The Self-Directed Search (SDS) Professional* user's *guide-1994 edition.* Odessa, FL: Psychological Assessment Resources.

HOLLAND, P. W., & RUBIN, D. B. (Eds.). (1982). *Test equating.* New York: Academic Press.

HOLLAND, P. W., & THAYER, D. T. (1988). Differential item performance and the Mantel-Haenszel procedure. In H. Wainer & H. Braun (Eds.), *Test validity* (pp. 129–145). Hillsdale, NJ: Erlbaum.

HOLLAND, P. W., & WAINER, H. (Eds.). (1993). *Differential item functioning: Theory and Practice.* Hillsdale, NJ: Erlbaum.

HOLLANDER, P. (1982). Legal context of educational testing. In A.K. Wigdor & W.R. Gamer (Eds.), *Ability testing: Uses, consequences, and controversies* (pp.195–231). Washington, DC: National Academic Press.

HOLLENBECK, G. R, &. KAUFMAN, A. S. (1973). Factor analysis of the Wechsler Preschool and Primary Scale of Intelligence (WPPSI). *Journal of Clinical Psychology, 29,* 41–45.

HOLLENBECK, J. R., & WHITEMER, E. M. (1988). Criterion-related validation for small sample contexts: An integrated approach to synthetic validity. *Journal of Applied Psychology, 73, 536–544.*

HOLLINGSHEAD, A. B. (1957). *Two-factor index of social position.* Unpublished manuscript, Yale University, Department of Sociology, New Haven, CT.

HOLMSTROM, R. W., SLLBER, D. E., & KARP, S. A. (1990). Development of the Apperceptive Personality Test. *Journal of Personality Assessment, 54,* 252–264.

HOLTZMAN, W. H. (1961). *Guide to administration and scoring: Holtzman Inkblot Technique.* New York: Psychological Corporation.

HOLTZMAN, W. H. (Ed.). (1970). *Computer-assisted instruction, testing, and guidance.* New York: Harper & Row.

HOLTZMAN, W. H. (1975). New developments in Holtzman Inkblot Technique. In P. McReynolds (Ed.), *Advances in psychological assessment* (Vol. 3, pp. 243–274). San Francisco: Jossey-Bass.

HOLTZMAN, W. H. (1986). Holtzman Inkblot Technique (HIT). In A. I. Rabin (Ed.), *Assessment with projective techniques: A concise introduction,* (pp. 47–83). New York: Springer.

HOLTZMAN, W. H. (1988). *Beyond the Rorschach. Journal of Personality Assessment, 52, 578–609.*

HOLTZMAN, W. H., MOSELEY, E. C., REINEHR, R. C., & ABBOTT, E. (1963). Comparison of the group method and the standard individual version of the Holtzman Inkblot Technique. *Journal of Clinical Psychology, 19,* 441–449.

HOLTZMAN, W. H., THORPE, J. S., SWARTZ, J. D., & HERRON, E. W. (1961). *Inkblot perception and personality—Holtzman Inkblot Technique.* Austin: University of Texas Press.

HONTS, C. R. (1994). Psychophysiological detection of deception. *Current Directions in Psychological Science, 3,* 77–82.

HONZIK, M. P. (1967). Environmental correlates of mental growth: Prediction from the family setting at 21 months. *Child Development, 38,* 337–364.

HONZIK, M. P, MACFARLANE, J. W., &. ALLEN, L. (1948). The stability of mental test performance between two and eighteen years. *Journal of Experimental Education, 17,* 309–324.

HOOD, A. B., & JOHNSON, R. W. (1997). *Assessment in counseling: A guide to the use of psychological assessment procedures* (2nd ed.). Alexandria, VA: American Counseling Association.

HOOPER, F. H. (1973). Cognitive assessment across the life-span: Methodological implications of the organismic approach. In J. R. Nesselroade & H. W. Reese (Eds.), *Life span developmental psychology: Methodological issues* (pp. 299–316). New York: Academic Press.

HOOPER, S. R., & WILLIS, W. C. (1989). *Neuropsychological foundations, conceptual models, and issues in clinical differentiation.* New York: Springer-Verlag.

HOPKINS, K. D., & STANLEY, J. C. (1981). *Educational and psychological measurement and evaluation* (6th ed.). Englewood Cliffs, NJ: Prentice Hall.

HORN, J. L. (1976). Human abilities: A review of research and theory in the early 1970s. *Annual Review of Psychology,* 27, 437–485.

HORN, J. L., & CATTELL, R. B. (1966). Refinement and test of the theory of fluid and crystallized general intelligences. *Journal of Educational Psychology, 57,* 253–270.

HORN, J. L., & KNAPP, J. R. (1973). On the subjective character of the empirical base of Guilford's structure-of-intellect model. *Psychological Bulletin,* 80, 33–43.

HORN, J. L., WANBERG, K. W., & FOSTER, F. M. (1990). *Guide to the Alcohol Use Inventory (AUI).* Minneapolis, MN: National Computer Systems.

HOROWITZ, F. D. (1994). The nature-nurture controversy in social and historical perspective. In F. Kessel (Ed.), *Psychology, science, and human affairs Essays in honor of William Bevan* (pp. 84–99). Boulder, CO: Westview Press.

HOROWITZ, F. D., & O'BRIEN, M. (Eds.). (1985). *The gifted and talented: Developmental perspectives.* Washington, DC: American Psychological Association.

HOROWITZ, F. D., & O'BRIEN, M. O. (Eds.). (1989). Children and their development: Knowledge base, research agenda, and social policy application [Special issue]. *American Psychologist, 44* (2).

HORST, P. (1954). A technique for the development of a differential prediction battery. *Psychological Monographs, 68 (9, Whole No. 380).*

HOUGH, L. M., EATON, N. K., DUNNETTE, M. D., KAMP, J. D., & MCCLOY, R. A. (1990). Criterion-related validities of personality constructs and the effect of response distortion on those validities. *Journal of Applied Psychology Monograph, 75,* 581–595.

HOUGH, L., & PAULLIN, C. (1994). Construct-oriented scale construction: The rational approach. In G. S. Stokes, M. D. Mumford, & W. A. Owens (Eds.), *Biodata handbook: Theory, research, and use of biographical information in selection and performance prediction* (pp. 109–145). Palo Alto, CA: Consulting Psychologists Press.

HOUSE, J. D. (1995). The predictive relationship between academic self-concept, achievement expectancies, and grade performance in college calculus. *Journal of Social Psychology, 135,* 111–112.

HOWARD, A., & BRAY, D. W. (1988). *Managerial lives in transition: Advancing age and changing times.* New York: Guilford Press.

HOWELL, D. C. (1997). *Statistical methods for psychology* (4th ed.). Belmont, CA: Duxbury Press.

HOWELL, K. W., & RUEDA, R. (1996). Achievement testing with culturally and linguistically diverse students. In L. A. Suzuki, P. J. Meller, & J. G. Ponterotto (Eds.), *Handbook of multicultural assessment: Clinical, psychological, and educational applications* (pp. 253–290). San Francisco: Jossey-Bass.

HRNCIR, E. J., SPELLER, G. M., & WEST, M. (1985). What are we testing? *Developmental Psychology, 21,* 226–232.

HU, S., & OAKLAND, T. (1991). Global and regional perspectives on testing children and youth: An empirical study. *International Journal of Psychology, 26,* 329–344.

HUGHES, J. (1990). Assessment of social skills: Sociometric and behavioral approaches. In C. R. Reynolds & R. W. Kamphaus (Eds.), *Handbook of psychological and educational assessment of children: Personality, behavior, and context* (pp. 423–444). New York: Guilford Press.

HULL, C. L. (1928). *Aptitude testing.* Yonkers, NY: World Book.

HUMPHREY, D. H., & DAHLSTROM, W. G. (1995). The impact ot changing from the MMPI to the MMPI-2 on profile configurations. *Journal of Personality Assessment, 64,* 428–439.

Humphreys, L. G. (1952). Individual differences. *Annual Review of Psychology, 3,* 131–150.

Humphreys, L. G. (1962). The organization of human abilities. *American Psychologist, 17,* 475–483.

Humphreys, L. G. (1970). A skeptical look at the factor pure test. In C. Lunneborg (Ed.), *Current problems and techniques in multivariate psychology* (pp. 23–32). Seattle: University of Washington Press.

Humphreys, L. G. (1973). Statistical definitions of test validity for minority groups. *Journal of Applied Psychology, 58,* 1–4.

Humphreys, L. G. (1979). The construct of general intelligence. *Intelligence, 3,* 105–120.

Humphreys, L. G., Rich, S. A., & Davey, T. C. (1985). A Piagetian test of general intelligence. *Developmental Psychology, 21,* 872–877.

Hunt, E. (1987). Science, technology, and intelligence. In R. R. Ronning, J. A. Glover, J. C. Conoley, & J. C. Witt (Eds.), *The influence of cognitive psychology on testing* (pp. 11–40). Hillsdale, NJ: Erlbaum.

Hunt, J. McV. (1976). The utility of ordinal scales inspired by Piaget's observations. *Merrill-Palmer Quarterly, 22,* 31–45.

Hunt, J. McV. (1981). Experiential roots of intention, initiative, and trust. In H. I. Day (Ed.), *Advances in intrinsic motivation and aesthetics* (pp. 169–202). New York: Plenum Press.

Hunt, J. McV., & Kirk, G. E. (1974). Criterion-referenced tests of school readiness: A paradigm with illustrations. *Genetic Psychology Monographs, 90,* 143–182.

Hunter, J. E. (1986). Cognitive ability, cognitive aptitudes, job knowledge, and job performance. *Journal of Vocational Behavior, 29,* 340–362.

Hunter, J. E., & Hunter, R. F. (1984). Validity and utility of alternative predictors of job performance. *Psychological Bulletin, 96,* 72–98.

Hunter, J. E., & Schmidt, F. L. (1976). Critical analysis of the statistical and ethical implications of various definitions of *test bias. Psychological Bulletin, 83,* 1053–1071.

Hunter, J. E., & Schmidt, F. L. (1981). Fitting people into jobs: The impact of personnel selection on national productivity. In M. A. Dunnette & E. A. Fleishman (Eds.), *Human performance and productivity: Vol. 1. Human capability assessment* (pp. 233–284). Hillsdale, NJ: Erlbaum.

Hunter, J. E., & Schmidt, F. L. (1990). *Methods of meta-analysis: Correcting error and bias in research findings.* Newbury Park, CA: Sage.

Hunter, J. E., Schmidt, F. L., & Hunter, R. (1979). Differential validity of employment tests by race: A comprehensive review and analysis. *Psychological Bulletin, 86,* 721–735.

Hunter, J. E., Schmidt, F. L., & Judiesch, M. K. (1990). Individual differences in output variability as a function of job complexity. *Journal of Applied Psychology, 75,* 28–42.

Hunter, J. E., Schmidt, F. L., & Rauschenberger, J. M. (1977). Fairness of psychological tests: Implications of four definitions tor selection utility and minority hiring. *Journal of Applied Psychology, 62,* 245–260.

Hunter, J. E., Schmidt, F. L., &. Rauschenberger, J. (1984). Methodological, statistical, and ethical issues in the study of bias in psychological tests. In C. E. Reynolds & R. T. Brown (Eds.), *Perspectives on bias in mental testing* (pp. 41–99). New York: Plenum Press.

Hurt, S. W., Reznikoff, M., &. Clarkin, J. F. (1991). *Psychological assessment, psychiatric diagnosis, and treatment planning.* New York: Brunner-Mazel.

HUSÉN, T. (1951). The influence of schooling upon IQ. *Theoria, 17,* 61–88.

HY, L. X., & LOEVINGER, J. (1996). *Measuring ego development* (2nd ed.). Mahwah, NJ: Erlbaum.

INHELDER, B., DE CAPRONA, D., & CORNU-WELLS, A. (Eds.). (1987). *Piaget today.* Hove, England: Erlbaum.

INTELLIGENCE AND ITS MEASUREMENT: A SYMPOSIUM. (1921). *Journal of Educational Psychology, 12,* 123–147, 195–216.

IRETON, H., THWING, E., & GRAVEM, H. (1970). Infant mental development and neurological status, family socioeconomic status, and intelligence at age four. *Child Development, 41,* 937–945.

IRONSON, G. H., GUION, R. M., & OSTRANDER, M. (1982). Adverse impact from a psychometric perspective. *Journal of Applied Psychology, 67,* 419–432.

IRVINE, S. H. (1969a). Factor analyses of African abilities and attainments: Constructs across cultures. *Psychological Bulletin, 71,* 20–32.

IRVINE, S. H. (1969b). Figural tests of reasoning in Africa: Studies in the use of Raven's matrices across cultures. *International Journal of Psychology, 4,* 217–228.

IRVINE, S. H. (1983). Testing in Africa and America. In S. H. Irvine & J. W. Berry (Eds.), *Human assessment and cultural factors* (pp. 45–58). New York: Plenum Press.

IRVINE, S. H., & BERRY, J. W. (Eds.). (1988). *Human abilities in cultural contexts.* New York: Cambridge University Press.

IRVINE, S. H., & CARROLL, W. K. (1980). Testing and assessment among cultures: Issues in methodology and theory. In H. C. Triandis et al.(Eds.), *Handbook of cross-cultural psychology* (Vol. 2, pp. 181–244). Boston: Allyn & Bacon.

ISAACS, M., & CHEN, K. (1990). Presence/absence of an observer in a word association test. *Journal of Personality Assessment*, 55, 41–51.

IVNIK, R. J., MALEC, J. E, SMITH, G. E., TANGALOS, E. G., PETERSEN, R. C., KORMEN, E., & KURLAND, L. T. (1992). Mayo's older Americans normative studies: WAIS-R norms for ages 56 to 97. *Clinical Neuropsychologist,* 6(Suppl.), 1–30.

IZARD, C. E., KAGAN, J., & ZAJONC, R. B. (Eds.). (1989). *Emotions, cognition, and behavior.* New York: Cambridge University Press.

JACKSON, D. N. (1970). A sequential system for personality scale development. In C. D. Spielberger (Ed.), *Current topics in clinical and community psychology* (Vol. 2, pp. 61–96). New York: Academic Press.

JACKSON, D. N. (1971). The dynamics of structured personality tests. *Psychological Review, 78,* 229–248.

JACKSON, D. N. (1973). Structured personality assessment. In B. B. Wolman (Ed.), *Handbook of general psychology* (pp. 775–792). Englewood Cliffs, NJ: Prentice Hall.

JACKSON, D. N. (1976). *Jackson Personality Inventory: Manual.* Port Huron, MI: Research Psychologists Press.

JACKSON, D. N. (1977). *Jackson Vocational Interest Survey manual.* Port Huron, MI: Research Psychologists Press.

JACKSON, D. N. (1985). Computer-based personality testing. *Computers in Human Behavior, 1,* 225–264.

JACKSON, D. N. (1986a). *Career Directions Inventory manual.* Port Huron, MI: Research Psychologists Press.

JACKSON, D. N. (1986b). The process of responding in personality assessment. In A. Angleitner & J. S. Wiggins (Eds.), *Personality assessment via questionnaires: Current issues in theory and measurement* (pp. 123–142). Berlin: Springer-Verlag.

JACKSON, D. N. (1989a). *Basic Personality Inventory: BPI manual.* Port Huron, MI: Sigma Assessment Systems.

JACKSON, D. N. (1989b). *Personality Research Form manual* (3rd ed.). Port Huron, MI: Sigma Assessment Systems.

JACKSON, D. N. (1991). Computer-assisted personality test interpretation: The dawn of discovery. In T. B. Gutkin & S. L. Wise (Eds.), *The computer and the decision-making process* (pp. 1–10). Hillsdale, NJ: Erlbaum.

JACKSON, D. N. (1994a). *Jackson Personality Inventory-Revised: Manual*. Port Huron, MI: Sigma Assessment Systems.

JACKSON, D. N. (1994b). *Multidimensional Aptitude Battery* (MAB): *Manual*. Port Huron, ML: Sigma Assessment Systems. (1st ed., 1984)

JACKSON, D. N. (1995). *JVIS occupations guide*. Port Huron, Ml: Sigma Assessment Systems.

JACKSON, D. N., GUTHRIE, G. M., ASTILLA, E., & ELWOOD, B. (1983). The cross-cultural generalization of personality construct measures. In S. H. Irvine & J. W. Berry (Eds.), *Human assessment and cultural factors* (pp. 365–375). New York: Plenum Press.

JACKSON, D. N., & MESSICK, S. (1958). Content and style in personality assessment. *Psychological Bulletin, 55, 243–252.*

JACKSON, D. N., & MESSICK, S. (1962). Response styles and the assessment of psychopathology. In S. Messick & J. Ross (Eds.), *Measurement in personality and cognition* (pp. 129–155). New York: Wiley.

JACKSON, D. N., & PAUNONEN, S. V. (1980). Personality structure and assessment. *Annual Review of Psychology, 31,* 503–551.

JACKSON, D. N., & WILLIAMS, D. R. (1975). Occupational classification in terms of interest patterns. *Journal of Vocational Behavior, 6,* 269–280.

JACOB, S., & HARTSHORNE, T.S. (1991). *Ethics and law for school psychologists.* Brandon, VT: Clinical Psychology Publishing Co.

JACOBS, A., &. BARRON, R. (1968). Falsification of the Guilford-Zimmerman Temperament Survey: II. Making a poor impression. *Psychological Reports, 23,* 1271–1277.

JACOBS, P. I., & VANDEVENTER, M. (1971). The learning and transfer of double-classification skills: A replication and extension. *Journal of Experimental Child Psychology, 12,* 140–157.

JACOBSON, J. W., &. MULICK, J. A. (Eds.). (1996). *Manual of diagnosis and professional practice in mental retardation*. Washington, DC: American Psychological Association.

JAEGER, R. M. (1973). The national test-equating study in reading (The Anchor Test Study). NCME *Measurement in Education, 4* (4), 1–8.

JAEGER, R. M. (Ed.) (1977). Applications of latent trait models [Special issue]. *Journal of Educational Measurement, 14* (2).

JAEGER, R. M. (1989). Certification of student competence. In R. L. Linn (Ed.), *Educational measurement* (3rd ed., pp. 485–514). New York: American Council on Education/Macmillan.

JAMES, L. A., &. JAMES, L. R. (1989). Integrating work environment perceptions: Explorations into the measurement of meaning. *Journal of Applied Psychology, 74,* 739–751.

JAMES, L. R. (1973). Criterion models and construct validity for criteria. *Psychological Bulletin, 80,* 75–83.

JAMES, L. R. (1980). The unmeasured variable problem in path analysis. *Journal of Applied Psychology, 65,* 415–421.

JAMES, L. R., DEMAREE, R. G., MULAIK, S. A., & LADD, R. T. (1992). Validity generalization in the context of situational models. *Journal of Applied Psychology, 77,* 3–14.

James, L. R., Mulaik, S. A., & Brett, J. M. (1982). *Causal analysis: Assumptions, models, and data*. Beverly Hills, CA: Sage Publications.

Jaynes, J. H., & Wlodkowski, R. J. (1990). *Eager to learn: Helping children become motivated and love learning.* San Francisco: Jossey-Bass.

Jenkins, J. J., & Russell, W. A. (1960). Systematic changes in word association norms: 1910–1952. *Journal of Abnormal Psychology, 60,* 293–304.

Jensen, A. R. (1968). Social class and verbal learning. In M. Deutsch, I. Katz, & A. R. Jensen (Eds.), *Social class, race, and psychological development* (pp. 115–174). New York: Holt, Rinehart & Winston.

Jensen, A. R. (1969). How much can we boost IQ and scholastic achievement? *Harvard Educational Review,* 39, 1–123.

Jensen, A. R. (1973). *Educability and group differences*. London: Methuen.

Jensen, A. R. (1984). The black-white difference on the K-ABC: Implications for future tests. *Journal of Special Education, 18,* 377–408.

Jitendra, A. K., Kameenui, E. J., & Carnine, D. W. (1994). An exploratory evaluation of dynamic assessment and the role of basals on comprehension of mathematical operations. *Education and Treatment of Children, 17,* 139–162.

Johansson, C. B. (1984). Career Assessment *Inventory: The Vocational Version* (2nd ed.). Minneapolis, MN: National Computer Systems.

Johansson, C. B. (1986). *Career Assessment Inventory: The Enhanced Version.* Minneapolis, MN: National Computer Systems.

John, O. P., Angleitner, A., & Ostendorf, F. (1988). The lexical approach to personality: A historical review of trait taxonomic research. *European Journal of Personality,* 2, 171–203.

Johnson, A. P. (1951). Notes on a suggested index of item validity: The U-L index. *Journal of Educational Psychology, 42, 499–504.*

Johnson, D. L., Swank, P., Howie, V. M„ Baldwin, C. D., Owen, M., & Luttman, D. (1993). Does the HOME add to the prediction of child intelligence over and above SES? *Journal of Genetic Psychology, 154,* 33–40.

Johnson, E. G. (1992). The design of the National Assessment of Educational Progress. *Journal of Educational Measurement, 29,* 95–110.

Johnson, N. L., & Gold, S. N. (1995). The Defense Mechanism Profile: A sentence completion test. In H. R. Conte & R. Plutchik (Eds.), *Ego defenses: Theory and measurement* (pp. 247–262). New York: Wiley.

Joint Committee on Testing Practices (JCTP). (1988). *Code of fair testing practices in education*. Washington, DC: Author. (Information about the Joint Committee is available from the Joint Committee on Testing Practices, American Psychological Association, 750 First Street, NE, Washington, DC 20002.)

Jonassen, D. H., & Grabowski, B. L. (1993). *Handbook of individual differences, learning, and instruction*. Hillsdale, NJ: Erlbaum.

Jones, L. E., & Koehly, L. M. (1993). Multidimensional scaling. In G. Keren & C. Lewis (Eds.), A *handbook for data analysis in the behavioral sciences: Methodological issues* (pp. 95–163). Hillsdale, NJ: Erlbaum.

Jones, L. V., & Appelbaum, M. I. (1989). Psychometric methods. *Annual Review of Psychology, 40,* 23–43.

Jones, P. B., &. Sabers, D. L. (1992). Examining test data using multivariate procedures. In M. Zeidner & R. Most (Eds.), *Psychological testing: An inside view* (pp. 297–339). Palo Alto, CA: Consulting Psychologists Press.

Jones, R. R., Reid, J. B., &. Patterson, G. R. (1975). Naturalistic observation in clinical assessment. In P. McReynolds (Ed.), *Advances in psychological assessment* (Vol. 3, pp. 42–95). San Francisco: Jossey-Bass.

JÖRESKOG, K. G., &. SÖRBOM, D. (1986). *LISREL: Analysis of linear structural relationships by maximum likelihood, instrumental variables, and least squares methods* (4th ed.). Mooresville, IN: Scientific Software.

JÖRESKOG, K. G., & SÖRBOM, D. (1989). *LISREL 7 User's Guide.* Mooresville, IN: Scientific Software.

JÖRESKOG, K. G., & SÖRBOM, D. (1993). *LISREL 8 structural equation modeling with the S1MPL1S command language.* Hillsdale, NJ: Erlbaum.

JUNG, C. G. (1910). The association method. *American Journal of Psychology, 21,* 219–269.

JUNG, C. G. (1971). *Psychological types* (H. G. Baynes, Trans, revised by R. F. C. Hull). Princeton, NJ: Princeton University Press. (Original work published 1921)

KAGAN, J. (1965). Impulsive and reflective children: Significance of conceptual tempo. In J. Krumboltz (Ed.), *Learning and the educational process* (pp. 133–161). Chicago: Rand McNally.

KAGAN, J., & FREEMAN, M. (1963). Relation of childhood intelligence, maternal behaviors, and social class to behavior during adolescence. *Child Development, 34,* 899–911.

KAGAN, J., SONTAG, L. W., BAKER, C. T., & NELSON, V. L. (1958). Personality and IQ *change. Journal of Abnormal and Social Psychology, 56, 261–266.*

KAHN, J. V. (1987). Uses of the scales with mentally retarded populations. In I. C. Užgiris & J. McV. Hunt (Eds.), *Infant performance and experience: New findings with the ordinal scales* (pp. 252–280). Champaign: University of Illinois Press.

KAISER, H. E (1958). A modified stanine scale. *Journal of Experimental Education,* 26, 261.

KAISER, H. E, & MICHAEL, W. B. (1975). Domain validity and generalizability. *Educational and Psychological Measurement, 35,* 31–35.

KAMINER, Y., FEINSTEIN, C., & SEIFER, R. (1995). Is there a need for observationally based assessment of affective symptomatology in child and adolescent psychiatry? *Adolescence, 30,* 483–489.

KAMPHAUS, R. W. (1990). K-ABC theory in historical and current contexts. *Journal of Psychoeducational* Assessment, 8, 356–368.

KAMPHAUS, R. W. *(1993). Clinical* ASSESSMENT *of children's intelligence: A handbook for professional practice. Boston:* Allyn & Bacon.

KAMPHAUS, R. W., & FRICK, P. J. (1996). *Clinical assessment of child and adolescent personality and behavior.* Boston: Allyn & Bacon.

KAMPHAUS, R. W., KAUFMAN, A. S., &. HARRISON, P. L. (1990). Clinical assessment practice with the Kaufman Assessment Battery for Children (K-ABC). In C. R. Reynolds & R. W. Kamphaus (Eds.), Handbook *of psychological and educational assessment of children: Intelligence and achievement,* (pp. 259–276). New York: Guilford Press.

KAMPHAUS, R. W., & REYNOLDS, C. R. (1987). *Clinical and research applications of the K-ABC.* Circle Pines, MN: American Guidance Service.

KANE, J. S., & LAWLER, E. E., III. (1978). Methods of peer assessment. *Psychological Bulletin,* 85, 555–586.

KANFER, R., ACKERMAN, P. L., & CUDECK, R. (Eds.). (1989). *Abilities, motivation, and* methodology (The Minnesota Symposium on Learning and Individual Differences). Hillsdale, NJ: Erlbaum.

KANFER, R., ACKERMAN, P. L., MURTHA, T., & GOFF, M. (1995). Personality and intelligence in industrial and organizational psychology. In D. H. Saklofske & M. Zeidner (Eds.), *International handbook of personality and intelligence* (pp. 577–602). New York: Plenum Press.

KANTOR, J. E., & CARRETTA, T. R. (1988). Aircrew selection systems. *Aviation, Space, and Environmental Medicine, 59*, 32–38.

KAPES, J. T., MASTIE, M. M., & WHITFIELD, E. A. (Eds.). (1994). A *counselor's guide to career assessment instruments* (3rd ed.). Alexandria, VA: National Career Development Association.

KAPLAN, M. F., & ERON, L. D. (1965). Test sophistication and faking in the TAT situation. *Journal of Projective Techniques, 29*, 498–503.

KARLSEN, B. (1992). *LAAP, Language Arts Assessment Portfolio: Teacher's guide* (Levels I—III). Circle Pines, MN: American Guidance Service.

KARNES, F. A., &. BROWN, K. E. (1980). Factor analysis of WISC-R for the gifted. *Journal of Educational Psychology, 72*, 197–199.

KATZ, M. R. (1974). Career decision-making: A computer-based System of Interactive Guidance and Information (SIGI). *Proceedings of the 1973 Invitational Conference on Testing Problems, Educational Testing Service*, 43–69.

KATZ, M. R. (1993). *Computer-assisted career decision making: The guide in the machine.* Hillsdale, NJ: Erlbaum.

KATZ, S., &. LAUTENSCHLAGER, G. J. (1995). The SAT reading task in question: Reply to Freedle and Kostin. *Psychological Science, 6*, 126–127.

KAUFMAN, A. S. (1971). Piaget and Gesell: A psychometric analysis of tests built from their tasks. *Child Development, 42*, 1341–1360.

KAUFMAN, A. S. (1975). Factor analysis of the WISC-R at eleven age levels between 6 1/2 and 16 1/2 years. *Journal of Counseling and Clinical Psychology, 43*, 135–147.

KAUFMAN, A. S. (1979). *Intelligent testing with the WISC-R*. New York: Wiley.

KAUFMAN, A. S. (1990). *Assessing adolescent and adult intelligence.* Boston: Allyn & Bacon.

KAUFMAN, A. S. (1994). *Intelligent testing with the WISC-III*. New York: Wiley.

KAUFMAN, A. S., & HOLLENBECK, G. P. (1974). Comparative structure of the WPPSI for blacks and whites. *Journal of Clinical Psychology, 30*, 316–319.

KAUFMAN, A. S., & KAUFMAN, N. L. (1972). Tests built from Piaget's and Gesell's tasks as predictors of first-grade achievement. *Child Development, 43*, 521–535.

KAUFMAN, A. S., & KAUFMAN, N. L. (1977). *Clinical evaluation of young children with the McCarthy Scales.* New York: Grune & Stratton.

KAUFMAN, A. S., & KAUFMAN, N. L. (1983a). *Kaufman* Assessment *Battery for Children: Administration and scoring manual*. Circle Pines, MN: American Guidance Service.

KAUFMAN, A. S., & KAUFMAN, N. L. (1983b). *Kaufman Assessment Battery for Children: Interpretive manual*. Circle Pines, MN: American Guidance Service.

KAUFMAN, A. S., & KAUFMAN, N. L. (1985). *Kaufman Test of Educational Achievement: Comprehensive Form manual*. Circle Pines, MN: American Guidance Service.

KAUFMAN, A. S., &. KAUFMAN, N. L. (1990). *Kaufman Brief Intelligence Test: Manual*. Circle Pines, MN: American Guidance Service.

KAUFMAN, A. S., & KAUFMAN, N. L. (1993). *Kaufman Adolescent and Adult Intelligence Test: Manual*. Circle Pines, MN: American Guidance Service.

KAUSLER, D. H. (1994). *Learning and memory in normal aging.* San Diego, CA: Academic Press.

KAVALE, K. A., & FORNESS, S. R. (1984). A meta-analysis of the validity of Wechsler Scale profiles and recategorizations: Patterns or parodies? Learning *Disability Quarterly*, 7, 136–156.

KAVRUCK, S. (1956). Thirty-three years of test research: A short history of test development in the U. S. Civil Service Commission. *American Psychologist, 11*, 329–333.

KEHOE, J. F. (1992). Review of the Career Assessment Inventory, Second Edition [Vocational version]. *Eleventh Mental Measurements Yearbook,* 149.

KEFIOE, J. E, &. TENOPYR, M. L. (1994). Adjustment in assessment scores and their usage: A taxonomy and evaluation of methods. *Psychological Assessment*, 6, 291–303.

KEISER, R. E., & PRATHER, E. N. (1990). What is the TAT? A review of ten years of research. *Journal of Personality* Assessment, 55, 800–803.

KEITH, T. Z. (1985). Questioning the K-ABC: What does it measure? *School Psychology Review, 14,* 9–20.

KEITH, T. Z., & DUNBAR, S. B. (1984). Hierarchical factor analysis of the K-ABC: Testing alternate models. *Journal of Special Education, 18,* 367–375.

KELLER, L. S., & BUTCHER, J. N. (1991). *Assessment of chronic pain patients with the MMP1-2.* Minneapolis: University of Minnesota Press.

KELLEY, C., & MEYERS, J. E. (1993). *The Cross-Cultural Adaptability Inventory.* Minneapolis, MN: National Computer Systems.

KELLEY, M. F., & SURBECK, E. (1991). History of preschool assessment. In B. A. Bracken (Ed.), *The psychoeducational assessment of preschool children* (2nd ed., pp. 1–17). Boston: Allyn & Bacon.

KELLEY, T. L. (1928). *Crossroads in the mind of man: A study of differentiable mental abilities.* Stanford, CA: Stanford University Press.

KELLEY, T. L. (1935). *Essential traits of mental life.* Cambridge, MA: Harvard University Press.

KELLEY, T. L. (1939). The selection of upper and lower groups for the validation of test items. *Journal of Educational Psychology,* 30, 17–24.

KELLEY, T. L. (1943). Cumulative significance of a number of independent experiments: Reply to A. E. Traxler and R. N. Hilkert. *School and Society, 57,* 482–484.

KELLY, G. A. (1955). *The psychology of personal constructs.* New York: Norton.

KELLY, G. A. (1963). A *theory of personality.* New York: Norton.

KELLY, G. A. (1970). A summary statement of a cognitively oriented comprehensive theory of behavior. In J. C. Mancuso (Ed.), *Readings for a cognitive theory of personality* (pp. 27–58). New York: Holt, Rinehart & Winston.

KELLY, M. P, & MELTON, G. B. (1993). Legal and ethical issues. In J. L. Culbertson & D. J. Willis (Eds.), *Testing young children:* A *reference guide for developmental, psychoeducational, and psychosocial assessments* (pp. 408–425). Austin, TX: PRO-ED.

KELZ, J. W. (1966). The development and evaluation of a measure of counselor effectiveness. *Personnel* and *Guidance Journal, 44,* 511–516.

KENRICK, D. T., & FUNDER, D. C. (1988). Profiting from controversy: Lessons from the person-situation debate. *American Psychologist, 43,* 23–34.

KENT, G. H., & ROSANOFF, A. J. (1910). A study of association in insanity. *American Journal of Insanity, 67,* 37–96, 317–390.

KENT, R. N., &. FOSTER, S. L. (1977). Direct observational procedures: Methodological issues in naturalistic settings. In A. R. Ciminero, K. S. Calhoun, & H. E. Adams (Eds.), *Handbook of behavioral assessment* (pp. 279–328). New York: Wiley.

KERLINGER, F. N. (1986). *Foundations of behavioral research* (3rd ed.). New York: Holt, Rinehart & Winston.

KEYSER, D. J., & SWEETLAND, R. C. (Eds.). (1984–1994). *Test critiques.* Austin, TX: PRO-ED.

KHAN, S. B. (1970). Development of mental abilities: An investigation of the "differentiation hypothesis." *Canadian Journal of Psychology, 24,* 199–205.

KHAN, S. B. (1972). Learning and the development of verbal ability. *American Educational Research Journal,* 9, 607–614.

KHAN, S. B., ALVI, S. A., SHAUKAT, N., & HUSSAIN, M. A. (1990). A study of the validity of Holland's theory in a non-Western culture. *Journal of Vocational Behavior,* 36, 132–146.

KIM, J.-O., & MUELLER, C. W. (1978a). *Factor analysis: Statistical methods and practical issues.* Newbury Park, CA: Sage.

KIM, J.-O., & MUELLER, C. W. (1978b). *Introduction to factor analysis: What it is and how to do it.* Newbury Park, CA: Sage.

KINDER, B. N. (1992). The problems of R in clinical settings and in research: Suggestions for the future. *Journal of Personality Assessment,* 58, 252–259.

KING, L. A., &. KING, D. W. (1990). Role conflict and role ambiguity: A critical assessment of construct validity. *Psychological Bulletin, 107,* 48–64.

KING, W. L., &. SEEGMILLER, B. (1973). Performance of 14- to 22-month-old black, first-born male infants on two tests of cognitive development: The Bayley Scales and the Infant Psychological Development Scale. *Developmental Psychology, 8,* 317–326.

KINSLINGER, H. J. (1966). Application of projective techniques in personnel psychology since 1940. *Psychological Bulletin,* 66, 134–149.

KIRCHER, J. C., & RASKIN, D. C. (1992). Polygraph techniques: History, controversies, and prospects. In P. Suedfeld & P. E. Tetlock (Eds.), *Psychology and social policy* (pp. 295–308). New York: Hemisphere.

KIRCHNER, W. K. (1966). A note on the effect of privacy in taking typing tests. *Journal of Applied Psychology, 50,* 373–374.

KIRNAN, J. R, & GEISINGER, K. F. (1986). Review of the General Aptitude Test Battery. In D. J. Keyser & R. C. Sweetland (Eds.), *Test critiques* (Vol. 5, pp. 150–167). Kansas City, MO: Test Corporation of America.

KIRSCH, I. S., JUNGEBLUT, A., JENKINS, L., & KOLSTAD, A. (1993). *Adult literacy in America: A first look at the results of the National Adult Literacy Survey.* Washington, DC: US Department of Education.

KITAYAMA, S., & MARCUS, H. R. (Eds.) (1994). *Emotion and culture: Empirical studies of mutual influences.* Washington, DC: American Psychological Association.

KLEIGER, J. H. (1992). A conceptual critique of the EA:es comparison in the Comprehensive Rorschach System. *Psychological* Assessment, *4,* 288–296.

KLEINMUNTZ, B. (1990). Why we still use our heads instead of formulas: Toward an integrative approach. *Psychological Bulletin, 107,* 296–310.

KLINE, P. (1993). *An easy guide to factor analysis.* New York: Routledge.

KLINE, P. (2000). *The handbook of psychological testing.* Florence, KY: Psychology Press.

KLINE, R. B. (1994). Test review: New objective rating scales for child assessment. I. Parent-and teacher-informant inventories of the Behavioral Assessment System for Children, the Child Behavior Checklist, and the Teacher Report Form. *Journal of Psychoeducational Assessment, 12,* 289–306.

KLINE, R. B., LACHAR, D., &. BOERSMA, D. C. (1993). Identification of special education needs with the Personality Inventory for Children (PIC): A hierarchical classification model. *Psychological Assessment, 5,* 307–316.

KLINE, R. B., LACHAR, D., &. GDOWSKI, C. L. (1992). Clinical validity of a Personality Inventory for Children (PIC) profile typology. *Journal of Personality Assessment, 58,* 591–605.

KLINE, R. B., SNYDER, J., & CASTELLANOS, M. (1996). Lessons from the Kaufman Assessment Battery for Children (K-ABC): Toward a new cognitive assessment model. *Psychological Assessment, 8,* 7–17.

KLINEBERG, O. (1928). An experimental study of speed and other factors in "racial" differences. *Archives of Psychology,* No. 93.

KLINGER, E. (1966). Fantasy need achievement as a motivational construct. *Psychological Bulletin, 66,* 291–308.

KLOPFER, W. G. (1983). Writing psychological reports. In C. E. Walker (Ed.), *The handbook of clinical psychology* (Vol. 1, pp. 501–527). Homewood, IL: Dow Jones-Irwin.

KLOPFER, W. G., & TAULBEE, E. S. (1976). Projective tests. *Annual Review of Psychology, 27,* 543–568.

KNAPP, D. J., & CAMPBELL, J. P. (1993). *Building a joint-service classification research roadmap: Criterion-related issues* (AL/HR-TP-1993–0028). Brooks AFB, TX: Armstrong Laboratory.

KNAPP, D. J., RUSSELL, T. L., & CAMPBELL, J. P. (1993). *Building a joint-service classification research roadmap: Job analysis methodologies* (Interim report HumRRO IR-PRD-93–15). Brooks AFB, TX: Armstrong Laboratory.

KNAPP, R. R. (1960). The effects of time limits on the intelligence test performance of Mexican and American subjects. *Journal of Educational Psychology, 51,* 14–20.

KNOBLOCK, H., & PASAMANICK, B. (1963). Predicting intellectual potential in infancy. *American Journal of Diseases of Children, 106,* 43–51.

KNOBLOCH, H., & PASAMANICK, B. (1966). Prospective studies on the epidemiology of reproductive casualty: Methods, findings, and some implications. *Merrill-Palmer Quarterly, 12,* 27–43.

KNOBLOCH, H., & PASAMANICK, B. (Eds.). (1974). *Gessell and Amatmda's developmental diagnosis* (3rd ed.). New York: Harper & Row.

KNOBLOCH, H., STEVENS, F., &. MALONE, A. F. (1980). *Manual of developmental diagnosis: The administration and interpretation of revised Gesell and Amatruda Developmental and Neurologic Examination.* Philadelphia: Harper & Row.

KNOELL, M., & HARRIS, C. W. (1952). A factor analysis of spelling ability. *Journal of Educational Research, 46,* 95–111.

KNOFF, H. M. (1989). Review of the Personality Inventory for Children, Revised Format. *Tenth Mental Measurements Yearbook,* 625–630.

KNOFF, H. M. (1990). Evaluation of projective drawings. In C. R. Reynolds & R. W. Kamphaus (Eds.), *Handbook of psychological assessment of children: Personality, behavior, and context* (pp. 89–146). New York: Guilford Press.

KNOFF, H. M. (1992). Assessment of social-emotional functioning and adaptive behavior. In E. Vazquez Nutall, I. Romero, & J. Kalesnik (Eds.), *Assessing and screening preschoolers: Psychological and educational dimensions* (pp. 121–143). Boston: Allyn & Bacon.

KNOFF, H. M. (1993). The utility of human figure drawings in personality and intellectual assessment: Why ask why? *School Psychology Quarterly, 8,* 191–196.

KNOX, H. A. (1914). A scale based on the work at Ellis Island for estimating mental defect. *Journal of the American Medical Association, 62,* 741–747.

KOCH, H. L. (1966). *Twins and twin relations.* Chicago: University of Chicago Press.

KOGAN, N. (1976). *Cognitive styles in infancy and early childhood.* Hillsdale, NJ: Erlbaum.

KOGAN, N., & BLOCK, J. (1991). Field dependence-independence from early childhood through adolescence: Personality and socialization aspects. In S. Wagner & J. Demick (Eds.), *Field dependence-independence: Cognitive style across the life span* (pp. 177–207). Hillsdale, NJ: Erlbaum.

KOLB, B., & WHISHAW, I. Q. (1990). *Fundamentals of human neuropsychology* (3rd ed.). New York: Freeman.

KOPPITZ, E. M. (1964). *The Bender Gestalt Test for young children.* Orlando, FL: Grune & Stratton.

KOPPITZ, E. M. (1968). *Psychological evaluation of childretds human figure drawings.* Boston: Allyn &. Bacon.

KOPPITZ, E. M. (1975). *The Bender Gestalt Test for young children: Research and application, 1963–1973.* Orlando, FL: Grune &. Stratton.

KOPPITZ, E. M. (1984). *Psychological evaluation of human figure drawings by middle school pupils.* Orlando, FL: Grune & Stratton.

KOTSONIS, M. E., & PATTERSON, C. J. (1980). Comprehension-monitoring skills in learning-disabled children. *Developmental Psychology, 16,* 541–542.

KOZLOWSKI, S. W., J., KLRSCH, M. P, & CHAO, G. T. (1986). Job knowledge, ratee familiarity, and halo effect: An exploration. *Journal of Applied Psychology, 71,* 45–49.

KRAEPELIN, E. (1892). *Über die Beeinflüssung einfacher psychischer Vorgänge durch einige Arzneimittel.* Jena: Fischer.

KRAEPELIN, E. (1895). Der psychologische Versuch in der Psychiatrie. *Psychologische Arbeiten, 1,* 1–91.

KRALL, V. (1986). Projective play techniques. In A. I. Rabin (Ed.), *Projective techniques for adolescents and children* (pp. 264–278). New York: Springer.

KRAMER, J. H. (1990). Guidelines for interpreting WAIS-R subtest scores. *Psychological Assessment, 2,* 202–205.

KRAMER, J. H. (1993). Interpretation of individual subtest scores on the WISC-III. *Psychological Assessment, 5,* 193–196.

KRAMER, J. J., & MITCHELL, J. V., JR. (Eds.). (1985). Computer-based assessment and interpretation: Prospects, promise, and pitfalls [Special issue]. *Computers in Human Behavior, 1* (3/4).

KRATOCHWILL, T. R., DOLL, E. J., & DICKSON, W. P. (1991). Use of computer technology in behavioral assessments. In T. B. Gutkin & S. L. Wise (Eds.), *The computer and the decision-making process* (pp. 125–154). Hillsdale, NJ: Erlbaum.

KRAVETS, M., & WAX, I. (1992). *The K & W guide: Colleges and the learning disabled student.* New York: Harper Collins.

KROGER, R. O., & WOOD, L. A. (1993). Reification, "faking," and the Big Five. *American Psychologist, 48,* 1297–1298.

KROHNE, H. W. AND LAUX, L. (1982). *Achievement, Stress and Anxiety.* Washington, DC: Hemisphere.

KRUG, S. E. (Ed.). (1988). *Psychware sourcebook* (3rd ed.). Kansas City, MO: Test Corporation of America.

KRUG, S. E. (Ed.). (1993). *Psychware sourcebook* (4th ed.). Champaign, IL: Metritech.

KRUGLANSKI, A. W. (1989). The psychology of being right: The problem of accuracy in social perception and cognition. *Psychological Bulletin, 106,* 395–409.

KRUMBOLTZ, J. D. (1991). *Manual for the Career Beliefs Inventory.* Palo Alto, CA: Consulting Psychologists Press.

KUDER, G. F. (1966). The Occupational Interest Survey. *Personnel and Guidance Journal, 45,* 72–77.

KUDER, G. F., & DIAMOND, E. E. (1979). *Kuder Occupational Interest Survey: General manual.* Chicago: Science Research Associates.

KUDER, G. E, & RICHARDSON, M. W. (1937). The theory of estimation of test reliability. *Psychometrika, 2,* 151–160.

KUDER, F., & ZYTOWSKI, D. G. (1991). *Kuder Occupational Interest* Survey *Form DD: General manual* (3rd ed.), Monterey, CA: CTB Macmillan/McGraw-Hill.

KUHLMANN, F. (1912). A revision of the Binet-Simon system for measuring the intelligence of children. *Journal of Psycho-Asthenics, Monograph Supplement, 1,* 1–41.

KULIKOWICH, J. M., &. ALEXANDER, A. (1994). Evaluating students' errors on cognitive tasks: Applications of polytomous item response theory and log-linear modeling. In C. R. Reynolds (Ed.), *Cognitive assessment: A multidisciplinary perspective* (pp. 137–154). New York: Plenum Press.

KUMMEROW, J. M. (Ed.). (1991). *New directions in career planning and the workplace: Practical strategies for counselors.* Palo Alto, CA: Davies-Black.

KURTZ, A. K. (1948). A research test of the Rorschach test. *Personnel Psychology, 1,* 41–51.

LACHAR, D. (1982). *Personality Inventory for Children (PIC): Revised format manual supplement.* Los Angeles: Western Psychological Services.

LACHAR, D., &. GDOWSKI, C. L. (1979). *Actuarial assessment of child and adolescent personality: An interpretive gidde for the Personality Inventory for Children profile.* Los Angeles: Western Psychological Services.

LACHAR, D., & GRUBER, C. P. (1993). Development of the Personality Inventory for Youth: A self-report companion to the Personality Inventory for Children. *Journal of Personality Assessment, 61,* 81–98.

LACHAR, D., & GRUBER, C. P. (1995a). *Personality Inventory for Youth (PIY) manual: Administration and scoring guide.* Los Angeles: Western Psychological Services.

LACHAR, D., & GRUBER, C. P. (1995b). *Personality Inventory for Youth (PIY) manual: Technical guide.* Los Angeles: Western Psychological Services.

LADUCA, A. (1994). Validation of professional licensure examinations: Professions theory, test design, and construct validity. *Evaluation & the Health Professions, 17,* 178–197.

LAFAVE, L. (1966). Essay vs. multiple-choice: Which test is preferable? *Psychology in the Schools, 3, 65–69.*

LAH, M. I. (1989). Sentence completion tests. In C. S. Newmark (Eel.), *Major psychological assessment instruments* (Vol. 2, pp. 133–163). Boston: Allyn & Bacon.

LALLI, J. S., & GOH, H. (1993). Naturalistic observations in community settings. In J. Reichle & D. R Wacker (Eds.), *Communicative alternatives to challenging behavior: integrating functional assessment and intervention strategies* (pp. 11–39). Baltimore: Paul H. Brookes.

LAMBERT, N. M. (1990). Consideration of the Das-Naglieri Cognitive Assessment System. *Journal of Psychoeducational* Assessment, 8, 338–343.

LAMBERT, N. (1991). The crisis in measurement literacy in psychology and education. *Educational Psychologist, 26,* 23–35.

LAMBERT, N., NIHIRA, K., & LELAND, H. (1993). *AAMR Adaptive Behavior Scale-School-Second Edition: Examiner's manual.* Austin, TX: PRO-ED.

LANDFIELD, A. W., & EPTING, F. R. (1987). *Personal construct psychology: Clinical and personality assessment.* New York: Human Sciences Press.

LANDY, F. J., & FARR, J. L. (1980). Performance rating. *Psychological Bulletin, 87,* 72–107.

LANDY, F. J., & FARR, J. L. (1983). *The measurement of work performance.* New York: Academic Press.

LANDY, F. J., SHANKSTER, L. J., &. KOHLER, S. S. (1994). Personnel selection and placement. *Annual Review of Psychology, 45,* 261–296.

LANDY, F., SHANKSTER-CAWLEY, L., & KOHLER MORAN, S. (1995). Advancing personnel selection and placement methods. In A. Howard (Ed.), *The changing nature of work* (pp. 252–289). San Francisco: Jossey-Bass.

LANG, W. S. (1992). Review of the TEMAS (Tell-Me-A-Story). *Eleventh Mental Measurements Yearbook,* 925–926.

LANNING, K. (1991). *Consistency, scalability, and personality measurement.* New York: Springer-Verlag.

LANYON, R. I. (1966). A free-choice version of the EPPS. *Journal of Clinical Psychology,* 22, 202–205.

LANYON, R. I. & GOODSTEIN, L. D. (1997). *Personality assessment* (3rd ed.). New York: Wiley.

LAOSA, L. M., SWARTZ, J. D., & DIAZ-GUERRERO, R. (1974). Perceptual-cognitive and personality development of Mexican and Anglo-American children as measured by human figure drawings. *Developmental Psychology, 10,* 131–139.

LARKIN, J. H., MCDERMOTT, J., SIMON, D. F., & SIMON, H. A. (1980a). Expert and novice performance in solving physics problems. *Science*, 208, 1335–1342.

LARKIN, J. H„ MCDERMOTT, J., SIMON, D. F, & SIMON, H. A. (1980b). Models of competence in solving physics problems. *Cognitive Science, 4,* 317–345.

LARKIN, K. C., & WEISS, D. J. (1974). *An empirical investigation of computer-administered pyramidal ability testing* (Res. Rep. 74–3). Minneapolis: University of Minnesota, Department of Psychology, Psychometric Methods Program.

LAST, J., & BRUHN, A. R. (1991). *The Cotnprehensive Early Memories Scoring System— Revised.* 17 pages. Available from the second author.

LASSITER, K. S., & BARDOS, A. N. (1995). The relationship between young children's academic achievement and measures of intelligence. *Psychology in the Schools*, *32*(3), 170–177.

LAURENT, J., SWERDLIK, M., & RYBURN, M. (1992). Review of validity research on the Stanford-Binet Intelligence Scale: Fourth Edition. *Psychological* Assessment, *4,* 102–112.

LAUTENSCHLAGER, G. J. (1994). Accuracy and faking of background data. In G. S. Stokes, M. D. Mumford, &. W. A. Owens (Eds.), *Biodata handbook: Theory, research, and use of biographical information in selection and performance prediction* (pp. 391–419). Palo Alto, CA: Consulting Psychologists Press.

LAVE, J. (1988). *Cognition in practice: Mind, mathematics, and culture in everyday life.* Cambridge, England: Cambridge University Press.

LAWRENCE, S. W., JR. (1962). The effects of anxiety, achievement motivation, and task importance upon performance on an intelligence test. *Journal of Educational Psychology,* 53, 150–156.

LAZARUS, A. A. (1981). *The practice of multimodal therapy.* New York: McGraw-Hill.

LEARK, R. A., DUPUY, T. R., GREENBERG, L. M., CORMAN, C. L., & KINDSCHI, C. (1996). T.O.V.A. *Test of Variables of Attention : Professional manuals Version 7.0.* Los Alamitos, CA: University Attention Disorders.

LECKLITER, I. N., MATARAZZO, J. D., & SLLVERSTEIN, A. B. (1986). A literature review of factor analytic studies of the WAIS-R. *Journal of Clinical Psychology, 42,* 332–342.

LEE, R., & FOLEY, P. P. (1986). Is the validity of a test constant throughout the score range? *Journal of Applied Psychology, 71,* 641–644.

LEE, Y., JUSSIM, L. J., & MCCAULEY, C. R. (1995). *Stereotype accuracy: Toward appreciating group differences.* Washington, DC: American Psychological Association.

LEFCOURT, H. M. (1991). Locus of control. In J. P. Robinson, P. R. Shaver, & L. S. Wrightsman (Eds.), *Measures of personality and social psychological attitudes* (pp. 413–499). San Diego, CA: Academic Press.

LEFCOURT, H. M., VON BAEYER, C. L., WARE, E. E., & COX, D. V. (1979). The multidimensional-multiattributional causality scale: The development of a goal specific locus of control scale. *Canadian Journal of Behavioural Science, 11,* 286–304.

LEICHSENRING, F. (1991). Discriminating schizophrenics from borderline patients: Study with the Holtzman Inkblot Technique. *Psychopathology, 24,* 225–231.

LENNEY, E. (1991). Sex roles: The measurement of masculinity, femininity, and androgyny. In J. P. Robinson, P. R. Shaver, & L. S. Wrightsman (Eds.), *Measures of personality and social psychological attitudes* (pp. 573–660). San Diego, CA: Academic Press.

LENNON, R.T. (1956). Assumptions underlying the use of content validity. *Educational and Psychological Measurement,* 16, pp. 294–304.

LENNON, R. T. (1966a). A comparison of results of three intelligence tests. In C. I. Chase & H. G. Ludlow (Eds.), *Readings in educational and psychological measurement* (pp. 198–205. Boston: Houghton Mifflin.

LENNON, R. T. (1966b). Norms: 1963. In A. Anastasi (Ed.), *Testing problems in perspective* (pp. 243–250). Washington, DC: American Council on Education.

LENS, W,, ATKINSON, J. W., & YIP, A. G. (1979). *Academic achievement in high school related to "intelligence" and motivation as measured in sixth, ninth, and twelfth grade boys and girls.* Unpublished manuscript, University of Michigan, Ann Arbor.

LERNER, B. (1980a). Employment discrimination: Adverse impact, validity, and equality. In P. B. Kurland & C. Casper (Eds.), *1979 Supreme Court Review* (pp. 17–49). Chicago: University of Chicago Press.

LERNER, B. (1980b). The war on testing: Detroit Edison in perspective. *Personnel Psychology,* 33, 11–16.

LERNER, P. M. (1991). *Psychoanalytic theory and the Rorschach.* New York: Analytic Press. LERNER, P. M. (1994). Current status of the Rorschach. *Contemporary Psychology, 39,* 724–725.

LEVIN, J. D. (1992). *Theories of the self.* Washington, DC: Hemisphere.

LEVY, L. (1963). *Psychological interpretation.* New York: Holt, Rinehart & Winston. LEWIS, M. (1973). Infant intelligence tests: Their use and misuse. *Human Development, 16,* 108–118.

LEWIS, M. (1976). What do we mean when we say "infant intelligence scores?" A sociopolitical question. In M. Lewis (Ed.), *Origins of intelligence: Infancy and early childhood* (pp. 1–17). New York: Plenum Press.

LEWIS, M., & MCGURK, H. (1972). Evaluation of infant intelligence: Infant intelligence scores—true or false? *Science, 178* (4066), 1174–1177.

LEZAK, M. D. (1995). *Neuropsychological assessment* (3rd ed.). New York: Oxford University Press.

LIBEN, L. S. (Ed.). (1983). *Piaget and the foundations of knowledge* (The Jean Piaget Symposium Series, No. 10). Hillsdale, NJ: Erlbaum.

LIDZ, C. S. (1981). *Improving assessment of schoolchildren.* San Francisco: Jossey-Bass.

LIDZ, C. S. (Ed.). (1987). *Dynamic assessment: An interactive approach to evaluating learning potential.* New York: Guilford Press.

LIDZ, C. S. (1991). *Practitioner's guide to dynamic assessment. New York: Guilford Press.*

LIDZ, C. S. (1995). Dynamic assessment and the legacy of L. S. Vygotsky. *School Psychology International, 16,* 143–153.

LIDZ, C. S. (1997). Dynamic assessment approaches. In D. P. Flanagan, J. L. Genshaft, & P. L. Harrison (Eds.), *Contemporary intellectual assessment: Theories, tests, and issues* (pp. 281–296). New York: Guilford.

LIKERT, R. (1932). A technique for the measurement of attitudes. *Archives of Psychology,* No. 140.

LIKERT, R., & QUASHA, W. H. (1995). *Revised Minnesota Paper Form Board Test: Manual* (2nd ed.). San Antonio, TX: Psychological Corporation.

LIM, R. G., & DRASGOW, F. (1990). Evaluation of two methods for estimating item response theory parameters when assessing differential item functioning. *Journal of Applied Psychology, 75,* 164–174.

LINDEN, M. J., & WHIMBEY, A. (1990). *Analytical writing and thin king: Facing the tests.* Hillsdale, NJ: Erlbaum.

LINDSLEY, D. B. (1955). The psychology of lie detection. In G. J. Dudycha et al., (Eds.) *Psychology for law enforcement officers* (chap. 4). Springfield, IL: Charles C Thomas.

LINDZEY, G. (1977). *Projective techniques and cross-cultural research.* New York: Irvington. (Original work published 1961)

LINDZEY, G., &. HERMAN, P. S. (1955). Thematic Apperception Test: A note on reliability and situational validity. *Journal of Projective Techniques, 19,* 36–42.

LINN, R. L. (1975). Test bias and the prediction of grades in law school. *Journal of Legal Education, 27,* 293–323.

LINN, R. L. (1978). Single-group validity, differential validity, and differential prediction. *Journal of Applied Psychology, 63,* 507–512.

LINN, R. L. (1989). Review of the Boehm Test of Basic Concepts—Revised. *Tenth Mental Measurements Yearbook,* 99–101.

LINN, R. L., & DRASGOW, F. (1987). Implications of the Golden Rule settlement for test construction. *Educational Measurement: Issues & Practice, 6,* 13–17.

LINN, R. L., & GRONLUND, N. E. (1995). *Measurement and assessment in teaching* (7th ed.). Upper Saddle River, NJ: Prentice Hall.

LINN, R. L., &. WERTS, C. E. (1971). Considerations for studies of test bias. *Journal of Educational Measurement, 8,* 1–4.

LIPGAR, R. M. (1992). The problem of R in the Rorschach: The value of varying responses. *Journal of Personality Assessment, 58,* 223–230.

LIPSEY, M. W., & WILSON, D. B. (1993). The efficacy of psychological, educational, and behavioral treatment: Confirmation from meta-analysis. *American Psychologist, 48,* 1181–1209.

LITTELL, W. M. (1960). The Wechsler Intelligence Scale for Children: Review of a decade of research. *Psychological Bulletin, 57,* 132–156.

LIVINGSTON, S. A., & ZIEKY, M. J. (1982). *Passing scores: A manual for setting standards of performance on educational and occupational tests.* Princeton, NJ: Educational Testing Service.

LOBELLO, S. G., &. GULGOZ, S. (1991). Factor analysis of the Wechsler Preschool and Primary Scale of Intelligence—Revised. *Psychological Assessment, 3,* 130–132.

LOEHLIN, J. C. (1992). *Latent variable models: An introduction to factor, path, and structural analysis (*2nd ed.*).* Hillsdale, NJ: Erlbaum.

LOEHLIN, J., LLNDZEY, G., & SPUHLER, J. N. (1975). *Race, differences in intelligence.* New York: Freeman.

LOEVINGER, J. (1966a). The meaning and measurement of ego development. *American Psychologist, 21,* 195–206.

LOEVINGER, J. (1966b). A theory of test response. In A. Anastasi (Ed.), *Testing problems in perspective* (pp. 545–556). Washington, DC: American Council on Education.

LOEVINGER, J. (1976). *Ego development.* San Francisco: Jossey-Bass.

LOEVINGER, J. (1985). Revision of the Sentence Completion Test for ego development. *Journal of Personality and Social Psychology, 48,* 420–427.

LOEVINGER, J. (1987). *Paradigms of personality.* New York: Freeman.

LOEVINGER, J. (1993). Measurement of personality: True or false? *Psychological Inquiry, 4,* 1–16.

LOEVINGER, J. (1994). Has psychology lost its conscience? *Journal of Personality Assessment, 62,* 2–8.

LOEVINGER, J., &. OSSORIO, A. G. (1958). Evaluation in therapy by self-report: A paradox. *American Psychologist, 13, 366.*

LOEVINGER, J., & WESSLER, R. (1970). *Measuring ego development: Vol. 1. Construction and use of a sentence completion test.* San Francisco: Jossey-Bass.

LOEVINGER, J., WESSLER, R., & REDMORE, C. (1970). *Measuring ego development: Vol. 2. Scoring manual for women and girls.* San Francisco: Jossey-Bass.

LOFTUS, E. F. (1993). The reality of repressed memories. *American Psychologist, 48,* 518–537.

LOKAN, J. J., & TAYLOR, K. F. (Eds.). (1986). *Holland in Australia: A vocational choice theory in research and practice.* Melbourne: Australian Council for Educational Research.

LONNER, W. J., & ADAMS, H. L. (1972). Interest patterns of psychologists in nine Western nations. *Journal of Applied Psychology, 56,* 141–151.

LONNER, W. J., & BERRY, J. W. (Eds.). (1986). *Field methods in cross-cultural research.* Beverly Hills, CA: Sage.

LORD, F. M. (1952). The relation of the reliability of multiple-choice tests to the distribution of item difficulties. *Psychometrika, 17,* 181–194.

LORD, F. M. (1970). Some test theory for tailored testing. In W. H. Holtzman (Ed.), *Computer-assisted instruction, testing, and guidance* (pp. 139–183). New York: Harper &. Row.

LORD, F. M. (1971a). The self-scoring flexilevel test. *Journal of Educational Measurement, 8,* 147–151.

LORD, F. M. (1971b). A theoretical study of the measurement effectiveness of flexilevel tests. *Educational and Psychological Measurement, 31,* 805–813.

LORD, F. M. (1971c). A theoretical study of two-stage testing. *Psychometrika, 36,* 227–241.

LORD, F. M. (1980). *Applications of item response theory to practical testing problems.* Hillsdale, NJ: Erlbaum.

LORET, P. G., SEDER, A., BIANCHINI, J. C., & VALE, C. A. (1974). *Anchor Test Study: Equivalence and norms tables for selected reading achievement tests.* Washington, DC: U.S. Government Printing Office.

LORGE, I. (1945). Schooling makes a difference. *Teachers College Record, 46,* 483–492.

LOWMAN, R. L. (1989). *Pre-employment screening for psychopathology: A guide to professional practice. Sarasota,* FL: Professional Resource Press.

LOWMAN, R. L. (1991). *The clinical practice of career assessment: Interests, abilities, and personality.* Washington, DC: American Psychological Association.

LOWMAN, R. L. (1993). *Counseling and psychotherapy of work dysfunctions.* Washington, DC: American Psychological Association.

LOYD, B. H. (1995). Review of the Family Environment Scale, Second Edition. *Twelfth Mental Measurements Yearbook,* 385–386.

LU, C., & SUEN, H. K. (1995). Assessment approaches and cognitive styles. *Journal of Educational Measurement, 32,* 1–17.

LUBIN, B., LARSEN, R. M., & MATARAZZO, J. D. (1984). Patterns of psychological test usage in the United States: 1935–1982. *American Psychologist, 39,* 451–454.

LUBINSKI, D., &. BENBOW, C. P. (1995). An opportunity for empiricism *[Review of Multiple intelligences: The theory and practice]. Contemporary Psychology, 40, 935–940.*

LUBINSKI, D., & DAWIS, R. V. (1992). Aptitudes, skills, and proficiencies. In M. D. Dunnette & L. M. Hough (Eds.), *Handbook of industrial and organizational psychology* (2nd ed., Vol. 3, pp. 1–59). Palo Alto, CA: Consulting Psychologists Press.

LUKAS, S. (1993). *Where to start and what to ask: An assessment handbook.* New York: W. W. Norton.

LUKHELE, R., THISSEN, D., & WAINER, H. (1994). On the relative value of multiple-choice, constructed response, and examinee-selected items on two achievement tests. *Journal of Educational Measurement, 31,* 234–250.

LURIA, A. R. (1966). *Human brain and psychological processes.* New York: Harper & Row.

LURIA, A. R. (1973). *The working brain.* New York: Basic Books.

LURIA, A. R. (1980). *Higher cortical functions in man* (2nd ed.). New York: Basic Books.

LUTEY, C., &. COPELAND, E. P. (1982). Cognitive assessment of the school-age child. In C. R. Reynolds & T. B. Gutkin (Eds.), *The handbook of school psychology* (pp. 121–155). New York: Wiley.

LYKKEN, D. T. (1981). *A tremor in the blood: Uses and abuses of the lie detector test.* New York: McGraw-Hill.

LYKKEN, D. T. (1992), Controversy: The fight-or-flight response in *Homo scientificus.* In P. Suedfeld & P. E. Tetlock (Eds.), *Psychology and social policy* (pp. 309–325). New York: Hemisphere.

LYON, M. A., & MACDONALD, N. T. (1990). Academic self-concept as a predictor of achievement for a sample of elementary school students. *Psychological Reports, 66,* 1135–1142.

MABRY, L. (1995). Review of the Metropolitan Readiness Tests, Fifth Edition. *Twelfth Mental Measurements Yearbook,* 611–612.

MACCALLUM, R. C., & BROWNE, M. W. (1993). The use of causal indicators in covariance structure models: Some practical issues. *Psychological Bulletin, 114,* 533–541.

MACCALLUM, R. C., WEGENER, D. T., UCHINO, B. N., & FABRIGAR, L. R. (1993). The problem of equivalent models in applications of covariance structure analysis. *Psychological Bulletin, 114,* 185–189.

MACHOVER, K. (1949). *Personality projection in the drawing of the human figure. A method of personality investigation.* Springfield, IL: Charles C Thomas.

MACLENNAN, R. N. (1992). *Personality Research Form (PRF): Annotated research bibliography with author and subject indexes.* Port Huron, MI: Sigma Assessment Systems.

MACMANN, G. M., & BARNETT, D. W. (1994a). Some additional lessons from the Wechsler scales: A rejoinder to Kaufman and Keith. *School Psychology Quarterly, 9, 223–236.*

MACMANN, G. M., &. BARNETT, D. W. (1994b). Structural analysis of correlated factors: Lessons from verbal-performance dichotomy of the Wechsler scales. *School Psychology Quarterly, 9,* 161–197.

MACMILLAN, D. L., GRESHAM, F. M., & SIPERSTEIN, G. N. (1993). Conceptual and psychometric concerns about the 1992 AAMR definition of mental retardation. *American Journal on Mental Retardation, 98, 325–335.*

MADDI, S. R. (1989). *Personality theories: A comparative analysis* (5th ed.). Chicago: Dorsey Press.

MADDUX, J. E. (Ed.). (1995). *Self-efficacy, Adaptation, and adjustment: Theory, research, and application.* New York: Plenum Press.

MAEL, F. A. (1991). A conceptual rationale for the domain and attributes of biodata items. *Personnel Psychology, 44,* 763–792.

MAHONEY, M. J. (1991). *Human change processes: The scientific foundations of psychotherapy.* New York: Basic Books.

MAHURIN, R. K. (1992). Review of the Computer Programmer Aptitude Battery. *Eleventh Mental Measurements Yearbook,* 225–227.

MAIER, M. H. (1972). *Effects of educational level on prediction of training success with ACB* (Tech. Res. Note 225). Alexandria, VA: U.S. Army Research Institute for the Behavioral and Social Sciences.

Maier, M. H., & Fuchs, E. F. (1973). *Effectiveness of selection and classification testing* (Res. Rep. 1179). Alexandria, VA: U.S. Army Research Institute for the Behavioral and Social Sciences.

Maier, M. H., & Hirshfeld, S. F. (1978). *Criterion-referenced job proficiency testing: A large scale application* (Res. Rep. 1193). Alexandria, VA: U. S. Army Research Institute for the Behavioral and Social Sciences.

Malgady, R. G., Rogler, L. H., & Costantino, G. (1987). Ethnocultural and linguistic bias in mental health evaluation of Hispanics. *American Psychologist, 42,* 228–234.

Maller, S. J., & Braden, J. P. (1993). The construct and criterion-related validity of the WISC-III with deaf adolescents. *Journal of Psychoeducational Assessment, W1SC-Ill Monograph,* 105–113.

Maloney, M. P., & Ward, M. P. (1976). *Psychological assessment: A conceptual approach*. New York: Oxford University Press.

Mandler, G., & Sarason, S. B. (1952). A study of anxiety and learning. *Journal of Abnormal and Social Psychology, 47,* 166–173.

Manoleas, P. (Ed.). (1995). *The cross-cultural practice of clinical case management. Binghamton,* NY: Haworth Press.

Manuele-adkins, C. (1989). Review of The Self-Directed Search: A guide to educational and vocational planning—1985 Revision. *Tenth Mental Measurements Yearbook,* 738–740.

Marco, G. L. (1992). Review of the Computer Literacy and Computer Science Tests. *Eleventh Mental Measurements Yearbook,* 220–222.

Marín, G., & Marín, B. V. (1991). *Research with Hispanic populations.* Newbury Park: CA: Sage.

Marks, P. A., Seeman, W., & Haller, D. L. (1974). *The actuarial use of the MMPI with adolescents and adults.* Baltimore: Williams & Wilkins.

Markus, H., & Wurf, E. (1987). The dynamic self-concept: A social psychological perspective. *Annual Review of Psychology,* 38, 299–337.

Marsh, D. T., Linberg, L. M., & Smeltzer, J. K. (1991). Human figure drawings of adjudicated and non adjudicated adolescents. *Journal of Personality* Assessment, 57, 77–86.

Marsh, H. W. (1990a). Causal ordering of academic achievement: A multiwave, longitudinal panel analysis. *Journal of Educational Psychology, 82,* 646–656.

Marsh, H. W., (1990b). The structure of academic self-concept: The Marsh/Shavelson model. *Journal of Educational Psychology, 82,* 623–636.

Marsh, H. W., Byrne, B. M., & Shavelson, R. J. (1992). A multidimensional, hierarchical self-concept. In T. M. Brinthaupt & R. P. Lipka (Eds.), *The self: Definitional and methodological issues* (pp. 44–95). Albany: State University of New York Press.

Marsh, H. W., & Shavelson, R. (1985). Self-concept: Its multifaceted, hierarchical structure. *Educational Psychologist, 20,* 107–123.

Martin, S. L., and Raju, N. S. (1992). Determining cutoff scores that optimize utility: A recognition of recruiting costs. *Journal of Applied Psychology,* 77, 15–23.

Maruish, M. E. (Ed.). (1994). *The use of psychological testing for treatment planning and outcome assessment.* Hillsdale, NJ: Erlbaum.

Maruish, M. E., & Moses, J. A. (Eds.). (1997). *Clinical neuropsychology: Theoretical foundations for practitioners. Mahwah,* NJ: Erlbaum.

Mash, E. J., & Terdal, L. G. (Eds.). (1988). *Behavioral assessment of childhood disorders: Selected core problems* (2nd ed.). New York: Guilford Press.

Masling, J. (1959). The effects of warm and cold interaction on the administration and scoring of an intelligence test. *Journal of Consulting Psychology, 23,* 336–341.

MASLING, J. (1960). The influence of situational and interpersonal variables in projective testing. *Psychological Bulletin, 57*, 65–85.

MASLING, J. (1965). Differential indoctrination of examiners and Rorschach responses. *Journal of* Consulting *Psychology, 29*, 198–201.

MATARAZZO, J. D. (1972). *Wechsler's measurement and appraisal of adult intelligence (*5th ed.*)*. Baltimore: Williams & Wilkins.

MATARAZZO, J. D. (1983). Computerized psychological testing. *Science, 221*, 323.

MATARAZZO, J. D. (1986a). Computerized clinical psychological test interpretation: Unvalidated plus all mean and no sigma. *American Psychologist, 41*, 14–24.

MATARAZZO, J. D. (1986b). Response to Fowler and Butcher on Matarazzo. *American Psychologist, 41, 96*.

MATARAZZO, J. D. (1990). Psychological assessment versus psychological testing: Validation from Binet to the school, clinic, and courtroom. *American Psychologist, 45*, 999–1017.

MATHUR, P., & PALIWAL, A.K. (1986). Some personality factors related to accident behaviour: A study on textile mill workers. *Journal of the Indian Academy of Applied Psychology*, 12, 16–27.

MATSON, J. L. (1995). Comments on Gresham, MacMillan, and Siperstein's paper 'Critical analysis of the 1992 AAMR definition: Implications for school psychology'. *School Psychology Quarterly, 10*, 20–23.

MATTHEWS, G., JONES, D. M., & CHAMBERLAIN, A. G. (1992). Predictors of individual differences in mail-coding skills and their variation with ability level. *Journal of Applied Psychology*, 77, 406–418.

MAY, T. M. (1990). An evolving relationship. *Counseling Psychologist, 18*, 266–270.

MAYER, J. D., &. SALOVEY, P (1993). The intelligence of emotional intelligence. *Intelligence, 17*, 433–442.

MAZE, M., & MAYALL, D. (Eds.). (1995). *The enhanced guide for occupational exploration*. Indianapolis, IN: JIST.

MAZZEO, J., DRUESNE, B., RAFFELD, P. C., CHECKETTS, K. T., & MUHLSTEIN, A. (1991). *Comparability of computer and paper-and-pencil scores for two* CLEP *general examinations* (College Board Rep. No. 91–5; ETS Res. Rep. No. 92–14). Princeton, NJ: Educational Testing Service.

MCALLISTER, L. W. (1996). A *practical guide to CPI interpretation* (3rd ed.). Palo Alto, CA: Consulting Psychologists Press.

MCANDREW, F. T. (1993). *Environmental psychology*. Pacific Grove, CA: Brooks/Cole.

MCARTHUR, D. S., & ROBERTS, G. E. (1982). *Roberts Apperception Test for Children: Manual*. Los Angeles: Western Psychological Services.

MCBRIDE, J. R., & MARTIN, J. T. (1983). Reliability and validity of adaptive tests in a military setting. In, D. J. Weiss (Ed.), *New horizons in testing* (pp. 223–236). Orlando, FI: Academic Press.

MCCALL, R. B. (1976). Toward an epigenetic conception of mental development in the first three years of life. In M. Lewis (Ed.), *Origins of intelligence: Infancy and early childhood* (pp. 97–121). New York: Plenum Press.

MCCALL, R. B. (1981). Nature-nurture and the two realms of development: A proposed integration with respect to mental development. *Child Development, 52*, 1–12.

MCCALL, R. B., APPELBAUM, M. I., & HOGARTY, P. S. (1973). Developmental changes in mental performance. *Monographs of the Society for Research in Child Development, 38* (3, Serial No. 150).

MCCALL, R. B., EICHORN, D. H., & HOGARTY, P. S. (1977). Transitions in early mental development. *Monographs of the Society for Research in Child Development, 42* (3, Serial No. 171).

McCALL, R. B., HOGARTY, P. S., & HURLBURT, N. (1972). Transitions in infant sensorimotor development and the prediction of childhood IQ. *American Psychologist, 27,* 728–748.

McCALL, W. A. (1922). *How to measure in education.* New York: Macmillan.

McCALLUM, R. S. (1985). Review of Peabody Picture Vocabulary Test—Revised. *Ninth Mental Measurements Yearbook,* Vol. 2, 1126–1127.

McCALLUM, R. S. (1990). Determining the factor structure of the Stanford-Binet: Fourth Edition—The right choice. *Journal of Psychoeducational Assessment, 8,* 436–442.

McCARDLE, J. J. (1989). A structural modeling experiment with multiple growth functions. In R. Kanfer, P. L. Ackerman, & R. Cudek (Eds.), *Abilities, motivation, and tnethodology* (pp. 203–237). Hillsdale, NJ: Erlbaum.

McCARTHY, D. (1944). A study of the reliability of the Goodenough drawing test of intelligence. *Journal of Psychology, 18,* 201–216.

McCARTHY, D. (1972). *Manual for the McCarthy Scales of Children's Abilities.* New York: Psychological Corporation.

McCLELLAND, D. C. (1966). Longitudinal trends in the relation of thought to action. *Journal of Consulting Psychology, 30,* 479–483.

McCLELLAND, D. C. (1976). *The achieving society.* New York: Irvington. (Original work published 1961)

McCLELLAND, D. C. (1985). *Human motivation.* Glenview, IL: Scott, Foresman.

McCLELLAND, D. C., ATKINSON, J. W., CLARK, R. A., & LOWELL, E. L. (1976). *The achievement motive.* New York: Irvington. (Original work published 1953)

McCORMICK, E. J. (1979). *Job analysis: Methods and applications.* New York: AMACOM.

McCORMICK, E. J. (1983). Job and task analysis. In M. D. Dunnette (Ed.), *Handbook of industrial and organizational psychology* (pp. 651–696). New York: Wiley.

McCORMICK, E. J., &. ILGEN, D. (1980). *Industrial psychology* (7th ed.). Englewood Cliffs, NJ: Prentice Hall.

McCORMICK, E. J., JEANNERET, P. R., & MECHAM, R. C. (1972). A study of job characteristics and job dimensions as based on the Position Analysis Questionnaire (PAQ). *Journal of Applied Psychology,* 56, 347–368.

McCRAE, R. R., COSTA, JR., P. T. & MARTIN, T. A. (2005). The NEO–PI–3: A more readable revised NEO personality inventory. *Journal of Personality Assessment,* 84(3), 261-270, DOI: 10.1207/s15327752jpa8403_05. Retrieved June 8, 2016, from *http://dx.doi.org/10.1207/s15327752jpa8403_05*

McCRAE, R. R., &. JOHN, O. P. (1992). An introduction to the five-factor model and its applications. *Journal of Personality,* 60, 175–215.

McCUSKER, P. J. (1994). Validation of Kaufman, Ishikuma, and Kaufman-Packer's Wechsler Adult Intelligence Scale—Revised short forms on a clinical sample. *Psychological Assessment, 6,* 246–248.

McDANIEL, M. A., WHETZEL, D. L., SCHMIDT, F. L., & MAURER, S. D. (1994). The validity of employment interviews: A comprehensive review and meta-analysis. *Journal of Applied Psychology,* 79, 599–616.

McDERMOTT, P. A., FANTUZZO, J. W., & GLUTTING, J. J. (1990). Just say no to subtest analysis: A critique on Wechsler theory and practice. *Journal of Psychoeducational Assessment, 8,* 290–302.

McDERMOTT, P. A., FANTUZZO, J. W., GLUTTING, J. J., WATKINS, M. W., & BAGGALEY, A. R. (1992). Illusions of meaning in the ipsative assessment of children's ability. *Journal of Special Education, 25,* 504–526.

McDERMOTT, P. A., GLUTTING, J. J., JONES, J. N., &. NOONAN, J. V. (1989). Typology and prevailing composition of core profiles in the WAIS-R standardization sample. *Psychological Assessment, 1,* 118–125.

McDowell, C., & Acklin, M, W. (1996). Standardizing procedures for calculating Rorschach interrater reliability: Conceptual and empirical foundations. *Journal of Personality Assessment, 66,* 308–320.

McGee, M. G. (1979). Human spatial abilities: Psychometric studies and environmental, genetic, hormonal, and neurological influence. *Psychological Bulletin, 86,* 889–918.

McGrew, K. S. (1994). *Clinical interpretation of the Woodcock-Johnson Tests of Cognitive Ability—Revised.* Boston: Allyn &. Bacon.

McGrew, K. S., Werder, J. K., & Woodcock, R. W. (1991). *Woodcock-Johnson: Technical manual.* Allen, TX: DLM.

McGrew, M. W., & Teglasi, H. (1990). Formal characteristics of Thematic Apperception Test stories as indices of emotional disturbance in children. *Journal of Personality Assessment, 54,* 639–655.

McHenry, J. J., Hough, L. M., Toquam, J. L., Hanson, M. A., & Ashworth, S. (1990). Project A validity results: The relationship between predictor and criterion domains. *Personnel Psychology, 43,* 335–354.

McIntyre, R. M., Smith , D. E., & Hassett, C. E. (1984). Accuracy of performance ratings as affected by rater training and perceived purpose of rating. *Journal of Applied Psychology, 69,* 147–156.

McKenna, F. P. (1984). Measures of field dependence: Cognitive style or cognitive ability? *Journal of Personality and Social Psychology, 47,* 593–603.

McKeown, B. & Thomas, D. (1988). Q *methodology.* Newbury Park, CA: Sage.

McNeely, S. (1995). Review of the Alcohol Use Inventory. *Twelfth Mental Measurements Yearbook,* 66–67.

McReynolds, R (1975). Historical antecedents of personality assessment. In P. McReynolds (Ed.), *Advances in psychological assessment* (Vol. 3, pp. 477–532). San Francisco: Jossey-Bass.

McReynolds, P. (1986). History of assessment in clinical and educational settings. In R. O. Nelson & S. C. Hayes (Eds.), *Conceptual foundations of behavioral assessment* (pp. 42–80). New York: Guilford Press.

McReynolds, P., & DeVoge, S. (1978). Use of improvisational techniques in assessment. In P. McReynolds (Ed.), *Advances in psychological assessment* (Vol. 4, pp. 222–227). San Francisco: Jossey-Bass.

Mead, A. D., &. Drasgow, F. (1993). Equivalence of computerized and paper-and-pencil cognitive ability tests: A meta-analysis. *Psychological Bulletin, 114,* 449–458.

Meehl, P. E. (1945). An investigation of a general normality or control factor in personality testing. *Psychological Monographs, 59*(4, Whole No. 274).

Meehl, P. E. (1954). *Clinical versus statistical prediction: A theoretical analysis and a review of the evidence. Minneapolis: University of Minnesota Press.*

Meehl, P. E. (1956). Wanted—a good cookbook. *American Psychologist, 11,* 263–272.

Meehl, P. E. (1992). Factors and taxa, traits and types, differences of degree and differences in kind. *Journal of Personality, 60,* 117–174.

Meehl, P. E. (1995). Extension of the MAXCOV-HITMAX taxonomic procedure to situations of sizable nuisance covariance. In D. Lubinski & R. V. Dawis (Eds.), *Assessing individual differences in human behavior: New concepts, methods, and findings* (pp. 81–92). Palo Alto, CA: Davies-Black.

Meehl, P. E., & Golden, R. (1982). Taxometric methods. In P. Kendall & J. N. Butcher (Eds.), *Handbook of research methods in clinical psychology* (pp. 127–181). New York: Wiley.

MEEHL, P. E., & ROSEN, A. (1955). Antecedent probability and the efficiency of psychometric signs, patterns, or cutting scores. *Psychological Bulletin, 52,* 194–216.

MEEHL, P. E., & YONCE, L. J. (1994). Taxometric analysis: I. Detecting taxonicity with two quantitative indicators using means above and below a sliding cut (MAMBAC procedure). *Psychological Reports, 74,* 1059–1274.

MEEKER, M., MEEKER, R., & ROID, G. H. (1985). *Structure of Intellect Learning Abilities Test (SOI-LA): Manual.* Los Angeles: Western Psychological Services.

MEGARGEE, E. I. (1966). The relation of response length to the Holtzman Inkblot Technique. *Journal of Consulting Psychology, 30,* 415–419.

MEHRYAR, A. H., TASHAKKORI, A., YOUSEFI, F., &. KHAJAVI, F. (1987). The application of the Goodenough-Harris Draw-A-Man Test to a group of Iranian children in the city of Shiraz. *British Journal of Educational Psychology, 57,* 401–406.

MEIER, M. J. (1985). Review of Halstead-Reitan Neuropsychological Test Battery. *Ninth Mental Measurements Yearbook,* Vol. 1, 646–649.

MEIER, S. T. (1993). Revitalizing the measurement curriculum: Four approaches for emphasis in graduate education. *American Psychologist, 48,* 886–891.

MELLENBERGH, G. J. (1994). Generalized linear item response theory. *Psychological* Bulletin, 115, 300–307.

MELOY, J. R., & SINGER, J. (1991). A psychoanalytic view of the Rorschach Comprehensive System "special scores ." *Journal of Personality Assessment, 56,* 202–217.

MELTZOFF, J. (1951). The effect of mental set and item structure upon responses to a projective test. *Journal of Abnormal and Social Psychology, 46,* 177–189.

MENNE, J. W., MCCARTHY, W., & MENNE, J. (1976). A systems approach to the content validation of employee selection procedures. *Public Personnel Management, 5,* 387–396.

MERENDA, P F. (1995). Substantive issues in the Soroka v. Dayton-Hudson case. *Psychological Reports,* 77, 595–606.

MERLUZZI, T. V. (1991). Representation of information about self and other: A multidimensional scaling analysis. In M. J. Horowitz (Ed.), *Person schemas and maladaptive interpersonal patterns* (pp. 155–166). Chicago: University of Chicago Press.

MERRELL, K. (2003). *Behavioral, social, and emotional assessment of children and adolescents.* Florence, KY: Psychology Press.

MESSER, D. J., MCCARTHY, M. E., MCQUISTON, S., MACTURK, R. H., YARROW, L. J., & VLETZE, P. M. (1986). Relation between mastery behavior in infancy and competence in early childhood. *Developmental Psychology,* 22, 366-372.

MESSER, S. B. (1976). Reflection-impulsivity: A review. *Psychological Bulletin, 83,* 1026–1052.

MESSICK, S. (1980a). *The effectiveness of coaching for the SAT: Review and reanalysis of research from the fifties to the FTC.* Princeton, NJ: Educational Testing Service.

MESSICK, S. (1980b). Test validity and the ethics of assessment. *American Psychologist,* 35, 1012–1027.

MESSICK, S. (1981). The controversy over coaching: Issues of effectiveness and equity. In B. F. Green (Ed.), *Issues in testing: Coaching, disclosure, and ethnic bias* (pp. 21–53). San Francisco: Jossey-Bass.

MESSICK, S. (1988). The once and future issues of validity: Assessing the meaning and consequences of measurement. In H. Wainer & H. Braun (Eds.), *Test validity* (pp. 33–45). Hillsdale, NJ: Erlbaum.

MESSICK, S. (1989). Validity. In R. L. Linn (Ed.), *Educational measurement* (3rd ed., pp. 13–103). New York: American Council on Education/Macmillan.

MESSICK, S. (1992). Multiple intelligences or multilevel intelligence? Selective emphasis on distinctive properties of hierarchy: On Gardner's *Frames of mind* and Sternberg's *Beyond IQ* in the context of theory and research on the structure of human abilities. *Psychological Inquiry, 3* (4), 365–384.

MESSICK, S. (1995). Validity of psychological assessment: Validation of inferences from persons' responses and performances as scientific inquiry into score meaning. *American Psychologist, 50,* 741–749.

MESSICK, S., Et al. (1976). *Individuality in learning.* San Francisco: Jossey-Bass.

MESSICK, S., BEATON, A., & LORD, F. (1983). *National* Assessment *of Educational Progress reconsidered: A new design for a new era.* Princeton, NJ: National Assessment of Educational Progress.

MESSICK, S., & JUNGEBLUT, A. (1981). Time and method in coaching for the SAT. *Psychological Bulletin, 89,* 191–216.

MEYER, G. J. (1992). Response frequency problems in the Rorschach: Clinical and research implications with suggestions for the future. *Journal of Personality Assessment, 58,* 231–244.

MEYER, G. J. (1993). The impact of response frequency on the Rorschach constellation indices and on their validity with diagnostic and MMPI-2 criteria. *Journal of Personality* Assessment, 60, 153–180.

MEYER, P., &. DAVIS, S. (1992). *The CPI applications guide.* Palo Alto, CA: Consulting Psychologists Press.

MEYERS, J. F. (1992). *Soroka v. Dayton Hudson Corp.*—Is the door closing on pre-employment testing of applicants? *Employee Relations Law Journal, 17,* 645–653.

MIDDLETON, H. A., KEENE, R. G., &. BROWN, G. W. (1990). Convergent and discriminant validities of the Scales of Independent Behavior and the Revised Vineland Adaptive Behavior Scales. *American Journal on Mental Retardation, 94,* 669–673.

MILLER, A. (1991a). *Personality types: A modern synthesis.* Calgary, Alberta, Canada: University of Calgary Press.

MILLER, A. (1991b). Personality types, learning styles, and educational goals. *Educational Psychology, 11,* 217–238.

MILLER, L. T., & LEE, C. J. (1993). Construct validation of the Peabody Picture Vocabulary Test-Revised: A structural equation model of the acquisition order of words. *Psychological Assessment, 5,* 438–441.

MILLER, P. C., LEFCOURT, H. M., & WARE, E. E. (1983). The construction and development of the Miller Marital Locus of Control Scale. *Canadian Journal of Behavioural Science, 15,* 266–279.

MILLER, R, J. (1973). Cross-cultural research in the perception of pictorial materials. *Psychological Bulletin, 80,* 135–150.

MILLER, T. L. (Ed.). (1984). Special issue: Kaufman Assessment Battery for Children. *Journal of Special Education, 18* (3), 211–444.

MILLER-JONES, D. (1989). Culture and testing. *American Psychologist, 44,* 360–366.

MILLMAN, J., BISHOP, C. H., & EBEL, R. (1965). An analysis of test-wiseness. *Educational and Psychological Measurement, 25,* 707–726.

MILLMAN, J., &. GREENE, J. (1989). The Specification and development of tests of achievement and ability. In R. L. Linn (Ed.), *Educational measurement* (3rd ed., pp. 335–366). New York: American Council on Education/Macmillan.

MILLON, T. (1969). *Modern psychological pathology: A biosocial approach to maladaptive learning and functioning.* Philadelphia: Saunders.

MILLON, T. (1981). *Disorders of personality, DSM-III: Axis II.* New York: Wiley.

MILLON, T. (1990). *Toward a new personology: An evolutionary model.* New York: Wiley.

MILLON, T. (1994). *Millon* Index *of Personality Styles (MIPS) manual*. San Antonio, TX: Psychological Corporation.

MILLON, T. (with Davis, R. D., and Millon, C. M., Wenger, A., Van Zuilen, M. H., Fuchs, M., & Millon, R. B.). (1996). *Disorders of personality: DSM-*IV *and beyond* (2nd ed.). New York: Wiley.

MILLON, T., GREEN, C. J., & MEAGHER, R. B., JR. (1982). *Millon Adolescent Personality Inventory manual*. Minneapolis, MN: National Computer Systems.

MILLON, T., MILLON, C., & DAVIS, R. (1993). *Millon Adolescent Clinical Inventory (MACI) manual. Minneapolis,* MN: National Computer Systems.

MILLON, T., MILLON, C., & DAVIS, R. (1994). MCM*I-II manual: Millon Clinical Multiaxial Inventory-III*. Minneapolis, MN: National Computer Systems.

MISCHEL, W. (1968). *Personality and assessment*. New York: Wiley.

MISCHEL, W. (1969). Continuity and change in personality. *American Psychologist, 24,* 1012–1018.

MISCHEL, W. (1973). Toward a cognitive social learning reconceptualization of personality. *Psychological Review, 80,* 252–283.

MISCHEL, W. (1977). On the future of personality measurement. *American Psychologist, 32,* 246–254.

MISCHEL, W. (1979). On the interface of cognition and personality: Beyond the person-situation debate. *American Psychologist, 34,* 740–754.

MISCHEL, W., &. PEAKE, P. K. (1982). Beyond deja vu in the search for cross-situational consistency. *Psychological Review, 89,* 730–755.

MISLEVY, R. J. (1993). A framework for studying differences between multiple-choice and free-response test items. In R. E. Bennett & W. C. Ward (Eds.), *Construction versus choice in cognitive measurement: Issues in constructed response, performance testing, and portfolio assessment* (pp. 75–106). Hillsdale, NJ: Erlbaum.

MISTRY, J., & ROGOFF, B. (1985). A cultural perspective on the development of talent. In F. D. Horowitz & M. O'Brien (Eds.), *The gifted and talented: Developmental perspectives.* Washington, DC: American Psychological Association.

MITCHELL, B. C. (1967). Predictive validity of the Metropolitan Readiness Tests and the Murphy-Durrell Reading Readiness Analysis for white and negro pupils. *Educational and Psychological Measurement, 27,* 1047–1054.

MLTCHELL, T. W., & KLIMOSKI, R. J. (1986). Estimating the validity of cross-validity estimation. *Journal of Applied Psychology, 71,* 311–317.

MOEN, P, ELDER, G. H., JR., & LÜSCHER, K. (Eds.). (1995). *Examining lives in context: Perspectives on the ecology of human development*. Washington, DC: American Psychological Association.

MOLLENKOPF, W. G. (1950a). An experimental study of the effects on item-analysis data of changing item placement and test time limit. *Psychometrika, 15,* 291–317.

MOLLENKOPF, W. G. (1950b). Predicted differences and differences between predictions. *Psychometrika, 15,* 409–417.

MOORE, B. S., & ISEN, A. M. (Eds.).(1990). *Affect and social behavior.* New York: Cambridge University Press.

MOORE, H. W., & UNSINGER, P. C. (Eds.). (1987). *The police assessment center.* Springfield, IL: Charles C Thomas.

MOORE, M. S., & MCLAUGHLIN, L. (1992). Assessment of the preschool child with visual impairment. In E. Vazquez Nutall, I. Romero, & J. Kalesnik (Eds.), *Assessing and screening preschoolers: Psychological and educational dimensions* (pp. 345–368). Boston: Allyn & Bacon.

MOOS, R. H. (1974). *Evaluating treatment environments: A social ecological approach*. New York: Wiley.

MOOS, R. (1993a). *The Family* Environment *Scale: An annotated bibliography.* Palo Alto, CA: Stanford University and VA Medical Center, Center for Health Care Evaluation.

MOOS, R. (1993b). *The Group Environment Scale: An annotated bibliography.* Palo Alto, CA: Stanford University and VA Medical Center, Center for Health Care Evaluation.

MOOS, R. (1993c). *The Work Environment Scale: An annotated bibliography.* Palo Alto, CA: Stanford University and VA Medical Center, Center for Health Care Evaluation.

MOOS, R. H. (1994a). *The Social Climate Scales: A user's guide.* Palo Alto, CA: Consulting Psychologists Press.

MOOS, R. H. (1994b). *Work Environment Scale manual: Development, applications, research* (3rd ed.). Palo Alto, CA: Consulting Psychologists Press.

MOOS, R. H., &. MOOS, B. S. (1994). *Family Environment Scale manual: Development,* applications, *research* (3rd ed.). Palo Alto, CA: Consulting Psychologists Press.

MOOS, R. H., & SPINRAD, S. (1984). *The social climate scales: An annotated blibliography, 1979–1983.* Palo Alto, CA: Consulting Psychologists Press.

MORELAND, K. L. (1985). Validation of computer-based test interpretations: Problems and prospects. *Journal of Consulting and Clinical Psychology, 53,* 816–825.

MORELAND, K. L. (1987). Computer-based test interpretation: Advice to the consumer. *Applied Psychology: An International Review, 36(3/4), 385–399.*

MORELAND, K. L. (1992). Computer-assisted psychological assessment. In M. Zeidner &. R. Most (Eds.), *Psychological testing:* An *inside view* (pp. 343–376). Palo Alto, CA: Consulting Psychologists Press.

MORELAND, K. L., EYDE, L. D., ROBERTSON, G. J., PRIMOFF, E. S., & MOST, R. B. (1995). Assessment of test user qualifications: A research-based measurement procedure. *American Psychologist, 50,* 14–23.

MORENO, J. L. (1953). *Who shall survive? Foundations of sociometry, group psychotherapy, and sociodrama* (2nd ed.). New York: Beacon House.

MORENO, K. E., WETZEL, C. D., MCBRIDE, J. R., & WEISS, D. J. (1984). Relationship between corresponding Armed Services Vocational Aptitude Battery (ASVAB) and computerized adaptive testing (CAT) subtests. *Applied Psychological Measurement, 8,* 155–163.

MOREY, L. C. (1991). *Personality Assessment Inventory: Professional manual.* Odessa, FL: Psychological Assessment Resources.

MORGAN, G. A., & HARMON, R. J. (1984). Developmental transformations in mastery motivation. In R. N. Emde & R. J. Harmon (Eds.), *Continuities and discontinuities in development* (pp. 263–291). New York: Plenum Press.

MORGAN, W. G. (1995). Origin and history of the Thematic Apperception Test images. *Journal of Personality Assessment, 65,* 237–254.

MORRIS, J. H., SHERMAN, J. D., & MANSFIELD, E. R. (1986). Failures to detect moderating effects with ordinary least squares-moderated multiple regressions: Some reasons and a remedy. *Psychological Bulletin,* 99, 282–288.

MORRISON, J. (1995). *The first interview: Revised for DSM-IV.* New York: Guilford Press.

MORRISON, T. L., EDWARDS, D. W, & WEISSMAN, H. N. (1994). The MMPI and MMPI-2 as predictors of psychiatric diagnosis in an outpatient sample. *Journal of Personality Assessment, 62,* 17–30.

MOSES, J. L. (1985). Using clinical methods in a high-level management assessment center. In H. J. Bernardin & D. A. Bownas (Eds.), *Personality assessment in organizations* (pp. 177–192). New York: Praeger.

MOSSHOLDER, K. W., &. ARVEY, R. D. (1984). Synthetic validity: A conceptual and comparative review. *Journal of Applied Psychology, 69*, 322–333.

MUELLER, D. J. (1986). *Measuring social attitudes: A handbook for researchers and practitioners.* New York: Teachers College Press.

MUELLER, R. O. (1995). Review of the Work Environment Scale, Second Edition. *Twelfth Mental Measurements Yearbook,* 1121–1122.

MULAIK, S. A., JAMES, L. R., VAN ALSTINE, J., BENNETT, N., LIND, S., & STILWELL, C. D. (1989). Evaluation of goodness-of-fit indices for structural equation models. *Psychological Bulletin, 105*, 430–445.

MULCAHY, R. F., SHORT, R. H., & ANDREWS, J. (Eds.). (1991). *Enhancing learning and thinking.* New York: Praeger.

MULLEN, J. D., & ROTH, B. M. (1991). *Decision making: Its logic and practice.* Savage, MD: Rowman &. Littlefield.

MULLEN, Y. (1992). Assessment of the preschool child with hearing impairment. In E. Vazquez Nutall, I. Romero, & J. Kalesnik (Eds.), *Assessing and screening preschoolers: Psychological and educational dimensions* (pp. 327–343). Boston: Allyn & Bacon.

MUMFORD, M. D., & STOKES, G. S. (1992). Developmental determinants of individual action: Theory and practice in applying background measures. In M. D. Dunnette & L. M. Hough, (Eds.), *Handbook of industrial and organizational psychology,* (2nd ed., Vol. 3, pp. 61–138). Palo Alto, CA: Consulting Psychologist Press.

MUMFORD, M. D., STOKES, G. S., & OWENS, W. A. (1990). *Patterns of life adaptation: The ecology of human individuality.* Hillsdale, NJ: Erlbaum.

MURPHY, G., & KOVACH, J. R. (1972). *Historical introduction to modern psychology* (3rd ed.). San Diego, CA: Harcourt, Brace, Jovanovich.

MURPHY, K. R. (1992). Review of the Test of Nonverbal Intelligence, Second Edition. *Eleventh Mental Measurements Yearbook,* pp. 969–970.

MURPHY, K. R. (1993). *Honesty in the workplace.* Pacific Grove, CA: Brooks/Cole.

MURPHY, K. R., & ANHALT, R. L. (1992). Is halo error a property of the rater, ratees, or the specific behaviors observed? *Journal of Applied Psychology,* 77, 494–500.

MURPHY, K. R., & BALZER, W. K. (1989). Rater errors and rating accuracy. *Journal of Applied Psychology, 74*, 619–624.

MURRAY, H. A., et al. (1938). *Explorations in personality: A clinical and experimental study of fifty men of college age.* New York: Oxford University Press.

MURRAY, H. A., et al. (1943). *Thematic Apperception Test: Manual.* Cambridge, MA: Harvard University Press.

MURRAY, H. A., & MACKINNON, D. W. (1946). Assessment of OSS personnel. *Journal of Consulting Psychology, 10*, 76–80.

MURSTEIN, B. I. (1963). *Theory and research in projective techniques (emphasizing the TAT).* New York: Wiley.

MURSTEIN, B. I. (1972). Normative written TAT responses for a college sample. *Journal of Personality Assessment,* 36, 213–217.

MUSSEN, P. H., & NAYLOR, H. K. (1954). The relationships between overt and fantasy aggression. *Journal of Abnormal and Social Psychology, 49*, 235–240.

MYERS, H. F., WOHLFORD, P., GUZMAN, L. P., & ECHEMENDIA, R. J. (Eds.). (1991). *Ethnic minority perspective on clinical training and services in psychology.* Washington, DC: American Psychological Association.

MYERS, I. B. (1962). *Manual: The* Myers-Briggs *Type Indicator.* Princeton, NJ: Educational Testing Service.

MYERS, I. B., & MCCAULLEY, M. H. (1985). *Manual: A guide to the development and use of the Myers-Briggs Type Indicator. Palo Alto,* CA: Consulting Psychologists Press.

Nadien, M. B. (1989). *Adult years and aging.* Dubuque, IA: Kendall/Hunt.

Naglieri, J. A. (1988). *Draw A Person: A quantitative scoring system—Manual.* San Antonio, TX: Psychological Corporation.

Naglieri, J. A., &. Das, J. P. (1990). Planning, attention, simultaneous, and successive (PASS) cognitive processes as a model for intelligence. *Journal of Psychoeducational Assessment, 8,* 303–337.

Naglieri, J. A., & Das, J. P. (1997a). *Das-Naglieri Cognitive Assessment System: Administration and scoring manual. Itasca,* IL: Riverside.

Naglieri, J. A., & Das, J. P. (1997b). *Das-Naglieri Cognitive Assessment System: Interpretive handbook.* Itasca, IL: Riverside.

Naglieri, J. A., &. Pfeiffer, S. I. (1992). Performance of disruptive behavior disordered and normal samples on the Draw A Person: Screening Procedure for Emotional Disturbance. *Psychological Assessment, 4,* 156–159.

Naglieri, J. A., & Prewett, P. N. (1990). Nonverbal intelligence measures: A selected review of instruments and their use. In C. R. Reynolds & R. W. Kamphaus (Eds.), *Handbook of psychological and educational assessment of children: Intelligence and achievement* (pp. 348–370). New York: Guilford Press.

Nathan, B. R. (1986). The halo effect: It is a unitary concept! *Journal of Occupational Psychology, 59,* 41–44.

National Assessment of Educational Progress (NAEP). (1985). *The reading report card: Progress toward excellence in our schools (NAEP Report 15-R-01).* Princeton, NJ: Author.

National Commission on Testing and Public Policy. (1990). *From gatekeeper to gateway: Transforming testing in America. Chestnut Hill,* MA: Boston College and Author.

National Council on Education Standards and Testing. (1992). *Raising staitdards for American education: A Report to Congress, the Secretary of Education, the National Education Goals Panel, and the American People.* Washington, Dc: Author.

National Research Council, (1991). Measuring Job Competency. *Performance Assessment for the Workplace, Volume II: Technical Issues.* Washington, DC: The National Academies Press. Doi:10.17226/1898.

Naylor, J. C., & Shine, L. C. (1965). A table for determining the increase in mean criterion score obtained by using a selection device. *Journal of Industrial Psychology, 3,* 33–42.

Neimark, E. D. (1987). *Adventures in thinking.* San Diego, CA: Harcourt Brace Jovanovich. (Ed.).

Neimeyer, G. J. (1989). Applications of repertory grid technique to vocational assessment. *Journal of Counseling and Development, 67,* 585–589.

Neimeyer, G. J. (Ed.) (1993). *Constructivist assessment: A casebook.* Thousand Oaks, CA: Sage.

Neimeyer, G. J., & Neimeyer, R. A. (Eds.). (1990). Advances in *personal construct psychology* (Vol. 1). Greenwich, CT: JAI Press.

Neimeyer, R. A., & Mahoney, M. J. (Eds.). (1995). *Constructivism in psychotherapy.* Washington, DC: American Psychological Association.

Neimeyer, R. A., &. Neimeyer, G. J. (Eds.). (1992). *Advances in personal construct psychology* (Vol. 2). Greenwich, CT: JAI Press.

Neisser, U. (1976). General, academic, and artificial intelligence. In L. B. Resnick (Ed.), *The nature of intelligence* (pp. 135–144). Hillsdale, NJ: Erlbaum.

Neisser, U. (1979). The concept of intelligence. *Intelligence,* 3, 217–227.

Neisser, U., Boodoo, G., Bouchard, T. J., Jr., Boykin, A. W., Brody, N., Ceci, S. J., Halpern, D. F., Loehlin, J. C., Perloff, R., Sternberg, R.j., & Urbina, S. (1996). Intelligence: Knowns and unknowns. *American Psychologist, 51,* 77–101.

NELSON, R. O., & HAYES, S. C. (1986). the Nature of Behavioral Assessment. In R. O. Nelson & S. C. Hayes (Eds.), *Conceptual foundations of behavioral assessment* (pp. 3–41). New York: Guilford Press.

NESSELROADE, J. R., & REESE, H. W. (eds.). (1973). *Life-span developmental psychology: Methodological issues.* New York: Academic Press.

NESSELROADE, J. R., & VON EYE, A. (eds.). (1985). *Individual development and social change: Exploratory analysis.* Orlando, FL: Academic Press.

NESTER, M. A. (1994). Psychometric testing and reasonable accommodation for persons with disabilities. In S. M. Bruyère & J. O'Keeffe (Eds.), *Implications of the Americans with Disabilities Act for psychology* (pp. 25–36). Washington, DC: American Psychological Association.

NETTER, B. E. C., &. VLGLIONE, D. J., JR. (1994). An empirical study of malingering schizophrenia on the Rorschach. *Journal of Personality* Assessment, 62, 45–57.

NEUFELDT, S. A., IVERSEN, J. N., & JUNTUNEN, C. L. (1995). *Supervision strategies for the first practicum.* Alexandria, VA: American Counseling Association,

NEVILL, D. D., & SUPER, D. E. (1989). *The Values Scale: Theory, application, and research—Manual* (2nd ed.). Palo Alto, CA: Consulting Psychologists Press.

NEVO, B. (1985). Face validity revisited. *Journal of Educational Measurement, 22,* 287–293.

NEVO, B. (1992). Examinee feedback: Practical guidelines. In M. Zeidner & R. Most (Eds.), *Psychological testing:* An *inside view* (pp. 377–398). Palo Alto, CA: Consulting Psychologists Press.

NEVO, B., & JÄGER, R. S. (eds.). (1993). *Educational and psychological testing: The test taker's outlook.* Göttingen, Germany: Hogrefe & Huber.

NEVO, B., & SFEZ, J. (1985). Examinees' feedback questionnaires. Assessment *and Evaluation in Higher Education, 10,* 236–249.

NEVO, O., & NEVO, B. (1983). What do you do when asked to answer humorously? *Journal of Personality and Social Psychology, 44,* 188–194.

NEWELL, A., & SIMON, H. A. (1972). *Human problem solving.* Englewood Cliffs, NJ: Prentice Hall.

NEWLAND, T. E. (1979). The Blind Learning Aptitude Test. *Journal of Visual Impairment and Blindness, 73,* 134–139.

NIAZ, M. (1987). Mobility-fixity dimension in Witkin's theory of field-dependence/independence and its implications for problem solving in science. *Perceptual and* Motor *Skills, 65,* 755–764.

NICHOLS, D. S. (1992). Review of the Minnesota Multiphasic Personality Inventory-2. *Eleventh Mental Measurements Yearbook,* 562–565.

NICHOLS, D. S., & GREENE, R. L. (1995). MMP1–2 *structural summary: Interpretive manual.* Odessa, FL: Psychological Assessment Resources.

NICHOLS, J. G. (1979). Quality and equality in intellectual development: The role of motivation in education. *American Psychologist, 34,* 1071–1084.

NICHOLS, P. L., & BROMAN, S. H. (1974). Familial resemblance in infant mental development. *Developmental Psychology, 10,* 442–446.

NICHOLSON, C. L., & ALCORN, C. L. (1994). *Educational applications of the WISC-III: A handbook of interpretive strategies and remedial recommendations.* Los Angeles: Western Psychological Services.

NICKERSON, R. S. (1988). On improving thinking through instruction. *Review of Research in Education, 15,* 3–57.

NIHIRA, K., LELAND, H., & LAMBERT, N. (1993). *AAMR Adaptive Scale—Residential and Community—Second Edition: Examiner's Manual. Austin, TX: PRO-ED.*
The Ninth Mental Measurements Yearbook. (1985). Lincoln, NE: Buros Institute of Mental Measurements.

NISBET, J. D. (1957). Symposium: Contributions to intelligence testing and the theory of intelligence: IV. Intelligence and age: Retesting with twenty-four years' interval. *British Journal of Educational Psychology, 27,* 190–198.

NITKO, A. J. (1984). Defining "criterion-referenced test." In R. A. Berk (Ed.), *A guide to criterion-referenced test construction* (pp. 8–28). Baltimore: Johns Hopkins University Press.

NITKO, A. J. (1989). Designing tests that are integrated with instruction. In R. L. Linn (Ed.), *Educational measurement* (3rd ed., pp. 447–474). New York: American Council on Education/Macmillan.

NORRIS, L., SCHOTT, P. S., SHATKIN, L., & BENNETT, M. F. (1986). *The development and field testing of SIGI PLUS* (ETS Res. Mem., 86–6). Princeton, NJ: Educational Testing Service.

NOVICK, M. R., & LEWIS, C. (1967). Coefficient alpha and the reliability of composite measurements. *Psychometrika, 32,* 1–13.

NOVY, D. M. (1992). Gender comparability of Forms 81 of the Washington University Sentence Completion Test. *Educational and Psychological Measurement, 52,* 491–497.

NOVY, D. M., & FRANCIS, D. J. (1992). Psychometric properties of the Washington University Sentence Completion Test. *Educational and Psychological Measurement, 52,* 1029–1039.

NOVY, D. M., GAA, J. P., FRANKIEWICZ, R. G., LIBERMAN, D., &. AMERIKANER, M. (1992). The association between patterns of family functioning and ego development of the juvenile offender. *Adolescence, 27,* 25–35.

NOWICKI, S., JR., & DUKE, M. P. (1983). The Nowicki-Strickland life-span locus of control scales: Construct validation. In H. M. Lefcourt (Ed.), *Research with the locus of control construct* (Vol. 2, pp. 13–51). Orlando, FL: Academic Press.

NUGENT, J. K., LESTER, B. M., & BRAZELTON, T. B. (eds.). (1991). *The cultural context of infancy, Vol. 2: Multicultural and interdisciplinary approaches to parent-infant relations.* Norwood, NJ: Ablex.

OAKLAND, T., GLUTTING, J., &. HORTON, C. (1996). *Student Styles* Questionnaire: *Manual.* San Antonio, TX: Psychological Corporation.

OAKLAND, T., & HAMBLETON, R. K. (eds.). (1995). *International perspectives on academic assessment.* Boston: Kluwer.

OAKLAND, T., & HU, S. (1992). The top 10 tests used with children and youth world wide. *Bulletin of the International Test Commission, 19,* 99–120.

O'BRIEN, W. H., &. HAYNES, S. N. (1993). Behavioral assessment in the psychiatric setting. In A. S. Bellack & M. Hersen (Eds.), *Handbook of behavior therapy in the psychiatric setting* (pp. 39–71). New York: Plenum Press.

OBRZUT, J. E., & BOLIEK, C. A. (1986). Thematic approaches to personality assessment with children and adolescents. In H. M. Knoff (Ed.), *The assessment of child and adolescent personality* (pp. 173–198). New York: Guilford Press.

OETTING, E. R., &. DEFFENBACHER, J. L. (1980). *Text Anxiety Profile manual.* Fort Collins, CO: Rocky Mountain Behavioral Science Institute.

OFFICE OF TECHNOLOGY ASSESSMENT. (1992). *Testing in American schools: Asking the right questions* (OTA-SET-520). Washington, DC: U.S. Government Printing Office.

OGILVIE, D. M., &. ASHMORE, R. D. (1991). Self-with-other representation as a unit of analysis in self-concept research. In R. C. Curtis (Ed.), *The relational self* (pp. 282–314). New York: Guilford Press.

OLES, H. J., & DAVIS, G. D. (1977). Publishers violate APA standards on test distribution. *Psychological Reports, 41,* 713–714.

OLKIN, I., & FINN, J. D. (1995). Correlations redux. *Psychological Bulletin, 118,* 155–164.

OLLENDICK, T. H., & HERSEN, M. (eds.). (1993). *Handbook of child and adolescent assessment*. Boston: Allyn & Bacon.

OLSAT, 7th ed.: Technical Manual. (1997). San Antonio, TX: Harcourt Brace.

OLSON, J. M., & ZANNA, M. P. (1993). Attitudes and attitude change. *Annual Review of Psychology, 44,* 117–154.

OLSON-BUCHANAN, J. B., DRASGOW, E, MOBERG, P. J., MEAD, A. D., & KEENAN, P. *(1996). The Conflict Resolution Skills Assessment: Model-based, multimedia measurement*. Manuscript submitted for publication.

OLTON, R. M., &. CRUTCHFIELD, R. S. (1969). Developing the skills of productive thinking. In P. H. Mussen, J. Langer, & M. Covington (Eds.), *Trends and issues in developmental psychology* (pp. 68–91). New York: Holt, Rinehart & Winston.

On Your Own: Preparing for a Stattdardized Test (videodisk). (1987). Princeton, NJ: Educational Testing Service.

ONES, D. S., VLSWESVARAN, C., & SCHMIDT, F. L. (1993). Comprehensive meta-analysis of integrity test validities: Findings and implications for personnel selection and theories of job performance. *Journal of Applied Psychology Monographs,* 78, 679–703.

OOSTERHOF, A. C. (1976). Similarity of various item discrimination indices. *Journal of Educational Measurement, 13,* 145–150.

OOSTERVELD, P. (1994). Confirmatory factor analysis of the Self-Directed Search test: A multitrait-multimethod approach. *Personality and Individual Differences, 17,* 565–569.

OOSTERWEGEL, A., &. OPPENHEIMER, L. (1993). *The self-system: developmental changes between and within self-concepts.* Hillsdale, NJ: Erlbaum.

ORLANSKY, M. D. (1988). Assessment of visually impaired infants and preschool children. In T. D. Wachs &. R. Sheehan (Eds.), Assessment *of young developmentally* disabled *children* (pp. 93–107). New York: Plenum Press.

ORTAR, G. (1963). Is a verbal test cross-cultural? *Scripta Hierosolymitana, 13,* 219–235.

ORTAR, G. (1972). Some principles for adaptation of psychological tests. In L. J. Cronbach & P. J. D. Drenth (Eds.), *Mental tests and cultural adaptation* (pp. 111–120). The Hague: Mouton.

OSGOOD, C. E., SUCI, G. J., & TANNENBAUM, P. H. (1957). *The measurement of mean' ing.* Urbana: University of Illinois Press.

OSIPOW, S. H. (1973). *Theories of career development* (2nd ed.). New York: Appleton Century-Crofts.

OSS ASSESSMENT STAFF. (1948). *ASSESSMENT of men: Selection of personnel for the Office of Strategic Services.* New York: Rinehart.

OSTERLIND, S. J. (1983). *Test item bias.* Newbury Park, CA: Sage.

OSTROM, T. M., BOND, C. E, JR., KROSNICK, J. A., & SEDIKIDES, C. (1994). Attitude scales: How we measure the unmeasureable. In S. Shavitt & T. C. Brock (Eds.), *Persuasion: Psychological insights and perspectives* (pp. 15–42). Boston: Allyn & Bacon.

OWENS, W. A. (1953). Age and mental abilities: A longitudinal study. *Genetic Psychology Monographs, 48,* 3–54.

OWENS, W. A. (1966). Age and mental abilities: A second adult follow-up. *Journal of Educational Psychology, 57,* 311–325.

OWENS, W. A. (1983). Background data. In M. D. Dunnette (Ed.), *Handbook of industrial and organizational psychology* (pp. 609–644). New York: Wiley.

OWENS, W. A., &. SCHOENFELDT, L. F. (1979). Toward a classification of persons [Monograph]. *Journal of Applied Psychology, 64, 569–607.*

OWINGS, R. A., PETERSEN, G. A., BRANSFORD, J. D., MORRIS, C. D., & STEIN, B. S. (1980). Spontaneous monitoring and regulation of learning: A comparison of successful and less successful fifth graders. *Journal of Educational Psychology, 72*, 250–256.

Ownby, R. L. (1991). *Psychological reports: A guide to report writing in professional psychology (2nd ed.). Brandon*, VT: Clinical Psychology Publishing Co.

Ozer, D. J. (1993). The Q-sort method and the study of personality development. In D. C. Funder, R. D. Parke, C. Tomlinson-Keasey, & K. Widaman (Eds.), *Studying lives through time: Personality and development* (pp. 147–168). Washington, DC: American Psychological Association.

Ozer, D. J., & Reise, S. P. (1994). Personality assessment. *Annual Review of Psychology, 45*, 357–388.

Paajanen, G. E., Hansen, T. L., & Mclellan, R. A. (1993). *PDI Employment Inventory and PDI Customer Service Inventory manual. Minneapolis*, MN: Personnel Decisions.

Page, E. B. (1985). Review of Kaufman Assessment Battery for Children. *Ninth Mental Measurements Yearbook*, Vol. 1, 773–777.

Paget, K. D. (1991). Fundamentals of family assessment. In B. A. Bracken (Ed.), *The psychoeducational assessment of preschool children* (2nd ed., pp. 514–528). Boston: Allyn & Bacon.

Palermo, D. S., & Jenkins, J. J. (1963). Frequency of superordinate responses to a word association test as a function of age. *Journal of Verbal Learning and Verbal Behavior, 1*, 378–383.

Palisin, H. (1986). Preschool temperament and performance on achievement tests. *Developmental Psychology, 22*, 766–770.

Palmore, E. (Ed.) (1970). *Normal aging.* Durham, NC: Duke University Press.

Palomares, R. S., Crowley, S. L., Worchel, F. E, Olson, T. K., & Rae, W. A. (1991). The factor analytic structure of the Roberts Apperception Test for Children: A comparison of the standardization sample with a sample of chronically ill children. *Journal of Personality Assessment, 56*, 414–425.

Panell,r.c.,&laabs,g. J. (1979). Construction of a criterion-referenced, diagnostic test for an individualized instruction program. *Journal of Applied Psychology, 64*, 255–261.

Paniagua, F. A. (1994). *Assessing and treating culturally diverse clients: A practical guide.* Thousand Oaks, CA: Sage.

Parker, K. C. H., Hanson, R. K., & Hunsley, J. (1988). MMPI, Rorschach, and WAIS: A meta-analytic comparison of reliability, stability, and validity. *Psychological Bulletin, 103*, 367–373.

Parker, R. M. (1991a). *Occupational Aptitude Survey and Interest Schedule, Second Edition (OASIS-2)—Aptitude Survey: Examiner's manual*. Austin, TX: PRO-ED.

Parker, R. M. (1991b). *Occupational Aptitude Survey and Interest Schedule, Second Edition* (OASIS-2)—*Interest Schedule: Examiner's manual*. Austin, TX: PRO-ED.

Parkerson, J. A., Lomax, R. G., Schiller, D. P., & Walberg, H. J. (1984). Exploring causal models of educational achievement, *Journal of Educational Psychology*, 76, 638–646.

Pascal, G. R., & Suttell, B. J. (1951). *The Bender-Gestalt Test: Quantification and validity for adults.* New York: Grune & Stratton.

Pascual-leone, J., & Ijaz, H. (1991). Mental capacity testing as a form of intellectual-developmental assessment. In R. P. Samuda, S. L. Kong, J. Cummins, J. Pascual-Leone, & J. Lewis (Eds.), *Assessment and placement of minority students* (pp. 143–171). Toronto: Hogrefe.

Pashley, P. J. (1992). *Graphical IRT-based DIF analyses* (Res. Rep. No. 92–66). Princeton, NJ: Educational Testing Service.

PAUL, G. L., & ERIKSEN, C. W. (1964). Effects of test anxiety on "real-life" examinations. *Journal of Personality, 32,* 480–494.

PAULHUS, D. L. (1983). Sphere-specific measures of perceived control. *Journal of Personality and Social Psychology, 44,* 1253–1265.

PAULHUS, D. L. (1984). Two-component models of socially desirable responding. *Journal of Personality and Social Psychology, 46,* 598–609.

PAULHUS, D. L. (1986). Self-deception and impression management in test responses. In A. Angleitner & J. S. Wiggins (Eds.), *Personality assessment via questionnaires: Current issues in theory and measurement* (pp. 143–165). Berlin: Springer-Verlag.

PAULHUS, D. L. (1991). Measurement and control of response bias. In J. P. Robinson, P. R. Shaver, & L. S. Wrightsman (Eds.), Measures *of personality and social psychological attitudes.* San Diego, CA: Academic Press.

PAULHUS, D. L., & BRUCE, M. N. (1992). The effect of acquaintanceship on the validity of personality impressions: A longitudinal study. *Journal of Personality and Social Psychology, 63,* 816–824.

PAULHUS, D. L., & REID, D. B. (1991). Enhancement and denial in socially desirable responding. *Journal of Personality and Social Psychology, 60,* 307–317.

PAULMAN, R. G. AND KENNELLY, K. J. (1984). Test Anxiety and Ineffective Test Taking: Different Names, Same Construct? *Journal of Educational Psychology,* 76(2), pp. 279.

PAUNONEN, S. V. (1993, August). *Sense, nonsense, and the Big Five Factors of Personality.* Paper presented at the convention of the American Psychological Association, Toronto, Canada.

PAUNONEN, S. V., JACKSON, D. N., TRZEBINSKI, J., & FORSTERLING, F. (1992). Personality structure across cultures: A multimethod evaluation. *Journal of Personality and Social Psychology, 62, 447–456.*

PAYNE, R. N. (1985). Review of the SCL-90-R. *Ninth Mental Measurements Yearbook,* Vol. 2, 1326–1329.

PEARLMAN, K., SCHMIDT, F. L., & HUNTER, J. E. (1980). Validity generalization results for tests used to predict job proficiency and training success in clerical occupations. *Journal of Applied Psychology,* 65, 373–406.

PEARSON, K. (1901). On lines and planes of closest fit to systems of points in space. *Philosophical Magazine (Series 6), 2, 559–572.*

PEDERSEN, P. B. (1987). *Handbook of cross-cultural counseling and therapy.* Westport, CT: Greenwood.

PEDERSEN, P. B., & IVEY, A. (1993). *Culture-centered counseling and interviewing skills: A practical guide.* Westport, CT: Greenwood.

PEEL, E. A. (1951). A note on practice effects in intelligence tests. *British Journal of Educational Psychology, 21,* 122–125.

PEEL, E. A. (1952). Practice effects between three consecutive tests of intelligence. *British Journal of Educational Psychology, 22,* 196–199.

PELLEGRINO, J. W., & GLASER, R. (1979). Cognitive correlates and components in the analysis of individual differences. *Intelligence,* 3, 187–214.

PELLEGRINO, J. W., MUMAW, R. J., & SHUTE, V. J. (1985). Analyses of Spatial aptitude and expertise. In S. E. Embretson (Ed.), *Test design: Developments in psychology and psychometrics* (pp. 45–76). Orlando, FL: Academic Press.

PEMBERTON, C. L. (1952). The closure factors related to temperament. *Journal of Personality, 21,* 159–175.

PENNER, L. A., BATSCHE, G. M., KNOFF, H. M., & NELSON, D. L. (Eds.). (1993). *The challettge in mathematics and science education: Psychology's response. Washington, DC: American Psychological Association.*

PENNINGTON, B. F. (1991). *Diagnosing learning disorders: A neuropsychological framework*. New York: Guilford Press.

PENNOCK-ROMÁN, M. (1990). *Test validity and language background: A study of HispanicAmerican students at six universities.* New York: College Entrance Examination Board.

PERRY, G. G., & KINDER, B. N. (1990). The susceptibility of the Rorschach to malingering: A critical review. *Journal of Personality Assessment, 54,* 47–57.

PERRY, W. (1993). Rorschach for the '90s: An interpretation milestone. *Journal of Personality* Assessment, 60, 418–420.

PETERSEN, N. S., KOLEN, M. J., & HOOVER, H. D. (1989). Scaling, norming, and equating. In R. L. Linn (Ed.), *Educational measurement* (3rd ed., pp. 221–262). New York: American Council on Education/Macmillan.

PETERSEN, N. S., & NOVICK, M. R. (1976). An evaluation of some models for culture-fair selection. *Journal of Educational Measurement, 13,* 3–29.

PETERSON, C. A. (1994). Book review: The Eleventh Mental Measurements Yearbook. *Journal of Personality* Assessment, 63, 394–397.

PETERSON, D. (1968). *The clinical study of social behavior.* New York: Appleton-Century Crofts.

PETERSON, G. W,, SAMPSON, J. R, JR., & REARDON, R. C. (1991). Career *development and services: A cognitive approach*. Pacific Grove, CA: Brooks/Cole.

PETERSON, J. (1926). *Early conceptions and tests of intelligence.* Yonkers, NY: World Book.

PETERSON, N. G., HOUGH, L. M., DUNNETTE, M. D., ROSSE, R. L., HOUSTON, J. S., TOQUAM, J. L., &. WING, H. (1990). Project A: Specification of the predictor domain and development of new selection/classification tests. *Personnel Psychology, 43,* 247–276.

PETRILA, J. & OTTO, R. K. (1995). *Law and mental health professionals: Florida.* Washington, DC: American Psychological Association.

PHILIPPE, J. (1894). Jastrow—exposition d'anthropologie de Chicago—testes psychologiques, etc. *Année Psychologique, 1,* 522–526.

PLACENTINI, J. (1993). Checklists and rating scales. In T. H. Ollendick & M. Hersen *(Eds.), Handbook of child and adolescent assessment* (pp. 82–97). Boston: Allyn & Bacon.

PIAGET, J. (1972). Intellectual evolution from adolescence to adulthood. *Human Development, 15,* 1–12.

PLCKMAN, A. J. (1994). *The complete guide to outplacement counseling.* Hillsdale, NJ: Erlbaum.

PIEDMONT, R. L., MCCRAE, R. R., & COSTA, P. T., JR. (1992). An assessment of the Edwards Personal Preference Schedule from the perspective of the Five-Factor Model. *Journal of Personality Assessment, 58,* 67–78.

PLETROFESA, J. J., & SPLETE, H. (1975). *Career development: Theory and research.* Orlando, FL: Grune & Stratton.

PLNARD, A., & LAURENDEAU, M. (1964). A scale of mental development based on the theory of Piaget: Description of a project. *Journal of Research in Science Teaching, 2,* 253–260.

PLNDER, C. C. (1973). Statistical accuracy and practical utility in the use of moderator variables. *Journal of Applied Psychology, 57,* 214–221.

PLNNEAU, S. R. (1961). *Changes in intelligence quotient from infancy to maturity.* Boston: Houghton Mifflin.

PLOTROWSKI, C. (1984). The status of projective techniques: Or, "Wishing won't make it go away." *Journal of* Clinical *Psychology, 40,* 1495–1502.

PLOTROWSKI, C., & KELLER, J. W. (1992). Psychological testing in applied settings: A literature review from 1982–1992. *Journal of Training & Practice in Professional Psychology, 6,* 74–82.

PLOTROWSKI, C., SHERRY, D., & KELLER, J. W. (1985). Psychodiagnostic test usage: A survey of the Society for Personality Assessment. *Journal of Personality Assessment, 49,* 115–119.

PLOTROWSKI, C., & ZALEWSKI, C. (1993). Training in psychodiagnostic testing in APA-approved PsyD and PhD clinical psychology programs. *Journal of Personality* Assessment, *61,* 393–405.

PLAKE, B. S. (1980). A comparison of a statistical and a subjective procedure to ascertain item validity: One step in the test validation process. *Educational and Psychological Measurement, 40,* 397–404.

PLANT, W. T., & MINIUM, E. W. (1967). Differential personality development in young adults of markedly different aptitude levels. *Journal of Educational Psychology, 58,* 141–152.

PLOMIN, R., DEFRIES, J. C., & FULKER, D. W. (1988). *Nature and nurture during infancy and early childhood*. New York: Cambridge University Press.

PLOMIN, R., & MCCLEARN, G. E. (Eds.). (1993). *Nature, nurture, and psychology.* Washington, DC: American Psychological Association.

PLOMIN, R., & READE, R. (1991). Human behavioral genetics. *Annual Review of Psychology, 42,* 161–190.

POON, L. W. (Ed.). (1986). *Handbook for clinical memory assessment of older adidts.* Washington, DC: American Psychological Association.

POPE, K. S. (1992). Responsibilities in providing psychological test feedback to clients. *Psychological Assessment, 4,* 268–271.

POPE, K. S. BUTCHER, J. N. & SEELEN, J. (1993). *The MMPI, MMPl-2, and MMP1-A in court: A practical guide for expert witnesses and attorneys.* Washington, DC: American Psychological Association.

POPE, K. S., & VASQUEZ, M.J.T. (1991). *Ethics in psychotherapy and counseling: A pratical guide for psychologists.* San Francisco: Jossey-Bass.

POPE, M. (1995). Review of the Kuder General Interest Survey, Form E. *Twelfth Mental Measurements Yearbook,* 543–545.

POPHAM, W. J. (1984). Specifying the domain of content or behaviors. In R. A. Berk (Ed.), A *guide to criterion-referenced test construction* (pp. 29–48). Baltimore: Johns Hopkins University Press.

POPHAM, W. J., &. HLUSEK, T. R. (1969). Implications of criterion referenced measurement. *Journal of Educational Measurement,* 6, 1–9.

PORTEGAL, M. (Ed.). (1982). *Spatial abilities: Developmental and physiological foundations.* Orlando, FL: Academic Press.

PORTEUS, S. D. (1931). *The psychology of a primitive people.* New York: Longmans, Green.

POSTMAN, L., & KEPPEL, G. (1970). *Norms of word association*. New York: Academic Press.

POTH, R. L., & BARNETT, D. W. (1988). Establishing the limits of interpretive confidence: A validity study of two preschool developmental scales. *School Psychology Review, 17,* 322–330.

POWELL, D. H., KAPLAN, E. F., WHITLA, D., WEINTRAUB, S., CATLIN, R., & FUNKENSTEIN, H. H. (1993). *MicroCog Assessment of Cognitive Functioning: Manual.* San Antonio, TX: Psychological Corporation.

POWELL, D. H., & WHITLA, D. K. (1994a). Normal cognitive aging: Toward empirical perspectives. *Current Directions in Psychological Science,* 3, 27–31.

POWELL, D. H., & WHITLA, D. K. (1994b). *Profiles in cognitive aging.* Cambridge, MA: Flarvard University Press.

POWERS, D. E. (1983). *Effects of coaching on GRE Aptitude Test scores* (GRE Board Res. Rep. GREB No. 81–3R). Princeton, NJ: Educational Testing Service.

POWERS, D. E. (1986). Relations of test item characteristics to test preparation/test practice effects: A quantitative summary. *Psychological Bulletin, 100,* 67–77.

POWERS, D. E. 1993. Coaching for the SAT: A summary of the summaries and an update. *Educational Measurement: Issues and Practice,* 12(2), 24–30.

POWERS, D. E., & SWINTON, S. S. (1984). Effects of self-study for coachable test item types. *Journal of Educational Psychology, 76,* 266–278.

PREDIGER, D. J. (1982). Dimensions underlying Holland's hexagon: Missing link between interests and occupations? *Journal of Vocational Behavior, 21,* 259–287.

PREDIGER, D. J. (1993). *Multicultural assessment standards: A* compilation *for counselors.* Alexandria, VA: American Counseling Association.

PREDIGER, D. (1996). Alternative dimensions for the Tracey-Rounds interest sphere. *Journal of Vocational Behavior, 48, 59–67.*

PREDIGER, D. J., & VANSICKLE, T. R. (1992). Locating occupations on Holland's hexagon: Beyond RIASEC. *Journal of Vocational Behavior, 40,* 111–128.

PRIMOFF, E. S. (1959). Empirical validations of the J-coefficient. *Personnel Psychology, 12,* 413–418.

PRIMOFF, E. S. (1975). *How to prepare and conduct job element examinations.* Washington, DC: U.S. Government Printing Office.

PRIMOFF, E. S., &. EYDE, L. D. (1988). Job element analysis. In S. Gael (Ed.), *The job analysis handbook for business, industry, and government* (Vol. 2, pp. 807–824). New York: Wiley.

PRINCE, J. P. (1995). *Strong Interest Inventory resource: Strategies for group and individual interpretations in college settings.* Palo Alto, CA: Consulting Psychologists Press.

Privacy and Behavioral Research. (1967). Washington, DC: U.S. Government Printing Office.

PROCTER, M. (1993). Measuring attitudes. In N. Gilbert (Ed.), *Researching social life* (pp. 116–134). London: Sage.

PROVENCE, S., ERIKSON, J., VATER, S., & PALMERI, S. (1995a). *Infant-Toddler Developmental Assessment—Family centered assessment of young childrett at risk: The IDA readings.* Chicago: Riverside.

PROVENCE, S., ERIKSON, J., VATER, S., & PALMERI, S. (1995b). *Infant-Toddler Developmental Assessment: Foundations and study guide.* Chicago: Riverside.

PROVENCE, S., ERIKSON, J., VATER, S., & PALMERI, S. (1995c). *Infant-Toddler Developmental Assessment—IDA administration manual: Procedures summary—Provence Birth- to-Three Developmental Profile.* Chicago: Riverside.

PSYCHOLOGICAL CORPORATION. (1991a). *Counselor's Manual for Interpreting the Career Interest Inventory.* San Antonio, TX: Author.

PSYCHOLOGICAL CORPORATION. (1991b). *Differential Aptitude Tests, Fifth Edition/ Career Interest Inventory: Counselor's manual.* San Antonio, TX: Author.

PSYCHOLOGICAL CORPORATION. (1992a). *Differential Aptitude Tests, Fifth Edition: Technical manual. SAN ANTONIO, TX: AUTHOR.*

PSYCHOLOGICAL CORPORATION. (1992b). *Wechsler Individual Achievement Test—WIAT: Manual.* San Antonio, TX: Author.

PULAKOS, E. D. (1986). The development of training programs to increase accuracy with different rating tasks. *Organizational Behavior and Human Decision Processes, 38,* 76–91.

QUAN, B., PARK, T. A., SANDAHL, G., & WOLFE, J. H. (1984). *Microcomputer network for computerized adaptive testing CAT* (Tech. Rep. 84–33). San Diego, CA: Navy Personnel Research and Development Center.

RABIN, A. I. (ed.). (1981). *Assessment with projective techniques: A concise introduction*. New York: Springer.

RABIN, A. I. (ed.). (1986). *Projective techniques for adolescents and children*. New York: Springer.

RABIN, A. I., & GUERTIN, W. H. (1951). Research with the Wechsler-Bellevue Test: 1945–1950. *Psychological* Bulletin, *48,* 211–248.

RABIN, A. I., & ZLOTOGORSKI, Z. (1981). Completion methods: Word association, sentence, and story completion. In A. I. Rabin (Ed.), *Assessment with projective techniques: A concise introduction* (pp. 121–149). New York: Springer.

RADCLIFFE, J. A. (1966). A note on questionnaire faking with the 16PFQ and MPI. *Australian Journal of Psychology, 18,* 154–157.

RAGGIO, D. J., & MASSINGALE, T. W. (1990). Comparability of the Vineland Social Maturity Scale and the Vineland Adaptive Behavior Scale—Survey form with infants evaluated for developmental delay. *Perceptual and Motor Skills, 71,* 415–418.

RAJU, N. S., BURKE, M. J., & NORMAND, J. (1990). A new approach to utility analysis. *Journal of Applied Psychology, 75,* 3–12.

RAMSEYER, G. C., & CASHEN, V. M. (1971). The effect of practice sessions on the use of separate answer sheets by first and second graders. *Journal of Educational Measurement, 8,* 177–181.

RAND, Y., TANNENBAUM, A. J., &. FEUERSTEIN, R. (1979). Effects of instrumental enrichment on the psychoeducational development of low-functioning adolescents. *Journal of Educational Psychology, 71,* 751–763.

RANDAHL, G. J., HANSEN, J. C., & HAVERKAMP, B. E. (1993). Instrumental behaviors following test administration and interpretation: Exploration validity of the Strong *Interest Inventory. Journal of Counseling and Development, 71, 435–439*.

RAPAPORT, D., et al. (1968). *Diagnostic psychological testing* (rev. ed. edited by R. R. Holt). New York: International Universities Press. (Original work published 1946)

RASCH, G. (1966). An individualistic approach to item analysis. In P. F. Lazarsfeld & N. W. Henry (Eds.), *Readings in mathematical social sciences* (pp. 89–107). Cambridge, MA: MIT Press.

RASKIN, E. (1985). Counseling implications of field dependence-independence in an educational setting. In M. Bertini, L. Pizzamiglio, & S. Wapner (Eds.), *Field dependence in psychological theory, research, and application: Two symposia in memory of Herman A.* witkin (pp. 107–113). Hillsdale, NJ: Erlbaum.

RAVEN, J. (1983). The Progressive Matrices and Mill Hill Vocabulary Scale in Western Societies. In S. H. Irvine & J. W. Berry (Eds.), *Human assessment and cultural factors* (pp. 107–114). New York: Plenum Press.

RAVEN, J., RAVEN, J. C., & COURT, J. H. (1995). *Manual for Raven's Progressive Matrices and vocabulary scales—Section 1: General Overview (1995 Edition)*. Oxford, England: Oxford Psychologists Press.

RECKASE, RECKASE, M. D. (1989). Adaptive testing: The evolution of a good idea. Educational Measurement: Issues & Practice, 8, 11–15.

REED, R., ROTATORI, A. F., & DAY, G. F. (1990). Career and vocational assessment. In A. F. Rotatori, R. A. Fox, D. Sexton, & J. Miller (Eds.), *Comprehensive assessment in special education: Approaches, procedures, and concerns* (pp. 341–386). Springfield, IL: Charles C Thomas.

REESE, H. W. (Ed.). (1987). *Advances in child development and behavior* (Vol. 20). Orlando, FL: Academic Press.

REEVES, D., &. WEDDING, D. (1994). *The clinical assessment of memory: A practical guide*. New York: Springer.

REICHENBERG-HACKETT, W. (1953). Changes in Goodenough drawings after a gratifying experience. *American Journal of Orthopsychiatry, 23,* 501–517.

REILLY, R. R. (1973). A note on minority group test bias studies. *Psychological Bulletin, 80,* 130–132.

REINEHR, R. C. (1992). Review of Differential Ability Scales. *Eleventh Mental Measurements Yearbook,* 282–283.

REINERT, G. (1970). Comparative factor analytic studies of intelligence throughout the human life-span. In L. R. Goulet & P. B. Baltes (Eds.), *Life-span developmental psychology: Research and theory* (pp. 467–484). New York: Academic Press.

REISE, S. P., & OLIVER, C. J. (1994). Development of a California Q-set indicator of primary psychopathy. *Journal of Personality* Assessment, 62, 130–144.

REISS, S. (1994). Issues in defining mental retardation. *American Journal on Mental Retardation,* 99, 1–7.

REITAN, R. M. (1955). Certain differential effects of left and right cerebral lesions in human adults. *Journal of Comparative and Physiological Psychology, 48,* 474–477.

REITAN, R. M. (1966). A research program on the psychological effects of brain lesions in human beings. In N. R. Ellis (Ed.), *International review of research in mental retardation* (Vol. 1, pp. 153–218). Orlando, FL: Academic Press.

REITAN, R. M., & WOLFSON, D. (1993). *The Halstead-Reitan Neuropsychological Test Battery: Theory and clinical interpretation (2nd ed.).* Tucson, AZ: Neuropsychology Press.

RENNINGER, K. A., HIDI, S., & KRAPP, A. (eds.). (1992). *The role of interest in learning and development*. Hillsdale, NJ: Erlbaum.

RENTZ, R. R., & BASHAW, W. L. (1977). The National Reference Scale for reading: An application of the Rasch model. *Journal of Educational Measurement, 14,* 161–179.

REPP, A. C., & FELCE, D. (1990). A microcomputer system used for evaluative and experimental behavioural research in mental handicap. *Mental Handicap Research, 3,* 21–32.

RESCHLY, D. J. (1988). Larry P! Larry P.! Why the California sky fell on IQ testing. *Journal of School Psychology, 26,* 199–205.

RESNICK, L. B. (Ed.). (1976). *The nature of intelligence.* Hillsdale, NJ: Erlbaum.

RESNICK, L. B., & GLASER, R. (1976). Problem solving and intelligence. In L. B. Resnick (Ed.), *The nature of intelligence* (pp. 205–230). Hillsdale, NJ: Erlbaum.

RESNICK, L. B., & NECHES, R. (1984). Factors affecting individual differences in learning ability. In R. J. Sternberg (Ed.), *Handbook of human intelligence* (Vol. 2, pp. 275–323). Hillsdale, NJ: Erlbaum.

RESNICK, L. B., &. RESNICK, D. P. (1992). Assessing the thinking curriculum: New tools for educational reform. In B. R. Gifford & M. C. O'Connor (Eds.), *Changing assessments: Alternative views of aptitude, achievement and instruction* (pp. 37–75). Boston: Kluwer.

RETZLAFF, P. (1992). Review of the State-Trait Anger Expression Inventory, Research Edition. *Eleventh Mental Measurements Yearbook,* 869–870.

RETZLAFF, P. (1995). *Tactical psychotherapy of the personality disorders: An MCM III-based approach*. Boston: Allyn & Bacon.

REYNOLDS, C. R. (1982). Methods for detecting construct and predictive bias. In R. A. Berk (Ed.), *Handbook of* methods *for detecting test bias* (pp. 199–227). Baltimore: Johns Hopkins University Press.

REYNOLDS, C. R. (1986). Vineland Adaptive Behavior Scales, 1984 Edition. *Journal of Educational Measurement, 23,* 389–391.

REYNOLDS, C. R. (1990). Conceptual and technical problems in learning disability diagnosis. In C. R. Reynolds & R. W. Kamphaus (Eds.), *Handbook of psychological and educational assessment of children: Intelligence and achievement* (pp. 571–593). New York: Guilford Press.

REYNOLDS, C. R. (1992a). Review of the Millon Clinical Multiaxial Inventory-II *Eleventh Mental Measurements Yearbook, 533–535.*

REYNOLDS, C. R. (1992b). Two key concepts in the diagnosis of learning disabilities and the habilitation of learning. *Learning Disability Quarterly, 15, 2–12.*

REYNOLDS, C. R., & BROWN, R. T. (1984). *Perspectives on bias in mental testing.* New York: Plenum Press.

REYNOLDS, C. R. & KAMPHAUS, R. W. (eds.). (1990a). *Handbook of psychological and educational assessment of children: Intelligence and achievement.* New York: Guilford Press.

REYNOLDS, C. R., & KAMPHAUS, R. W. (eds.). (1990b). *Handbook of psychological and educational assessment of children: Personality, behavior, and context.* New York: Guilford Press.

REYNOLDS, C. R., & KAMPHAUS, R. W. (1992). *Behavior Assessment System for Children: Manual.* Circle Pines, MN: American Guidance Service.

REYNOLDS, S. B. (1989). Review of the Multidimensional Aptitude Battery. *Tenth Mental Measurements Yearbook, 522–523.*

REZMOVIC, E. L., & REZMOVIC, V. (1980). Empirical validation of psychological constructs: A secondary analysis. *Psychological Bidletin,* 87, 66–71.

RICHARDSON, J. P. E., ANGLE, R. W., HASHER, L., LOGIE, R. H., & STOLTUS, E. R. (1996). *Working memory and human cognition.* New York: Oxford University Press.

RITCHIE, R. J. (1994). Using the assessment center method to predict senior management potential. *Consulting Psychology Journal: Practice and Research, 46,* 16–23.

RLTZLER, B. (1993a). Test review: TEMAS (Tell-Me-A-Story). *Journal of Psychoeducational Assessment, 11,* 381–389.

RLTZLER, B. (1993b). Thanks for the memories! *Journal of Personality* Assessment, 60, 208–210.

RLTZLER, B., & ALTER, B. (1986). Rorschach teaching in APA-approved clinical graduate programs: Ten years later. *Journal of Personality Assessment,* 50, 44–49.

Riverside 2000: Technical Summary I. (1994). Chicago, IL: Riverside.

ROBERTS, G. E. (1994). *Interpretive handbook for the Roberts Apperception Test for Children.* Los Angeles, CA: Western Psychological Services.

ROBINSON, C., &. FLEBER, N. (1988). Cognitive assessment of motorically impaired infants and preschoolers. In T. D. Wachs & R. Sheehan (Eds.), Assessment *of young developmentally disabled children* (pp. 127–161). New York: Plenum Press.

ROBINSON, J. P., SHAVER, P. R., & WRIGHTSMAN, L. S. (Eds.). (1991). Measures *of personality and social psychological attitudes.* San Diego, CA: Academic Press.

ROBINSON, S. P. (1993). The politics of multiple-choice versus free-response assessment. In R. E. Bennett & W. C. Ward (Eds.), *Construction versus choice in cognitive measurement: Issues in constructed response, performance testing, and portfolio assessment* (pp. 313–323). Hillsdale, NJ: Erlbaum.

ROCK, D. A., BENNETT, R. E., & JIRELE, T. (1988). Factor structure of the Graduate Record Examination's General Test in handicapped and non-handicapped groups. *Journal of Applied Psychology,* 73, 382–392.

RODGER, A. G. (1936). The application of six group intelligence tests to the same children, and the effects of practice. *British Journal of Educational Psychology,* 6, 291–305.

ROECKER, C. E. (1995). Well stated well met [Review of the book *Intelligent testing with the WISC-III]. Contemporary Psychology, 40, 659–660.*

ROGERS, C. R., & DYMOND, R. F. (Eds.). (1954). *Psychotherapy and personality change.* Chicago: University of Chicago Press.

ROGERS, R. (1995). *Diagnostic and structured interviewing: A handbook for psychologists. Odessa, FL: Psychological Assessment Resources.*

ROGOFF, B, (1990). *Apprenticeship in thinking: Cognitive development in social context.* New York: Oxford University Press.

ROGOFF, B., & CHAVAJAY, P. (1995). What's become of research on the cultural basis of cognitive development? *American Psychologist,* 50, 859–877.

ROGOFF, B., & LAVE, J. (Eds.). (1984). *Everyday cognition: Its development in social context.* Cambridge, MA: Harvard University Press.

ROGOFF, B., & MORELLI, G. (1989). Perspectives on children's development from cultural psychology. *American Psychologist, 44,* 343–348.

ROGOSA, D. (1979). Causal models in longitudinal research: Rationale, formulation, and interpretation. In J. R. Nesselroade & P. B. Bakes (Eds.), *Longitudinal research in the study of behavior development* (pp. 263–302). New York: Academic Press.

ROGOSA, D. (1980). A critique of cross-lagged correlation. *Psychological Bulletin, 88,* 245–258.

ROID, G. H. (1984). Generating the test items. In R. A. Berk (Ed.), A *guide to criterion referenced test construction* (pp. 49–77). Baltimore: Johns Hopkins University Press.

ROID, G. H. (1986). Computer technology in testing. In B. S. Plake & J. C. Witt (Eds.), *The future of testing* (pp. 29–69). Hillsdale, NJ: Erlbaum.

ROID, G. H., & GORSUCH, R. L. (1984). Development and clinical use of test-interpretive programs on microcomputers. In M. D. Schwartz (Ed.), *Using computers in clinical practice* (pp. 141–149). New York: Haworth.

ROID, G. H., & MILLER, L. J. (1997). *Examiner's manual: Leiter International Performance Scale-Revised.* Wood Dale, IL: Stoelting.

RONAN, G. F., COLAVITO, V. A., & HAMMONTREE, S. R. (1993). Personal problem' solving system for scoring TAT responses: Preliminary validity and reliability data. *Journal of Personality* Assessment, 61, 28–40.

RONAN, G. F., DATE, A. L., & WEISBROD, M. (1995). Personal problem-solving scoring of the TAT: Sensitivity to training. *Journal of Personality Assessment, 64,* 119–131.

RONNING, R. R., GLOVER, J. A., CONOLEY, J. C., & WITT, J. C. (Eds.). (1987). *The influence of cognitive psychology on testing.* Hillsdale, NJ: Erlbaum.

ROONEY, J. P. (1987). Golden Rule on "Golden Rule." *Educational Measurement: Issues & Practice, 6, 9–12.*

ROPER, B. L., BEN-PORATH, Y. S., & BUTCHER, J. N. (1991). Comparability of computerized adaptive and conventional testing with the MMPI-2. *Journal of Personality Assessment, 57,* 278–290.

ROPER, B. L., BEN-PORATH, Y. S., & BUTCHER, J. N. (1995). Comparability and validity of computerized adaptive testing with the MMPI-2. *Journal of Personality Assessment, 65,* 358–371.

RORER, L. G. (1965). The great response-style myth. *Psychological Bulletin,* 63, 129–156.

RORER, L. G., HOFFMAN, P. J., & HSIEH, K. (1966). Utilities as base rate multipliers in the determination of optimum cutting scores for the discrimination of groups of unequal size and variance. *Journal of Applied Psychology, 50,* 364–368.

RORSCHACH, H. (1942). *Psychodiagnostics: A diagnostic test based on perception* (P. Lemkau & B. Kronenberg, Trans.). Berne: Huber. (1st German ed. published 1921; U. S. distributor, Grune & Stratton)

ROSENBERG, M. (1965). *Society and the adolescent self-image.* Princeton, NJ: Princeton University Press.

ROSENTHAL, A. C. (1985). Review of Assessment in infancy: Ordinal Scales of Psychological Development. *Ninth Mental Measurements Yearbook,* Vol. 1, 85–86.

ROSENTHAL, R. (1966). *Experimenter effects in behavioral research.* New York: Appleton Century-Crofts.

ROSENTHAL, R. (1991). *Meta-analytic procedures for social research* (rev. ed.). Newbury Park, CA: Sage.

ROSENTHAL, R., & ROSNOW, R. L. (Eds.). (1969). *Artifact in behavioral research.* New York: Academic Press.

ROSENZWEIG, S. (1950). *Revised scoring manual for the Rosettzweig Picture-Frustration Study, Form for Adults.* St. Louis, MO: Author.

ROSENZWEIG, S. (1960). The Rosenzweig Picture-Frustration Study, Children's Form. In A. I. Rabin & M. Haworth (Eds.), *Projective techniques with children* (pp. 149–176). Orlando, FL: Grune &. Stratton.

ROSENZWEIG, S. (1970). Sex differences in reaction to frustration among adolescents. In J. Zubin & A. M. Freedman (Eds.), *Psychopathology of adolescence* (pp. 90–107). Orlando, FL: Grune & Stratton.

ROSENZWEIG, S. (1976a). Aggressive behavior and the Rosenzweig Picture-Frustration (P-F) Study. *Journal of Clinical Psychology, 32,* 885–891.

ROSENZWEIG, S. (1976b). *Manual for the Rosenzweig Picture-Frustration Study, Adolescent Form.* St. Louis, MO: Author.

ROSENZWEIG, S. *(1977). Manual for the Children's Form of the Rosenzweig Picture-Frustration Study.* St. Louis, MO: Rana House.

ROSENZWEIG, S. (1978a). *ADULT Form supplement to the basic manual of the Rosenzweig Picture-Frustration (P-F) Study.* St. Louis, MO: Rana House.

ROSENZWEIG, S. (1978b). *Aggressive behavior and the Rosenzweig Picture-Frustration.* New York: Praeger.

ROSENZWEIG, S. (1978c). An investigation of the reliability of the Rosenzweig Picture-Frustration (P-F) Study, Children's Form. *Journal of Personality* Assessment, *42,* 483–488.

ROSENZWEIG, S. (1978d). *The Rosenzweig Picture-Frustration (P-F) Study: Basic manual.* St. Louis, MO: Rana House.

ROSENZWEIG, S. (1981a). *Adolescent Form supplement to the basic manual of the Rosenzweig Picture-Frustration (P-F) Study. St. Louis,* MO: Rana House.

ROSENZWEIG, S. (1981b). *Children's Form supplement to the basic manual of the Rosenzweig Picture-Frustration (P-F) Study. St. Louis,* MO: Rana House.

ROSENZWEIG, S. (1988). Revised norms for the Children's Form of the Rosenzweig Picture-Frustration (P-F) Study, with updated reference list. *Journal of Clinical Child Psychology, 17,* 326–328.

ROSENZWEIG, S., & ADELMAN, S. (1977). Construct validity of the Picture-Frustration Study. *Journal of Personality Assessment, 41,* 578–588.

ROSS, B. M. (1991). *Remembering the personal past: Descriptions of autobiographical memory.* New York: Oxford University Press.

ROTHSTEIN, H. R., SCHMIDT, F. L., ERWIN, F. W., OWENS, W. A., & SPARKS, C. P. (1990). Biographical data in employment selection: Can validities be made generalizable? *Journal of Applied Psychology, 75,* 175–184.

ROTTER, J. B. (1966). Generalized expectancies for internal versus external control of reinforcement. *Psychological Monographs, 80* (1, Whole No. 609).

ROTTER, J. B., LAH, M. I., & RAFFERTY, J. E. (1992). *Rotter Incomplete Sentences Blank manual.* San Antonio, TX: Psychological Corporation.

ROTTER, J. B., & RAFFERTY, J. E. (1950). *Manual: The Rotter Incomplete Sentences Blank*. San Antonio, TX: Psychological Corporation.

ROUNDS, J. (1995). Vocational interests: Evaluating structural hypotheses. In D. Lubin ski & R. V. Dawis (Eds.), *Assessing individual differences in human behavior: New concepts, methods, and findings* (pp. 177–232). Palo Alto, CA: Davies-Black.

ROUNDS, J., & TRACEY, T. J. (1996). Cross-cultural structural equivalence of RIASEC models and measures. *Journal of Counseling Psychology, 43*, 310–329.

ROURKE, B. P. (ed.). (1990). *Neuropsychological validation of learning disability subtypes*. New York: Guilford Press.

ROVEE-COLLIER, C., & LIPSITT, L. P. (Eds.). (1992). *Advances in infancy research* (Vol. 7). Norwood, NJ: Ablex.

ROWE, D. C. (1987). Resolving the person-situation debate: Invitation to an interdisciplinary dialogue. *American Psychologist, 42*, 218–227.

ROWE, H. A. H. (Ed.). (1991). *Intelligence: Reconceptualization and measurement*. Hillsdale, NJ: Erlbaum.

RUBIN, D. C. (Ed.). (1986). *Autobiographical memory*. New York: Cambridge University Press.

RULON, P. J. (1939). A simplified procedure for determining the reliability of a test of split-halves. Harvard Educational Review, 9, 99–103.

RUMSEY, M. G., WALKER, C. B., & HARRIS, J. H. (Eds.). (1994). Personnel *selection arid classification*. Hillsdale, NJ: Erlbaum.

RUNCO, M. A. (1991). *Divergent thinking*. Norwood, NJ: Ablex.

RUNCO, M. A. (ed.). (1994). *Problem finding, problem solving, and creativity. Norwood*, NJ: Ablex.

RUNYON, R. T., & HABER, A. (1991). *Fundamentals of behavioral statistics* (7th ed.). New York: McGraw-Hill.

RUSHTON, J. R (1984). The altruistic personality: Evidence from laboratory, naturalistic, and self-report perspectives. In E. Straub, D. Bar-Tal, J. Karylowski, & J. Reykowski (Eds.), *Development and maintenance of prosocial behavior* (pp. 271–290). New York: Plenum Press.

RUSSELL, C. J., MATTSON, J., DEVLIN, S. E., & ATWATER, D. (1990). Predictive validity of biodata items generated from retrospective life experience essays. *Journal of Applied Psychology, 75*, 569–580.

RUSSELL, E. W., & STARKEY, R. I. (1993). *Halstead Russell Neuropsychological Evaluation System (HRNES): Manual*. Los Angeles: Western Psychological Services.

RUSSELL, M. T., &. KAROL, D. (1994). *Administrator's manual for the* 16PF *Fifth Edition*. Champaign, IL: Institute for Personality and Ability Testing.

RUSSELL, T. L., REYNOLDS, D. H., & CAMPBELL, J. P. (1994). *Building a joint-service classification research roadmap: Individual differences measurement (AL/HR-TP-1994-0009). Brooks AFB*, TX: Armstrong Laboratory.

RUST, J., & GOLOMBOK, S. (2009). *Modern psychometrics: The science of psychological assessment*. London: Routledge.

RUTTER, M., & RUTTER, M. (1993). *Developing minds: Challenge and continuity across the life span*. New York: Basic Books.

RYAN, J. J., & BOHAC, D. L. (1994). Neurodiagnostic implications of unique profiles of the Wechsler Adult Intelligence Scale-Revised. *Psychological Assessment, 6*, 360–363.

RYAN, J. J., PAOLO, A. M., & BRUNGARDT, T. M. (1990). Standardization of the Wechsler Adult Intelligence Scale—Revised for persons 75 years and older. *Psychological Assessment, 2*, 404–411.

SAAL, F. E., DOWNEY, R. G., & LAKEY, M. A. (1980). Rating the ratings: Assessing the psychometric quality of rating data. *Psychological Bulletin, 88,* 413–428.

SACCHI, C., & RLCHAUD DE MINZI, M. C. (1989). The Holtzman Inkblot Technique in preadolescent personality. *British Journal of Projective Psychology, 34(2),* 2–11.

SACKETT, P. R. (1994). Integrity testing for personnel selection. *Current Directions in Psychological Science, 3,* 73–76.

SACKETT, P. R., &. WLLK, S. L. (1994). Within-group norming and other forms of score adjustment in preemployment testing. *American Psychologist, 49,* 929–954.

SACKS, E. L. (1952). Intelligence scores as a function of experimentally established social relationships between the child and examiner. *Journal of Abnormal and Social Psychology, 47,* 354–358.

SADACCA, R., CAMPBELL, J. P., DIFAZIO, A. S., SCHULTZ, S. R., & WHITE, L. A. (1990). Scaling performance utility to enhance selection/classification decisions. *Personnel Psychology, 43,* 367–378,

SAKLOFSKE, D. H., &. ZEIDNER, M. (Eds.). (1995). *International handbook of personality and intelligence.* New York: Plenum Press.

SALOVEY, P, & MAYER, J. D. (1990). Emotional intelligence. *Imagination, Cognition, and Personality,* 9, 185–211.

SALOVEY, R, & SLUYTER, D. J. (eds.). (1997). *Emotional development and emotional intelligence: Educational implications.* New York: Basic Books.

SAMEJIMA, F. (1969). Estimation of latent ability using a response pattern of graded scores. *Psychcrmetric Monograph,* No. 17.

SAMUDA, R. J. (1975). *Psychological testing of American minorities: Issues and consequences.* New York: Dodd, Mead.

SAMUDA, R. J., KONG, S. L., CUMMINS, J., LEWIS, J., & PASCUAL-LEONE, J. (1991). *Assessment and placement of minority students. Kirkland,* WA: Hogrefe & Huber Publishers.

SANDOVAL, J. H., & MLILLE, M. P. W. (1980). Accuracy judgments of WISC-R item difficulty for minority groups. *Journal of Consulting and Clinical Psychology, 48,* 249–253.

SARASON, I. G. (1961). Test anxiety and the intellectual performance of college students. *Journal of Educational Psychology,* 52, 201–206.

SARASON, I. G. (ed.). (1980). *Test anxiety: Theory, research, and applications. Hillsdale,* NJ: Erlbaum.

SARASON, S. B. (1954). *The clinical interactim, with special reference to the Rorschach.* New York: Harper.

SARASON, S. B., DAVIDSON, K. S., LIGHTHALL, F. F., WAITE, R. R., & RUEBUSH, K. (1960). Anxiety *in elementary school children.* New York: Wiley.

SARASON, S. B., HILL, K. T., & ZLMBARDO, P. (1964). A longitudinal study of the relation of test anxiety to performance on intelligence and achievement tests. Monographs *of the Society for Research in Child Development,* 29 (7, Serial No. 98).

SATTLER, J. M. (1970). Racial "experimenter effects" in experimentation, testing, and interviewing. *Psychological Bulletin,* 73, 137–160.

SATTLER, J. M. (1982). Assessment *of children's intelligence and special abilities* (2nd ed.). Boston: Allyn &. Bacon.

SATTLER, J. M. (1988). Assessment *of children* (3rd ed.). San Diego, CA: Author.

SATTLER, J. M. (1992). Assessment *of children: WISC-III and WPPSIR supplement.* San Diego, CA: Author.

SATTLER, J. M., & THEYE, F. (1967). Procedural, situational, and interpersonal variables in individual intelligence testing. *Psychological Bulletin, 68,* 347–360.

SAUDARGAS, R. A. (1989). Review of the Classroom Environment Scale, Second Edition. *Tenth Mental Measurements Yearbook*, 173–174.

SAUNDERS, D. R. (1956). *Moderator variables in prediction. Educational and Psychological Measurement, 16*, 209–222.

SAVICKAS, M. L., & LENT, R. W. (Eds.). (1994). *Convergence in career development theories: Implications for science and practice.* Palo Alto, CA: CPP Books.

SAX, G. (1991). *The Fields Teaching Tests.* Seattle: University of Washington.

SAXE, L. (1994). Detection of deception: Polygraph and integrity tests. *Current Directiorrs* in *Psychological Science, 3*, 69–73.

SCARPATI, S. (1991). Current perspectives in the assessment of the handicapped. In R. K. Hambleton & J. N. Zaal (Eds.), *Advances in educational and psychological testing: Theory and applications* (pp. 251–276). Boston: Kluwer.

SCHAEFER, C. E., GITLIN, K., & SANDGRUND, A. (1991). *Play diagnosis and assessment*. New York: Wiley.

SCHAFER, W. O. (1992). Review of the Computer Programmer Aptitude Battery. *Eleventh Mental* Measurements *Yearbook*, 227–228.

SCHAIE, J. P. (1978). Review of the Gerontological Apperception Test. *Eighth Mental Measurements Yearbook*, Vol. l, 829–830.

SCHAIE, K. W. (1965). A general model for the study of developmental problems. *Psychological Bulletin, 64*, 92–107.

SCHAIE, K. W. (1973). Methodological problems in descriptive developmental research on adulthood and aging. In J. R. Nesselroade & H. W. Reese (Eds.), *Life-span developmental psychology: Methodological issues* (pp. 253–280). New York: Academic Press.

SCHAIE, K. W. (1978). Review of the Senior Apperception Technique. *Eighth Mental Measurements Yearbook*, Vol. 1, 1060.

SCHAIE, K. W. (1988a). Internal validity threats in studies of adult cognitive develop ment. In M. L. Howe & C. J. Brainard (Eds.), *Cognitive development in adulthood: Progress in cognitive development research* (pp. 241–272). New York: Springer-Verlag.

SCHAIE, K. W. (1988b). *Manual for the Schaie-Thurstone Adult Mental Abilities Test* (STAMAT). Palo Alto, CA: Consulting Psychologists Press.

SCHAIE, K. W. (1994). The course of adult intellectual development. *American* Psychologist, *49*, 304–313.

SCHAIE, K. W., &. GRIBBIN, K. (1975). Adult development and aging. *Annual Review of Psychology, 26*, 65–96.

SCHAIE, K. W., & HERTZOG, C. (1986). Toward a comprehensive model of adult intellectual development: Contributions of the Seattle Longitudinal Study. In R. J. Sternberg (Ed.), *Advances in the psychology of human intelligence* (Vol. 3, pp. 79–118). Hillsdale, NJ: Erlbaum.

SCHAIE, K. W., WILLIS, S. L., & CASKIE, G. I. (2004). The Seattle Longitudinal Study: Relationship Between Personality and Cognition. *Aging Neuropsychology and Cognition, 11*(2–3), 304–324. Retrieved June 7, 2016, from *http://www.ncbi.nlm.nih.gov/pmc/articles/PMC1474018/*.

SCHATZ, J., & HAMDAN-ALLEN, G. (1995). Effects of age and IQ on adaptive behavior domains for children with autism. *Journal of Autism and Developmental Disorders, 25*, 51–60.

SCHERICH, H. H., & HANNA,G. S. (1977). Passage-dependence data in the selection of reading comprehension test items. *Educational arid Psychological Measurement, 37*, 991–997.

SCHEUNEMAN, J. D. (1982). A posteriori analyses of biased items. In R. A. Berk (Ed.), *Handbook of methods for detecting test bias* (pp. 180–198). Baltimore: Johns Hopkins University Press.

SCHEUNEMAN, J., GERRITZ, K., & EMBRETSON, S. (1991). *Effects of prose complexity on achievement test item difficulty* (Res. Rep. No. 91–43). Princeton, NJ: Educational Testing Service.

SCHMID, J., & LEIMAN, J. (1957). The development of hierarchical factor solutions. *Psychometrika, 22,* 53–61.

SCHMIDT, F. L. (1985). Review of Wonderlic Personnel Test. *Ninth Mental Measurements Yearbook,* Vol. 2, 1755–1757.

SCHMIDT, F. L. (1992). What do data really mean? Research findings, meta-analysis, and cumulative knowledge in psychology. *American Psychologist, 47,* 1173–1181.

SCHMIDT, F. L. (1996). Statistical significance testing and cumulative knowledge in psychology: Implications for training of researchers. *Psychological Methods, 1,* 115–129.

SCHMIDT, F. L., BERNER, J. G., & HUNTER, J. E. (1973). Racial differences in validity of employment tests: Reality or illusion? *Journal of Applied Psychology, 58,* 5–9.

SCHMIDT, F. L. GAST-ROSENBERG, L., & HUNTER, J. E. (1980). Validity generalization results for computer programmers. *Journal of Applied Psychology, 65,* 643–661.

SCHMIDT, F. L., &. HUNTER, J. E. (1977). Development of a general solution to the problem of validity generalization. *Journal of Applied Psychology, 62,* 529–540.

SCHMIDT, F. L., & HUNTER, J. E. (1992). Development of a casual model of processes determining job performance. *Current Directions in Psychological Science, 1,* 89–92.

SCHMIDT, F. L., HUNTER, J. E,, MCKENZIE, R. C., & MULDROW, T. W. (1979). Impact of valid selection procedures on work-force productivity. *Journal of Applied Psychology, 64,* 609–626.

SCHMIDT, F. L., HUNTER, J. E., & OUTERBRIDGE, A. N. (1986). Impact of job experience and ability on job knowledge, work sample performance, and supervisory ratings on job performance. *Journal of Applied Psychology, 71,* 432–439.

SCHMIDT, F. L., HUNTER, J. E., & PEARLMAN, K. (1981). Task differences as moderators of aptitude test validity in selection: A red herring. *Journal of Applied Psychology, 66,* 166–185.

SCHMIDT, F. L., HUNTER, J. E., PEARLMAN, K., & HIRSH, H. R. (1985). Forty questions about validity generalization and meta-analysis. *Personnel Psychology, 38,* 697–798.

SCHMIDT, F. L., HUNTER, J. E., PEARLMAN, K., & SHANE, G. S. (1979). Further tests of the Schmidt-Hunter Bayesian validity generalization model. *Personnel Psychology, 32,* 257–281.

SCHMIDT, F. L., HUNTER, J. E., & URRY, V. W. (1976). Statistical power in criterion-related validation studies. *Journal of Applied Psychology, 61,* 473–485.

SCHMIDT, F. L., LAW, K., HUNTER, J. E., ROTHSTEIN, H. R., PEARLMAN, K., & MCDANIEL, M. (1993). Refinements in validity generalization methods: Implications for the situational specificity hypothesis. *Journal of Applied Psychology, 78,* 3–12.

SCHMIDT, F. L., ONES, D. S., & HUNTER, J. E. (1992). Personnel selection. *Annual Review of Psychology, 43,* 627–670.

SCHMIDT, F. L., PEARLMAN, K., & HUNTER, J. E. (1980). The validity and fairness of employment and educational tests for Hispanic Americans: A review and analysis. *Personnel Psychology, 33,* 705–724.

SCHMITT, N. (1995). Review of the Differential Aptitude Tests, Fifth Edition. *Twelfth Mental Measurements Yearbook,* 304–305.

SCHMITT, N., BORMAN, W. C., et al. (Eds.). (1993). *Personnel selection in organizations.* San Francisco: Jossey-Bass.

SCHMITT, N., MELLON, P. M., & BYLENGA, C. (1978). Sex differences in validity for academic and employment criteria, and different types of predictors. *Journal of Applied Psychology, 63,* 145–150.

SCHNEIDER, W., & WEINERT, F. E. (Eds.). (1990). *Interaction among aptitudes, strategies, and knowledge in cognitive performance.* New York: Springer-Verlag.

SCHOENFELDT, L. F. (1985). Review of Wonderlic Personnel Test. *Ninth Mental Measurements Yearbook,* Vol. 2, 1755–1758.

SCHOENFELDT, L. F., & MENDOZA, J. L. (1991). The use of the computer in the practice of industrial/organizational psychology. In T. B. Gutkin &. S. L. Wise (Eds.), *The computer and the decision-making process* (pp. 155–176). Hillsdale, NJ: Erlbaum.

SCHOENFELDT, L. F., & MENDOZA, J. L. (1994). Developing and using factorially derived biographical scales. In G. S. Stokes, M. D. Mumford, & W. A. Owens (Eds.), *Biodata handbook: Theory, research, and use of biographical information in selection and performance prediction* (pp. 147–169). Palo Alto, CA: Consulting Psychologists Press.

SCHOENFELDT, L. F., SCHOENFELDT, B. B., ACKER, S. R., & PERLSON, M. R. (1976). Content validity revisited: Test development of a content-oriented test of industrial reading. *Journal of Applied Psychology, 61,* 581–588.

SCHOGGEN, P. (1989). *Behavior settings; A revision and extension of Roger G. Barker's "Ecological psychology."* Stanford, CA: Stanford University Press.

SCHULER, H., FARR, J. L., &. SMITH, M. (Eds.). (1993). *Personnel selection and assessment: Individual and organizational perspectives.* Hillsdale, NJ: Erlbaum.

SCHULZ, R., & EWEN, R. B. (1993). *Adult development and aging: Myths and emerging realities* (2nd ed.) New York: Macmillan.

SCHWARTZ, M. M., COHEN, B. D., & PAVLIK, W. B. (1964). The effects of subject- and experimenter-induced defensive response sets on Picture-Frustration Test reactions. *Journal of Projective Techniques, 28,* 341–345.

SCHWARTZ, R. H. (1992). Is Holland's theory worthy of so much attention, or should vocational psychology move on? *Journal of Vocational Behavior, 40,* 179–187.

SCHWARTZ, S. H. (1992). Universals in the content and structure of values: Theoretical advances and empirical tests in 20 countries. *Advances in Experimental Social Psychology, 25,* 1–65.

SCHWARTZ, S. H. (1994). Are there universal aspects in the structure and contents of human values? *Journal of Social Issues, 50* (4), 19–45.

SCHWARTZ, S. H., & SAGIV, L. (1995). Identifying culture-specifics in the content and structure of values. *Journal of Cross-Cultural Psychology, 26,* 92–116.

SCHWARZ, R A., &. KRUG, R. E. *(1972). Ability testing in developing countries: A handbook of principles and techniques.* New York: Praeger.

SCHWARZER, R. (Ed.). (1992). *Self-efficacy: Thought control of action.* Washington, DC: Hemisphere.

SCIENCE RESEARCH ASSOCIATES. (1990). CRT *Skills Test: Examiner's manual.* Rosemont, IL: Author.

SCOTTISH COUNCIL FOR RESEARCH IN EDUCATION (1949). *The trend of Scottish intelligence.* London: University of London Press.

SCRUGGS, C. (1994). [Review of Work Keys Assessments], In J. T. Kapes, M. M. Mastie, & E. A. Whitfield (Eds.), A *counselor's guide to career assessment instruments* (3rd ed., pp. 126–130). Alexandria, VA: National Career Development Association.

SEASHORE, H. G. (1962). Women are more predictable than men. *Journal of Counseling Psychology,* 9, 261–270.

SEASHORE, H. G., WESMAN, A. G., & DOPPELT, J. E. (1950). The standardization of the Wechsler Intelligence Scale for Children. *Journal of Consulting Psychology, 14,* 99–110.

SECHREST, L. (1963). Incremental validity: A recommendation. *Educational and Psychological Measurement, 23,* 153–158.

SEGALL, M. H. (1983). On the search for the independent variable in cross-cultural psychology. In S. H. Irvine & J. W. Berry (Eds.), *Human assessment and cultural factors* (pp. 127–137). New York: Plenum Press.

SEGALL, M. H., CAMPBELL, D. T., & HERSKOVITS, M. J. (1966). *The influence of culture on visual perception.* Indianapolis, IN: Bobbs-Merrill.

SEGUIN, E. (1907). *Idiocy: Its treatment by the physiological method.* New York: Columbia University, Bureau of Publications. Teachers College. (Original work published 1866)

The Seventh Mental Measurements Yearbook. (1972). Highland Park, NJ: Gryphon Press.

SEXTON, D., KELLEY, M. F., & SURBECK, E. (1990). Piagetian-based assessment. In A. F. Rotatori, R. A. Fox, D. Sexton, & J. Miller (Eds.), *Comprehensive assessment in special education: Approaches, procedures, and concerns* (pp. 54–88). Springfield, IL: Charles C Thomas.

SEXTON, M. E. (1987). The correlates of sensorimotor functioning in infancy. In I. C. Užgiris &J. McV. Hunt (Eds.), *Infant performance and experience: New findings with the ordinal scales* (pp. 230–251). Champaign: University of Illinois Press.

SHAFFER, M. B. (1985). Review of the Children's Apperception Test. *Ninth Mental Measurements Yearbook,* Vol. 1, 316–317.

SHAH, C. R, & BOYDEN, M. F. H. (1991). Assessment of auditory functioning. In B. A. Bracken (Ed.), *The psychoeducational assessment of preschool children* (2nd ed., pp. 341–378). Boston: Allyn & Bacon.

SHANKWEILER, D., CRAIN, S., KATZ, L., FOWLER, A. E., LIBERMAN, A. M., BRADY, S. A., THORNTON, R., LUNDQUIST, E., DREYER, L., FLETCHER, J. M., STUEBING, K. K., SHAYWITZ, S. E., & SHAYWITZ, B. A. (1995). Cognitive profiles of reading-disabled children: Comparison of language skills in phonology, morphology, and syntax. *Psychological Science, 6,* 149–156.

SHAPIRA, Z., & DUNBAR, R. L. M. (1980). Testing Mintzberg's managerial roles classification using an in-basket simulation. *Journal of Applied Psychology, 65,* 87–95.

SHAPIRO, D. L. (1991). *Forensic psychological assessment: An integrative approach.* BOSTON:Allyn & Bacon.

SHARF, J. C. (1994). The impact of legal and equal employment opportunity issues on personal history inquiries. In G. S. Stokes, M. D. Mumford, & W. A. Owens (Eds.), *Biodata handbook: Theory, research, and use of biographical information in selection and performance prediction* (pp. 351–390). Palo Alto, CA: Consulting Psychologists Press.

SHARP, S. E. (1898–1899). Individual psychology: A study in psychological method. *American Journal of Psychology, 10,* 329–391.

SHAVELSON, R. J., & BOLUS, R. (1982). Self-concept: The interplay ot theory and methods. *Journal of Educational Psychology, 74,* 3–17.

SHAVELSON, R. J., HUBNER, J. J., & STANTON, G. C. (1976). Self-concept: Validation of construct interpretations. *Review of Educational Research, 46,* 407–441.

SHAVELSON, R. J., & WEBB, N. M. (1991). *Generalizability theory: A primer.* Newbury Park, CA: Sage.

SHAW, M. E., & WRIGHT, J. M. (1967). *Scales for the measurement of attitudes.* New York: McGraw-Hill.

SHAW, S. R., SWERDLIK, M. E., & LAURENT, J. (1993). Review of the WISC-III. *Journal of Psychoeducational* Assessment (Monograph Series: Advances in Psychoeducational Assessment). Germantown, TN: Psychoeducational Corporation.

SHEA, S. C. (1988). *Psychiatric interviewing: The art of understanding.* Philadelphia: Saunders.

SHEDLER, J., MAYMAN, M., & MANIS, M. (1993). The illusion of mental health. American *Psychologist, 48,* 111 7–1131.

SHEEHAN, E. P. (1995). Review of the Work Environment Scale, Second Edition. *Twelfth Mental Measurements Yearbook,* 1122–1123.

SHEEHAN, K., & MLSLEVY, R. J. (1989). *Integrating cognitive and psychometric models to* measure *document literacy* (Res. Rep. No. 89–51). Princeton, NJ: Educational Testing Service.

SHELDON, W., &. STEVENS, S. S. (1970). *The varieties of temperament: A psychology of constitutional differences. New York:* Hafner. (Original work published 1942)

SHEPARD, J. W. (1989). Review of the Jackson Vocational Interest Survey. Tenth *Mental Measurements Yearbook,* 403–404.

SHEPARD, L. A. (1984). Setting performance standards. In R. A. Berk (Ed.), A *guide to criterion-referenced test construction* (pp. 169–198). Baltimore: Johns Hopkins University Press.

SHERMAN, S. W., &. ROBINSON, N. M. *(Eds.). (1982). Ability testing of handicapped people: Dilemma for government, science, and the public.* Washington, DC: National Academy Press.

SHINN, M. R. (1989). *Curriculum-based measurement: Assessing special children.* New York: Guilford Press.

SHINN, M. R., & BAKER, S. K. (1996). The use of curriculum-based measurement with diverse learners. In L. A. Suzuki, P. J. Meller, & J. G. Ponterotto (Eds.), *Handbook of multicultural assessment: Clinical, psychological, and educational applications* (pp. 179–222). San Francisco: Jossey-Bass.

SHINN, M. R., ROSENFIELD, S., & KNUTSON, N. (1989). Curriculum-based assessment: A comparison of models. *School Psychology Review, 18,* 299–316.

SHOCK, N. W., GREULICH, R. C., ANDRES, R., ARENBERG, D., COSTA, P. T., JR., LAKATTA, E. G., & TOBIN, J. D. (1984). *Normal human aging: The Baltimore Longitudinal Study of Aging.* Washington, DC: U.S. Government Printing Office. (NIH Publication No. 84–2450)

SHORE, C. W., & MARION, R. (1972). *Suitability of using common selection test standards for Negro and white airmen* (AFHRL-TR-72–53). Lackland Air Force Base, TX: Air Force Human Resources Laboratory, Personnel Research Division.

SHORE, T. H., SHORE, L. M., & THORNTON, G. C., III. (1992). Construct validity of self- and peer evaluations of performance dimensions in an assessment center. *Journal of Applied Psychology,* 77, 42–54.

SHUMAN, D. W. (1990). *Law and mental health professionals: Texas.* Washington, DC: American Psychological Association.

SHUMAN, D. W. (1993). *Law and mental health professionals: Texas supplement.* Washington, DC: American Psychological Association.

SHURRAGER, H. C., & SHURRAGER, P. S. (1964). *Haptic Intelligence Scale for adult blind.* Chicago: Stoelting.

SHWEDER, R. A., &. SULLIVAN, M. A. (1993). Cultural psychology: Who needs it? Annual *Review of Psychology, 44,* 497–523.

SHYE, S. (1988). Inductive and deductive reasoning: A structural reanalysis of ability tests. *Journal of Applied Psychology,* 73, 308–311.

SIGEL, I. E. (1963). How intelligence tests limit understanding of intelligence. Merrill *Palmer Quarterly, 9*, 39–56.

Sigi: a Computer-based System of Interactive Guidance and Informatiort. (1974–1975). Princeton, NJ: Educational Testing Service.

SILVERMAN, I., & SHULMAN, A. D. (1970). A conceptual model of artifact in attitude change studies. Sociometry, 33, 97–107.

SILVERMAN, L. H. (1959). A Q-sort Study of the validity of evaluations made from projective techniques. *Psychological Monographs,* 73(7, Whole No. 477).

SILVERSTEIN, A. B. (1982a). Alternative multiple-group solutions for the WISC and the WISC-R. *Journal of Clinical Psychology,* 38, 166–168.

SILVERSTEIN, A. B. (1982b). Factor structure of the Wechsler Adult Intelligence Scale— Revised. *Journal of Consulting and Clinical Psychology, 50*, 661–664.

SILVERSTEIN, A. B. (1986). Nonstandard standard scores on the Vineland Adaptive Behavior Scales: A cautionary note. *American Journal on Mental Deficiency, 91*, 1–4.

SILVERSTEIN, A. B. (1989). Review of the Multidimensional Aptitude Battery. *Tenth Mental Measurements Yearbook*, 523–524.

SILVERSTEIN, A. B. (1990). Short forms of individual intelligence tests. *Psychological Assessment*, 2, 3–11.

SIMON, H. A. (1976). Identifying basic abilities underlying intelligent performance of complex tasks. In L. B. Resnick (Ed.), *The nature of intelligence* (pp. 65–98). Hillsdale, NJ: Erlbaum.

SIMON, H. A. (1990). Invariants of human behavior. *Annual Review of Psychology, 41*, 1–19.

SIMON, H. A. (1994). Focus on attention: The linkage between cognition and emotion. In W. Spaulding (Ed.), *Nebraska Symposium on Motivation: Vol. 41. Integrative views of motivation, cognition, and emotion* (pp. 1–21). Lincoln: University of Nebraska Press.

SINES, J. O. (1985). Review of Roberts Apperception Test for Children. *Ninth Mental Measurements Yearbook,* Vol. 2, 1290–1291.

SINGER, J. A., & SALOVEY, P. (1993). *The remembered self: Emotion and* memory *in personality.* New York: Free Press.

SIRECI, S. G., THISSEN, D., & WAINER, H. (1991). On the reliability of testlet-based tests. *Journal of Educational Measurement, 28*, 237–247.

SIVAN, A. B. (1991). *Benton Visual Retention Test Fifth Edition: Manual.* San Antonio, TX: Psychological Corporation.

SKINNER, E. A. (1995). *Perceived control, motivation, and coping.* Thousand Oaks, CA: Sage.

SKOLNICK, A. (1966). Motivational imagery and behavior over twenty years. *Journal of Consulting Psychology, 30*, 463–478.

SLAVIK, S. (1991). Early memories as a guide to client movement through life. *Canadian Journal of Counseling, 25*, 331–337.

SLEEK, S. (1995, June). APA's national college to begin issuing credentials. APA Monitor, p. 24.

SMITH, C. P. (1992). Reliability issues. In C. P. Smith (Ed.), *Motivation and personality: Handbook of thematic content analysis* (pp. 126–139). New York: Cambridge University Press.

SMITH, C. P. (Ed.), (with Atkinson, J. W., McClelland, D. C., & Veroff, J.). (1992). *Motivation and personality: Handbook of thematic content analysis.* New York: Cambridge University Press.

SMITH, C. R. (1989). Review of the Classroom Environment Scale, Second Edition. *Tenth Mental Measurements Yearbook*, 174–177.

SMITH, G. (1991). Assessing family interaction by the collaborative drawing technique. In C. E. Schaefer, K. Gitlin, & A. Sandgrund (Eds.), *Play diagnosis and assessment* (pp. 599–607). New York: Wiley.

SMITH, J., HARRE, R., & VAN LANGENHOVE, L. (Eds.). (1995). *Rethinking psychology.* Thousand Oaks, CA: Sage.

SMITH, P. B., &. BOND, M. H. (1993). *Social psychology across cultures: Analysis and perspectives.* London: Harvester Wheatsheaf.

SMITTLE, P. (1990). Assessment's next wave: The computerized placement tests. *College Board Review,* No. *156,* 22–27.

SNIDER, J. G., & OSGOOD, C. E. (Eds.). (1969). *Semantic differential technique: A source book.* Chicago: Aldine.

SNOW, J. H. (1992). Review of the Luria-Nebraska Neuropsychological Battery: Forms I and II. *Eleventh Mental Measurements Yearbook,* 484–486.

SNOW, R. E. (1989). Toward assessment of cognitive and conative structures in learning. *Educational Researcher, 18* (9), 8–14.

SNOW, R. E. (1990). *Progress and propaganda in learning assessment [Review of the book Dynamic assessment: An interactional approach to evaluating learning potential]. Contemporary Psychology, 35, 1134–1136.*

SNOW, R. E. (1992). Aptitude theory: Yesterday, today, and tomorrow. *Educational Psychologist, 27,* 5–32.

SNOW, R. E. (1993). Construct validity and constructed response tests. In R. E. Bennett & W. C. Ward (Eds.), *Construction versus choice in cognitive measurement: Issues in constructed response, performance testing, and portfolio assessment* (pp. 45–60). Hillsdale, NJ: Erlbaum.

SNOW, R. E., & LOHMAN, D. F. (1989). Implications of cognitive psychology for educational measurement. In R. L. Linn (Ed.), *Educational measurement* (3rd ed., pp. 263–331). New York: American Council on Education/Macmillan.

SNYDER, C. R., & LARSON, G. R. (1972). A further look at student acceptance of general personality interpretations. *Journal of Consulting and Clinical Psychology, 38,* 384–388.

SOCIETY FOR INDUSTRIAL AND ORGANIZATIONAL PSYCHOLOGY. (1987). *Principles for the validation and use of personnel selection procedures* (3rd ed.). College Park, MD: Author.

SOMMER, R. (1894). *Diagnostik der Geisteskrankheiten für praktische Ärzte und Studierende.* Wien & Leipzig: Urban & Schwarzenberg.

SONDEREGGER, T. B. (Ed.). (1992). *Nebraska Symposium on Motivation: Psychology and aging.* Lincoln: University of Nebraska Press.

SONTAG, L. W., BAKER, C. T., & NELSON, V. L. (1958). Mental growth and personality development: A longitudinal study. *Monographs of the Society for Research in Child Development, 23* (2, Serial No. 68).

SPANGLER, W. D. (1992). Validity of questionnaire and TAT measures of need for achievement: Meta-analyses. *Psychological Bulletin, 112,* 140–154.

SPARROW, S. S., BALLA, D. A., & CICCHETTI, D. V. (1984a). *Vineland Adaptive Behavior Scales: Interview Edition Expanded Form Manual.* Circle Pines, MN: American Guidance Service.

SPARROW, S. S., BALLA, D. A., & CICCHETTI, D. V. (1984b). *Vineland Adaptive Behavior Scales: Interview Edition Survey Form Manual.* Circle Pines, MN: American Guidance Service.

SPAULDING, W. D. (Ed.). (1994). *Integrative views of motivation, cognition, and emotion.* Lincoln, NE: University of Nebraska Press.

SPEARMAN, C. (1904). "General intelligence" objectively determined and measured. *American Journal of Psychology, 15,* 201–293.

SPEARMAN, C. (1927). *The abilities of man*. New York: Macmillan.

SPENGLER, P. M., & STROHMER, D. C. (1994). Clinical judgmental biases: The moderating roles of counselor cognitive complexity and counselor client preferences. *Journal of Counseling Psychology, 41*, 8–17.

SPIELBERGER, C. D. (Ed.). (1972). *Anxiety: Current trends in theory and research* (Vol. 2). Orlando, FL: Academic Press.

SPIELBERGER, C. D. (1985). Assessment of state and trait anxiety: Conceptual and methodological issues. *Southern Psychologist, 2*, 6–16.

SPIELBERGER, C. D. (1988). *State-Trait Anger Expression Inventory manual*. Odessa, FL: Psychological Assessment Resources.

SPIELBERGER, C. D. (1989). *State-Trait Anxiety Inventory: A comprehensive bibliography*. Palo Alto, CA: Consulting Psychologists Press.

SPIELBERGER, C.D. (1966). Theory and research on anxiety. In: C.D. Spielberger ed. Anxiety and behavior. New York: Academic Press.

SPIELBERGER, C. D., et al. (1980). *Test Anxiety Inventory: Preliminary professional manual*. Palo Alto, CA: Consulting Psychologists Press.

SPIELBERGER, C. D., et al. (1983). *Manual for the State-Trait Anxiety Inventory (STAI, Form Y)*. Palo Alto, CA: Consulting Psychologists Press.

SPIELBERGER, C. D., ANTON, W. D., & BEDELL, J. (1976). The nature and treatment of test anxiety. In M. Zuckerman &. C. D. Spielberger (Eds.), *Emotions and anxiety: New concepts, methods, and applications* (pp. 317–345). New York: LEA/Wiley.

SPIELBERGER, C., & DIAZ-GUERRERO, R. (Eds.). (1990). *Cross-cultural anxiety* (Vol. 4). Bristol, PA: Hemisphere.

SPIELBERGER, C. D., GONZALEZ, H. P., & FLETCHER, T. (1979). Test anxiety reduction, learning strategies, and academic performance. In H. F. O'Neil, Jr. &. C. D. Spielberger (Eds.), *Cognitive and affective learning strategies* (pp. 111–131). New York: Academic Press.

SPIELBERGER, C. D., GONZALEZ, H. P, TAYLOR, C. J., ALGAZE, B., & ANTON, W. D. (1978). Examination stress and test anxiety. In C. D. Spielberger & I. G. Sarason (Eds.), *Stress and anxiety* (Vol. 5, pp. 167–191). New York: Hemisphere.

SPIELBERGER, C. D. (1980). "Test Anxiety Inventory: Preliminary Professional Manual," Consulting Psychologists Press, Palo Alto, CA

SPIELBERGER, C. D., JOHNSON, E. H., RUSSELL, S. F., CRANE, R. J., JACOBS, G. A., & WORDEN, T. J. (1985). The experience and expression of anger: Construction and validation of an anger expression scale. In M. A. Chesney & R. H. Rosenman (Eds.), Anger *and hostility in cardiovascular and behavioral disorders* (pp. 5–30). New York: McGraw-Hill/Hemisphere.

SPIELBERGER, C. D., & SYDEMAN, S. J. (1994). State-Trait Anxiety Inventory and State-Trait Anger Expression Inventory. In M. Maruish (Ed.), *The use of psychological testing for treatment planning and outcome assessment* (pp. 292–321). Hillsdale, NJ: Erlbaum.

SPIELBERGER, C.D. AND VAGG, R.P. 1995. *Test Anxiety*. Bristol: Taylor & Francis.

SPITERI, S. P. (n.d.). *Word association testing and thesaurus construction*. Retrieved June 11, 2016, from http://en.wikipedia.org/wiki/Projective_test.

SPITZ, H. H. (1986). *The raising of intelligence: Selected history of attempts to raise retarded intelligence*. Hillsdale, NJ: Erlbaum.

SPRANGER, E. (1928). *Types of men* (P J. W. Pigors, Trans.). Halle: Niemeyer.

SPREEN, O., & STRAUSS, E. (1991). *A compendium of neuropsychological tests: Administration, norms, and commentary*. New York: Oxford University Press.

SPRUILL, J. (1991). A comparison of the Wechsler Adult Intelligence Scale-Revised with the Stanford-Binet (4th edition) for mentally retarded adults. *Psychological Assessment*, 3, 133–135.

STAABS, G. VON (1991). *The Scenotest* (J. A. Smith, Trans.). Toronto: Hogrefe & Huber. (Original work published 1964)

STAMOULIS, D. T., &. HAUENSTEIN, N. M. A. (1993). Rater training and rating accuracy: Training for dimensional accuracy versus training for ratee differentiation. *Journal of Applied Psychology, 78,* 994–1003.

STANLEY, J. C. (Ed.). (1972). Preschool programs for the disadvantaged: Five experimental approaches to early childhood education. Baltimore: Johns Hopkins University Press.

STANLEY, J. C. (Ed.). (1973). *Compensatory education for children, ages two to eight.* Baltimore: Johns Hopkins University Press.

STARR, B. J., &. KATKIN, E. S. (1969). The clinician as aberrant actuary: Illusory correlation and the Incomplete Sentences Blank. *Journal of Abnormal Psychology, 74,* 670–675.

STEELE, C. (Chair). (1995, August). *Defying the Bell Curve—Social factors that inhibit and facilitate academic performance of women and minorities.* Symposium at the annual convention of the American Psychological Association, New York.

STEELE, C., SPENCER, S., &. ARONSON, J. (1995, August) Inhibiting the expression of intelligence: The role of stereotype vulnerability. In C. Steele (Chair), *Defying the Bell Curve* (Symposium conducted at the annual convention of the American Psychological Association, New York).

STEPHENSON, W. (1953). *The study of behavior: Q-technique and its methodology.* Chicago: University of Chicago Press.

STERNBERG, R. J. (1977). *Intelligence, information processiitg, and analogical reasoning: The componential analysis of human abilities.* Hillsdale, NJ: Erlbaum.

STERNBERG, R. J. (1980). Representation and process in linear syllogistic reasoning. *Journal of Experimental Psychology, General, 109,* 119–159.

STERNBERG, R. J. (1981). Testing and cognitive psychology. *American Psychologist, 36,* 1001–1011.

STERNBERG, R. J. (Ed.). (1982–1989). *Advances in the psychology of human imelligence* (Vols. 1–5). Hillsdale, NJ: Erlbaum.

STERNBERG, R. J. (1984). What cognitive psychology can (and cannot) do for test development. In B. S. Plake (Ed.), *Social and technical issues in testing: Implications for test construction and usage* (pp. 39–60). Hillsdale, NJ: Erlbaum.

STERNBERG, R. J. (1985a). *Beyond IQ: A triarchic theory of human intelligence.* New York: Cambridge University Press.

STERNBERG, R. J. (Ed.). (1985b). *Human abilities: An information-processing approach.* New York: Freeman.

STERNBERG, R. J. (1986). *Intelligence applied: Understanding and increasing your intellectual skills.* San Diego, CA: Harcourt Brace Jovanovich.

STERNBERG, R. J. (1988). Mental self-government: A theory of intellectual styles and their development. *Human Development, 31,* 197–224.

STERNBERG, R. J. (1989). *The triarchic mind: A new theory of human intelligence.* New York: Penguin.

STERNBERG, R. J. (1990). *Metaphors of mind: Conceptions of the nature of* intelligence. New York: Cambridge University Press.

STERNBERG, R. J. (1993). Rocky's back again: A review of the WISC-III. *Journal of Psychoeducational* Assessment (Monograph Series: Advances in Psychoeducational Assessment). Germantown, TN: Psychoeducational Corporation.

STERNBERG, R. J. (1994a). The PRSVL model of person-context interaction in the study of human potential. In M. G. Rumsey, C. B. Walker, & J. H. Harris (Eds.), *Personnel selection and classification* (pp. 317–332). Hillsdale, NJ: Erlbaum.

STERNBERG, R. J. (1994b). Thinking styles: Theory and assessment at the interface between intelligence and personality. In R. J. Sternberg & P. Ruzgis (Eds.), *Personality and intelligence* (pp. 169–187). New York: Cambridge University Press.

STERNBERG, R. J., & DETTERMAN, D. K. (Eds.). (1979). *Human intelligence: Perspectives on its theory and measurement*. Norwood, NJ: Ablex.

STERNBERG, R. J., & DETTERMAN, D. K. (eds.). (1986). *WHAT is intelligence? Contemporary viewpoints on its nature and definitions.* Norwood, *NJ: Ablex.*

STERNBERG, R. J., & FRENSCH, P. A. (Eds.). (1991). *Complex problem solving: Principles and mechanisms.* Hillsdale, NJ: Erlbaum.

STERNBERG, R. J., & RUZGIS, P. (Eds.). (1994). *Personality and intelligence.* New York: Cambridge University Press.

STERNBERG, R. J., & WAGNER, R. K. (Eds.). (1986). *Practical intelligence: Origins of competence in the everyday world*. New York. Cambridge University Press.

STERNBERG, R. J., WAGNER, R. K., WILLIAMS, W. M., & HORVATH, J. A. (1995). Testing common sense. *American Psychologist, 50,* 912–927.

STERNBERG, R. J., & WEIL, E. M. (1980). An aptitude X strategy interaction in linear syllogistic reasoning. *Journal of Educational Psychology, 72,* 226–239.

STEVENS, J. H., JR., & BAKEMAN, R. (1985). A factor analytic study of the HOME scale for infants. *Developmental Psychology, 21,* 1196–1203.

STEVENS, M. J., & CAMPION, M. A. (1994). *Teamwork-KSA Test: Examiner's manual.* Rosemont, IL: SRA-McGraw-Hill/London House.

STICHT, T. G. (Ed.). (1975). *Reading for working: A functional literacy anthology.* Alexandria, VA: Human Resources Research Organization.

STOKES, G. S., MUMFORD, M. D., & OWENS, W. A. (Eds.). (1994). *Biodata handbook: Theory, research, and use of biographical information in selection and performance prediction*. Palo Alto, CA: Consulting Psychologists Press.

STOKOLS, D. (1995). The paradox of environmental psychology. *American Psychologist, 50,* 821–837.

STOKOLS, D., & ALTMAN, I. (Eds.). (1987). *Handbook of environmental psychology* (Vols. 1&. 2). New York: Wiley.

STOLOFF, M. L., & COUCH, J. V. (Eds.). (1992). *Computer use in psychology: A directory of software* (3rd ed.). Washington, DC: American Psychological Association.

STONE, B. J., GRIDLEY, B. E., &. GYURKE, J. S. (1991). Confirmatory factor analysis of the WPPSI-R at the extreme end of the age range. *Journal of Psychoeducational Assess*-merit, 9, 263–270.

STONE, E. F., & HOLLENBECK, J. R. (1989). Clarifying some controversial issues surrounding statistical procedures for detecting moderators: Empirical evidence and related matters. *Journal of Applied Psychology, 74,* 3–10.

STONER, G. (1995). Review of the Metropolitan Readiness Tests, Fifth Edition. *Twelfth* Mental Measurements *Yearbook,* 612–614.

STORANDT, M., & VANDENBOS, G. R. (eds.). (1994). *Neuropsychological assessment of dementia and depression in older adults: A clinician's guide.* Washington, DC: American Psychological Association.

STOTT, L. H. & BALL, S. (1965). Infant and preschool mental tests: Review and evaluation. *Monographs of the Society for Research in Child Development,* 30 (3, Serial No. 101).

STRAUSS, A. A., & LEHTINEN, L. E. (1947). *Psychopathology and education of the brain-injured child*. New York: Grune & Stratton.

STREINER, D. L., & NORMAN, G. R. (1995). *Health measurement scales: A practical guide to their development* and *use* (2nd ed.). Oxford, England: Oxford University Press.

STRICKER, G., DAVIS-RUSSELL, E., BOURG, E., DURAN, E., HAMMOND, W. R., MCHOLLAND, W. R., POLITE, K., & VAUGHN, B. E. (Eds.). (1990). *Toward ethnic diversification in psychology education and training.* Washington, DC: American Psychological Association.

STRICKER, L. J. (1966). Compulsivity as a moderator variable: A replication and extension. *Journal of Applied Psychology, 50*, 331–335.

STRICKER, L. J. (1969). "Test-wiseness" on personality scales. *Journal of Applied Psychology Monograph, 53(3,* Part 2).

STRICKER, L. J. (1982). Interpersonal Competence Instrument: Development and preliminary findings. *Applied Psychological Measurement, 6,* 69–81.

STRICKER, L. J. (1984). Test disclosure and retest performance on the SAT. *Applied Psychological Measurement, 8,* 81–87.

STRICKER, L. J. (1985). *Measuring social status with occupational information: A simple method* (Res. Rep. 85–18). Princeton, NJ: Educational Testing Service.

STRICKER, L. JR., &. ROCK, D. A. (1990). Interpersonal competence, social intelligence, and general ability. *Personality and htdividual Differences, 11,* 833–839.

Structural Equation Modeling: a Multidisciplinary Journal. Vol. 1. (1994). Hillsdale, NJ: Erlbaum.

STRUNK, W., JR., & WHITE, E. B. (1979). *The elements of style* (3rd ed.). Boston: Allyn & Bacon.

STURGIS, E. T., & GRAMLING, S. (1988). Psychophysiological assessment. In A. S. Bellack &. M. Hersen (Eds.), *Behavioral assessment: A practical handbook* (3rd ed., pp. 213–251). New York: Pergamon Press.

SUBKOVIAK, M. J. (1984). Estimating the reliability of mastery-nonmastery classifications. In R. A. Berk (Ed.), A *guide to criterion-referenced test construction* (pp. 267–291). Baltimore: Johns Hopkins University Press.

SUBOTNIK, R. F., & ARNOLD, K. D. (Eds.). (1994). *Beyond Terman: Contemporary longitudinal studies of giftedness and talent.* Norwood, NJ: Ablex.

SUGARMAN, S. (1987). *Piaget's construction of the child's reality.* New York: Cambridge University Press.

SULLIVAN, P. M., & BURLEY, S. K. (1990). Mental testing of the hearing-impaired child. In C. R. Reynolds &. R. W. Kamphaus (Eds.), *Handbook of psychological and educational* assessment *of children: Intelligence and achievement* (pp. 761–788). New York: Guilford Press.

SULLIVAN, R M., & SCHULTE, L. E. (1992). Factor analysis of WISC-R with deaf and hard-of-hearing children. *Psychological Assessment, 4,* 537–540.

SULSKY, L. M., & BALZER, W. K. (1988). Meaning and measurement of performance rating accuracy: Some methodological and theoretical concerns. *Journal of Applied Psychology,* 73, 1–10.

SULSKY, L. M., & DAY, D. V. (1992). Frame-of-reference training and cognitive categorization: An empirical investigation of rater memory issues. *Journal of Applied Psychology, 77,* 501–510.

SULSKY, L. M., & DAY, D. V. (1994). Effects of frame-of-reference training on ratér accuracy under alternative time delays. *Journal of Applied Psychology, 79, 535–543.*

SUPER, D. E. (1953). A theory of vocational development. *American Psychologist, 8,* 185–190.

SUPER, D. E. (1957). The psychology of careers: An introduction to vocational development. New York: Harper & Row.

SUPER, D. E. (1980). A life-span, life-space approach to career development. *Journal of Vocational Behavior, 16, 282–298.*

SUPER, D. E. (1985). Coming of age in Middletown: Careers in the making. *American Psychologist, 40,* 405–415.

SUPER, D. E. (1990). A life-span, life-space approach to career development. In D. Brown, Brooks, Et Al. (Eds.), *Career choice and development: Applying contemporary theories to practice* (2nd ed., pp. 197–261). San Francisco: Jossey-Bass.

SUPER, D. E., et al. (1970). *Computer-assisted counseling.* New York: Teachers College Press.

SUPER, D. E., & BOHN, M. J., JR. (1970). *Occupational psychology.* Belmont, CA: Wadsworth.

SUPER, D. E., CRITES, J. O., HUMMEL, R. C., MOSER, H. R, OVERSTREET, P. L., & WARNATH, C. (1957). *Vocational development: A framework for research.* New York: Teachers College Press.

SUPER, D. E., & OVERSTREET, P. L. (1960). *The vocational maturity of ninth grade boys.* New York: Teachers College Press.

SUPER, D. E., & SVERKO, B. (Eds.). (1995). *Life roles, values, and careers: International findings of the Work Importance Study.* San Francisco: Jossey-Bass.

SUZUKI, L. A., MELLER, P. J., &. PONTEROTTO, J. G. (Eds.). (1996). *Handbook of multicultural assessment: Clinical, psychological, and educational applications.* San Francisco: Jossey-Bass.

SWANSON, H. L., & KEOGH, B. (Eds.). (1990). *Learning disabilities: Theoretical and research issues.* Hillsdale, NJ: Erlbaum.

SWANSON, J. L. (1992). The structure of vocational interests for African-American college students. *Journal of Vocational Behavior, 40,* 144–157.

SWARTZ, J. D. (1973). Gamble's review of the Holtzman Inkblot Technique: Corrections and clarifications. *Psychological Bulletin, 79,* 378–379.

SWARTZ, J. D. (1992). The HIT and the HIT 25: Comments and clarifications. *Journal of Personality Assessment, 58,* 432–433.

SWARTZ, J. D., & HOLTZMAN, W. H. (1963). Group method of administration for the Holtzman Inkblot Technique. *Journal of Clinical Psychology,* 19, 433–441.

SWEZEY, R. W., & PEARLSTEIN, R. B. (1975). *Guidebook for developing criterion-referenced tests.* Arlington, VA: U.S. Army Research Institute for the Behavioral and Social Sciences.

SWINTON, S. S., & POWERS, D. E. (1985). *The impact of self-study on GRE test performance* (Res. Rep. 85–12). Princeton, NJ: Educational Testing Service.

SYMONDS, P. M. (1931). *Diagnosing personality and conduct.* New York: Century.

SZYMULA, G. (1990). Vocational assessment. In C. Schiro-Geist (Ed.), *Vocational counseling for special populations* (pp. 65–97). Springfield, IL: Charles C Thomas.

TABE (1994). *Complete battery, Forms 7 & 8. Examiner's manual.* Monterey, CA: CTB/ McGraw-Hill.

TAIT, M., PADGETT, M. Y., & BALDWIN, T. T. (1989). Job and life satisfaction: A reevaluation of the strength of the relationship and gender effects as a function of the date of the study. *Journal of Applied Psychology, 74,* 502–507.

TALLENT, N. (1992). *The practice of psychological* assessment. Englewood Cliffs, NJ: Prentice Hall.

TALLENT, N. (1993). *Psychological report writing* (4th ed.). Englewood Cliffs, NJ: Prentice Hall.

TASBIHSAZAN, R., NETTELBECK, T., & KIRBY, N. (2003). Predictive validity of the Fagan test of infant intelligence. *British Journal of Developmental Psychology, 21*(4), 585–597.

TAYLOR, H. C., & RUSSELL, J. T. (1939). The relationship of validity coefficients to the practical effectiveness of tests in selection. Discussion and tables. *Journal of Applied Psychology, 23,* 565–578.

TAYLOR, S. E. (1990). Health psychology: The science and the field. *American Psychologist, 45,* 40–50.

TCS/2 *technical report*. (1993). *Test of Cognitive Skills*. Monterey, CA: CTB Macmillan/ McGraw-Hill.

TEETER, P. A. (1985). Review of Adjective Check List. *Ninth Mental Measurements Yearbook*, Vol. 1, 50–52.

TEGLASI, H. (1993). *Clinical use of story telling: Emphasizing the T.A.T. with children and adolescents*. Boston: Allyn & Bacon.

TELLEGEN, A., & BEN-PORATH, Y. S. (1992). The new uniform T scores for the MMPI-2: Rationale, derivation, and appraisal. *Psychological* Assessment, 4, 145–155.

TELLEGEN, A., & BEN-PORATH, Y. S. (1993). Code-type comparability of the MMPI and MMPI-2: Analysis of recent findings and criticisms. *Journal of Personality Assessment, 61*, 489–500.

TELZROW, C. F. (1990). Does PASS pass the test? A critique of the Das-Naglieri Cognitive Assessment System. *Journal of Psychoeducational Assessment, 8*, 344–355.

TENOPYR, M. L. (1986). Needed directions for measurement in work settings. In B. S. Plake &. J. C. Witt (Eds.), *The future of testing* (pp. 269–288). Hillsdale, NJ: Erlbaum.

TENOPYR, M. L. (1989). Review of the Kuder Occupational Interest Survey, Revised (Form DD). *Tenth Mental Measurements Yearbook*, 427–429.

TENOPYR, M. L. (1995, August). *Measurement at the crossroads*. Presidential address (Div. 5) presented at the annual convention of the American Psychological Association, New York.

The Tenth Mental Measurements Yearbook. (1989). Lincoln, NE: Buros Institute of Mental Measurements.

TERMAN, L. M. (1916). *The measurement of intelligence*. Boston: Houghton Mifflin.

TERMAN, L. M. (1921). Intelligence and its measurement: A symposium–II. *Journal of Educational Psychology*, *12*(3), 127.

TERMAN, L. M., et al. (1925). *Genetic studies of genius: Vol. I. Mental and physical traits of a thousand gifted children*. Stanford University, CA: Stanford University Press.

TERMAN, L. M., &. MERRILL, M. A. (1937). *Measuring intelligence*. Boston: Houghton Mifflin.

TERMAN, L. M., & MERRILL, M. A. (1960). *Stanford-Binet Intelligence Scale: Manual for the third revision, Form L-M*. Boston: Houghton Mifflin.

TERMAN, L. M., & MERRILL, M. A. (1973). *Stanford-Binet Intelligence Scale: 1972 norms edition*. Boston: Houghton Mifflin.

Tests in print II. (1974). Lincoln, NE: Buros Institute of Mental Measurements.

Tests in print III. (1983). Lincoln, NE: Buros Institute of Mental Measurements.

Tests in print IV (Vols. 1–2). (1994). Lincoln, NE: Buros Institute of Mental Measurements.

TETT, R. R, JACKSON, D. N., & ROTHSTEIN, M. (1991). Personality measures as predictors of job performance: A meta-analytic review. *Personnel Psychology, 44*, 703–742.

THARINGER, D. J., & STARK, K. (1990). A qualitative versus quantitative approach to evaluating the Draw-A-Person and Kinetic Family Drawing: A study of mood- and anxiety-disorder children. *Psychological Assessment, 2*, 365–375.

THOMAS, H. (1970). Psychological assessment instruments for use with human infants. *Merrill-Palmer Quarterly of Behavioral Development, 16*, 179–223.

THOMPSON, A. S., & LINDEMAN, R. H. (1981). *Career Development Inventory: Vol. I. User's manual*. Palo Alto, CA: Consulting Psychologists Press.

THOMPSON, A. S., & LINDEMAN, R. H. (1984). *Career Development Inventory: Vol. 2. Technical manual*. Palo Alto, CA: Consulting Psychologists Press.

THOMPSON, D. (1995). Review of the Kuder General Interest Survey, Form E. *Twelfth Mental Measurements Yearbook, 545–546.*

THOMSON, G. H. (1948). *The factorial analysis of human ability.* (3rd ed.). Boston: Floughton Mifflin.

THORNDIKE, R. L. (1933). The effect of interval between test and retest on the constancy of the IQ .*Journal of Educational Psychology, 24,* 543–549.

THORNDIKE, R. L. (1940). "Constancy" of the IQ. *Psychological Bulletin, 37,* 167–186.

THORNDIKE, R. L. (1963). *The concepts of over-and under-achievement.* New York: Teachers College Press.

THORNDIKE, R. L. (1977). Causation of Binet IQ decrements. *Journal of Educational Measurement, 14,* 197–202.

THORNDIKE, R. L., HAGEN, E. P, &. SATTLER, J. M. (1986a). *The Stanford-Binet Intelligence Scale: Fourth Edition, Guide for administering and scoring.* Chicago: Riverside.

THORNDIKE, R. L., HAGEN, E. P., & SATTLER, J. M. (1986b). *The Stanford-Binet Intelligence Scale: Fourth Edition, Technical manual.* Chicago: Riverside.

THORNDIKE, R. M. (1990). Would the real factors of the Stanford-Binet Fourth Edition please come forward? *Journal of Psychoeducational* Assessment, 8, 412–435.

THORNTON, G. C., III, & BYHAM, W. C. (1982). Assessment *cetiters and managerial performance,* Orlando, FL: Academic Press.

THORNTON, G. C., III, & ZORICH, S. (1980). Training to improve observer accuracy. *Journal of Applied Psychology, 65,* 351–354.

THURSTONE, L. L. (1925). A method of scaling psychological and educational tests. *Journal of Educational Psychology, 16,* 433–451.

THURSTONE, L. L. (1938). Primary mental abilities. *Psychometric Monographs,* No. 1.

THURSTONE, L. L. (1944). A factorial study of perception. *Psychometric Monographs,* No. 4.

THURSTONE, L. L. (1947a). The calibration of test items. *American Psychologist, 2,* 103–104.

THURSTONE, L. L. (1947b). *Multiple factor analysis.* Chicago: University of Chicago Press.

THURSTONE, L. L. (1950). *Some primary abilities in visual thinking* (No. 59). Chicago: University of Chicago, Psychometric Laboratory.

THURSTONE, L. L. (1959). *The measurement of values.* Chicago: University of Chicago Press.

THURSTONE, L. L., & CHAVE, E. J. (1929). *The measurement of attitude.* Chicago: University of Chicago Press.

THURSTONE, L. L., AND THURSTONE, T. G. (1941). Factorial studies of intelligence. *Psychometric Monographs, No. 2.*

TIEDEMAN, D. V. (1994). "The guide is where?" [Review of the book *Computer-assisted career decision making: The guide in the machine]. Contemporary Psychology, 39, 87–88.*

TIMMONS, L. A., LANYON, R. I., ALMER, E. R., &. CURRAN, P. J. (1993). Development and validation of sentence completion test indices of malingering during examination for disability. *American Journal of Forensic Psychology, 11* (3), 23–38.

TITTLE, C. K. (1982). Use of judgmental methods in item bias studies. In R. A. Berk (Ed.), *Handbook of methods for detecting test bias* (pp. 31–63). Baltimore: Johns Hopkins University Press.

TITTLE, C. K., & ZYTOWSKI, D. G. (Eds.). (1978). *Sex-fair interest measurement: Research and implications.* Washington, DC: National Institute of Education.

TOBEY, L. H., & BRUHN, A. R. (1992). Early memories and the criminally dangerous. *Journal of Personality Assessment, 59,* 137–152.

TOPP, R. 1989. Effect of relaxation or exercise on undergraduates' test anxiety. *Perceptual and Motor Skills* 69, 35–41.

TOPPING, D. M., CROWELL, D. C., & KOBAYASHI, V. N. (Eds.). (1989). *Thinking across cultures: The Third International Conference on Thinking.* Hillsdale, NJ: Erlbaum.

TORDY, G. R., EYDE, L. D., PRIMOFF, E. S., & HARDT, R. H. (1976). *Job analysis of the position of New York State trooper: An application of the Job Element Method.* Albany: New York State Police.

TOUYZ, S., BYRNE, D., & GLLANDAS, A. (Eds.). (1994). *Neuropsychology in clinical practice.* San Diego, CA: Academic Press.

TRACEY, T. J., & ROUNDS, J. B. (1993). Evaluating Holland's and Gati's vocational interest models: A structural meta-analysis. *Psychological Bulletin, 113,* 229–246.

TRACEY, T. J. G., & ROUNDS, J. (1996). The spherical representation of vocational interests. *Journal of Vocational Behavior, 48,* 3–41.

TRAUB, R. E. (1993). On the equivalence of the traits assessed by multiple-choice and constructed-response tests. In R. E. Bennett & W. C. Ward (Eds.), *Construction versus choice in cognitive measurement: Issues in constructed response, performance testing, and portfolio assessment* (pp. 29–44). Hillsdale, NJ: Erlbaum.

TRAXLER, A. E., & HLLKERT, R. N. (1942). Effect of type of desk on results of machine-scored tests. *School and Society, 56,* 277–296.

TRENT, T., &. LAURENCE, J. H. (Eds.). (1993). *Adaptability screening for the Armed Forces.* Washington, DC: Office of Assistant Secretary of Defense.

TREVISAN, M. S., SAX, G., & MICHAEL, W. B. (1991). The effects of the number of options per item and student ability on test validity and reliability. *Educational and Psychological Measurement, 51,* 829–837.

TREVISAN, M. S., SAX, G., & MICHAEL, W. B. (1994). Estimating the optimum number of options per item using an incremental option paradigm. *Educational and Psychological Measurement, 54,* 86–91.

TRIANDIS, H. C., DUNNETTE, M. D., & HOUGH, L. (Eds.). (1994). *Handbook of industrial and organizational psychology* (2nd ed., Vol. 4). Palo Alto, CA: Consulting Psychologists Press.

TRICKETT, E. J., & MOOS, R. H. (1995). *Classroom Environment Scale manual: Development, applications, research* (3rd ed.). Palo Alto, CA: Consulting Psychologists Press.

TRIMBLE, J. E., LONNER, W. J., & BOUCHER, J. D. (1983). Stalking the wily emic: Alternatives to cross-cultural measurement. In S. H. Irvine & J. W. Berry (Eds.), *Human assessment and cultural factors* (pp. 259–273). New York: Plenum Press.

TRIVEDI, S., & RAGHAVAN, R. (1991). Multi-phasic questionnaire profile of alcoholics and related factors. *Drug and Alcohol Dependence,* 29(1), 1–4.

TRYON, G. S. (1980). The measurement and treatment of test anxiety. *Review of Educational Research, 50,* 343–372.

TRYON, R. C. (1935). A theory of *psychological components*—an alternative to "mathematical factors." *Psychological Review, 42,* 425–454.

TRYON, W. W. (ed.). (1985). *Behavioral assessment in behavioral medicine.* New York: Springer.

TRYON, W. W. (1991). *Activity measurement in psychology and medicine.* New York: Plenum Press.

TRYON, W. W. (1996). *Confidence interval testing: An alternative to null hypothesis testing. Manuscript submitted tor publication.*

TSUDZUKI, A., HATA, Y., & KUZE, T. (1957). [A study of rapport between examiner and subject.] Japanese *Journal of Psychology, 27,* 22–28.

Tuddenham, R. D. (1948). Soldier intelligence in World Wars I and II. *American Psychologist, 3*, 54–56.

Tuddenham, R. D., Blumenkrantz, J., & Wilkin, W. R. (1968). Age changes on AGCT: A longitudinal study of average adults. *Journal of Consulting and Clinical Psychology, 32*, 659–663.

Turco, T. L. (1989). Review of the Bracken Basic Concept Scale. Tenth *Mental Measurements Yearbook*, 102–104.

Turkheimer, E., Haley, A., Waldron, M., D'Onofrio, B., & Gottesman, I. I. (2003). Socioeconomic status modifies heritability of IQ in young children. *Psychological science*, 14(6), 623–628. Retrieved June 7, 2016, from *https://www.researchgate.net/profile/Andreana_Haley/publication/8997472_Socioeconomic_status_modifies_heritability_of_IQ_in_young_children/links/0deec516b9271c1c48000000.pdf*

Turnbull, W. W. (1985). *Student change, program change: Why the* SAT *scores kept falling* (College Board Rep. 85–2). New York: College Entrance Examination Board.

The Twelfth Mental Measurements Yearbook. (1995). Lincoln: Buros Institute of Mental Measurements.

Tyler, B., & Miller, K. (1986). The use of tests by psychologists: Report on a survey of BPS members. *Bulletin of the British Psychological Society, 39*, 405–410.

Tziner, A., Ronen, S., Hacohen, D. (1993). A four-year validation study of an assessment center in a financial corporation. *Journal of Organizational Behavior, 14*, 225–237.

Uguroglu, M. E., &. Walberg, H. J. (1979). Motivation and achievement: A quantitative synthesis. *American Educational Research Journal, 16*, 375–389.

Uniform Guidelines on Employee Selection Procedures. (1978). *Federal Register, 43* (166), 38296–38309.

U.S. Department of Defense. (1982). *Profile of American youth: 1980 nationwide administration of the Armed Services Vocational Aptitude Battery*. Washington, DC: Office of the Assistant Secretary of Defense (Manpower, Reserve Affairs, and Logistics).

U.S. Department of Labor. (1970). *Manual for the USES General Aptitude Test Battery, Section III: Development. Washington, DC: U.S. Government Printing Office.*

U.S. Department of Labor. (1979). *Manual for the USES General Aptitude Test Battery: Section II. Occupational aptitude pattern structure*. Washington, DC: U.S. Government Printing Office.

U.S. Department of Labor. (1980). *Manual for the USES General Aptitude Test Battery: Section II-A. Development of the occupational aptitude pattern structure*. Washington, DC: U.S. Government Printing Office.

U.S. Department of Labor. (1983a). *The dimensionality of the General Aptitude Test Battery (GATB) and the dominance of general factors over specific factors in the prediction of job performance (USES Test Res. Rep. No. 44)*. Washington, DC: U.S. Government Printing Office.

U.S. Department of Labor. (1983b). *The economic benefits of personnel selection using ability tests* (USES Test Res. Rep. No. 47). Washington, DC: U.S. Government Printing Office.

U.S. Department of Labor. (1983c). *Overview of validity generalization (USES Test* Res. Rep. No. 43). Washington, DC: U.S. Government Printing Office.

U.S. Department of Labor. (1983d). *Test validation for 12,000 jobs: An application of job classification and validity generalization analysis to the General Aptitude*

Test Battery (USES Test Res. Rep. No. 45). Washington, DC: U.S. Government Printing Office.

U.S. Department of Labor Employment and Training Administration. (1991). *Dictionary of occupational titles* (4th rev. ed.). Washington, DC: Author.

Update on the New Gre General Test. (1995, Summer). *GRE Board Newsletter, 10, 2–3.*

Urbina, S. (1995). Review of the Basic Personality Inventory. *Twelfth Mental Measurements Yearbook,* pp. 105–106.

Urbina, S. (1997). *Study guide: Psychological testing, Seventh edition.* Upper Saddle River, NJ: Prentice Hall.

Užgiris, I. C., & Hunt, J. Mcv. (1975). *Assessment in infancy: Ordinal Scales of Psychological Development.* Urbana, IL: University of Illinois Press.

Užgiris, I. C., & Hunt, J. Mcv. (Eds.). (1987). *Infant performance and experience: New findings with the ordinal scales.* Champaign: University of Illinois Press.

Vacc, N. A. (1992). Review of the Career Assessment Inventory, Second Edition (Vocational version). *Eleventh Mental Measurements Yearbook,* 150–151.

Vaidya, S., & Chansky, N. (1980). Cognitive development and cognitive style in mathematics achievement. *Journal of Educational Psychology,* 72, 326–330.

Vaillant, G. E., & McCullough, L. (1987). The Washington University Sentence completion Test compared with other measures of adult ego development. *American Journal of Psychiatry, 144, 1189–1194.*

Valciukas, J. A. (1995). *Forensic neuropsychology: Conceptual foundations and clinical practice.* New York: Haworth Press.

Valencia, R. R. (1990). Clinical assessment of young children with the McCarthy Scales of Children's Abilities. In C. R. Reynolds & R. W. Kamphaus (Eds.), *Handbook of psychological and educational assessment of children: Intelligence and achievement* (pp. 209–258). New York: Guilford Press.

Valencia, R. R., & Lopez, R. (1992). Assessment of racial and ethnic minority students: Problems and prospects. In M. Zeidner & R. Most (Eds.), *Psychological testing: An inside view* (pp. 399–439). Palo Alto, CA: Consulting Psychologists Press.

Valencia, R. R., & Rankin, R. J. (1985). Evidence of content bias on the McCarthy Scales with Mexican-American children: Implications for test translation and nonbiased assessment. *Journal of Educational Psychology,* 77, 197–207.

Vance, H. B. (Ed.). (1993). *Best practices in assessment for school and clinical settings.* Brandon, VT: Clinical Psychology.

Van Der Made-van Bekkum, I. J. (1971). *Dutch word association norms.* Amsterdam: Swets & Zeitlinger.

Vanderploeg, R. D. (ed.). (1994a). *Clinician's guide to neuropsychological assessment.* Hillsdale, NJ: Erlbaum.

Vanderploeg, R. D. (1994b). Estimating premorbid level of functioning. In R. D. Vanderploeg (Ed.), *Clinicians guide to neuropsychological assessment* (pp. 43–68). Hillsdale, NJ: Erlbaum.

Van De Vijver, F., & Hambleton, R. K. (1996). Translating tests: Some practical guidelines. *European Psychologist, 1,* 89–99.

Van Gorp, W. G. (1992). Review of the Luria-Nebraska Neuropsychological Battery: Forms I and II. *Eleventh Mental Measurements Yearbook,* 486–488.

Van Someren, M., Barnard, Y., & Sandberg, J. (1994). *The think aloud method: A practical guide to modeling cognitive processes. San Diego, CA: Academic Press.*

Vazquez Nutall, E., Romero, I., & Kalesnik, J. (eds.). (1992). *Assessing and screening preschoolers: Psychological and educational dimensions (pp. 43–54).* Boston: Allyn &. Bacon.

VERHOEVE, M. A. (1993). *JVIS applications handbook: A user's guide for the Jackson Vocational Interest Survey.* Port Huron, MI: Sigma Assessment Systems.

VERNON, P. E. (1960). *The structure of human abilities* (Rev. ed.). London: Methuen.

VERNON, P. E. (1969). *Intelligence and cultural environment*. London: Methuen.

VLGLIONE, D. J., JR. (1985). Review of the Rosenzweig Picture-Frustration Study. *Ninth Mental Measurements Yearbook,* Vol. 2, 1295–1297.

VLGLIONE, D. J. (1989). Rorschach science and art. *Journal of Personality Assessment,* 53, 195–197.

VINCENT, K. R., &. HARMAN, M. J. (1991). The Exner Rorschach: An analysis of its clinical validity. *Journal of Clinical Psychology, 47, 596–599.*

VLNITSKY, M. (1973). A forty-year follow-up on the vocational interests of psychologists and their relationship to career development. *American Psychologist, 28,* 1000–1009.

VLTZ, P. C. (1990). The use of stories in moral development: New psychological reasons for an old education method. *American Psychologist, 45,* 709–720.

WACHS, T. D., & SHEEHAN, R. (eds.). (1988). Assessment *of young developmentally disabled children*. New York: Plenum Press.

WACHTER, K. W., & STRAF, M. L. (Eds.). (1990). *The future of meta-analysis.* New York: Russell Sage Foundation.

WAGNER, E. E. (1985). Review of the Rosenzweig Picture-Frustration Study. *Ninth* Mental *Measurements Yearbook,* Vol. 2, 1297–1298.

WAHLSTROM, M., &. BOERSMAN, F. J. (1968). The influence of test-wiseness upon achievement. *Educational and Psychological Measurement, 28,* 413–420.

WAINER, H. (1993a). Measurement problems. *Journal of Educational Measurement, 30* (1), 1–21.

WAINER, H. (1993b). Some practical considerations when converting a linearly administered test to an adaptive format. *Educational Measurement: Issues and Practice, 12* (1), 15–20.

WAINER, H., DORANS, N. J., FLAUGHER, R., GREEN, B. E, JR., MISLEVY, R. J., STEINBERG, L., & THISSEN, D. (1990). *Computerized adaptive testing: A primer.* Hillsdale, NJ: Erlbaum.

WAINER, H., & KIELY, G. L. (1987). Item clusters and computerized adaptive testing: A case for testlets. *Journal of Educational Measurement, 24,* 185–201.

WAINER, H., &. LEWIS, C. (1990). Toward a psychometrics for testlets. *Journal of Educational Measurement, 27,* 1–14.

WAITE, R. R., SARASON, S. B., LIGHTHALL, F. E, & DAVIDSON, K. S. (1958). A study of anxiety and learning in children. *Journal of Abnormal and Social Psychology,* 57, 267–270.

WALD, A. (1947). *Sequential analysis.* New York: Wiley.

WALD, A. (1950). *Statistical decision function*. New York: Wiley.

WALKER, B. S., & SPENGLER, P. M. (1995). Clinical judgment of major depression in AIDS patients: The effects of clinician complexity and stereotyping. *Professional Psychology: Research and Practice, 26,* 269–273.

WALLACE, S. R. (1965). Criteria for what? *American Psychologist, 20,* 411–417.

WALLER, N. G., LYKKEN, D. T., & TELLEGEN, A. (1995). Occupational interests, leisure time interests, and personality: Three domains or one? Findings from the Minnesota Twin Registry. in D. Lubinski & R. V. Dawis (Eds.), *Assessing individual differences in human behavior: New concepts, methods, and findings* (pp. 233–259). Palo Alto, CA: Davies-Black.

WALLER, N. G., & WALDMAN, I. D. (1990). A reexamination of the WAIS-R factor structure. *Psychological Assessment, 2,* 139–144.

WALSH, W. B., & BETZ, N. E. (1995). *Tests and* assessment (3rd ed.). Englewood Cliffs, NJ: Prentice Hall.

WALSH, W. B., & OSIPOW, S. H. (Eds.). (1993). Career counseling for women. Hillsdale, NJ: Erlbaum.

WANG, M. C., REYNOLDS, M. C., & WALBERG, H. J. (eds.). (1991). *Handbook of special education: Research and practice, Vol. 4: Emerging programs.* Elmsford, NY: Pergamon Press.

WARD, W. C., KLINE, R. G., &. FLAUGHER, J. (1986). *College Board Computerized Placement Tests: Validation of an adaptive test of basic skills* (ETS Res. Rep. *86–29*). Princeton, NJ: Educational Testing Service.

WARNER, W. L., MEEKER, M., & EELLS, K. (1949). *Social class in America: A manual of procedure for the measurement of social status.* Chicago: Science Research Associates.

WASIK, B. H., & WASIK, J. L. (1971). Performance of culturally deprived children on Concept Assessment Kit-Conservation. *Child Development, 42,* 1586–1590.

WATKINS, C. E. (1991). What have surveys taught us about the teaching and practice of psychological assessment? *Journal of Personality Assessment, 56,* 426–437.

WATKINS, C. E., CAMPBELL, V. L., & NIEBERDING, R. (1994). The practice of vocational assessment by counseling psychologists. *Counseling Psychologist, 22,* 115–128.

WATKINS, C. E., JR., CAMPBELL, V. L., NIEBERDING, R., & HALLMARK, R. (1995). Contemporary practice of psychological assessment by clinical psychologists. *Professional Psychology: Research and Practice, 26,* 54–60.

WATKINS, M. W., & MCDERMOTT, P. A. (1991). Psychodiagnostic computing: From interpretive programs to expert systems. In T. B. Gutkin & S. L. Wise (Eds.), *The computer and the decision-making process* (pp. 11–42). Hillsdale, NJ: Erlbaum.

WATSON, S. (1992). Review of the Test of Nonverbal Intelligence, Second Edition. *Eleventh Mental Measurements Yearbook, 970–972.*

WEBB, E. J., CAMPBELL, D. T., SCHWARTZ, R. D., SECHREST, L., & GROVE, J. B. (1981). *Nonreactive measures in the social sciences* (2nd ed.). Boston: Houghton Mifflin.

WEBSTER, E. C. (1982). *The employment interview: A social judgment process.* Schomberg, Canada: S. I. P. Publications.

WECHSLER, D. (1939). *The measurement of adult intelligence.* Baltimore: Williams & Wilkins.

WECHSLER, D. (1958). *The measurement and appraisal of adult intelligence* (4th ed.). Baltimore: Williams & Wilkins.

WECHSLER, D. (1981). *WAIS-R manual: Wechsler Adult Intelligence Scale—Revised.* San Antonio, TX: Psychological Corporation.

WECHSLER, D. (1989). *WPPSl-R: Manual.* San Antonio, TX: Psychological Corporation.

WECHSLER, D. (1991). *W1SC-III: Manual.* San Antonio, TX: Psychological Corporation.

WEDDING, D., & FAUST, D. (1989). Clinical judgement and decision making in neuropsychology. *Archives of Clinical Neuropsychology, 4,* 233–265.

WEEKLEY, J. A., FRANK, B., O'CONNOR, E. J., & PETERS, L. H. (1985). A comparison of three methods of estimating the standard deviation of performance in dollars, *journal of Applied Psychology, 70,* 122–126.

WEINER, I. B. (1994a). Rorschach assessment. In M. E. Maruish (Ed.), *The use of psychological testing for treatment planning and outcome assessment* (pp. 249–278). Hillsdale, NJ: Erlbaum.

WEINER, I. B. (1994b). The Rorschach Inkblot Method (RIM) is not a test: Implications for theory and practice. *Journal of Personality Assessment, 62,* 498–504.

WEINER, I. B. (1995a). How to anticipate ethical and legal challenges in personality assessments. In J. N. Butcher (Ed.), *Clinical personality assessment: Practical approaches* (pp. 95–103). New York: Oxford University Press,

WEINER, I. B. (1995b). Methodological considerations in Rorschach research. *Psychological Assessment, 7*, 330–337.

WEINER, I. B., & HESS, A. K. (Eds.). (1987). *Handbook of forensic psychology.* New York: Wiley.

WEISS, D. J. (1974). *Strategies of adaptive ability measurement* (Res. Rep. 74–5). Minneapolis: University of Minnesota, Department of Psychology, Psychometric Methods Program.

WEISS, D. J. (1982). Improving measurement quality and efficiency with adaptive testing. *Applied Psychological Measurement, 6*, 473–492.

WEISS, D. J. (ed.). (1983). *New horizons in testing: Latent trait test theory and computerized adaptive testing.* Orlando, FL: Academic Press.

WEISS, D. J., & BETZ, N. E. (1973). *Ability measurement: Conventional or adaptive*? (Res. Rep. 73–1). Minneapolis: University of Minnesota, Department of Psychology, Psychometric Methods Program.

WEISS, D. J., & DAVISON, M. L. (1981). Test theory and methods. *Annual Review of Psychology, 32*, 629–658.

WEISS, D. J., & VALE, C. D. (1987). Computerized adaptive testing for measuring abilities and other psychological variables. In J. N. Butcher (Ed.), *Computerized psychological assessment* (pp. 325–343). New York: Basic Books.

WEISS, D. S., ZILBERG, N. J., & GENEVRO, J. L. (1989). Psychometric properties of Loevinger's Sentence Completion Test in an adult psychiatric outpatient sample. *Journal of Personality Assessment*, 53, 478–486.

WEISSENBERG, P, & GRUENFELD, L. W. (1966). Relationships among leadership dimensions and cognitive style. *Journal of Applied Psychology, 50*, 392–395.

WELSH, G. S. (1956). Factor dimensions A and R. In G. S. Welsh & W. G. Dahlstrom (Eds.), *Basic readings on the MMPI in psychology and medicine* (pp. 264–281). Minneapolis: University of Minnesota Press.

WELSH, G. S. (1975a). Adjective Check List descriptions of Freud and Jung. *Journal of Personality Assessment, 39*, 160–168.

WELSH, G. S. (1975b). *Creativity and intelligence: A personality approach.* Chapel Hill: University of North Carolina, Institute for Research in Social Science.

WELSH, J. R., JR., WATSON, T. W., & REE, M. J. (1990). *Armed Services Vocational Aptitude Battery (ASVAB): Predicting military criteria from general and specific abilities (AFHRL-TR-90–63). Brooks AFB, TX: U.S. Air Force Human Resources Laboratory.*

WERNER, E. E., HONZIK, M. P, & SMITH, R. S. (1968). Prediction of intelligence and achievement at ten years from twenty months pediatric and psychologic examinations. *Child Development, 39*, 1063–1075.

WERNER, H., & STRAUSS, A. A. (1941). Pathology of figure-background relation in the child. *Journal of Abnormal and Social Psychology, 36*, 236–248.

WERNER, H., & STRAUSS, A. A. (1943). Impairment in thought processes of brain-injured children. *American Journal of Mental Deficiency, 47*, 291–295.

WESMAN, A. G. (1949). Effect of speed on item-test correlation coefficients. *Educational and Psychological Measurement, 9*, 51–57.

WESMAN, A. G. (1952). Faking personality test scores in a simulated employment situation. *Journal of Applied Psychology, 36*, 112–113.

WEST, R. (1991). *Computing for psychologists: Statistical analysis using SPSS and MINITAB.* Langhorn, PA: Gordon & Breach.

WESTEN, D. (1991). Clinical assessment of object relations using the TAT. *Journal of Personality Assessment, 56*, 56–74.

WESTEN, D., LOHR, N., SILK, K. R., GOLD, L., & KERBER, K. (1990). Object relations and social cognition in borderlines, major depressives, and normals: A thematic apperception analysis. *Psychological* Assessment, 2, 355–364.

WESTENBERG, P. M., & BLOCK, J. (1993). Ego development and individual differences in personality. *Journal of Personality and Social Psychology, 65*, 792–800.

WETZLER, S. (1990). The Millon Clinical Multiaxial Inventory (MCMI): A review. *Journal of Personality Assessment, 55*, 445–464.

WHIMBEY, A. (1975). *Intelligence can be taught*. New York: Dutton.

WHIMBEY, A. (1977). Teaching sequential thought: The cognitive-skills approach. *Phi Delta Kappan, 59*, 255–259.

WHIMBEY, A. (1980). Students can learn to be better problem solvers. *Educational Leadership, 37*, 560–565.

WHIMBEY, A. (1990). *Thinking through math word problems: Strategies for intermediate elementary school students*. Hillsdale, NJ: Erlbaum.

WHIMBEY, A., & DENENBERG, V. H. (1966). Programming life histories: Creating individual differences by the experimental control of early experiences. *Multivariate Behavioral Research, 1*, 279–286.

WHITE, B. L. (1978). *Experience and environment: Major influences on the development of the young child (Vol. 2)*. Englewood Cliffs, NJ: Prentice Hall.

WHITE, P. A. (1990). Ideas about causation in philosophy and psychology. *Psychological Bulletin, 108*, 3–18.

WHITE, R. F. (ed.). (1992). *Clinical syndromes in adult neuropsychology: The practitioner's handbook*. Amsterdam: Elsevier.

WHITEMAN, M. (1964). Intelligence and learning. *Merrill-Palmer Quarterly, 10*, 297–309.

WHITEN, A. (ed.). (1991). *Natural theories of mind: Evolution, development, and simulation of everyday mind-reading*. Oxford, England: Basil Blackwell.

WHITING, B. B. (1976). The problem of the packaged variable. In K. Riegel & J. Meacham (Eds.), *The developing individual in a changing world* (Vol. 1, pp. 303–309). The Hague: Mouton.

WHITWORTH, J. R., & SUTTON, D. L. (1993). *WISC-III compilation: What to do now that you know the score*. Novato, CA: Academic Therapy Publications.

WHYTE, W. F. (1991). *Social theory for action: How individuals and organizations learn to change*. Newbury Park, CA: Sage.

WICKES, T. A., JR. (1956). Examiner influence in a testing situation. *Journal of Consulting Psychology, 20*, 23–26.

WIGDOR, A. K. (1982). Psychological testing and the law of employment discrimination. In A. K. Wigdor & W. R. Garner (Eds.), *Ability testing: Uses, consequences, and controversies* (Pt.2, pp. 39–69). Washington, DC: National Academy Press.

WIGDOR, A. K., & GARNER, W. R.(Eds.). (1982). *Ability testing: Uses, consequences, and controversies* (Pts. 1 &. 2). Washington, DC: National Academy Press.

WIGDOR, A. K., &. GREEN, B. E, JR. (1991a). *Performance assessment for the workplace* (Vol. 1). Washington, DC: National Academy Press.

WIGDOR, A. K., & GREEN, B. F., JR. (1991b). *Performance assessment for the workplace: Vol. 2. Technical issues*. Washington, DC: National Academy Press.

WIGDOR, A. K., &. SACKETT, P. R. (1993). Employment testing and public policy: The case of the General Aptitude Test Battery. In H. Schuler, J. L. Farr, & M. Smith (Eds.), *Personnel selection and assessment: Individual and organizational perspectives* (pp. 183–204). Hillsdale, NJ: Erlbaum.

WIGGINS, G. P. (1993). Assessing *student performance: Exploring the purpose and limits of testing.* San Francisco: Jossey-Bass.

WIGGINS, J. S. (1959). Interrelationships among MMPI measures of dissimulation under standard and social desirability instructions. *Journal of Consulting Psychology,* 23, 419–427.

WIGGINS, J. S. (1962). Strategic, method, and stylistic variance in the MMPI. *Psychological Bulletin, 59,* 224–242.

WIGGINS, J. S. (1966). Social desirability estimation and "faking good" well. *Educational and Psychological Measurement, 26,* 329–341.

WIGGINS, J. S. (1988). *Personality and prediction: Principles of personality assessment.* Malabar, FL: S. A. Krieger. (Original work published 1973)

WIGGINS, J. S. (1989). Review of the Myers-Briggs Type Indicator. *Tenth* Mental *Measurements Yearbook,* 536–538.

WIGGINS, J. S. (1996). An informal history of the interpersonal circumplex tradition. *Journal of Personality Assessment,* 66, 217–233.

WIGGINS, J. S., & PINCUS, A. L. (1992). Personality: Structure and Assessment. *Annual Review of Psychology, 43,* 493–504.

WIGGINS, N. (1966). Individual viewpoints of social desirability. *Psychological Bulletin, 66,* 68–77.

WIIG, E. H. (1985). Review of Peabody Picture Vocabulary Test—Revised. *Ninth Mental Measurements Yearbook,* Vol. 2, 1127–1128.

WILLETT, J. B., & SAYER, A. G. (1994). Using covariance structure analysis to detect correlates and predictors of individual change over time. *Psychological Bulletin, 116,* 363–381.

WILLIAMS, A. (1995). *Visual and active supervision: Roles, focus, technique.* New York: Norton.

WILLIAMS, C. L., BUTCHER, J. N., BEN-PORATH, Y. S., & GRAHAM, J. R. (1992). *MMPI-A Content scales: Assessing psychopathology in adolescents. Minneapolis: University of Minnesota Press.*

WILLIAMS, H. G. (1991). Assessment of gross motor functioning. In B. A. Bracken (Ed.), *The psychoeducational assessment of preschool children* (2nd ed., pp. 284–316). Boston: Allyn & Bacon.

WILLIAMS, M. (1960). The effect of past experience on mental performance in the elderly. *British Journal of Medical Psychology,* 33, 215–219.

WILLINGHAM, W. W. (1988). Testing handicapped people: The validity issue. In H. Wainer & H. Braun (Eds.), *Test validity* (pp. 89–103). Hillsdale, NJ: Erlbaum.

WILLINGHAM, W. W., RAGOSTA, M., BENNETT, R. E., BRAUN, H., ROCK, D. A., & POWERS, D. E. (1988). *Testing handicapped people.* Boston: Allyn & Bacon.

WILLIS, J. (1970). Group versus individual intelligence tests in one sample of emotionally disturbed children. *Psychological Reports, 27,* 819–822.

WILLIS, S. L., BLIESZNER, R., & BALTES, R B. (1981). Intellectual training research in aging: Modification of performance on the fluid ability of figural relations. *Journal of Educational Psychology, 73,* 41–50.

WILLIS, S. L., &L SCHAIE, K. W. (1986). Practical intelligence in later adulthood. In R. J. Sternberg & R. K. Wagner (Eds.), *Practical intelligence: Origins of competence in the everyday world* (pp. 236–268). New York: Cambridge University Press.

WILLOCK, B. (1992). Projection, transitional phenomena, and the Rorschach. *Journal of Personality Assessment, 59,* 99–116.

WILLSON, V. L. (1994). Cognitive modeling of individual responses in test design. In R. Reynolds (Ed.), *Cognitive assessment: A multidisciplinary perspective* (pp. 155–173). New York: Plenum Press.

WILSON, R. S., & MATHENY, A. R, JR. (1983). Assessment of temperament in infant twins. *Developmental Psychology, 19,* 172–183.

WILSON, S. L. (1991). Microcomputer-based psychological assessment: An advance in helping severely physically disabled people. In P. L. Dann, S. H. Irvine, & J. M. Collis (Eds.), *Advances in computer-based human assessment* (pp. 171–187). Dordrecht, The Netherlands: Kluwer.

WINK, P. (1991). Two faces of narcissism. *Journal of Personality and Social Psychology, 61, 590–597.*

WINK, P. (1992). Three narcissism scales for the California Q-set. *Journal of Personality* Assessment, 58, 51–66.

WINK, P, & PIELSON, R. (1993). Personality change in women and their partners. *Journal of Personality and Social Psychology, 65,* 597–605.

WINTER, D. A. (1992). *Personal construct psychology in clinical practice: Theory, research, and applications.* New York: Routledge, Chapman & Hall.

WIRT, R. D., & LACHAR, D. (1981). The Personality Inventory for Children: Development and clinical applications. In P. McReynolds (Ed.), *Advances in psychological assessment* (Vol. 5, pp. 353–392). San Francisco: Jossey-Bass.

WIRT, R. D., LACHAR, D., KLINEDINST, J. K., & SEAT, P. D. (1991). *Multidimensional description of child personality: A manual for the Personality Inventory for Children 1990 Edition.* Los Angeles: Western Psychological Services.

WLRTZ, W. (Chair). (1977). *On further examination: Report of the Advisory Panel on the Scholastic Aptitude Test Score Decline.* New York: College Entrance Examination Board.

WISE, L. L., MCHENRY, J., & CAMPBELL, J. P. (1990). Identifying optimal predictor composites and testing for generalizability across jobs and performance factors. *Personnel Psychology, 43,* 355–366.

WISE, P. S. (1989). *The use of assessment techniques by applied psychologists.* Belmont, CA: Wadsworth.

WISKOFF, M. F., & SCHRATZ, M. K. (1989). Computerized adaptive testing of a vocational aptitude battery. In R. F. Dillon & J. W. Pellegrino (Eds.), *Testing: Theoretical and applied perspectives* (pp. 66–96). New York: Praeger.

WISSLER, C. (1901). The correlation of mental and physical traits. *Psychological Monographs, 3(6,* Whole No. 16).

WITKIN, H. A., DYK, R. B., FATERSON, H. F, GOODENOUGH, D. R., & KARP, S. A. (1974). *Psychological differentiation: Studies in development.* New York: Wiley. (Original work published in 1962)

WITKIN, H. A., & GOODENOUGH, D. R. (1977). Field dependence and interpersonal behavior. *Psychological Bulletin, 84,* 661–689.

WITKIN, H. A., &. GOODENOUGH, D. R. (1981). *Cognitive styles: Essence and Origins—Field dependence and independence.* New York: International Universities Press.

WITKIN, H. A., LEWIS, H.B., HERTZMAN, M., MACHOVER, K., MEISSNER, P. B., & WAPNER, S. (1972). *Personality through perception: An experimental and clinical study.* Westport, CT: Greenwood Press. (Original work published 1954)

WITKIN, H. A., OLTMAN, P. K., RASKIN, E., & KARP, S. A. (1971). A *manual for the Embedded Figures Tests.* Palo Alto, CA: Consulting Psychologists Press.

WITKIN, H. A., PRICE-WILLIAMS, D., BERTINI, M., CHRISTIANSEN, B., OLTMAN, P. K., RAMIREZ, M., & VAN MEEL, J. (1974). Social conformity and psychological differentiation. *International Journal of Psychology,* 9, 11–29.

WITT, J. C. ELLIOTT, S. N., GRESHAM, F. M., & KRAMER, J. J. (1988). *Assessment of special children: Tests and the problem-solving process.* Glenview, IL: Scott, Foresman.

WITT, J. C., HEFFER, R. W., & PFEIFFER, J. (1990). Structured rating scales: A review of sell-report and informant rating processes, procedures, and issues. In C. R. Reynolds R. W. Kamphaus (Eds.), *Handbook of psychological and educational assessment of children: Personality, behavior, and context (pp. 364–394).* New York: Guilford Press.

WOLF, D. P. (1993). *Assessment as an episode of learning. In* R. E. Bennett & W. C. Ward (Eds.), *Construction versus choice in cognitive measurement: Issues in constructed response, performance testing, and portfolio assessment (pp. 213–240).* Hillsdale, NJ: Erlbaum.

WOLF, F. M. (1986). *Meta-analysis: Quantitative methods for research synthesis.* Newbury Park, CA: Sage.

WOLF, T. H. (1973). *Alfred Binet.* Chicago: University of Chicago Press.

WOLK, R. L., & WOLK, R. B. (1971). *Manual: Gerontological Apperception Test.* New York: Human Sciences Press.

WOMER, F. B. (1970). *What is National Assessment?* Ann Arbor, MI: National Assessment of Educational Progress.

WOMER, M. (1972). Culture and the concept of intelligence: A case in Uganda. *Journal of Cross-Cultural Psychology,* 3, 327–328.

WONDERLIC PERSONNEL TEST, INC. (1992). *Wonderlic Personnel Test & Scholastic Level Exam: User's manual.* Libertyville, IL: Author.

WOOD, J. M., NEZWORSKI, M. T., & STEJSKAL, W. J. (1996a). The Comprehensive System tor the Rorschach: A critical examination. *Psychological Science,* 7, 3–10.

WOOD, J. M., NEZWORSKI, M. T., & STEJSKAL, W. J. (1996b). Thinking critically about the Comprehensive System for the Rorschach: A reply to Exner. *Psychological Science,* 14–17.

WOODCOCK, R. W., & JOHNSON, M. B. (1989, 1990). *Woodcock-Johnson Psycho-Educational Battery—Revised.* Allen, TX: DLM Teaching Resources.

WOOTEN, K. C., BARNER, B. O., & SILVER, N. C. (1994). The influence of cognitive style upon work environment preferences. *Perceptual and Motor Skills,* 79, 307–314.

WORCHEL, F. F., & DUPREE, J. L. (1990). Projective storytelling techniques. In C. R. Reynolds & R. W. Kamphaus (Eds.), *Handbook of psychological and educational assessment of children: Personality, behavior, and context* (pp. 70–88). New York: Guilford Press.

WORTHEN, B. R. (1995). Review of the Strong Interest Inventory (Fourth Edition). *Twelfth Mental Measurements Yearbook,* 999–1002.

WRIGHT, B. D. (1977). Solving measurement problems with the Rasch model. *Journal of Educational Measurement, 14,* 97–116.

WRIGHT, B. D., & STONE, M. H. (1979). *Best test design: Rasch measurement.* Chicago: Mesa Press.

WULACH, J. S. (1991). *Law and mental health professionals: New Jersey.* Washington, DC: American Psychological Association.

WYLIE, R. C. (1989). *Measures of self-concept.* Lincoln: University of Nebraska Press.

YAMA, M. E (1990). The usefulness of human figure drawings as an index of overall adjustment. *Journal of Personality* Assessment, *54,* 78–86.

YARROW, L. J., MACTURK, R. H., VIETZE, P. M., MCCARTHY, M. E., KLEIN, R. R, & MCQUISTON, S. (1984). Developmental course of parental stimulation and its relationship to mastery motivation during infancy. *Developmental Psychology, 20,* 492–503.

YARROW, L. J., MCQUISTON, S., MACTURK, R. H., MCCARTHY, M. E,, KLEIN, R., & VIETZE, P. M. (1983). Assessment of mastery motivation during the first year of life: Contemporaneous and cross-age relationships. *Developmental Psychology, 19,* 159–171.

YARROW, L. J., & MESSER, D. J. (1983). Motivation and cognition in infancy. In M. Lewis (Ed.), *Origins of intelligence: Infancy and early childhood* (2nd ed., pp. 451–477). New York: Plenum Press.

YARROW, L. J., &. PEDERSEN, F. A. (1976). The interplay between cognition and motivation in infancy. In M. Lewis (Ed.), *Origins of intelligence: Infancy and early childhood* (pp. 379–399). New York: Plenum Press.

YATES, A. J. et al. (1953–1954). Symposium on the effects of coaching and practice in intelligence tests. *British Journal of Educational Psychology, 23,* 147–162; *24,* 1–8, 57–63.

YERKES, R. M. (Ed.). (1921). Psychological examining in the United States Army. *Memoirs of the National Academy of Sciences,* Vol. 15.

YORK, K. L., & JOHN, O. P. (1992). The four faces of Eve: A typological analysis of women's personality at midlife. *Journal of Personality and Social Psychology, 63,* 494–508.

YOUNG, F. W. (1984). Scaling. *Annual Review of Psychology, 35, 55–81.*

YSSELDYKE, J. E. (1989). Review of the Bracken Basic Concept Scale. *Tenth Mental Measurements Yearbook,* 104–105.

YUKL, G., & VAN FLEET, D. D. (1992). Theory and research on leadership in organizations. In M. D. Dunnette & L. M. Hough (Eds.), *Handbook of industrial and organizational psychology* (2nd ed., Vol. 3, pp. 147–197). Palo Alto, CA: Consulting Psychologists Press.

ZACHARY, R. A. (1990). Wechsler's Intelligence Scales: Theoretical and practical considerations. *Journal of Psychoeducational Assessment, 8,* 276–289.

ZARSKE, J. A. (1985). Review of Adjective Check List. *Ninth Mental Measurements Yearbook,* Vol. 1, 52–53.

ZEDECK, S. (1971). Problems with the use of "moderator" variables. *Psychological Bulletin, 76,* 295–310.

ZEICHMEISTER, E. B., & JOHNSON, J. E. (1992). *Critical thinking: A functional approach*. Pacific Grove, CA: Brooks/Cole.

ZEIDNER, J., & JOHNSON, C. D. (1991). Classification efficiency and systems design. *Journal of the Washington Academy of Sciences, 81,* 110–128.

ZEIDNER, M. (1987). Test of the cultural bias hypothesis: Some Israeli findings. *Journal of Applied Psychology, 72,* 38–48.

ZEIDNER, M. (1988). Cultural fairness in aptitude testing revisited: A cross-cultural parallel. *Professional Psychology, Research and Practice, 19,* 257–262.

ZEIDNER, M. (1993). Essay versus multiple-choice type classroom exams: The student's perspective. In B. Nevo & R. S. Jager (Eds.), *Educational and psychological testing: The test taker's outlook* (pp. 67–82). Toronto, Canada: Hogrete & Huber.

ZEIDNER, M. (1995). Personality trait correlates of intelligence. In D. H. Saklofske & M. Zeidner (Eds.), *International handbook of personality and intelligence* (pp. 299–319). New York: Plenum Press.

ZEIDNER, M. (1998). *Test anxiety: The state of the art*. New York: Plenum.

ZELNIKER, T. (1989). Cognitive style and dimensions of information processing. In T. Globerson & T. Zelniker (Eds.), *Cognitive style and cognitive development* (pp. 172–191). Norwood, NJ: Ablex.

ZENDERLAND, L. (1987). The debate over diagnosis: Henry Hebert Goddard and the medical acceptance of intelligence testing. In M. M. Sokal (Ed.), *Psychological testing and American society, 1890–1930* (pp. 46–74). New Brunswick, NJ: Rutgers University Press.

ZIGLER, E., & MUENCHOW, S. (1992). *Head Start: The inside story of America's most successful educational experiment*. New York: Basic Books.

ZIGLER, E., & STYFCO, S. J. (Eds.). (1993). *Head Start and beyond*. New Haven, CT: Yale University Press.

ZIGLER, E., & VALENTINE, J. (Eds.). (1980). *Project Head Start: A legacy of the war on poverty.* New York: Free Press.

ZIMMERMAN, B. J., & ROSENTHAL, T. L. (1974a). Conserving and retaining equalities and inequalities through observation and correction. *Developmental Psychology, 10,* 260–268.

ZIMMERMAN, B. J., &. ROSENTHAL, T. L. (1974b). Observational learning of rule-governed behavior by children. *Psychological Bulletin, 81,* 29–42.

ZIMMERMAN, I. L., & WOO-SAM, J. (1972). Research with the Wechsler Intelligence Scale for Children: 1960–1970 [Special Monograph Suppl.] *Psychology in the Schools,* 9, 232–271.

ZUCKERMAN, M., KUHLMAN, D. M., JOIREMAN, J., TETA, E, & KRAFT, M. (1993). A comparison of three structural models for personality: The big three, the big five, and the alternative five. *Journal of Personality and Social Psychology, 65,* 757–768.

ZYTOWSKI, D. G. (1992). Three generations: The continuing evolution of Frederic Kuder's interest inventories. *Journal of Counseling and Development, 71,* 245–248.

ZYTOWSKI, D. G., & BORGEN, F. H. (1983). Assessment. In B. Walsh & S. H. Osipow (Eds.), *Handbook of vocational psychology: Vol. 2. Applications* (pp. 5–45). Hillsdale, NJ: Erlbaum.

ZYTOWSKI, D. G., & WARMAN, R. E. (1982). The changing use of tests in counseling. *Measurement and Evaluation in Guidance, 15,* 147–152.

Acknowledgments

Figure 1.1: Source: AERA, APA, NCME (1985). Topics from *Standards for Educational and Psychological Testing.* Copyright © 1985 by the American Psychological Association. Reprinted by permission.

Table 3.6: Source: The Psychological Corporation (1972). *Differential Aptitude Tests—Fourth Edition.* Percentage of Cases of Each I.Q. Interval in Normal Distributions with Mean of 100 and Different Standard Deviations. Copyright © 1972, 1982 by The Psychological Corporation. "Differential Aptitude Tests" and "DAT" are registered trademarks of The Psychological Corporation. Reprinted by permission.

Pages 24–25: Source: W. H. Angoff (1962). Scales with nonmeaningful origins and units of measurement. *Educational and Psychological Measurement,* **22,** 32-33. Copyright © 1962. Reprinted by permission of Sage Publications.

Table 3.7: Source: The Psychological Corporation (1992). *Differential Aptitude Tests—Fifth Edition,* p. 152. Copyright © 1992 The Psychological Corporation. "Differential Aptitude Tests" and "DAT" are registered trademarks of The Psychological Corporation. Adapted by permission.

Figure 3.7: Source: J. C. Flanagan (1947). Scientific development of the use of human resources: Progress in the Army Air Forces. *Science*, **105**, 58. Copyright ©1947 American Association for the Advancement of Science. Reprinted by permission.

Figure 4.6: Data from The Psychological Corporation (1990). Individual Report, *Differential Aptitude Tests—Fifth Edition.* Copyright © 1990 by The Psychological Corporation. "Differential Aptitude Tests" and "DAT" are registered trademarks of The Psychological Corporation. Reprinted by permission.

Table 5.1: Source: D. T. Campbell and D. W. Fiske (1959). Convergent and discriminant validation by the multitrait-multimethod matrix. *Psychological Bulletin,* **56,** 82. Reprinted by permission of the American Psychological Association.

Table 6.3: Source: H. E. Brogden (1951). Increased efficiency of selection resulting from replacement of a single predictor with several differential predictors.

Educational and Psychological Measurement, **11,** 182. Copyright © 1951. Reprinted by permission of Sage Publications.

Figure 7.2: Source: P. J. Pashley (1992). *Research Report No. 92-66: Graphical IRT-Based DIF Analyses.* Copyright © 1992 by Educational Testing Service. All rights reserved. Adapted and reproduced under license.

Figure 9.1: Source: Bayley (1993). *Bayley Scales of Infant Development—Second Edition,* 143, 145, 150. Copyright © 1993 by The Psychological Corporation. "Bayley Scales of Infant Development" is a registered trademark of The Psychological Corporation. Adapted by permission. All rights reserved.

Figure 9.2: Source: J. Fagan and D. Detterman (1992). The Fagan Test of Infant Intelligence: A technical summary. *Journal of Applied Developmental Psychology,* **13,** 189. Reprinted by permission of Ablex Publishing Corp.

Table 9.1: Source: American Association on Mental Retardation (1992). *Mental retardation: Deftnition, classification and* systems *of support,* 26. Reprinted by permission.

Table 9.2: Source: S. S. Sparrow, D. A. Balla, & D. V. Cicchetti (1984). *The Vineland Adaptative Behavior Scales: Interview edition expanded form manual,* 3. Copyright © 1984, 1985 by American Guidance Service, Inc., 4201 Woodland Road, Circle Pines, MN 55014-1796. Adapted and reprinted by permission. All rights reserved.

Figure 9.3: Source: B. B. Burgenmeister, L. H. Blum, & I. Lorge (1972). *Columbia Mental Maturity Scale: Guide for Administering and Interpreting,* 3rd ed., 11. Copyright © 1954, 1959, 1972 by Harcourt Brace & Company. Reprinted by permission. All rights reserved.

Figure 9.4: Typical Materials for Use in the Leiter International Performance Scale (Revised). Courtesy of Stoelting Co., Wood Dale, IL.

Figure 9.5: Source: Raven, J. C. *Standard Progressive Matrices.* Reprinted by permission of J. C. Raven Ltd.

Figure 9.6: *Goodenough-Harris Drawing Test.* Reprinted by permission of Dale B. Harris.

Figure 10.3: Source: R. L. Thorndike and E. P. Hagen (1993). *Cognitive Abilities Test* (CogAT), Form 5, Practice Test for Levels A-H. "Cognitive Abilities Test" and "CogAT" are registered trademarks of The Riverside Publishing Co. Copyright © 1993. Reprinted by permission of The Riverside Publishing Company.

Figure 11.5: Source: J. P. Guilford (1988). Some changes in the Structure of Intellect Model. *Educational and Psychological Measurement,* **48,** 3. Copyright © 1988. Reprinted by permission of Sage Publications.

Figure 11.6: Source: P. E. Vernon (1960). *The structure of human abilities,* rev. ed., 22. London: Methuen. Reprinted by permission of Routledge, London.

Figure 12.2: Source: K. W. Schaie (1994). The course of adult intellectual development. *American Psychologist* (April), 308. Copyright © 1994 by the American Psychological Association. Reprinted by permission of the author and publisher.

Page 294, Chap. 13: *Minnesota Multiphasic Personality Inventory-2 (MMPI-2).* Copyright © 1942, 1943 (renewed 1970), 1989 by the Regents of the University of Minnesota. Reprinted by permission of University of Minnesota Press.

Figure 13.1: University of Minnesota (1989). *Minnesota Multiphasic Inventory-2 (MMPI-2) Profile Form for* Basic *Scales.* Copyright © 1989 by the Regents of the University of Minnesota. "Minnesota Multiphasic Inventory-2" and "MMPI-2" are registered trademarks of the University of Minnesota. The scores are from the Annotated Sample of The Minnesota Report (tm): Adult Clinical System—Revised, p. 7. Copyright © 1989, 1993 by the Regents of the University of Minnesota. Reprinted by permission. All rights reserved.

Table 13.1: P. T. Costa, Jr., & R. R. McCrae (1992b). *Revised NEO Personality Inventory (NEO PI-R) and NEO Five-Factor Inventory (NEO-FFI) professional manual,* 2. Copyright © 1992 by Psychological Assessment Resources, Inc. Reprinted by permission.

Table 13.2: Source: Millon et al. (1994). *Scales of the Millon Clinical Multiaxial Inventory-III,* 2. Copyright © 1994 by DICANDRIEN, INC. Reprinted by permission of National Computer Systems, Minneapolis, MN.

Table 13.3: Source: D. N. Jackson (1989). *Personality research Form manual,* 6-7. © 1989 Sigma Assessment Systems, Inc., P. O. Box 610984, Port Huron, MI 48061-0984, (800) 265-1285. Reprinted by permission.

Figures 14.1 and 14.2: Source: L. W. Harmon et al. (1994). *Strong Interest Inventory: Applications and technical guide,* pages 236 and 51. Modified and reproduced by special permission of the Publisher, Consulting Psychologists Press, Inc., Palo Alto, CA 94303 from the **Strong Interest Inventory of the Strong Vocational Interest Blanks, Form T317.** Copyright 1933, 1938, 1945, 1946, 1966, 1968, 1974, 1981, 1985, 1994 by the Board of Trustees of the Leland Stanford Junior University. All rights reserved. Printed under license from Stanford University Press, Stanford, California 94305. Further reproduction is prohibited without the Publisher's written consent.

Table 14.1: Source: J. B. Rotter (1966). Generalized expectancies for internal versus external control of reinforcement. *Psychological Monographs,* 80 (1, Whole No. 609), p. 11. Copyright © 1966 by the American Psychological Association. Reprinted by permission of the author and publisher.

Figure 15.2: Copyright © 1982 by Western Psychological Services. Reprinted by permission.

Figure 15.3: Source: S. Rosenzweig (1976). *Rosenzweig Picture-Frustration Study, Children's Form.* Copyright © 1976, renewed by Saul Rosenzweig. Reprinted by permission.

Figure 15.4: *The Scenotest.* Copyright © 1991 by Hogrefe & Huber Publishers, Seattle, Toronto, Gottingen, Bern. Reprinted by permission.

Figure 16.1: Source: L. L. Thurstone (1950). *Some primary abilities in visual thinking* (No. 59), p. 7. Chicago: University of Chicago, Psychometric Laboratory.

Figure 16.2: Source: Group Embedded Figures Test. Modified and reproduced by special permission of the Publisher, Consulting Psychologists Press, Inc., Palo Alto, CA 94303 from **Group Embedded Figures Test** by Phillip K. Oltman, Evelyn Raskin, &. Herman A. Witkin. Copyright © 1971 by Consulting Psychologists Press, Inc. All rights reserved. Further reproduction is prohibited without the Publisher's written consent.

Figure 17.2: Source: Crawford Small Parts Dexterity Test. Copyright © by The Psychological Corporation. Reprinted by permission.

Figure 17.3: Sample Items from the Bennett Mechanical Comprehension Test. Copyright © 1967–1970, 1994 by The Psychological Corporation. Reprinted by permission. All rights reserved.

Figures 17.4 and 17.5: Photographs and materials Courtesy of American Guidance Service, Inc.

Name Index

C

D

H

I

N

O

P

Q

R

Subject Index

A

B

C

D

Q

R

S

T

U

V